Handbook of
INCOME
DISTRIBUTION

INTRODUCTION TO THE SERIES

The aim of the *Handbooks in Economics* series is to produce Handbooks for various branches of economics, each of which is a definitive source, reference, and teaching supplement for use by professional researchers and advanced graduate students. Each Handbook provides self-contained surveys of the current state of a branch of economics in the form of chapters prepared by leading specialists on various aspects of this branch of economics. These surveys summarize not only received results but also newer developments, from recent journal articles and discussion papers. Some original material is also included, but the main goal is to provide comprehensive and accessible surveys. The Handbooks are intended to provide not only useful reference volumes for professional collections but also possible supplementary readings for advanced courses for graduate students in economics.

Kenneth J. Arrow and Michael D. Intriligator

Handbook of
INCOME
DISTRIBUTION

Volume 2B

First edition

Edited by

ANTHONY B. ATKINSON
Nuffield College, Oxford, UK

FRANÇOIS BOURGUIGNON
Paris School of Economics, Paris, France

Amsterdam • Boston • Heidelberg • London • New York • Oxford
Paris • San Diego • San Francisco • Singapore • Sydney • Tokyo
North-Holland is an imprint of Elsevier

North-Holland is an imprint of Elsevier

The Boulevard, Langford Lane, Kidlington, Oxford OX5 1GB, UK
Radarweg 29, PO Box 211, 1000 AE Amsterdam, The Netherlands

British Library Cataloguing in Publication Data
A catalogue record for this book is available from the British Library

Library of Congress Cataloging-in-Publication Data
A catalog record for this book is available from the Library of Congress

ISBN: 978-0-444-59428-0 (Vol. 2A)
ISBN: 978-0-444-59429-7 (Vol. 2B)

For information on all North-Holland publications
visit our website at http://store.elsevier.com/

Working together
to grow libraries in
developing countries

www.elsevier.com • www.bookaid.org

Printed in the United Kingdom
Last digit is the print number: 10 9 8 7 6 5 4 3

CONTENTS

Volume 2B

Part III.   Explanations   **1227**

14.   Inequality in Macroeconomics   **1229**

15.   Wealth and Inheritance in the Long Run   **1303**

CONTRIBUTORS

Rolf Aaberge
Statistics Norway, Research Department and University of Oslo, Department of Economics, ESOP, Oslo, Norway

Daron Acemoglu
Massachusetts Institute of Technology, Cambridge, MA, USA

Facundo Alvaredo
EMod/OMI-Oxford University, Paris School of Economics, and CONICET, Oxford, UK

Sudhir Anand
Department of Economics, University of Oxford, Oxford, UK; and Department of Global Health and Population, Harvard School of Public Health, Boston, MA, USA

Andrea Brandolini
Bank of Italy, Directorate General for Economics, Statistics, and Research, Rome, Italy

Daniele Checchi
Department of Economics, University of Milan, Milano, Italy and IZA, Bonn, Germany

Pierre-André Chiappori
Department of Economics, Columbia University, NY, USA

Andrew E. Clark
Paris School of Economics—CNRS, Paris, France

Frank A. Cowell
STICERD, London School of Economics, London, UK

Conchita D'Ambrosio
INSIDE, Université du Luxembourg, Walferdange, Luxembourg

Koen Decancq
Centre for Social Policy Herman Deleeck, University of Antwerp, Antwerp; Department of Economics, Katholieke Universiteit Leuven, Leuven, and CORE, Université catholique de Louvain, Louvain-la-Neuve, Belgium

Jean-Yves Duclos
IZA, Département d'économique and CIRPÉE, Université Laval, Quebec, QC, Canada

Francesco Figari
University of Insubria, Varese, Italy, and Institute for Social and Economic Research (ISER), University of Essex, Colchester, UK

Emmanuel Flachaire
Aix-Marseille Université, AMSE & IUF, Marseille, France

Marc Fleurbaey
Princeton University, Princeton, NJ, USA

Michael F. Förster
OECD, Paris, France

Leonardo Gasparini
CEDLAS-FCE-Universidad Nacional de La Plata, and CONICET, La Plata, Argentina

István György Tóth
Tárki Social Research Institute, Budapest, Hungary

Markus Jäntti
Swedish Institute for Social Research (SOFI), Stockholm University, Stockholm, Sweden

Stephen P. Jenkins
Department of Social Policy, London School of Economics, London; ISER, University of Essex, Colchester, UK, and IZA, Bonn, Bonn, Germany

Ravi Kanbur
Cornell University, Ithaca, NY, USA

Ive Marx
Herman Deleeck Centre for Social Policy, University of Antwerp, Antwerp, and Institute for the Study of Labor, IZA, Bonn, Germany

Costas Meghir
Department of Economics, Yale University, New Haven, CT, USA

Dominique Meurs
University Paris Ouest Nanterre, EconomiX and Ined, France

Salvatore Morelli
CSEF, University of Naples, Federico II, Naples, Italy, and INET Oxford, University of Oxford, Oxford, UK

Suresh Naidu
Columbia University, NY, USA

Brian Nolan
Department of Social Policy and Intervention and Institute for New Economic Thinking at the Oxford Martin School, University of Oxford, UK

Owen O'Donnell
Erasmus School of Economics & Tinbergen Institute, Erasmus University Rotterdam, Rotterdam, The Netherlands, and School of Economics and Area Studies, University of Macedonia, Thessaloniki, Greece

Javier Olivera
Institute for Research on Socio-Economic Inequality, RU INSIDE, University of Luxembourg, Luxembourg, Luxembourg

Alari Paulus
Institute for Social and Economic Research (ISER), University of Essex, Colchester, UK

Thomas Piketty
Paris School of Economics, Paris, France

Sophie Ponthieux
Institut national de la statistique et des études économiques, France

Vincenzo Quadrini
University of Southern California, CEPR, Los Angeles, CA, USA

Martin Ravallion
Department of Economics, Georgetown University, Washington, DC, USA

Pascual Restrepo
Massachusetts Institute of Technology, Cambridge, MA, USA

José-Víctor Ríos-Rull
University of Minnesota, Federal Reserve Bank of Minneapolis, CAERP, CEPR, NBER, Minneapolis, MN, USA

James A. Robinson
Harvard University, Cambridge, MA, USA

John E. Roemer
Yale University, New Haven, CT, USA

Jesper Roine
Stockholm Institute of Transition Economics, Stockholm School of Economics, Stockholm, Sweden

Wiemer Salverda
Amsterdam Institute for Advanced Labour Studies (AIAS), and Amsterdam Centre for Inequality Studies (AMCIS), University of Amsterdam, Amsterdam, The Netherlands

Agnar Sandmo
Department of Economics, Norwegian School of Economics (NHH), Bergen, Norway

Erik Schokkaert
Department of Economics, Katholieke Universiteit Leuven, Leuven, and CORE, Université catholique de Louvain, Louvain-la-Neuve, Belgium

Paul Segal
King's International Development Institute, King's College London, London, UK

Timothy Smeeding
University of Wisconsin, Madison, WI, USA

Holly Sutherland
Institute for Social and Economic Research (ISER), University of Essex, Colchester, UK

André-Marie Taptué
Département d'économique and CIRPÉE, Université Laval, Quebec, QC, Canada

Jeffrey Thompson
Federal Reserve Board of Governors, Washington, DC, USA

Alain Trannoy
Aix-Marseille University, EHESS and CNRS, France

Eddy Van Doorslaer
Erasmus School of Economics, Tinbergen Institute & Institute for Health Policy and Management, Erasmus University Rotterdam, Rotterdam, The Netherlands

Tom Van Ourti
Erasmus School of Economics & Tinbergen Institute, Erasmus University Rotterdam, Rotterdam, The Netherlands

Daniel Waldenström
Department of Economics, Uppsala University, Uppsala, Sweden

Gabriel Zucman
London School of Economics, London, UK

INTRODUCTION: INCOME DISTRIBUTION TODAY

Anthony B. Atkinson*, François Bourguignon[†]
*Nuffield College, Oxford, UK
[†]Paris School of Economics, Paris, France

1. SETTING THE SCENE

When the first volume of the *Handbook of Income Distribution* was published in 2000, the subject of income inequality was not in the mainstream of economic debate—despite the long history of engagement with this issue by earlier leading economists—see Chapter 1 by Agnar Sandmo. Fifteen years later, inequality has become very much centre stage. Rising income inequality has attracted the attention of the U.S. President, of international bodies such as the IMF and the OECD, and of participants in the Davos meeting.

This volume of the Handbook aims to cover the advances made in the past 15 years in our understanding of the extent, causes, and consequences of inequality. In this respect, the second volume should be seen as complementing, not supplanting, the first volume. We have encouraged authors to concentrate on the developments that have taken place since 2000, and the chapters should be read in conjunction with those in volume I. In this Introduction, we give a flavor of the issues discussed and some personal reflections on the state of the subject.

In our Introduction to volume I of the Handbook, we said that "income distribution may be considered the normative economic issue 'par excellence'" (Atkinson and Bourguignon, 2000, p. 41). People are concerned about economic inequality because they feel it to be socially unjust or unfair. It violates principles of social justice. The nature of these principles is of course much debated and there is disagreement about what constitutes an unacceptable level of inequality. People focus on different dimensions. But the concern is with inequality intrinsically. At the same time, there is a second set of—instrumental—concerns with the consequences of inequality. The societal consequences were highlighted by Joseph Stiglitz when he entitled his 2012 book, *The price of inequality*, where he says "the impact of inequality on societies is now increasingly well understood—higher crime, health problems, and mental illness, lower educational achievements, social cohesion and life expectancy" (inside cover). The social, political and cultural impacts of inequality have been the subject of the GINI (Growing

Inequalities' Impacts) research project (Salverda et al., 2014; Nolan et al., 2014). In the second volume of the Handbook, some of these consequences feature, notably those regarding health in Chapter 17 by Owen O'Donnell, Eddy Van Doorslaer, and Tom Van Ourti. But the wider societal impact of inequality is not the principal focus of the chapters that follow. This still leaves much to be discussed. Inequality is of instrumental importance within the field of economics itself. As we said in volume I, "income distribution assists our understanding of various fields of economics" (2000, p. 4). Now, as then, we believe that the study of economic inequality should be at the heart of economic analysis.

Upon reflecting the issues covered in this volume, this Introduction considers successively: (a) the concepts and approaches to economic inequality measurement, or the various facets of inequality (Section 2); (b) the care needed with data on inequality (Section 3); (c) the explanations of changes in various dimensions of economic inequality, most notably the distribution of income, earnings and wealth and the links with macroeconomics (Section 4); and (d) the policies available to influence those changes or to correct those distributions (Section 5).

We plunge straight into the subject matter with Figure 1, which depicts the evolution of economic inequality in the United States over the past century. The data are taken from the Chartbook of Economic Inequality (Atkinson and Morelli, 2014),[1] but are presented in four panels to highlight different dimensions of the distribution of income.[2] The pictures provide a good basis for describing what is covered in this Handbook and for identifying some of the issues that are missing. The fact that most of the lines in the different panels are rising to the right is the main reason why inequality is on the agenda. At the same time, the long run of historical data on inequality shows us that there have been periods in the past when inequality fell and when poverty was reduced. Indeed the past 100 years has seen a broadly U-shaped pattern. The series shown in Figure 1 also allow us to underline at the outset the crucial, and often overlooked, point that observed differences in income are not necessarily an indicator of the existence of inequality. Earnings at the top decile (shown in Panel C), for example, may have risen on account of increased costs of acquiring educational qualifications, and not represent any rise in inequality of lifetime incomes. For this reason, it is important to ask what we mean by "inequality."

---

[1] An alternative colored graph can be found here: http://www.chartbookofeconomicinequality.com/wp-content/uploads/StaticGraphs/USA_staticgraph_coloured.pdf.

[2] We are following here the advice of Schwabish (2014) to avoid "spaghetti" charts.

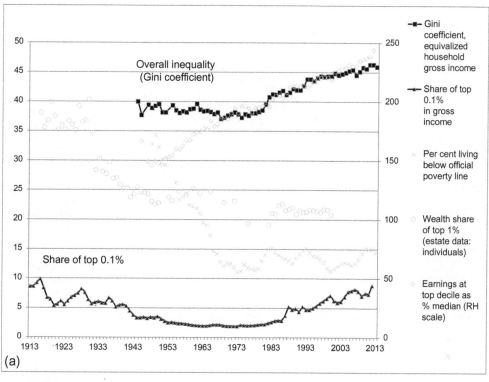

(a)

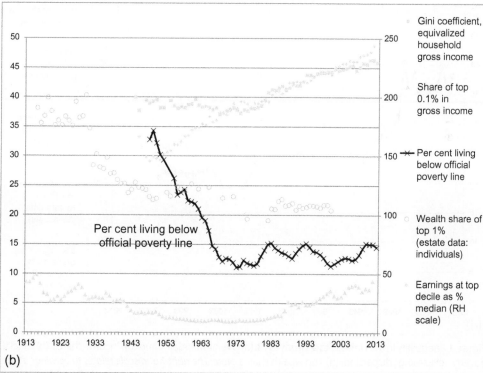

(b)

Figure 1 (See legend on next page.)

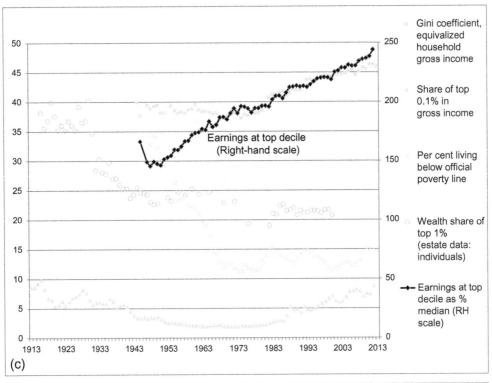

Figure 1 Inequality in the United States from 1913. (a) Overall inequality and top income shares. (b) Official poverty. (c) Earnings dispersion. (d) Top wealth shares. *Note: The right-hand scale relates to earnings at the top decile, and all other series are measured on the left-hand scale. Atkinson and Morelli (2014).*

Box Sources of Data for Figure 1

Overall inequality: Gini coefficient of gross equalized household income from the U.S. Bureau of the Census, Income, Poverty, and Health Insurance Coverage in the United States: 2013 (table A-3, Selected measures of equivalence-adjusted income dispersion), where it has been assumed that half of the recorded change between 1992 and 1993 was due to the change in methods (and therefore 1.15 percentage points have been added to the values from 1992 back to 1967), this series is linked backward at 1967 to the series from 1944 given by Budd (1970, table 6).

   Top income shares: The share in total gross income (excluding capital gains) of the top 0.1% is based on the work of Piketty and Saez (2003); updated figures are taken from the Web site of Emmanuel Saez:

   http://eml.berkeley.edu/~saez/.

   Poverty: The proportion of the population below the official poverty line before 1959 from Fisher (1986) and from 1959 from the U.S. Bureau of the Census Web site, Historical Poverty Tables, Table 2 and Table B1 from the U.S. Bureau of the Census, Income, Poverty, and Health Insurance Coverage in the United States: 2013.

   Individual earnings: The series for the top decile of earnings, expressed as a percentage of the median, is based on the Current Population Survey (CPS) from the OECD iLibrary, linked at 1973 to the estimates of Karoly (1992, table 2B.2), and at 1963 to the estimates in Atkinson (2008, table T.10) from the CPS tabulations.

   Wealth: The share in total personal wealth of the top 1% of adult individuals is based on estate data from Kopczuk and Saez (2004, table B1).

2. DIFFERENT FACETS OF INEQUALITY

There is much discussion of inequality but there is also much confusion, as the term means different things to different people. Inequality arises in many spheres of human activity. People have unequal political power. People may be unequal before the law. In these two volumes, we are concerned with one particular dimension: economic inequality.

   Even limiting attention to economic inequality, there are many interpretations and careful distinctions have to be drawn. It is convenient to first make a distinction between monetary and nonmonetary inequality. The former, refers to standard dollar-valued magnitudes associated with the economic activity of an individual or a household (earnings, income, consumption expenditures, and wealth). Nonmonetary inequality, also referred to here as "beyond income" inequality, addresses broader dimensions of economic life such as well-being or capability.

2.1 Monetary Inequality

Restricting inequality to monetary magnitudes does not prevent confusion. In the media, one often hears statements like "the wealth of the richest *x* billionaires would feed all the poor in a particular country." But this confuses wealth, which is a stock, with income or consumption, which are flows. Flows have to be specified as occurring over a certain period, so that the figures for overall inequality in Figure 1a relate to annual income. Wealth, shown in Figure 1d, is in contrast measured at a point in time. If billionaires gave away all their wealth this year to feed poor families, then they would not appear in the Forbes list next year. If, on the other hand, they gave away the income from their wealth, then the gift would be smaller but they could go on doing it year after year.

There is often confusion between income and earnings. Articles in the academic literature may contain in their titles the words "distribution of income," but they are often actually about the distribution of earnings, and earnings are only part of income. Often too they look only at those in work, and tell nothing about the inequality of income among pensioners or the unemployed. The distinction between earnings and income is made clearly in Chapter 18 by Wiemer Salverda and Daniele Checchi. They observe that there appear to be two largely separate literatures, one concerned with earnings and one with income distribution; their chapter plays an important role in bridging this divide. As they note, it is a question not only of "inequality of what?" but also of "inequality among whom?" Earnings are typically considered on an individual basis. The earnings at the top decile (the person 10% from the top) shown in Figure 1c are those of individual workers, whereas the income measured by overall inequality is the total income of the household.

A person may have zero earnings, and no other income, but live in a household which is comfortably off. Such a situation does of course raise interesting questions—both for the analysis of inequality and in real life. What is the distribution within the household? The curve highlighted in the upper part of Figure 1a refers to the inequality of equivalized household income, which imputes to each member the total income of the household divided by the size of the household corrected by a factor that takes into account economies of scale as well as age-dependent needs. This assumes that all household members enjoy the same well-being. The topic of intrahousehold inequality is addressed in Chapter 16 by Pierre-André Chiappori and Costas Meghir. As they stress, both the level of inequality and the trend over time may be quite different. This issue is particularly relevant to gender inequality, which is the subject of Chapter 12 by Dominique Meurs and Sophie Ponthieux.

Overall inequality is summarized in Figure 1 in terms of the Gini coefficient, and this is the statistic most commonly published by statistical agencies. The typical explanation of the coefficient is geometric: the Gini coefficient is equal to the ratio of the area between the Lorenz curve and the diagonal to the area of the whole triangle under the diagonal. As illustrated in Figure 2, the Lorenz curve shows the proportion of income received by the bottom F percent as a function of F. Where the Lorenz curve is close to the diagonal (curve A in Figure 2), the Gini coefficient is small; where the Lorenz curve hugs the horizontal axis (curve B), the coefficient is closer to 1. If we are comparing two Lorenz

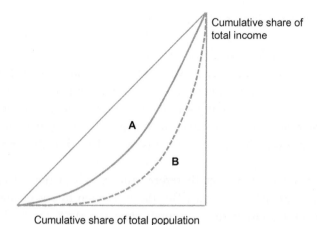

Cumulative share of total population

Figure 2 Lorenz curves. *Note: The Gini coefficient of the distribution A is equal to the ratio to the whole triangle of the area between the curve A and the diagonal.*

curves that do not cross, as with A and B, then one (in this case, A) definitely has a lower Gini coefficient. In this case we have Lorenz dominance, and A scores better than B on a wide variety of inequality measures (Atkinson, 1970). The converse is not true. The fact that the Gini coefficient is lower does not imply that the Lorenz curve is everywhere higher: the curves may intersect. The Gini coefficient can also be described in terms of the mean difference. A Gini coefficient of G percent means that, if we take any two households from the population at random, the expected difference is 2G percent times the mean. So that a rise in the Gini coefficient from 30% to 40% implies that the expected difference has gone up from 60% to 80% of the mean. Another useful way of thinking, suggested by Sen (1976), is in terms of "distributionally adjusted" national income, which with the Gini coefficient is (100G) percent of national income. So that a rise in the Gini coefficient from 30% to 40% is equivalent to reducing national income by 14% (i.e., $(100 - 40)/(100 - 30) = 6/7$ of its previous value).

We may be interested, not just in overall inequality, but also in the top and bottom of the distribution. The top income shares, for which we have the longest run of data in Figure 1, stretching back in the United States to 1913, show the share of total gross income (i.e., before deducting the taxes paid) accruing to the top 0.1%. Figures like these, or the share of the top 1%, have appeared on the placards at demonstrations, such as those of the Occupy Movement. At the bottom of the scale, the poverty figures record the number of people living below the official line, which in the United States dates back to the War on Poverty launched by President Johnson in the 1960s. The evolution of top income shares receives particular attention in Chapter 7 by Jesper Roine and Daniel Waldenström on long-run trends. Chapter 8 by Salvatore Morelli, Timothy Smeeding, and Jeffrey Thompson discusses whether top shares are proxies for overall inequality. This chapter and Chapter 9 by Facundo Alvaredo and Leonardo Gasparini on the post-1970 trends provide evidence about both top and bottom of the scale. In a different sense, the concentration of people at the top and at the bottom of the distribution, or by complement the size of the "middle class," leads to the concept of "polarization," another concept, discussed in Chapter 5 by Jean-Yves Duclos and André-Marie Taptué. There are still many other ways to measure inequality than the Gini or percentage shares, whether it refers to income, earnings, consumption, or wealth. Likewise, there are many ways of expressing social welfare as a combination of some inequality measure and the mean income of a population. These were extensively reviewed in the first volume of this Handbook.

The panels in Figure 1 present therefore quite a rich picture of inequality in the United States over the past 100 years. But there is much that is missing. Figure 1 is a sequence of snapshots, rather than a movie. The top 0.1% in the United States in 1913 were those in the top group in that particular year; some of these people would have fallen out of the group by 1914. The statistics presented in Figure 1 tell us nothing about such mobility, which is the subject of Chapter 10 by Markus Jäntti and Stephen Jenkins. As they explain, there are two aspects. First, there is the subject of how an individual's income changes from one year to the next during their lifetime; on the other hand, there is the subject of income change between generations of parents and children. Such a distinction between intragenerational and intergenerational income mobility reflects the division in the existing literature, but one of the features of their chapter is that it draws out the elements of the measurement of income mobility that are common to both topics. They also raise the measurement issues associated with the inherently multidimensioned information about incomes over time; many of these issues are the counterpart of those that arise when one considers multidimensionality at a point in time (see in the next section).

Figure 1 shows evidence about the distribution of income within one country, but inequality is local and global as well as national. To begin with, money income has different purchasing power depending on local prices, and geographical variation can have a significant impact, as has been shown in the work of Moretti (2013) on the college wage premium in the United States. Spatial inequality is highlighted by Ravi Kanbur in Chapter 20. As he notes, "the spatial dimension of inequality is a key concern in the policy discourse, because it intersects with and interacts with disparities between subnational entities and jurisdictions. These entities sometimes have defined ethnic or linguistic characteristics, and in Federal structures have constitutional identities which naturally lead to a subnational perspective on national inequality." Inequality equally intersects with concerns about globalization, which is the main subject of Chapter 20. The world distribution of income is the subject of Chapter 11 by Sudhir Anand and Paul Segal—see also Bourguignon (2013).

We have referred above to the important topic of gender inequality. This is treated in Chapter 12, where the authors note that much of the literature is concerned with the gender gap in earnings. As they say, this is important, but only part of the story, since there is gender inequality in other forms of income and among those not in paid work, and all these inequalities interact with each other. See also Chapter 20 where Kanbur discusses globalization and gender inequality. Another important missing topic is that of inequality by race and ethnicity. It is a serious omission that we have not included a chapter on discrimination, although we should note that ethnic cleavages are one of the motivations for the theoretical analysis of polarization in Chapter 5.

In introducing considerations such as gender and ethnicity, we are, however, going beyond straight income inequality as pictured in Figure 1. We are abandoning the anonymity that lies behind a Gini coefficient or a top 1% income share. We are asking how unequal income is across various well-identified groups. This is adding a dimension to the inequality concept. Two populations A and B may have the same overall inequality of earnings but the distribution of earnings may be exactly the same for men and women in A, whereas it may be more favorable to men in B. Two countries may have the same share of the top 1%, but in one country they may be all men. World poverty may have fallen, but the number in a particular ethnic group below the poverty line may have risen.

2.2 "Beyond Income" Inequality

Much of the reflection about inequality over the past 15 years or so has been concerned with extending the concept to "beyond income" inequality. As Sen et al. (2010) proposed to incorporate nonmarket dimensions into the measure of social progress, thus going "Beyond GDP," the point here is also to take nonincome dimensions onboard when measuring inequality.

In addition to the quite remarkable perspective it offers on two centuries of economic thought on income distribution and redistribution, the chapter on the history of economic thought (Chapter 1) reminds us that there may be a historical bias in the way economists see and think about income distribution and inequality. This bias is likely to be as present today as it was in the past. Classical economists focused on functional income distribution among land, labor, and capital because they viewed the society they were living in as made up of classes deriving their income from different factors. This view does not fit well our own world, even though factor rewards and the functional income distribution still features today in macroeconomic distribution theories. Another interesting feature of Chapter 1 is the long-lasting reliance in normative economics on utilitarianism. It is only relatively recently, i.e., the 1970s, and very much under the influence of Rawls and Sen, which economists have begun to distance themselves from this approach and to consider alternatives.

It is noteworthy that this line of thought developed very much as a major extension of the previous literature on income inequality measurement, a literature that is comparatively young in a historical perspective. Several features of the income inequality measurement "paradigm" as it developed say between 1920 (Pigou, 1920; Dalton, 1920)[3] and the 1980s are worth stressing as it provides a point of reference for modern researchers who seek to extend this paradigm to a higher level of generality in terms of the definition of economic inequality. A first feature is that most properties of inequality indicators, their interpretation in terms of social welfare, and their analogy with risk analysis are now well understood. To be sure, work remains to be done on the income inequality measurement agenda. This volume of the Handbook gives two examples of it: polarization (Chapter 5) and the introduction of statistical methods in the measurement of income inequality (Chapter 8 by Frank Cowell and Emmanuel Flachaire). But considerable progress has been made. A second feature is that this was done rather quickly after the contributions by Kolm (1966, 1971), Atkinson (1970), and Sen (1973). A third feature is that, despite a possible analogy with utilitarianism, the paradigm was explicitly presented as nonutilitarian, even in the generalized sense of a social welfare function, thus breaking with an important and powerful school of economic thought on social issues. Finally, as the paradigm started to develop, its very relevance was questioned. "Equality of what?" asked Sen (1980), suggesting that the income focus was severely restrictive and even questioning the welfare basis for inequality measurement.

Four chapters in this volume of the Handbook deal in different ways with this extension of the income inequality measurement paradigm. The following simple framework is intended to help identify their main contribution, as well as the general issues in moving from income to other, more general, definitions of economic inequality. We first introduce the concept of "functionings," in the sense of Sen, of individual i, denoted by the vector a_i. Functionings include various aspects of life enjoyment: material consumption, health, job market status, housing and environment quality, etc. Among them, let us single out material consumption, as measured by money income, y_i, so that $a_i = (y_i, x_i)$ where x_i stands for nonmaterial consumption functionings. Let the preferences of individual i among those functionings be described by an ordinal utility $u_i(y_i, x_i)$ function, normalized to unity for some reference bundle $a°$. Let the "satisfaction" of individual i be an increasing function $S[u_i(y_i, x_i), b_i]$ where b_i stands for a set of individual characteristics that can influence the satisfaction that individual i derives from (y_i, x_i). Finally, assume that the economic environment, the technology and social habits are such that the vector of functionings must belong to an individual-specific set Q_i defined by y_i, x_i, and z_i, where z_i is a vector of attributes of individual i, which may differ from b_i. A person may, for example, be able to function at home but not in a formal labor market setting or may come from a social background that broadens her economic opportunities. The set Q_i thus describes the set of functionings individual i can reach, given her characteristics. This may include the standard budget constraint as well as the production function that permits the

---

[3] They gave their name to the Pigou–Dalton transfer principle, according to which a distribution is less unequal than another if it can be reached by a sequence of mean-preserving equalizing transfers of income.

transformation into functionings of the goods and services bought on the market. Let (y_i^*, x_i^*) be the bundle of functionings preferred by individual i in the set of possibilities, Q_i. Of course both y_i^* and x_i^* are individual-specific functions of z_i. It is also natural to assume that this preferred vector is also the observed vector of functionings. The corresponding satisfaction of individual i is $V_i = S[u_i(y_i^*, x_i^*), b_i]$, where the second argument allows for the fact that two individuals may get different levels of satisfaction from the same functioning bundles.

With the aid of this notation, it is then possible to describe the various approaches in the recent literature to extend the measurement of inequality beyond money income and to see their advantages and limitations.[4] They are discussed in Chapter 2 by Koen Decancq, Marc Fleurbaey, and Eric Schokkaert on inequality and well-being, Chapter 3 by Rolf Aaberge and Andrea Brandolini on multidimensional inequality, and Chapter 4 by John Roemer and Alain Trannoy on inequality of opportunity.

2.2.1 Defining Inequality on Functionings: Multidimensional Inequality Measurement

Inequality is to be defined on the collection of vectors (y_i^*, x_i^*) in the population. Various approaches can then be used with varying degrees of generality. The most obvious way to proceed is to aggregate the various dimensions into a single scalar and apply standard unidimensional inequality measurement to this scalar. The aggregator function, defined as $A(x,y)$, may be arbitrary, satisfying some basic properties, or it may be related to the framework set out in Section 2.2, in which case it is equivalent to assuming that all individuals have the same preferences, u, and the same characteristics b, so that they have the same satisfaction function, $S(u(x_i,y_i), b)$, of a functioning bundle (x_i,y_i). Alternatively, this function of (x_i,y_i) may be the preferences of the social evaluator. In any case, all individuals are assumed to apply the same trade-offs among the various functionings. Such a normative aggregation approach lies behind several specific multidimensional inequality measures based on some functional form for the aggregator function, as in Maasoumi (1986). The new inequality-extended Human Development Index used in the Development Program of the United Nations (UNDP) (Foster et al., 2005; Alkire and Foster, 2010), or the recent efforts by OECD to measure multidimensional living standards taking account of inequality, unemployment, and health (OECD, 2014) are examples of this approach. The recent poverty measurement literature based on the counting of deprivations follows the same logic. Deprivations are grouped by functioning, then the number of deprivations and the extent of deprivation in the various functionings are aggregated to

---

[4] It also allows us to distinguish the approach adopted in the inequality measurement literature of defining social welfare in terms of incomes y_i from an utilitarian approach where social welfare is defined over u_i (or $S[u_i,b_i]$).

generate an overall poverty indicator for individual i—see Alkire and Foster (2011) and Chapter 3.

Instead of using specific measures and specific aggregator functions, $A(x,y)$ or $S(u(x,y),b)$, it is possible to generalize social welfare dominance analysis in income inequality measurement—the counterpart to Lorenz dominance of income distributions (Kolm, 1977). Following Atkinson and Bourguignon (1982), a partial ordering of distributions of the bundles (y_i^*, x_i^*) in a population may be obtained by considering all the aggregator functions within some class of functions (see, for example, Duclos et al., 2011). As, however, is brought out in Chapter 3 by Aaberge and Brandolini, it is not straightforward to generalize the Pigou–Dalton principle of transfers to the multidimensional case. Moreover, we should not lose sight of the fact that nonmaterial functionings may require different treatment. The choice of aggregator function has to reflect the specific characteristics of, say, health as a variable. For example, health may be measured in ordinal rather than cardinal form, as is discussed by Allison and Foster (2004) and Duclos and Echevin (2011).

2.2.2 Individual Preferences and the Income Equivalent Approach

Interpreted in terms of individual preferences, the preceding approach imposes identical preferences on all individuals. If ordinal preferences are observed, then a particular individual-specific aggregator function can be used which has the dimension of income—see chapter 4 of Fleurbaey and Blanchet (2013). With a reference vector x° of nonincome functionings, the equivalent income corresponding to an observed bundle (y_i, x_i) is given by the solution $\mathring{y}_i$ of the equation: $u_i(\mathring{y}_i, x^\circ) = u_i(y_i, x_i)$. Such a solution does exist if $u_i( )$ is reasonably assumed to be continuous and monotonically increasing. The equivalent income is thus a function of the bundle (y_i, x_i) conditional on x°. It can be handled exactly in the same way as income is dealt with in income inequality measures. Of course, the issue is whether it is possible to estimate individual preferences $u_i(y,x)$. In Decancq et al. (2014), this is done using subjective satisfaction data and relating these data to income and observed functionings for individuals with common characteristics in some subset of (b_i). Another issue is the choice of the reference nonincome bundle, x°, since inequality measures will be conditional on that bundle—see Chapter 2.

2.2.3 Defining Inequality Using Subjective Satisfaction

Going further along the chain, another approach at measuring inequality is to focus directly on satisfaction levels, $V_i = S[u_i(y_i^*, x_i^*), b_i]$, as directly observed in satisfaction surveys. This is equivalent to using the individual-specific aggregator function, $u_i(y_i^*, x_i^*)$, as well as the satisfaction function $S(u,b_i)$. Several authors have followed this route, showing for instance that, unlike for observed income, inequality of "happiness" tended to go down over time in most developed countries and, as for income, to be smaller in richer than in poorer countries—see for instance Veenhoven

(2005), Stevenson and Wolfers (2008) on the United States, Ovaska and Takashima (2010), Becchetti et al. (2011), and Clark et al. (2012).

Since life satisfaction is generally recorded on an ordinal scale, there are evident problems in converting such measures to a cardinal scale and employing standard inequality indicators. For this reason, an alternative approach based on dominance criteria has been proposed by Dutta and Foster (2013). On the conceptual side, the issue arises as to the interpretation to be given to life satisfaction data. In particular, they may actually reveal the satisfaction of an individual relatively to his or her past experience and future expectations, and also possibly in relation to other individuals. If so they are improper for the measurement of "economic inequality." In terms of the notation introduced above, it is doubtful whether the individual characteristics b_i, which determine how ordinal preferences are cardinalized into satisfaction, should be taken into account in measuring economic inequality. The same bundle of functionings enjoyed by two individuals having the same preferences may yield different levels of satisfaction if one of them has a rather positive and the other a negative attitude toward life in general. A more detailed account of the interpretation to be given to subjective satisfaction data is offered in Chapter 13 by Andrew Clark and Conchita d'Ambrosio.

2.2.4 Inequality of Capabilities

Instead of defining inequality on the observed bundle of functionings (y_i^*, x_i^*), resulting from the choice of individual i in his/her choice set, Q_i, one could move upstream and consider the inequality of these choice sets, as in the capability approach. The first step is to identify these sets, as different from the particular point (y_i^*, x_i^*) actually achieved in the set. Presumably, this could be done by considering the set generated by all the functioning bundles observed for persons with the same vector as attributes, z. Assuming that such identification has been made, the second step would consist of defining an inequality measure on these sets rather than scalars, as with income, or vectors as with multidimensional inequality. In practice, the measurement of inequality based on capabilities has been reduced to emphasizing a few components of the vector of individual characteristics, z_i, that indirectly define the size of the set Q_i. Typically, these are variables like education, health, or the availability of material resources. These three variables are combined linearly at the aggregate national level to define the familiar Human Development Index used by the UNDP to measure the inequality of functionings between any pair of countries. Several attempts have been made to incorporate a larger set of variables at the individual level in specific countries (see, for instance, Anand et al. (2007).

2.2.5 Inequality of Opportunities

Inequality of opportunity is defined as that part of the inequality in optimal functionings, (y_i^*, x_i^*), that is, due to differences in individual characteristics, z_i, or possibly in a subset of these variables. Among these characteristics, a distinction is made between variables, on the one hand, that are outside the control of individuals, which are called the "circumstances" faced by the individual, and variables, on the other hand, which may be assumed under his/her control. Then the inequality of opportunity can be measured by the inequality that exists in the (y,x) space across groups of people facing the same circumstances. Those groups are called "types" by Roemer (1998). The simplest measure is obtained by considering the inequality of the mean vector (y, x) among the various types. More elaborate measures would compare the distributions (y,x), rather than means, across types. In Chapter 4, Roemer and Trannoy discuss methods for doing so when focusing on income distribution only. The implementation of this approach requires assumptions to be made about what may be considered as "circumstances" (gender, ethnicity, family background, ...) and what may be assumed under the control of an individual (school achievement, for instance). Moreover, there are necessarily unobserved circumstances, so that one can at best measure the income inequality due to observed circumstances. A particular case frequently used is when one considers only one component of z_i, like ethnicity. In the space of earnings, the inequality of opportunity then corresponds to the familiar concept of wage discrimination, as is discussed for gender in Chapter 12.

Inequality in terms of opportunity or capability is both defined on an "*ex ante* basis," that is among groups of people with some common characteristics, and irrespective of differences in individual achievements in the space of functionings. (In contrast, inequality of outcomes, be they income, earnings, consumption spending or even "satisfaction," is an *ex post* inequality concept.) Practically, the main difference between the measurement of the inequality of capability and opportunity is that the former focuses on the inequality in the vectors of attributes, z_i, whereas the simplest approach to the latter considers the inequality between mean outcomes (y,x) across various "types" defined by identical "circumstances," z. A second difference may lie in the individual characteristics selected to differentiate people, determinants of the set of possible functionings on the side of capabilities, and exclusively circumstances outside the control of individuals on the side of opportunity. Recently, there have been a number of attempts at measuring the inequality of opportunity in several countries—for instance, Brunori et al. (2013) have put together estimates obtained for a set of 40 countries using earnings as outcome and family background as circumstances. A related literature, although with more antecedents, is concerned with intergenerational income and more generally social mobility—see Chapter 10. Here too, the issue is to measure the contribution of an observed circumstance, the parents' social status, the inequality of a particular functioning, and the children's social status.

Overall, "beyond income" inequality measurement touches upon the very fundamentals of economic inequality and a number of important conceptual advances have been made since the pathbreaking work by Rawls and Sen. Data limitations, the frequent difficulty of translating conceptual parameters into actual figures, and quite often the complexity of the analytical instruments being proposed have limited the empirical applications, but the area is promising for future research. A priority should be the search for simpler ways of making use of the conceptual advances in describing the multiple dimensions of economic inequality without reducing them to a single number.

3. DATA ON INEQUALITY

We began this chapter with the concrete example of Figure 1 in order to highlight the centrality of data. In all fields of economics, data play a key role, but in a field as politically charged as inequality, it is especially important to be careful with the quality of data. When faced with charts like those in Figure 1, showing the evolution of inequality, one should not take them simply on trust. One should ask: what data are there? Where do they come from? Are they fit for purpose? In what follows, we concentrate on data on monetary inequality, particularly income, but similar questions arise with data on nonmonetary variables such as material deprivation or happiness.

3.1 Care with Data

There are two dangers. The first is the inappropriate use of data. All too often, people make claims that inequality is increasing, or decreasing, on the basis of comparing data at two different dates that are not comparable. Or country A is claimed to be performing better than country B on the basis of statistics derived from sources that cannot be compared. The share of the top 10% in total wealth may be obtained in one country from a household survey and in the other from the records of administering a wealth tax. The other danger is that of going to the other extreme and rejecting all evidence about inequality on the grounds and that it can only be measured imperfectly. That is a counsel of despair.

In our view, all forms of possible evidence should be brought to bear, but we need to take full account of their strengths and of their weaknesses. Here there have been remarkable advances. When one of us (ABA) started research on poverty in Britain in the late 1960s, the British government had decided not to allow access to the household records. The only materials were published tabulations. This changed in the 1970s. The first volume of the Handbook, published in 2000, could draw on the household survey data that had become much more widely available. Not only were there many more surveys being conducted, typically by statistical agencies, but also researchers more commonly had access to the microdata. Although this change is far from universal, it has allowed scholars to assemble internationally comparable datasets, notably the Luxembourg Income Study (LIS) founded by Tim Smeeding, Lee Rainwater, and Gaston Schaber in 1983, and the World Bank's PovcalNet covering some 850 household surveys from 127 countries.

In the decade and a half since the first volume, there have been at least four major departures. The first is the rapid growth of experimental research in economics, represented here by Chapter 13 by Andrew Clark and Conchita d'Ambrosio, where the authors show how data generated in experiments, together with survey evidence, can throw light on the subtleties of attitudes to inequality. The second is the much greater access to distributional data from administrative records. When the European Union Statistics on Income and Living Conditions (EU-SILC) replaced the European Community Household Panel from 2003, the regulations allowed flexibility as to the source of data and increasingly Member States have drawn information from administrative sources. The third is the renewed interest in historical data. Inspired by Piketty (2001), there has been a considerable investment in the construction of long-run time series, notably covering top income shares, as made available in the World Top Incomes Database administered by Facundo Alvaredo. Finally, the fourth improvement is the increasing standardization of the collection of data across countries, which permits more rigorous comparative work. EU-SILC is an example in Europe; the Program for the Improvement of Surveys and the Measurement of Living Conditions in Latin America and the Caribbean is another example. Even though more efforts are needed, cross-country comparisons today definitely make more sense than was the case one or two decades ago.

These developments mean that we now are much better informed about the extent of economic inequality and the trends over time, as is clear from reading the surveys of the evidence in Part II. The historical research is examined in Chapter 7 on long-run trends in the distributions of income and wealth, covering more than 25 countries and going back in some cases to the eighteenth century. The post-1970 evolution is the subject of Chapters 8 and 9. The former covers inequality and poverty in OECD and Middle Income countries, demonstrating that "data have come a long way" since the chapter by Gottschalk and Smeeding (2000) in volume I. The latter covers developing countries, where again there has been great progress in the measurement of inequality and poverty. Chapter 11 investigates the world distribution of income and global poverty.

The availability of data is, moreover, one key ingredient in the study of the causes of economic inequality, which is the focus of Part III. In many cases, these investigations are based on statistical analysis of country panel datasets on inequality (derived by pooling time series of observations for each of a number of countries). Differences over time and differences across countries are used to explore the multiple causes of inequality. This is the explicit concern of Chapter 19 by Michael Förster and István Tóth, and it underlies much of the analysis of Chapter 18 on the distribution of earnings by Wiemer Salverda and Daniele Checchi. In Chapter 21, the econometric analysis of the relationship among democracy, redistribution, and inequality by Daron Acemoglu, Suresh Naidu, Pascual Restrepo, and James Robinson uses international databases on inequality. It is on such international databases, now widely used, that we concentrate here, since they illustrate many of the issues.

3.2 International Databases on Income Inequality

In considering international income distribution databases, as listed and discussed in Chapter 19, a key distinction is between primary databases that rely directly on micro-data, standardized as much as possible to ensure comparability across countries and time periods, and secondary databases that compile estimates of income distribution indicators from available published sources. Examples of the former include LIS, the EU-SILC—which also coordinates the data collection in the countries covered—the OECD income distribution database, SEDLAC covering Latin America and the Caribbean and the World Bank's POVCAL/WYD. Secondary databases include the World Income Inequality Database (WIID) assembled by UNU-WIDER (an updated version of the dataset originally constructed by Deininger and Squire (1996) at the World Bank), and the "All the Ginis you ever wanted" database put together by Branko Milanovic (2013), also at the World Bank. The latter states clearly that "this dataset consists only of the Gini coefficients that have been calculated from actual household surveys," and a second important distinction is between databases, like "All the Ginis," that are restricted to actual observations and those databases that impute missing values of specific indicators for some countries and for some time periods. Aiming at "the widest possible coverage across countries and over time," the Standardized World Income Inequality Database (SWIID) "uses a custom missing-data algorithm to standardize the United Nations University's WIID and many, many additional observations" (SWIID Web site and documentation). The University of Texas Inequality Project (UTIP) Estimated Household Income Inequality Data Set is derived from the econometric relationship between the UTIP-UNIDO dataset on industrial pay, other conditioning variables, and the World Bank's Deininger-Squire dataset on income inequality.

The original World Bank Deininger and Squire (1996) database was scrutinized by Atkinson and Brandolini (2001), who showed the risks of reaching inconsistent conclusions using secondary databases, or, more generally, comparing income distribution indicators across countries or time periods that relied on different definitions of income or the statistical unit. While recognizing the value of such databases, they cautioned against their uncritical use and set out a number of principles which should guide the construction of secondary databases. Progress has been made since then. In a paper reviewing the WIID database for a special issue of the *Journal of Economic Inequality*, edited by Ferreira and Lustig (2015), on income inequality databases, Jenkins (2014) repeated the comparison made by Atkinson and Brandolini between the database and consistent estimates obtained from LIS for a sample of rich countries in the early 1990s, using WIID version 2c (2008) and found that differences had been reduced (and a new WIID version 3.0B was subsequently released in 2014). Yet, he reiterated that "one cannot simply use the WIID data 'as is'" (Jenkins, 2014, p. 15). As this kind of benchmarking has not been made for developing countries, it is not unlikely that inconsistencies are more frequent there. One should not use data from secondary databases without first making a careful inspection.

3.3 A Checklist of Questions

When using data on income inequality, what questions should one ask? Here, we give a checklist covering some of the most important. These issues, and many others, are discussed in the Canberra Group Handbook on Household Income Statistics (United Nations Economic Commission for Europe, 2011), which is the second edition of a handbook produced in 2001 by an International Expert Group on Household Income Statistics established in 1996 at the initiative of the Australian Bureau of Statistics. In describing it as a "checklist," we are not suggesting that there is a single right answer. The appropriate choice depends on the context and may differ between countries at different stages of development. The choice depends on the purpose of the analysis. But it is essential that the user be aware of what data they are employing.

3.3.1 Inequality of What?

In some countries statistical offices collect data on household income, whereas in others consumption expenditure data are collected. The Povcal database comprises both countries that report income inequality and others that report inequality in consumption expenditure. LIS avoids this heterogeneity by using income surveys for all countries. Income may be defined in a variety of ways: posttax (or disposable) income, pretax income allowing for deductions, such as interest paid (confusingly, this is often called "net income" in official statistics), or pretax income before deductions. As implemented, the income concept may follow more or less closely the definition adopted by the International Conference of Labour Statisticians (and the second edition of the Canberra Handbook), which covers all receipts whether in monetary form or in kind, apart from irregular or windfall receipts. Important issues here (as for the definition of consumption) are the inclusion or exclusion of imputed rent for owner-occupied housing, of home production, and of in-kind benefits.

Income and expenditure relate typically to a year, but may be measured over different time periods. This is particularly important in the case of earnings, as discussed in Chapter 18. The reference period may be the latest pay period or earnings that may relate to normal monthly earnings, excluding irregular bonuses, or they may be total annual earnings. They may be expressed per hour, and this may allow a decomposition into wage and leisure inequalities. The issue of timing also affects the population covered. People may be present for part of the year, and the inclusion or exclusion of such part-year incomes, or earnings, affects the measured degree of inequality. Another issue related to the comparability of earnings data across countries is the status of payroll charges and social security contributions. Earnings are net of all these charges in some cases and gross of contributions paid by employees in other cases, whereas payroll charges paid by employers are rarely recorded. From that point of view, progress in constructing international databases on income distribution has not been paralleled by the same effort for individual earnings.

An additional issue of importance with existing datasets on income inequality is the difference in the cost of living across geographical areas in the same country. Such data do not exist in all countries. Yet, these differences may be sizable and may have a major impact on the estimation of inequality. Uncertainty about the rural–urban cost of living differential has led the managers of the Povcal database in the World Bank to report separately on the distribution of income in rural and urban areas in both China and India and differences in reported estimates of income inequality in China are often due to different assumptions about the rural/urban cost of living ratio. Differences in the cost of living across cities—if only with respect to housing rents—in developed countries generate the same kind of imprecision (we have already cited the work of Moretti, 2013).

3.3.2 Among Whom?

Data on inequality may refer to differences between households, between inner families, between tax units, or between individuals. Much empirical evidence relates to households, and surveys are typically conducted on this basis. Such a measure however tells us nothing about the distribution within the household—the subject of Chapter 16. Where there are several generations of adults within the household, inequality may be concealed. The same applies to the inner family, in that the aggregation of the income (or consumption) of a couple conceals gender inequality—the subject of Chapter 12. In this context, it is interesting that a number of countries have moved to individual taxation under the personal income tax. From such administrative data, we can learn, for example, that women were seriously underrepresented among the top 1%. In Canada, in 2010, women accounted for only 21% of those with gross incomes in the top 1% (Statistics Canada, 2013); in the United Kingdom, in 2011, the corresponding figure was 17% (Atkinson et al., forthcoming).

Households and other units have differing size and composition, and adjustments have to be made using equivalence scales. Here, there is a variety of practice and some harmonization across primary databases would be welcome. For instance, the "equivalization" procedure differs between LIS ("Key Figures" webpage) and the OECD income distribution database, which use the square root of the total family size as an equivalence scale, and Povcal which uses the total family size, and imputes the total household per capita to each household member. In other words, the equivalence elasticity is set to 0.5 in the first case and to 1 in the second. These choices can make developing and emerging countries appear more unequal in comparison with developed countries, were the definition of income the same in both groups. To reestablish comparability, it would not be difficult for all the databases to provide estimates of income distribution indicators with both equivalence elasticities—something that is done in the SEDLAC database for Latin America. At the same time, it is not clear that economies of scale in consumption and therefore the equivalence scale should be the same across countries at different development levels.

Except where the reference unit is the individual, there is the further question of the weighting of observations—an issue that is often neglected, and not always documented. If we observe income at the household level, it does not follow that each household should be regarded as one unit regardless of size. Weighting is a separate issue from the choice of equivalence scale. The income of a household may be corrected by an equivalence scale that allows for economies of scale within the household but that does not mean that it should be weighted by the number of equivalent units. Weighting by the number of individuals may be judged more appropriate. This has, of course, the consequence that total income attributed to the multiperson households is greater.

3.3.3 Data Sources

Each source of data has strengths and weaknesses. Historically, evidence on income inequality, such as that used by Kuznets (1955), came from administrative records, of which the most important were the statistics derived from personal income taxation. The income tax data have serious limitations—the incomplete coverage of those below the tax threshold, the underreporting of income, and the impact of lawful tax avoidance and income shifting—which are discussed extensively in Chapters 7 to 9. They must therefore be used with caution. The same applies to the source that is now more widely used: household surveys.

In the case of household surveys, differences in survey questionnaires and in the methodology of correcting for nonresponse or missing observation reduce the comparability of inequality indicators. In his review of LIS, Ravallion (2014) emphasizes the issue of nonresponse and missing income data. Nonresponse by sampled households is in some cases handled by redrawing a comparable household in the same stratum, and in other cases by simply reweighting responding households. But there is a risk of a bias if nonresponse is relatively frequent and not random with regards to income. This bias is likely to be substantial if the very top of the distribution is simply not sampled, as it is often the case in developing countries—as shown by Korinek et al. (2006). The frequency of nonresponse might usefully be reported by statistical offices. The same applies to missing income values for responding households. In some cases, a value for total income or for an income component is imputed based on observed characteristics of households and household members. In others, no correction is made with the effect of the corresponding observation being taken out of the sample on which the income distribution is estimated. Again, in both cases, there is a clear problem if missing values are income-dependent.

3.3.4 Relation with National Accounts

Data from administrative records or from household surveys have to be viewed in relation to the national income accounts, which provide an important point of reference. Indeed, in the case of income tax data covering only part of the population, the national accounts are the standard source of the independent income control totals. In the case of household surveys, the issue may arise at the level of total household income, as has been extensively discussed in the literature on world income inequality—see Chapter 11. It may arise when some average income component in a survey appears to be relatively more underestimated in comparison with National Accounts than other components, provided that a full-fledged household account is available. In some cases, the statistical office scales up that income component so as to establish consistency with the National Accounts total. But where this is not distributed as total income, or where the discrepancy is due to underreporting as well as nonreporting, this may drastically modify most income distribution indicators. This kind of correction is now rarely done in advanced countries, but is still applied in some emerging countries, especially for property income, most often grossly underreported in household surveys. The database managed by the Economic Commission for Latin America and the Caribbean includes such an adjustment. In Chile, for instance, all income components in the CASEN survey (salaries, self-employment income, property income, transfers, and imputed rents) are scaled up (or down in the case of imputed rent) so as to match National Accounts. The only exception is for property income, for which the gap is imputed entirely to the top quintile of the distribution. As there are differences in the definition of income in surveys and in National Accounts, such a correction introduces additional noise in the distribution data that appear later in cross-country databases. Bourguignon (2014) indeed shows that the size of the adjustment may be substantial.

3.4 Implications of Data Heterogeneity

The consequences of the heterogeneity of income distributions indicators in cross-country databases for economic analysis and policy are important. In the first place, they make benchmarking across countries or time periods a fuzzy exercise. Not being able to check unambiguously that inequality has increased or decreased in a given country or to compare such an evolution to what has occurred in neighboring countries is a serious handicap for policy making and for the democratic debate in general. Relying on the most transparent and comparable measurement apparatus of income inequality is absolutely essential.

A second consequence of the imprecision and the lack of comparability of income distribution indicators is the weakening of standard econometric analyses of the consequences of income inequality. A noisy regressor introduces a bias in any regression. At the limit, if the noise is too big the estimated coefficient of that regressor goes to zero and income distribution is deemed unimportant in explaining, for instance, the pace of economic growth, political instability, or crime. Consider, for example, the widely cited study of Ostry et al. (2014), who test the influence of inequality and the extent of redistribution, as measured by the difference between the inequality of gross and net incomes, on growth. They find that "lower net inequality is robustly correlated with faster and more durable growth, for a given level of redistribution [and that] redistribution appears generally benign in terms of its impact on growth; only in extreme cases is there some evidence that it may have direct negative effects on growth. Thus, the combined direct and indirect effects of redistribution—including the growth effects of the resulting lower inequality—are on average pro-growth" (2014, p. 4). As the authors clearly recognize, these conclusions must be taken with care if one expects substantial measurement error in the difference between net and gross income inequality, and one should therefore look at the underlying source.[5] The study makes use of version 3.1 of the SWIID database created by Solt (2009). The SWIID data are indeed extensive, providing Gini coefficients for gross and net income for some 175 countries for years in the period 1960–2010. There are more than 4500 observations in the version 3.1 of the database. At the same time, many of these observations are imputed: many countries in the sample lack regular observation of both gross and net income inequality.[6] The author of the SWIID database is to be commended for providing the standard deviations of imputed values, but a two standard deviation range for the Gini coefficient in Bhutan, for example, in 2012 of 24–45% (from SWIID version 4.0) means that there is limited information content, as does the range for Malaysia in 2012 of 32–61%. This means in turn that users need to take account of the underlying data quality and that studies that fail to do so are open to question, as is emphasized by Solt (2009). (Version 4.0 of the SWIID is set up to facilitate the application of the multiple imputation approach to parameter estimation, and we understand that version 5.0 goes further in that direction.)[7]

Another consequence of the inconsistency of the income distribution indicators found in cross-country databases is the likely inaccuracy of global income distribution indicators, which cumulate the measurement errors to be found in national income distribution indicators. Global income inequality estimates are certainly extremely noisy, as suggested by the discussion in Chapter 11, although the imprecision of national income distribution indicators is only one part of the problem. The inequality between countries represents a high share of total global inequality so that another major source of ambiguity lies in the estimates of the mean income of national populations relatively to each other. In both cases, moreover, it is clear that big countries play a major role, whereas the

---

[5] Chapter 21 by Acemoglu et al. in this volume uses the same database on income inequality with two important differences. On the one hand, they use only net income inequality rather than the difference between net and gross, necessarily more imprecise. On the other hand, the inequality appears on the left-hand side of their regression equation so that measurement errors do not create estimation biases.

[6] SWIID provides estimates of redistribution in countries where the source data include at least three observations of net inequality and at least three observations of market inequality (and excludes some countries that meet this criterion but the two are not contemporaneous). Ostry et al. (2014) also provide estimates of the relationship among growth, inequality, and redistribution restricted to that sample.

[7] Such improvements in datasets are much to be welcomed. At the same time, they mean that we should revisit the conclusions drawn in studies based on earlier versions. It also underlines the importance of recording the version of the dataset used and of maintaining archives.

imprecision on the degree of inequality or the mean income within small countries has very little impact on global inequality. This is well illustrated in Chapter 11 where the difference in the rate of growth of the mean individual standard of living in India as reported in the household surveys and in National Accounts is shown to have a significant impact on trends in global inequality. More work is needed to evaluate the degree of imprecision of global inequality estimates due to these different causes—imprecision of national income distribution data, of national means, and of course purchasing power parity estimates—so as to estimate confidence intervals and being able to check whether or not estimated changes are significant. The same applies to global poverty measurement, in particular when it is defined on the basis of a common absolute poverty line.

3.5 The Way Forward

What is the way forward? How can we improve our ability to make international comparisons of distribution and distribution trends, whether for benchmarking, econometric analysis, or global distribution estimates? In comparing income distribution across countries and over time, one would ideally like to access microdata and compute the appropriate summary measures controlling for the definition of the income unit (household or individual), income (gross, net, consumption expenditures, including or not in kind transfers, imputed rents, . . .). But, of course, this would be a herculean task. Hence, there is an obvious need for a first treatment of the data done once for all by the database managers rather than by every user of the database. This requires that data be standardized, as much as possible, in agreement with some consensual definition of income and income units. The "Key Figures" on the LIS Web site obey that logic, while access to the original microdata (and to the STATA or SPSS programs that generate the Key Figures) allows users to depart from this core definition.

Progress in this direction can best be made by following the route of national accounts, with the analogue of the UN System of National Accounts being developed, building on the work of the Canberra Group on Household Income Statistics and on regional initiatives such as the European Union social indicators (Atkinson and Marlier, 2010). Guidelines could then be agreed for the assembly and analysis of distributional data. But in the case of income distribution analysis, a further step is necessary, since a key element is that of access to the microdata. What is required is the possibility for outsiders to access the microdata themselves, under conditions that guarantee confidentiality as in LIS. The same kind of architecture could be developed in other regions or possibly within an international institution like the World Bank. Such guidelines and agreed access to income distribution microdata would not however solve the data problems inherent to the unavoidable incompleteness of the surveys. Moreover, these problems, notably those of securing adequate response rates, may in the future become more severe. From that point of view, complementing standard survey-based analysis with administrative sources has proved to be extremely promising in the recent years.

A number of European countries have moved in this direction, with their EU-SILC data being collected in this manner (although this does raise issues of comparability with the data from countries that rely solely on household surveys). The use being made of the top income database based on tax data in developed countries is a sign of the importance of complementary data—see the discussion in Chapter 8. Combining both sources is not an easy task. The reference unit is not always the same, household in one case, tax unit in the other. Income concepts may differ across the two types of source. Moreover, it is not clear whether top income individuals are absent from household surveys—the nonresponse issue alluded to above—or whether they are present but with underreported income. The correction to be made to inequality indicators is not the same in the two cases—see Alvaredo and Londoño Velez (2013). More generally, the required adjustments may differ across countries.

In line with the discussion in Section 2, one may also wonder whether cross-country inequality databases should not go "beyond income" and incorporate other dimensions relevant to economic inequality. Without getting into the difficulty of measuring the inequality of capabilities or opportunities, some components of a broader definition of inequality can easily be measured, and the dimensions extended. This is the case, in particular, of inequality across gender. Such a database, based on Labour Force Surveys, does exist for OECD countries at the OECD and also for some emerging countries in LIS' "Key Figures." It should not be a major effort for most other primary databases relying on household or labor force surveys covering a larger set of countries to report summary statistics on gender earnings ratios. More generally, primary databases could try to go "beyond income" by reporting summary statistics on the joint distribution of income variables and other individual or household attributes available in standard surveys. Education, gender, and ethnicity are the most obvious examples.

Going beyond the exploitation of standard income focused surveys is problematic because relevant attributes are typically covered in different surveys. For instance, the Demographic and Health Surveys (DHS) in developing countries cover self-reported health status, fertility, infant mortality at the individual or household level. Yet, they do not collect direct information on monetary resources, so that nonincome functionings cannot be considered jointly with income. Matching techniques with household income or consumption surveys could be used to impute an income to households in the DHS but then it is difficult to deal with the inherent imprecision. On the other hand, there are numerous international databases that combine income inequality data with other dimensions of functionings. In the field of health, this was achieved by the Globalization-Health Nexus database put together by Cornia et al. (2008). The problem with these databases, however, is that the nonincome indicators are essentially aggregate so that those databases generally give no information on the inequality of the corresponding nonincome attributes, and, of course, still less on their joint distribution with other attributes, including income or earnings. From that point of view, generalizing and standardizing poverty surveys that include questions on various types of deprivation may be the simplest way of monitoring one aspect of "beyond income" inequality.

4. TAKING ECONOMIC THEORY SERIOUSLY

Data are one important ingredient in studying economic inequality; the second important ingredient is provided by economic theory, which underpins the search for explanations of inequality in Part III. Here again, we make a plea for taking seriously the building blocks that are utilized. One cannot simply take an economic model off the shelf and apply it in an unthinking way to the problem at hand. Likewise, theorists must keep an attentive eye on basic empirical facts and make sure their representation of the way multiple economic mechanisms combine to generate specific properties of the degree of inequality in an economy fits these facts. In what follows, we illustrate and discuss this twofold requirement for identifying the mechanisms that perpetuate or modify inequality by focusing on the role of technical progress, human capital, and wealth accumulation within a largely macroeconomic framework. As can be seen from Chapters 15 and 16, models that incorporate these particular mechanisms are indeed central in the present theoretical reflections on economic inequality, including the accent recently put on the top of the income and wealth distribution. Much of the recent reflection on the possible causes of the observed rise in inequality actually bears upon macroeconomic factors.

In this section, we focus on the determinants of market incomes: wages and capital incomes. These subjects, particularly wages, are covered extensively in other Handbooks, such as the *Handbook of Labour Economics*, and in designing this volume we have sought to avoid overlap. For the same reason, we have devoted more space to this aspect in this Introduction, as a contribution to bridge-building across fields of economics. We should also underline that while wages and the return to capital are important elements in determining the distribution of household income, their impact depends on a variety of social and institutional mechanisms, such as household formation and demographics, and on the redistributive incidence of public policy (see Section 5).

4.1 The Race Between Technology/Globalization and Education

In the Introduction to volume I, we set out the application of supply and demand analysis—perhaps the simplest of economic theories—to the explanation of rising earnings dispersion. Jan Tinbergen (1975) famously described a "race" between increased demand for educated workers and the expansion of the educated population. Where demand—driven by new technology or by globalization—outstrips supply, then the premium for education rises. As typically portrayed, as in Figure 3, the supply and demand equilibrium is shifting up over time. The wage premium for higher-educated workers is rising because technological progress is biased in their favor—the skill-bias technical change (SBTC) hypothesis—or because increased global competition favors more

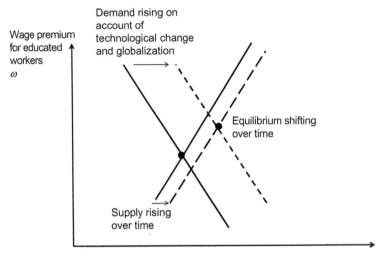

Figure 3 The "race" between technology/globalization and education.

educated workers. In what follows, we refer mainly to the SBTC hypothesis, but this does not mean that we discount the role of international trade.

First year economics appears to explain what is observed in the real world. However, second year economics teaches us that a race is a dynamic process and its outcome depends on how one specifies the underlying adjustments. Suppose, as seems reasonable, that at any moment, t, the ratio of higher-educated to basic-educated workers is fixed at $h(t)$ and that the relative wage, ω, clears the labor market. With aggregate output a function of the two kinds of labor, with a constant elasticity of substitution σ, the wage premium is determined by

$$\omega = A\left[\alpha_h/\alpha_b\right]^{(1-1/\sigma)} h^{-1/\sigma} \tag{1}$$

where A is a constant and α_i denotes the productivity of workers of type i (h for higher-educated and b for basic-educated). If over time skill-biased technical change (SBTC) raises the square bracket, and if (a condition that is often forgotten) the elasticity σ is greater than 1, then the wage premium rises for any given $h(t)$. In general, however, h will rise in response to the rising premium. If the growth rate of a variable x is denoted by $G(x)$, and the growth rate of the square bracket is a constant, g, then we can write

$$G(\omega) = (1 - (1/\sigma))g - (1/\sigma)G(h) \tag{2}$$

Suppose that the growth rate of h responds to the difference between the wage premium and the cost of acquiring education with an elasticity β; moreover, suppose that the cost of education, in terms of the wage of basic-educated workers, is equal to a fee, F, plus the cost of postponing earnings by T years, given by e^{rT}, where r is the annual cost of borrowing, i.e.,

$$G(h) = \beta\{\omega - F - e^{rT}\} \tag{3}$$

So that, combining (2) and (3)

$$G(\omega) = (1 - 1/\sigma)g - (1/\sigma)\beta\{\omega - F - e^{rT}\} \tag{4}$$

and for positive ω the relative wage converges to a value

$$\omega^* = F + e^{rT} + g(\sigma - 1)/\beta \tag{5}$$

From this, we can see that SBTC (and $\sigma > 1$) does not lead to an ever-increasing wage premium. The move to a new, constant, rate of technological progress leads to an increase in wage dispersion but we should not expect this to continue, since supply adjusts.

We have set out this theory for two reasons. The first is that, when looking at the data, we need to distinguish between a continuing upward trend and an upward shift in the degree of wage dispersion. If, empirically, wage dispersion has ceased to increase, this does not mean that SBTC (or globalization) has come to an end.[8] Indeed, from (5), we can see that g falling to zero would imply that the wage premium fell back to its earlier value. The second reason for the explicit model of dynamics is that economic theory is valuable because it points to other mechanisms that may be important. From (5), we can see immediately that the same forces—SBTC or globalization—can have differing effects in different countries depending on the speed of adjustment of supply (via β). This is one response to the challenge to the SBTC explanation made by Lemieux: "if technological change is the explanation for growing inequality, how can it be that other advanced economies subject to the same technological change do not experience an increase in inequality?" (2008, p. 23). A country where the labor market is more responsive will see a smaller increase in wage dispersion. From (5), we can also see that wage dispersion may increase on account of increases in the cost of education. Raising student fees leads, with these market responses, to a higher wage premium. Such a rise in wage dispersion does not however imply a rise in inequality—when viewed over the life time as a whole.

4.2 Steady States and Transitional Dynamics

This condensed presentation of the supply and demand model of wage inequality shows the power of theory. At the same time, it raises questions as to whether the available models actually capture what is being observed and provide a reasonable basis for projecting the future development and drawing policy implications. On the one hand, there is the issue of the relative strength of the various mechanisms simultaneously at play—e.g., biased technical change, educational choices, supply of skills, capital accumulation

---

[8] The model has been discussed in terms of technological change, but similar considerations apply where demand is shifting on account of globalization.

and allocation, etc. On the other hand, there is the issue of the time scale, which is a key aspect that we would like to highlight—both here and, later, when we discuss the distribution of wealth.

To be tractable, the analysis generally focuses on the steady-state or long-run equilibrium properties of these models, without necessarily mentioning how long the long run is. In Chapter 14, Vincenzo Quadrini and Victor Rios-Rull thus warn the reader that: "for simplicity of exposition, we limit the analysis here to steady-state comparisons with the caveat that in the real economy, the distribution will take a long time to converge to a new steady state." However, to bring theory to bear on the observed evolution of the distribution of income and on policy, tackling transitional phases is essential. In distributional analysis, the fact that accumulation of human and physical capital, the factors the most likely to modify the distribution of income, takes time at both the individual and the aggregate level means that it may take a long time for the economy to adjust to an exogenous shock. After all, if a shock modifies the incentive to get tertiary education, it will take around 40 years—or the duration of active life—before the full effect is felt, or in other words all workers in the labor force have faced the new trade-off between education and work. In between, many other things may change.

To illustrate this point, consider the dynamics of the preceding model in adjusting to a steady state, where again we focus on SBTC. This requires modeling with a little more detail the behavior of h, the ratio of the skilled, L_h, to the unskilled, L_b, labor force. Assume the population is stationary so that a proportion n of the labor force is exiting every year and an equal proportion is entering. For a stationary population, n would be the inverse of the duration of active life, roughly 2.5%. The important point is that most of the change in the skill structure of the labor force goes through its progressive renewal and modifying educational choices made by the entrants. More precisely, assume that the dynamics of the skill structure of the labor force is given by:

$$\Delta L_h = n\left[1 + \beta\left(\omega - F - e^{rT}\right)\right]L_h - nL_h$$

$$\Delta L_b = nL - n\left[1 + \beta\left(\omega - F - e^{rT}\right)\right]L_h - nL_b$$

where L is the total labor force $(L_h + L_b)$. In other words, the rate of growth of the skilled labor force depends on the net benefit from acquiring a skill from more schooling, whereas the growth of the unskilled labor force is driven by those entrants who have decided not to stay in school. Dividing these two equations respectively by L_h and L_b and subtracting the latter from the former yields:

$$G(h) = n(1 + h)\beta\left(\omega - F - e^{rT}\right) \tag{3'}$$

which is a slight modification of (3). Then the dynamics of the economy when skill-biased technical change (SBTC) takes place, and the productivity ratio (a_h/a_b) increases at the constant rate g, is given by (3') and:

$$G(\omega) = (1 - (1/\sigma))g - (1/\sigma)G(h) \qquad (2)$$

Note that, with this modification of the labor supply dynamics, no steady state exists in the (2)–(3′) model as long as g is strictly positive. Simulating this dynamic system with $\sigma = 1.2$, $h(0) = 3$, $n = 1/42$, $F = 1.9$, $r = 2.5\%$, $T = 4$, $\beta = 1$, and with no SBTC ($g = 0\%$) yields an initial steady state. Then, in year 1, the rate of SBTC rises to $g = 3\%$, and the economy evolves according to the trajectories shown in Figure 4 for the wage skill ratio or skill premium, ω, and for the size of the skilled labor force relatively to the number of unskilled workers, h. As before, the wage skill ratio rises, but—there being no steady state with positive g—it then falls back to the starting level.

Three features are of interest in Figure 4. The first is that, as expected, the wage skill ratio increases and then turns back down as the relative supply of skilled labor increases. Yet, this stabilization takes approximately 30 years to materialize. Even after 50 years, the curve has only just begun to turn down. The second feature is that the overall increase in the skill premium is rather modest, 3.1% in Figure 4. Such a limited increase is due of course to the labor supply response or the value of the elasticity β. Without such a response, the skill premium after 30 years of SBTC at the rate of 3% would have been 12% higher than initially. The third interesting feature in Figure 4 is the behavior of the skilled share of the labor force, which keeps increasing even when the wage skill premium has stabilized. In the presence of SBTC, such a persistent increase in the proportion of

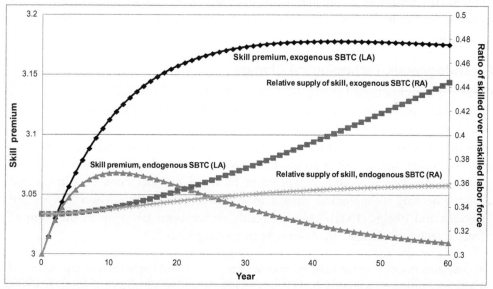

Figure 4 Skill-biased technical change: simulated trajectories of the skill premium and the relative supply of skilled labor with exogenous or endogenous rate of skill-biased technical progress. *Note: The skill premium is shown on the left-hand axis; the relative supply of skilled workers on the right-hand axis.*

skilled workers in the labor force is indeed needed to stabilize the wage skill premium and occurs because the long-run equilibrium premium is above the cost of acquiring a skill relatively to the unskilled wage level, unlike the case at the initial equilibrium.

Economic theory is thus important to understand switches from a long-run equilibrium to another but also the nonsteady-state behavior. In this respect, note that the transition modeled above depends on the way expectations are formed. Equation (3) and (3′) are implicitly based on static expectations about the skill premium. Rational expectations are somewhat irrelevant in the present framework as the cause of the increase in the skill premium is not necessarily known by economic agents. But adaptive expectations might yield another time path. Likewise, a stronger supply response, β, to a change in the skill premium makes the transition shorter, and the new long-run wage skill ratio smaller.

From the point of view of the inequality of earnings, Figure 4 shows that two forces are at play. On the one hand, the increase in the wage differential increases inequality in the sense that the Lorenz curve shifts outward. On the other hand, the fact that more people get skilled has an ambiguous effect on the distribution of earnings. As the average earnings increases, both low-skill and high-skill people lose relatively to the average—the bottom of the Lorenz curve shifts outward but the opposite occurs at the top. The relationship between these two ratios, ω and h, and the overall inequality as summarized by the Gini coefficient is discussed in Chapter 18. Note however, that this analysis refers to the distribution of earnings. Implications of the joint dynamics of technology and education for the inequality of income might be different because of various mechanisms including endogamy, joint labor force participation within couples or fertility differentials.

4.3 Endogenous Technological Change

To this point, technological change has been assumed to be exogenous, but the change in relative wages may induce a change in the degree of bias. In 1932, Sir John Hicks reasoned in his *The Theory of Wages* that "a change in the relative prices of the factors of production is itself a spur to invention, and to invention of a particular kind—directed to economizing the use of a factor that has become relatively expensive" (1932, pp. 124–125). This was later formalized in terms of the bias between capital- and labor-augmenting technological change by Kennedy (1964), Samuelson (1965), and Drandakis and Phelps (1965).[9] More recently, it has been taken up in the form of "directed technical change" by Acemoglu (for example, 2002).

---

[9] We may note that the induced technical progress literature identified the key role of the elasticity of substitution in determining the stability of the dynamic process governing the degree of bias: the condition for stability of the steady state in the model of Drandakis and Phelps (1965) is that the elasticity of substitution between capital and labor be less than 1. But the wage dispersion literature takes it for granted that the elasticity is greater than 1, which would be relevant if the same models were to be applied to the bias between skilled and unskilled workers.

Where technological progress is endogenous, this may substantially modify the trajectory of the economy. Following Acemoglu (2002), assume that the bias of technical progress is determined by the relative profitability of improving the productivity of the two factors of production. This profitability depends itself on two effects: a price effect, defined as the price of the technical bias—here the ratio $\omega/(a_h/a_b)$—and a market size effect according to which technical progress should favor the factor relatively the most abundant—i.e., the relative supply of skilled labor, h. Assuming that these two effects are multiplicative, and within the same CES framework as in (1), the relative profitability of investing in productivity gains of skilled labor thus depends on (Acemoglu, 2002, p. 790):

$$\frac{h\omega}{a_h/a_b} = A\left(\frac{a_h}{a_b}\right)^{-1/\sigma} h^{1-(1/\sigma)}$$

Then, the dynamics of the productivity differential can be specified as:

$$\Delta\left(\frac{a_h}{a_b}\right) = g \cdot \left(\frac{a_h}{a_b}\right) = \gamma\left[A\left(\frac{a_h}{a_b}\right)^{-1/\sigma} h^{1-(1/\sigma)} - c\right] \tag{6}$$

where c stands for the relative cost of developing technical progress in one factor in comparison with the other and γ is the response rate of actual technical change to the economic incentive.

Adding Equation (6) to the preceding model (2)–(3′) modifies substantially the dynamics of the skill premium and relative labor supply. In the simulation shown in Figure 4, c is chosen so that (6) is initially stationary. Then an exogenous drop in the cost parameter, c, in year 1 triggers SBTC, initially at a rate identical to the exogenous rate, g, in the previous simulation (the response rate, γ, is taken to be 1). If the new trajectory is initially similar to the one obtained before, a divergence occurs after a few years. The rate of growth of the skill premium declines and a turning point is reached after 10 years. Then the skill premium starts falling as SBTC attenuates due to the negative price effect. If the relative supply of skilled labor keeps increasing—because the skill premium keeps being above its initial value—its rate of growth is much smaller than in the previous simulation. Interestingly enough, the new steady state to which the economy is very slowly converging displays the same wage skill premium as initially, but a larger relative supply of skill. In other words, in the very long run the fact that the cost of improving the relative productivity of skilled workers has fallen simply resulted in an increase in relatively more people being skilled. In the short run, however, the skill premium moved up.

This analysis demonstrates the value of theory in understanding the mechanisms behind the evolution of a simple aggregate inequality indicator like the wage skill premium. It shows the need to consider transitional paths between equilibria, not just steady states, as well as the multiplicity of mechanisms influencing specific economic magnitudes to interpret their observed evolution.

4.4 Beyond Supply and Demand

The supply and demand story assumes that all agents act as price-takers: that we have perfect competition. As was observed by Michael Kalecki, "perfect competition—when its real nature, that of a handy model, is forgotten—becomes a dangerous myth" (1971, p. 3). In the real world, there are firms that have market power, as do collective organizations such as trade unions, and market power affects the operation of the labor market. The relative bargaining power of different actors determines the way in which economic rents are shared and hence the distribution of income. Power in turn is affected by the legal rights of workers, their representatives, and of employers. Such considerations turn the spotlight on governments, where the trend of recent decades has been to scale back the rights of workers, but also on employers. Where employers have market power, they can make choices regarding their employment practices, such as, for example, adopting the policy of paying "a living wage" or of limiting the range between top and bottom pay in their enterprise.

Bargaining power is not limited to firms and unions, as is shown by search and matching models of the labor market that involve individual workers and employers. Frictions in the labor market mean that, while *ex ante* competition may drive down the expected value of filling a job vacancy to the cost of its creation, *ex post* the matching of a worker to a vacancy creates a positive surplus. Without a positive surplus, no jobs are created. The worker offered a job has a degree of bargaining power, since if he or she rejects the job offer, the employer has to return to the pool with the risk that no match can be secured. The magnitude of the risk, and hence the worker's leverage, depends on the tightness of the overall labor market; the worker's leverage also depends on the cost of remaining unemployed. The impact on the distribution of earnings depends on how bargaining power varies across jobs, but the important point is that market forces, even in a globalized world, impose only upper and lower limits on differentials. This becomes particularly important when there are multiple possible market outcomes. Atkinson (2008) suggests a behavioral model of changing pay norms, where there is more than one locally stable equilibrium consistent with profit-maximizing behavior by employers. What has been observed in recent decades may be a shift from one equilibrium to another with much wider pay dispersion, particularly at the top.

There is therefore considerable scope for social institutions and social norms to influence the degree of pay dispersion, as is discussed in Chapters 18 and 19. In the latter, Förster and Tóth note that "while it is widely recognized that institutions matter as an important factor for identifying the multiple causes of inequality ... the weight attached to this factor in econometric studies has for a long time been limited" (p. 1801). As is stressed by Salverda and Checchi in Chapter 18, there is a pressing need to bring together the two rather separate literatures on supply/demand explanations and on institutions.

4.5 Bringing Back Capital

The SBTC explanation of rising wage dispersion focuses on the labor market, but—as the presence of the term e^{rT} in Equation (3) hints—we need to consider, not just the labor market, but also the capital market. Stated in terms of the aggregate production function, we have to consider not just $F(L_b, L_h)$, where L_b denotes basic-educated labor and L_h denotes higher-educated labor, but $F(K, L_b, L_h)$, where K is capital. We have to consider, not just the ratio of skilled to unskilled wages, but also the relative shares of wages and profits—the classical problem of distribution. Indeed, as in the classical analysis, we should extend the production function to include land and natural resources, N, giving output as $F(K, L_b, L_h, N)$.

The extension to three, or more, factors means that substitutability and complementarity becomes more complex, with richer potential outcomes for the distribution of income. The interesting possibilities include capital being a substitute for basic-educated workers but a complement to higher-educated workers. Such models, in the line of Krusell et al. (2000) are among those discussed in Chapter 14 by Quadrini and Rios-Rull. An alternative has been proposed by Summers in his Feldstein Lecture (2013). As Summers notes, capital can now be seen as playing two roles: not only directly via the first argument of the production function but also indirectly insofar as it supplants human labor through robotization. Denoting the first use of capital by K_1 and the second by K_2, the aggregate two-factor production function becomes $F(K_1, AL + BK_2)$, where A and B depend on the level of technology. The production function is such that capital is always employed in the first use, but may or may not be used to supplement labor. The condition under which robots, or other forms of automation, are used to replace human labor depends, as one would expect, on the relative costs of labor and capital. Where there is perfect competition, K_2 is zero where the ratio of the wage, w, to the rate of return, r, is less than A/B, and where K_2 is positive, then $w/r = A/B$. The ratio of the wage share to the capital share in the latter case is $(A/B)/(K/L)$ and falls with the capital–labor ratio.

We can therefore tell a story of macroeconomic development where initially the Solow model applies: the capital stock is below the level at which w/r exceeds A/B. In this context, a rising capital–labor ratio leads to rising wages and a falling rate of return. The capital share rises if and only if the elasticity of substitution between capital and labor is greater than 1 (about which there is debate—see Acemoglu and Robinson, 2014, footnote 12). Beyond a certain point, however, the wage/rate of return ratio reaches A/B, and K_2 begins to be positive. We then see further growth in the economy, as capital per head rises, but the wage/rate of return ratio remains unchanged. There is no longer any gain to wage-earners, since they are increasingly being replaced by robots/automation. What is more, the capital share rises, independently of the elasticity of substitution. It is as though the elasticity of substitution is increased discontinuously to infinity. In this way, the textbook Solow growth model can be modified in a simple way to highlight the central distributional dilemma: that the benefits from growth now increasingly accrue through rising profits. This outcome was indeed stressed some 50 years ago by James Meade in his *Efficiency, equality and the ownership of property* (1964), where he argued with considerable prescience that automation would lead to rising inequality.

4.6 The Distribution of Wealth

The distribution of wealth is the subject of the long-run studies in Chapter 7 by Roine and Waldenström and Chapter 15 by Piketty and Zucman. Both chapters show that the concentration of wealth was very high in the eighteenth to nineteenth centuries up until the First World War, dropped during the twentieth century, but has been rising again in the late twentieth and early twenty-first centuries. Chapter 15 shows that in France, the United Kingdom, and other countries, there has been a return of inheritance.

In Chapter 15, Piketty and Zucman begin by saying that

> to properly analyze the concentration of wealth and its implications, it is critical to study top wealth shares jointly with the macroeconomic wealth/income and inheritance/wealth ratios. In so doing, this chapter attempts to build bridges between income distribution and macroeconomics.

Building such a bridge is indeed one of our aims in this Introduction, and, with this in mind, we return to the question of the timescale for the macroeconomic magnitudes. Denoting aggregate capital by w_t, aggregate income by y_t, and their ratio by β_t, we have:

$$\beta_{t+1} = \frac{\beta_t + s_t}{1 + g_t} \tag{7}$$

where s_t and g_t are respectively the net saving rate and the growth rate of income at time t. Assuming that those two rates are constant, the steady-state equilibrium of the economy is given by $\beta^* = s/g$. With s equal to 10% and g equal to 3% per annum, the equilibrium capital–income ratio is 3.33. But, then, suppose that growth decelerates and the economy's constant growth rate falls to 2%. The economy will then converge toward a new equilibrium with a capital–income ratio equal now to 5. How long though will it take to get to this new equilibrium? As a matter of fact, the process described by (7) is quite slow. A simple simulation shows that, in going from 3.33 to 5, it will take almost 30 years for the capital–income ratio to reach 4, the double to reach 4.5 and more than a century to reach 4.8. As was shown many years ago by Ryuzo Sato (1963), the adjustment time in the neoclassical growth model can be extremely long.[10] With such a transitional phase, relying on the steady-state properties of a theoretical model may be misleading for economic or policy analysis, even with a horizon of a decade. The direction of changes expected at equilibrium

---

[10] As was pointed out by Sato (1966), the conclusions reached regarding convergence times are sensitive to the precise assumptions made concerning savings and technical change; the key issue is that transition path should be examined.

because of some exogenous modification or some policy changes is most likely to be felt along the whole transitional trajectory but their size might have to be substantially scaled down at the beginning of the transition. A tax on capital that reduces the saving rate by 1 percentage point, from 10% to 9%, for example, would lead to a drop in the steady-state capital–income ratio of 10%, but only 2.3% after 10 years and 4% after 20 years.

Let us now turn to the *distribution* of wealth. In that case, focusing on steady-states—or the golden rule—leads in some sense to the simple dismissal of distributional issues. Chapter 14 shows that any distribution of wealth combined with any distribution of work abilities is consistent with the steady-state equilibrium of the neoclassical model with dynastic agents, provided that aggregate wealth and aggregate effective labor satisfy some consistency relationship that involves the (common) rate of time preference of agents— the same kind of result holds trivially in endogenous growth models of the AK type, see Bertola et al. (2006, chapter 3). This is fine but possibly of limited practical relevance. Assume indeed that an economy initially at a steady state with a distribution D of wealth is then subject to some shock, for example, a technological shock or an income tax, that modifies its aggregate long-run equilibrium. Then, in moving toward this new equilibrium, the distribution D will change and, at the new equilibrium, there will be a new distribution D'. The fact that this new aggregate equilibrium may be supported by another distribution than D' is not the relevant point. What we are interested in is the change from D to D' and this is certainly not indeterminate. Likewise, the indeterminacy of distribution in a steady state does not mean that redistribution has no macroeconomic effect and no impact on the primary distribution of income. As long as redistribution cannot be lump sum, it will modify both the steady-state equilibrium and the distribution of primary and disposable income.

The models in Chapter 15 of the distribution of wealth are rather different and have different long-run properties. The treatment of time is again important. To be precise, let us take the unit of time as the lifetime (identical for all), with the present value of inherited wealth of individual i denoted by w_{it}. It is assumed that lifetime savings are a constant proportion of the aggregate of wealth and income:

$$w_{it+1} = S_{it}(w_{it} + y_{it}), \text{ with } y_{it} = y_{Lt} + Rw_{it} \tag{8}$$

where y_{Lt} is the lifetime labor income, assumed to be identical across individuals, R is the rate of return over the lifetime, and S_{it}, the individual saving rate defined on wealth plus lifetime income. S_{it} is assumed to be independently and identically randomly distributed around some mean value, S, across periods. Aggregating the accumulation equation over all individuals in a generation yields:

$$w_{t+1} = S(w_t + y_t), \text{ with } y_t = y_{Lt} + Rw_t \tag{9}$$

Combining (8) and (9) and assuming that the aggregate economy has converged to a steady state, it is shown in Chapter 15 that the dynamic behavior of the wealth of individual i, relatively to the mean wealth of the population, z_{it}, is given by the following multiplicative stochastic difference equation:

$$z_{it+1} = \frac{S_{it}}{S}[(1 - \varphi + \varphi z_{it}], \text{ with } \varphi = S\frac{1+R}{1+G} \tag{10}$$

where G is the rate of growth over a lifetime.[11] Under the condition that $\varphi < 1$, the steady-state stochastic distribution of z_{it} has a Pareto upper tail, with a Pareto coefficient that decreases with φ, where a smaller coefficient corresponds to greater concentration of wealth. Denoting the annual rate of interest by r and the annual rate of growth by g, and assuming a lifetime of H years, φ can be expressed as $Se^{(r-g)H}$. It follows that long-run wealth concentration increases with $r - g$; it is also clear that concentration increases with the savings rate, S. Both elements have a role to play.

Suppose, instead, that one adopts an *intragenerational* perspective, with the time unit as the year rather than a lifetime, and assumes that people save a proportion of their current income, s_{it}, drawn randomly from some distribution with expected value s. Then (8) and (9) are transformed into:

$$w_{it+1} = w_{it} + s_{it}(y_t + rw_{it}); w_{t+1} = w_t + s(y_t + rw_t) \tag{11}$$

where y_t is now the common annual wage income. Assuming a steady state with growth rate, g, and using the same kind of derivation as above, the stochastic difference equation (10) becomes[12]

$$z_{it+1} = z_{it}\left[\frac{1}{1+g} + \frac{s_{it}}{s}\frac{rs}{1+g}\right] + \frac{s_{it}}{s}\frac{g-rs}{1+g} \tag{12}$$

Under the assumption that $E(rs/(1+g))(s_{it}/s) + (1/(1+g)) < 1$ or $rs < g$, the distribution of z_{it} converges toward a steady-state distribution with a Pareto upper tail, with a

---

[11] The derivation of that equation goes as follows. At a steady state: $w_{t+1} = (1 + G)w_t$. From (8) and (9), it then follows that $z_{it+1} = (S_{it}/S)S((1+R)/(1+G))z_{it} + S_{it}(y_{Lt}/w_{t+1})$. But (9) implies at a steady state that: $w_{t+1} = S[y_{Lt} + (1+R)\cdot(w_{t+1}/1+G)]$. Then: $S(y_{Lt}/w_{t+1}) = 1 - S((1+R)/(1+G))$ and (10) follows.

[12] As before, at the steady state, $w_{t+1} = (1+g)w_t$. From (11), we obtain:

$$z_{it+1} = \frac{z_{it}}{1+g} + \frac{s_{it}}{s}\frac{rs}{1+g}z_{it} + \frac{s_{it}y_t}{w_{t+1}}. \tag{13}$$

Then, the second part of (11) becomes:

$$w_{t+1} = \frac{w_{t+1}}{1+g} + sr\frac{w_{t+1}}{1+g} + sy_t.$$

This implies:

$$\frac{y_t}{w_{t+1}} = \frac{g-rs}{s(1+g)}$$

and then plugging that expression back into (13) leads to (12).

Pareto coefficient that decreases, and a wealth concentration that increases, with $rs/(1+g)$. This refers to the distribution of current wealth, since there is a fresh drawing of s_{it} each period of life. (The independence assumption has therefore quite different implications.) In this model, it is the balance between rs and g that determines the long-run distribution, as in the early models of Meade (1964) and in the primogeniture version of Stiglitz (1969).[13]

Which model is the most appropriate? With the long horizon adopted to study the evolution of the distribution of income and wealth in Chapters 7 and 15, it would seem that the intergenerational framework is the most appropriate. It can also be argued that the assumption about randomness, with persistent lifetime good or bad luck, captures better our distributional concerns. Against this, it is the distribution of current wealth that is observed (as, for example, in Figure 1). It has, however, been shown by Benhabib, Bisin, and Zhu that when a model of lifetime wealth accumulation, with a realization fixed for any household during its lifetime, is embedded in a model of the current distribution of wealth, then "the power tail of the stationary distribution of wealth in the population is as thick as the thickest tail across the wealth distribution by age" (2011, p. 132). Put loosely, the upper tail of the current distribution tends to be dominated by the most unequal generation. But, it remains the case that the full effect of an increase in $r-g$ from today onward is bound to be observed only some generations from now. As a matter of fact, the inegalitarian effect that will be observed in the second or even third generation might be very limited and $r-g$ may change again in the distant future.

The conclusions that we draw are twofold. The first is that, as in the discussion of mobility in Chapter 10, it is necessary to consider both the intra- and the intergenerational dimensions, and that in both cases a better understanding of the transitional periods seems crucial. The second is that the evolution of the distribution of wealth depends on savings behavior, on the rate of return, and on the rate of growth. In this context, we should not forget that there were two arms to Kuznets (1955) Presidential Address, in which he sought to explain why inequality was at that time falling despite the existence of long-term forces leading to higher inequality. One arm was the theory of structural change that has come to characterize his approach, but the other was the concentration of savings in the upper income groups. This led him to conclude that "the basic factor militating against the rise in upper income shares that would be produced by the cumulative effects of concentration of savings, is the dynamism of a growing and free economic society" (1955, p. 11).

---

[13] It is $rs-g$ that formed the basis for the time-series analysis of the share of the top 1% of wealth-holding in Great Britain over the period 1923–1972 carried out by Atkinson and Harrison (1978, chapter 9). They showed the significance of two variables likely to influence the rate of accumulation (rs): the share price index and the rate of estate taxation.

5. THE ROLE OF POLICY

The role of policy is considered in many of the chapters, but this is the explicit focus of the final part of the Handbook.

5.1 Policy Objectives

Here, we should begin by observing that the past 15 years has seen a major change in the extent to which there has been official adoption of distributional objectives. This development is the culmination of a series of shifts in attitudes toward policy, notably with regard to the abolition of poverty. In Chapter 22, Martin Ravallion traces, with a broad geographical and historical sweep, the evolution of thinking on poverty and antipoverty policy.

The most evident manifestation of this change has been the adoption at a world level of the Millennium Development Goals (MDGs). The goals were ratified by world leaders in 2000 at the U.N. Millennium Assembly, and the first on the list was the halving between 1990 and 2015 of the proportion of people whose income was less than $1 a day (later $1.25 a day). At a national level, countries have adopted their own goals, such as the national social target for poverty reduction in Ireland aiming to reduce consistent poverty. In the United Kingdom, the Child Poverty Act 2010 requires the government to produce a poverty strategy every 3 years setting out actions to end child poverty. At a regional level, the European Union adopted in 2010, as part of the Europe 2020 program, the objective of reducing by 20 million the number of people in or at risk of poverty and social exclusion. These have been translated to varying degrees into national targets (Social Protection Committee, 2014).

It is not clear whether the same kind of change is occurring in the field of inequality reducing policies. Due to the rise in inequality, and possibly to the recent crisis, it is certainly the case that the public spotlight is focused on inequality and some announcements have been made by politicians that important measures would be taken to fight inequality. Yet, few explicit targets have been set and no ambitious measure has been taken or is being seriously considered in advanced countries that would make a major dent in the existing income inequality.

5.2 Impact of Policy to Date

What grounds are there then for optimism if one is concerned with present levels of economic inequality? Can we point to past experience where inequality has been reduced? The first obvious, but important, point is that inequality is not increasing everywhere. Globally, the recent past has been more encouraging, as is well summarized in Chapter 9 by Alvaredo and Gasparini:

The available evidence suggests that on average the levels of national income inequality in the developing world increased in the 1980s and 1990s, and declined in the 2000s. There was a remarkable fall in income poverty since the early 1980s, driven by the exceptional performance of China over the whole period, and the generalized improvement in living standards in all the regions of the developing world in the 2000s.

They caution that the decline in the 2000s was not universal: in 15% the fall was less than 2.5 percentage points, and in 20% of cases the Gini coefficient increased. The latter included two populous countries: China and Indonesia. The decline was most evident in Latin America, where they say

> *This remarkable decline appears to be driven by a large set of factors, including the improved macroeconomic conditions that fostered employment, the petering out of the unequalizing effects of the reforms in the 1990s, the expansion of coverage in basic education, stronger labour institutions, the recovery of some countries from severe unequalizing crises and a more progressive allocation of government spending, in particular monetary transfers.*

In other words, policy was relevant in influencing both market incomes and redistribution. In the case of Brazil, they conclude that the two major determinants were the decline in wage inequality, due to the expansion of the supply of educated workers and to the substantial increase in the minimum wage, and the expansion of cash transfers, notably the *Bolsa Família*. Despite this noticeable progress, however, it remains the case that Brazil, like most other countries in Latin America, is extremely unequal by world standards—with the exception of several countries in sub-Saharan Africa. The drop in inequality observed during the 2000s compensated for the increase that took place during the 1980s and part of the 1990s. Over the very long run, progress remains limited. Moreover, it must be kept in mind that top income earners are undersampled in the developing countries' household surveys so that it is not impossible that reported inequality figures miss the same increase at the top of the distribution as has been observed in many developed countries.[14]

Although lower than in Latin America, inequality is sizable in many emerging Asian countries and it is increasing. In discussing how far the policies pursued in several Latin American countries could be applied in an Asian context, Kanbur notes in Chapter 20 that

> *the additional expenditure on conditional cash transfers requires revenues, and the progressivity of the tax system is another major determinant of how globalization related increases in inequality can be mitigated. But progressivity is also important in addressing the rise in very high incomes the world over, especially in Asia. Asian tax systems do not generally score highly on progressivity. In fact, it is argued that raising progressivity of taxation would have a bigger impact on inequality than elsewhere in the world.*

---

[14] Alvaredo and Gasparini warn the reader in Chapter 9 that in the household surveys on which they are drawing there is substantial understatement of the top incomes. Cornia notes, in his analysis of recent distributive changes in Latin America, that "given the scarcity of information on capital incomes and the income of the 'working rich' in household surveys [it is not possible] to establish formally whether the distributive changes . . . concern also the top percentiles of the income distribution" (2014, p. 7).

What about the richer countries? In terms of reducing the inequality of market incomes, the standard policy response is educational expansion, as would be indicated by the supply and demand explanation for rising wage dispersion (as discussed in Section 4). The review of cross-country time series evidence by Förster and Tóth in Chapter 19 concludes that most evidence points to an equalizing impact of educational expansion:

> none of the studies covering the set of OECD/EU countries suggest a dis-equalising role of the growth in average educational attainment over the past three decades, but to the contrary, in their majority rather an equalising one. Human capital can be seen as a complement to technology. Increases in human capital and in the supply of skills are necessary to decrease and eventually reverse the pressure to higher inequality that stems from technological change.

The impact of labor market policy is reviewed in Chapter 18 by Salverda and Checchi who conclude that their empirical results

> are consistent with the main findings in the literature. . . . They confirm that the presence and stringency of a minimum wage reduces earnings inequality, also setting an (implicit) control on the distribution of working hours, which seems to be the main channel of inequality reduction of the bargaining activity of unions. Less common in the literature is the finding of a negative impact of both active and passive labour market policies.

The reason that the overall distributive effect of labor market regulations and institutions can be insignificant, as found by Förster and Tóth in their cross-country analysis, is that the employment and wage dispersion effects can operate in opposite directions.

When it comes to redistributive tax and transfer policy, Förster and Tóth conclude in Chapter 19 that:
- Policies are inequality reducing, but the effects vary across countries;
- Transfers are typically more effective than taxation;
- There has been a reduction in the redistributive effectiveness since the 1990s;
- Behavioral responses may offset but do not in general outweigh the first-round effects.

The last of these conclusions is particularly important. For understandable reasons, much of the analysis of public policy by economists in recent decades has focused on negative behavioral responses. Understandable, since the toolkit of economists is designed to illuminate these responses and the second-round effects are often missed in the public debate. At the same time, the analysis seems often to lose sight of the purpose for which transfers are paid. As put by Ive Marx, Brian Nolan and Javier Olivera in Chapter 23, "no advanced economy achieved a low level of inequality and/or relative income poverty with a low level of social spending, regardless of how well that country performed on other dimensions that matter for poverty, notably employment." The GINI project concluded that

> The best performers among the rich countries in terms of employment and economic and social cohesion have one thing in common: a large welfare state that invests in people, stimulating them and supporting them to be active and adequately protecting them when everything else fails. This continues to offer the best prospect for rich countries pursuing growth with equity.
> **Salverda et al. (2014, p. 349).**

But it is also clear, as these authors bring out, that it is not only the aggregate but also the design of spending that matters. It is for this reason that the construction of policy reforms has to be based on analysis of the contribution that they can make to distributive and efficiency objectives, and to this end an important development has been that of micro-simulation modeling, as surveyed in Chapter 24 by Francesco Figari, Alari Paulus and Holly Sutherland. These models build on the improvements in data availability described in Section 1—their construction requires access to microdata. They also require in-depth knowledge of the institutional details of public policy and how it operates in reality. As is discussed in Chapter 24, there is a considerable challenge in modeling noncompliance and—the less commonly discussed—other side of the coin, which is the non-take-up of benefits to which people are entitled. In melding microdata and institutional detail, the microsimulation models provide an important bridge between the theoretical analysis of policy design and the implementation of policy in the form of legislation and administration.

5.3 Prospects for Future Policy

Given their high level of inequality and the limited development of redistribution in many developing countries, the scope for progress in redistributive policies and in pre-redistribution opportunity equalizing policies is considerable. This is especially true in middle income or emerging countries where state capacity is sufficient to manage effective redistribution instruments.

What should make things easier for emerging countries' governments wishing to strengthen their redistribution system is, on the one hand, that they can learn from the experience of developed countries and, on the other hand, that modern technology permits better monitoring and control of individual incomes. Beyond some level of income, it is difficult today to function without a bank account and a credit/debit card, so that individual transactions are recorded. Approaching 50% of all households in Latin America hold a bank account and this proportion is rising so that the tax authority's capacity of auditing taxpayers suspected of underreporting their income is necessarily increasing. Yet, the income tax is severely underdeveloped in most emerging countries, where it represents most often less than 2% of GDP. Brazil is an exception but with an income tax amounting to 6% of GDP, it is still lower than the 9% average rate observed in OECD countries. Modern technology also makes easier the transfer of income to people at the bottom of the distribution. Smart payment cards in particular assist in avoiding suspicious leakages. There is therefore scope for extending redistribution and making use of policies in the field of education, social protection, minimum pensions, or minimum wage that are currently seldom used or at a very low scale despite their huge equalizing potential in most countries. As a result, the extent of redistribution in emerging countries, evaluated with the same microsimulation tools as described in Chapter 24, appears much smaller than in developed countries. For instance, the fall in the Gini coefficient when moving from market income—including replacement income like public or private pensions—to disposable income averages 3 percentage points in Latin American countries where such simulation has been performed (Lustig, 2014), whereas it oscillates around 10 percentage points for rich countries (Immervoll et al., 2009).

Of course, having the capacity to redistribute will lead to a substantial redistribution only if there is the political willingness to do so, or if the political system permits a majority to impose some redistribution, as could be expected in a democracy. In the empirical work undertaken in Chapter 21, Acemoglu et al. find that a transition to democracy indeed tends to raise the average tax rate in a country. Yet, no significant effect is found on income inequality as such. This may suggest that the political system is more complex than the mere distinction between democracies and nondemocracies would imply; or, as the authors note, may reflect the poorer quality of the income inequality data, an aspect we discussed in Section 3.

In contrast, OECD countries may be closer to their frontier in terms of the trade-off between less inequality and a higher degree of aggregate economic efficiency. The distance depends however on the institutional features of taxes and transfers—aspects to which economists have devoted too little attention (Atkinson, 1999)—and there may be scope for new and innovative ideas, as discussed in the final part of this section. The frontier itself may have been affected itself by the globalization process, its requirement for more competitiveness and, through factor mobility, its weakening of redistributive instruments like the progressivity of income taxation, including capital or capital income. At the same time, the same forces of globalization may have increased the need for social protection, just as they did in the early days of the welfare state toward the end of the nineteenth century. Today, as then, the extent to which redistribution takes place depends on the political context. It may also be the case that the perception of inequality in the society today may not coincide with the evolution of inequality as measured by statisticians and economists. In the United States, for instance, the feeling that income mobility matters more than income inequality and the (unfounded) belief that income mobility is and remains high in comparison with other countries may make the public opinion insensitive to the mounting objective income and wealth inequality. Clearly, this cannot continue forever. At some stage, beliefs will change and it is not unlikely that this process is under way—as McCall (2013) seems to detect in the changing discourse on inequality in the U.S. media.

5.4 Thinking Outside the Box

At the beginning of this Introduction, we evoked the increasing attention being paid by policymakers to rising income inequality. To date, the response in terms of policy proposals has been along conventional lines, notably investment in education and reform of redistribution. In our view, these are important, but if progress is to be made, then we

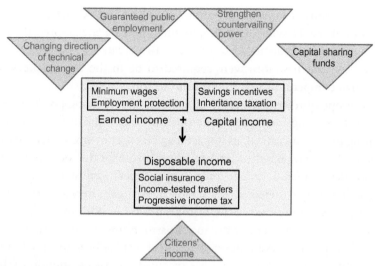

Figure 5 Thinking outside the box.

need to think outside of the box. We must consider ideas that—while far from new—are not on the current policy agenda.

The standard labor market policies—shown inside the box in Figure 5—clearly have a major role to play, and there have been moves to strengthen minimum wages, in order to reduce wage dispersion. As we have noted, however, central is the conjunction of wages and employment, and the latter has proved a hard nut to crack. In our view, one of the crucial elements is the direction of technical progress. Rather than concentrating on factor-augmentation, as in much of the literature, our discussion in Section 4.3 suggests that we should instead focus on the interaction between labor and capital, and specifically the supplantation of labor by capital. Given that much of the innovation is funded directly by public bodies, or subsidized through tax or other concessions, it would be possible to influence this trade-off. This is the first of the "out of the box" alternatives shown in Figure 5. The second concerns public employment. The fact that the present-day market economy does not deliver full employment suggests that we should learn from policy responses in other cases of market failure, notably in financial markets. Here, the government has intervened as a lender of last resort, and the obvious parallel is that the government should act as the employer of last resort. The state should guarantee to everyone seeking it employment at the minimum wage. Such a proposal may seem to some readers outlandish and infeasible on fiscal grounds, but to others it may appear no more outlandish or fiscally irresponsible than the policy that financial institutions are too big to fail. After all, such policies have already been pursued. It is an initiative of this type which was taken by the Indian government when it launched the Mahatma Gandhi National Rural Employment Guarantee Act in 2005. Public employment has formed part of active labor market programs in a number of countries. In the United States, it was authorized under the Humphrey–Hawkins Full Employment and Balanced Growth Act of 1978, which allowed the Federal Government to create a "reservoir of public employment," where these jobs were required to be in the lower ranges of skill and pay to minimize competition with the private sector.

The third proposal refers back to the discussion of bargaining power in Section 4.4. To the extent that rising inequality is the outcome of a shift in the balance of market power favoring profits and capital, its impact may be offset by strengthening the counter-vailing powers. This may take the form of a stronger role for the social partners, or it may involve more determined action to protect consumers against monopolistic pricing. Again such actions may be rejected as too radical, but again they are not so far removed from current policy. In the case of the European Union, both the promotion of com-petition and the encouragement of the social partners are already accepted objectives.

The fourth proposal draws attention to an aspect that has been missing from the policy arena—the capital market—but which has received increasing attention following the debate surrounding Piketty (2014). For macroeconomic reasons outlined in Section 4.6, and given the return of inherited capital in a number of richer countries, capital income is potentially of increasing significance, as it was in the past. The particular proposal is indeed far from new. It goes back at least to the eighteenth century English-man/Frenchman/American Thomas Paine, who in 1797 in his *Agrarian Justice* proposed:[15]

> To create a national fund, out of which there shall be paid to every person, when arrived at the age of twenty-one years, the sum of fifteen pounds sterling, as a compensation in part, for the loss of his or her natural inheritance, by the introduction of the system of landed property.

The proposal of Paine for a capital element payable on reaching the age of majority has its modern counterpart in various schemes for asset-based egalitarianism (as proposed, for example, by Ackerman and Alstott, 1999). The creation of a sovereign wealth fund, as already well established in a number of countries, would offer the possibility of a minimum inheritance for all.

The fifth proposal—which also has shades of Paine—is for a citizen's income, or the payment of a guaranteed minimum income to all individuals. Such an income is some-times described as "unconditional"; however, conditions are naturally attached. As described in Figure 5, a condition would be that of citizenship. An alternative, advocated in Atkinson (1995, 1996) is that of a *participation income*, paid not on the basis of citizenship but of participation in the society in question, through employment, past employment (on retirement), caring for dependants, being available for work when unemployed, in

---

[15] The text can be downloaded from the Official Web site of the U.S. Social Security Administration. The Web site carries the caution: "this is an archival or historical document and may not reflect current policies or procedures."

approved education or training, and with appropriate provisions for those who are sick, injured, or disabled. The participation income would represent a radical departure from the targeted income-tested transfers that have been the preoccupation of policymakers in recent decades. It would be individual-based, rather than involving a family means-test. It would recognize the fluidity of the employment relationship in the twenty-first century labor market.

No doubt there will be many objections to these final policy proposals, but we hope that the chapters contained in volume II of the Handbook will stimulate new ideas in this important field.

ACKNOWLEDGMENTS

In writing this Introduction, we have drawn heavily on the Handbook chapters. This will be evident from the frequency of cross-references, although we have tried to stop short of the point at which such references become tedious to the reader. We are most grateful to Rolf Aaberge, Facundo Alvaredo, Andrew Berg, Andrea Brandolini, Daniele Checchi, Pierre-André Chiappori, Andrew Clark, Koen Decancq, Jean-Yves Duclos, Francesco Figari, Michael Förster, Marc Fleurbaey, Stephen Jenkins, Salvatore Morelli, Dominique Meurs, Brian Nolan, Jonathan Ostry, Alari Paulus, Sophie Ponthieux, Thomas Piketty, Victor Rios-Rull, Wiemer Salverda, Tim Smeeding, Frederick Solt, Holly Sutherland, István Tóth, Alain Trannoy, and Daniel Waldenström for their very helpful comments on the draft of the Introduction, but none of them should be held responsible in any way for its contents. We thank Maarit Kivilo for her help with the bibliography. Atkinson's research for the Introduction was carried out as part of the EMoD program supported by INET at the Oxford Martin School.

REFERENCES

Acemoglu, D., 2002. Directed technical change. Rev. Econ. Stud. 69 (4), 781–809.

Acemoglu, D., Robinson, J.A., 2014. The Rise and Fall of General Laws of Capitalism. working paper, Cambridge, MA. http://economics.mit.edu/files/9834.

Ackerman, B., Alstott, A., 1999. The Stakeholder Society. Yale University Press, New Haven.

Alkire, S., Foster, J., 2010. Designing the Inequality-Adjusted Human Development Index (HDI): OPHI Working Paper 37. University of Oxford.

Alkire, S., Foster, J., 2011. Counting and multidimensional poverty measurement. J. Public Econ. 95 (7–8), 476–487.

Allison, R.A., Foster, J., 2004. Measuring health inequality using qualitative data. J. Health Econ. 23 (3), 505–524.

Alvaredo, F., Londoño Velez, J., 2013. High Incomes and Personal Taxation in a Developing Economy: Colombia 1993-2010: Center for Equity, Working Paper No. 12. Tulane University.

Anand, P., Santos, C., Smith, R., 2007. The Measurement of Capabilities: Discussion Paper 67. The Open University.

Atkinson, A.B., 1970. On the measurement of inequality. J. Econ. Theory 2, 244–263.

Atkinson, A.B., 1995. Beveridge, the national minimum and its future in a European context. In: Atkinson, A.B. (Ed.), Incomes and the Welfare State. Cambridge University Press, Cambridge, pp. 290–304.

Atkinson, A.B., 1996. The case for a participation income. Polit. Q. 67 (1), 67–70.

Atkinson, A.B., 1999. The Economic Consequences of Rolling Back the Welfare State. MIT Press, Cambridge, MA.

Atkinson, A.B., 2008. The Changing Distribution of Earnings in OECD Countries. Oxford University Press, Oxford.

Atkinson, A.B., Bourguignon, F., 1982. The comparison of multi-dimensioned distributions of economic status. Rev. Econ. Stud. 49 (2), 183–201.

Atkinson, A.B., Bourguignon, F., 2000. Income distribution and economics. In: Atkinson, A.B., Bourguignon, F. (Eds.), Handbook of Income Distribution, vol. 1. Elsevier, Amsterdam.

Atkinson, A.B., Brandolini, A., 2001. Promise and pitfalls in the use of "secondary" data-sets: income inequality in OECD countries as a case study. J. Econ. Lit. 34 (3), 771–799.

Atkinson, A.B., Harrison, A.J., 1978. Distribution of Personal Wealth in Britain. Cambridge University Press, Cambridge.

Atkinson, A.B., Marlier, E., 2010. Indicators of poverty and social exclusion in a global context. J. Policy Anal. Manage. 29 (2), 285–304.

Atkinson, A.B., Morelli, S., 2014. Chartbook of Economic Inequality: Economic Inequality Over the Long Run. INET Oxford. http://www.chartbookofeconomicinequality.com/.

Atkinson, A.B., Casarico, A., Voitchovsky, S., forthcoming. Top incomes and the glass ceiling. Working Paper, INET Oxford.

Becchetti, L., Massari, R., Naticchioni, P., 2011. The Drivers of Happiness Inequality: Suggestions for Promoting Social Cohesion: Working Papers 2011-06. Universita' di Cassino.

Benhabib, J., Bisin, A., Zhu, S., 2011. The distribution of wealth and fiscal policy in economies with finitely lived agents. Econometrica 79 (1), 123–157.

Bertola, G., Foellmi, R., Zweimuller, J., 2006. Income Distribution in Macroeconomic Models. Princeton University Press, Princeton.

Bourguignon, F., 2014. Appraising income inequality databases in Latin America. mimeo, J. Econ. Inequal. (forthcoming).

Bourguignon, F., 2013. La mondialisation de l'inégalité. Le Seuil, Paris (Expanded English version, The Globalization of Inequality, forthcoming, Princeton University Press).

Brunori, P., Ferreira, F., Peragine, V., 2013. Inequality of Opportunity, Income Inequality and Economic Mobility: Some International Comparisons: IZA Discussion Paper 7155. Institute for the Study of Labor (IZA).

Budd, E.C., 1970. Postwar changes in the size distribution of income in the US. Am. Econ. Rev. Pap. Proc. 60, 247–260.

Canada, Statistics, 2013. High-Income Trends Among Canadian Taxfilers, 1982 to 2010, Release January 28, 2013.

Clark, A., Flèche, S., Senik, C., 2012. The Great Happiness Moderation: IZA Discussion Paper 6761. Institute for the Study of Labor (IZA).

Cornia, G.A. (Ed.), 2014. Falling Inequality in Latin America: Policy Changes and Lessons. Oxford University Press, Oxford.

Cornia, A., Rosignoli, S., Tiberti, L., 2008. Globalization and Health Impact Pathways and Recent Evidence: Research Paper No. 2008/74. UNU-WIDER, Helsinki.

Dalton, H., 1920. The measurement of the inequality of incomes. Econ. J. 30 (119), 348–461.

Decancq, K., Fleurbaey, M., Maniquet, F., 2014. Multidimensional Poverty Measurement with Individual Preferences: Princeton University William S. Dietrich II Economic Theory Center Research Paper 058. Princeton University.

Deininger, K., Squire, L., 1996. A new data set measuring income inequality. World Bank Econ. Rev. 10 (3), 565–591.

Drandakis, E., Phelps, E.S., 1965. A model of induced invention, growth and distribution. Econ. J. 76 (304), 823–840.

Duclos, J.-Y., Echevin, D., 2011. Health and income: a robust comparison of Canada and the US. J. Health Econ. 30, 293–302.

Duclos, J.-Y., Sahn, D.E., Younger, S.D., 2011. Partial multidimensional inequality orderings. J. Public Econ. 98, 225–238.

Dutta, I., Foster, J., 2013. Inequality of happiness in the US: 1972–2010. Rev. Income Wealth 59 (3), 393–415.

Ferreira, F., Lustig, N. (Eds.), 2015. International databases on inequality. Special issue of the J. Econ. Inequal., forthcoming.

Fisher, G., 1986. Estimates of the Poverty Population Under the Current Official Definition for Years Before 1959. Office of the Assistant Secretary for Planning and Evaluation, U.S. Department of Health and Human Services (Mimeograph).

Fleurbaey, M., Blanchet, D., 2013. Beyond GDP: Measuring Welfare and Assessing Sustainability. Oxford University Press, Oxford.

Foster, J., Lopez-Calva, L., Szekely, M., 2005. Measuring the distribution of human development: methodology and an application to Mexico. J. Hum. Dev. 6 (1), 5–29.

Hicks, J.R., 1932. The Theory of Wages. Macmillan, London.

Immervoll, H., Levy, H., Nogueira, J.R., O'Donoghue, D., Bezera de Siqueira, R., 2009. The impact of Brazil's tax and benefit system on inequality and poverty. In: Klasen, S., Nowak-Lehmann, F. (Eds.), Poverty, Inequality and Policy in Latin America. In: CES-Ifo Seminar Series, The MIT Press, Cambridge, MA, pp. 271–302.

Jenkins, S., 2014. World Income Inequality Database: an assessment, mimeo. Final version forthcoming in J. Econ. Inequal.

Kalecki, M., 1971. Selected Essays on the Dynamics of the Capitalist Economy 1933-1970. Cambridge University Press, Cambridge.

Karoly, L., 1992. The Trend in Inequality Among Families, Individuals, and Workers in the United States: A Twenty-Five-Year Perspective. Rand, Santa Monica.

Kennedy, C., 1964. Induced bias in innovation and the theory of distribution. Econ. J. 74 (295), 541–547.

Kolm, S.-Ch, 1966. The optimal production of justice. In: Guitton, H., Margolis, J. (Eds.), Public Economics. Proceedings of an IEA conference held in Biarritz, published (1969). Macmillan, London, pp. 145–200.

Kolm, S.-Ch., 1971. Justice et équité. Cepremap, Paris (English translation, Justice and Equity, MIT Press, 1988).

Kolm, S.-Ch., 1977. Multi-dimensional Egalitarianism. Q. J. Econ. 91 (1), 1–13.

Kopczuk, W., Saez, E., 2004. Top wealth shares in the US, 1916-2000: evidence from the Estate Tax returns. Natl. Tax J. 57, 445–487 (longer version in NBER Working Paper 10399).

Korinek, A., Mistiaen, J., Ravallion, M., 2006. Survey nonresponse and the distribution of income. J. Econ. Inequal. 4 (1), 33–55.

Krusell, P., Ohanian, L., Rios-Rull, V., Violante, G., 2000. Capital skill complementarity and inequality: a macroeconomic analysis. Econometrica 68 (5), 1029–1053.

Kuznets, S., 1955. Economic growth and income inequality. Am. Econ. Rev. 45 (1), 1–28.

Lemieux, T., 2008. The changing nature of wage inequality. J. Popul. Econ. 21 (1), 21–48.

Lustig, N., 2014. Taxes, Transfers, Inequality and the Poor in the Developing World, Presentation at the USAID, Washington, DC, May 15, 2014.

Maasoumi, E., 1986. The measurement and decomposition of multi-dimensional inequality. Econometrica 54 (4), 991–997.

McCall, L., 2013. The Undeserving Rich: American Beliefs About Inequality, Opportunity, and Redistribution. Cambridge University Press, Cambridge.

Meade, J.E., 1964. Efficiency, Equality and the Ownership of Property. Allen and Unwin, London.

Milanovic, B., 2013. All the Ginis You Ever Wanted. World Bank website, http://econ.worldbank.org/WBSITE/EXTERNAL/EXTDEC/EXTRESEARCH/0,contentMDK:22301380~pagePK:64214825~piPK:64214943~theSitePK:469382,00.html.

Moretti, E., 2013. Real wage inequality. Am. Econ. J. Appl. Econ. 5, 65–103.

Nolan, B., Salverda, W., Checchi, D., Marx, I., McKnight, A., Tóth, I., van de Werfhorst, H. (Eds.), 2014. Changing Inequalities and Societal Impacts in Rich Countries. Oxford University Press, Oxford.

OECD, 2014. All on Board: Making Inclusive Growth Happen. OECD, Paris.

Ostry, J., Berg, A., Tsangarides, C.G., 2014. Redistribution, Inequality, and Growth: IMF Discussion Note, SDN 14/02. International Monetary Fund, Washington, D.C.

Ovaska, T., Takashima, R., 2010. Does a rising tide lift all the boats? Explaining the national inequality of happiness. J. Econ. Issues 44 (1), 205–224.

Paine, T., 1797. Agrarian Justice, Printed by W. Adlard, Paris. Reprinted and sold by J. Adlard and J. Parsons, London.

Pigou, A.C., 1920. The Economics of Welfare. Macmillan and Co., London.

Piketty, T., 2001. Les hauts revenus en France. Grasset, Paris.

Piketty, T., 2014. Capital in the 21st Century. Harvard University Press, Cambridge, MA.

Piketty, T., Saez, E., 2003. Income inequality in the United States, 1913–1998. Q. J. Econ. 118, 1–39.

Ravallion, M., 2014. The Luxembourg Income Study. J. Econ. Inequal. (forthcoming).

Roemer, J., 1998. The Equality of Opportunities. Harvard University Press, Cambridge.

Salverda, W., Nolan, B., Checchi, D., Marx, I., McKnight, A., Tóth, I., van de Werfhorst, H. (Eds.), 2014. Changing Inequalities in Rich Countries. Oxford University Press, Oxford.

Samuelson, P.A., 1965. A theory of induced innovations along Kennedy-Weizsäcker lines. Rev. Econ. Stat. 47 (4), 444–464.

Sato, R., 1963. Fiscal policy in a neo-classical growth model: an analysis of the time required for equilibrating adjustment. Rev. Econ. Stud. 30 (1), 16–23.

Sato, K., 1966. On the adjustment time in neo-classical models. Rev. Econ. Stud. 33 (3), 263–268.

Schwabish, J.A., 2014. An economist's guide to visualizing data. J. Econ. Perspect. 28 (1), 209–234.

Sen, A., 1973. On Economic Inequality. Clarendon Press, Oxford (Expanded edition with a substantial annexe by James Foster and Amartya Sen, Oxford University Press, 1997).

Sen, A., 1976. Real national income. Rev. Econ. Stud. 43 (1), 19–39.

Sen, A., 1980. Equality of what? In: McMurrin, S. (Ed.), Tanner Lectures on Human Values, vol. 1. Cambridge University Press, Cambridge, pp. 195–220.

Sen, A., Stiglitz, J., Fitoussi, J.-P., 2010. Mismeasuring Our Lives: Why GDP Doesn't Add Up. The New Press, New York.

Social Protection Committee, 2014. Social Europe—Many Ways, One Objective. Publications Office of the European Union, Luxembourg.

Solt, F., 2009. Standardizing the World Income Inequality Database. Soc. Sci. Q. 90 (2), 231–242.

Stevenson, B., Wolfers, J., 2008. Happiness inequality in the US. J. Leg. Stud. 37, 33–79.

Stiglitz, J.E., 1969. Distribution of income and wealth among individuals. Econometrica 37 (3), 382–397.

Stiglitz, J., 2012. The Price of Inequality. W. W. Norton & Company, New York.

Summers, L., 2013. Economic possibilities for our children, pp. 1–13, The 2013 Martin Feldstein Lecture. NBER Reporter, No. 4.

Tinbergen, J., 1975. Income Distribution: Analysis and Policies. North-Holland, Amsterdam.

United Nations Economic Commission for Europe, 2011. Canberra Group Handbook on Household Income Statistics, 2nd edition. United Nations, New York and Geneva.

Veenhoven, R., 2005. Return of inequality in modern society? Test by dispersion of life-satisfaction across time and nations. J. Happiness Stud. 6, 457–487.

ACKNOWLEDGMENTS

First, we would like to thank Ken Arrow and Mike Intriligator for having persuaded us back in 2010 that the time was ripe for a new volume. How prescient their advice was!

In the course of preparing the new Handbook volume, we have incurred many debts. Without the—more than 50—authors, there would be no Handbook, and we would like to thank them sincerely for the cooperative spirit in which they have produced such excellent chapters. We much appreciate the way in which they responded to several rounds of comments from the editors and (usually) met deadlines. Part of preparation took the form of an Author's conference, entitled "Recent Advances in the Economics of Income Distribution" that was held on April 4–7, 2013 at the Paris School of Economics. We are most grateful for the support that was provided to this conference by the Agence National de la Recherche (Projet INDURA INEG 2011), Cornell University, the UK Economic and Social Research Council and DFID (Grant ES/1033114/1), Ouvrir la science économique (Opening Economics), and the Paris School of Economics.

Throughout all this, a key organizing role has been played by Véronique Guillotin of the Paris School of Economics, and we thank her most warmly.

Tony Atkinson
François Bourguignon

PART III

Explanations

CHAPTER 14

Inequality in Macroeconomics

Vincenzo Quadrini*, José-Víctor Ríos-Rull[†]
*University of Southern California, CEPR, Los Angeles, CA, USA
[†]University of Minnesota, Federal Reserve Bank of Minneapolis, CAERP, CEPR, NBER, Minneapolis, MN, USA

Contents

Handbook of Income Distribution, Volume 2B
ISSN 1574-0056, http://dx.doi.org/10.1016/B978-0-444-59429-7.00015-7

Abstract

We revise some of the main ways in which the study of aggregate performance of an economy overlaps with the study of inequality.

Keywords

Macromodels of inequality, Inequality dynamics, Inequality and financial markets, Political economy of inequality

JEL Classification Codes

E2, D31, B22

In a handbook devoted to income distribution, a chapter devoted to macroeconomics should start by clarifying the role of macroeconomics. Two of the main concerns about macroeconomics are aggregation and general equilibrium. The first ensures that the various sections of the economy aggregate, that is, by adding the incomes, wealth, and other variables of all households, we obtain the economywide value of these variables. The second macroeconomic concern is general equilibrium, that is, how changes in any section of the economy propagate to other sections of the economy via implied adjustments in prices and tax rates that are necessary to clear markets and balance the government's budget constraint. Although a large body of macroeconomic research abstracts from distributional considerations among individuals and households, a significant strand of studies are also concerned about the interaction between distribution and aggregate outcomes. In this chapter we will explore the possible interactions between distribution and the aggregate dynamics of the economy.

Since Bertola (2000) (the macroeconomics chapter in Volume 1 of this handbook series), many changes have taken place in the way macroeconomists deal with income inequality. One important change is that interest has shifted away from the study of the relation between inequality and long-term growth and has focused more on other aspects of macroeconomic performance. Perhaps the main reason for this change is that, in general, there is less concern about long-term growth. Now, the more popular view is that all advanced economies grow by about 2% annually. The main question is, what does it take for less-developed countries to accelerate the process of development and join the group of rich countries? As a result of these changes, macroeconomists have two main concerns with regard to inequality. One is what determines the joint distribution of earnings (or labor income) and wealth, and the other is how the explicit account of empirically sound inequality shapes the answers to the standard questions in macroeconomics. The models typically used feature a large number of agents that differ in earnings, wealth, and, in some cases, other characteristics. Consequently, we find it convenient to separate the two main branches of macroeconomic studies in this vein: the branch primarily interested in understanding the sources or causes of inequality and the branch concerned with the consequences of inequality for the aggregate performance of the economy. Such a distinction is not always applicable, yet it provides a natural organization of the literature. We will also find it occasionally convenient to separate studies that are primarily interested in economic growth from those focusing on business cycles.

The outline of the chapter is as follows. We start in Section 14.1 with some facts on the U.S. income and wealth distribution that are relevant from a macroeconomic point of view. We look at both cross-sectional evidence and the changes observed in the last few decades. Although some of these facts are analyzed in more detail in other chapters of this handbook (for example, Chapters 7–9), it will be useful to summarize them here as they are the reference for some of the theories we will review in this chapter.

After summarizing the main empirical facts about the income and wealth distribution, we take a look in Section 14.2 at how macroeconomists make sense of these facts. First, we show how the distribution of wealth is determined given an exogenous process for earnings. After reviewing the models used by macroeconomists to examine this question and their success in replicating the wealth distribution observed in the data, we turn to models of endogenous determination of earnings. We look at models of human capital investment to determine why some people are more successful than others, in the sense of earning higher labor incomes. Thus, we will look at earnings inequality not as a purely stochastic process (luck) but as an outcome of different mechanisms such as investment in human capital (for example, education) or the higher relative demand of certain skills (affecting the relative prices of certain skills compared with other skills). The section concludes with a look at how occupational choices can also determine labor earnings. This section is concerned with inequality as a permanent or steady-state phenomenon, and the occupational choice part is informed by the bad employment performance of the Great Recession, which includes business-cycle aspects.

Next we turn to the dynamics of inequality. Section 14.3 studies how inequality may change both over the business cycle and over a longer horizon. Here we consider a simple model in which factor shares—of capital and labor—can change.

Section 14.4 deals with what is possibly one of the most exciting ways in which macroeconomics and inequality interact: the role of financial markets or, more specifically, financial frictions. We start by looking at how the ability to borrow shapes the income and wealth distribution (and the allocation efficiency) by reallocating investment funds to entrepreneurs that are efficient and reliable, but not always both. We then turn to how wealth inequality is shaped by borrowing ability even when the rate of return of savings is equated across households. First, we look at how the sheer ability to borrow shapes inequality, and then we consider endogenous theories of borrowing where financial frictions arise from the institutional environment. We also look at various extensions of these ideas where the frictions are endogenous. In addition to exploring the effects of financial frictions on inequality, we look at the long-term effects on the performance of the economy, including some issues that have become of concern to macroeconomists, such as implications for global imbalances.

In Section 14.5 we analyze how the political system interacts with inequality to yield different policies that have an impact on the aggregate performance of the economy. People have different views about the desirability of alternative economic policies that depend on the position of individuals in the economywide distribution of income. The aggregation of individual preferences leads to the choice of particular policies. As the distribution of income changes, so does the choice of policies, which in turn affect the aggregate performance of the economy.

Section 14.6 concludes the chapter with a global assessment of what may be behind some of the changes observed in the last few decades.

Finally, a note of caution and a disclaimer. Throughout the chapter, we make use of various theoretical models that, for expositional purposes, are kept simple. Although this makes the intuitions of the basic mechanisms easy to understand, it also implies that these models may not be completely suited to address quantitative questions. Therefore, even if we often illustrate the properties of the model quantitatively, we should be careful in interpreting the simulation numbers as they are often intended to provide a qualitative, rather than quantitative, assessment of the model. The disclaimer is about the necessary incompleteness of this chapter. As much as we have tried to provide a general presentation of the studies that deal with inequality in macroeconomics, covering all possible subjects is impossible. There are many topics that we do not review. For example, we exclude studies that introduce behavioral elements in macroeconomic analysis. In part, this is motivated by our limited expertise in these subjects. We have also avoided for the most part the study of inequality in developing countries. We have marginally touched on issues such as the impact of the rise in inequality on the U.S. economy, the macroeconomic causes for the rising inequality, and globalization and inequality among others. Perhaps, more importantly, we have only scratched the surface of how income inequality translates into consumption inequality, which is what most economists think is what really matters. The topic of income inequality is quite vast, and different authors would write it quite differently; in fact, Thomas Piketty's chapter in this volume includes some macro modeling of the wealth distribution with a very different flavor than this chapter.

14.1. SOME FACTS ON THE INCOME AND WEALTH DISTRIBUTION

Here we outline some general features of the Lorenz curves for earnings and wealth and their correlation and persistence over a medium span of 5–10 years for both individuals and across generations. We draw data from Díaz-Giménez et al. (2011), Kuhn (2014), and Budría et al. (2001) for the United States.[1] The data come from the Survey of Consumer Finances (SCF). Although the facts are for the U.S. economy, they may apply in varying degrees to other countries. In general, the United States is a more extreme version of the other developed countries in the sense that it is characterized by higher inequality.

Table 14.1 shows the shares of earnings (the part of the income that can be attributed to labor), income (earnings plus capital income plus government transfers before taxes), and wealth (both financial and real assets, but not defined benefits pensions). See Díaz-Giménez et al. (2011) for details about the definition of these variables. As we can see, a large number of households have zero or negative earnings, almost two-thirds of all earnings come from the top quintile, and the top 1% receive almost 20% of all earnings. Our definition of earnings includes part of self-employment income that is imputed as labor income.[2] Because self-employment income can be negative, several households have zero or even negative earnings in our sample. Negative earnings contribute to a much higher Gini index compared to other measures provided in the literature, such as those that result from using earnings data from the Current Population Survey (CPS). However, correcting the CPS data by tax information could lead to Gini indexes that exceed 0.6 (see Alvaredo, 2011 and the discussion in Chapter 9). Wealth is more concentrated than income, and the poorest quintile holds negative wealth. Furthermore, more than 85% of the wealth is held by the richest quintile and more than one-third of all wealth by the richest 1%. Table 14.2 shows a few measures of dispersion that are useful to keep in mind.

The properties of the distribution of earnings, income, and wealth (total (Wea) and excluding housing (N–H–W)) have changed in the last few years. Tables 14.3–14.5 show the values of a few measures of concentration for 1998, 2007, and 2010. For earnings, the Ginis, the coefficient of variations, the various ratios involving the median and the shares of top groups have all increased, most of them monotonically. For income, the picture presented by the SCF is muddier. The Gini seems unchanged, with some measures indicating an increase in inequality and others a decrease. The same seems to have happened for wealth. While the Gini, the ratio of the 90th percentile to the median and of the

---

[1] In Krueger et al. (2010) various macroeconomists study inequality in a variety of other countries with a similar way of looking at the data as we do in this chapter.

[2] In fact, owing to the recession, the overall fraction of business income attributed to labor is larger in 2010 (93.4%) and in earlier waves of the SCF when it was around 85%. See Díaz-Giménez et al. (2011) for details on how to calculate such fraction.

Table 14.1 Distribution of earnings and net worth in the U.S. economy

	Bottom (%)			Quintiles					Top (%)			All
	0–1	1–5	5–10	1st	2nd	3rd	4th	5th	90–95	95–99	99–100	0–100
Shares of total sample sorted by earnings (%)												
Earnings	−0.1	0	0	−0.1	3.5	11	20.6	65.0	12.1	18.3	18.0	100
Income	0.8	0.4	0.9	6.5	8.5	10.5	17.8	56.7	10.3	16.5	15.9	100
Net worth	4.5	0.5	0.7	11.6	13	6.3	9.9	59.1	8.6	21.2	20.2	100
Shares of total sample sorted by net worth (%)												
Earnings	0.9	2.8	2.3	8.4	10.7	14.6	17.5	48.8	10.3	15.7	10.8	100.0
Income	0.8	2.6	2.2	8.4	10.0	13.9	17.6	50.1	10.2	15.3	12.2	100.0
Net worth	−0.3	−0.3	−0.1	−0.7	0.7	3.3	10.0	86.7	13.5	26.8	34.1	100.0

Data are from the 2010 Survey of Consumer Finances. Income includes all transfers including food stamps. Earnings are defined as the part of income earned by labor. Farm and business incomes are assigned split between labor (93.4%) and capital (6.6%) (a much lower capital share than in other years).
Source: Kuhn (2014).

Table 14.2 Concentration and skewness of the distributions for 2010

	Earnings	Income	Wealth
Coefficient of variation	3.26	3.45	6.35
Variance of the logs	1.41	0.92	4.65
Gini index	0.65	0.55	0.85
Top 1%/lowest 40%	210	67	47,534
Location of mean (%)	70	73	83
Mean/median	1.85	1.70	6.42

Source: Kuhn (2014).

Table 14.3 Changes in concentration

	Ginis				Coeff. of Variation			
	Ear	Inc	Wea	N–H–W	Ear	Inc	Wea	N–H–W
1998	0.61	0.55	0.80	0.86	2.86	3.56	6.47	7.93
2007	0.64	0.57	0.82	0.88	3.60	4.32	6.01	7.59
2010	0.65	0.55	0.85	0.89	3.26	3.45	6.35	7.70

Source: Kuhn (2014).

Table 14.4 Changes of relevant ratios involving the medians

	Median to 30th percentile				90th percentile to Median				Mean to Median			
	Ear	Inc	Wea	N–H–W	Ear	Inc	Wea	N–H–W	Ear	Inc	Wea	N–H–W
1998	2.80	1.71	4.00	4.54	3.18	2.87	6.88	12.56	1.57	1.62	3.95	7.66
2007	2.77	1.68	4.54	4.73	3.41	3.00	7.55	15.73	1.72	1.77	4.60	10.39
2010	3.30	1.64	5.24	4.11	3.79	3.10	12.37	23.33	1.85	1.71	6.42	13.18

Source: Kuhn (2014).

Table 14.5 Percentages of Total Earnings, Income, and Wealth of Selected Groups

	SCF Earnings			SCF Income			SCF Wealth		
	Top 10%	Top 1%	Top 0.1%	Top 10%	Top 1%	Top 0.1%	Top 10%	Top 1%	Top 0.1%
1998	43.5	16.1	1.7	42.8	17.4	6.1	68.6	33.9	12.5
2007	47.0	18.7	1.9	46.9	21.0	7.8	71.4	33.6	12.4
2010	48.4	18.0	1.7	44.5	17.2	5.6	74.4	34.1	12.3

Source: Kuhn (2014).

mean to the median have all gone up, the shares of the top 10%, 1% and 0.1%, have either remained stable or have gone down.

The modest evidence for an increase in inequality in income and wealth contrasts drastically with the picture reported by Piketty and Saez (2003), Piketty (2014), and Saez and Zucman (2014), who have used tax data. They have documented a big increase in inequality in the last few years in both income and wealth. Their evidence for income is direct as it comes straight from tax returns. The evidence for the evolution of wealth concentration in Saez and Zucman (2014) is indirect; it imputes the value of the assets that generate the reported capital income using the capitalization method with the rates of return for each class of assets that are obtained in the Flow of Funds. Yet it is quite persuasive. They suggest that the discrepancies that result between using the SCF and using tax data is due mostly to the top 0.1% of the top wealth holders. The SCF excludes the richest 400 households (the Forbes 400), and it is quite possible that even within income strata, response rates to the SCF voluntary questionnaire vary by income. The two sets of data are complementary, and the SCF is working hard to improve how it represents the very richest. There is likely to be a major update of the SCF that tries hard to improve in these dimensions. Hopefully, such improvements in the SCF will be available in the next few months, and we will get a much better picture of the characteristics of the very rich.

Turning to consumption inequality, there are some doubts about whether it has also increased. Using data from the Consumer Expenditure Survey, Krueger and Perri (2006) have documented that consumption inequality has increased only slightly. However, Attanasio et al. (2004) and Aguiar and Bils (2011) claim that the increase in consumption inequality has been more significant. One of the reasons these studies reach different conclusions is because they use different survey data. Krueger and Perri (2006) use data in which consumption comes from survey collecting interviews, and Attanasio et al. (2004) use diary data. In addition, Aguiar and Bils (2011) have argued that the observed reduction in the quality of the consumption data in terms of how much of aggregate consumption is recovered in the interviews is concentrated among goods that are mostly purchased by rich people and among the high income groups, and both features point to a larger increase in the underlying consumption inequality than what is obtained by using the data without special adjustments.

To summarize, over the last 10–20 years, the evidence points to a sizable increase in inequality.

14.2. MODELING THE SOURCES OF MACRO INEQUALITY

In this section we show what macroeconomics has to say about inequality. We start by exploring in Section 14.2.1 the implications of existing macro models for the distribution of wealth. Most of the models reviewed in this section start from the assumption that the process for earnings is exogenous: it can be stochastic, but it cannot be affected by individual decisions. In Section 14.2.1.3 we describe some of the theories in which the process for earnings is endogenous in the sense of being affected by individual choices. Because individual choices respond to policies, these models have interesting predictions about the impact of economic policies on the distribution of earnings.

14.2.1 Theories of Wealth Inequality Given the Process for Earnings

We start this section by emphasizing the limits of the neoclassical growth model with infinitely lived agents and complete markets in predicting wealth inequality. After reviewing the prediction of the overlapping generations model, we analyze models with incomplete markets. As we will see, the consideration of market incompleteness allows for more precise predictions about the distribution of wealth for given processes of individual earnings.

14.2.1.1 The Irrelevance of Income and Wealth Inequality in the Neoclassical Model

The deterministic neoclassical growth model says very little about income and wealth inequality. Note that we mean the neoclassical growth model in its modern meaning of incorporating fully optimizing saving behavior.[3] In an important article by Chatterjee (1994), reiterated later by Caselli and Ventura (2000), it is shown that any initial distribution of wealth is essentially self-perpetuating. To see this, consider the typical problem of a household $i \in \{1, \ldots, I\}$. Using recursive notation with primes denoting next period variables, the household's problem can be written as

$$v^i(a) = \max_{c,d'} u^i(c) + \beta_i v^i(a'), \tag{14.1}$$

$$\text{subject to} \quad c + d' = a(1 + r) + \varepsilon_i w. \tag{14.2}$$

Here, $u^i(c)$ is a standard utility function (differentiable, strictly concave), $\beta_i \in [0, 1]$ is the discount factor, and ε_i is the household's endowment of efficient units of labor, which we assume constant for now. The necessary condition for optimality is

$$u_c^i(c_i) = \beta_i \, (1 + r') \, u_c^i(c_i'), \tag{14.3}$$

where $u_c^i(c_i)$ is the marginal utility of consumption. In steady state, the allocation is constant over time, $c_i = c_i'$, and $r = r'$, which requires that the rate of return on savings is equal to the rate of time preference in every period, that is, $\beta_i = (1 + r)^{-1}$. One implication is that, if households have interior first order conditions so that Equation (14.3) is satisfied with equality, then $\beta_i = \beta$ for all i. Otherwise, some households would reduce their assets as much as they can until they reach some lower bound that depends on the borrowing ability.

Because the rate of return in the neoclassical growth model is given by the marginal productivity of capital, we have that

---

[3] As such, the standard analysis of Stiglitz (1969) does not apply, since there saving behavior is postulated and not derived from first principles.

$$\beta^{-1} = 1 + r = F_K(K, N) - \delta, \tag{14.4}$$

where K is aggregate capital, $N = \sum_i \varepsilon_i$ is the aggregate effective labor (hours worked weighted by their efficiency), F is the production function, and δ is the constant rate of capital depreciation. In the neoclassical growth model, physical capital is the only form of wealth, so the following has to hold:

$$K = \sum_i a_i \tag{14.5}$$

where a_i are the assets held by household i. Note that these last three equations are the only ones imposed by the theory. It turns out that any distribution of wealth $\{a_i\}_{i=1}^I$ that satisfies Equations (14.4) and (14.5) is a steady state of this economy in which each individual household i consumes its income, $c_i = ar + \varepsilon_i w$. This is the sense in which the theory poses no constraints whatsoever on the distribution of a. Note that this is true no matter how efficiency units of labor (and hence earnings) are distributed across households. Nonseparability between consumption and leisure does not change this finding.

Small details qualify the behavior of the system outside a steady state. Under constant relative risk-aversion (CRRA) preferences, Equation (14.3) can be written as $\left(\frac{c_i'}{c_i}\right)^\sigma = \beta_i(1 + r')$, where $1/\sigma$ is the intertemporal elasticity of substitution. Depending on the joint distribution of earnings and wealth, the evolution of the wealth distribution is dictated by this equation and the budget constraint.

What other possibilities does the neoclassical growth model or its variants offer? Not many. Consider heterogeneity in the per period utility function. We have already noted that this does not change any steady-state consideration. Outside the steady state, the model just takes the initial wealth distribution and uses the first order conditions and the budget constraints to propagate the wealth distribution into the future, essentially dispersing or concentrating the wealth distribution without much endogenous action on the part of the model.

What about stochastic versions of these economies? With complete markets, all idiosyncratic uncertainty disappears (it is insured away), whereas the aggregate uncertainty is borne by those who are more willing to bear it. If such ability to bear the risk is increasing in wealth, then the model could generate some redistribution in response to aggregate shocks. But abstracting from aggregate uncertainty, we will see that the irrelevance result no longer applies when markets are incomplete (and agents continue to face idiosyncratic shocks). Before exploring the implications of incomplete markets, however, we briefly review the overlapping generations model.

14.2.1.2 Overlapping Generations Models and Wealth Inequality

In overlapping generations models, new households are born every period and live up to a certain number of periods J (they may also die earlier with some probability).[4] In what follows, we abstract from differences among households in any given age cohort and assume that the heterogeneity is only between cohorts. Households in age cohort j have earnings ε_j, which we take as exogenous. This specification can accommodate retirement and, with some extra work, government-provided Social Security (see Section 14.2.2 for theories of the determination of age-specific earnings). In a steady state, households solve the following problem:

$$\max_{\{c_j,\, a_{j+1}\}_{j=1}^{J}} \sum_{j=1}^{J} \beta_j u(c_j), \tag{14.6}$$

$$\text{subject to } \quad c_j + a_{j+1} = a_j(1+r) + w\varepsilon_j, \tag{14.7}$$

$$a_1 = 0, \tag{14.8}$$

$$a_{J+1} \geq 0. \tag{14.9}$$

Here, β_j is the specific weight that households place in the age-j utility. Note that households are born with no assets and cannot die with debts. Steady-state factor prices are r and w. The solution of the problem includes age-specific consumptions, c_j, and asset holdings, a_j, that satisfy the Euler equation

$$u_c(c_j) = \frac{\beta_{j+1}}{\beta_j}(1+r)u_c(c_{j+1}). \tag{14.10}$$

Steady-state factor prices are equal to the marginal productivities of a neoclassical production function with respect to aggregate capital, $K = \sum_{j=1}^{J} A_j$, and labor, $N = \sum_{j=1}^{J} \varepsilon_j$. We are using capital A_j to denote the assets of households of age j of which there are many, making it an aggregate variable which explains the use of capital letters.

When mapping these models to the data, we calibrate the earnings profile to have an inverse U shape as in the data (even after including Social Security payments). If we pose a constant discount rate, that is, we substitute β_j with β^j in Equation (14.6), as most researchers do, the model generates wealth holdings with an inverse U shape that typically peaks a little beyond 60 years of age. From that point on, the model predicts a slow but certain depletion of assets until death. Because in equilibrium household wealth has to add up to capital, households have to save during their finite lifetime to accumulate the whole capital stock. Although the prediction of the overlapping generations model in terms of lifetime wealth is broadly consistent with the data, the prediction for lifetime consumption is not. The strong incentive to save, together with the Euler equation,

---

[4] Sometimes the literature uses the term "overlapping generations model" for environments in which new agents are born every period and die with some probability at any point in the future. We refer to this particular environment as the Blanchard–Yaari model (Blanchard, 1985; Yaari, 1965), which is very similar mathematically to the infinitely lived model.

implies that $c_{j+1} > c_j$ for all j. In the data, however, consumption is also hump shaped. Various approaches are proposed in the literature to get around this shortcoming. They include demographic shifters, nonseparable leisure in the utility function (Auerbach and Kotlikoff, 1987; Ríos-Rull, 1996), existence of both durable goods and incomplete financial markets (Fernandez-Villaverde and Krueger, 2011), borrowing constraints and low rates of return (Gourinchas and Parker, 2002), and others.

With stochastic mortality, the model produces identical predictions as long as there is a market for annuities (which are available even if scarcely used). To see why, consider the probability of surviving between ages j and $j+1$, which we denote by φ_j. The survival probability multiplies the discount factor $\frac{\beta_{j+1}}{\beta_j}$, capturing the fact that the household gets utility only if alive.[5] Fairly priced (i.e., issued at zero expected cost) annuities imply that households save by purchasing them, and one unit of savings today yields $\frac{1}{\varphi_j}(1+r)$ units of the good tomorrow if the household survives and zero otherwise. Clearly, this asset dominates noncontingent investment of savings and the budget constraint (14.7) becomes

$$c_j + \frac{a_{j+1}}{\varphi_j} = a_j(1+r) + w. \tag{14.11}$$

It can be verified that with these modifications to discounting and the budget constraint, we obtain the same first order conditions as in Equation (14.10).

If we assume that there are no annuities, as in Hansen and Imrohoroglu (2008), we have to make some assumption about the allocation of the assets left by the deceased households. There are various options. One possibility is to assume that any household is like a pharaoh and assets are buried with their owners. The predictions of the model change a little relative to the basic model because there is now a smaller amount of total wealth due to the lower rate of return tilting the allocation toward young ages. Other options include the assumption that there is a 100% estate tax (with implications identical to that of the pharaoh model except for the use of public revenues) or that the assets of the deceased go to those in a certain age group. If the assets are distributed equally among the households of certain age groups, the wealth distribution will present a hike at the age at which households inherit, which is not a feature of the data. A more attractive alternative that has not been directly explored is to build direct links between a dead household and a randomly chosen younger household that inherits the assets. In this case, there will be limited within-cohort inequality that results from differences in the timing of the death and the wealth of the ancestors.

What about versions of overlapping generations economies with aggregate shocks? With aggregate shocks, even if there are markets for one-period-ahead state-contingent

---

[5] In this model, there is nothing that the household can do to affect survival, so the relative value of being alive or dead is irrelevant. With a CRRA utility function with more curvature than log, the utility is negative and, implicitly, our formulation seems to indicate that the household would rather be dead than alive.

assets, there could be incomplete insurance because households that are not alive cannot insure each other. The answers depend first on the size of the shocks. For (small) business-cycle type shocks, there are no great differences between the allocations implied by complete or incomplete markets. Ríos-Rull (1996) and Ríos-Rull (1994) find that the allocations are almost identical with and without typical business-cycle shocks. Larger and persistent shocks are a different matter. For example, Krueger and Kubler (2006) study the role of Social Security in reducing market incompleteness across generations and do not find large effects. Glover et al. (2011) study the redistributional implications of the (most recent) recession and find that the loss of output and consequent drop in the price of assets affect the old generations more than the young ones. The intuition for this result is that the recent crisis has been associated with large drops in asset prices, including housing, and old generations own more assets than the young.

If markets for the insurance of idiosyncratic risks are not present and households can save only by holding noncontingent assets, the situation changes dramatically and the model has very tight predictions. We will see this in the next section.

14.2.1.3 Stationary Theories of Earnings and Wealth Inequality

When households do not have access to insurance against shocks, the accumulation of riskless assets acts as a mechanism that allows households to smooth consumption—saving in good times when earnings are above the mean and dissaving in bad times. This means that in environments in which households are subject to uninsurable risks, those that have been lucky and have enjoyed good realizations of the shocks are wealthier than those that faced adverse realizations. This type of ex post inequality has been widely studied in models in which the risk was on endowments or earnings and agents could save only in the form of non-state-contingent assets. The basic theory was first developed in Bewley (1977), and the general equilibrium and quantitative properties were studied later by İmrohoroğlu (1989), Huggett (1993), and Aiyagari (1994). These ideas have important applications such as those in Carroll (1997) and Gourinchas and Parker (2002).

Successive studies have extended these models to improve the ability to generate greater wealth inequality. Among these approaches are the addition of special earning risks (Castañeda et al., 2003), entrepreneurial risks (Angeletos, 2007; Buera, 2009; Cagetti and De Nardi, 2006; Quadrini, 2000), endogenous accumulation of human capital (Terajima, 2006), and stochastic discounting (Krusell and Smith, 1998). Because in these models inequality is endogenous, the degree of wealth concentration can be affected by policies. This opened the way to studies that investigate the importance of taxation policies for wealth inequality. Examples are Díaz-Giménez and Pijoan-Mas (2011), Cagetti and De Nardi (2009), and Benhabib et al. (2011).

We start by reviewing how to pose the process for earnings (Section 14.2.1.3.1), and then we describe the main features of the Aiyagari model (Section 14.2.1.3.2).

14.2.1.3.1 Stochastic Representation of Earnings

A large body of literature tries to provide a parsimonious representation of the stochastic processes for wages or earnings. This literature uses panel data to estimate a univariate process for labor income or earnings, sometimes at the level of individual earners and sometimes at the household level (which is more in line with the data used in Tables 14.1 and 14.2).[6] (See, for example, Guvenen, 2009 or Guvenen and Kuruşçu, 2010; Guvenen and Kuruşçu, 2012.)

One important feature to take into account, as we will see below, is that the most common data sets do not include the very rich. The SCF is designed to provide a better picture of the rich but, unfortunately, it has no panel dimension and therefore cannot be used to separate individual effects from shocks and other interesting property that affects the most appropriate representation of earnings as a stochastic process. A comparison between the properties of the cross section in both data sets gives an idea of the differences in the sample. Recent work using either tax data (Atkinson et al., 2011; DeBacker et al., 2011) or Social Security data (Guvenen et al., 2012) looks very promising in terms of including both the very top earners and information about the persistence of their earnings.

14.2.1.3.2 The Aiyagari (1994) Model

Consider an economy populated by many, in fact a continuum, of infinitely lived agents that can be of finitely many types $i \in I$. They are subject to shocks that cannot be insured. Without loss of generality, we pose that there are finitely many possible realizations of the shock $m \in M$ and that it follows a Markov chain with (possibly type-specific) transition matrix $\Gamma^i_{m,m'}$. For compactness, we write Γ to denote a block diagonal matrix in which each block is $\Gamma^i_{m,m'}$. For the most part, the shock refers to the agents' endowment of efficiency units of labor, so we denote the shock by $s \in S = \{s^1, s^2, \ldots, s^M\}$.

Households do not care for leisure and assess consumption streams through a per period utility function $u^i(c)$ with intertemporal discount factor β_i. The utility function and the discounting may be type specific.

We start by considering the most primitive financial structure in which households have access to saving only in one-period noncontingent assets, and they cannot borrow. To map the model to a real economy and to consider its empirical implications, we build the model economy on top of a neoclassical growth model with exogenous labor supply. With a Cobb–Douglas production function, the prices of capital (rental rate of capital) and labor (wage) depend only on the capital-labor ratio. Because the aggregate labor supply is constant, prices depend only on aggregate capital K, and we can express them as $r(K)$ and $w(K)$.

---

[6] The process could also be for wages, but given the low variability of individual variance of hours worked for primary earners, wages and earnings have similar properties.

We consider only steady-state equilibria in which households face a constant interest rate r and a constant wage w per efficiency unit of labor. This approach is common in these types of studies because it greatly simplifies the computational burden. In fact, by focusing on steady states, when we solve the individual problem we can ignore the evolution of the aggregate states and we only need to keep track of the individual states (household's type i, asset position a, and realization of the idiosyncratic shock m). Of course, by doing so we have to exclude from the analysis changes that affect the whole economy, such as aggregate productivity shocks or structural changes. The consideration of aggregate and recurrent shocks represents a major computational complication (see, for example, Krusell and Smith, 1998). However, if we restrict ourselves to explore the implications of a one-time completely unexpected shock (a somewhat oxymoronic term) or structural change, then the computation remains tractable. For simplicity of exposition, we limit the analysis here to steady-state comparisons with the caveat that in the real economy, the distribution will take a long time to converge to a new steady state.

The household's problem can be written as

$$v^i(m, a; K) = \max_{c, a'} u^i(c) + \beta_i \sum_{m'} \Gamma^i_{m, m'} v^i(m', a'; K), \tag{14.12}$$

$$\text{s.t.} \quad c + a' = w s^m + a(1 + r), \tag{14.13}$$

$$a' \geq 0, \tag{14.14}$$

where the superscript i denotes the household's type. Because this does not vary over time, we wrote it outside the arguments of the value function. The first order condition is given by

$$u^i_c(c) \geq \beta_i(1 + r) \sum_{m'} \Gamma_{m, m'} u^i_c(c'), \quad \text{with equality if } a'_i > 0. \tag{14.15}$$

Standard results show that this problem is well behaved and the solution is given by a function $a'_i(m, a; K)$. Moreover, when $\beta_i^{-1} < (1 + r)$, it is easy to show that for all i and m, there is a level of wealth $\bar{a}$ such that $a'_i(m, \bar{a}) < \bar{a}$. This means that there is a maximum level of wealth accumulated by an individual household. Thus, the set of possible asset holdings is the compact set $A = [0, \bar{a}]$.

To describe the economy, we could use a list of households with their types, shocks, and assets along with their names, but it is easier to use a measure x. This measure tells us how agents have certain characteristics in the space (i, m, a). Then, aggregate capital, which is just the sum of the assets of all households, can be written as

$$K = \int a \, dx. \tag{14.16}$$

The measure x gives us all the information that we need. For example, the total amount of efficiency units of labor or aggregate labor input is equal to

$$N = \int s^m dx, \tag{14.17}$$

and the variances of both wealth and earnings are

$$\sigma_k^2 = \int (a - K)^2 dx, \tag{14.18}$$

$$\sigma_N^2 = \int (s^m - N)^2 dx. \tag{14.19}$$

To calculate the Gini index for wealth, we need to compute the Lorenz curve and then calculate its integral. Note that any point of the Lorenez curve, for example, its value at 0.99 denoted by $\ell_{0.99}$, is one minus the share of wealth held by the richest 1%. To compute $\ell_{0.99}$, we start by finding the threshold of wealth that separates the richest 1% from the rest of households. Once we have found the threshold, we compute the wealth held by those households with wealth above the threshold relative to total wealth. The Gini index is simply twice the area between the Lorenz curve and the triangle below the diagonal between 0 and 1. (See Figure 14.6, for instance.) Other inequality statistics are also readily obtained from x, including those pertaining to the joint distribution of earnings and wealth and their intertemporal persistence.

The Aiyagari model has unique predictions about wealth and income inequality for any specification of the process of earnings. Therefore, the determination of the properties of the earning process becomes the central issue in the application of this model to the data. Should we think of people as being all ex ante equal in the sense that there is only one i type and they differ only in the realization of the shock? Or should we think of people consisting of different ex ante types? In either case, how do we determine which process to use? We now turn to this issue.

As we have seen in Section 14.1, the distribution of wealth in the United States is highly skewed, with about one-third of all the wealth in the hands of a mere 1% of households. How did those households become so wealthy? In order to become rich, households need both motive and opportunity. The reason for the opportunity is clear: at some point, the households had to have high enough earnings to be able to save and accumulate high levels of wealth. Motive is also important: why should households save rather than consume if they are impatient? If high earnings are not going to be around forever, then prudent households would want to save for the bad times that are likely to lie ahead. The issue is whether motives and opportunities are big enough to generate the wealth concentration observed in the United States.

To choose the actual parameterization of the earnings process for the model, we first need a Markovian process for earnings. If the focus is on the U.S. economy, one possibility is to specify a process estimated using the Panel Study of Income Dynamics (PSID). This is what Aiyagari (1994) did in his seminal paper, which relied on existing empirical studies such as Abowd and Card (1987) and Heaton and Lucas (1996).

The results are disappointing. The first row of Table 14.6 shows the shares of wealth of key groups in the U.S. data, and the second row displays those same shares as predicted by a model in which the earning process is calibrated using PSID data. The red line in Figure 14.4 shows the associated Lorenz curve. There is very little inequality compared with the inequality observed in the U.S. economy. The shares of wealth of the top 1% and the top quintile generated by the model are 4% and 27%, respectively, whereas in the United States these shares are 34% and 87%. The use of alternative estimates of the earning process, such as those provided by Storesletten et al. (2001), improves the performance of the model but only marginally.

The model fails to replicate the high concentration of wealth observed in the data for many possible reasons. One obvious explanation is that the model misses important pieces; for example, the model ignores life-cycle heterogeneity with all the demographic complications of actual lives. Or it ignores the permanent characteristics of people as well as education and human capital acquisition. It also ignores the fact that lives are affected by many other types of shocks such as health or unforeseen expenditures.

Castañeda et al. (2003) take a different approach and argue that the reason for the failure is the misrepresentation of the process of earnings. The PSID sample does not include very rich households. A comparison of its data with that of the SCF in which the emphasis is on wealthy people shows a large mismatch. The PSID does a better job at including people outside the top 10% of income earners and asset holders, but it is not appropriate to capture the dynamic properties of the incomes earned by the top of the distribution. Based on this observation, Castañeda et al. (2003) propose to ignore the PSID and focus instead on the specification of a process for earnings where the cross-sectional dispersion is similar to the SCF but its persistence is engineered so that it replicates the main features of the wealth inequality.

The third row of Table 14.6 displays the wealth distribution of an economy where the earning process has been calibrated following the above criteria. As we can see from the table, the model replicates quite well (by construction) the empirical data. Comparing the two processes for earnings (at least in the parsimonious representation used in Díaz et al., 2003) is very useful. The version of their economy designed to replicate the properties of the original Aiyagari economy has three values for earnings that are essentially symmetric, as are the persistence properties of the process: the earnings of agents in the middle and top thirds are $1.28\times$ and $1.63\times$, respectively, the earnings of those of the bottom third. Households in both, the top and the bottom thirds, have a one-third probability of moving out of their current situation by the next period. This society is very equal. Moreover, encountering bad luck, that is, being sent to the bottom third, is not really that bad. Clearly, because there are few motives to save money in this society, households soon stop doing so and consume all of their income.

The process that replicates the U.S. wealth distribution is extremely different from the process just described. The bottom of the society is now almost *half* of all households. Moreover, once at the bottom, less than 1% of these households move up each year.

Table 14.6 Concentration of wealth of various economies

Economy	1st	2nd	3rd	4th	5th	Top 10%	Top 5%	Top 1%	Gini
2010 U.S. Data	−0.7	0.7	3.3	10.0	86.7	74.4	60.9	34.1	0.85
PSID Ear–Pers	3.7	10.1	17.0	25.1	44.1	26.7	15.5	4.0	0.41
SCF Ear–Wea	0.0	0.0	0.3	4.5	95.2	78.3	53.2	14.7	0.87
Emp–Unemp	10.4	16.2	19.6	23.4	30.4	16.8	9.1	2.3	0.19
Stochastic β	1.7	6.5	12.5	21.1	59.3	40.3	25.3	6.7	0.56

Aiyagari (1994) used the PSID Ear–Pers calibration, Castañeda et al. (2003) used the SCF Ear–Wea calibration, and Krusell and Smith (1998) used both the Emp–Unemp and the Stochastic β calibrations.
U.S. data source Kuhn (2014).

Households that make up the middle class, almost one-half of the population, earn 5 × more than those at the bottom and have an equal chance (1%) of moving up or down. Only 6% of the households are in the top earnings group, and their earnings are huge: 47 × those of the poor and 9 × those of the middle class. More than 8% of these households will move down in a given year. Although these particular values are somewhat arbitrary, they give an accurate sense of how extreme both motives and opportunities have to be in order to induce the U.S. wealth disparities in a model in which agents differ only in the realization of a common earnings process.

Krusell and Smith (1998) pursue a very different approach to get a suitable wealth distribution. Instead of tracking the behavior of earnings, they pose a simple employment/unemployment process to generate earnings inequality, and they assume that the discount rate of individual agents is also stochastic. Therefore, in addition to the idiosyncratic shock to earnings, they consider a second idiosyncratic shock to the discount rate. The earnings process alone generates almost no inequality because the only way to get rich is through remaining employed but without earning more than other employed workers. In the extension with stochastic discounting, they assume that β can take three values, $\{0.9858, 0.9894, 0.9930\}$, with a symmetric distribution that satisfies the following properties: (i) the average duration of the extremes is 50 years (so it lasts the length of the adult life of a person); (ii) the transition from extreme to extreme requires a spell in the middle; and (iii) the (stationary) size of the middle group is 80%. Interestingly, the model with stochastic discounting yields disarmingly similar inequality indexes as in the data (see the last row of Table 14.6).

Various papers used life-cycle models with idiosyncratic risk to study wealth inequality. An important early contribution is Huggett (1996). De Nardi (2004), Cagetti and De Nardi (2006), and Cagetti and De Nardi (2009) study the role of bequest, estate taxation, and entrepreneurship in shaping the wealth distribution.

14.2.2 Theories of Earnings Inequality

So far we have described how macroeconomists think of the distribution of wealth given the distribution of earnings. But what about the distribution of earnings itself? Where is it coming from? In general, we can think of the differences in earnings as resulting from a combination of heterogeneity in (i) innate abilities or ex ante luck that persists for the lifetime of the agent; (ii) ex post luck due to the realization of shocks that are not under the control of the agent; (iii) effort or occupational choice; and (iv) investment in human capital. In the model considered in the previous section, the heterogeneity in earnings was only a consequence of innate heterogeneity (captured by the agents' type) and ex post luck (captured by the Markov process for skills). In this section we make the earnings endogenous by allowing for the optimal choice of effort and investment in human capital. An important consequence of endogenizing the earning process is that the distribution of earnings can be affected by several factors including financial market development (which, for example, facilitates access to the financing of investment in human capital) and taxation policies (which, for example, affect the marginal decision of effort and investment in human capital).

Next we briefly describe three aspects of models with endogenous earnings: models in which earnings are the result of explicit choices of either learning by doing or learning by not doing, including education (Section 14.2.2.1); models in which not all types of labor are perfect substitutes (Section 14.2.2.3); and models with occupational choices in which agents decide which occupation to take (Section 14.2.2.5).

14.2.2.1 Human Capital Investments

A common approach to endogenizing the process for earnings is the assumption that human capital is endogenous and depends on the individual investment chosen by agents. If the return from the investment is stochastic, then agents will be characterized ex post by different levels of human capital and, therefore, unequal earnings. An interesting feature of this setup is that it generates a positive relation between the aggregate performance of the economy and the degree of inequality. More specifically, higher investment in human capital leads to higher income or growth or both, but also to higher inequality because investment amplifies the impact of idiosyncratic shocks.

We illustrate this point with a simple model without taking a stand on the issue of what type of investment yields higher human capital. The investment can be either the result of time and hence forgone output or leisure, or the result of effort that generates a disutility, or the result of investment in goods. In this sense and at this level of abstraction, it accommodates both learning by direct investment in schooling or more general human capital investment such as that pioneered by Ben-Porath (1967). It also captures the key mechanisms formalized in more recent studies such as Guvenen et al. (2009), Manuelli and Seshadri (2010), and Huggett et al. (2011). For an extensive discussion of the life-cycle human capital model, see von Weizsäcker (1993).

Consider an economy with a continuum of risk-neutral workers, each characterized by human capital h. Production, which in this simple model corresponds to earnings, is equal to the worker's human capital h. Individual human capital can be enhanced with investment captured by the variable y. Investment is costly in terms of either utility or output (given risk neutrality, they are essentially the same). We assume that the cost takes the form $\frac{\alpha y^2 h}{2}$ and human capital evolves according to

$$h' = h(1 + y\varepsilon'),$$

where ε' is an i.i.d. random variable with $\mathbb{E}\varepsilon' = \bar{\varepsilon}$. To simplify notation, we denote by $g(y, \varepsilon') = 1 + y\varepsilon'$ the gross growth rate of human capital.

Because the outcome of the investment is stochastic, the model generates a complex distribution of human capital among workers. In the long run, the distribution will be degenerate because at the individual level h follows a random walk. To make the distribution stationary and keep the model simple, we assume that workers die with probability λ in each period and are replaced by the same mass of newborn workers. To allow for ex ante heterogeneity or innate abilities, we also assume that newborn agents are heterogeneous in initial human capital. In particular, there are I types of newborn agents indexed by $i \in \{1, \ldots, I\}$, each of size x_0^i and with initial human capital h_0^i. The initial distribution of newborn agents satisfies $\sum_i x_0^i = \lambda$.

Because of the linearity assumption, it will be convenient to normalize by h the optimization problem solved by a worker. We can then write the problem recursively as

$$\omega = \max_y \left\{ 1 - \frac{\alpha y^2}{2} + \beta(1 - \lambda)\mathbb{E}[g(y, \varepsilon')\omega'] \right\}, \tag{14.20}$$

where ω is the expected lifetime utility normalized by human capital h. The non-normalized lifetime utility is ωh. Of course, the linearity of the accumulation function is crucial here. If the new human capital was a Cobb–Douglas function of old human capital, as in the Ben-Porath (1967) model, the analysis would be more complex analytically.

The first order condition gives

$$\alpha y = \beta(1 - \lambda)\bar{\varepsilon}\omega', \tag{14.21}$$

where $\bar{\varepsilon}$ is the average value of the stochastic variable ε.

Because the first order condition is independent of h, the investment variable y is constant over time, which in turn implies that the normalized lifetime utility for the worker, ω, is constant. Therefore, y and ω can be determined by the two equations that define the value for the worker and the optimal investment, that is,

$$\omega = 1 - \frac{\alpha y^2}{2} + \beta(1 - \lambda)(1 + y\bar{\varepsilon})\omega, \tag{14.22}$$

$$\alpha y = \beta(1 - \lambda)\omega\bar{\varepsilon}. \tag{14.23}$$

Given the distribution of human capital for newborn workers x_0 and the investment variable y, we can determine the economywide distribution of human capital (equal to the distribution of earnings) and compute a cross-sectional index of inequality. We focus on the square of the coefficient of variation, that is,

$$\text{Inequality index} \equiv \frac{\text{Var}(h)}{\text{Ave}(h)^2},$$

which can be calculated exactly in a steady-state equilibrium.

Before we do this, note that the mass or measure of agents of age $j+1$ is given by $\sum_i x_j^i = \sum_i x_0^i (1-\lambda)^j$ and the average human capital is equal to

$$\text{Ave}(h) = \sum_i x_0^i \sum_{j=0}^{\infty} (1-\lambda)^j \mathbb{E}_j h_j^i. \tag{14.24}$$

The index j denotes the age of the worker and i the cohort of newly born agents with human capital h_0^i. The population size of newborn agents of type i is x_0^i, and the total mass of newborn agents is $\sum_i x_0^i = \lambda$. Because workers survive with probability $1-\lambda$, the fraction who is still alive after j periods is $(1-\lambda)^j$.

The cross-sectional variance of h is calculated using the formula

$$\text{Var}(h) = \sum_i x_0^i \sum_{j=0}^{\infty} (1-\lambda)^j \mathbb{E}_j \left[h_j^i - \text{Ave}(h) \right]^2, \tag{14.25}$$

which has an interpretation similar to the formula used to compute the average h. Of course, for the variance to be finite, we have to impose some parameter restrictions. In particular, we need to impose that the death probability λ is sufficiently large and the return on human capital accumulation $\mathbb{E}[\varepsilon']$ is not too big.

Using Equations (14.24) and (14.25), Appendix A shows that the average human capital and the inequality index take the forms

$$\text{Ave}(h) = \frac{\lambda \bar{h}_0}{1 - (1-\lambda)\mathbb{E}[g(\gamma, \varepsilon)]}, \tag{14.26}$$

$$\text{Inequality index} = \left[\frac{\sum_i x_0^i (h_0^i)^2}{\bar{h}_0^2} \right] \frac{[1 - (1-\lambda)\mathbb{E}g(\gamma, \varepsilon)]^2}{1 - (1-\lambda)\mathbb{E}g(\gamma, \varepsilon)^2} - 1, \tag{14.27}$$

where $\bar{h}_0$ is the aggregate human capital of newborn agents.

We can see from Equation (14.26) that the average human capital and, therefore, aggregate output are strictly increasing in the investment variable γ. This is intuitive given the structure of the model.

As far as the inequality index is concerned, Equation (14.27) shows that this results from the product of two terms. The first term in parentheses captures the ex ante inequality, that is, the distribution of human capital at birth. If all agents are born with the same human capital, this term is 1. However, if the initial endowment is heterogeneous (heterogeneity in innate abilities), then this term is bigger than 1. The second term in parentheses captures the inequality generated by investment. It is easy to show that this term, and therefore, the inequality index, are strictly increasing in y. Because the average value of h is also strictly increasing in y, we have established that there is a positive relation between macroeconomic performance and inequality. The intuition for this dependence is simple. If $y=0$, human capital for all workers will be equal to h_0^i and the inequality index is fully determined by the ex ante heterogeneity. As y becomes positive, inequality increases for two reasons. First, because the growth rate $g(y, \varepsilon)$ is stochastic, human capital will differ *within* the same age-cohort of workers. Second, because each age-cohort experiences growth, the average human capital will differ *between* different age-cohorts.[7] Both mechanisms are amplified by the growth rate of human capital, which increases in the investment y.

Using this model, we can analyze how changes that have an impact on the incentives to invest in human capital affect macroeconomic performance and inequality simultaneously. An example is a change in income taxes.

Suppose that the government taxes income at rate τ. The equilibrium conditions (14.22) and (14.23) become

$$\omega = 1 - \tau - \frac{\alpha y^2}{2} + \beta(1 - \lambda)(1 + y\bar{\varepsilon})\omega, \tag{14.28}$$

$$\alpha y = \beta(1 - \lambda)\omega\bar{\varepsilon}. \tag{14.29}$$

A bit of algebra shows that y is strictly decreasing in τ. Effectively, the tax reduces the value of human capital, ω, which in turn must be associated with a reduction in y (see Equation 14.29). Then, we can see from Equations (14.26) and (14.27) that higher taxes reduce inequality but also reduce the average human capital. This mechanism captures, in stylized form, the idea of Guvenen et al. (2009) used to explain cross-country wage inequality. They argue that higher taxation of labor accounts for the wage compression and lower productivity in Europe relative to the United States. Note also that the effects of higher labor taxation in the short run would differ from those in the long run in environments like this. In this particular model, taxation has no short-run disincentive effects (they would exist, however, if leisure were valued). Taxation does have long-run effects because agents would invest less in human capital. Empirical studies based only on short-run data would miss these effects.

14.2.2.2 *Human Capital Investment Versus Learning by Doing*

The stylized model considered in the previous section can easily be extended to include learning by doing. To do so, we can simply interpret the variable y as the fraction of time spent investing (in human capital) and $1 - y$ the fraction of time spent producing. Output is produced according to the function $h(1 - \alpha y^2/2)$, which is strictly decreasing and

---

[7] This is in addition to the differences in initial human capital among the I types of newborn agents.

concave in the time spent investing. The equation determining the evolution of human capital becomes

$$h' = h(1 + y\varepsilon') + \chi(1 - y).$$

The first term captures the time spent investing, whereas the second results from learning by producing. The analysis conducted so far extends trivially to this case. In particular, the two Equations (14.22) and (14.23) become

$$\omega = 1 - \frac{\alpha y^2}{2} + \beta(1 - \lambda)[(1 + y\bar{\varepsilon}) + \chi(1 - y)]\omega, \tag{14.30}$$

$$\alpha y = \beta(1 - \lambda)\omega(\bar{\varepsilon} - \chi). \tag{14.31}$$

A further extension is to assume that the return from learning by doing is stochastic, that is, χ is a stochastic variable. Also, we could consider the special case in which the evolution of human capital is determined only by learning by doing. This case is obtained by setting $\varepsilon = 0$. These extensions do not change the basic properties of the model illustrated in the previous subsection, including the analysis of the short- and long-run effects of labor income taxation.

14.2.2.3 Prices of Skills

So far we have presented a model in which there is only one type of human capital or skills. Individuals have different levels of human capital and, therefore, earn different incomes. In reality, different types of skills are combined together with physical capital to produce goods and services. If those skills are not additive, they have a relative price that may be changing, implying that the distribution of income also depends on those relative prices, which in turn depend on the relative supplies and demands of the various skills.

To fix these ideas, suppose that there are three types of agents according to their skill types, H_1, H_2, and H_3. Production takes place through the technology

$$(H_1 + AH_2)^\theta H_3^{1-\theta}.$$

Assuming that markets are competitive, the prices of the three types of skills are equal to their marginal productivities, that is,

$$W_1 = \theta(H_1 + AH_2)^{\theta-1} H_3^{1-\theta},$$
$$W_2 = \theta A(H_1 + AH_2)^{\theta-1} H_3^{1-\theta},$$
$$W_3 = (1 - \theta)(H_1 + AH_2)^\theta H_3^{-\theta}.$$

In this example, the relative prices for the three types of skills depend on three factors: (i) the relative supplies of the skill types; (ii) the parameter A determining the productivity of H_2 relative to H_1; (iii) the parameter θ determining the relative productivity between the aggregation of H_1 and H_2 on one side and H_3 on the other. For example, an increase in the parameter A, keeping constant the relative supplies of the three skills, increases the productivity of H_2 and H_3 but reduces the marginal productivity of H_1. This changes the distribution of income between the three groups. The change in A could be the result of particular technological progress. As we will see in Section 14.3, a similar idea has been used by Krusell et al. (2000) to explain the increase in the skill premium observed in the United States since 1980.

14.2.2.4 Search and Inequality

Where does workers' luck come from? Some economists think it is from the arbitrariness of the process that matches workers to jobs. The idea is that some firms are better than others, and these firms end up paying more for essentially identical workers. The argument relies on two considerations. The first is that certain frictions make it difficult for firms to get a worker. The second is that wages depend on the characteristics of both workers and firms.

We can discuss these ideas with the help of the basic labor market model (see Pissarides, 1990) in which firms are created through the random matching of job vacancies and unemployed workers. Workers have linear utility $\mathbb{E}_0 \sum_{t=0}^{\infty} \beta^t c_t$. Risk neutrality implies that the interest rate is constant and equal to $r = 1/\beta - 1$.

A firm is created by paying a cost κ_0 that entails a draw of a productivity level z from the distribution $F(z)$. After the initial draw, z stays constant over time. Then the firm has to post a vacancy at cost κ_1. If matched with an unemployed worker, the firm produces output z starting in the next period until the match is separated, which happens exogenously with probability λ. The firm can use only one worker. The number of newly formed matches is determined by the function $M(v, u)$, where v is the number of vacancies and u is the number of unemployed workers. The probability that a vacancy is filled is $q = M(v, u)/v$, and the probability that an unemployed worker finds occupation is $p = M(v, u)/u$. The second ingredient of this model is that wages are determined through Nash bargaining, where we denote by η the bargaining power of workers. A worker attached to a firm with productivity z is paid the wage $w(z)$ and the firm earns $z - w(z)$.

The value of a firm that has a worker can be written recursively as

$$J^1(z) = \{z - w(z) + \beta(1-\lambda)J^1(z)\}, \tag{14.32}$$

which implies that the value is $J^1(z) = \frac{z - w(z)}{1 - \beta(1-\lambda)}$. A newly created firm has value

$$J^0(z) = \{-\kappa_1 + \beta(1-\lambda)[qJ^1(z) + (1-q)J^0(z)]\}, \tag{14.33}$$

which can also be expressed as $J^0(z) = \dfrac{-\kappa_1 + \beta(1-\lambda)\dfrac{(z-w(z))q}{1-\beta(1-\lambda)}}{1-\beta(1-\lambda)(1-q)}$.

The value of a worker employed by a firm with productivity z is

$$W(z) = w(z) + \beta[(1-\lambda)W(z) + \lambda U], \tag{14.34}$$

where U is the value if the worker does not have a job. Such value is given by

$$U = \bar{u} + \beta\left\{ p\int W(z)F(\mathrm{d}z) + (1-p)U \right\}, \tag{14.35}$$

where $\bar{u}$ is the flow utility for the unemployed worker.

To derive the bargaining problem, let's define the following functions:

$$\hat{J}(z, w) = z - w + \beta(1-\lambda)J^1(z), \tag{14.36}$$

$$\hat{W}(z, w) = w + \beta[(1-\lambda)W(z) + \lambda U]. \tag{14.37}$$

These functions are, respectively, the value of a firm and the value of an employed worker, given an arbitrary wage w paid in the current period and future wages determined by the function $w(z)$. The actual wage function $w(z)$ is the solution to the problem

$$\max_{w} \left[\hat{J}(z, w) - J^0(z)\right]^{1-\eta}\left[\hat{W}(z) - U\right]^{\eta}. \tag{14.38}$$

Notice that the terms inside the brackets describe, respectively, what the firm and the worker would lose if they do not reach an agreement and break the match. Parameter η captures the bargaining power of workers. To reach an equilibrium, a couple of additional conditions are needed. One is free entry of firms, that is, the expected value of creating a firm, $\int J^0(z)F(dz)$, equals its cost, κ_0. To get a steady-state equilibrium, total firm creation has to be sufficient to create enough vacancies to replace the jobs of workers that join unemployment from job separation.

It is easy to see that the wage is an increasing function of z. In this fashion, a theory of wage inequality can arise from the sheer luck of matching with a very productive firm, even though there is nothing inherently different between two workers in different firms. Hornstein et al. (2011) proposed a new method to assess the quantitative importance of the wage dispersion induced by search frictions and found that it is very small. In fact, the actual dispersion is 20 × larger than the dispersion generated by the type of search frictions described here. To understand this finding, think of an intermediate step between a worker being matched with a firm and before the actual bargaining process takes place. In this step, the worker could forecast what the wage will be and could potentially choose whether to take the job or keep searching. The minimum wage makes the worker indifferent between accepting the job and continuing searching. Such a wage can be compared with the average wage that workers get. Hornstein et al. (2011) found that for empirically sound values of the parameters, the difference between the minimum and the average wages generated by search frictions was tiny.

14.2.2.5 Occupational Choice and Earnings Inequality

Workers' choice of occupation has recently come to the fore as a source of income inequality. Income inequality may occur not only because workers accumulate different levels of human capital, but also because they work in different occupations. As evidenced by Kambourov and Manovskii (2009b), among others, human capital is largely occupation specific. We will discuss how occupation choices can directly affect the return to human capital and wage growth. In another vein, some workers' occupations may make them more sensitive to cyclical dynamics and unemployment. As in Wiczer (2013), the occupation specificity of human capital makes workers less flexible in response to specific shocks during the business cycle, and this generates inequality across occupations in terms of unemployment rates, unemployment duration, and earnings.

To see the pathways through which occupation choices may affect earnings inequality, consider a simple model with occupations indexed by $j = \{1, \ldots, J\}$. Human capital is only imperfectly transferable between occupations. Therefore, the human capital of a worker with current human capital h in occupation j that switches to occupation ℓ becomes $h' = \omega(h, j, \ell)$.

This is the basic framework with which Kambourov and Manovskii (2009a) connected occupational mobility to wage inequality. Workers who remain in the same occupation experience the same wage growth. Workers who switch occupations lose human capital, that is, experience negative growth in earnings. Let's normalize $h = 1$ for experienced workers. When a new employee arrives, the human capital is $\omega_{j,\ell} = \omega(1, j, \ell)$, and it takes one period to become experienced. Let $g(j, \ell)$ be the probability that a worker switches from j to ℓ, and x_j is the measure of workers in occupation j. The variance of wages is

$$\mathrm{var}(w) = \sum_j x_j \sum_\ell g(j, \ell) \left(\omega_{j,\ell} - \mathbb{E}w \right)^2.$$

Clearly, without switching occupations, the variance would be zero. But, occupational switching is not infrequent and has, in fact, been rising concurrently with the recent rise in earnings inequality—the probability of switching occupations rose by 19% from the 1970s to the 1990s.[8] Kambourov and Manovskii (2009a) connect the former to the latter, posing a common cause for both. If occupation-specific shocks are on the rise, they will affect wage inequality through two channels. Directly, they will increase the dispersion in wages of those attached to an occupation, but shocks will also increase switching and create more wage inequality. Because these shocks are difficult to observe directly, Kambourov and Manovskii (2009a) use the occupational switching behavior of workers to inform the underlying process that would generate such behavior; as switching rose,

---

[8] This probability uses the 1970 Census occupations definitions at the three-digit level and PSID data.

the shocks must have also amplified. With this identification logic, occupational switching accounts for 30% of the overall rise in earnings inequality.

Unobserved, occupation-specific shocks are certainly not the only hypothesis for why workers move to different occupations. Several authors, e.g., Papageorgiou (2009) and Yamaguchi (2012), propose that workers' wages depend on occupation-specific match quality that is learned only through the course of the match. In these papers, earnings inequality is exacerbated by occupational mismatch, which slows the wage growth for some workers. On the other hand, aggregate factors such as business-cycle pressures and unemployment may also increase occupational switching. Indeed, unemployed workers are $3\times$ more likely than employed workers to switch occupations. In this vein, we introduce a simple model with unemployment and search as motives to switch occupations.

The critical object to be determined in this environment is the stochastic finding rate, $\{p_{j,\ell}\}$, at which workers with occupation j find a job in occupation ℓ. Denote by $P=\{p_{j,\ell}\}_{j,\ell\in\{1,\dots,J\}}$ the collection of all such finding rates. Denote by $g(j,\ell)$ the fraction of time spent searching for occupation ℓ by a worker with previous occupation j. We assume that looking for jobs in a particular area has decreasing returns at rate $\varphi<1$, so that not all workers from occupation j shift to the same type of new occupation ℓ. This simplification could be a stand-in for any number of more realistic elements of a model such as heterogeneous preferences. Clearly, the allocation of searching time determines the realized finding rate.

The characteristics of the equilibrium are going to depend on the type of wage-setting rule we use, but here we consider the simplest case in which workers earn their marginal product. Hence, the wage of a worker who has just switched occupations is $\omega_{j,\ell}$ and 1 for an experienced worker.

Let W be the value function for an employed worker and U for an unemployed worker. These functions are defined recursively as

$$W(\ell, P) = \omega_{\ell,\ell} + \beta(1-\lambda)\mathbb{E}\,W(\ell, P') + \beta\lambda\mathbb{E}\,U(\ell, P'),$$

$$U(j, P) = \max_{g(j,\ell)} \sum_{\ell=1,\dots,J} g(j,\ell)^{\varphi} p_{j,\ell}\big(\omega_{j,\ell} + \beta\mathbb{E}W(\ell, P')\big) + \left(1 - \sum_{\ell=1,\dots,J} g(j,\ell)^{\varphi} p_{j,\ell}\right)$$
$$\times (\overline{u} + \beta\mathbb{E}U(j, P')).$$

In this case, $g(j,\ell)$ is chosen so that, given wages and finding rates, the marginal return to search time satisfies

$$g(j,j)^{\varphi-1} p_{j,j}\{1 - \overline{u} + \beta\mathbb{E}[W(j, P') - U(j, P')]\}$$
$$= g(j,\ell)^{\varphi-1} p_{j,\ell}\{\omega_{j,\ell} - \overline{u} + \beta\mathbb{E}[W(\ell, P') - U(j, P')]\}, \quad \forall \ell.$$

To get a taste of the dynamics, suppose that $p_{j,j}$ falls. The indifference condition holds that search time toward this occupation falls so that $g(j,j)^{\varphi-1}$ will rise. This increases earnings inequality through two channels: (1) the increase in the unemployment rate among type j workers and (2) more of the new matches go to different occupations, where they produce only $\omega_{j,\ell} < 1$.

The model we have presented has the essential elements of that explored in Wiczer (2013) and, in tying it to data, he shows that recessions often bring a correlated change in P that hurts some occupations much more than others. In such a case, workers from the affected occupations can be unemployed for very long durations and keep the level of unemployment high for a long time. To allow for this result, Wiczer (2013) builds upon Kambourov and Manovskii (2009a) by introducing search frictions, so that the job finding rate is endogenous and affected by business-cycle conditions. As in the case of a typical matching function, the finding rate is reduced by *congestion*.

To extend our framework to endogenous matching frictions, following Wiczer (2013) let $p_{j,\ell} = p(z_\ell, g(j, \ell))$, where z_ℓ is a shock affecting hiring in occupation ℓ and the more workers looking for the same types of job lowers the finding rate, $\frac{\partial p}{\partial g} < 0$. Then, when $p_{j,j}$ falls, the probability of successfully switching occupations also falls. Whereas Kambourov and Manovskii (2009a) find their shocks to reconcile switching behavior, Wiczer (2013) maps his shocks to measured value added by occupation. Looking directly at productivity allows Wiczer (2013) to address business cycles in which unemployment and earnings dispersion across occupations increases even though search frictions prevent workers from mass switches into new jobs.

How to identify "occupations" in the data is still an open question. Whereas Wiczer (2013) uses two-digit occupation codes, Carrillo-Tudela and Visschers (2013) take a similar model but with a finer definition of occupation that highlights the interaction between occupation-specific skills and other job characteristics such as location. Hence, the position of a machinist in Detroit may be even more volatile than machinists in general. Both papers generate significant volatility in unemployment and earnings over the business cycle beyond search models that abstract from occupational heterogeneity.

14.3. THE DYNAMICS OF INEQUALITY

So far we have looked at how to build theories of inequality in earnings and wealth that aggregate into a macro model. Now we turn to the analysis of factors that affect the dynamics of inequality. We first consider in Section 14.3.1 changes in inequality that take place over the business cycle, and in Section 14.3.2 we analyze the dynamics over a longer horizon.

14.3.1 Inequality and the Business Cycle

A well-established feature of the business cycle is that the labor share of income is highly countercyclical. As shown in Figure 14.1, the labor share in the U.S. economy tends to increase during recessions. The figure also shows a declining trend in the labor share since

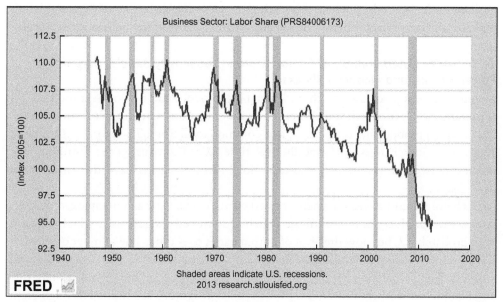

Figure 14.1 Labor share in the U.S. business sector as defined by the Bureau of Labor Statistics. *Source: U.S. Department of Labor: Bureau of Labor Statistics.*

the early 1980s. To the extent that agents are heterogeneous in the sources of their income—that is, some agents earn primarily capital incomes whereas others earn primarily labor income—there is significant redistribution over the business cycle.

To capture the cyclical properties of the labor share, we have to deviate from the standard neoclassical model with a Cobb–Douglas production function, because in this model the labor share is constant. In this section, we review some models in which the compensation of workers is determined through bargaining between employers and workers. Because the bargaining strength of workers depends on macroeconomic conditions, this mechanism has the potential to generate a labor income share that changes over the business cycle.

We start in Section 14.3.1.1 by using the search and matching model developed in Section 14.2.2.4 modified to allow for the study of the determination of the labor share. The modification associates the creation of firms with actual investors, which gives an explicit separation of labor and capital income. We look at two versions of this model: a simple one and another in which investors use both debt and external financing with bonds. An important property of this model is that shocks that affect the bargaining position of workers also affect the distribution of income as well as the macroeconomic impact of these shocks. We will consider two types of shocks: standard productivity shocks and shocks that affect access to credit. Then in Section 14.3.1.2, we will review the financial accelerator model in which the distribution is also interconnected with the business cycle. We will conclude this section by discussing the ability of these models to replicate the empirical properties of the data beyond the contemporaneous correlation.

14.3.1.1 The Determination of Factor Shares: Productivity Shocks, Bargaining Power Shocks, and Financial Shocks

Consider a version of the search and matching model described in Section 14.2.2.4 (Pissarides, 1987) in which the owners of firms—investors—are distinct from workers, but in which productivity is stochastic and common to all firms. Therefore, z is the same across firms and changes stochastically over time. We will focus on the distribution of income between investors and workers. Both types of agents have the same utility $\mathbb{E}_0 \sum_{t=0}^{\infty} \beta^t c_t$.

As before, a firm is created when a posted vacancy is filled by an unemployed worker. A new firm produces output until the match is destroyed exogenously, which happens with probability λ, but now the level of output varies over time. The number of matches is determined by the matching function $M(v, u)$, where v is vacancies and u is unemployed workers. The probability that a vacancy is filled is $q = M(v, u)/v$, and the probability that an unemployed worker finds a job is $p = M(v, u)/u$. Wages are determined through Nash bargaining, where we denote by η the bargaining power of workers. We also consider the possibility that the bargaining power η may be stochastic. With these stochastic terms we rewrite the value functions for investors as

$$J^1(z, \eta) = z - w(z, \eta) + \beta(1 - \lambda)\mathbb{E}J^1(z', \eta'|z, \eta), \tag{14.39}$$

$$J^0(z, \eta) = -\kappa_1 + \beta(1 - \lambda)\left[q\mathbb{E}J^1(z', \eta'|z, \eta) + (1 - q)\mathbb{E}J^0(z', \eta'|z, \eta)\right], \tag{14.40}$$

and for workers

$$W(z, \eta) = w(z, \eta) + \beta\mathbb{E}[(1 - \lambda)W(z', \eta') + \lambda U(z', \eta')], \tag{14.41}$$

$$U(z, \eta) = \bar{u} + \beta\mathbb{E}[pW(z', \eta') + (1 - p)U(z', \eta')]. \tag{14.42}$$

After some rearrangement, the values for the firm and the worker can be written as

$$J^1(z, \eta) - J^0(z, \eta) = (1 - \eta)S(z, \eta), \tag{14.43}$$

$$W(z, \eta) - U(z, \eta) = \eta S(z, \eta), \tag{14.44}$$

where $S(z, \eta) = J^1(z, \eta) - J^0(z, \eta) + W(z, \eta) - U(z, \eta)$ is the bargaining surplus that is split between the contractual parties, proportional to their relative bargaining power. The surplus function can be written recursively as

$$S(z, \eta) = z - \bar{u} + (1 - \lambda)\beta\mathbb{E}S(z', \eta') - \eta\beta p\mathbb{E}S(z'\eta'). \tag{14.45}$$

Using the free-entry condition $\kappa_1 = q\beta\mathbb{E}S(z', \eta')$, the sharing rules (14.43) and (14.44), and the functions (14.39), (14.41), and (14.42), we can derive the following expression for the wage:

$$w(z, \eta) = (1 - \eta)\bar{u} + \eta z + \frac{\eta p \kappa_1}{q}.$$

14.3.1.1.1 Shocks to Productivity

Figure 14.2 plots the impulse responses of employment and the investor's share of income to a positive productivity shock under the heading baseline model. An economic boom is characterized by a larger share of income going to investors. However, the quantitative effects in terms of income distribution and employment are not large. The weak employment response is a well-known property of the matching model (see Costain and Reiter, 2008 or Shimer, 2005). What is interesting is that the inability of the model to generate large employment fluctuations is related to the inability of the model to generate large movements in the distribution of income. Because wages respond too quickly to

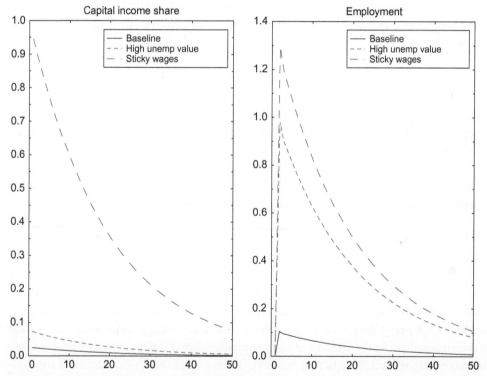

Figure 14.2 Impulse response to productivity shock. The common parameters to all versions of the model are $\beta = 0.985$, $\alpha = 0.5$, $\mathbb{E}z = 1$, $\rho_z = 0.95$, $\sigma_z = 0.01$. The remaining parameters $\bar{u}$, κ, λ, and A are chosen to achieve the following steady-state targets: a replacement rate of unemployment of 50% (95% in the model with high unemployment value), 10% unemployment rate, 93% probability of filling a vacancy, 70% probability of finding a job. The resulting values are $\bar{u} = 0.473$ (0.944 in the model with high unemployment value), $\kappa = 0.316$ (0.034 in the model with high unemployment value), $\lambda = 0.103$, and $A = 0.807$.

productivity, the share of income going to investors increases only slightly. As a result, the incentive to create new vacancies does not increase much. However, if wages would respond less, the increase in the share of income going to investors and the increase in employment would be bigger.

Recognizing the direct link between distribution and employment, several authors have proposed some mechanisms for generating smoother responses of wages and, therefore, larger fluctuations in income shares. Here we summarize three of these approaches. The first approach, proposed by Hagedorn and Manovskii (2008), is to assume that the flow utility received by workers when unemployed is not much smaller than the flow utility from working. In terms of the model, this is obtained by choosing a large value for the parameter $\bar{u}$, that is, the flow utility in the unemployment state. Although many consider this assumption implausible, the paper illustrates how this feature could bring the model closer to the data. The second approach proposed by Gertler and Trigari (2009) is to assume that wages are sticky. To illustrate these two cases, we first assign a higher value for the parameter $\bar{u}$ so that the replacement rate from unemployment is 95%. The impulse responses for this case, plotted in Figure 14.2, are labeled "High unemp. value." The figure also plots the impulse responses when the wage is exogenously fixed at the steady state with flexible wages (an extreme case of wage rigidity). As can be seen, both assumptions generate much higher volatility of employment and income distribution between investors and workers. This shows that inequality and macroeconomic volatility are closely interconnected: more volatile income distribution over the business cycle is associated with greater macroeconomic volatility. A third approach is explored in Duras (2013). The idea is that in periods with high productivity or output, the cost for workers to break the match is higher than in normal times. This weakens workers' bargaining position, alleviating the upward pressure on wages when productivity rises.

14.3.1.1.2 Shocks to Bargaining Power

Although it has been customary to assume that macroeconomic fluctuations are driven by productivity shocks, economic disturbances have many other possible sources. Here we summarize the effects of shocks that have a direct impact on the distribution of income, in particular, shocks that directly affect the bargaining power of workers, that is, the bargaining share η. When η decreases, a larger share of income will go to investors, increasing income inequality. At the same time, as investors appropriate a larger share of the surplus, they have a higher incentive to hire workers, thereby inducing a macroeconomic expansion. A similar approach has been studied by Ríos-Rull and Santaeulàlia-Llopis (2010) in the context of a neoclassical model.

14.3.1.1.3 Financial Shocks

The next step is to show that similar effects to those generated by shocks to bargaining power can be generated by the expansion and contraction of financial markets. The presentation of this case follows Monacelli et al. (2011).

Consider another slight modification of the search and matching model presented earlier, where we allow firms to borrow at the gross rate r. Borrowing, however, is subject to the constraint $b' \leq \varphi \mathbb{E} J'(b')$, where φ is stochastic. This variable captures the possible changes to the tightness of credit markets.

The firm enters the period with debt b. Given the new debt b' and the wage w, the dividends paid to investors are $d = z - w + b'/R - b$, where $R = (1+r)/(1-\lambda)$ is the gross interest rate paid by the firm conditional on survival. We assume that, in the event of exit, the firm defaults on the outstanding debt. Anticipating this, the lender charges the gross interest rate $R = (1+r)/(1-\lambda)$ so that the expected return from the loan is r. Notice that investors are shareholders and bondholders at the same time. We write the value functions exclusively as functions of debt, ignoring the potential variability of both productivity and bargaining power (that is, we now assume that z and η are constant).

The equity value of the firm can be written recursively as

$$J(b) = \max_{b'} \left\{ z - g(b) - b + \frac{b'}{R} + \beta(1-\lambda)\mathbb{E} J'(b') \right\} \qquad (14.46)$$

$$\text{subject to} \quad b' \leq \varphi \mathbb{E} J'(b'),$$

where $w = g(b)$ denotes the (to be determined) wage paid to the worker. As we will see, the wage will depend on the debt. Notice that we have also used a prime to denote the next period value of equity, because this also depends on the next period aggregate states, specifically, the unemployment rate and credit market conditions. To avoid cumbersome notation, we do not include the aggregate states as explicit arguments of the functions defined here. Instead we use the prime to distinguish current versus future functions.

The value of an employed worker is

$$W(b) = g(b) + \beta \mathbb{E}[(1-\lambda)W'(b') + \lambda U'], \qquad (14.47)$$

which is defined once we know the wage $g(b)$. The function U' is the value of being unemployed and is defined recursively as

$$U = \bar{u} + \beta \mathbb{E}[p W'(b') + (1-p)U'],$$

where p is the probability that an unemployed worker finds a job and $\bar{u}$ is the flow utility for an unemployed worker. Although the value of an employed worker depends on the aggregate states and the individual debt b, the value of being unemployed depends only on the aggregate states, because all firms choose the same level of debt in equilibrium. Thus, if an unemployed worker finds a job in the next period, the value of being employed is $W'(b')$.

The determination of the current wage solves the same problem as in Equation (14.38). We should take into account, however, that this solution also depends on b and on the function that determines future wages. Therefore, we write the solution of the bargaining problem as $w = \psi(g; b)$, where g is the function determining future wages. The equilibrium solution to the bargaining problem is the fixed point to the functional equation $g(b) = \psi(g; b)$.

Also in this case, the values for the firm and the worker satisfy

$$J(b) = (1 - \eta)S(b), \tag{14.48}$$

$$W(b) - U = \eta S(b), \tag{14.49}$$

where the surplus is defined as $S(b) = J(b) + W(b) - U$. This can be written recursively as

$$S(b) = z - a - b + \frac{b'}{R} + (1 - \lambda)\beta\mathbb{E}S'(b') - \eta\beta p\mathbb{E}S'(B'). \tag{14.50}$$

When a vacancy is filled, the newly created firm starts producing and pays wages in the next period. The only decision made in the current period is the debt b'. Therefore, the value of a vacancy just filled with a worker is

$$Q = \max_{b'}\left\{\frac{b'}{1 + r} + \beta(1 - \eta)ES'(b')\right\} \tag{14.51}$$

subject to $b' \leq \varphi(1 - \eta)\mathbb{E}S'(b')$.

Because the new firm becomes an incumbent starting in the next period, $S'(b')$ is the surplus of an incumbent firm defined in Equation (14.50). Notice that in the choice of b', a new firm faces a problem similar to that of incumbent firms (see problem 14.46). Even if the new firm has no initial debt and it does not pay wages, it will choose the same stock of debt b' as incumbent firms. We can then focus on a "representative" firm and in equilibrium $B = b$.

The value of posting a vacancy is equal to $V = qQ - \kappa$. Because in this version of the model there are no firm-specific productivity draws, $\kappa = \kappa_0 + \kappa_1$. As long as the value of a vacancy is positive, more vacancies will be posted. Free entry implies that $V = 0$ and in equilibrium we have

$$qQ = \kappa. \tag{14.52}$$

We now characterize the optimal choice of debt, that is, problem (14.46). Denoting by μ the Lagrange multiplier associated with the enforcement constraint, the first order condition is

$$\eta - R[1 + (1 - \eta)\varphi]\mu = 0. \tag{14.53}$$

In deriving this expression, we have used the property of the model for which the choice of b' does not depend on the existing debt b and, therefore, $\frac{\partial S(b)}{\partial b} = -1$. We have also used the equilibrium condition $\beta R(1 - \lambda) = \beta(1 + r) = 1$.

Looking at the first order condition, we can see that the enforcement constraint is binding (that is, $\mu > 0$) if $\eta \in (0, 1)$. Thus, provided that workers have some bargaining power, the firm always chooses the maximum debt and the borrowing limit binds. In this way, bargaining introduces a mechanism through which the financial structure is determined (Modigliani and Miller, 1958 does not apply). The reason is clear: by using outside finance, the firm is able to reduce the surplus that is bargained with the worker, increasing the possible rewards to equity.

To gather some intuition about the economic interpretation of the multiplier μ, it will be convenient to rearrange the first order condition as

$$\mu = \underbrace{\left(\frac{1}{1+(1-\eta)\varphi}\right)}_{\substack{\text{Total change} \\ \text{in debt}}} \times \underbrace{\left(\frac{1}{R} - \frac{1-\eta}{R}\right)}_{\substack{\text{Marginal gain} \\ \text{from borrowing}}} .$$

The multiplier results from the product of two terms. The first term is the change in next period liabilities b' allowed by a marginal relaxation of the enforcement constraint, that is, $b' = \varphi(1-\eta)\mathbb{E}S(b') + \bar{a}$, where $\bar{a} = 0$ is a constant. This is obtained by marginally changing $\bar{a}$. In fact, using the implicit function theorem, we obtain $\frac{\partial b'}{\partial \bar{a}} = \frac{1}{1+(1-\eta)\varphi}$, which is the first term.

The second term is the actualized net gain from increasing the next period liabilities b' by one unit (marginal change). If the firm increases b' by one unit, it receives $1/R$ units of consumption today in the form of additional dividends. In the next period, the firm has to repay one unit. However, the effective cost for the firm is lower than 1, because the higher debt allows the firm to reduce the next period wage by η, that is, the part of the surplus going to the worker. Thus, the effective repayment incurred by the firm is $1 - \eta$. This cost is discounted by $R = (1+r)/(1-\lambda)$ because the debt is repaid only if the match is not separated, which happens with probability $1 - \lambda$. Thus, the multiplier μ is equal to the total change in debt (first term) multiplied by the gain from a marginal increase in borrowing (second term).

Using the property for which the enforcement constraint is binding, that is, $\varphi EJ(b') = b'$, Appendix B shows that the wage can be written as

$$w = (1-\eta)\bar{u} + \eta(z - B) + \frac{\eta[p + (1-\lambda)\varphi]\kappa}{q(1+\varphi)}. \tag{14.54}$$

This equation makes clear that the initial debt B acts like a reduction in output in the determination of wages. Instead of getting a fraction η of output, the worker gets a fraction η of output "net" of debt. Thus, for a given bargaining power η, the larger the debt the lower the wage received by the worker. This motivates the firm to maximize the debt, as we have already seen from the first order condition.

Figure 14.3 plots the impulse responses to a credit shock, that is, a shock that raises φ and increases the credit available to firms. The credit expansion generates an increase in the capital income share and an increase in employment. Thus, changes in financial markets could alter the distribution of income and, with it, affect the incentives to create jobs. This is another example of how the distribution of income and macroeconomic performance are directly interconnected.

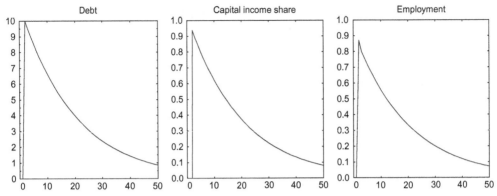

Figure 14.3 Impulse response to credit shock. The parameters are $\beta=0.985$, $\alpha=0.5$, $\mathbb{E}z=1$, $\rho_z=0.95$, $\sigma_z=0.01$, $\bar{u}=0.473$, $\kappa=0.316$, $\lambda=0.103$, and $A=0.807$, $\bar{\varphi}=0.0022$, $\rho_\varphi=0.95$, $\sigma_\varphi=100$.

14.3.1.2 Financial Accelerator and Inequality

A well-established tradition in macroeconomics introduces financial market frictions in business-cycle models. The key ingredients are based on two assumptions: market incompleteness and heterogeneity. Although not often emphasized, inequality plays a central role in these models. For example, in the seminal work of Bernanke and Gertler (1989) and (Kiyotaki and Moore (1997), entrepreneurial net worth is central to the amplification of aggregate shocks. When more resources are in the hands of constrained producers (i.e., these agents are richer), they can expand production and enhance macroeconomic activities. This can happen because they earn higher incomes or because their assets are worth more following asset price appreciations. Thus, these models posit a close connection between profit shares and the business cycle.

These models share some similarities with the matching models reviewed above: when a larger share of output goes to investors/entrepreneurs, the economy expands. At the same time, as the economy expands, a larger share of output or wealth (or both) is allocated to entrepreneurs. The mechanism of transmission, however, is different. In the matching model, the mechanism is the higher profitability of employment or investment. In the financial accelerator model, instead, it is the relaxation of the borrowing constraints. For a detailed review of the most common models used in the literature to explore the importance of financial frictions for macroeconomic fluctuations, see Quadrini (2011).[9]

---

[9] In addition to cyclical movements in the shares of income that go to labor and capital, there are cyclical movements in the shares of income earned by different groups of households. Castañeda et al. (1998) find that movements in unemployment rates by skill groups as well as movements in factor shares account for the bulk of the cyclical share of income earned by the various quintiles of households.

14.3.2 Low Frequency Movements in Inequality

We discuss here some theoretical ideas that have been proposed in the literature to explain some of the trends in the distribution of income that have occurred since the early 1980s. In Section 14.3.2.1 we look at the reduction in labor share, and in the following two sections we look at the increased inequality in wages and earnings. In Section 14.3.2.2 we examine the potential role of increased competition for human capital and in Section 14.3.2.3 the changes in the prices of skills due to skills-biased technical changes.

14.3.2.1 Labor Share's Reduction Since the Early 1980s

In a recent paper, Karabarbounis and Neiman (2014) document that labor share has significantly declined since the early 1980s for a majority of countries and industries. They pose a constant elasticity of substitution (CES) production function with nonunitary elasticity of substitution between labor and capital and argue that the well-documented decline in the relative price of investment goods (see Cummins and Violante, 2002; Gordon, 1990; Krusell et al., 2000) induced firms to substitute away from labor and toward capital. The consequence was the reduction in the price of labor. They conclude that roughly half of the observed decline in the labor share can be attributed to this mechanism.

To see how this mechanism works, consider the following aggregate production function:

$$Yt = F(K_t, N_t) = \left[\alpha_k (A_{K_t} K_t)^{\frac{\sigma-1}{\sigma}} + (1-\alpha_k)(A_{N_t} N_t)^{\frac{\sigma-1}{\sigma}} \right]^{\frac{\sigma}{\sigma-1}}, \qquad (14.55)$$

where σ denotes the elasticity of substitution between capital and labor in production, α_k is a distribution parameter, and A_{K_t} and A_{N_t} denote, respectively, capital-augmenting and labor-augmenting technology processes. As σ approaches 1, this becomes a Cobb–Douglas production function. Under perfect competition, marginal productivities yield factor prices and one can easily obtain expressions for labor share that crucially depend on the elasticity of substitution σ.

Karabarbounis and Neiman (2014) estimate σ by using only trends in the relative price of investment and the labor share in a cross section of countries. They find a value of 1.25. With this value, the decline in the (observable) relative price of investment accounts for 60% of the observed reduction in labor share. The remaining reduction can be imputed to larger increases in capital-augmenting technology relative to labor-augmenting technology, and to changes in noncompetitive factors (the most important, perhaps, are the permanent changes in the bargaining power of workers relative to firms along the lines of the models discussed earlier). Additional explanations arise from changes in the sectoral composition of output toward industries with higher capital share (which does not really seem to be the case), in part associated with globalization or the increase in the share of output that is traded with other countries, especially developing countries.

14.3.2.2 Increased Wage Inequality: The Role of Competition for Skills

There has been a big increase in earnings dispersion that is well documented in the literature. A glimpse of it can be seen in Tables 14.3 and 14.4. We now explore a possible explanation based on increased competition for skills in the context of human capital accumulation. We have already seen in Section 14.2.2.1 that human capital accumulation could be an important mechanism through which income becomes heterogeneous and that the higher the incentive to invest in human capital, the greater the degree of income inequality. We now look at one of the mechanisms that could affect the incentive to invest in human capital: competition for skills.

To study the importance of competition, we explore yet another version of the matching model described above by adding investment in human capital. We ignore here the possibility of firms to raise debt and limit the analysis to the version of the model without aggregate shocks. However, we now assume that output depends on the human capital of the worker, denoted by h. The production technology has a structure similar to the model presented in Section 14.2.2.1. The key feature of the model we look at now is that human capital investment requires both an output loss or pecuniary cost within the firm denoted by y and a utility cost for the worker that we assume quadratic, $\frac{\alpha y^2 h}{2}$. Given y, human capital evolves stochastically according to

$$h' = h(1 + y\varepsilon'),$$

where ε is an i.i.d. random variable. The gross growth rate of human capital is denoted by $g(y, \varepsilon') = 1 + y\varepsilon'$.

Because the outcome of the investment is stochastic, the model generates a complex distribution of human capital among workers. In the long run, the distribution will be degenerate because at the individual level, h follows a random walk. We assume that workers die with probability λ and that a match breaks down only when a worker dies. Thus, λ represents at the same time the death probability of a worker and the probability of separation of a match. In this way, the distribution becomes stationary and converges to a steady state.

There are contractual frictions that derive from the ability of the worker to control the investment y after bargaining over the wage. The worker unilaterally chooses an investment y that may be, and indeed is, different from the investment that maximizes the surplus of the match. This would be the investment that the worker would choose if he had been able to commit. Of course, when the firm bargains the wage, it anticipates the investment that the worker will choose in absence of commitment.

Let's define a few items. We can write the values of the investor and the worker in normalized form, that is, rescaled by human capital h. Then, the value for the investor can be written as

$$j = h - y - w + \beta(1-\lambda)\mathbb{E}g(y, \varepsilon')j', \tag{14.56}$$

where $j = J/h$ and w is the wage per unit of human capital. The total wage received by the worker is wh. The value for the worker is

$$\omega = w - \frac{\alpha y^2}{2} + \beta(1-\lambda)\mathbb{E}g(y, \varepsilon')\omega', \tag{14.57}$$

where $\omega = W/h$.

The value of being unemployed is

$$u = \bar{u} + \beta(1-\lambda)[p\omega' + (1-p)u'], \tag{14.58}$$

where $u = U/h$.

Even though in equilibrium, employed workers do not lose their occupation, u is important because it affects the threat value in bargaining. In a steady state we have $v = v'$, $\omega = \omega'$, $u = u'$.

The optimal investment y chosen by the worker maximizes the worker's value, that is,

$$\max_{y} \left\{ w - \frac{\alpha y^2}{2} + \beta(1-\lambda)\mathbb{E}g(y, \varepsilon')\omega' \right\},$$

with the first order condition given by

$$y = \beta(1-\lambda)\omega'\mathbb{E}\varepsilon'. \tag{14.59}$$

The important part to remember is that bargaining happens before the worker chooses her investment, which means that the surpluses that enter the problem take the investment y as determined by condition (14.59). From this condition we can see that y depends on ω' but not on the current value of ω, which implies that y is not affected by the outcome of the wage bargaining in the current period. Effectively, the current bargaining problem takes y as given and solves

$$\max_{w} \left\{ j^{1-\eta}(\omega - u)^{\eta} \right\}. \tag{14.60}$$

The first order condition implies that the parties split the net surplus, $s = j + \omega - u$, according to the bargaining weight η, that is,

$$j = (1-\eta)s,$$
$$\omega = \eta s + u.$$

As a comparison, we can also characterize the optimal investment when the worker commits to a particular y chosen to maximize the surplus of the match. In this case, the bargaining problem maximizes the objective (Equation 14.60) over both w and y. The first order condition with respect to w does not change, whereas the first order condition with respect to y becomes

$$1 + \alpha y = \beta(1 - \lambda)(j' + \omega')\mathbb{E}\varepsilon'. \tag{14.61}$$

Compared with the optimality condition when the investment is controlled by the worker, Equation (14.59), we observe that the left-hand side and right-hand side terms in Equation (14.61) are both bigger. Therefore, the optimal choice of y with commitment could be smaller or bigger. However, provided that α is sufficiently small, that is, the cost for the worker is not too large, the investment without commitment will be bigger.

14.3.2.2.1 General Equilibrium and the Impact of Competition

So far we have not worried about what happens outside the match, but there is a free entry condition that determines how many vacancies are posted. This is given by

$$q\beta j = \kappa, \tag{14.62}$$

where κ is the normalized cost of a vacancy.[10] One way of thinking about increased competition is that the entry cost κ is lower. We then have the following proposition.

Proposition 3.1 *The degree of competition κ affects the steady-state value of y only in the environment without worker commitment.*

This result has a simple intuition: A lower κ is associated with a higher probability that an unemployed worker finds an occupation. As a result, the value of being unemployed increases. Inasmuch as this represents the threat value in bargaining, the worker can extract a higher wage w, which in turn increases the incentive to invest.

We can now show how an increase in competition (lower κ) affects inequality and aggregate outcomes simultaneously. In particular, we have that lower κ generates: (i) more risk taking and greater income inequality and (ii) higher aggregate income. The first effect can be seen from the first order condition (14.59). A lower entry cost increases the number of vacancies and, therefore, the value of finding another occupation if the worker quits. This allows the worker to bargain a higher wage, which in turn increases the employment value ω. We can then see from Equation (14.59) that a higher value of ω is associated with a higher y. As we have seen in Section 14.2.2.1, a higher y implies greater inequality. The second property—the increase in aggregate income—is obvious because a higher y implies higher aggregate human capital. Thus, there is a trade-off between inequality and aggregate income.

Cooley et al. (2012) use a model with similar features but where the accumulation of human capital takes place in the financial sector. They show that greater competition for skills in the financial industry increased the incentive to invest in human capital and generated greater income inequality within and between sectors. This seems consistent with the recent increase in inequality, with income more concentrated at the very top of the

---

[10] For simplicity we are assuming that the cost of vacancies is proportional to the amount of human capital.

distribution and in certain professions, namely, managerial occupations in the financial sector. This pattern is also observed in the United Kingdom, as documented by Bell and Van Reenen (2010).

The idea that competition may increase inequality may go against the common wisdom that wealth is very concentrated because those who control wealth are able to protect it by limiting competition. From this the call is for increased enforcement of competition to reduce inequality. Of course, this does not mean that the theory described above is not valid. It depends on the particular environment we are studying: in certain sectors competition may lead to more inequality, in other sectors to lower inequality.

The degree of competition is just one way of affecting the equilibrium properties of aggregate income and inequality. Taxes are also important. In the context of this model, higher taxes discourage human capital investment (because the after-tax return from investing is lower), but this could be mitigated by the tax deductibility of the investment. Because the costs (curtailment of future earnings) and benefits (tax deductibility) occur at different stages of life when the individual has different incomes, the degree of progressivity becomes more important than the overall taxation. However, to the extent that taxes reduce investment, they also lower inequality (because lower investment reduces the volatility of individual incomes).

14.3.2.3 Skill-Biased Technical Change

In addition to increased competition for skills, which ends up rewarding those who are more skilled, a natural explanation for the increased earnings inequality is skill-biased technical change (Katz and Murphy, 1992). Although this term refers in general to changes in the distribution of earnings as a whole, it is often applied more specifically to the premium that college-educated people command compared with those without a college degree. This is motivated by the fact that the college wage premium, defined as the mean log wages of college graduates relative to high school graduates, has increased from 0.3 to 0.6 (see Goldin and Katz, 2009).

To illustrate how skill-biased technical change may have contributed to the increased earnings inequality, consider the following production function:

$$Y_t = F(A_{s,t}S_t, A_{u,t}U_t), \tag{14.63}$$

where S stands for the number of skilled workers (with a college education) and U stands for the number of uneducated workers (without a college education). $A_{s,t}$ and $A_{u,t}$ are exogenous technical coefficients that could change over time. Under perfect competition in the labor market, wages are marginal productivities, that is

$$w_{s,t} = A_{s,t} \frac{\partial F(A_{s,t}S_t, A_{u,t}U_t)}{\partial S_t}, \tag{14.64}$$

$$w_{u,t} = A_{u,t} \frac{\partial F(A_{s,t} S_t, A_{u,t} U_t)}{\partial U_t}. \tag{14.65}$$

The skill wage premium is defined as

$$\frac{w_{s,t}}{w_{u,t}} = \frac{A_{s,t} \dfrac{\partial F_t}{\partial S}}{A_{u,t} \dfrac{\partial F_t}{\partial U}}. \tag{14.66}$$

Absent large changes in the relative quantities of skilled and unskilled workers, we can assume that $\frac{\partial F_{t+1}}{\partial S} / \frac{\partial F_{t+1}}{\partial U}$ is very close to $\frac{\partial F_t}{\partial S} / \frac{\partial F_t}{\partial U}$, and the same goes for the marginal productivity of the unskilled. Consequently, we have that the change in the skill wage premium is given by

$$\frac{\dfrac{w_{s,t+1}}{w_{u,t+1}}}{\dfrac{w_{s,t}}{w_{u,t}}} \sim \frac{\dfrac{A_{s,t+1}}{A_{u,t+1}}}{\dfrac{A_{s,t}}{A_{u,t}}} = \frac{A_{s,t+1}}{A_{s,t}} \frac{A_{s,t}}{A_{u,t+1}} \frac{A_{u,t}}{A_{u,t}}. \tag{14.67}$$

This implies that the increase in the wage premium is owing to faster growth in the technology coefficient A_{s_t} relative to the growth of A_{u_t}, hence, the commonly used term "skill-biased technical change." But is there something more tangible than just an exogenous and largely unobserved technological change, or can we track it down to something observable?

Krusell et al. (2000) argued that we can relate these changes to something observable. Gordon (1990) and later Cummins and Violante (2002) have documented that the price of equipment (which is the main part of capital) in terms of consumption goods has gone down dramatically during the period of the rising skill premium. At the same time, the quantity of equipment has gone up significantly relative to output. This is a measurable form of technical change. Combine this with the notion that equipment or capital and skilled labor are complements, whereas unskilled labor is a substitute, and we have an actual channel through which technical progress is skill biased. The formulation in Krusell et al. (2000) does not have factor-specific technical change because all the effects of skill-biased technical change are in the increased quantity of equipment and can be written as

$$Y_t = K_t^\alpha \left[\mu U_t^\sigma + (1-\mu)\left(\lambda E_t^\rho + (1-\lambda) S_t^\rho\right)^{\frac{\sigma}{\rho}} \right]^{\frac{1-\alpha}{\sigma}}, \tag{14.68}$$

where K_t stands for structures (buildings) that play no role as they enter the production function in a Cobb–Douglas form, U_t and S_t are again unskilled and skilled labor, and E_t is equipment. Using observed measures of inputs, they estimated the elasticities of substitution ρ and σ and the share parameters α, λ, and μ, and found that unskilled labor is indeed a substitute for the aggregate of equipment and skilled labor, with both items being complementary to each other. They also found that this specification accounts very well for the observed wage premium under perfect competition for factor inputs.

Other forms of technical innovation indirectly generate skill-biased technical change. Suppose that technical change, regardless of its final effects on total productivity, is sometimes more dramatic than other change. The introduction of information technology could be one of these instances even if its impact on productivity is not as clear (Solow, 1987). Yet, the adaptation to this new technology may be easier for educated people. This is the approach taken by Greenwood and Yorukoglu (1974), Caselli (1999), and Galor and Moav (2000). Alternatively, suppose that information technology reduces information and monitoring costs within firms, allowing for reorganizations with fewer vertical layers and with workers performing a wider range of tasks. This gives educated workers an advantage. See, for example, Milgrom and Roberts (1990) and Garicano and Rossi-Hansberg (2004). Yet another form of skilled-biased technical change is an increase in competition for skills, as in the previous section, which could be the result of the technical change. In the context of the model studied earlier, the technical change can take the form of a lower vacancy cost κ. The lower κ increases the demand of skilled workers, which in turn increases the incentive to accumulate skills.

The technological innovations introduced in the 1970s seem to have affected the economy in other respects. Greenwood and Jovanovic (1999) and Hobijn and Jovanovic (2001) assume that new information technologies required a level of restructuring that incumbent firms could not face. As a result, their stock market value dropped. This is another form of redistribution in the sense that the owners of incumbent firms lost market value to the owners of new firms. Acemoglu (1998) has proposed a theory of the technical change itself being the result of a surge in college graduates.

The rise of superstars is another possible mechanism that increases the concentration of income. Rosen (1981) viewed the increase in earnings dispersion among people in some occupations as the result of an increase in their ability to reach more users of rare skills. Although this applies naturally to the case of artists and athletes, it also applies more generally to other types of skills. For example, Gabaix and Landier (2008) propose a theory of CEO pay where the value of managerial superstars is enhanced by the increase in the size of firms.

14.3.2.3.1 Skill-Biased Technical Change and Human Capital Accumulation

How does human capital investment interact with skill-biased technical change? Heckman et al. (1998) provide an answer that relies on the difference between observed wages and the price of skills that is due to the unpaid on the job investment of the Ben-Porath (1967) type models. They find no special role to capital in generating the increase in the skill wage premium. Instead, they find that the endogenous response of both more college attendance and the allocation of time to invest in further skills is sufficient to account for the patterns in the data. Guvenen and Kuruşçu (2010) also explore the inter-action of skill-biased technical change and human capital accumulation emphasizing dif-ferences across people in the ability to acquire human capital. Guvenen and Kuruşçu (2010) argue that increased biased technical change immediately induces an increase in investment by talented individuals that first depresses the skill wage premium and then raises it and that is consistent with the observed bad performance of median wages and with the lack of increase in consumption inequality.

14.4. INEQUALITY AND FINANCIAL MARKETS

A large body of work links, theoretically, inequality and financial markets. The lack of complete markets helps to shape inequality through two channels. In Section 14.4.1 we study how the limited access to borrowing prevents poor households from undertaking valuable investments. This limited access keeps them and their descendants from climb-ing the social ladder. In Section 14.4.2 we study environments in which access to bor-rowing affects inequality, even when there are no household-specific investments.

In the environments studied in the first two sections, the borrowing limits are set exogenously. In Section 14.4.3 we start exploring endogenous theories of the borrowing limit by looking at environments in which the ability to borrow is limited by the incen-tive to default. In doing so, we follow the ideas suggested in Kehoe and Levine (1993). In Section 14.4.4 we review recent papers in which the limits to borrow come from the legal ability to default on debts allowed by the U.S. bankruptcy code. In Section 14.4.5 we explore various extensions of these models. Finally, in Section 14.4.6 we briefly discuss the literature that links the long-term performance of an aggregate economy with the ability of households to borrow.

14.4.1 Financial Markets and Investment Possibilities

Agents with available funds are not necessarily those with the best opportunities to use the funds. It is then socially desirable that the funds are channeled from the former to the latter, which is the primary role played by financial markets. Financial market imperfec-tions, however, limit the volume of funds that can be transferred, and as a result the allocation is inefficient.

Financial market imperfections can take different forms. In a simple overlapping gen-erations model in which the only decision that agents make is how much to invest in the education of their children, the lack of borrowing possibilities implies that investments with a rate of return higher than the risk-free rate will not be undertaken. A similar mech-anism operates when there are borrowing possibilities but investments are risky and there are no insurance possibilities. This implies that investing agents may be left with very little consumption if they are unlucky. As a result, risk-averse agents may choose not to undertake investments.

To illustrate the importance of financial market frictions, consider an environment in which agents can save but cannot borrow, similar to that of Aiyagari (1994) developed in Section 14.2.1.3.2. The difference now is that the amount of efficiency units of labor is not random but is the result of investment. Consequently, two different investment strategies are available: households can save in the financial asset a (which in this model is backed by real capital), or they can invest in their own human capital so that $s' = \varphi(s, y)$, where y is the amount invested. The household's problem can be written as

$$v(s, a) = \max_{c, y, d'} u(c) + \beta v(s', d'; K),$$
(14.69)

$$\text{subject to}$$
(14.70)

$$c + d' + y = ws + a(1 + r),$$
(14.71)

$$s' = \varphi(s, y),$$
(14.72)

$$d' \geq 0.$$
(14.73)

If constraint (14.73) is not binding, the first order conditions of this problem imply

$$w\varphi_y(s, y) = 1 + r,$$
(14.74)

that is, the rate of return of the two types of investment is equalized. Moreover, imagine for simplicity that $\varphi(s, y) = \varphi(y)$; then in a steady state, all agents will have the same labor income. An interesting feature of this model is that convergence will arise immediately. That is, all households will have within a period the same labor income, because all agents will make the same investment in human capital. Differences in initial wealth perpetuate. For more general human capital production functions, we can get similar results, with the speed of convergence depending on the decreasing returns in s but not on y.

How would the analysis change when constraint (14.73) is binding? It all depends on the shape of function $\varphi(s, y)$. Let's start with the case $\varphi(s, y) = \varphi(y)$. Assuming that the function $\varphi(y)$ is strictly concave and $\varphi_y(y)$ approaches infinity as y approaches zero, all households will make some investment and the first order condition is

$$u_c(c) = \beta \varphi_y(y) u_c(c')w'.$$
(14.75)

This equation looks very similar to the Euler equation in the standard representative agent growth model, in which there is curvature in the production function. Consequently, no matter how poor they start out, all agents will slowly but steadily converge to a level of human capital that satisfies $\varphi_y(y)w = \beta^{-1}$. So the economy converges to equal labor income, even if the wealth distribution can be very unequal. Policies that subsidize investment in human capital could speed up the equalization process but will not change the eventual convergence outcome.

A lot of concern remains about *poverty traps*, that is, situations in which households that start with insufficient initial resources never abandon their poverty status. For this situation to happen, some special assumptions are needed. In particular, $\varphi(y)$ cannot be strictly concave. The typical assumption is to have a state of discontinuity such as a minimum expenditure that is needed to increase human capital. One example is the investment required for educational advancement. In this case, households compare the two options: whether to invest in education or not. If initial household wealth is very low, they may be unable to invest and still have positive consumption. But even households with slightly higher initial wealth may find that educational investment is feasible but not worth it, because it requires that initial consumption is way too low and the cost in utility terms too high. Clearly, in cases like these, government intervention can be fruitful because it is able to circumvent households' inability to borrow. The government can tax richer households today and transfer resources to the poorer households, or it can borrow, transfer resources to the poor households, and tax them later after they have acquired more education. A policy that makes education compulsory even at the cost of severe current disutility will not be optimal because poor households could have chosen to do it themselves if this choice were preferable.

Another possibility in which the structure of financial markets matters is to have a stochastic return to the investment technology. Consider a version of Equation (14.72) where higher investments in y yield a high expected value of s' but also a high variance. If the household had access to insurance markets, then it would happily undertake the investment, but if not, its risk aversion would prevent it from doing so. Again, in this case, certain government interventions that provide some form of insurance could be desirable.

14.4.2 Changes in the Borrowing Constraint

One way of assessing the role of financial constraints is to see what happens when they are relaxed. The Aiyagari (1994) model described in Section 14.2.1.3.1 assumes that financial markets are extremely underdeveloped: only one asset needs to be backed by physical capital, and there are no borrowing possibilities. What would happen if the financial constraints were to be relaxed, that is, what if we allowed for some noncontingent borrowing?

Table 14.7 shows the steady-state wealth distribution under various borrowing limits that go from a quarter of per-household yearly GDP to 1-year GDP. Figure 14.4 shows their associated Lorenz curves. We can see from the figure that, regardless of the calibration of the earnings process, inequality increases substantially with the relaxation of the borrowing constraint, in some cases to implausible levels (we cannot imagine an actual economy in which more than 60% of the population have negative financial assets). The Gini indices go up substantially, with one economy displaying a value above one, which is possible when we allow for negative values for the variable of interest. Looser borrowing constraints are associated with greater inequality because the poorest households want

Table 14.7 Distribution of wealth for various borrowing limits (in terms of per household yearly output)

Borrowing Constraint	Quintiles					Top 10%	Top 5%	Top 1%	Gini
	1st	2nd	3rd	4th	5th				
Low concentration of wealth economy (PSID)									
0.00	3.75	10.14	16.97	25.06	44.08	26.73	15.51	3.99	0.41
−0.25	2.39	8.82	15.21	24.10	49.48	30.90	17.81	4.44	0.46
−0.50	0.82	7.77	14.72	24.56	52.13	32.52	18.62	4.69	0.50
−1.00	−2.98	5.37	13.60	26.11	57.90	35.88	20.73	5.32	0.60
High concentration of wealth Aiyagari economy (SCF)									
0.00	0.00	0.00	0.50	4.78	94.72	76.96	51.77	14.54	0.86
−0.25	−1.72	−1.72	−0.23	3.56	100.11	81.47	54.83	15.50	0.93
−0.50	−3.50	−3.50	−0.88	2.89	104.99	85.16	57.03	16.19	0.99
−1.0	−7.21	−7.10	−1.87	2.88	113.30	90.75	60.68	16.94	1.11

to borrow more. This result arises from the impatient nature of households in the general equilibrium. More specifically, households have a precautionary motive to save for the future when markets are incomplete, and on average they will never stop saving and will perpetually accumulate assets. But in a general equilibrium, the excess savings, which in aggregate takes the form of higher accumulation of capital, will drive down the marginal product of capital and, therefore, the return from savings. Consequently, in the steady-state equilibrium we have that $\beta^{-1} > 1 + r$, that is, households are more impatient than the return of their savings.[11] This result creates an incentive to anticipate consumption when the realization of earnings is low, which is made possible by the greater availability of credit (looser borrowing limit). This mechanism generates a greater concentration of wealth, as shown in Figure 14.4 and Table 14.7.

Another possibility is that improvements in the financial market allow agents not only to borrow more but also to buy insurance. In this case, agents could acquire assets or take liabilities with payments contingent on the realizations of idiosyncratic shocks. One

[11] To better understand why β^{-1} must be bigger than $1 + r$ in a steady-state general equilibrium, consider the following. Suppose that in a steady state $\beta^{-1} = 1 + r$. Given r, we can determine the stock of capital K from the equilibrium condition that equalizes the interest rate to the marginal product of capital. Lower interest rates must be associated with higher stocks of capital since the marginal product of capital is decreasing in K. Because agents face uninsurable risks, they save for precautionary reasons and, when $\beta^{-1} = 1 + r$, the average wealth accumulated by agents grows without bound (although individual wealth goes up and down stochastically, the average growth is positive). But in equilibrium the accumulated wealth is equal to K. Therefore, if wealth increases, K also increases, reducing the marginal product of capital and, with it, the interest rate r. As the interest rate declines, households save less until the average growth rate of wealth for the aggregate economy is zero. We therefore conclude that in a steady-state equilibrium, $1 + r$ must be lower than β^{-1}.

consequence is that households will no longer save for precautionary motives, because they can completely insure their individual consumption. Furthermore, there would not be too much aggregate savings, as in the economy without insurance. So the economy would slowly reduce savings until the interest rate became equal to the rate of time preference. Individual consumption could differ across households, as consumption depends on the initial distribution of physical and human wealth, as in Chatterjee (1994) (see Section 14.2.1.1).

Another important question is, how much borrowing can be sustained? In a model without leisure choice, the maximum sustainable debt is the one that can be paid in all states of nature. The worst state of the world is the lowest possible value of s, which we refer to as $\underline{s}$. A household that receives the lowest realization of earnings forever has the capability to pay a maximum amount of interest $\underline{s}w$. Thus, the maximum sustainable debt

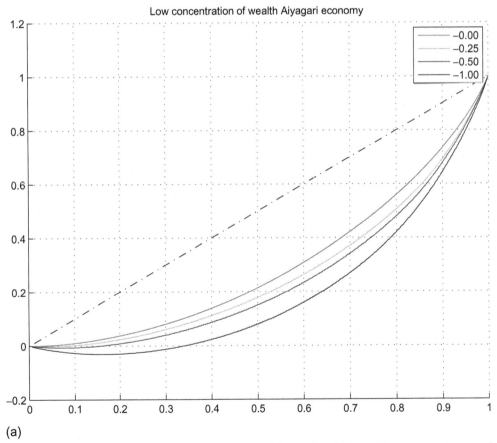

(a)

Figure 14.4 Lorenz curves for various economies and borrowing limits. (a) Low concentration of wealth economy (PSID) calibrated as in Aiyagari (1994).

(Continued)

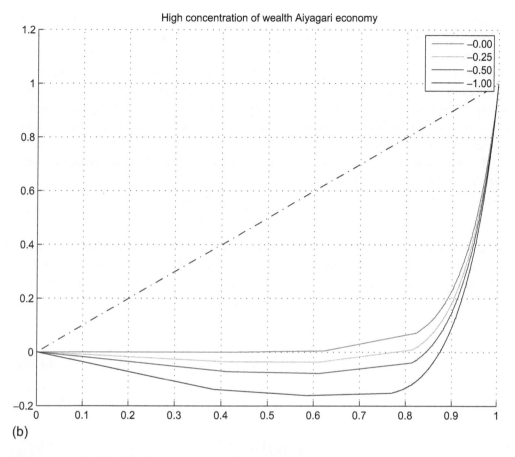

Figure 14.4—Cont'd (b) High concentration of wealth economy (SCF) calibrated as in Castañeda et al. (2003).

is $\frac{sw}{r}$, because the interest on this debt is exactly $\underline{s}$. Sometimes this is called the solvency constraint. Any debt larger than this value has a positive probability of not being paid.

14.4.3 Limits in the Ability to Borrow

So far, we have considered environments in which the access to credit markets is arbitrarily limited and there are no markets for contingencies. But why not? What limits the set of contracts that people can sign?

In a well-known and influential paper, Kehoe and Levine (1993) postulated that the ability of households to borrow is limited by their willingness to pay back when the alternative is to give up access to credit markets. In addition, a subset of the assets (physical or human or both) or endowments of the households can be seized, but not necessarily all of them. For example, future labor income may be outside of the reach of creditors.

Their approach does not preclude the existence of contingent markets. We would like to emphasize two features of this approach. The first feature is that it is the institutional environment that determines the set of contracts that are available. We think that this is an enormous advance compared with the literature that relies on exogenous borrowing limits. The second feature is that only the contracts that can be enforced ex post are available in the market. Therefore, once signed, there is complete compliance in the execution of these contracts. This feature is perhaps less appealing, as we see actual ex post reneging on formal contracts.

To show how this works, we could again slightly modify the Aiyagari economy. Let's first define the following object:

$$\overline{V}(s, a) = \max_{d' \geq 0} u\big(a(1 + r) + sw - d'\big) + \beta \sum_{s'} \Gamma_{s,s'} \overline{V}(s', d'), \tag{14.76}$$

which is the household's value without having access to borrowing. Moreover, with some abuse of notation, let's define $\overline{V}(s) = \overline{V}(s, 0)$ as the value attainable when the initial assets are zero. Clearly, this limit depends on the value of the shock s. Now consider the following problem:

$$v(s, a) = \max_{c, y, d'} u(c) + \beta_i v(s', d'; K), \tag{14.77}$$

$$\text{s.t.} \quad c + d' + y = ws + a(1 + r), \tag{14.78}$$

$$d' \geq \underline{a}(s), \tag{14.79}$$

where $\underline{a}(s)$ is such that

$$v\big(s, \underline{a}(s)\big) = \overline{V}(s). \tag{14.80}$$

In words, households can borrow up to the level in which they would be better off in an autarkic state, that is, in a state in which they start from zero assets and never borrow again. Notice that it is quite possible that in this situation high-income people have more difficulties borrowing than low-income people, and this is because $\overline{V}(s^H) > \overline{V}(s^\ell)$ when $s^H > s^\ell$. Notice also that $\underline{a}(s)$ is an endogenous variable. We do not know its value before solving for the equilibrium of this economy.

We have written problem (14.77) under the implicit assumption that assets can never be confiscated. If the legal system were such that assets could be taken away in absence of compliance, we could substitute Equation (14.79) with

$$d' \geq \underline{\underline{a}}(s), \tag{14.81}$$

where $\underline{\underline{a}}(s)$ is such that $v\big(s, \underline{\underline{a}}(s)\big) = \overline{\overline{V}}(s)$ and $\overline{\overline{V}}(s) = u(sw) + \beta \sum_{s'} \Gamma_{s,s'} \overline{\overline{V}}(s')$. Essentially, the borrowing limit could be the amount that makes the agent indifferent between paying back the lender or defaulting and being forever unable to save or borrow.

In this model, all contracts are carried out, that is, loans and state-contingent contracts are always honored. In reality, however, many people file for bankruptcy. For example, in the 12 months between April 1, 2012, and March 31, 2013, 779,306 people filed for bankruptcy in the United States.[12] In some countries including the United States and Canada, debts are typically discharged after filing, whereas in other countries, such as Hungary, Romania, and Spain, there is no legal procedure to handle personal bankruptcy, and people are always liable for previous debts. The rest of the countries lie somewhere in between these extremes.

One possible strategy to deal with the pervasiveness of bankruptcy is to model it as a contingency fully negotiated ex ante by the parties. This strategy is hard to justify, however, because filing for bankruptcy is a legal procedure that can be completed unilaterally by the debtor. Hence, it is a right that cannot be forfeited. We need, then, to have explicit models that explicitly incorporate bankruptcy filings. One approach, followed within the optimal contracting tradition, is to assume that there are information asymmetries and costly state verification, as in Townsend (1979). The costly state verification model has been widely applied in macroeconomics, for example, in Bernanke and Gertler (1989), Bernanke et al. (1999), and Carlstrom and Fuerst (1995). In these models, default arises in equilibrium even if agents sign fully optimal contracts. In the next section, we will describe other approaches that are more in line with the literature that excludes the applicability of fully optimal contracts.

14.4.4 Endogenous Financial Markets Under Actual Bankruptcy Laws

During the last few years, considerable work has been done to bring together models with imperfect insurance and models with a legal system that allows agents to file for bankruptcy in a way that is similar to that of Chapter 7 in the U.S. bankruptcy code (Chatterjee et al., 2007; Livshits et al., 2007). We now present a version of these models and describe how their implications for the income and wealth distribution change compared with the basic Aiyagari model. These studies take advantage of a feature of the legal system that lists people who have filed for bankruptcy in public records for a certain number of years. The literature interprets the implications of the listing as limiting accessibility to borrowing for the duration of the public record.

Consider the following household problem, yet another variant of the basic Aiyagari problem:

$$v(s, a, 1) = \max_{c, d' \geq 0} u(ws + a(1 + r) - d') + \beta \sum_{s'} \Gamma_{s, s'} [(1 - \delta)v(s', d', 1) + \delta v(s', d', 0)],$$

$$(14.82)$$

[12] See U.S. courts, http://www.uscourts.gov/.

$$v(s, a, 0) = \max \left\{ u(sw) + \beta \sum_{s'} \Gamma_{s,s'} v(s', 0, 1), \quad \max_{c, d'} u(c) + \beta \sum_{s'} \Gamma_{s,s'} v(s', d', 0), \right\}$$

(14.83)

$$\text{s.t.} \quad c + q(s, d')d' = ws + a.$$

(14.84)

The function $v(s, a, h)$ is the household's value function, with the last argument $h \in \{0, 1\}$ denoting the household's credit history. When $h = 1$, the household's credit history is bad in the sense that the agent has defaulted in the near past and is prevented from having access to credit. Problem (14.82) depicts this case, showing that in the following period, its credit history may turn out to be good, $h = 0$, with parameter δ controlling the expected duration of market exclusion.

Problem (14.83) is of interest when the credit history is good, $h = 0$, and we have written it compactly, implicitly assuming that the household is in debt, $a < 0$. Here, the agent has two options: to file for bankruptcy or not. If the agent files, three things happen: household consumption equals current labor income, sw, credit history turns bad next period, $h' = 1$, and the household is prevented from saving. The latter property is a feature of the bankruptcy code, as the agent is not permitted to keep assets after filing for bankruptcy.[13] If the household does not file for bankruptcy, it can borrow or save as it wishes. Note, however, that we have written the budget constraint (14.84) differently from previous problems. The left-hand side, the uses of funds, has the asset position at the beginning of the following period multiplied by $q(s, d')$. This is the household-specific inverse of the interest rate. Lenders accurately forecast that the agent may file for bankruptcy and charge an extra premium so that in expected value they get the market return. The function $q(s, d')$ is an equilibrium object. If the household chooses to save, $d' \geq 0$, and the inverse of the interest rate is that of the safe asset: $q(s, d') = (1 + r)^{-1}$.

The optimal solution to the problem of a household with negative assets is to default for a range of its earnings. The set of earnings for which the household defaults increases with the stock of debt.

The solution to this problem has two interesting properties. First, inasmuch as default is costly (the household will not be able to borrow for a while), the household would not default if the debt is very small. Second, in some circumstances, the household may be too poor to default, opting instead to borrow even more for a sufficiently low realization of earnings. Consequently, the equilibrium of this model requires that the inverse of the interest rate $q(s, d')$ is such that lenders break even in expected value, which in turn implies that interest rates are increasing in the amount borrowed and in the likelihood of bad earnings realizations.

---

[13] In the United States, the agent can keep a maximum amount of assets, and this amount varies across states. Here, we have assumed zero retainable. In the discussion from which we are abstracting are other subtleties of the bankruptcy code, such as the requirement that labor income is below the state median's income.

This structure has proved useful in making sense simultaneously of the extent of unsecured borrowing in the United States as well as the frequency of bankruptcy filings, especially if the model is enhanced with a few bells and whistles such as expenditure shocks.

14.4.4.1 A Weakness of This Approach

Why are households refused credit when they have a bad credit history? Nothing in the law requires this. In fact, the opposite is true: in the United States, a bankruptcy filing under Chapter 7, the relevant case, precludes additional filings over a period of years, making a recent filer appear to be a better creditor than somebody with a clean slate.

This question has three possible answers, but none are completely satisfactory. First, a Nash equilibrium with a coordination problem can be constructed when lenders believe that agents with bad credit histories will not pay back and hence they will not lend, whereas prospective borrowers might as well choose to default, because they do not receive credit. Although this is indeed a Nash equilibrium, it is one that is always present in the event of lending, and there is no argument for why it happens only with a bad credit history. Another possibility is to construct a trigger strategy whereby lenders coordinate not to lend during a punishment period in the event of default. But like all triggers, this is not an equilibrium of the limit of finite economies. Hence, it is not a Markov equilibrium. Many economists are comfortable with trigger strategy equilibria, whereas others are not. The last rationale for exclusion of those with bad credit is to postulate the existence of a regulator that prevents lenders from lending to those with bad credit, something that is not actually done by any of the banking regulators.

14.4.5 Credit Scoring

Chatterjee et al. (2008) and Chatterjee et al. (2004) propose a solution to the weakness of models based on exogenous exclusion after bankruptcy filings. These papers note that in the United States, there is pervasive use of credit scores, which are assessments of reliability made by independent companies. The authors then pose a model in which two types of people differ in some fundamental attribute associated with reliability that is not directly observable by outsiders—for instance, patience or even good driving habits. The credit score is then used as the market assessment of being a good type, meaning the type that is more likely to pay back debts or be reliable. In this context, both types of agents fall under the model of borrowing in which there are multiple types. The key here is that both types of agents—both the patient and the impatient agents—want to repay their debts to signal that they are patient, which allows them to have access to better borrowing terms. In this context, filing for bankruptcy increases the market-assessed likelihood that an agent is of the bad type, which translates to a severe worsening of loan terms, if not an outright exclusion of future credit. Moreover, because the market is assessing traits that are relevant not only for the repayment of credit but also for other things (e.g., cheap property insurance, access to rental property, personal relationships), timely repayment of debts carries a strong incentive that allows for the possibility of many contracts to be carried out, even if the law lacks the necessary teeth to enforce these contracts.

14.4.6 Financial Development and Long-Run Dynamics

We now look at the extent to which access to financial markets can help us to understand the long-run dynamics of the economy. In Section 14.4.6.1 we briefly focus on long-term growth, and in Section 14.4.6.2 we discuss how the evolution of financial markets can also help us understand the issue of global imbalances, that is, the emergence of large and persistent balance of payments deficits.

14.4.6.1 Long-Run Growth and Financial Development

The Schumpeterian view places entrepreneurship at the center stage of economic development. Owing to financial constraints and the lack of insurance markets, however, entrepreneurial investment is suboptimal. Essentially, when financial markets are not well developed, resources cannot be redistributed from those who control the resources but do not have the best uses of these resources to those who have the best investment opportunities but lack the funds. This efficiency problem is especially severe when the distribution of resources is particularly concentrated. We may then end up with a situation in which the poor become (relatively) poorer because they cannot take advantage of investment opportunities and the economy as a whole grows less. Examples of studies that emphasize the importance of inequality for growth in the presence of financial constraints are Galor and Zeira (1993), Banerjee and Newman (1993), and Aghion and Bolton (1997). Because these studies were already reviewed by Bertola (2000) in a previous edition of the Handbook, we do not repeat their description in this chapter.

A more recent literature, however, also emphasizes that market incompleteness—that is, environments in which the trade of state-contingent claims is limited—could have both positive and negative effects on capital accumulation. In a world with only uninsurable and exogenous earning shocks as in Aiyagari (1994), market incompleteness generates more capital accumulation and, therefore, more growth. When risky income is endogenous, however, as in Angeletos (2007), market incompleteness may discourage investment. See also Meh and Quadrini (2006).

Another group of studies that investigates the relation between inequality and macroeconomic performance emphasizes the importance of social conflict and expropriation. Greater inequality often associated with underdeveloped financial markets means that a larger group of individuals are at the bottom of the distribution and face poor economic conditions compared with the rest of the population. Faced with poor economic conditions and the feeling that the prospects for economic improvement are impaired by the excessive concentration of wealth, the resentment toward the rich starts to rise, which creates incentives to expropriate either by stealing or through revolutions. The risk of expropriation has two negative effects. First, it acts as an investment tax that discourages investment. Second, agents devote more resources to protect property rights instead of using the resources for productive and growth-enhancing activities. Benhabib and Rustichini (1996) develop a model that formalizes this idea. Although not explicitly considered in this paper, financial underdevelopment could contribute to this because it makes it more difficult for poor people to escape from poverty.

Another theory of inequality affecting growth is developed in Murphy et al. (1989). This paper assumes that some technologies have increasing returns. These technologies become profitable only if the domestic market is sufficiently large, that is, enough demand exists for the goods produced with the new technologies. If wealth is highly concentrated, the domestic market remains small (because not enough consumers can afford these goods). As a result, growth-enhancing technologies will not be implemented. The paper does not explicitly explore the role of financial markets; however, to the extent that financial underdevelopment creates the conditions for greater concentration of wealth, the mechanism described in this paper becomes more relevant in economies in which the financial structure is relatively underdeveloped.

Kumhof and Rancière (2010) have proposed an explanation for the recent crisis based on the changes in income distribution pinpointing similarity with the Great Depression. The idea is that, because of an exogenous shock that affected the ability of the rich to grab earnings, income became more concentrated, and as a result, the poor started to borrow more, increasing the debt-to-income ratio in the economy. Eventually, the increase in borrowing triggered the crisis.

We conclude this section by citing the work of Greenwood and Jovanovic (1990). Although this paper does not deal directly with inequality, it shows that improvements in financial markets (in this particular case, through the information gathered by financial intermediaries) have important effects on economic growth. As we have seen in previous chapters, market incompleteness also creates inequality. Therefore, once complemented with the previous analysis, this paper could also be relevant for understanding the link between financial market development, inequality, and growth. Also important is the work of Greenwood et al. (2010).

14.4.6.2 Global Imbalances

We have not talked much about cross-country inequality because this topic is usually a concern for development-oriented economists. However, inequality may be shaped by the increase in trade that is properly known as globalization, which is due to the reduction in the trade barriers for both technological and policy reasons. We have already referred, if only obliquely, to a mechanism by which more trade across countries could affect inequality: opening to trade changes the relative price of skills and may be behind part of the recent increase in the wage-skill gap. But an increase in trade shapes inequality both within and between countries through other, more subtle mechanisms. In this section we illustrate some potential mechanisms through which inequality is linked to globalization. Further analysis of the role of globalization for inequality is conducted in Chapter 20.

The process of international globalization is commonly presented as taking the form of higher trade in goods and services (imports and exports) as a fraction of GDP. But there is another side to it. Several advanced countries, the United States in particular, have experienced over the last 30 years a persistent deficit in the balance of payments as a result of imports being higher than exports, with the consequent deterioration in their net foreign asset positions. On the other hand, oil-producing countries and several emerging countries, China in particular, have been accumulating positive net foreign asset positions. "Global imbalances" is the term often used to refer to the situation in which some countries accumulate large negative net foreign asset positions whereas others accumulate positive net foreign asset positions. This situation has affected inequality, but to understand the impact on inequality we first need a theory of why imbalances could emerge in the wave of globalization.

Mendoza et al. (2007) provide one such theory. They claim that sustained deficits cannot be explained solely with traditional trade forces (different factor prices, technological advantages, or lower transportation costs). We also need to understand the differential saving behavior of countries that in equilibrium lead to different rates of returns on savings (insofar as international financial markets are somewhat segmented). This is possible even if countries have identical preferences and production technologies, but agents in each country differ in the extent to which they are capable of insuring their individual risks. This can be illustrated with the now familiar Aiyagari economy.

Suppose that we compare two economies, both slightly modified versions of the Aiyagari environment described above, that differ only in the process for earnings, one being more volatile than the other. It is important to point out that the assumption that countries differ in the volatility of earnings is a shortcut to capture other, more micro-founded differences. For example, in Mendoza et al. (2007), countries do not differ in the underlying process for earnings but in the sophistication of financial markets. Agents (consumers and firms) in countries with more advanced financial markets have a better opportunity to insure their idiosyncratic risk. Because in terms of savings the implication of higher insurance is similar to lower variability of earnings, here we illustrate the mechanism by assuming lower earning volatility. In some applications the higher ability to insure could derive from government policies (for example, the provision of public-funded health insurance). In some cases, the differences could come from more uncertainty about the underlying process for earnings. For example, a country that is experiencing a process of transformation (such as China, during the last three decades) is also possibly characterized by greater uncertainty at the individual level. Independently of the actual sources (greater ability to insure or greater underlying uncertainty), it should be clear that the example provided here is just a shortcut to illustrate something more fundamental such as differences in the characteristics of the financial system.[14]

---

[14] See Mendoza et al. (2007) for more details on how differences in the financial system can lead to lower ability to insure.

Table 14.8 Two economies before and after being able to borrow from each other

Economy	Before: autarky		After: mobility	
	Low var	High var	Low var	High var
Capital to output ratio	3.34	3.88	3.67	3.67
Interest rate (%)	4.02	1.27	2.24	2.24
Wealth to output ratio	3.34	3.88	0.39	6.95
Gini index of wealth	0.41	0.59	0.50	0.39
Coeff. of var wealth	0.76	1.09	0.88	0.96
1st quantile	3.40	0.00	0.40	0.00
2nd quantile	10.21	0.69	6.06	3.35
3rd quantile	17.11	15.50	17.58	17.45
4th quantile	25.16	30.21	25.94	21.00
5th quantile	44.15	53.60	50.01	58.20
Top 10% (cumulative)	26.73	33.28	30.37	29.63
Top 5% (cumulative)	15.51	19.72	18.09	17.21
Top 1%	3.99	5.19	4.25	4.32

To this end, we use two different processes for earnings. The first process is what we used above for the version of the model that we called PSID economy or low-variability economy. The second process is what we used in the high-variability economy, a version of the SCF economy with a slightly less extreme good state. Besides the process for earnings, the two economies are alike in all other dimensions.

The first two columns of Table 14.8 display the steady states of these two economies under autarky. The first column, the low-variability economy, has a capital-to-output ratio of 3.34, implying an annual interest rate of 4.02%. Because in this economy wealth can only take the form of capital, total wealth is also 3.34 × output, and this is what households choose to hold to accommodate the shocks to earnings given the 4.02% interest rate. The second column of Table 14.8 refers to the economy with higher income variability also in the autarky regime. Households choose to hold more wealth (3.88 × output) to bear the high risk. Two things to note are that the interest rate is now much lower, 1.27%, and that output is slightly higher because of the higher capital.

The determination of the equilibrium is depicted in panel (a) of Figure 14.5. This figure plots the aggregate (steady-state) supply of savings as an increasing, concave function of the interest rate.[15] The demand for savings is downward sloping because of the diminishing marginal productivity of capital. Country 1 has a lower volatility of

---

[15] Aggregate savings converge to infinity as the interest rate approaches the rate of time preference from below, because agents need an infinite amount of precautionary savings to attain a nonstochastic consumption profile.

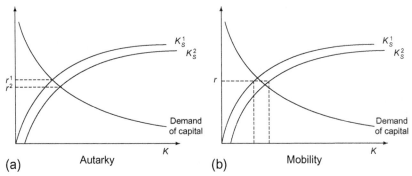

Figure 14.5 Steady-state equilibria with heterogeneous earning risks.

individual earnings and hence a lower supply of savings for each interest rate. As a result, the equilibrium in autarky implies a higher interest rate and a lower total capital.

Imagine now that households in these two economies can start owning capital in the other country, that is, the countries become financially integrated. After a brief period of transition that depends on the ease with which physical capital can flow or be reallocated, the interest rate in both countries will be equalized. This implies that the low-variability economy will experience a reduction in the interest rate and the high-variability economy will experience an increase in the interest rate. Then, in the country in which the interest rate decreases (low-variability economy), savings will fall, whereas in the country in which the interest rate increases (high-variability economy), savings will rise. The result is that households in the high-variability economy end up owning part of the capital installed in the low-variability economy. In this way, global imbalances may emerge as the low-variability economy dis-saves. Effectively, the low-variability economy consumes and invests more than it produces, with the difference covered by imports in excess of exports (trade deficit).

This process takes a long time until the aggregate savings of households in each country no longer change. This new steady state is depicted in panel (b) of Figure 14.5. The world interest rate is somewhere between the pre-liberalization interest rates in the two countries. Compared with autarky, the interest rate and the supply of savings fall in country 1 and rise in country 2, and hence the country with lower volatility of earnings ends up with a negative foreign asset position. Moreover, the capital stock rises relative to its autarky level in country 1 and falls in country 2. Thus, financial globalization leads capital to flow from economies with more risk to those with lower risk.

For analytical simplicity, we have modeled this process as the outcome of countries that differ in their earnings risk. However, as emphasized above, this is just a shortcut to capture other types of differences across countries that ultimately lead to different exposure to risk. It could very well be the case that the underlying risk is identical across countries but that the lower risk in one country is just the result of more-developed financial markets, which allow for higher insurability of risk. Formally, in the first country there are more markets for state-contingent claims. This is the approach taken in Mendoza et al. (2007), and the end result is similar to the case of differential processes for earnings: the country with a higher ability to insure saves less and has a higher interest rate than the country with less-developed financial markets. When the two countries integrate, it is the more financially developed country that accumulates negative foreign assets, whereas the less financially developed country accumulates positive foreign assets.

Therefore, financial market differences can affect the distribution of wealth across countries: in the long run, countries that are more financially sophisticated become poorer relative to countries that are less financially sophisticated (compared to the pre-liberalization era). This, however, does not mean that liberalization is welfare reducing for developed countries and welfare improving for less-developed countries. In Mendoza et al. (2007) we found, somewhat surprisingly, that liberalization was welfare improving for developed countries but slightly welfare reducing for less-developed countries (based on an equally weighted welfare function). In our example displayed in Table 14.8, the international redistribution of wealth is quite large, with the low-variability country ending up with barely 5% of total wealth. Yet, it started with almost half. The large international redistribution of wealth follows from the assumption that there are large differences in risk between the two countries. In reality, especially among integrated countries, the differences in risk may not be that big. Also, when a country accumulates too many foreign liabilities, there could be an incentive to default on these liabilities. This imposes a limit on the redistribution of wealth that can be generated across countries through this mechanism. Nevertheless, this example suggests that differences in savings could generate significant inequality in wealth across countries.

Cross-country financial market heterogeneity also plays a central role in Caballero et al. (2008) for explaining global imbalances. The mechanism proposed in this paper does not rely on risk but on the availability of saving instruments. The idea is that in certain countries, savers have difficulty storing their savings in high return assets. The implications for global imbalances, however, are similar to Mendoza et al. (2007). The two mechanisms are complementary ways of thinking about how the characteristics of financial systems can shape the distribution of wealth across countries in a globalized world. Interestingly, these contributions illustrate another mechanism through which financial globalization redistributes wealth. When productive inputs are not perfectly reproducible (as in the case of land), liberalization also leads to the equalization in the prices of these assets. Because under autarky these assets were cheaper in financially developed countries, these countries experience capital gains, whereas countries with less-developed financial markets experience capital losses.

The process of international redistribution of wealth also has consequences for the internal wealth distribution within each country. We see how wealth concentration increases in the low-variability country as measured by either the Gini index of the coefficient of variation of wealth or even by the shares held by the richest households (see Table 14.8). The opposite process happens in the less financially developed country, where the wealth distribution becomes more equal after international financial integration. Perhaps this process has contributed, at least in part, to the increased wealth concentration in the United States that we documented earlier.

14.5. THE POLITICAL ECONOMY CHANNEL

We have already seen in the previous sections some channels through which the distribution of income and wealth is interconnected with the aggregate performance of the economy. In this section, we discuss one particular channel through which inequality affects economic activities, that is, through the political and institutional system. Because many policies have redistributive consequences, the degree of inequality plays a central role in the choice of policies because societies with more unequal distributions of resources might demand greater redistribution. Because redistributive policies are often distortionary, the result is that more unequal societies tend to experience lower income or growth (or both).

Many contributions emphasize this mechanism, starting with Meltzer and Richard (1981). Examples are Persson and Tabellini (1994), Alesina and Rodrik (1994), Krusell and Ríos-Rull (1996), and Krusell et al. (1997). Many of these contributions, however, ignore individual uncertainty, which in a dynamic environment could play an important role in affecting the demand for redistribution as well as the distortions associated with redistributive policies. The goal of this section is to present a simple framework that illustrates the central idea of the early literature. It shows how the consideration of idiosyncratic uncertainty enriches the analysis and makes the relation between inequality and redistribution more complex than in these early studies.

14.5.1 A Simple Two-Period Model

Suppose that there is a continuum of agents who are alive for two periods. Agents value consumption, c_t, but dislike working, h_t, according to the utility function

$$u\left(c_t - \frac{h_t^2}{2}\right).$$

There are two sources of income: endowment, η_t, and labor, h_t. Individual endowments evolve according to

$$\ln\left(\eta_{t+1}\right) = \rho \cdot \ln\left(\eta_t\right) + \varepsilon_{t+1},$$

where $\varepsilon_{t+1} \sim N(0, (1-\rho^2) \cdot \sigma^2)$. This implies that the economywide distribution of log-endowments is normal with mean zero and variance σ^2, that is, $\ln(\eta_t) \sim N(0, \sigma^2)$. By changing ρ we change the persistence of endowments, but we keep the economywide distribution (inequality) constant. This parameter determines the degree of mobility: higher values of ρ imply lower mobility.

Before continuing, it will be helpful to derive some of the key moments of the cross-sectional distribution of endowments. Because endowments are log-normally distributed, that is, $\eta \sim LN(0, \sigma^2)$, the mean and the median are, respectively,

$$\text{Mean}(\eta_t) = e^{\frac{\sigma^2}{2}}, \quad \text{Median}(\eta_t) = 1.$$

These are unconditional moments. Also convenient is to derive the expected next-period endowment for an individual with current endowment η_t^i. The conditional mean is

$$\mathbb{E}\left[\eta_{t+1}^i \mid \eta_t^i\right] = e^{\rho \ln(\eta_t^i) + \frac{(1-\rho^2)\sigma^2}{2}}.$$

This conditional expectation will play an important role in the analysis of the model. Here we observe that if $\rho = 0$, the expected next-period endowment is the same for all agents. For an agent with median endowment, that is, $e_t^m = 1$, the conditional expectation becomes

$$\mathbb{E}\left[\eta_{t+1} \mid \eta_t^m\right] = e^{\frac{(1-\rho^2)\sigma^2}{2}}.$$

We can then compute the ratio of the next period economywide average endowment over the next period endowment expected by an agent whose current endowment is the median value. This is equal to

$$\frac{\text{Mean}(\eta_{t+1})}{\mathbb{E}\left[\eta_{t+1} \mid \eta_t^m\right]} = e^{\frac{\rho^2 \sigma^2}{2}}.$$

This expression makes it clear that the difference between the average endowment and the endowment expected by the agent with the median endowment in the current period depends on the persistent parameter ρ. The difference becomes zero if there is no persistence, that is, $\rho = 0$, and it is maximal when $\rho = 1$. Although the parameter ρ affects the ratio between the average endowment and the expected endowment by the median agent, ex post inequality does not depend on ρ. In fact, we have that

$$\frac{\text{Mean}(\eta_{t+1})}{\eta_{t+1}^m} = e^{\frac{\sigma^2}{2}}.$$

We will use these moments below, after completing the description of the model.

The government taxes incomes, from endowment and labor, at rate τ_t and redistributes the revenues as lump-sum transfers. The budget constraint for the government is

$$T_t = \tau_t \int_i \left(\eta_t^i + h_t^i\right) di,$$

where i is the index for an individual agent.

Agents do not save and solve a static optimization problem. Given the tax rate and the transfer, an individual agent i maximizes the period utility by choosing the labor supply h_t^i, subject to the following budget constraint:

$$c_t^i = \left(\eta_t^i + h_t^i\right)(1 - \tau_t) + T_t.$$

Taking first order conditions with respect to h_t for an individual worker with endowment η_t^i, we get the supply of labor $h_t = 1 - \tau_t$. Substituting in the utility function and using the equation that defines the government transfers, we get the indirect utility for period t:

$$U^i(\tau_t) = u\left(\tau_t \int_\eta \eta dF_t + \tau_t(1 - \tau_t) + \eta_t^i(1 - \tau_t) + \frac{(1 - \tau_t)^2}{2}\right).$$

Now suppose that agents vote for the next period tax rate τ_{t+1}. The tax rate preferred by an agent with current endowment η_t^i maximizes the expected next period indirect utility, that is,

$$\max_{\tau_{t+1}} \mathbb{E}_t\left[u\left(\tau_{t+1}\int_\eta \eta dF_{t+1} + \tau_{t+1}(1 - \tau_{t+1}) + \eta_{t+1}^i(1 - \tau_{t+1}) + \frac{(1 - \tau_{t+1})^2}{2}\right)\eta_t^i\right],$$

where we have denoted by $F(\eta)$ the distribution of endowments. Because the log-endowments are normally distributed, $F(\eta)$ is a log-normal distribution.

Notice that the voter forms expectations about the future endowment conditional on the current endowment. Of course, the higher is the persistence, the higher the dependence of the expected value from the current value.

Taking the first order condition, we derive

$$\tau_{t+1}^i = \int_\eta \eta dF_{t+1} - \mathbb{E}\left[\eta_{t+1}^i | \eta_t^i\right] - \frac{\text{Cov}\left(dU_{t+1}^i, \eta_{t+1}^i | \eta_t^i\right)}{\mathbb{E}\left[dU_{t+1}^i | \eta_t^i\right]}, \tag{14.85}$$

where dU_{t+1}^i denotes the derivative of the indirect utility for agent i with respect to the next-period tax rate. Notice that this term also depends on the tax rate. The above condition implicitly determines the tax rate.

The first term on the right-hand side of Equation (14.85) is the mean value of the economywide endowment, which is equal to $e^{\frac{\sigma^2}{2}}$. This term is the same for all agents. The second term is the expected endowment of agent i given the current endowment. This term is increasing in η_t^i, unless $\rho \leq 0$, which is excluded by assumption. Therefore, ignoring the third term, the preferred tax rate decreases with the current endowment.

The third term captures the role of risk aversion. Because the utility function is strictly concave and its derivative is strictly decreasing, $dU_{t+1}^i(.)$ decreases with the realization of next period endowment η_{t+1}^i, implying that the covariance term is negative. Therefore, preferences for taxes increase with the concavity of the utility function. This is the effect of risk aversion.

14.5.1.1 The Case of Risk Neutrality

Because the third term in the first order condition (14.85) is itself a function of τ_{t+1}^i, it is difficult to derive an analytical expression for the tax rate. Therefore, we first specialize to the case with risk–neutral agents so that $\mathrm{Cov}(dU_{t+1}^i, \eta_{t+1}^i | \eta_t^i) = 0$ and the preferred tax rate reduces to the first two terms in Equation (14.85). We can then establish that the preferred tax rate is monotonically decreasing in the current endowment η_t^i and the equilibrium tax rate is the one preferred by the agent with the median endowment. Using the fact that endowments are log-normally distributed and the log-endowment of the median voter is zero, the conditional expectation of the median voter for the next period endowment is $\mathbb{E}\left[\eta_{t+1} | \eta_t^m\right] = e^{\frac{(1-\rho^2)\sigma^2}{2}}$, whereas the economywide average is $\int_\eta \eta\, dF_{t+1} = e^{\frac{\sigma^2}{2}}$. Substituting in the preferred tax rate, we obtain the equilibrium tax rate

$$\tau_{t+1}\left(e_t^m\right) = e^{\frac{\sigma^2}{2}} - e^{\frac{(1-\rho^2)\sigma^2}{2}}. \tag{14.86}$$

The first two terms capture the standard politico-economy theory: because the average endowment, $e^{\frac{\sigma^2}{2}}$, is bigger than the median endowment, $e^{\frac{(1-\rho^2)\sigma^2}{2}}$, there is demand for redistribution. If we increase inequality by raising σ, the demand for redistribution increases. Because the optimal effort chosen by all agents is $h = 1 - \tau$, higher taxes discourage effort with negative effects on aggregate production. In some of the models proposed in the literature, taxes distort the accumulation of capital instead of effort, but the idea is similar.

The mechanism described above links inequality to redistribution and macroeconomic activity and captures the key features of the model studied in Meltzer and Richard (1981). In addition to this mechanism, the model presented here emphasizes the role of mobility captured by the parameter ρ. If we reduce ρ so that the economy experiences higher mobility, the cross-sectional inequality does not change. In fact, the ratio of average endowment and median endowment remains $e^{\frac{\sigma^2}{2}}$. However, the tax rate preferred by the median voter declines, as we can see from Equation (14.86). Even if the median voter has low endowment in the current period, what matters for next period taxes is the future endowment. If mobility is high, the median voter does not expect to keep the low endowment in the future. Thus, it is not optimal to choose high tax rates. In the limiting case with $\rho = 0$, the expected future endowment for all agents will be the average endowment and, in expected terms, the future benefit of redistribution is zero for all agents.

The importance of mobility for political preferences has received less attention than cross-sectional inequality. But the simple model presented here shows that mobility is also an important factor in the determination of political preferences. More importantly, if inequality and mobility are not independent, either across countries or across times, by focusing only on inequality we may reach inaccurate conclusions. Suppose, for example, that an increase in cross-sectional inequality, σ, is associated with a decrease in ρ, that is, with an increase in mobility. Therefore, we have two contrasting effects: the increase in σ leads to higher taxes, whereas the decrease in ρ leads to lower taxes.

This example may help to explain why, in certain episodes of increasing inequality, such as in the United States before the recent crisis, we do not see a significant increase in demand for redistribution. Perhaps the reason is that voters perceive higher mobility as coincident with greater inequality. Then, thanks to the perceived mobility, voters do not demand higher taxes and the economy continues to perform well even if income becomes more concentrated. However, if the performance of the economy changes and voters start to perceive lower mobility, they will start demanding more redistribution, which will further deteriorate the performance of the economy. This idea has been developed in Quadrini (1999) in a model that features two equilibria. The first equilibrium is characterized by high growth, high inequality, and low redistribution. The second equilibrium is characterized by low growth, low inequality, and high redistribution.[16] The idea that the prospect of upward mobility reduces the demand for redistribution has also been studied in Benabou and Ok (2001).

14.5.1.2 The Case of Risk Aversion
We now assume that the utility function is concave and takes the following form:

$$u\left(c_t - \frac{h_t^2}{2}\right) = \frac{\left(c_t - \frac{h_t^2}{2}\right)^{1-\nu}}{1-\nu},$$

where the parameter ν captures the curvature of the utility function.

Figure 14.6 plots the preferred tax rate as a function of current endowment η_t^i for different values of ν. As can be seen from the figure, the preferred tax rate is monotonically decreasing in current endowment, and therefore, the median voter theorem also applies in the case of risk-averse agents. Furthermore, we see that, for each endowment level η_t^i, the preferred tax rate increases with risk aversion.

Figure 14.7 plots the preferred tax rate as a function of current endowment for different degrees of mobility and risk aversion. The first panel is for the case of risk neutrality. In this case, we see that lower mobility (ρ changes from 0.5 to 0.9) increases the equilibrium tax rate, that is, the tax rate preferred by the median voter, which in the figure is identified by the vertical line. These are the properties we have shown analytically in the previous subsection. However, when agents are risk averse, lower mobility reduces

---

[16] The increase in inequality in the United States is not a recent phenomenon. However, voters and politicians started to focus more on this issue after the recent crisis. During the good times in which financial markets were expanding, low-income households had access to credit, allowing them to own houses. For many this appeared as a new opportunity (mobility). However, with the crisis and the credit market and the freeze, these opportunities dried up and many households lost faith in the possibility of improving their current position (mobility). Not surprisingly, they turned to the government for help and asked for more populist policies.

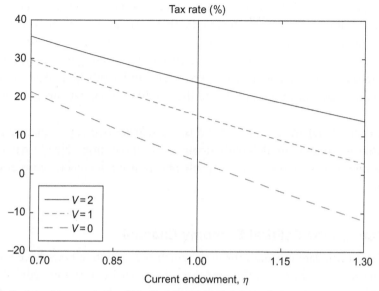

Figure 14.6 Preferred tax rates for different degrees of risk aversion. The inequality and mobility parameters are $\sigma = 0.5$ and $\rho = 0.5$. The vertical line denotes the median endowment.

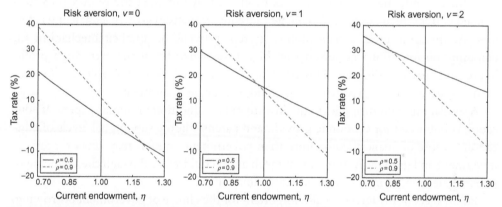

Figure 14.7 Preferred tax rates for different degrees of mobility, $\rho \in \{0.5, 0.9\}$, and risk aversion, $v \in \{0, 1, 2\}$. The inequality parameter is $\sigma = 0.5$. The vertical line denotes the median endowment.

the equilibrium tax rate. The reason is that, conditional on the current endowment, lower mobility means that agents face lower risk. In fact, with $\rho = 1$, next period endowment is equal to current endowment. Thus, there is less demand for insurance.

This example shows that mobility affects equilibrium policies through two mechanisms. The first mechanism works through the impact of mobility on the redistributive gains from next period taxes. When mobility is low, the expected redistributive gains are high. These gains vanish if mobility is perfect, that is, $\rho = 0$. The second mechanism works through the impact of mobility on individual risk. Given the current endowment, higher mobility (lower ρ) increases the conditional volatility of next period endowment and the median agent faces higher risk. Thus, greater redistribution is preferred if preferences are concave. This second mechanism is irrelevant when agents are risk neutral but becomes important when agents are risk averse. For a sufficiently high degree of risk aversion, the second mechanism dominates and the equilibrium tax rate declines with lower mobility.

Corbae et al. (2009) and Bachmann and Bai (2013) are two papers that study infinite horizon political economy models with income taxes and uninsurable idiosyncratic risks. Thus, these two papers are potentially capable of capturing the mechanisms described in this section.

14.5.2 More on the Political Economy Channel

Some theories formulate channels through which redistributive taxes have a beneficial effect on the macroeconomy in the presence of financial constraints. For example, in the Schumpeterian view where entrepreneurship is central to economic growth, financial constraints and the absence of insurance markets make entrepreneurial investment suboptimal. Under these conditions, redistribution may provide extra resources to constrained entrepreneurs and could facilitate more investments in growth-enhancing activities. At the same time, a redistributive system provides an implicit mechanism for consumption smoothing (a person pays high taxes when he or she earns high profits but receives payments in case of losses). Therefore, it provides insurance. Thus, if entrepreneurs are risk averse, redistribution could encourage investment.

A similar mechanism applies to the investment in education or human capital. If education is important for economic growth, and parents choose suboptimal levels of education because of financial constraints, then government transfers may allow for greater investment and growth. A more direct mechanism could work through the financing of public education, as in Glomm and Ravikumar (1992).

Political economy forces are also important for the choice of government borrowing. Azzimonti et al. (2014) propose a theory of public debt where greater income inequality could increase the incentive of the government to borrow more if the higher inequality is associated with greater individual risk. This is because higher risk increases the demand for safe assets, which are undersupplied when markets are incomplete. If financial markets are integrated, the increase in inequality (risk) in a few countries could induce a worldwide increase in public debt. In this way, the paper proposes one of the possible mechanisms for explaining the rising public debt observed in most of the industrialized countries since the early 1980s.

We close this section by mentioning that, although a large branch of the political economy literature has been developed on the assumption that voters are self-motivated and agree on their views of the world, so that their assessment of a policy is based on how much they benefit, some authors have proposed alternative frameworks. Especially interesting is Piketty (1995). This study develops a model in which agents prefer different policies not because they are selfish but because they have different beliefs. All voters care about social welfare, but some believe that luck is more important in generating income, whereas others believe that effort is more important. These beliefs evolve over time based on personal experience, but they never converge. Thus, at any point in time, preferences are heterogeneous. Although not explicitly explored in the original article, it is possible to introduce factors that could change the distribution of beliefs and with them the properties of the macro economy. This could be an interesting direction for future research.

14.6. CONCLUSION

In this chapter we have discussed a variety of topics that lie in the somewhat fuzzy intersection of income distribution and macroeconomics. The choice of topics and approaches has surely been idiosyncratic, reflecting our tastes, interests, and expertise, and we have left out many topics from behavioral and nonoptimizing models to issues in development, to the analysis of the impact of the rise of inequality on the U.S. economy. We have also touched other aspects only superficially, such as the role of globalization on the economy. In addition, we have only looked marginally at the implications of income inequality for consumption inequality or even for inequality in the duration of life,[17] which is in the end what really matters to determine the welfare costs of inequality.

We are very aware that a very different chapter covering the same could be written by other authors (in fact, the next chapter includes an example of this by providing some very different ideas of macro modeling of the wealth distribution). But we hope that this chapter has provided an idea of how macroeconomics is explicitly incorporating the analysis of inequality to improve our understanding of the dynamics of the aggregate economy, and also of how the discipline that macroeconomics brings to the table—that all pieces have to be mutually consistent and that dynamics is at the core of economics—shapes the way we think about income and wealth inequality.

ACKNOWLEDGMENTS

We are grateful for the comments from many people over the years. Many people contributed direct comments about and calculations for this paper. They include the editors for this handbook, but also Makoto Nakajima, Mariacristina De Nardi, Josep Pijoan-Mas, and Thomas Piketty. Others, such as David Wiczer and Moritz Kuhn, made even more direct contributions. We received research assistance from Kai Ding and Gero Dolfus, comments by Sergio Salgado and Annaliina Soikkanen, and editorial help from Joan Gieseke.

[17] Pijoan-Mas and Ríos-Rull (2014) argue that the welfare cost of inequality in life spans dwarfs that of inequality in consumption.

We thank all of them. Ríos-Rull thanks the National Science Foundation for grant SES-1156228. The views expressed herein are those of the authors and not necessarily those of the Federal Reserve Bank of Minneapolis or the Federal Reserve System.

APPENDIX A. DERIVATION OF THE INEQUALITY INDEX

In each period, there are different cohorts of workers who have been employed for j periods. They also differ in terms of initial human capital h_0^k at birth. Because workers die with probability λ, the fraction of workers in the j cohort (composed of workers who survive for j periods) is equal to $\sum_k x_0^k (1 - \lambda)^j$. Denote by h_j^k the human capital of a worker born with initial human capital h_0^k of age $j + 1$. Because human capital grows at the gross rate $g(\gamma, \varepsilon)$, we have that $h_j^k = h_0^k \prod_{t=1}^{j} g(\gamma, \varepsilon_t)$. Of course, this differs across workers of the same cohort because the growth rate is stochastic. The average human capital is then computed as

$$\bar{h} = \sum_k x_0^k \sum_{j=0}^{\infty} (1 - \lambda)^j \mathbb{E} h_j^k, \tag{A1}$$

where $\mathbb{E}$ averages the human capital of all agents in the $j - k$ cohort. Because growth rates are serially independent, we have that $\mathbb{E} h_j^k = h_0^k \mathbb{E} g(\gamma, \varepsilon)^j$. Substituting in the above expression and solving we get

$$\bar{h} = \frac{\bar{h}_0}{1 - (1 - \lambda) \mathbb{E} g(\gamma, \varepsilon)},$$

where $\bar{h}_0 = \sum_k x_0^k h_0^k$ is the aggregate human capital of newborn agents.

We now turn to the variance, which is calculated as

$$\mathrm{Var}(h) = \sum_k x_0^k \sum_{j=0}^{\infty} (1 - \lambda)^j \mathbb{E} \left(h_j^k - \bar{h} \right)^2.$$

This can be rewritten as

$$\mathrm{Var}(h) = \sum_k x_0^k \sum_{j=0}^{\infty} (1 - \lambda)^j \left[\mathbb{E} \left(h_j^k \right)^2 - \bar{h}^2 \right].$$

This can be further rewritten as

$$\mathrm{Var}(h) = \sum_k x_0^k \left(h_0^k \right)^2 \sum_{j=0}^{\infty} (1 - \lambda)^j \mathbb{E} \left(\frac{h_j^k}{h_0^k} \right)^2 - \bar{h}^2.$$

The term h_j^k / h_0^k is independent of the initial human capital h_0^k. Taking into account the serial independence of the growth rates, we have that $\mathbb{E}\left(h_j^k / h_0^k\right)^2 = \left[\mathbb{E}g(\gamma, \varepsilon)^2\right]^j$. Substituting and solving, we have

$$\text{Var}(h) = \left(\sum_k x_0^k \left(h_0^k\right)^2\right) \left(\frac{1}{1-(1-\lambda)\mathbb{E}g(\gamma, \varepsilon)^2}\right) - \bar{h}^2.$$

To compute the inequality index, we simply divide the variance by $\bar{h}^2$, where $\bar{h}$ is given by Equation (A1). This returns the inequality index (14.27).

APPENDIX B. WAGE EQUATION WITH ENDOGENOUS DEBT

Consider the value of a filled vacancy defined in Equation (14.51). Using the binding enforcement $B' = \varphi(1-\eta)\mathbb{E}S'(B')$ to eliminate B', this value becomes

$$Q = (1+\varphi)\beta(1-\eta)\mathbb{E}S'(B').$$

Notice that at this stage we are imposing $b = B$ and $b' = B'$, which hold in a symmetric equilibrium.

Next we use the free entry condition $V = qQ - \kappa = 0$. Eliminating Q using the above expression and solving for the expected value of the surplus, we obtain

$$\mathbb{E}S'(B') = \frac{\kappa}{q(1+\varphi)\beta(1-\eta)}. \tag{B1}$$

Substituting into the definition of the surplus—Equation (14.50)—and taking into account that $b' = \varphi(1-\eta)\mathbb{E}S'(B')$, we get

$$S(B) = z - \bar{u} - B + \frac{[1-\lambda-p\eta+\varphi(1-\lambda)(1-\eta)]\kappa}{q(1+\varphi)(1-\eta)}. \tag{B2}$$

Now consider the net value for a worker,

$$W(B) - U = w - \bar{u} + \eta(1-\lambda-p)\beta\mathbb{E}S'(B').$$

Substituting $W(B) - U = \eta S(B)$ in the left-hand side and eliminating $\mathbb{E}S'(B')$ in the right-hand side using Equation (B1), we obtain

$$\eta S(B) = w - \bar{u} + \frac{\eta(1-\lambda-p)\kappa}{q(1+\varphi)(1-\eta)}. \tag{B3}$$

Finally, combining Equations (B2) and (B3) and solving for the wage, we get

$$w = (1-\eta)\bar{u} + \eta(z-b) + \frac{\eta[p+(1-\lambda)\varphi]\kappa}{q(1+\varphi)},$$

which is the expression reported in (14.54).

REFERENCES

Abowd, J.M., Card, D., 1987. Intertemporal labor supply and long-term employment contracts. Am. Econ. Rev. 77 (1), 50–68.

Acemoglu, D., 1998. Why do new technologies complement skills? Directed technical change and wage inequality. Q. J. Econ. 113 (4), 1055–1089.

Aghion, P., Bolton, P., 1997. A theory of trickle-down growth and development. Rev. Econ. Stud. 64 (2), 151–172.

Aguiar, M.A., Bils, M., 2011. Has consumption inequality mirrored income inequality? Working Paper 16807, National Bureau of Economic Research.

Aiyagari, S.R., 1994. Uninsured idiosyncratic risk and aggregate saving. Q. J. Econ. 109 (3), 659–684.

Alesina, A., Rodrik, D., 1994. Distributive politics and economic growth. Q. J. Econ. 109 (2), 465–490.

Alvaredo, F., 2011. A note on the relationship between top income shares and the Gini coefficient. Econ. Lett. 110 (3), 274–277.

Angeletos, G.-M., 2007. Uninsured idiosyncratic investment risk and aggregate saving. Rev. Econ. Dyn. 10 (1), 1–30.

Atkinson, A.B., Piketty, T., Saez, E., 2011. Top incomes in the long run of history. J. Econ. Lit. 49 (1), 3–71.

Attanasio, O., Battistin, E., Ichimura, H., 2004. What really happened to consumption inequality in the U.S.? Working Paper 10338, National Bureau of Economic Research.

Auerbach, A.J., Kotlikoff, L.J., 1987. Dynamic Fiscal Policy. Cambridge University Press, Cambridge.

Azzimonti, M., de Francisco, E., Quadrini, V., 2014. Financial globalization, inequality, and the rising public debt. Am. Econ. Rev. 104 (8), 2267–2302.

Bachmann, R., Bai, J.H., 2013. Politico-economic inequality and the comovement of government purchases. Rev. Econ. Dyn. 16 (4), 565–580.

Banerjee, A., Newman, A., 1993. Occupational choice and the process of development. J. Polit. Econ. 101 (2), 274–298.

Bell, B., Van Reenen, J., 2010. Bankers' pay and extreme wage inequality in the UK. Economic Performance Special Papers CEPSP21, Centre for Economic Performance, London School of Economics and Political Science.

Benabou, R., Ok, E.A., 2001. Social mobility and the demand for redistribution: the Poum hypothesis. Q. J. Econ. 116 (2), 447–487.

Benhabib, J., Rustichini, A., 1996. Social conflict and growth. J. Econ. Growth 1 (1), 125–142.

Benhabib, J., Bisin, A., Zhu, S., 2011. The distribution of wealth and fiscal policy in economies with finitely lived agents. Econometrica 79 (1), 123–157.

Ben-Porath, Y., 1967. The production of human capital and the life cycle of earnings. J. Polit. Econ. 75 (4), 352–365.

Bernanke, B., Gertler, M., 1989. Agency costs, net worth, and business fluctuations. Am. Econ. Rev. 79 (1), 14–31.

Bernanke, B.S., Gertler, M., Gilchrist, S., 1999. The financial accelerator in a quantitative business-cycle framework. In: Taylor, J.B., Woodford, M. (Eds.), Handbook of Macroeconomics, vol. 1. Elsevier, Amsterdam, pp. 1341–1393 (Chapter 21).

Bertola, G., 2000. Macroeconomics of distribution and growth. In: Atkinson, A., Bourguignon, F. (Eds.), Handbook of Income Distribution, vol. 1. Elsevier, Amsterdam, pp. 477–540 (Chapter 9).

Bewley, T., 1977. The permanent income hypothesis: a theoretical formulation. J. Econ. Theory 16 (2), 252–292.

Blanchard, O.J., 1985. Debt, deficits, and finite horizons. J. Polit. Econ. 93 (2), 223–247.

Budría, S., Díaz-Gimenez, J., Quadrini, V., Ríos-Rull, J.-V., 2001. New facts on the U.S. distribution of earnings, income and wealth. Unpublished Manuscript.

Buera, F.J., 2009. A dynamic model of entrepreneurship with borrowing constraints: theory and evidence. Ann. Finance 5 (3), 443–464.

Caballero, R.J., Farhi, E., Gourinchas, P.-O., 2008. An equilibrium model of "global imbalances" and low interest rates. Am. Econ. Rev. 98 (1), 358–393.

Cagetti, M., De Nardi, M., 2006. Entrepreneurship, frictions, and wealth. J. Polit. Econ. 114 (5), 835–869.

Cagetti, M., De Nardi, M., 2009. Estate taxation, entrepreneurship, and wealth. Am. Econ. Rev. 99 (1), 85–111.

Carlstrom, C.T., Fuerst, T.S., 1995. Interest rate rules vs. money growth rules: a welfare comparison in a cash-in-advance economy. J. Monet. Econ. 36 (2), 247–267.

Carrillo-Tudela, C., Visschers, L., 2013. Unemployment and endogenous reallocation over the business cycle. IZA Discussion Paper 7124, Institute for the Study of Labor (IZA).

Carroll, C.D., 1997. Buffer-stock saving and the life-cycle/permanent income hypothesis. Q. J. Econ. 112 (1), 1–55.

Caselli, F., 1999. Technological revolutions. Am. Econ. Rev. 89 (1), 78–102.

Caselli, F., Ventura, J., 2000. A representative consumer theory of distribution. Am. Econ. Rev. 90 (4), 909–926.

Castañeda, A., Díaz-Giménez, J., Ríos-Rull, J.-V., 1998. Exploring the income distribution business-cycle dynamics. J. Monet. Econ. 42 (1), 93–130.

Castañeda, A., Díaz-Giménez, J., Ríos-Rull, J.-V., 2003. Accounting for the U.S. earnings and wealth inequality. J. Polit. Econ. 111 (4), 818–857.

Chatterjee, S., 1994. Transitional dynamics and the distribution of wealth in a neoclassical growth model. J. Public Econ. 54 (1), 97–119.

Chatterjee, S., Corbae, D., Ríos-Rull, J.-V., 2004. A Competitive Theory of Credit Scoring. University of Pennsylvania, CAERP.

Chatterjee, S., Corbae, D., Nakajima, M., Ríos-Rull, J.-V., 2007. A quantitative theory of unsecured consumer credit with risk of default. Econometrica 75 (6), 1525–1589.

Chatterjee, S., Corbae, D., Ríos-Rull, J.-V., 2008. A finite-life private-information theory of unsecured consumer debt. J. Econ. Theory 142 (1), 149–177.

Cooley, T., Marimon, R., Quadrini, V., 2012. Risky investments with limited commitment. Working Paper 19594, National Bureau of Economic Research.

Corbae, D., D'Erasmo, P., Kuruscu, B., 2009. Politico-economic consequences of rising wage inequality. J. Monet. Econ. 56 (1), 43–61.

Costain, J.S., Reiter, M., 2008. Business cycles, unemployment insurance, and the calibration of matching models. J. Econ. Dyn. Control. 32 (4), 1120–1155.

Cummins, J.G., Violante, G.L., 2002. Investment-specific technical change in the United States (1947–2000): measurement and macroeconomic consequences. Rev. Econ. Dyn. 5 (2), 243–284.

De Nardi, M., 2004. Wealth inequality and intergenerational links. Rev. Econ. Stud. 71 (3), 743–768.

DeBacker, J., Heim, B., Panousi, V., Vidangos, I., 2011. Rising inequality: transitory or permanent? New evidence from a panel of U.S. household income 1987–2006. Finance and Economics Discussion Series 2011-60, Board of Governors of the Federal Reserve System (U.S.).

Díaz, A., Pijoan-Mas, J., Ríos-Rull, J.-V., 2003. Precautionary savings and wealth distribution under habit formation preferences. J. Monet. Econ. 50 (6), 1257–1291.

Díaz-Giménez, J., Pijoan-Mas, J., 2011. Flat tax reforms: investment expensing and progressivity. Discussion Paper No. 8238, Centre for Economic Policy Research.

Díaz-Giménez, J., Glover, A., Ríos-Rull, J.-V., 2011. Facts on the distributions of earnings, income, and wealth in the United States: 2007 update. Q. Rev. (Federal Reserve Bank of Minneapolis) 34 (1), 2–31.

Duras, J., 2013. Amplification of Shocks in a Model with Labor and Goods Market Search. University of Minnesota.

Fernandez-Villaverde, J., Krueger, D., 2011. Consumption and saving over the life cycle: how important are consumer durables? Macroecon. Dyn. 15 (5), 725–770.

Gabaix, X., Landier, A., 2008. Why has CEO pay increased so much? Q. J. Econ. 123 (1), 49–100.

Galor, O., Moav, O., 2000. Ability-biased technological transition, wage inequality, and economic growth. Q. J. Econ. 115 (2), 469–497.

Galor, O., Zeira, J., 1993. Income distribution and macroeconomics. Rev. Econ. Stud. 60 (1), 6035–6052.

Garicano, L., Rossi-Hansberg, E., 2004. Inequality and the organization of knowledge. Am. Econ. Rev. 94 (2), 197–202.

Gertler, M., Trigari, A., 2009. Unemployment fluctuations with staggered Nash wage bargaining. J. Polit. Econ. 117 (1), 38–86.

Glomm, G., Ravikumar, B., 1992. Public versus private investment in human capital: endogenous growth and income inequality. J. Polit. Econ. 100 (4), 818–834.

Glover, A., Heathcote, J., Krueger, D., Ríos-Rull, J.-V., 2011. Inter-generational redistribution in the Great Recession. Working Paper 16924, National Bureau of Economic Research.

Goldin, C., Katz, L.F., 2009. The Race Between Education and Technology. Belknap Press, Cambridge, MA.

Gordon, R.J., 1990. The measurement of durable goods prices. National Bureau of Economic Research Monograph Series, University of Chicago Press, Chicago, IL.

Gourinchas, P.-O., Parker, J.A., 2002. Consumption over the life cycle. Econometrica 70 (1), 47–89.

Greenwood, J., Jovanovic, B., 1990. Financial development, growth, and the distribution of income. J. Polit. Econ. 98 (5), 1076–1107.

Greenwood, J., Jovanovic, B., 1999. The information-technology revolution and the stock market. Am. Econ. Rev. Pap. Proc. 89 (2), 116–122.

Greenwood, J., Yorukoglu, M., 1997. Carnegie-Rochester conference series on public policy. J. Monet. Econ. 46 (2), 49–95.

Greenwood, J., Sanchez, J.M., Wang, C., 2010. Financing development: the role of information costs. Am. Econ. Rev. 100 (4), 1875–1891.

Guvenen, F., 2009. An empirical investigation of labor income processes. Rev. Econ. Dyn. 12 (1), 58–79.

Guvenen, F., Kuruşcu, B., 2010. A quantitative analysis of the evolution of the U.S. wage distribution, 1970–2000. In: Acemoglu, D., Rogoff, K., Woodford, M. (Eds.), NBER Macroeconomics Annual, vol. 24, pp. 227–276.

Guvenen, F., Kuruşcu, B., 2012. Understanding the evolution of the U.S. wage distribution: a theoretical analysis. J. Eur. Econ. Assoc. 10 (3), 489–517.

Guvenen, F., Kuruşcu, B., Ozkan, S., 2009. Taxation of human capital and wage inequality: a cross-country analysis. Federal Reserve Bank of Minneapolis, Research Department Staff Report 438.

Guvenen, F., Ozkan, S., Song, J., 2012. The nature of countercyclical income risk. Working Paper 18035, National Bureau of Economic Research.

Hagedorn, M., Manovskii, I., 2008. The cyclical behavior of equilibrium unemployment and vacancies revisited. Am. Econ. Rev. 98 (4), 1692–1706.

Hansen, G.D., Imrohoroglu, S., 2008. Consumption over the life cycle: the role of annuities. Rev. Econ. Dyn. 11 (3), 566–583.

Heaton, J., Lucas, D.J., 1996. Evaluating the effects of incomplete markets on risk sharing and asset pricing. J. Polit. Econ. 104 (3), 443–487.

Heckman, J., Lochner, L., Taber, C., 1998. Explaining rising wage inequality: explorations with a dynamic general equilibrium model of labor earnings with heterogeneous agents. Rev. Econ. Dyn. 1 (1), 1–58.

Hobijn, B., Jovanovic, B., 2001. The information-technology revolution and the stock market: evidence. Am. Econ. Rev. 91 (5), 1203–1220.

Hornstein, A., Krusell, P., Violante, G., 2011. Frictional wage dispersion in search models: a quantitative assessment. Am. Econ. Rev. 101 (7), 2873–2898.

Huggett, M., 1993. The risk-free rate in heterogeneous-agent, incomplete-insurance economies. J. Econ. Dyn. Control. 17 (5), 953–969.

Huggett, M., 1996. Wealth distribution in life-cycle economies. J. Monet. Econ. 38 (3), 469–494.

Huggett, M., Ventura, G., Yaron, A., 2011. Sources of lifetime inequality. Am. Econ. Rev. 101 (7), 2923–2954.

İmrohoroğlu, A., 1989. Cost of business cycles with indivisibilities and liquidity constraints. J. Polit. Econ. 97 (6), 1364–1383.

Kambourov, G., Manovskii, I., 2009a. Occupational mobility and wage inequality. Rev. Econ. Stud. 76 (2), 731–759.

Kambourov, G., Manovskii, I., 2009b. Occupational specificity of human capital. Int. Econ. Rev. 50 (1), 63–115.

Karabarbounis, L., Neiman, B., 2014. The global decline of the labor share. Q. J. Econ. 129 (1), 61–103.

Katz, L.F., Murphy, K.M., 1992. Changes in relative wages, 1963–1987: supply and demand factors. Q. J. Econ. 107 (1), 35–78.

Kehoe, T., Levine, D., 1993. Debt-constrained asset markets. Rev. Econ. Stud. 60 (4), 865–888.

Kiyotaki, N., Moore, J., 1997. Credit cycles. J. Polit. Econ. 105 (2), 211–248.

Krueger, D., Kubler, F., 2006. Pareto-improving social security reform when financial markets are incomplete!? Am. Econ. Rev. 96 (3), 737–755.

Krueger, D., Perri, F., 2006. Does income inequality lead to consumption inequality? Evidence and theory. Rev. Econ. Stud. 73 (1), 163–193.

Krueger, D., Perri, F., Pistaferri, L., Violante, G.L., 2010. Cross-sectional facts for macroeconomists. Rev. Econ. Dyn. 13 (1), 1–14.

Krusell, P., Ríos-Rull, J.-V., 1996. Vested interests in a positive theory of stagnation and growth. Rev. Econ. Stud. 63 (215), 301–331.

Krusell, P., Smith Jr., A.A., 1998. Income and wealth heterogeneity in the macroeconomy. J. Polit. Econ. 106 (5), 867–896.

Krusell, P., Quadrini, V., Ríos-Rull, J.-V., 1997. Politico-economic equilibrium and economic growth. J. Econ. Dyn. Control. 21 (1), 243–272.

Krusell, P., Ohanian, L.E., Ríos-Rull, J.-V., Violante, G.L., 2000. Capital-skill complementarity and inequality: a macroeconomic analysis. Econometrica 68 (5), 1029–1054.

Kuhn, M., 2014. Trends in income and wealth inequality. University of Bonn, Working Paper.

Kumhof, M., Rancière, R., 2010. Inequality, leverage and crises. IMF Working Paper WP/10/268.

Livshits, I., MacGee, J., Tertilt, M., 2007. Consumer bankruptcy: a fresh start. Am. Econ. Rev. 97 (1), 402–418.

Manuelli, R.E., Seshadri, A., 2010. Human capital and the wealth of nations. Unpublished Manuscript, University of Wisconsin-Madison.

Meh, C.A., Quadrini, V., 2006. Endogenous market incompleteness with investment risks. J. Econ. Dyn. Control 30 (11), 2143–2165.

Meltzer, A.H., Richard, S.F., 1981. A rational theory of the size of government. J. Polit. Econ. 89 (5), 914–927.

Mendoza, E.G., Quadrini, V., Ríos-Rull, J.-V., 2007. Financial integration, financial deepness and global imbalances. Working Paper 12909, National Bureau of Economic Research.

Milgrom, P., Roberts, J., 1990. The economics of modern manufacturing: technology, strategy, and organization. Am. Econ. Rev. 80 (3), 511–528.

Modigliani, F., Miller, M.H., 1958. The cost of capital, corporate finance and the theory of investment. Am. Econ. Rev. 48 (3), 261–279.

Monacelli, T., Quadrini, V., Trigari, A., 2011. Financial markets and unemployment. Working Paper 17389, National Bureau of Economic Research.

Murphy, K.M., Shleifer, A., Vishny, R., 1989. Income distribution, market size, and industrialization. Q. J. Econ. 104 (3), 537–564.

Papageorgiou, T., 2009. Learning your comparative advantages. 2009 Meeting Papers 1150, Society for Economic Dynamics.

Persson, T., Tabellini, G., 1994. Is inequality harmful for growth? Am. Econ. Rev. 84 (3), 600–621.

Pijoan-Mas, J., Ríos-Rull, J.-V., 2014. The Welfare Cost of Inequality in Life Expectancies. University of Minnesota.

Piketty, T., 1995. Social mobility and redistributive politics. Q. J. Econ. 110 (3), 551–584.

Piketty, T., 2014. Capital in the Twenty-First Century. Harvard University Press, Cambridge, MA. ISBN 9780674369559.

Piketty, T., Saez, E., 2003. Income inequality in the United States, 1913–1998. Q. J. Econ. 118 (1), 1–39. Longer updated version published in: Atkinson, A.B., Piketty, T. (Eds.), Top Incomes over the Twentieth Century: A Contrast between European and English-Speaking Countries. Oxford University Press, Oxford, 2007.

Pissarides, C.A., 1987. Search, wage bargains and cycles. Rev. Econ. Stud. 54 (3), 473–483.

Pissarides, C.A., 1990. Equilibrium Unemployment Theory. Basil Blackwell, Oxford.

Quadrini, V., 1999. Growth, learning and redistributive policies. J. Public Econ. 74 (2), 263–297.

Quadrini, V., 2000. Entrepreneurship, saving, and social mobility. Rev. Econ. Dyn. 3 (1), 1–40.

Quadrini, V., 2011. Financial frictions in macroeconomic fluctuations. Econ. Q. 97 (3Q), 209–254.

Ríos-Rull, J.-V., 1994. On the quantitative importance of market completeness. J. Monet. Econ. 34 (3), 463–496.

Ríos-Rull, J.-V., 1996. Life-cycle economies and aggregate fluctuations. Rev. Econ. Stud. 63 (3), 465–489.

Ríos-Rull, J.-V., Santaeulàlia-Llopis, R., 2010. Redistributive shocks and productivity shocks. J. Monet. Econ. 57 (8), 931–948.

Rosen, S., 1981. The economics of superstars. Am. Econ. Rev. 71 (5), 845–858.

Saez, E., Zucman, G., 2014. The distribution of US wealth, capital income and returns since 1913. Unpublished Manuscript, University of California, Berkeley.

Shimer, R., 2005. The cyclical behavior of equilibrium unemployment and vacancies. Am. Econ. Rev. 95 (1), 25–49.

Solow, R., 1987. We'd Better Watch Out. New York Times Book Review, p. 36, July.

Stiglitz, J.E., 1969. Distribution of income and wealth among individuals. Econometrica 37 (3), 382–397.

Storesletten, K., Telmer, C.I., Yaron, A., 2001. How important are idiosyncratic shocks? Evidence from labor supply. Am. Econ. Rev. Pap. Proc. 91 (2), 413–417.

Terajima, Y., 2006. Education and self-employment: changes in earnings and wealth inequality. Bank of Canada Working Paper 2006-40.

Townsend, R.M., 1979. Optimal contracts and competitive markets with costly state verification. J. Econ. Theory 21 (2), 265–293.

von Weizsäcker, R.K., 1993. A Theory of Earnings Distribution. Cambridge University Press, Cambridge.

Wiczer, D., 2013. Long-term unemployment: attached and mismatched? Unpublished Manuscript, University of Minnesota.

Yaari, M.E., 1965. Uncertain lifetime, life insurance and the theory of the consumer. Rev. Econ. Stud. 32 (2), 137–150.

Yamaguchi, S., 2012. Tasks and heterogeneous human capital. J. Labor Econ. 30 (1), 1–53.

CHAPTER 15

Wealth and Inheritance in the Long Run

Thomas Piketty*, Gabriel Zucman†
*Paris School of Economics, Paris, France
†London School of Economics, London, UK

Contents

Handbook of Income Distribution, Volume 2B
ISSN 1574-0056, http://dx.doi.org/10.1016/B978-0-444-59429-7.00016-9

Abstract

This chapter offers an overview of the empirical and theoretical research on the long-run evolution of wealth and inheritance. Wealth–income ratios, inherited wealth, and wealth inequalities were high in the eighteenth to nineteenth centuries up until World War I, then sharply dropped during the twentieth century following World War shocks, and have been rising again in the late twentieth and early twenty-first centuries. We discuss the models that can account for these facts. We show that over a wide range of models, the long-run magnitude and concentration of wealth and inheritance are an increasing function of $\bar{r} - g$ where $\bar{r}$ is the net-of-tax rate of return on wealth and g is the economy's growth rate. This suggests that current trends toward rising wealth–income ratios and wealth inequality might continue during the twenty-first century, both because of the slowdown of population and productivity growth, and because of rising international competition to attract capital.

Keywords

Wealth, Inheritance, Distribution, Growth, Rate of return, Pareto coefficient

JEL Classification Codes

E10, D30, D31, D32

15.1. INTRODUCTION

Economists have long recognized that the magnitude and distribution of wealth play an important role in the distribution of income—both across factors of production (labor and capital) and across individuals. In this chapter, we ask three simple questions: (1) What do we know about historical patterns in the magnitude of wealth and inheritance relative to income? (2) How does the distribution of wealth vary in the long run and across countries? (3) And what are the models that can account for these facts?

In surveying the literature on these issues, we will focus the analysis on three inter-related ratios. The first is the aggregate wealth-to-income ratio, that is the ratio between marketable—nonhuman—wealth and national income. The second is the share of aggregate wealth held by the richest individuals, say the top 10% or top 1%. The last is the ratio between the stock of inherited wealth and aggregate wealth (or between the annual flow of bequests and national income). As we shall see, to properly analyze the concentration of wealth and its implications, it is critical to study top wealth shares jointly with the macroeconomic wealth–income and inheritance–wealth ratios. In so doing, this chapter attempts to build bridges between income distribution and macroeconomics.

The wealth-to-income ratio, top wealth shares, and the share of inheritance in the economy have all been the subject of considerable interest and controversy—but usually on the basis of limited data. For a long time, economics textbooks have presented the wealth–income ratio as stable over time—one of the Kaldor facts.[1] There is, however, no strong theoretical reason why it should be so: With a flexible production function, any ratio can be a steady state. And until recently, we lacked comprehensive national balance sheets with harmonized definitions for wealth that could be used to vindicate the constant-ratio thesis. Recent research shows that wealth–income ratios, as well as the share of capital in national income, are actually much less stable in the long run than what is commonly assumed.

Following the Kuznets curve hypothesis, first formulated in the 1950s, another common view among economists has been that income inequality—and possibly wealth inequality as well—should first rise and then decline with economic development, as a growing fraction of the population joins high-productivity sectors and benefits from industrial growth.[2] However, following the rise in inequality that has occurred in most developed countries since the 1970s–1980s, this optimistic view has become less popular.[3] As a consequence, most economists are now fairly skeptical about universal laws regarding the long-run evolution of inequality.

Last, regarding the inheritance share in total wealth accumulation, there seems to exist a general presumption that it should tend to decline over time. Although this is rarely formulated explicitly, one possible mechanism could be the rise of human capital (leading maybe to a rise of the labor share in income and saving), or the rise in life-cycle wealth accumulation (itself possibly due to the rise of life expectancy). Until recently, however, there was limited empirical evidence on the share of inherited wealth available to test these hypotheses. The 1980s saw a famous controversy between Modigliani (a life-cycle advocate, who argued that the share of inherited wealth was as little as 20–30% of U.S. aggregate wealth) and Kotlikoff–Summers (who instead

---

[1] See, e.g., Kaldor (1961) and Jones and Romer (2010).

[2] See Kuznets (1953).

[3] See Atkinson et al. (2011). See also Chapter 7 in Handbook of Income Distribution, volume 2A by Roine and Waldenstrom (2015).

argued that the inheritance share was as large as 80%, if not larger). Particularly confusing was the fact that both sides claimed to look at the same data, namely U.S. data from the 1960s–1970s.[4]

Because many of the key predictions about wealth and inheritance were formulated a long time ago—often in the 1950s–1960s, or sometime in the 1970s–1980s—and usually on the basis of a relatively small amount of long-run evidence, it is high time to take a fresh look at them again on the basis of the more reliable evidence now available.

We begin by reviewing in Section 15.2 what we know about the historical evolution of the wealth–income ratio β. In most countries, this ratio has been following a U-shaped pattern over the 1910–2010 period, with a large decline between the 1910s and the 1950s, and a gradual recovery since the 1950s. The pattern is particularly spectacular in Europe, where the aggregate wealth–income ratio was as large as 600–700% during the eighteenth, nineteenth, and early twentieth centuries, then dropped to as little as 200–300% in the mid-twentieth century. It is now back to about 500–600% in the early twenty-first century. These same orders of magnitude also seem to apply to Japan, though the historical data is less complete than for Europe. The U-shaped pattern also exists—but is less marked—in the United States.

In Section 15.3, we turn to the long-run changes in wealth concentration. We also find a U-shaped pattern over the past century, but the dynamics have been quite different in Europe and in the United States. In Europe, the recent increase in wealth inequality appears to be more limited than the rise of the aggregate wealth–income ratio, so that European wealth seems to be significantly less concentrated in the early twenty-first century than a century ago. The top 10% wealth share used to be as large as 90%, whereas it is around 60–70% today (which is already quite large—and in particular a lot larger than the concentration of labor income). In the United States, by contrast, wealth concentration appears to have almost returned to its early twentieth century level. Although Europe was substantially more unequal than the United States until World War I, the situation has reversed over the course of the twentieth century. Whether the gap between both economies will keep widening in the twenty-first century is an open issue.

In Section 15.4, we describe the existing evidence regarding the evolution of the share φ of inherited wealth in aggregate wealth. This is an area in which available historical series are scarce and a lot of data has yet to be collected. However existing evidence—coming mostly from France, Germany, the United Kingdom, and Sweden—suggests that the inheritance share has also followed a U-shaped pattern over the past century. Modigliani's estimates—with a large majority of wealth coming from life-cycle savings—might have been right for the immediate postwar period (though somewhat exaggerated). But Kotlikoff–Summers' estimates—with inheritance

---

[4] See Kotlikoff and Summers (1981, 1988) and Modigliani (1986, 1988). Modigliani's theory of life-cycle saving was first formulated in the 1950s–1960s; see the references given in Modigliani (1986).

accounting for a significant majority of wealth—appear to be closer to what we generally observe in the long run, both in the nineteenth, twentieth, and early twenty-first centuries. Here again, there could be some interesting differences between Europe and the United States (possibly running in the opposite direction than for wealth concentration). Unfortunately the fragility of available U.S. data makes it difficult to conclude at this stage.

We then discuss in Section 15.5 the theoretical mechanisms that can be used to account for the historical evidence and to analyze future prospects. Some of the evolutions documented in Sections 15.2–15.4 are due to shocks. In particular, the large U-shaped pattern of wealth–income and inheritance-income ratios observed over the 1910–2010 period is largely due to the wars (which hit Europe and Japan much more than the United States). Here the main theoretical lesson is simply that capital accumulation takes time, and that the world wars of the twentieth century have had a long-lasting impact on basic economic ratios. This, in a way, is not too surprising and follows from simple arithmetic. With a 10% saving rate and a fixed income, it takes 50 years to accumulate the equivalent of 5 years of income in capital stock. With income growth, the recovery process takes even more time.

The more interesting and difficult part of the story is to understand the forces that determine the new steady-state levels toward which each economy tends to converge once it has recovered from shocks. In Section 15.5, we show that over a wide range of models, the long-run magnitude and concentration of wealth and inheritance are a decreasing function of g and an increasing function of $\bar{r}$, where g is the economy's growth rate and $\bar{r}$ is the net-of-tax rate of return to wealth. That is, under plausible assumptions, our three interrelated sets of ratios—the wealth–income ratio, the concentration of wealth, and the share of inherited wealth—all tend to take higher steady-state values when the long-run growth rate is lower or when the net-of-tax rate of return is higher. In particular, a higher $\bar{r} - g$ tends to magnify steady-state wealth inequalities. We argue that these theoretical predictions are broadly consistent with both the time-series and the cross-country evidence. This also suggests that the current trends toward rising wealth–income ratios and wealth inequality might continue during the twenty-first century, both because of population and productivity growth slowdown, and because of rising international competition to attract capital.

Owing to data availability constraints, the historical evolutions analyzed in this chapter relate for the most part to today's rich countries (Europe, North America, and Japan). However, to the extent that the theoretical mechanisms unveiled by the experience of rich countries also apply elsewhere, the findings presented here are also of interest for today's emerging economies. In Section 15.5, we discuss the prospects for the global evolution of wealth–income ratios, wealth concentration, and the share of inherited wealth in the coming decades. Finally, Section 15.6 offers concluding comments and stresses the need for more research in this area.

15.2. THE LONG-RUN EVOLUTION OF WEALTH–INCOME RATIOS

15.2.1 Concepts, Data Sources, and Methods

15.2.1.1 Country Balance Sheets

Prior to World War I, there was a vibrant tradition of national wealth accounting: economists, statisticians, and social arithmeticians were much more interested in computing the stock of national wealth than the flows of national income and output. The first national balance sheets were established in the late seventeenth and early eighteenth centuries by Petty (1664) and King (1696) in the United Kingdom, and Boisguillebert (1695) and Vauban (1707) in France. National wealth estimates then became plentiful in the nineteenth and early twentieth century, with the work of Colquhoun (1815), Giffen (1889), and Bowley (1920) in the United Kingdom, de Foville (1893) and Colson (1903) in France, Helfferich (1913) in Germany, King (1915) in the United States, and dozens of other economists.

The focus on wealth, however, largely disappeared in the interwar. The shock of World War I, the Great Depression, and the coming of Keynesian economics led to attention being switched from stocks to flows, with balance sheets being neglected. The first systematic attempt to collect historical balance sheets is due to Goldsmith (1985, 1991). Building upon recent progress made in the measurement of wealth, and pushing forward Goldsmith's pioneering attempt, Piketty and Zucman (2014) construct aggregate wealth and income series for the top eight rich economies. Other recent papers that look at specific countries include Atkinson (2013) for the United Kingdom and Ohlsson et al. (2013) for Sweden. In this section, we rely on the data collected by Piketty and Zucman (2014)—and closely follow the discussion therein—to present the long-run evolution of wealth–income ratios in the main developed economies.

In determining what is to be counted as wealth, we follow the U.N. System of National Accounts (SNA). For the 1970–2010 period, the data come from official national accounts that comply with the latest international guidelines (SNA, 1993, 2008). For the previous periods, Piketty and Zucman (2014) draw on the vast national wealth accounting tradition to construct homogenous income and wealth series that use the same concepts and definitions as in the most recent official accounts. The historical data themselves were established by a large number of scholars and statistical administrations using a wide variety of sources, including land, housing and wealth censuses, financial surveys, corporate book accounts, and the like. Although historical balance sheets are far from perfect, their methods are well documented and they are usually internally consistent. It was also somewhat easier to estimate national wealth around 1900–1910 than it is today: the structure of property was simpler, with less financial intermediation and cross-border positions.[5]

---

[5] A detailed analysis of conceptual and methodological issues regarding wealth measurement, as well as extensive country-specific references on historical balance sheets, are provided by Piketty and Zucman (2014).

15.2.1.2 Concepts and Definitions: Wealth Versus Capital

We define private wealth, W_t, as the net wealth (assets minus liabilities) of households.[6] Following SNA guidelines, assets include all the nonfinancial assets—land, buildings, machines, etc.—and financial assets—including life insurance and pensions funds—over which ownership rights can be enforced and that provide economic benefits to their owners. Pay-as-you-go Social Security pension wealth is excluded, just as all other claims on future government expenditures and transfers (such as education expenses for one's children or health benefits). Durable goods owned by households, such as cars and furniture, are excluded as well.[7] As a general rule, all assets and liabilities are valued at their prevailing market prices. Corporations are included in private wealth through the market value of equities and corporate bonds. Unquoted shares are typically valued on the basis of observed market prices for comparable, publicly traded companies.

Similarly, public (or government) wealth, W_{gt}, is the net wealth of public administrations and government agencies. In available balance sheets, public nonfinancial assets such as administrative buildings, schools, and hospitals are valued by cumulating past investment flows and upgrading them using observed real estate prices.

Market-value national wealth, W_{nt}, is the sum of private and public wealth:

$$W_{nt} = W_t + W_{gt}$$

and national wealth can also be decomposed into domestic capital and net foreign assets:

$$W_{nt} = K_t + NFA_t$$

In turn, domestic capital K_t can be written as the sum of agricultural land, housing, and other domestic capital (including the market value of corporations, and the value of other nonfinancial assets held by the private and public sectors, net of their liabilities).

Regarding income, the definitions and notations are standard. Note that we always use net-of-depreciation income and output concepts. National income Y_t is the sum of net domestic output and net foreign income: $Y_t = Y_{dt} + r_t \cdot NFA_t$.[8] Domestic output can be thought of as coming from some aggregate production function that uses domestic capital and labor as inputs: $Y_{dt} = F(K_t, L_t)$.

---

[6] Private wealth also includes the assets and liabilities held by nonprofit institutions serving households (NPISH). The main reason for doing so is that the frontier between individuals and private foundations is not always clear. In any case, the net wealth of NPISH is usually small, and always less than 10% of total net private wealth: currently it is about 1% in France, 3–4% in Japan, and 6–7% in the United States; see Piketty and Zucman (2014, Appendix Table A65). Note also that the household sector includes all unincorporated businesses.

[7] The value of durable goods appears to be relatively stable over time (about 30–50% of national income, i.e., 5–10% of net private wealth). See for instance Piketty and Zucman (2014, Appendix Table US.6f) for the long-run evolution of durable goods in the United States.

[8] National income also includes net foreign labor income and net foreign production taxes—both of which are usually negligible.

One might prefer to think about output as deriving from a two-sector production process (housing and nonhousing sectors), or more generally from n sectors. In the real world, the capital stock K_t comprises thousands of various assets valued at different prices (just like output Y_{dt} is defined as the sum of thousands of goods and services valued at different prices). We find it more natural, however, to start with a one-sector formulation. Since the same capital assets (i.e., buildings) are often used for housing and office space, it would be quite artificial to start by dividing capital and output into two parts. We will later on discuss the pros and cons of the one-sector model and the need to appeal to two-sector models and relative asset price movements to properly account for observed changes in the aggregate wealth–income ratio.

Another choice that needs to be discussed is the focus on market values for national wealth and capital. We see market values as a useful and well-defined starting point. But one might prefer to look at book values, for example, for short-run growth accounting exercises. Book values exceed market values when Tobin's Q is less than 1, and conversely when Tobin's Q is larger than 1. In the long run, however, the choice of book versus market value does not much affect the analysis (see Piketty and Zucman, 2014, for a detailed discussion).

We are interested in the evolution of the private wealth–national income ratio $\beta_t = W_t / Y_t$ and of the national wealth–national income ratio $\beta_{nt} = W_{nt} / Y_t$. In a closed economy, and more generally in an open economy with a zero net foreign position, the national wealth–national income ratio β_{nt} is the same as the domestic capital–output ratio $\beta_{kt} = K_t / Y_{dt}$.[9] If public wealth is equal to zero, then both ratios are also equal to the private wealth–national income ratio $\beta_t = \beta_{nt} = \beta_{kt}$. At the global level, the world wealth–income ratio is always equal to the world capital–output ratio.

15.2.2 The Very Long-Run: Britain and France, 1700–2010

Figures 15.1 and 15.2 present the very long-run evidence available for Britain and France regarding the national wealth–national income ratio β_{nt}. Net public wealth—either positive or negative—is usually a relatively small fraction of national wealth, so that the evolution of β_{nt} mostly reflects the evolution of the private wealth–national income ratio β_t (more on this below).[10]

---

[9] In principle, one can imagine a country with a zero net foreign asset position (so that $W_{nt} = K_t$) but nonzero net foreign income flows (so that $Y_t \neq Y_{dt}$). In this case the national wealth–national income ratio β_{nt} will slightly differ from the domestic capital–output ratio β_{kt}. In practice today, differences between Y_t and Y_{dt} are very small—national income Y_t is usually between 97% and 103% of domestic output Y_{dt} (see Piketty and Zucman, 2014, Appendix Figure A57). Net foreign asset positions are usually small as well, so that β_{kt} turns out to be usually close to β_{nt} in the 1970–2010 period (see Piketty and Zucman, 2014, Appendix Figure A67).

[10] For an historical account of the changing decomposition of national wealth into private and public wealth in Britain and France since the eighteenth century, see Piketty (2014, Chapter 3).

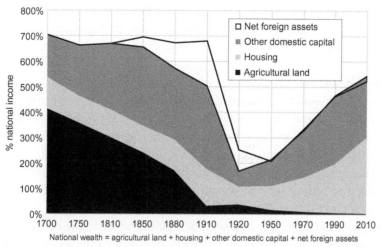

Figure 15.1 The changing level and nature of national wealth: United Kingdom 1700–2010.

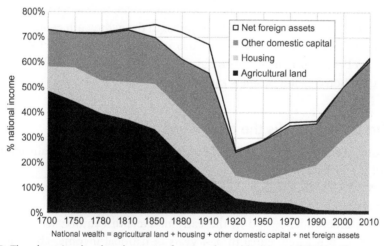

Figure 15.2 The changing level and nature of national wealth: France 1700–2010.

The evolutions are remarkably similar in the two countries. First, the wealth–income ratio has followed a spectacular U-shaped pattern. Aggregate wealth was worth about 6–7 years of national income during the eighteenth to nineteenth centuries on both sides of the channel, up until the eve of World War I. Raw data sources available for these two centuries are not sufficiently precise to make fine comparisons between the two countries or over time, but the orders of magnitude appear to be reliable and roughly stable (they come from a large number of independent estimates). Aggregate wealth then collapsed to as little as 2–3 years of national income in the aftermath of the two World Wars. Since the 1950s, there has been a gradual recovery in both countries. Aggregate wealth is back to about 5–6 years of national income in the 2000s to 2010s, just a bit below the pre-World War I level.

The other important finding that emerges from Figures 15.1 and 15.2 is that the composition of national wealth has changed in similar ways in both countries. Agricultural land, which made the majority of national capital in the eighteenth century, has been gradually replaced by real estate and other domestic capital, which is for the most part business capital (i.e., structures and equipment used by private firms). The nature of wealth has changed entirely reflecting a dramatic change in the structure of economic activity, and yet the total value of wealth is more or less the same as what it used to be before the Industrial Revolution.

Net foreign assets also made a large part of national capital in the late nineteenth century and on the eve of World War I: as much as 2 years of national capital in the case of Britain and over a year in the case of France. Net foreign-asset positions were brought back to zero in both countries following World War I and II shocks (including the loss of the colonial empires). In the late twentieth and early twenty-first centuries, net foreign positions are close to zero in both countries, just as in the eighteenth century. In the very long run, net foreign assets do not matter too much for the dynamics of the capital/income ratio in Britain or France. The main structural change is the replacement of agricultural land by housing and business capital.[11]

15.2.3 Old Europe Versus the New World

It is interesting to contrast the case of Old Europe—as illustrated by Britain and France—with that of the United States.

As Figure 15.3 shows, the aggregate value of wealth in the eighteenth to nineteenth centuries was markedly smaller in the New World than in Europe. At the time of the Declaration of Independence and in the early nineteenth century, national wealth in the United States was barely equal to 3–4 years of national income, about half that of Britain or France. Although available estimates are fragile, the order of magnitude again

---

[11] It is worth stressing that should we divide aggregate wealth by disposable household income (rather than national income), then today's ratios would be around 700–800% in Britain or France and would slightly surpass eighteenth to nineteenth century levels. This mechanically follows from the fact that disposable income was above 90% in the eighteenth to nineteenth centuries and is about 70–80% of disposable income in the late twentieth to early twenty-first century. The rising gap between disposable and household income reflects the rise of government-provided services, in particular in health and education. To the extent that these services are mostly useful (in their absence households would have to purchase them on the market), it is more justified for the purpose of historical and international comparisons to focus on ratios using national income as a denominator. For wealth–income ratios using disposable income as a denominator, see Piketty and Zucman (2014, Appendix, Figure A9).

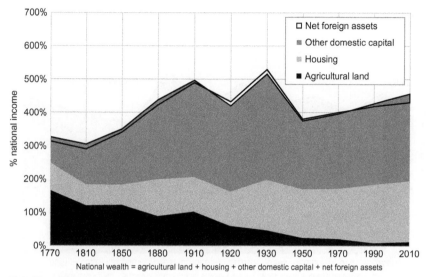

Figure 15.3 The changing level and nature of national wealth: United States 1770–2010.

appears to be robust. In Section 15.5, we will attempt to account for this interesting contrast. At this stage, we simply note that there are two obvious—and potentially complementary—factors that can play a role: first, there had been less time to save and accumulate wealth in the New World than in the Old World; second, there was so much land in the New World that it was almost worthless (its market value per acre was much less than in Europe).

The gap between the United States and Europe gradually reduces over the course of the nineteenth century, but still remains substantial. Around 1900–1910, national wealth is about 5 years of national income in the United States (see Figure 15.3) versus about 7 years in Britain and France. During the twentieth century, the U.S. wealth–income ratio also follows a U-shaped pattern, but less marked than in Europe. National wealth falls less sharply in the United States than in Europe following World War shocks, which seems rather intuitive. Interestingly, European wealth–income ratios have again surpassed U.S. ratios in the late twentieth and early twenty-first centuries.

This brief overview of wealth in the New World and Europe would be rather incomplete if we did not mention the issue of slavery. As one can see from Figure 15.4, the aggregate market value of slaves was fairly substantial in the United States until 1865: about 1–1.5 years of national income according to the best available historical sources. There were few slaves in Northern states, but in the South the value of the slave stock was so large that it approximately compensated—from the viewpoint of slave owners—the lower value of land as compared to the Old World (see Figure 15.5).

It is rather dubious, however, to include the market value of slaves into national capital. Slavery can be viewed as the most extreme form of debt: it should be counted as an

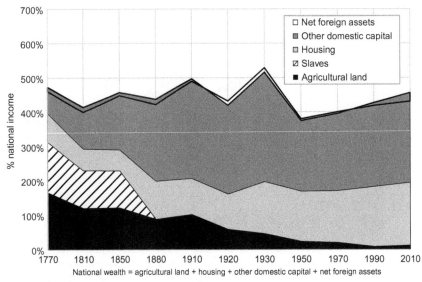

Figure 15.4 The changing level and nature of wealth: United States 1770–2010 (including slaves).

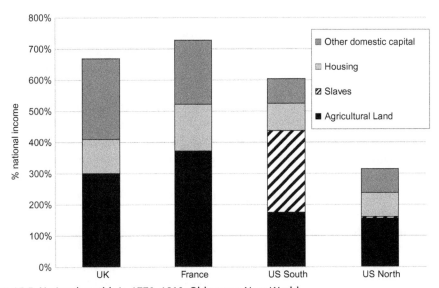

Figure 15.5 National wealth in 1770–1810: Old versus New World.

asset for the owners and a liability for the slaves, so that net national wealth should be unaffected. In the extreme case where a tiny elite owns the rest of the population, the total value of slaves—the total value of "human capital"—could be a lot larger than that of nonhuman capital (since the share of human labor in income is typically larger than

50%). If the rate of return r is equalized across all assets, then the aggregate value of human capital—expressed in proportion to national income—will be equal to $\beta_h = (1-\alpha)/r$, whereas the value of nonhuman capital will be given by $\beta_n = \alpha/r$, where α is the capital share and $1-\alpha$ the labor share implied by the production technology.[12] So for instance with $r=5\%$, $\alpha=30\%$, $1-\alpha=70\%$, the value of the human capital stock will be as large as $\beta_h = (1-\alpha)/r = 1400\%$ (14 years of national income), and the value of the nonhuman capital stock will be $\beta_n = \alpha/r = 600\%$ (6 years of national income). Outside of slave societies, however, it is unclear whether it makes much sense to compute the market value of human capital and to add it to nonhuman capital.

The computations reported on Figures 15.4 and 15.5 illustrate the ambiguous relationship of the New World with wealth, inequality, and property. To some extent, America is the land of opportunity, the place where wealth accumulated in the past does not matter too much. But it is also the place where a new form of wealth and class structure—arguably more extreme and violent than the class structure prevailing in Europe—flourished, whereby part of the population owned another part.

Available historical series suggest that the sharp U-shaped pattern for the wealth–income ratio in Britain and France is fairly representative of Europe as a whole. For Germany, the wealth–income ratio was approximately the same as for Britain and France in the late nineteenth and early twentieth centuries, then fell to a very low level in the aftermath of the World Wars, and finally has been rising regularly since the 1950s (see Figure 15.6). Although the German wealth–income ratio is still below that of the United Kingdom and France, the speed of the recovery over the past few decades has been similar.[13] On Figure 15.7, we compare the European wealth–income ratio (obtained as a simple average of Britain, France, Germany, and Italy, the latter being available only for the most recent decades) to the U.S. one. The European wealth–income ratio was substantially above that of the United States until World War I, then fell significantly below in the aftermath of World War II, and surpassed it again in the late twentieth and early twenty-first centuries (see Figure 15.7).

---

[12] That is, $1-\alpha$ is the marginal product of labor times the labor (slave) stock. The formula $\beta_h = (1-\alpha)/r$ implicitly assumes that the fraction of output that is needed to feed and maintain the slave stock is negligible (otherwise it would just need to be deducted from $1-\alpha$), and that labor productivity is unaffected by the slavery condition (this is a controversial issue).

[13] The factors that can explain the lower German wealth–income ratio are the following. Real estate prices have increased far less in Germany than in Britain or France, which could be due in part to the lasting impact of German reunification and to stronger rent regulations. This could also be temporary. Next, the lower market value of German firms could be due to a stakeholder effect. Finally, the return to the German foreign portfolio, where a large part of German savings were directed, was particularly low in the most recent period. See Piketty and Zucman (2014, Section V.C) and Piketty (2014, Chapter 3).

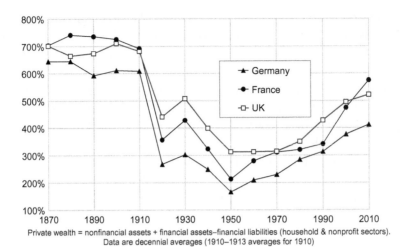

Figure 15.6 Private wealth/national income ratios in Europe, 1870–2010.

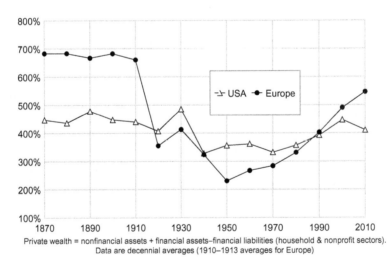

Figure 15.7 Private wealth/national income ratios 1870–2010: Europe versus United States.

15.2.4 The Return of High Wealth–Income Ratios in Rich Countries

Turning now to the 1970–2010 period, for which we have annual series covering most rich countries, the rise of wealth–income ratios, particularly private wealth–national income ratios, appears to be a general phenomenon. In the top eight developed economies, private wealth is between 2 and 3.5 years of national income around 1970, and between 4 and 7 years of national income around 2010 (see Figure 15.8). Although there are chaotic short-run fluctuations (reflecting the short-run volatility of asset prices),

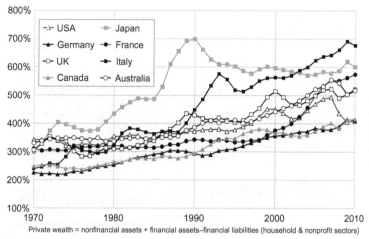

Private wealth = nonfinancial assets + financial assets−financial liabilities (household & nonprofit sectors)

Figure 15.8 Private wealth/national income ratios, 1970–2010.

the long-run trend is clear. Take Japan. The huge asset price bubble of the late 1980s should not obscure the 1970–2010 rise of the wealth–income ratio, fairly comparable in magnitude to what we observe in Europe. (For instance, the Japanese and Italian patterns are relatively close: both countries go from about 2–3 years of national income in private wealth around 1970 to 6–7 years by 2010.)

Although we do not have national wealth estimates for Japan for the late nineteenth and early twentieth centuries, there are reasons to believe that the Japanese wealth–income ratio has also followed a U-shaped evolution in the long run, fairly similar to that observed in Europe over the twentieth century. That is, it seems likely that the wealth–income ratio was relatively high in the early twentieth century, fell to low levels in the aftermath of World War II, and then followed the recovery process that we see in Figure 15.8.[14]

To some extent, the rise of private wealth–national income ratios in rich countries since the 1970s is related to the decline of public wealth (see Figure 15.9). Public wealth has declined virtually everywhere owing both to the rise of public debt and the privatization of public assets. In some countries, such as Italy, public wealth has become strongly negative. The rise in private wealth, however, is quantitatively much larger than the decline in public wealth. As a result, national wealth—the sum of private and public wealth—has increased substantially, from 250–400% of national income in 1970 to 400–650% in 2010 (see Figure 15.10). In Italy, for instance, net government wealth fell by the equivalent of about 1 year of national income, but net private wealth rose by over

[14] The early twentieth century Japanese inheritance tax data reported by Morigushi and Saez (2008) are consistent with this interpretation.

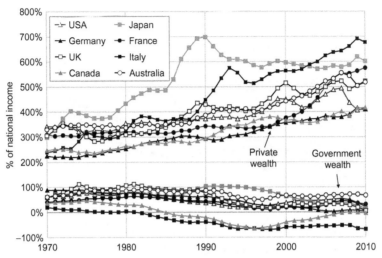

Figure 15.9 Private versus government wealth, 1970–2010.

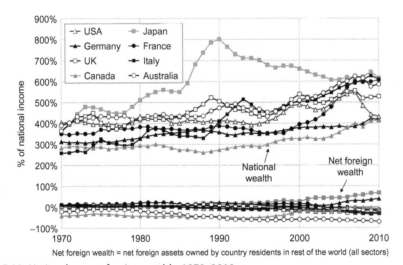

Net foreign wealth = net foreign assets owned by country residents in rest of the world (all sectors)

Figure 15.10 National versus foreign wealth, 1970–2010.

4 years of national income, so that national wealth increased by the equivalent of over 3 years of national income.

Figure 15.10 also depicts the evolution of net foreign wealth. Net foreign asset positions are generally small compared to national wealth. In other words, the evolution of national wealth–national income ratios mostly reflects the evolution of domestic capital–output ratios. There are two caveats, however. First, gross cross-border positions have risen a lot in recent decades, which can generate large portfolio valuation effects at the country level. Second, Japan and Germany have accumulated significant net foreign wealth (with net positions around 40% and 70% of national income, respectively, in 2010). Although these are still much smaller than the positions held by France and Britain on the eve of World War I (around 100% and 200% of national income, respectively), they are becoming relatively large (and were rising fast in the case of Germany in the first half of the 2010s, due to the large German trade surpluses).

15.3. THE LONG-RUN EVOLUTION OF WEALTH CONCENTRATION
15.3.1 Concepts, Data Sources, and Methods

We now turn to the evidence on the long-run evolution of wealth concentration. This question can be studied with different data sources (see Davies and Shorrocks, 1999, for a detailed discussion). Ideally, one would want to use annual wealth tax declarations for the entire population. Annual wealth taxes, however, often do to exist, and when they do, the data generally do not cover long periods of time.

The key source used to study the long-run evolution of wealth inequality has traditionally been inheritance and estate tax declarations.[15] By definition, estates and inheritance returns only provide information about wealth at death. The standard way to use inheritance tax data to study wealth concentration was invented over a century ago. Shortly before World War I, a number of British and French economists developed what is known as the mortality multiplier technique, whereby wealth-at-death is weighted by the inverse of the mortality rate of the given age and wealth group in order to generate estimates for the distribution of wealth among the living.[16] This approach was later followed in the United States by Lampman (1962) and Kopczuk and Saez (2004), who use estate tax data covering the 1916–1956 and 1916–2000 periods, respectively, and in the United Kingdom by Atkinson and Harrison (1978), who exploit inheritance tax data covering the 1922–1976 period.

To measure historical trends in the distribution of wealth, one can also use individual income tax returns and capitalize the dividends, interest, rents, and other forms of capital income declared on such returns. The capitalization technique was pioneered by King (1927), Stewart (1939), Atkinson and Harrison (1978), and Greenwood (1983), who used it to estimate the distribution of wealth in the United Kingdom and in the United States for some years in isolation. To obtain reliable results, it is critical to have detailed income data, preferably at the micro level, and to carefully reconcile the tax data with household balance sheets, so as to compute the correct capitalization factors. Drawing

---

[15] The difference between inheritance and estate taxes is that inheritance taxes are computed at the level of each inheritor, whereas estate taxes are computed at the level of the total estate (total wealth left by the decedent). The raw data coming from these two forms of taxes on wealth transfers are similar.

[16] See Mallet (1908), Séaillès (1910), Strutt (1910), Mallet and Strutt (1915), and Stamp (1919).

on the very detailed U.S. income tax data and Flow of Funds balance sheets, Saez and Zucman (2014) use the capitalization technique to estimate the distribution of U.S. wealth annually since 1913.

For the recent period, one can also use wealth surveys. Surveys, however, are never available on a long-run basis and raise serious difficulties regarding self-reporting biases, especially at the top of the distribution. Tax sources also raise difficulties at the top, especially for the recent period, given the large rise of offshore wealth (Zucman, 2013). Generally speaking, it is certainly more difficult for the recent period to accurately measure the concentration of wealth than the aggregate value of wealth, and one should be aware of this limitation. One needs to be pragmatic and combine the various available data sources (including the global wealth rankings published by magazines such as *Forbes*, which we will refer to in Section 15.5).

The historical series that we analyze in this chapter combines works by many different authors (more details below), who mostly relied on estate and inheritance tax data. They all relate to the inequality of wealth among the living.

We focus on simple concentration indicators, such as the share of aggregate wealth going to the top 10% individuals with the highest net wealth and the share going to the top 1%. In every country and historical period for which we have data, the share of aggregate wealth going to the bottom 50% is extremely small (usually less than 5%). So a decline in the top 10% wealth share can for the most part be interpreted as a rise in the share going to the middle 40%. Note also that wealth concentration is usually almost as large within each age group as for the population taken as a whole.[17]

15.3.2 The European Pattern: France, Britain, and Sweden, 1810–2010

15.3.2.1 France

We start with the case of France, the country for which the longest time series is available. French inheritance tax data is exceptionally good, for one simple reason. As early as 1791, shortly after the abolition of the tax privileges of the aristocracy, the French National Assembly introduced a universal inheritance tax, which has remained in force since then. This inheritance tax was universal because it applied both to bequests and to inter-vivos gifts, at any level of wealth, and for nearly all types of property (both tangible and financial assets). The key characteristic of the tax is that the successors of all decedents with positive wealth, as well as all donees receiving a positive gift, have always been required to file a return, no matter how small the estate was, and no matter whether any tax was ultimately owed.

In other countries, available data are less long run and/or less systematic. In the United Kingdom, one has to wait until 1894 for the unification of inheritance taxation (until this date the rules were different for personal and real estate taxes), and until the early 1920s

---

[17] See, e.g., Atkinson (1983) and Saez and Zucman (2014).

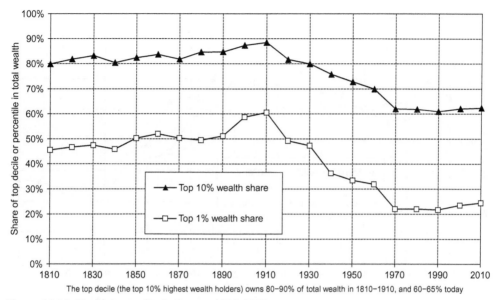

Figure 15.11 Wealth inequality in France, 1810–2010.

for unified statistics to be established by the U.K. tax administration. In the United States, one has to wait until 1916 for the creation of a federal estate tax and the publication of federal statistics on inheritance.

In addition, individual-level inheritance tax declarations have been well preserved in French national archives since the time of the revolution, so that one can use tax registers to collect large representative micro samples. Together with the tabulations by inheritance brackets published by the French tax administration, this allows for a consistent study of wealth inequality over a two-century-long period (see Piketty et al., 2006, 2013).

The main results are summarized on Figures 15.11 and 15.12.[18] First, wealth concentration was very high—and rising—in France during the nineteenth and early twentieth centuries. There was no decline in wealth concentration prior to World War I, quite the contrary: the trend toward rising wealth concentration did accelerate during the 1870–1913 period. The orders of magnitude are quite striking: in 1913, the top 10% wealth share is about 90%, and the top 1% share alone is around 60%. In Paris, which hosts about 5% of the population but as much as 25% of aggregate wealth, wealth is even more concentrated: more than two-thirds of the population has zero or negligible wealth, and 1% of the population owns 70% of the wealth.

---

[18] The updated series used for Figures 15.11 and 15.12 are based on the historical estimates presented by Piketty et al. (2006) and more recent fiscal data. See Piketty (2014, Chapter 10, Figures 10.1–10.2).

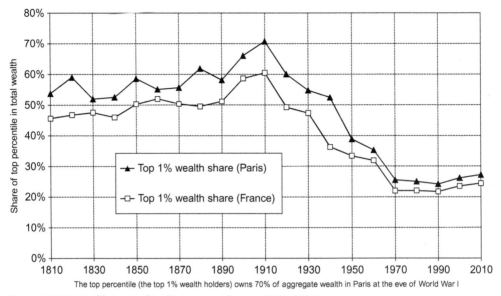

Figure 15.12 Wealth inequality: Paris versus France, 1810–2010.

Looking at Figures 15.11 and 15.12, one naturally wonders whether wealth concentration would have kept increasing without the 1914–1945 shocks. It might have stabilized at a very high level, but it could also have started to decline at some point. In any case, it is clear that the war shocks induced a violent regime change.

The other interesting fact is that wealth concentration has started to increase again in France since the 1970s–1980s—but it is still much lower than on the eve of World War I. According to the most recent data, the top 10% wealth share is slightly above 60%. Given the relatively low quality of today's wealth data, especially regarding top global wealth holders, one should be cautious about this estimate. It could well be that we somewhat underestimate the recent rise and the current level of wealth concentration.[19] In any case, a share of 60% for the top decile is already high, especially compared to the concentration of labor income: the top 10% of labor earners typically receive less than 30% of aggregate labor income.

15.3.2.2 Britain

Although the data sources for other countries are not as systematic and comprehensive as the French sources, existing evidence suggests that the French pattern extends to other European countries. For the United Kingdom, on Figure 15.13, we have combined historical estimates provided by various authors—particularly Atkinson and Harrison (1978)

[19] In contrast, the nineteenth and early twentieth centuries estimates are probably more precise (the tax rates were so low at that time that there was little incentive to hide wealth).

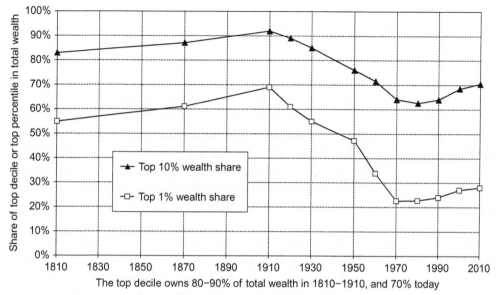

Figure 15.13 Wealth inequality in the United Kingdom, 1810–2010.

and Lindert (1986)—as well as more recent estimates using inheritance tax data. These series are not fully homogenous (in particular, the nineteenth century computations are based on samples of private probate records and are not entirely comparable to the twentieth-century inheritance tax data), but they deliver a consistent picture. Wealth concentration was high and rising during the nineteenth century up until World War I, then fell abruptly following the 1914–1945 shocks, and has been rising again since the 1980s.

According to these estimates, wealth concentration was also somewhat larger in the United Kingdom than in France in the nineteenth and early twentieth centuries. Yet the gap is much smaller than what French contemporary observers claimed. Around 1880–1910, it was very common among French republican elites to describe France as a "country of little property owners" (*un pays de petits propriétaires*), in contrast to aristocratic Britain. Therefore, the argument goes, there was no need to introduce progressive taxation in France (this should be left to Britain). The data show that on the eve of World War I the concentration of wealth was almost as extreme on both sides of the channel: the top 10% owns about 90% of wealth in both countries, and the top 1% owns 70% of wealth in Britain, versus 60% in France. It is true that aristocratic landed estates were more present in the United Kingdom (and to some extent still are today). But given that the share of agricultural land in national wealth dropped to low levels during the nineteenth century (see Figures 15.1 and 15.2), this does not matter much. At the end of the day, whether the country is a republic or a monarchy seems to have little impact on wealth concentration in the long run.

15.3.2.3 Sweden

Although widely regarded as an egalitarian haven today, Sweden was just as unequal as France and Britain in the nineteenth and early twentieth centuries. This is illustrated by Figure 15.13, where we plot some of the estimates constructed by Roine and Waldenstrom (2009) and Waldenstrom (2009).

The concentration of wealth is quite similar across European countries, both for the more ancient and the more recent estimates. Beyond national specificities, a European pattern emerges: the top 10% wealth share went from about 90% around 1900–1910 to about 60–70% in 2000–2010, with a recent rebound. In other words, about 20–30% of national wealth has been redistributed away from the top 10% to the bottom 90%. Since most of this redistribution benefited the middle 40% (the bottom 50% still hardly owns any wealth), this evolution can be described as the rise of a patrimonial middle class (Figure 15.14).

In the case of Sweden, Roine and Waldenstrom (2009) have also computed a corrected top 1% of wealth shares using estimates of offshore wealth held abroad by rich Swedes. They find that under plausible assumptions the top 1% share would shift from about 20% of aggregate wealth to over 30% (i.e., approximately the levels observed in the United Kingdom, and not too far away from the level observed in the United States). This illustrates the limitations of our ability to measure recent trends and levels, given the rising importance of tax havens.

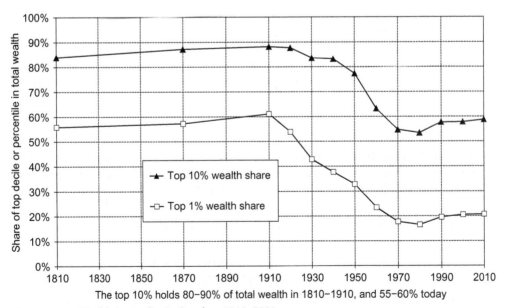

The top 10% holds 80–90% of total wealth in 1810–1910, and 55–60% today

Figure 15.14 Wealth inequality in Sweden, 1810–2010.

15.3.3 The Great Inequality Reversal: Europe Versus the United States, 1810–2010

Comparing wealth concentration in Europe and the United States, the main finding is a fairly spectacular reversal. In the nineteenth century, the United States was to some extent the land of equality (at least for white men): the concentration of wealth was much less extreme than in Europe (except in the South). Over the course of the twentieth century, this ordering was reversed: wealth concentration has become significantly higher in the United States. This is illustrated by Figure 15.15, where we combine the estimates due to Lindert (2000) for the nineteenth century with those of Saez and Zucman (2014) for the twentieth and twenty-first centuries to form long-run U.S. series, and by Figure 15.16, where we compare the United States to Europe (defined as the arithmetic average of France, Britain, and Sweden).

The reversal comes from the fact that Europe has become significantly less unequal over the course of the twentieth century, whereas the United States has not. The United States has almost returned to its early twentieth-century wealth concentration level: at its peak in the late 1920s, the 10% wealth share was about 80%, in 2012 it is about 75%; similarly the top 1% share peaked at about 45% and is back to around 40% today. Note, however, that the United States never reached the extreme level of wealth concentration of nineteenth- and early twentieth-century Europe (with a top decile of 90% or more). The United States has always had a patrimonial middle class, although one of varying importance. The share of wealth held by the middle class appears to have been shrinking since the 1980s.

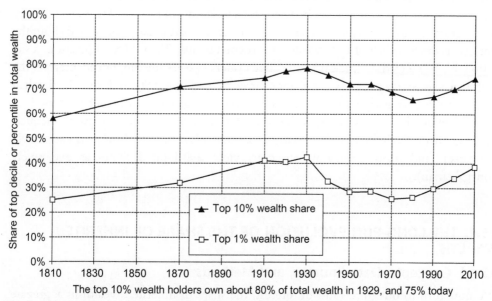

Figure 15.15 Wealth inequality in the United States, 1810–2010.

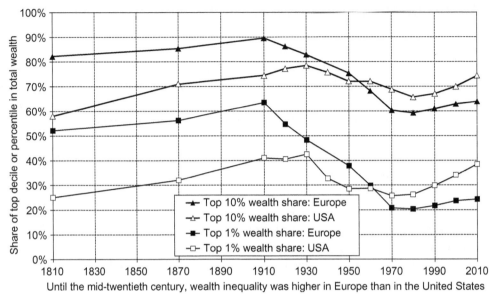

Figure 15.16 Wealth inequality: Europe and the United States, 1810–2010.

U.S. economists of the early twentieth century were very concerned about the pos-sibility that their country becomes as unequal as Old Europe. Irving Fisher, then pres-ident of the American Economic Association, gave his presidential address in 1919 on this topic. He argued that the concentration of income and wealth was becoming as dan-gerously excessive in America as it had been for a long time in Europe. He called for steep tax progressivity to counteract this tendency. Fisher was particularly concerned about the fact that as much as half of U.S. wealth was owned by just 2% of U.S. population, a sit-uation that he viewed as "undemocratic" (see Fisher, 1920). One can indeed interpret the spectacular rise of tax progressivity that occurred in the United States during the first half of the twentieth century as an attempt to preserve the egalitarian, democratic American ethos (celebrated a century before by Tocqueville and others). Attitudes toward inequal-ity are dramatically different today. Many U.S. observers now view Europe as excessively egalitarian (and many European observers view the United States as excessively nonegalitarian).

15.4. THE LONG-RUN EVOLUTION OF THE SHARE OF INHERITED WEALTH

15.4.1 Concepts, Data Sources, and Methods

We now turn to our third ratio of interest, the share of inherited wealth in aggregate wealth. We should make clear at the outset that this is an area where available evidence is scarce and incomplete. Measuring the share of inherited wealth requires a lot more data than the measurement of aggregate wealth–income ratios or even wealth concentration. It is also an area where it is important to be particularly careful about concepts and definitions. Purely definitional conflicts have caused substantial confusion in the past. Therefore it is critical to start from there.

15.4.1.1 Basic Notions and Definitions

The most natural way to define the share of inherited wealth in aggregate wealth is to cumulate past inheritance flows. That is, assume that we observe the aggregate wealth stock W_t at time t in a given country, and that we would like to define and estimate the aggregate inherited wealth stock $W_{Bt} \leq W_t$ (and conversely aggregate self-made wealth, which we simply define as $W_{St} = W_t - W_{Bt}$). Assume that we observe the annual flow of inheritance B_s that occurred in any year $s \leq t$. At first sight, it might seem natural to define the stock of inherited wealth W_{Bt} as the sum of past inheritance flows:

$$W_{Bt} = \int_{s \leq t} B_s \cdot ds$$

However, there are several practical and conceptual difficulties with this ambiguous definition, which need to be addressed before the formula can be applied to actual data. First, it is critical to include in this sum not only past bequest flows B_s (wealth transmissions at death) but also inter vivos gift flows V_s (wealth transmissions inter vivos). That is, one should define W_{Bt} as $W_{Bt} = \int_{s \leq t} B_s^* \cdot ds$, with $B_s^* = B_s + V_s$.

Alternatively, if one cannot observe directly the gift flow V_s, one should replace the observed bequest flow B_s by some gross level $B_s^* = (1 + v_s) \cdot B_s$, where $v_s = V_s / B_s$ is an estimate of the gift/bequest flow ratio. In countries where adequate data is available, the gift–bequest ratio is at least 10–20%, and is often higher than 50%, especially in the recent period.[20] It is thus critical to include gifts in one way or another. In countries where fiscal data on gifts are insufficient, one should at least try to estimate $1 + v_s$ using surveys (which often suffers from severe downward biases) and harder administrative evidence from other countries.

Next, to properly apply this definition, one should only take into account the fraction of the aggregate inheritance flow $B_{st} \leq B_s$ that was received at time s by individuals who are still alive at time t. The problem is that doing so properly requires very detailed individual-level information. At any time t, there are always individuals who received inheritance a very long time ago (say, 60 years ago) but who are still alive (because they inherited at a very young age and/or are enjoying a very long life). Conversely, a fraction

---

[20] See below. Usually one only includes formal, monetary capital gifts, and one ignores informal presents and in-kind gifts. In particular in-kind gifts made to minors living with their parents (i.e., the fact that minor children are usually catered by their parents) are generally left aside.

of the inheritance flow received a short time ago (say, 10 years ago) should not be counted (because the relevant inheritors are already dead, e.g., they inherited at an old age or died young). In practice, however, such unusual events tend to balance each other, so that a standard simplifying assumption is to cumulate the full inheritance flows observed the previous H years, where H is the average generation length, that is, the average age at which parents have children (typically $H = 30$ years). Therefore we obtain the following simplified definition:

$$W_{Bt} = \int_{t-30 \leq s \leq t} (1 + v_s) \cdot B_s \cdot ds$$

15.4.1.2 The Kotlikoff–Summers–Modigliani Controversy

Assume now that these two difficulties can be addressed (i.e., that we can properly estimate the factor $1 + v_s$ and the average generation length H). There are more substantial difficulties ahead. First, to properly compute W_{Bt}, one needs to be able to observe inheritance flows B_s^* over a relatively long time period (typically, the previous 30 years). In the famous Kotlikoff–Summers–Modigliani (KSM) controversy, both Kotlikoff and Summers (1981) and Modigliani (1986, 1988) used estimates of the U.S. inheritance flow for only 1 year (and a relatively ancient year: 1962), see also Kotlikoff (1988). They simply assumed that this estimate could be used for other years. Namely, they assumed that the inheritance flow–national income ratio (which we note $b_{ys} = B_s^*/Y_s$) is stable over time. One problem with this assumption is that it might not be verified. As we shall see below, extensive historical data on inheritances recently collected in France show that the b_{ys} ratio has changed tremendously over the past two centuries, from about 20–25% of national income in the nineteenth and early twentieth centuries, down to less than 5% at mid-twentieth century, back to about 15% in the early twenty-first century (Piketty, 2011). So one cannot simply use one year of data and assume that we are in a steady state: One needs a long-run time series on the inheritance flow in order to estimate the aggregate stock of inherited wealth.

Next, one needs to decide the extent to which past inheritance flows need to be upgraded or capitalized. This is the main source of disagreement and confusion in the KSM controversy.

Modigliani (1986, 1988) chooses zero capitalization. That is, he simply defines the stock of inherited wealth W_{Bt}^M as the raw sum of past inheritance flows with no adjustment whatsoever (except for the GDP price index):

$$W_{Bt}^M = \int_{t-30 \leq s \leq t} B_s^* \cdot ds$$

Assume a fixed inheritance flow–national income ratio $b_y = B_s^*/Y_s$, growth rate g (so that $Y_t = Y_s \cdot e^{g(t-s)}$), generation length H, and aggregate private wealth–national income ratio

$\beta = W_t / Y_t$. Then, according to the Modigliani definition, the steady-state formulas for the stock of inherited wealth relative to national income W^M_{Bt}/Y_t and for the share of inherited wealth $\varphi^M_t = W^M_{Bt}/W_t$ are given by

$$W^M_{Bt}/Y_t = \frac{1}{Y_t} \int_{t-30 \leq s \leq t} B^*_s \cdot ds = \frac{1 - e^{-gH}}{g} \cdot b_y$$

$$\varphi^M_t = W^M_{Bt}/W_t = \frac{1 - e^{-gH}}{g} \cdot \frac{b_y}{\beta}$$

In contrast, Kotlikoff and Summers (1981, 1988) choose to capitalize past inheritance flows by using the economy's average rate of return to wealth (assuming it is constant and equal to r). Following the Kotlikoff–Summers definition, the steady-state formulas for the stock of inherited wealth relative to national income W^{KS}_{Bt}/Y_t and for the share of inherited wealth $\varphi^{KS}_t = W^{KS}_{Bt}/W_t$ are given by

$$W^{KS}_{Bt}/Y_t = \frac{1}{Y_t} \int_{t-30 \leq s \leq t} e^{r(t-s)} \cdot B^*_s \cdot ds = \frac{e^{(r-g)H} - 1}{r - g} \cdot b_y$$

$$\varphi^{KS}_t = W^{KS}_{Bt}/W_t = \frac{e^{(r-g)H} - 1}{r - g} \cdot \frac{b_y}{\beta}$$

In the special case where growth rates and rates of return are negligible (i.e., infinitely close to zero), then both definitions coincide. That is, if $g=0$ and $r-g=0$, then $(1 - e^{-gH})/g = (e^{(r-g)H} - 1)/(r-g) = H$, so that $W^M_{Bt}/Y_t = W^{KS}_{Bt}/Y_t = Hb_y$ and $\varphi^M_t = \varphi^{KS}_t = Hb_y/\beta$.

   Thus, in case growth and capitalization effects can be neglected, one simply needs to multiply the annual inheritance flow by generation length. If the annual inheritance flow is equal to $b_y = 10\%$ of national income, and generation length is equal to $H=30$ years, then the stock of inherited wealth is equal to $W^M_{Bt} = W^{KS}_{Bt} = 300\%$ of national income according to both definitions. In case aggregate wealth amounts to $\beta = 400\%$ of national income, then the inheritance share is equal to $\varphi^M_t = \varphi^{KS}_t = 75\%$ of aggregate wealth.

   However, in the general case where g and $r-g$ are significantly different from zero, the two definitions can lead to widely different conclusions. For instance, with $g=2\%$, $r=4\%$, and $H=30$, we have the following capitalization factors: $(1 - e^{-gH})/(g \cdot H) = 0.75$ and $(e^{(r-g)H} - 1)/((r-g) \cdot H) = 1.37$. In this example, for a given inheritance flow $b_y = 10\%$ and aggregate wealth–income ratio $\beta = 400\%$, we obtain $\varphi^M_t = 56\%$ and $\varphi^{KS}_t = 103\%$. About half of wealth comes from inheritance according to the Modigliani definition, and all of it according to the Kotlikoff–Summers definition.

   This is the main reason why Modigliani and Kotlikoff–Summers disagree so much about the inheritance share. They both use the same (relatively fragile) estimate for the United States b_y in 1962. But Modigliani does not capitalize past inheritance flows and concludes that the inheritance share is as low as 20–30%. Kotlikoff–Summers do capitalize the same flows and conclude that the inheritance share is as large as 80–90% (or even larger than 100%). Both sides also disagree somewhat about the measurement of b_y, but the main source of disagreement comes from this capitalization effect.[21]

15.4.1.3 The Limitations of KSM Definitions

Which of the two definitions is most justified? In our view, both are problematic. It is wholly inappropriate not to capitalize at all past inheritance flows. But full capitalization is also inadequate.

The key problem with the KSM representative-agent approach is that it fails to recognize that the wealth accumulation process always involves two different kinds of people and wealth trajectories. In every economy, there are inheritors (people who typically consume part of the return to their inherited wealth) and there are savers (people who do not inherit much but do accumulate wealth through labor income savings). This is an important feature of the real world that must be taken into account for a proper understanding of the aggregate wealth accumulation process.

The Modigliani definition is particularly problematic as it simply fails to recognize that inherited wealth produces flow returns. This mechanically leads to artificially low numbers for the inheritance share φ_t^M (as low as 20–40%), and to artificially high numbers for the life-cycle share in wealth accumulation, which Modigliani defines as $1 - \varphi_t^M$ (up to 60–80%). As Blinder (1988) argues, "a Rockefeller with zero lifetime labor income and consuming only part of his inherited wealth income would appear to be a life-cycle saver in Modigliani's definition, which seems weird to me." One can easily construct illustrative examples of economies where all wealth comes from inheritance (with dynasties of the sort described by Blinder), but where Modigliani would still find an inheritance share well below 50%, simply because of his definition. This makes little sense.[22]

The Kotlikoff–Summers definition is conceptually more satisfactory than Modigliani's. But it suffers from the opposite drawback in the sense that it mechanically leads to artificially high numbers for the inheritance share φ_t^{KS}. In particular, φ_t^{KS} can easily be larger than 100%, even though there are life-cycle savers and self-made wealth accumulators in the economy, and a significant fraction of aggregate wealth accumulation comes from them. This will arise whenever the cumulated return to inherited wealth

---

[21] In effect, Modigliani favors a b_y ratio around 5–6%, whereas Kotlikoff–Summers find it more realistic to use a b_y ratio around 7–8%. Given the data sources they use, it is likely that both sides tend to somewhat underestimate the true ratio. See the discussion below for the case of France and other European countries.

[22] It is worth stressing that the return to inherited wealth (and the possibility to save and accumulate more wealth out of the return to inherited wealth) is a highly relevant economic issue not only for high-wealth dynasties of the sort referred to by Blinder, but also for middle-wealth dynasties. For instance, it is easier to save if one has inherited a house and has no rent to pay. An inheritor saving less than the rental value of his inherited home would be described as a life-cycle saver according to Modigliani's definition, which again seems odd.

consumed by inheritors exceeds the savers' wealth accumulation from their labor savings. In the real world, this condition seems to hold not only in prototype rentier societies such as Paris 1872–1937 (see Piketty et al., 2013), but also in countries and time periods when aggregate inheritance flow is relatively low. For instance, aggregate French series show that the capitalized bequest share φ_t^{KS} has been larger than 100% throughout the twentieth century, including in the 1950s–1970s, a period where a very significant amount of new self-made wealth was accumulated (Piketty, 2011).

In sum, the Modigliani definition leads to estimates of the inheritance share that are artificially close to 0%, whereas the Kotlikoff–Summers leads to inheritance shares that tend to be structurally above 100%. Neither of them offers an adequate way to look at the data.

15.4.1.4 The PPVR Definition

In an ideal world with perfect data, the conceptually consistent way to define the share of inherited wealth in aggregate wealth is the following. It has first been formalized and applied to Parisian wealth data by Piketty et al. (2013), so we refer to it as the PPVR definition.

The basic idea is to split the population into two groups. First, there are "inheritors" (or "rentiers"), whose assets are worth less than the capitalized value of the wealth they inherited (over time they consume more than their labor income). The second group is composed of "savers" (or "self-made individuals"), whose assets are worth more than the capitalized value of the wealth they inherited (they consume less than their labor income). Aggregate inherited wealth can then be defined as the sum of inheritors' wealth plus the inherited fraction of savers' wealth, and self-made wealth as the noninherited fraction of savers' wealth. By construction, inherited and self-made wealth are less than 100% and sum to aggregate wealth, which is certainly a desirable property. Although the definition is fairly straightforward, it differs considerably from the standard KSM definitions based on representative agent models. The PPVR definition is conceptually more consistent and provides a more meaningful way to look at the data and to analyze the structure of wealth accumulation processes. In effect, it amounts to defining inherited wealth at the individual level as the minimum between current wealth and capitalized inheritance.

More precisely, consider an economy with population N_t at time t. Take a given individual i with wealth w_{ti} at time t. Assume he or she received bequest b_{ti}^0 at time $t_i < t$. Note $b_{ti}^* = b_{ti}^0 \cdot e^{r(t-t_i)}$ the capitalized value of b_{ti}^0 at time t (where $e^{r(t-ti)}$ is the cumulated rate of return between time t_i and time t). Individual i is said to be an "inheritor" (or a "rentier") if $w_{ti} < b_{ti}^*$ and a "saver" (or a "self-made individual") if $w_{ti} \geq b_{ti}^*$. We define the set of inheritors as $N_t^r = \{i \, \text{s.t.} \, w_{ti} < b_{ti}^*\}$ and the set of savers as $N_t^s = \{i \, \text{s.t.} \, w_{ti} \geq b_{ti}^*\}$.

We note $\rho_t = N_t^r / N_t$ and $1 - \rho_t = N_t^s / N_t$ as the corresponding population shares of inheritors and savers; $w_t^r = E(w_{ti} | w_{ti} < b_{ti}^*)$ and $w_t^s = E(w_{ti} | w_{ti} \geq b_{ti}^*)$ as the average wealth levels of both groups; $br_t^* = E(b_{ti}^* | w_{ti} < b_{ti}^*)$ and $bs_t^* = E(b_{ti}^* | w_{ti} \geq b_{ti}^*)$ as the levels of their average capitalized bequest; and $\pi_t = \rho_t \cdot w_t^r / w_t$ and $1 - \pi_t = (1 - \rho_t) \cdot w_t^s / w_t$ as the share of inheritors and savers in aggregate wealth.

We define the total share φ_t of inherited wealth in aggregate wealth as the sum of inheritors' wealth plus the inherited fraction of savers' wealth, and the share $1 - \varphi_t$ of self-made wealth as the noninherited fraction of savers' wealth:

$$\varphi_t = \left[\rho_t \cdot w_t^r + (1 - \rho_t) \cdot b_t^{s*} \right] / w_t = \pi_t + (1 - \rho_t) \cdot b_t^{s*} / w_t$$

$$1 - \varphi_t = (1 - \rho_t) \cdot \left(w_t^s - b_t^{s*} \right) / w_t = 1 - \pi_t - (1 - \rho_t) \cdot b_t^{s*} / w_t$$

The downside of this definition is that it is more demanding in terms of data availability. Although Modigliani and Kotlikoff–Summers could compute inheritance shares in aggregate wealth by using aggregate data only, the PPVR definition requires micro data. Namely, we need data on the joint distribution $G_t(w_{ti}, b_{ti}^*)$ of current wealth w_{ti} and capitalized inherited wealth b_{ti}^* in order to compute ρ_t, π_t, and φ_t. This does require high-quality, individual-level data on wealth and inheritance over two generations, which is often difficult to obtain. It is worth stressing, however, that we do not need to know anything about the individual labor income or consumption paths (y_{Lsi}, c_{si}, $s < t$) followed by individual i up to the time of observation.[23]

For plausible joint distributions $G_t(w_{ti}, b_{ti}^*)$, the PPVR inheritance share φ_t will typically fall somewhere in the interval $[\varphi_t^M, \varphi_t^{KS}]$. There is, however, no theoretical reason why it should be so in general. Imagine, for instance, an economy where inheritors consume their bequests the very day they receive them, and never save afterward, so that wealth accumulation entirely comes from the savers, who never received any bequest (or negligible amounts) and who patiently accumulate savings from their labor income. Then with our definition $\varphi_t = 0\%$: in this economy, 100% of wealth accumulation comes from savings, and nothing at all comes from inheritance.

However, with the Modigliani and Kotlikoff–Summers definitions, the inheritance shares φ_t^M and φ_t^{KS} could be arbitrarily large.

---

[23] Of course, more data are better. If we also have (or estimate) labor income or consumption paths, then one can compute lifetime individual savings rate s_{Bti}, that is, the share of lifetime resources that was not consumed up to time t: $s_{Bti} = w_{ti} / (b_{ti}^* + y_{Lti}^*) = 1 - c_{ti}^* / (b_{ti}^* + y_{Lti}^*)$ with $y_{Lti}^* = \int\limits_{s<t} y_{Lsi} e^{r(t-s)} ds = $ capitalized value at time t of past labor income flows, and $c_{ti}^* = \int\limits_{s<t} c_{si} e^{r(t-s)} ds = $ capitalized value at time t of past consumption flows. By definition, inheritors are individuals who consumed more than their labor income (i.e., $w_{ti} < b_{ti}^* \leftrightarrow c_{ti}^* > y_{Lti}^*$), while savers are individuals who consumed less than their labor income (i.e., $w_{ti} \geq b_{ti}^* \leftrightarrow c_{ti}^* \leq y_{Lti}^*$). But the point is that we only need to observe an individual's wealth (w_{ti}) and capitalized inheritance (b_{ti}^*) to determine whether he or she is an inheritor or a saver, and in order to compute the share of inherited wealth.

15.4.1.5 A Simplified Definition: Inheritance Flows versus Saving Flows

When available micro data is not sufficient to apply the PPVR definition, one can also use a simplified, approximate definition based on the comparison between inheritance flows and saving flows.

Assume that all we have is macro data on inheritance flows $b_{yt} = B_t/Y_t$ and savings flows $s_t = S_t/Y_t$. Suppose for simplicity that both flows are constant over time: $b_{yt} = b_y$ and $s_t = s$. We want to estimate the share $\varphi = W_B/W$ of inherited wealth in aggregate wealth. The difficulty is that we typically do not know which part of the aggregate saving rate s comes from the return to inherited wealth, and which part comes from labor income (or from the return to past savings). Ideally, one would like to distinguish between the savings of inheritors and self-made individuals (defined along the lines explained above), but this requires micro data over two generations. In the absence of such data, a natural starting point would be to assume that the propensity to save is on average the same whatever the income sources. That is, a fraction $\varphi \cdot \alpha$ of the saving rate s should be attributed to the return to inherited wealth, and a fraction $1 - \alpha + (1 - \varphi) \cdot \alpha$ should be attributed to labor income (and to the return to past savings), where $\alpha = Y_K/Y$ is the capital share in national income and $1 - \alpha = Y_L/Y$ is the labor share. Assuming again that we are in steady state, we obtain the following simplified formula for the share of inherited wealth in aggregate wealth:

$$\varphi = \frac{b_y + \varphi \cdot \alpha \cdot s}{b_y + s},$$

$$\text{i.e., } \varphi = \frac{b_y}{b_y + (1 - \alpha) \cdot s}.$$

Intuitively, this formula simply compares the size of the inheritance and saving flows. Because all wealth must originate from one of the two flows, it is the most natural way to estimate the share of inherited wealth in total wealth.[24]

There are a number of caveats with this simplified formula. First, real-world economies are generally out of steady state, so it is important to compute average values of b_y, s, and α over relatively long periods of time (typically over the past H years, with $H = 30$ years). If one has time-series estimates of the inheritance flow b_{ys}, capital share α_s, and saving rate s_s, then one can use the following full formula, which capitalizes past inheritance and savings flows at rate $r - g$:

---

[24] Similar formulas based on the comparison of inheritance and saving flows have been used by DeLong (2003) and Davies et al. (2012, pp. 123–124). One important difference is that these authors do not take into account the fact that the savings flow partly comes from the return to inherited wealth. We return to this point in Section **15.5.4**.

$$\varphi = \frac{\displaystyle\int_{t-H\le s\le t} e^{(r-g)(t-s)}\cdot b_{ys}\cdot ds}{\displaystyle\int_{t-H\le s\le t} e^{(r-g)(t-s)}\cdot \left(b_{ys} + (1-\alpha_s)\cdot s_s\right)\cdot ds}.$$

With constant flows, the full formula boils down to $\varphi = \frac{b_y}{b_y + (1-\alpha)\cdot s}$.

Second, one should bear in mind that the simplified formula $\varphi = b_y/(b_y + (1-\alpha)\cdot s)$ is an approximate formula. In general, as we show below, it tends to underestimate the true share of inheritance, as computed from micro data using the PPVR definition. The reason is that individuals who have only labor income tend to save less (in proportion to their total income) than those who have large inherited wealth and capital income, which. in turn, seems to be related to the fact that wealth (and particularly inherited wealth) is more concentrated than labor income.

On the positive side, simplified estimates of φ seem to follow micro-based estimates relatively closely (much more closely than KSM estimates, which are either far too small or far too large), and they are much less demanding in terms of data. One only needs to estimate macro flows. Another key advantage of the simplified definition over KSM definitions is that it does not depend upon the sensitive choice of the rate of return or the rate of capital gains or losses. Whatever these rates might be, they should apply equally to inherited and self-made wealth (at least as a first approximation), so one can simply compare inheritance and saving flows.

15.4.2 The Long-Run Evolution of Inheritance in France 1820–2010

15.4.2.1 The Inheritance Flow–National Income Ratio b_{yt}

What do we empirically know about the historical evolution of inheritance? We start by presenting the evidence on the dynamics of the inheritance to national income ratio b_{yt} in France, a country for which, as we have seen in Section 15.3, historical data sources are exceptionally good (Piketty, 2011). The main conclusion is that b_{yt} has followed a spectacular U-shaped pattern over the twentieth century. The inheritance flow was relatively stable, around 20–25% of national income throughout the 1820–1910 period (with a slight upward trend), before being divided by a factor of about 5–6 between 1910 and the 1950s, and then multiplied by a factor of about 3–4 between the 1950s and the 2000s (see Figure 15.17).

These are enormous historical variations, but they appear to be well-founded empirically. In particular, the patterns for b_{yt} are similar with two independent measures of the inheritance flow. The first, what we call the fiscal flow, uses bequest and gift tax data and makes allowances for tax-exempt assets such as life insurance. The second measure, what we call the economic flow, combines estimates of private wealth W_t, mortality tables, and observed age–wealth profile, using the following accounting equation:

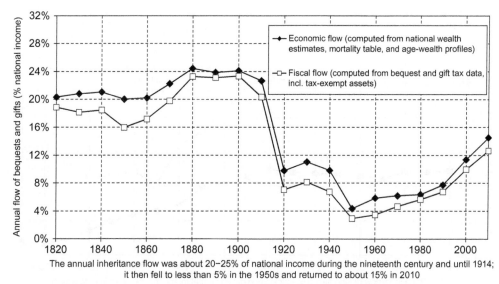

The annual inheritance flow was about 20–25% of national income during the nineteenth century and until 1914; it then fell to less than 5% in the 1950s and returned to about 15% in 2010

Figure 15.17 The annual inheritance flow as a fraction of national income, France 1820–2010.

$$B_t^* = (1 + v_t) \cdot \mu_t \cdot m_t \cdot W_t,$$

where $m_t =$ mortality rate (number of adult decedents divided by total adult population), $\mu_t =$ ratio between average adult wealth at death and average adult wealth for the entire population, and $v_t = V_t/B_t =$ estimate of the gift/bequest flow ratio.

The gap between the fiscal and economic flows can be interpreted as capturing tax evasion and other measurement errors. It is approximately constant over time and relatively small, so that the two series deliver consistent long-run patterns (see Figure 15.17).

The economic flow series allow—by construction—for a straightforward decomposition of the various effects at play in the evolution of b_{yt}. In the above equation, dividing both terms by Y_t we get

$$b_{yt} = B_t^*/Y_t = (1 + v_t) \cdot \mu_t \cdot m_t \cdot \beta_t.$$

Similarly, dividing by W_t we can define the rate of wealth transmission b_{wt} as

$$b_{wt} = B_t^*/W_t = (1 + v_t) \cdot \mu_t \cdot m_t = \mu_t^* \cdot m_t$$
$$\text{with} \mu_t^* = (1 + v_t) \cdot \mu_t = \text{gift-corrected ratio}$$

If $\mu_t = 1$ (i.e., decedents have the same average wealth as the living) and $v_t = 0$ (no gift), then the rate of wealth transmission is simply equal to the mortality rate: $b_{wt} = m_t$ (and $b_{yt} = m_t \cdot \beta_t$). If $\mu_t = 0$ (i.e., decedents die with zero wealth, such as in Modigliani's pure life-cycle theory of wealth accumulation) and $v_t = 0$ (no gift), then there is no inheritance at all: $b_{wt} = b_{yt} = 0$.

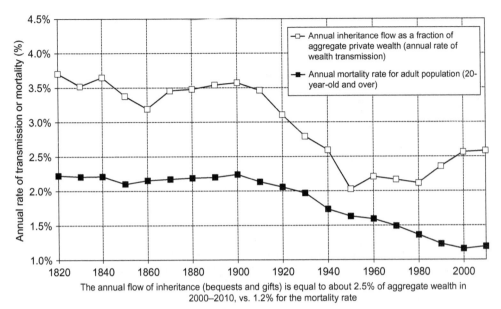

Figure 15.18 Inheritance flow versus mortality rate, France 1820–2010.

Using these accounting equations, we can see that the U-shaped pattern followed by the French inheritance-income ratio b_{yt} is the product of two U-shaped evolutions. First, it partly comes from the U-shaped evolution of the private wealth–income ratio β_t. The U-shaped evolution of b_{yt}, however, is almost twice as marked at that of β_t. The wealth–income ratio was divided by a factor of about 2–3 between 1910 and 1950 (from 600–700% to 200–300%, see Figure 15.2), whereas the inheritance flow was divided by a factor around 5–6 (from 20–25% to about 4%, see Figure 15.17). The explanation is that the rate of wealth transmission $b_{wt} = \mu_t^* \cdot m_t$ has also been following a U-shaped pattern: it was almost divided by 2 between 1910 and 1950 (from over 3.5% to just 2%), and it has been rising again to about 2.5% in 2010 (see Figure 15.18).

The U-shaped pattern followed by b_{wt}, in turn, entirely comes from μ_t^*. The relative wealth of decedents was at its lowest historical level in the aftermath of World War II (which, as we shall see below, is largely due to the fact that it was too late for older cohorts to recover from the shocks and reaccumulate wealth after the war). Given that aggregate wealth was also at its lowest historical level, the combination of these two factors explains the exceptionally low level of the inheritance flow in the 1950s–1960s. By contrast, the mortality rate m_t has been constantly diminishing: this long-run downward trend is the mechanical consequence of the rise in life expectancy (for a given cohort size).[25]

---

[25] The mortality rate, however, is about to rise somewhat in coming decades in France owing to the aging of the baby boomers (see Piketty, 2011). This effect will be even stronger in countries where cohort size has declined in recent decades (such as Germany or Japan) and will tend to push inheritance flows toward even higher levels.

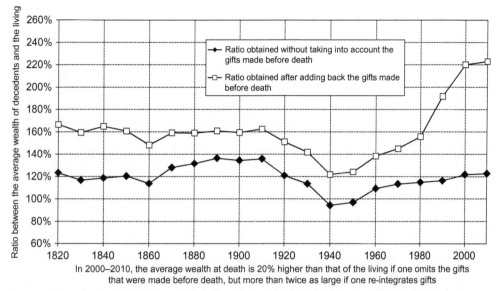

Figure 15.19 The ratio between average wealth at death and average wealth of the living, France 1820–2010.

In the recent decades, a very large part of the rise in $\mu_t^* = (1 + v_t) \cdot \mu_t$ comes from the rise in the gift–bequest ratio v_t, which used to be about 20% during most of the nineteenth to twentieth centuries, and has gradually risen to as much as 80% in recent decades (see Figure 15.19). That is, the gift flow is currently almost as large as the bequest flow.

Although there is still much uncertainty about the reasons behind the rise in gifts, the evidence suggests that it started before the introduction of new tax incentives for gifts in the 1990s–2000s, and has more to do with the growing awareness by wealthy parents that they will die old and that they ought to transmit part of their wealth inter-vivos if they want their children to fully benefit from it.

In any case, one should not underestimate the importance of gifts. In particular, one should not infer from a declining age–wealth profile at old ages or a relatively low relative wealth of decedents that inheritance is unimportant: this could simply reflect the fact that decedents have already given away a large part of their wealth.

15.4.2.2 The Inheritance Stock-Aggregate Wealth Ratio φ_t

How do the annual inheritance flows transmit into cumulated inheritance stocks? Given the data limitations we face, we show on Figure 15.20 two alternative estimates for the share φ_t of total inherited wealth in aggregate French wealth between 1850 and 2010. According to both measures, there is again a clear U-shaped pattern. The share of inherited wealth φ_t was as large as 80–90% of aggregate wealth in 1850–1910, down to as little as 35–45% around 1970, and back up to 65–75% by 2010.

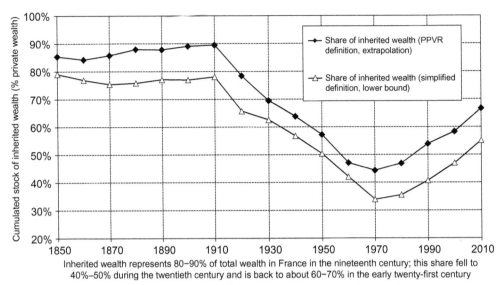

Inherited wealth represents 80–90% of total wealth in France in the nineteenth century; this share fell to 40%–50% during the twentieth century and is back to about 60–70% in the early twenty-first century

Figure 15.20 The cumulated stock of inherited wealth as a fraction of aggregate private wealth, France 1850–2010.

The higher series, which we see as the most reliable, was obtained by applying the micro-based PPVR definition (see Section 15.4.1.4). The limitation here is that the set of micro data on wealth over two generations that has been collected in French historical archives is more complete for Paris than for the rest of France (see Piketty et al., 2006, 2013). For years with missing data for the rest of France, the estimates reported on Figure 15.20 were extrapolated on the basis of the Parisian data. Ongoing data collection suggests that the final estimates will not be too different from the approximate estimates reported here.

The lower series, which we see as a lower bound, comes from the simplified definition based on the comparison of inheritance and saving flows (see Section 15.4.1.5).[26] The key advantage of this simplified definition is that it requires much less data: it can readily be computed from the inheritance flow series b_{yt} that were reported above. It delivers estimates of the inheritance share φ_t that are always somewhat below the micro-based estimates, with a gap that appears to be approximately constant. The gap seems to be due to the fact that the simplified definition attributes too much saving to pure labor earners with little inheritance.

In both series, the share φ_t of total inherited wealth in aggregate wealth reaches its lowest historical point in the 1970s, whereas the inheritance flow b_{yt} reaches its lowest point in the immediate aftermath of World War II. The reason is that the stock of

---

[26] The series was computed as $\varphi = b_y / (b_y + (1 - \alpha) \cdot s)$ using 30-year averages for saving rates, capital shares, and inheritance flows.

inherited wealth comes from cumulating the inheritance flows of the previous decades—hence the time lag.

15.4.3 Evidence from Other Countries

What do we know about the importance of inheritance in countries other than France? A recent wave of research attempts to construct estimates of the inheritance flow–national income ratio b_{yt} in a number of European countries. The series constructed by Atkinson (2013) for Britain and Schinke (2013) for Germany show that b_{yt} has also followed a U-shaped pattern in these two countries over the past century (see Figure 15.21). Data limitations, however, make it difficult at this stage to make precise comparisons between countries.

For Britain, the inheritance flow b_{yt} of the late nineteenth to early twentieth centuries seems to be similar to that of France, namely about 20–25% of national income. The flow then falls following the 1914–1945 shocks, albeit less spectacularly than in France, and recovers in recent decades. Karagiannaki (2011), in a study of inheritance in the United Kingdom from 1984 to 2005, also finds a marked increase in that period. The rebound, however, seems to be less strong in Britain than in France, so that the inheritance flow appears smaller than in France today. We do not know yet whether this finding is robust. Available British series are pure "fiscal flow" series (as opposed to French series, for which we have both an "economic" and a "fiscal" estimate). As pointed out by Atkinson (2013), the main reason for the weaker British rebound in recent decades is that the gift–bequest ratio v_t has not increased at all according to fiscal data (v_t has remained relatively flat at a

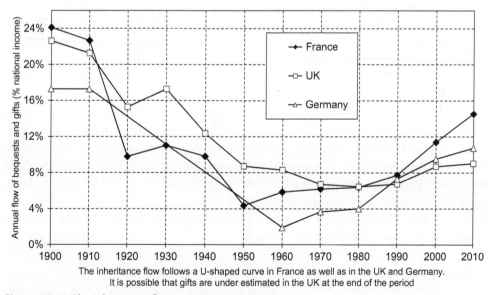

The inheritance flow follows a U-shaped curve in France as well as in the UK and Germany.
It is possible that gifts are under estimated in the UK at the end of the period

Figure 15.21 The inheritance flow in Europe, 1900–2010.

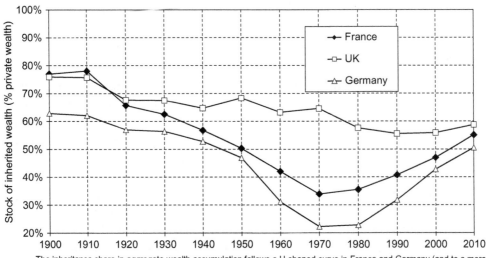

The inheritance share in aggregate wealth accumulation follows a U-shaped curve in France and Germany (and to a more limited extent in the UK and Germany). It is possible that gifts are underestimated in the UK at the end of the period

Figure 15.22 The inheritance stock in Europe, 1900–2010.

low level, around 10–20%). According to Atkinson, this could be due to substantial underreporting of gifts to tax authorities.

Germany also exhibits a U-shaped pattern of inheritance flow b_{yt} that seems to be broadly as sharp as in France. In particular, just as in France, the strong German rebound in recent decades comes with a large rise in the gift–bequest ratio v_t during the 1990s– 2000s (v_t is above 50–60% in the 2000s). The overall levels of b_{yt} are generally lower in Germany than in France, which given the lower aggregate wealth–income ratio β_t is not surprising. Should we compare the rates of wealth transmission (i.e., $b_{wt} = b_{yt}/\beta_t$), then the levels would be roughly the same in both countries in 2000–2010.

We report on Figure 15.22 the corresponding estimates for the share φ_t of total inherited wealth in aggregate wealth, using the simplified definition $\varphi = b_y/(b_y + (1 - \alpha)s)$. For Germany, the inheritance share φ_t appears to be generally smaller than in France. In particular, it reaches very low levels in the 1960s–1970s, owing to the extremely low inheritance flows in Germany in the immediate postwar period, and to large saving rates. In recent decades, the German φ_t has been rising fast and seems to catch up with France's. In the United Kingdom, the inheritance share φ_t apparently never fell to the low levels observed in France and Germany in the 1950s, and seems to be always higher than on the Continent. The reason, for the recent period, is that the United Kingdom has had relatively low saving rates since the 1970s.[27]

---

[27] In effect, British saving rates in recent decades are insufficient to explain the large rise in the aggregate wealth–income ratio, which can only be accounted for by large capital gain (Piketty and Zucman, 2014). The simplified definition of φ_t based on the comparison between inheritance and saving flows assumes the same capital gains for inherited and self-made wealth.

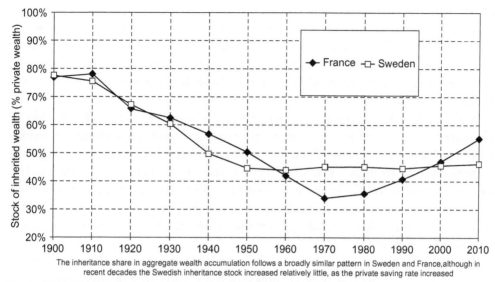

The inheritance share in aggregate wealth accumulation follows a broadly similar pattern in Sweden and France, although in recent decades the Swedish inheritance stock increased relatively little, as the private saving rate increased

Figure 15.23 The inheritance stock in France and Sweden, 1900–2010.

Recent historical research suggests that inheritance flows have also followed U-shaped patterns in Sweden (see Ohlsson et al., 2013). Here b_{yt} appears to be smaller than in France, but this again seems largely due to lower β_t ratios. When we look at the implied b_{wt} and φ_t ratios, which in a way are the most meaningful ratios to study, then both the levels and shape are relatively similar across European countries. As shown by Figure 15.23, the share of inherited wealth followed the same evolution in Sweden and France in the twentieth century (the main difference is that it seems to have increased a bit less in Sweden than in France in recent decades, because of a rise in the private saving rate). We stress again, however, that a lot more data needs to be collected—and to some extent is currently being collected—on the historical evolution of inheritance before we can make proper international comparisons.

Prior to the recent inheritance flow estimates surveyed above, a first wave of research, surveyed by Davies and Shorrocks (1999), mostly focused on the United States, with conflicting results—the famous Modigliani–Kotlikoff–Summers controversy. More recently, Kopczuk and Edlund (2009) observe that in estate tax data, the share of women among the very wealthy in the United States peaked in the late 1960s (at nearly one-half) and then declined to about one-third. They argue that this pattern reflects changes in the importance of inheritance, as women are less likely to be entrepreneurs. Wolff and Gittleman (2013) analyze Survey of Consumer Finances (SCF) data and find little evidence of a rise in inheritances since the late 1980s. Looking at *Forbes'* data, Kaplan and Rauh (2013) find that Americans in the Forbes 400 are less likely to have inherited their wealth today than in the 1980s. It is unclear, however, whether this result reflects a true economic phenomenon or illustrates the limits of *Forbes* and other wealth rankings.

Inherited wealth holdings are probably harder to spot than self-made wealth, first because inheritors' portfolios tend to be more diversified, and also because inheritors may not like to be in the press, while entrepreneurs usually enjoy it and do not attempt to dissimulate their wealth nearly as much. The conclusions about the relative importance of inherited versus self-made wealth obtained by analyzing *Forbes* list data may thus be relatively fragile.

In the end, there remain important uncertainties about the historical evolution of inheritance in the United States. There are reasons to believe that inheritance has historically been less important in the United States than in Europe, because population growth has been much larger (more on this below). It is unclear whether this still applies today, however. Given the relatively low U.S. saving rates in recent decades, it is possible that even moderate inheritance flows imply a relatively large share φ_t of total inherited wealth in aggregate wealth (at least according to the simplified definition of φ based on the comparison between b_y and s).

One difficulty is that U.S. fiscal data on bequests and gifts are relatively low quality (in particular because the federal estate tax only covers few decedents; in 2012 only about 1 decedent out of 1000 pays the estate tax). One can use survey data (e.g., from the SCF) to estimate the relative wealth of decedents μ_t and compute the economic inheritance flow $b_{yt} = (1 + v_t) \cdot \mu_t \cdot \beta_t$. One key problem is that one needs to find ways to estimate the gift–bequest ratio v_t, which is not easy to do in the absence of high-quality fiscal data. Self-reported retrospective data on bequest and gift receipts usually suffer from large downward biases and should be treated with caution. In countries where there exists exhaustive administrative data on bequests and gifts (such as France, and to some extent Germany), survey-based self-reported flows appear to be less than 50% of fiscal flows. This may contribute to explain the low level of inheritance receipts found by Wolff and Gittleman (2013).[28]

15.5. ACCOUNTING FOR THE EVIDENCE: MODELS AND PREDICTIONS

15.5.1 Shocks Versus Steady States

How can we account for the historical evidence on the evolution of the aggregate wealth–income ratio, the concentration of wealth, and the share of inherited wealth? In this section, we describe the theoretical models that have been developed to address this question. While we still lack a comprehensive model able to rigorously and

---

[28] One additional challenge in this study is that inherited assets are generally valued using asset prices at the time the assets were transmitted: no capital gain is included—which probably contributes to a relatively low estimated inheritance share in total U.S. wealth (about 20%, just like in Modigliani's estimates). A comparison between inheritance flows and saving flows (using the simplified formula) would likely lead to more balanced results.

quantitatively assess the various effects at play, the literature makes it possible to highlight some of the key forces.

We are primarily concerned here about the determinants of long-run steady states. In practice, as should be clear from the historical series presented above, real-world economies often face major shocks and changes in fundamental parameters, so that we observe large deviations from steady states. In particular, the large decline in the aggregate wealth–income ratios β_t between 1910 and 1950 is due to the shocks induced by the two World Wars. By using detailed series on saving flows and war destructions, one can estimate the relative importance of the various factors at play (Piketty and Zucman, 2014). In the case of France and Germany, three factors of comparable magnitude each account for approximately one-third of the total 1910–1950 fall of β_t: insufficient national savings (a large part of private saving was absorbed by public deficits); war destructions; and the fall of relative assets prices (real estate and equity prices were historically low in 1950–1960, partly due to policies such as rent control and nationalization). In the case of Britain, war destructions were relatively minor, and the other two factors each account for about half of the fall in the ratio of wealth to income (war-induced public deficits were particularly large).[29]

In thinking about the future, is the concept of a steady state a relevant point of reference? Historical evidence suggests that it is. Whereas the dynamics of wealth and inequality has been chaotic in the twentieth century, eighteenth- and nineteenth-century United Kingdom and France can certainly be analyzed as being in a steady state characterized by low-growth, high wealth–income ratios, high levels of wealth concentration, and inheritance flows. This is true despite the fact that there were huge changes in the nature of wealth and of economic activity (from agriculture to industry).[30] The shocks of the twentieth century put an end to this steady state, and it seems justified to ask: if countries are to converge to a new steady state in the twenty-first century (that is, if the shocks of the twentieth century do not happen again), which long-term ratios will they reach?

We show that over a wide range of models, the long-run magnitude and concentration of wealth and inheritance are a decreasing function of g and an increasing function of $\bar{r}$, where g is the economy's growth rate and $\bar{r}$ is the net-of-tax rate of return to wealth. That is, under plausible assumptions, both the wealth–income ratio and the concentration of wealth tend to take higher steady-state values when the long-run growth rate is lower and when the net-of-tax rate of return is higher. In particular, a higher $\bar{r} - g$ tends to magnify steady-state wealth inequalities. Although there does not exist yet any

---

[29] For detailed decompositions of private and national wealth accumulation over the various subperiods, see Piketty and Zucman (2014).

[30] In particular, private wealth/income ratios and inheritance flows seemed quite stable in nineteenth-century France (with perhaps a slight upward trend at the end of the century), despite major structural economic changes. This suggests that although the importance of inheritance and wealth may rise and fall in response to the waves of innovation, a steady-state analysis is a fruitful perspective.

rigorous calibrations of these theoretical models, we argue that these predictions are broadly consistent with both the time–series and cross-country evidence. These findings also suggest that the current trends toward rising wealth–income ratios and wealth inequality might continue during the twenty-first century, both because of population and productivity-growth slowdown, and because of rising international competition to attract capital.

15.5.2 The Steady-State Wealth–Income Ratio: $\beta = s/g$

The most useful steady-state formula to analyze the long-run evolution of wealth–income and capital–output ratios is the Harrod–Domar–Solow steady-state formula:

$$\beta_t \to \beta = s/g.$$

With $s=$ long-run (net-of-depreciation) saving rate, $g=$ long-run growth rate.[31]

The steady-state formula $\beta = s/g$ is a pure accounting equation. By definition, it holds in the steady state of any micro-founded, one-good model of capital accumulation, independently of the exact nature of saving motives. It simply comes from the wealth-accumulation equation $W_{t+1} = W_t + S_t$, which can be rewritten in terms of wealth–income ratio $\beta_t = W_t/Y_t$:

$$\beta_{t+1} = \frac{\beta_t + s_t}{1 + g_t}$$

With $1 + g_t = Y_{t+1}/Y_t =$ growth rate of national income, $s_t = S_t/Y_t =$ net saving rate.

It follows immediately that if $s_t \to s$ and $g_t \to g$, then $\beta_t \to \beta = s/g$.

The Harrod–Domar–Solow says something trivial but important in a low-growth economy, the sum of capital accumulated in the past can become very large, as long as the saving rate remains sizable.

For instance, if the long-run saving rate is $s = 10\%$, and if the economy permanently grows at rate $g = 2\%$, then in the long run the wealth–income ratio has to be equal to $\beta = 500\%$, because it is the only ratio such that wealth rises at the same rate as income: $s/\beta = 2\% = g$. If the long-run growth rate declines to $g = 1\%$, and the economy keeps saving at rate $s = 10\%$, then the long-run wealth–income ratio will be equal to $\beta = 1000\%$.

In the long run, output growth g is the sum of productivity and population growth. In the standard one-good growth model, output is given by $Y_t = F(K_t, L_t)$, where K_t is non-human capital input and L_t is human labor input (i.e., efficient labor supply). L_t can be written as the product of raw-labor supply N_t and labor productivity parameter h_t. That is, $L_t = N_t \cdot h_t$, with $N_t = N_0 \cdot (1+n)^t$ (n is the population growth rate) and $h_t = h_0 \cdot (1+h)^t$ (h is

---

[31] When one uses gross-of-depreciation saving rates rather than net rates, the steady-state formula writes $\beta = s/(g + \delta)$ with s the gross saving rate, and δ the depreciation rate expressed as a proportion of the wealth stock.

the productivity growth rate). The economy's long-run growth rate g is given by the growth rate of L_t. Therefore it is equal to $1+g=(1+n)\cdot(1+h)$, i.e., $g\approx n+h$.[32] The long-run g depends both on demographic parameters (in particular, fertility rates) and on productivity-enhancing activities (in particular, the pace of innovation).

The long-run saving rate s also depends on many forces: s captures the strength of the various psychological and economic motives for saving and wealth accumulation (dynastic, life cycle, precautionary, prestige, taste for bequests, etc.). The motives and tastes for saving vary a lot across individuals and potentially across countries. Whether savings come primarily from a life cycle or a bequest motive, the $\beta=s/g$ formula will hold in steady state. In case saving is exogenous (as in the Solow model), the long-run wealth–income ratio will obviously be a decreasing function of the income growth rate g. This conclusion, however, is also true in a broad class of micro-founded, general equilibrium models of capital accumulation in which s can be endogenous and can depend on g. That is the case, in particular, in the infinite-horizon, dynastic model (in which s is determined by the rate of time preference and the concavity of the utility function), in "bequest-in-the-utility-function" models (in which the long-run saving rate s is determined by the strength of the bequest or wealth taste), and in most endogenous growth models (see box below). In all cases, for given preference parameters, the long-run $\beta=s/g$ tends to be higher when the growth rate is lower. A growth slowdown—coming from a decrease in population or productivity growth—tends to lead to higher capital–output and wealth–income ratios.

Box: The steady-state wealth–income ratio in macro models
Dynastic Model

Assume that output is given by $Y_t=F(K_t, L_t)$, where K_t is the capital stock and L_t is efficient labor and grows exogenously at rate g. Output is either consumed or added to the capital stock. We assume a closed economy, so the wealth–income ratio is the same as the capital–output ratio. In the infinite-horizon, dynastic model, each dynasty maximizes

$$V=\int_{t\geq s} e^{-\theta t}U(c_t)$$

where θ is the rate of time preference and $U(c_t)=c^{1-\gamma}(1-\gamma)$ is a standard utility function with a constant intertemporal elasticity of substitution equal to $1/\gamma$. This elasticity of substitution is often found to be small, typically between 0.2 and 0.5, and is in any case smaller than one. Therefore γ is typically bigger than one.

Continued

---

[32] To obtain the exact equality $g=n+h$, one needs to use instantaneous (continuous-time) growth rates rather than annual (discrete-time) growth rates. That is, with $N_t=N_0\cdot e^{nt}$ (with $n=$population growth rate) and $h_t=h_0\cdot e^{ht}$, we have $L_t=N_t\cdot h_t=L_0\cdot e^{gt}$, with $g=n+h$.

The first-order condition describing the optimal consumption path of each dynasty is: $dc_t/dt = (r-\theta) \cdot c_t/\gamma$, i.e., utility-maximizing agents want their consumption path to grow at rate $g_c = (r-\theta)/\gamma$. This is a steady state if and only if $g_c = g$, i.e., $r = \theta + \gamma g$, what is known as the modified Golden Rule of capital accumulation. The long-run rate of return $r = \theta + \gamma g$ is entirely determined by preference parameters and the growth rate and is larger than g.

The steady-state saving rate is equal to $s = \alpha \cdot g/r = \alpha \cdot g/(\theta + \gamma g)$, where $\alpha = r \cdot \beta$ is the capital share. Intuitively, a fraction g/r of capital income is saved in the long run, so that dynastic wealth grows at the same rate g as national income. The saving rate $s = s(g)$ is an increasing function of the growth rate, but rises less fast than g, so that the steady-state wealth–income ratio $\beta = s/g$ is a decreasing function of the growth rate.

For instance, with a Cobb–Douglas production function (in which case the capital share is entirely set by technology and is constantly equal to α), the wealth–income ratio is given by $\beta = \alpha/r = \alpha/(\theta + \gamma \cdot g)$ and takes its maximum value $\overline{\beta} = \alpha/\theta$ for $g = 0$.

One unrealistic feature of the dynastic model is that it assumes an infinite long-run elasticity of capital supply with respect to the net-of-tax rate of return, which mechanically entails extreme consequences for optimal capital tax policy (namely, zero tax). The "bequest-in-the-utility-function" model provides a less extreme and more flexible conceptual framework in order to analyze the wealth accumulation process.

Wealth-in-the-Utility-Function Model

Consider a dynamic economy with a discrete set of generations $0, 1, \ldots, t, \ldots$, zero population growth, and exogenous labor productivity growth at rate $g > 0$. Each generation has measure $N_t = N$, lives one period, and is replaced by the next generation. Each individual living in generation t receives bequest $b_t = w_t \geq 0$ from generation $t-1$ at the beginning of period t, inelastically supplies one unit of labor during his lifetime (so that labor supply $L_t = N_t = N$), and earns labor income y_{Lt}. At the end of period, he then splits lifetime resources (the sum of labor income and capitalized bequests received) into consumption c_t and bequests left $b_{t+1} = w_{t+1} \geq 0$, according to the following budget constraint:

$$c_t + b_{t+1} \leq y_t = y_{Lt} + (1 + r_t) b_t$$

The simplest case is when the utility function is defined directly over consumption c_t and the increase in wealth $\Delta w_t = w_{t+1} - w_t$ and takes a simple Cobb–Douglas form: $V(c, \Delta w) = c^{1-s} \Delta w^s$. (Intuitively, this corresponds to a form of "moral" preferences where individuals feel that they cannot possibly leave less wealth to their children than what they have received from their parents, and derive utility from the increase in wealth, maybe because this is a signal of their ability or virtue.) Utility maximization then leads to a fixed saving rate: $w_{t+1} = w_t + s y_t$. By multiplying per capita values by population $N_t = N$ we have the same linear transition equation at the aggregate level: $W_{t+1} = W_t + s Y_t$. The long-run wealth–income ratio is given by $\beta_t \to \beta = s/g$. It depends on the strength of the bequest motive and on the rate of productivity growth.

With other functional forms for the utility function, e.g., with $V = V(c, w)$, or with heterogenous labor productivities or saving tastes across individuals, one simply needs to replace the parameter s by the properly defined average wealth or bequest taste parameter. For instance, with $V(c, w) = c^{1-s} w^s$, utility maximization leads to $w_{t+1} = s \cdot (w_t + y_t)$ and

Continued

$\beta_t \to \beta = s/(g+1-s) = \widetilde{s}/g$, with $\widetilde{s} = s(1+\beta) - \beta$ the conventional saving rate (i.e., defined relative to income). See Section 15.5.4.1 for a simple application of this model to the analysis of the steady-state distribution of wealth.

Endogenous Growth Models

In endogenous growth models with imperfect international capital flows, the growth rate might rise with the saving rate, but it will usually rise less than proportionally. It is only in what is known as the AK closed-economy model that the growth rate rises proportionally with the saving rate. To see this, assume zero population growth ($n=0$) and a Cobb–Douglas production function $Y = K^\alpha \cdot (A_L \cdot L)^{1-\alpha}$. Further assume that the productivity parameter is endogenously determined by an economy-wide capital accumulation externality, such that $A_L = A_0 \cdot K$. Then we have $Y = A \cdot K$, with $A = (A_0 \cdot L_0)^{1-\alpha}$. For a given saving rate $s > 0$, the growth rate is given by $g = g(s) = s \cdot A$. The growth rate rises proportionally with the saving rate, so that the wealth–income ratio is entirely set by technology: $\beta = s/g = 1/A$ is a constant.

In more general endogenous growth models, the rate of productivity growth depends not only on the pace of capital accumulation, but also—and probably more importantly—on the intensity of innovation activities, the importance of education spendings, the position on the international technological frontier, and a myriad of other policies and institutions, so that the resulting growth rate rises less than proportionally with the saving rate.

The slowdown of income growth is the central force explaining the rise of wealth–income ratios in rich countries over the 1970–2010 period, particularly in Europe and Japan, where population growth has slowed markedly (and where saving rates are still high relative to the United States). As Piketty and Zucman (2014) show, the cumulation of saving flows explains the 1970–2010 evolution of β in the main rich countries relatively well. An additional explanatory factor over this time period is the gradual recovery of relative asset prices. In the very long run, however, relative asset-price movements tend to compensate each other, and the one-good capital accumulation model seems to do a good job at explaining the evolution of wealth–income ratios.

It is worth stressing that the $\beta = s/g$ formula works both in closed-economy and open-economy settings. The only difference is that wealth–income and capital–output ratios are the same in closed-economy settings but can differ in open-economy environments. In the closed-economy case, private wealth is equal to domestic capital: $W_t = K_t$.[33] National income Y_t is equal to domestic output $Y_{dt} = F(K_t, L_t)$. Saving is equal to domestic investment, and the private wealth–national income ratio $\beta_t = W_t/Y_t$ is the same as the domestic capital–output ratio $\beta_{kt} = K_t/Y_{dt}$.

In the open economy case, countries with higher saving rates $s_a > s_b$ accumulate higher wealth ratios $\beta_a = s_a/g > \beta_b = s_b/g$ and invest some their wealth in countries with

---

[33] For simplicity we assume away government wealth and saving.

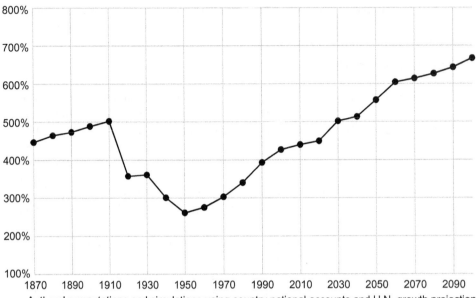

Authors' computations and simulations using country national accounts and U.N. growth projections

Figure 15.24 World wealth/national income ratio, 1870–2100.

lower saving rates, so that the capital–output ratio is the same everywhere (assuming perfect capital mobility). Noting N_a and N_b the population of countries a and b, $N = N_a + N_b$ the world population, $Y = Y_a + Y_b$ the world output, and $s = (s_a \cdot Y_a + s_b \cdot Y_b)/Y$ the world saving rate, and assuming that each country's effective labor supply is proportional to population and grows at rate g, then the long-run wealth–income and capital–output ratio at the world level will be equal to $\beta = s/g$. With perfect capital mobility, each country will operate with the same capital–output ratio $\beta = s/g$. Country a with wealth $\beta_a > \beta$ will invest its extra wealth $\beta_a - \beta$ in country b with wealth $\beta_b < \beta$. Both countries have the same per capita output $y = Y/N$, but country a has a permanently higher per capita national income $y_a = y + r \cdot (\beta_a - \beta) > y$, while country b has a permanently lower per capita national income $y_b = y - r \cdot (\beta - \beta_b) < y$. In the case of Britain and France at the eve of World War I, the net foreign wealth position $\beta_a - \beta$ was of the order of 100–200%, the return on net foreign assets was about $r = 5\%$, so that national income was about 5–10% larger than domestic output.

At the world level, wealth–income and capital–output ratios always coincide (by definition). The long-run ratio is governed by the steady-state condition $\beta = s/g$. In the very long run, if the growth rate slows down at the global level (in particular due to the possible stabilization of world population), then the global β might rise. We report on Figure 15.24 one possible evolution of the world wealth–income ratio in the twenty-first century, assuming that the world-income growth rate stabilizes at about 1.5% and world saving rate at about 12%. Under these (arguably specific and uncertain) assumptions, the world β would rise to about 700–800% by the end of the twenty-first century.

15.5.3 The Steady-State Capital Share: $\alpha = r \cdot \beta = a \cdot \beta^{\frac{\sigma-1}{\sigma}}$

How does the evolution of the capital–income ratio β relate to the evolution of the capital share $\alpha_t = r_t \cdot \beta_t$ (where r_t is the average rate of return)? All depends on whether the capital–labor elasticity of substitution σ is larger or smaller than one.

Take a CES production function $Y = F(K, L) = \left(a \cdot K^{\frac{\sigma-1}{\sigma}} + (1-a) \cdot L^{\frac{\sigma-1}{\sigma}} \right)^{\frac{\sigma-1}{\sigma}}$. The rate of return is given by $r = F_K = a\beta^{-1/\sigma}$ (with $\beta = K/Y$), and the capital share is given by $\alpha = r \cdot \beta = a \cdot \beta^{\frac{\sigma-1}{\sigma}}$. If $\sigma > 1$, then as β_t rises, the fall of the marginal product of capital r_t is smaller than the rise of β_t, so that the capital share $\alpha_t = r_t \cdot \beta_t$ is an increasing function of β_t. Conversely, if $\sigma < 1$, the fall of r_t is bigger than the rise of β_t, so that the capital share is a decreasing function of β_t.[34]

As $\sigma \to \infty$, the production function becomes linear, that is, the return to capital is independent of the quantity of capital: this is like a robot economy where capital can produce output on its own. Conversely, as $\sigma \to 0$, the production function becomes putty clay, that is, the return to capital falls to zero if the quantity of capital is slightly above the fixed-proportion technology.

A special case is when the capital–labor elasticity of substitution σ is exactly equal to one: changes in r and in β exactly compensate each other so that the capital share is constant. This is the Cobb–Douglas case $F(K, L) = K^\alpha L^{1-\alpha}$. The capital share is entirely set by technology: $\alpha_t = r_t \cdot \beta_t = \alpha$. A higher capital–output ratio β_t is exactly compensated by a lower capital return $r_t = \alpha/\beta_t$, so that the product of the two is constant.

There is a large literature trying to estimate the elasticity of substitution between labor and capital, reviewed in Antras (2004) and Chirinko (2008); see also Karabarbounis and Neiman (2014). The range of estimates is wide. Historical evidence suggests that the elasticity of substitution σ may have risen over the development process. In the eighteenth to nineteenth centuries, it is likely that σ was less than one, particularly in the agricultural sector. An elasticity less than one would explain why countries with large quantities of land (e.g., the United States) had lower aggregate land values than countries with little land (the Old World). Indeed, when $\sigma < 1$, price effects dominate volume effects: when land is very abundant, the price of land is extremely low, and the product of the two is small. An elasticity less than 1 is exactly what one would accept in an economy in which

---

[34] Because we include all forms of capital assets into our aggregate capital concept K, the aggregate elasticity of substitution σ should be interpreted as resulting from both supply forces (producers shift between technologies with different capital intensities) and demand forces (consumers shift between goods and services with different capital intensities, including housing services versus other goods and services).

capital takes essentially one form only (land), as in the eighteenth and early nineteenth centuries. When there is too much of the single capital good, it becomes almost useless.

Conversely, in the twentieth century, capital shares α have tended to move in the same direction as capital–income ratios β. This fact suggests that the elasticity of substitution σ has been larger than one. Since the mid-1970s, in particular, we do observe a significant rise of capital shares α_t in rich countries (Figure 15.25). Admittedly, the rise in capital shares α_t was less marked than the rise of capital–income ratios β_t—in other words, the average return to wealth $r_t = \alpha_t / \beta_t$ has declined (Figure 15.26). But this decline is

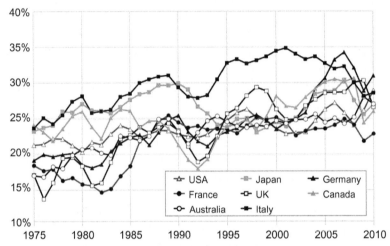

Figure 15.25 Capital shares in factor-price national income, 1975–2010.

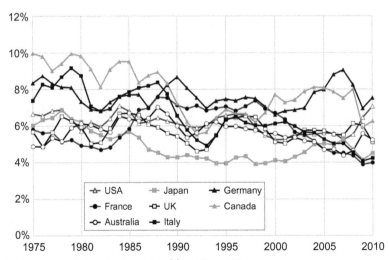

Figure 15.26 Average return on private wealth, 1975–2010.

exactly what one should expect in any economic model: when there is more capital, the rate of return to capital must go down. The interesting question is whether the average return r_t declines less or more than β_t increases. The data gathered by Piketty and Zucman (2014) suggest that r_t has declined less, i.e., that the capital share has increased, consistent with an elasticity $\sigma > 1$. This result is intuitive: an elasticity larger than one is what one would expect in a sophisticated economy with different uses for capital (not only land, but also robots, housing, intangible capital, etc.). The elasticity might even increase with globalization, as it becomes easier to move different forms of capital across borders.

Importantly, the elasticity does not need to be hugely superior to one in order to account for the observed trends. With an elasticity σ around 1.2–1.6, a doubling of capital–output ratio β can lead to a large rise in the capital share α. With large changes in β, one can obtain substantial movements in the capital share with a production function that is only moderately more flexible than the standard Cobb–Douglas function. For instance, with $\sigma = 1.5$, the capital share rises from $\alpha = 28\%$ to $\alpha = 36\%$ if the wealth–income ratio jumps from $\beta = 2.5$ to $\beta = 5$, which is roughly what has happened in rich countries since the 1970s. The capital share would reach $\alpha = 42\%$ in case further capital accumulation takes place and the wealth–income ratio attains $\beta = 8$. In case the production function becomes even more flexible over time (say, $\sigma = 1.8$), the capital share would then be as large as $\alpha = 53\%$.[35] The bottom line is that we certainly do not need to go all the way toward a robot economy ($\sigma = \infty$) in order to generate very large movements in the capital share.

15.5.4 The Steady-State Level of Wealth Concentration: $Ineq = Ineq\ (\bar{r}-g)$

The possibility that the capital–income ratio β—and maybe the capital share α—might rise to high levels entails very different welfare consequences depending on who owns capital. As we have seen in Section 15.3, wealth is always significantly more concentrated than income, but wealth has also become less concentrated since the nineteenth to early twentieth century, at least in Europe. The top 10% wealth holders used to own about 90% of aggregate wealth in Europe prior to World War I, whereas they currently own about 60–70% of aggregate wealth.

What model do we have to analyze the steady-state level of wealth concentration? There is a large literature devoted to this question. Early references include Champernowne (1953), Vaughan (1979), and Laitner (1979). Stiglitz (1969) is the first attempt to analyze the steady-state distribution of wealth in the neoclassical growth model. In his and similar models of wealth accumulation, there is at the same time both convergence of the macro-variables to their steady-state values and of the distribution of wealth to its steady-state form. Dynamic wealth-accumulation models with random

---

[35] With $a = 0.21$ and $\sigma = 1.5$, $\alpha = a \cdot \beta^{\frac{\sigma-1}{\sigma}}$ goes from 28% to 36% and 42% as β rises from 2.5 to 5 and 8. With $\sigma = 1.8$, α rises to 53% if $\beta = 8$.

idiosyncratic shocks have the additional property that a higher $\bar{r} - g$ differential (where $\bar{r}$ is the net-of-tax rate of return to wealth and g is the economy's growth rate) tends to magnify steady-state wealth inequalities. This is particularly easy to see in dynamic model with random multiplicative shocks, where the steady-state distribution of wealth has a Pareto shape, with a Pareto exponent that is directly determined by $\bar{r} - g$ (for a given structure of shocks).

15.5.4.1 An Illustrative Example with Closed-Form Formulas

To illustrate this point, consider the following model with discrete time $t = 0, 1, 2, \ldots$. The model can be interpreted as an annual model (with each period lasting $H = 1$ year), or a generational model (with each period lasting $H = 30$ years), in which case saving tastes can be interpreted as bequest tastes. Suppose a stationary population $N_t = [0, 1]$ made of a continuum of agents of size one, so that aggregate and average variables are the same for wealth and national income: $W_t = w_t$ and $Y_t = y_t$. Effective labor input $L_t = N_t \cdot h_t = h_0 \cdot (1 + g)^t$ grows at some exogenous, annual productivity rate g. Domestic output is given by some production function $Y_{dt} = F(K_t, L_t)$.

We suppose that each individual $i \in [0, 1]$ receives the same labor income $y_{Lti} = y_{Lt}$ and has the same annual rate of return $r_{ti} = r_t$. Each agent chooses c_{ti} and w_{t+1i} so as to maximize a utility function of the form $V(c_{ti}, w_{ti}) = c_{ti}^{1-s_{ti}} w_{ti}^{s_{ti}}$, with wealth (or bequest) taste parameter s_{ti} and budget constraint $c_{ti} + w_{t+1i} \leq y_{Lt} + (1 + r_t) \cdot w_{ti}$. Random shocks only come from idiosyncratic variations in the saving taste parameters s_{ti}, which are supposed to be drawn according to some i.i.d. random process with mean $s = E(s_{ti}) < 1$.[36]

With the simple Cobb–Douglas specification for the utility function, utility maximization implies that consumption c_{ti} is a fraction $1 - s_{ti}$ of $y_{Lt} + (1 + r_t) \cdot w_{ti}$, the total resources (income plus wealth) available at time t. Plugging this formula into the budget constraint, we have the following individual-level transition equation for wealth:

$$w_{t+1i} = s_{ti} \cdot [y_{Lt} + (1 + r_t) \cdot w_{ti}] \tag{15.1}$$

At the aggregate level, since by definition national income is equal to $y_t = y_{Lt} + r_t \cdot w_t$, we have

$$w_{t+1} = s \cdot [y_{Lt} + (1 + r_t) \cdot w_t] = s \cdot [y_t + w_t] \tag{15.2}$$

dividing by $y_{t+1} \approx (1 + g) \cdot y_t$ and denoting $\alpha_t = r_t \cdot \beta_t$ the capital share and $(1 - \alpha_t) = y_{Lt}/y_t$ the labor share, we have the following transition equation for the wealth–income ratio $\beta_t = w_t / y_t$:

---

[36] For a class of dynamic stochastic models with more general structures of preferences and shocks, see Piketty and Saez (2013).

$$\beta_{t+1} = s \cdot \frac{1-\alpha_t}{1+g} + s \cdot \frac{1+r_t}{1+g} \cdot \beta_t = \frac{s}{1+g} \cdot (1+\beta_t) \qquad (15.3)$$

In the open-economy case, the world rate of return $r_t = r$ is given. From the above equation one can easily see that β_t converges toward a finite limit β if and only if

$$\omega = s \cdot \frac{1+r}{1+g} < 1$$

In case $\omega > 1$, then $\beta_t \to \infty$. In the long run, the economy is no longer a small open economy, and the world rate of return will have to fall so that $\omega < 1$.

In the closed-economy case, β_t always converges toward a finite limit, and the long-run rate of return r is equal to the marginal product of capital and depends negatively upon β. With a CES production function, for example, we have $r = F_K = \alpha \cdot \beta^{-1/\sigma}$ (see Section 15.5.3).

Setting $\beta_{t+1} = \beta_t$ in Equation (15.3), we obtain the steady-state wealth–income ratio:

$$\beta_t \to \beta = s/(g+1-s) = \tilde{s}/g$$

where $\tilde{s} = s(1+\beta) - \beta$ is the steady-state saving rate expressed as a fraction of national income.

Noting $z_{ti} = w_{ti}/w_t$ the normalized individual wealth, and dividing both sides of Equation (15.1) by $w_{t+1} \approx (1+g) \cdot w_t$, the individual-level transition equation for wealth can be rewritten as follows[37]:

$$z_{t+1i} = \frac{s_{ti}}{s} \cdot [(1-\omega) + \omega \cdot z_{ti}] \qquad (15.4)$$

Standard convergence results (e.g., Hopenhayn and Prescott, 1992, Theorem 2, p. 1397) then imply that the distribution $\psi_t(z)$ of relative wealth will converge toward a unique steady-state distribution $\psi(z)$ with a Pareto shape and a Pareto exponent that depends on the variance of taste shocks s_{ti} and on the ω coefficient.

For instance, assume simple binomial taste shocks: $s_{ti} = s_0 = 0$ with probability $1-p$, and $s_{ti} = s_1 > 0$ with probability p (with $s = p \cdot s_1$ and $\omega < 1 < \omega/p$). The long-run distribution function $1 - \Psi_t(z) = \text{proba}(z_{ti} \geq z)$ will converge for high z toward

$$1 - \Phi(z) \approx \left(\frac{\lambda}{z}\right)^a,$$

with a constant term λ

---

[37] Note that $y_{Lt} = (1-\alpha) \cdot y_t$, where $\alpha = r \cdot \beta = r \cdot s/(1+g-s)$ is the long-run capital share. Note also that the individual-level transition equation given below holds only in the long run (i.e., when the aggregate wealth–income ratio has already converged).

$$\lambda = \frac{1-\omega}{\omega-p},$$

a Pareto coefficient a

$$a = \frac{\log(1/p)}{\log(\omega/p)} > 1, \qquad (15.5)$$

and an inverted Pareto coefficient b

$$b = \frac{a}{a-1} = \frac{\log(1/p)}{\log(1/\omega)} > 1.$$

To see this, note that the long-run distribution with $\omega < 1 < \omega/p$ looks as follows: $z = 0$ with probability $1-p$, $z = \frac{1-\omega}{p}$ with probability $(1-p)\cdot p$, ..., and $z = z_k = \frac{1-\omega}{\omega-p}\cdot\left[\left(\frac{\omega}{p}\right)^k - 1\right]$ with probability $(1-p)\cdot p^k$. As $k \to +\infty$, $z_k \approx \frac{1-\omega}{\omega-p}\cdot\left(\frac{\omega}{p}\right)^k$ The cumulated distribution is given by $1 - \Phi(z_k) = \text{proba}(z \geq z_k) = \sum_{k' \geq k}(1-p)\cdot p^{k'} = p^k$. It follows that as $z \to +\infty$, $\log[1 - \Phi(z)] \approx a\cdot[\log(\lambda) - \log(z)]$, i.e., $1 - \Phi(z) \approx (\lambda/z)^a$. In case $\omega/p < 1$, then $z_k = \frac{1-\omega}{p-\omega}\cdot\left[1 - \left(\frac{\omega}{p}\right)^k\right]$ has a finite upper bound $z_1 = \frac{1-\omega}{p-\omega}$.[38]

As ω rises, a declines and b rises, which means that the steady-state distribution of wealth is more and more concentrated.[39] Intuitively, an increase in $\omega = s\cdot\frac{1+r}{1+g}$ means that the multiplicative wealth inequality effect becomes larger as compared to the equalizing labor income effect, so that steady-state wealth inequalities get amplified.

In the extreme case where $\omega \to 1^-$ (for given $p < \omega$), $a \to 1^+$ and $b \to +\infty$ (infinite inequality). That is, the multiplicative wealth inequality effect becomes infinite as compared to the equalizing labor-income effect. The same occurs as $p \to 0^+$ (for given $\omega > p$): an infinitely small group gets infinitely large random shocks.[40] Explosive wealth inequality paths can also occur in case the taste parameter s_{ti} is higher on average for individuals with high initial wealth.[41]

---

[38] See Piketty and Saez (2013, working paper version, pp. 51–52).

[39] A higher inverted Pareto coefficient b (or, equivalently, a lower Pareto coefficient a) implies a fatter upper tail of the distribution and higher inequality. On the historical evolution of Pareto coefficients, see Atkinson et al. (2011, pp. 13–14 and 50–58).

[40] In the binomial model, one can directly compute the "empirical" inverted Pareto coefficient $b' = \frac{E(z|z \geq z_k)}{z_k} \to \frac{1-p}{1-\omega}$ as $k \to +\infty$. Note that $b' \simeq b$ if $p, \omega \simeq 1$, but that the two coefficients generally differ because the true distribution is discrete, while the Pareto law approximation is continuous.

[41] Kuznets (1953) and Meade (1964) were particularly concerned about this potentially powerful unequalizing force.

15.5.4.2 Pareto Formulas in Multiplicative Random Shocks Models

More generally, one can show that all models with multiplicative random shocks in the wealth accumulation process give rise to distributions with Pareto upper tails, whether the shocks are binomial or multinomial, and whether they come from tastes or other factors. For instance, the shock can come from the rank of birth, such as in the primogeniture model of Stiglitz (1969),[42] or from the number of children (Cowell, 1998),[43] or from rates of return (Benhabib et al., 2011, 2013; Nirei, 2009). Whenever the transition equation for wealth can be rewritten so as take a multiplicative form

$$z_{t+1i} = \omega_{ti} \cdot z_{ti} + \varepsilon_{ti}$$

where ω_{ti} is an i.i.d. multiplicative shock with mean $\omega = E(\omega_{ti}) < 1$, and ε_{ti} an additive shock (possibly random), then the steady-state distribution has a Pareto upper tail with coefficient a, which must solve the following equation:

$$E\left(\omega_{ti}^a\right) = 1.$$

A special case is when $p \cdot (\omega/p)^a = 1$, that is $a = \log(1/p)/\log(\omega/p)$, the formula given in Equation (15.5) above. More generally, as long as $\omega_{ti} > 1$ with some positive probability, there exists a unique $a > 1$, so that $E(\omega_{ti}^a) = 1$. One can easily see that for a given average $\omega = E(\omega_{ti}) < 1$, $a \to 1$ (and thus wealth inequality tends to infinity) if the variance of shocks goes to infinity, and $a \to \infty$ if the variance goes to zero.

Which kind of shocks have mattered most in the historical dynamics of the distribution of wealth? Many different kinds of individual-level random shocks play an important role in practice, and it is difficult to estimate the relative importance of each of them. One robust conclusion, however, is that for a given variance of shocks, steady-state wealth concentration is always a rising function of $r - g$. That is, due to cumulative dynamic effects, relatively small changes in $r - g$ (say, from $r - g = 2\%$ per year to $r - g = 3\%$ per year) can make a huge difference in terms of long-run wealth inequality.

For instance, if we interpret each period of the discrete-time model described above as lasting H years (with $H = 30$ years = generation length), and if r and g denote instantaneous rates, then the multiplicative factor ω can be rewritten as

---

[42] With primogeniture (binomial shock), the formula is exactly the same as before. See, e.g., Atkinson and Harrison (1978, p. 213), who generalize the Stiglitz (1969) formula and get: $a = \log(1+n)/\log(1+sr)$, with s the saving rate out of capital income. This is the same formula as $a = \log(1/p)/\log(\omega/p)$: with population growth rate per generation $= 1 + n$, the probability that a good shock occurs—namely, being the eldest son—is given by $p = 1/(1+n)$. Menchik (1980), however, provides evidence on estate division in the United States, showing that equal sharing is the rule.

[43] The Cowell result is more complicated because families with many children do not return to zero (unless infinite number of children), so there is no closed form formula for the Pareto coefficient a, which must solve the following equation: $\sum \dfrac{p_k \cdot k}{2} \left(\dfrac{2 \cdot \omega}{k}\right)^a = 1$, where $p_k =$ fraction of parents who have k children, with $k = 1, 2, 3$, etc., and $\omega =$ average generational rate of wealth reproduction.

$$\omega = s \cdot \frac{1+R}{1+G} = s \cdot e^{(r-g)H}$$

with $1+R = e^{rH}$ the generational rate of return and $1+G = e^{gH}$ the generational growth rate. If $r-g$ rises from $r-g = 2\%$ to $r-g = 3\%$, then with $s = 20\%$ and $H = 30$ years, $\omega = s \cdot e^{(r-g)H}$ rises from $\omega = 0.36$ to $\omega = 0.49$. For a given binomial shock structure $p = 10\%$, this implies that the resulting inverted Pareto coefficient $b = (\log(1/p))/(\log(1/\omega))$ shifts from $b = 2.28$ to $b = 3.25$. This corresponds to a shift from an economy with moderate wealth inequality (say, with a top 1% wealth share around 20–30%) to an economy with very high wealth inequality (say, with a top 1% wealth share around 50–60%).

Last, if we introduce taxation into the dynamic wealth accumulation model, then one naturally needs to replace r by the after-tax rate of return $\bar{r} = (1-\tau) \cdot r$, where τ is the equivalent comprehensive tax rate on capital income, including all taxes on both flows and stocks. That is, what matters for long-run wealth concentration is the differential $\bar{r} - g$ between the net-of-tax rate of return and the growth rate. This implies that differences in capital tax rates and tax progressivity over time and across countries can explain large differences in wealth concentration.[44]

15.5.4.3 On the Long-Run Evolution of $\bar{r} - g$

The fact that steady-state wealth inequality is a steeply increasing function of $\bar{r} - g$ can help explain some of the historical patterns analyzed in Section 15.3.

First, it is worth emphasizing that during most of history, the gap $\bar{r} - g$ was large, typically of the order of 4–5% per year. The reason is that growth rates were close to zero until the industrial revolution (typically less than 0.1–0.2% per year), while the rate of return to wealth was generally of the order of 4–5% per year, in particular for agricultural land, by far the most important asset.[45] We have plotted on Figure 15.27 the world GDP growth rates since Antiquity (computed from Maddison, 2010) and estimates of the average return to wealth (from Piketty, 2014). Tax rates were negligible prior to the twentieth century, so that after-tax rates of return were virtually identical to pretax rates of return, and the $\bar{r} - g$ gap was as large as the $r - g$ gap (Figure 15.28).

The very large $\bar{r} - g$ gap until the late nineteenth to early twentieth century is in our view the primary candidate explanation as to why the concentration of wealth has been so large during most of human history. Although the rise of growth rates from less than 0.5% per year before the eighteenth century to about 1–1.5% per year during the eighteenth to

---

[44] For instance, simulation results suggest that differences in top inheritance tax rates can potentially explain a large fraction of the gap in wealth concentration between countries such as Germany and France (see Dell, 2005).

[45] In traditional agrarian societies, e.g., in eighteenth-century Britain or France, the market value of agricultural land was typically around 20–25 years of annual land rent, which corresponds to a rate of return of about 4–5%. Returns on more risky assets such as financial loans were sometime much higher. See Piketty (2014).

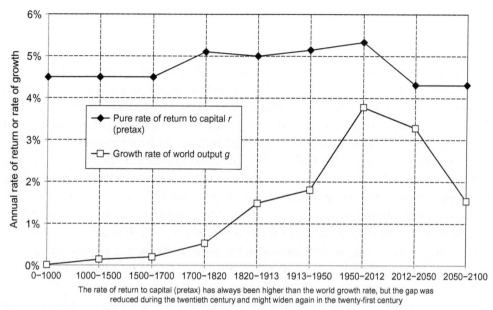

The rate of return to capital (pretax) has always been higher than the world growth rate, but the gap was reduced during the twentieth century and might widen again in the twenty-first century

Figure 15.27 Rate of return versus growth rate at the world level, from antiquity until 2100.

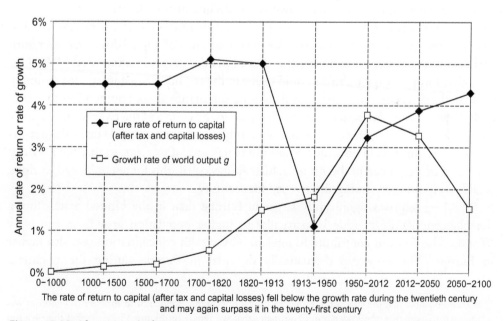

The rate of return to capital (after tax and capital losses) fell below the growth rate during the twentieth century and may again surpass it in the twenty-first century

Figure 15.28 After tax rate of return versus growth rate at the world level, from antiquity until 2100.

nineteenth centuries was sufficient to make a huge difference in terms of population and living standards, it had a relatively limited impact on the $\bar{r} - g$ gap: $\bar{r}$ remained much bigger than g.[46]

The spectacular fall of the $\bar{r} - g$ gap in the course of the twentieth century can also help understand the structural decline of wealth concentration, and in particular why wealth concentration did not return to the extreme levels observed before the World Wars. The fall of the $\bar{r} - g$ gap during the twentieth century has two components: a large rise in g and a large decline in $\bar{r}$. Both, however, might well turn out to be temporary.

Start with the rise in g. The world GDP growth rate was almost 4% during the second half of the twentieth century. This is due partly to a general catch up process in per capita GDP levels (first in Europe and Japan between 1950 and 1980, and then in China and other emerging countries starting around 1980–1990), and partly to unprecedented population growth rates (which account for about half of world GDP growth rates over the past century). According to UN demographic projections, world population growth rates should sharply decline and converge to 0% during the second half of the twenty-first century. Long run per capita growth rates are notoriously difficult to predict: they might be around 1.5% per year (as posited on Figure 15.27 for the second half of the twenty-first century), but some authors—such as Gordon (2012)—believe that they could be less than 1%. In any case, it seems plausible that the exceptional growth rates of the twentieth century will not happen again—at least regarding the demographic component—and that g will indeed gradually decline during the twenty-first century.

Looking now at $\bar{r}$, we also see a spectacular decline during the twentieth century. If we take into account both the capital losses (fall in relative asset prices and physical destructions) and the rise in taxation, the net-of-tax, net-of-capital-losses rate of return $\bar{r}$ fell below the growth rate during the entire twentieth century after World War I.

Other forms of capital shocks could occur in the twenty-first century. But assuming no new shock occurs, and assuming that rising international tax competition to attract capital leads all forms of capital taxes to disappear in the course of the twenty-first century (arguably a plausible scenario, although obviously not the only possible one), the net-of-tax rate of return $\bar{r}$ will converge toward the pretax rate of return r, so that the $\bar{r} - g$ gap will again be very large in the future. Other things equal, this force could lead to rising wealth concentration during the twenty-first century.

The $\bar{r} - g$ gap was significantly larger in Europe than in the United States during the nineteenth century (due in particular to higher population growth in the New World). This fact can contribute to explain why wealth concentration was also higher in Europe. The $\bar{r} - g$ gap dramatically declined in Europe during the twentieth

---

[46] It is also possible that the rise of the return to capital during the eighteenth to nineteenth centuries was somewhat larger than the lower-bound estimates that we report on Figure 15.27, so that the $r - g$ gap perhaps did not decline at all. See Piketty (2014) for a more elaborate discussion.

century—substantially more than the United States, which can, in turn, explain why wealth has become structurally less concentrated than in the United States. The higher level of labor income inequality in the United States in recent decades, as well as the sharp drop in tax progressivity, also contribute to higher wealth concentration in the United States (see Saez and Zucman, 2014). Note, however, that the United States is still characterized by higher population growth (as compared to Europe and Japan), and that this tends to push in the opposite direction (i.e., less wealth concentration). So whether the wealth inequality gap with Europe will keep widening in coming decades is very much an open issue at this stage.

More generally, we should stress that although the general historical pattern of $\bar{r} - g$ (both over time and across countries) seems consistent with the evolution of wealth concentration, other factors do also certainly play an important role in wealth inequality.

One such factor is the magnitude of idiosyncratic shocks to rates of return r_{ti}, and the possibility that average rates of return $r(w) = E(r_{ti}|w_{ti} = w)$ vary with the initial wealth levels. Existing evidence on returns to university endowments suggests that larger endowments indeed tend to get substantially larger rates of returns, possibly due to scale economies in portfolio management (Piketty 2014, Chapter 12). The same pattern is found for the universe of U.S. foundations (Saez and Zucman, 2014). Evidence from *Forbes* global wealth rankings also suggests that higher wealth holders tend to get higher returns. Over the 1987–2013 period, the top fractiles (defined in proportion to world adult population) of the *Forbes* global billionaire list have been growing on average at about 6–7% per year in real terms, when average adult wealth at the global level was rising at slightly more than 2% per year (see Table 15.1).

Whatever the exact mechanism might be, this seems to indicate that the world distribution of wealth is becoming increasingly concentrated, at least at the top of the distribution. It should be stressed again, however, that available data is of relatively low quality. Little is known about how the global wealth rankings published by magazines

Table 15.1 The growth rate of top global wealth, 1987–2013

Average real growth rate per year (after deduction of inflation)	1987–2013
The top 1/(100 million) highest wealth holders (about 30 adults out of 3 billions in 1980s, and 45 adults out of 4.5 billions in 2010s)	6.8%
The top 1/(20 million) highest wealth holders (about 150 adults out of 3 billions in 1980s, and 225 adults out of 4.5 billions in 2010s)	6.4%
Average world wealth per adult	2.1%
Average world income per adult	1.4%
World adult population	1.9%
World GDP	3.3%

Between 1987 and 2013, the highest global wealth fractiles have grown at 6–7% per year, versus 2.1% for average world wealth and 1.4% for average world income. All growth rates are net of inflation (2.3% per year between 1987 and 2013).

are constructed, and it is likely that they suffer from various biases. They also focus on such a narrow fraction of the population that they are of limited utility for a comprehensive study of the global distribution of wealth. For instance, what happens above $1 billion does not necessarily tell us much about what happens between $10 and 100 million. This is a research area where a lot of progress needs to be made.

15.5.5 The Steady-State Level of the Inheritance Share: $\varphi = \varphi(g)$

15.5.5.1 The Impact of Saving Motives, Growth, and Life Expectancy

The return of high wealth–income ratios β does not necessarily imply the return of inheritance. From a purely logical standpoint, it is perfectly possible that the steady-state $\beta = s/g$ rises (say, because g goes down and s remains relatively high, as we have observed in Europe and Japan over the recent decades), but that all saving flows come from life-cycle wealth accumulation and pension funds, so that the inheritance share φ is equal to zero. Empirically, however, this does not seem to be the case. From the (imperfect) data that we have, it seems that the rise in the aggregate wealth–income ratio β has been accompanied by a rise in the inheritance share φ, at least in Europe.

This suggests that the taste for leaving bequests (and/or the other reasons for dying with positive wealth, such as precautionary motives and imperfect annuity markets) did not decline over time. Empirical evidence shows that the distribution of saving motives varies a lot across individuals. It could also be that the distribution of saving motives is partly determined by the inequality of wealth. Bequests might partly be a luxury good, in the sense that individuals with higher relative wealth also have higher bequest taste on average. Conversely, the magnitude of bequest motives has an impact on the steady-state level of wealth inequality. Take, for instance, the dynamic wealth accumulation model described above. In that model we implicitly assume that individuals leave wealth to the next generation. If they did not, the dynamic cumulative process would start at zero all over again at each generation, so that steady-state wealth inequality would tend to be smaller.

Now, assume that we take as given the distribution of bequest motives and saving parameters. Are there reasons to believe that changes in the long-run growth rate g or in the demographic parameters (such as life expectancy) can have an impact on the inheritance share φ in total wealth accumulation?

This question has been addressed by a number of authors, such as Laitner (2001) and DeLong (2003).[47] According to DeLong, the share of inheritance in total wealth accumulation should be higher in low-growth societies, because the annual volume of new savings is relatively small in such economics (so that in effect most wealth originates from inheritance). Using our notations, the inheritance share $\varphi = \varphi(g)$ is a decreasing function of the growth rate g.

---

[47] See also Davies et al. (2012, pp. 123–124).

This intuition is interesting (and partly correct) but incomplete. In low-growth societies, such as preindustrial societies, the annual volume of new savings—for a given aggregate β—is indeed low in steady state: $s = g \cdot \beta$. In contrast, the flow of inheritances is given by: $b_y = \mu \cdot m \cdot \beta$ (see Section 15.4). Therefore, for given μ and m, inheritance flows tend to dominate saving flows in low-growth economies, and conversely in high-growth economies.

For instance, if $\mu = 1$, $m = 2\%$, and $\beta = 600\%$, the inheritance flow is equal to $b_y = 12\%$. The inheritance flow b_y is four times bigger than the saving flow $s = 3\%$ if $g = 0.5\%$, it is equal to the saving flow $s = 12\%$ if $g = 2\%$, and it is 2.5 times smaller than the saving flow $s = 30\%$ if $g = 5\%$. Therefore—the argument goes—inherited wealth represents the bulk of aggregate wealth in low-growth, preindustrial societies; makes about half of aggregate wealth in medium-growth, mature economies; and a small fraction of aggregate wealth in high-growth, booming economies.

This intuition, however, is incomplete, for two reasons. First, as we already pointed out in Section 15.4, saving flows partly come from the return to inherited wealth, and this needs to be taken into account. Next, the μ parameter, i.e., the relative wealth of decedents, is endogenous and might well depend on the growth rate g, as well as on demographic parameters such as life expectancy and the mortality rate m. In the pure life-cycle model where agents die with zero wealth, μ is always equal to zero, and so is the inheritance share φ, independently of the growth rate g, no matter how small g is. For given (positive) bequest tastes and saving parameters, however, one can show that in steady state, $\mu = \mu(g, m)$ tends to be higher when growth rates g and mortality rates m are lower.

15.5.5.2 A Simple Benchmark Model of Aging Wealth and Endogenous μ

To see this point more clearly, it is necessary to put more demographic structure into the analysis. Here we follow a simplified version of the framework introduced by Piketty (2011).

Consider a continuous-time, overlapping-generations model with a stationary population $N_t = [0, 1]$ (zero population growth). Each individual i becomes adult at age $a = A$, has exactly one child at age $a = H$, and dies at age $a = D$. We assume away inter-vivos gifts, so that each individual inherits wealth solely when his or her parent dies, that is, at age $a = I = D - H$.

For example, if $A = 20$, $H = 30$, and $D = 60$, everybody inherits at age $I = D - H = 30$ years old. But if $D = 80$, then everybody inherits at age $I = D - H = 50$ years old.

Given that population N_t is assumed to be stationary, the (adult) mortality rate m_t is also stationary, and is simply equal to the inverse of (adult) life expectancy: $m_t = m = \frac{1}{D-A}$.[48]

---

[48] It is more natural to focus upon adults because minors usually have very little income or wealth (assuming that $I > A$, i.e., $D - A > H$, which is the case in modern societies).

For example, if $A=20$ and $D=60$, the mortality rate is $m=1/40=2.5\%$. If $D=80$, the mortality rate is $m=1/60=1.7\%$. That is, in a society where life expectancy rises from 60 to 80 years old, the steady-state mortality rate among adults is reduced by a third. In the extreme case where life expectancy rises indefinitely, the steady-state mortality rate becomes increasingly small: one almost never dies.

Does this imply that the inheritance flow $b_y=\mu\cdot m\cdot\beta$ will become increasingly small in aging societies? Not necessarily: even in aging societies, one ultimately dies. Most importantly, one tends to die with higher and higher relative wealth. That is, wealth also tends to get older in aging societies, so that the decline in the mortality rate m can be compensated by a rise in relative decedent wealth μ (which, as we have seen, has been the case in France).

Assume for simplicity that all agents have on average the same uniform saving rate s on all their incomes throughout their life (reflecting their taste for bequests and other saving motives such a precautionary wealth accumulation) and a flat age-income profile (including pay-as-you-go pensions). Then one can show that the steady-state $\mu=\mu(g)$ ratio is given by the following formula:

$$\mu(g)=\frac{1-e^{-(g-s\cdot r)(D-A)}}{1-e^{-(g-s\cdot r)H}}=\frac{1-e^{-(1-\alpha)g(D-A)}}{1-e^{-(1-\alpha)gH}}.$$

With $\alpha=r\cdot\beta=r\cdot s/g=$ capital share in national income.

In other words, the relative wealth of decedents $\mu(g)$ is a decreasing function of the growth rate g (and an increasing function of the rate of return r or of the capital share α).[49] If one introduces taxes into the model, one can easily show that μ is a decreasing function of the growth rate g and an increasing function of net-of-tax rate of return $\bar{r}$ (or the net-of-tax capital share $\bar{\alpha}$).[50]

The intuition for this formula, which can be extended to more general saving models, is the following. With high growth rates, today's incomes are large as compared to past incomes, so the young generations are able to accumulate almost as much wealth as the older cohorts, in spite of the fact that the latter have already started to accumulate in the past, and in some cases have already received their bequests. Generally speaking, high growth rates g are favorable to the young generations (who are just starting to accumulate wealth, and who therefore rely entirely on the new saving flows out of current incomes), and tend to push for lower relative decedent wealth μ. High rates of return $\bar{r}$, by contrast,

---

[49] This steady-state formula applies both to the closed-economy and open-economy cases. The only difference is that the rate of return r is endogenously determined by the marginal product of domestic capital accumulation in the closed economy case (e.g., $r=F_K=a\cdot\beta^{-1/\sigma}$ with a CES production function), while it is a free parameter in the open economy setup (in which case the formula can be viewed as $\mu=\mu(g,r)$).

[50] With taxes, $\bar{r}$ also becomes a free parameter in the closed-economy model, so the formula should always be viewed as $\mu=\mu(g,\bar{r})$.

are more favorable to older cohorts, because this makes the wealth holdings that they have accumulated or inherited in the past grow faster, and tend to pusher for higher μ.

In the extreme case where $g \to \infty$, then $\mu \to 1$ (this directly follows from flat saving rates and age-labor income profiles).

Conversely, in the other extreme case where $g \to 0$, then $\mu \to \bar{\mu} = \frac{D-A}{H} > 1$.

It is worth noting that this maximal value $\bar{\mu}$ rises in proportion to life expectancy $D - A$ (for given generation length H). Intuitively, with $g \approx 0$ and uniform saving, most of wealth originates from inheritance, so that young agents are relatively poor until inheritance age $I = D - H$, and most of the wealth concentrates between age $D - H$ and D, so that relative decedent wealth $\mu \approx \bar{\mu} = \frac{D-A}{H}$.[51]

That is, as life expectancy $D - A$ rises, wealth gets more and more concentrated at high ages. This is true for any growth rate, and all the more for low growth rates. In aging societies, one inherits later in life,[52] but one inherits bigger amounts. With $g \approx 0$, one can see that both effects exactly compensate each other, in the sense that the steady-state inheritance flow b_y is entirely independent of life expectancy. That is, with $m = \frac{1}{D-A}$ and $\bar{\mu} = \frac{D-A}{H}$, we have $b_y = \bar{\mu} \cdot m \cdot \beta = \frac{\beta}{H}$, independently from $D - A$. For a given wealth–income ratio $\beta = 600\%$ and generation length $H = 30$ years, the steady-state annual inheritance flow is equal to $b_y = 20\%$ of national income, whether life expectancy is equal to $D = 60$ years or $D = 80$ years.

Strictly speaking, this is true only for infinitely small growth $g \approx 0$. However, by using the above formula one can see that for low growth rates (say, $g \approx 1$–1.5%) then the steady-state inheritance flow is relatively close to $b_y = \frac{\beta}{H}$ and is almost independent of life expectancy. It is only for high growth rates—above 2–3% per year—that the steady-state inheritance flow is reduced substantially.

15.5.5.3 Simulating the Benchmark Model

Available historical evidence shows that the slowdown of growth is the central economic mechanism explaining why the inheritance flow seems to be returning in the early twenty-first century to approximately the same level $b_y \approx 20\%$ as that observed during the nineteenth and early twentieth centuries.

By simulating a simple uniform-saving model for the French economy over the 1820–2010 period (starting from the observed age–wealth pattern in 1820, and using observed aggregate saving rates, growth rates, mortality rates, capital shocks and age–labor

---

[51] In the extreme case where young agents have zero wealth and agents above age $I = D - H$ have average wealth $\bar{w}$, then average wealth among the living is equal to $w = \frac{(D-I) \cdot \bar{w}}{D-A}$ and, so that $\bar{\mu} = \frac{\bar{w}}{w} = \frac{D-A}{H}$. See Piketty (2011), Propositions 1–3.

[52] Although in practice, this is partly undone by the rise of inter vivos gifts, as we have seen above.

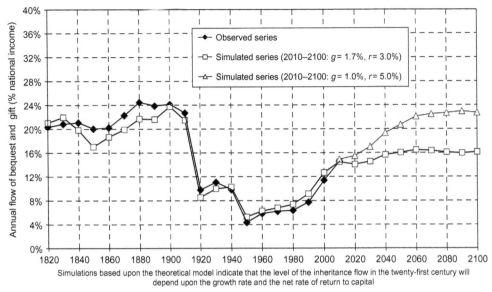

Simulations based upon the theoretical model indicate that the level of the inheritance flow in the twenty-first century will depend upon the growth rate and the net rate of return to capital

Figure 15.29 Observed and simulated inheritance flow, France 1820–2100.

income profiles over the entire period), one can reasonably well reproduce the dynamics of the age–wealth profile and hence of the μ ratio and the inheritance flow b_y over almost two centuries (see Figure 15.29).

We can then use this same model to simulate the future evolution of the inheritance flow in coming decades. As one can see on Figure 15.29, a lot depends on future values of the growth rate g and the net-of-tax rate of return $\bar{r}$ over the 2010–2100 period. Assuming $g = 1.7\%$ (which corresponds to the average growth rate observed in France between 1980 and 2010) and $\bar{r} = 3.0\%$ (which approximatively corresponds to net-of-tax average real rate of return observed in 2010), then b_y should stabilize around 16–17% in coming decades. If growth slows $g = 1.0\%$ and the net-of-tax rate of return rises to $\bar{r} = 5.0\%$ (e.g., because of a rise of the global capital share and rate of return, or because of a gradual repeal of capital taxes), b_y would keep increasing toward 22–23% over the course of the twenty-first century. The flow of inheritance would approximately return to its nineteenth and early twentieth centuries level.

In Figure 15.30, we use these projections to compute the corresponding share φ of cumulated inheritance in the aggregate wealth stock (using the PPVR definition and the same extrapolations as those described above). In the first scenario, φ stabilizes around 80%; in the second scenario, it stabilizes around 90% of aggregate wealth.

These simulations, however, are not fully satisfactory, first because a lot more data should be collected on inheritance flows in other countries, and next because one should ideally try to analyze and simulate both the flow of inheritance and the inequality of

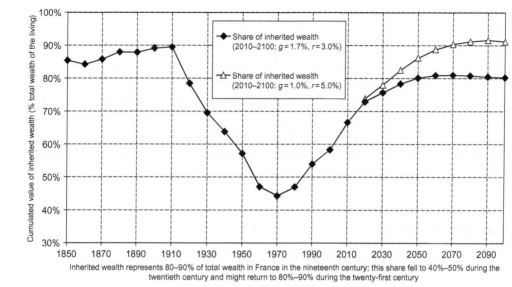

Figure 15.30 The share of inherited wealth in total wealth, France 1850–2100.

wealth. The computations presented here assume uniform saving and solely attempt to reproduce the age-average wealth profile, without taking into account within-cohort wealth inequality. This is a major limitation.

15.6. CONCLUDING COMMENTS AND RESEARCH PROSPECTS

In this chapter, we have surveyed the empirical and theoretical literature on the long-run evolution of wealth and inheritance in relation to output and income. The magnitude and concentration of wealth and inheritance (relative to national income) were very high in the eighteenth to nineteenth centuries up until World War I, then dropped precipitously during the twentieth century following World War shocks, and have been rising again in the late twentieth and early twenty-first centuries. We have showed that over a wide range of models, the long-run magnitude and concentration of wealth and inheritance are an increasing function of $\bar{r} - g$, where $\bar{r}$ is the net-of-tax rate of return to wealth and g is the economy's growth rate, and we have argued that these predictions are broadly consistent with historical patterns. These findings suggest that current trends toward rising wealth–income ratios and wealth inequality might continue during the twenty-first century, both because of the slowdown of population and productivity growth, and because of increasing international competition to attract capital.

We should stress, however, that this is an area where a lot of progress still needs to be made. Future research should particularly focus on the following issues. First, it becomes more and more important to study the dynamics of the wealth distribution from a global perspective.[53] In order to do so, it is critical to take into account existing macro data on aggregate wealth and foreign wealth holdings. Given the large movements in aggregate wealth–income ratios across countries, such macro-level variations are likely to have a strong impact on the global dynamics of the individual-level distribution of wealth. It is also critical to use existing estimates of offshore wealth and to analyze how much tax havens are likely to affect global distributional trends (see Zucman, 2014). Next, a lot more historical and international data needs to be collected on inheritance flows. Last, there is a strong need of a better articulation between empirical and theoretical research. A lot more work has yet to be done before we are able to develop rigorous and credible calibrations of dynamic theoretical models of wealth accumulation and distribution.

ACKNOWLEDGMENTS

We are grateful to the editors and to Daniel Waldenstrom for helpful comments. All series and figures presented in this chapter are available in an online data appendix.

REFERENCES

Antras, P., 2004. Is the U.S. aggregate production function Cobb-Douglas? New estimates of the elasticity of substitution. B.E. J. Macroecon. 4 (1) article 4.

Atkinson, A., 1983. The Economics of Inequality. Clarendon Press, Oxford, 330 pp.

Atkinson, A.B., 2013. Wealth and Inheritance in Britain from 1896 to the Present. Working Paper.

Atkinson, A., Harrison, A.J., 1978. Distribution of Personal Wealth in Britain, 1923–1972. Cambridge University Press, Cambridge, 330 pp.

Atkinson, A.B., Piketty, T., Saez, E., 2011. Top incomes in the long run of history. J. Econ. Lit. 49 (1), 3–71.

Benhabib, J., Bisin, A., Zhu, S., 2011. The distribution of wealth and fiscal policy in economies with finitely lived agents. Econometrica 79 (1), 123–157.

Benhabib, J., Bisin, A., Zhu, S., 2013. The Wealth Distribution in Bewley Models with Investment Risk. NYU, New York.

Blinder, A., 1988. Comments on Modigliani and Kotlikoff-Summers. In: Kessler, D., Masson, A. (Eds.), Modelling the Accumulation and Distribution of Wealth. Oxford University Press, Oxford, pp. 68–76.

Boisguillebert, P., 1695. Le détail de la France, Paris, 215 pp. Reprinted in E. Daire, Economistes financiers du 18e siècle, Paris: Guillaumin, 1843.

Bowley, A.L., 1920. The Change in the Distribution of National Income, 1880–1913. Clarendon Press, Oxford.

Champernowne, D.G., 1953. A model of income distribution. Econ. J. 63 (250), 318–351.

Chirinko, R., 2008. σ: the long and short of it. J. Macroecon. 30, 671–686.

Colquhoun, P., 1815. A Treatise on the Wealth. Power and Resources of the British Empire, London, 561 pp.

Colson, C., 1903. Cours d'économie politique. Gauthier-Villars, Paris, 1918, 1927 (several editions).

Cowell, F., 1998. Inheritance and the Distribution of Wealth. LSE, London.

Davies, J.B., Shorrocks, A.F., 1999. The distribution of wealth. In: Atkinson, A.B., Bourguignon, F. (Eds.), Handbook of Income Distribution, vol. 1. pp. 605–675 (Chapter 11).

---

[53] See the important pioneering work of Davies et al. (2010, 2012).

Davies, J.B., Sandström, S., Shorrocks, A., Wolff, E.N., 2010. The level and distribution of global household wealth. Econ. J. 121, 223–254.

Davies, J.B., Lluberas, R., Shorrocks, A., 2012. Global Wealth Data-book. Credit Suisse. https://www.credit-suisse.com/ch/en/news-and-expertise/research/credit-suisse-research-institute/publications.html.

Dell, F., 2005. Top incomes in Germany and Switzerland over the twentieth century. J. Eur. Econ. Assoc. 3, 412–421.

de Foville, A., 1893. The wealth of France and of other countries. J. R. Stat. Soc. 56 (4), 597–626.

DeLong, J.B., 2003. Bequests: an historical perspective. In: Munnel, A. (Ed.), The Role and Impact of Gifts and Estates. Brookings Institution, Washington, DC.

Edlund, L., Kopczuk, W., 2009. Women, wealth and mobility. Am. Econ. Rev. 99 (1), 146–178.

Fisher, I., 1920. Economists in public service. Am. Econ. Rev. 9, 5–21.

Giffen, R., 1889. The Growth of Capital. G. Bell and sons, London, 169 pp.

Goldsmith, R.W., 1985. Comparative National Balance Sheets: A Study of Twenty Countries, 1688–1978. The University of Chicago Press, Chicago, 353 pp.

Goldsmith, R.W., 1991. Pre-Modern Financial Systems. Cambridge University Press, Cambridge, 348 pp.

Gordon, R.J., 2012. Is U.S. Economic Growth Over? Faltering Innovation Confronts the Six Headwinds. NBER Working Paper 18315.

Greenwood, D., 1983. An estimation of U.S. family wealth and its distribution from microdata, 1973. Rev. Income Wealth 29, 23–43.

Helfferich, K., 1913. Deutschlands Volkswholhstand, 1888–1913. G. Stilke, Berlin.

Hopehnayn, H., Prescott, E., 1992. Stochastic monotonicity and stationary distributions for dynamic economies. Econometrica 60 (6), 1387–1406.

Jones, C.I., Romer, P.M., 2010. The new Kaldor facts: ideas, institutions, population, and human capital. Am. Econ. J. 2 (1), 224–245.

Kaldor, N., 1961. Capital accumulation and economic growth. In: Lutz, F.A., Hague, D.C. (Eds.), The Theory of Capital. Saint Martins Press, New York.

Karabarbounis, L., Neiman, B., 2014. The global decline of the labor share. Q. J. Econ. 129 (1), 61–103.

King, G., 1696. Natural and Political Observations and Conclusions Upon the State and Condition of England, 1696. pp. 29–73, 45 pp., Published in Chalmers 1804.

King, W.I., 1915. The Wealth and Income of the People of the United States. McMillan Press, New York, 278 pp.

King, W.I., 1927. Wealth distribution in the Continental United States at the close of 1921. J. Am. Stat. Assoc. 22, 135–153.

Kaplan, S.N., Rauh, J., 2013. Family, education, and sources of wealth among the richest Americans, 1982–2012. Am. Econ. Rev. 103 (3), 158–166.

Karagiannaki, E., 2011. Recent Trends in the Size and the Distribution of Inherited Wealth in the UK. London School of Economics, London, CASE Paper 146.

Kopczuk, W., Saez, E., 2004. Top wealth shares in the United States, 1916–2000: evidence from estate tax returns. Natl. Tax J. 57 (2), 445–487.

Kotlikoff, L., 1988. Intergenerational transfers and savings. J. Econ. Perspect. 2 (2), 41–58.

Kotlikoff, L., Summers, L., 1981. The role of intergenerational transfers in aggregate capital accumulation. J. Polit. Econ. 89, 706–732.

Kuznets, S., 1953. Shares of upper income groups in income and savings, 1913–1948. National Bureau of Economic Research, Cambridge, MA, 707 pp.

Lampman, R.J., 1962. The share of top wealth-holders in national wealth 1922–1956. Princeton University Press, Princeton.

Laitner, J., 1979. Bequest behaviour and the national distribution of wealth. Rev. Econ. Stud. 46 (3), 467–483.

Laitner, J., 2001. Secular changes in wealth inequality and inheritance. Econ. J. 111 (474), 691–721.

Lindert, P., 1986. Unequal English wealth since 1688. J. Polit. Econ. 94 (6), 1127–1162.

Lindert, P., 2000. Three centuries of inequality in Britain and America. In: Atkinson, A.B., Bourguignon, F. (Eds.), Handbook of Income Distribution, vol. 1. Elsevier/North Holland, Amsterdam, pp. 167–216.

Maddison, A., 2010. Historical Statistics of the World Economy: 1–2008 AD. www.ggcc.net/maddisonupdated tables.

Mallet, B., 1908. A method of estimating capital wealth from the estate duty statistics. J. R. Stat. Soc. 71 (1), 65–101.

Mallet, B., Strutt, H.C., 1915. The multiplier and capital wealth. J. R. Stat. Soc. 78 (4), 555–599.

Meade, J.E., 1964. Efficiency, Equality and the Ownership of Property. Allen and Unwin, London.

Menchik, P.L., 1980. Primogeniture, equal sharing, and the U.S. distribution of wealth. Q. J. Econ. 94 (2), 299–316.

Modigliani, F., 1986. Life cycle, individual thrift and the wealth of nations. Am. Econ. Rev. 76 (3), 297–313.

Modigliani, F., 1988. The role of intergenerational transfers and lifecycle savings in the accumulation of wealth. J. Econ. Perspect. 2 (2), 15–40.

Morigushi, C., Saez, E., 2008. The evolution of income concentration in Japan, 1886–2005: evidence from income tax statistics. Rev. Econ. Stat. 90 (4), 713–734.

Nirei, M., 2009. Pareto Distributions in Economic Growth Models. Hitotsubashi University, Tokyo, Working Paper.

Ohlsson, H., Roine, J., Waldenstrom, D., 2013. Inherited Wealth over the Path of Development: Sweden 1810-2010. Mimeo, Uppsala.

Petty, W., 1664. Verbum Sapienti. 26 pp. Published as an addendum to Petty, W., 1691. The Political Anatomy of Ireland. London, 266 pp. Reprinted in The Economic Writings of Sir William Petty, Hull, C.H. (Ed.), 2 vols., Cambridge University Press, 1989.

Piketty, T., 2011. On the long-run evolution of inheritance: France 1820–2050. Q. J. Econ. 126 (3), 1071–1131.

Piketty, T., 2014. Capital in the 21st Century. Harvard University Press, Cambridge.

Piketty, T., Saez, E., 2013. A theory of optimal inheritance taxation. Econometrica 81 (5), 1851–1886.

Piketty, T., Zucman, G., 2014. Capital is back: wealth-income ratios in rich countries 1700–2010. Q. J. Econ. 129 (3), 1255–1310.

Piketty, T., Postel-Vinay, G., Rosentha, J.-L., 2006. Wealth concentration in a developing economy: Paris and France, 1807–1994. Am. Econ. Rev. 96 (1), 236–256.

Piketty, T., Postel-Vinay, G., Rosenthal, J.-L., 2013. Inherited versus self-made wealth: theory and evidence from a rentier society (1872–1927). Explor. Econ. Hist. 51, 21–40.

Roine, J., Waldenstrom, D., 2009. Wealth concentration over the path of development: Sweden, 1873–2006. Scand. J. Econ. 111, 151–187.

Saez, E., Zucman, G., 2014. Wealth Inequality in the United States since 1913: Evidence from Capitalized Income Tax Data. Working Paper.

Schinke, C., 2013. Inheritance in Germany 1911 to 2009. PSE Working Paper.

Séaillès, J., 1910. La répartition des fortunes en France. Editions Felix Alcan, Paris, 143 pp.

Stamp, J.C., 1919. The wealth and income of the chief powers. J. R. Stat. Soc. 82 (4), 441–507.

Stewart, C., 1939. Income capitalization as a method of estimating the distribution of wealth by size group. Studies in Income and Wealth, vol. 3. National Bureau of Economic Research, New York.

Stiglitz, J.E., 1969. Distribution of income and wealth among individuals. Econometrica 37 (3), 382–397.

Strutt, H.C., 1910. Notes on the distribution of estates in France and the United Kingdom. J. R. Stat. Soc. 73 (6), 634–644.

Vauban, S., 1707. Projet d'une dixme royale. Librairie Félix Alcan, Paris, 267 pp. Reprinted in E. Daire, Economistes financiers du 18e siècle, Paris: Guillaumin, 1843.

Vaughan, R.N., 1979. Class behaviour and the distribution of wealth. Rev. Econ. Stud. 46 (3), 447–465.

Waldenstrom, D., 2009. Lifting All Boats? The Evolution of Income and Wealth Inequality over the Path of Development. PhD Dissertation, Lunds universitet, Lund.

Wolff, E., Gittleman, M., 2013. Inheritances and the distribution of wealth or whatever happened to the great inheritance boom? J. Econ. Inequal. 1–30, available online at http://dx.doi.org/10.1007/s10888-013-9261-8.

Zucman, G., 2013. The missing wealth of nations: are Europe and the U.S. net debtors or net creditors? Q. J. Econ. 128 (3), 1321–1364.

Zucman, G., 2014. Taxing Across Borders: Tracking Personal Wealth and Corporate Profits. J. Econ. Perspect. forthcoming.

CHAPTER 16

Intrahousehold Inequality

Pierre-André Chiappori[*], Costas Meghir[†]
[*]Department of Economics, Columbia University, NY, USA
[†]Department of Economics, Yale University, New Haven, CT, USA

Contents

Abstract

Studies of inequality often ignore resource allocation within the household. In doing so they miss an important element of the distribution of welfare that can vary dramatically depending on overall environmental and economic factors. Thus, measures of inequality that ignore intrahousehold allocations are both incomplete and misleading. We discuss determinants of intrahousehold allocation of resources and welfare. We show how the sharing rule, which characterizes the within-household allocations, can be identified from data on household consumption and labor supply. We also argue that a measure based on estimates of the sharing rule is inadequate as an approach that seeks to understand how welfare is distributed in the population because it ignores public goods and the allocation of time to market work, leisure, and household production. We discuss a money metric alternative, that fully characterizes the utility level reached by the agent. We then review the current literature on the estimation of the sharing rule based on a number of approaches, including the use of distribution factors as well as preference restrictions.

Keywords

Collective model, Income distribution, Economics of the family, Labor supply, Household behavior

JEL Classification Codes

D1, D11, D12, D13, D31, D6, H41

16.1. INTRODUCTION

16.1.1 Inequality Between Individuals

Consider an economy with identical couples, each of whom has a total income of 100. Individuals privately consume a unique, perfectly divisible commodity; there exist neither externalities nor economies of scale, so that, in each couple, the sum of individual consumptions equals the couple's total income. Inequality, as measured in a standard way, is nil. Assume, now, that some of these couples divorce, and that after divorce husbands each receive an income of 75, while each wife gets 25. The new income distribution, again by standard criteria, is now unequal; in particular, the presence of lower-income singles (the divorced wives) increases both inequality and poverty.

From a deeper perspective, however, the conclusion just stated is far from granted. It entirely relies on an implicit assumption—namely, that the predivorce distribution of income *within households* was equal. Most of the time, such an assumption has little or no empirical justification; and from a theoretical viewpoint, it is actually quite unlikely to hold—few serious models of household behavior would predict an equal distribution of income while married if the post-divorce allocation is highly skewed. Still, it is crucial. Assume, for the sake of the argument, that the distribution of resources within married couples simply mimics what it would be in case of divorce (he gets 75, she gets 25)—not an unreasonable assumption, given that in our (admittedly simplistic) structure this is the only individually rational allocation. Then the claim that inequality increased after the wave of divorces is simply wrong. Inequality, at least across individuals, has not changed; each agent has exactly the same income, consumption and welfare than before. And the surge in measured poverty is just as spurious. There are exactly as many poor women after than there were before; it is just that, in the predivorce situation, the standard measures missed them.

The previous example, extreme as it may be, illustrates a basic point that this chapter will try to emphasize—namely, that any attempt at measuring inequality (or its evolution

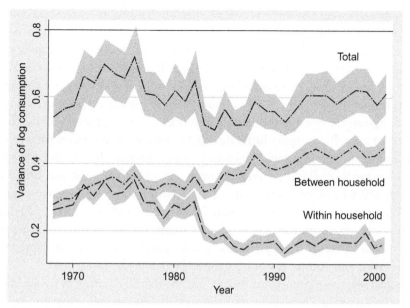

Figure 16.1 Trends in the variance of log consumption, UK. *Source: Lise and Seitz (2011).*

over time) that ignores allocation of resources within the family is unreliable at best, and deeply flawed at worst, especially when the basic demographics regarding family composition evolve over the period under consideration. This point had already been emphasized in the literature; for instance, Haddad and Kanbur (1990) have showed, on Philippine data, that standard measures of inequality in calorie adequacy would be understated by 30–40% if intrahousehold inequality was ignored. As a more recent illustration, consider the graph in Figure 16.1, due to Lise and Seitz (2011), that plots the evolution of inequality across households, within households, and across individuals in the United Kingdom over the last decades, as estimated from a collective model of labor supply. The main conclusion is that the standard approach, based on adult equivalence scales, underestimates the initial level of cross-sectional consumption inequality by 50%. Moreover, it gives a deeply flawed picture of the evolution of inequality over the last decades. While the usual story—a large surge in inequality between 1970 and 2000—applies to inequality across households, it is compensated by a considerable reduction of intrahousehold inequality, so that total inequality (across *individuals*) remains more or less constant over the period.[1]

---

[1] This conclusion must be qualified in view of the population under consideration. Indeed, the sample excludes all households with children, all persons aged under 22 or over 65, all persons who were self-employed, and the top 1% of the earnings distribution (which is, in any case, not well covered by the Family Expenditure Survey); so the conclusions are only valid for that particular subpopulation. Still, it is suggestive of the general claim that ignoring intrahousehold allocation may severely bias our views regarding inequality.

All this strongly suggests, at the very least, that much more attention should be paid to intrahousehold inequality, from both a theoretical and an empirical viewpoint. Analyzing intrahousehold inequality, however, raises a host of specific problems. Some are of a conceptual nature. A large fraction of household expenditures relate to public commodities, that is, goods that are jointly consumed by the household, without exclusion restrictions; moreover, in many cases these public commodities are internally produced within the household. Spouses may have different preferences regarding public goods; therefore, the fraction of household expenditures devoted to public consumption has a potentially important impact on intrahousehold inequality, that cannot be disregarded. Similar questions arise for intrahousehold production, with the additional twist that time spent by each spouse should also be taken into account. How should such public productions and consumptions be taken into account in our inequality measures? Although the impact of public goods on inequality is by no means a new problem, it is particularly stringent in our context, if only because public goods and domestic production are among the main (economic) reasons for the existence of the household.

As we shall see, these conceptual issues affect the standard notion of inequality in two ways. Besides shedding a new light on its measurement, they also revive some old discussions about its foundations. In particular, the role of public goods raises questions about which type on inequality we should concentrate on: income? (private) consumption? utility? The problem is far from innocuous: in the presence of public goods, it is relatively easy to generate examples in which a change in prices and incomes results in a decrease in a person's private consumption and an increase in the spouse's, whereas utilities evolve in the opposite way (welfare declines for the person whose private consumption increases and conversely). In such a context, the impact of the change on intrahousehold inequality is not clearly defined: It all depends on what exactly we are interested in.

Empirical problems are equally challenging. As always in economics, preferences are not directly observed and have to be recovered from observable data (demand, labor supply). But, in addition, the allocation of resources within the household cannot (in general) be directly observed; it has to be recovered from the household's (aggregate) behavior. It follows that when deciding which aspect of inequality should be considered, one cannot abstract from identification issues: there is little interest in concentrating on a notion that is not identifiable in practice. An interesting paradox, in this respect, is provided by a standard result of household economics, namely, that in some circumstances, a continuum of different models generate the same observable behavior (so they are observationally indistinguishable). In some cases, these models correspond to different intrahousehold allocations of resources, but to the same allocation of utility (in the language of the theory, the indeterminacy is welfare-irrelevant). In other words, the main justification for concentrating on inequality in income or consumption rather than in utility—namely, the fact that the former are observed, but not the latter—is sometimes partially reversed.

These questions obviously arise whenever inequality is assessed on a utilitarian basis. However, even an alternative approach in terms of capabilities could hardly disregard them. Issues related to individual preferences for public goods would be less problematic in that case; what matters, from a capabilities perspective, is more an individual's potential access to the public goods than the utility the individual actually derives from their consumption. But the difficulties in recovering individual private consumptions (especially when it comes to nutrition or other fundamental needs) would become all the more crucial. All in all, the problems raised by intrahousehold allocation should be central to any analysis of inequality, even though specific aspects may be more damaging for some approaches than for others.

What recent developments in the literature clearly indicate, however, is that while these problems are serious, they are by no means insuperable. Although intrahousehold allocation is not (fully) observable, it can be recovered using specific, identifying assumptions that will be discussed later; that is the path followed by Lise and Seitz, but also by Chiappori et al. (2002), Dunbar et al. (2013), Browning et al. (2013), and many others in the literature. Clear progress has been made on this front over the last decades. One goal of this chapter is to briefly review these advances.

A first step is to adopt an explicit model of household decision making that clarifies the notion of inequality within the household. Obviously, such models must explicitly recognize that household members each have their own preferences—if only because omitting individuals does not seem a promising way of analyzing inequality between them. An additional requirement is empirical tractability. To be usable, a model of household behavior should fulfill a double requirement: testability (i.e., it should generate a set of empirically testable restrictions that fully characterize the model, in the sense that any given behavior is compatible with the model if and only if these conditions are satisfied) and identifiability (it should be feasible, possibly under additional assumption, to recover the structure of the model—in our case, individual preferences and the decision process—from the sole observation of household behavior). Lastly, the model should provide (or be compatible with) an "upstream" theory of the generation of intrahousehold inequality; that is, we need to explain, and ideally predict, how the intrahousehold distribution of resources—and ultimately of power—responds to changes in the household's socioeconomic environment.

Most of the recent advances use one particular class of models, based on the collective approach (see Chiappori, 1988, 1992).[2] Although other (nonunitary) perspectives have been adopted in the literature, none of the alternatives has (so far) convincingly addressed the double requirement of testability and identifiability just evoked.

---

[2] For a more detailed presentation, the reader is referred to Browning et al. (2014).

16.1.2 Modeling Household Decision Making: The Collective Model

The basic axiom of the collective approach is Pareto efficiency: Whatever decision the household is making, no alternative choice would have been preferred by *all* members. Whereas this assumption is undoubtedly restrictive, its scope remains quite large. It encompasses as particular cases many models that have been proposed in the literature, including:

- "Unitary" models, which posit that the household behaves like a single decision maker; this includes simple dictatorship (possibly by a "benevolent patriarch," as in Becker, 1974) to the existence of some household welfare function (as in Samuelson, 1956).
- Models based on cooperative game theory, and particularly bargaining theory (at least in a context of symmetric information), as pioneered by Manser and Brown (1980) and McElroy and Horney (1981).
- Model based on market equilibrium, as analyzed by Grossbard-Shechtman (1993), Gersbach and Haller (2001), Edlund and Korn (2002), and others.
- More specific models, such as Lundberg and Pollak's "separate spheres" (1993) framework.

On the other hand, the collective framework excludes models based on noncooperative game theory (at least in the presence of public good), such as those considered by Ulph (2006), Browning et al. (2010), Lechene and Preston (2011), and many others, as well as models of inefficient bargaining a la Basu (2006).

The efficiency assumption is standard in many economic contexts and has often been applied to household behavior. Still, it needs careful justification. Within a static context, this assumption amounts to the requirement that married partners will find a way to take advantage of opportunities that make both of them better off. Because of proximity and durability of the relation, both partners are in general aware of the preferences and actions of each other. They can act cooperatively by reaching some binding agreement. Enforcement of such agreements can be achieved through mutual care and trust, by social norms and by formal legal contracts. Alternatively, the agreement can be supported by repeated interactions, including the possibility of punishment. A large literature in game theory, based on several "folk theorems," suggests that in such situations, efficiency should prevail.[3] At the very least, efficiency can be considered as a natural benchmark.

Another potential issue with a collective approach to inequality issues is of a more conceptual nature. By definition, the collective approach is axiomatic; it assumes specific properties of the outcome (efficiency), and leaves aside the specific process by which this outcome has been generated. It has sometimes been argued that one should judge differently situations that generate the same allocations (and the same utility levels) but

---

[3] Note, however, that folk theorems essentially apply to infinitely repeated interactions.

which are reached by different processes. In that case, the collective approach has to be further specialized, and this may be (and has been) done in several directions.[4]

Finally, an obvious but crucial advantage of the collective model is that it has been by now fully characterized. We have a set of necessary and sufficient conditions for a demand function to stem from a collective framework (Chiappori and Ekeland 2006); exclusion restrictions have been derived under which individual preferences and the decision process (as summarized by the Pareto weights) can be recovered from the sole observation of household behavior (Chiappori and Ekeland, 2009a,b). To the best of our knowledge, this is the only model of the household for which similar results have been derived.[5]

The next section describes the basic model. We then discuss the conceptual issues linked with intrahousehold inequality, first in the case where all commodities are privately consumed, then in the presence of public goods, finally for the case of domestic production. We then discuss the determinants of intrahousehold allocations followed by a section on identification of preferences and the sharing rule. Finally, we discuss issues related to identification. In the following section we give an overview of empirical findings and then we conclude with a brief discussion of future directions of research.

16.2. THE COLLECTIVE MODEL: CONCEPTS, DEFINITIONS, AND AXIOMS

In what follows, we consider a K-person household that can consume several commodities; these may include standard consumption goods and services, but also leisure, future or contingent goods, and the like. Formally, N of these commodities are publicly consumed within the household. The market purchase of public good j is denoted Q_j; the N-vector of public goods is given by Q. Similarly, private goods are denoted q_i with the n-vector q. Each private good bought is divided between the members so that member a $(a = 1, \ldots, K)$ receives q_i^a of good i, with $\sum_a q_i^a = q_i$. The vector of private goods that a receives is q^a, with $\sum_a q^a = q$. An *allocation* is an $N + Kn$-vector $(Q, q^1, \ldots, q^K)$. The associated market prices are given by the N-vector P and the n-vector p for public and private goods, respectively.

We assume that each married person has her or his own preferences over the allocation of family resources. The most general version of the model would consider utilities of the form $U^a(Q, q^1, \ldots, q^K)$, implying that a is concerned directly with all members' consumptions. Here, however, tractability requires additional structure. In what follows, we therefore assume that preferences are of the *caring* type. That is, each individual a has a felicity function $u^a(Q, q^a)$; and a's utility takes the form:

---

[4] See Browning et al. (2014).

[5] Browning et al. (2008) and Lechene and Preston (2011) provide a set of necessary conditions for noncooperative models. However, whether these conditions are sufficient is not known; moreover, no general identification result has been derived so far.

$$U^a\left(Q, q^1, \ldots, q^K\right) = W^a\left(u^1\left(Q, q^1\right), \ldots, u^K\left(Q, q^K\right)\right), \qquad (16.1)$$

where $W^a(.,.)$ is a monotone increasing function. The weak separability of these "social" preferences represents an important moral principle; a is indifferent between bundles (q^b, Q) that b consumes whenever b is indifferent. In this sense, caring is distinguished from paternalism. Caring rules out direct externalities between members because a's evaluation of her private consumption q^a does not depend directly on the private goods that b consumes.

Lastly, a particular but widely used version of caring is *egotistic* preferences, whereby members only care about their own (private and public) consumption; then individual preferences can be represented by felicities (i.e., utilities of the form $u^a(Q, q^a)$).[6] Note that such egotistic preferences *for consumption* do not exclude noneconomic aspects, such as love, companionship, or others. That is, a person's utility may be affected by the *presence* of other persons, but not by their *consumption*. Technically, the "true" preferences are of the form $F^a(u^a(Q, q^a))$, where F^a may depend on marital status and on the spouse's characteristics. Note that the F^as will typically play a crucial role in the decision to marry and in the choice of a partner. However, it is irrelevant for the characterization of married individuals' preferences over consumption bundles.

Efficiency has a simple translation; namely, the household behaves as if it was maximizing a weighted sum of utilities of its members. Technically, the program is thus (assuming egotistic preferences):

$$\max_{(Q, q^1, \ldots, q^K)} \sum_a \mu^a u^a\left(Q, q^a\right) \qquad (P)$$

under the budget constraint:

$$\sum_i P_i Q_i + \sum_j p_j \left(q_j^1 + \cdots + q_j^K\right) = y^1 + \cdots + y^K = y$$

where y^a denotes a's (nonlabor) income. Here, μ^a is the *Pareto weight* of member a; one may, for instance, adopt the normalization $\sum_a \mu^a = 1$. In the particular case where μ^a is constant, the program above describes a *unitary* model, whereas household behavior is described by the maximization of some (price-independent) utility. In general, however, μ^a may vary with prices and individual incomes; the maximand in (P) is therefore price dependent, and we are not in a unitary framework in general.

This program can readily be extended to caring preferences; one must simply replace $u^a(Q, q^a)$ with $W^a(u^1(Q, q^1), \ldots, u^K(Q, q^K))$ in (P). In what follows, however, (P) plays a

---

[6] Throughout the chapter, we assume, for convenience, that utility functions $u^a(\cdot)$, $a = 1, K$ are continuously differentiable and strictly quasi-concave.

very special role, because any allocation that is efficient for caring preferences must be efficient for the underlying, egotistic felicities, as stated by the following result:

Proposition 1

Assume that some allocation is Pareto efficient for the caring utilities $W^1, \ldots, W^K$. Then it solves (P) for some $(\mu^1, \ldots, \mu^K)$.

Proof

Suppose there exists an alternative allocation that gives a larger value to u^a for all $a = 1, \ldots, K$. But then that allocation also gives a higher value to all $W^a s$, a contradiction.

The converse is not true, because a very unequal solution to (P) may fail to be Pareto efficient for caring preferences: transferring resources from well-endowed but caring individuals to the poorly endowed ones may be Pareto improving. Still, any property of the solutions to a program of the form (P) must be satisfied by any Pareto-efficient allocation with caring preferences.

A major advantage of the formulation (P) is that the Pareto weights have a natural interpretation in terms of respective decision powers. The notion of "power" in households may be difficult to define formally, even in a simplified framework such as ours. Still, it seems natural to expect that when two people bargain, a person's gain increases with the person's power. This somewhat hazy notion is captured very effectively by the Pareto weights. Clearly, if μ^a in (P) is zero, then a has no say on the final allocation, whereas if μ^a is large, then a effectively gets her way. A key property of (P) is precisely that increasing μ^a will result in a move along the Pareto frontier, in the direction of higher utility for a. If we restrict ourselves to economic considerations, we may thus consider that the Pareto weight μ^a reflects a's power, in the sense that a larger μ^a corresponds to more power (and better outcomes) being enjoyed by a.

If $\left(\overline{Q}(p, P, y), \overline{q}^1(p, P, y), \ldots, \overline{q}^K(p, P, y) \right)$ denotes the solution to (P), we define the *collective indirect utility* of a as the utility reached by a at the end of the decision process; formally:

$$V^a(p, P, y) = u^a \left(\overline{Q}(p, P, y), \overline{q}^a(p, P, y) \right)$$

Note that, unlike the unitary setting, in the collective framework a member's collective indirect utility depends not only on the member's preferences but also on the decision process (hence the adjective "collective"). This notion is crucial for welfare analysis, as we shall see below.

Finally, an important concept is the notion of "distribution factors." A distribution factor is any variable that (i) does not affect preferences or the budget constraint, but (ii) may influence the decision process, therefore the Pareto weights. Think, for instance, of a bargaining model in which the agents' respective threat points may vary. A change in the threat point of one member will typically influence the outcome of the bargaining process, even if the household's budget constraint is unaffected. In particular, several tests of household behavior consider the income pooling property. The basic intuition is straightforward: in a unitary framework, whereby households behave like single decision makers (and maximize a unique, income-independent utility), only total household income should matter. Individual contributions to total income have no influence on behavior: they are pooled in the right-hand side of the household's budget constraint. For instance, paying a benefit to the wife rather than to the husband cannot possibly impact the household's demand. As we will see later, this property has been repeatedly rejected by the data. The most natural interpretation for such rejections (although not the only one) is that individual incomes may impact the decision process (in addition to their aggregate contribution to the budget constraint). Technically, if $(y^1, \ldots, y^K)$ is the vector of individual incomes and $y = \sum_a y^a$, whereas total income y is *not* a distribution factor (it enters the budget constraints), the $(K-1)$ ratios $y^1/y, \ldots, y^{K-1}/y$ are.[7] Of course, such a setting by no means implies that each individual consumes exactly his or her income. On the contrary, empirical evidence strongly suggests that transfers between family members are paramount. Whether these transfers are progressive or regressive, that is, whether they increase or decrease intrahousehold inequality, is in the end an empirical question. Whether it can be answered ultimately depends on the extent to which these transfers can be either observed or identified, an issue to which the end of this survey is dedicated.

In what follows, the vector of distribution factors will be denoted $z = (z_1, \ldots, z_S)$; Pareto weights and collective indirect utilities, therefore, have the general form $\mu^a(p, P, y, z)$ and $V^a(p, P, y, z)$.

16.3. MODELING HOUSEHOLD BEHAVIOR: THE COLLECTIVE MODEL

16.3.1 Private Goods Only: The Sharing Rule

We first consider a special case in which all commodities are privately consumed. Then the household can be considered as a small economy without externalities or public goods. From the second welfare theorem, any Pareto efficient allocation can be decentralized by adequate transfers; formally, we have the following result:

Proposition 2

Assume an allocation $(\bar{q}^1, \ldots, \bar{q}^K)$ is Pareto efficient. There then exist K nonnegative functions $(\rho^1, \ldots, \rho^K)$ of prices, total income, and distribution factors, with $\sum_k \rho^k(p, y, z) = y$, such that agent a solves

$$\max_{q^a} u^a(q^a) \tag{D}$$

---

[7] In practice, distribution factors must also be *uncorrelated* with unobserved components of preferences, which, in the case of individual incomes, can generate subtle exogeneity problems. See Browning et al. (2014) for a detailed discussion.

under the budget constraint

$$\sum_{i=1}^{n} p_i q_i^a = \rho^a.$$

Conversely, for any nonnegative functions $(\rho^1, \ldots, \rho^K)$, such that $\sum_k \rho_k(p, y, z) = y$, an allocation that solves (D) for all a is Pareto efficient.

In words, in a private-goods setting, any efficient decision can be described as a two-stage process. In the first stage, agents jointly decide on the allocation of household aggregate income y between agents (and agent a gets ρ^a); in the second stage, agents freely spend the shares they have received. The decision process (bargaining, for instance) takes place in the first stage; its outcome is given by the functions $(\rho^1, \ldots, \rho^K)$, which are called the *sharing rule* of the household. From a welfare perspective, there exists a one-to-one, increasing correspondence between Pareto weights and the sharing rule, at least when the Pareto set is strictly convex: when prices and incomes are constant, increasing the weight of one individual (keeping the other weights unchanged) always results in a larger share for that individual. The converse is also true. Finally, the collective, indirect utility takes a simple form, namely

$$V^a(p, y) = v^a(p, \rho^a(p, y)),$$

where v^a is the standard, indirect utility of agent a. We therefore have the following result:

Proposition 3
When all commodities are privately consumed, then for any given price vector there exists a one-to-one correspondence between the sharing rule and the indirect utility.

In particular, a member's collective indirect utility can be directly computed from the knowledge of that person's preferences and sharing rule; given the preferences, the sharing rule is a sufficient statistic for the entire decision process.

Regarding the issue of intrahousehold inequality, the key remark is that the sharing rule contains all the information required: Because all agents face the same prices, the sharing rule fully summarizes intrahousehold allocation of resources. As such, it is directly relevant for intrahousehold inequality. Specifically, let $I(y_1, \ldots, y_n)$ be some inequality index (as a function of individual incomes). Then the intrahousehold index of inequality is

$$I_I(p, y) = I\big(\rho^1(p, y), \ldots, \rho^K(p, y)\big).$$

16.3.2 Public and Private Commodities

Convenient as the previous notion may be, it still relies on a strong assumption, namely that all commodities are privately consumed. Relaxing this assumption is obviously necessary, if only because the existence of public consumption is one of the motives of household formation.

Different notions have been considered in the literature. The notion of *conditional sharing rule* (CSR), initially introduced by Blundell et al. (2005), refers to a two-stage process, whereby in stage one the household decides the consumption of public goods and the distribution of remaining income between members. In stage two all members spend their allotted amount on private consumptions to maximize individual utility *conditional on* the level of public consumption decided in stage one. As before, any efficient decision can be represented as stemming from a two-stage process of that type. The converse, however, is not true: for any given level of public consumptions, almost all CSRs lead to inefficient allocations. Moreover, the monotonic relationship between sharing rule and Pareto weights is lost. In particular, increasing a's weight does not necessarily result in a larger value for a's CSR; the intuition being that more weight to one agent may result in a different allocation of public expenditures, which may or may not result in an increase in the agent's private consumption. Lastly, and more importantly for our purpose, the CSR may give a biased estimate of intrahousehold inequality, because it simply disregards public consumption. That this pattern could be problematic is easy to see. Assume that one spouse (say the wife) cares a lot for a public good, whereas her husband cares very little. If the structure of household demand entails a significant fraction of expenditures being devoted to that public good, one can expect this pattern to have an impact on any inequality measure within the household. Disregarding public consumption altogether is therefore not an adequate approach.

A second approach relies on an old result in public economics, stating that in the presence of public goods, any efficient allocation can be decentralized using personal (or Lindahl) prices for the public good. This result establishes a nice duality between private and public goods: for the former, agents face identical prices and purchase different quantities (the sum of which is the household's aggregate demand), whereas for the latter the quantity is the same for all but prices are individual specific (and add up to market prices).[8] Again, the household behaves as if it was using a two-stage process. In stage one the household chooses a vector of individual prices for the public goods and an allocation of total income between members; in stage two members all spend their income on private and public consumptions under a budget constraint entailing their Lindahl prices. Formally, member a solves

$$\max_{q^a} u^a(Q, q^a) \qquad \text{(DP)}$$

under the budget constraint

---

[8] See Chiappori and Ekeland (2009b) for a general presentation. For applications, see for instance Donni (2009) and Cherchye et al. (2007, 2009) for a revealed preferences perspective.

$$\sum_{i=1}^{n} p_i q_i^a + \sum_{j=1}^{N} P_j^a Q_j^a = \rho^{*a}$$

where P_j^a is the Lindahl price of good j for agent a. The vector $\rho^* = (\rho^{*1}, \ldots, \rho^{*K})$, with $\sum_a \rho^{*a} = y$, defines a generalized sharing rule (GSR).

From an inequality perspective, this notion raises interesting issues. One could choose to adopt ρ^* as a description of intrahousehold inequality; indeed, agents now maximize utility under a budget constraint in which ρ^* describes available income. In particular, ρ^* is a much better indicator of the distribution of resources than the CSR $\tilde{\rho}$, because it takes into account both private and public consumptions.

However, the welfare of agent a is *not* fully described by ρ^{*a}; one also needs to know the vector P^a of a's personal prices. Technically, the collective indirect utility of a is

$$V^a(p, P, y, z) = v^a(p, P^a, \rho^{*a}(p, P, y, z)),$$

which depends on both ρ^{*a} and P^a. This implies that the sole knowledge of the GSR is not sufficient to recover the welfare level reached by a given agent, even if her preferences are known; indeed, one also needs to know the prices, which depend on *all* preferences. In particular, we believe that the level of inequality within the household cannot be analyzed from the sole knowledge of the GSR. Agents now face different personal prices, and this should be taken into account. Of course, this conclusion was expected; it simply reflects a basic but crucial insight, namely that if agents "care differently" about the public goods (as indicated by personal prices, which reflect individual marginal willingness to pay), then variations in the quantity of these public goods have an impact on intrahousehold inequality.

Finally, Chiappori and Meghir (2014) have recently proposed the concept of Money Metric Welfare Index (MMWI). Formally, the MMWI of agent a, $m^a(p, P, y, z)$, is defined by

$$v^a(p, P, m^a(p, P, y, z)) = V^a(p, P, y, z).$$

Equivalently, if c^a denotes the expenditure function of agent a, then

$$m^a(p, P, y, z) = c^a(p, P, V^a(p, P, y, z)).$$

In words, m^a is the monetary amount that agent a would need to reach the utility-level $V^a(p, P, y)$, *if she was to pay the full price of each public good* (i.e., if she faced the price vector P instead of the personalized prices P^a). The basic intuition is simple enough. The index is defined as the monetary amount that would be needed to reach the same utility level at some reference prices. A natural benchmark is to use the current market price for all goods, private and public. In particular, there exists a direct relationship between the MMWI and the standard notion of *equivalent income*,[9] although to the best of our

---

[9] See for instance Fleurbaey et al. (2014).

knowledge, equivalent income has mostly been applied so far to private goods.[10] Both approaches rely on the notion that referring to a common price vector can facilitate inter-personal comparisons of welfare.

Unlike the GSR, the MMWI fully characterizes the utility level reached by the agent. That is, knowing an agent's preferences, there is a one-to-one relationship between her utility and her MMWI, and this relationship does *not* depend on the partner's character-istics. In the pure private goods case, the MMWI coincides with the sharing rule; it generalizes this notion to a general setting without losing its main advantage, namely the one-to-one relationship with welfare. Finally, it can readily be extended to allow for labor supply and domestic production; the reader is referred to Chiappori and Meghir (2014) for a detailed presentation.

16.3.3 An Example

The previous concepts can be illustrated on a very simple example, borrowed from Chiappori and Meghir (2014). Assume two agents a and b, two commodities—one private q, one public Q—and Cobb–Douglas preferences:

$$u^a = \frac{1}{1+\alpha}\log q^a + \frac{\alpha}{1+\alpha}\log Q$$

$$u^b = \frac{1}{1+\beta}\log q^b + \frac{\beta}{1+\beta}\log Q$$

corresponding to the indirect utilities

$$v^a = \log y - \frac{\alpha}{1+\alpha}\log P - \log(1+\alpha) + \frac{\alpha}{1+\alpha}\log\alpha$$

$$v^b = \log y - \frac{\beta}{1+\beta}\log P - \log(1+\beta) + \frac{\beta}{1+\beta}\log\beta.$$

Let μ be b's Pareto weight; then the couple's consumption is given by

$$q^a = \frac{1}{(1+\alpha)(1+\mu)}y, \quad q^b = \frac{\mu}{(1+\beta)(1+\mu)}y$$

$$\text{and } Q = \frac{\alpha(1+\beta)+\mu\beta(1+\alpha)}{(1+\alpha)(1+\beta)(1+\mu)}\frac{y}{P},$$

generating utilities equal to

$$V^a = \log y - \frac{\alpha}{1+\alpha}\log P - \log((1+\alpha)(1+\mu)) + \frac{\alpha}{1+\alpha}\log\left(\frac{\alpha(1+\beta)+\mu\beta(1+\alpha)}{1+\beta}\right)$$

---

[10] See, however, Hammond (1995) and Fleurbaey and Gaulier (2009).

$$V^b = \log y - \frac{\beta}{1+\beta} \log P$$
$$- \log(1+\beta)(1+\mu) + \frac{1}{1+\beta}\log\mu + \frac{\beta}{1+\beta}\log\left(\frac{\alpha(1+\beta)+\mu\beta(1+\alpha)}{1+\alpha}\right).$$

In this context, straightforward calculations allow to see that

1. The CSR coincides with private consumption

$$\tilde{\rho}^a = \frac{1}{(1+\alpha)(1+\mu)}y, \quad \tilde{\rho}^b = \frac{\mu}{(1+\beta)(1+\mu)}y$$

2. Lindahl prices are

$$P^a = \frac{\alpha(1+\beta)}{\alpha(1+\beta)+\mu\beta(1+\alpha)}P$$

$$P^b = \frac{\mu\beta(1+\alpha)}{\alpha(1+\beta)+\mu\beta(1+\alpha)}P$$

and the GSR is

$$\rho^{*a} = \frac{y}{1+\mu}$$

$$\rho^{*b} = \frac{\mu y}{1+\mu}$$

3. The two MMWIs are given by

$$m^a = \left(\frac{\alpha(1+\beta)+\mu\beta(1+\alpha)}{\alpha(1+\beta)}\right)^{\frac{\alpha}{1+\alpha}}\frac{y}{1+\mu} = \left(\frac{\alpha(1+\beta)+\mu\beta(1+\alpha)}{\alpha(1+\beta)}\right)^{\frac{\alpha}{1+\alpha}}\rho^{*a}$$

$$m^b = \left(\frac{\alpha(1+\beta)+\mu\beta(1+\alpha)}{\mu\beta(1+\alpha)}\right)^{\frac{\beta}{1+\beta}}\frac{\mu y}{1+\mu} = \left(\frac{\alpha(1+\beta)+\mu\beta(1+\alpha)}{\mu\beta(1+\alpha)}\right)^{\frac{\beta}{1+\beta}}\rho^{*b}.$$

Assume now that $\mu=1$, but agents have different preferences for the public good. For instance, $\alpha=2$ while $\beta=0.5$, implying that the wife (or husband) puts two-thirds of the weight on the public (private) consumption. In this setting, we can analyze intrahousehold inequality using three possible indicators.

1. If we concentrate on private consumption (or equivalently on the CSR), we find that

$$\tilde{\rho}^a = \frac{1}{6}y, \quad \tilde{\rho}^b = \frac{1}{3}y$$

and we conclude that member b is much better off than a.

2. This conclusion is clearly unsatisfactory, because it disregards the fact that half the budget is spent on the public good, which benefits a more than b. Indeed, the GSR is

$$\rho^{*a} = \frac{y}{2} = \rho^{*b}$$

and we conclude that for this indicator, the household is perfectly equal: the benefits of public expenditures exactly compensate differences in private consumptions.

3. The later conclusion is, however, too optimistic, as it omits the fact that a "pays" twice as much for the public good than b does (here, $P^a = \frac{2}{3}P$ while $P^b = \frac{1}{3}P$). Taking this last aspect into account, the respective MMWIs are

$$m^a = 0.655y, \quad m^b = 0.72y$$

Again, b is better off than a (although by much less than with the first measure). In addition, one may note that

$$m^a + m^b = 1.375y.$$

Individual MMWIs add up to more than total income, reflecting the gain generated by the publicness of one commodity.

16.3.4 Domestic Production

Finally, the previous analysis can readily be extended to domestic production. Here, we only consider the case where all commodities are privately consumed; for a more general presentation along similar lines, the reader is referred to Chiappori and Meghir (2014). The household production technology is thus described by a production function that gives the possible vector of outputs $q = f(x, \tau)$, that can be produced given a vector of market purchases x and the time $\tau = (\tau^a, a = 1, K)$ spent in household production by each of the members.

We first disregard the time spent by each member on domestic production. This setting is thus identical to the general model of household production of Browning et al. (2013).[11] Pareto efficiency translates into the program

$$\max \sum \mu^a u^a(q^a)$$

$$\sum_a q_i^a = f_i(x^i),$$

$$p'\left(\sum_i x^i\right) = y,$$

where

---

[11] For empirical applications, these authors use a linear technology a la Barten.

$$q^a = \left(q_i^a\right), \quad i = 1, n$$

$$x^i = \left(x_j^i\right), \quad j = 1, k.$$

As before, this program can be decentralized, although decentralization now requires specific (shadow) prices for the produced goods. Specifically, let η_i, λ be the respective Lagrange multipliers of the production constraints in (16.2), and define

$$\pi_i = \frac{\eta_i}{\lambda}.$$

Let $((q^{a*}), a = 1, \ldots, K, x^*)$ denote the solutions, and define the sharing rule by

$$\rho^a = \pi' q^{a*}.$$

Then the program is equivalent to a two-stage process, in which q^{a*} solves

$$\max u^a(q^a)$$

under the budget constraint

$$\pi' q^a = \rho^a$$

and x^* solves the profit maximization problem

$$\max \sum_i \pi_i f_i(x^i) - \sum_{i,j} p_j x_j^i,$$

or, equivalently, the cost minimization problem

$$\min p'x$$

$$f(x) = \sum_a q^{a*}.$$

In that case, again, individual welfare is adequately measured by the sharing rule.

Extending this model to domestic labor supply is straightforward. The Pareto program is now

$$\max \sum \mu^a u^a(q^a, L^a)$$

$$\sum_a q_i^a = f_i(x^i, \tau_i)$$

$$p'\left(\sum_i x^i\right) + \sum_a w_a\left(L^a + \sum_i \tau_i^a\right) = y + \sum_a w_a T = Y,$$

where

$$\tau_i = \left(\tau_i^a\right), \quad a = 1, K.$$

Prices for internally produced goods are defined as before. The sharing rule is now

$$\rho^a = \pi' q^{a*} + w_a L^{a*}, \quad a = 1, K,$$

where L^{a*} denotes a's optimal leisure. The program can be decentralized as follows. For each a, (q^{a*}, L^{a*}) solve

$$\max u^a(q^a, L^a),$$

$$\pi' q^a + w_a L^a = \rho^a,$$

and x^*, τ^{a*} solves

$$\max \sum_i \pi_i f_i(x^i, \tau_i) - \sum_{i,j} p_j x_j^i - \sum_{i,a} w_a \tau_i^a.$$

or equivalently,

$$\min \sum_{i,j} p_j x_j^i + \sum_{i,a} w_a \tau_i^a \tag{16.2}$$

under

$$f_i(x^i, \tau_i^a) = \sum_a q_i^{a*}, \quad i = 1, n.$$

In practice, several variants of this basic framework can be considered, depending on whether the internally produced goods are marketable, and whether market labor supplies are available via an interior or a corner solution. These technical issues are not without importance. For instance, a standard issue in family economics is whether a change in the respective powers of the various members has an impact on the intrahousehold allocation of domestic work. In the model just described, if the produced commodities are marketable and all individuals work on the market, then the πs and the ws must coincide with market prices and wages; they are therefore exogenous, and individual, domestic labor supplies are fully defined by the program (16.2), which does not depend on Pareto weights. We conclude that, in that case, powers have no impact on domestic work, which is fully determined by efficiency considerations. Clearly, this argument must be modified when either the πs or the ws are endogenous (as will be the case if, respectively, the commodity is not marketable or a person does not participate in the labor market). The reader is referred to Browning et al. (2014) for a precise discussion, as well as to the Chapter 12 in this handbook.

16.4. THE DETERMINANTS OF INTRAHOUSEHOLD ALLOCATION

The second task assigned to theory is to explain the allocation of powers, hence of resources, within the household. As such, it must address issues related to household formation and dissolution, as well as the interaction between the household and its environment, that is, which external factors may impact the intrahousehold decision process. In what follows, we concentrate on two types of approaches, respectively based on cooperative bargaining and matching or search theory. In a sense, this distinction reflects the classic dichotomy between partial and general equilibrium. Bargaining models analyze, for a given household, how the particular situation of each member may affect the household decision; much emphasis is put on individual "threat points," generally considered as exogenous. Matching and search models, on the other hand, describe a global equilibrium on the "market for marriage" as a whole. Although the decision process may in some cases entail bargaining (in search models, or in matching with a finite set of agents), the crucial distinction is that the threat points are now *endogenous*—their determination is part of the equilibrium conditions.

16.4.1 Bargaining Models

Any bargaining model requires a specific setting: In addition to the framework described above (K agents, with specific utility functions), one has to define a *threat point* T^a for each individual a. Intuitively, a person's threat point describes the utility level this person could reach in the absence of an agreement with the partner. Typically, bargaining models assume that the outcome of the decision process is Pareto efficient and individually rational, in the sense that individuals never receive less than their threat point. Bargaining theory is used to determine how the threat points influence the location of the chosen point on the Pareto frontier. Clearly, if the point $T = (T^1, \ldots, T^K)$ is outside of the Pareto set, then no agreement can be reached, because at least one member would lose by agreeing. However, if T belongs to the interior of the Pareto set so that all agents can gain from the relationship, the model picks a particular point on the Pareto utility frontier. Note that the crucial role played by threat points—a common feature of all bargaining models—has a very natural interpretation in terms of distribution factors. Indeed, *any variable that is relevant for threat points only is a potential distribution factor*. For example, the nature of divorce settlements, the generosity of single-parent benefits, or the probability of remarriage do not directly change a household's budget constraint (as long as it does not dissolve), but may affect the respective threat points of individuals within it. Then bargaining theory implies that they will influence the intrahousehold distribution of power in households and, ultimately, household behavior. Equivalently, one could say that these variables are distribution factors that affect the Pareto weights.

In practice, models based on bargaining must make a number of basic choices. One is the bargaining concept to be used. Whereas most studies refer to Nash bargaining, some either adopt Kalai–Smorodinski or refer to a noncooperative bargaining model. Second, one must choose a relevant threat point. This part is crucial; indeed, a result due to Chiappori et al. (2012) states that *any* Pareto efficient allocation can be derived as the

Nash bargaining solution for an *ad hoc* definition of the threat points. Hence any additional information provided by the bargaining concepts (besides the sole efficiency assumption) must come from specific hypotheses on the threat points, that is, on what is meant by the sentence "no agreement is reached." Several ideas have been used in the literature. One is to refer to divorce as the "no agreement" situation. Then the threat point is defined as the maximum utility a person could reach after divorce. Such an idea seems well adapted when one is interested, say, in the effects of laws governing divorce on intrahousehold allocation. It is probably less natural when minor decisions are at stake: Choosing who will walk the dog, for example, is unlikely to involve threats of divorce.[12] Another interesting illustration would concern public policies that affect single parents, or the guaranteed employment programs that exist in some Indian states. Haddad and Kanbur (1992) convincingly argue that the main impact of the program was to change the opportunities available to the wife outside of marriage.

A second idea relies on the presence of public goods and the fact that noncooperative behavior typically leads to inefficient outcomes. The idea, then, is to take the noncooperative outcome as the threat point: In the absence of an agreement, both members provide the public good(s) egotistically, not taking into account the impact of their decision on the other member's welfare. This version captures the idea that the person who would suffer more from this lack of cooperation (the person who has the higher valuation for the public good) is likely to be more willing to compromise in order to reach an agreement. A variant, proposed by Lundberg and Pollak (1993), is based on the notion of "separate spheres." The idea is that each partner is assigned a set of public goods to which they alone can contribute; this is their "sphere" of responsibility or expertise. These spheres are determined by social norms. Then the threats consist of continued marriage in which the partners act noncooperatively and each chooses independently the level of public goods under their domain.

Finally, it must be reminded that assumptions on threat points tend to be strong, not grounded on strong theoretical arguments, and often not independently testable. This suggests that models based on bargaining should be used parsimoniously and with care.

16.4.2 Equilibrium Models

Alternatively, one can consider the "market for marriage" as a whole from a general perspective. Two types of models can be found in the literature, that make opposite assumptions on the role of frictions in the matching game. Specifically, models based on matching (with transferable or imperfectly transferable utility, TU and ITU, respectively) assume away frictions and consider perfectly smooth markets, while models based on

---

[12] An additional difficulty is empirical. The estimation of utility in case of divorce is delicate, because most data sets allow us to estimate (at best) an ordinal representation of preferences, whereas Nash bargaining requires a cardinal representation. See Chiappori (1991).

search emphasize the importance of frictions in the emergence of marital patterns. While matching and search-based approaches use different technologies, their scope and outcomes are largely similar for what we are concerned with here. In what follows, for the sake of brevity, we therefore concentrate on matching models. Moreover, we only discuss models based on TU. The nontransferable utility framework, which assumes away any transfer between members, is not relevant here. And although more general approaches based on ITU have recently been developed (see Chiappori, 2012), the distinction between TU and ITU can basically be disregarded for our current discussion.

Consider the two populations of men and women: Each individual is defined by a vector of characteristics, denoted $x \in X$ for women and $y \in Y$ for men. Both sets are endowed with a finite measure, denoted μ_X and μ_Y, respectively. When matched, Mrs. x and Mr. y jointly generate a surplus $s(x, y)$, which can be derived from a more structural framework (e.g., a collective model). A *matching* is defined by (i) a measure μ on the set $X \times Y$, the marginals of which coincide with μ_X and μ_Y, and (ii) two functions $u(x)$ and $v(y)$ such that $u(x) + v(y) = s(x, y)$ on the support of μ. Intuitively, the measure μ defines who marries whom, whereas the functions determine how the surplus is divided within couples who are matched with positive probability: She gets $u(x)$, he gets $v(y)$. A matching is *stable* if (i) no married person would prefer being single and (ii) no pair of currently unmarried persons would both prefer forming a new couple. Technically, this is equivalent to

$$u(x) + v(y) \geq s(x, y) \quad \forall (x, y). \tag{16.3}$$

The functions $u(x)$ and $v(y)$ are crucial, inasmuch as they fully determine the intrahousehold inequality. The key feature of matching models is that these functions are *endogenous*. They are determined (or constrained) as part of the equilibrium, and depend on the whole matching game structure; in particular, the allocation within any given couple depends on the entire distribution of characteristics in the two populations. In that sense, the model does provide an endogenous determination of intrahousehold inequality. Note, however, that in this abstract presentation, their exact interpretation is undetermined; depending on the framework, $u(x)$ can be a monetary amount, the consumption of some commodity or the utility generated by the consumption of bundles of private and public commodities. For instance, the simple framework used by Chiappori and Weiss (2007) consider an economy with two commodities, one private and one public within the household, and agents with Cobb–Douglas preferences $u^a = q^a Q$; x and y are one-dimensional and denote male and female income. In this TU framework, any efficient allocation maximizes the *sum* of utilities; that is, a (x, y) couple solves

$$\max_{q^1, q^2, Q} \left(q^1 + q^2\right) Q \quad \text{under} \quad q^1 + q^2 + Q = x + y \tag{16.4}$$

and the surplus $s(x, y)$ is the value of this program, namely $(x + y)^2 / 4$. Here, $u(x)$ and $v(y)$ are utilities, although there exists a one-to-one correspondence between utilities and transfers (because $Q = (x + y)/2$, we have that $q^1 = 2u(x)/(x + y), q^2 = 2v(y)/(x + y)$).

From a mathematical point of view, a basic result states that, if a matching is stable, then the corresponding measure maximizes total surplus over the set of measures whose marginals coincide with μ_X and μ_Y. That is, the measure μ must solve

$$\max_{\mu} \int_{X \times Y} s(x, y) d\mu(x, y) \tag{16.5}$$

under the marginal conditions. This maximization problem is linear in its unknown μ. Therefore, it admits a dual, which can be written as

$$\min_{u, v} \int_{X} u(x) d\mu_X(x) + \int_{Y} v(y) d\mu_Y(y) \tag{16.6}$$

under the constraints

$$u(x) + v(y) \geq s(x, y) \quad \forall (x, y) \tag{16.7}$$

Here, functions u and v are the dual variables of the program. But, crucially, they can be interpreted as describing the utility reached by each individual at optimal matching. In particular, they define the allocation of surplus between (matched) spouses. Note that conditions of the dual program (16.7) are exactly the stability conditions (16.3).

From the standard duality results, a solution to the dual exists if and only if the primal has a solution, and the values are then the same. It follows that the existence of a stable match (that is, of functions u and v satisfying (16.3)) boils down to the existence of a solution to the linear maximization problem (16.5). This allows us to establish existence under very general conditions; see, for instance, Chiappori et al. (2010).

Regarding uniqueness, if the sets X and Y are finite, then the us and vs are not pinned down, although the equilibrium conditions generate constraints. However, with continuous, atomless populations, the functions are in general fully determined by the equilibrium conditions. The intuition is straightforward: in the continuous case, each individual has almost perfect substitutes, and (local) competition determines exactly the surplus sharing that must exist at equilibrium. Finally, stochastic versions of these models can be considered, in which some of the individual characteristics are unobserved (to the econometrician); see, for instance, the recent survey by Chiappori and Salanié (2014).

16.5. IDENTIFICATION

Whereas the conceptual tools just presented help clarify some of the issues involved, their empirical content must be very carefully considered. As stated previously, there is no point in putting much emphasis on a concept that cannot possibly be identified from existing data. This section summarizes the main results obtained on this issue over the last two decades; for a more detailed presentation, the reader is referred to Chiappori and Ekeland (2009a).

We divide the presentation into three subsections. One considers the "pure" identification problem. Assume that the entire demand function of a household can be observed; what can be recovered from such data (and such data only)? Next, we introduce additional identifying assumptions. Broadly speaking, these postulate a relationship between an individual's preferences as a single person and as being part of a household; in other words, we admit that some information about spouses' utilities can be derived from the observation of the behavior of single persons. Lastly, we introduce a general, market-wide perspective and ask whether (and how) equilibrium conditions on the marriage market can help identify the intrahousehold allocation process.

16.5.1 "Pure" Identification in the Collective Model

Identification issues in the collective model have been extensively studied during the recent years; the interested reader is referred to Chiappori and Ekeland (2009a,b) for an exhaustive presentation. In what follows, we briefly summarize some key findings.

We start with the basic framework described above, assuming egotistic preferences of the type $u^a(Q, q^a)$; also, for the sake of brevity, we assume only two persons (spouses) in the household, although the generalization to any number is straightforward. In what follows, we assume that we observe the household's "aggregate" demand, that is, the vector $(q, Q) \in \mathbb{R}^{n+N}$ (where $q_i = \sum_a q_i^a, i=1, \ldots, n$) as a function of prices (p, P) and total income y, plus possibly a vector of distribution factors z. Remember that the *collective indirect utility* of agent a is defined as the utility level a will reach at the end of the decision process, as a function of (p, P, y, z).

16.5.1.1 Main Identification Result

Assume, first, that we observe the demand function of some household. This demand is aggregated at the household level. This means what we observe is the household's total demand for any private commodity, together with its demand for public goods. However, in general, we are not able to observe the internal allocation of the private goods between household members. When is this information sufficient to recover the underlying structure, that is, the preferences and the decision process (as summarized by the Pareto weights)?

A first answer is provided as a result from Chiappori and Ekeland (2009a). It states that generically, all that is needed is one exclusion restriction per agent. In other words, for any agent a, there should be some commodity that a does *not* consume (and which does not enter a's egotistic utility). Then the *local* knowledge of the household demand allows us to exactly (locally) identify each agent's collective indirect utility, irrespective of the number of private and public goods. Formally, this is stated as

Theorem 1

(Chiappori and Ekeland, 2009a) Assume $N + n \geq 4$. Consider a point $(\bar{p}, \bar{P}, \bar{y})$ such that the CSR satisfies the condition

$$\frac{\partial \rho^a}{\partial \gamma}(\bar{p}, \overline{Q}, \bar{\gamma}) \neq 0, \quad a = 1, 2,$$

where $\overline{Q} = Q(\bar{p}, \overline{P}, \bar{\gamma})$. Assume that for each member, there exists at least one good not consumed by this member (but consumed by the other). Then generically there exists an open neighborhood of $(\bar{p}, \overline{P}, \bar{\gamma})$ on which the indirect collective utility of each member is exactly (ordinally) identifiable from household demand. For any cardinalization of indirect collective utilities, the Pareto weights are exactly identifiable.

For a precise proof, see Chiappori and Ekeland (2009a) Proposition 7 on page 781. The underlying intuition is that if commodity i is not consumed by agent γ, then any impact of its price on that agent's behavior can only operate through the decision process—the Pareto weights. The resulting conditions, which are reminiscent of separability restrictions in standard consumer theory, are sufficient in general to fully recover the (ordinal) indirect collective utility of each member, as well as, for any choice of cardinalization, the corresponding Pareto weights.

The specific nature of the identification result can be simply illustrated on a Cobb–Douglas example, as described later on. Before considering it, a few remarks are in order. First, the identification result stated in Theorem 1 is only local. This is important because additional constraints of a global nature (such as nonnegativity restrictions on consumption), which are not considered in this result, typically provide additional identification power; a precise illustration will be given below. Second, the result does not require distribution factors. Again, the latter would allow a stronger identification result. Indeed, Chiappori and Ekeland show that, in the presence of distribution factors, the exclusivity requirement can be relaxed; one only needs either one excluded good (instead of two) or an *assignable* commodity.[13] Third, identification requires the observation of the household demand as a function of prices and income; in particular, price variations are crucial. Although this fact is not surprising (even in standard consumer theory, preferences cannot be recovered from demand without price variations) it has important empirical applications, because data entailing significant (and credibly exogenous) price variations are not easy to find. However, recent approaches relax this requirement by imposing additional structure on the decision process; they will be discussed below.

Fourth, the identification result above is only generic: it may fail to hold in particular cases, although such cases are not robust to "small variations." Quite interestingly, one of the situations in which identification does not obtain is the unitary model. To see why, consider program (P) above, and assume that the Pareto weights μ^a are all constant. For

---

[13] A good is assignable when it is consumed by both members, and the consumption of each member is independently observed.

one thing, we are in a unitary context: the household maximizes the sum $\sum_a \mu^a u^a(Q, q^a)$, which is a *price-* and *income-independent* utility. More importantly, Hicks's aggregation theorem applies. If we define U by

$$U(Q, q) = \overset{\max}{\underset{a}{\sum}} q^a = q \sum_a \mu^a u^a(Q, q^a) \tag{16.8}$$

then the household maximizes U under the budget constraint. By standard integration, U can be recovered from the household demand. However, this is not sufficient to identify individual preferences: there exists a continuum of different sets of individual utilities that generate the same U by (16.8). The paradox here is that the unitary model, which used to be the dominant framework for empirical works on household behavior, belongs to the small (actually nongeneric) class of frameworks for which individual welfare cannot be identified from household demand.

Lastly, it is important to note that what is identified is the *indirect collective utility* of each member. From a welfare perspective, this is the only relevant concept, because it fully characterizes the utility reached by each agent. However, the inequality measures described above require more, namely, an assessment of the intrahousehold allocation of income. We now consider to what extent the latter can be recovered from the indirect collective utility.

16.5.1.2 Private Goods and the Sharing Rule
We start with the case in which all commodities are private. In that case, the various concepts (CSR, GSR, MMWI) coincide with the sharing rule, and the collective indirect utility takes the form

$$V^a(p, y) = v^a(p, \rho^a(p, y)),$$

where, as above, v^a is a's indirect utility and ρ is the sharing rule. If we assume that the first (respectively the second) good is exclusively consumed by the second (first) agent, the collective indirect utility of each agent is identified (as always, up to some increasing transform).

16.5.1.2.1 Local Identification
A first result states that the sharing rule is *not* fully identified from the knowledge of the collective indirect utility, at least locally; identification only obtains up to an additive function of the prices of the nonexclusive goods. Formally, assume that one observes the functions $(q_1, \ldots q_n)$ of (p, y), with $p \in \mathbb{R}^n$ and

$$q_1(p, y) = \chi_1^a(p, \rho(p, y))$$

$$q_2(p, y) = \chi_2^b(p, y - \rho(p, y)) \tag{16.9}$$

$$q_i(p, y) = \chi_i^a(p, \rho(p, y)) + \chi_i^b(p, y - \rho(p, y)), \quad i = 3, \ldots, n,$$

where the functions χ_i^s and ρ are unknown. Then

Proposition 4

(Chiappori and Ekeland, 2009a) Assume $n \geq 3$, and let $\left(\overline{\chi}_1^a, \ldots, \overline{\chi}_n^b, \overline{\rho}\right)$ solve for (16.9). For any other solution $(\chi_1^a, \ldots, \chi_n^b, \rho)$, there exist a $\varphi : \mathbb{R}^{n-2} \to \mathbb{R}$ such that

$$\rho(p, y) = \overline{\rho}(p, y) + \varphi(p_3, \ldots, p_n),$$

$$\chi_i^a(p, \rho) = \overline{\chi}_i^a(p, \rho - \varphi(p_3, \ldots, p_n)), \tag{16.10}$$

$$\chi_j^b(p, \rho) = \overline{\chi}_j^b(p, \rho + \varphi(p_3, \ldots, p_n)).$$

Moreover, overidentifying restrictions are generated.

The basic conclusion is that the sharing rule is identified up to an additive function, which cannot be pinned down unless either all commodities are assignable or individual preferences are known (for instance, from data on singles) or other (global) restrictions are used as described below. To see why, consider the simple case of three private commodities; two of these are exclusive (for members a and b, respectively), whereas the third is consumed by both. Individual consumptions of commodity 3 are not observed, and its price is taken as numeraire. In practice, we observe two demand functions q_1^a and q_2^b that satisfy

$$q_1^a(p_1, p_2, y) = \widetilde{q}^a(p_1, \rho(p_1, p_2, y)) \tag{16.11}$$

$$q_2^b(p_1, p_2, y) = \widetilde{q}^b(p_2, y - \rho(p_1, p_2, y)) \tag{16.12}$$

where $\widetilde{q}^s$ denotes the Marshallian demand by person s. Now, for some constant K, define ρ_K, u_K^a and u_K^b by

$$\rho_K(p_1, p_2, y) = \rho(p_1, p_2, y) + K,$$

$$u_K^a\left(q_1^a, q_3^a\right) = u_K^a\left(q_1^a, q_3^a - K\right),$$

$$u_K^b\left(q_2^b, q_3^b\right) = u_K^b\left(q_2^b, q_3^b + K\right).$$

It is easy to check that the Marshallian demands derived from ρ_K, u_K^a and u_K^b satisfy (16.11) and (16.12). The intuition is illustrated in Figure 16.2 in the case of a. Switching from ρ and u^a to ρ_K and u_K^a does two things. First, the sharing rule and the intercept of the budget constraint are shifted downward by K. Second, all indifference curves are also shifted downward by the same amount. When only demand for commodity 1 (on the horizontal axis) is observable, these models are empirically indistinguishable. Lastly, with several, nonexclusive goods, this construct is still possible, and the constant may in addition vary with nonexclusive prices in an arbitrary way.

Two remarks can be made about this result. One is that the indetermination is not welfare relevant; one can easily check that the different solutions correspond to the same collective indirect utilities for each agent. This is the paradox evoked in introduction. Unlike standard consumer theory, there is no longer an equivalence between identifying direct and indirect utilities. Indirect utilities are identified as soon as the exclusion restrictions are satisfied, but they may correspond to various, welfare-equivalent direct utilities, each of them associated with a specific sharing rule.

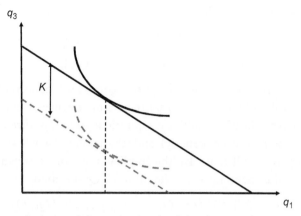

Figure 16.2 Welfare equivalence of alternative levels of the sharing rule.

16.5.1.2.2 Global Restrictions

The second remark is that the nonidentification result is only local. In particular, it disregards additional, global restrictions such as nonnegativity constraints. If these are added, then more can be identified. For instance, consider (16.10), and add the restrictions that

$$\rho(p, 0) = 0 \quad \forall p,$$

which stems from nonnegativity of consumption at very low income levels. Then φ is exactly pinned down:

$$\varphi(p_3, \ldots, p_n) = -\overline{\rho}(p, 0)$$

and additional, overidentifying restrictions are generated (e.g., $\partial \overline{\rho}(p, 0)/\partial p_i = 0$ for $i = 1, 2$).

    This result should be related to recent work on the estimation of the sharing rules based on a revealed preference approach (see, for instance, Cherchye et al., 2012). Because the revealed preference approach is global by nature, it can generate bounds on the sharing rule, which can actually be quite narrow. In all cases, the global restrictions are generated at one end of the distribution of expenditures, so their use for identifying the sharing rule outside this range should be submitted to the usual caution. Still, they tend to considerably reduce the scope of the nonidentification conclusion.

16.5.1.3 Public Goods Only

We now consider the opposite polar case, in which all commodities (but the exclusive ones) are public. That is, utilities are now of the form

$$U^a(Q_1, Q_3, \ldots, Q_N) \quad \text{and} \quad U^b(Q_2, Q_3, \ldots, Q_N).$$

Note that the exclusive commodities 1 and 2 can be considered as either public or private.

In that case, the collective indirect utility has a simple form, namely,

$$V^a(P, y) = U^a(Q_1, Q_3, \ldots, Q_N),$$

$$V^b(P, y) = U^b(Q_2, Q_3, \ldots, Q_N).$$

The crucial remark is that the demands for public goods (as functions of prices and total income) are empirically observed. An important consequence is that, in general, the knowledge of indirect collective utilities is equivalent to that of direct utilities. To see why, normalize y to be 1 (by homogeneity), and take a point at which the Jacobian matrix $D_P(Q_1, Q_2, \ldots, Q_N)$ is of full rank. By the implicit function theorem, we can locally invert the function, thus defining P as a function of Q; but then,

$$U^a(Q_1, Q_3, \ldots, Q_N) = V^a(P_1(Q_1, Q_2, \ldots, Q_N), \ldots, P_N(Q_1, Q_2, \ldots, Q_N), 1),$$

$$U^b(Q_2, Q_3, \ldots, Q_N) = V^b(P_1(Q_1, Q_2, \ldots, Q_N), \ldots, P_N(Q_1, Q_2, \ldots, Q_N), 1),$$

which proves identification. In addition, overidentifying restrictions are generated. In particular, we see that in this context Lindahl prices for all goods (therefore the MMWIs) are exactly identified. Somewhat paradoxically, the pure public good case appears to be the one in which identification is least problematic.

16.5.1.4 The General Case

Finally, the general case is a direct generalization of the two particular cases just described. The aforementioned exclusion restrictions guarantee identification of the collective indirect utility of each agent. Then the exact intrahousehold allocation is locally identified up to an additive function of the prices of the nonexclusive private goods. Moreover, global restrictions (e.g., nonnegativity) allow exact identification in general. The interested reader is referred to Chiappori and Ekeland (2009a,b) for detailed statements.

16.5.1.5 A Linear Expenditure System Example

The previous discussions can be illustrated on a simple example, borrowed from Chiappori and Ekeland (2009a). Consider individual preferences of the LES type:

$$U^s(q^s, Q) = \sum_{i=1}^{n} \alpha_i^s \log \left(q_i^s - c_i^s \right) + \sum_{j=n+1}^{N} \alpha_j^s \log \left(Q_j - C_j \right), \quad s = a, b,$$

where the parameters α_i^s are normalized by the condition $\sum_{i=1}^{N} \alpha_i^s = 1$ for all s, whereas the parameters c_i^s and C_j are unconstrained. Here, commodities 1 to n are private, whereas commodities $n+1$ to N are public. Also, given the LES form, it is convenient to assume that the household maximizes the weighted sum $\mu U^a + (1 - \mu)U^b$, where the Pareto weight μ has the simple, linear form:

$$\mu = \mu^0 + \mu^y y + \mu^z z, \quad s = a, b.$$

16.5.1.5.1 Household Demand

The couple solve the program

$$\max \left(\mu^0 + \mu^y y + \mu^z z\right) \left(\sum_{i=1}^{n} \alpha_i^a \log \left(q_i^a - c_i^a\right) + \sum_{j=n+1}^{N} \alpha_j^a \log \left(Q_j - C_j\right) \right)$$
$$+ \left(1 - \left(\mu^0 + \mu^y y + \mu^z z\right)\right) \left(\sum_{i=1}^{n} \alpha_i^b \log \left(q_i^b - c_i^b\right) + \sum_{j=n+1}^{N} \alpha_j^b \log \left(Q_j - C_j\right) \right)$$

under the budget constraint. Individual demands for private goods are given by

$$p_i q_i^a = p_i c_i^a + \alpha_i^a \left(\mu^0 + \mu^y y + \mu^z z\right) \left(y - \sum_{i,s} p_i c_i^s - \sum_j P_j C_j \right)$$

$$p_i q_i^b = p_i c_i^b + \alpha_i^b \left[1 - \left(\mu^0 + \mu^y y + \mu^z z\right)\right] \left(y - \sum_{i,s} p_i c_i^s - \sum_j P_j C_j 0 \right)$$

generating the aggregate demand

$$p_i q_i = p_i c_i + \left[\alpha_i^a \left(\mu^0 + \mu^y y + \mu^z z\right) + \alpha_i^b \left(1 - \left(\mu^0 + \mu^y y + \mu^z z\right)\right)\right] Y \qquad (16.13)$$

and for public goods

$$P_j Q_j = P_j C_j + \left[\alpha_j^a \left(\mu^0 + \mu^y y + \mu^z z\right) + \alpha_j^b \left(1 - \left(\mu^0 + \mu^y y + \mu^z z\right)\right)\right] Y,$$

where $c_i = c_i^a + c_i^b$ and $Y = (y - \sum_{i,s} p_i c_i^s - \sum_j P_j C_j)$. The household demand is thus a direct generalization of the standard LES, with additional quadratic terms in y^2 and cross terms in $y p_i$ and $y P_j$, plus terms involving the distribution factor z.

A first remark is that c_i^a and c_i^b cannot be individually identified from group demand, because the latter only involves their sum c_i. As a consequence, the various generalizations of the sharing rule will only be identified up to one additive constant, a result mentioned earlier. Also, the constant is welfare irrelevant; indeed, the collective indirect utilities of the wife and the husband are (up to an increasing transform)

$$W^a(p, P, y, z) = \log Y + \log \left(\mu^0 + \mu^y y + \mu^z z\right)$$
$$- \sum_i \alpha_i^a \log p_i - \sum_j \alpha_j^a \log P_j$$

$$W^b(p, P, y, z) = \log Y + \log \left(1 - \left(\mu^0 + \mu^y y + \mu^z z\right)\right)$$
$$- \sum_i \alpha_i^b \log p_i - \sum_j \alpha_j^b \log P_j$$

which does not depend on each c_i^s separately. Second, the form of aggregate demands is such that private and public goods have exactly the same structure. We, therefore, simplify our notations by defining

$$\xi_i = q_i \text{ for } i \leq n, \xi_i = Q_i \text{ for } n < i \leq N$$

and similarly

$$\gamma_i = c_i \text{ for } i \leq n, \gamma_i = C_i \text{ for } n < i \leq N,$$

$$\pi_i = p_i \text{ for } i \leq n, \pi_i = P_i \text{ for } n < i \leq N,$$

so that the group demand has the simple form

$$\pi_i \xi_i = \pi_i \gamma_i + \left[\alpha_i^a \left(\mu^0 + \mu^y y + \mu^z z \right) + \alpha_i^b \left(1 - \left(\mu^0 + \mu^y y + \mu^z z \right) \right) \right] Y \tag{16.14}$$

leading to collective indirect utilities of the form

$$W^a(p, P, y, z) = \log Y + \log \left(\mu^0 + \mu^y y + \mu^z z \right) - \sum_i \alpha_i^a \log \pi_i,$$

$$W^b(p, P, y, z) = \log Y + \log \left(1 - \left(\mu^0 + \mu^y y + \mu^z z \right) \right) - \sum_i \alpha_i^b \log \pi_i.$$

It is clear on this form that the distinction between private and public goods can be ignored. This illustrates an important remark: while the ex ante knowledge of the public versus the private nature of each good is necessary for the identifiability result to hold in general, for many parametric forms it is actually not needed.

16.5.1.5.2 Identifiability: The General Case

The question now is whether the empirical estimation of the form (16.14) allows us to recover the relevant parameters, namely, the α_i^s, the γ^i, and the μ^α. We start by rewriting (16.14) as

$$\pi_i \xi_i = \pi_i \gamma_i + \left(\begin{array}{c} \alpha_i^b + \left(\alpha_i^a - \alpha_i^b \right) \mu^0 \\ + \left(\alpha_i^a - \alpha_i^b \right) \left(\mu^y y + \mu^z z \right) \end{array} \right) \left(y - \sum_m \pi_m \gamma^m \right) \tag{16.15}$$

The right-hand side of (16.15) can in principle be econometrically identified; we can thus recover the coefficients of the right hand side variables, i.e., y, y^2, yz, the π_m, and the products $y\pi_m$ and $z\pi_m$. For any i and any $m \neq i$, the ratio of the coefficient of y by that of π_m gives γ^m; the γ^m are therefore vastly overidentified. However, the remaining coefficients are identifiable only up to an arbitrary choice of two of them. Indeed, an empirical estimation of the right-hand side of (16.15) can only recover for each j the respective coefficients of y, y^2, and yz, that is the three expressions

$$K_y^j = \alpha_j^b + \left(\alpha_j^a - \alpha_j^b \right) \mu^0$$

$$K_{yy}^j = \left(\alpha_j^a - \alpha_j^b \right) \mu^y$$

$$K_{yz}^j = \left(\alpha_j^a - \alpha_j^b \right) \mu^z \tag{16.16}$$

Now, pick up two arbitrary values for μ^0 and μ^y, with $\mu^y \neq 0$. The last two expressions give $(\alpha_j^a - \alpha_j^b)$ and μ^z; the first gives α_j^b therefore α_j^a.

As expected, a continuum of different models generate the same aggregate demand. Moreover, these differences are welfare relevant, in the sense that the individual welfare gains of a given reform (say, a change in prices and incomes) will be evaluated differently by different models. In practice, the collective indirect utilities recovered above are not invariant across the various structural models compatible with a given aggregate demand.

A unitary version of the model obtains when the Pareto weights are constant: $\mu^y = \mu^z = 0$. Then $K_{yz}^j = 0$ for all j (because distribution factors cannot matter), and $K_{yy}^j = 0$ for all j (demand must be linear in y, as a quadratic term would violate Slutsky). We are left with $K_y^j = \alpha_j^b + (\alpha_j^a - \alpha_j^b)\mu^0$, and it is obviously impossible to identify independently α_j^a, α_j^b, and μ^0; as expected, the unitary framework is not identifiable.

16.5.1.5.3 Identification Under Exclusion

We now show that in the nonunitary version of the collective framework, an exclusion assumption per member is sufficient to exactly recover all of the (welfare-relevant) coefficients. Assume that member a does not consume commodity 1, and member b does not consume commodity 2; that is, $\alpha_1^a = \alpha_2^b = 0$. Then equations (16.15) give

$$\alpha_1^b(1 - \mu^0) = K_y^1, \quad -\alpha_1^b\mu^y = K_{yy}^1, \quad -\alpha_1^b\mu^z = K_{yz}^1$$

and

$$\alpha_2^a\mu^0 = K_y^2, \quad \alpha_2^a\mu^y = K_{yy}^2, \quad \alpha_2^a\mu^z = K_{yz}^2.$$

Combining the first two equations of each block and assuming $\mu^y \neq 0$, we get

$$\frac{1 - \mu^0}{\mu^y} = -\frac{K_y^1}{K_{yy}^1} \quad \text{and} \quad \frac{\mu^0}{\mu^y} = \frac{K_y^2}{K_{yy}^2};$$

therefore, assuming $K_y^2 K_{yy}^1 - K_y^1 K_{yy}^2 \neq 0$,

$$\frac{1 - \mu^0}{\mu^0} = -\frac{K_y^1 K_{yy}^2}{K_y^2 K_{yy}^1} \quad \text{and} \quad \mu^0 = \frac{K_y^2 K_{yy}^1}{K_y^2 K_{yy}^1 - K_y^1 K_{yy}^2}$$

It follows that

$$\mu^y = \frac{K_{yy}^2}{K_y^2}\mu^0 = \frac{K_{yy}^2 K_{yy}^1}{K_y^2 K_{yy}^1 - K_y^1 K_{yy}^2}$$

and all other coefficients can be computed as above. It follows that the collective indirect utility of each member can be exactly recovered, which allows for unambiguous welfare statements. As mentioned above, identifiability is only generic in the sense that it requires $K_y^2 K_{yy}^1 - K_y^1 K_{yy}^2 \neq 0$. Clearly, the set of parameters values violating this condition is of zero measure. Also, identifiability requires $\mu^y \neq 0$; in particular, *it does not hold true* in the unitary version, in which $\mu^y = \mu^z = 0$. Indeed, the same exclusion restrictions property as above only allow us to recover $\alpha_1^b(1 - \mu^0) = K_y^1$ and $\alpha_2^a \mu^0 = K_y^2$; this is not sufficient to identify μ^0, let alone the α_j^i for $j \geq 3$. This confirms that the unitary version of the model is not identified even under the exclusivity assumptions that guarantee generic identifiability in the general version.

Finally, one can readily check the previous claim that the MMWIs are not identified. Indeed, the MMWI m^s of s is defined by

$$v^s(\pi, m^s) = \log\left(m^s - \sum_k \pi_k \gamma_k^s\right) - \sum_i \alpha_i^s \log \pi_i = W^s(\pi, y, z),$$

where

$$v^s(\pi, P, y) = \log\left(y - \sum_k \pi_k \gamma_k^s\right) - \sum_{i=1}^n \alpha_i^s \log \pi_i$$

and

$$W^s(\pi, z) = \log\left(y - \sum_{i,k} \pi_i \gamma_i^k\right) + \log\left(\mu^0 + \mu^y y + \mu^z z\right) - \sum_i \alpha_i^s \log \pi_i.$$

This gives

$$m^s(\pi, y, z) = \left(\mu^0 + \mu^y y + \mu^z z\right)\left(y - \sum_i \pi_i\left(\sum_k \gamma_i^k\right)\right) + \sum_i \pi_i \gamma_i^s.$$

For any private commodity i, the sums $\sum_k \gamma_i^k$ are identified, but the individual γ_i^s are not; therefore, m^s is identified up to an additive function of the prices of private, nonexclusive goods.

16.5.2 Comparing Different Family Sizes

A second approach enlarges the set of usable information by allowing comparisons between families of different compositions. A first idea is to assume some relationship between individual preferences when married and single. In that sense, the "pure" approach just described relies on an extreme version. This is because it does not postulate *any* link between utilities when married and single; hence, knowledge of an individual's preferences when single brings no information about her tastes within the household. At the other extreme, some models assume that preferences are unaffected by marital status, at least ordinally. This means that if $u_S^a(Q, q^a)$ denotes a's utility when single, then her utility when married takes the form

$$u^a(Q, q^a) = F\left(u_S^a(Q, q^a)\right),$$

where F is an increasing transform. Thus, marriage can directly affect a person's utility level, but not the person's marginal rates of substitution between various commodities. Note that if we assume preferences are unaffected by marital status, then the MMWI defined above has a natural interpretation; namely, it is the level of income that would be needed by the individual, *if single*, to reach the same utility level as what she currently gets within marriage. It must however be stressed that the assumption of constant preferences across marital status is not needed for the *definition* of the index, but only for this particular interpretation.

Various, intermediate approaches can be found in the literature. One, mostly used in a labor supply context, only assumes that some preference parameters are common to singles and households, and can therefore be estimated separately on a sample of singles. In general, this is sufficient to identify (or calibrate) the remaining parameters (relevant for marriage-specific preferences and the Pareto weights) on observed labor supplies of men and women in a sample of couples. This approach has been adopted in a series of papers recently published in the *Review of Economics of the Household* (Bargain et al., 2006; Beninger et al., 2006; Myck et al., 2006; Vermeulen et al., 2006). For instance, consider a model of labor supply in a couple in which the utility of agent a takes the form

$$u^a\left(q^a, L^a, L^b\right) = \alpha^a \ln\left(q^a - \overline{q}^a\right) + \beta^a \ln\left(L^a - \overline{L}^a\right) + \gamma^a \ln\left(L^a - \overline{L}^a\right) \ln\left(L^b - \overline{L}^b\right),$$

where L denotes leisure; note that this form is more general than the ones considered above, because it allows for (positive) externalities of leisure within the couple.[14] The α and β parameters are assumed to be independent of marital status and are therefore identified from a sample of singles; the γs and the Pareto weights are then calibrated from data on households.

An intermediate approach, that relies on the notion of domestic production, has recently been proposed by Browning et al. (2013). It posits that agents, when they get married, keep the same preferences but can access a different (and generally more productive) technology. That is, while the basic rates of substitution between *consumed* commodities remains unaffected by marriage (or cohabitation), the relationship between purchases and consumptions is not; therefore, the structure of demand, including for exclusive commodities (consumed only by one member) is different from what it would be for singles. More generally, one can, following Dunbar et al. (2013), only assume that preferences are unaffected by family composition (e.g., that parents' preferences regarding their own consumption does not depend on the number of children). These approaches are described in the next section.

---

[14] Equivalently, this approach considers both leisures as public goods within the household.

16.5.3 Identifying from Market Equilibrium

Lastly, a series of recent contributions are aimed at taking to data the aforementioned equilibrium approaches. The basic, theoretical intuition is quite straightforward: the equilibrium conditions on the marriage market (with or without search frictions, but with intrahousehold transfers) either constrain or exactly pin down intrahousehold allocations. Several papers propose an empirical implementation of this idea. A first set of works only consider matching patterns; the marriage market equilibrium is then exclusively characterized by a matrix of intermarriages between various categories, which can be defined by age, education, income, or any combination of these. On the matching front, following the initial contribution by Choo and Siow (2006), Chiappori et al. (2011) have shown how a structural, parametric model can be (over)identified from such patterns, under the assumption that, while the surplus generated by marriage may (and does) vary over time, its supermodularity (which drives the extent of assortative matching in the population) is constant.[15] According to their estimate, while the gains from marriage have globally decreased over the last decades, the decline has been much smaller for educated couples. Moreover, the share of household resources received has increased for college-educated wives, resulting in a strong increase in their "marital college premium" (defined as the additional gain provided by a university education on the marriage market). This is compatible with the theoretical analysis of Chiappori et al. (2009), who argued that the asymmetry between male and female marital college premiums could explain (at least in part) the higher demand for university training by women. Alternatively, Jacquemet and Robin (2011) and Goussé (2013) analyze marital patterns from a search perspective.

A clear limitation of these approaches is that the sole observation of marital patterns conveys only limited information on the form of the marital surplus (therefore on distribution). For instance, knowing that matching is assortative tells us only that the surplus is supermodular. The previous approaches, therefore, must rely on strong and largely untestable assumptions on the precise form of the heterogeneity distribution across couples. Adding information on the total surplus would greatly enhance the identification power of these models. But such information is precisely what collective models can provide based on observed behavior. The intuition, here, is that the observation of, say, labor supply patterns of married couples (which reflects intrahousehold transfers), together with that of marital patterns, should allow us to fully identify a general matching model in a very robust way. This line of research is pursued, in a series of paper, by Chiappori et al. (2014).

---

[15] For a general presentation of the econometrics of matching models, see the survey by Chiappori and Salanié (2014).

16.6. EMPIRICAL FINDINGS

In this section we review some empirical work based on the collective model and emphasizing the identification of the sharing rule.

The first-generation models used information on private and assignable goods such as consumption of clothing or individual leisure to identify the sharing rule up to a constant. These models adopt mainly two approaches for identification. The first approach refers to what we called "pure" identification, that is it recovers the derivatives of the sharing rule with no further information than observed consumption bundles of the household. As discussed above, while some identifying conditions can be relaxed by using distribution factors, these models cannot identify separately the level of sharing (how much goes to each household member) from preferences. There exists a continuum of allocations of resources, each associated to a utility function for each household member, that fit the data equally well; across these allocations, income inequality within the household is different, although the allocation of welfare to each member remains the same.

To identify the way overall resources are allocated and thus measure inequality, one needs more information, either in terms of identifying assumptions on the behavior of the sharing rule (such as nonnegativity conditions discussed earlier) or assumptions on preferences. One possibility is to compare the behavior of married and single individuals by making assumptions about the way preferences change with marriage. Other approaches involve specific restrictions on preferences. We show how some of these approaches have been used in the literature. Finally, we also consider the information content of revealed preference restrictions. These extend the revealed preference arguments for individual choice to the case of collective households. Clearly this is a much more complicated setup than standard revealed preference restrictions for individuals or for unitary households because the aggregate household does not necessarily behave like a rational single agent. We discuss what can be learned from revealed preference in this context.

However, the issue of identification of the sharing rule is deeper than what is suggested by the use of the restrictions above and has to do with the way people make agreements at the point of marriage and the level of commitment associated with these agreements. In other words, fundamentally the sharing rule is identified from behavior without having to impose possibly *ad hoc* restrictions. Identification requires extending the model to include marital decisions in an equilibrium context. Indeed a marriage market equilibrium will define the sharing rule, and conditions in the marriage market can allow us to identify it. This effectively introduces dynamics, which then allows one to delve deeper into the extent of commitment and what this means about within-household inequality. Characterizing the theoretical and empirical power of using marriage-market data to better understand intrahousehold allocations is a relatively new and active area of research, particularly when limited commitment is allowed for.

Before we discuss the empirical literature we need to introduce a distinction between the concept of identifiably of preferences and the sharing rule on the one hand and econometric identification on the other. The identifiability results discussed earlier in the chapter relate to our ability to recover individual preferences and the sharing rule given *we know* the household level demand functions exactly. Empirical analysis is concerned with estimating these household demands from empirical data to be able to then recover the sharing rule. This issue brings forth all the standard econometric concerns, such as the role of unobserved heterogeneity, the endogeneity of wages, prices and income, corner solutions (particularly in labor supply), and the like. One of the hardest issues concerns the way that unobserved heterogeneity enters household demands, particularly if such unobservables are correlated with observables. The specific issue arises from the fact that, in general, unobserved heterogeneity in preferences will imply unobservables in the sharing rule. In most specifications this will mean that unobservables are not separable from observables, which has implications for econometric identification. For example, Blundell et al. (2007) used linearity to bypass the difficulties implied by unobserved heterogeneity in preferences. Here we are not offering any general solution to the problem, but we need to point out that, before we even consider identification of the sharing rule, an empirical approach would have to solve the standard econometric identification issues, which in this context may be severe.[16]

16.6.1 "Pure" Identification of the Sharing Rule

In this first generation of collective models we can point to three main empirical studies. The first is by Browning et al. (1994); the second is by Chiappori et al. (2002); and the third is by Blundell et al. (2007). All three share a similar approach to identification: they assume efficiency and an assignable good. However, the details of the empirical approach differ.

In Browning et al. (1994), the authors use a sample of couples drawn from the Canadian FAMEX and estimate a model for the demand of men's and women's clothing, and identify the sharing rule, up to a constant. Identification relies on two assumptions: first, clothing is an assignable good, which effectively means that we can observe male and female clothing and that only the person using the clothing derives any utility from it. In other words, clothing does not include a public good element. Second, they assume that the distribution of a partner's income does not affect preferences, but they may enter the sharing rule, reflecting bargaining positions. Given these assumptions, they identify a sharing rule as a function of the age difference of the partners, total household expenditure (thus allowing wealth effects in the way resources are shared), and most importantly, the share of income attributable to the female partner. It turns out that the way resources are distributed between couples is not very sensitive to the proportion of income for which they are accountable. For example, going from a share of income of 25–75% raises

---

[16] For recent attempts in this direction (including a discussion of the specific difficulties it raises), see for instance Lewbel and Pendakur (2013) and Chiappori and Kim (2013).

the share of household expenditure by a significant but small 2.3%. The age difference and the level of expenditure also matter with relatively older individuals gaining more and wealthier households allocating more to the wife.

The Browning et al. (1994) paper shows the potential of the approach and the richness of the empirical results that can be obtained by judicious use of information reflecting bargaining power of households. However, the main determinant of female bargaining power in their model is the relative magnitude of female income. A higher share of income may reflect her relative skills or, alternatively, it may reflect her decision to forgo leisure and work more; in other words, this distribution factor is indeed endogenous. In principle, this fact does not harm identification provided that labor supply is separable from consumption: Controlling for total expenditures, individual consumption should then be independent of labor supply (therefore of labor income). However, separability is a strong assumption, that has been empirically criticized. The next two papers address exactly this issue by endogenizing labor supply.

The empirical relevance of the discussion above for within-household inequality and allocation of resources is illustrated by Chiappori et al. (2002). They use data from the PSID to estimate a collective labor supply model, where the sharing rule is identified (up to a constant) based on distribution factors. These include the sex ratio (males/females) in the state as measured by the 1990 census as well as by dummy variables indicating the nature of divorce laws.[17] Measuring the sex ratio is, of course, very tricky, both because we need to define the relevant marriage market and because timing may matter. In a full commitment model, for example, the sex ratio at the time of marriage is what is going to matter. However, the sex ratio is unlikely to change vastly over time, and it is probably a good idea to define marriage markets quite broadly rather than too narrowly. The authors also report using the county-level sex ratio with the state level as an instrument, which had little impact on their results. In their model, labor supply is evaluated over one whole year and they consider a sample where both are working. So the relevant group are individuals with sufficient attachment to the labor market to want to work at least some part of the year. In their model, the sharing rule is allowed to be a function of the wages of both partners, nonlabor income, and the distribution factors. Allowing both wages to enter is important: It has been empirically observed that both wages matter when estimating family labor supply (see, e.g., Blundell and Walker, 1986) a fact that in a unitary context has been interpreted as nonseparability in household preferences between male and female leisure. Here this nonseparability is interpreted as being driven by the impact of the sharing rule on individual labor supply in a collective setting. The

---

[17] The intuition underlying the CFL paper—that a relative scarcity of women and/or more favorable divorce laws should improve the wife's Pareto weight—can be supported by an explicit matching model, with some nuances (e.g., changes in divorce laws affect differently women already married and women getting married after the change in law). On these issues, see Chiappori et al. (2013).

fact that the restrictions from the collective model are not rejected strengthens this interpretation.

The results suggest that marriage and labor market conditions can lead to large differences in the allocation of household resources within a couple. For example, a $1 increase in the female hourly wage rate leads to a transfer at the means of $1600 to the husband, implying that most of the extra income goes to him. However, a $1 increase in his hourly wage rate leads only to $600 transfer to her, implying he keeps the lion's share and does not behave as altruistically (to use the authors' words) as she does. The wage effects are of particular interest because changes in wages and in male–female wage differentials may be a key driver of within-household allocation of resources. Unfortunately, these results are not precisely estimated; we revisit this issue below in our discussion of Blundell et al. (2007) and of Lise and Seitz (2011). Anyhow, a result that stands out in Chiappori et al. (2002) is the impact of the sex ratio. Based on this result, an increase of one percentage point in the sex ratio leads to $2160 transfer to the wife. Noting that the range of the sex ratio in their data is 0.46–0.57, the implication is that from the least favorable to the most favorable marriage market, the transfer can differ by as much as $23,000. Of course, this does not all translate into an increase in consumption because the income effect on labor supply will imply a change in the amount of hours worked, with women who live in marriage markets more favorable for them working less. To obtain a summary of divorce laws, the authors constructed an index ranging from 1 to 4 and indicating the extent to which the divorce laws are favorable to women. Here the effects are particularly strong as well. A one-point increase in the index leads to a transfer of $4310 to the wife, which again is shared between consumption and leisure.

These results are important because they show the extent to which within-household allocation of resources can be sensitive to external conditions affecting the bargaining power of the members of the couple. Noting, for example, that average household income in this data is $48,000, the change that can be induced just because of (admittedly extreme) changes in the sex ratio can amount to almost half of household income.

However, there are a number of empirical issues that were not addressed by the papers already discussed. First, we need to be concerned that the allocation of women across states with different sex ratios is not random with respect to their unobserved preferences for labor supply. This can bias the results if women who live in areas abundant with men tend to have lower labor market attachment. Second, we need to address the issue of precision in the estimation of wage effects, an issue that persists in the Blundell et al. (2007) paper we will discuss below. CLF instrument wages, but the instruments are necessarily quite weak: they rely on a polynomial in age and education as an instrument while (correctly) controlling linearly for education and age in the labor supply function. This leaves higher-order nonlinearity in the profile of wages with respect to age and education to act as excluded instruments that is both difficult to justify theoretically and, at the same time, is not very informative. To solve these empirical issues we will require exogenous events that change wages and the marriage market, something that a newer generation of collective models is now addressing, such as the paper by Attanasio and Lechene (2014) who use experimental variation in female income induced by the Conditional Cash Transfer (PROGRESA) experiment in Mexico to obtain exogenous variation in the relative bargaining position of males and females.

Beyond these difficulties there is one further important issue that the papers we discussed fail to address, namely nonparticipation of women. Given that many women do not work allowing for this possibility and understanding how resources are allocated despite the fact she is not producing in the formal market is a key concern. The Blundell et al. (2007) paper addresses the question of identification and estimation of a collective labor supply model that allows for male and female non participation in the labour market. In addition, it considers the case where the male labor supply decision is discrete (work or not). This restriction is imposed to accommodate the fact that in the United Kingdom (where the data is drawn from) the male hours of work distribution seem discontinuous between 0 and about 35 h per week, with the entire mass of workers concentrated in the full time range. This restriction is not entirely satisfactory, but it may do better justice to the data than assuming hours of work are freely chosen. Thus, the resulting model is one where females make choices both on the intensive and the extensive margin, whereas males choose only on the extensive margin. The authors prove identification of the sharing rule; however, this is only identified (nonparametrically) if at least one of the two household members work. Parametric restrictions provide the rest. In the empirical implementation Blundell et al. (2007) deal with the endogeneity of the wage rate by exploiting the changes in wage inequality across cohorts and education groups. Econometric identification relies on the assumption that whereas the structure of wages changed across education groups and cohorts—a testable assumption—preferences remained unchanged. This implies that changes in work behavior across cohorts and education groups can be attributed to changes in the incentive structure, which is the identification strategy employed by Blundell et al. (1998).

The empirical analysis is conducted on a sample of married couples, observed between 1978 and 2001 in the UK Family Expenditure Survey. The assumptions imposed for identification (over and above efficiency) required only private goods and one assignable good. The assignable good is leisure. Because expenditures on children are not separately observable in the data, and because these are effectively public, the authors exclude all couples with children and then assume that the observed aggregate household consumption reflects the sum of private consumption of each of the two members of the household.

The model implies two different sharing rules depending on whether the husband works or not. They differ by a monotonic transformation, which in their empirical specification acts as an attenuation factor, implying that the husband only gets a fraction of transfers when he is not working. This fraction is 0.71, implying that the derivatives of the sharing rule (as well as the level) are attenuated by that amount when he is not working. Their empirical approach does not use any distribution factors that can be excluded from preferences: the sharing rule depends on male wages, female wages, and unearned income as well as education and age. It turns out that empirically the effect of the female wage on the sharing rule is not well identified. However, the effect of the male wage is precisely estimated. It implies that 88% of an increase in male-market earnings translates into a transfer to the husband if he is working. Inasmuch as there is no intensive margin for the male decision, this translates to a direct impact on his consumption, if he continues to work. If he does not work, the same change in potential earnings translates to a transfer equal to 62% of the potential increase (0.71×0.88). These results imply that when the earnings of a working husband increase, the resulting increase in the consumption of the wife is only small; if potential earnings increase (and he is not working) her consumption declines substantially and he enjoys more of the household resources. Finally, the wife keeps 73% of increases in unearned income. Nevertheless, unearned income is a relatively low fraction of household income.

These results again illustrate that external factors (here the relative wages) can influence the allocation of resources substantially. Unfortunately Blundell et al. (2007) do not provide precise estimates of the effects of female wages, and this hinders an understanding of how the change in the wage structure affected within household allocations. The source of lack of precision is the relatively small sample size where the man does not work. Moreover, allowing both wages and nonlabor income to be endogenous, while important for obtaining consistent estimates that make sense, does affect precision substantially. The paper does demonstrate that one does not need (in principle) distribution factors for identification. However, looking at the empirical problem from the perspective of Chiappori et al. (2002), other environmental factors may be very important in determining allocations and, if they are omitted, they could bias the results. On the other hand, if included they can be allowed to affect preferences as well. Identification does not require they affect the sharing rule alone.

This first generation of models showed the potential of the collective model for identifying allocations of resources within the black box of the household. However there are key issues that had not been dealt with. First, taxes and welfare were ignored. At one level this is an empirical specification issue because ignoring taxes can bias the estimates of the preference parameters. But at a more fundamental level by not taking into account the tax and welfare system we omit one of the most important factors affecting (and sometimes designed to affect) within household allocations. Estimating models that allow for taxes and welfare can then explain how changes in the policy and the market environment can affect the allocation of resources.

The next fundamental issue is that the models described above can only identify the derivatives of the sharing rule, that is, how sharing changes when distribution factors, prices, and unearned income change. This precludes any discussion of the levels of inequality of resources and hence does not allow us to put into perspective the implication of changes that occur over time.

Adding taxes and welfare does not pose any important conceptual problems. In practice it involves allowing for more complex budget sets and solving the model to take into account nonlinear budget sets. An interesting issue is that the welfare and tax system may create a further interdependence in the decisions of husband and wife, over and above that induced by the sharing rule. These issues are considered, for instance, in Donni (2003), who uses a "pure" identification strategy of the type just described, and by Beninger et al. (2006), Myck et al. (2006), and Vermeulen et al. (2006) who use information from singles and couples.

Extending the model to allow identification of the level of the sharing rule does, however, pose conceptual problems. Fundamentally, the sharing rule is identified by the equilibrium in the marriage market. However, barring the use of a complete marriage market equilibrium model one can obtain information on the level of inequality with alternative auxiliary assumptions. One possibility is to use information on singles. This involves restricting the way preferences change with marriage. This is an approach used by Lise and Seitz in an early version of their paper. Another possibility is to assume something about the sharing rule at one point of the wage space, for example, that all resources are shared equally when wages are equal, which is the assumption made in the published version of Lise and Seitz (2011). Finally, one can make assumptions about the functional forms of demand, as in Dunbar et al. (2013). We now look into these empirical studies.

16.6.2 Intrahousehold Inequality Over Time and the Sharing Rule: Lise and Seitz (2011)

Lise and Seitz (2011) use the collective model to first estimate overall consumption inequality (at the individual level) and to then decompose this to between household and within household. The important economic fact is that the distribution of wages in the United Kingdom changed dramatically over the period they consider (1968–2001) both within and between education groups (see Gosling et al., 2000). Moreover, the structure of the marriage market has also changed with increased degrees of marital sorting over time. They thus set up a model of male and female labor supply with many (but discrete) choices of hours worked for both members of the household. Hours can take values from 0 to 65 in 5-h intervals. In many ways their empirical framework is similar to that of Blundell et al. (2007): They use couples with no children drawn from the UK Family Expenditure Survey over many years. However, they depart in a number of important ways. First, they allow for taxes and account for the impact of joint taxation over the period that this was in effect in the UK (up to 1989). Also they allow for a richer choice set for the male and they impose further structure so as to identify the level of the sharing rule as well as its derivatives. Finally they account for public goods when they define consumption, although they are taken as separable from private consumption and leisure.

Whereas the logic underlying the identification of the derivatives of the sharing rule is similar to that of Blundell et al. (2007), identification of the location (level) of the sharing rule empirically is based on the identifying assumption that when individuals have the same potential earnings they share resources equally. In earlier versions of the paper it was instead assumed that preferences of married and single individuals are identical; both these assumptions can identify the model. The point at which one pins down the sharing rule is welfare irrelevant, because the preference specification adapts to leave welfare unchanged when the location of sharing is fixed. In principle, just normalizing the location parameter will not cause any bias but will, of course, lead to a specific level of inequality. On the other hand, using information from singles has the advantage that it uses a restriction grounded in some explicit assumption on preferences (marriage does not affect marginal utilities) but, if wrong, will bias all results.

Over the period considered in the paper (1968–2001), earnings inequality increased rapidly. There has been a steady increase in both the potential earnings' and actual earnings' share of women relative to men and a decline in male employment while female employment increased at the start of the period later remaining constant. Consumption inequality increased rapidly in the period between 1980 and 1990, but was basically stable the rest of the time. When Lise and Seitz interpret these results under the prism of their collective model, they uncover some interesting facts: while between-household inequality of consumption increases, within-household inequality of consumption declines to such an extent that the overall inequality of consumption remains more or less the same over time. When they consider a different measure of resources, namely full consumption, which includes the value of leisure enjoyed by each member, they find similar but less stark results. First, between-household inequality still increases, but much less dramatically because the decline in consumption for those households who have workless members is compensated by the value of leisure. Second again they find that within-household inequality declines as before, but much less. Obviously none of these consumption measures is ideal and a money-metric measure of welfare may be better. However, these results illustrate exactly the potential importance of finding credible ways to understand inequality (and poverty) within households. This is more so given that who marries whom is endogenous and in part drives the way that within-household inequality is determined and has implications for between-household inequality is determined.

16.6.3 Intrahousehold Inequality and Children

While intrahousehold inequality may be of general interest because it tells us about allocation of resources within a household and can reveal hidden poverty and inequality, the whole issue acquires special importance when it comes to allocations of consumption to children. Thus is because child consumption and more generally investments in children have long-term implications for the intergenerational transmission of poverty. Yet little or no empirical work had been done to understand how resources are allocated to children and the extent to which reallocations of income from the male spouse to the female can affect the shares directed to children. A theoretical framework for the analysis of this question has been developed by Blundell et al. (2005). In a recent important paper, Dunbar et al. (2013) address this issue empirically using data from Malawi. In their model, each child is represented as having his or her own utility function. This creates a very special difficulty regarding the assumption, used for identification in studies such as Browning et al. (2013), namely that preferences of singles and married individuals are the same. Here, such a strategy is no longer available because children are never seen living as singles. Moreover, in data from Malawi that the authors use, there is not enough price variation—another requirement of the Browning et al. approach. Thus, identification is obtained by making assumptions on the structure and shape of the Engel curves.

The identification strategy first requires either one assignable private good or one exclusive good per person. Remember that an exclusive good is exclusively consumed by one household member type (for example, child clothing is consumed only by children), whereas an assignable good is such that each member's consumption of this good is observable.[18] Of course, there can be many other purely private goods (such as food) for which we do not observe the amounts of individual consumption: This fact does not hamper identification.

The assignability assumption is not sufficient to identify the share of resources of each household member; additional assumptions are therefore needed. Dunbar et al. (2013) assume, first, that resource shares are invariant to total expenditure. In addition, they make two alternative assumptions on preferences: either the demand for goods is similar across household types (i.e., households with one, two, or more children) or they are similar across types of goods within a household type. An extreme form of the assumption is that preferences do not vary across types of household; since shadow prices vary across households because of the partially public nature of goods, this extreme assumption is essentially equivalent to assuming that the assignable good used for identification is irresponsive to prices. Another extreme form of this assumption is that preferences over the assignable good are identical across different household member types (male, female, and children). However, Dunbar et al. (2013) show that identification only requires that some aspect of the demand functions be the same either across household member types

[18] It should be stressed that a good is private when its consumption does not alter the *preferences* of other household members over goods consumption. As the authors put it, smoking by one household member may annoy the others, but it can still be taken as private if it does not in itself alter their consumption of goods.

or across household types. Thus, in one case, they assume that all household members share the same shape of Engel curves for the assignable good. In another case they assume that preferences are the same across types of household (number of children), conditional on a deflator of income. This deflator reflects the different shadow prices that different-sized households face and is the way that preferences for the assignable good are allowed to vary across types. The key point is that the authors need to define similarity so that identification is delivered without sacrificing theoretical consistency (integrability) of the demand functions.

Dunbar et al. (2013) estimate their model on data from Malawi, probably in one of the first such studies with development data. In a sense their framework is very well adapted to this context because wages and/or prices, which are at the heart of some other iden-tification strategies and are not observed in that case. Their approach relies on measuring expenditures and having an assignable good for which they use clothing and footwear. The results they obtain are both astounding and an excellent illustration of the impor-tance of looking within the household. They find that the male obtains about 45–50% of household resources. His share seems to be insensitive to the number of chil-dren present. The mother's share declines with the second child, but then remains more or less constant, with the consumption share of children declining.

Even more pertinent are the implied poverty rates. Male poverty rates are at their highest in one-child households and seem to decline in households with more children. However, the important result concerns poverty rates for women and children: Com-pared to the male poverty rate of around 69%, there are 79% poor women and 95% poor children in one-child households. In larger households, the male poverty rate is about 55% whereas the female poverty rate is 89% and nearly all children are poor. Hence their approach not only offers a more complete picture of poverty but reveals the extent of child poverty, which is crucial to development. Without such an approach, child poverty would not be apparent to the extent that it is in reality. Although the authors did not focus on gender differences between children, which may be another important dimension, this line of research can easily be extended in that direction; it offers an obvious mech-anism for trying to understand how resources are allocated by gender.

A potential limitation of this approach is the fixed nature of the sharing rule. While the authors spend a lot of time explaining the upsides of not relying on distribution factors (essentially, they avoid having to take a position on whether they affect preferences or not), the absence of an underlying model of what the resource share should depend on and how it can be affected by exogenous driving forces may in some cases be prob-lematic. In models where the sharing rule is allowed to depend on wages or institutional features we have some understanding of how policy can be used to target individuals. In the Dunbar et al. model this aspect is missing. However, this is not an integral part of the approach, and richer models can be identified.

16.6.4 Revealed Preference Restrictions and the Identification of the Sharing Rule

The approach to the identification of the sharing rule has exploited the structure of the demand functions and the way that income affects observed outcomes when the collective model is true. This leads to a set of differential equations that when solved provide the derivatives of the sharing rule. As already discussed, this is not sufficient for identifying the level of the sharing rule.

A different approach is that of revealed preference. In the context of the single-agent utility maximization model the axioms of revealed preference allow one to test nonparametrically whether a particular set of choices can be rationalized by utility maximization and if they can, to bound the underlying demand functions. Such an approach has been developed and implemented for the unitary model by Blundell et al. (2003, 2008) and is based on the original work of Afriat (1973) and Varian (1982). In the collective framework the aggregate household demands will in general violate the revealed preference restrictions corresponding to the unitary model simply because as the budget constraint changes (wages, prices, incomes, etc.) individuals make different choices and the Pareto weights change. This insight was developed by Browning and Chiappori (1998), who showed that the aggregate household demands have to possess a Slutsky matrix that can be decomposed into a symmetric matrix plus a matrix with rank equal to the number of decision makers (whose demands are aggregated) minus 1. The fact that the pattern of choices is restricted implies that there should also be revealed preference type restrictions, as noticed by Chiappori (1988), who provides an early example in a labor supply context. Indeed these restrictions have been fully developed by Cherchye et al. (2007). In a further development Cherchye et al. (2012) show how the revealed preference restrictions can be used to bound the sharing rule without imposing any restrictions other than Pareto efficiency of intrahousehold allocations. The main result is based on the following principle: Suppose that a set of observed demands are collectively rationalizable in the sense that the observed choices are consistent with the existence of admissible individual demand functions. Then it has to be that any alternative choices that could lead to a Pareto improvement within the household should be infeasible at current market prices and for any allocation of income within the household such that each person receives a nonnegative share. More specifically, consider the set of demands that individual 1 reveals, based on all possible admissible demand functions for that person. They must cost more than person 1's share of total household income; similarly for person 2. The least-costly bundle that would lead to a Pareto improvement provides the upper bound for a person's share. Adding up the shares to total income and the assumption that the shares cannot be negative determines the lower bound. The difficulty in implementing this principle is the fact that we need to search over all possible admissible individual demand functions.

This principle turns out to generate nontrivial upper and lower bounds for the sharing rule. Importantly, no restriction is needed for such bounds other than Pareto optimality: All or some goods may be either private, in part public, and in part private or completely private. Moreover, we do not need to specify which goods (if any) are purely private, but if such information were to be available it can be used to tighten the bounds.

Cherchye et al. apply their approach to the PSID from 1999, when expenditures on individual consumption goods became available, until 2009. The sample consists of childless couples where both are working. Utility depends on leisure, food and other goods, which include health and transportation. Leisure is assumed to be assignable, but no assumption is made on the other goods. This is important because in this case, at least in general, neither the level nor the derivatives of the sharing rule are point identified.

To implement their approach they start by estimating three different versions of an aggregate household demand system: a nonparametric system, the QUAIDS demand system (Banks et al., 1997) and a QUAIDS demand system where the substitution matrix is restricted to be symmetric plus rank one, which imposes that the demands are consistent with the collective model. Given this demand system they apply their algorithm to bound the sharing rule for different values of the full household income, wages, and prices. Their empirical results are remarkable. First, the bounds are very narrow with the nonparametric demand system implying 12% median difference between upper and lower bounds and the fully restrictive demand system implying only 3%. Going from the nonparametric demand system to the unrestricted QUAIDS system, the tightening is due to imposing the parametric restrictions that may or may not be valid—the authors provide no evidence on that matter. However, assuming the parametric restrictions are valid, the further step of going from QUAIDS to restricted QUAIDS is just imposing restrictions that are implied by the problem and hence serve only to make the bounds sharp(er). Thus, when Pareto efficiency is imposed, the median difference between the upper and lower bound tightens from about 9% to 3%, a substantial improvement. It would have been useful to use a shape-constrained nonparametric demand system (see Blundell et al., 2012) avoiding the parametric restrictions, but using the Pareto constraints as implied by the model.

Using their bounds they establish that the female share is a normal good, that is, as full-household income grows so does the female share; interestingly, this finding confirms results previously derived in different contexts. Moreover they show that in percentage terms the average female share is very closely bounded around 50%, although there is substantial heterogeneity around that point. However, it is impressive how tightly bounded the sharing rule is throughout the distribution. In interpreting this result, one needs to be careful because it is full income that is being shared equally. This measure of income includes both leisure and consumption. Thus the share of a woman with a high wage who does not work will include her leisure and her consumption; hence a 50% share may in certain cases hide very unequal levels of consumption of all other goods.

In the final part of the analysis, the authors use their estimates to carry out a poverty analysis. The idea here is similar to that in Dunbar et al. (2013) described earlier: They compare poverty rates implied by household-level income and those implied by individual allocations. The household poverty line is 60% of median household income whereas the individual poverty line is set at half this amount. This, of course, is an income-based and not a welfare-based measure and ignores any household economies of scale. This point notwithstanding, the individual rates are higher: while household poverty is 11%, individual poverty is bounded between 16% and 21%, the lower bound being above the household number. Interestingly the bounds do not differ by gender by any substantive amount.

The Cherchye et al. study breaks new ground and shows the power of the collective approach. Specifically it reinforces the identifiability results substantially by showing not only that the levels of the sharing rule can be identified, but more importantly in our view, that the entire sharing rule can also be bounded without much more than within-household Pareto efficiency. Nevertheless, there is still a long and important agenda in this research. First, empirically we need to understand better how to deal with heterogeneity in preferences within such a nonparametric framework as well as with endogeneity of prices and wages. The entire analysis of Cherchye et al. is based on the assumption that wages and prices are exogenous. This is internally consistent with the absence of heterogeneity and shocks, but is broadly unsatisfactory. For example, there is a vast labor supply literature dealing with endogenous wage rates. Moreover, prices of goods may not be exogenous if there are aggregate shocks to the demand functions. While these seem to be side issues as far as the central identifiability of the collective model is concerned, they are important for the ultimate empirical credibility of the approach.

16.7. CONCLUSION

Understanding intrahousehold inequality and, more broadly, intrahousehold allocations is crucial for understanding the effects of policy and for targeting programs designed to alleviate poverty. The implications are far reaching and they span simple questions of who will benefit from certain programs to deeper questions about child poverty and even child development. It is now well understood that treating households as an individual unit does not just provide an incomplete picture of standards of living but can be seriously misleading when we try and understand behavior and its reactions to the environment. In our review we have discussed both the questions underlying the notion of intrahousehold inequality as well as the extent of our ability to identify what goes on in the household from typically observed data. In this context we have argued that it is important to be able to observe variables that shift the bargaining power of spouses without affecting preferences as well as other approaches to peeking inside the household black box. It is evident from this discussion that better data would be important; and nothing is more important than detailed consumption and time use data. A renewed emphasis on such data is called for, given the importance of the issues at hand. A better understanding of what may constitute distribution factors and indeed experimental evidence would be an important way to support research into intrahousehold allocations.

However, beyond the above, research is now advancing into the dynamics of intrahousehold allocations and being linked to marriage markets. It is now becoming clear how the conditions at the time of marriage can affect intrahousehold allocations. Indeed, under full commitment, current distribution factors may have little to do with current allocations. On the other hand, full commitment is a very strong and some may argue an implausible assumption. Thus, research is also advancing in understanding how allocations are determined when commitment is limited. In such limited commitment environments changes in the institutional framework, such as the structure of the welfare system or divorce laws, may have important implications for intrahousehold inequality as well as for the formation and dissolution of marriages. We thus are acquiring a rich theoretical and empirical framework that will allow us to better understand how individual welfare is determined within the context of the family. Important contributions in understanding the dynamics of intrahousehold allocations and of household formation include papers by Mazzocco (2007) and Voena (2013). We are convinced that this is a crucial direction for future research.

ACKNOWLEDGMENTS

P.-A. C. gratefully acknowledges financial support from the NSF (grant 1124277). C. M. is grateful for financial support by the Cowles foundation and the Institution for Social and Policy Studies at Yale. Moreover, we thank Tony Atkinson, Francois Bourguignon, and Marc Fleurbaey for useful comments on a previous version. The usual disclaimer applies.

REFERENCES

Afriat, S.N., 1973. On a system of inequalities in demand analysis: an extension of the classical method. Int. Econ. Rev. 14, 460–472.

Attanasio, O., Lechene, V., 2014. Efficient responses to targeted cash transfers. J. Polit. Econ. 122 (1), 178–222.

Banks, J., Blundell, R.W., Lewbel, A., 1997. Quadratic Engel curves and consumer demand. Rev. Econ. Stat. 79 (4), 527–539.

Bargain, O., Beblo, M., Beninger, D., Blundell, R., Carrasco, R., Chiuri, M.-C., Laisney, F., Lechene, V., Moreau, N., Myck, M., Ruiz-Castillo, J., Vermeulen, F., 2006. Does the representation of household behavior matter for welfare analysis of tax-benefit policies? An introduction. Rev. Econ. Househ. 4, 99–111.

Basu, K., 2006. Gender and say: a model of household behavior with endogenously-determined balance of power. Econ. J. 116, 558–580.

Becker, G.S., 1974. A theory of social interactions. J. Polit. Econ. 82 (6), 1063–1093.

Beninger, D., Bargain, O., Beblo, M., Blundell, R., Carrasco, R., Chiuri, M.-C., Laisney, F., Lechene, V., Longobardi, E., Moreau, N., Myck, M., Ruiz-Castillo, J., Vermeulen, F., 2006. Evaluating the move to a linear tax system in Germany and other European countries. Rev. Econ. Househ. 4, 159–180.

Blundell, R.W., Walker, I., 1986. A life-cycle consistent empirical model of family labour supply using cross-section data. Rev. Econ. Stud. 53 (4, Econometrics Special Issue), 539–558.

Blundell, R.W., Duncan, A., Meghir, C., 1998. Estimating labor supply responses using tax reforms. Econometrica 66 (4), 827–861.

Blundell, R.W., Browning, M., Crawford, I.A., 2003. Nonparametric Engel curves and revealed preference. Econometrica 71 (1), 205–240.

Blundell, R.W., Chiappori, P.A., Meghir, C., 2005. Collective labor supply with children. J. Polit. Econ. 113 (6), 1277–1306.

Blundell, R.W., Chiappori, P.-A., Magnac, T., Meghir, C., 2007. Collective labour supply: heterogeneity and non-participation. Rev. Econ. Stud. 74 (2), 417–445.

Blundell, R.W., Browning, M., Crawford, I.A., 2008. Best nonparametric bounds on demand responses. Econometrica 76 (6), 1227–1262.

Blundell, R., Horowitz, J.L., Parey, M., 2012. Measuring the price responsiveness of gasoline demand: economic shape restrictions and nonparametric demand estimation. Quant. Econ. 3 (1), 29–51.

Browning, M., Chiappori, P.A., 1998. Efficient intra-household allocations: a general characterization and empirical tests. Econometrica 66 (6), 1241–1278.

Browning, M., Chiappori, P.A., Lechene, V., 2010. Distributional effects in household models: separate spheres and income pooling. Econ. J. 120 (545), 786–799.

Browning, M., Chiappori, P.A., Lewbel, A., 2013. Estimating consumption economies of scale, adult equivalence scales, and household bargaining power. Rev. Econ. Stud. 80 (4), 1267–1303.

Browning, M., Chiappori, P.A., Weiss, Y., 2014. Family Economics. Cambridge University Press, New York.

Browning, M., Bourguignon, F. Chiappori, P-A., Lechene, V. 1994. Income and outcomes. J. Polit. Econ. 102 (6), 1067–1096.

Cherchye, L., de Rock, B., Vermeulen, F., 2007. The collective model of household consumption: a nonparametric characterization. Econometrica 75 (2), 553–574.

Cherchye, L., De Rock, B., Vermeulen, F., 2009. Opening the black box of intrahousehold decision making: theory and nonparametric empirical tests of general collective consumption models. J. Polit. Econ. 117 (6), 1074–1104.

Cherchye, L.J.H., de Rock, B., Lewbel, A., Vermeulen, F.M.P., 2012. Sharing Rule Identification for General Collective Consumption Models, Tilburg University, Center for Economic Research, Discussion Paper 2012–041.

Chiappori, P.-A., 1988. Rational household labor supply. Econometrica 56 (1), 63–90.

Chiappori, P.-A., 1991. Nash-bargained household decisions: a rejoinder. Int. Econ. Rev. 32 (3), 761–762.

Chiappori, P.-A., 1992. Collective labor supply and welfare. J. Polit. Econ. 100 (3), 437–467.

Chiappori, P.-A., 2012. Modèles d'appariement en conomie: quelques avances recentes. Texte de la Confrence Jean-Jacques Laffont Revue Economique 63 (2012/3), 437–452.

Chiappori, P.-A., Ekeland, I., 2006. The microeconomics of group behavior: general characteriation. J. Econ. Theor. 130 (1), 1–26.

Chiappori, P.-A., Ekeland, I., 2009a. The micro economics of efficient group behavior: identification. Econometrica 77 (3), 763–799.

Chiappori, P.-A., Ekeland, I., 2009b. The economics and mathematics of aggregation. Foundations and Trends in Microeconomics. Now Publishers, Hanover, USA.

Chiappori, P.-A., Kim, J.-H., 2013. Identifying Heterogeneous Sharing Rules. Mimeo, Columbia University, New York.

Chiappori, P.-A., Meghir, C., 2014. Intrahousehold Welfare, mimeo.

Chiappori, P.-A., Salanié, B., 2014. The econometrics of matching models. J. Econ. Lit., forthcoming.

Chiappori, P.-A., Weiss, Y., 2007. Divorce, remarriage and child support. J. Labor Econ. 25 (1), 37–74.

Chiappori, P-A., Costa-Dias, M., Meghir, C., 2014. Marriage Market, Labor Supply and Education Choice. Mimeo, Columbia University, New York.

Chiappori, P.-A., Donni, O., Komunjer, I., 2012. Learning from a Piece of Pi. Rev. Econ. Stud. 79 (1), 162–195.

Chiappori, P.-A., Fortin, B., Lacroix, G., 2002. Marriage market, divorce legislation, and household labor supply. J. Polit. Econ. 110 (1), 37–72.

Chiappori, P.A., Iyigun, M., Weiss, Y., 2009. Investment in schooling and the marriage market. Am. Econ. Rev. 99 (5), 1689–1717.

Chiappori, P.-A., Salanie, B., Weiss, Y., 2011. Partner Choice and the Marital College Premium. Columbia University Academic Commons.

Chiappori, P.-A., McCann, R., Nesheim, L., 2010. Hedonic price equilibria, stable matching, and optimal transport: equivalence, topology, and uniqueness. Econ. Theor. 42 (2), 317–354.

Chiappori, P.A., Iyigun, M., Lafortune, J., Weiss, Y., 2013. Changing the Rules Midway: The Impact of Granting Alimony Rights on Existing and Newly-Formed Partnerships. Mimeo, Columbia University, New York.

Choo, E., Siow, A., 2006. Who marries whom and why. J. Polit. Econ. 114 (1), 175–201.

Donni, O., 2003. Collective household labor supply: non-participation and income taxation. J. Public Econ. 87, 1179–1198.

Donni, O., 2009. A simple approach to investigate intrahousehold allocation of private and public goods. Rev. Econ. Stat. 91, 617–628.

Dunbar, G.R., Lewbel, A., Pendakur, K., 2013. Children's resources in collective households: identification, estimation, and an application to child poverty in Malawi. Am. Econ. Rev. 103 (1), 438–471 (34).

Edlund, L., Korn, E., 2002. A theory of prostitution. J. Polit. Econ. 110 (1), 181–214.

Fleurbaey, M., Gautier, G., 2009. International comparisons of living standards by equivalent incomes. Scand. J. Econ. 111, 597–624.

Fleurbaey, M., Decancq, K., Schokkaert, E., 2014. Inequality, Income and Well-Being. Elsevier, Amsterdam, this Handbook.

Gersbach, H., Haller, H., 2001. Collective decisions and competitive markets. Rev. Econ. Stud. 68, 347–368.

Gosling, A., Machin, S. Meghir, C., 2000. The changing distribution of male wages in the U.K. Rev. Econ. Stud. 67 (4), 635–666.

Goussé, M., 2013. Marriage Market and Intra-Household Allocation: Evolution of Preferences and Transfers in the UK from 1991 to 2008, mimeo Sciences Po.

Grossbard-Shechtman, S., 1993. On the Economics of Marriage: A Theory of Marriage, Labor, and Divorce. Westview Press, Boulder.

Haddad, L., Kanbur, R., 1990. How serious is the neglect of intrahousehold inequality. Econ. J. 100, 866–881.

Haddad, L., Kanbur, R., 1992. Intrahousehold inequality and the theory of targeting. Eur. Econ. Rev. 36, 372–378.

Hammond, P.J., 1994. Money metric measures of individual and social welfare allowing for environmental externalities. In: Eichhorn, W. (Ed.), Models and Measurement of Welfare and Inequality. Springer, Berlin.

Jacquemet, N., Robin, J.-M., 2011. Marriage with labor supply. CES Working Papers 2011.50.

Lechene, V., Preston, I., 2011. Noncooperative household demand. J. Econ. Theor. 146 (2), 504–527.

Lewbel, A., Pendakur, K., 2013. Unobserved Preference Heterogeneity in Demand Using Generalized Random Coefficients. Boston College, Mimeo.

Lise, J., Seitz, S., 2011. Consumption inequality and intrahousehold allocations. Rev. Econ. Stud. 78 (1), 328–355.

Lundberg, S., Pollak, R.A., 1993. Separate spheres bargaining and the marriage market. J. Polit. Econ. 101 (6), 988–1010.

Manser, M., Brown, M., 1980. Marriage and household decision-making: a bargaining analysis. Int. Econ. Rev. 21 (1980), 31–44.

Mazzocco, M., 2007. Household intertemporal behaviour: a collective characterization and a test of commitment. Rev. Econ. Stud. 74 (3), 857–895.

Mcelroy, M.B., Horney, M.J., 1981. Nash-bargained household decisions: toward a generalization of the theory of demand. Int. Econ. Rev. 22, 333–349.

Myck, M., Bargain, O., Beblo, M., Beninger, D., Blundell, R., Carrasco, R., Chiuri, M.-C., Laisney, F., Lechene, V., Longobardi, E., Moreau, N., Ruiz-Castillo, J., Vermeulen, F., 2006. The working families' tax credit and some European tax reforms in a collective setting. Rev. Econ. Househ. 4, 129–158.

Samuelson, P.A., 1956. Social indifference curves. Q. J. Econ. 70 (1), 1–22.

Ulph, D., 2006. Un modèle non-coopératif de Nash appliqué à l'étude du comportement de consommation du ménage. Actualité économique: revue d'analyse économique 82, 53–86.

Varian, H., 1982. The nonparametric approach to demand analysis. Econometrica 50, 945–974.

Vermeulen, F., Bargain, O., Beblo, M., Beninger, D., Blundell, R., Carrasco, R., Chiuri, M.-C., Laisney, F., Lechene, V., Moreau, N., Myck, M., Ruiz-Castillo, J., 2006. Collective models of labor supply with nonconvex budget sets and nonparticipation: a calibration approach. Rev. Econ. Househ. 4, 113–127.

Voena, A., 2013. Yours, Mine and Ours: Do Divorce Laws Affect the Intertemporal Behavior of Married Couples? mimeo University of Chicago.

CHAPTER 17

Health and Inequality

Owen O'Donnell[*,†], Eddy Van Doorslaer[‡], Tom Van Ourti[*]
[*]Erasmus School of Economics & Tinbergen Institute, Erasmus University Rotterdam, Rotterdam, The Netherlands
[†]School of Economics and Area Studies, University of Macedonia, Thessaloniki, Greece
[‡]Erasmus School of Economics, Tinbergen Institute & Institute for Health Policy and Management, Erasmus University Rotterdam, Rotterdam, The Netherlands

Contents

Handbook of Income Distribution, Volume 2B
ISSN 1574-0056, http://dx.doi.org/10.1016/B978-0-444-59429-7.00018-2

Abstract

We examine the relationship between income and health with the purpose of establishing the extent to which the distribution of health in a population contributes to income inequality and is itself a product of that inequality. The evidence supports a substantial impact of ill-health on income, mainly operating through employment, although the magnitude of ill-health's contribution to income inequality is difficult to gauge. Variation in exposure to health risks early in life could be an important mechanism through which health may generate and possibly sustain economic inequality. If material advantage can be exercised within the domain of health, then economic inequality will generate health inequality. In high-income countries, the evidence that income (wealth) does have a causal impact on health in adulthood is weak. But this may simply reflect the difficulty of identifying a relationship that, should it exist, is likely to emerge over a lifetime as poor material living conditions slowly take their toll on health. There is little credible evidence to support the claim that the economic inequality in society threatens the health of all its members or that relative income is a determinant of health.

JEL Classification Codes

D31, I14, J3

Keywords

Income, Wealth, Health, Inequality

17.1. INTRODUCTION

The financially better-off also tend to be in better health. This holds between and within countries, both developed and developing, and it has been evident for a considerable period of time (Hibbs, 1915; Van Doorslaer et al., 1997; Woodbury, 1924). There is an income gradient in mortality, as well as in a variety of measures of morbidity and disability. The income–health relationship is not confined to a health gap between the poor and the rest, however. Health continues to rise with income among the nonpoor.

The strength, ubiquity, and persistence of the positive relationship between income and health make it of considerable interest for those studying distributions of income, health, and well-being. Understanding the mechanisms that generate the income–health nexus can help account for inequality, as well as identify inequity, in each of those distributions. This chapter examines the strength and nature of the relationships between income and health with the purpose of establishing the extent to which the distribution of health in a population contributes to economic inequality and is itself a product of that inequality.

The distribution of health is potentially both a cause and a consequence of the distribution of income. Differences in health can generate differences in income, most obviously by restricting earnings capacity. But health inequality may itself reflect economic inequality if health-enhancing goods, such as medical care and nutritious food, are allocated by price. The potentially bidirectional relationship between health and income is relevant both to the positive explanation of the distribution of income and to its normative evaluation. A full understanding of how income differences across individuals are generated requires identification of the extent to which health constrains income. This positive exercise feeds into the normative one of evaluating the distribution of income because the inequity of income inequality surely depends on its causes. The ethical judgment of income distribution is also contingent on its consequences. If money can buy health, then there may be greater aversion to inequality in the distribution of income than there would be if the rich were merely able to afford smarter clothes and faster cars.

The relationship between income and health is not only of interest to those concerned with the distribution of income. From the public health perspective, attention is drawn to observed increases in health with income, as opposed to the corresponding decrease in income with ill-health. Public health scientists tend to interpret the income gradient in health as a symptom of inequity in the distribution of health (Commission on the Social Determinants of Health, 2008), while economists are inclined to view the gradient as reflecting the operation of the labor market in which the sick and disabled are constrained in their capacity to generate earnings (Deaton, 2002; Smith, 1999, 2004). Resolution of this debate is obviously crucial to the formation of the appropriate policy response to the gradient. If it mainly reflects the impact of ill-health on income, then the proposal to use income redistribution as an instrument of health policy (Commission on the Social Determinants of Health, 2008; Navarro, 2001) would be entirely inappropriate (Deaton, 2002).

The inclusion of this chapter in the Handbook is partly motivated by insights into the explanation and evaluation of income distribution that can be gained through the study of the income–health relationship, but it also reflects a trend away from the more narrow focus on differences in income to the more encompassing analysis of inequality in well-being.

Health and income are typically cited as the most important determinants of well-being and are the most common arguments of multidimensional measures of inequality (see Chapters 2 and 3). For given degrees of inequality in the marginal distributions of income and health, most would consider that inequality in well-being is greater when the poor also tend to be in worse health. Understanding the nature of the relationship between income and health is central to determining the degree of inequality in well-being.

17.1.1 Health to Income

There are multiple mechanisms through which health may affect income distribution, with the labor market obviously being an important one. Differences in productivity deriving from variation in physical and mental capacities related to illness and disability are also potentially important determinants of earnings. Differences in the nature of work and infrastructures may mean that physical disability represents a greater constraint on earnings in low-income settings, and mental health problems are relatively more important in developed countries. Discrimination may further widen any disparity in earnings between the disabled and able-bodied. Institutional constraints on wage flexibility may result in unemployment of less healthy individuals who are less productive or face discrimination. On the supply side, ill-health may shift preferences away from work, and this may be reinforced by reduced financial incentives arising from a lower offer wage and entitlement to disability insurance (DI). The latter will cushion the earnings loss arising from disability and so compress the income distribution, but this will be offset if the financial incentives induce withdrawal from employment at a given degree of disability, which may strengthen the earnings–health relationship, if not the income–health relationship, in high-income countries relative to low-income countries. Beyond its effect on the distribution of personal income, health may impact the distribution of household income through the formation and maintenance of marriage partnerships and spousal earnings given needs for informal care.

The impact of health on income may operate with a very long lag. Poor health in childhood may disrupt schooling. Exposure to health risks *in utero* and illness in infanthood may impair cognitive functioning and reduce the efficiency of education in producing knowledge and skills. Childhood health problems may be persistent, such that less healthy young adults enter the labor market with less human capital and lower prospects for lifetime earnings. Early-life health conditions may impact income not only through human-capital acquisition but also by triggering health problems in adulthood (Barker, 1995) that interfere with work. If exposure to health risks in early life is related to economic circumstances, then childhood health could be partly responsible for the transmission of these circumstances across generations (Currie, 2009). According to this proposition, poorer mothers with less education deliver less healthy babies and raise sicker children who acquire less human capital and suffer persistent health problems, both of which constrain earnings and increase the likelihood of parenting a child with health problems. If this theory is empirically significant, then it would place health policy at the very heart of social policy.

17.1.2 Income and Income Inequality to Health

The distribution of income may have consequences for population health through two broad mechanisms. First, the health of an individual may depend on his or her (parents') level of income. If health is a normal good, then demand for it rises with income, and the relationship should be stronger in countries that rely more on the market to allocate health resources, in particular medical care. Second, some claim that the health of an individual is contingent not only on his own income but also on the economic inequality within the society in which he lives (Wilkinson, 1996; Wilkinson and Pickett, 2010). Aggregate data show a clear negative association between measures of population health and income inequality. One proposed mechanism is that psychosocial stress arising from the stigma attached to low relative incomes is physiologically damaging. But the negative relationship between average health and income dispersion could also arise from decreasing health returns to absolute income (Gravelle, 1998; Rodgers, 1979). We weigh the evidence that not only income but also income inequality has a causal impact on health and so affects the distribution of health in a population.

17.1.3 Scope of the Chapter

The literature on the socioeconomic determinants of health is immense and comes from epidemiology, sociology, demography, and psychology, as well as economics. We confine attention to the relationship between income and health, which has been the focus of the economics discipline. Our goal is to establish what is known about the relationship from empirical analyses, and we do not cover the normative literature on health inequality. The evidence we assemble is relevant to the ethical judgment of distributions of income, health, and well-being, but we do not discuss how such normative evaluations might be conducted. Interested readers can consult the excellent discussion of some of the normative issues by Fleurbaey and Schokkaert (2011), as well as Chapters 2 and 4. Relatedly, we do not cover the burgeoning literature on the measurement of income-related health inequality (Erreygers and Van Ourti, 2011; Van Doorslaer and Van Ourti, 2011). Inequality in both income and health could also be analyzed using measures of multidimensional inequality, which are discussed in Chapter 3.

Population health is a standard covariate in empirical growth models, and its contribution to growth has been the focus of a substantial literature aiming to estimate the economic returns from health investments (Barro, 2003, 2013; Commission on Macroeconomics and Health, 2001). We do not cover this literature on the relationship between average income and health because it says nothing about the distribution of each variable across individuals. We do cover evidence on the impact of individual health on income and of income on health, looking at low-income, as well as high-income, countries. But the balance is tilted toward a focus on the latter. Comprehensively covering the very large literature on the impact of health (and nutritional status) on earnings in low-income settings (Strauss and Thomas, 1998) would be too unwieldy. We refer to this literature mainly to establish whether the income–health relationships observed in this setting differ from those in high-income economies that we consider in more detail.

Although we have referred until now to the relationship between income and health, our scope is a little broader. We also consider the relationships between wealth and health. Wealth is an economic outcome of intrinsic interest and is arguably a more appropriate indicator of the economic status of older individuals who provide much of the action in terms of variation in health. The health–wealth effect is likely to differ from the health–income effect. Health may affect income largely through labor market returns. This will feed through to the distribution of wealth, but, in addition, ill-health may threaten wealth through asset depletion to pay for medical and nursing care.

17.1.4 Organization of the Chapter

We begin by illustrating the strong positive relationship between health and income, using data from three countries—China, the Netherlands (NL), and the United States (USA)—that differ greatly with respect to level of development, economic inequality, labor market structures, and social welfare institutions. For each country, we show the contribution (in a purely statistical sense) that health differences make to income inequality, and, from the other side, the extent to which income variation accounts for health inequality. Having established the strength of the association between income and health, in sections 17.3 and 17.4, we turn to the mechanisms potentially responsible for the relationship and the extent to which it arises from a causal effect of health on income and vice versa. Section 17.3 identifies a number of routes through which health may impact income and wealth, paying particular attention to how economic inequality may be generated by health differences. The pathways considered are wages, work, human capital, early-life health risks, occupation, marriage, and medical expenditures. Evidence relevant to each broad pathway and more specific mechanisms is reviewed. Section 17.4 looks at the relation from the other direction: income (wealth) to health. Much of this discussion concerns whether income (wealth) has a causal impact on health over and above that of other socioeconomic characteristics, such as education and occupation, and after controlling for correlated determinants, such as time preferences and risk attitudes. Section 17.5 considers the logic and empirical support for the hypothesis that health is determined by economic inequality and by relative, as opposed to absolute, income. Finally, section 17.6 briefly summarizes the lessons that can be drawn from the literature about the nature of the income–health relationship and discusses what these imply for the normative evaluation of the distributions of income, health, and well-being.

17.2. HEALTH AND INCOME: A FIRST PASS

To whet the appetite, we illustrate the strength of the relationship between health and income in the USA, the NL, and China.[1] Our purpose is simply to show that there is a substantial and ubiquitous relationship that deserves attention and to assess its potential relevance to the explanation of inequalities in the distributions of income and health. The three countries are chosen primarily because of their differences. One is large, rich, and unequal, and it does not (yet) have universal health insurance coverage. Another is small, rich, and egalitarian, and it provides universal health coverage and extensive social protection, including DI, typical of northern continental Europe. The third is very large, much poorer (but rapidly becoming less poor), and less healthy than the other two, with increasing economic inequality and limited health and DI coverage. Differences in the wealth and economic structures of these countries, as well as their health and welfare institutions, might be expected to be reflected in the distributions of income and health, as well as the association between them.

Figure 17.1 illustrates the income gradient in self-assessed health (SAH) (Smith, 2004)—the most common survey measure of general health that invites a respondent to select one of four (China) or five (NL and USA) labels as the best description of his or her health. We focus on the percentage of individuals reporting less than *good* health, which always corresponds to the bottom two categories of SAH, by age-specific quartile groups of household per capita income.[2] In the USA, this percentage rises monotonically as income falls at all ages except among the oldest (70+). Even the poorest elderly, whose income should not depend on their current health, are more than twice as likely as their richest contemporaries to report less than *good* health. The pattern is similar in the Netherlands but for the absence of a gradient among young adults and a weaker gradient among the elderly. In both countries, the gradient increases until middle age and

---

[1] The US data are from the 2008 well-being module of the American Life Panel (ALP), which is nationally representative and implemented by RAND over the internet (https://mmicdata.rand.org/alp/). The Dutch data are from the 2011/2012 wave of the Longitudinal Internet Studies for the Social sciences (LISS), which is also nationally representative and has a similar protocol to the ALP (http://www.lissdata.nl/lissdata/). The Chinese data are from the 2006 wave of the Chinese Health and Nutrition Survey (CHNS) (http://www.cpc.unc.edu/projects/china/), which is representative of nine provinces (Heilongjiang, Liaoning, Shandong, Henan, Jiangsu, Hubei, Hunan, Guizhou, and Guangxi) that account for 41.7% of the total population of the country (National Bureau of Statistics of China, 2007). The sampled provinces are mainly located in the central-eastern, more developed and populated part of the country, although the eastern seaboard and the megacities located there are excluded. Clearly the CHNS is not nationally representative. By excluding both the poor western part of the country and the eastern seaboard, it likely understates the degree of economic and health inequality. Nevertheless, there is substantial variation in terms of GDP per capita and life expectancy across the provinces that are covered, and there is at least one province in each of the four economic regions of the country.

[2] We assign household per capita income to every household member and calculate the age-specific quartile groups of individuals.

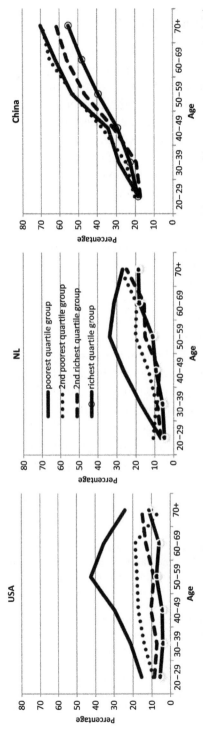

Figure 17.1 Percentage of individuals reporting less than *good* health by age-specific quartile groups of household per capita income in United States (USA), the Netherlands (NL), and China. *Notes: Authors' calculations from 2006 CHNS (China), 2011 LISS (NL), and 2008 ALP (USA). ALP and LISS respondents report health as being excellent, very good, good, fair (ALP)/moderate (LISS), or poor. CHNS respondents report health relative to others of their own age as very good, good, fair, or poor. Household income is before payment of taxes and Social Security contributions and after receipt of transfers. Income is annual for ALP and monthly for LISS and CHNS, with all incomes in local currencies. Per capita income assigned to each household member.*

narrows beyond that when retirement becomes more prevalent. This is consistent with employment being an important characteristic linking health to income. At the peak of the gradient between the ages of 50 and 59, more than 40% of the poorest Americans report their health to be less than *good*, compared with less than 10% of their richest compatriots. The inequality is narrower in the Netherlands, but the poor middle aged are still around three-and-a-half times more likely to report less than *good* health than are those in the top quartile group of the income distribution.

In China, the main health disparity is not between the poorest quartile group and the rest, as it is in the USA and the Netherlands, but, if anything, it is between the richest quartile group and those less privileged. There is no narrowing of the gradient in old age in China. In fact, health differences are greatest in the oldest age group, which is consistent with sizable inequalities in pension entitlements and health insurance coverage among the Chinese elderly but may also reflect the fact that the Chinese survey asks respondents to report health relative to others of the same age (see note to Figure 17.1).

Figure 17.2 shows the flip side of the relationship between individual health and income, with individual income measured by household per capita income. In all three countries, those in (at least) *very good* health have substantially higher incomes than those in *poor* health. In the USA at all ages, mean household per capita income falls as health drops from one category to the next. The health gradient in income peaks in the prime years of working life (40–49), when the mean income of those reporting *excellent* or *very good* health is around three-and-a-half times greater than the income of those in poor health. Even in old age, those with the best health have almost twice the incomes of those with the worst health. The health-related income gaps are narrower in the Netherlands. Even at the ages (50–59 years) where the disparity is greatest, those in the best health do not receive twice the income of those in the worst. The relative income differences by health in China are similar in magnitude to those in the Netherlands, except in old age when the gap widens, rather than narrows.

The individual health–income relationship remains strong after controlling for some potential correlates of both. Table 17.1 shows estimates from least squares regressions of the logarithm of household equivalent income of each individual for SAH, gender, age, ethnicity, education, and region (USA and China).[3] Conditional on these characteristics, in the US sample, the mean income of those reporting *very good* or *excellent* health is approximately 66–69% greater than that of someone reporting *poor* health (left panel, first column). This is larger than the relative income difference between those with the middle (post-high school vocational) and lowest (high school graduate or less) level of education, although it is not quite as large as the difference between university graduates and those with no more than high school education. Controlling for employment status has a very large impact on income differences by health. In the USA, the mean income of those

---

[3] Definitions of household equivalent income and the covariates are provided in Table A1.

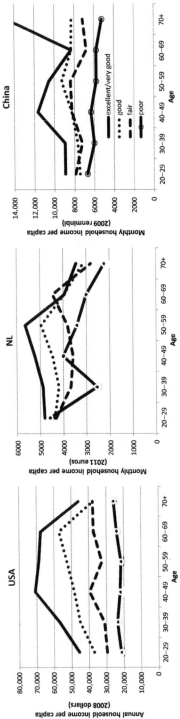

Figure 17.2 Mean household per capita income by self-assessed health and age in the United States (USA), the Netherlands (NL), and China.
Notes: As in Figure 17.1, the unit of analysis is the individual.

Table 17.1 Least squares regressions of log household equivalent income and decompositions of income inequality (relative Gini) in the United States, the Netherlands, and China

| | Without control for employment status | | | | | | With control for employment status | | | | | |
| | United States | | Netherlands | | China | | United States | | Netherlands | | China | |
	OLS coeff.	Inequality contribution	OLS coeff.	Inequality contribution	OLS coeff.	Inequality contribution	OLS coeff.	Inequality contribution	OLS coeff.	Inequality contribution	OLS coeff.	Inequality contribution
Health (SAH) (reference = poor)												
Moderate/fair	0.208**	6.5%	0.146**	3.6%	0.197***	3.0%	0.013	4.0%	0.092	2.8%	0.184***	2.5%
Good	0.508***		0.235***		0.244***		0.206***		0.152**		0.221***	
Very good	0.688***		0.314***		0.389***		0.334***		0.232***		0.362***	
Excellent	0.663***		0.369***				0.316***		0.268***			
Education (reference = low)												
Middle	0.445***	18.0%	0.069***	14.2%	0.370***	13.9%	0.390***	15.2%	0.040**	12.1%	0.314***	11.1%
High	0.882***		0.344***		0.754***		0.764***		0.305***		0.641***	
Gender (reference = female)	0.138***	1.8%	0.060***	1.5%	0.021	0.3%	0.103***	1.2%	0.036***	0.8%	−0.042*	0.4%
Ethnicity	0.449***	6.7%	0.062**	0.4%	0.078**	0.6%	0.392***	5.6%	0.034	0.2%	0.051	0.3%
(reference = minority)												
Age (reference = 20–29 years)												
30–39 years	0.195***	7.8%	−0.009	4.8%	0.048	2.5%	0.158***	8.0%	−0.060*	4.3%	−0.020	3.0%
40–49 years	0.392***		0.023		0.097**		0.354***		−0.036		0.023	
50–59 years	0.496***		0.161***		0.106**		0.513***		0.127***		−0.017	
60–69 years	0.585***		0.081**		−0.059		0.617***		0.132***		−0.247***	
70+ years	0.474***		−0.032		−0.098*		0.508***		0.041		−0.311***	
Region		3.6%		NA		8.0%		3.0%		NA		6.0%
Employment status (reference = employed)												
Unemployed							−0.782***	11.1%	−0.322***	7.7%	−0.527***	8.2%
Disabled							−0.892***		−0.248***		−0.361**	
Retired							−0.259***		−0.175***		−0.401***	
Not working							−0.440***		−0.244***		−0.345***	
Unexplained (OLS residual)		55.7%		75.6%		71.8%		51.9%		72.0%		68.1%
Relative Gini	0.456		0.292		0.472		0.456		0.292		0.472	
Number of observations	5050		4137		7694		5050		4137		7694	

Notes: Unit of analysis is the individual. Household equivalent income allocated to each individual in the household aged >19. Column headed "OLS coeff." gives coefficients from least squares regression of log household equivalent income on individual characteristics. "Inequality contribution" is the estimated contribution of the factor to inequality across individuals in household equivalent income computed from the Shapley value decomposition of the relative Gini index. SAH = self-assessed health. Definitions and means of the dependent variables and covariates are provided in Table A1. Reference category for ethnicity is not belonging to the main ethnic group (white (USA), Dutch (NL), and Han (China). Coefficients of regions (USA) and provinces (China) are not shown to save space. Region identifiers are not made available with the Dutch data. *, **, *** indicate significance at 10%, 5%, and 1% levels.

with at least *very good* health relative to those in *poor* health is reduced by half to 32–33% (right panel, first column). A large part of the strong relationship between income and health appears to be mediated through employment.

Multivariate analysis confirms what is suggested by Figure 17.2—that income gaps by levels of health are narrower in the Netherlands and China than in the USA. Without being conditional on employment, the Dutch reporting at least *very good* health have incomes approximately 31–37% higher than their compatriots in *poor* health. This is much lower than the respective relative disparity in the US sample. But being conditional on employment has a much smaller impact than it does in the USA, reducing the difference by around a quarter to 23–27%, which is only slightly less than the relative income difference of 30% between those with the highest and lowest levels of education. The more modest effect of being conditional on employment may be a reflection of the more generous DI in the Netherlands, which is evident in the coefficients on DI status. Being conditional on employment has little or no impact in the Chinese sample. Those reporting *very good* health have incomes approximately 36% higher than those in *poor* health. This is because employment differs less by health in China (see Figure 17.4).

Large differences in income by health do not necessarily imply that health statistically explains, let alone causally determines, a substantial part of income inequality. Whether it does depends on the degree of health variation that exists in the population, in addition to its partial correlation with income. The percentage of respondents reporting *poor* health is only 1.5% in the Dutch sample, rising to 3% in the USA and to 7% in the Chinese

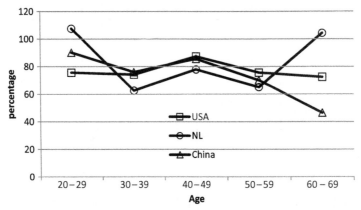

Figure 17.3 Mean earnings in bottom two categories of self-assessed health as a percentage of mean earnings in the top two categories, for China, the Netherlands, and the USA. *Notes: Authors' calculations from CHNS 2006 (China), LISS 2011 (Netherlands), ALP 2008 (USA). Samples restricted to those in work. Earnings include gross earnings/salary income from employment and profits from self-employment in the past year in the Netherlands and the USA, and gross wages, including bonuses and subsidies, in the last month in China. Self-assessed health is reported from five categories in NL and USA and from four in China. See notes to Figure 17.1.*

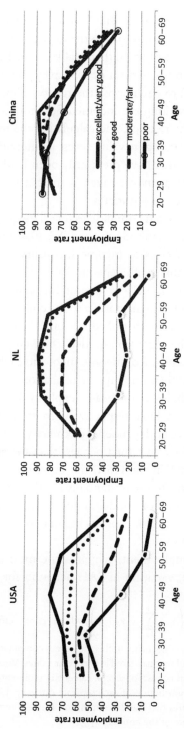

Figure 17.4 Employment rates by self-assessed health and age in China, the Netherlands, and the USA. *Notes: Authors' calculations from 2006 CHNS (China), 2011 LISS (NL), and 2008 ALP (USA). Employment includes full- and part-time work. For details of SAH by country, see notes to Figure 17.1.*

(Table A1). Differences in income between those with *poor* and higher levels of health may therefore make only modest contributions to the explanation of income inequality.

To give an impression of the contribution that health can make to the explanation of income inequality, we apply a simple version of a Shapley value approach (Sastre and Trannoy, 2002; Shorrocks, 2013) to decompose the relative Gini index estimated from the three datasets. This involves writing the income of each individual as the predicted value from the regression, plus the residual, and calculating the marginal impact on the Gini of neutralizing a variable by fixing its value across all individuals. This impact will vary depending on the covariates that have previously been held constant. The contribution of a variable to inequality is given by its average marginal impact across all possible sequences of neutralizing the set of all covariates.[4]

As would be expected, the estimated Gini indices reveal inequality to be lowest in the Netherlands (0.29) and of similar magnitude in the USA (0.46) and China (0.47). The percentage contributions of the factors to income inequality are reported adjacent to the respective column of regression coefficients in Table 17.1. Without conditioning on employment status, SAH explains 6.5% of income inequality in the US sample (left panel, second column). This is similar in magnitude to the contribution of race, a little less than that of age, and about one-third of that of education. The decomposition obviously depends on the specification of the regression model. Once employment status is added to the controls, health only explains 4% of income inequality, which is half of the contribution of age and a little more than one quarter of that of education.

Without conditioning on employment, health explains 3.6% and 3.0% of income inequality in the Netherlands and China, respectively. In each country, this is substantially more than the contribution of both gender and ethnicity. The health contribution is around 20% higher than that of age in China but less than the age contribution in the Netherlands. In both countries, as in the USA, the contribution of variation in SAH to the explanation of income inequality is substantially less than that of education. As predicted by the estimates of the regression models, controlling for employment status has less impact on the extent to which health explains income inequality in the Netherlands and China than it does in the USA.

Without conditioning on employment, which is the most obvious route through which health influences income, variation in SAH accounts for 6.5%, 3.6%, and 3.0%

---

[4] Income of individual i is given by $\exp\left(\hat{\gamma}_0 + \sum_{k=1}^{K} x_{ki}\hat{\gamma}_k + \hat{e}_i\right)$, where $\hat{\gamma}_k$ are coefficients from the OLS regression of log income and $\hat{e}_i$ is the residual. Inequality in this measure is computed and compared for different combinations of the regressors (x_{ki}) and residuals fixed at particular values. We compute the aggregate contribution of a factor, such as SAH, that consists of several categories represented by dummy variables, and we do not attempt to establish the contribution of each separate category. Use of the relative Gini and a regression model of log income ensures that the decomposition is insensitive to the values at which the regressors are fixed and to the estimate of the constant ($\hat{\gamma}_0$).

of income inequality in the USA, the Netherlands, and China respectively. Although these contributions appear modest, one must bear in mind that most inequality remains unexplained by an admittedly rather restricted set of factors in all three countries. SAH accounts for almost 15% of the explained income inequality in the USA and the Netherlands and just over 10% in China. In addition, SAH is only one measure of health and varies only over four or five categories. It is inevitable that such a variable will not be able to account for a substantial proportion of the variation in continuous incomes. Differential reporting of health may also result in SAH understating the correlation between income and health (Bago d'Uva et al., 2008). While it is established that SAH is an informative summary measure of health, the addition of more health measures, particularly continuous ones and those capturing disabilities, to the decomposition analysis would inevitably increase the proportion of income inequality that is explained by health variation.

Based on the regression and decomposition analysis presented, nothing can be inferred about causality—its direction or even existence. One can just as well look at health differences that are explained by income variation. Table 17.2 presents estimates from interval regressions of transformations of SAH on household equivalent income and the same covariates used in the income regressions (Doorslaer and Jones, 2003).[5] This health measure lies between 0 (minimum health) and 1 (maximum health). In the USA, the difference in predicted health between the richest and poorest quartile groups of household equivalent income is about 1.8 times greater than the difference between the youngest and oldest age group and between the highest and lowest education categories (left panel, first column). As could be anticipated from the narrower income gaps by health in the Netherlands, observed in Table 17.1, the health differences by income are also smaller than those in the USA (Table 17.2, middle panel). Still, the health disparity between the richest and poorest income groups is more than twice the difference between the top and bottom education groups. In China, the health differences by income are also substantially larger than the differences by education.[6]

Table 17.2 also presents results from Shapley value decompositions of inequality in transformed SAH. There are two notable differences from the decomposition of income

[5] Thresholds separating different categories of SAH are taken from external data. For China, we use the Chinese visual analog scale estimated from the World Health Organization Multi-Country Survey on Health and Responsiveness (Üstün et al., 2003), which gives thresholds 0 (minimum health), 0.50, 0.80, 0.91, and 1 (maximum health) corresponding to four categories of SAH. For the USA and the Netherlands, we obtain the thresholds 0, 0.428, 0.756, 0.897, 0.947, and 1 from the Canadian Health Utility Index (Feeny et al., 2002), with those thresholds dividing five categories of SAH.

[6] Conditioning on employment status reduces the health difference between the richest and poorest by about two-fifths in the USA. Doing so results in a smaller reduction in the income gradient in health in the Netherlands, which remains about twice the education gradient. Conditioning on employment has little impact in the Chinese sample.

Table 17.2 Interval regressions of self-assessed health (SAH) and decompositions of inequality (absolute Gini) in predicted SAH for the United States, the Netherlands, and China

	United States				Netherlands				China			
	Regression coeff.	Inequality contribution			Regression coeff.	Inequality contribution			Regression coeff.	Inequality contribution		
	Baseline	Baseline	With employment	With employment and health behavior	Baseline	Baseline	With employment	With employment and health behavior	Baseline	Baseline	With employment	With employment and health behavior
Income quartile group (reference = poorest 25%)												
2nd poorest	0.038**	44.0%	21.7%	14.3%	0.016***	34.5%	17.7%	13.8%	0.010**	10.5%	9.2%	8.8%
2nd richest	0.057***				0.024***				0.022***			
Richest	0.075***				0.036***				0.030***			
Education (reference = low)												
Middle	0.020***	25.9%	18.7%	9.6%	0.009**	15.9%	9.4%	6.4%	0.006	3.1%	2.6%	2.5%
High	0.042***				0.015***				0.011**			
Gender (reference = female)	0.001	0.2%	0.5%	0.1%	0.005*	3.5%	2.5%	1.9%	0.024***	8.6%	7.2%	7.4%
Ethnicity (reference = minority)	0.012***	4.4%	2.9%	1.9%	0.011**	3.1%	1.7%	1.3%	−0.002	0.1%	0.1%	0.1%
Age (reference = 20–29 years)												
30–39 years	−0.012**	20.4%	7.8%	4.4%	−0.01***	43.1%	26.3%	19.4%	−0.016***	63.8%	57.9%	55.9%
40–49 years	−0.035***				−0.035***				−0.041***			
50–59 years	−0.051***				−0.051***				−0.083***			
60–69 years	−0.054***				−0.048***				−0.111***			
70+ years	−0.042***				−0.055***				−0.148***			
Region		5.2%	4.8%	3.5%		NA	NA	NA		13.9%	13.1%	12.3%
Employment status			43.7%	34.2%		NA	42.5%	37.9%			9.9%	10.0%
Health behavior			31.9%	34.2%		NA	19.2%					3.0%
Absolute Gini		0.024	0.028	0.033		0.014	0.018	0.020		0.030	0.031	0.031
Number of observations	5050				4137				7694			

Notes: Unit of analysis is the individual. Column headed "Regression coeff." gives the coefficient from the interval regression of SAH with thresholds of categories as defined in footnote 5. "Inequality contribution" is the estimated percentage contribution of the factor to inequality in predicted health (obtained from the respective interval regression) computed from the Shapley value decomposition of the absolute Gini index. The latter takes values between 0 and 0.25, with those bounds indicating minimum and maximum health inequality, respectively. Definitions and means of the dependent variables and covariates are provided in Table A1. Reference category for ethnicity as in notes to Table 17.1. Region/province coefficients are shown only for the baseline specification. Extended specifications sequentially add employment status (as Table 17.1) and proxies for health behaviors—smoking and weight. Smoking is measured by an indicator of ever having smoked in the USA and NL and currently being a smoker in China. Weight is summarized by a dummy for normal or overweight ($18.5 < BMI < 27.5$ for China and $18.5 < BMI < 30$ for the USA and the Netherlands) and another for obesity ($BMI > 30$ for the USA and the Netherlands, and $BMI > 27.5$ for China). For underweight, $BMI < 18.5$ is the reference. ⋆, ⋆⋆ and ⋆⋆⋆ indicate significance at the 10%, 5% and 1% levels respectively.

inequality. First, the categorical nature of SAH, modeled by interval regression, means that unexplained variation in health cannot be captured by the decomposition. All contributions refer to the percentage of the explained variation that is accounted for by a factor. Second, the absolute, rather than relative, Gini index (Yitzhaki, 1983) is a more appropriate measure of inequality in a bounded variable such as transformed SAH (Erreygers, 2009; Lambert and Zheng, 2011).[7]

Income quartile groups account for 45% of the explained inequality in SAH in the USA (left panel, second column). This is roughly equal to the contributions of age and education combined. Further evidence that employment is central to the association between health and income in the USA is provided by the fall in the income contribution by more than half, such that it becomes only slightly more important than education in explaining health inequality when employment status is added to the interval regression of SAH and so the decomposition (left panel, third column). Adding proxies for health behavior, in the form of indicators of weight and smoking, reduces the income contribution by about one-third more, which is suggestive of differences in lifestyle being an important reason why health differs by income.

In the Netherlands, income variation accounts for 35% of the explained inequality in SAH, which is more than twice the contribution of education. Adding employment status reduces the contribution of income by half, but it remains roughly twice that of education. Entering health behavior into the decomposition has a more modest impact. In China, income differences account for much less of the explained variation in health— around 9% irrespective of whether employment or health behavior is controlled for. As is also evident in Figure 17.1, health inequality in China appears to be driven mainly by age, which is perhaps surprising given that only the Chinese survey asks respondents to report their health relative to that of someone of the same age. On the other hand, a very steep decline in health with age in China would be anticipated from the lack of health insurance coverage, particularly for the elderly in rural locations, at the time of the survey, as well as from events experienced in the twentieth century.

Our empirical illustration demonstrates that there is a strong relationship between income and health. Income differences by health are large. Correspondingly, health disparities by income are wide. The relationship is stronger in the USA than in the Netherlands and China. The dissimilarities of the latter two countries imply that the strength of the relationship is not explained by a simple factor, such as the informality of the economy, universality of health insurance coverage, or generosity of welfare, but is likely a product of many such factors. Employment status, particularly in the USA among the three countries examined, is key to the relationship between income

---

[7] Given that the interval regression model has an additive specification and we use an inequality index that is invariant to equal additions, neither the constant nor the values to which factors are set when neutralized will affect the decomposition results.

and health. But it is unlikely to be the only mechanism. Even after controlling for employment, income differs greatly by health, and thus, health varies substantially with income.

A single health variable, self-assessed health, accounts for 6.5% of total income inequality and 14.6% of explained inequality in the USA. These estimates suggest the distribution of health in the population has a potentially important, although not central, role in explaining income inequality. But one could equally claim that variation in economic circumstances is key to the explanation of the health distribution. Indeed, income differences explain almost half of the inequality in predicted (self-assessed) health in the USA.[8]

While descriptive multivariate analysis and decompositions are useful in determining the strength of relationships, they tell us nothing about causality. Nevertheless, we hope to have convinced the reader that the association between income and health is sufficiently strong and pervasive such that it deserves to be probed by those seeking a better understanding of the distribution of income, as well as others aiming to account for disparities in health. In the next two sections, in turn, we consider the impact that health has on the distribution of income and the effect that income has on the distribution of health.

17.3. HEALTH DETERMINATION OF ECONOMIC INEQUALITY

17.3.1 Overview

How might the distribution of health determine the distribution of income? The most obvious effect is through physical and mental capacity for work. We begin this section by considering how health may impact productivity and wages. We then turn to the relationship between health and the quantity of work. Labor supply may be reduced at both the extensive margin, with illness in middle age tilting the balance in favor of early retirement, and the intensive margin, with part-time work becoming a more attractive proposition for some with a debilitating illness. In high-income countries, the employment effect on earnings will be directly cushioned by DI, but resultant moral hazard will indirectly contribute to the effect. Earnings losses may be exacerbated by discrimination, but legislation designed to prevent this may increase the impact on employment by constraining wage flexibility. Labor supply may be constrained by current sickness and influenced over the longer term by any downward revision of life expectancy following the onset of a major illness.

In addition to the immediate impact of ill-health on earnings, there may be important lifetime effects operating through education, occupation, and marriage. Illness in childhood can constrain opportunities for education and its efficiency in producing knowledge and skills. With few education qualifications, a frail young adult will be limited in his or her choice of occupation. The less healthy may also be constrained in their choice of partners. If there is sorting, such that the least healthy marry others of less than

---

[8] Of course, income would explain a much smaller proportion of the greater inequality in actual health.

average health or remain unmarried, then the contribution of health to inequality in household incomes will be even greater than its contribution to inequality in individual incomes. Ill-health may not only directly constrain the work effort of the disabled person, but it may also indirectly affect the labor supply of the spouse, who may face conflicting demands on his or her time to both replace lost earnings and provide informal care.

Health may impact the distribution of wealth, both directly and indirectly, through income and the accumulation of savings. Because the latter effect is cumulative, the contribution of health to inequality in wealth should be even greater than that to inequality in incomes. The healthy, expecting to live for longer, may save a larger fraction of their higher incomes, further increasing wealth disparities by health. When health insurance is incomplete and medical care must be paid for from an individual's own resources, illness can directly deplete wealth.

In the subsequent subsections, we consider the potential effects of health on income through wages, work, human capital, occupation, and household formation or spousal earnings. In each case, we elucidate the potential mechanisms and evaluate the evidence relevant to establishing the extent to which health differences contribute to economic inequality.

17.3.2 Health and Wages

Individuals in poor health have substantially lower earnings than those in good health. Figure 17.3 shows mean gross earnings of employees in the bottom two categories of SAH as a percentage of the mean in the two top categories for China, the Netherlands, and the USA, as estimated from the data sources in Section 17.2. Although there are discrepancies at the youngest and oldest age groups, mainly due to the small sample of individuals working and in less than *good* health in the Netherlands at these ages, among those working between the ages of 30 and 60, the earnings of individuals in the worst health are 15–40% below those in the best health in the three countries. In the middle age range, the health gradient in earnings is largest in the Netherlands, which may reflect both qualification for partial DI, which acts as an earnings subsidy, and the high rate of part-time employment. The relative earnings of the least healthy individuals decline most rapidly with age in China, where lower pension coverage leaves many with little option but to continue working despite deteriorating earnings capacity.

17.3.2.1 Productivity

Deterioration in health will often decrease labor market productivity and earnings capacity. But the multidimensionality of health and variation in the capacities and skills required for different occupations are reasons to expect a great deal of heterogeneity in the response of wages to health problems. A mobility-impeding disability obviously constrains the productivity of a manual worker much more than it does that of an office worker. Technology, particularly that which enables remote work and reduces the need for commuting, is making the productivity of workers who draw more on their brains than their brawn even less contingent on physical functioning. But the productivity of such workers is dependent on retaining cognitive functioning and is potentially vulnerable to mental health problems. Thus, the estimated effects of health on wages, derived from measures of different dimensions of health for individuals with different demographic and occupation characteristics, should display substantial variability.

The relationship between productivity and physical health is likely to be strongest in developing countries where there is a preponderance of low-skilled manual work.[9] Identifying the economic returns from health investments has been the motivation for macro studies, revealing a strong positive correlation between economic growth and initial population health (Barro, 2003, 2013),[10] and micro studies of the relationship between wages and health across individuals in developing countries (Strauss and Thomas, 1998). Our focus is not on the impact of health on average income. Rather, we are interested in the extent to which the distribution of health affects the dispersion in incomes.

In low-income settings, the relationship between health and productivity can sustain, exacerbate, and, in theory, even generate inequality. The crux of the argument is that health constrains productivity, and wages provide the means, through nutrition, to sustain health. A negative shock to either health or wages can generate a downward spiral into a nutrition-based poverty trap (Dasgupta, 1993, 1997). The theory of nutrition-based efficiency wages (Bliss and Stern, 1978; Dasgupta and Ray, 1986; Leibenstein, 1957; Mirlees, 1975; Stiglitz, 1976) generates the prediction of increased inequality as a result of the interdependence of nutritional status and productivity. As nutrition rises above the critical threshold of physiological sustenance, the marginal increases in productivity rise substantially, and diminishing returns eventually set in. This nonconvexity results in involuntary unemployment because the savings in labor costs from employing the poorly nourished unemployed at lower wages would be more than offset by the resulting loss in productivity. Individuals with initially fewer assets, who can invest less in health, are more likely to be involuntarily unemployed (Dasgupta and Ray, 1986). The poor are more likely to be malnourished and sick, and because they are sicker, they are more likely to be unemployed and so fall into destitution. Thus, inequality is exacerbated.

The relevance of this theory has been challenged by the observation that one of its central assumptions—that poor households are constrained to spend almost all their resources on food—is inconsistent with the observed behavior of the poor (Banerjee and Duflo, 2011). Starvation is not perennially present even in very low-income

---

[9] Strauss and Thomas (1998) note that the wage elasticity with respect to height (an indicator of health status) was almost eight times larger in Brazil (in the mid-1970s) than it was in the USA (in the early 1990s).

[10] Barro (2013) maps an extension of the neoclassical growth model that incorporates health, in addition to human capital, and sets a resulting research agenda, including the examination of how health and health policies may impact the evolution of income inequality.

countries (Strauss and Thomas, 1998). Ill-health may, however, be a source of a poverty trap and a contributor to inequality. For the income- and asset-poor with little formal or informal insurance options, the loss of productivity and earnings precipitated by illness results in reduced consumption opportunities and consequently nutritional deprivation, which further harms health and constrains productivity. The economic impact of illness is likely to be greatest on poor individuals because their livelihoods rest most on their health and because they have fewer assets that can be used to protect consumption and maintain nutritional status when illness strikes. Even if health shocks were evenly distributed across the population, their differential effects would increase economic inequality.

There is a vast body of evidence concerning the impact of health and nutrition on productivity and wages in low- and middle-income countries. The main motivation for this research is to evaluate the case for investment in health and nutrition programs as an instrument of development policy. Reviewing this literature would take us well beyond the scope of this chapter. In any case, a number of reviews already exist (Commission on Macroeconomics and Health, 2001; Deolalikar, 1988; Schultz, 2005, 2010; Strauss and Thomas, 1998; Thomas and Frenkenberg, 2002). Strauss and Thomas (1998) conclude that there is no robust, consistent evidence from nonexperimental studies that ill-health reduces productivity and wages, although it does reduce labor supply. In interpreting this conclusion, one needs to bear in mind that the wage response to ill-health can only be studied among employees. This misses the large informal sector of the economy in which the productivity of self-employed, mainly agricultural, workers could be expected to depend on health (Dasgupta, 1997). Evidence of an effect of nutrition, as opposed to health, is stronger. Strauss and Thomas (1998) are convinced that the positive impact of nutritional status (height and body size) on wages and micronutrients (particularly iron) clearly raises productivity. Calorie intake, when accurately measured, is found to have a positive effect on wages, at least among those initially malnourished.

17.3.2.2 Discrimination

Not all disabilities impede productivity; at least, not in all occupations. Nonetheless, equally productive disabled individuals may be paid less than their able-bodied counterparts because they are perceived to be less productive, or simply because of prejudice.

Discrimination against the disabled, as against other minority groups, comes in two varieties. What economists refer to as *taste discrimination* would be more commonly recognized as prejudice, and it arises from a preference of employers, or other employees, to keep disabled workers at a distance. Since Becker (1957), this has been modeled as a marginal cost, on top of the wage, that a prejudiced employer incurs in employing a member of the minority group. Such an employer will only hire a disabled person at a wage below his or her marginal product. Whether this discriminatory behavior is sustainable in a competitive market depends on the prevalence of prejudice relative to the supply of disabled labor (Becker, 1957). Under competitive conditions, nonprejudiced firms can undercut their prejudiced rivals, and discrimination will be competed away (Cain, 1986), unless prejudice arises from customers (Kahn, 1991).

This model was developed with the central purpose of explaining and understanding the consequences of discrimination against ethnic minorities. Although some disabilities, or rather handicaps, may still carry a social stigma, most are unlikely to make others, or at least a majority of others, uncomfortable. Stereotyping, or *statistical discrimination* (Aigner and Cain, 1977; Arrow, 1973; Phelps, 1972), seems a more probable source of bias against disabled individuals. In making appointments and wage offers, it is optimal for an employer to supplement information obtained from a noisy signal of productivity, such as a test score or qualifications, with knowledge of the average productivity of a group to which the applicant is observed to belong. Presuming disabled individuals are, on average, less productive, a disabled person would be offered a lower wage than a nondisabled applicant who performed no better with respect to the assessment criteria.

This theory does not help us explain earnings differentials between the disabled and nondisabled over and above those attributable to productivity differences. But it can explain part of the reason for the productivity deficit. If test scores or qualifications are a noisier signal of productivity for the disabled, perhaps because the tests are designed to discriminate between able-bodied applicants, then employers will put less weight on these criteria and more on the observed disability. Faced with a lower return, this group will invest less in human capital. Inequality will be greater than it would be if employers where blind to disability status, or legislation successfully forced them to act as if they were.

Besides its inability to explain earnings differentials beyond those attributable to productivity, the relevance of statistical discrimination as an explanation for health-related wage differences depends upon the extent to which these differences exist across easily recognizable disabilities with known average productivity differentials. A blind man is easily recognized and categorized. Someone with a heart condition is not. Even if all health conditions were observable, perhaps because applicants were required to declare them, how much would employers know about even average productivity specific to them? Rather than responding to an immediately recognizable disability group, employers might have only a partial, perhaps unconsciously biased, understanding of the productivity implication of an incompletely comprehensible health condition.

Empirical identification of discrimination against the disabled is difficult because disability, being an impairment of functioning, will certainly reduce productivity in many jobs. Getting hold of data that make it possible to control for real differences in productivity, and so isolate wage differences attributable to discrimination, is a tall order. Studies that control for little or no differences in health (Kidd et al., 2000) cannot credibly claim to identify discrimination against the disabled. But controlling for impaired functioning while comparing wage differences between the disabled and nondisabled seems to be like asking to have one's cake and eat it. One approach is to concentrate on the wage differences between individuals with easily observed disabilities, such as blindness, paralysis, or loss of a limb, which may be more likely to evoke prejudice, and others who may be completely able-bodied or disabled by an unobservable condition, such as a back pain or heart problems. US data from the 1970s and 1980s reveal that one-third to one-half of the wage differential between these groups is unexplained by wage determinants, including a battery of health indicators intended to capture differences in functional impairments (Baldwin and Johnson, 1994; Johnson and Lambrinos, 1985). This finding is indicative of substantial discrimination only if the controls are sufficient to mop up any productivity differentials. DeLeire (2001) suggests another approach which involves assuming there are no unobserved productivity differences between individuals who report a health problem but no work limitation arising from this and others reporting no health problem. In that case, all of the wage difference between these two groups can be attributed to discrimination. This can be taken as indicative of the discrimination against those with a work-limiting disability under the further assumption that the degree of discrimination is independent of the productivity loss arising from disability. Under these assumptions, only 7–11% of the wage difference not explained by observable characteristics between US males with a work-limiting disability and those with no disability could be attributed to discrimination.[11] It is difficult to hazard a guess as to whether this estimate lies closer to the truth than the larger earlier one, given that both rest on rather strong assumptions.

17.3.2.3 Nonwage Costs and Nonpecuniary Benefits

The previous two subsections considered wage variation arising from health-related differences in (perceived) productivity. The employer was assumed powerless to correct productivity differentials. A richer model of the demand for disabled labor relaxes this assumption. The productivity of someone bound to a wheelchair is contingent on adjustments made to the workplace—ramps, elevators, adjustable desk, etc. Installation of such facilities involves incurring a fixed cost that pays off through raising the marginal product of disabled workers (Acemoglu and Angrist, 2001). Treating labor as a quasi-fixed factor, with the simplifying assumption that there are fixed costs associated with employing disabled but not able-bodied workers, and supposing that workplace modifications close the productivity gap between disabled and able-bodied workers, the wage paid to the former will be lower by the amount of the (discounted) fixed costs (Acemoglu and Angrist, 2001). Wage differentials need not reflect only productivity differences or discrimination. Even with perfect measures of productivity, an empirical test of discriminatory behavior would be difficult. A second implication of this model is that employers are likely to be particularly apprehensive about appointing disabled workers. Fixed costs incurred

---

[11] The analysis is done for 1984 and 1993. Jones et al. (2006) apply the same approach to UK data and also find a small discrimination effect.

up-front must be compared with expectations of future marginal products and wages. A risk-averse employer will opt for labor with a higher proportion of variable costs.

Health-related wage variation could also arise from a willingness of employees to trade wage for nonwage benefits. The onset of a chronic condition would be expected to increase the value attached to employer-provided health insurance (Currie and Madrian, 1999). A worker suffering from a long-term illness would be more likely to accept a wage cut, or to forgo a pay rise, for fear of not being able to obtain insurance in a better paying job. Note that such health-related wage differentials do not imply differences in well-being. The individual is choosing to accept a lower price for his labor in return for obtaining a lower price for health insurance. Nevertheless, this would be an additional mechanism through which health differences may contribute to inequality in measured income, at last in countries with employment-based health insurance.

17.3.2.4 Evidence

Theory identifies mechanisms through which ill-health may reduce wages. But how large is the effect? Is health-induced variation large or small relative to overall wage inequality? The usual econometric demons—selection, omitted variables, reverse causality and measurement error—hinder attempts to answer these empirical questions. Evaluation of the evidence largely comes down to assessing the extent to which these problems have been overcome or avoided. Ill-health is likely to be a major reason for labor-force withdrawal (see next section). Estimation of the impact of health on wages from a cross section of workers or a balanced panel of individuals in continuous employment will overlook those whose wage opportunities were reduced most by ill-health and decided to stop working. Correction of this selection bias requires modeling employment, in addition to wages, with health allowed to impact both. With panel data, there may also be health-related attrition: those experiencing a marked deterioration in health might be more likely to drop out of the sample. Recognizing that individuals can influence their health through lifestyle, for example, leads to the realization that the same unobservable factors, such as time preferences, risk attitudes, and schooling quality, that influence job choices and thus wages may also condition investments in health. If panel data are available, then differencing can be used to purge the time-invariant unobservables correlated with health, or efficiency gains may be sought by using averages of assumed exogenous time-varying covariates to instrument health (Hausman and Taylor, 1981). Neither of these solutions is sufficient to remove bias if there is direct dependence of health on the wage. This is implied by Grossman's seminal model of health determination (Grossman, 1972a,b), according to which the wage influences both the costs of, and the returns to, investments in health (see Section 17.4.1). Correcting or avoiding the threat of simultaneity bias requires identification from exogenous variation in health that does not arise from wage differences. Prices of medical care and, in a developing country context, the local disease environment have been used as instruments for measuring health (Strauss and Thomas, 1998). However, it can be difficult to find variation in prices that is not endogenous to the choice of medical care provider, and geographic variation may be a rather weak instrument (Currie and Madrian, 1999). Disease exposure is often correlated with weather and agricultural conditions that would be expected to impact wages directly.

Currie and Madrian (1999) provide a comprehensive review of the US evidence on the health impact on wages (and on labor supply) up to the end of the twentieth century. They note three main deficiencies in this evidence base. First, estimates are sensitive to the measure of health, and variability in the measures adopted impedes comparability across studies. We would add that this sensitivity does not merely reflect inconsistency in the measurement of health but is due to intrinsic heterogeneity in the effect depending on the nature of the health condition. Second, few studies attempted to correct for the potential endogeneity of health, and those that did relied on rather dubious exclusion restrictions. Third, most of the evidence available referred to white (US) males. Picking up from where Currie and Madrian (1999) left off, in the remainder of this subsection, we focus on the evidence published since 1999, using data from high-income countries. The latter two criticisms have, to an extent, been addressed in the more recent literature. The increasing availability of panel data, particularly on older populations that experience the most variability in health, as well as population level administrative data, has reduced reliance on instruments to deal with endogeneity. Although many studies still tend to focus on males, there are many exceptions, and the evidence comes from a wider spread of countries. All studies cited are summarized in Table 17.3 for evidence relating to the USA and Table 17.4 for studies that use data from European and other high-income countries.

A fixed effects estimate obtained from retrospective life history data collected in the first wave (1992–1993) of the US Health and Retirement Study (HRS) suggests that a work limitation lasting at least 3 months reduces the wage rate by 4.2% for males and twice that for females aged 50–60 (Pelkowski and Berger, 2004). Given that 7–9% of individuals in this age range report such a health condition, these estimates suggest that ill-health makes a substantial, though not dramatic, contribution to wage inequality. Using 25 years of longitudinal data from the US Panel Study of Income Dynamics (PSID), Charles (2003) obtains a fixed effects estimate (corrected for selection into employment) only half as large for men for a similar measure of ill-health experienced by almost one-third of the sample at some time during the panel. This would suggest a much more modest contribution of ill-health to wage inequality. The lower estimate obtained by Charles may be attributable not only to the use of panel data, rather than retrospective, but also to estimation using a younger sample. An analysis of the same dataset and health measure, taking account of simultaneity as well as selection and unobservable heterogeneity, finds that below the age of 35 and above the age of 62 there is little difference between the wage profiles of individuals in good and bad health

Table 17.3 US evidence of health effects on labor market outcomes

			Study details				Effect of ill-health on			
Authors	Data	Sample	Health measure[a]	% in ill-health	Biases addressed	Estimator	Wage[b]	Employment[c]	Hours[d]	Earnings/income
Bound et al. (2010)	HRS 1992–1998 (4 waves)	Single men 50–62 years (baseline)	Latent: SAH instrumented by ADLs		SEL, UH, ME (JB)	DP model by SML		1 SD ↓ from average health @ 60 years → Pr (labor force exit) ↑ 8 ppt		
French (2005)	PSID 1968–1997	20–70 years	Work-limiting physical impairment or nervous condition	30 years: 6% 70 years: 40%	SEL, UH, SIM	FE with SEL and MSM	<35 and >62 years: no effect 35–62 years: ↓ 8–17%	<38 years: no effect 62 years: ↓ 45 ppt 66 years: ↓ 20 ppt	<40 years: no effect >40 years: 20–27% ↓	
Smith (2004)	HRS 1992–2000 (5 waves)	50–62 years	Major/minor new diagnosis	Major (minor): 20% (30%) incidence over 8 years	UH	OLS FD		Major: ↓ 15 ppt Minor: ↓ 4 ppt		Major: ↓ $4000 Minor: ↓ $500 (household annual income)
Pelkowski and Berger (2004)	HRS 1992–3 (life history data)	50–62 years	Work-limiting condition ≥ 3 months	Males: 8.7% Females: 7.3% (lifetime incidence)	SEL	Heckman selection	Males: ↓ 6.4% Females: ↓ 7.2%	Males: ↓ Females: ↓	Males: ↓ 6.3% Females: ↓ 3.9%	Males and females: ↓ 52% (lifetime earnings)
Charles (2003)	PSID 1968–1993	Men 22–64 years	Work-limiting physical impairment	31.6% (disabled at any time over panel)	SEL, UH	FE with Heckman selection	↓ 2%		↓ 6.7%[e]	↓ 15% (annual earnings)
Blau and Gilleskie (2001)	HRS 1992–94 (2 waves)	Men 50–62 years	SAH, work-limiting disability, major/minor diagnoses, ADLs		SEL, ATT, UH, SIM	FIML		Excellent→poor SAH: ↑ labor-force exit 5.7 ppt Work-limiting disability: ↑ labor-force exit 5.5 ppt		
Bound et al. (1999)	HRS 1992–1996 (3 waves)	50–62 years	SAH instrumented by ADLs (effect for SAH ≥ good → < good)		SEL, UH, ME (JB)	SML		Males: ↓ 55 ppt Females: ↓ 46 ppt		
McClellan (1998)	HRS 1992–94 (2 waves)	50–62 years	Major/minor new diagnosis, accident	Major: 3.5–6.3% Minor: 18.5–22% Accident: 5.3–8.7%	UH	OLS FD		Major: ↓ 17.5–26.3 ppt Minor: ↓ 1.8–5.1 ppt Accident: 0–↓ 2.1 ppt	[e]Major: ↓ 13.1–35% Minor: 0–↓ 3.8% Accident: ↓ 4.3–9.6%	

Notes: Table excludes earlier (pre-1998) studies summarized in tables presented in Currie and Madrian (1999). JB, justification bias; ME, measurement error; SIM, simultaneity bias; SEL, selection bias; UH, unobservable heterogeneity (OVB bias). See Table A2 for explanation other acronyms, including those of datasets and variables.

[a]Effects on outcomes are with respect to this health measure.

[b]Impact on hourly wage for those in employment.

[c]Impact on probability of employment unless otherwise stated.

[d]Relative impact on annual work hours.

[e]Assuming average annual work hours of 1800.

Table 17.4 European and rest-of-world evidence of health effects on labor market outcomes

			Study details					Effect of ill-health on		
Authors	Country	Data	Sample	Health measure[a]	% in ill-health	Biases addressed	Estimator	Wage[b]	Employment[c]	Earnings/income
García Gómez et al. (2013)	Netherlands	Administrative 1998–2005	18–64 years	Urgent, unscheduled hospital admission ≥3 nights	0.85%	UH, ME (JB)	DID and matching		↓ 7.1 ppt	↓ 4.8% (in work ↓ 2.9%, on DI ↓ 32.7%) (income)
Halla and Zweimuller, 2013	Austria	Administrative 2000–2007	Private employees 25–50 years	Commuting accident ≥1 sick day	0.67%	UH, ME (JB)	DID and matching	↓ 1.4% (daily wage)	↓ 3.3 ppt	
García-Gómez (2011)	9 EU countries	ECHP 1994–2001 (8 waves)	16–64 years	ΔSAH = top 2→bottom 3, onset chronic illness/disability		UH	DID and matching		ΔSAH: ↓ >5 ppt in 5/9 countries Chronic: ↓ >4 ppt in 6/9 countries	
Jackle and Himmler (2010)	Germany	GSOEP 1995–2006	18–65 years	ΔSAH = top 2→bottom 5	Males: 12.5% Females: 13.3%	SEL, UH, ME, SIM	Semykina and Wooldridge (2010)	Males: ↓ 4.8%. Females: no effect	Males: ↓ 0.5 ppt Females: ↓ 1.5 ppt[d]	
Brown et al. (2010)	UK	BHPS 1991–2004 (14 waves)	18–65 years	SAH instrumented by health problems and reported limited activity		SEL, ME (JB), UH (Mundlak)	2 stage: GOP of SAH→ML of wage and employment probability	No signif. effect	ΔSAH (very good/good→poor/very poor): ↓ 11 ppt	
Jones et al. (2010)	UK	BHPS 1991–2002 (12 waves)	50–60/65 years	Reported limited activity and SAH instrumented by health problems	Limited activity: Males: 15.6% Females: 13.9%	UH (RE) ME (JB) when use instrumented SAH)	2 stage: GOP of SAH→ML of retirement hazard		Effects on retirement hazard: Limited activity – ↑3.5 (M), ↑5.8 (F)[e] ΔSAH (excellent→poor/very poor): ↑ 4.9 (M), ↑ 7.2 (F) (large relative to nonhealth effects)	
Lindeboom and Kerkhofs (2009)	Netherlands	CERRA 1993–95 (2 waves)	Male 43–63 years, employed, household head	Work limitation instrumented by health problems	14%	UH (RE), ME (JB), SIM				
Cai (2009)	Australia	HILDA 2003	Males	SAH (top 3→bottom 2)	10.3% (bottom 2 SAH)	SEL, SIM	FIML	↓17–20%		
Disney et al. (2006)	UK	BHPS 1991–98 (8 waves)	25–64 years 50–60/64 years	SAH instrumented by health problems and reported limited activity		UH (FE (logit) and RE (hazard)), ME (JB)	2 stage: ordered probit of SAH→FE logit		↓ (large relative to nonhealth effects)	

Continued

Table 17.4 European and rest-of-world evidence of health effects on labor market outcomes—cont'd

Authors	Country	Data	Sample	Health measure	% in ill-health	Biases addressed	Estimator	Effect of ill-health on		
								Wage	Employment	Earnings/income
García Gómez and Lopez-Nicolas (2006)	Spain	ECHP 1994–2001 (8 waves)	16–64 years	ΔSAH = top 2 → bottom 3	8.1%	UH	(or RE hazard) of employment DID and matching		↓ 5 ppt	Earnings ↓ €1740 Personal income ↓ €1033 Household income ↓ €1927
Moller Dano (2005)	Denmark	Administrative 1981–2000	20–54 years	Road accident casualty admitted to hospital	1.4%	UH, ME (JB)	DID and matching		Males: ↓ 11.8 ppt Females: no effect	Earnings: M ↓ 12%, F no effect
Au et al. (2005)	Canada	CNPHS 1994–2001 (4 waves)	50–64 years	SAH instrumented with HUI3 or health conditions		ME (JB)	2 stage: Ordered Probit SAH → LPM of employment		1 SD ↓ health: Males ↓ 25 ppt Females ↓ 19–21 ppt	Income: no effect
Contoyannis and Rice (2001)	UK	BHPS 1991–96 (6 waves)	16+ finished schooling	SAH, GHQ (psychological ill-health)	SAH < good: Males: 16% Females: 19%	UH	Hausman and Taylor (1981)	ΔSAH (excellent → <good): M/F: no effect F in work ↓ 2.8% GHQ: M ↓, F no effect		
Kerkhofs et al. (1999)	Netherlands	CERRA 1993–1995 (2 waves)	Male 43–63 years, employed, household head	Work limitation instrumented by health problems (HSCL)		UH, ME (JB)	2 stage: FE of work limitation → ML of employment hazard		↓ (ill-health dominant effect on exit through DI)	
Riphan (1999)	Germany	GSOEP 1984–94 (10 waves)	40–59 years	ΔSAH ↓ 5 points on 10-point scale	3.1%		Logit (employment), unconditional DID (earnings/income)		↓ 6 ppt	Earnings: growth ↓ 1.9 ppt Household income: growth ↓ 5.2 ppt

Notes: Table excludes studies published pre-1999. JB, justification bias; ME, measurement error; SIM, simultaneity bias; SEL, selection bias; UH, unobservable heterogeneity (OVB bias). See Table A2 for explanation other acronyms, including those of datasets and variables.

[a] Effects on outcomes are with respect to this health measure.

[b] Impact on hourly wage for those in employment.

[c] Impact on probability of employment unless otherwise stated.

[d] Estimates from one of estimators used to correct for selectivity bias. Estimates from other estimators vary greatly, reaching effects of 16–19% points.

[e] Despite the large impact of a health shock on the retirement hazard, few individuals experience such a shock, and early retirement is simulated to be only 11% above what it would be in the absence of the shocks incurred.

(French, 2005). But in the prime ages of working life, individuals with a work limitation can command wages around 8–17% below the wages of those in good health.

Using UK panel data and the Hausman and Taylor (1981) estimator, Contoyannis and Rice (2001) find a significant effect of psychological health, but not general SAH, on wages for males, but no interpretation of the magnitude of the effect is given. For females in full-time employment, there is a significant effect of SAH; moving from less than *good* health to *excellent* health is estimated to result in a rather modest wage increase of less than 3%.

A cross-section analysis of data on Australian men that attempts to allow for full simultaneity finds a large effect of SAH on wages (Cai, 2009). But the instruments used (health conditions and behavior) are of dubious validity, and exploitation of the panel dimension of the data using a fixed effects estimator results in a large reduction of the estimate and loss of its significance.[12] Jackle and Himmler (2010) also resort to instruments in order to deal with endogeneity arising from more than correlated time-invariant unobservables in their analysis of German panel data. They assume that past doctor visits determine health but not labor-force participation or wages conditional on this. The rationale is that past medical care is the investment response to previous health shocks and need not be correlated with current labor market outcomes given current health. This may be so, but it does not allow for the possibility that individuals visit a doctor to obtain a sick note to justify work absence. For males, a worsening in reported health from *excellent* to *poor* is estimated to result in a 4.8% drop in the hourly wage. For females, there is no significant effect.

Although differences in health indicators and estimators still make it difficult to compare estimates, we tentatively conclude that ill-health does reduce wages in high-income economies, but the effect is more likely modest than substantial. Because most studies estimate the wage response to ill-health while controlling for occupation, this conclusion refers to the degree to which the wage adjusts within a given job. A larger wage effect may arise through ill-health induced changes in occupation. We examine this effect in Section 17.3.5.

17.3.3 Health and Work

As would be expected, employment rates vary a great deal with health. This is illustrated in Figure 17.4 for China, the Netherlands, and the USA. In the two high-income countries, already in young adulthood, individuals reporting *poor* health are much less likely to be working than their contemporaries reporting better health. The difference in employment by health widens until middle age, after which early retirement begins to reduce

---

[12] The author attributes this to greater measurement error in health changes and failure of the fixed effects estimator to deal with correlated idiosyncratic errors. Alternatively, it could be that the IV estimate is upwardly biased by invalid instruments.

labor-force participation of even those in good health and the employment gap narrows.[13] The relationship between employment and health is different in China in two respects. First, there is little or no difference in employment by health in young adulthood. Second, while a gap opens up at older ages, it never becomes as wide as that observed in the Netherlands and the USA. This is partly an artefact of self-assessed health being reported in four, rather than five, categories in the Chinese survey. But this is not the whole story. In the USA around the age of 50, the employment rate difference between those reporting *fair* health and those reporting *excellent* or *very good* health is about twice as large as the difference between those reporting *poor* health and those reporting *very good* health in China at the same age. The relationship between employment and health is weaker in China. This is not what one would expect given the differences in the structures of the economies and the greater role of manual labor in China. It may be that the more generous social protection in the high-income countries allows individuals experiencing health problems to more easily withdraw from the labor market.

In this section, we consider a number of mechanisms through which health may impact on employment, including the incentive effects of DI.

17.3.3.1 Incapacity and Involuntary Unemployment

The impact of ill-health on work may seem obvious. If you are sick, you cannot work. For relatively short term, acute illnesses, this is a reasonably adequate description of the effect. But it is an effect that could only explain temporary interruptions to earnings and income. Any substantial contribution of the distribution of health to the distribution of income is unlikely to operate through short-term sickness. A few chronic medical conditions are completely incapacitating. But most reduce capacity for work to some degree. Ill-health may reduce productivity, but it is unlikely that the marginal product is pushed to zero in all possible jobs. The wage could fall below the level at which work is considered worthwhile, but that is a choice rather than a *fait accompli*.

This reasoning rests on the assumption that wages are perfectly flexible. Evidence of a moderate impact of health on wages (see Section 17.3.2.4) may reflect institutional constraints on wage flexibility. Equal pay and antidiscrimination laws typically make it illegal for employers to pay disabled workers less than their able-bodied colleagues doing the same job. This may succeed in constraining health-related wage inequality but exacerbate disparities in employment.

The 1990 Americans with Disabilities Act (ADA) compels employers to accommodate disabled workers through adjustments to the workplace and outlaws discrimination against the disabled in hiring, firing, and pay. In theory, the impact on employment of the

---

[13] It is surprising that the total employment rate at ages 50–59 in the Netherlands sample is higher than that in the US sample. This may partly reflect the difference in years, but it seems that the ALP is underestimating the rate in the USA.

disabled is ambiguous. The threat of legal action for discrimination in hiring would tend to increase employment, while increased accommodation and hiring costs would reduce employment. Acemoglu and Angrist (2001) argue that the negative effects are likely to dominate. Before and after legislation, trends in employment are consistent with this prediction (Acemoglu and Angrist, 2001; DeLeire, 2000). Employment of disabled individuals was also reduced immediately after the introduction of the UK Disability Discrimination Act in 1996, which imposed similar obligations on employers as the ADA, before it recovered somewhat (Bell and Heitmueller, 2009). Digging deeper into the effect in the USA, Hotchkiss (2004) reveals that it is not due to individuals always classified as disabled being more likely to leave employment or less likely to enter employment. Rather, it is due to nonparticipants in the labor market reclassifying themselves as disabled after the passing of the legislation. Whether antidiscrimination legislation makes it more difficult for disabled individuals to obtain work may still be an open question. What seems clear is that there is no evidence that major legislation makes it easier for disabled individuals to gain employment.

17.3.3.2 Disability Insurance
Any illness-induced reduction in the offer wage makes labor-force participation less financially attractive. If the decline in health is sufficient to qualify for DI, then financial disincentives to work are compounded. Qualification for DI is not unambiguous (Diamond and Sheshinski, 1995). It is typically not determined by the presence of a precisely defined medical condition but is assessed on the basis of the vague concept of "capability of performing paid work," perhaps taking account of workplace conditions and occupation. There is subjectivity in whether a person considers himself incapable of work, as well as whether the adjudication officer agrees. Financial incentives can tilt the balance in favor of applying for DI. For a given degree of work incapacity, withdrawal from employment is more likely when social protection is available to cushion the resulting loss of income (Autor and Duggan, 2006; Bound and Burkhauser, 1999; Gruber, 2000; Parsons, 1980).

By increasing the likelihood of labor-force withdrawal but compensating for the resulting income loss, the existence and generosity of DI may simultaneously strengthen the relationship between health and earnings, and it may weaken the relationship between health and income.[14] For a given distribution of health, income would be expected to be more equally distributed in countries with generous DI. But the equalizing effect of social protection may be weakened by a moral hazard effect that is stronger for individuals with lower earnings potential. If, as is usually the case, the replacement rate

---

[14] Hurd and Kapteyn (2003) find that income change is more sensitive to the level of self-assessed health of individuals aged 51–64 in the Netherlands, which has more generous DI, than in the USA. A possible explanation is that the moral hazard effect outweighs the income replacement effect of DI. Individuals in poor health are more likely to withdraw from employment in the Netherlands at prime working ages, consistent with what is observed in Figure 17.4.

is decreasing with predisability earnings, the financial disincentive to continue in employment will be greatest for lower-paid workers. As a result of these differential incentives, onset of a given disability is more likely to result in employment withdrawal and loss of earnings (only partially replaced by DI) of lower-paid workers. This differential moral hazard effect will tend to increase income inequality relative to the hypothetical situation in which the financial incentives arising from DI have no impact on employment. But in the complete absence of DI and the income protection it provides, income inequality would be likely to be even greater. In addition to the strength of the differential moral hazard effect, the extent to which DI reduces income inequality will depend on the incidence of disability. The equalizing effect will be greater if, as is likely, the poor are more likely to become disabled. The lower paid are more likely to both benefit from social DI and respond to its financial disincentives to work.

DI rolls have been rising over much of the past 30 years in many high-income countries (OECD, 2010; Wise, 2012). Steep downward trends in mortality rates, accompanied by a compression of disability, if not disease, into fewer years before death (Crimmins and Beltran-Sanchez, 2011; Cutler et al., 2013; Milligan and Wise, 2012), suggest that this is not because populations are becoming less healthy. Looser eligibility criteria and increased returns from claiming DI relative to those available from work are considered to be the chief culprits (Autor and Duggan, 2006; Bound and Burkhauser, 1999; OECD, 2010; Wise, 2012). We will not evaluate the evidence concerning the strength of the moral hazard effect of DI (Bound and Burkhauser, 1999) but concentrate on the proposition that it interacts with increased economic inequality arising from structural changes in the economy to reduce labor-force participation of low-skilled, low-paid workers (Autor and Duggan, 2003, 2006).

The falling relative wages and employment opportunities experienced by low-skilled workers in the USA and other high-income countries since the 1980s increases the attractiveness of DI for this group (Autor and Duggan, 2003; Black et al., 2002). Dependence of DI awards on ability to engage in gainful employment results in DI applications tending to rise in an economic downturn (Autor and Duggan, 2006) and suspicion that some governments deliberately use DI to disguise long-term unemployment. After the loosening of the Social Security Disability Insurance (SSDI) eligibility criteria in the USA in the mid-1980s, the sensitivity of applications to adverse economic conditions increased by at least twofold, and high school dropouts became twice as likely to exit the labor force on the occurrence of a negative shock to the economy (Autor and Duggan, 2003). The effect is compounded by the indexing of the SSDI benefit formula to average wage growth. As a result, the replacement rate has increased for individuals whose wage growth lagged the average, as has been the case for low-paid workers in the USA over the past 30 years (Autor and Duggan, 2003, 2006). The replacement rate was further increased by rising real expenditures on Medicare, the health insurance program for the elderly that SSDI beneficiaries are given entitlement to before reaching the age of 65. Taking into account these fringe benefits, the DI replacement rate for a 50- to 61-year-old male at the 10th percentile of the earnings distribution increased from 68% in 1984 to 86% in 2002 (Autor and Duggan, 2006). At the 90th percentile, the increase was much more modest, from 18% to 22%. As would be expected given these differential incentives, SSDI enrolment rates are much higher and have increased much more rapidly for low-skilled individuals. For male high school dropouts aged 55–64, the rate increased by 5% points between 1984 and 2004 to reach almost 20% (Autor and Duggan, 2006). The increase was only 1% point (to reach 3.7%) for the college educated.

In the USA, reduced earnings prospects relative to the average and increased DI replacement income relative to those reduced earnings, separately and in combination, have reduced the incentives for low-skilled workers with health problems to continue working. Increased reliance of this disadvantaged group on DI may be both a consequence of rising economic inequality and, given the replacement ratio is less than one, a contributor to it. This process may also operate in Europe, which also witnessed increased wage inequality and, at times, rising DI rolls since the 1980s.

17.3.3.3 Preferences

In addition to an indirect effect through DI, ill-health may shift the reservation wage directly by changing preferences for consumption relative to leisure. The direction of the effect is ambiguous. Ill-health would be expected to increase the disutility of work. But it may also reduce the marginal utility of a number of leisure activities, such as sport. The direction of the effect on the marginal utility of consumption is even more difficult to predict. A disabled person may derive less, or no, pleasure from some goods, including sports equipment or travel, but become more dependent on others, such as pharmaceuticals, heating, and private as opposed to public transport. Comparing the relationship between subjective well-being and consumption—proxied by permanent income— for older Americans with and without chronic illness, Finkelstein et al. (2013) infer that the marginal utility of consumption decreases with ill-health. If we assume that the increased disutility of work dominates, such that the marginal utility of leisure rises, this gives a clear prediction that the marginal rate of substitution of leisure for consumption rises when health falls. The reservation wage rises and labor-force withdrawal becomes more likely.[15] More direct evidence suggests that a work-limiting health problem is equivalent to aging around 4 years in the extent to which it increases the willingness of older (58+) Americans to trade consumption for leisure (Gustman and Steinmeier, 1986a,b).[16]

---

[15] The evidence from Finkelstein et al. (2013) is obtained from a sample of nonworking, elderly individuals, and thus, one cannot necessarily infer from this how ill-health affects preferences for consumption relative to leisure.

[16] For other estimates of health-specific utility function parameters in models of health and retirement, see Sickles and Yazbeck (1998) and Bound et al. (2010).

While these estimates support the plausible proposition that ill-health shifts preferences away from work, one should be careful not to overlook the multidimensionality
of health. A physical disability may reduce the marginal utility of many leisure pastimes as
much as, or more than, it raises the disutility of work. A chronic illness such as diabetes
may have little or no impact on preferences for leisure relative to consumption. The
empirical content of a prediction that preferences for work increase with a characteristic
we conveniently refer to as *health* is blurred if that characteristic, or at least the means of
measuring it, is not well defined. In the social sciences, we are rather attached to the concept of health, despite finding it difficult to define what we mean by it (Twaddle, 1974).
Estimates of the impact of ill-health on work–leisure preferences are likely to vary with
the dimensions of health examined and the indicators used to measure them.

17.3.3.4 Life Expectancy

Expected longevity is an additional mechanism through which differences in health may
contribute to observed differences in income and wealth in a cross section. In the standard
life cycle model of consumption with no bequest motive in which there is dissaving
before death, a longer length of life is predicted to increase labor supply (and saving)
at any given age (Chang, 1991; Hammermesh, 1984). This is basically a wealth effect.
Increased lifespan implies greater lifetime potential income. The resulting increase in
demand for consumption prompts a rise in labor supply.[17] We may refer to this as the
horizon effect. Individuals in poor health work less because they do not have to provide
for an extended old age. For a given degree of functional impairment, illnesses that
are life-threatening, or at least life-shortening, should be observed to reduce earnings
by more than chronic disabilities that present no threat to longevity (McClellan, 1998).

Recognizing that the length of life is uncertain and annuity markets are incomplete
gives rise to an offsetting effect. Through the mortality risk on savings, or the prospect of
dying before being able to enjoy the fruits of one's savings, variation in survival probability affects the marginal return on savings and, consequently, the marginal rate of
substitution between consumption and leisure (Chang, 1991; Kalemli-Ozcan and
Weil, 2010). Through this *uncertainty effect*, a reduction in the probability of death raises
the return on and, thus, level of savings, making it possible to reduce labor supply, perhaps by retiring earlier, even when there is a longer expected length of life to be provided
for. The chances of this *uncertainty effect* dominating the *horizon effect* decrease with the
initial mortality rate (Kalemli-Ozcan and Weil, 2010). In high-income countries, one
expects ill-health and reduced longevity to be associated with lower earnings (and
wealth).

---

[17] Similarly, increased loss of time due to sickness within any period of life is predicted to reduce labor supply
in that period, although increases in the expectation and uncertainty of future sickness are predicted to
increase current work effort (O'Donnell, 1995).

17.3.3.5 Evidence

Apart from the ambiguous effects of preferences and longevity, theory gives the clear prediction that ill-health reduces work effort. Under reasonable assumptions for high-income economies, the effects of preferences and longevity go in the same direction. But what is the size of the overall effect of ill-health on employment?[18]

Most studies address this question using samples of older individuals. Effectively, they estimate the impact of health on (early) retirement. In general, health is found to be an important determinant of retirement (Currie and Madrian, 1999; Lindeboom, 2012). How important depends on the measure of health and estimator adopted, as well as the context.

Estimating the effect of health on employment is complicated by econometric obstacles similar to those confronted when trying to identify the impact of health on wages, only the measurement error problem becomes particularly thorny. Most studies have relied on survey data and self-reported measures of ill-health. One would expect the reporting of health to be endogenous to employment. Put most crudely, individuals who have decided not to work may lie about their capacity to work either to reduce the stigma attached to voluntary inactivity or because they are claiming DI. But the phenomenon need not be so blatant. The threshold of functioning at which an individual considers himself to be incapable of work may be influenced, possibly subconsciously, by financial incentives to work, job stimulus, length of working life, contact with others claiming DI, and so on. Reported ill-health may reflect motivations for not working. This so-called *justification bias* has been a major concern in the literature (Bound, 1991). The evidence tends to suggest that it leads to substantial overestimation of the effect of ill-health on employment (Bazzoli, 1985; Bound et al., 2010; Lindeboom, 2012; Lindeboom and Kerkhofs, 2009), although there are dissenting findings (Dwyer and Mitchell, 1999; Stern, 1989).

Replacing reported work incapacity with more objective indicators of chronic illnesses or future mortality reduces the risk of justification bias but increases classical measurement error and may result in underestimation of the effect (Bound, 1991). Instrumenting reported work limitations with more objective health indicators is arguably a better approach (Bound, 1991; Bound et al., 2010; Stern, 1989) but requires that the indicators are free of the justification bias, which may be a strong assumption given these are often also self-reported.

---

[18] We address this question in the context of high-income countries. In low-income countries with less formal labor markets, identification of the impact of health on employment and earnings is more challenging. The literature tends to focus on the extent to which households can smooth consumption over health shocks in the absence of formal health and disability insurance (Gertler and Gruber, 2001; Mohanan, 2013; Townsend, 1994). Reviewing that literature would take us beyond the scope of our objectives.

All studies from North America and Europe that attempt to deal with justification bias by treating self-reported health as endogenous confirm that health is an important determinant of labor-force participation (Au et al., 2005; Blau and Gilleskie, 2001; Bound et al., 1999; Brown et al., 2010; Disney et al., 2006; Dwyer and Mitchell, 1999; Jones et al., 2010; Kerkhofs et al., 1999; Lindeboom and Kerkhofs, 2009; Sickles and Taubman, 1986; Stern, 1989).[19] Health also emerges as a strong determinant of retirement in structural life cycle models of older US males (Bound et al., 2010; French, 2005; Sickles and Yazbeck, 1998). Bound et al. (2010) find that, although responding to justification bias by instrumenting self-reported health with objective indicators greatly reduces the health effect, this effect remains very large. Before the early retirement age, an older single male in bad health is five times more likely to withdraw from the labor force than an equivalent in good health.[20] When US workers reach 62, the age at which Social Security pensions can first be claimed and financial incentives shift in favor of retirement, the probability of withdrawal rises from 0.1 to 0.17 for those in poor health and from 0.025 to 0.049 for those in good health. In absolute terms, those in poor health react more to the financial incentives such that the difference in employment probabilities widens when it becomes financially more advantageous to retire. Ill-health and financial incentives interact. Financial incentives appear to tilt the balance toward considering a health problem to be incapacitating. From a low level of health, marginal deteriorations in health have a large effect. At age 62, when the health of a worker in poor health decreases by one-half of a standard deviation, the probability of that worker's labor-force exit increases from 0.17 to 0.27; this change is 10 times larger than the change in probability for a comparable worker in average health.

Extending the scope of analysis beyond older US males, French (2005) finds a very strong health effect that varies across the lifecycle. Below the age of 40, there is no difference in the employment rate of men in good and bad health. At 40, an incapacitating physical or nervous condition is estimated to reduce employment probability by 5% points for a stereotypical male. The effect reaches a peak of 60 points at age 58 before declining to 45 points at age 62 and 20 points at age 66. In responding to these very large effects, one needs to bear in mind that they are not corrected for justification bias. Despite the very large estimated health effect, the author argues that it is modest in terms of the proportion of the total decline in older male labor-force participation that can be attributed to population health. The percentage of males reporting an incapacity rises from 20% at age 55 to 37% at age 70. Applying the estimated health effect, this decline in health can explain only 7% of the 74% fall in labor-force participation between these ages. This

---

[19] All mentioned studies that are not included in the tables presented in Currie and Madrian (1999) are summarized in Table 17.3 for the USA and Table 17.4 for elsewhere.

[20] Health is modeled as a latent variable. "Good health" refers to an average score and "bad health" to a score one standard deviation below the average.

may be so, but the estimates of both French (2005) and Bound et al. (2010) imply that ill-health can account for a substantial fraction of labor-force withdrawal before the early retirement age of 62.

Establishing a substantial effect of health on employment only takes us part way toward our objective of gauging the contribution of health to the distribution of income. We need to know the earnings and, ultimately, income consequences of illness-induced loss of employment. Reviewing the earlier US evidence, Currie and Madrian (1999) conclude that ill-health has a large negative effect on earnings, which operates mainly through reduced hours of work, including nonparticipation, rather than reduced wages.

From the US HRS life history data, Pelkowski and Berger (2004) find that 7–9% of individuals over the age of 50 have experienced a work limitation at some time that, on average, is estimated to result in the loss of half of their potential future earnings. By far the greatest part of this substantial loss is from the reduced likelihood of working, which falls to around half of its counterfactual value. Taken at face value, these estimates suggest that health is a major determinant of earnings differences. Caution should be exercised in their interpretation, however. A major concern is the retrospective nature of the data, which may be vulnerable to recall, as well as justification, bias. There could be a tendency to report health events that did have labor market consequences and to recall changes in labor outcomes that coincided with periods of illness.

Charles (2003), using the US PSID, finds that annual earnings of initially employed individuals fall, on average, by 15% around the time of onset of disability. Given that almost one-third of the panel experiences a work limitation at least once, this suggests that ill-health is an important contributor to cross-sectional inequality in earnings. But earnings do not remain as depressed as they are immediately following the onset of ill-health. Some illnesses recede and disabilities can be adapted to through retraining. Within 2 years of the onset of disability, about half of the earnings loss is recovered. Subsequently, earnings continue to trend upward, rather slowly, toward the level at which they would have been without the worker having experienced the disability. These findings suggest that Pelkowski and Berger (2004) substantially overestimate lifetime earnings losses by extrapolating from the contemporaneous impact of ill-health on earnings.

While the PSID study provides valuable insight into the impact of ill-health on earnings, it is weakened by reliance on self-reported work limitation with no correction for justification bias. The steepest drops in earnings occur in the period between 1 and 2 years prior to the reporting of a work limitation. One interpretation is that health is declining and impeding labor outcomes prior to the point at which a health problem is reported. But another is that decreasing returns to and motivation for work lead to the reporting of a disability, perhaps to justify entry to DI.

Besides its vulnerability to justification bias, another limitation of the reported work capacity measure is that it focuses on functional impairment and does not discriminate other dimensions of health, such as longevity. This is not sufficiently recognized in part of the literature, which tends to presume that the ideal measure of health would be one that accurately informs of work capacity (Bazzoli, 1985; Bound, 1991; Lindeboom, 2012). Implicitly, the assumption is that there is only one mechanism through which health impacts employment—physical and mental capacity to perform work-related tasks. Recognizing the other mechanisms identified in the preceding subsections, health conditions that differ with respect to their implications for current functional impairment, prospects of recovery, survival chances, and so on can be expected to have differential impacts on work.

McClellan (1998) makes an interesting distinction between three types of health outcomes. *Major health events*, such as a severe heart attack or a stroke, imply both acute and long-term functional impairment and reduced life expectancy. Onset of a *chronic illness*, such as a heart condition or diabetes, does not dramatically affect current functioning but may affect labor supply through expectations given prospects of a degenerative disease and long-term impairment. At the other extreme, *accidents* have an immediate impact on functioning but are less likely to have any effect on preferences or health expectations in the long term. Using the first two waves of the US HRS, McClellan finds evidence consistent with the nature of the health event having an independent effect on employment over and above that of the degree of functional limitation arising from it. For a given change in functioning (measured by Activities of Daily Living (ADL)), the reduction in the employment probability is 40 points greater when it is precipitated by a major health event. The employment probability falls by 14% and 35% points for males incurring a new chronic illness with moderate and major reductions in functioning, respectively. Accidents are not significantly associated with a decline in employment. McClellan interprets this as indicative of employment effects being muted when the health event does not have consequences for long-term health expectations.[21]

Smith (2004) extends this type of analysis by using more waves of the HRS to look at longer term effects. Onset of a major health condition (i.e., cancer, heart disease, lung disease) is associated with an immediate reduction of 15% points in the employment probability of males among whom just over half were working at baseline. After 8 years, those contracting such an illness are 27 points less likely to be working. The short- and long-term effects for those succumbing to a minor chronic illness (i.e., hypertension, diabetes, arthritis, heart attack, angina, and stroke) are reductions of 4% and 11% points, respectively. The average loss in annual household income immediately following the onset of a major chronic illness is $4000, which rises to $6250 after 8 years. Cumulating these losses gives a total loss of income over 8 years of $37,000. The cumulative income loss associated with a minor condition is almost $9000.

---

[21] It could also be that the number of survey participants experiencing an accident does not provide sufficient power to precisely estimate the effect. Using population data, Moller Dano (2005) and Halla and Zweimuller (2013) do find significant effects of accidents on employment (see below).

Although this evidence of sustained reductions in employment and income appears to contradict that of Charles (2003), it does not once the older age of the HRS sample is recognized, and the heterogeneity in the effects estimated by Charles is scrutinized. Men that become chronically disabled, defined as reporting a work limitation in every period after the initial onset, experience an estimated initial earnings loss of 21% with little or no recovery over time. The initial loss is also greater and the recovery absent for older men. So, both studies find substantial permanent losses of income for older males succumbing to a chronic condition.

Bound et al. (1999) focus on the implications of the dynamic evolution of health for the continued labor-force participation of older (50+) US workers. They find that it is health deterioration, rather than the health level arrived at, that most affects labor-force exit. Employment is not simply dependent on current functional capacity because there can be adaptation to impairments. A drop to any given level of health implies lower expectations of future health that may have an independent effect on the decision to continue in employment. Disney et al. (2006) take the same approach with British data and find a different pattern of behavior. Controlling for past health, lower current health still increases the likelihood of job exit. But for any given level of current health, a lower level of past health also raises the probability of retirement. A possible interpretation of this result is that individuals take time to revise their health expectations downward. Only when health is persistently lower is the decision made to retire, which may be difficult to revoke.

Cross-country comparisons can be useful for exploring the extent to which the employment and income responses to ill-health appear to be influenced by employment and social policies. García-Gómez (2011) compares the likelihood of continuing in employment following a sustained drop in SAH in nine EU countries. She finds the employment effects are largest in Ireland, a country in which DI claimants are not allowed to engage in any form of paid work, followed by Denmark and the Netherlands, where replacement rates are highest and, as in Ireland, there is no quota on the percentage of employees that must be registered disabled. In France and Italy, the two countries that impose the highest quotas on disabled employees, there is no significant impact on employment. These findings suggest, but do not confirm, that the employment (and income) effect of ill-health is highly contingent on policies influencing both the demand and supply of disabled labor.

Rather than attempt to identify the health effect from data on self-reported general health, which is difficult to interpret and potentially endogenous, or reported work incapacity, which is possibly even more endogenous due to justification bias, three European studies have concentrated on more narrowly defined health events that are abrupt and unforeseen and so more plausibly exogenous to lifecycle planning of health and labor supply (García Gómez et al., 2013; Halla and Zweimuller, 2013; Moller Dano, 2005). Unlike structural models that aim to estimate the endogenously determined lifecycle profiles of health and labor supply (Bound et al., 2010; French, 2005; Sickles and Yazbeck, 1998), the objective of these studies is to exploit some unanticipated shift in the health profile to estimate the response of employment and income. Two of the studies use accidents (Halla and Zweimuller, 2013; Moller Dano, 2005), and the third relies on urgent and unscheduled hospital admissions (García Gómez et al., 2013). Implementation of this strategy is made feasible by the availability of population, or near population, data from administrative registers providing sufficient observations of relatively rare health events for which matches can be found from millions of control observations. Use of administrative records greatly reduces measurement error and avoids the justification bias that plagues estimates based on reported health. All three of the studies combine matching, which deals with observable differences, with taking difference-in-differences to eliminate correlation of the health event with time-invariant unobservables.

These studies consistently find that a health shock reduces the probability of employment. The estimates range from a 3.3% point reduction as a result of a commuting accident in Austria (Halla and Zweimuller, 2013), through a 7.1 point drop due to an acute hospital admission in the Netherlands (García Gómez et al., 2013), to a 11.8 point fall following a road accident experienced by men in Denmark (Moller Dano, 2005).[22] That the estimates differ in magnitude is to be expected given the narrow definition of the health events from which they are identified. Commuting accidents mostly give rise to musculoskeletal impairments, and diseases of the circulatory, digestive, and respiratory systems are all important causes of acute hospital admissions. Such different conditions would be expected to have different effects. A focus on specific health events that occur suddenly enhances the internal validity of these studies, but generalization to other forms of health deterioration cannot be presumed. There is no avoiding the multidimensionality of health and the consequent heterogeneity in its effects.

These studies confirm that ill-health causes employment to fall, a conclusion that could be made with less certitude from more weakly identified estimates. A less predictable finding is that the effect is persistent. All three studies find that the probability of employment remains reduced by a health shock for at least 5 years following its occurrence. This contrasts with what Charles (2003) finds for prime working-age US men. The difference is most likely attributable to the lack of incentives for DI recipients in continental Europe to move off the roll.

In Austria and the Netherlands, but not in Denmark, the impact on employment is greater for women. In the same two countries, the effects are greater on older persons and blue collar (Austria) or low-income (the Netherlands) workers. This is consistent with evidence from the UK showing that older poor individuals are more likely exit the labor force by entering disability insurance (Banks, 2006). It is also consistent with

---

[22] There is no significant impact of a road accident on the employment probability of women.

US evidence from the PSID that earnings losses from ill-health are larger and more sustained for nonwhites and the poorly educated (Charles, 2003), characteristics associated with working in industries and occupations in which productivity is more contingent on physical health and that identify low-skilled workers for whom, as observed in Section 17.3.3.2, labor market opportunities have deteriorated and dependence on DI has increased. The less privileged may not only be more likely to be struck by ill-health, but their employment and incomes are also more contingent on their health. Ill-health may increase economic inequality through both its skewed incidence and its differential effect.

In the Netherlands, an acute hospital admission results in an average reduction of around 5% in personal income 2 years after the health shock, with little or no recovery over the following 4 years (García Gómez et al., 2013). For individuals who remain in employment, income falls by only 3%, indicative of very modest reductions in wages and hours of work at the intensive margin. Those moving onto DI experience an income loss of one-third, which is broadly consistent with the DI replacement rate. Although this is a substantial drop, the moral hazard effects of providing more complete income protection are likely to be large in a country where at one time 10% of the working-age population was on DI. But Denmark does offer even greater insurance, with an average 12% average drop in male earnings maintained for 6 years after a road accident offset by a rise in transfer income such that there is no significant change in total income (Moller Dano, 2005). This does not imply that there is complete insurance. Presumably, the 12% who lose employment do experience income losses, but this is not reported. For women, there is no significant drop in earnings or loss of income. These findings are consistent with the income consequences of ill-health being muted in a country, such as Denmark, with a generous welfare state. But one should keep in mind that it is the effect of a road accident that is estimated. According to McClellan (1998), accidents should have the mildest economic consequences because the induced health change may be temporary, and longer term functioning and survival expectations may be little affected. This is the limitation of the described approach. Although one can be confident that the estimate does accurately capture the effect of the health change studied, the rarity of the narrowly defined event reduces the relevance of the evidence to the broader question of the extent to which the overall variation in health contributes to observed economic inequality in the population.

17.3.4 Early-Life Health Determinants of Later-Life Economic Inequality

The focus on the income effects of ill-health in adulthood until this point risks missing much of the action. A rapidly growing literature, to which Janet Currie and James Heckman are leading contributors, argues that early-life—even prebirth—and childhood conditions, including health, explain much of the variation in economic outcomes across adults (Almond and Curric, 2012; Cunha et al., 2006; Currie, 2009; Heckman, 2007; Heckman et al., 2006). It has been estimated that a staggering 50% of inequality in the present value of lifetime earnings in the USA can be explained by factors known at age 18 (Cunha and Heckman, 2009). Although most, such as parental occupation, are not directly health-related, exposure to health risks in the womb, infancy, and childhood is a potentially important component of these economically significant conditions. Ill-health in early life may directly constrain health capital in later life and impede the accumulation of nonhealth human capital. Both effects would reduce earnings potential.

One may distinguish three broad mechanisms through which early-life health may impact on economic outcomes in adulthood, differentiated by the life stage in which they become manifest. Nutritional deprivation and exposure to health risks *in utero* and in infancy can directly impair cognitive functioning and lead to childhood health problems that interfere with the acquisition of cognitive, and possibly noncognitive, skills. A second route is through education. Ill-health in childhood and adolescence may restrict opportunities to acquire education, and impaired cognitive functioning arising from insults to health in infancy may reduce the efficiency of schooling in producing educational qualifications. The third mechanism operates through health capital, as opposed to other forms of human capital. Ill-health may persist from childhood to adulthood. More dramatically, exposure to health risks in the womb may do lasting physiological damage, which becomes manifest with the onset of disease in middle age. Earnings may subsequently fall, as is clear from the evidence reviewed in the previous section.

In the following subsections, we discuss each of these three broad mechanisms by which infant and childhood health may constrain economic success in adulthood. This takes us into territory that has traditionally been the domain of psychology and epidemiology but in which economists are increasingly daring to venture. We end the section by summarizing and evaluating the evidence on the extent to which adult economic outcomes are determined by early-life health conditions. We do not provide detailed reviews of the rapidly growing literatures, which have already been provided by researchers with far greater expertise (Almond and Currie, 2011, 2012; Cunha et al., 2006; Currie, 2009). Our focus is on what the literature has to say about the contribution of health to income inequality and to understanding the association between income and health in adulthood.

17.3.4.1 Health, Cognitive, and Noncognitive Capabilities

There is abundant evidence that cognitive functioning is a strong predictor of wages (Cawley et al., 2001; Herrnstein and Murray, 1994; Jencks, 1979). We are interested in whether cognitive functioning measured during childhood determines economic success later in life and whether childhood cognitive function is in part determined by health in infancy. Case and Paxson (2008) provide indirect evidence of the first relationship. Using longitudinal data from the UK, they show the strong positive correlation between earnings and adult height.[23] This relationship is well established, but it falls greatly in magnitude and becomes insignificant when cognitive functioning in childhood, which is shown to be a strong predictor of wages, is controlled for. The change resulting from the cognition control is consistent with early-life nutrition producing both cognition and height and only the former impacting on earnings. After dealing with bias arising from cognition measured in adolescence being a product of (endogenously chosen) schooling, Heckman et al. (2006) find that cognitive functioning is an important determinant of schooling, employment, occupation, and wages.

So, cognitive functioning in childhood has economic consequences. Do we know that cognition itself is contingent on health in infancy? Through animal experiments, neuroscience has identified the biological and neurological processes that link undernutrition, as well as nutrient deficiency and exposure to toxins, *in utero* and infancy to impeded development of the brain (Grantham-McGregor et al., 2007). Birth weight, which is an indicator of exposure to health risks *in utero*, particularly nutritional deprivation, is the most frequently used indicator of the health of humans at birth. Epidemiological studies confirm that low birth weight is associated with low IQ (Breslau et al., 1994), along with a host of other child health problems including asthma (Nepomnyaschy and Reichman, 2006), behavioral problems including attention deficit hyperactivity disorder (ADHD) (Hayes and Sharif, 2009; Loe et al., 2011), slower motor and social development (Hediger et al., 2002), and depression (Costello et al., 2007). While consistent with the neuroscience, one cannot read too much into a simple correlation because low birth weight could reflect the behavior of the pregnant mother correlated with later investments in the child that influence cognitive functioning. Variation in birth weight within siblings and twins has been used to reduce the risk of such bias. This approach has produced evidence that the smaller sibling or twin tends to have a lower IQ at age 7 in Scotland (Lawlor et al., 2006) and on entrance to the military in Norway (Black et al., 2007). The latter finding is more difficult to interpret because IQ in young adulthood could reflect differential investment in education.

In low- and middle-income countries, where the nutritional and micronutrient deficiencies are obviously much more pronounced, there is clearer evidence from randomly assigned nutrition supplementation programs that better nutrition improves cognitive functioning and raises educational attainment (Grantham-McGregor et al., 1991, 2007; Pollitt et al., 1993; Walker et al., 2005). Currie (2009) cites evidence showing that even in the US children of mothers included (not randomly) in a nutritional program during pregnancy achieve higher test scores.

Heckman and his collaborators present evidence demonstrating that noncognitive skills developed in childhood are as important, possibly even more important, than

---

[23] In the USA and the UK, someone who is 1 in. taller has, on average, 1.5–2% higher earnings (Case and Paxson, 2008).

cognitive functioning in explaining economic outcomes in adulthood (Cunha and Heckman, 2009; Heckman, 2007; Heckman et al., 2006). Noncognitive capabilities refer to personality traits, such as self-esteem, perseverance, dependency, consistency, patience, and optimism, which may be considered to be determinants or aspects of preferences over risk and the timing of consumption. Currie (2009) points out that some noncognitive skills are closely related to, or are highly contingent on, mental health conditions. She cites a number of studies presenting evidence that child behavioral problems, such as ADHD and aggression, are strong predictors of lower cognitive functioning, educational attainment, and economic outcomes. Most of the studies control only for observables, but Currie and Stabile (2006) use sibling fixed effects and find that children in both the USA and Canada with high ADHD scores at younger ages had lower cognitive functioning (math and reading test scores) at age 11 and were more likely to be admitted into special education and to have repeated a grade. Given that behavioral mental health problems are so prevalent in children, they are potentially an important part of the link between child health and adult economic circumstances.

Although the evidence base does need strengthening, we believe that there are sufficient conceptual grounds for expecting health in infancy and early childhood to emerge as an important constraint on the formation of cognitive and noncognitive skills that are increasingly recognized as important determinants of labor market success. Within the framework developed by Cunha and Heckman (2008), the importance of these skills in the generation and reproduction of economic inequality derives from the fact that they are malleable. Skills are produced through parental investments, the level and efficiency of which are likely to depend on the socioeconomic environment of the child's family and neighborhood. Heckman (2007) hypothesizes that there may be complementarities between investments in health and cognition. Bad luck of the draw that leaves a child with a deficit of one may make it more difficult to raise the other through investments. An early-life health shock could leave a child frail, with limited capacity to respond to the stimuli that can raise cognitive functioning. Facing a higher price for a marginal gain in functioning, parents may invest less in the development of the child's skills. Thus, sickly kids may be doubly penalized with a deficit in both health and human capital.

17.3.4.2 Education

Education is a potential conduit that links income to health not only over the life cycle but also across generations. Health problems in childhood may directly constrain the acquisition of education, as well as weaken incentives for investment in schooling, with long-run consequences for income. If the children of poorer and less healthy parents are more likely to experience illness, then the interference of health capital in the acquisition of other forms of human capital could contribute to the intergenerational transmission of income (Currie, 2009). Health determination of income distribution may operate with a very long lag.

According to life course epidemiology (Kuh and Ben-Shlomo, 1997; Kuh and Wadsworth, 1993; Wadsworth and Kuh, 1997), childhood illness, which may arise from social deprivation, not only has a permanent effect on health, but it also interferes with education. As a result, occupational opportunities are limited in young adulthood, which may further reduce adult health, and lifetime earnings potential is constrained. Health and income in adulthood are correlated because they are both determined by childhood illness.

The most straightforward way in which health may impact education is through the interruption of schooling. In low-income countries, this could be an important constraint. In high-income countries, it seems less relevant. Currie (2009), citing Grossman and Kaestner (1997), notes that differences in school absence rates between healthy and unhealthy US kids are too small to lead to a strong correlation between health and educational attainment. Any impact of child ill-health on knowledge and skills acquisition more likely operates through the channel examined in the last subsection constrained cognitive functioning and impaired efficiency of learning.

Using a cohort of Britons born in 1958 and controlling for childhood socioeconomic status (SES), Case et al. (2005) find that a health problem in childhood is correlated with lower educational attainment. But poor health and low education could both result from parents who make little investment in the human capital of their offspring. A partial solution is to go one stage back in the child's development when parental behavior can exercise less influence and examine the association between birth weight and educational attainment. We noted above the evidence of the impact of birth weight on cognition. If this is the channel, we now need to establish the next link in the chain, to educational outcomes. There are many epidemiological and social science studies showing that children with very low, or even low, birth weight tend to perform poorly in school (Case et al., 2005; Currie and Hyson, 1999; Hille et al., 1994; Kirkegaard et al., 2006; Saigal et al., 1991). The causality of the relationship is given credence by sibling and twin difference studies of sufficiently large samples from high-income countries across three continents. These studies show lower educational attainment by the children who were smaller at birth (Behrman and Rosenzweig, 2004; Black et al., 2007; Johnson and Schoeni, 2011; Lin and Liu, 2009; Oreopoulos et al., 2008; Royer, 2009). There is, however, variation in the magnitudes of the estimates. For example, using US PSID data, Johnson and Schoeni (2011) find that low birth weight increases the probability of dropping out of high school by one-third, with part of the effect appearing to operate through impaired cognitive functioning. Royer (2009), using data on twins who both became mothers in California, finds a rather small average effect.[24] A claimed feasible 250 g increase in birth weight would raise schooling by only 0.04 of a year.

---

[24] A priori, restriction of the sample to twin pairs who both became mothers risks selection bias, although analysis conducted by the author suggests that this is not large.

A couple of US studies only find significant or substantial effects for children born into poor families or neighborhoods (Conley and Bennett, 2001; Currie and Moretti, 2007). This is consistent with wealthier parents being able to compensate for a health disadvantage in early life, when poorer parents lack the means to invest in medical care or other health and educational inputs. Other studies conducted with British (Currie and Hyson, 1999), Norwegian (Black et al., 2007), and Canadian (Oreopoulos et al., 2008) data find no evidence of this heterogeneity. Hasty attribution of this discrepancy to the equalizing effect of universal health care coverage in Europe and Canada, but not in the USA, would be foolhardy. The 1958 British cohort would have had access to only rudimentary medical interventions for the treatment of low weight babies by today's standards (Almond and Currie, 2012). But it could be that little treatment was available for both rich and poor low-birth-weight babies in 1950s Britain. The pertinent question is whether the gradient observed in the more recent US data arises from differential access to effective medical care and possibly other corrective interventions. It may also be that the incentives parents have to make investments that compensate for poor child health differ between the rich and the poor. A particularly tight budget constraint may not allow investment in all offspring. It can then be optimal to concentrate investments on the child with the best chance at the expense of the child the parents observe to be frail and likely to struggle in life in any case (Almond and Currie, 2012).[25]

There is emerging evidence of a link between measures of school performance, or educational attainment, and *in utero* exposure to health risks through disease (Almond, 2006; Kelly, 2011), radiation (Almond et al., 2009), and maternal alcohol consumption (Nilsson, 2009). This is arguably a more convincing strategy to identify the effect of early-life health on education than that of twin differences because it uses variation in infant health risks that is external to the family environment and so is more plausibly exogenous to factors that also impact on schooling. Even more convincing is evidence that treatment of children for disease raises school attendance (Bleakley, 2007; Miguel and Kremer, 2004).

The evidence is convincing that health status at the time of birth impacts positively on educational attainment. How does this effect operate? Does fetal distress permanently damage cognitive functioning, which interferes with knowledge acquisition and skills development throughout school? Or do children who are frail at birth subsequently develop health conditions and illnesses at preschool ages that delay development and place the child at a disadvantage throughout his or her schooling? Or do health problems

---

[25] In general, the investment response will depend on the technology of human-capital production and the parental aversion to inequality across children (Almond and Currie, 2011). When technology is such that early-life health shocks can only be partially offset by later childhood investments, it can be optimal to reinforce the shock by withdrawing investment in the frail child irrespective of the degree of inequality aversion. This is more likely to occur as household income falls. See Appendix C and footnote 7 in Almond and Currie (2011).

in the preschool and early school years lead to additional health problems in later school life at ages when qualifications must be obtained? Currie et al. (2010) are able to address these types of questions by using rich Canadian data following children from birth into young adulthood. Controlling for sibling fixed effects, birth weight, and congenital and perinatal abnormalities, which always have effects, major physical health conditions and injuries in the preschool (0–3) and early school (4–8) years impact on educational attainment only because they raise the probability of experiencing similar conditions in later school years. The process is different with respect to mental health conditions. Behavioral problems at all ages, including the preschool years, directly reduce educational attainment. From this and other evidence, Almond and Currie (2012) conclude that there is an important effect of early-life health on human-capital acquisition and later-life outcomes. Exposure to adverse conditions *in utero* appears to exert a stronger effect than postnatal health, although mental health conditions identified in the preschool years have lasting effects.

Besides a *technological* effect of childhood ill-health on the acquisition of education, if the reduction in health is permanent, then there may be an *incentive* effect operating through life expectancy. A longer life may raise education by lengthening the period over which the return on this investment can be reaped (Ben-Porath, 1967). This further strengthens the extent to which dispersion in health implies dispersion in earnings potential. There is an inequality increasing concentration of health and human capital in the same individuals.

17.3.4.3 Fetal Origins Hypothesis

Early-life health potentially determines later-life economic outcomes not only via education and skills acquisition but more directly through health problems that interfere with productive work in adulthood. The *fetal origins hypothesis*, proposed by David Barker, is that chronic diseases, principally coronary heart diseases but also related diseases such as type 2 diabetes, originate in nutritional deprivation in gestation and infancy (Barker, 1992, 1995; Barker et al., 1993). Nutrition-induced stresses placed on the fetus at critical stages of development alter the physiology of vital organs, particularly the heart, which makes them susceptible to failure in middle and old age, inducing the onset of chronic disease.[26] Metabolism can also be detrimentally affected by *in utero* nutritional deprivation such that the risk of obesity is raised.

One cause of fetal stress that has been exploited to estimate long-term economic effects is *in utero* exposure to the 1918–1919 Spanish flu (Almond, 2006), which has been shown to increase the incidence of stroke, diabetes, and hearing, seeing, and mobility impairments (Almond and Mazumder, 2005), as well as cardiovascular disease

---

[26] The theory is not free of sceptics in medicine and epidemiology. See, for example, Paneth and Susser (1995) who call for clearer elucidation of precise physiological mechanisms and their testing.

(Mazumder et al., 2010). As is clear from the evidence reviewed in Section 17.3.3.5, chronic illnesses such as these have negative impacts on employment and earnings. Economic consequences of the *fetal origins hypothesis* are a topic that is increasingly receiving attention (Almond and Currie, 2011, 2012; Currie, 2009). We discuss some of the evidence in Section 17.3.4.4.

17.3.4.4 Economic Consequences of Early-Life Ill-Health

The previous three subsections establish that ill-health in early life and childhood constrains the acquisition of nonhealth human capital and directly impinges on adult health. With these disadvantages, one expects adults who were sick, or exposed to health risks as infants and children to be less well-off. What is the evidence that frailty of health at the beginning of life leads to economic disadvantage later in life?

Analyses of the 1958 British birth cohort establish that low birth weight is not only associated with lower educational attainment but also with lower employment, greater likelihood of being engaged in manual labor, and lower wages (Case et al., 2005; Currie and Hyson, 1999). Sibling and twin fixed effects studies produce evidence that lower birth weight reduces wages in Minnesota (Behrman and Rosenzweig, 2004) and reduces employment and earnings in the USA (Johnson and Schoeni, 2011).[27] It also reduces earnings (but not employment) in Norway (Black et al., 2007).[28] In addition, low birth weight increases welfare dependency in Canada (Currie et al., 2010; Oreopoulos et al., 2008) and may (Currie and Moretti, 2007) or may not (Royer, 2009) increase the likelihood of living in a poor neighborhood of California.

Johnson and Schoeni (2011) find that only around 10% of the effect of low birth weight on earnings operates through years of schooling.[29] The fact that most of the health effect does not operate via human capital is consistent with the findings of other studies (Luo and Waite, 2005; Persico et al., 2004; Smith, 2009). Using the 1970 British Cohort Study, Conti et al. (2010a,b) do not find any selection into postcompulsory schooling on the basis of child health for males and only a weak effect for females, although there is very strong selection on cognitive and noncognitive skills. There is a direct effect of child health on wages for males, but the weak wage effect for females does run via education.

---

[27] Low birth weight is estimated to reduce labor-force participation by 5% points and earnings (given employment) by around 15%.

[28] A 10% increase in birth weight is estimated to raise earnings of the full-time employed by 1%, an effect equivalent to that of about 3 months of education.

[29] In interpreting this finding, one should bear in mind that birth weight is estimated to have a small and insignificant impact on years of education. Rather, its stronger impacts are on the probability of high school graduation and on test scores. If these intermediate outcomes were considered, then, presumably, the proportion of the effect of birth weight on earnings that operates through human capital would be revealed to be greater.

The health measures employed by Conti et al. are height and head circumference at age 10. Although these measures should pick up nutritional deprivation at early ages, they will miss many other child health conditions. Estimating the long-term economic impact of child health, more generally defined, is made difficult by the scarcity of suitable longitudinal data and the challenge of measuring the general health status of children. Using the US PSID, Smith (2009) estimates that an adult retrospectively reporting *excellent* or *very good* health in childhood earns 24% more than his or her sibling who reports less than *good* health in childhood. There are no differences in education, so again most of the effect, if we are prepared to label the earnings difference as such, does not appear to operate through human capital.

In an intriguing paper, Almond (2006) finds dramatic effects of *in utero* exposure to the 1919 Spanish flu on economic outcomes. Earnings of male workers were reduced by 5–9%. Applying standard estimates of the return to education to the impact on schooling (length reduced by 5 months, on average, and high school graduation probability down by 13–15%), the indirect effect through education explains around one-half of the earnings effect. So, although there is support for the *pathways model* of life course epidemiology that proposes that the infant health effect operates (partly) through education (Hertzman et al., 2001; Kuh et al., 2003), this does not tell the full story. There appears to be a substantial direct effect of fetal conditions on earnings.

Welfare payments, which include DI, are higher for those exposed to the flu. There is also evidence of a substantial effect through occupation. For men, exposure results in a drop of around 6% on a hierarchical index of occupational status. Total income is reduced by about 6.4% for men, and the probability of being poor is increased by as much as 15% points.[30] Identification of these effects from prebirth conditions cuts through the endogeneity problems that plague the evidence on the economic consequences of ill-health reviewed in Section 17.3.3.5. The limitation is that the link between health and economic outcomes is less transparent. The identification requires a leap of faith that it is the Spanish flu and not some other peculiarity of the 1919 birth cohort that is responsible for the effects.[31]

---

[30] Poverty is defined as an income below 150% of the poverty line. The effects presented here for occupation and income are computed as the average of the effects for the 3 census years presented in Table 17.1, each of which is scaled by a one-third infection rate and expressed relative to the control group means in Table 17.2 in Almond (2006).

[31] Additional evidence of the long-term economic effects of early-life health conditions includes Nilsson's (2009) finding that increased *in utero* exposure to alcohol due to mothers drinking more following a liberalization of licensing laws in Sweden not only reduced years of schooling but also decreased earnings and increased welfare dependency. Based on the effects of a program to eradicate hookworm in the American South in the first quarter of the twentieth century, Bleakley (2007) estimates that infection with the disease in childhood reduced the probability of school enrollment by 20% and reduced wages by around 40%.

Subject to this caveat, this study has important implications for the interpretation of income distribution and its association with health. Sizable differences in incomes, and in its education and occupation determinants, appear to be attributable to differences in health conditions at the very beginning of life. Policies that can improve the early-life conditions of the most vulnerable infants can potentially compress the distribution of income decades later by ensuring that there are fewer physically frail individuals who can become the most economically deprived. Almond (2006) draws attention to the tremendous racial disparity in early-life conditions in the USA, where nonwhites are exposed to twice the infant mortality rate of whites. His estimates suggest that this health inequality may not only be a consequence of current economic inequality but also a potentially important cause of future economic inequality.

Overall, the evidence points to the health environment in which a child is conceived and delivered exerting a lifelong effect on economic opportunities. Currie (2009) notes that it is difficult to gauge the magnitude of the effect, given the variety of health risks and measures that have been employed by researchers and the differing study contexts. However, the evidence would seem sufficient to conclude that it is not a negligible effect. A further tentative conclusion is that the effect of health risks in infanthood on economic outcomes, via adult health, is stronger than the effect that operates via educational attainment. This is sometimes claimed as support for the *fetal origins hypothesis*. Strictly, it is not. The hypothesis claims a direct causal link between fetal health and the onset of chronic disease in middle age. Yet, a number of the studies purported to find evidence consistent with the hypothesis examine younger adults, and the health measures used often do not identify the cardiovascular conditions that are triggered by fetal stress according to the theory. Adult health can also be related to health conditions in childhood because illness is persistent and cumulative, which is a feature of the *accumulation model* of epidemiology (Kuh et al., 2003; Riley, 1989).

It is safe to conclude that health in early life is relevant to economic circumstances in adult life. Establishing precisely why and to what extent is a challenging research agenda to be tackled by both economists and epidemiologists.

17.3.5 Health and Occupation

The *life course model* identifies entry into the labor market as an important stage at which the relationship between health and SES is strengthened (Kuh and Wadsworth, 1993). Frail young adults face a narrower choice of entry-level jobs both because their education has been constrained by ill-health and because persistent health conditions directly impede productivity or provoke discrimination. The evidence reviewed in the previous section suggests that the direct productivity effect is stronger than the education effect. The income gradient in health may then partly reflect selection of the less healthy into lower-paid jobs, as well as sickness impeding movement up the career ladder.

This mechanism has been the focus of the epidemiological literature that has considered the extent to which causality runs from health to SES. The literature generally concludes that health-related occupation selection and social mobility are of insufficient magnitudes to make important contributions to the observed socioeconomic gradient in health (Chandola et al., 2003; Power et al., 1996, 1998). In this literature, SES is typically measured by occupation, social class, or employment grade. What is found is that, although job changes are related to health, movements of the more healthy into "better jobs" are insufficient to explain the observed health disparity across the occupational hierarchy (Chandola et al., 2003). The same need not follow with respect to the explanation of health differences across more economic dimensions of SES, such as earnings or income (Adda et al., 2003). As is hopefully clear by now, ill-health can impact on income through many channels other than occupation, and thus, even if this is not an important mechanism, it certainly does not follow that the income (rather than the occupation) gradient in health is mainly attributable to causality from income to health, rather than vice versa. Researchers from the economics discipline are generally more sympathetic to the selection hypothesis (Deaton, 2002, forthcoming; Smith, 2004). In particular, they recognize and emphasize the potential evolution of an individual's career and health based on his early-life health and other experiences, as discussed in the previous section (Case and Paxson, 2011).

The health-related selection of occupation need not necessarily steepen the income gradient in health. If productivity varies with health, and productivity is unobservable, then wages will vary with health only if the latter is observable (Strauss and Thomas, 1998). If health is not observable, then the healthy would be expected to sort into occupations in which productivity is less difficult to observe. Particularly in low-income countries, the healthy may stick to self-employment in which there is no issue of productivity verification and earnings are not set at some average over higher and lower levels of productivity. But such occupations may offer lower earnings potential, perhaps because there is less capital per unit of labor. Wage differences by health would be more compressed than in a situation in which there was no sorting.

The evidence reviewed in Section 17.3.2.4 generally provides estimates of the impact of health on the wage rate conditional on occupation. But there could be an additional effect on earnings through occupation itself. The evidence on job change after the onset of a health condition is relatively sparse. Now rather old data reveal that around one quarter of males and one-fifth of females in the USA with a work-limiting health problem report having moved to jobs more compatible with their conditions (Daly and Bound, 1996). Older workers and high school dropouts are less likely to change jobs. Charles (2003) argues that older workers are less likely to retrain for the purpose of accommodating a disability, because they have less time remaining to reap a return on this investment. He finds evidence consistent with this hypothesis in the US PSID. The low-educated may be less likely to adapt because they lack the general human capital that raises the efficiency of specific investments. It is more difficult to move from manual to nonmanual labor if basic reading and writing skills are lacking. This may partly explain why lower-educated, lower-skilled, and lower-paid workers are more likely to exit the labor force when struck down by a disability (Banks, 2006; García Gómez et al., 2013; Halla and Zweimuller, 2013) and, in the USA, are less likely to recover earnings lost after the initial onset of a disability (Charles, 2003).

17.3.6 Health and Household Income

The impact of health on the distribution of household incomes may differ from that on the distribution of individual incomes for two principal reasons. First, health may affect the formation and dissolution of households. Second, the illness of one household member may provoke a response from the labor supply of others.

Poor health may make it more difficult to find a partner. Limitations in functioning, caring needs, and reduced expected longevity may make a disabled or chronically ill person a less attractive proposition in what some economists refer to as the *marriage market*. On top of the direct effect, there may be a reinforcing indirect effect operating through the impact of health on human-capital accumulation and earnings potential; marrying a sicker person, on average, means marrying a poorer person. The marriage vows of "in sickness and in health" appear to recognize the threat that illness poses to marriage. If less healthy people do have fewer opportunities to find and keep a partner, then one would expect that there will be health-related sorting. Then lower than average earnings of a disabled or sickly person will be compounded, not compensated, by the earnings of his or her spouse.

Although the idea that health influences marriage prospects has been around for some time (Carter and Glick, 1976; Sheps, 1961), there is little convincing evidence with which to judge its empirical validity. In part, this is because of the difficulty of separating healthy selection into marriage from the potentially beneficial effect of marriage on health (Goldman, 1993). Longitudinal data are required. Fu and Goldman (1994) find little evidence that health predicts the marriage behavior of young American adults. For US women there is evidence of health selection, however. Among young women not in full-time employment, those in better health are more likely to marry and less likely to break up (Waldron et al., 1996), and in a Californian sample of siblings, the sister with the lower birth weight is 3% points less likely to be married when she gives birth (Currie and Moretti, 2007).

Recognition of potential health gains from marriage introduces the possibility that there is negative health selection into the institution. The less healthy have more to gain from marriage. Lillard and Panis (1996) find evidence of such adverse selection among US men; the less healthy (re)marry sooner and remain married for longer. However, there is also selection on unobservables correlated with good health, and this dominates so that married men are healthier than their unmarried counterparts.

Within a household, ill-health of one partner could provoke two conflicting motivations for labor market activity of the other partner. On the one hand, reduced earnings of the disabled partner will generate an income effect that will motivate the spouse to replace those lost earnings through increased work effort. This is the added worker effect that is familiar in the unemployment literature. On the other hand, the disabled person's productivity may be reduced not only in the labor market, but also within the household. Limitations in functioning may reduce capacity to wash, dress, and feed oneself. Meeting these caring needs will place demands on the spouse's time. *A priori*, one cannot say which effect will dominate.

There appears to be a gender difference in the relative magnitude of the two effects, but the direction of this bias is not always consistent. Most US evidence finds that women are more likely to participate in employment when their husbands fall ill, but, if anything, male spouses are less likely to participate (Berger, 1983; Berger and Fleisher, 1984; Charles, 1999; Van Houtven and Coe, 2010). Coile (2004) finds no effect on the female spouse and only a small increase in the employment of men whose wives fall ill, however. The employment response of the spouse has also been found to depend on the type of health condition and the initial labor supply of the spouse (Blau and Riphahn, 1999; Siegel, 2006).

There is evidence from Germany (Riphan, 1999), Spain (García Gómez and Lopez-Nicolas, 2006), and the Netherlands (García Gómez et al., 2013) that ill-health reduces household income by more than the fall in the personal income of the person experiencing the health shock. For example, the Dutch study finds that an acute hospital admission reduces household income by 50% more than the reduction in income of the person admitted to hospital.

17.3.7 Health and Wealth

The impact of health on economic inequality may go beyond wage and income distributions to wealth distribution.[32] If ill-health reduces income through one or more of the mechanisms identified in the previous subsections, then opportunities to accumulate wealth over a lifetime will be constrained. Because the effect is accumulated, permanent differences in health will create greater variance in wealth than in income. In addition, ill-health may force depletion of wealth to pay for medical or nursing care. Less obviously, health may affect wealth through life expectancy and consequent saving incentives. The *horizon* and *uncertainty* effects of increased longevity both raise saving, while they have contradictory effects on labor supply (see Section 17.3.3.4). Those expecting to live

---

[32] Identification of the distribution of wealth itself can require taking an account of the distribution of health, or rather mortality. When one only observes the wealth of the deceased in the form of inheritances, then mortality multipliers need to be applied in order to infer the distribution of wealth among the living. Differential mortality may be taken into account (Atkinson and Harrison, 1978).

for longer will accumulate more wealth both to provide for an extended old age and because they face a lower risk of dying before having the opportunity to enjoy their savings.

Consistent with these mechanisms, the relationship between health and wealth is particularly strong. PSID data reveal that the median wealth in 1994 of a household whose head was in *excellent* health 10 years earlier was 268% greater than the median wealth of a household whose head had been in *poor* health (Smith, 1999). This wealth inequality grew both with the lapse of time since the difference in heath was recorded and with age, consistent with differential rates of wealth accumulation by health. A number of US studies have examined whether the strong positive relationship between health and wealth is due to causality from health to wealth, causality from wealth to health, or simply a spurious correlation.

The much-cited paper by Adams et al. (2003) analyzes panel data on a sample of the US population aged 70+ (Asset and Health Dynamics among the Oldest Old—AHEAD). Their focus on the elderly eliminates differential earnings as a mechanism through which health may contribute to differences in wealth accumulation. The null of no causation from both current and previous health, indicated by 19 conditions and SAH, to the change in wealth is rejected.[33] The authors' rigorous analysis leads them to emphasize that, although the result is consistent with a causal effect from health to wealth, they cannot rule out the possibility that it reflects model misspecification and/or time-invariant unobservable factors driving the evolution of both health and wealth.

Michaud and van Soest (2008) overcome both limitations and provide even more conclusive evidence of a causal effect from health to wealth. They use the HRS and allow for causality operating contemporaneously and with lags in both directions, along with unobservable heterogeneity. Health is measured by an index constructed from principal components analysis of SAH, major and minor conditions, ADL, depression score, and body mass index. The health of both the husband and the wife are found to impact on household wealth. The effect of the wife's health is immediate, but that of the husband's health is delayed.[34] This assumption is due to a gender difference in the type of ill-health that impacts on wealth. For both sexes there is a delayed impact of physical ill-health. But only the mental health of females has an impact on wealth that is immediate. Evidence of the causal impact of health on wealth is stronger for households that lack health insurance

---

[33] The null is rejected for total, liquid, and nonliquid wealth for couples in which both partners survive and single households (except nonliquid wealth). The null is not rejected in a number of cases for couples experiencing a death (see Adams et al., 2003, Table 11).

[34] Instruments are required in models that allow contemporaneous effects. The onset of major health conditions (cancer, heart condition, lung disease, and stroke) is used under the assumption that these critical illnesses only impact wealth though health and are not contemporaneously affected by changes in wealth. Essentially, this is the same identification assumption used by Smith (2004) and Wu (2003).

coverage, particularly those in which the wife succumbs to mental ill-health, suggesting that depletion of assets to pay for medical care is an important part of the effect.

Although the Michaud and van Soest study gives us good reason to believe that there is an effect of health on wealth, at least in the older US population, its use of a health index has the disadvantage of not producing an estimate of easily interpretable magnitude. Without allowing for unobservables that condition the evolution of both health and wealth, Smith (2004) estimates, using HRS data, that the income loss, medical expenses, and consequent forgoing of interest arising from the onset of a major health condition (see Section 17.3.3.5) accumulate over 8 years to an average loss of wealth of almost $50,000. Most of this lost wealth is due to reduced earnings. Consequently, the wealth loss is considerably lower ($11,350) for the older AHEAD cohort analyzed by Adams et al. The wealth loss resulting from the onset of a minor health condition is also much smaller ($11,500). Recognizing that one-fifth of Americans aged 50+ experience the onset of a major health condition over an 8-year period and a further 30% incur a minor condition, Smith argues that the consequent wealth losses represent substantial effects of health on the distribution of wealth. Consistent with Michaud and van Soest (2008), the magnitude of the effect that does not operate though earnings losses is larger when the wife experiences the illness (Wu, 2003).[35] This effect relationship is explained by assets being run down to pay for general living expenses when the wife is no longer fit to perform household chores. Accordingly, it is not observed when the husband's health deteriorates.

Overall, the evidence is convincing that health constrains the accumulation of wealth, and illness speeds its depletion. The magnitude of the effect is likely to differ with the nature of the health condition and the means of financing both pensions and medical care.[36] In the USA, for which most evidence is available, the effect seems substantial. Variation in both health levels and rates of health depreciation with age may make substantial contributions to interhousehold inequality in wealth holdings.

17.3.8 Summary

Understanding the effects of health on income and wealth is important for the explanation of distributions of income and wealth and the interpretation of the economic

---

[35] This evidence comes from analysis of only the first two waves of the HRS and the contemporaneous relationship between changes in health and changes in wealth.

[36] Hurd and Kapteyn (2003) propose and confirm that the relationship between wealth and health at older ages is weaker in a country such as the Netherlands, where a greater share of retirement income is obtained from annuities, than in a country such as the USA, where savings and assets are more important sources of financing consumption in old age. Differential financing of medical care, and not only the source of retirement incomes, may contribute to this result. One expects a stronger correlation between wealth and health in countries, such as the USA, with less comprehensive public health insurance and where, until the 2010 Affordable Care Act, private insurance premiums could be related to pre-existing conditions.

gradient in health. We have identified a number of pathways through which health potentially impacts income and wealth, and the evidence suggests that many of these are empirically important. Ill-health can lead to a fall in wages at the margin, but wages are more likely to drop through job changes. In high-income economies, policies that constrain wage flexibility, such as effective minimum wage laws and antidiscrimination legislation, which has been strengthened considerably in relation to disability in Europe and the USA from the 1990s onward, can limit the downward pressure on wages, but this effect often comes at the cost of reducing employment opportunities for disabled individuals. Legislation frequently obligates employers to adapt workplace and employment conditions to accommodate disabled workers, and the responses of employers may vary across sectors and occupations. Changes toward a more disability-friendly workplace are evident to those of us working in white collar and professional occupations. Employers faced with difficulties in recruiting skilled workers may offer an accommodating work environment and flexible hours to secure a competitive advantage. In lower-paid sectors, employment decisions have become more short-term, however, and firms may be even less willing to invest in accommodating low-skilled workers with health problems. Although we are not aware of any evidence of such a heterogeneous employer response, it is a hypothesis worthy of investigation, not least because it implies that increasing general labor market inequality would generate an even greater increase in inequality between disabled workers with different skill sets.

Policy further conditions the labor market response to ill-health through DI, which protects incomes but increases the impact on employment through a sizable incentive effect. From the perspective of public finances, the moral hazard of DI is a legitimate and substantial concern. However, the increased responsiveness of employment to ill-health does not necessarily imply welfare loss. For individuals suffering health conditions that make work extremely uncomfortable, DI may, indeed should, allow these workers to withdraw from the labor force. In lower-income economies with less social protection, ill-health may have a smaller impact on employment, and perhaps even on money income, but it could contribute more to inequality in well-being, because the necessity to continue working with a disability reduces worker utility, both immediately through the discomfort of work and in the long term through reduced health. This point serves as a reminder that, although the focus of this chapter is on the relationship between two central dimensions of well-being, income and health, we are ultimately interested in the implications of this relationship for the distribution of well-being itself.

The impact of ill-health on household income can be substantially larger than that on the earnings of the disabled person, because of a spillover effect on the labor supply of the spouse. In addition, illness may reduce the likelihood of forming and maintaining marriage partnerships, although the evidence on this point is mixed. Through these two mechanisms, the contribution of ill-health to inequality in household incomes need not be less and may even be greater than its contribution to inequality in personal incomes. Beyond DI, policy can attenuate the contribution of ill-health to inequality in household disposable incomes through the tax and benefit system. High marginal tax rates, resulting from tax credits and other income-tested transfers, will moderate any increased inequality in gross household earnings arising from the distribution of health.

Perhaps the most important conclusion emerging from the literature, and emphasized by others (Almond and Currie, 2012; Currie, 2009; Heckman, 2007), is that ill-health can have a very long reach from exposure to health risks in childhood to constrained economic opportunities in adulthood. By constraining human-capital acquisition through education and skills formation, as well as persistent and delayed effects on health in adulthood, early-life and childhood health experiences can be important determinants of both income distribution and the observed income gradient in adult health.

A good deal of evidence supports the mechanisms through which health may impact income and wealth, but inferring the magnitude of each effect is far from easy. This is because, even with respect to a particular mechanism, there is not a single effect but many. Health is not unidimensional. Different dimensions of health will impact income and wealth through different routes and to different degrees. Using a general measure of health, such as self-assessed health, may provide some average effect over different types of health problems, but the usefulness of this average is questionable. Relatedly, measurement error in health variables has been a substantial obstacle to obtaining credible estimates of health on labor market outcomes. But this problem is receding. Longitudinal surveys, such as the HRS and its equivalents, increasingly contain detailed measures of specific health conditions, allowing researchers to exploit the timing of illness onset in order to identify the economic consequences of intrinsically interesting changes in health with precise medical meanings. Also promising is the increasing access of researchers to linked administrative registers on hospital admissions, social insurance, and tax files, which drastically reduce measurement error and provide very large samples from which the effects of specific medical conditions can be identified.

Ill-health reduces income and wealth. The contribution of health to economic inequality depends upon how it is distributed. If health variation is random, then it adds to the dispersion of income (wealth). In this case, the additional economic inequality may not be considered socially objectionable. Losing income as a consequence of illness may be seen as unlucky but not unjust, and insurance may be called for on grounds of efficiency. The consequences for economic inequality—both the nature of the impact and its normative interpretation—are quite different if ill-health is not distributed by the roll of the dice, however. The next section examines whether income and wealth exert causal effects on health. Irrespective of whether such effects exist, if individuals with lower potential incomes are more likely to fall sick, then the income distribution is skewed even more to the disadvantage of the poor. For example, assume that low education both reduces income and increases the likelihood of sickness. The poor are more likely to get sick, and because they are sick, they become even poorer. The income distribution gets stretched by the unequal incidence of illness and its impact on income. Economic inequality is generated by biases that place the socially underprivileged at a health disadvantage and then impose an economic penalty for this status. Thus, inequality is more likely to be considered morally objectionable than it would be if it arose from even-handed luck in the distribution of illness.

In addition to the uneven incidence of illness, the effect of health on economic inequality is likely exacerbated by heterogeneity in the impact of health on income across the income distribution. The employment and earnings of low-skilled, low-paid workers is more contingent on their health than is the case for higher-paid professionals. Not only do the socially disadvantaged face a higher incidence of illness, but they are also more economically vulnerable to it. DI provides a safety net, but its disincentive effects are stronger for the low-paid, and they are more responsive to these incentives, because labor market opportunities have been deteriorating for this group since the 1980s. As a result, the loss of employment following ill-health is both a contributor to economic inequality and a consequence of it.

We conjecture that ill-health contributes to economic inequality not merely by adding noise to the distribution of income (wealth) but by further reducing the incomes (wealth) of those who would be located toward the bottom of the distribution in any case. This could occur even without low income or wealth reducing health. We now turn to the question of whether there is a causal effect from the economic to the health domain of well-being.

17.4. ECONOMIC DETERMINATION OF HEALTH INEQUALITY

17.4.1 Overview

If, as one would expect, health is a normal good, then the financially better-off will demand more of it. Whether this inflated demand is realized will depend on how health-enhancing and health-depleting goods are allocated. If medical care is delivered through the market, then the rich will be both willing and able to afford more effective treatment when illness strikes. But few countries, particularly high-income ones, leave the distribution of health care entirely to the market. Public provision of care to the poor and elderly, or even universal provision of care to the entire population, should constrain health differences that arise from variation in the individual's willingness and ability to pay for medicine. But other goods that are beneficial to health, such as quality housing, safe neighborhoods, and education, are at least partially allocated by the market and provide an opportunity for income to "buy" health. The direction of the relationship is not, however, unambiguous. Whether inequality in health reflects economic inequality will depend on the extent to which the greater demand of richer individuals for health is offset by their higher demand for the pleasures of alcohol, smoking, and rich foods that higher income makes affordable.

Whether the better-off should be expected to be in better health will also depend on the source of their economic advantage. If it arises from higher earnings potential, then the health effect is ambiguous. This insight emerges from Grossman's (1972a) health-capital model according to which health is demanded for a direct utility benefit—feeling sick is uncomfortable—and a production benefit—less time is lost to sickness and so more is available for work. Health is produced by investment in medical care, exercise, healthy eating, and so on. In the pure investment version of the model, which incorporates the production benefit only, a wage increase has two conflicting effects on health. A higher wage implies a higher value for a given increase in productive time, which would lead higher-waged individuals to invest more in health. But the marginal cost of the time input into health investment also increases. More earnings are lost visiting the doctor, jogging, and so on. The net effect is positive, provided that market goods, such as medical care and nutritious food, are used in the production of health in addition to the individual's own time input (Grossman, 2000). But in the pure consumption version of the model, which confines attention to the direct utility benefit of health, the fact that the time cost of producing health is less than the total cost is not sufficient to create a positive substitution effect from a wage increase. The relative intensity with which time is used in the production of health must be less than the relative time input into the production of other commodities that generate utility. Otherwise, a wage increase implies a rise in the relative price of health. Maintaining one's health is likely to be more time-intensive than many other activities that generate sources of utility, and thus, a negative pure wage effect certainly cannot be ruled out.

Empirically determining the extent to which economic advantage bestows health advantage is complicated greatly by the multitude of mechanisms, identified in the previous section, through which health impacts economic circumstances, as well as the plethora of *unobservables*, such as risk attitudes, time preferences, and genetics, that can influence investments in health and other human and financial capital. Fixed effects methods deal with the latter problem but are powerless against the former simultaneity problem, and early attempts to tackle both problems tended to rely on instruments of questionable validity.[37] Since the beginning of the twenty-first century, researchers have increasingly studied changes in the health response due to more plausibly exogenous sources of variation in income or wealth, such as sudden policy reforms, stock market volatility, or windfall gains. The weakness of this strategy is that it employs a form of economic variation that, while exogenous, does not correspond to the variation that can plausibly impact health. The problem is exacerbated by the fact that health does not respond immediately to a change in demand. Even if a windfall gain from a stock market

---

[37] For example, Ettner (1996) instruments the wage rate with work experience and state unemployment rate, and unearned income with parental and spousal education. Work experience may be correlated with the evolution of health, and parental education could have a direct effect on health.

boom, inheritance, or lottery win does induce a rise in an individual's desired level of health, achieving this improved health will take years of investment in preventive medical care, diet, and so on. Even long panels may be insufficient to observe this process. There is a greater chance of identifying the income effect on health determinants than on health itself.

Many chronic health problems are also unlikely to be provoked by sudden changes in income or wealth, but they may, in part, result from long-term exposure to unhealthy living conditions experienced by the poor. The time lag in such an effect, along with the obvious endogeneity issues, make its identification challenging. Most of the existing evidence does not relate to such long-term relationships, and this lack of applicable data must be kept in mind when interpreting the evidence from shorter-term variation that tends to show no, or a weak, effect of income or wealth on health, at least in higher-income countries.

In this section, we begin our review of the evidence by examining the impact of income and wealth on health in adulthood. Most of this evidence comes from high-income countries. We then turn to mechanisms and look at the evidence that economic resources impact health behavior and utilization of medical care. The penultimate subsection examines the evidence for an impact of household economic circumstances on child health. Much of this evidence has been collected from low- and middle-income countries, or it refers to low-income populations in high-income countries.[38]

17.4.2 Income and Wealth Effects on Adult Health
17.4.2.1 Causality Tests
Perhaps the most influential examination of the economic determinants of health conducted since the turn of the century is the study by Adams et al. (2003). Adams and colleagues recognize the difficulty of finding plausibly exogenous instruments for economic circumstances that provide variation relevant to mechanisms of causation. So, they concentrate on the less demanding task of testing for the absence of causal income and wealth effects (and other dimensions of SES) on health among elderly (70+) Americans (see Table 17.5 for details of this study and other evidence relating to the USA). Their focus on an elderly sample neatly sidesteps the reverse causality from health to earnings that would likely occur in a sample of working-age individuals, and this complication is further avoided by adopting the concept of Granger (1969) causality and testing whether, conditional on lagged health, current health is uncorrelated with lagged income (wealth). This involves imposition of an assumption that there is no contemporaneous impact of income (or wealth) on health. The authors argue this plausible and strive to weaken it

---

[38] We purposefully do not cover macro studies that attempt to identify the impact of country GDP on the mortality rate (see Pritchett and Summers, 1996), because such studies tell us nothing about whether income is a determinant of health within any country.

Table 17.5 US evidence of income and wealth effects on adult health and health behavior

Authors	Data	Sample	Income/ wealth measure[a]	Measures of health/ health behavior	Estimator	IV for income/ wealth	Effect on health	Effect on health behavior or medical care use	Remarks
Carman (2013)	PSID 1984–2007	Adults	Inheritance	SAH	FE ordered logit	Inheritance	Overall—none Males—negative		Positive effect of anticipated inheritance
McInerney et al. (2013)	HRS 2006 and 2008	Adults 50+	Drop in nonhousing wealth	CES–D depression score, anxiety, medication, SAH	IV in 1st differences	Interview date post 2008 stock market crash	↑ CES–D ↑1.4 ppt prob. depressed ↓ prob. of *good health*	↑ prob. antidepressant use for large wealth losses	
Schwandt (2013)	HRS 1992–2008	Retirees reporting wealth, income and stocks	Change in stock value as % lifetime wealth	Onset health conditions (hypertension, heart disease, stroke, etc.), SAH, CES-D depression score, survival	OLS on change in health (2SLS in robustness checks)	Identification of change in S&P 500 index	↓ onset health conditions ↑ reported change in SAH ↓ CES–D, ↑ survival ↓ hypertension, heart disease, stroke, psychiatric problems No signif. effect on diabetes, cancer, lung disease, arthritis		
Van Kippersluis and Galama (2013)	HRS 1992–2010	50 +	Household wealth	Smoking and drinking	IV FE	Inheritances		↑ moderate, not excessive, drinking. ↑ smoking	
Kim and Ruhm (2012)	HRS 1992–2006	50–60 at baseline	Inheritances (above and below $10,000)	Mortality, SAH, ADL, CES–D	Discrete time hazard (logit), LPM As Adams et al. (2003)	Inheritance also used as IV for household income	Mortality—no effect Health—no robust evidence of effects		Effects on medical care and behavior explored
Stowasser et al. (2012)	HRS and AHEAD 1992–2008	50 +	Liquid and nonliquid wealth income	As Adams et al. (2003)	As Adams et al. (2003)		Noncausality rejected for many conditions		Rejection of noncausality does not→causality

Table 17.5 US evidence of income and wealth effects on adult health and health behavior—cont'd

Authors	Data	Sample	Income/ wealth measure	Measures of health/ health behavior	Estimator	IV for income/ wealth	Effect on health	Effect on health behavior or medical care use	Remarks
Goda et al. (2011)	AHEAD 1993–1995	70+ at baseline	Social Security (SS) income	Use of home care or nursing home	IV probit	SS notch		↑ home care, ↓ nursing home care	
Salm (2011)	US Vital statistics 1900–1917	Union Army Veterans	Pensions	Age-adjusted mortality, by cause of death	Weibull prop. hazard		11.5–29.6% ↓ mortality		Mortality reductions strongest for infectious disease related deaths
Cawley et al. (2010)	NHIS 1990–1992, 1994–1996	55+	Household income	BMI, over- and underweight, obesity	2SLS	SS notch (5–7% income loss)	No effects	No effects	
Michaud and van Soest (2008)	HRS 1992–2002 (6 waves)	Couples 51–61 at baseline	Liquid and nonliquid wealth	Health index constructed from SAH, conditions, ADL, CES-D, BMI	Dynamic panel GMM	Inheritances when allow contemporaneous effect	No effects		Models w/o unobserved heterogeneity or with too few lags →different estimates
Schmeiser (2009)	NLSY 1979	Low-income 25–43 years	Family income	BMI and obesity	2SLS, 2 SQR, FE	EITC		Females: ↑ BMI and ↑ prob. obese Males: no effects	
Smith (2007)	PSID 1984–1999	Adults	Household income, total and stock market wealth ↓ Social Security income	Onset of new health conditions/disease	Probit		No effects		No effect of either positive or negative wealth change
Moran and Simon (2006)	AHEAD 1993/94	70+		Use of prescription drugs	OLS and IV	SS Notch	–	↓ prescription drug use among low income	

Table 17.5 US evidence of income and wealth effects on adult health and health behavior—cont'd

Authors	Data	Sample	Income/ wealth measure	Measures of health/ health behavior	Estimator	IV for income/ wealth	Effect on health	Effect on health behavior or medical care use[a]	Remarks
Snyder and Evans (2006)	MCOD NHIS 1986–1994	65+	Family income	5-year mortality rates	DID and RDD	SS Notch	↑ mortality		
Adams et al. (2003)	AHEAD 1994–1998	70+	Liquid and nonliquid wealth, household income	Mortality, acute and chronic conditions, SAH, ADL, BMI, smoking	Probit and ordered probit		Non-causality not rejected except for mental health and some chronic conditions	Noncausality rejected only for smoking (males) and BMI (females)	UH not eliminated
Meer et al. (2003)	PSID 1984–1999	Household heads	Net wealth (not pension wealth)	SAH	Two-stage probit	Gifts or inheritances > $10,000	No effect	–	
Deaton and Paxson (2001)	CPS 1976–96	25–85	Equivalent family income	Mortality	OLS and IV	Schooling and cohort dummies	Long term (middle age): ↓ mortality Short-term (young men): ↑ mortality	–	
Ettner (1996)	NSFH 1987, SIPP 1986–1997, NHIS 1988	18–65	Family income	SAH, work and functional limitations, bed days, alcohol consumption, depressive symptoms	OLS and 2SLS	Work experience and state unemp. rate, parental and spousal education	Strong and large ↑ physical and mental health	No effects	Dubious IVs

Note: See Appendix for explanation of dataset, variable, and estimator acronyms.

[a]Effect on health/health behavior is with respect to health measure defined in this column.

further by conditioning on a battery of health conditions that are presumed, in a medical sense, to be precursors of the illness that income (wealth) is hypothesized to affect.

In this study, the null stating that lagged income (wealth) does not predict health is not rejected for most conditions, including acute, sudden-onset conditions and mortality. The authors interpret this result as consistent with the absence of a causal effect of income and wealth on most health outcomes.[39] The hypothesis of no causal effect of wealth is rejected for the incidence of mental health problems, and the results for chronic and degenerative diseases are mixed. The authors argue that, because the treatment of mental and chronic illnesses are often not (fully) covered by Medicare, the ability of the individual to pay for such care may be a causal factor in the determination of these conditions.[40]

Stowasser et al. (2012) revisit the analysis by applying the same Granger causality tests to the original data source extended to a longer observation period, younger cohorts at a given age and younger ages (50+ rather than 70+). The last extension generates some variation in health insurance status that was not present in the older, Medicare-eligible sample included in the original study. With these changes, the null that health is conditionally independent of lagged income and wealth is rejected for a much larger number of conditions, leaving only a minority of conditions for which it is not rejected. This result is problematic for the approach because rejection of the null can arise either due to a true causal effect or a common correlation with omitted unobservables. So, while the original study tends toward the conclusion of no causal effect of income or wealth on health, analysis of more data leaves one in the unfortunate situation of being unable to make any conclusions about the existence of the causal effect.

17.4.2.2 Causal Effects

Panel data methods can be used to deal with time-invariant unobservable determinants of health and income that cloud the conclusions that can be drawn from Granger causality analysis, although this is not straightforward because it uses the nonlinear estimators appropriate for modeling categorical health measures when dynamics and long-term relationships are taken into account. Estimating a dynamic random effects model of SAH with British data, Contoyannis et al. (2004) find that health varies with income averaged over time but not with current income (see Table 17.6 for all studies providing evidence from Europe). This result might be interpreted as indicating that health responds to changes in permanent income but not to transitory income shocks. As such, it is consistent with the above-mentioned argument that sudden income surprises observed over a

---

[39] Considering that correlation through omitted common determinants is not ruled out, this interpretation of the test outcome is based on the presumption that there is no offsetting bias from unobserved heterogeneity that might confound a true causal effect enough for the net association to be insignificantly different from zero (Heckman, 2003; Stowasser et al., 2012).

[40] Adda et al. (2003) question the plausibility of this interpretation because they find similar results using the same tests applied to Swedish and UK cohorts that are fully covered.

Table 17.6 European evidence of income and wealth effects on adult health and health behavior

Authors	Country and data	Sample	Income/wealth measure[a]	Measures of health/ health behavior	Estimator	Effect on health	Effect on health behavior or medical care use	Remarks
Apouey and Clark (2013)	UK BHPS 1997–2005	Adults	Lottery winnings	SAH, mental health (GHQ), physical health problems, smoking, social drinking	FE OLS	Mental health ↑ SAH and physical health— no effects	↑ smoking and drinking	
Van Kippersluis and Galama (2013)	UK BHPS 1997–2008	Adults	Household wealth instrumented by lottery win	Smoking and drinking	IV FE		↑ in moderate, not excessive drinking No effect on smoking	
Adda et al. (2009)	UK FES, GHS, and HSE 1978–2003, HMD 1978–1998	Synthetic cohorts 30–60 years	Equivalent household income (cohort averaged)	Mortality, SAH, chronic illness, blood pressure, cardiovascular/ respiratory diseases. Smoking and drinking	GMM	Mortality ↑ Health/morbidity—no effects	Smoking/ drinking ↑	Assume no effect of cohort health shocks on income
Gardner and Oswald (2007)	UK BHPS 1996–2003	Adults	Lottery winnings 1000–120,000 GBP	Mental health (GHQ)	OLS	↑ mental health (↓ 1.4/36 GHQ points) 2 years after win		Estimates derived from only 137 wins >1000 GBP
Frijters et al. (2005)	Germany SOEP 1984–2002 (west) and 1990–2002 (east)	18+	Household income	Health satisfaction (1–10)	FE ordered logit	Significant but small ↑ health; in East Germany is small effect for males only	–	No exogenous income variation for West Germans
Lindahl (2005)	Sweden SLLS 1968, 1974, 1981	Adults	Disposable family income (tax register) instrumented by lottery win	Health index, mortality, overweight	2SLS and probit	10% ↑ in income → ↑ health index 0.04–0.09 SD and ↓ 2–3 ppt prob. death within 10 years	No effect on overweight	IV estimates for mortality by large. No effects for older (60+)

Continued

Table 17.6 European evidence of income and wealth effects on adult health and health behavior—cont'd

Authors	Country and data	Sample	Income/wealth measure	Measures of health/health behavior	Estimator	Effect on health	Effect on health behavior or medical care use	Remarks
Contoyannis et al. (2004)	UK BHPS 1991–1999	16+	Household income (current = annual permanent = mean over panel)	SAH	Dynamic RE ordered probit	↑ health larger for permanent than current income. Larger effect for men than women		Cannot separate UH from permanent income in mean income effect
Deaton and Paxson (2004)	England and Wales FES 1971–1998	25–85	Gross income per adult equivalent (cohort average)	Mortality and tobacco expenditure (cohort averages)	OLS	No coherent, stable effects	—	Tenuous identifying assumption of time-invariant age effect on mortality
Jensen and Richter (2004)	Russia RLMS 1995–1996	Pensioner households	Pension income	Mortality, ADL, calorie and protein intake, medication	FE	Pension arrear ↑ 2-year mortality for men by 6%	↓ nutrition, medication, and checkups	
Adda et al. (2003)	Sweden ULF	28–84	Household income	As in Adams et al. (2003)	As in Adams et al. (2003)	Noncausality rejected only rejected for similar conditions to Adams et al	Noncausality rejected from smoking and BMIs	

Note: See Appendix for explanation of dataset, variable, and estimator acronyms.
[a]Effect on health/health behavior is with respect to health measure defined in this column.

short period may not provide variation in economic circumstances relevant to the determination of health. Sustained differences in income that influence long-term behavior seem more relevant to the evolution of health. However, caution is called for because it is not possible to separate the effect of individual income averaged over a panel from that of time-invariant correlated unobservables.

Frijters et al. (2005) exploit the largely exogenous income variation generated by the reunification of Germany in 1990 that resulted in sudden large income gains for nearly all residents of the former East Germany. Reverse causality cannot be eliminated because the East German component of the panel only started in 1990, and so reunification cannot be used as an instrument. Fixed effects models of reported health satisfaction reveal positive effects of income on health in the West, but, surprisingly, in the East where the income variation was much greater, these effects are only observed for males. However, all estimated effects are very small. Taking into account that the estimates are potentially upwardly biased by the failure to eliminate reverse causality, this study suggests that income does not have a substantial causal impact on health (satisfaction) in Germany.

Using data aggregated at the level of birth cohorts, Deaton and Paxson (2001) find strong negative effects of income on all-cause US mortality in the period 1976–1996. The effects appear strongest in middle age and in young men. But these findings are not uncontroversial. It is difficult to rule out reverse causality in cohort models, and the authors' use of education as an instrument for income is easily criticized. Moreover, the same authors do not find any coherent or stable effects of cohort income on cohort mortality in England and Wales (1971–1998) (Deaton and Paxson, 2004). They conclude that the observed correlated cohort income growth and mortality decline in both countries does not necessarily reflect a causal effect of the former on the latter, but it more plausibly arises from technological advances and the emergence of new diseases, such as AIDS, that affect age groups differentially. In this case, the main identifying assumption of the cohort approach—that age effects on mortality are constant through time—is invalid. This rather negative conclusion has not kept others from adopting a similar approach. Adda et al. (2009) study the health effect of permanent income innovations arising from structural changes in the UK economy in the 1980s and 1990s that are assumed to be exogenous. They find that cohort incomes have little effect on a wide range of health outcomes, but they do lead to *increases* in mortality: a 1% increase in income is estimated to lead to 0.7–1 more deaths per 100,000 persons among the prime-aged (30–60) population in any given year. This result is in sharp contrast to Deaton and Paxson's finding of no mortality effect for the UK, and a negative effect of income on mortality for the USA. The authors claim their finding is consistent with substantial evidence that population health is countercyclical (Ruhm, 2000, 2003), although they are identifying the health effect of permanent income shocks, not transitory changes.

The countercyclicality of health is consistent with accumulating evidence from the USA of deterioration in individual health coinciding with the receipt of income. Evans and Moore (2011) find that mortality increases immediately following the arrival of monthly Social Security payments, regular wage payments for military personnel, tax rebates, and dividend payments. The increase in mortality is large and occurs for many causes of death connected to short-term behavior—like heart attacks and traffic accidents—but not for cancer deaths, which suggests that the effects derive from increased risky behavior. For example, the daily mortality of seniors is half a percentage point higher in the week after Social Security pay checks arrive compared to the week before. Mortality in younger populations is even more responsive to income receipt. Dobkin and Puller (2007) find elevated drug-related hospital admissions (23%) and within-hospital mortality (22%) in California in the first few days of the month for recipients on federal DI programs paid on the first of the month.

Health deterioration in response to payment of a given level of income is not necessarily inconsistent with health improvement arising from a permanently higher level of income. Higher income may afford both a smoother consumption profile and a lifestyle that is freer of health-threatening binging on alcohol or drugs. Although the evidence on the health response to the receipt of income rightly makes one wary of the health consequences of increased intermittent cash payments to certain groups, it tells us nothing about how the level of income impacts health.

Identification of the health effect of windfalls arising from prizes, lottery wins, investment returns, or inheritances is attractive because the gains are unanticipated and so are more plausibly exogenous to the evolution of health. Smith (2007) exploits large wealth gains accumulated by US stockholders during the stock market run-ups of the late 1980s and 1990s to estimate effects on the onset of major and minor chronic conditions, while conditioning on baseline health, income, and wealth. He does not deal with unobserved heterogeneity and so uses the language of prediction, not causation. Wealth changes (positive or negative) do not predict health changes.

Using the same PSID data but instrumenting wealth by inheritances, Meer et al. (2003) also find no significant effect on health. The same negative result emerges from three studies that test for a response of health to inheritance-induced changes in wealth using data on older (50+) individuals from the HRS (Carman, 2013; Kim and Ruhm, 2012; Michaud and van Soest, 2008). Allowing for a rich lag structure and unobserved heterogeneity, Michaud and van Soest (2008), as was noted in Section 17.3.7, find a significant effect of health on wealth, but they find *no* evidence of a causal effect of (contemporaneous or lagged) wealth on either SAH or chronic conditions.[41] Carman (2013) finds that health is only correlated with inheritances that are anticipated, the exogeneity of which may be doubted.

In stark contrast, Schwandt (2013) provides evidence of a positive wealth effect on health among relatively well-off retirees observed in the US HRS. In this admirably

---

[41] Inheritances are only used as an instrument for wealth in the models that test for a contemporaneous effect.

careful and detailed study, the author constructs a claimed exogenous measure of wealth shocks from the rate of change in the S&P 500 stock market index over a 2-year period applied to the household's share of lifetime wealth held in stocks. The use of this measure presumes that it is the proportionate, and not the absolute, change in wealth that potentially impacts health. Thus, a psychophysiological response to a relative change in wealth, perhaps operating through stress, will generate more health variation in relatively wealthy, stock-holding retirees with health insurance than will a change in absolute wealth, given that the absolute change in wealth is not large enough to influence their ability to purchase health-preserving goods, such as medical care. Schwandt (2013) estimates that a shock (positive or negative) corresponding to 5% of lifetime wealth, which is within the range observed in the data, is positively associated with a change of 1–2% of a standard deviation in a variety of health measures, including onset of new health conditions, reported change in self-assessed health, mental health, and, for negative wealth shocks, even survival. Consistent with the hypothesis of a mechanism operating through stress, the study shows a significant impact on hypertension and, to a lesser extent, heart disease, stroke, and psychiatric problems, but no significant effect on conditions that are likely to evolve more gradually, such as diabetes, arthritis, cancer, and lung disease, although this may also be attributable to the lower incidence of some of the latter conditions. A further clue to a possible mechanism is provided by comparing the estimated health effects of a wealth shock with the cross-sectional correlation of health and wealth. For aggregate health conditions, mental health, hypertension, and heart disease, the magnitude of the estimated effect is greater than the respective correlation. For chronic conditions that take longer to develop, the opposite is true. This is consistent with an abrupt change in wealth of the otherwise well-off triggering a health change that is quite different in nature and aetiology from the health differences by wealth observed in that population.

Zooming in on the October 2008 stock market crash, McInerney et al. (2013) present further evidence from the HRS on the impact of large wealth losses on mental health.[42] The crash reduced wealth and increased depressive symptoms, as well as the use of antidepressants. The effects are nontrivial: for instance, a loss of $50,000 in the value of non-housing wealth is estimated to increase the likelihood of feeling depressed by 1.4% points (8% in relative terms). Although one may expect some recovery from these immediate and substantial declines in mental health as result of adaptation, the evidence from

---

[42] There is striking and persistent evidence from analyses of aggregated data showing that mortality tends to follow the business cycle, increasing during booms and declining during recessions (Ruhm, 2000, 2003). Although this evidence is not necessarily directly relevant to an explanation of the strong positive cross-sectional correlation between income and health, it does appear inconsistent with income gains causally raising health. The health benefits of recessions have been contested in research covering the post-2007 Great Recession period by McInerney and Mellor (2012), Stevens et al. (2011), Tekin et al. (2013), as well as Ruhm (2013) himself.

Schwandt (2013) would suggest that the mental stress may provoke the onset of risk factors for physical illness.

The main threat to identifying the short-term health effect of a wealth shock arising from share prices is the possibility that health risks differ systematically with the fraction of wealth held in stocks. Schwandt (2013) provides some analysis that suggests this is not driving his results. However, a dynamic model of joint decisions over financial and health investments, which has a good fit with the relationships observed in PSID data, does predict that individuals facing greater health risks will diversify by holding less risky financial investments (Hugonnier et al., 2013). This model also predicts that investments in health rise steeply with wealth. While resting on strong behavioral assumptions, it provides insight into the joint evolution of health and wealth and could potentially be useful for pinpointing strategies for convincingly identifying the wealth effect on health.

A few European studies find evidence of positive health effects resulting from lottery wins. Using a Swedish panel and instrumenting a measure of permanent income (average income over 15 years) with average lottery winnings, Lindahl (2005) estimates that an income increase of 10% generates a fall in morbidity and a rather spectacular 2–3% point decrease in the probability of dying within 5–10 years. One may be sceptical of the credibility of such a large effect, which exceeds even the raw correlation between income and mortality. Using British data, Gardner and Oswald (2007) find that 2 years after a win of between £1000 and £120,000, the GHQ index of mental health increased by 1.4 points, on a scale of 36 points. The effect is only significant for males and, surprisingly, for higher-income individuals. Using a few more waves of the same data, Apouey and Clark (2013) find that lottery winnings have no significant effect on SAH, but a large positive effect on mental health.

Although the exogeneity of windfalls is certainly valuable, one may question the relevance of the resulting evidence to an understanding of the large differences in morbidity and mortality between the rich and the poor that are likely to arise from sustained differences in health behavior, and perhaps access to medical care, over many years. Economic shocks observed in data with a limited longitudinal span are potentially useful in identifying short-term health responses, but they can tell us little or nothing about the mechanisms responsible for the gradient in health conditions that emerge over the life cycle.

Pension policies have provided a final source of income variation from which researchers have attempted to identify effects on health. Jensen and Richter (2004) study the effect of losses in pension income in Russia during a major crisis period (1995–1996) (Table 17.6). Delayed pension payments had a dramatic impact on living standards, with income declining by up to 24% and poverty rates tripling to over 50%. For males, the loss of pension income increased the likelihood of death within 2 years by 5.8% points, and raised functional impairment (ADL) and the probability of experiencing chest pain. These effects are likely to have materialized from substantial and significant reductions in both calorie and protein intake, as well as reduced use of medication for chronic conditions and preventive checkups. There were no effects on women's health or mortality.

Back in the USA, Snyder and Evans (2006) report evidence suggesting that reduced pension income *raises* health (Table 17.5). They exploit a notch in Social Security payments that resulted in those born after January 1, 1917, receiving sharply lower retirement incomes than contemporaries with identical earnings histories born slightly earlier. There was little time to adjust to the income loss because the legislative changes happened late in their working lives. In any case, most of those affected did not realize the impact of the changes until after retirement. The authors find that the decrease in pensions reduced mortality and rationalize this surprising result by a claimed positive health effect of increased postretirement (part-time) work effort in response to the income loss.

The contradictory evidence from the USA and Russia is most plausibly attributable to differences in how the level of income around pensions fluctuated. There is evidence of large mortality reductions (particularly for the poor) resulting from increases in pensions paid to US Union Army veterans at the beginning of the twentieth century (Salm, 2011), when both incomes and health were obviously much lower than in the period studied by Snyder and Evans.

17.4.3 Income and Wealth Effects on Health Behavior

The evidence reviewed in the previous section does not support a strong, or even any, causal effect of income, or wealth, on health. But this may simply reflect the difficulty of observing, even in moderately long panels, the health consequences of changes in health behavior and utilization of medical care that may only materialize in the long term. In this and the following section, we assume that there are health effects of smoking, drinking, forgoing effective health care, and so on, and we examine whether there is evidence that economic circumstances impact on these health determinants.

Particularly in the USA, more affluent individuals are generally less likely to smoke, drink heavily, be overweight, or use illegal drugs, and they are more likely to exercise and engage in preventive care (Cutler and Lleras-Muney, 2010; Cutler et al., 2011a,b). But simple correlations obviously tell us nothing about the presence or direction of causality. Some of the evidence reviewed by Cawley and Ruhm (2011) shows that income and/or wealth increases consumption of tobacco and alcohol. This holds for the response to income shocks in the UK captured by cohort income (Adda et al., 2009) and lottery winnings (Apouey and Clark, 2013) (see Table 17.6). In the USA, Kim and Ruhm (2012) find that wealth gains from inheritances only raise moderate drinking and have no effect on smoking (Table 17.5).

The evidence for income and wealth effects on obesity is mixed but certainly does not support a strong causal effect in either direction. Kim and Ruhm (2012) find some indication of wealth gains reducing the likelihood of being overweight, which is consistent with Swedish evidence based on lottery winnings (Lindahl, 2005). Cawley et al. (2010) use US National Health Interview survey data and the Social Security notch as an IV for income and find no impact of income on weight or obesity. Exploiting variation across US states in the generosity of the Earned Income Tax Credit (EITC), Schmeiser (2009) finds no effect of income on weight for men and a positive effect for women: an additional $1000 per year is associated with a gain of no more than 1.80 pounds (0.82 kg).

Galama and van Kippersluis (2010) extend Grossman's (1972a,b) health–capital model with the aim of understanding how health behavior may differ by wealth. They distinguish between healthy consumption, which reduces the rate of depreciation of health (e.g., good housing, vitamins, muesli) and unhealthy consumption, which increases health depreciation (e.g., cigarettes, excessive alcohol, etc.). Wealth has a positive effect on healthy consumption both because of a pure wealth effect and because higher wealth raises health investment, which is assumed to exhibit diminishing returns, so that depreciated health is more expensive to replace through medical care.[43] The effect on unhealthy consumption is ambiguous because the wealth and price effects go in opposite directions. The wealthy are less inclined to run down their health because of the higher marginal cost of replacement. The model predicts that, under arguably plausible assumptions, the wealthy will be more likely to engage in moderately unhealthy consumption (wealth effect dominates) and less likely to partake in severely unhealthy consumption (price effect dominates).

Van Kippersluis and Galama (2013) test these predictions with wealth gains instrumented by lottery winnings in British (BHPS) data (Table 17.6), as in Apouey and Clark (2013), and by inheritances in US (HRS) data (Table 17.5), as in Kim and Ruhm (2012). Unlike the earlier studies, they use fixed effects models to deal with unobserved heterogeneity and find robust evidence that wealth increases the probability of drinking alcohol, but it has no effect on the number of drinks and heavy drinking. This is consistent with the direct wealth effect dominating for behavior that is moderately unhealthy, although indulgence in a glass of good claret over dinner may actually be beneficial to one's health. Their results for smoking are inconclusive: a lottery win in the UK does not increase smoking, which is inconsistent with Apouey and Clark (2013), but inheritance receipt in the USA does immediately increase both the prevalence and intensity of smoking, which is inconsistent with Kim and Ruhm (2012), who look at longer term effects, and also with the prediction of the theory.

Income opens consumption opportunities. For unhealthy consumption to explain income-related health inequality, tobacco, alcohol, fatty foods, and so on would have

---

[43] The assumption that health investment technology exhibits diminishing returns is a departure from Grossman's model that assumes constant returns. With diminishing returns, because greater wealth raises the demand for health and the level of investment, the marginal cost of producing a unit of health by investing in medical care is greater at higher levels of wealth. This higher marginal cost gives the wealthy an added incentive to look after their health.

to be grossly inferior goods. There is no evidence of this. This is not to say that health behavior is not an important contributor to the social, as opposed to economic, gradient in health. On the contrary, health behavior can account for a large proportion of the differences in health across education groups (Cutler and Lleras-Muney, 2010; Cutler et al., 2011a,b). But it is likely to be the preferences and knowledge of higher education groups, and not their wealth, that lead them to adopt healthier lifestyles.

17.4.4 Income Effects on Medical Care

As pointed out earlier, the potential for medical care to contribute to health differences by income is constrained in many high-income countries by the dominance of public health insurance. The income gradient in utilization of medical care should be stronger in countries, such as the USA, that give the market greater more influence on the financing of the health system. But public health care seldom completely crowds out private care, and even within the European social health insurance and national health service systems, specialist care is often distributed in favor of the better-off (Van Doorslaer et al., 2000, 2004, 2006). But while the income elasticity of demand for medical care has been the subject of numerous studies, the literature provides surprisingly little evidence of a causal effect of income on utilization.[44]

The Kim and Ruhm (2012) study using the US HRS finds that wealth gains from inheritances raise utilization of many types of medical services and out-of-pocket spending. Using a sample of the old (70+) US population whose drug expenses were not covered by Medicare at the time, Moran and Simon (2006) find a large and statistically significant effect of income instrumented by the Social Security notch on prescription drug utilization, though only for households that have low education and do not have high income (<75th percentile) (Table 17.5). Their estimates of income elasticity are all above 1. Goda et al. (2011) extend the analysis to estimating the impact of income on utilization of long-term care, which is also not fully covered by Medicare, and they find that a positive permanent income shock lowers nursing home use but increases the utilization of paid home care services. It is important to bear in mind that the estimated positive income effects on both drug and long-term care utilization pertain only to the elderly who had been low-wage workers, because the Social Security notch had only a weak impact on the pensions of older cohorts who had been higher earners.

These three studies of the older US population confirm what one would expect. Medical care is a normal good. Where universal public health insurance coverage is absent, individuals who can afford more and better health care will purchase it.

---

[44] Virtually every textbook in health economics devotes a chapter to the demand for medical care, including estimates of income elasticity (e.g., Sloan and Hsieh, 2012). We do not cover the literature on the effect of income on the demand for health insurance, which would take us some distance from the income–health nexus. It is well-known that uptake of insurance is very much income-related.

17.4.5 Income Effects on Child Health

In Section 17.3.4, we conclude that early-life health conditions have an economically significant effect on economic well-being in adulthood. Currie (2009) proposes that child health is a potentially important contributor to the intergenerational transmission of education and economic status. The idea is that less educated, poor parents are more likely to give birth to and rear less healthy children. Childhood ill-health interferes with human-capital acquisition and directly constrains health capital in adulthood, which further reduces earnings potential. A cycle of poverty is propelled by childhood ill-health. Poverty begets childhood illness, which generates poverty later in life. If true, this would give health a role not only in the creation of inequality, through health shocks that increase income dispersion, but in its perpetuation across generations. Whether parental income does constrain child health is therefore an important question to be addressed not only from a health perspective but also from that of economic inequality.

We focus here on the evidence that parental economic circumstances constrain child health and skip consideration of the mechanisms through which an effect may arise. Almond and Currie (2012) use Cunha and Heckman's (2007) model of investment in cognitive and noncognitive skills of children to provide a framework for thinking about the evolution of children's human capital, including health. Further development of this model to formally incorporate health may provide insight into the impact of parental income on child health.

From a review of the evidence, Currie (2009) concludes that, while there is little doubt that children from less privileged backgrounds are less healthy, there is insufficient evidence to conclude that, in a high-income country context, this arises from a causal effect. Identification of a causal effect of parental income on child health should, nonetheless, be easier than the identification of the (own) income effect on adult health. The reason is that reverse causality is less of an issue because children generally do not earn income, at least in high-income countries. This has been one of the main motivations for researchers to examine the impact of parental income on child health. Of course, reverse causality is not entirely eliminated, because the illness of a child may interfere with his or her parents' work activity, and correlated unobservables remain a substantial problem.

17.4.5.1 Evidence from High-Income Countries

The correlation between family income and children's general health strengthens as children grow older in the USA (Case et al., 2002) and Canada (Currie and Stabile, 2003), suggesting that the disadvantages associated with parental income accumulate as children age. The steepening of the gradient with age can be due to poorer children being hit by more health shocks and/or having more difficulty recovering from illness, given constrained access to medical care. In the USA, the strengthening of the gradient is due to a combination of these effects (Case et al., 2002; Condliffe and Link, 2008), whereas in Canada, consistent with its universal health care system, it is only due to poor children becoming sick more frequently (Currie and Stabile, 2003).[45]

These findings are not generally confirmed for other countries. Khanam et al. (2009) find that there is a gradient in Australia that strengthens with age when similar covariates to those used by Case et al. (2002) are included. However, the gradient disappears when they include a richer set of controls, in particular maternal health, suggesting that there may be no causal effect. Reinhold and Jürges (2012) find that the parental income gradient in child health in Germany is as strong as it is in the USA, but it does not steepen as children grow older, which could be attributed to the constraining effect of universal health care.

The UK evidence is mixed, with Currie et al. (2007) and Case et al. (2008) arriving at different conclusions from analyses of the same survey. Currie et al. (2007) find a significant family income gradient in child general health that increases between ages 0–3 and 4–8 and decreases afterward. Case et al. (2008) add 3 years of data and find that the gradient keeps increasing until age 12. Analyses of a rich data set from one region of England reveal a gradient that does not increase between birth and age 7 and almost disappears with an expanded set of controls, including parental behaviors and health (Burgess et al., 2004; Propper et al., 2007) Using a nationally representative sample, Apouey and Geoffard (2013) find a gradient that persists up to the age of 17 but no evidence that utilization of health care, housing conditions, nutrition, or clothing are important mechanisms for generating it.

In North America and Europe, children from poorer households are less healthy. Whether this arises from an effect of parental income or some other characteristic of the family associated with both income and child health cannot be established from the studies cited above. Using reform-induced variation in the US Earned Income Tax Credit (EITC), Hoynes et al. (2012) estimate that increased maternal income reduces the incidence of low birth weight and increases mean birth weight. For single low-educated mothers, an increase of $1000 in the EITC generates a 6.7–10.8% reduction in the incidence of low birth weight (see Table 17.7 for this and other studies providing causal evidence in this and next subsection). The effect appears to be mediated through slightly greater use of prenatal care and much more substantial reductions in smoking and drinking during pregnancy.[46] These estimates suggest sizeable gains in infant health from income increases among low-income populations.[47] A much more

---

[45] Allin and Stabile (2012) find no evidence that health care utilization is an important factor for generating the gradient in Canada.

[46] A $1000 credit received by a low-educated single mother is estimated to increase the propensity to use prenatal care by 0.65% points (from a baseline of 96%) and to reduce the likelihood of smoking by 1.2% points (baseline of 30%) and of consuming alcohol by 1.1% points (baseline of 3.3%). It is not clear why increased income reduces smoking and drinking, although one might suppose that it has to do with reduced financial stress.

[47] There is also evidence of the child health impact of targeted programs such as food stamps (Almond et al., 2011) or food and nutrition vouchers (Hoynes et al., 2011). These are not considered here because of their conditional nature, although Hoynes and Schanzenbach (2009) claim that recipients of food stamps behave as if the benefits were paid in cash.

Table 17.7 Evidence of income effects on child health and related health behavior

Authors	Country and data	Sample	Income measure	Measures of health/health behavior	Estimator	Effect on health	Effect on health behavior and medical care	Remarks
Mocan et al. (2013)	US Natal Detail Files and CPS Annual Demographic Files 1989–2004	Singleton births to unmarried mothers >19 years	Weekly earnings instrumented by measure of skilled-biased technology shocks	Birth weight, gestation age, prenatal care, smoking and drinking during pregnancy	Two sample IV	Small ↑ birth weight and gestational age babies of low education (≤high school) mothers unlikely to be on Medicaid	↑ prenatal care for low educ. mothers not on Medicaid No effect on smoking or drinking	Effects are very small. Doubling of income ↑ birth weight by 100 g and ↑ gestational age by 0.7 weeks No effects for high education mothers or those likely to be on Medicaid
Hoynes et al. (2012)	US Vital Statistics Natality Data 1983–1999	Infants of low-income mothers	Change in maternal income due to EITC reform	LBW, smoking, drinking, prenatal care use	DID	$1000 → 6.7–10.8% ↓ LBW	$1000 → prenatal care ↑ 0.65 ppt smoking ↓ 1.2 ppt drinking ↓	
Amarante et al. (2011)	Uruguay mortality, natality, Social Security registers 2003–2007	All newborns	Unconditional cash transfer = 50–100% prepayment income to low-income women	LBW, maternal smoking, nutrition	DID, FE, and RDD	15% ↓ LBW (1.5 ppt of baseline 10 ppt)	1.1 ppt ↑ maternal nutrition, ↓ smoking during pregnancy, ↓ % children born to unmarried parents	Transfer paid women in bottom income decile
Fernald and Hidrobo (2011)	Ecuador, 2003–2006	Children 12–35 months	Unconditional cash transfer = $15 per month (6–10% mean household exp.) to low-income women	HAZ score, hemoglobin concentration, vitamin A and iron supplements	Randomized experiment	No effects	↑ vitamin A and iron supplements in rural areas	Transfers paid to women in poorest 40%
Agüero et al. (2009)	South Africa KIDS 1993, 1998, 2004	Children	Unconditional cash transfer paid to women	HAZ scores	GPSM	Large cash transfer early in life ↑ HAZ		

Table 17.7 Evidence of income effects on child health and related health behavior—cont'd

Authors	Country and data	Sample	Income measure	Measures of health/health behavior	Estimator	Effect on health	Effect on health behavior and medical care	Remarks
Paxson and Schady (2010)	Rural Ecuador 2003–2006	Children 36–83 months	as Fernald and Hidrobo (2011)	Hemoglobin level, HAZ, fine motor control, deworming treatment	Randomized experiment	Poorest quartile: ↑ hemoglobin Other quartiles: no effects	↑ deworming treatments	as Fernald and Hidrobo (2011)
Case (2004)	South Africa Langeberg Survey 1999	Children	Pension receipt	height	OLS	↑ height of black and colored kids		
Duflo (2000, 2003)	South Africa SALDRU 1993	Children 6–60 months	Woman's receipt of pension	HAZ and WHZ scores	2SLS (IV = pension eligibility)	↑ HAZ and WHZ of girls by 1.2 SD after 2 years		No effect on boys. No effect of pension paid to male on either girls or boys.

Note: See Appendix for explanation of dataset, variable, and estimator acronyms.

modest effect is estimated from data on 14 million US births between 1989 and 2004 that uses a census division year-specific index of skill-biased technological change to instrument mothers' earnings (Mocan et al., 2013). For low-educated (i.e., no more than high school diploma) unmarried mothers who are unlikely to be on Medicaid (public health insurance for low-income households), increased earnings raise utilization of prenatal care, as well as birth weight and gestational age. The fact that there are no significant effects on births to high-educated mothers and to all mothers who are likely to be covered by Medicaid suggests that low income constrains access to maternity care for those lacking insurance coverage. However, the effects are very small. A doubling of earnings would raise birth weight by only 100 grams and gestational age by only two-thirds of a week.

17.4.5.2 Evidence from Low- and Middle-Income Countries

One would expect health in general, and child health in particular, to be more contingent on income in low-income settings where the nutritional needs to sustain health are often not met and universal health insurance coverage is absent, with most medical care paid for out-of-pocket. Indeed, the economic gradient in health is particularly steep in low- and middle-income countries and is evident in critical indicators, such as infant mortality (Commission on the Social Determinants of Health, 2008). The evidence that the gradient in child health does derive, at least in part, from the causal impact of economic circumstances on health is much more clear-cut than that from high-income countries (see Table 17.7 for studies cited in this section).[48]

Duflo (2000, 2003) examines whether the extension of pensions to black South Africans in the early 1990s had an impact on the nutritional status of children. An effect may have been anticipated because more than a quarter of black children under five lived with a pension recipient by the end of the period studied. The analysis reveals that pensions paid to women have substantial positive effects on the weight and height of girls but no significant effects on the nutritional status of boys, and pensions paid to males have no effect.[49] The effects are very large. Payment of a pension to a woman

---

[48] A number of studies have exploited macroeconomic shocks to identify the impact of income on health and (infant) mortality in nations of the developing world, including Mexico (Cutler et al., 2002), Peru (Paxson and Schady, 2005), India (Bhalotra, 2010), Colombia (Miller and Urdinola, 2010), and 59 other countries (Baird et al., 2011). Although these studies are able to identify health effects at the individual level, they are unable to trace the income consequences of the macro shocks at this level. They tend to find substantial negative effects of aggregate income on mortality, but tell us little about the extent to which variation in income across individuals generates inequality in health.

[49] The effect on weight-for-height z-score, which should respond immediately to improved nutrition, is identified by comparing children living in households with elderly relatives eligible for pensions (>59 for females and >64 for males) with others with older relatives that did not quite reach the age of pension qualification. The effect on height-for-age z-score, which reflects longer term nutritional intake, is identified by comparing the height deficits of younger and older children living in households with an elderly person eligible for a pension relative to those in other households. A smaller deficit among younger children is consistent with a positive impact of income on height because the younger children lived in households benefiting from the pension extension for a larger proportion of their lives.

is estimated to raise both weight and height of girls by 1.2 standard deviations over a 2-year period (Duflo, 2003). The income gain was also large with pension benefits being around twice the median per capita income in the rural areas at the time. These results suggest that income can have very large positive effects on child health in low-income settings, but whether this effect materializes crucially depends on who receives the income.[50] Consistent with this, an unconditional cash grant paid to child caregivers (mostly women) in South Africa has been demonstrated to significantly boost child height (Agüero et al., 2009). On the basis of the observed relationship between adult height and earnings, the projected discounted return to the grant is estimated to be as much as 50%.

The evidence is mixed for income effects on child health in poor populations, as obtained from unconditional cash transfer programs in Latin America, however.[51] Ecuador's *Bono de Desarrollo Humano* (BDH) pays $15 per month—equivalent to 6–10% of average household expenditure in the target group—to mothers of children below the age of 17 in the poorest two-fifths of the population, but this additional income has been found to have no significant impact on the health (height and hemoglobin concentrations) of children aged 1–3 years (Fernald and Hidrobo, 2011), and among older children aged 3–7 years, there are only modest effects (on hemoglobin and deworming treatments) for the poorest (Paxson and Schady, 2010).[52] Uruguay's PANES program targets poorer households, restricting payment of the generous monthly cash transfer—equivalent to 50% of average preprogram income for recipient households and up to 100% of income for households with a recent birth—to households in the bottom decile. It is estimated to reduce the incidence of low birth weight by 1.5% points relative to a baseline of 10% (Amarante et al., 2011). This effect appears to materialize through improved maternal nutrition, reduced smoking during pregnancy, a large reduction in the proportion of children born to unmarried parents, and a modest reduction in maternal labor supply. The larger health impact relative to that of the general cash transfer in Ecuador is plausibly explained by the greater magnitude of the payment and its direction to (relatively) poorer households.

[50] The health gains from pension income in South Africa are not confined to children. Case (2004) finds that the extra income brought by the presence of a pension in a household (equal to 2.5 times the median income in the sample analyzed) improves the health status of all adults in households in which income is pooled.

[51] Conditional transfer schemes are less interesting for our purpose because payments are made conditional upon behavior (e.g., school attendance, medical care receipt, attendance of preventative health services, health, and nutrition education) that are intended to have a direct impact on health. While many of these programs have proven highly effective, Gertler (2004), Rivera et al. (2004), and Fernald et al. (2008) have shown it is difficult to separate the pure income effect from the incentive effect.

[52] In rural areas, vitamin A and iron supplementation did increase, and language development improved among children aged 1–3 years (Fernald and Hidrobo, 2011).

17.4.6 Conclusion

In this section, we set out to determine the extent to which differences in economic circumstances contribute to health inequality across individuals. Do the poor experience worse health because they are poor? Answering this question is difficult because worse health would be expected to be associated with lower income even without being caused by it. This has driven researchers to search for phenomena that generate variation in income or wealth without being caused by or associated with health. In high-income countries, this research enterprise has tended to produce evidence indicative of no impact of income on health in adulthood, or effects that are small in comparison to the observed income-health gradient, suggesting that the association does not derive from financial resources impinging on health. An exception is US evidence of deterioration in health, particularly as reflected in indicators related to stress and mental status, in response to stock market losses. To an extent, the general finding of little or no effect is plausible. Variation in health arises from differences in the health stock with which we are endowed (genetics), the extent to which we look after this endowment (lifestyle and living conditions), the opportunities to repair it when it gets damaged (medical care), and luck. Financial resources cannot influence the first and last determinants. Most high-income countries offer universal health care coverage irrespective of ability to pay, which greatly weakens the economic impact on the third determinant. That leaves lifestyle and living conditions. Most research concentrates on the former, and, within this, on what we do that is bad for our health, rather than what we do that is good for it. It would be perverse if greater ability to afford indulgencies in unhealthy behavior, such as smoking and drinking, explained why the better-off are in better health. In fact, the rich tend to lead less unhealthy lives, but that is not because they are economically privileged. More likely, it has to do with their education advantage.

The ability of money to buy health in the developed world is limited. Mental health appears to respond to economic circumstances, with losses producing larger deteriorations in mental well-being than gains generate improvements. But there is little evidence that physical health problems are provoked by worsened personal finances. However, we suspect that there is much that current research is missing.

Identification of the effect of one stock variable (financial wealth) on another (health capital) is far from easy. There is a risk that identification strategies that focus on very local effects of windfall gains from lottery wins, inheritances, or tax/benefit reforms throw away effects that accumulate over the life cycle together with the bathwater containing the common unobservables. The determinant that is more permanent—living conditions—tends to get overlooked in research conducted by economists. This includes housing and features of the built and social environment that vary with the economic status of neighborhoods: pollution, leisure facilities, open spaces, food quality, and crime. Money can afford improved housing quality and relocation but it takes a very large economic shock to achieve this. Chronic poverty can entail damp walls, confined spaces, disruptive neighbors, polluted air, and a threat of violence that gradually, or perhaps suddenly, take a toll on health.

The health experience of the chronically poor has no influence on the estimated impact of wealth on health in some research, such as that identifying variation in inheritances or stock prices. Other evidence, such as that based on lottery wins, does potentially capture exposure among the poor, but the sudden and often moderate gains in cash involved may not be sufficient to substantially change living conditions, and even if they are, the observation period is unlikely to be sufficiently long to detect impacts on chronic health problems that may only slowly respond to material circumstances. We are hesitant to conclude that lack of evidence of an impact of wealth on adult physical health in much of the developed world means that there is no effect.

One can be more confident that the worse health of poorer children, which is unfortunately still observed in many high-income countries, is not simply a reflection of health constraining earnings. It may also arise from the fact that poorer parents are also less educated, and this lower level of education impacts child health. As would be anticipated, the strongest evidence that economic conditions determine inequalities in (child) health comes from the developing world. But even here more income does not necessarily bring better health. Money may be able to buy health when nutritional status is low and many cannot afford medical care, but the money must be given to those that value health highly. There is some evidence that women prioritize child health more than men.

17.5. ECONOMIC INEQUALITY AS A DETERMINANT OF HEALTH

17.5.1 Overview

More than 20 years ago, Wilkinson (1990, 1992) introduced the hypothesis that income inequality is harmful to health. He showed that countries with higher-income inequality have lower life expectancy, and others soon confirmed a negative association with other measures of population health (Steckel, 1995; Waldmann, 1992). According to one variant of the hypothesis, this cross-country association reflects a causal effect of income inequality on individual health via psychosocial mechanisms: striving to keep up with the Joneses in societies with higher levels of income inequality raises levels of stress. Income redistribution can potentially raise average health not only because of any greater responsiveness of health to income at lower levels of income, if indeed there is a causal effect of income on health, but also because narrower disparities in income are good for everyone's health, including that of the rich.

The validity of this hypothesis has been heavily debated (Gravelle, 1998; Smith, 1999; Wilkinson and Pickett, 2006), and associated claims that economic inequality is responsible for a host of societal ills beyond poor health, including violence, teenage pregnancy, obesity, mistrust, and high incarceration rates (Wilkinson and Pickett, 2010), has attracted much attention and been subject to a good deal of criticism (Saunders and Evans, 2010; Snowdon, 2010). In the present context, establishing whether there is a health cost of economic inequality is relevant to the evaluation of the strength of an instrumental argument for reducing inequality.

We focus here on the mechanisms through which income inequality can potentially impact health, and we pay close attention to whether empirical analyses are capable of testing the hypotheses. We restrict our attention to the impact of inequality on morbidity and mortality, and we neglect studies of homicides, for which there is general agreement on the importance of income inequality (Deaton, 2003; Lynch et al., 2004b). We also steer clear of the happiness literature that has paid a great deal of attention to income inequality (Alesina et al., 2004; Clark et al., 2008).

In the next subsection, we demonstrate the stylized fact that population health is negatively associated with income inequality, and we outline the mechanisms through which income inequality might threaten the health of all individuals. We then consider alternative theories that can explain the negative association between population health and income inequality at the aggregate level without inequality being a threat to the health of all individuals in a society. We then turn to the evidence.

17.5.2 Basic Hypothesis: Inequality Threatens Everyone's Health

Population health rises with per capita income but at a decreasing rate (Preston, 1975). Among high-income countries, where this so-called *Preston curve* flattens out, population health has been found to be negatively correlated with income inequality (Wilkinson, 1992, 1996; Wilkinson and Pickett, 2010). There is only weak evidence of this in Figure 17.5, which is based on the same data on life expectancy, as well as measures of inequality employed in a popular publication that advances the inequality hypothesis (Wilkinson and Pickett, 2010). In these data, the relationship appears to be driven by the low inequality and high life expectancy of Japan and Sweden, and the high inequality and low life expectancy of the USA and Portugal. Among the bulk of countries with life expectancies of 78–80 years, there appears to be no relationship with income inequality.[53]

A negative correlation between income inequality and average health, presuming it exists, has been attributed to the falling potency of further, material gains in generating health once the average standard of living reaches a threshold beyond which income differences become more relevant to the determination of health (Wilkinson and Pickett, 2010).[54] Two causal mechanisms through which income inequality may threaten the

---

[53] Some have criticized the criteria used by Wilkinson and Pickett (2010) to select the countries included in the figure, and to exclude others (Saunders and Evans, 2010; Snowdon, 2010). The authors defended their country selections in the second edition of their book, however (Wilkinson and Pickett, 2010).

[54] The literature tends to presume that there is a positive effect of the income level on health.

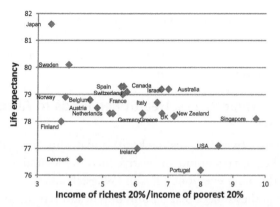

Figure 17.5 Life expectancy and income inequality in high-income countries. *Notes: Data are from Wilkinson and Pickett (2010) who, in turn, took them from UN Human Development Reports. Life expectancy is at birth averaged over males and females in 2004. Income inequality is measured by the ratio of income received by the richest 20% of households to the income of the poorest 20% averaged over the years 2003–2006.*

health of all individuals—rich and poor—have been proposed. The first stresses the importance of the public provision of health-determining goods, while the second focuses on social capital. Some stress a third psychosocial mechanism mentioned above (Wilkinson, 1992). Given that this theory does not propose that income inequality affects health throughout the distribution of income, but rather that the health of less well-off individuals suffers because of their relative deprivation, we cover this assertion in the next section.

The public provision of goods would create a pathway from income inequality to individual health if inequality impacts on the provision of goods that determine health, such as curative and preventive health care, education, and sanitation. Income inequality might lead to more heterogeneous preferences, which will reduce the average value (and thus the provision) of publicly provided goods (Alesina et al., 1999; Deaton, 2003; Thorbecke and Charumilind, 2002). But income inequality could also lead to increased public provision because a more skewed income distribution will reduce the income of the median voter relative to the mean and increase the redistributive effect of public provisions financed by nonregressive taxation (Meltzer and Richard, 1981). Following Sen (1999), Deaton (2003, forthcoming) argues that the focus should be on the health consequences of political, rather than economic, inequalities. He notes that in nineteenth-century Britain, and in the USA and India in the twentieth century, sub-stantial improvements in public health were realized after the extension of political rights.

Social capital—cohesion and trust among citizens (Putnam et al., 1993)—is argued to be a consequence of economic inequality and a determinant of health via social and psy-chosocial support, informal insurance mechanisms, and information diffusion (d'Hombres et al., 2010; Kawachi and Kennedy, 1997; Kennedy et al., 1998; Ronconi et al., 2012). This hypothesis has received a fair amount of attention in the literature, but whether this attention is justified depends on the assumption that income inequality reduces social cohesion, as opposed to lower social cohesion raising income inequality, which is an equally plausible explanation.

17.5.3 Alternative Hypotheses: Health Responds to Absolute or Relative Income

A negative association between population health and income inequality could arise from the dependence of health on absolute or relative income, without this necessarily implying that inequality threatens everyone's health (Wagstaff and van Doorslaer, 2000). The absolute income hypothesis states that diminishing health returns to income at the individual health level explain the negative association between average population health and income inequality at the aggregate level (Gravelle, 1998; Gravelle et al., 2002; Rodgers, 1979; Wildman et al., 2003). If the health-income relationship is concave then an increase in the spread of the income distribution will bring down mean health because the health loss to those becoming poorer is larger than the health gain to those becoming richer. Income redistribution could raise average population health but this would occur without the health of any individual, given his or her income, being directly affected by the level of economic inequality in society. The literature reviewed in Section 17.4 provides only limited evidence of a causal impact of income on health in high-income countries, but some evidence indicates that the effect is stronger among the poor, and there does appear to be an income effect in low-income countries. If there are health returns to income, they would appear to be diminishing. But even if there is no (diminishing) causal effect of income on health, a negative statistical association between average health and income inequality will be observed when there is a concave statistical relationship between health and income across individuals.

According to the relative income hypothesis, one's health depends on how one's income fares relative to others. When there are diminishing health returns to the difference between individual income and some aggregate, such as the mean, there will be a negative association between average health and income inequality. These hypotheses are distinguished—unfortunately, often not explicitly—from the above-mentioned income inequality hypothesis by the assertion that income inequality only matters to the extent that it increases the number of individuals who have an income deficit relative to some reference level. It is only the health of these individuals that is claimed to be damaged by inequality. In contrast, the income inequality hypothesis postulates that income inequality is a common factor impacting on the health of everyone.

Health is presumed to depend on relative income because of psychosocial effects. It is not so much possession of more material goods that matters for health, but rather the stress, depression, anxiety, shame, and distrust brought on by judging one's standard of living to fall short of that enjoyed by others. These emotional responses are claimed to trigger health-damaging psychoneuroendocrine reactions, such as increased cortisol production (Wilkinson, 1992). Some have even hypothesized that this psychosocial–biological effect may be hardwired into humans through our evolutionary experience (Wilkinson, 2001). Hunter-gatherer societies were extremely egalitarian, and humans might not yet be well adapted to the social inequalities that have arisen in settlement societies. Consistent with the psychosocial–biological mechanism, experiments have found that manipulating baboons, which also have stable, although obviously much simpler, hierarchical societies, into lower social positions induces stress (Sapolsky, 2005). It has been hypothesized that low relative economic status may impact negatively on health through epigenetic responses, as well (Wilkinson and Pickett, 2010).[55] Wilkinson and Pickett cite evidence of the maternal nursing behavior of rats affecting the offspring's epigenome at a (glucocortoid) receptor known to regulate stress responses (Weaver et al., 2004). They propose that, if this also occurs among humans, then increased stress and cortisol levels experienced throughout life could be due to early-life epigenetic processes. These authors do not elaborate on why exposure to such processes may be related to low (parental) socioeconomic position, although there is evidence of associations between epigenetic differences and SES, which is proxied by income position, occupation, education, and housing tenure among adults (McGuinness et al., 2012) and children (Borghol et al., 2012). Understanding of the epidemiological implications of epigenetic processes is still limited (Relton and Davey Smith, 2012), and it would certainly be premature to presume that they contribute to health differences across socioeconomic environments.

Why psychosocial responses should be confined to inequality in the income dimension has been questioned (Deaton, 2003, 2013). It seems quite conceivable that they might be triggered, perhaps more strongly so, by comparisons of occupation, education, housing, and so on. While describing the mechanism in the previous paragraphs, we (and the authors cited) have often resorted to terms such as social hierarchy. The most influential research on health and social position—the Whitehall studies (Marmot et al., 1978, 1991)—has used occupational grade as the discriminating indicator. The evidence obtained from animal studies cannot, of course, inform us about effects in the income dimension. In reviewing the evidence below, we focus on the health effects of relative income, but this is because of the context of this chapter and not because we believe other dimensions of SES to be of lesser importance to health.

Less frequently cited than the psychosocial mechanism is the idea that pecuniary externalities, arising from the pricing of health-enhancing goods, reduce average health in regions that are more unequal (Miller and Paxson, 2006). Take the case of healthy

---

[55] Although still very much in its infancy, epigenetics is the field of medical science that studies (possibly heritable) random or environment-induced changes in gene expression that are not driven by changes in the underlying DNA sequence (Ebrahim, 2012).

foods. When the quality and availability of healthy food is comparable across regions, but more expensive in rich areas, then poor individuals in these areas will have worse health than their equivalents in poorer areas. Health depends negatively on the individual's income deficit from the regional average because of the price effect on the cost of maintaining health. But there could be an offsetting effect through collectively and locally financed health-enhancing goods, which may include some medical care. The larger tax base of wealthier neighborhoods will increase the supply and quality of health care, which will raise the health of a poor person in the rich region compared with his equivalent in a poor region.

There are three variants of the relative hypothesis—relative income, relative deprivation, and relative position—distinguished (again, often not explicitly) by the functional form linking health to income differences (Wagstaff and van Doorslaer, 2000). The *relative income* hypothesis proposes that the magnitude of the difference between income and that of a reference group is what ultimately matters for health (Deaton, 2001a,b, 2003; Deaton and Paxson, 2004). The average income of the group is mostly used as the point of reference, but other aggregations seem equally plausible, and there is no theoretical guidance on this. The reference group is likely to be unobservable or, at best, observed with error, and this will lead to income inequality reentering the picture even when it exerts no causal effect on individual health (Deaton, 2001b, 2003). The *relative deprivation* hypothesis posits that health is responsive to the difference between income and all larger incomes within the same reference group (Deaton, 2001b; Eibner and Evans, 2005; Yitzhaki, 1979).[56] Lower incomes are assumed to be irrelevant for health, and so the point of reference is individual-specific. The *relative position* hypothesis suggests that the magnitude of income differences is unimportant and that health responds only to rank in the income distribution. This hypothesis is closest to the aforementioned theories that stress the importance of social hierarchy. It might also be used to justify choice of a rank-based measure of income-related health inequality, such as the concentration index (Wagstaff et al., 1991).

17.5.4 Evidence

17.5.4.1 Empirical Challenges

Tests have been performed using data at three levels of aggregation: country, region, and individual. The majority of studies, and most of the early ones, have relied on country-level data, although early US studies used state-level data. Individual-level data is required to discriminate between the five hypotheses (income inequality, absolute income, relative income, relative deprivation, and relative position) because income inequality will

---

[56] Gravelle and Sutton (2009) also study the opposite situation of individuals caring about being richer than others.

correlate with average population health under all of them (Deaton, 2003; Lynch et al., 2004b; Mackenbach, 2002; Wagstaff and van Doorslaer, 2000).

The relative hypotheses provoke many unanswered questions with respect to the reference groups: how are they formed, does each individual have a unique reference, and how are they to be defined in the data? Testing is further complicated by the potential for position in relation to the reference to be endogenous through choices of group membership. Data quality and the reliability of measures of income inequality are other major issues (Deaton, 2003; West, 1997). Estimates of income inequality or relative income at town or village levels may be derived from relatively few observations and so lack precision (Leigh et al., 2009).

A major problem for analyses identifying effects from cross-country or regional variation is that time-invariant unobservable determinants of health may be correlated with income inequality. Fixed effects methods are unlikely to prove successful at aggregated levels because income inequality tends to evolve rather slowly, and measurement error bias is compounded (Babones, 2008). In addition, fixed effect estimators only identify short run effects and may fail to detect inequality effects operating with a lag. Reverse causality is unlikely to be a major problem at more aggregated levels, but through one or more of the mechanisms identified in Section 17.3, relative income could certainly be a function of health. This would tend to induce bias toward concluding that low relative income exerts a negative impact on health. These limitations must be kept in mind in interpreting the evidence.

We differentiate the evidence by the nature of the hypothesis tested and the level of data aggregation. Given that the impact of income on health is covered in Section 17.4, we do not explicitly consider evidence for the absolute income hypothesis, although we do note what happens to the health–income inequality relationship when individual income is controlled for. Studies published since previous reviews and a few key earlier papers are summarized in Tables 17.8–17.10.

17.5.4.2 Income Inequality Hypothesis

Previous reviews have concluded that the evidence does not point to income inequality as an important determinant of individual health, and this seems to hold for both morbidity and mortality (Deaton, 2003; Leigh et al., 2009; Lynch et al., 2004b; Subramanian and Kawachi, 2004; Wagstaff and van Doorslaer, 2000).[57] They also infer from the literature that state-level income inequality associates negatively with health in the USA, but this is not true in other countries, and this difference most likely reflects racial composition at the state level, although this interpretation is disputed (Subramanian and Kawachi, 2004). There is agreement on the importance of appropriately defining

---

[57] Wilkinson and Pickett, 2006 dissent, referring mainly to studies using country-level or state-level analyses to infer that income inequality is important for health.

Table 17.8 Cross-country evidence on population health-income inequality association

Authors	Countries/region and period	Data	Estimator	(Partial) correlation with income inequality
Pascual et al. (2005)	12 EU countries 1994–2001	ECHP and OECD	Linear RE and FE	LE −, U5MR +
Cantarero et al. (2005)	12 EU countries 1994–2001	ECHP and OECD	Linear RE and FE	LE −, U5MR +
Babones (2008)	134 countries 1970–1995	WIID and World Bank	OLS, FD	LE −, IMR +, murder rate ns
Biggs et al. (2010)	22 Latin American countries 1960–2007	WDID, GTD, WIID, SEDLAC	Linear FE	LE ns, IMR ns
Wilkinson and Pickett (2010)	25 rich income countries 2000, 2001, 2002, 2003, 2004	UNHDR, WDID, IOT, WHO	Bivariate association	LE −, IMR +, mental health −, obesity +
Regidor et al. (2012)	21 OECD countries 1995, 2000, 2005	OECD	Bivariate association	1995 IMR +, 2005 IMR ns
Avendano (2012)	34 OECD countries 1960–2008	WIID, OECD	Poisson FE	IMR ns
Tacke and Waldmann (2013)	93 countries 1999–2005	WIID, WDID, GHN	OLS	LE −, IMR +, U5MR +

Notes: LE − indicates that life expectancy is negatively correlated with income inequality. IMR + indicates the infant mortality is positively correlated with income inequality. Acronyms of other health indicators, datasets, and estimators are explained in Table A2. ns indicates no significant association.

reference groups: when references are defined with respect to smaller geographic units, such as towns or cities, there is less evidence of an association between income inequality and health.

17.5.4.2.1 Cross-Country Data

The positive cross-country association between mortality and income inequality is well documented and has been confirmed for 12 European countries (Cantarero et al., 2005; Pascual et al., 2005), 25 high-income countries (Wilkinson and Pickett, 2010), and across many countries worldwide (Babones, 2008; Tacke and Waldmann, 2013) (Table 17.8). But the positive association between infant mortality and income inequality across OECD countries evident in 1995 was no longer apparent in 2005 data (Regidor et al., 2012). It also appears that the relationship between population health and income inequality is reversed across low-income countries (Nilsson and Bergh, 2013).

Table 17.9 US cross-region evidence of population health-income inequality association

Authors	Regional unit and period	Data	Estimator	Health measure	(Partial) correlation with income inequality
Ash and Robinson (2009)	287 MSA 1990	CMF, STF	WLS	Age-adjusted mortality ratio	Varies with size of MSA
Deaton and Lubotsky (2009)	287 MSA 1980, 1990	CMF, PUMS	WLS	Age-adjusted mortality ratio	No robust association (conditional on racial composition)
Wilkinson and Pickett (2010)	50 states 1999–2002	Census and CHS, NHANES, BRFSS	Bivariate association	LE, infant deaths, obesity	LE −, IMR +, obesity +
Yang et al. (2012)	3072 counties 1998–2002	CMF	QR	Age-adjusted mortality ratio	+ with effect increasing in magnitude until 80th percentile of mortality

Notes: −/+ indicates negative/positive association of health indicator with income inequality. See Table A2 for explanation of acronyms. MSA is Metropolitan Statistical Area.

The association between population health, measured by life expectancy or infant mortality, and income inequality that is observed across countries is not evident in time variation within countries, even when exploiting very long time series. For example, there is no association between income inequality and mortality between 1900 and 1998 in the USA (Lynch et al., 2004a). Data for Australia, Canada, New Zealand, the USA, and eight European countries display no associations between the within-country evolution of either life expectancy or infant mortality and the income share of the richest 10% (contemporaneous and lagged) between 1903 and 2003 (Leigh and Jencks, 2007). There is also no relationship in the data for 22 Latin American countries between 1960 and 2007 (Biggs et al., 2010). There is an association between the change in income inequality, on the one hand, and the change in life expectancy or infant mortality, on the other hand, for over 90 countries between 1975 and 1995, but this disappears when the change in GDP per capita is controlled for (Babones, 2008). Finally, Avendano (2012) finds no association between within-country variation in infant mortality and income inequality over 4 decades for 34 OECD countries. This finding remains unchanged after allowing for country-specific (linear) time trends or allowing for a lag of 15 years between changes in income inequality and changes in infant mortality.

Table 17.10 Individual-level evidence of association between health and income, relative income, and income inequality

Authors	Country, region, period	Data	Estimator	Findings
Gerdtham and Johannesson (2004)	Sweden, 284 municipalities 1980–1986	ULF, NCD, and NITS register data	Cox proportional hazard	10–17 yr. survival: + AI, ns RI, ns INEQ
Li and Zhu (2006)	China 180 communities 1993	CHNS	Probit	*Excellent/good* SAH: + AI, ns RD, ns RP, ∩ INEQ Physical conditions: ~AI, ns RD, ns RP, ~ INEQ (physical conditions = ADL)
Jones and Wildman (2008)	UK 1991–2001	BHPS	OLS, FE, RE	*Good* SAH: + AI, ns RD GHQ: ~ AI, ~ RD
Lorgelly and Lindley (2008)	UK 19 regions 1991–2002	BHPS	Pooled, RE, and Mundlak ordered probit	Better SAH: + AI, ns RI, ns INEQ
Petrou and Kupek (2008)	UK 2003	HSE	WLS	EQ-5D: + SC
Gravelle and Sutton (2009)	UK 11 areas 1979–2000	GHS	Pooled binary and ordered probit	Better SAH: + AI, ~ RI, ~ INEQ Long-term illness: − AI, ~ RI; ~ INEQ
Hildebrand and Kerm (2009)	11 EU countries, 52 EU regions 1994–2001	ECHP	Linear FE	better SAH: ~ AI, ~ RI, − INEQ (effect size negligible)
Theodossiou and Zangelidis (2009)	6 EU countries 2004	SOCIOLD	Linear IV	Worse ADL: − AI, + RD Better SAH: + AI, ns RD Mental health: + AI, − RD
d'Hombres et al. (2010)	8 former Soviet countries 2001	LLH	Probit, OLS, GMM	Better SAH: + SC
Karlsson et al. (2010)	21 low-/middle-/high-income countries	FORS, WIID	Pooled ordered probit	Better SAH: + AI, + RI, − INEQ in rich countries (= better ADL)

Table 17.10 Individual-level evidence of association between health and income, relative income, and income inequality—cont'd

Authors	Country, region, period	Data	Estimator	Findings
Mangyo and Park (2011)	China 2004	CIDJ	OLS	Better SAH: + RI, − RD, + RP (= mental health)
van Groezen et al. (2011)	10 EU 2004	SHARE	OLS	Better SAH: + SC
Fang and Rizzo (2012)	China 54 cities and counties 1997–2006	CHNS	FE logit	Better SAH: − INEQ (effect size larger for poorer)
Grönqvist et al. (2012)	Sweden municipalities 1987–2004	Hospital admissions register	Linear FE	Hospital admission: ns INEQ (= sickness leave and mortality)
Lillard et al. (2012)	Australia, Germany, UK, USA	CNEF	Ordered probit	Better SAH: − INEQ
Ronconi et al. (2012)	Argentina 1997	Encuesta de Desarrollo Social	Bivariate probit	Better SAH: + SC
Nilsson and Bergh (2013)	Zambia 155 constituencies, 72 districts, 9 provinces 2004	LCMS IV	OLS and 2SLS	HAZ: + AI, − RI (constituency reference), + RI (provincial reference), + INEQ

Notes: AI, absolute income; RI, relative income; INEQ, income inequality; RD, relative deprivation; RP, relative position; SC, social capital. Read "XXX: AI+" as the health indicator XXX is significantly positively associated with absolute income. Same for RI, INEQ, RD, RP, and SC. Similarly: − indicates negative association; ns indicates no significant association; ~ AI indicates no consistent evidence in favor of or against AI hypothesis (respectively for INEQ, RI, RD, RP, and SC hypotheses); ∩ INEQ indicates an inverse U shape relationship with income inequality. When indicated in the second column, regional unit indicates the level at which income inequality and references for relativities are defined. When not indicated inequality/relativities is at national level. See Table A2 for explanation of other acronyms.

The absence of any evidence that population health moves with changes in income inequality strongly suggests that the static cross-country relationship does not derive from a causal effect of income inequality on health.

17.5.4.2.2 Regional and Cohort Level Data

Conditional on average regional income, life expectancy is sometimes negatively associated with regional income inequality. The negative relationship holds across US states but not at lower levels of aggregation (metropolitan areas, cities)[58] and the evidence is

[58] There is a significant US county level association between income inequality and mortality (Yang et al., 2012).

mixed in other countries (Deaton, 2003; Leigh et al., 2009; Lynch et al., 2004a; Subramanian and Kawachi, 2004; Wagstaff and van Doorslaer, 2000; Wilkinson and Pickett, 2006). The state-level association in the USA could either indicate a causal mechanism or greater aggregation bias at that level. Inclusion of state-level variables eliminates (or dramatically reduces) the association, although these may be mediators rather than confounders (Subramanian and Kawachi, 2004; Wilkinson and Pickett, 2006). The racial composition of US states, a control that knocks out the effect of income inequality, might itself be related to the provision and quality of publicly provided health care (Ash and Robinson, 2009; Deaton and Lubotsky, 2009) (Table 17.9). That state-level income inequality loses much of its explanatory power for mortality after conditioning on measures of social cohesion and interpersonal trust has been interpreted as indicative of a mechanism operating through social capital (Kawachi et al., 1997). Missing from this argument is evidence of a causal effect of income inequality on social capital.

USA and UK birth cohort studies find no association between mortality and income inequality (Deaton and Paxson, 2001, 2004).

17.5.4.2.3 Individual-Level Data
There is little support for an association between *individual* mortality and income inequality conditional on individual income. This holds both in studies exploiting regional variation in income inequality, which risk confounding from regional health effects, and in studies exploiting within-country time variation in income inequality, which risk confounding from time trends (Deaton, 2003; Lynch et al., 2004a,b; Subramanian and Kawachi, 2004; Wagstaff and van Doorslaer, 2000). Morbidity measures, which are more commonly available at the individual level, also have no association with income inequality outside the USA. There is evidence that income inequality at the state level, but again not lower levels, is negatively correlated with the physical and mental health of the poorest individuals in the USA. But this could simply result from state-level income inequality picking up the effect of state-level differences in public policies toward the poor (Mellor and Milyo, 2002) (Table 17.10).

Analyses of individual-level (pseudo) panel data find no association between mortality or morbidity and income inequality. Using high-quality Swedish administrative data with more than 10 years of follow up on income and vital status, Gerdtham and Johannesson (2004) find no effect of municipality-level income inequality on mortality after conditioning on individual income and average municipality income. There is also no relationship of income inequality with SAH revealed by analyses of 12 years of British panel data allowing for unobserved heterogeneity (Lorgelly and Lindley, 2008) and 22 years of British repeated cross-section data (Gravelle and Sutton, 2009). Neither is mental health correlated with income inequality in Australian panel data (Bechtel et al., 2012).

Cross-country studies of individual-level data largely corroborate the negative finding. There are statistically significant, but economically negligible, effects of regional and nationwide income inequality on SAH in panel data on 11 European countries between 1994 and 2001 (Hildebrand and Kerm, 2009). Combining micro data from Australia, Germany, the UK, and the USA with country-level tax records on the income share of the richest percentile (Atkinson et al., 2011), Lillard et al. (2012) find that a higher-income share of the rich is associated with worse SAH, but once time trends are accounted for, the pattern reverses or disappears. The authors also find no evidence that income inequality during the first 20 years of life impacts on current SAH.

Pooling cross-section data for 21 countries, and subject to imposing the same relationship between health and individual income across all those countries, Karlsson et al. (2010) find that health is negatively correlated with income inequality in high-income countries, but there is no relationship in middle- and low-income countries. However, with point-in-time cross-country variation, one can never be sure that the income inequality effect is distinguished from health variation across countries for any other reason. In China, SAH has been found to be positively associated with community-level income inequality at relatively low levels of inequality, but the association turns negative at higher inequality (Li and Zhu, 2006). Correcting for unobserved heterogeneity using panel data, the negative relationship persists and is stronger for poorer individuals (Fang and Rizzo, 2012). While consistent with the income inequality hypothesis, it is possible that this finding is driven by nonlinearity between income and health that is not fully captured in the specification adopted. Child undernutrition in a much lower-income country, Zambia, has been found to be negatively correlated with economic inequality (Nilsson and Bergh, 2013).

If there is health-related migration across regions with differing levels of inequality, perhaps because of differences in medical care, then estimates from the regression of individual health on regional inequality will be biased. One study avoids this by using the random assignment of refugees to a first area of residence in Sweden (Grönqvist et al., 2012). Despite the fact that the range of income inequality across years and municipalities is—perhaps surprisingly—of similar magnitude in Sweden, as it is in the USA or the UK, hospitalizations, sickness leave and mortality were all found to be unrelated to municipality income inequality. Because refugees are likely to be much poorer and to have quite different references from the general population, one may doubt whether this analysis reveals much about either the income inequality or relative hypotheses that can be generalized.

Finally, some studies find that higher levels of social capital are associated with better individual health (Petrou and Kupek, 2008; van Groezen et al., 2011), and others confirm this when using instruments to deal with potential endogeneity of measures of social capital (d'Hombres et al., 2010; Ronconi et al., 2012). None of these studies test whether social capital itself responds to income inequality.

17.5.4.3 Relative Hypotheses

The only study that seeks to test all the relative hypotheses (income, deprivation, and position) rejects all three in favor of the absolute income hypothesis as an explanation of variation in SAH, using UK longitudinal data (Lorgelly and Lindley, 2008). Inconsistent with the relative income hypothesis, conditional on individual income, mortality is found to be lower among individuals living in Swedish municipalities with higher average incomes (Gerdtham and Johannesson, 2004). In contrast, mortality risk, especially for black males, is positively correlated with community average income in the USA (Miller and Paxson, 2006). Data on SAH from 11 European countries are consistent with the relative income hypothesis for males, although the negative correlation of health with average regional income is very small in magnitude, but, if anything, women report slightly better health when regional income is higher (Hildebrand and Kerm, 2009). There is little evidence in favor of the relative income hypothesis in the UK data on SAH (Gravelle and Sutton, 2009).

Analyses of data from Australia (Bechtel et al., 2012), China (Li and Zhu, 2006), and the UK (Gravelle and Sutton, 2009; Jones and Wildman, 2008) find little or no evidence consistent with the relative deprivation hypothesis.[59] Although one of the UK studies finds that mental health does fall slightly with relative deprivation (Jones and Wildman, 2008), which is consistent with other evidence that mental health, but not physical health or longevity, is negatively associated with relative deprivation (Adjaye-Gbewonyo and Kawachi, 2012). One analysis of the US data on mortality and SAH does find evidence consistent with the relative deprivation hypothesis when reference groups are defined narrowly (based on race, state, education, and age) rather than more broadly (state only), as is the case with most other studies (Eibner and Evans, 2005).

17.5.5 Conclusion

The claim that income inequality is harmful to health has provoked much empirical research. This research has delivered little credible evidence to support the hypothesis that income inequality negatively impacts the health of all individuals in society, however. Average population health is negatively associated with income inequality across high- and middle-income countries, but there is no association through time or across regions within countries, except in the USA where state-level differences in health seem to be related to racial composition and possibly also social capital. Individual-level data on morbidity and mortality from high-income countries display no significant, nonnegligible relationship to income inequality after controlling for individual income. Few studies have designs capable of testing the hypotheses that relative income, deprivation,

---

[59] There is a significant negative relationship in some Australian data, but the magnitude is negligible (Bechtel et al., 2012).

or economic position causally impact health. The evidence that exists shows little support for these hypotheses, except maybe for a negative impact of relative deprivation on mental health. But research has yet to fully separate relative from absolute income effects, investigate the strong possibility that health determines relative economic status, and create an appropriate definition, and thus potential endogeneity, for reference groups.[60]

The lack of evidence might reflect a lack of well-defined theory and, consequently, precision in the way in which empirical analyses relate to hypotheses. Several potential mechanisms, including public provision of goods, social capital, psychosocial mechanisms, and pecuniary externalities, have been proposed, but all lack a precise description of how income inequality and/or relative income impact health. The distinction between the hypotheses is not clear; the relative hypotheses are often claimed to imply an effect of income inequality on the health of all individuals, and it is not clear whether the three relative hypotheses are intended to derive from distinct mechanisms. Psychosocial effects are often loosely cited as the main potential mechanism without specification of how, and for whom, relative economic status provokes stress. Further, it is not clear why priority should be given to relative income, as opposed to some other dimension of socioeconomic position, as a cause of psychosocial stress.

A cheap call for research designs capable of identifying the impact of income inequality on health would be unhelpful. Sound identification of a causal effect of income on health is difficult enough. Obtaining exogenous variation in income inequality is an even more daunting task. Rather than further searching for a significant effect of income inequality on health, a more fruitful research agenda would be to directly investigate the causal mechanisms through which health may be related to income inequality. For example, studies have shown that individual health and social capital are associated, but whether this is the result of causality has not received sufficient attention.

17.6. CONCLUSION

This chapter has examined three propositions: health differences generate income inequality, income differences generate health inequality, and income inequality damages health. Grossly simplifying a host of arguments and a vast body of evidence, our verdicts on these three charges are "guilty," "not proven," and "not guilty," respectively.[61] More cautious assessments of the weight of evidence are provided in the conclusions

---

[60] Some studies have allowed respondents to define their own reference groups (Karlsson et al., 2010; Mangyo and Park, 2011; Theodossiou and Zangelidis, 2009), although this introduces an obvious endogeneity.

[61] "Not proven" is a verdict available to the courts under Scots law. It is issued when the jury or judge is not convinced of the innocence of the accused but finds the evidence insufficient to prove guilt.

to Sections 17.3–17.5, respectively. Rather than repeat the arguments that lead us to these conclusions, here we restrict attention to their normative and research implications.

Chief among the multitude of mechanisms through which ill-health can impinge on income is the loss of earnings arising from reduced productivity combined with institutional inflexibilities that result in adjustment through employment rather than wages, or marginal changes in work intensity. In high-income countries, ill-health is a major cause of labor-force withdrawal in middle age. On pure efficiency grounds, disability insurance (DI) is called for to weaken the dependence of income on health and thus compress the income distribution. But there is a strong moral hazard effect that makes employment even more sensitive to ill-health. Achieving the optimal balance between income replacement and work incentives is perhaps the greatest challenge for policy that seeks to constrain income inequality arising from ill-health. The task is made even more difficult by increasing economic inequality itself, in the context of which DI can further weaken the labor market attachment of the low-skilled facing deteriorating opportunities. Research needs to move beyond identifying the impact of ill-health on exiting from employment to the design of programs and incentives that can help individuals experiencing health problems remain in work.

Early-life experience might be another major route through which health impacts the distribution of income. Exposure to health risks *in utero* and ill-health in infanthood appear to impact earnings capacity both by interfering with the accumulation of human capital and skills and by triggering illnesses in adulthood that disrupt employment. The currently observed income distribution is, to some degree, the product of health events that occurred during the childhood of the current adult population. This contribution to economic inequality will be particularly strong if, as appears to be the case, disadvantaged children, who would have grown up to be poorer in any case, face greater health risks. Policies directed at childhood circumstances, including those intended to break the link between parental socioeconomic status and health, may not only be preferred normatively in pursuit of the goal of equal opportunity (see Chapter 4), but they might also be favored simply for their effectiveness in influencing the distribution of income among adults. However, much of this line of argument is still supposition. The evidence that childhood health is influenced by economic background and determines adult economic outcomes is persuasive but not yet concrete. Fortunately, the pace of progress in this field makes it unnecessary to call for more research on the contribution of early-life health to economic inequality.

Our "not proven" verdict on the contribution of income (and wealth) to health inequality arises from the potential difficulty in detecting an effect if one did, in fact, exist. At least in high-income countries with near-universal health insurance coverage and in which the burden of disease is mostly chronic, economic circumstances are likely to exert a toll on health, if at all, over a lifetime. The empirical strategies that have been employed, such as fixed effects and instrumenting with transitory financial shocks, are incapable of identifying the long-run effects that may be operating. Finding random permanent shocks to health from which to estimate the health impact on income is easier than stumbling across exogenous events that permanently change income and allow its effect on health to be identified. The empirical task would undoubtedly be more manageable if there was more theory available to identify precise mechanisms through which income (wealth) might plausibly impact health. The lack of theory is understandable. Economists are trained to explain the distribution of income, not health. Forty years after Grossman (1972a) introduced the concept of the health production function, it remains a black box. Although all too often cited to motivate study of the relationship between health and some socioeconomic factor, it is seldom more fully specified to make the mechanism of any effect explicit.

Rather than further identifying a reduced form effect of income or wealth on health, we believe it is more fruitful to focus on plausible inputs to the health production function that can be influenced by economic status. For example, establishing the health effect of damp, squalid housing is more feasible than finding the health effect of the income that affords superior quality housing. This is not merely a call for empirical pragmatism. Provided that redistribution policy is motivated, in part, by (health) specific egalitarianism—and we attribute the extensive involvement of governments in the provision of health insurance and medical care as being motivated not only by the correction of market failures but also by concern for the distribution of health—it might be more efficient to enable poor people to live in less unhealthy conditions, rather than redistributing cash to them. Once basic nutritional needs are satisfied and access to medical care has been divorced from the ability to pay, the path leading from income to health seems a very long one.

If one switches attention from the distribution of health to that of well-being, then the association between income and health may be used to justify greater redistribution of income, even in the absence of any causal effect. Assuming well-being increases with both income and health, the positive correlation between them increases inequality in well-being by more than is implied by the inequality in their marginal distributions (Deaton, 2013). Redistribution of income toward those in worse health would reduce inequality in well-being both by compensating for sickness and, on average, by reaching poorer individuals (Deaton, 2002).[62] According to this argument, redistribution is partially motivated by one dimension of well-being (income) compensating for deficiency in another (health). This is not how health-related income transfers are typically justified. The disabled are paid transfers because their earnings capacity is impaired and/or they have higher costs of living. The transfers are made because ill-health has a causal impact on economic living standards. The ethical argument makes a case for income redistribution to the sick simply because they are sick. Courts awarding damages for injuries

---

[62] A still more effective redistribution policy might be one that operates through a factor, perhaps education, that exerts a causal impact on both income and health (Deaton, 2002).

irrespective of their consequences for earnings or living costs are consistent with these ethics. But government social policies typically are not. Transfers compensate for financial losses, not reductions in other dimensions of welfare.

With respect to the charge that income inequality threatens health, a case could be made for revising the verdict from "not guilty" to "not proven." It is fundamentally difficult to separate any potential effect of income inequality on the individual's health from that of physical, environmental, social, cultural, or economic determinants of health that operate on the level at which income inequality is measured. Identifying the impact of relative income on health is even more challenging than doing so for absolute income given the added complexity of defining and measuring the reference point. But the limitations are not only empirical. There is a lack of precision in the theoretical arguments as to why economic inequality should impact negatively on health.

The conclusions offered above are based on evidence from high-income countries. In low-income countries, in which a substantial fraction of the population may live close to subsistence and only the economically privileged can afford effective medical care, ill-health is not only an important cause of economic inequality but a consequence of it. But it is the absolute living conditions of the poor, and not their relative deprivation, that takes the toll on health.

ACKNOWLEDGMENTS

We thank the editors, Tony Atkinson and François Bourguignon, for their encouragement and detailed comments on drafts of this chapter. Thanks are also due to Hans van Kippersluis and participants of the NH Handbook of Income Distribution conference, particularly Andrew Clark, for suggestions. Hale Koc and Hao Zhang provided excellent research assistance. We are grateful to various organizations for collecting and providing data (see Appendix). We acknowledge support from the National Institute on Aging, under Grant R01AG037398.

APPENDIX

Table A1 Descriptions and means of variables used in analyses in Section 17.2

		Mean		
	Description	USA	Netherlands	China
Self-assessed health (SAH)[a]				
Poor[a]	1 if self-assessed health is *poor*, 0 otherwise	0.031	0.015	0.066
Moderate/fair	1 if self-assessed health is *moderate/fair*, 0 otherwise	0.123	0.156	0.336
Good	1 if self-assessed health is *good*, 0 otherwise	0.339	0.622	0.474
Very good	1 if self-assessed health is *very good*, 0 otherwise	0.394	0.168	0.124

Table A1 Descriptions and means of variables used in analyses in Section 17.2—cont'd

	Description	Mean USA	Mean Netherlands	Mean China
Excellent	1 if self-assessed health is *excellent*, 0 otherwise	0.112	0.039	
ln(income)[b]	Natural logarithm of equivalent gross household income in national currency	10.142	7.786	9.140

Education[c]

	Description	USA	Netherlands	China
Low[a]	1 if upper secondary education or less, 0 otherwise	0.271	0.413	0.726
Middle	1 if postsecondary nontertiary education, 0 otherwise	0.341	0.245	0.138
high	1 if tertiary education, 0 otherwise	0.388	0.342	0.136
Gender: male	1 if male, 0 if female	0.403	0.470	0.463
Ethnicity: main group	1 for largest ethnic group [white (USA)/ Dutch (NL)/Han (China)], 0 otherwise	0.737	0.879	0.880

Age (years)

	Description	USA	Netherlands	China
20–29[d]	1 if age is 20–29 years, 0 otherwise	0.183	0.099	0.087
30–39	1 if age is 30–39, 0 otherwise	0.197	0.148	0.191
40–49	1 if age is 40–49, 0 otherwise	0.203	0.188	0.239
50–59	1 if age is 50–59, 0 otherwise	0.217	0.211	0.246
60–69	1 if age is 60–69, 0 otherwise	0.135	0.218	0.148
70+	1 if age is 70+, 0 otherwise	0.066	0.136	0.089

Employment status

	Description	USA	Netherlands	China
Employed[d]	1 if employed, 0 otherwise	0.564	0.548	0.650
Unemployed	1 if not working and report being unemployed, 0 otherwise	0.107	0.028	0.032
Disabled	1 if not working and report being disabled, 0 otherwise	0.070	0.044	0.005
Retired	1 if not working and report being retired, 0 otherwise	0.134	0.226	0.141
Not working	1 if not working and do not report being unemployed/disabled/retired	0.124	0.154	0.172
Number of observations		5.050	4.137	7.694

[a]In the USA and Dutch surveys, respondents report their health in general as being *excellent, very good, good, fair* (USA)/ *moderate* (NL), or *poor*. In the Chinese survey, respondents report their health *relative to others of their own age* as *very good, good, fair*, or *poor*.

[b]Gross household income is before payment of taxes and social security contributions and after receipt of transfers. Annual income for USA and monthly income for NL and China. Household income equivalized through division by the square root of household size, with the result being assigned to each household member.

[c]Education has been classified using the International Standard Classification of Education (ISCED) for the USA and the Netherlands, with low education referring to ISCED < 4, middle education to ISCED = 4, and higher education to ISCED > 4 (UNESCO Institute for Statistics). For China, low education refers to a primary or junior high school degree, middle education to a senior high school degree, and high education to vocational higher education and university higher education.

[d]Reference category in the least squares and interval regressions in Tables 17.1 and 17.2.

Table A2 Acronyms used in tables
Name/definition

Datasets

BHPS	British Household Panel Study
BRFSS	Behavioral risk factor surveillance system
CERRA	Leiden University Center for Research on Retirement and Aging Panel
CHS	US National Centre for Health Statistics
CIDJ	Chinese Inequality and Distributive Justice survey project
CMF	Compressed Mortality File of the National Centre for Health Statistics
CNEF	Cross-national equivalent file
ECHP	European Community Household Panel
FORS	Future of Retirement Survey
FSUH	Financial Survey of Urban Housing
GHN	Globalization-Health Nexus database
GHS	General Household Survey
GSOEP	German Socioeconomic Panel
GTD	WHO Global Tuberculosis Database
HRS	Health and Retirement Study
HSE	Health Survey of England
IOT	International Obesity Taskforce
LCMS	Living Condition Monitoring Study
LLH	Living Conditions, Lifestyle, and Health survey
NCD	Swedish National Cause of Death Statistics
NHANES	National Health and Nutrition Examination Survey
NITS	Swedish National Income Tax Statistics
OECD	OECD Health Data
PSID	Panel Study of Income Dynamics
PUMS	US Census Public Use Micro Sample
RHS	Retirement History Study
SALDRU	South African Labour & Development Research Unit survey
SEDLAC	Socio-Economic Database for Latin America and the Caribbean
SHARE	Survey of Health, Ageing and Retirement in Europe
SOCIOLD	Socioeconomic and occupational effects on the health inequality of the older workforce
STF	US Census Summary Tape File 3C
ULF	Statistics Sweden's Survey of Living Conditions
UNHDR	United Nations Development Report
WDID	World Bank World Development Indicators
WHO	Various databases
WIID	WIDER World Income Inequality Database

Table A2 Acronyms used in tables—cont'd
                    Name/definition

Health measures

ADL	Activities of Daily Living
U5MR	Under-5 mortality rate
GHQ	General health questionnaire (psychological health)
HAZ	Height-for-age z-score
HSCL	Hopkins Symptoms Checklist
IMR	Infant mortality
LE	Life expectancy
Major diagnosis	Cancer, heart disease, lung disease (McClellan, 1998—minor)
Minor diagnosis	Hypertension, diabetes, stroke (McClellan, 1998—major), arthritis, back pain
MR	Mortality rate
SAH	Self-assessed health
SB	Stillbirth rate
WHZ	Weight-for-height z-score

Estimators

DID	Difference-in-differences
DP	Dynamic programming
FD	First difference
FE	Fixed effects
GMM	Generalized method of moments
GOP	Generalized ordered probit
GPSM	Generalized propensity score matching
IV	Instrumental variables
LPM	Linear probability model
MSM	Method of simulated moments
OLS	Ordinary least squares
QR	Quantile regression
RE	Random effects
SML	Simulated maximum likelihood
2SLS	Two-stage least squares
2SQR	Two-stage quantile regression
WLS	Weighted least squares

DATA SOURCES

We use data from the Chinese Health and Nutrition Survey (CHNS), the Netherlands Longitudinal Internet Studies for the Social Sciences (LISS), and the ALP. We thank the organizations that collected and provided these data.

The LISS panel data were collected by CentERdata (Tilburg University, The Netherlands) through its MESS project funded by the Netherlands Organization for Scientific Research.

RAND ALP are proprietary capabilities of the RAND Corporation. They were developed by RAND with its own funds and with the support of numerous clients and grantors who have commissioned social science and economics research and analysis at RAND.

The National Institute of Nutrition and Food Safety, China Center for Disease Control and Prevention, Carolina Population Center, the University of North Carolina at Chapel Hill, the NIH (R01-HD30880, DK056350, and R01-HD38700) and the Fogarty International Center, all contributed to the collection of the CHNS.

We thank the *Equality Trust Fund* for providing the data to reconstruct the first figure in Section 17.5.

REFERENCES

Acemoglu, D., Angrist, J.D., 2001. Consequences of employment protection? The case of the Americans with Disability Act. J. Polit. Econ. 109 (5), 915–957.

Adams, P., Hurd, M.D., Mcfadden, D., Merrill, A., Ribeiro, T., 2003. Healthy, wealthy, and wise? Tests for direct causal paths between health and socioeconomic status. J. Econom. 112 (1), 3–56.

Adda, J., Chandola, T., Marmot, M., 2003. Socio-economic status and health: causality and pathways. J. Econom. 112 (1), 57–64.

Adda, J., Gaudecker, H., Banks, J., 2009. The impact of income shocks on health: evidence from cohort data. J. Eur. Econ. Assoc. 7 (6), 1361–1399.

Adjaye-Gbewonyo, K., Kawachi, I., 2012. Use of the Yitzhaki Index as a test of relative deprivation for health outcomes: a review of recent literature. Soc. Sci. Med. 75 (1), 129–137.

Agüero, J., Carter, M., Woolard, I., 2009. The Impact of Unconditional Cash Transfers on Nutrition: The South African Child Support Grant. University of Cape Town, Cape Town.

Aigner, D.J., Cain, G.G., 1977. Statistical theories of discrimination in labor markets. Ind. Labor. Relat. Rev. 30 (2), 175–187.

Alesina, A., Baqir, R., Easterly, W., 1999. Public goods and ethnic divisions. Q. J. Econ. 114 (4), 1243–1284.

Alesina, A., Di Tella, R., MacCulloch, R., 2004. Inequality and happiness: are Europeans and Americans different? J. Public Econ. 88 (9–10), 2009–2042.

Allin, S., Stabile, M., 2012. Socioeconomic status and child health: what is the role of health care, health conditions, injuries and maternal health? Health Econ. Policy Law 7 (2), 227.

Almond, D., 2006. Is the 1918 influenza pandemic over? Long-term effects of in utero influenza exposure in the post-1940 U.S. population. J. Polit. Econ. 114 (4), 672–712.

Almond, D., Currie, J., 2011. Killing me softly: the fetal origins hypothesis. J. Econ. Perspect. 25 (3), 153–172.

Almond, D., Currie, J., 2012. Chapter 15—human capital development before age five. In: Ashenfelter, O., Card, D. (Eds.), Handbook of Labor Economics. Elsevier, Amsterdam, pp. 1315–1486.

Almond, D., Mazumder, B., 2005. The 1918 influenza pandemic and subsequent health outcomes: an analysis of SIPP data. Am. Econ. Rev. 95, 258–262.

Almond, D., Edlund, L., Palme, M., 2009. Chernobyl's subclinical legacy: prenatal exposure to radioactive fallout and school outcomes in Sweden. Q. J. Econ. 124 (4), 1729–1772.

Almond, D., Hoynes, H.W., Schanzenbach, D.W., 2011. Inside the war on poverty: the impact of food stamps on birth outcomes. Rev. Econ. Stat. 93 (2), 387–403.

Amarante, V., Manacorda, M., Miguel, E., Vigorito, A., 2011. Do Cash Transfers Improve Birth Outcomes? Evidence from Matched Vital Statistics, Social Security and Program Data. CEPR Discussion Paper No. DP8740, CEPR, London.

Apouey, B., Clark, A., 2013. Winning big but feeling no better? The effect of lottery prizes on physical and mental health. Centre for Economic Performance, London, LSE Discussion Paper No. 1228.

Apouey, B., Geoffard, P., 2013. Family income and child health in the UK. J. Health Econ. 32 (4), 715–727.

Arrow, K.J., 1973. The theory of discrimination. In: Ashenfelter, O., Rees, A. (Eds.), Discrimination in Labor Markets. Princeton University Press, Princeton, NJ.

Ash, M., Robinson, D.E., 2009. Inequality, race, and mortality in U.S. cities: a political and econometric review of Deaton and Lubotsky (56:6, 1139–1153, 2003). Soc. Sci. Med. 68 (11), 1909–1913.

Atkinson, A.B., Harrison, A.J., 1978. Distribution of Personal Wealth in Britain, 1923–1972. Cambridge University Press, Cambridge.

Atkinson, A.B., Piketty, T., Saez, E., 2011. Top incomes in the long run of history. J. Econ. Lit. 49 (1), 3–71.

Au, D.W.H., Crossley, T.F., Schellhorn, M., 2005. The effect of health changes and long-term health on the work activity of older Canadians. Health Econ. 14 (10), 999–1018.

Autor, D.H., Duggan, M.G., 2003. The rise in the disability rolls and the decline in unemployment. Q. J. Econ. 118 (1), 157–205.

Autor, D.H., Duggan, M.G., 2006. The growth in the social security disability rolls: a fiscal crisis unfolding. J. Econ. Perspect. 20 (3), 71–96.

Avendano, M., 2012. Correlation or causation? Income inequality and infant mortality in fixed effects models in the period 1960–2008 in 34 OECD countries. Soc. Sci. Med. 75 (4), 754–760.

Babones, S.J., 2008. Income inequality and population health: correlation and causality. Soc. Sci. Med. 66 (7), 1614–1626.

Bago D'Uva, T., Van Doorslaer, E., Lindeboom, M., O'Donnell, O., 2008. Does reporting heterogeneity bias measurement of health disparities? Health Econ. 17 (3), 351–375.

Baird, S., Friedman, J., Schady, N., 2011. Aggregate income shocks and infant mortality in the developing world. Rev. Econ. Stat. 93 (3), 847–856.

Baldwin, M., Johnson, W.G., 1994. Labor market discrimination against men with disabilities. J. Hum. Resour. 29 (1), 1–19.

Banerjee, A.V., Duflo, E., 2011. Poor Economics. Public Affairs, New York.

Banks, J., 2006. Economic capabilities, choices and outcomes at older ages. Fisc. Stud. 27 (3), 281–311.

Barker, D.J.P. (Ed.), 1992. Fetal and Infant Origins of Adult Disease. BMJ Publishing Group, London.

Barker, D.J., 1995. Fetal origins of coronary heart disease. Br. Med. J. 311, 171–174.

Barker, D.J.P., Godfrey, K.M., Gluckman, P.D., Harding, J.E., Owens, J.A., Robinson, J.S., 1993. Fetal nutrition and cardiovascular disease in adult life. Lancet 341 (8850), 938–941.

Barro, R.J., 2003. Determinants of economic growth in a panel of countries. Ann. Econ. Finance 4, 231–274.

Barro, R.J., 2013. Health and economic growth. Ann. Econ. Finance 14 (2), 329–366.

Bazzoli, G., 1985. The early retirement decision: new empirical evidence on the influence of health. J. Hum. Resour. 20, 214–234.

Bechtel, L., Lordan, G., Rao, D.S.P., 2012. Income inequality and mental health? Empirical evidence from Australia. Health Econ. 21, 4–17.

Becker, G., 1957. The Economics of Discrimination. University of Chicago Press, Chicago.

Behrman, J.R., Rosenzweig, M.R., 2004. Returns to birthweight. Rev. Econ. Stat. 86 (2), 586–601.

Bell, D., Heitmueller, A., 2009. The Disability Discrimination Act in the UK: helping or hindering employment among the disabled? J. Health Econ. 28 (2), 465–480.

Ben-Porath, Y., 1967. The production of human capital and the life cycle of earnings. J. Polit. Econ. 75, 352–365.

Berger, M.C., 1983. Labour supply and spouse's health: the effects of illness, disability and mortality. Soc. Sci. Q. 64, 494–509.

Berger, M.C., Fleisher, B.M., 1984. Husband's health and wife's labor supply. J. Health Econ. 3, 63–75.

Bhalotra, S., 2010. Fatal fluctuations? Cyclicality in infant mortality in India. J. Dev. Econ. 93 (1), 7–19.

Biggs, B., King, L., Basu, S., Stuckler, D., 2010. Is wealthier always healthier? The impact of national income level, inequality, and poverty on public health in Latin America. Soc. Sci. Med. 71 (2), 266–273.

Black, D., Kermit, D., Sanders, S., 2002. The impact of economic conditions on participation in disability programs: evidence from the coal boom and bust. Am. Econ. Rev. 92 (1), 27–50.

Black, S.E., Devereux, P.J., Salvanes, K.G., 2007. From the cradle to the labor market? The effect of birth weight on adult outcomes. Q. J. Econ. 122 (1), 409–439.

Blau, D., Gilleskie, D., 2001. The effect of health on employment transitions of older men. Worker Well-being in a Changing Labor Market Research in Labor Economics, vol. 20 JAI Press, Amsterdam, pp. 35–65.

Blau, D.M., Riphahn, R.T., 1999. Labor force transitions of older married couples in Germany. Labour Econ. 6 (2), 229–252.

Bleakley, H., 2007. Disease and development: evidence from hookworm eradication in the south. Q. J. Econ. 122 (1), 73–117.

Bliss, C., Stern, N., 1978. Productivity, wages and nutrition: part I: the theory. J. Dev. Econ. 5 (4), 331–362.

Borghol, N., Suderman, M., Mcardle, W., Racine, A., Hallett, M., Pembrey, M., Hertzman, C., Power, C., Szyf, M., 2012. Associations with early-life socio-economic position in adult DNA methylation. Int. J. Epidemiol. 41 (1), 62–74.

Bound, J., 1991. Self reported versus objective measures of health in retirement models. J. Hum. Resour. 26, 107–137.

Bound, J., Burkhauser, R.V., 1999. Chapter 51: economic analysis of transfer programs targeted on people with disabilities. In: Ashenfelter, O., Card, D. (Eds.), Handbook of Labor Economics. Elsevier, Amsterdam, pp. 3417–3528.

Bound, J., Schoenbaum, M., Stinebrickner, T.R., Waidmann, T., 1999. The dynamic effects of health on the labor force transitions of older workers. Labour Econ. 6 (2), 179–202.

Bound, J., Stinebrickner, T., Waidmann, T., 2010. Health, economic resources and the work decisions of older men. J. Econom. 156 (1), 106–129.

Breslau, N., Deldotto, J.E., Brown, G.G., Kumar, S., Ezhuthachan, S., Hufnagle, K.G., Peterson, E.L., 1994. A gradient relationship between low birth weight and IQ at age 6 years. Arch. Pediatr. Adolesc. Med. 148 (4), 377–383.

Brown, S., Roberts, J., Taylor, K., 2010. Reservation wages, labour market participation and health. J. R. Stat. Soc. A Stat. Soc. 173 (3), 501–529.

Burgess, S., Propper, C., Rigg, J.A., 2004. The Impact of Low Income on Child Health: Evidence from a Birth Cohort Study. Centre for Analysis of Social Exclusion, London, LSE CASE Paper 85.

Cai, L., 2009. Effects of health on wages of Australian men. Econ. Rec. 85 (270), 290–306.

Cain, G., 1986. The economic analysis of labor market discrimination: a survey. In: Ashenfelter, O., Layard, R. (Eds.), Handbook of Labor Economics. In: vol. I. North Holland, Amsterdam.

Cantarero, D., Pascual, M., María Sarabia, J., 2005. Effects of income inequality on population health: new evidence from the European community household panel. Appl. Econ. 37 (1), 87–91.

Carman, K.G., 2013. Inheritances, intergenerational transfers, and the accumulation of health. Am. Econ. Rev. Papers & Proc. 103 (3), 451–455.

Carter, H., Glick, P., 1976. Marriage and Divorce: A Social and Economic Study. Harvard University Press, Cambridge, MA.

Case, A., 2004. Does money protect health status? Evidence from South African pensions. Perspectives on the Economics of Aging, University of Chicago Press, Chicago, IL, pp. 287–312.

Case, A., Paxson, C., 2008. Stature and status: height, ability, and labor market outcomes. J. Polit. Econ. 116 (3), 499–532.

Case, A., Paxson, C., 2011. The long reach of childhood health and circumstance: evidence from the Whitehall II study. Econ. J. 121 (554), F183–F204.

Case, A., Lubotsky, D., Paxson, C., 2002. Economic status and health in childhood: the origins of the gradient. Am. Econ. Rev. 92 (5), 1308–1334.

Case, A., Fertig, A., Paxson, C., 2005. The lasting impact of childhood health and circumstance. J. Health Econ. 24, 365–389.

Case, A., Lee, D., Paxson, C., 2008. The income gradient in children's health: a comment on Currie, Shields, and Wheatley Price. J. Health Econ. 27 (3), 801–807.

Cawley, J., Ruhm, C.J., 2011. The economics of risky health behaviors 1. Handb. Health Econom., vol. 2, p. 95.

Cawley, J., Heckman, J.J., Vytlacil, E.J., 2001. Three observations on wages and measured cognitive ability. Labour Econ. 8 (4), 419–442.

Cawley, J., Moran, J., Simon, K., 2010. The impact of income on the weight of elderly Americans. Health Econ. 19 (8), 979.

Chandola, T., Bartley, M., Sacker, A., Jenkinson, C., Marmot, M., 2003. Health selection in the Whitehall II study. Soc. Sci. Med. 56 (10), 2059–2072.

Chang, F., 1991. Uncertain lifetimes, retirement and economic welfare. Economica 58 (230), 215–232.

Charles, K.K., 1999. Sickness in the Family: Health Shocks and Spousal Labor Supply. University of Michigan, Ann Arbor.

Charles, K.K., 2003. The longitudinal structure of earnings losses among work-limited disabled workers. J. Hum. Resour. 38 (3), 618–646.

Clark, A.E., Frijters, P., Shields, M.A., 2008. Relative income, happiness, and utility: an explanation for the Easterlin paradox and other puzzles. J. Econ. Lit. 46 (1), 95–144.

Coile, C.C., 2004. Health Shocks and Couples' Labor Supply Decisions. NBER Working Paper No. 10810, NBER, Cambridge, MA.

Commission on Macroeconomics and Health, 2001. Macroeconomics and Health: Investing in Health for Economic Development. World Health Organisation, Geneva.

Commission on the Social Determinants of Health, 2008. Closing the gap in a generation: health equity through action on the social determinants of health. Final Report of the Commission on Social Determinants of Health, World Health Organization, Geneva.

Condliffe, S., Link, C.R., 2008. The relationship between economic status and child health: evidence from the United States. Am. Econ. Rev. 98 (4), 1605–1618.

Conley, D., Bennett, N.G., 2001. Birth weight and income: interactions across generations. J. Health Soc. Behav. 42 (4), 450–465.

Conti, G., Heckman, J.J., Urzua, S., 2010a. Early endowments, education, and health. Unpublished manuscript, University of Chicago, Department of Economics, Chicago, p. 162.

Conti, G., Heckman, J., Urzua, S., 2010b. The education–health gradient. Am. Econ. Rev. 100, 234–238, Papers and proceedings.

Contoyannis, P., Rice, N., 2001. The impact of health on wages: evidence from the British Household Panel Survey. Emp. Econ. 26 (4), 599–622.

Contoyannis, P., Jones, A.M., Rice, N., 2004. The dynamics of health in the British Household Panel Survey. J. Appl. Econ. 19 (4), 473–503.

Costello, E.J., Worthman, C., Erkanli, A., Angold, A., 2007. Prediction from low birth weight to female adolescent depression: a test of competing hypotheses. Arch. Gen. Psychiatry 64 (3), 338–344.

Crimmins, E.M., Beltran-Sanchez, H., 2011. Mortality and morbidity trends: is there compression of morbidity? J. Gerontol. B 66B (1), 75–86.

Cunha, F., Heckman, J., 2007. The technology of skill formation. Am. Econ. Rev. 97 (2), 31–47.

Cunha, F., Heckman, J., 2008. A new framework for the analysis of inequality. Macroecon. Dyn. 12 (Suppl. S2), 315.

Cunha, F., Heckman, J.J., 2009. The economics and psychology of inequality and human development. J. Eur. Econ. Assoc. 7 (2–3), 320–364.

Cunha, F., Heckman, J.J., Lochner, L., Masterov, D.V., 2006. Chapter 12: interpreting the evidence on life cycle skill formation. In: Hanushek, E., Welch, F. (Eds.), Handbook of the Economics of Education. Elsevier, Amsterdam, pp. 697–812.

Currie, J., 2009. Healthy, wealthy, and wise: socioeconomic status, poor health in childhood, and human capital development. J. Econ. Lit. 47 (1), 87–122.

Currie, J., Hyson, R., 1999. Is the impact of health shocks cushioned by socioeconomic status? The case of low birthweight. Am. Econ. Rev. 89 (2), 245–250.

Currie, J., Madrian, B.C., 1999. Chapter 50: health, health insurance and the labor market. In: Ashenfelter, O.C., Card, D. (Eds.), Handbook of Labor Economics. Elsevier, Amsterdam, pp. 3309–3416.

Currie, J., Moretti, E., 2007. Biology as destiny? Short- and long-run determinants of intergenerational transmission of birth weight. J. Labor Econ. 25 (2), 231–264.

Currie, J., Stabile, M., 2003. Socioeconomic status and child health: why is the relationship stronger for older children. Am. Econ. Rev. 93 (5), 1813–1823.

Currie, J., Stabile, M., 2006. Child mental health and human capital accumulation: the case of ADHD. J. Health Econ. 25 (6), 1094–1118.

Currie, A., Shields, M.A., Price, S.W., 2007. The child health/family income gradient: evidence from England. J. Health Econ. 26 (2), 213–232.

Currie, J., Stabile, M., Manivong, P., Roos, L.L., 2010. Child health and young adult outcomes. J. Hum. Resour. 45 (3), 517–548.

Cutler, D.M., Lleras-Muney, A., 2010. Understanding differences in health behaviors by education. J. Health Econ. 29 (1), 1–28.

Cutler, D.M., Knaul, F., Lozano, R., Méndez, O., Zurita, B., 2002. Financial crisis, health outcomes and ageing: Mexico in the 1980s and 1990s. J. Public Econ. 84 (2), 279–303.

Cutler, D.M., Lange, F., Meara, E., Richards-Shubik, S., Ruhm, C.J., 2011a. Rising educational gradients in mortality: the role of behavioral factors. J. Health Econ. 30 (6), 1174–1187.

Cutler, D., Lleras-Muney, A., Vogl, T., 2011b. Chapter 7: socioeconomic status and health: dimensions and mechanisms. In: Glied, S., Smith, P.C. (Eds.), Oxford Handbook of Health Economics. Oxford University Press, Oxford, pp. 124–163.

Cutler, D., Ghosh, K., Landrum, M.B., 2013. Evidence for significant compression of morbidity in the elderly US population. NBER Working Paper No. 19268, NBER, Cambridge, MA.

Daly, M.C., Bound, J., 1996. Worker adaptation and employer accommodation following the onset of a health impairment. J. Gerontol. 51, S53–S60.

Dasgupta, P., 1993. An Inquiry into Well-Being and Destitution. Oxford University Press, Oxford.

Dasgupta, P., 1997. Nutritional status, the capacity for work, and poverty traps. J. Econom. 77 (1), 5–37.

Dasgupta, P., Ray, D., 1986. Inequality as a determinant of malnutrition and unemployment: theory. Econ. J. 96 (384), 1011–1034.

Deaton, A., 2001a. Inequalities in income and inequalities in health. In: Welch, F. (Ed.), The Causes and Consequences of Increasing Inequality. Chicago University Press, Chicago, pp. 285–313.

Deaton, A., 2001b. Relative Deprivation, Inequality, and Mortality. National Bureau of Economic Research, Cambridge, MA.

Deaton, A., 2002. Policy implications of the gradient of health and wealth. Health Aff. 21 (2), 13–30.

Deaton, A., 2003. Health, inequality, and economic development. J. Econ. Lit. 41 (1), 113–158.

Deaton, A., 2013. What does the empirical evidence on SES and health tell us about inequity and about policy? In: Eyal, N., Hurst, S.A., Norheim, O.F., Wikler, D. (Eds.), Inequalities in Health: Concepts, Measures and Ethics. Oxford University Press, New York.

Deaton, A., Lubotsky, D., 2009. Income inequality and mortality in U.S. cities: weighing the evidence. A response to ash. Soc. Sci. Med. 68 (11), 1914–1917.

Deaton, A., Paxson, C., 2001. Mortality, education, income, and inequality among American cohorts. In: Wise, D. (Ed.), Themes in the Economics of Aging. University of Chicago Press, Chicago, IL, pp. 129–170.

Deaton, A., Paxson, C., 2004. Mortality, income, and income inequality over time in Britain and the United States. In: Wise, D. (Ed.), Perspectives on the Economics of Ageing. University of Chicago Press, Chicago, IL, pp. 247–285.

Deleire, T., 2000. The wage and employment effects of the Americans with Disabilities Act. J. Hum. Resour. 35 (4), 693–715.

Deleire, T., 2001. Changes in wage discrimination against people with disabilities: 1984–93. J. Hum. Resour. 36 (1), 144–158.

Deolalikar, A.B., 1988. Nutrition and labor productivity in agriculture: estimates for rural South India. Rev. Econ. Stat. 70 (3), 406–413.

D'Hombres, B., Rocco, L., Suhrcke, M., McKee, M., 2010. Does social capital determine health? Evidence from eight transition countries. Health Econ. 19 (1), 56–74.

Diamond, P., Sheshinski, E., 1995. Economic aspects of optimal disability benefits. J. Public Econ. 57 (1), 1–23.

Disney, R., Emmerson, C., Wakefield, M., 2006. Ill health and retirement in Britain: a panel data-based analysis. J. Health Econ. 25 (4), 621–649.

Dobkin, C., Puller, S., 2007. The effects of government transfers on monthly cycles in drug abuse, hospitalization and mortality. J. Pub. Econ. 91, 2137–2151.

Doorslaer, E.V., Jones, A.M., 2003. Inequalities in self-reported health: validation of a new approach to measurement. J. Health Econ. 22 (1), 61–87.

Duflo, E., 2000. Child health and household resources in South Africa: evidence from the old age pension program. Am. Econ. Rev. 90 (2), 393–398.

Duflo, E., 2003. Grandmothers and granddaughters: old-age pensions and intrahousehold allocation in South Africa. World Bank Econ. Rev. 17 (1), 1–25.

Dwyer, D.S., Mitchell, O.S., 1999. Health problems as determinants of retirement: are self-rated measures endogenous? J. Health Econ. 18 (2), 173–193.

Ebrahim, S., 2012. Epigenetics: the next big thing. Int. J. Epidemiol. 41 (1), 1–3.

Eibner, C., Evans, W.N., 2005. Relative deprivation, poor health habits, and mortality. J. Hum. Resour. XL (3), 591–620.

Erreygers, G., 2009. Can a single indicator measure both attainment and shortfall inequality? J. Health Econ. 28 (4), 885–893.

Erreygers, G., Van Ourti, T., 2011. Measuring socioeconomic inequality in health, health care and health financing by means of rank-dependent indices: a recipe for good practice. J. Health Econ. 30 (4), 685–694.

Ettner, S.L., 1996. New evidence on the relationship between income and health. J. Health Econ. 15 (1), 67–85.

Evans, W.N., Moore, T.J., 2011. The short-term mortality consequences of income receipt. J. Public Econ. 95 (11), 1410–1424.

Fang, H., Rizzo, J.A., 2012. Does inequality in China affect health differently in high-versus low-income households? Appl. Econ. 44 (9), 1081–1090.

Feeny, D., Furlong, W., Torrance, G.W., Goldsmith, C.H., Zhu, Z., Depauw, S., Denton, M., Boyle, M., 2002. Multiattribute and single-attribute utility functions for the health utilities index mark 3 system. Med. Care 40 (2), 113–128.

Fernald, L.C., Hidrobo, M., 2011. Effect of Ecuador's cash transfer program (*Bono de Desarrollo Humano*) on child development in infants and toddlers: a randomized effectiveness trial. Soc. Sci. Med. 72 (9), 1437–1446.

Fernald, L.C., Gertler, P.J., Neufeld, L.M., 2008. Role of cash in conditional cash transfer programmes for child health, growth, and development: an analysis of Mexico's Oportunidades. Lancet 371 (9615), 828–837.

Finkelstein, A., Luttmer, E.F.P., Notowidigdo, M.J., 2013. What good is wealth without health? The effect of health on the marginal utility of consumption. J. Eur. Econ. Assoc. 11 (s1), 221–258.

Fleurbaey, M., Schokkaert, E., 2011. Chapter Sixteen—equity in health and health care. In: Pauly, M.V., Mcguire, T.G., Barros, P.P. (Eds.), Handbook of Health Economics. In: vol. 2. Elsevier, Amsterdam, pp. 1003–1092.

French, E., 2005. The effects of health, wealth, and wages on labour supply and retirement behaviour. Rev. Econ. Stud. 72 (2), 395–427.

Frijters, P., Shields, M.A., Haisken-DeNew, J.P., 2005. The effect of income on health: evidence from a large scale natural experiment. J. Health Econ. 24, 997–1017.

Fu, H., Goldman, N., 1994. Are healthier people more likely to marry? An event history analysis based on the NLSY. Working Paper 94-5, Office of Population Research, Princeton University, New Jersey.

Galama, T.J., Van Kippersluis, H., 2010. A Theory of Socioeconomic Disparities in Health over the Life Cycle. Tinbergen Institute, Amsterdam, Discussion Paper No. 2010-08-24.

García Gómez, P., Lopez-Nicolas, A., 2006. Health shocks, employment and income in the Spanish labour market. Health Econ. 9, 997–1009.

García Gómez, P., Van Kippersluis, H., O'Donnell, O., Van Doorslaer, E., 2013. Long term and spillover effects of health on employment and income. J. Hum. Resour. 48 (4), 873–909.

García-Gómez, P., 2011. Institutions, health shocks and labour market outcomes across Europe. J. Health Econ. 30 (1), 200–213.

Gardner, J., Oswald, A.J., 2007. Money and mental wellbeing: a longitudinal study of medium-sized lottery wins. J. Health Econ. 26 (1), 49–60.

Gerdtham, U., Johannesson, M., 2004. Absolute income, relative income, income inequality, and mortality. J. Hum. Resour. XXXIX (1), 228–247.

Gertler, P., 2004. Do conditional cash transfers improve child health? Evidence from PROGRESA's control randomized experiment. Am. Econ. Rev. 94 (2), 336–341.

Gertler, P., Gruber, J., 2001. Insuring consumption against illness. Am. Econ. Rev. 92 (1), 51–70.

Goda, G.S., Golberstein, E., Grabowski, D.C., 2011. Income and the utilization of long-term care services: evidence from the social security benefit notch. J. Health Econ. 30 (4), 719–729.

Goldman, N., 1993. Marriage selection and mortality patterns: inferences and fallacies. Demography 30 (2), 189–208.

Granger, C.W.J., 1969. Investigating causal relations by econometric models and cross-spectral methods. Econometrica 37 (3), 424–438.

Grantham-Mcgregor, S.M., Powell, C.A., Walker, S.P., Himes, J.H., 1991. Nutritional supplementation, psychosocial stimulation, and mental development of stunted children: the Jamaican Study. Lancet 338 (8758), 1–5.

Grantham-Mcgregor, S., Cheung, Y.B., Cueto, S., Glewwe, P., Richter, L., Strupp, B., 2007. Developmental potential in the first 5 years for children in developing countries. Lancet 369, 60–70.

Gravelle, H., 1998. How much of the relation between population mortality and unequal distribution of income is a statistical artefact? Br. Med. J. 316, 382–385.

Gravelle, H., Sutton, M., 2009. Income, relative income, and self-reported health in Britain 1979–2000. Health Econ. 18 (2), 125–145.

Gravelle, H., Wildman, J., Sutton, M., 2002. Income, income inequality and health: what can we learn from aggregate data? Soc. Sci. Med. 54 (4), 577–589.

Grönqvist, H., Johansson, P., Niknami, S., 2012. Income inequality and health: lessons from a refugee residential assignment program. J. Health Econ. 31 (4), 617–629.

Grossman, M., 1972a. The Demand for Health: A Theoretical and Empirical Investigation. NBER, New York.

Grossman, M., 1972b. On the concept of health capital and the demand for health. J. Polit. Econ. 80 (2), 223–255.

Grossman, M., 2000. The human capital model. In: Culyer, A., Newhouse, J. (Eds.), North Holland Handbook in Health Economics. North Holland, Amsterdam, Netherlands, pp. 1804–1862.

Grossman, M., Kaestner, R., 1997. Effects of education on health. In: Behrman, J.R., Stacey, N. (Eds.), The Social Benefits of Education. University of Michigan Press, Ann Arbor, pp. 69–123.

Gruber, J., 2000. Disability insurance benefits and labor supply. J. Polit. Econ. 108 (6), 1162–1183.

Gustman, A.L., Steinmeier, T.L., 1986a. A disaggregated, structural analysis of retirement by race, difficulty of work and health. Rev. Econ. Stat. 68 (3), 509–513.

Gustman, A.L., Steinmeier, T.L., 1986b. A structural retirement model. Econometrica 54 (3), 555–584.

Halla, M., Zweimuller, M., 2013. The effect of health on income: quasi-experimental evidence from commuting accidents. Labour Econ. 24, 23–38.

Hammermesh, D., 1984. Life-cycle effects on consumption and retirement. J. Labor Econ. 2 (3), 353–370.

Hausman, J., Taylor, W., 1981. Panel data and unobservable individual effects. Econometrica 49, 1377–1398.

Hayes, B., Sharif, F., 2009. Behavioural and emotional outcome of very low birth weight infants—literature review. J. Matern. Fetal Neonatal Med. 22 (10), 849–856.

Heckman, J., 2003. Conditioning, causality and policy analysis. J. Econom. 112 (1), 73–78.

Heckman, J.J., 2007. The economics, technology, and neuroscience of human capability formation. Proc. Natl. Acad. Sci. U.S.A. 104 (33), 13250–13255.

Heckman, J.J., Stixrud, J., Urzua, S., 2006. The effects of cognitive and noncognitive abilities on labor market outcomes and social behavior. J. Labor Econ. 24 (3), 411–482.

Hediger, M.L., Overpeck, M.D., Ruan, W.J., Troendle, J.F., 2002. Birthweight and gestational age effects on motor and social development. Paediatr. Perinat. Epidemiol. 16, 33–46.

Herrnstein, R.J., Murray, C.A., 1994. The Bell Curve: Intelligence and Class Structure in American Life. Free Press, New York.

Hertzman, C., Power, C., Matthews, S., 2001. Using an interactive framework of society and lifecourse to explain self-rated health in early adulthood. Soc. Sci. Med. 53, 1575–1585.

Hibbs, H., 1915. The influence of economic and industrial conditions on infant mortality. Q. J. Econ. 30, 127–151.

Hildebrand, V., Kerm, P.V., 2009. Income inequality and self-rated health status: evidence from the European community household panel. Demography 46 (4), 805–825.

Hille, E.T.M., Ouden, A.L.D., Bauer, L., Oudenrijn, C.V.D., Brand, R., Verloove-Vanhorick, S.P., 1994. School performance at nine years of age in very premature and very low birth weight infants: perinatal risk factors and predictors at five years of age. J. Pediatr. 125 (3), 426–434.

Hotchkiss, J.L., 2004. A closer look at the employment impact of the Americans with Disabilities Act. J. Hum. Resour. 39 (4), 887–911.

Hoynes, H.W., Schanzenbach, D.W., 2009. Consumption responses to in-kind transfers: evidence from the introduction of the food stamp program. Am. Econ. J. Appl. Econ. 1 (4), 109–139.

Hoynes, H., Page, M., Stevens, A.H., 2011. Can targeted transfers improve birth outcomes? Evidence from the introduction of the WIC program. J. Public Econ. 95 (7), 813–827.

Hoynes, H.W., Miller, D.L., Simon, D., 2012. Income, the Earned Income Tax Credit, and Infant Health. NBER, Cambridge, MA, Working Paper No. 18206.

Hugonnier, J., Pelgrin, F., St-Amour, P., 2013. Health and (other) asset holdings. Rev. Econ. Stud. 80, 663–710.

Hurd, M., Kapteyn, A., 2003. Health, wealth, and the role of institutions. J. Hum. Resour. 38 (2), 386–415.

Jackle, R., Himmler, O., 2010. Health and wages. J. Hum. Resour. 45 (2), 364–406.

Jencks, C., 1979. Who Gets Ahead? The Determinants of Economic Success in America. Basic Books, New York.

Jensen, R.T., Richter, K., 2004. The health implications of social security failure: evidence from the Russian pension crisis. J. Public Econ. 88 (1), 209–236.

Johnson, W.G., Lambrinos, J., 1985. Wage discrimination against handicapped men and women. J. Hum. Resour. 20 (2), 264–277.

Johnson, R., Schoeni, R., 2011. The influence of early-life events on human capital, health status, and labor market outcomes over the life course. BE J. Econ. Anal. Policy 11 (3), 1–55.

Jones, A.M., Wildman, J., 2008. Health, income and relative deprivation: evidence from the BHPS. J. Health Econ. 27 (2), 308–324.

Jones, M.K., Latreille, P.L., Sloane, P.J., 2006. Disability, gender, and the British labour market. Oxf. Econ. Papers 58 (3), 407–449.

Jones, A.M., Rice, N., Roberts, J., 2010. Sick of work or too sick to work? Evidence on self-reported health shocks and early retirement from the BHPS. Econ. Model. 27 (4), 866–880.

Kahn, L., 1991. Customer discrimination and affirmative action. Econ. Inq. 29, 555–571.

Kalemli-Ozcan, S., Weil, D., 2010. Mortality change, the uncertainty effect and retirement. J. Econ. Growth 15 (1), 65–91.

Karlsson, M., Nilsson, T., Lyttkens, C.H., Leeson, G., 2010. Income inequality and health: importance of a cross-country perspective. Soc. Sci. Med. 70 (6), 875–885.

Kawachi, I., Kennedy, B.P., 1997. Health and social cohesion: why care about income inequality? Br. Med. J. 314 (7086), 1037–1040.

Kawachi, I., Kennedy, B.P., Lochner, K., Prothrow-Stith, D., 1997. Social capital, income inequality and mortality. Am. J. Public Health 87 (9), 1491–1498.

Kelly, E., 2011. The scourge of Asian flu: in utero exposure to pandemic influenza and the development of a cohort of British children. J. Hum. Resour. 21 (4), 669–694.

Kennedy, B., Kawachi, I., Glass, R., Prothrow-Smith, D., 1998. Income distribution, socioeconomic status, and self rated health in the United States: multilevel analysis. Br. Med. J. 317, 917–921.

Kerkhofs, M., Lindeboom, M., Theeuwes, J., 1999. Retirement, financial incentives and health. Labour Econ. 6 (2), 203–227.

Khanam, R., Nghiem, H.S., Connelly, L.B., 2009. Child health and the income gradient: evidence from Australia. J. Health Econ. 28 (4), 805–817.

Kidd, M.P., Sloane, P.J., Ferko, I., 2000. Disability and the labour market: an analysis of British males. J. Health Econ. 19 (6), 961–981.

Kim, B., Ruhm, C.J., 2012. Inheritances, health and death. Health Econ. 21 (2), 127–144.

Kirkegaard, I., Obel, C., Hedegaard, M., Henriksen, T.B., 2006. Gestational age and birth weight in relation to school performance of 10-year-old children: a follow-up study of children born after 32 completed weeks. Pediatrics 118 (4), 1600–1606.

Kuh, D., Ben-Shlomo, Y. (Eds.), 1997. A Lifecourse Approach to Chronic Disease Epidemiology: Tracing the Origins of Ill-Health from Early to Adult Life. Oxford University Press, Oxford.

Kuh, D.J.L., Wadsworth, M.E.J., 1993. Physical health status at 36 years in a British national birth cohort. Soc. Sci. Med. 37 (7), 905–916.

Kuh, D., Ben-Shlomo, Y., et al., 2003. Life course epidemiology. J. Epidemiol. Commun. Health 57 (10), 778–783.

Lambert, P., Zheng, B., 2011. On the consistent measurement of attainment and shortfall inequality. J. Health Econ. 30 (1), 214–219.

Lawlor, D.A., Clark, H., Davey Smith, G., Leon, D.A., 2006. Intrauterine growth and intelligence within sibling pairs: findings from the Aberdeen children of the 1950s cohort. Pediatrics 117 (5), E894–E902.

Leibenstein, H., 1957. The theory of underemployment in backward economies. J. Polit. Econ. 65 (2), 91–103.

Leigh, A., Jencks, C., 2007. Inequality and mortality: long-run evidence from a panel of countries. J. Health Econ. 26 (1), 1–24.

Leigh, A., Jencks, C., Smeeding, T., 2009. Health and economic inequality. In: Salverda, W., Nolan, B., Smeeding, T. (Eds.), Oxford Handbook of Economic Inequality. Oxford University Press, Oxford, pp. 384–405.

Li, H., Zhu, Y., 2006. Income, income inequality, and health: evidence from China. J. Comp. Econ. 34 (4), 668–693.

Lillard, L., Panis, C.A., 1996. Marital status and mortality: the role of health. Demography 33, 313–327.

Lillard, D.R., Burkhauser, R.V., Hahn, M.H., Wilkins, R., 2012. Does the income share of the top 1 percent predict self-reported health status of the 99 percent? Evidence from four countries. In: 10th International German Socio-Economic Panel User Conference 2012.

Lin, M., Liu, J., 2009. Do lower birth weight babies have lower grades? Twin fixed effect and instrumental variable evidence from Taiwan. Soc. Sci. Med. 68 (10), 1780–1787.

Lindahl, M., 2005. Estimating the effect of income on health and mortality using lottery prizes as an exogenous source of variation in income. J. Hum. Resour. 40 (1), 144–168.

Lindeboom, M., 2012. Health and work of older workers. In: Jones, A.M. (Ed.), The Elgar Companion to Health Economics, second ed. Edward Elgar, Cheltenham, pp. 26–35.

Lindeboom, M., Kerkhofs, M., 2009. Health and work of the elderly: subjective health measures, reporting errors and endogeneity in the relationship between health and work. J. Appl. Econom. 24 (6), 1024–1046.

Loe, I.M., Lee, E.S., Luna, B., Feldman, H.M., 2011. Behavior problems of 9–16 year old preterm children: biological, sociodemographic, and intellectual contributions. Early Hum. Dev. 87, 247–252.

Lorgelly, P.K., Lindley, J., 2008. What is the relationship between income inequality and health? Evidence from the BHPS. Health Econ. 17 (2), 249–265.

Luo, Y., Waite, L.J., 2005. The impact of childhood and adult SES on physical, mental, and cognitive well-being on later life. J. Gerontol. 60B (2), S93–S101.

Lynch, J., Smith, G.D., Harper, S., Hillemeier, M., 2004a. Is income inequality a determinant of population health? Part 2. U.S. national and regional trends in income inequality and age- and cause-specific mortality. Milbank Q. 82 (2), 355–400.

Lynch, J., Smith, G.D., Harper, S., Hillemeier, M., Ross, N., Kaplan, G.A., Wolfson, M., 2004b. Is income inequality a determinant of population health? Part 1. A systematic review. Milbank Q. 82 (1), 5–99.

Mackenbach, J.P., 2002. Income inequality and population health. BMJ 324 (7328), 1–2.

Mangyo, E., Park, A., 2011. Relative deprivation and health. J. Hum. Resour. 46 (3), 459–481.

Marmot, M., Rose, G., Shipley, M., Hamilton, P., 1978. Employment grade and coronary heart disease in British civil servants. J. Epidemiol. Commun. Health 32, 244–249.

Marmot, M., Davey Smith, G., Stansfeld, S., Patel, C., North, F., Head, J., White, I., Brunner, E.J., Feeney, A., 1991. Health inequalities among British civil servants: the Whitehall II study. Lancet 337, 1387–1393.

Mazumder, B., Almond, D., Park, K., Crimmins, E.M., Finch, C.E., 2010. Lingering prenatal effects of the 1918 influenza pandemic on cardiovascular disease. J. Dev. Orig. Health Dis. 1 (1), 26.

McClellan, M., 1998. Health events, health insurance, and labor supply: evidence from the Health & Retirement Study. In: Wise, D. (Ed.), Frontiers in the Economics of Aging. University of Chicago Press, Chicago, IL.

Mcguinness, D., Mcglynn, L.M., Johnson, P.C., Macintyre, A., Batty, G.D., Burns, H., Cavanagh, J., Deans, K.A., Ford, I., Mcconnachie, A., Mcginty, A., Mclean, J.S., Millar, K., Packard, C.J., Sattar, N.A., Tannahill, C., Velupillai, Y.N., Shiels, P.G., 2012. Socio-economic status is associated with epigenetic differences in the pSoBid cohort. Int. J. Epidemiol. 41 (1), 151–160.

Mcinerney, M., Mellor, J.M., 2012. Recessions and seniors' health, health behaviors, and healthcare use: analysis of the Medicare Current Beneficiary Survey. J. Health Econ. 31 (5), 744–751.

Mcinerney, M., Mellor, J.M., Hersch Nicholas, L., 2013. Recession depression: mental health effects of the 2008 stock market crash. J. Health Econ. 32 (6), 1090–1104.

Meer, J., Miller, D.L., Rosen, H.S., 2003. Exploring the health–wealth nexus. J. Health Econ. 22 (5), 713–730.

Mellor, J.M., Milyo, J., 2002. Income inequality and health status in the United States: evidence from the Current Population Survey. J. Hum. Resour. 37 (3), 510–539.

Meltzer, A.H., Richard, S.F., 1981. A rational theory of the size of government. J. Polit. Econ. 89 (5), 914–927.

Michaud, P., Van Soest, A., 2008. Health and wealth of elderly couples: causality tests using dynamic panel data models. J. Health Econ. 27 (5), 1312–1325.

Miguel, E., Kremer, M., 2004. Worms: identifying impacts on education and health in the presence of treatment externalities. Econometrica 72 (1), 159–217.

Miller, D.L., Paxson, C., 2006. Relative income, race, and mortality. J. Health Econ. 25 (5), 979–1003.

Miller, G., Urdinola, B.P., 2010. Cyclicality, mortality, and the value of time: the case of coffee price fluctuations and child survival in Colombia. J. Polit. Econ. 118 (1), 113.

Milligan, K.S., Wise, D.A., 2012. Introduction and summary. In: Wise, D.A. (Ed.), Social Security Programs and Retirement Around the World: Historical Trends in Mortality and Health, Employment, and Disability Insurance Participation and Reforms. The University of Chicago Press, Chicago.

Mirlees, J.A., 1975. Pure theory of underdeveloped economies. In: Reynolds, L.G. (Ed.), Agriculture in Development Theory. Yale University Press, New Haven, CT.

Mocan, N., Raschke, C., Unel, B., 2013. The Impact of Mothers' Earnings on Health Inputs and Infant Health. NBER, Cambridge, MA, Working Paper 19434.

Mohanan, M., 2013. Causal effects of health shocks on consumption and debt: quasi-experimental evidence from bus accident injuries. Rev. Econ. Stat. 95 (2), 673–681.

Moller Dano, A., 2005. Road injuries and long-run effects on income and employment. Health Econ. 14 (9), 955–970.

Moran, J.R., Simon, K.I., 2006. Income and the use of prescription drugs by the elderly evidence from the notch cohorts. J. Hum. Resour. 41 (2), 411–432.

National Bureau of Statistics of China, 2007. China Statistical Yearbook 2007. China Statistics Press, Beijing. http://www.stats.gov.cn/tjsj/ndsj/2007/indexeh.htm.

Navarro, V., 2001. World Health Report 2000: responses to Murray and Frenk. Lancet 357 (9269), 1701–1702.

Nepomnyaschy, L., Reichman, N.E., 2006. Low birthweight and asthma among young urban children. Am. J. Public Health 96, 1604–1610.

Nilsson, P., 2009. The Long-Term Effects of Early Childhood Lead Exposure: Evidence from the Phase-Out of Leaded Gasoline. Uppsala University, Uppsala.

Nilsson, T., Bergh, A., 2013. Income inequality, health and development: in search of a pattern. In: Rosa Dias, P., O'Donnell, O. (Eds.), Health and Inequality. Emerald, Bingley, UK.

O'Donnell, O., 1995. Labour supply and saving decisions with uncertainty over sickness. J. Health Econ. 14 (4), 491–504.

Oecd, 2010. Sickness, Disability and Work: Breaking the Barriers: A Synthesis of Findings Across OECD Countries. OECD Publishing, Paris.

Oreopoulos, P., Stabile, M., Walld, R., Roos, L.L., 2008. Short-, medium-, and long-term consequences of poor infant health: an analysis using siblings and twins. J. Hum. Resour. 43 (1), 88–138.

Paneth, N., Susser, M., 1995. Early origin of coronary heart disease (the "Barker hypothesis"). Br. Med. J. 310 (6977), 411–412.

Parsons, D.O., 1980. The decline in male labor force participation. J. Polit. Econ. 88 (1), 117–134.

Pascual, M., Cantarero, D., Sarabia, J., 2005. Income inequality and health: do the equivalence scales matter? Atlantic Econ. J. 33 (2), 169–178.

Paxson, C., Schady, N., 2005. Child health and economic crisis in Peru. World Bank Econ. Rev. 19 (2), 203–223.

Paxson, C., Schady, N., 2010. Does money matter? The effects of cash transfers on child development in rural Ecuador. Econ. Dev. Cult. Change 59 (1), 187–229.

Pelkowski, J.M., Berger, M.C., 2004. The impact of health on employment, wages, and hours worked over the life cycle. Q. Rev. Econ. Finance 44 (1), 102–121.

Persico, N., Postlewaite, A., Silverman, D., 2004. The effect of adolescent experience on labor market outcomes: the case of height. J. Polit. Econ. 112 (5), 1019–1053.

Petrou, S., Kupek, E., 2008. Social capital and its relationship with measures of health status: evidence from the Health Survey for England 2003. Health Econ. 17 (1), 127–143.

Phelps, E.S., 1972. The statistical theory of racism and sexism. Am. Econ. Rev. 62, 659–661.

Pollitt, E., Gorman, K.S., Engle, P.L., Martorell, R., Rivera, J., 1993. Early Supplementary Feeding and Cognition: Effects Over Two Decades. University of Chicago Press, Chicago.

Power, C., Matthews, S., Manor, O., 1996. Inequalities in self rated health in the 1958 birth cohort: lifetime social circumstances or social mobility? Br. Med. J. 313 (7055), 449–453.

Power, C., Matthews, S., Manor, O., 1998. Inequality in self-rated health: explanations from different stages of life. Lancet 351, 1009–1014.

Preston, S.H., 1975. The changing relation between mortality and level of economic development. Popul. Stud. 29 (2), 231–248.

Pritchett, L., Summers, L.H., 1996. Wealthier is healthier. J. Hum. Resour. 31 (4), 841–868.

Propper, C., Rigg, J., Burgess, S., 2007. Child health: evidence on the roles of family income and maternal mental health from a UK birth cohort. Health Econ. 16 (11), 1245–1269.

Putnam, R.D., Leonardi, R., Nanetti, R., 1993. Making Democracy Work: Civic Traditions in Modern Italy. Princeton University Press, Princeton, NJ.

Regidor, E., Martínez, D., Santos, J.M., Calle, M.E., Ortega, P., Astasio, P., 2012. New findings do not support the neomaterialist theory of the relation between income inequality and infant mortality. Soc. Sci. Med. 75 (4), 752–753.

Reinhold, S., Jürges, H., 2012. Parental income and child health in Germany. Health Econ. 21 (5), 562–579.

Relton, C.L., Davey Smith, G., 2012. Is epidemiology ready for epigenetics? Int. J. Epidemiol. 41 (1), 5–9.

Riley, J.C., 1989. Sickness, Recovery and Death: A History and Forecast of Ill-Health. Macmillan, Basingstoke.

Riphan, R., 1999. Income and employment effects of health shocks. A test case for the German welfare state. J. Popul. Econ. 12 (3), 363–389.

Rivera, J.A., Sotres-Alvarez, D., Habicht, J., Shamah, T., Villalpando, S., 2004. Impact of the Mexican program for education, health, and nutrition (Progresa) on rates of growth and anemia in infants and young children. JAMA 291 (21), 2563–2570.

Rodgers, G.B., 1979. Income and inequality as determinants of mortality: an international cross-section analysis. Popul. Stud. 33, 343–351.

Ronconi, L., Brown, T.T., Scheffler, R.M., 2012. Social capital and self-rated health in Argentina. Health Econ. 21 (2), 201–208.

Royer, H., 2009. Separated at girth: estimating the long-run and intergenerational effects of birthweight using twins. Am. Econ. J. 1 (1), 49–85.

Ruhm, C.J., 2000. Are recessions good for your health? Q. J. Econ. 115 (2), 617–650.

Ruhm, C.J., 2003. Good times make you sick. J. Health Econ. 22 (4), 637–658.

Ruhm, C.J., 2013. Recessions, healthy no more? NBER Working Paper 19287, Cambridge, MA.

Saigal, S., Szatmari, P., Rosenbaum, P., Campbell, D., King, S., 1991. Cognitive abilities and school performance of extremely low birth weight children and matched term control children at age 8 years: a regional study. J. Pediatr. 118 (5), 751–760.

Salm, M., 2011. The effect of pensions on longevity: evidence from Union Army Veterans. Econ. J. 121 (552), 595–619.

Sapolsky, R.M., 2005. The influence of social hierarchy on primate health. Science 308 (5722), 648–652.

Sastre, M., Trannoy, A., 2002. Shapley inequality decomposition by factor components: some methodological issues. J. Econ. 9 (1), 51–89.

Saunders, P.R., Evans, N., 2010. Beware False Prophets: Equality, the Good Society and the Spirit Level. Policy Exchange, London.

Schmeiser, M.D., 2009. Expanding wallets and waistlines: the impact of family income on the BMI of women and men eligible for the Earned Income Tax Credit. Health Econ. 18 (11), 1277–1294.

Schultz, T.P., 2005. Productive Benefits of Health: Evidence from Low-Income Countries. Yale University, New Haven.

Schultz, T.P., 2010. Health human capital and economic development. J. Afr. Econ. 19 (Suppl. 3), iii12–iii80.

Schwandt, H., 2013. Wealth Shocks and Health Outcomes. Center for Health and Wellbeing, Princeton University, Mimeo. http://www.princeton.edu/~schwandt/.

Semykina, A., Wooldridge, J.M., 2010. Estimating panel data models in the presence of endogeneity and selection. J. Econometrics 157 (2), 375–380.

Sen, A., 1999. Development as Freedom. Knopf, New York.

Sheps, M.C., 1961. Marriage and mortality. Am. J. Public Health 51, 547–555.

Shorrocks, A., 2013. Decomposition procedures for distributional analysis: a unified framework based on the Shapley value. J. Econ. Inequal. 11 (1), 99–126.

Sickles, R.C., Taubman, P., 1986. An analysis of the health and retirement status of the elderly. Econometrica 54 (6), 1339–1356.

Sickles, R.C., Yazbeck, A., 1998. On the dynamics of demand for leisure and the production of health. J. Bus. Econ. Stat. 16 (2), 187–197.

Siegel, M., 2006. Measuring the effect of husband's health on wife's labour supply. Health Econ. 15, 579–601.

Sloan, F.A., Hsieh, C-R., 2012. Health Economics. MIT Press, Cambridge, MA.

Smith, J., 1999. Healthy bodies and thick wallets: the dual relation between health and socioeconomic status. J. Econ. Perspect. 13, 145–166.

Smith, J.P., 2004. Unraveling the SES: health connection. Popul. Dev. Rev. 30, 108–132.

Smith, J.P., 2007. The impact of socioeconomic status on health over the life-course. J. Hum. Resour. XLII (4), 739–764.

Smith, J.P., 2009. The impact of childhood health on adult labor market outcomes. Rev. Econ. Stat. 91 (3), 478–489.

Snowdon, C., 2010. The Spirit Level Delusion: Fact-Checking the Left's New Theory of Everything. Little Dice, Ripon.

Snyder, S.E., Evans, W.N., 2006. The effect of income on mortality: evidence from the social security notch. Rev. Econ. Stat. 88 (3), 482–495.

Steckel, R.H., 1995. Stature and the standard of living. J. Econ. Lit. 33 (4), 1903–1940.

Stern, S., 1989. Measuring the effect of disability on labor force participation. J. Hum. Resour. 24, 361–395.

Stevens, A.H., Miller, D.L., Page, M.E., Filipski, M., 2011. The Best of Times, the Worst of Times: Understanding Pro-Cyclical Mortality. NBER Working Paper No. 17657, National Bureau of Economic Research, Cambridge, MA.

Stiglitz, J.E., 1976. The efficiency wage hypothesis, surplus labour, and the distribution of income in L.D.C. s. Oxf. Econ. Papers 28 (2), 185–207.

Stowasser, T., Heiss, F., Mcfadden, D.L., Winter, J., 2012. "Healthy, Wealthy and Wise?" Revisited: an analysis of the causal pathways from socio-economic status to health. In: Wise, D.A. (Ed.), Investigations in the Economics of Aging. University of Chicago Press, Chicago, pp. 267–317.

Strauss, J., Thomas, D., 1998. Health, nutrition, and economic development. J. Econ. Lit. 36 (2), 766–817.

Subramanian, S.V., Kawachi, I., 2004. Income inequality and health: what have we learned so far? Epidemiol. Rev. 26 (1), 78–91.

Tacke, T., Waldmann, R.J., 2013. Infant mortality, relative income and public policy. Appl. Econ. 45 (22), 3240–3254.

Tekin, E., McClellan, C., Minyard, K.J., 2013. Health and Health Behaviors During the Worst of Times: Evidence from the Great Recession. NBER Working Paper No. 19234, Cambridge, MA.

Theodossiou, I., Zangelidis, A., 2009. The social gradient in health: the effect of absolute income and subjective social status assessment on the individual's health in Europe. Econ. Hum. Biol. 7 (2), 229–237.

Thomas, D., Frenkenberg, E., 2002. Health, nutrition and prosperity: a microeconomic perspective. Bull. World Health Organ. 80 (2), 106–113.

Thorbecke, E., Charumilind, C., 2002. Economic inequality and its socioeconomic impact. World Dev. 30 (9), 1477–1495.

Townsend, R.M., 1994. Risk and insurance in village India. Econometrica 62 (3), 539–591.

Twaddle, A., 1974. The concept of health status. Soc. Sci. Med. 8, 29–38.

UNESCO Institute for Statistics, ISCED, International Standard Classification of Education. Available http://www.uis.unesco.org.

Üstün, T., Chatterji, S., Villanueva, M., Bendib, L., Çelik, C., Sadana, R., Valentine, N., Ortiz, J., Tandon, A., Salomon, J., Cao, Y., Xie, W., Özaltin, E., Mathers, C., Murray, C., 2003. WHO multi-country survey study on health and responsiveness, 2000–2001. In: Murray, C.J.L., Evans, D.B. (Eds.), Health Systems Performance Assessment: Debates, Methods and Empiricism. World Health Organization, Geneva, pp. 761–796.

Van Doorslaer, E., Van Ourti, T., 2011. Measuring inequality and inequity in health and health care. In: Glied, S., Smith, P.C. (Eds.), Oxford Handbook of Health Economics. Oxford University Press, Oxford, pp. 837–869.

Van Doorslaer, E., Wagstaff, A., Bleichrodt, H., Calonge, S., Gerdtham, U.G., Gerfin, M., Geurts, J., Gross, L., Hakkinen, U., Leu, R.E., O'Donnell, O., Propper, C., Puffer, F., Rodriguez, M., Sundberg, G., Winkelhake, O., 1997. Income-related inequalities in health: some international comparisons. J. Health Econ. 16 (1), 93–112.

Van Doorslaer, E., Wagstaff, A., Van Der Burg, H., Christiansen, T., De Graeve, D., Duchesne, I., Gerdtham, U., Gerfin, M., Geurts, J., Gross, L., 2000. Equity in the delivery of health care in Europe and the US. J. Health Econ. 19 (5), 553–583.

Van Doorslaer, E., Koolman, X., Jones, A.M., 2004. Explaining income-related inequalities in doctor utilization in Europe. Health Econ. 13 (7), 629–647.

Van Doorslaer, E., Masseria, C., Koolman, X., 2006. Inequalities in access to medical care by income in developed countries. Can. Med. Assoc. J. 174 (2), 177–183.

Van Groezen, B., Jadoenandansing, R., Pasini, G., 2011. Social capital and health across European countries. Appl. Econ. Lett. 18 (12), 1167–1170.

Van Houtven, C., Coe, N., 2010. Spousal Health Shocks and the Timing of the Retirement Decision in the Face of Forward-Looking Financial Incentives. Center for Retirement Research at Boston College, Boston, Working Paper WP 2010-7.

Van Kippersluis, H., Galama, T.J., 2013. Why the Rich Drink More But Smoke Less: The Impact of Wealth on Health Behaviors. DP 13-035/V, Tinbergen Institute, Amsterdam/Rotterdam.

Wadsworth, M., Kuh, D., 1997. Childhood influences on adult health: a review of recent work for the British 1946 Birth Cohort Study, the MRC National Survey of Health and Development. Paediatr. Perinat. Epidemiol. 11, 2–20.

Wagstaff, A., Van Doorslaer, E., 2000. income inequality and health: what does the literature tell us? Annu. Rev. Public Health 21 (1), 543–567.

Wagstaff, A., Paci, P., Vandoorslaer, E., 1991. On the measurement of inequalities in health. Soc. Sci. Med. 33 (5), 545–557.

Waldmann, R.J., 1992. Income distribution and infant mortality. Q. J. Econ. 107, 1283–1302.

Waldron, I., Hughes, M.E., Brooks, T.L., 1996. Marriage protection and marriage selection—prospective evidence for reciprocal effects of marital status and health. Soc. Sci. Med. 43 (1), 113–123.

Walker, S.P., Chang, S.M., Powell, C.A., Grantham-Mcgregor, S.M., 2005. Effects of early childhood psychosocial stimulation and nutritional supplementation on cognition and education in growth-stunted Jamaican children: prospective cohort study. Lancet 366, 1804–1807.

Weaver, I.C.G., Cervoni, N., Champagne, F.A., D'Alessio, A.C., Sharma, S., Seckl, J.R., Dymov, S., Szyf, M., Meaney, M.J., 2004. Epigenetic programming by maternal behavior. Nat. Neurosci. 7 (8), 847–854.

West, P., 1997. Unhealthy societies: the afflictions of inequality (book). Sociol. Health Illn. 19 (5), 668–670.

Wildman, J., Gravelle, H., Sutton, M., 2003. Health and income inequality: attempting to avoid the aggregation problem. Appl. Econ. 35 (9), 999–1004.

Wilkinson, R.G., 1990. Income distribution and mortality: a 'natural' experiment. Sociol. Health Illn. 12 (4), 391–412.

Wilkinson, R.G., 1992. Income distribution and life expectancy. Br. Med. J. 304, 165–168.

Wilkinson, R.G., 1996. Unhealthy Societies: the Afflictions of Inequality. Routledge, London.

Wilkinson, R.G., 2001. Mind the Gap: Hierarchies, Health and Human Evolution. Yale University Press, New Haven.

Wilkinson, R.G., Pickett, K.E., 2006. Income inequality and population health: a review and explanation of the evidence. Soc. Sci. Med. 62 (7), 1768–1784.

Wilkinson, R.G., Pickett, K., 2010. The Spirit Level: Why Equality Is Better for Everyone. Penguin Books, London/New York.

Wise, D.A. (Ed.), 2012. Social Security Programs and Retirement Around the World: Historical Trends in Mortality and Health, Employment, and Disability Insurance Participation and Reforms. The University of Chicago Press, Chicago.

Woodbury, R.M., 1924. Economic factors in infant mortality. J. Am. Stat. Assoc. 19, 137–155.

Wu, S., 2003. The effects of health events on the economics status of married couples. J. Hum. Resour. 38 (1), 219–230.

Yang, T., Chen, V.Y., Shoff, C., Matthews, S.A., 2012. Using quantile regression to examine the effects of inequality across the mortality distribution in the U.S. counties. Soc. Sci. Med. 74 (12), 1900–1910.

Yitzhaki, S., 1979. Relative deprivation and the Gini coefficient. Q. J. Econ. 93 (2), 321–324.

Yitzhaki, S., 1983. On an extension of the Gini inequality index. Int. Econ. Rev. 24 (3), 617–628.

CHAPTER 18

Labor Market Institutions and the Dispersion of Wage Earnings

Wiemer Salverda*,†, Daniele Checchi‡

*Amsterdam Institute for Advanced Labour Studies (AIAS), University of Amsterdam, Amsterdam, The Netherlands
†Amsterdam Centre for Inequality Studies (AMCIS), University of Amsterdam, Amsterdam, The Netherlands
‡Department of Economics, University of Milan, Milano, Italy and IZA, Bonn, Germany

Contents

Handbook of Income Distribution, Volume 2B
ISSN 1574-0056, http://dx.doi.org/10.1016/B978-0-444-59429-7.00019-4

Abstract

Considering the contribution of the distribution of individual wages and earnings to that of household incomes we find two separate literatures that should be brought together, and bring "new institutions" into play. Growing female employment, rising dual-earnership and part-time employment underline its relevance. We discuss the measurement of wage inequality, data sources, and stylized facts of wage dispersion for rich countries. The literature explaining the dispersion of wage rates and the role of institutions is evaluated, from the early 1980s to the recent literature on job polarization and tasks as well as on the minimum wage. Distinguishing between supply-and-demand approaches and institutional ones, we find supply and demand challenged by the empirical measurement of technological change and a risk of ad hoc additions, without realizing their institutional preconditions. The institutional approach faces an abundance of institutions without a clear conceptual delineation of institutions and their interactions. Empirical cross-country analysis of the correlation between institutional measures and wage inequality incorporates unemployment and working hours dynamics, discussing the problems of matching individuals to their relevant institutional framework. Minimum wage legislation and active labor market policies come out negatively correlated to earnings inequality in US and EU countries.

Keywords

Labor market institutions, Household labor supply, Hourly wages, Hours worked, Annual earnings, Dispersion, Inequality measures, Household incomes, Minimum wage, Unions, Employment protection

JEL Classification Codes

D02, D13, D31, J22, J31, J51, J52

18.1. INTRODUCTION

This is not "simply" a study of the literature regarding wage inequality in the labor market, even apart from the fact that the literature is immense. The income distribution is the focus of the present handbook and provides the ultimate rationale for considering the dispersion of wage earnings here. It is natural therefore to consider the distribution of individual wages and earnings in the labor market in light of what it may contribute to the distribution of household incomes, which are the common unit of analysis for the income distribution. One may surmise that the subject of how wage inequality and income inequality relate has gained relevance—and also complexity—as the growing labor market participation of women and the concomitant rise of dual-earner households make societies move away from the single-earner breadwinner model, in which labor market earnings closely resemble household income.[1] The recent literature on household joblessness provides further encouragement. Nevertheless, the two strands of study, of wage dispersion on the one hand and household income distribution on the other, are miles apart. There is a growing literature aiming to measure the distance between the two distributions and attempting to bring them together, but it is still small and also rather diverse. More importantly, there is very little in this literature that also accounts for the role of institutions with respect to the interrelationship between the two distributions, though that role will be significant as one can infer from the burgeoning literature on institutions and female labor supply. In addition, these are often new institutions (e.g., parental leave, child care arrangements, job entitlements during maternity leave, and/ or changing from full-time to part-time employment), which seem deserving of attention together with the traditional labor market institutions (LMIs) (minimum wage, employment protection, union density, etc.).

However, understanding institutions in relation to wage dispersion is our overarching purpose—and a very demanding purpose in its own right. It would require a bridge too far to also try to overcome the gap and incorporate the income distribution in our approach. Instead we will take a swift look at said literature and the stylized facts of the subject, and we will do so at the start of our argument to make the best of it as a heuristic device for our ensuing discussion of wage dispersion and institutions. Thus, we hope to make a contribution on which future analysis can expand by providing a building block that can be used subsequently for constructing a unified economic theory of income distribution, a theory that is still missing (Atkinson and Bourguignon, 2000, 26). By the way, that building block itself needs to account for the very fact that neither a unified theory of earnings dispersion is available. We intend to do that by reviewing the literature on institutions and earnings distribution in a framework that may be relevant also for further use in studying the household income distribution.

Concretely, we explicitly include in our focus the distribution of *annual* earnings from labor as the income distribution is commonly measured and analyzed on an annual basis.[2] This entails, first, that we study both wage rates and (annual) hours of work—which

---

[1] In a world of joint within-household labor supply, the two distributions will deviate from each other unless households supply the same number of hours, and wage rates are identical across household members.

[2] We will be more precise about such concepts in Section 18.3.

taken together make up annual earnings—as well as the dispersion of both and their inter-relationship. Thus, we aim to go beyond, e.g., Blau and Kahn (1999), who address the effects of wage-setting institutions on wage inequality as well as on employment, but for the latter restrict themselves to aggregate employment effects and ignore its dispersion over individuals and households as well as its relationship to wage dispersion. It implies that one needs to consider the role that institutions play not only in relation to the wage rate, the hours worked, and the individual probability of employment, but ultimately also in relation to the household distribution of employment—what we can call a double-edged employment perspective. At the same time, this brings into play the role of unemployment and joblessness (zero hours), the frequency of which may also be affected by institutions. More generally, individual institutions that primarily concern one of these aspects, say the wage rate, will need to be considered also in relation to the other aspects. The separate effects may differ and in the end it is their joint effect that counts.[3]

Second, we will contemplate the relevance and the effects of LMIs from this distribution point of view. Particularly, we will on the one hand leave aside the literature that focuses on wage dispersion in relation to the matching of workers to given jobs (e.g., Mortensen, 2005, on search, or Rosen, 1986, on compensating differentials). We also leave out the literature on other important facets of inequality such as earnings mobility or its role as a work and career incentive. On the other hand we will look—to the extent that we can—for institutions that may affect the distribution of employment over households (e.g., equal treatment, working-hours nondiscrimination, child care provisions or tax measures) or the supply of hours over the year (e.g., temp agency work, temporary contracts). Thus, different institutions from the usual suspects may come into play, for example, new rules and regulations regarding part-time jobs and pay, or the "reconciliation of work and family life," while at the same time those usual suspects will be checked for their effects in this domain. The "new" institutions will need to be considered in their own right but, naturally, also in relation to the previous ones. We need to be careful, though, that the assortment of institutions under scrutiny be manageable; as in modern society labor market behavior has become so central to human existence that virtually any institution might be thought to have an effect.

In our take on the literature, we aim to be careful in considering the role of institutions not in isolation of the "normal" economy. That is, we may compare, for example, the meticulous evaluation of the literature by Katz and Autor (1999), who first discuss the role of supply and demand and after that turn to institutions, or the warning given by Blau and Kahn (1999, 1416) with regard to international comparative studies of the effects of institutions "that many things besides the institutions in question may differ across countries, so we cannot be certain if the institutions are really responsible for the observed differences in outcomes." Similarly, we need to remain aware of noninstitutional effects

---

[3] Interestingly, Olivetti and Petrongolo (2008) consider the interaction of hours and wages from a different perspective, focusing on the effect on the gender pay gap of the number of women being employed.

influencing market labor supply, such as, e.g., technical progress in household production (cf. Kahn, 2005). More generally, we sympathize with Manning (2011), who prefers to phrase his recent overview not in terms of canonical models, where "precision relates to the models and not the world and can easily become spurious precision when the models are very abstract with assumptions designed more for analytical tractability than realism" (2011, 975). In our view, the distribution of earnings is very much a phenomenon of crucial importance in "the world." Though we aim to broaden the scope to include the dispersion of employment, we do not and cannot possibly pursue this in a general equilibrium format. Further to this, being aware of significant differences among countries, we leave open the possibility that one size may not fit all.

In addition, we like to stress that the time period effectively covered in the chapter is determined by the literature that we aim to address. Though that period may seem long to some as we begin our coverage at the end of the 1960s for certain countries, it is important to realize that the trends found may be selective. The long-run historical perspectives adopted in the top-incomes literature (Alvaredo et al., 2013) or in Atkinson's (2008) internationally comparative study of the earnings distribution suggest that preceding trends may diverge, sometimes radically, and might throw a different light on the mechanisms at work. Ultimately, this may tell a different story, but the study of this is in its infancy.

Before continuing, we mention a caveat regarding the two concepts of "dispersion" and "inequality," which we have used indiscriminately to indicate the squeeze or stretch of a distribution. A major reason for many to pay attention to the dispersion is that a large part of it coincides with social or economic inequality as it is commonly understood. However, more precisely, the dispersion is thought to relate to a range of observations, wages, or incomes in this case, that are not all the same and therefore are unequal in a mechanical, mathematical sense of the word. Inequality, by contrast, provides a qualifier to such observations that makes them unequal in the sense of analyses providing an explanatory interpretation of the observations, either individual or aggregated. So, strictly speaking, dispersion and inequality are different concepts. Not all mechanical differences will also be inequalities from an analytical point of view, for example, differences in individual earnings that reflect differences in efforts. Conversely, not all analytical inequalities will also be mechanical differences, for example, individual earnings that are identical in spite of differences in efforts. Having said this we will continue to use the two words interchangeably as this chapter is aimed at evaluating a set of such qualifying analyses. Note, finally, that measures of dispersion or of inequality (Gini coefficient, etc.) are identical, and are usually called measures of inequality—terms that we will also use in this chapter.

Some of the above references indicate the existence of various literature overviews that are relevant to our study of earnings inequality, which are found in the first volume of the *Handbook of Income Distribution*, all volumes of the *Handbook of Labor Economics*, and the *Oxford Handbook of Economic Inequality*. We will not redo these, but gratefully build on them when it is useful to do so. Note that not only economists but also political and social scientists have studied the subject (Alderson and Nielsen, 2002; Becher and Pontusson,

2011; DiPrete, 2007; Golden and Wallerstein, 2011; Kenworthy and Pontusson, 2005; Oliver, 2008; Wallerstein, 1999). We will also allude to some of their results.

Our contribution takes the general level of inequality as its starting point but cannot escape digging below that surface. Thus, for example, we may touch upon the tails of the distribution—top incomes, (in-work) poverty—where much of the action is. However, for a deeper understanding of those tails as well as the complementing middle we refer to the treatment of polarization (Chapter 5), top incomes (Chapter 7), and in-work poverty (Chapter 23) elsewhere in this handbook. More generally, the labor market also figures as one of the multiple causes of inequality in Chapter 19. On another dimension, our contribution stops short of the within-household distribution (see Chapter 16) or any further analysis of gender inequality (see Chapter 12). Finally, this chapter will cover those countries that have well-developed, comprehensive formal labor markets. This restricts the selection of the literature to analyses that concern the United States, Canada, Japan, Korea, Australia, New Zealand, the member states of the European Union, and some other European countries such as Iceland, Norway, and Switzerland.

18.1.1 Lay Out

The layout of the chapter is as follows. First, in Section 18.2, we will briefly discuss the literature that regards the link between wage dispersion and the household income distribution, considering the distributions of earnings and employment from both the individual and the household perspectives, and presenting some stylized facts. In Section 18.3 we discuss the measurement of wage inequality with some relevant data sources and present some stylized facts of wage dispersion for a selection of countries. Next, in Section 18.4, we discuss theories aimed at explaining the dispersion of wage rates and the role of institutions. Section 18.5 then addresses the role of LMIs empirically, with the help of a model that that incorporates several features advocated in the preceding sections, such as a focus on earnings, i.e., the product of wage rate and annual efforts, and that inserts as explanatory variables a number of "new institutions" related to household labor supply. In addition, we use recent internationally comparative data. Finally, we conclude in Section 18.6 by summarizing the main findings and considering issues warranting further research.

18.2. EARNINGS DISTRIBUTION AND INCOME DISTRIBUTION: A SHORT TALE OF TWO LONG LITERATURES

In spite of recent declines in the labor share in GDP or national income,[4] the income that people generate in the labor market is obviously the most frequent and most important

---

[4] We leave aside here the relationship between the labor share in GDP (declining in many countries) and the income distribution. Compare, e.g., Atkinson (2009), Glyn (2009), Checchi and Garcia-Peñalosa (2008), and OECD (2012).

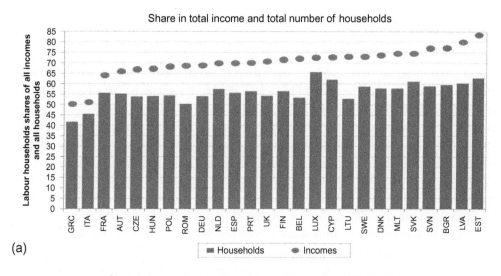

(a)

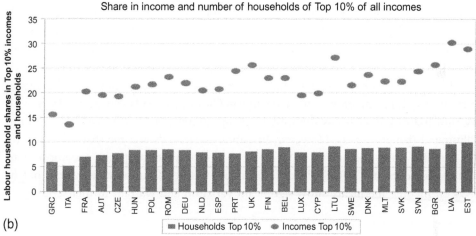

(b)

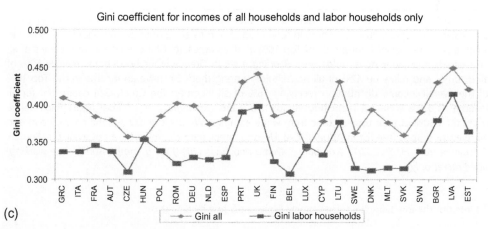

(c)

Figure 18.1 See legend on next page.

part of household incomes, and the inequality of labor earnings seems an important determinant of income inequality at face value. Figure 18.1 portrays in three panels the role of "labor households," which are defined as households receiving more than half their total income from wage earnings, across 26 countries of the European Union. Panel (a) ranks the countries by the income share of labor households (the markers), and the same ranking is adopted for the other panels. Panel (a) indicates that labor households receive the majority of all incomes, ranging from slightly over 50% in Greece and Italy up to a maximum of 84% in Estonia. They comprise significantly smaller shares of all households, however, ranging from less than half in Greece and Italy[5] to 66% in Luxembourg. Clearly, these households' mean incomes are above average in all countries. This is borne out by panel (b), which indicates similar shares with a focus on the Top 10% of all incomes in a country. The income share always exceeds the household share and does so by far: on average the income share is 14% points higher than the household share. This contrast with the Bottom 90% (not shown): here the gaps between the two shares are modest, and they can be positive as well as negative; the resulting cross-country average is almost nil. At the same time, in panel (c), the Gini coefficients for all households always exceed that for labor households and they move in striking parallel in various countries characterized by high labor-income inequality such as the United Kingdom, Portugal, Lithuania, Bulgaria, Latvia, and Estonia (overall correlation is 0.75). The Gini levels do not follow the smooth ranking of increasing income shares but vary substantially (correlation 0.23). Therefore, rather dissimilar Gini coefficients can go together with very similar income shares as the middle group, ranging from Germany to Belgium, as illustrated (panel c vs. a). However, for labor households income shares in the Top 10% and the Gini coefficient show a more similar pattern (panel c compared to panel b) (correlation 0.56). So income from labor is highly important indeed, but its effects on income inequality show significant variation and warrant further scrutiny.

Figure 18.1 Importance of labor households and their annual incomes, 26 European countries ranked by total income share, 2010. (a) Share in total income and total number of households. (b) Share in income and number of households of Top 10% of all incomes. (c) Gini coefficient for incomes of all households and labor households only. *Reading note*: In Greece labor households receive 50% of all incomes and make up 42% of all households; among them 6% have an income in the Top 10% of the overall income distribution receiving 16% of all incomes; the Greek Gini coefficient for all incomes is 0.408 while for labor households it is 0.336. *Explanatory note*: Labor households derive more than 50% of their total income from wage earnings. We use the ISO 3-alpha country codes in all relevant graphs (see list in Appendix A). Unfortunately, data for Ireland are not available. *Source: Calculated from EU-SILC 2011 (compare Salverda and Haas (2014) for a comparison for the working-age bracket only).*

[5] Note that the low household share largely explains the low income share.

Another measure of inequality, the income share of the top decile of the distribution, tells basically the same story for all incomes as the Gini and the top share are highly correlated (0.91) (compare Leigh, 2009). However, the gap between all incomes and labor incomes is more substantial here—the correlation of the two top shares is only 0.32—and suggests that the role of high levels of household earnings differs significantly between countries. The linkage between the dispersion of wages and the income distribution is clearly important and also warrants further research.

Though the literature on the two distributions is not absent and perhaps even growing, it is not the subject of a strong strand. Instead, one may surmise, there are two largely separate, extensive literatures, one addressing (individual) wage inequality in the labor market and the other (household) income inequality in society. As Gottschalk and Danziger (2005, 253) observe "Labor economists have tended to focus on changes in the distribution of wage rates, the most restrictive income concept, since they are interested in changes in market and institutional forces that have altered the prices paid to labor of different types. At the other extreme, policy analysts have focused on changes in the distribution of the broadest income concept, family income adjusted for family size. This reflects their interest in changes in resources available to different groups, including the poor." It confirms that the conclusion drawn 8 years before by Gottschalk and Smeeding (1997, 676), that "an overall framework would simultaneously model the generation of all sources of income . . . as well as the formation of income sharing units" and be considered "the next big step that must be taken," was still a tall order when Gottschalk and Danziger made their contribution. Yet another 5 years later, Jiří Večerník (2010, 2) observed that "there seems to be a gulf between the analysis of personal earnings and household income." It seems a foregone conclusion that for the combination of individual wage and earnings inequality and household earnings and income inequality, the unified economic theory of income distribution, hoped for by Atkinson and Bourguignon (2000, 26), is not yet forthcoming though interesting contributions may be found below.[6]

This divide has a technical aspect that deserves some attention. The dispersion of wages is commonly conceived as the distribution of hourly wages, i.e., wage rates. The income distribution, by contrast, focuses on annual incomes, and therewith annual earnings, which are the product of hourly wages and annual hours worked. Next to the wage distribution, this brings into play the distribution of hours worked during the year, which, in turn, are the product of jobs and hours on the job. These hours have become a significant dimension of employment in many countries because of the growing importance of part-time employment and temporary jobs. Their presence adds to the traditional effect on annual hours that is exerted by the turnover during the year of people who join or leave

---

[6] However, for a number of developing countries (which are not the subject of this chapter) a valuable attempt with interesting results has been made by Bourguignon et al. (2004) in decomposing household income inequality changes along the relevant dimension of labor market behavior and outcomes.

employment.[7] As a result we deem it essential to distinguish between various distributions: *wages* (which are hourly), *earnings* (which are annual), *employment* (which concerns annual hours worked), and *incomes* (which include other sources than earnings).

A second difference is that the wage distribution is commonly conceived in *gross* terms, that is pretax, whereas on the income side there is a strong focus on *disposable* incomes—after transfers and taxes—which are often also standardized (equivalized) for the size and composition of the receiving household.[8] The third difference is that the dispersion of wages rests on the individual as the unit of analysis whereas the income distribution is based on the household, which can be a combination of individuals. Thus, for linking the two distributions, the individuals from the one side need to be linked to their households on the other side. Importantly, this puts the limelight on the distribution of employment and corresponding earnings over households. There is a significant literature on the other side of this employment coin, the nonemployment or joblessness of households, especially in comparison to individual joblessness, which was started by Paul Gregg and Jonathan Wadsworth in the mid-1990s (Gregg et al., 1996, 1998 and Gregg and Wadsworth, 2008). However, this literature is not often linked to the distribution of incomes albeit it may be linked to poverty (De Graaf-Zijl and Nolan, 2011).

18.2.1 Individual or Household Incomes?

Before discussing the main points found in the literature we present a few stylized facts that may demonstrate the relevance of considering the link between the two distributions. First, we consider the employment side of the matter. A core message from the joblessness literature is that in many countries individual workless rates have fallen over the past 20 years, but household-based workless rates have not (Gregg et al., 2010, 161). Or to put it the other way around, the growth in (individual) employment-to-population ratios has not been mirrored in a corresponding increase in what can be termed the "household employment rate." The implication is that much of the additional jobs growth has gone to households already containing a worker. Figure 18.2 illustrates this for a number of European countries since the mid-1990s: most of the decline in individual unemployment has gone to households already engaged in employment and much less has contributed to a lowering of the number of people living in jobless households.

---

[7] Including temporary employment of less than 1 year this is reflected in the difference between the distributions of the full-year and the part-year employed. For example, Salverda et al. (2013), in Figure 2.11, shows for the Netherlands that the P90:P10 percentile ratio is halved when attention shifts from all earners to full-year earners only.

[8] Equivalization serves to account for the demands that household members put on income as well as the economies of scale of jointly managing a household (Atkinson et al., 1995; Förster, 1994; OECD, 2009). Note that applying equivalization not only to disposable incomes but also to market incomes and gross incomes (e.g., OECD, 2011; and various contributions to the special issue of the Review of Economic Dynamics), may affect the perception of labor market outcomes on the one hand and changes between these three distributions on the other hand.

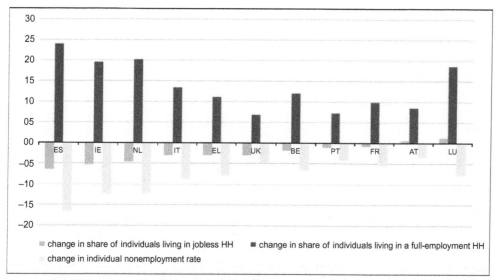

Figure 18.2 Changes (percentage points) in individual and household employment, 11 European countries, 1995–2008. *Reading note*: In Spain the share among individuals of those in work who are also members of a household where everyone is in work increased by 24% points between 1995 and 2008; the share for those living in households without work declined by 7% points; the share of individuals without work declined by 16.5% points. *Explanatory note*: In full-employment households everyone is in work; this includes single-person households. Employment follows the ILO definition and includes the self-employed. Persons aged 18–24 whose status is "inactive" are considered to be full-time students and excluded. For country codes see Appendix A. *Source: Eurostat—Corluy and Vandenbroucke, 2013, Figure 1 (based on the European Labour Force Survey).*

Figure 18.3 adds a particularly sharp example of the divergence between the two rates of employment for prime-age adults for the United Kingdom, one for persons (the traditional individual employment-to-population ratio), the other for households (the percentage of relevant households that have at least one employed person among their members). The former rate always exceeds the latter, and the gap between the two has grown rapidly from 2% points at the end of the 1970s to 13% points since the early 1990s.[9] Often such developments have gone hand in hand with an expansion of part-time employment. The correlation of individuals' levels of pay to their numbers of hours worked can tell us whether this hours-of-work dimension enhances or mitigates inequality. A positive correlation implies a more unequal distribution of annual earnings than of hourly earnings among individuals. The correlation has tended upward significantly and turned from negative to

[9] Atkinson (1993, 335 ff) discusses an 11.5% point decline in the family (adult) employment rate for the United Kingdom between 1975 and 1985 and infers that half the increase in inequality can be attributed to this "shift in work."

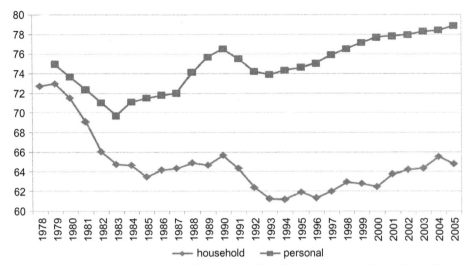

Figure 18.3 Employment rates (%) for individuals aged 25–59 and their households, United Kingdom, 1978–2005. *Reading note*: The share among individuals aged 25–59 who are in work grew from 75% in 1979 to 79% in 2005; the share of households corresponding to these individuals where at least one person is employed, declined from 73% to 65%. Source: *Derived from Blundell and Etheridge (2010), Figures 2.1 and 2.3 (based on Labor Force Survey and Family Expenditure Survey).*

positive in some countries although it still is negative in other countries. The correlation seems particularly strong for British women (Figure 18.4).

Compared to single-breadwinner households this complicates the relationship between the wage distribution and the income distribution. At the same time it makes the scrutiny of that relationship all the more important. Thus the role of dual-earner and multiple-earner households has expanded and is now substantial in many European countries as is indicated in Figure 18.5. With the exception of Italy and Greece, dual-earner and multiple-earner households are the majority among households, and evidently, employees in those households make up an even larger share of all employees. In particular, the role of multiple-earner households varies substantially across countries, from 4% of all households in Greece to 27% in Bulgaria.

In a world of full-time-working single-earner households, the correspondence between wage dispersion and income distribution seems pretty straightforward: a high individual wage directly implies a high household income. This traditional situation may provide another explanation, for lack of a problem, why the literature on the linkage between the two distributions seems underdeveloped. The formation of households and their labor supply may affect the distribution of incomes depending on the correlation of earnings levels between the earners in a household. A positive correlation will enhance household earnings inequality, in addition to the frequency of the occurrence of joint earnings. Changes in mating behavior or in partners' employment participation or both at the same time will be behind this. Figure 18.6 indicates the rise in the correlation

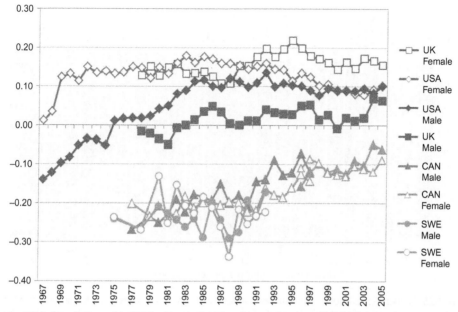

Figure 18.4 Correlation of individual wage level and annual hours worked, by gender, ages 25–59, United States, United Kingdom, Canada and Sweden, 1967–2005. *Reading note*: The correlation between the annual hours worked and earnings per hour among US males changed from −0.10 in 1967 to +0.10 in 2005. Source: *Blundell and Etheridge (2010), Brzozowski et al. (2010), Domeij and Floden (2010), and Heathcote et al. (2010).*

between such earners for the United States. It has roughly doubled over 1975–1990, which is less than half the 40-year period, and remained largely stable since. However, the level and evolution of this may differ between countries and, apparently, over time. Conversely, household joint labor supply may also affect the dispersion of wages, if additional earners would operate their labor supply at a less extensive margin of pay or working hours, given that a main income is already secured in the household, or if they would trade off pay and hours for a scenario combining paid labor with other activities, such as household care or participation in education.

In the end, household formation and the two distributions will all be endogenous to each other, and household formation should be added to the list of "stages for comprehending the distribution of income: aggregate factor incomes, differences in earnings and in capital incomes, the role of the corporate sector and of financial institutions, and the distributional impact of the state" (Atkinson, 2007a, 20).

18.2.2 A Cursory Review of the Literature Related to Household Incomes Distribution and LMIs

The literature on the linkage between the two distributions is diverse and cannot be viewed yet as a strong and coherent strand. More than occasionally contributions to

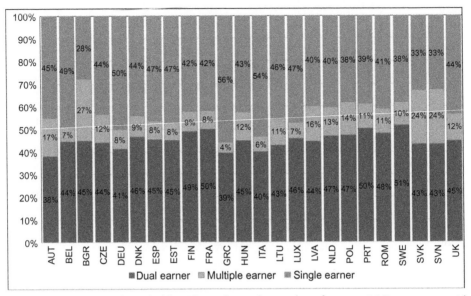

Figure 18.5 Working-age households with employees by number of earners, 26 European countries, 2010. *Reading note*: In Austria 38% of households with at least one member in employment have two persons employed, 17% have three or more persons employed, and 45% have one person employed (including single-person households). *Explanatory note*: Earners need to have positive hours and earnings as well. The household main earner is aged below 65, Students as identified in the data set are excluded. Naturally, female employment participation, traditionally large in what are now former communist countries, is an important determinant. Source: *Salverda and Haas (2014, Figure 3.9)*.

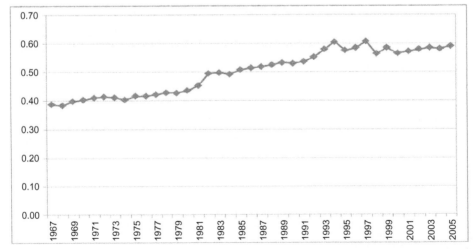

Figure 18.6 Correlation of earnings between married partners, United States, 1967–2005. *Reading note*: Correlation of earnings levels between married partners in households from less than 0.40 to around 0.60. Source: *Heathcote et al. (2010)*.

the subject are found in papers dedicated to other issues than the income distribution, such as the design of transfer programs (e.g., Liebman, 1998). Our own reading of the literature on household incomes distribution leads us to conclude that it pays little attention to the role of LMIs, which is, after all, the focus of our chapter. This is the very reason that we only touch on the household context of the dispersion of wages here. Checchi and Garcia Peñalosa (2008, 2010) do address LMIs and income inequality. In a comparative cross-country and macroeconomic perspective, they show the relevance of institutions especially in terms of their effects on the level of unemployment (i.e., zero hours and earnings) which, in turn, contributes significantly to the level of income inequality.[10] We will elaborate on elements of their approach later in the chapter. Certainly, some contributions investigate the effects on the income distribution of one particular institution, the minimum wage—itself the subject of a large literature for its effects on the dispersion of wages. Charles Brown (1999, Section 9.2) in his survey of that literature observes that many families have several earners, so that a minimum-wage worker can be part of a relatively affluent family and adds that the level of the minimum wage will be of little help in reducing income inequality, basing his argument on simple statistics that show the poor fraction among low-wage workers is low and that many poor families have no workers. Neumark and Wascher (2008) sum up many of their own and other contributions to the minimum-wage literature. In their view the combined evidence of income and employment effects for the United States is best summarized as "indicating that an increase in the minimum wage largely results in a redistribution of income among low-income families" (p. 189), as some may see their income rise and others may see their employment and therewith their income diminish. However, Arindrajit Dube (2013) finds sizable minimum-wage elasticities for the bottom quantiles of the equivalized family income distribution and argues from an evaluation of the existing literature, including works by Neumark and Wascher, that the finding is consistent with that.

There is, however, another emerging literature that studies the role of institutions in connection with the household incomes distribution, especially new institutions of relevance such as parental leave, tax credits, including the American EITC or the British WTC, or entitlements to remain in the same job (e.g., Brewer et al., 2006; Dingeldey, 2001; Dupuy and Fernández-Kranz, 2011; Eissa and Hoynes, 2004, 2006; Mandel and Semyonov, 2005; Thévenon, 2013; Thévenon and Solaz, 2013; Vlasblom et al., 2001). However, mostly it preoccupies itself with the employment effects and ignores the income side, and it is strongly focused on particular aspects of inequality as, for example, female labor supply or the motherhood gap in employment participation, and does not consider the aggregate picture of inequality nor the effects on earnings inequality or the

---

[10] OECD (2011) also advocates including the unemployed zeros in studying the contribution of the earnings distribution to the income distribution.

interrelationship between the two distributions.[11] We leave that literature out here, though we will try in the material to come to incorporate some of those new institutional measures in our broader framework. Note, finally, that we leave out the demographically motivated literature that focuses exclusively on the contribution to income inequality of household structure and composition (e.g., Brandolini and D'Alessio, 2001; Burtless, 2009; Peichl et al., 2010); nevertheless we do include contributions considering this in a broader framework that encompasses earnings inequality (e.g., Burtless, 1999).

In the collection of contributions there seem to be two main approaches (see Table 18.A7 in Appendix D for a summary of the relevant literature). The first approach is based on a direct comparison of the different distributions, and the second approach is based on a decomposition of income inequality that focuses on the sources of income, particularly earnings. The latter shows substantial variation in its choice of the measure of income that is decomposed (mainly established aggregate measures of inequality such as the Gini coefficient, but also newly devised ones such as the "polarization index" designed by Corluy and Vandenbroucke, 2013).[12] More importantly, this literature also varies in the precise technique of decomposition that is applied, which matters as the technique affects the outcome. In the literature there is no single generally accepted way of decomposing, which hampers the establishment of stylized facts.[13] This situation partly motivates the first, comparative approach. In addition to this, it can be observed that the decomposition approach takes one of the two distributions as its starting point and does not consider the effects on the other distribution. Thus it remains unclear when, e.g., growing female employment participation increases household earnings inequality if it also raises individual earnings inequality. We briefly discuss each of the two main approaches.

18.2.2.1 Comparing Distributions

One of the first contributions was made by Gottschalk and Smeeding (1997). They discuss various types of distributions and inequality measures on both the earnings and the income side, but largely in isolation of each other. Their conclusion is that "[b]etter structural models of income distribution and redistribution that can be applied across nations are badly needed. Ideally, an overall framework would simultaneously model the generation of all sources of income (labor income, capital income, private transfers,

---

[11] Liebman (1998, Table 2) finds a slight increase in the incomes shares of the lowest and the second quintiles in total income in the mid-1990s as a result of EITC; nevertheless, these shares remain well below those obtained 20 years earlier. Note also that Hyslop (2001) and Schwartz (2010) look specifically at the contribution of the association of partners' earnings to inequality on the earnings side.

[12] Note that this considers the distribution of employment over households and not the distribution of employment over pay, occupations, or tasks as discussed in Chapter 5.

[13] Gottschalk and Smeeding (1997, 669) express doubts regarding decompositions and point to the rather different outcomes in the literature. Equally, Gottschalk and Danziger (2005, 249) state that they "do not attempt to decompose the change in family income into its component parts because there are many ways to do so and there is no consensus on the most appropriate decomposition." See Shorrocks (1983) for dire warnings and Kimhi (2011) for a recent critique, but also Cowell and Fiorio (2011) for a possible way out.

public transfers, and all forms of taxation) as well as the formation of income sharing units" (p. 676). That is still a tall order today. In the absence of such a framework, decomposition leaves us with "purely accounting exercises" (p. 668).

Burtless (1999) compares the distributions of annual individual earnings distributions on the one hand and personal equivalized incomes on the other hand for the United States between 1979 and 1996. With the help of simple counterfactual exercises regarding the personal income distribution when holding the levels of earnings inequality constant, he finds that two-thirds of the observed increase in overall income inequality would have occurred leaving only one third for the changes in earnings. Within the latter share he attributes 13% of the increase to the growing correlation between male and female earnings in families. Also the increasing share of single-adult families among the population has contributed because the greater inequality within that group.

Reed and Cancian (2001) also simulate counterfactual distributions for the United States over the period 1969–1999, instead of pursuing a decomposition approach. They argue that this simulation allows using multiple measures of inequality, looking at different points in the distribution, and incorporating changes in the marriage rate. They find that changes in the distribution of female earnings account for most of the growth in family income throughout the distribution and disproportionately more at the bottom, leading to a decrease in inequality. By contrast, changes in male earnings account for over 60% of the growth in the Gini coefficient of the family income distribution.

Gottschalk and Danziger (2005) analyze in an interconnected way the evolution of inequality in four different percentile distributions: hourly individual wage rates, annual individual earnings (and therewith annual hours), annual family earnings, and annual family adjusted total income. The first two distributions are at one side of the earnings–incomes gulf, the other two at the other side. Interestingly, they bridge the gulf by ranking individuals for their annual earnings according to the total earnings of their households (p. 247) using consistent samples of individuals. Earnings exclude the self-employed and the analysis splits throughout between men and women. The focus is the American evolution over the last quarter of the previous century using CPS data.[14]

Atkinson and Brandolini (2006), though, for the most part considering trends in wage dispersion, compare the Gini of the individual annual earnings dispersion to the Gini of adjusted disposable household income for a set of eight countries: Canada, Finland, Germany, the Netherlands, Norway, Sweden, the United Kingdom, and the United

---

[14] Gottschalk and Danziger's approach is very apt in an intertemporal perspective but difficult to interpret in a cross section as it ranks male and female earners according to their respective households, which must be largely overlapping sets that concentrate higher up the income distribution, to the extent that both male and female in a household do have earnings. A disadvantage is that they do not discuss the role of singles nor of possible third earners within the household. They find that "for females, changes in hours more than offset the rise in wage inequality. The acceleration in male wage and earnings inequality during the early 1980s disappears when earnings of other family members are included" (p. 253). Thus, the household is found to mitigate inequality growth in the labor market.

States, using LIS data from around the year 2000. They draw the comparison on an annual basis and include part-time and part-year earnings, but they leave the distribution of employment out from their analysis, and, consequently, they also do not compare directly to the hourly wage rates, the traditional pay inequality in the labor market. In addition, they do not compare individuals and households on the basis of an identical ranking as is done by Gottschalk and Danziger. They find that the Nordic and Continental countries have similar Gini values for earnings and for incomes respectively, whereas both are higher for Canada and the United States; the United Kingdom is found to be European on earnings and North American on incomes (p. 58).

Lane Kenworthy (2008) observes that "if every household had one employed person, the distribution of earnings among households would be determined solely by the distribution of earnings among employed individuals" (p. 9). He mentions the possibility that households have different numbers of earners, adding that this number is mainly determined by the number of adults in the household. However, he leaves this aside in the analysis and focuses on the dichotomy between "some earner(s) or none" (p. 9). Using LIS data for 12 countries (Australia, Canada, Denmark, Finland, France, Germany, Italy, the Netherlands, Norway, Sweden, the United Kingdom, and the United States), he finds pretaxed, pretransfer household income inequality to be strongly related to the inequality in individual earnings of full-time employed individuals, all equivalized for household size and composition. The association to the incidence of households with zero earnings (for the head of household) is less, and to marital homogamy, defined as the correlation between spouses' annual earnings, it is smaller still. The total employment rate and the part-time employment rate appear to play no role.

Večerník (2010), also using LIS data, considers employees only and does so in conjunction with their households. His focus is the effects of transition in four CEE countries, in a comparison with Germany and Austria. He specifically draws other earners than the spouses in a household into the comparison, and effectively distinguishes between dual-earner and multiple-earner households. He shows that the latter category of employees can make an important contribution to household earnings, that earnings inequality among this group is very high in all countries, and that the contribution to overall inequality can also be very substantial. Slovakia combines the highest earnings share (19%) with a lower Gini coefficient than elsewhere, and a major contribution to overall inequality (39%). This contrasts strongly with Germany where both the income share and the contribution to overall inequality are the lowest (4% and 8%) and the within-group inequality is the highest (0.93). It seems to suggest that the population of other earners may have a very different character in Western Europe than in the East.[15]

---

[15] Večerník (2013), studying the evolution of the two distributions in the Czech Republic between 1988 and 2009, again with the help of regressions on both sides, finds an important role on both sides for education which runs via the employment and earnings of women as marital partners.

Finally, Salverda and Haas (2014), using EU-SILC data, build on some of the above approaches comparing decile distributions and the top-to-bottom inequality ratios (the shares or means of the tenth top decile relative to that of the first decile) in a cross section of 25 EU countries in 2010. They show how the dual-earner households and especially the multiple-earner households concentrate toward the top of the household earnings distribution: on average, across EU countries only one-tenth of households in the top decile are single-earner households whereas almost 90% are in the bottom decile (compare Figure 18.5 for the average picture). Unsurprisingly, dual-earner and multiple-earner households reach the top by combining wage levels often from well below the top of the earnings distribution, in contrast to the few single-earners whose households make it to the top. On average over the countries, the main earner's earnings are only 60% of a single earner's in a dual-earner household and less than 50% in a multiple-earner household. Salverda and Haas draw a comparison of the household earnings distribution with two different ways of distributing the individual earners: one ranked according to their households' earnings, the other ranked by their own individual earnings. They find that households add to household earnings inequality primarily by the combination of the activities of their members, although at the same time that combination mitigates the individual labor market inequalities in both hours worked and levels of pay: workers with higher earnings or longer hours combine with those working or earning less. At the same time, in international comparison the variation in hours is modest—clearly, one can only work so many hours regardless of the country—and the main difference reflected in the comparative level of household earnings inequality is, after all, the traditional inequality of the individual's own wages in the labor market.

Figure 18.7 compares household total earnings to individual wages in panel (a), and to hours worked in panel (b). The lower level of individual earnings inequality and annual-hours that is attained if persons are ranked by their households (lines 3 and 6) instead of as individuals in the way they appear in the labor market (lines 2 and 5), shows the mitigating effects of households compared to the labor market. Households earnings and hours (lines 1 and 4) are more unequally distributed due to the adding up of individual earnings, which, however, are attained at lower and higher levels. When compared to panel (a), panel (b) also shows that the inequalities in hours are substantially smaller than in earnings within as well as across countries. This is understandable as there are only so many hours in a year and the number of employees combined in a household is modest in practice.

18.2.2.2 Decompositions of Household Income Inequality

The second relevant approach in the literature is based on decompositions of income inequality, especially by sources of income which enables scrutinising the contribution that earnings or employment make to inequality. There is significant variation among the decomposition studies: their nature and the variable decomposed, and also the

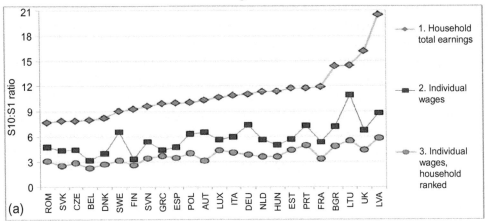

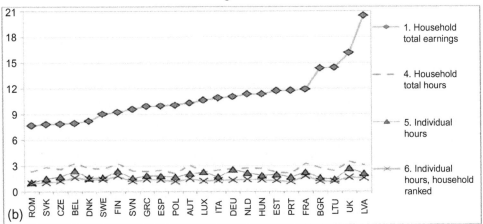

Figure 18.7 Top-to-bottom ratios (S10:S1) for employed individuals and their households, 26 European countries, 2010. (a) Annual earnings distributions. (b) Annual working-hours distributions. *Reading note*: In Romania average household total annual earnings in the 10th decile of such earnings are 8 times higher than in the 1st decile; annual earnings of individuals in the 10th decile of such earnings are 5 times higher than in the 1st decile if persons are individually ranked, and only 3 times if they are ranked according to their households total annual earnings. *Explanatory note*: The sample concerns households receiving their main income from earnings. The top-to-bottom ratio is between the average level of the tenth decile to the first decile. Source: *Salverda and Haas (2014, Table 3.2).*

technique of decomposition (see Fortin et al., 2011 for an overview). The results may depend on the choice.

In one of the first studies, Shorrocks (1983) using the American PSID over 1968–1977 concludes that "Dollar for dollar capital income and taxes have more distributional impact than earnings, which in turn exceeds the impact of transfer income" (which is defined to include retirement pensions and annuities).

Van Weeren and Van Praag (1983) use a special data set covering seven European countries (Belgium, Denmark, France, [West] Germany, Italy, the Netherlands, and the UK) in 1979 to decompose income inequality into subgroups. Interestingly, they look, inter alia, at the employment status of the head of household as well as the number of persons contributing to household income. At the time both characteristics make the largest contribution to inequality in Denmark, although employment makes the smallest contribution in the Netherlands and the number of earners in the UK.

Blackburn and Bloom (1987) draw a careful comparison of the family annual earnings distribution and the individual annual earnings distribution for the United States over the years 1967–1985. Using various aggregate inequality measures they find that annual earnings inequality has hardly changed, although income inequality has. Descriptively splitting the distribution in five parts, the change seems largely concentrated in what they term the "upper class," family with earnings over and above 225% of the median. From a time-series regression analysis they conclude that particularly the growth of nonprincipal earners in those households contributes to this growth. Blackburn and Bloom (1995) draw an international comparison at various points during the 1980s. For the United States, Canada, and Australia they find that income inequality increased among married-couple families and that the increases are closely associated with increases in the inequality of husbands' earnings. Evidence of an increase in married-couple income inequality is found also for France and the United Kingdom, but not for Sweden or the Netherlands. In various countries, that increased inequality of family income is closely associated with an increased correlation between husbands' and wives' earnings. A more detailed examination in Canada and the United States suggests that this increase cannot be explained by an increase in the similarity of husbands' and wives' observable labor market characteristics in either country. Rather, it is explained partly by changes in the interspousal correlation between unobservable factors that influence labor market outcomes.

Karoly and Burtless (1995) follow Lerman and Yitzhaki (1984) in decomposing the evolution of the Gini coefficient of American distribution of personal equivalized incomes between 1959 and 1989, basing themselves on census and CPS data. They find largely the same results as Burtless (1999) does for his more recent period. A large part of the reduction in income inequality before 1969 is attributed to the decline in earnings inequality among male heads of families. After 1969 the same group is responsible for more than one-third of the increase in inequality. Since 1979, the improved earnings of women have increased inequality as they were concentrated in families with high incomes.

Cancian and Schoeni (1998) consider 10 countries using LIS data for the 1980s. They find that the labor-force participation of wives married to high-earning husbands increased more than for those married to middle-earning men.[16] At the same time,

---

[16] They do not decompose strictly speaking but use a simple split of the coefficient of variation between married partners to look at the contribution of wives to inequality among this category; they therefore do not address the income distribution as a whole.

the mitigating effect of wives' earnings actually increased slightly in all countries. In their view an unprecedented increase in the correlation of earnings between the partners would be needed to make the effect disequalizing.

Evelyn Lehrer (2000) finds from the US National Survey of Families and Households that between 1973 and 1992–1994 the equalizing influence of the wife's contribution grew substantially stronger—partly due to a decrease in the dispersion of female earnings relative to that of male earnings. This seems to contrast with Karoly and Burtless (1995); however, her finding relates to married couples and their earnings only, not to the full personal income distribution.

Del Boca and Pasqua (2003) consider husbands and wives in Italy between 1977 and 1998 using regional differences and the absence of wives' incomes as a counterfactual. The added worker effect is found in households especially in the North where there is more acceptance and more choice of working hours and more child care support available. Here the reduction in the dispersion of wives' earnings seems to have offset increases in the dispersion of husbands' earnings as well as the increased correlation in the earnings between the spouses between 1989 and 1998.

Johnson and Wilkins (2003), following DiNardo et al. (1996), studying Australian inequality over the period 1975–1999, find changes in the distribution of work across families—for example, an increase in both two-earner families and no-earner families—were the single-most important source of the increase in private-income inequality, with such changes on their own accounting for half the increase in inequality.

Daly and Valetta (2006), using CPS data for the United States and adopting partly the method of Burtless (1999), in combination with the decomposition technique proposed by DiNardo et al. (1996), find a more substantial contribution (50–80%) of men's earnings to increased American inequality between 1969 and 1989 than does Burtless. This increase was counteracted by the growing employment participation of women. They explain the larger role of males as their methodology can account for growing inactivity and unemployment.

The *Review of Economic Dynamics*' Special Issue of 2010[17] presents an interesting and important inventory of various dimensions of economic inequality, including the distributions on both sides of the individual earnings versus household incomes divide as well as the distributions of wages versus that of hours. The set of papers for seven countries contains useful descriptives of the distributions. In addition, some decomposition

---

[17] Relevant to the set of countries covered here are Canada: Brzozowski et al. (2010), Germany: Fuchs-Schündeln et al. (2010), Italy: Japelli and Pistaferri (2010), Spain: Pijoan-Mas and Sánchez-Marcos (2010), Sweden: Domeij and Floden (2010), UK: Blundell and Etherigde (2010), and finally United States: Heathcote et al. (2010). In spite of the fully comparative set-up from the start, there are still some incomparableness left, especially with regard to annual individual earnings and to the household earnings distribution which is not always given on the same basis (pregovernment, pretax, after-tax or equivalized disposable income).

exercises are done on the log-variance of either earnings or hours. These decompositions concern a limited but important range of characteristics (gender, education, age, experience, region, family structure). They appear to explain little of the evolution and, in virtually all cases, leave most of the action to the residual. Of particular interest is Figure 18.8, where panel (a) specifies the variance of log individual hourly wages and panel (b) that of individual annual hours worked. The two are at different levels, the latter nowadays being much lower than the former, and their evolution seems to trend in opposite directions, clearly up for the former and declining for the latter. For annual earnings—seldom known from the contributions—the implication is a more substantial variance, which then feeds into household earnings.

Lu et al. (2011) study Canadian developments in the family earnings distribution (equivalized) from 1980 to 2005 using census data for those 2 years and 1995. They again adopt the decomposition approach developed by DiNardo et al. (1996). For 1980–1995 they find substantial increases in family earnings inequality, but for 1995–2005 some decrease. Changes in the earnings structure, such as those attributed to educational attainment, and changes in family composition (fewer married couples, more single individuals and lone parents) have been key factors contributing to growing family earnings inequality. Substantial changes in family characteristics (including a surprising decline in educational homogamy and the implied mating of women below their level) have had the most important counteracting effects as has continued growth in women's employment rates. Interestingly, the authors take a special look at the Top 1% of the distribution, mention that it has increased substantially between 1995 and 2005 in contrast with declining family earnings inequality; however, they do not further highlight this in their analysis.

Larrimore (2013), again focusing on American CPS data, now for 1979–2007, and with the help of a shift-share decomposition, finds important differences between the three subsequent decades: changes in the correlation of spouses' earnings accounted for income inequality growth in the 1980s but not in the 1990s (consistent with Figure 18.6). During the 2000s changes in the earnings of male household heads diminished income inequality, and the continued growth in income inequality was due to growing female earnings inequality and declining employment of both genders.

Finally, the most extensive decomposition study seems to be the one reported by Brewer et al. (2009) and Brewer and Wren-Lewis (2012). For the National Equality Panel (Hills et al., 2010) they have dissected the trends in British inequality over the long period 1968–2006 in many respects using a regression-based decomposition technique developed by Fields (2003) and Yun (2006).[18] The results are presented in Figure 18.9. Total inequality of all households (line with white markers) moves to a higher level over the 1980s, from less than 100 to more than 160. The contribution that

---

[18] Unfortunately they compare gross earnings to equivalised disposable household incomes, but they do decompose between (aggregate) taxes and benefits.

Log hourly earnings

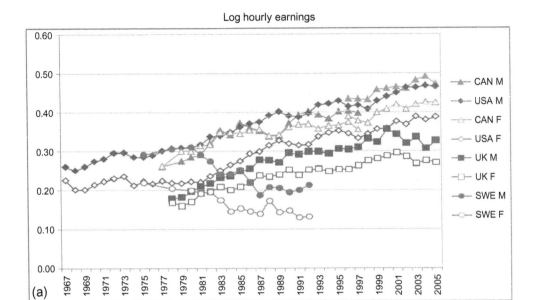

(a)

Annual hours worked

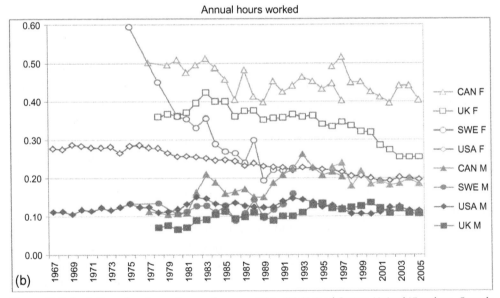

(b)

Figure 18.8 Evolution of variance, by gender, ages 25 to 59, United States, United Kingdom, Canada and Sweden, 2010. (a) Log hourly earnings. (b) Annual hours worked. *Reading note*: The variance of log hourly earnings of US males increased from 0.26 in 1967 to 0.47 in 2005. *Explanatory note*: F—females, M—males. Source: *Blundell and Etheridge (2010), Brzozowski et al. (2010), Domeij and Floden (2010), and Heathcote et al. (2010).*

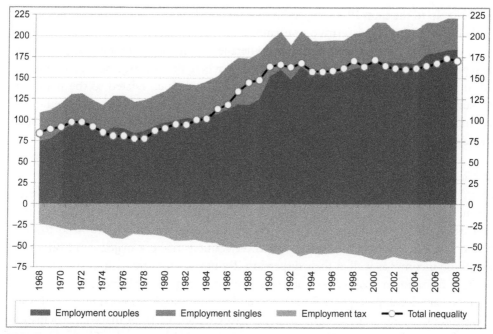

Figure 18.9 Contributions of household earnings to total net-equivalized household income inequality, United Kingdom, 1968–2008. *Reading note*: The line of total inequality results from adding up the contributions to inequality from couples and singles in employment and subtracting the tax they pay. *Explanatory note*: Inequalities are measured as the variance of logs (×1000). Contributions do not exactly add up as nonemployee categories receiving market income, pension have been left out. These contributions happen to partly cancel out but their aggregate has grown from 0 points in 1968 to 19 points out of the total of 171 that is shown for 2008. Source: *Brewer and Wren-Lewis (2012, Table 5)*.

household gross earnings makes to this is split between the single-earner and dual-earner households respectively and the total of taxes paid by both (stacked shaded areas). The role of singles has remained unchanged on balance, with a temporary increase during the 1980s. Dual earners run largely parallel to total inequality; their growth is also somewhat concentrated to the 1980s though it continued after that at a slower pace. Taken together single and dual earners lag the inequality growth of the 1980s somewhat. That gap is filled by incomes from self-employment, investment, and pensions whose role more than doubled during the 1980s (not shown).[19] The net effect of earnings is less as taxation (the negative area which needs to be deducted) has also increased. After an

---

[19] The relative role of benefits (including tax credits) grows until the mid-1980s but is almost halved subsequently.

initial rise up to the mid-1970s the rise is more gradual and extends over the period as a whole but hardly changes relative to earnings.

At the end of this overview a careful and detailed comparison of these results, including replication studies, seems advisable to find out where they diverge or even contradict and to seek an explanation whether differences are real—i.e., related to the period or the sample that is the focus—or artificial—i.e., due to the data set, the method of decomposition, or the approach to equivalization. Unfortunately, however useful, such a meta-analysis is entirely outside the scope of our contribution.

18.2.2.3 A Heuristic Help for the Role of Institutions and Earnings

Though we cannot and will not pursue a comprehensive approach to wage dispersion and income distribution, we may still ask what we can learn from the above and take with us for the contemplation of wage dispersion and institutions. We need to keep in mind, first and foremost, that labor market earnings make a major contribution to household incomes as well as their dispersion. By implication, the lack of such earnings resulting from unemployment or joblessness makes a large contribution, too.

Important developments are found that tend to diminish the direct influence of wage dispersion on the income distribution as the growing female labor market participation and at the same time enhance the role of household joint labor supply. This complicates the relationship between the two distributions, and it may also affect the labor market behavior of labor supply. Anyway, it brings into play a collection of new institutions that may affect both employment, hours worked, and pay, as well as their concentration across households. This may influence the level of wage inequality. It seems advisable to take the new institutions into account in addition to the traditional ones arising from labor market analysis on its own.

Another important inference to draw is the importance of considering hours and their dispersion in addition to wages. The inclusion of hours is important for several reasons. They are needed to arrive at the full picture of the earnings input that the labor market makes into household incomes. The hours dispersion differs significantly between the sexes, between countries, and also changes over time. In addition, the growing role of part-time and temporary jobs in itself makes this a more important dimension, and one that may also play a role in determining the dispersion of pay given the correlation between hours and pay. There may also be different trade-offs between hours and pay in different countries. At the same time, the role of hours may be relatively less important; it is more modest because of natural constraints than that of pay in an international comparison.

Second, it seems safe to conclude that one size does not fit all (countries). Significant differences are found, especially between different periods, and these seem to get more attention the further behind the period is (witness Larrimore's most detailed account of such periodization in his 2013 publication).

Interestingly, comparable decompositions of important characteristics such as gender, age, education, and family type seem to play an amazingly small and also often flat role in virtually all countries, leaving a large role to residuals, which may point to national idiosyncrasies.

18.3. WAGE DISPERSION: MEASUREMENT AND STYLIZED FACTS

Before we turn to the analysis of wage inequality and institutions in Section 18.4 we discuss here first the ways to measure these and then present what seem to be the current stylized facts of the literature concerning wage inequality. Section 18.3.1 starts with a discussion of the issues involved in measuring wage inequality and a quick presentation of data sources. This is followed by a presentation of the "stylized facts," which we define as the state-of-the-art knowledge of wage inequality currently accepted by scholars as necessitating explanation in spite of their different views and approaches. These facts regard, first, the aggregate level of inequality, referring to the most comprehensive distribution at the national level. For this we discuss outcomes according to different measures of inequality as well as for different definitions of the wage variable. Second, Section 18.3.2 considers disaggregate inequality, which highlights specific parts of the distribution—such as the tails or the middle—on the one hand, and inequalities among various subsamples of the population according to demographic or labor market criteria on the other hand. Then (in Section 18.3.3) we provide some new empirical evidence from a cross-section comparison of 30 countries for the most recent year available, which we elaborate on when our empirical approach in Section 18.3.4 concludes.

18.3.1 Measuring Wage Inequality and Data Sources

Blackburn and Bloom (1987) have argued in detail the need of precision for measures and definitions of wage inequality.[20] Following their suggestions, we need to pay attention to at least four dimensions:

---

[20] "The often-contradictory conclusions reached by studies of recent trends in income and earnings inequality are largely explained by the reliance of researchers on a remarkably wide range of conventions of data analysis. For example, the list of important dimensions in which previous studies vary includes: the time period covered; the way family units are defined; the population to which the studies of individual earnings generalize (e.g., all earners, private nonagricultural workers, male earners, wage and salary workers, full-time, year-round workers, etc.); the measures of earnings and income (e.g., total family income, equivalent family income, total family earnings, wage and salary income, etc.); the unit of time for the measurement of earnings (e.g., annual, weekly, or hourly); the nature of the earnings measure (e.g., usual earnings or average earnings); measures of inequality (e.g., the Gini coefficient, income-class shares, variance of logarithms, coefficient of variation, mean logarithmic deviation, etc.); the use of individual or grouped income/earnings data; the treatment of sample weights; the treatment of observations with imputed incomes; the handling of top-coded values of income and earnings; and other criteria for including observations in the sample, such as the age of the respondent and whether the respondent was working at the time of the survey or in the year preceding the survey" Blackburn and Bloom (1987, 603).

(1)   the measure of inequality

(2)   the definition of the wage variable (including its time dimension)

(3)   the selection of the sample of the population that is being covered

(4)   the nature of the data sources.

Clearly, the study of wage inequality adds several significant issues of measurement to those of long-term concern to the study of inequality (e.g., Atkinson, 1970; Chapter 5; Jenkins and Van Kerm, 2009). We consecutively address these four issues before we turn to data sources, and to the stylized facts in the following section.

Before starting this we mention a general observation. Wages are defined here as "wage rates,"[21] preferably controlled for hours worked[22] and therewith for differences in workers' efforts, whereas we consider "earnings" or "wage earnings" as the product of those wage rates with the hours worked and therefore reflecting also differences in individual efforts. For convenience we say in general that we are addressing "wage inequality." However, this does not mean that we restrict ourselves to the inequality of wages rates only; to the contrary, we aim to also consider the dispersions of hours and earnings. When doing so we will try to be clear and not just mention wages but use the appropriate concepts: weekly, monthly, or annual hours or earnings.[23] Wage rates serve the clear analytical purpose of enabling comparisons between individuals on the basis of the same efforts made in terms of time dedicated to paid work, measured in hours. As already argued, hours are an increasingly important dimension of labor market functioning and inequality and will be given their due.

18.3.1.1 Measures of Inequality

Although the Gini coefficient is a very popular measure in the analysis of income inequality, it hardly figures in the analysis of wage inequality. Variance, mean log deviation, the Theil index, and standard deviation are used, however.[24] Unfortunately, because of their aggregate nature, these measures tell us little about where in the distribution the differences over time or across countries reside, though decomposition of these measures, as far

---

[21] "Wage rates" as hourly wages can be part of wage scales agreed between unions and employers, albeit implicitly, when the agreement also covers hours of work. However, actual individual earnings will often deviate from these scales because of bonuses, performance pay, labor market scarcities, etc. (see, e.g., Salverda, 2009).

[22] Note that this may add to measurement error.

[23] Here we differ from OECD (2011, 26), which follows a more complex scheme that risks creating confusion: Their "dispersion of hourly wages" equates to our dispersion of wages and their "wage dispersion" equates to our "distribution of annual earnings." "Labor income" is a concept encountered in the US inequality literature and is effectively considered as a wage rate; however, it actually amounts to a wage rate multiplied by the efforts (usually for full-time workers on a weekly basis).

[24] There is an extensive literature discussing the properties and validity of these measures, such as the violation by the standard deviation of the transfer principle—see, for example, Chapter 6 of this handbook or Jenkins and Van Kerm (2009). Compare, e.g., Karoly (1992) who considers empirical outcomes for a broad range of such measures for American wage inequality.

as possible, can certainly be helpful for understanding the underlying processes. In wage-inequality analysis it is the percentile ratios that play a remarkably important role: the P90: P10, P90:P50, and P50:P10 ratios, which mutually relate the 10th, 50th, and 90th percentiles to each other.[25] These ratios are directly helpful in focusing attention on particular parts of the wage distribution and they are intuitive at the same time. Their evolution over time reflects differential changes in wages at specific points of the distribution. As we will see below, up to this very day the debate on the effects of the minimum wage on wage inequality is framed almost exclusively in terms of these ratios. The ratios have also provided important leverage to the shift that has occurred in the debate about the role of technology as a determinant of growing wage inequality. Their popularity may relate also to an easier consistency with the analytical focus on the individual and his or her efforts in the labor market in contrast to income analysis.[26] Note that the ratios are based on the upper-boundary wage levels of the chosen percentiles (or deciles), and not on their means, sums, or shares in the total of wages. This implies certain limitations to the use of these ratios, and it seems advisable to add measures that broaden to averages, sums, or shares. For example, a top-to-bottom ratio between the means, sums, or shares of the top decile on the one hand and that of the bottom decile on the other hand (denoted as S10:S1) may find inequality growing much farther apart than the P90:P10 ratio would suggest, if important changes are actually occurring within the two tail deciles and affecting their within-spread.[27] Precisely that is the upshot of the recent analysis of top-income shares, where the sum and the share of the top decile, and its within-distribution over smaller fractions, are the very subject of study. In a similar vein, much of the current minimum-wage debate appears to be effectively analyzing changes found within (and perhaps even restricted to) the bottom decile of the wage distribution. Note that the OECD has recently introduced the top-to-bottom ratio in its income inequality and poverty database.[28] In addition to these quantile ratios, the ratio between the average wage and the median wage is sometimes also found as an indicator of wage inequality; the Kaitz index similarly relates the level of the minimum wage to the average wage in the analysis of minimum wage effects. One disadvantage of all such ratios, however, is that they cannot be decomposed (Lemieux, 2008, 23),[29] though they may be further split into ever smaller fractions.

---

[25] Also denoted as decile ratios: D9:D1, D9:D5, and D5:D1, between the 1st, 5th, and 9th deciles, the aforementioned percentiles being their upper boundaries. Comparisons for all percentiles encountered in the literature below may be considered a visual generalization of this type of measures.

[26] Relative to the individual employee the type of the household as a unit of analysis shows much more variation, which is difficult to square with the use of exact percentile income levels as it is accidental what type may be found at a particular income level.

[27] Compare the "poverty gap," which acts as an indicator of the within-spread of poverty.

[28] See http://www.oecd.org/els/soc/income-distribution-database.htm.

[29] However, Firpo et al. (2009) develop a decomposition method based on recentered influence function (RIF) regressions, which they actually apply to these ratios.

Some other indicators are available in the same family of disaggregate measures that can also relay information about wage inequality. These relate to parts of the distribution that are defined with the help of an external wage-level criterion. The most important one in practice, regularly published by the OECD, is the incidence of low-wage employment (see Gautié and Schmitt, 2010; Lucifora and Salverda, 2009). This is defined as the share of all employees in the wage distribution who are found having wages below the level of two-thirds of the median wage.[30] It is important to realize that this is a concept that relates to the analysis of the labor market, in contrast with in-work poverty that depends on the household-income position of the wage earners concerned; nonetheless the former is definitely relevant to the analysis of the latter. The concept of low pay is only infrequently used in US analyses of wage inequality where the in-work poverty concept is more frequent, perhaps because the poverty threshold is of such central concern in that country's public discourse.[31] The divergence between the two concepts signifies that workers may be poor—on the basis of their household situation—at wage levels that are well above the low-pay threshold, and vice versa, that workers receiving low pay may be found in households well above the poverty level.[32] Unsurprisingly, the evolution over time may differ between low pay and poverty wages. Figure 18.10 clearly points this out for the United States. Over the period 1995–2002 the share of employees earning poverty wages shows a particularly sharp decline, although the incidence of low pay remains unchanged. Household composition, household joint labor supply, and the evolution of prices determining the poverty lines can influence the former but not the latter, which depends on wage developments.

As an analogue to low-wage employment one can conceive of the incidence of pay at or below the minimum wage as another simple measure of wage inequality. Strikingly, in spite of decades of intense debate on the employment effects of the minimum wage such

[30] Although there is a clear and internationally endorsed measure of low pay this is not readily available for high pay. Salverda et al. (2001) define high pay as over and above 1.5 the median wage, but other definitions are also found in the literature. The OECD Earnings Database also specifies high pay—using the same definition—but so far only for a few countries. By implication, as long as the tails are not well defined there is also no clear measure available of the polarization of the wage distribution, which might easily be defined as what remains in the middle of the distribution after excluding low-wage and high-wage employment. Instead, polarization seems to be gauged more as a qualitative phenomenon from ad hoc visual inspections of real wage growth, as we will see later.

[31] We disregard the debate about the "experimental poverty measures": in principle, the same difference of focus attaches to the European concept of poverty (see Chapters 3, 8, 9, and 23).

[32] For 2011, the US low-pay threshold can be put at $11.89 per hour (EPI *State of Working America 2012*, Table 4C), which at 2000 h of work in a year would generate annual earnings of $21,340, well above the official poverty threshold for a single-person household ($11,702, <65 years) and only slightly below that for two-adult, two-children households ($22,811). The poverty thresholds range up to $50,059, depending on household size and composition, which is 2.3 times low-wage annual earnings. We disregard for a moment taxes and contributions and also that the poverty levels are rather low as underlined by the introduction of the Experimental and Supplemental Poverty Measures.

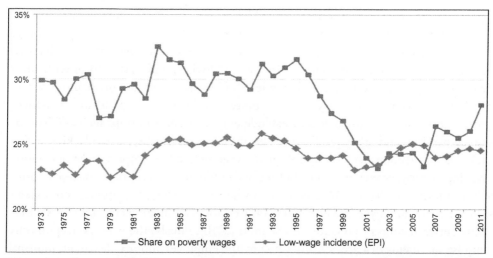

Figure 18.10 Shares (%) of workers earning a poverty wage or a low wage, United States, 1973–2011. *Reading note*: The percentage of all employees earning a poverty wage fluctuates around 30 until 1996 and then falls substantially; the percentage earning a low wage fluctuates around 25 from 1983 onward. *Explanatory note*: Poverty wages are earned by individuals whose household incomes are below the official poverty threshold; low wages are defined as being at or below two-thirds of the median wage: on authors' estimation for hourly earnings of all workers using linear interpolation in the decile distribution. Source: *Authors' calculation on EPI,* State of Working America 2012, *data underlying Figure 4E and C.*

statistical data are sporadic. Internationally, a possible explanation may be the nonuniversality of statutory minimum wages or their complex nature when, for example, it is less evident to whom they apply or not—a problem that is absent in measuring the low pay incidence.

Finally, as implictly suggested above, the share of top wages in the wage distribution—a direct corrollary to top-income shares—provides another possible statistic that can throw light on wage inequality. We will see later that pay at the top plays an increasingly important role in the wage-inequality debate.

18.3.1.2 Definitions of the Wage Variable[33]

Most of the literature restricts the definition of the wage variable to the payments received by employees from their employers, and we will follow that convention here. This excludes for reasons of principle both the unemployed and the self-employed (however, this does not mean that they should be excluded from the analysis of labor markets and wage inequality—compare our approach in Section 18.5). We will focus on gross

---

[33] For a deeper discussion of these definitory issues and the issues of composition and statistical observation considered next see Atkinson (2008), Chapter 2: *Taking Data Seriously: Where the Data Come From and How We Should Use Them.*

wages, including taxes and contributions, which are paid by the employee (also when the employer actually withholds them on behalf of the tax authorities). However, gross wages are not available for all countries all of the time though, fortunately, they now increasingly are (e.g., very recently France, Greece, and Switzerland started to provide gross wages; net wages will likely show a lower level of inequality because of tax progression). In addition, even gross wages are a more restricted concept than "employee compensation" in the sense that they exclude employer contributions such as for occupational pensions and other provisions. This is for the practical reason of lacking observations in most countries.[34] The full-gross wage defined as employee compensation including employee taxes and contributions seems the most appropriate concept in principle as it includes what can be called the "social wage." This encompasses entitlements financed out of employee and employer contributions and income tax, and varies significantly between countries (Gautié and Schmitt, 2010). Finally, the wage concept mostly comprises payments that are actually made by the employer and may leave out informal cash payments such as tips, in spite of their (suggested but often statistically unknown) importance for low-wage earners in some countries.

Given this definition of wages, there is one crucial dimension about which we aim to be as clear as possible. This regards their time dimension, which appears to greatly influence the apparent level of inequality. We have already touched on this above when mentioning the distinction between hourly wage rates and their multiplication by hours worked. Most of the US inequality debate has been framed in terms of full-time weekly wages if not full-time full-year wages (Acemoglu and Autor, 2011, 1049)—"earnings" in our definition. Though this seems largely a matter of data convenience, it may have important implications for comparisons. First, it ignores the incidence of part-time employment which varies significantly over time and across countries. Second, it overlooks the dispersion of full-time working hours itself, which can be considerable and may differ between countries.[35]

---

[34] Commonly, such contributions are not well known to the employee, and they are left out in household surveys as a consequence. They may differ considerably over the wage distribution and between countries. Among the stylized facts below, we will, however, mention an excellent example of information on the distribution of employee compensation.

[35] The OECD database on "Usual hours worked by weekly hours band," covering 28 countries, indicates that for 2012, on average, 76% of men and 65% of women worked 40 h or more in 2012, with a highly comparable cross-country pattern for the two genders. However, these shares vary from around 10% only in Denmark to almost 100% in Estonia, Greece, Hungary, Poland, and Slovenia. The evolution over time also differs. On average for the 13 countries with data for both 2012 and 1983, the share among male full-timers decreases from 81% to 66%, among women from 69% to 53%. In various European countries the shares working longer hours plummets: for example, in Denmark from 95% (men) and 85% (women) to 12% and 8%, respectively, in Germany from 100% and 99% to 73% and 64%, respectively. However, in the United States it remains unchanged at slightly above 90% and the growing number of women adapts upward to males. This female adaptation is also found in the United Kingdom, but not in various other countries, where the gap can even grow.

Third, different time periods for wages/earnings bring into play different, additional elements of pay such as bonuses and other special payments that are made with a lower frequency, for example, on an annual basis. Such payments usually have an increasing effect on inequality, which risks to be missed by a shorter time horizon—the use of an annual average of shorter-term wages can potentially mend this problem, but this is not standard practice.

Fourth, the use of time for the weighting of the observations bears on the level of inequality, too. This issue regards the working hours of the employee. Pay observations—including for hourly pay—can be taken simply over the head count of employees or alternatively over the count of hours worked, that is over employees weighted by their working hours. The latter boils down to full-time equivalent wage levels and lends part-time employees a lesser weight in determining the average and the quantiles. Evidently, such weighting reflects more closely the economics of the labor market and less the receiving side of labor's personal incomes, which affect their significance for household welfare and spending; both sides deserve consideration, and attention should not focus exclusively on one or the other.

Finally, there is yet another timing issue on the employee side: wages can concern all who are in work during a year or they may be restricted to those who work the full year, or alternatively all workers may be considered in terms of full-year equivalents. Covering all includes the people who enter or leave employment (or both) in the course of the year; in the full-year option they are left out, in the annualized full-year equivalent approach they will be weighted also by the part of the year in which they work. The share of part-year workers naturally differs between social groups, but it can differ also over countries and over time, because of the business cycle or because of a different or changing role of temporary jobs. New entrants in particular may have low wages and significantly affect inequality at the left-hand tail of the distribution. Finally, the part of the year they actually cover—say 3 months instead of four—will affect their earnings considerably and may have a significant effect at the margin on annual earnings inequality.[36]

To conclude, we do not think there is one best definition of the wage or earnings variable—it depends on the purpose of the analysis. We do think that definition and

---

[36] The time basis of the wage variable should be a matter of concern as it may cause major differences in the level of wage inequality. On an annual basis inequality may be five to six times larger than on an hourly basis (Karoly, 1993, Appendix B2B); the annual dispersion of hours worked explains the difference. Even on the much-used weekly basis there is a clear dispersion in the hours of work (Karoly, ibidem). Second, the dispersion of hours within categories in combination with their weight in the total will affect outcomes, cross section, and over time. For example, men's hours' dispersion seems much more compressed than women's and their compositional weights have developed strongly; in other words, full-time full-year working men are becoming steadily less representative of the wage distribution as a whole.

purpose should be explicit and mutually consistent and that shortcuts adopted for reasons of data covenience should be scrutinized for their hidden properties and potential effects on the outcomes.

18.3.1.3 Composition and Samples of the Population

Another issue worth mentioning is the part of the population that is covered by the analysis. A *pars pro toto* approach, that views a part of the population as representative of the whole, is particularly dangerous in inequality analysis. Subsets of the population may occupy very different positions in the overall distribution, and inequality may differ significantly between them. Their inclusion or exclusion can exert large marginal effects on the level of inequality even when they are relatively small compared to the whole population. Selection along dimensions such as gender, age, education, or experience on the side of the person, or industry, occupation, the nature of the employment contract and its protection, and the (part-time) working hours on the side of the job can greatly affect the aggregate outcome. The issue may seem obvious although it frequently is a source of error, confusion, or even distortion. For example, contributions may focus on men, on people working full time, on the working-age population, or on positive incomes only, as if assuming that all the rest of the population makes no difference to the general outcome nor to that of the selected group. Imagine that women increasingly occupy low-paid jobs while men are ousted and leave employment; both groups could potentially see their wage inequality fall, though overall it might actually increase. Another realistic example is from Krueger and Perri (2006), who draw conclusions about household consumption inequality for the United States as a whole on a (laudably specified) sample that leaves out non-working-age households, those without an income from labor, and rural households—which are groups that may substantially affect inequality at the margin. Finally, even if all the population is covered all the time, compositional shifts across categories may be highly relevant to the evolution of inequality and will need proper scrutiny. Vice versa, aggregate stability of inequality can go together with changes in inequality within many distinct categories; in the extreme case, even all categories could face inequality change in the same direction (together with shifts in their positions relative to each other). Finally, it is important to add the observation—found in the overview of the literature below—that the distinction of between-inequality and within-inequality (the residuals, after all) depends on the variables chosen as the basis for the decomposition. That choice will likely be inspired by what are considered to be the stylized facts; as a consequence, insufficient attention may be paid to the implications of large residuals and these may actually obtain an importance of their own as is underlined by some of the literature that we will be discussing.

18.3.1.4 Data Sources/Statistical Observation

Individual wages seem more cumbersome to observe statistically than household incomes. For incomes, the collection of taxes provides a strong and universal incentive for gathering administrative data. Such data usually combine considerable precision regarding the core variables with clear limitations for other variables such as personal characteristics, for example, educational attainment is of no direct importance to the tax authorities. This motivation may be less compelling for a comprehensive collection of wage data. Administrative data may be gathered for registering individual Social Security entitlements, but their nature and coverage will depend on the idiosyncracies of the entitlement rules; for example, the sampling may be restricted to those who can qualify for the entitlements in question (e.g., after a probation period, working a minimum of hours, excluding overtime earnings), or focus on their work histories and not their actual earnings, or cover their earnings up to a relevant threshold only. This may hamper their use particularly in international comparisons.

Dedicated surveys, by contrast, require a special effort and consequently are subject from the start to cost–benefit trade-offs, which will affect the range of variables, the population samples, and the time periods covered. This explains why surveys may concentrate on information that is easier to collect, and also that significant international differences occur in the availiability of data and in their coverage. As a result, one can understand the long-time focus in OECD data and American data, along with analyses of full-time workers[37]: collecting hours information on top of earnings information to enable determining hourly wages, or information on workers who have left during the year on top of those permanently employed or present at the time of the survey, is simply more demanding and costly. This may be the case particularly if the information is gathered from employers. Note, though, that ICT developments are greatly facilitating the transfer of firm data to statistical offices. Employers will, by their own interest, dispose of the most accurate information about pay. By contrast, if the information is gathered from households, the information on wages will be less precise, as respondents may not know the details of wage components or taxation and contributions, or respondents may actually be less well-informed than other members of the household. Equally, the information about hours of work may differ between employer sources and household sources, as the former will focus on legally formalized working time whereas the interest of the latter will be in the actual hours that a job involves, possibly including the necessary travel times. Interestingly, a concentration on full-time full-year workers may make little sense in a household survey as it will add to the costs. At the same time, employers will be less well informed about workers' personal characteristics such as educational attainment or the worker's household situation, and the availability and quality of that information from a household survey may be superior compared to employer surveys. Another advantage of administrative tax data can be their more comprehensive time coverage—tax is paid over the full year—whereas household surveys may have important

---

[37] Stretching all the way from the 1980s to Acemoglu and Autor (2011) included. Heathcote et al. (2010, 24) point out the inadequacy of this focus.

limitations, such as what time of the year the survey questions are asked—do the questions relate to the preceding year or the current one? Adding the dimension of hours to that of earnings can only complicate this.[38] Finally, administrative data will normally cover very large shares of the population and ascertain that all essential questions are answered, whereas other surveys can cover only much smaller samples and suffer from considerable nonresponse to questions,[39] generating less-accurate results also as a consequence of that. Nonresponse will be more important for the current focus on wages at the very top; unsurprisingly, tax data play a large role here though the top-coding of responses may still affect the availability of data, but that is no different for wages than for incomes. As administrative data will be available anyway, increasingly, the statistical offices are trying to use these instead of asking fresh questions to households or firms, and use those data for imputations in other surveys, blurring the distinction between the two types of information as a result. Naturally, both administrative and survey data are subject to changes over time. The tax system or Social Security rules may change and ask for new variables or drop existing ones. A survey may be adapted also because of costs, or simply because a new survey is started without paying due attention to the continuity with its precedessors.[40]

Having said this, the main data source in the literature is first and foremost the American Current Population Survey CPS. It is a household survey, started in the 1940s and providing tabulated data from then, that has made microdata available for research since the early 1960s (the more adequate CPS ORG—outgoing rotation groups—data being available since 1979 only). CPS comes in different "tastes": the March CPS or the May and/or ORG CPS, and one needs to be careful which one to use, partly depending on the purpose of its use. The March CPS is not good for hourly wages, whereas the CPS ORG does a better job here and also has a much larger sample size than the May CPS, which, in addition, may be seasonally affected while the ORG CPS data cover the full (preceding) year.[41] However, the practice of top-coding of labor incomes may reduce the usefulness of this source of data for studying earnings inequality.[42] Several other American data sources are sometimes used, such as the PSID (which we will use below

---

[38] Below we are forced to combine from EU-SILC survey-time working hours with preceding year information; the American PSID is subject to similar problems.

[39] Up to one-third of CPS wage observations may be imputed by the surveyors (John Schmitt at CEPR Washington, DC—personal conversation).

[40] The break between ECHP and EU-SILC is a case in point, but over its long duration the American CPS also shows several important changes.

[41] See also Lemieux (2008) for a detailed discussion.

[42] "For example, in the March CPS, reported wages and salaries were until recently top-coded at $150,000 a year, which is barely above the 95th percentile of the distribution of earnings in the tax data of Piketty and Saez ($125,471 in 2004). One well-known data set for which top-coding is not an issue is the Panel Study of Income Dynamics (PSID), which is unfortunately not ideal either for studying top-end inequality because of smaller sample sizes" (Lemieux, 2008, p. 32).

for better mimicking European SILC data) and the census, and also employer surveys such as the Employment Cost Index microdata (Pierce, 2001, 2010).

Second, on the EU side, increasingly two consecutive EU-wide (panel) surveys provide microdata for research: the European Community Household Survey (ECHP) and the Statistics on Income and Living Conditions EU-SILC. The ECHP covers the EU15 only, with the exception of the first years of Austria, Finland, and Sweden, who joined the EU in 1995. The survey performed eight annual waves in the years 1994–2001, generating annual data for the years 1993–2000. Sample sizes and degrees of panel attrition diverge substantially across countries depending on the value attached to the survey in the country.[43] The ECHP was discontinued and has been replaced with EU-SILC, which is still in force today. SILC has annual waves starting in 2003/2004 and extending to 2012 at the time of writing—again relaying full-year data for the preceding years (in most countries). SILC's country coverage follows the extension of EU membership and attains full coverage of EU-27 together with Iceland, Norway, Switzerland, and Turkey in 2007.[44] There are a host of small differences between countries in sampling, definitions, and the like, and these also change over the years. Importantly, the *gross* wage variable has been available for all countries since the wave of 2011, although up to then some countries provided net wages only (France, Italy, Switzerland).[45]

Another easily accessible and often-used international data set is the OECD's earnings database, which provides tabulated data. It has been built since the mid-1990s and now covers 34 countries,[46] albeit with rather uneven time coverage. Only seven countries go

---

[43] Particularly, the educational variable suffers from different national interpretations of the common data-gathering conventions in the course of the waves. In France and the Netherlands almost all responderts are misclassified at the lowest level of education from 1997 onward. At the same time the United Kingdom drastically alters its classification of educational attainment with a strong upward effect among the population as a result.

[44] Brandolini et al. (2011) consider SILC data in detail, and also attempt to aggregate over European countries. See epp.eurostat.ec.europa.eu/portal/page/portal/microdata/documents/SILC_IMPLEMENTATION_headezr.pdf

[45] The most advanced experiment in income and wealth data harmonization is known under the old name of Luxemburg Income Study-LIS (http://www.lisdatacenter.org/). LIS is home to two databases, the *Luxembourg Income Study Database* and the *Luxembourg Wealth Study Database*. The income data set contains information for 46 countries, in some cases going back to the 1970s. A parallel project was started at Cornell University, known as Cross-National Equivalent File-CNEF, 1970–2009, in collaboration with other research partners (see http://www.human.cornell.edu/pam/research/centers-programs/german-panel/cnef.cfm). The Cross-National Equivalent File 1970–2009 contains equivalently defined variables for the British Household Panel Study (BHPS), the Household Income and Labour Dynamics in Australia (HILDA), the Korea Labour and Income Panel Study (KLIPS) (new this year), the American PSID, the Russian Longitudinal Monitoring Survey (RLMS-HSE) (new this year), the Swiss Household Panel (SHP), the Canadian Survey of Labour and Income Dynamics (SLID), and the German Socio-Economic Panel (SOEP).

[46] The usual suspects from America, Asia, and Europe together with Chile, Iceland, Israel, and Turkey.

back in time before 1990, and complete coverage is very recent (2010). In most cases the data are provided by the national statistical offices, although in a few cases they are derived by the OECD from other surveys or provided by national experts. However, definitions and samples vary widely between countries, covering the entire set of possible differences that we have just discussed, ranging from all all individual employees to full-time, full-time full-year employees, and full-time equivalent employees, from hourly wages to weekly, monthly, and full-time equivalent annual earnings, and from gross to net after taxes and contributions. The latest version of the full database contains 90 different series endorsing 33 different definitions. It commonly details the outcomes also for the two genders. For the website version of the database, the OECD has chosen to present only one series per country, 33 in total. This reduces diversity to nine different definitions; the mode (20 series) concerns full-time employees' weekly or monthly gross earnings (which may be deemed reasonably comparable[47]) but only 11 of those go back in time before the year 2000. All definitory properties are admirably documented in the database and offer the user the opportunity to consider the differences and their potential effects. Nevertheless, the database is clearly not immune to the problems of secondary data sets that Atkinson and Brandolini (2001) have stressed for incomes, but which are equally important for wages and earnings.[48]

Finally, Atkinson (2008) provides the results of an in-depth study of the earnings distribution in 20 countries, inspired by the work of Harold Lydall (1968). He advocates a long-run picture on a year-by-year basis, showing that "drawing on isolated years . . . can be misleading." For each country an extensive appendix documents the available data sources and the properties of the data and the presents the evolution at various percentiles of the distribution, ranged separately for the lower and the upper half of the distribution. The series end in 2004 and stretch back in time to well before those of the OECD database. For 15 countries they start before 1960 and cover most of the postwar period and some of those (Canada, France, Germany, United States) go back to before the war.[49] This long time span helps to realize the particular nature of the more recent developments that are the subject of the debates considered in this chapter. Roughly speaking, strong declines in inequality over previous decades preceded the

---

[47] Often a week is taken as 4/13th of a month, or vice versa.

[48] They discuss other attempts of international data gathering apart from the OECD's, consider some of their use in the literature, and list the factors that influence what they call "a bewildering variety" of inequality outcomes. It is highly important to consider the variation and its implications when using the data for international comparisons of levels as well as evolution. Atkinson and Brandolini "caution strongly against mechanical use of such data sets." They also mention that country fixed effects may not provide a remedy and that even when data are uniformly defined the precise definition may have an effect on the conclusions that can be drawn. Atkinson (2008) extensively discusses similar issues with a focus on earnings, and adds important detail by wage definitions and time periods for 20 countries out of the OECD's 28.

[49] Atkinson and Morelli (2012) update the P90:P50 ratio to more recent years for most of these countries and add a few other countries.

increase on which the literature started to focus in the 1980s. Preferably, the analysis should be able to also explain the declines.

To conclude it seems natural that contributors to the literature are requested to specify their definitions, samples—including censoring or top-coding—as well as sources. Given the long history of using the CPS this is increasingly becoming standard practice in American contributions, but it certainly needs endorsement in international comparisons. Equally important, but not frequently practised, it seems highly advisable to consider the possible implications that data limitations and data choices made may have for the conclusions that are drawn.

18.3.2 Cross-Country Levels and Evolution of Wage Inequality

We now turn to the stylized facts of earnings inequality as we derive them from the literature. This is done in two steps. We start with the United States, which is the country having the best information and where the debate and the analysis of earnings inequality have developed most strongly, enabling us to spell out most of the issues at stake. We contemplate the variation in outcomes between different measures of inequality where feasible, between different definitions of the wage variable where necessary, and between different data sources where reasonably available. In addition to discussing aggregate outcomes, we take a look at some breakdowns—both of the earnings distribution itself and by segments of the (employee) population. Next to the United States, we continue with a consideration of various other countries aimed at comparing the inequality trends but also at identifying gaps in the available data that hamper comparability. In Section 18.3.3 we provide some new empirical evidence from a cross-section comparison of the EU countries and the United States for the most recent year available, based on EU-SILC and PSID, which we will use for our empirical approach in Section 18.5. We end with summary conclusions regarding the stylized facts in international comparison.

18.3.2.1 U.S. Earnings Inequality

Much of the American literature focuses on men or at least distinguishes between the sexes, treating them separately and seldom putting them together in the overarching distribution. This contrasts with other countries and seems a paradox as US female employment started growing earlier than elsewhere and also grew more fiercely in the sense of being predominantly full time and extending high up the overall earnings distribution (Salverda et al., 2001). It may be explained from the early start of the inequality debate in the United States at a time that data did not really allow putting them together. This split risks ignoring the genders' mutual interaction in labor supply and demand and overlooking also the contribution of the within-country doubling of the labor force between the late 1960 and mid-2000s, which has remained in the shadow of the worldwide Great Doubling, a term famously coined by Freeman (2006). For this reason and for the sake of international comparability, and also because it allows covering the recent years since the mid-2000s, we start with a quick look at the aggregate level of all employees irrespective of gender. That comprehensive picture is provided by Figure 18.11. Panel A indicates the overall percentile ratio, P90:P10, from two different sources, the EPI's *State of Working America* and the OECD's Gross Earnings Database. EPI covers hourly wages of all employees, presumably based on head count individuals and not full-time equivalents; the OECD data, by contrast, concern weekly earnings of full-time employees and therefore miss out on part-time employment.

Starting at exactly the same level in 1973, EPI shows a much stronger increase in the ratio between 1979 and 1988 than OECD, directly followed by a decline while the OECD series remains unchanged. At the end the inequality level according to EPI is well below the OECD's.[50] The conceptual difference between the two is important as it is found throughout the literature. Lemieux (2010) as well as Heathcote et al. (2010) provide state-of-the-art overviews of developments for many aspects of American earnings inequality from around 1970 to the mid-2000s, entirely based on hourly wages (but always split by gender).[51] Other important contributions (e.g., Acemoglu and Autor, 2011), by contrast, draw to an important extent on full-time weekly or full-time full-year workers (equally split by gender). Autor et al. (2008, Figures 2 and 3) draw a useful comparison between hourly and full-time full-year earnings inequality trends.

Panel (b) pictures the percentile ratios of the common split between the upper and the lower half of the distribution from the same two sources. It suggests that the difference between the sources and the definitions concentrates in the bottom half; in the upper half the two series are almost identical, which is understandable as in this case virtually all employees will be working full time. The divergence between the two halves is an important observation to retain. The panel also suggests, in accordance with much of the literature using the gender breakdown, that developments since the early 1990s have been different from before, because, on the one hand, lower-half inequality hardly changes in contrast to the preceding period, but upper-half inequality keeps on growing relentlessly, with ends far exceeding bottom-half inequality. With the EPI data, the divergence starts in 1992, with the OECD in 1995.

Finally, panel (c) adds a rather different way of presenting the evolution of inequality: the cumulative changes in real wage levels for each of the 100 percentiles over different time periods, using the work by Pierce (2010). This has become a convenient way of presenting the data in the polarization debate that we will report on later. The discontinuous periodization highlights apparent differences but may suffer from a certain arbitrariness at the same time. With its detail, this type of presentation seems to implicitly

---

[50] Our aim is not to seek an explanation; a possible one may reside in the variation in full-time hours across individuals. See Autor et al. (2008, Figure 3) for outcomes similar to panels (a) and (b).

[51] The two seem rather different at first sight; e.g., Lemieux finds much lower levels of the variance for both males and females; however, from 1979 to 2005 the trends are largely identical.

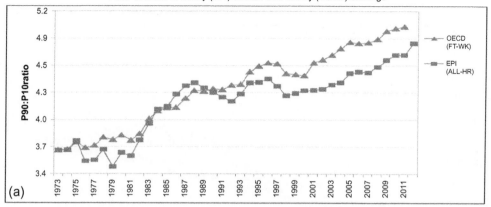

P90:P10 ratios of hourly (EPI) and full-time weekly (OECD) earnings

(a)

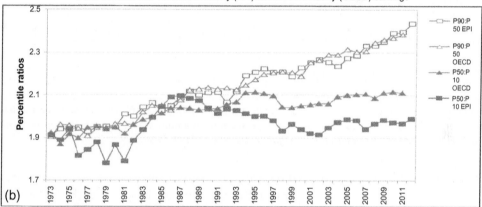

P90:P50 and P50:P10 ratios of hourly (EPI) and full-time weekly (OECD) earnings

(b)

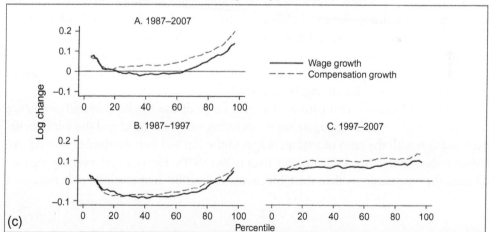

Wage and compensation growth by percentile, 1987–2007

(c)

Figure 18.11 Inequality of individual earnings, United States, 1973–2012. (a) P90:P10 ratios of hourly (EPI) and full-time weekly (OECD) earnings. (b) P90:P50 and P50:P10 ratios of hourly (EPI) and full-time weekly (OECD) earnings. (c) Wage and compensation growth by percentile, 1987–2007. Sources: *OECD Gross earnings: Decile ratios (26 October 2013), Economic Policy Institute EPI,* State of Working America 2012, *Washington: Real wage deciles, all workers, 2012 dollars (based on data from the CPS), and Pierce (2010, Figure 2.5) (based on Employment Cost Index data).*

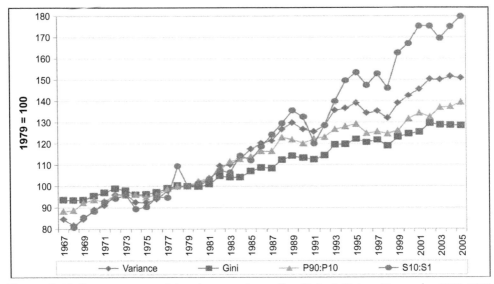

Figure 18.12 Four measures of hourly wage inequality: United States, Men only, 1967–2005, 1979 = 100. *Reading note*: S10:S1 is the ratio between average hourly wages in the top decile to the bottom decile. *Explanatory note*: Figures cover individuals aged 25–60 who work at least 260 h per year, with wages at least half of the legal federal minimum wage. Source: *Heathcote et al. (2010, Figure 4) and S10:S1 derived from Figure 7 (based on March CPS).*

criticize the use of more aggregated measures such as the Gini coefficient or the overall percentile ratio. The panel shows a much flatter pattern of changes over the 1990s than over the 1980s, when strong declines in real wages occur for most percentiles between the tails of the distribution. Nevertheless, real wage growth mostly increases with the wage level. Interestingly, the panel elaborates also on total compensation (dashed lines), which includes employer contributions on top of wages. This is a unique feature that will be mentioned only here. We may conclude from it that the comprehensive concept of earnings does not change the general patterns for the 1980s and 1990s though it reinforces inequality levels somewhat during both periods.[52]

Figure 18.12 draws a comparison (for men only) of the intuitive overall percentile ratio with the often-used aggregate measures of log wage variation and the Gini coefficient and also with the ratio of average wages in the top and bottom decile (S10:S1). All measures show much higher levels now than in the 1970s. However, the variance grows substantially more strongly than the Gini coefficient, while the percentile ratio fluctuates

---

[52] Congressional Budget Office (2012, Table 7) suggests (for annual earnings) that the relative top-up of cash wages and salaries with contributions to deferred compensation and employer contributions to health insurance and payroll taxes has grown over the quintiles of employee incomes.

between them, the S10:S1 ratio runs away from the rest after 1993.[53] The divergence between the S10:S1 ratio and the common P90:P10 ratio implies that the rapid rise has to do with the within distribution of the two tails, which none of the other three measures seem to be able to capture adequately. The top-incomes literature has already shown its importance at the top end, but the dispersion within the bottom decile merits equal attention.[54] Apparently, the strength of the increase in the dispersion depends on the measure chosen and also their periodic ups and downs do not fully coincide.

The top and bottom half split of Figure 18.11 has provided a first breakdown of the aggregate by focusing on parts of the distribution. The incidence of low pay or high pay, and the size of the remaining middle are indicators of the same sort. The former was already shown in Figure 18.10. It moves up from 23% in 1975 to 25% in the mid-1980s and has been rather stable at about that level since. Over the same period the share of those high-paid, defined as earnings exceeding 1.5 times the median hourly wage, increases from 21% to 25% in the mid-1980s and further to 28% (not shown). As a result the remainder in the middle shows a considerable fall before the mid-1980s (55–50%) and another slighter fall over the current crisis (49–47%). A narrower definition of high pay following the top-incomes literature is pursued by Lemieux (2010), who endorses a simple repair for the top-coding of earnings in the CPS[55] and presents percentiles distributions similar to those of Pierce above, which we reproduce in Figure 18.13. Starting in 1974 the period covered is significantly longer but still split into two parts, now on both sides of the year 1980. Separate distributions are given for men and women. Again developments are more positive and spread more evenly over most of the distribution during the second period after 1989 than before. The longer period covered up to 1989 shows a more skewed picture than Pierce's. Particularly, real wage change in the bottom 20% seems more negative now for men, although an increase in the lowest percentiles for women may help explain the surprisingly upward move found by Pierce. At the same time, it is clear that among men the high part of the distribution has run away from the rest with a steep gradient within the top decile. The top percentile ratios seem to support this (not shown). They are almost identical and trend upward together until the end of the 1990s when female inequality starts to lag behind. The bottom-half ratios run largely parallel to each other with the one for females indicating a substantially lower level of inequality. The more positive development of wages for women seem suggestive of a declining gender gap. This is borne out clearly by Heathcote et al. (2010, Figure 5) who, after a slight increase of the gap from 1967 to 1978, find a continuous decline after

---

[53] The evolution of the S10:S1 ratio seems to imply that the variance is a plausible measure to use here in spite of its sensitivity to outliers in the distribution.

[54] Since the mid-1980s the incidence of the minimum wage ranges entirely within this decile.

[55] Checking against the Pareto parameter-based approach of Piketty and Saez (2003) he concludes that results are the same.

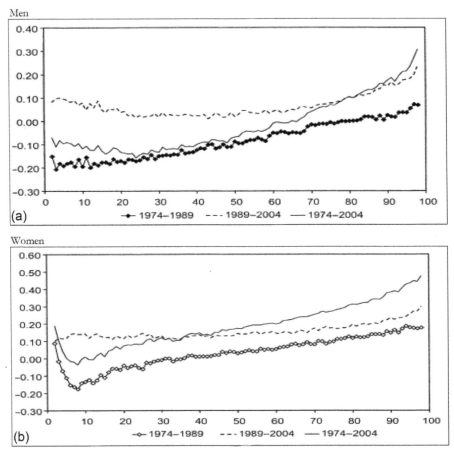

Figure 18.13 Percentage change in real hourly wages, by gender and percentiles, United States, 1974–2004. (a) Men and (b) women. Source: *Lemieux (2010, Figure 1.7).*

that year, sharply up to the mid-1990s and more modest since then. The current gap (30%) is much smaller than before but certainly not negligible.

Next to gender, educational attainment is the most important dimension for breaking down inequality. Its role has been a bone of contention in the literature from the start, as we will see later. Here Lemieux (2010) presents differentials for various levels of attainment relative to high school graduates (Figure 18.14). They appear to be mostly flat with slight declines at the lower levels but with the clear exception of the highest two levels, particularly the highest. These start growing away upward particularly over the 1980s and more modestly since. For men the top–bottom gap almost doubles. At the end of the period the differentials seem almost identical between the two sexes. Heathcote et al. (2010, Figure 5) present a college wage premium defined as the ratio between the average

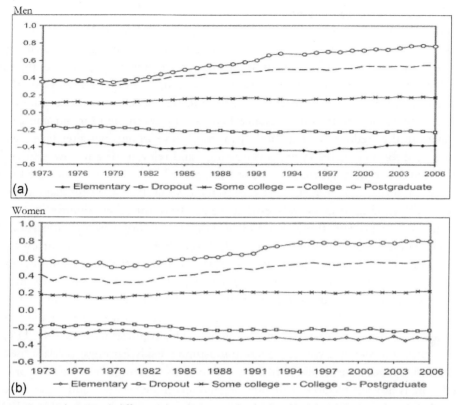

Figure 18.14 Educational differentials relative to the high-school level, by gender, United States, 1973–2006. (a) Men and (b) women. *Explanatory note*: Using a decomposition based solely on education and experience. Source: *Lemieux (2010), Figure 1.3.*

hourly wage of workers with at least 16 years of schooling, and the average wage of workers with fewer than 16 years of schooling. The premium increases significantly though more for men (52–92%) than for women (58–69%).

We stop here and refer for further detail of other dimensions of the earnings dispersion, such as experience or nationality/country of birth, to the literature itself. Before we continue we will stress again the important role of residuals. These outcomes for gender and education rest on simple decompositions, and most of the action appears to reside in the residuals, which develop largely in parallel to the growth in overall "raw" inequality (Heathcote et al., 2010, Figure 5). The implication is that other factors of influence need to be incorporated in the analysis and/or that idiosyncrasies, which may be immune to further analysis, play a nonnegligible role. Lemieux (2010, Figure 1.8) finds, interestingly, that the importance of residuals grows with the level of earnings, especially over the period 1974–1989.

18.3.2.2 Earnings Inequality in Other Countries

We now turn to inequality trends in other countries. The *Review of Economic Dynamics* (RED) (2010) is a special issue dedicated to cross-sectional facts regarding elements of economic inequality; it provides the most precise cross-country comparison of the earnings dispersion and several of its important facets, using as uniform a template of data treatment and presentation as possible.[56] Unfortunately, it has several drawbacks. The limited number of countries of relevance here is only seven, and for our comparison it is even further reduced as Italy and Spain focus on earnings net after taxes, which are unsuited for a comparison to gross earnings, and relevant data for Sweden end in 1992 when the country's financial crisis had just started. That leaves us with the United Kingdom, Canada, and Germany. We turn to these results first, and after that we turn to the OECD's earnings database to see what we can learn for other countries.

Figure 18.15 presents three measures of individual hourly earnings dispersion, for men and women together, as found in the RED contributions: the variance of log wages, Gini coefficient, and overall percentile ratio. All indicators for the three countries tend to rise over time. The British variance increases very rapidly up to a level 60% above the start of 1978, which well exceeds the other two measures (and also the variance in the United States), and subsequently falls over the 2000s. The other two measures for the United Kingdom also show a decline over that last period. This contrasts with the OECD's percentile ratio (not shown), which (covering full-time weekly earnings) is at a somewhat lower level but continues rising until 2006 and remains unchanged until 2011. For Canada the rise is also considerable, +20–40% depending on the measure, and continues until the end of the period. Mutual differences between the measures are smaller. The OECD's percentile ratio (not shown), again for full-time weekly earnings and available after the mid-1990s only, shows continued growth over the entire 2000s. Finally, in Germany, data are available from 1983, the rise of the three indicators concentrates in the period after unification. The variance shows a clear rise, and it is virtually identical for the percentile ratio—in contrast with the other two countries. Taken over the same 1983–2004 period, their growth is stronger than in the United Kingdom or Canada. The rise of the percentile ratio must rest on the use of hourly earnings as the trend of the OECD's ratio (not shown), which concerns full-time monthly earnings, is largely flat over the 1990s and early 2000s. However, the increase in the Gini coefficient is modest relative to the other indicators as well as the other countries.

---

[56] Brzezowski et al. for Canada: 1978–2005, Fuchs-Schundeln et al. for Germany: 1984–2005, Japelli and Pistaferri for Italy: 1980–2006, Pijoan-Mas et al. for Spain: 1994–2001, Domeij and Flodén for Sweden: 1978–2004 (effectively 1975–1992 only), Blundell and Etheridge for the United Kingdom: 1977–2005, and Heathcote et al. for the United States: 1967–2005 (but always split by gender). Unfortunately, Spanish data are net after taxes and will be left out here. Krueger et al. provide a summary overview in the Introduction. Individual earnings dispersion is addressed as part of the study of the household distribution of earnings (mentioned above, see, e.g., Figure 18.4).

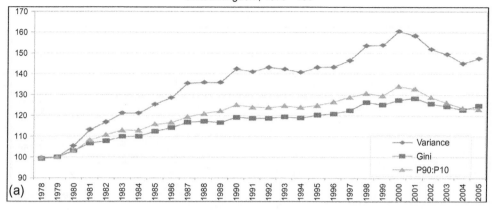

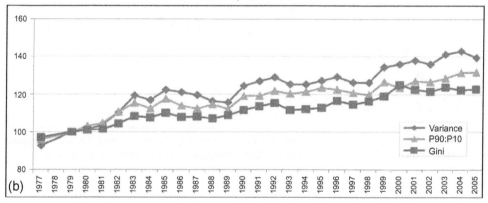

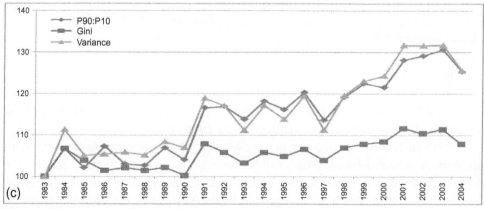

Figure 18.15 Dispersion of hourly wages, United Kingdom, Canada and Germany, late-1970s to mid-2000s. (a) United Kingdom, 1979 = 100. (b) Canada, 1979 = 100. (c) Germany, 1983 = 100. *Explanatory note*: Figures cover individuals aged 25–60. Derived from the data underlying Figures 3.1 (UK), 4 (Canada) and 6 (Germany) as posted on the RED website. Data sets concern for Canada the *Survey of Consumer Finances* SCF 1977–1997 and *Survey of Labor and Income Dynamics SLID* 1996–2005, for Germany the German Socioeconomic Panel GOEP, and for the UK the Family Expenditure Survey FES and Labor Force Survey LFS. Sources: *Brzozowski et al. (2010), Fuchs-Schündeln et al. (2010), and Blundell and Etheridge (2010).*

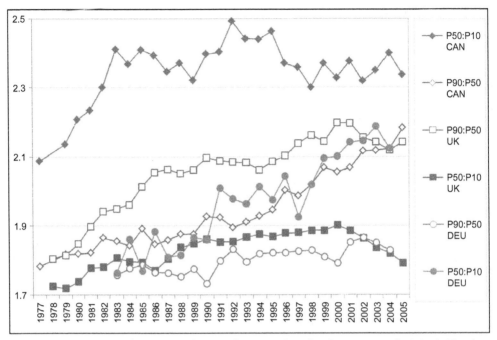

Figure 18.16 Lower and upper half inequalities in Canada, Germany, and United Kingdom, 1977–2005. Sources: *Blundell and Etheridge (2010), Brzozowski et al. (2010), and Fuchs-Schündeln et al. (2010).*

In Figure 18.16 we split the overall percentile ratio into its two contributing halves, P90:P50 and P50:P10. We a find strong divergence between the countries. The high levels and strong rise of the bottom-half ratios in Canada and Germany[57] are strikingly different from the United Kingdom; the German ratio moves up as much as the British but over a considerably shorter period. Canada and the United Kingdom share a decline in recent years though. Upper-half inequality rises very little in Germany and clearly less than in Canada and the United Kingdom. Generally, the pattern of the two British trends is very similar to the United States in Figure 18.11, whereas Canadian trends look surprisingly different. This clearly call for further scrutiny.[58]

Unfortunately, wage changes by percentile, which have come to play an important role in the American debate, are not available for other countries. The RED papers have also looked at the roles of gender and educational attainment. The gender pay gap for Canada is small from the start, comparable to the US gap at the end of the period

---

[57] For Germany this rise is absent in the OECD's (full-time) data, and therefore also in the overall ratio that was mentioned.

[58] Fortin and Lemieux (2014) conclude to a role of provincial minimum wages and natural-resources growth.

(30%), and it trends downward only very slowly. The German gap declines slightly more steeply and ends below (20%) the American level in the mid-2000s. The British gap, finally, declines somewhat more strongly; it is below the US level in the late 1970s but ends at about the same level. Note again that the decompositions made in the RED papers are based on gender, educational attainment, and experiences only and that in these three counties, as in the United States, residuals are quantitatively important and behind most of the increase in inequality.

With the help of the OECD's earnings database of percentile ratios, the evolution of individual earnings inequality can be described for a number of other countries (see Figure 18.17).[59] As already stated it is a secondary database, and it has to be used with great care. It comprises a wide array of wage definitions and concomitant samples of the employee population. We first select eight countries that focus on gross earnings of full-time workers (be it hourly, weekly, monthly, or annually[60]) and also have a long-run series. Given the diverging incidence of part-time employment, the full-time focus will be more or less representative of the country, but there is nothing we can do about that apart from being aware that in (various European) countries where part-time jobs have become more important and tend to be overrepresented in the low-wage segment of employment, the actual picture of inequality will plausibly be more pessimistic both in cross section and over time than found here for full-time workers only. With the exception of Japan and Finland over the period as a whole and Korea over its first half, overall inequalities in panel (a) seem to be trending upward, albeit to varying degrees and with different timings. Compared to the rest, Hungary and Korea show strong episodic changes, which apparently hang together with deep political change—the end of communism and of dictatorship respectively. The two halves of the distribution are pictured in panels (b) and (c). With the exception of Hungary and Korea, differences in trends seem to be relatively small. Lower-half inequality is usually less than upper-half inequality, and most of the overall rise can be attributed to the upper half. In the stable cases of Japan and Finland, lower-half inequality declines somewhat, but in all other countries it grows at some point in time. Comparable information about gender and educational differentials is not available.

Finally, Figure 18.18 assembles remaining short-run information on gross earnings. This concerns full-time workers with the exception of Denmark (all workers, headcount) and Norway (all workers, full-time equivalents). Countries seem to move into a closer band: higher-inequality countries move down (Portugal, Poland, Greece, Spain) while most of the rest moves upward. Breaking down into halves (not shown) the strong declines in Portugal and Poland are due primarily to the upper half, although lower-half

---

[59] See Blau and Kahn (2009) for a more detailed international analysis based on this data set.

[60] As a result levels cannot be precisely compared cross-country. Finland, the Netherlands, and Sweden sample full-year workers, which may partly explain their relatively low levels of inequality.

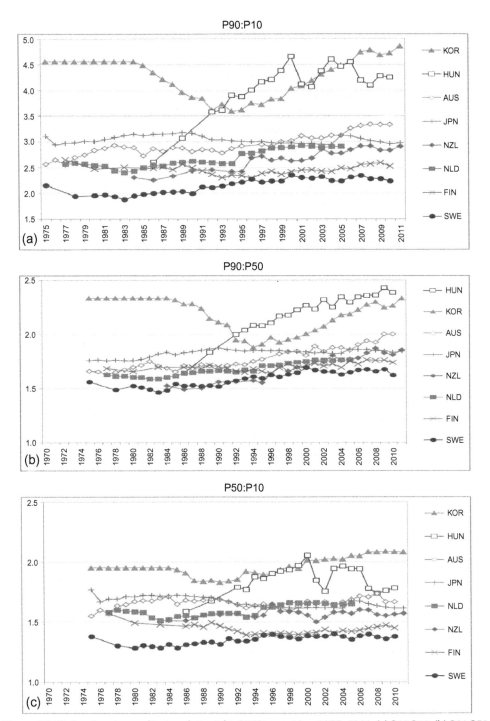

Figure 18.17 Earnings inequality trends in eight OECD countries, 1975–2011. (a) P90:P10. (b) P90:P50. (c) P50:P10. *Explanatory note*: full-time workers only; hourly earnings for NZL, weekly for AUS, monthly for HUN, JPN, ad KOR, full year for FIN, NLD and SWE. Source: *OECD Earnings decile ratios database*.

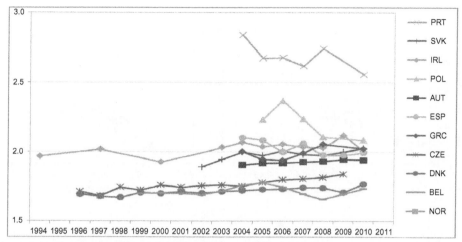

Figure 18.18 Short-run earnings inequality trends in 11 OECD countries, 1994–2011. *Explanatory note*: Gross earnings only; full-time workers except DNL (all, head count) and NOR (all, full-time equivalents). Source: *OECD Earnings decile ratios database.*

inequality also falls. Portugal combines extremely high levels in the upper half with low levels in the bottom half. For the rest, increases and decreases seem split roughly equally between the two halves.

18.3.3 Additional Evidence on Earnings Inequality in European Countries and the United States

From the data that we will be using in Section 18.5 we have derived a cross-section comparison for the most recent year, which provides a useful complement to the above stylized facts. It covers 27 EU countries, Iceland and Norway, as well as the United States. First, we consider a selection of inequality indicators, keeping in mind the household context that was discussed in Section 18.2. In the analysis of income inequality it is common practice to make use of the *Gini concentration index* or, to a lesser extent, of the *mean log deviation* (thanks to its property of decomposability). In earnings inequality analysis, by contrast, the most common indicator is the *standard deviation of log earnings* and/or the *decile or percentile ratio*. In Figure 18.19 we show that different measures provide largely similar country rankings in a cross-country perspective, whereas Table 18.1 provides the correlation indices for the same variables. As known from the literature the first two indices look at the bulk of the distribution, whereas the other two emphasize better what is happening at the tails (Cowell, 2000—see also Heshmati, 2004).[61]

---

[61] We speculate that the rather lower level of correlation found for the standard deviation may be attributable to top incomes.

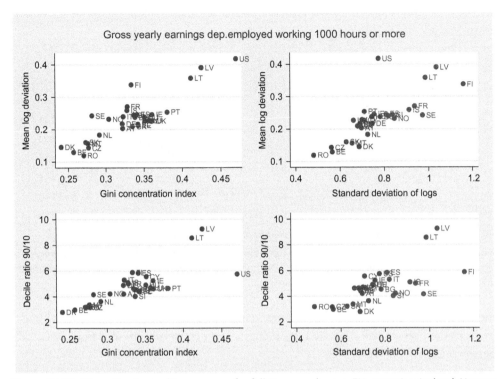

Figure 18.19 Alternative inequality measures for full-time employees, EU countries, Iceland, Norway, and United States, 2010. Note and Source: *See Table 18.1.*

Table 18.1 Cross-country correlation indices of various inequality measures, annual earnings of full-time employees, EU countries, Iceland, Norway, and United States, 2010

	Gini index	Mean log deviation	Standard deviation of logs	Percentile ratio 90/10
Gini concentration index	1.000			
Mean log deviation	0.871	1.000		
Standard deviation of logs	0.409	0.770	1.000	
Decile ratio 90/10	0.790	0.855	0.689	1.000

Explanatory note: Full time is defined as working 1000 h per year or more.
Source: Authors' calculations on EU-SILC 2010 and PSID 2011.

Inasmuch as the tails of the distribution may be affected by the increasingly diversified regimes in working hours, we prefer to work with the Gini concentration index, and we provide evidence of various inequality dimensions with the help of this measure. We start with a country overview, as reported in Table 18.2. The first column shows the level of inequality associated with labor earnings, which here include gross earnings from employees and the self-employed together with benefits received by the unemployed.

Table 18.2 Inequality measures for individual annual and hourly earnings and hours, EU countries, Iceland, Norway, and United States, 2010

	Gini of annual labor earnings (including self-employed and unemployment benefits)	Gini of annual gross earnings (hours > 1000) dependent employment	Gini of annual hours worked (positive values)	Gini of hourly gross wages dependent employment	Correlation of hours and hourly wages
Austria	0.376	0.322	0.167	0.325	−0.162
Belgium	0.332	0.257	0.173	0.266	−0.284
Bulgaria	0.422	0.338	0.084	0.318	−0.150
Cyprus	0.392	0.352	0.130	0.350	−0.077
Czech Republic	0.341	0.277	0.095	0.252	−0.124
Denmark	0.278	0.240	0.108	0.228	−0.190
Estonia	0.412	0.342	0.117	0.351	−0.208
Finland	0.361	0.333	0.156	0.340	−0.271
France	0.376	0.328	0.176	0.321	−0.201
Germany	0.420	0.322	0.181	0.307	0.038
Greece	0.485	0.335	0.146	0.338	−0.245
Hungary	0.392	0.351	0.084	0.317	−0.004
Iceland	0.338	0.328	0.172	0.337	−0.196
Ireland	0.448	0.361	0.210	0.374	−0.216
Italy	0.407	0.323	0.135	0.308	−0.230
Latvia	0.494	0.425	0.114	0.401	−0.124
Lithuania	0.494	0.412	0.099	0.403	−0.144
Luxembourg	0.428	0.357	0.166	0.355	−0.145
Malta	0.347	0.276	0.109	0.285	−0.156
Netherlands	0.359	0.292	0.174	0.290	−0.123
Norway	0.329	0.304	0.134	0.287	−0.115
Poland	0.464	0.342	0.122	0.354	−0.178
Portugal	0.453	0.380	0.104	0.374	−0.144
Romania	0.419	0.270	0.046	0.271	0.045
Slovak Republic	0.347	0.273	0.082	0.253	−0.084
Slovenia	0.397	0.337	0.073	0.314	−0.102
Spain	0.444	0.341	0.142	0.313	−0.209
Sweden	0.321	0.282	0.139	0.336	−0.295
United Kingdom	0.466	0.361	0.193	0.371	−0.094
United States	0.570	0.470	0.164	0.603	0.036
Average	0.408	0.332	0.133	0.331	−0.145

Source: See Table 18.1.

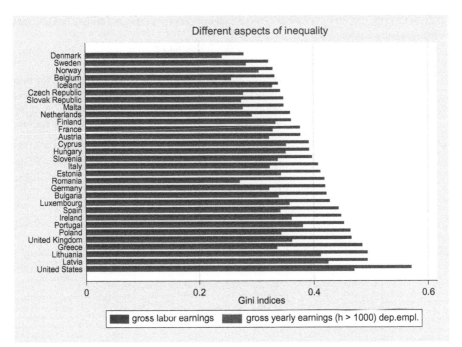

Figure 18.20 Inequality in annual labor earnings, EU countries, Iceland, Norway, and United States, 2010. Source: *See Table 18.1.*

The level found here always exceeds the one pictured in the second column for the earnings of full-time employees who comprise a subset of the population considered in the first column. Manifest country-rank reversals occur, plausibly due to a large share of self-employment (as in the case of Greece, Poland, or Romania—see Table 18.A1 in Appendix B) and/or the combination of the unemployment rate and the generosity of the welfare state (as in the case of the Nordic countries—see also Figure 18.20).

Where countries differ more is in the distribution of working hours: because the distribution of hours worked is much less unequal than the distribution of wages (compare second and third columns of Table 18.2), the inequality in hourly wages (computed dividing yearly earnings by worked hours) tends to mimic the inequality in yearly earnings (correlation coefficient is 0.90).[62] This is another important dimension of inequality in the labor market, because given the existing demand for labor inputs, this work can be accomplished by a variable number of individuals, according to existing labor standards

---

[62] The US exception is accounted for by the fact that hourly wages for European countries are deduced by dividing annual earnings by worked hours, and in the PSID the interviewees are directly asked about their hourly wage. Using the same accounting procedure would reduce the Gini index on hourly wage for the United States to a more reasonable 0.47.

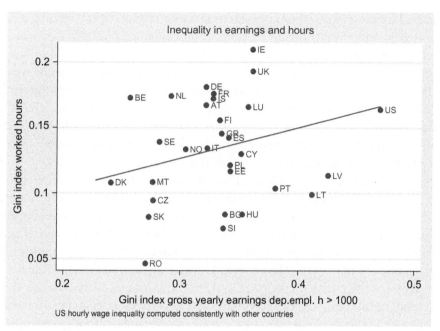

Figure 18.21 Inequality in earnings and hours, EU countries, Iceland, Norway, and United States, 2010. Source: *See Table 18.1.*

and cultural attitudes (regarding female participation, labor sharing within the couples, retirement rules, and so on).

As can be seen from Figure 18.21, the distribution of work may contribute to global earnings inequality, despite being the lowest in formerly planned economies (especially Romania, Czech and Slovak Republics, Hungary, and Slovenia). When a job is characterized by full-time working hours the contribution of working hours to inequality is minimal; by contrast, when flexibilization of the labor market allows for various regimes of working hours (as in Ireland or Great Britain, but consider also the Netherlands, where part-time jobs are widespread), it contributes to the observed inequality in individual annual earnings (which can be partially mitigated by household dynamics, as previously discussed in Section 18.2).[63] However, the picture obtained here by means of aggregate indices is purely impressionistic, as hours and hourly wages tend to be negatively correlated in many countries. As a consequence of the latter, a high inequality in hours

[63] These data on correlation between hours and hourly wages should be taken with caution, because the latter measure is obtained by dividing annual earnings by the former. As a consequence, hours and wages inequality are positively correlated. Thus, any measurement error in the latter generates a measurement error in the opposite direction for the former. However, unless different countries are hit by measurement errors in different (and systematic) ways, cross-country comparisons are still informative of the flexibility in adjustment.

accompanied by a high inequality in hourly wages may produce a low level of earnings inequality; note, however, that this is a possible outcome not a necessary one and that measurement error in hours enhances the risk of spurious correlation.

It is interesting to note that individual workers may react to lower wages by working longer hours—South Korea provides a clear example (Cheon et al., 2013, Figure 2.9). This is consistent with a standard model of labor supply where the income effect dominates the substitution effect. Competing explanations refer to a sort of Veblen's effect: partitioning workers by income layers, if consumption depends on consumption of richer people, an increase in the socioeconomic distance increases the hours worked (Bowles and Park, 2005). The empirical evidence does not contradict this viewpoint (see the final column of Table 18.2, where we have computed the correlation between hours and wages at the individual level). Although the correlation is negative almost everywhere, its intensity varies across countries: in some countries it exceeds 0.20 (notably Belgium, Finland, and Sweden), in other countries it does not differ from zero, suggesting an independent distribution of wages and hours (e.g., United Kingdom and United States as well as Germany—see also Bell and Freeman, 2001). Institutions may be responsible also for this outcome, because employers and workers may have different degrees of freedom in arranging working-hours regime and/or resorting to nonstandard labor contracts. Thus, the two dimensions of inequality (hours and wages) correlate with the same set of institutions, and for this reason in the econometric analysis of Section 18.5 we will allow for this decomposition. But even the correlation between hours and wages itself may be influenced by existing regulations, as it can be considered as evidence of a higher or lower flexibility: the evidence depicted in Figure 18.22 shows that the possibility of adjusting hours when wages are relatively low contributes to reducing earnings inequality.[64] For this reason, in the sequel we will study the correlation between this flexibility measures and LMIs.

The overall picture in terms of earnings inequality is well shown in Figure 18.20: inequality is higher in the so-called liberal market economies (United Kingdom, United States, and Ireland) to which one should add some "transition-to-market" economies (such as Poland, Lithuania, and Latvia) and the Mediterranean countries (Greece, Spain, and Portugal). At the other extreme we find the Nordic countries (except Finland). As Figure 18.23 shows in a clear way, the main determinants of this country ranking derive from the availability of employment opportunities, because countries characterized by high employment rates (including self-employment) are also the less unequal from the point of view of labor earnings. This is partly by construction: because we retain in our sample the entire labor force of the country, whenever the employment rate rises

---

[64] The United States does represent an outlier, but even after removing this observation, the correlation between the two variables in Figure 18.22 remains positive.

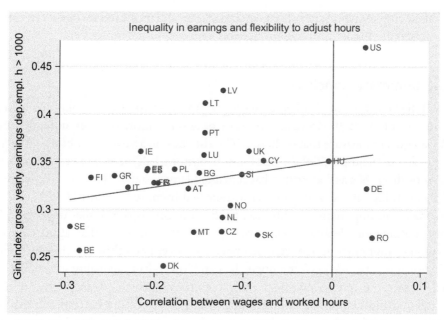

Figure 18.22 Inequality and flexibility for adjustment, EU countries, Iceland, Norway, and United States, 2010. Source: *See Table 18.1.*

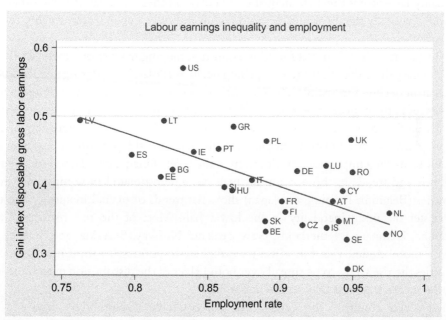

Figure 18.23 Inequality and employment, EU countries, Iceland, Norway, and United States, 2010. Source: *See Table 18.1.*

(and the unemployment rate consequently declines) the measured inequality in earnings declines (see the model proposed in Section 18.5).

18.3.4 Summary Conclusions

A key stylized fact for the United States is that hourly-earnings inequality has increased secularly over the last 40–45 years, not more or less, but more or even more, depending on the inequality measure that is chosen. The rise rests on a virtually continuous increase in inequality in the top half of the distribution; bottom-half inequality grew sharply until the end of the 1980s and after that has remained largely stable. The sharp upward evolution of earnings at the very top, that is reflected by now infamous Top 1% incomes share, makes an important contribution to the continuous rise of that upper half. This is borne out by more detailed changes based on all 100 percentiles that, at the same time, shows some emptying out between the upper and lower tails of the earnings distribution.

A similar divergence between upper-half and lower-half inequality in recent years is found also for the other English-speaking countries (Australia, Canada, Ireland, New Zealand, and the United Kingdom) though the stability of the bottom half may have started somewhat later than at the beginning of the 1990s, or was already there for most of the time. Note, however, that the absolute levels of inequality may differ substantially between these countries, both overall and in the two halves. In some cases bottom-half inequality far exceeds top-half inequality whereas in other countries it is the other way around—naturally the diverging evolution tends to inflate upper-half inequality relative to the bottom half.

The picture is less clear-cut for other countries, ranging from strong increases (Korea and Hungary since the 1990s) to compelling declines (Poland and Portugal in the 2000s; and a small decline for Spain). The comparison is complicated though by international differences in the concept of earnings and therewith in the sampling of the wage-earning population (by the way, also for Australia, Ireland, and New Zealand here above). The sampling often targets full-time employees only, ignoring the part-time ones, who may actually be making important contributions to the level of inequality. Therefore, inequality levels and trends in those countries may be underestimated in comparison. Some countries (Belgium, Finland, and Japan) show flat trends of overall inequality and tend to register declining inequality in the lower half. Most of the rest (Austria, Czech Republic, Denmark, Netherlands, New Zealand, Norway, Slovakia, and Sweden) do show a more modest rise, but a rise nevertheless. In contrast to the English-speaking countries the rise seems to be spread over both halves of the distribution even if the level and the increase are less than in the upper half.

For a few countries the gender pay gap could be consistently compared. This decreased strongly in the United States, more than in the United Kingdom, Canada, or Germany, and from a high level, so that currently, the gaps are of largely the same magnitude. In the US educational differentials between the better-to-best educated and the lower-to-least educated have grown significantly. No internationally comparable stylized facts are available for those differentials though one may assume that they will have grown in many cases albeit to different degrees.

A cross-section comparison of 27 EU countries, Iceland, Norway, and the United States underlines the importance of including the employment chances or, in other words, the distribution of individual hours worked, and not focusing exclusively on the distribution of earnings. The two distributions hang together and do so in different ways, partly depending on LMIs which may make the distribution of hours over individual employees more unequal, e.g., by allowing flexibilization or encouraging part-time hours. Naturally, the effect on household earnings depends on the combination of both hours and wage levels across the members of the household.

18.4. THEORETICAL APPROACHES TO WAGE DISPERSION AND THE ROLE OF INSTITUTIONS

18.4.1 The Wage Inequality Debate 1980–2000 and the Role of LMIs

We start this paragraph with a brief introduction of the evolution of the literature on wage dispersion up to 2000. We go back to the start of the literature on inequality in the 1980s to better understand the current situation and fill a lacuna in existing overviews. This is followed by a more detailed discussion of the study of LMIs in the rest of this introduction. After that we discuss recent contributions in two main directions: supply and demand (4.2) and institutions (4.5); we sum up our findings at the end (4.7).

The literature in which the contemporary discussion on the dispersion of wages is rooted took off seriously in the course of the 1980s, kicked off with a detailed picture of changing male and female inequalities in the United States by Peter Henle and Ryscavage (1980).[65] This literature focused initially on the factual question about whether inequality had increased or not, and it took some time before the factual doubts about that growth dissipated,[66] though factual questions have remained on the agenda throughout. It did not take long before the "why?" question started being asked and answers were sought in many directions—more often than not in different directions at the same time incurring a risk of *ad hocery*. From the start, some of these routes led to what in due course have become known as LMIs. For example, Plotnick (1982) attributed the (slow) increase in the variance of log (male) annual earnings—"earned income"

---

[65] Henle (1972) already showed an increase in earned income inequality over 1958–1970.

[66] Blackburn and Bloom (1987) compared studies with conflicting outcomes, spelling out important differences in sample choice and definitions, and were about the first to consider both men and women; they concluded that "the time profile of earnings inequality, measured across individual workers, has been quite flat since the late 1960s" (p. 604) combining a decrease in inequality among women with an increase among men.

as it was usually called—between 1958 and 1977 entirely to the differential effects of the level of unionization, the dispersion in weeks worked, the age distribution of workers, and the inequality of education. Dooley and Gottschalk (1984) looked for a demographic explanation (viz. cohort size and the baby boom), and Dooley and Gottschalk (1985) added—on the factual side—the insight that real earnings of men's earnings below a low-pay threshold were lagging behind.[67] Bluestone and Harrison (1982) launched the thesis of deindustrialization and expansion of low-wage employment, which in a later book (Bluestone and Harrison, 1988) turned into the famous "Great U-turn" of growing inequality. This lent political significance to the issue, which was particularly viewed as a polarization negatively affecting the middle class, which may sound familiar to current debates.[68]

Thus, education, institutions, demographics, and the composition of the economy made an appearance in the literature almost from the start. From the early 1990s, international trade and especially the competition with low-wage countries were added as other explanations (e.g., Wood, 1995). However, this is outside the focus on LMIs of the current chapter.[69] Though the interest in demographics may have waned (apart from the fact that gender has become a staple ingredient), the attentiveness to educational differentials, institutions, and the composition of the economy—industries and sectors at the time, occupations and tasks nowadays—has grown into a vast literature over the 1990s. The interest in education focused on the demand for skills in the economy on the one hand and their supply by the labor force on the other hand (e.g., Juhn et al., 1993). This has ushered in the thesis of "skill-biased technological change" (SBTC for short) (Bound and Johnson, 1989, 1992; Levy and Murnane, 1992) as the driving force behind the demand for skills. For some time this became the canonical model for explaining growing wage inequality. Evidently, the composition of the economy is not unrelated to this, if only because the skill structure differs between industries.

Technological change and economic composition together have become the supporting vector for the attention paid in the literature to supply and demand—or "market forces"—as explanatory factors for differences and changes in wage inequality. In their first overview of the literature, Levy and Murnane (1992) recommend future research to "get inside the black box of the firm" (p. 1374) and pursue the hedonic theory of labor demand that views a worker as possessing a fixed package of separate productive abilities and the wage as the sum of payments to them. The worker cannot separate these abilities and sell each to the highest bidder (Mandelbrot, 1962). As a result, the unit price

---

[67] The threshold was defined as $3, a good 40% above the Federal minimum wage in 1975.

[68] Harrison et al. (1986) brought the issue to the Congress; presidential candidates George W. Bush and Michael Dukakis discussed the status of the middle class and the nature of job growth in their campaigns of 1988 (Karoly, 1988, 13).

[69] Compare Machin (2008) for an evaluation, finding little support for this explanation.

of a productive ability may vary across sectors (Heckman and Sedlacek, 1985). Basically, Levy and Murnane seem to point in the direction of the route taken more recently by Acemoglu and Autor (2011) with their tasks-based approach. At the same time, it illustrates that technology is difficult to pin down empirically in economic studies and is usually subsumed in the unexplained part of modeling, also in the study of inequality. Although Levy and Murnane focus almost exclusively on the United States, Gottschalk and Smeeding (1997) broaden the horizon to include various European and other countries. They pay considerably more attention to institutions and signal important problems of conceptualization and measurement and stress that both market forces and institutional constraints cannot be missed in the analysis. Gottschalk and Joyce (1998) focus on the evolution of inequality in international comparison and conclude that market forces can be used to explain much of the cross-national differences that have been attributed in the literature to differences in LMIs. They hasten to add that this does not mean that institutional explanations do not matter but that the presumption should not be that they always provide binding constraints. Basing themselves on both direct and indirect evidence, Katz and Autor (1999, Section 5.5), in their comprehensive overview of the literature on wage structure and earnings inequality, view SBTC as perhaps the most important driver of the long-run growth in demand for more educated workers. They are less assertive about an acceleration in the trend. One important issue for further research they see is that the advantage of the better skilled may be transitory and for the long run depend on a continuing chain of technological changes or, alternatively, that 20th-century technological changes may happen to be systematically skill biased. Another question is whether the change is exogenous or may endogenously be affected by the supply of different skills.

Parallel to the market view, the institution-focused approach thrives. Fortin and Lemieux (1997) convincingly demonstrate its relevance basing themselves on both current American experience and effects of the Great Depression. There are some empirically obvious candidates for explaining wage inequality—the extent of union membership and the minimum wage given the clear declines in both the United States and the significant international differences, including the (de)centralized nature of wage bargaining. Freeman (1991) finds an important but not overwhelming role for unionization in relation to increasing inequality; by contrast, DiNardo and Lemieux (1997) explain two-thirds of the American-Canadian difference in male wage inequality growth from the faster decline of American unions; Blackburn et al. (1990) attribute only a small role to the declining minimum wage. DiNardo et al. (1996) find a substantial contribution to increasing wage inequality for the declining level of the minimum wage between 1879 and 1988. Though Levy and Murnane (1992) mention these institutions in their overview, they barely touch upon institutions—and then for the United States only—and apparently see no clear research agenda there. During the rest of the 1990s, however, the interest in institutions widens far beyond the above-mentioned. This receives great stimulus from international comparisons where differences in institutions can more easily get into the limelight. *Working under Different Rules* (Freeman, 1994), *Differences and Changes in Wage Structures* (Freeman and Katz, 1995), and Blau and Kahn (1996) bring together important empirical studies of a variety of countries. On a somewhat different tack from wage inequality, Freeman (1988) and Richard Layard and Stephen Nickell (1991) contribute on LMIs and macroeconomic performance in OECD countries. At the same time, Card and Krueger (1995a) dispel the consensus regarding the negative employment effects of the American minimum wage. As we will see later, these effects have remained a bone of contention up to this very day for their effects on employment, but much less for those on the wage distribution that are generally agreed to be compressing (Blau and Kahn, 1999). The *Handbook of Labour Economics*, Volume 3, concludes the 1990s by offering a rich palette of contributions on wage formation and inequality and institutions. Katz and Autor (1999) explicitly focus on earnings inequality and explanations from supply and demand on the one hand and from institutions on the other hand; Blau and Kahn (1999) treat LMIs in detail, and Brown (1999) specifically considers the minimum wage literature. Nickell and Layard (1999) also discuss the effects of LMIs but in relation to economic performance in general (the "natural rate of unemployment" and the later NAIRU), a different strand in the literature going back to Friedman (1968).

18.4.2 Defining and Analyzing LMIs

Given the importance of the subject for this chapter we will pay attention to the issue raised by the treatment of institutions before turning to the discussion of recent developments in the inequality literature in the next two sections. We distinguish between conceptualizing (method) and analyzing institutions and consider this at a general level in the present subsection, which boils down to the question of how economic analysis accounts for the existence of institutions. More specifically, their role in wage-inequality analysis is discussed in Section 18.4.5.

18.4.2.1 Method

First, the definition of institutions, and of LMIs in particular, seems in need of more precision, generically as well as in specific cases.[70] Too often in the literature they seem to be considered too obvious—and therewith perhaps too difficult—to warrant explicit definition. As Nickell and Layard (1999) say, "It is difficult to define precisely what we mean by labour market institutions, so we simply provide a list of those features of the labour market which we shall consider." In the words of Freeman (2007), "While economists do

---

[70] In the words of Freeman (2000, 11) "The absence of a general metric for measuring institutions at the national or firm level creates a problem for institutional economics. Measurement is, after all, the sine qua non of any scientific endeavour." See Autor (2013) for a similar worry regarding definitions and measurement for the tasks approach.

not have a single tight definition of an institution, per Justice Potter's famous statement about pornography, they know institutions when they see them, and they see them everywhere." Those who actually venture a definition come up with very broad ones, such as "A labour market institution is a system of laws, norms or conventions resulting from a collective choice and providing constraints or incentives that alter individual choices over labour and pay" (Boeri and Van Ours, 2008, 3), that may be begging important questions—in this case: Is the alteration of choice a practical matter or a theoretical issue? If the latter, this poses the risk that by definition any institution will imply a deviation from the theoretical ideal and also that institutions will be conceptually difficult to endogenize, meaning that an institution might endorse changes in behavior that have already taken place instead of causing such changes. It may also make the identification of institutions differ between different theories. Further to the restriction to laws, norms, or conventions: what about organizations? A trade union is an organization aimed at furthering the interests of its members.[71] Can a policy be an institution or not—as, e.g., active labor market policies are regarded an institution by Nickell and Layard (1999) and by Eichhorst et al. (2008)?

Institutions started their career in the inequality discussion as union density and the (de)centralized nature of wage bargaining. These are factors that can obviously influence individual wages, but they are neither law, nor regulation or rule, and seem closer to physical organization. The minimum wage, another institution also present from the start, is (often) in the law though. Not only in the inequality debate but more broadly, institutions have come to encompass a wide array of factors, and there seems to be no clear defining limit as to what can qualify as one or not. This makes institutions not only difficult to delineate but also tends to lend them a fundamentally *ad hoc* character. The selection of LMIs does not necessarily result from a systematic scrutiny but seems to reflect trial and error based on constrained and sometimes even biased knowledge. How otherwise to explain the immensely strong focus on unions while employer associations hardly figure, in spite of the fact that they are equally involved in collective bargaining and that "employer density"—the percentage of workers in a sector who are employed by the negotiating firms—and not union density may actually provide the basis for declaring a collective agreement generally binding.[72] The attention paid first to union density and only much later, when this appears to fail as an explanation, to the coverage of

---

[71] Checchi and Garcia Peñalosa (2008, 607) do distinguish "employee organizations outside the direct control of policy-makers" as one form of "collective intervention" encompassed in LMIs.

[72] Alan Manning (2011, 978–979) draws attention to employer collusion and points to research showing that "some institutions and laws in the labour market serve to aid collusion of employers to hold down wages." Though, in his view, it is clear that employers do not *en masse* collude, it would still seem logical to test centralized wage bargaining that results in protracted wage moderation for its potential as a form of nationwide monopsony.

collective bargaining, is another case in point.[73] Last but not least, it is difficult to understand, given the highly central role of educational differentials in the wage-inequality literature, that the educational system figures so little as an institution in this literature.[74]

In addition, in the literature, LMIs can be viewed as specific factors with an actual origin and presence in the labor market and only there (e.g., wage bargaining), but equally they may be factors that affect the labor market from outside that market (e.g., income taxation or the tax wedge). The latter definition, as a factor affecting the labor market irrespective of its origin, opens the door to a myriad of institutions and, unsurprisingly, many other factors have been added in the 30-year course of the debate. For example, Nickell and Layard (1999, 3047) include home ownership in their list of labor market "institutions" (their quotation marks), inspired by the finding of Oswald (1996) that it is one of the most important barriers to the geographical mobility of labor.[75] Freeman (2007) lists, without presumption of being exhaustive: mandated works councils, employment protection laws, minimum wages, extension of collective-bargaining coverage, lifetime employment, peak-level collective bargaining, wage flexibility, teams, job rotation, temporary employment contracts, social dialogue, apprenticeship programs, occupational health and safety rules, defined benefit, and defined contribution pension plans. To name a few other examples: Oliver (2008) draws attention to industrywide wage scales, Boeri (2011, 1183) adds regulations on working hours, Blau and Kahn (2002, 4) include the public-sector share of employment. Antidiscrimination measures easily come to mind as a further example,[76] and we will meet more below when we discuss recent contributions to the literature. Obviously, the discussion of earnings in relation to household income in the preceding section suggests new candidate institutions such as parental leave, child care provisions, or individual entitlements to the choice of working hours.

Second, the analysis of the effects of institutions still demand attention even if they were clearly defined, for several reasons: the actual significance of individual institutions and the type of effects they may have, their embedding in a larger set of institutions and also in the wider economy, and the potential pitfalls of international comparisons which have taken center stage in the literature.

---

[73] Availability of internationally comparative data was also a problem (e.g., Koeniger et al., 2007, 344).

[74] Leuven et al. (1997, 2004) criticize deriving skill levels from, inter alia, years of schooling in international comparisons. Nickell and Layard (1999, 3046) point to the same. Freeman and Schettkat (2001) and Mühlau and Horgan (2001) elaborate on the issue for the low skilled. Based on data from the International Adult Literacy Survey of the 1990s these contributions point out that the American low-skilled attain much lower levels of literary and numeracy than their counterparts in various European countries. At first glance the recent Survey of Adult Skills seems to underline the same 29 years later (OECD, 2013, 118–125).

[75] See also Blanchflower and Oswald (2013).

[76] Charles and Guryan (2007, 2008) explain one-quarter of the racial wage gap for blacks in the United States from employer prejudice.

In many studies institutions seem to be taken at face value and equated with what they look like *de jur*, and, naturally, it is their *de facto* implementary force or "bite" that counts (Eichhorst et al., 2008, 18). That bite may depend on its particular enforcement—laws and rules can be strictly enforced or they may be a dead letter to which no one pays attention. Enforcement may be automatic when it is the responsibility of a supervising inspectorate, or it may be costly and cumbersome if it is the responsibility of the individual who feels duped—minimum wages and other provisions diverge importantly in this respect (Benassi, 2011). Institutions may also be general provisions whose precise nature is filled in by actual policy. The minimum wage is again a case in point when the law establishes its mere existence while its actual (uprated) level is determined by policy making—the United States being the leading example.[77] For policies the bite is the heart of the matter.[78] Note that this further blurs the distinction between institution and policy. Institutions may also differ in the nature of their implementation: legally prohibiting or prescribing certain behavior, or economically encouraging or discouraging it, and consequently in the type of effects they may have. An example may be a prescriptive rule of employment protection versus a hiring subsidy for disadvantaged groups of active labor market policies. Note that the implementation of an institution may not be either black or white but can have different shades, a cross section within as well as between countries, and can also differ over time.[79] Evidently, the *de facto* significance of an institution may come close to actually measuring its effects, and this can pose a methodological problem.

Often the effects are scrutinized for *individual* institutions as there is no clear theory on their coherence or interactions as a (national) set (Eichhorst et al., 2008, 17, 24, 29). However, institutions may partly balance or reinforce each other, say a country with strong employment protection could be mitigating the possible upward pressure on wages by collective bargaining, or employment "at will" may be neutralized by individual contracts. It is easier to expand union membership if workers are protected from the threat of being fired. Diffusion of part-timers may reduce the quest of work leave permits. Generosity of unemployment benefit schemes may increase voluntary mobility and raise the demand for publicly provided training. Similar functions may be provided by different institutions. For example, Garnero et al. (2013) conclude to the functional

---

[77] See Boeri (2012) for a comparison of the effects of minimum-wage setting mechanisms, depending on the roles of unions and employers and the government in the process, across 66 countries.

[78] For the bite of the minimum wage see Kampelmann et al. (2013, 12–16) who discuss its relative money level in the wage distribution (Kaitz index) together with the share of minimum-wage employment in total employment. Eurostat's database on minimum wages ([earn_mw_cur] at http://epp.eurostat.ec.europa.eu/portal/page/portal/eurostat/home) is restricted to the former.

[79] For example, for involuntary dismissals, Dutch employers have the choice between following an administrative procedure, with no costs apart from the time it may take to settle, or going to court, which normally will be costly as it implies a severance payment. In recent decades the choice between the two routes has drastically shifted toward the latter option even though the administrative procedure has become more efficient (Salverda, 2008, 105).

equivalence with regard to earnings inequality of statutory minimum wages in some European countries and minimum-pay provisions of sector collective labor agreements combined with high bargaining coverage in other countries.[80] Gottschalk and Smeeding (1997, 647) warn for the risk of double counting the effects of institutions when considered in isolation (union density and the minimum wage in their example).

There may be deeper dangers in international comparisons. Institutions may catch the eye more readily than other international differences and be considered in relative isolation, enhancing the risk of their effects being overestimated. Blau and Kahn (1999) focus their overview on some 20 OECD countries stating that this selection permits utilizing "the similarity in educational levels, technology, living standards and cultures among these countries as de facto controls in examining the effects of institutions." Freeman (2007, 18) cautions against the methodological implications of the fact that the number of countries is small compared to that of institutions. Conversely, appearances may be deceptive and the potential dissimilarities of institutions that may look the same at first sight, need to be taken into account. We have already seen the possible divergence between educational attainment and skill levels in spite of the extensive efforts spent on a standardized measurement of educational systems (ISCED). Freeman's (2000) plea for a metric may be more demanding than thought but above all it may be necessary but not sufficient. The above observations about the enforcement and bite of institutions apply particularly in a comparative context, to prevent comparing apples with pears. More importantly, there may be deep-seated differences in the general economy as have been illustrated forcefully in recent years by, for example, the havoc wreaked by the larger propensity to consume by private households in the United States as compared to many other countries.[81]

In sum, the study of the role of institutions needs to account for the force of those institutions, their mutual interactions at the national level, supply and demand in the labor market, and also the broad structure of the economy. The latter potentially puts on the research agenda institutions that affect the economy more broadly such as those governing the flexibility of exchange rates[82] or international capital movements, which have undergone important liberalization in many European countries since the end of the 1970s and may have weakened employees and unions vis-à-vis employers. An important lesson of the minimum wage debate and the contribution made by Card and Krueger (1995a), who no longer started from the *a priori* of a negative effect on employment, is to prevent a stacking of the cards against institutions. As Freeman (2007, 2) observes, "many adherents to the

---

[80] The resulting levels may differ though.

[81] Glyn et al. (2003) find that the European–American services-employment gap resides largely in the distribution (retail) activities and personal-services sector and show "that the much lower European level of goods consumption per head of the population was the dominating influence in explaining the much lower levels of employment than in the US distribution" (p. 173).

[82] Blau and Kahn (1999, 1454) in their conclusions argue that exchange rates can adjust to compensate for institutional rigidities (and warn that introducing the euro may take away that opportunity, which has been borne out in the meantime).

claim (that labour institutions impair aggregate performance, authors) hold strong priors that labour markets operate nearly perfectly in the absence of institutions and let their priors dictate their modelling choices and interpretation of empirical results."

18.4.3 Why Do LMIs Exist?

The economic rationale and potentially beneficial effects of creating and/or preserving LMIs need to be accounted for from the start.[83] According to Freeman (2007) there are three ways in which institutions affect economic performance: by altering incentives, by facilitating efficient bargaining, and by increasing information, communication, and possibly trust. In his cursory review, the evidence shows that labor institutions reduce the dispersion of earnings and income inequality, which alters incentives, but finds controversial effects on other aggregate outcomes, such as employment and unemployment.[84] In his opinion, the modest effect would be attributable to the fact that "the political economy of institutional interventions rules out collective bargaining settlements and regulations that are truly expensive to an economy. No country would impose a minimum wage that disemployed a large fraction of the work force; and no union or employer would sign a collective bargaining agreement that forced the firm to close." In this perspective, a positive contribution of institutions would be observed whenever and wherever they solve transaction cost of individual bargaining, according to the prediction of the Coase theorem.

Regulations in the labor market as defined by Botero and coauthors (2004) emerge by government desires to protect the weaker side in a labor relationship.[85] They show that

---

[83] Some recent examples are Acemoglu (2003), who argues that LMIs stimulating wage compression in Europe may also incentivize investments in improving the productivity of the low skilled; Sutch (2010), who points to capital deepening and increased educational attainment as a consequence of the minimum wage (compare also Freeman, 1988); Nickell and Layard (1999), who consider that employee representation rights may induce management/worker cooperation and enhance productivity; or Atkinson (1999), who demonstrates that unemployment benefits, if accounting for their real-world rules, may actually be employment enhancing. A more fundamental, long-run perspective relates the origins of the welfare state, be it Beveridgean or Bismarckian, to the development of dependent employment.

[84] Similarly, Betcherman (2012) indicates four rationales for the existence of LMIs: "imperfect information, uneven market power (between employers and workers), discrimination, and inadequacies of the market to provide insurance for employment-related risks" (p. 2). According to him, the literature can be classified according to a positive view (that he calls *institutionalist*), when institutions solve coordination problems, and a negative view, that he calls *distortionary*, when institutions prevent economic efficiency.

[85] "Regulation of labour markets aiming to protect workers from employers takes four forms. First, governments forbid discrimination in the labour market and endow the workers with some 'basic rights' in the on-going employment relationships, such as maternity leaves or the minimum wage. Second, governments regulate employment relationships by, for example, restricting the range of feasible contracts and raising the costs of both laying off workers and increasing hours of work. Third, in response to the power of employers against workers, governments empower labour unions to represent workers collectively, and protect particular union strategies in negotiations with employers. Finally, governments themselves provide social insurance against unemployment, old age, disability, sickness and health, or death" (Botero et al., 2004, p. 1342).

the orientation of governments to the political left is often associated to more stringent labor market regulations (*political power theory*), but find the legal origin to be even more relevant to accounting for cross-country variation (especially when considering the transplantation of legal systems in the colonial era, much in line with sociological theories of path dependence—*legal origin theory*). According to the latter, common-law countries tend to rely more on markets and contracts, whereas civil-law (and socialist) countries on regulation (and state ownership): as a consequence, civil-law countries do regulate labor market more extensively than common law ones. The legal origin, possibly adopted for efficiency reasons in mother countries, becomes exogenous for former colonies, thus allowing a study of its causal impact on the origin of institutions.[86] Following this line of argument, several papers account for the endogenous emergence of some LMI as an (optimal) solution for at least of a subset of agents. A controversial contribution to this approach is given by Saint-Paul (2000), who aims to identify gainers and losers of a given institution. In his view, each institution creates a rent (i.e., a difference between the paid wage and the outside option), which is unevenly distributed in the workforce. Because the employed workers enjoy most of the benefits of these rents, they obviously represent the largest constituency advocating the preservation of institutions (*political insider mechanism*). This has to be traded-off against the rise of unemployment, which is associated to higher wages, and this represents the most serious threat to the continuation over time of an institutional setup. If we accept Saint-Paul's view that the most relevant conflict within the workforce is between the skilled and the unskilled, then "labour market rigidities mostly redistribute between skilled and unskilled labour" (Saint-Paul, 2000, p. 6). Ignoring within-group inequality, this means that institutions affect earnings inequality by affecting the skill premium and the (unskilled) unemployment rate. In this perspective, institutions emerge when the constituency represented by the employed unskilled dominates those of the skilled and of the unemployed (which is a different coalition than the one supporting fiscal redistribution, for example). The relationship between inequality and institutions becomes ambiguous: institutions create or enhance wage differences, but wage inequality may support the introduction of LMI as an alternative device for redistribution.[87] Similarly, different institutions may reinforce each other, revealing

---

[86] When they analyze the causal impact of legal indices on a measure of the skilled/unskilled differential, they find than only the "Social Security laws index" as an inequality enhancing causal impact (using the legal origin as instrument).

[87] "Inequality, i.e. the gap between the skilled and unskilled productivities, determines the intensity of internal conflict. As we have argued, it is because of that internal conflict that it pays the middle class coalition to opt for rigid LMIs. Therefore we expect that the support for rents will be greater, the greater the inequality. This is actually true over some range, if inequality is low enough. But past a certain threshold inequality reduces the support for rents, because at high inequality levels the cost of rigidity in terms of job loss is too big" (Saint-Paul, 2000, p. 8). See also Brügemann, 2012, who builds a model where stringent protection in the past actually reduces support for employment protection today.

the potential existence of a *politicoeconomic complementarity*, which contributes to explaining why empirically we observe clusters of institutions, often indicated as *social models* (Amable, 2003; Hall and Soskice, 2001). For reasons of viability, labor market reforms are more likely to emerge after a period of crisis, when the bias toward the status quo is weakened and the rise of unemployment allows the formation of alternative constituencies. A rather different view on rents in the labor contract, however, is offered by Manning (2011). According to him, rents are pervasive in the labor market, because of frictions in hiring and recruiting, separation costs due to investment in specific human capital, and collusive behavior on both sides (employers and employees). If imperfect competition is therefore taken as the relevant paradigm,[88] the regulation of this market (via wage bargaining or wage setting by public authorities, as in the case of minimum wage) acts as a second best device, which may achieve Pareto improvements (as in the case of the minimum wage under monopsony).

In a recent contribution, Aghion et al. (2011) frame the existence of labor market regulations as an incomplete and less-efficient substitute for the quality of labor relations. They rationalize their argument with a model of learning of the quality of labor relations: the unionization decision is seen as a costly experimentation device aimed at finding out more about cooperation at the workplace. Thus, the existence of legal provisions (such as a minimum wage) reduces the learning incentive. Because beliefs are gradually updated based on past experiences, the authors obtain the prediction of a coevolution of beliefs (as measured by the quality of labor relations perceived by top executives) and institutions (as measured by the stringency of minimum wage).[89] As a consequence, distrustful labor relations lead to low unionization and high demand for a direct state regulation of wages. In turn, state regulation crowds out the possibility for workers to experiment with negotiating and to learn about the potential cooperative nature of labor relations. This crowding-out effect can give rise to multiple equilibria: a "good" equilibrium characterized by cooperative labor relations and high-union density, leading to low-state regulation (the Nordic countries), and a "bad" equilibrium, characterized by distrustful labor relations, low-union density, and strong state regulation of the minimum wage (some of the Mediterranean countries, and especially France). Their empirical application covers 23 countries over the period 1980–2003, and shows that the quality of labor relations is negative correlated with either union density or state regulation of the minimum wage (while controlling for other institutional measures such as unemployment benefits and the tax wedge).

[88] "Many empirical observations (e.g., equilibrium wage dispersion, the gender pay gap, the effect of minimum wages on employment, employers paying for general training, costs of job loss for workers with no specific skills to list only a few) that are puzzles if one thinks the labour market is perfectly competitive are simply what one might expect if one thinks the labour market is characterized by pervasive imperfect competition" (Manning, 2011, 62).

[89] Although this prevents any causality analysis, it resembles the path dependence often advocated by sociologists in the analysis of institutions.

Also recently, Alesina et al. (2010) have proposed a model where the emergence of employment protection and minimum wage provision is accounted for by cultural traits, namely the strength of family ties. In their theoretical model, individuals are born with different preferences with respect to family ties: those characterized by weak ties are geographically or sectorally mobile and achieve an efficient allocation by being matched to jobs providing the highest productivity; however, those characterized by strong ties rationally select labor market rules (such as firing restrictions and minimum wages) that restrain the monopsonistic power of local employers while accepting a less-productive allocation. Another rationale of living close to family members is that it provides additional insurance against unforeseeable shocks (including unemployment). The authors prove the existence of two stable Nash equilibria: one where everybody chooses weak family ties, votes for labor market flexibility, and changes her or his initial location (high mobility); another where everyone chooses strong family ties, votes for stringent labor market regulation, and stays in the original (birth) location. In the latter case the labor market is monopsonistic because workers are immobile, and workers limit employers' power by means of labor regulations. Empirically, they show the existence of positive cross-country correlations between the strength of family ties and labor market rigidities. More convincingly, they also find that individuals who inherit stronger family ties (i.e., second-generation immigrants from countries that record high preferences for family values) are less mobile, have lower wages, are less often employed, and support more stringent labor market regulations.

In their historical review of the introduction of severance payment schemes in 183 countries, Holzmann et al. (2011) suggest three rationales for the introduction of such schemes: (1) as a primitive form of social benefits (anticipating the introduction of benefits for unemployment and retirement), thus providing an *answer to a demand for insurance*; (2) as an efficiency-enhancing human resource instrument (a sort of bonding between workers and firms, to minimize the loss of firm-specific knowledge) solving the *hold-up problem*; and (3) as a proper job-protection instrument, intended to enhance permanence in employment of main earners in the household.

If we restrict ourselves to the minimum wage, the historical account provided by Neumark and Wascher (2008) suggests that this institution has emerged as a counterbalance of power in the labor contract, preventing the exploitation of child labor (minimum-wage settlement power assigned to law courts in New Zealand in 1894 and in Australia 2 years later) or women (Fair Labor Standards Act, introduced at the federal level in the United States in 1938). Viewed in this perspective, the minimum wage would represent a device aimed at preventing a "race to the bottom" competition among firms, more than a measure aimed at sustaining the incomes of poor families.[90] Seen from

---

[90] In a similar vein, Agell and Lommerud (1993) proposed a model where setting higher wages promoted higher growth by eliminating low productivity enterprises.

the side of union leaders, minimum-wage legislation represents an improvement in the outside options of workers, inducing an increase in their bargaining power. The sum of these two effects may create an unusual coalition of large companies and worker unions supporting the introduction and/or the periodical updating of wage minima.[91]

18.4.4 Do LMIs Matter for the Economy?

In their overview of LMIs, Blau and Kahn (1999), with a careful discussion of the ratio-nale, draw some implications for studying the causalities. They look back at "an explosion of research" on the economic impact of institutions and conclude that institutions do appear to matter. In their view, the evidence across the literature that institutions affect the distribution of wages is more robust than for employment levels. Freeman (2001) supports this, saying that institutions identifiably affect the distribution, but that other effects on the macroeconomy and on efficiency are hard to discover and modest at best. Later he states even more forcefully that "institutions have a major impact on one impor-tant outcome: the distribution of income ... By contrast, despite considerable effort, researchers have not pinned down the effects, if any, of institutions on other aggregate economic outcomes, such as unemployment and employment" (Freeman, 2009, pp. 19–20; see also Freeman, 2005). Nickell and Layard (1999, p. 3078) seem more ret-icent about the role of institutions when they conclude that "[m]ost of the gross features of unemployment and wage distributions across the OECD in recent years seem expli-cable by supply and demand shifts and the role required of special institutional features such as unions and minimum wages is correspondingly minimal." These are not the last words about the role of institutions with regard to the dispersion of wages—let alone that of earnings incorporating the hours dimension which we deem of special interest here—as we will see when we turn to more recent contributions to the literature in the next two sections and to our empirical approach in Section 18.5.

So over the 1980s and 1990s a vast literature has grown, which seems to tend into two main directions: supply and demand on the one hand, institutions on the other. Each side acknowledges the relevance of the other, there is talk even of an SDI (supply-demand-institutions) model (Freeman and Katz, 1995; Katz and Autor, 1999; see also Lemieux, 2010) but little has grown out of that since, and in reality—understandably given the above-mentioned concerns—the prime focus of the market view and the institutional view seem to have grown more independent of each other. The flurry of institutions make them look overdetermined, and, by comparison, technological change—the driver of supply and demand—underdetermined. Over the 2000s many new arguments have been developed: polarization of the distribution, offshoring of productive activities, sharp growth in the upper tail of the distribution, top taxation, focus on tasks and skills, two-tier

---

[91] See their review of empirical evidence based on minimum wage voting across US states (Neumark and Wascher, 2008, chap. 8).

nature of reforms of institutions, growing importance of performance pay, rise of "new institutions," and, last but not least, new contributions have been made with regard to the minimum wage. These contributions seem firmly placed in either one or the other of the two main directions. In this respect the recent Volume 4 of the *Handbook of Labor Economics* repeats the preceding Volume 3. Acemoglu and Autor (2011) hardly even touch upon institutions in their conclusions, whereas Boeri (2011) focuses exclusively on aspects of institutions.

We think that Manning's (2011) approach of imperfect competition in the labor market, which aims to leave behind the thinking in terms of canonical models and departures from these, may indicate a third route that can provide a different and ultimately more unified perspective. From the starting point that rents are inevitable and pervasive—though it is unclear how large they are and who gets them—Manning (p. 996) suggests that their very existence creates a "breathing space" in the determination of wages and allows the observed multiplicity of institutions on efficiency grounds. He concludes (p. 1031) that "[o]ne's views of the likely effects of labour market regulation should be substantially altered once one recognizes the existence of imperfect competition."[92] An important corollary seems that institutions do not "cause the labour market to function differently from a spot market" (Blau and Kahn, 1999, p. 1400) but that this market should not be considered a spot market but instead needs institutions for its proper functioning from the very start. Thus, a better principle for analyzing supply and demand as well as institutions may be that institutions are equally pervasive: every act of supply and demand goes together with an institution of some kind, and their existence and effects shall be accounted for from the start.

18.4.5 Recent Theories Based on Demand and Supply of Labor Inputs

The review of theories of earnings inequality provided by Neal and Rosen (2000) a decade ago focused on the allocation of workers to jobs (the Roy model), on individual human capital accumulation (the Ben Porath model), on the search models (yielding variations in tenure—for a recent review see Rogerson et al., 2005 or Rogerson and Shimer, 2011), and on imperfect observability of either ability or effort (efficiency wage and contract theories). They adopted an individual perspective of wage determination, which did not allow great scope for the institutional framework to affect the resulting earnings distribution. In such a perspective, wage inequality can be considered as the outcome of changes in the relative demand and supply of labor inputs. Starting from the original paper by Katz and Murphy (1992) and the literature originated since then (reviewed in Katz and Autor, 1999), the so-called *canonical model* predicts that the wage differential between skilled and unskilled workers accommodates an expanding demand for skilled

---

[92] Note, however, his observation that the actual effects of (or, for that matter, the limits to) institutions are an empirical matter.

labor (SBTC, induced by introduction of computers in production) and a contraction of the demand for unskilled labor (due to increasing competition by developing countries). Demographic changes (variations in cohort size, immigration) and/or educational choices may partly attenuate (or even offset) these changes. The resulting dynamics of inequality can be predicted by tracking down these movements (Acemoglu, 2003).

In this framework, wage-setting institutions affect the flexibility of relative wages, creating a trade-off between wage differential and relative unemployment; when considering inter-industry wage differentials, it translates into lower employee quit rates and longer queues of job applicants.[93] Consider, for example, an increase in the relative demand for skilled labor (*upskilling*), at given supply of labor inputs. If the wage differential cannot adjust the relative excess demand for skilled labor (because minimum-wage legislation prevents a downfall of the unskilled wage and/or union bargaining prevents an excessive rise of the skill premium), then the unskilled workers will experience an increase in their relative unemployment rate. This effect will be more pronounced the higher the substitutability between labor types.

It did not take long into the new century before Card and DiNardo (2002) mounted a fierce critique of the thesis of skill-biased technological change. Their arguments are both theoretical and empirical. From a theoretical point of view, a constant SBTC rate does not yield a permanent skilled/unskilled wage differential, as long as the relative supply is sufficiently elastic (see Atkinson, 2007b). On the empirical side, they revisit the evolution of American wage inequality since 1967, almost back to the starting point of the literature but now extending to include more recent occurrences over the 1990s. This refers to the problem already mentioned that technological change lacks a positive identification in economic models but is commonly subsumed in the unexplained leftovers. To avoid the tautology that this implies, they look for independent empirical measures of technological change that can be incorporated in the model: the introduction of PCs and the Internet, the size of the IT sector in the economy, and the use of computers by individuals at work—particularly disaggregated by personal characteristics.[94] From this material, the general trend in technological change seems unabated over the 1990s, if not increasing because of the Internet. The disaggregated use of computers points, among other things, to a larger role among women than men, particularly among the less-educated women whereas the best-educated men have closed the gap to their female counterparts. From this, Card and DiNardo conclude that computer technology should have widened gender differentials for the most highly educated and narrowed them for the least educated.

---

[93] Katz and Autor (1999) also consider product market regulation, in that it creates differences in sectoral rents, which are partly appropriated by wage bargaining, thus contributing to the overall wage inequality.

[94] Note that DiNardo and Pischke (1997) show robust wage differentials for the use of pencils (in Germany) and draw attention to the possible selection effect that office tools tend to be used more by higher-paid workers.

On the inequality side, they argue from a fresh inspection of the data (using different samples, sources, and inequality measures), "viewed from 2002" as they say, that there has been a pattern of a strong episodic rise in inequality in the 1980s, preceded by near stability before and after, during the 1970s and 1990s respectively.[95] From a comparison of the two, demand and supply, they conclude to "a fundamental problem ... that rises in overall wage inequality have not persisted in the 1990s" and also to various puzzles, including the fact that the gender differential has diminished irrespective of education. In summary, they find the evidence for SBTC to be surprisingly weak. They do think there has been substantial technological change but deplore that this has diverted attention away from inequality trends that cannot be easily explained by this. The critique of SBTC is the main point of their contribution, not the design of an alternative explanation of inequality. However, Atkinson (2007b, 2008) points out that their critique of SBTC ignores the dynamics of the process and implicitly assumes a curve of skilled labor supply whose speed of adjustment is inversely related to the distance from an infinitely elastic one. International differences in the wage differential may reflect differences in the speed of that adjustment. Card and DiNardo end their contribution by teasing the reader with a quick exercise about the minimum wage that shows a strong correlation between the evolution of its real level and aggregate hourly wage inequality (P90:P10) over the entire period 1970–1999.

Autor et al. (2006, 2008) have shown that the period of rising earnings inequality in the US labor market during the 1970s and the 1980s has been replaced by *job polarization* (simultaneous growth of the share of employment in high-skill/high-wage occupations and low-skill/low-wage occupations) in the following two decades. Despite the fact that the emergence of polarization crucially hinges on the procedure according to which occupations are ranked (educational attainment, wage rank, task content), also many European countries feature similar patterns: the decline in blue-collar jobs (mostly held by uneducated men) and the expansion of service jobs (mostly held by women and youngsters). One suggested interpretation (Autor et al., 2003) points to the increase in productivity of information and communications technology (ICT), which would have replaced middle-skilled administrative, clerical, and productive tasks with computer-operated machines.

Autor et al. (2008) have taken up the challenge of what they call a "revisionist" literature of both the description and the explanation of US wage inequality since the 1970s. They object to the episodic interpretation of the rise in wage inequality; that is, they contrast this with ongoing inequality growth in the top half of the distribution combined with initially (1980s) increasing and subsequently (1990s) declining inequality

---

[95] Lemieux (2006a,b) finds a concentration of the increase in the 1980s together with a concentration of within-group inequality change among male and female college graduates and females with some college, implying an increasing concentration of wage inequality at the very top of the wage distribution. In addition, Lemieux (2006c) finds a role for changes in the composition of the labor force after the 1980s.

in the bottom half.[96] They view that initial lower-half increase as episodic indeed and incorporate the minimum wage as a potential explanatory factor in their approach; however, they find only a modest role when modeled together with relative supply and demand. For the 1990s they agree that the slowing down of inequality growth poses a problem for the SBTC thesis, but only for the "naïve" SBTC story as they call it, which is based on a dichotomy of high skills and low skills. They aim to improve on this by arguing a more detailed approach, based on the dispersion of occupations by their skill levels, measured as the mean years of schooling of an occupation's occupants (weighted by their hours worked), and distinguishing between different types of tasks that can be performed in an occupation, showing that this works out differently between the 1980s and the 1990s.

The occupations and tasks approach can be viewed as a step along the route for further research pointed out by Levy and Murnane (1992), opening up an important black box albeit at the level of industry and not of the firm.[97] In principle, though not always in practice, it also advances on the traditional SBTC approach by distinguishing between properties of the occupation and of the worker. Routine tasks were first stressed by Autor et al. (2003), polarization by Goos and Manning (2003, 2007). The approach aims to provide an answer to the problem posed to the SBTC thesis by the strong slowdown in wage inequality growth after the 1980s. It implies a significant shift in the SBTC thesis and the underlying empirics. Modern technology is complementary no longer to higher levels of skills and education but to nonroutine types of work. Although before workplace computerization was indiscriminately interpreted as skill biased and furthering the demand for higher skills, it is now taken to substitute for routine tasks that are defined as cognitive and manual activities that can be accomplished by following explicit rules. Therewith it reduces the demand for workers predominantly performing such activities, implying a more polarized effect on educational levels. Autor et al. (2003) focus on American employees, and the period 1960–1998 and combine CPS data with Dictionary of Occupational Titles (DOT) classifications. They analyze the shift in tasks that has resulted from both compositional changes across occupations and changes in task composition within occupations, and find strongly diverging trends: negative for routine cognitive tasks from the 1970s and routine manual tasks from the 1980s and strongly positive for nonroutine cognitive tasks whereas nonroutine manual tasks decline steadily and strongly over the entire period.[98] Note that they focus on employment effects and do not link the results to wage inequality,[99] though the implication is clear and to some extent spelled out in Autor et al. (2006): low-wage and high-wage employment both

---

[96] They agree to compositional effects (Lemieux, 2006a), but for the lower half of the distribution only.

[97] Dunne et al. (2004) find most of the action between and not within establishments in US manufacturing.

[98] The authors consider the latter tasks as orthogonal to computerization and therefore not impinging on their results.

[99] Interestingly, Goos and Manning (2007) fill that gap, showing—for 1983 only, the first possible year—that routine jobs are concentrated in the middle of the US wage distribution.

expand while jobs with intermediate pay contract. Notably, employment trends do not seem to differ between the 1980s and 1990s, though, naturally, the gaps between increasing and decreasing types of tasks become much wider.

Goos and Manning scrutinize the UK data for similar developments between the mid-1970s and the late 1990s, using a variety of data sets, samples, and methodological approaches. They find a clear polarization across the distribution of occupations and, linking to wages, also across the wage distribution. They check various tenets of the SBTC thesis. They discuss first whether labor supply may have contributed to the polarization, because of the rapid growth in female workers, and better-educated workers, but they find these changes unable to explain the polarization pattern. As to educational attainment, they find an increase in almost all occupations. This may be due to either rising requirements of the jobs or overeducation of the occupants. The data are insufficient to decide between the two hypotheses though the authors seem inclined to opt for the second one. On the demand side they touch upon other factors than technology that may have contributed: trade and especially the structure of product demand—though these are not necessarily fully independent from technology—but find no explanation for polarization either. From a counterfactual exercise of the wage distribution over the 1975–1999 period restricted to changes in the occupational distribution only they conclude that polarization can explain large fractions of the rise in wage inequality (51% lower half, 79% upper half). They underline the important implication that the contribution of within-job inequality is minor. This contrasts sharply with established explanations in terms of education and age where most of the action is within groups, and they point out that the between/within conclusion is sensitive to the choice of controls included in the earnings function. They leave open the explanation of inequality change in the lower half of the distribution which may be due to imperfect competition, including institutional changes such as declines in unionization or the minimum wage. Goos et al. (2009) show a polarization of employment by occupations for 16 European countries between 1993 and 2006; Goos et al. (2010, 2011, 2014) extend the analysis to include relative wages and also capture effects of product demand, induced by a lowering of relative prices in industries with routine tasks, and institutions. They find that relative occupational wage movements in Europe are not strongly correlated with technology and offshoring, which may be due to wage-setting institutions, and therefore consider relative wages as being exogenous. They conclude that the thesis of routine jobs is the most important explanatory factor for increasing polarization, and product demand shifts across industries mitigate it.

Dustmann et al. (2009) find increasing wage inequality for Germany in the upper half of the distribution over the 1980s and 1990s.[100] This is attributed partly to composition

---

[100] Spitz-Oener (2006) looks at the employment side of occupational polarization in Germany over the 1980s and 1990s.

changes and largely to technological change, as occupations at the top grow faster. For the lower half they find increasing inequality only in the 1990s, not before. For this they suggest possible episodic explanations such as a decline in unionization and an inflow into the country of low-skilled labor after the demise of the communist regime; the latter lends a role to the relative supply of skills. Following Autor et al. (2008) they conclude that the naïve or canonical SBTC hypothesis cannot explain these trends, but they find support for the "nuanced" tasks-focused hypothesis as they note that occupations in the middle of the distribution decline compared to those at the bottom. In summary, they believe that the German results add unifying evidence to the pattern of polarizing effects of technological change already found for the United States and the United Kingdom.

We conclude our discussion of this stream of the literature with its current culminating point, the overview and further development of the task-based approach to SBTC by Acemoglu and Autor (2011) for the latest *Handbook of Labor Economics* (Ashenfelter and Card, 2011).[101] Note, however, that Mishel et al. (2013) provide various arguments why the evidence for the job polarization of these is weak. Although the canonical model builds on the unity of skills, tasks, and job (better-educated/talented workers obtain skilled jobs where they perform more complex tasks), the task-based approach considers a job as a collection of tasks, which can be executed by workers of different abilities, though at different level of productivity, and even by machinery. The empirical classification of tasks is still in its infancy; they are classified according to three attributes: routine, abstract, manual. "Offshorability," meaning that the performance of certain tasks is internationally footloose, is added as another important job dimension, which can overlap with each of the three types of tasks.[102] This theoretical approach improves upon the canonical model by accounting for job polarization, real wage decline for some groups of workers (but not in a monotonic relationship with skill ranks), and offshoring as an alternative explanation of reductions in jobs to technical change.

---

[101] Autor (2013) adds a further overview of the literature stressing the need to develop a precise terminology and consistent measurement. He honorably concludes that "[t]he economics profession is very far from a full understanding of the interactions among rising worker skills, advancing technology, improvements in offshoring and trade opportunities, and shifting consumer demands in determining the division of labour, the growth of aggregate productivity, and the level and inequality of earnings within and between skill groups. The 'task approach' to labour markets does not come close to offering a solution to this vast intellectual puzzle" (p. 27). Surprisingly, he also sounds an optimistic note about the future of middle-skill jobs. Autor and Dorn (2013) make a further addition venturing consumer preferences as a second force next to technological change that can help explain polarization through the growth of low-skill services in the United States. However, one cannot be sure about the general validity of this approach as consumer preferences may differ significantly across countries.

[102] The concept of offshorability of jobs and its analysis in relation to wage inequality was developed during the 2000s by Levy and Murnane (2005), harking back to Blinder (2007), Lemieux (2008), and Blinder and Krueger (2009). Evidently, offshorability itself is conditional on both technological change and institutional preconditions.

Acemoglu and Autor's model considers a continuum of tasks (unit of work activity that produces output, similarly to occupations) and different levels of skills (capability to perform various tasks); given existing supply of skills in the labor market, profit maximizing firms allocate skills to tasks, given existing prices. Capital and/or offshoring may replace workers in performing tasks. The key assumption is the existence of comparative advantage of skills in executing tasks: more skilled workers are more productive in executing more complex tasks when compared to less-skilled workers. This structure creates a sort of *hierarchical sorting* associated to comparative advantage.

Wage flexibility ensures full employment of all workers. Given perfect substitutability among workers in task assignment, wages dynamics depend on the relative supply of skills (as in the canonical model) and on task assignment rules, which then allow for a potential competition in task execution posed by technological progress and/or offshorability. With their model they make a sharp prediction: "[I]f the relative market price of the tasks in which a skill group holds comparative advantage declines (holding the schedule of comparative advantage constant), the relative wage of that skill group should also decline—even if the group reallocates its labour to a different set of tasks (i.e., due to the change in its comparative advantage)" (p. 1152). The impact on the overall wage inequality is hard to predict, because the relative wages (high to medium skill and medium to low skill, when only three skill levels are considered) can move in opposite directions.

Acemoglu and Autor do not incorporate LMIs in their framework, which as they observe "depends crucially on competitive labour markets" (p. 1159) and can be thwarted by labor market imperfections of search and information and institutions such as collective bargaining by unions. The impact of certain LMIs may be enhanced by the way these affect the assignment of tasks to labor or capital as, for example, they may restrict the substitution of machines for labor for certain tasks, or conversely they may change the return to unionization, thus feeding back onto union density. The authors see this as an area for further research.

18.4.6 Recent Theories Based on LMIs

The other main current in the literature does take the existence and effects of LMIs into account. Also here, interesting contributions have been made throughout the 2000s. At the start of the new century, Blanchard and Wolfers (2000) launched their hypothesis that the internationally differential effects of institutions can be found particularly in countries' responses to shocks. This view can offer a solution to the problem that, on the one hand, shocks alone cannot explain country differences, and, on the other hand, institutions on their own cannot explain long-run country performances. Their focus is the macroeconomy and unemployment, not wage inequality. Blau and Kahn (2002) connect to the latter in much of their book, and later extend this further by accounting for demographic shocks (with Bertola, 2007). However, their strong focus on the international comparison of institutions may be the reason that they seem to overlook the shifting trend in the evolution of American wage inequality after the 1980s. The issue of this shift has been taken up by Lemieux (2008), for the United States. He objects to the consensus view on inequality growth that had taken root in the early 1990s which views this growth as secular and all-pervading. As we have seen his contribution (2010) extensively revisits the American data on the evolution of wage inequality, and pays particular attention to the very top of the wage distribution, improving on the traditional adjustment for top-coding. From this, he concludes that in the 1970s inequality change was not all-pervading, whereas it was in the 1980s (though it also already showed more convexity at the top than at the bottom), and that since the 1990s inequality growth has been concentrated at the top of the distribution. Growth in residual ("within") wage inequality is general in the 1980s, although later it is largely confined to the college-educated category. In particular, relative wages continue to grow for postgraduates and their annual returns to education compared to high-school returns double between the mid-1970s and the mid-2000s.

Lemieux (2008) also questions the consensus explanation of SBTC on the basis of this, but also because it leaves no room for a role of institutions in spite of the research that has shown the effects of unionization and wage-setting. He advocates an explanation that can account for both the above findings and the international differences and explores the possible contributions of institutions as well as of supply and demand.[103] He finds that deunionization can explain one-third of the expanding inequality in each of the two halves of the distribution, and is also consistent with the divergence of English-speaking countries, where top incomes grew much more, from other countries. In addition to this the decline in the minimum wage has augmented lower-half inequality in the 1980s.[104] On the side of supply and demand he thinks that more empirical research is needed before the tasks-based development of the SBTC thesis can be accepted as an explanation. That research should account for the fact that, contrary to what one would expect, the relative wages of occupations at the core of the IT revolution are suffering, and it should also answer the question why the process should not have occurred already during the 1980s. In addition, it should account for the growth of within-inequality at the top. For the latter he suggests modeling heterogeneous returns to education, which have

---

[103] His main objection to SBTC is that technology is widely available across countries, whereas inequality growth is recorded only in the Anglo-Saxon world. However, similar impacts are now also recorded in developing countries (Behar, 2013).

[104] Lemieux et al. (2009) add, as an additional institution, performance pay at the top—bonuses, stock options, etc.—and show that this can account for a large share of inequality growth above the 80th percentile of the wage distribution.

as a key implication that both the level and the within-dispersion of pay of the better educated can rise relative to the less educated at the same time.[105]

18.4.6.1 Top Incomes

Interestingly, Lemieux's conclusion about upper-tail growth is consistent with the findings in the top-incomes literature (Alvaredo et al., 2013; Atkinson and Piketty, 2007, 2010; Atkinson et al., 2011, especially the summary Chapter 12; Piketty and Saez, 2003, 2006). Often a strong rise in labor incomes at the top is found, particularly in the United States, but not only there.[106] This literature is suggestive of the role of yet another institution: income taxation, not as the traditional tax wedge but as marginal taxation at the top.[107] "Higher top marginal tax rates can reduce top reported earnings through three main channels. First, top earners may work less and hence earn less—the classical supply side channel. Second, top earners may substitute taxable cash compensation with other forms of compensation such as non-taxable fringe benefits, deferred stock-option or pension compensation—the tax-shifting channel. Third, because the marginal productivity of top earners, such as top executives, is not perfectly observed, top earners might be able to increase their pay by exerting effort to influence corporate boards. High top tax rates might discourage such efforts aimed at extracting higher compensation" (Atkinson et al., 2011). Thus, the rise in top incomes and pay may have been encouraged by the lowering of top marginal tax rates. However causation may also run in the opposite way, because the rise of capital incomes in recent decades may have produced pressure for tax reductions. In a recent series of papers, (e.g. Piketty and Saez, 2013) have proposed formal models where the relationship between taxation and earnings has been carefully scrutinized. Most of the argument is a supply-side story, in the presence of imperfections: a reduction in the degree of progressivity would stimulate more effort and bargaining of CEOs and high-rank cadres with stakeholders, thus raising earnings inequality. Piketty et al. (2011) show a strong negative correlation between the Top 1% share and the top tax rate for a set of 18 OECD countries since 1960; the correlation also holds for CEO pay after controlling for firm characteristics and performance. The element of luck in CEO pay seems to be more important when tax rates are lower. It may point to more aggressive pay bargaining in a situation of lower tax rates. The high top tax rates of the 1960s were then part of the institutional setup putting a brake on top compensation through bargaining or rent extraction effects. In their view, the SBTC explanation seems to be at odds with international differences in top pay shares as well as their correlation to tax rates.

---

[105] Slonimczyk (2013) links overeducation to the differential growth of inequality in the two halves of the distribution.

[106] For example for the Netherlands (in spite of stability of the top income share as a whole): see Salverda and Atkinson (2007) and Salverda (2013).

[107] DiPrete (2007) highlights the increase in external recruitment of CEOs and the concomitant growth of related institutions (governance and CEO pay benchmarking).

18.4.6.2 Minimum Wage[108]

New contributions to the literature of inequality and institutions are also found for various other individual LMIs. First and foremost, we consider the literature on the effects of the minimum wage—an old debate by now (as old as the Department of Labor (viz. 1913) according to some)[109] that nevertheless continues to attract passionate contributions. The combination of wage and employment effects taken together determines the effects on annual earnings and, ultimately, incomes. Especially the impacts of a minimum wage on employment remain a bone of contention—"the canonical issue in wider debates about the pros and cons of regulating labour markets" in the words of Manning (2011, p. 1026). A complication is that the employment effects likely relate to the level of the minimum wage and also differ between worker categories (e.g., Abowd et al., 1999; and also Philippon, 2001).

Neumark and Wascher (2008) hold a very critical attitude with respect to minimum wages. Exploiting cross-state and temporal variations in the United States, they conclude that minimum wages are ineffective in raising low wages and reduce employment opportunities for their earners.[110] However, Dolton and Bondibene (2011) analyze employment effects for 33 OECD countries over 1976–2008 and find that existing evidence of negative effects is not robust. Dube et al. (2010) generalize Card and Krueger's comparison of minimum-wage policy differences across US state borders and find no employment effects over 1990–2006, whereas Neumark et al. (2013) dispute their method and results. Allegretto et al. (2011) find no employment effects (including the hours dimension) distinguishable from zero over 1990–2009. Slonimczyk and Skott (2012) use US state variation to confirm their model predictions of a negative effect

---

[108] There is also an emerging literature on developing-country case studies, which confirm the inequality-reducing impact of minimum wage, both in the formal and informal sectors of the economy (e.g., Gindling and Terrell, 2009; Lemos, 2009).

[109] Note that the UK minimum wage, introduced very recently in comparison with the United States (1999 vs. 1938) has been a great source of new evidence thanks to the careful role of the Low Pay Commission—see Butcher (2011).

[110] "Based on the extensive research we have done, and our reading of the research done by others, we arrive at the following four main conclusions regarding the outcomes that are central to policy debate about minimum wages. First, minimum wages reduce employment opportunities for less-skilled workers, especially those who are most directly affected by the minimum wage. Second, although minimum wages compress the wage distribution, because of employment and hours declines among those whose wages are most affected by minimum wage increases, a higher minimum wage tends to reduce rather than to increase the earnings of the lowest-skilled individuals. Third, minimum wages do not, on net, reduce poverty or otherwise help low-income families, but primarily redistribute income among low-income families and may increase poverty. Fourth, minimum wages appear to have adverse longer-run effects on wages and earnings, in part because they hinder the acquisition of human capital. The latter two sets of conclusions, relating to the effects of minimum wages on the income distribution and on skills, come largely from U.S. evidence; correspondingly, our conclusions apply most strongly to the evaluation of minimum wage policies in the United States" (Neumark and Wascher, 2008, p. 6).

of minimum wages on the skill premium, owing to increasing overeducation of college-educated workers following an increase in mismatch. The overall effect is that a minimum wage would lead to a rise in both total and low-skill employment, accompanied by a fall in earnings inequality. Giuliano (2013) studies personnel data of a large US retail firm and finds no aggregate employment effect but composition effects that run contrary to standard theory. Interestingly, Dube et al. (2012) focus attention on effects on employment flows. In the view of Richard Sutch (2010), the disemployment effects of pricing low-skill jobs out of the market may create incentives to invest more in human capital.

Most of the recent discussion revolves around whether there are spillover effects on wages higher than the minimum. A higher statutory minimum wage in itself compresses the wage distribution as it prohibits paying lower wages. However, the higher minimum rise may send ripples up the wage distribution—in the most extreme case all wages could be increased to the same extent and the dispersion of wages would remain unchanged. The minimum wage debate of the 2000s has generated new contributions particularly on this spillover or knock-on issue. Wages higher up may be raised for several reasons (Stewart, 2012, 618): the higher price for low-skilled labor incites substitution demand for higher-skilled workers, realignment of the marginal product of minimum wage workers affects the marginal product of other workers, firms maintain within-firm pay differentials for motivation, and reservation wages increase more broadly in certain sectors.

During the 1990s, spillover effects were detected in various contributions. Card and Krueger (1995a, 295) conclude to no effect at or above the 25th percentile of the wage distribution, which is well above the relative position of the minimum wage. Lee (1999) endorses an approach that compares to an estimated "latent" wage distribution (in the absence of the minimum wage). He finds effects beyond the P50:P10 ratio on other percentile differentials across the entire distribution. At the end of the 1990s, the consensus view agreed to spillover effects though not extending high up the distribution (Brown, 1999, p. 2149).[111] Over the 2000s, views on this have changed. Neumark and Wascher (2008, Section 4.3.2) discuss the previous literature and observe that the percentile approach as used by Lee may conflate spillover effects with disemployment effects of the minimum wage: as some of the least-paid lose their jobs, wage levels may increase at all percentiles of the distribution. Neumark et al. (2004) do not link to the wage distribution but look instead at actual impacts on workers with wages up to eight times above the minimum wage, using US states with no rise in their minimum wages as controls. They find a wage elasticity with respect to the minimum wage of 0.25 at 1.5 times the minimum wage and much smaller effects above that level. Autor et al. (2010) are puzzled by Lee's effects on the upper half of the distribution and attribute these to an omission of variables and the insertion of the median wage on both sides of the equation (division bias). They stick to Lee's basic approach but propose econometric corrections

---

[111] Lee (1999) is not covered in Brown's (1999) overview.

and demonstrate the effects using a longer panel of US states with more variation in state minimum wages. They find substantial widening effects on the lower tail (P50:P10) of the decline in the real minimum wage over 1979–1988, but these effects remain well below those found earlier in the literature; they find only small effects for 1988–2009. Then they are puzzled by the large and increasing effects even at the 10th percentile in spite of the fact that currently the minimum wage is received by less than 10% of workers. They confront those effects with the possibility of mismeasurement and misreporting of lower wages in the data and conclude from a detailed analysis that it cannot be ruled out that all of the spillover found is actually the result of such data problems.

Stewart (2012) adopts the direct estimations of Neumark et al. (2004) over a range of fractions of the minimum wage extending up to six times the minimum wage using differences-in-differences for comparisons between these factions. In addition, he exploits comparisons between minimum wage upratings that have differed in size (including no change period before the introduction of the minimum wage in 1999) while accounting for differences in general wage growth. Using British data, he concludes to no spillover effects. As the level of the minimum wage is steadily below the 10th percentile, he draws the logical inference that the changes in the minimum wage have not affected lower-half wage inequality as measured by P50:P10. That seems fair enough, but it also puts on the table the strength of this inequality measure as evidently the minimum wage may significantly affect the within-distribution of the bottom decile. The top-to-bottom ration S10: S1 may be better suited to capture such effects. Butcher et al. (2012) revisit the effects on wage inequality and spillovers for the United Kingdom and do find spillover effects up to the first quartile of the distribution. In their view, decades of discussing the employment effects of the minimum wage—with very little to none as the consensus outcome—have been focusing on second-order effect, and instead they advocate developing a theoretical framework for thinking about its first-order effects on wage inequality, which, naturally, should be able to allow the possible absence of employment effects. They develop a non-competitive model with wage-posting instead of bargaining[112] with imperfectly elastic labor supply to the individual firm. The authors elaborate on their model to consider the spillover effects to wage levels above the minimum wage. They derive those from a comparison between the actual wage distribution at and above the minimum wage and a counterfactual latent wage distribution derived with the help of the distribution preceding the introduction of the minimum wage in 1999. They find higher levels for the former compared to the latter up to 40% above the minimum wage, which corresponds with the 25th percentile of the aggregate wage distribution.

---

[112] Wage bargaining cannot explain the frequent uniform payment of the same low wage to workers with rather different characteristics. Hall and Krueger (2010, p. 25) conclude that their findings from a special survey of wage posting and bargaining practices in the US labor market "is consistent with the view that a wage constrained by the minimum wage is inherently posted."

Finally, Garnero et al. (2013) show that statutory minimum wages (or equivalent systems) represented by sectoral minimum rates combined with high coverage of collective bargaining—see also Boeri (2012)—are very effective in reducing earnings inequality. They combine harmonized microdata from household surveys (EUSILC), data on national statutory minimum wages and coverage rates, and hand-collected information on minimum rates from more than 1100 sectoral-level agreements across 18 European countries over several years (2007–2009—see also Kampelmann et al., 2013). Alternative specifications confirm that institutional variants of setting a wage floor reduce both between and within-sectors wage inequalities.

18.4.6.3 Union Presence

Card et al. (2004) study the relationship between wage inequality and unionization in the United States, Canada, and the United Kingdom over the period 1980–2005, showing that within narrowly defined skill groups, wage inequality is always lower for union workers than for nonunion workers. For male workers, union coverage tends to be concentrated at the middle of the skill distribution, and union wages tend to be "flattened" relative to nonunion wages. As a result, unions have an equalizing effect on the dispersion of male wages across skill groups. For female workers, union coverage is concentrated near the top of the skill distribution, and there is no tendency for unions to flatten skill differentials across groups. The effect of deunionization on US wage inequality is stronger at the top end of the distribution than at the bottom, as shown by Lemieux (2008) when updating the DiNardo et al. (1996) decomposition. In addition, the increase of performance pay schemes may have enhanced the within-group wage inequality at the top end of US distribution.[113]

The decline in workers' bargaining power in the Anglo-Saxon world is recorded by several authors (see, for example, Levy and Temin, 2007), but we have not found any convincing decomposition of the relative contribution of each specific institutions. However, when taking the dynamics of the wage share in the domestic product as an overall indicator of workers' bargaining power, one would recognize a clear declining trend in most countries over the past decade, though some reversal can be recognized during the crisis period (ILO, 2008, 2010).[114]

---

[113] However, existing comparative evidence on differences in executive compensation between the United States and Europe suggests that this labor market is fully globalized, and pattern of remuneration are quite similar (except in the banking sector). See Conyon et al. (2011).

[114] "The slow growth in wages was accompanied by a decline in the share of GDP distributed to wages compared with profits. We estimate that every additional 1 per cent of annual growth of GDP has been associated on average with a 0.05 per cent decrease in the wage share. We also found that the wage share has declined faster in countries with a higher openness to international trade, possibly because openness places a lid on wage demands based on a fear of losing jobs to imports. Inequality among workers has also increased. Overall, more than two-thirds of the countries included in our sample experienced increases in wage inequality. This was both because top wages took off in some countries and because bottom wages fell relative to median wages in many other countries" (ILO, 2008, p. 59). See also Karabarbounis and Neiman (2013), who attribute the decline in wage share to the decline in the relative price of capital inputs.

A parallel decline in workers' bargaining power can underlie the decentralization of wage bargaining. Following recent changes in industrial relations in Denmark, Dahl et al. (2011) show the existence of a wage premium associated with firm-level bargaining relative to sector-level bargaining, and a higher return to skills under more decentralized wage-setting systems.[115]

18.4.6.4 Unemployment Benefit

Even if unemployment benefits and employment protection are negatively correlated in the data (Bertola and Boeri, 2003), in principle they do respond to the same problem of reducing the intertemporal variability of workers' earnings (Blanchard and Tirole, 2008).[116] This may explain why research has paid less attention to the contribution of unemployment schemes to inequality reduction. Corsini (2008) studies the dynamics of the college premium in 10 European countries over the last decade of previous century. He finds a positive impact of the generosity of unemployment benefit (but a negative correlation with duration), which is interpreted as the outcome of wage bargaining that takes into account the outside option.[117] If we shift to individual data analysis, the results of Paul Bingley et al. (2013) on Danish data show that access to unemployment insurance is associated with lower wage-growth heterogeneity over the life cycle and greater wage instability, changing the nature of wage inequality from permanent to transitory. Given data limitations, the authors are unable to control for moral hazard behavior of unemployed, who may be induced to lengthening their permanence in unemployment, thus increasing cross-sectional inequality.[118]

18.4.6.5 Employment Protection Legislation

Recent cross-country evidence has been summarized in the following way by World Bank (2012, 262): "Based on this wave of new research, the overall impact of EPL and minimum wages is smaller than the intensity of the debate would suggest." However, Martin and Scarpetta (2011) express a different view, arguing that EPL reduces workers' reallocation and prevents efficiency gains for highly productive workers, while avoiding

---

[115] Kenworthy (2001) discusses existing measures of wage-setting institutions.

[116] Chetty (2008) derives the optimal replacement rate for unemployment benefit schemes that depends on the reduced-form liquidity and moral hazard elasticities.

[117] Vroman (2007) discusses the correct measure of (average) unemployment compensation from aggregate public expenditure on subsidies, to be contrasted with standard OECD replacement rate and duration series, which are commonly used, despite their being completely hypothetical (because they are derived from microsimulation models) and do not correspond to actual payments to entitled unemployed workers.

[118] Using cyclical and across-US states variation, Farber and Valletta (2013) show that extending the duration of unemployment benefits (from a Federal requirement of a minimum of 26–99 weeks at the cyclical peak of late 2009) lengthens unemployment spells, via a reduction in exits from the labor force (and not in job finding due to reduced search effort).

job losses and/or real wage reductions for unskilled workers.[119] In their review they list a series of papers based on changes in dismissal regulation, which find mixed evidence of EPL impact on labor productivity (see, among others, Bassanini et al., 2009; Boeri and Jimeno, 2005; Kugler and Pica, 2008; Schivardi and Torrini, 2008). Productivity dynamics may translate one to one into wage dynamics in a competitive environment; in noncompetitive models, firing restrictions raise the bargaining power, creating artificial divisions among workers when groups of firms are exempted (see Leonardi and Pica, 2013). Similarly, EPL exemptions for firms may create artificial wage differences among workers, due to their differential cost, thus enhancing wage inequalities; for example, Karin Van der Wiel (2010) provides evidence referring to a policy reform of terms of notice in the Netherlands. A further connection between EPL and wage inequality can be found in comparative analysis: Bryson et al. (2012) show that higher labor (and product) market regulation is associated with lower use of incentive pay (ranging from 10% of covered workers in Portugal to 50% of the workforce in the United States). Inasmuch as incentive-pay schemes increase within-group earnings inequality (Lemieux et al., 2009), this induces a negative correlation at the aggregate level between earnings inequality and EPL indexes.

18.4.6.6 Labor Market Policies

Kluve (2010) provides an extensive meta-analysis based on a data set that comprises 137 active labor market program evaluations from 19 countries. Four main categories of ALMP are considered across European countries: (i) training programs, (ii) private-sector incentive schemes (such as wage subsidies to private firms and start-up grants), (iii) direct public employment programs, and (iv) "services and sanctions," a category comprising all measures aimed at increasing job search efficiency, such as counselling and monitoring, job-search assistance, and corresponding sanctions in case of noncompliance. His main finding is that traditional training programs have a modest significant positive impact on postprogram employment rates, but both private-sector incentive programs and services and sanctions show a significantly better performance. Evaluations of direct employment programs, on the other hand, are around 25% points less likely to estimate a significant positive impact on postprogram employment outcomes. Although effectiveness is here defined in terms of employment impact, they can be easily mapped one-to-one to wage inequality whenever the unemployed are taken into the picture.

---

[119] Similar results are found in Messina and Vallanti (2007). However results significantly differ when using aggregate or microdata. For example, using a German employer–employee matched data set. Bauer et al. (2007) do not find any evidence of variable enforcement of dismissal protection legislation on the employment dynamics in small establishments. Considering that labor churning is typically associated to increased earnings variability, their result would imply lack of correlation between employment protection and wage inequality. Analogous lack of significant impact of firing restrictions is found by in Martins (2009).

18.4.6.7 Stepwise Institutional Change

A new and different line of argument regarding institutions is nicely summarized by Boeri (2011). After reviewing existing institutional differences among European countries and stressing their persistence over time, he proposes a taxonomy of institutional changes (*reforms*), in terms of orientation and phasing-in. The orientation concerns the question whether they reduce (e.g., by making employment protection less strict and/or unemployment benefits less generous or by expanding the scope of activation programs) or increase the wedge (e.g., by increasing labor-supply-reducing taxes on relatively low-paid jobs) introduced by LMIs between supply and demand. Boeri accordingly classifies a reform as either decreasing or increasing the (institutional) wedge. The second characteristic relates to the phasing-in of reforms: this can be either complete or partial. In the former case, the change in the regulation eventually involves everybody. In the latter case, even at the steady state, the reform is confined to a subset of the population. The timing is also important. Even a complete phasing-in may involve a very long transitional period, so that the steady-state institutional configuration is attained beyond the planning horizon of management's potential involvement by the reform (Boeri, 2011, 1184). A two-tier reform is then defined as the case involving either a partial phasing-in or when its complete phasing-in requires more than 30 years, the average length of the working life in many countries. According to data collected over the period 1980–2007 for the European Union, the two-tier pattern is prevailing in most of the institutional dimensions. This has obvious implications in terms of earnings inequality, especially between insiders and new entrants (typically women and youngsters). With the help of a search model à la Pissarides-Mortensen, Boeri shows that institutions affect the threshold below which it is no longer convenient for either the employer or the employee to continue the work relationship. Even if the underlying inequality pattern depends on idiosyncratic shocks hitting individual productivity, the boundaries of the distribution of realized wages are institutionally determined, owing to variation in the equilibrium unemployment. According to the model an *increase in unemployment benefits* raises the reservation productivity at which matches are dissolved as the outside option of workers has improved: in equilibrium there is a higher probability of job loss, a lower job finding rate, higher unemployment and average wage.[120] Conversely an *increase in firing taxes* has the opposite effect of maintaining alive jobs with a lower match productivity. This reduces the gross job destruction rate and positively affects wages. An *increase in employment conditional incentives* (modeled as an employment subsidy) makes the labor market tighter, and increases the duration of jobs at the expenses of a decline in entry wages. Finally, an *increase in the activation scheme* reducing recruitment costs features higher

---

[120] For simplicity Boeri assumes that any unemployed person is entitled to the benefit, but actually this depends on the length of the contribution period and/or on belonging to specific categories (married/unmarried, with/without children, sector of employment, age).

job finding and job-loss rates, whereas the effects on unemployment and the average wage are ambiguous. When liberalizing (wedge-reducing) reforms are applied to only a fraction of workers (temporarily creating a dual labor market), then earnings inequality expands: insiders enjoy a surplus over outsiders at the same productivity levels, which is increasing in the difference in replacement rate offered to the unemployed (coming from long-tenured jobs with respect to those coming from short-tenured jobs), in the employment conditional incentive and in firing taxes, which matter more when workers have more bargaining power.

Returning to the more general, internationally comparative literature, developed by Blau and Kahn (2002) and others, we find the contribution of Koeniger et al. (2007) who look beyond cross-sectional differences at the comparative evolution of wage inequality over time, and extend to more OECD countries over a longer period, focused on overall wage inequality of males taken from the OECD database. They treat the various institutions (union density, union coordination/centralization, the minimum wage, employment protection, unemployment benefit generosity and duration, and the tax wedge) simultaneously and also model some interactions. On the demand side they control for the aggregate economy (unemployment rate), the relative supply of skills, international trade (import intensity), and technology (R&D intensity). They add some counterfactual simulations, including one that attributes US institutions to the other countries. They find compressing effects on the wage distribution of most institutions which explain at least as much as trade and technology do on the demand side. Applying American regulations would increase wage inequality in Continental Europe by 50–80%. The authors observe, however, that endogenizing the institutions, that means accounting for their dependence on supply and demand, will likely reduce the effects somewhat.

Finally, as we have observed above, the context of household (joint) labor supply potentially augments the number of institutions that need to be addressed, adding parental leave, maternity leave, part-time work regulations, and any other institution affecting the flexible use of working hours. Analyses of this (e.g., Dupuy and Fernández-Kranz, 2011; Thévenon and Solaz, 2013) are few, and they are focused on employment chances and/or pay penalties of gender/motherhood/family, not on the wage dispersion.

18.4.7 Summing Up

Over time the literature seems to have gone in two different directions that tend to grow further apart—not in the sense of interactions (one retorting to the other) but in the sense of integrating the approaches into one framework. Freeman (2007, p. 24) signaled the risk of creating the social science equivalent of "epicycles"—aimed at preserving Ptolemaic views on the earth as the center of the universe—for the institutional approach. However, the same danger may be looming for the supply-and-demand approach, which has been adding tasks, offshoring, and consumer preferences, in an attempt to dispel doubts about the relative demand of skills as a tautology. The institutional approach faces an abundance of institutions for which it lacks a clear criterion of choice; the supply-and-demand approach by contrast is challenged by the need for finding better empirical measures of technological change. However, a fortunate effect of the interactions just mentioned has been the great interest that is now taken in the very data on wage inequality. The take on the data's properties, advantages, and disadvantages has greatly improved over time. Consideration of the data at later points in time alter the stylized facts and also show that consensus explanations may be temporary and can break down when data for later periods become available and shine a different light on preceding periods. In spite of this, the prime aim of future work on both sides should be to integrate the other side into the framework. Pursuing that may be more a problem of empirical method for the institutional side, and on the demand-and-supply side the problem may be more on the theoretical side as long as institutions continue to be viewed as alien bodies. For both sides there is a perspective of work to do at the firm level. Matched employer-employee data (Cardoso, 2010; Lane, 2009) can help enlighten the role of both institutions and labor supply and demand (see, e.g., Andersson et al., 2006; Matano and Natichioni, 2011 for some interesting attempts). In addition, though much attention has been paid to data quality, a better grasp of the customary use of inequality measures seems desirable.

18.5. LMIs AND WAGE INEQUALITY: AN EMPIRICAL ASSESSMENT

In this section we present an accounting framework and an empirical model aiming to assess the contribution of LMIs to shaping earnings inequality. Here we face the problem of identifying who are benefiting from (or disadvantaged by) the action of a specific LMI. Before we have mentioned the stepwise changes introduced by many institutional reforms, which seem to create two-tier systems (Boeri, 2011), implying that the effect of institutions on earnings inequality may significantly differ across age cohorts. To deal with this, the ideal data set would be longitudinal, in order to be able to compute inequality measures over the lifetime of earnings, conditional of attrition in the sample creation. In addition, measuring institutions is not an easy task. Even if we restrict ourselves to the notion of institutions as rules inducing deviations from competitive market equilibria in economic transactions, these rules are still difficult to measure, because they often treat individuals differently or affect their behavior differently (think, for example, of taxes and benefits, which are almost always conditional to family composition—Boeri and Van Ours, 2008). Rules and norms change rather smoothly over time; in the definition used by Boeri (2011), reforms are rarely radical, and therefore it can take a significant amount of time before a minimum detectable effect may be observable. Despite these limitations, a significant literature has studied the correlation between institutional measures and earnings inequality measures (Alderson and Nielsen, 2002; Rueda and Pontusson, 2000; Wallerstein, 1999—more recently Kierzenkowski and Koske, 2012; Scheve and Stasavage, 2009). It exploits, in turn, cross-country and/or over-time variations of the institutions to arrive at estimates of the correlation with earnings inequality. In many instances, the dependent variable (the inequality measures) are derived from secondary sources, and do not always allow for measures that are fully comparable across countries (Atkinson and Brandolini, 2001). Some studies have computed their own inequality measures, relying on existing projects of data harmonization across countries (Atkinson, 2007a,b; Checchi and Garcia Peñalosa, 2008). We have followed here the same line of research, by computing appropriate indices of earnings inequality from SILC and PSID data sets, described in Section 18.3. Given the absence of natural experiments to obtain estimates of the causal impact of specific norms onto the relevant inequality measures, we will obtain at best correlations between institutional measures and inequalities. In Section 18.5.1, we consider a simple accounting scheme in order to discuss the correlation of market equilibria, institutions, and between-group inequality, whereas in Section 18.5.2 we provide a decomposition of the within-group earnings inequality and correlate these measures with proxies for institutions. In Section 18.5.3 we correlate inequality measured across age cohorts with past institutional measures, finding evidence of inequality-reducing impact of unions and minimum wages. Section 18.5.4 discusses the results.

A simple accounting scheme is plotted in Figure 18.24, which adopts the core of a scheme presented in OECD (2011) and elaborates on that. It describes the process of generating earnings inequality in an institutional framework. Starting components, individual wages, and hours worked are clearly affected by either the bargaining activity of unions (where/when present and active) and/or by existing regulations (minimum wage, regulation on worked hours). This determines individual labor earnings among the employees, but the total level of employment (and its split between dependent and self-employment) are conditioned by existing taxation as well as by employment protection (because so-called self-employment may disguise dependent employment conditions, especially in the case of a single purchaser). In addition, the generosity of public benefits to those laid-off or unemployed also contributes to reducing earnings inequality in the bottom part of the distribution. Although we will not proceed further with our analysis in that direction, one should keep in mind that the list of potential institutions affecting earnings inequality at large should consider the household dimension. Half of the sample of the workforce population is concentrated in households where two members are employed (either as dependent or self-employed). As long as their earnings are not perfectly correlated, cohabitation (and expected income sharing) works as a shock absorber. However, one-fourth of the population does not possess this insurance, as they are single-person households who by definition lack such shielding from the unemployment risk.

18.5.1 A Simple Scheme to Account for Between-Group Inequality

To frame our theoretical expectations before moving to the econometrics, let us consider a simple model that considers a partition of the population into groups. As such, it may be

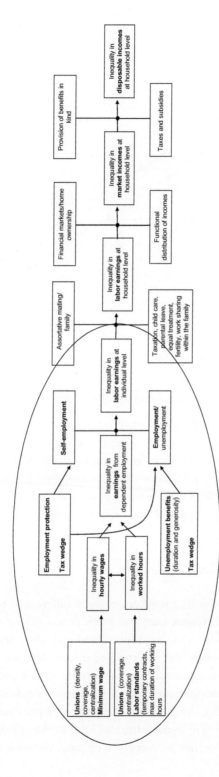

Figure 18.24 Accounting for the basic components of income inequality and the role of institutional measures. Source: *Adapted from OECD (2011, box 1).*

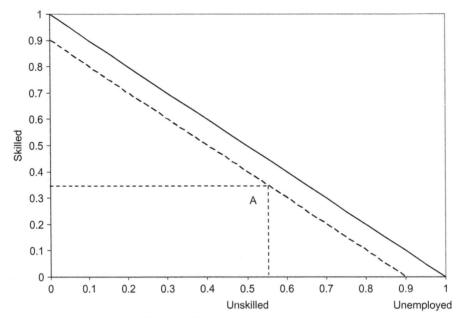

Figure 18.25 The distribution of the population.

considered appropriate to sketch the between-group component of inequality, whereas the between-component incorporates idiosyncratic components (including different marriage attitudes in each group), which are not necessarily connected to the institutional framework. This model builds on Atkinson and Bourguignon (2000) and Checchi and Garcia-Peñalosa (2008). If the workforce is composed by skilled and unskilled workers, a fraction of which may be unemployed, an inequality measure (Gini index) can be expressed (see Box 18.1)

$$\text{Gini}_{\text{earnings}} = f\left(\underset{\pm}{\alpha},\ \underset{+}{\sigma},\ \underset{\pm}{u},\ \underset{-}{\gamma}\right)$$

where α indicates the share of skilled workers, σ wage differential between skilled and unskilled wage, u the unemployment rate, and γ the generosity of the unemployment benefit. This ideal population can be represented on the unitary simplex (see Figure 18.25), which has its empirical counterpart in our data set (see Figure 18.26). Although it is intuitive that earnings inequality is increasing in skill premium and decreasing in the generosity of the unemployment support scheme (conditional on the replacement rate being less than 100%), the effects of the other two parameters are ambiguous. Inequality is increasing in the skill composition as long as the initial fraction of skilled worker is small enough and/or not extremely well paid vis-à-vis the other unskilled

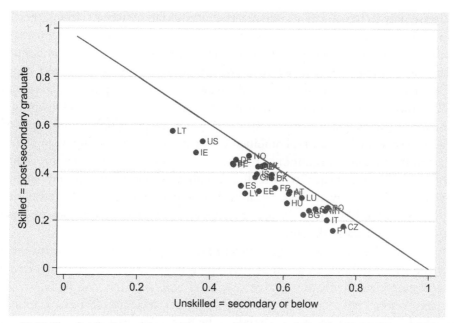

Figure 18.26 The distribution of the employee workforce (aged 20–55)—SILC 2010 and PSID 2011.

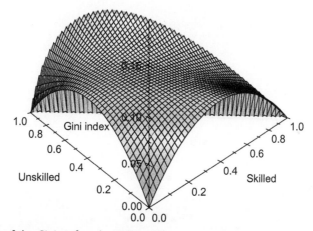

Figure 18.27 Plot of the Gini surface ($\gamma = 0.5$, $\sigma = 2$).

workers (i.e., the skill premium is small).[121] Eventually earnings inequality is increasing in unemployment rate in an intermediate range, while it exhibits negative correlation for high or low values (Figure 18.27).

---

[121] The ambiguous effect of α on Gini is not surprising because a change in α leads to Lorenz curves which cross each other, meaning that the change in the Gini will depend on how they cross each other; as a consequence other inequality measures may yield results in contradiction with the Gini index.

We are now in the position to discuss the relationship between earnings (between-groups) earnings inequality, market determinants, and LMIs. Among the four parameters identified by the model, one is partly independent from LMI. The skill composition of the employed (parameter α) depends on the interplay between demand and supply of skills. Demand for skill may be related to the technological development of an economy, which, in turns, relates to the international distribution of production and the possibility of off-shoring (Acemoglu and Autor, 2011, 2012). The supply of skills is the output of the educational system of a country, combined with expectations regarding wage premia. If we extend the notion of institutions to include educational systems, then this is the first determinant of wage inequality, which is nonlinearly related to earnings inequality (Leuven et al., 2004). Given intergenerational persistence in educational choice, the skill composition of the labor force changes rather smoothly across generations, and can be taken as given, at least in the short run.

By contrast, the return to skill (parameter σ) is jointly affected by competitive market forces and by institutions. In a competitive environment, this relative wage should be negatively correlated with the relative supply, as is slightly the case in Figure 18.28 (Katz and Autor, 1999). However there are significant deviations from such a relationship, which, among other factors, depend on the bargaining activity of unions (typically pursuing an egalitarian stance, aiming to tie wages to jobs and not to people—Visser and

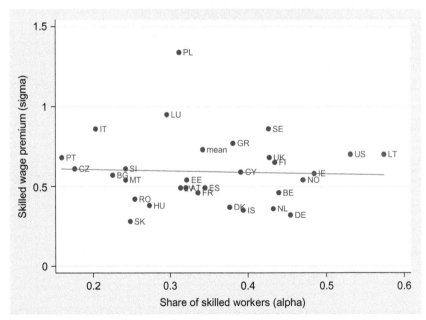

Figure 18.28 Return to skills and skill availability for dependent employees (aged 20–55)—SILC 2010 and PSID 2011.

Checchi, 2009; see also the role of wage scales described by Oliver, 2008) as well as the presence and coverage of minimum-wage legislation.

The unemployment benefit (parameter γ) has an uncontroversial effect of reducing earnings inequality when unemployed people are counted in. However, there is a general consensus that it has also a detrimental effect on the incentive to work, thereby raising the unemployment rate. Because the unemployment benefit can be thought of as a proxy for the outside option in wage bargaining or efficiency wage models, it also creates an upward wage push, which contributes to a positive correlation between benefit and unemployment. The overall effect is therefore $\frac{\partial \text{Gini}}{\partial \gamma} = \frac{\partial \text{Gini}}{\partial \gamma}\Big|_{u=\text{constant}} + \frac{\partial \text{Gini}}{\partial u} \cdot \frac{\partial u}{\partial \gamma}$ which can be either positive (for a high level of unemployment and/or a weak elasticity of unemployment to benefit) or negative (for a low level of unemployment and/or a high elasticity of unemployment to benefit). In our sample, the correlation tends to be positive (see Figure 18.29—however, this concerns short-run unemployment rates, whereas such a correlation should be studied using multiperiod unemployment rate in order to dispense with cyclical fluctuations). Once again, this is not the unique determinant of the unemployment rate (parameter u), because in a more general equilibrium model it depends on the state of the aggregate demand as well as on the average labor cost, which should incorporate the tax wedge. In addition, it may also be correlated with many other LMI variables, sometimes referred as determinants of the NAIRU (Nickell, 1997).

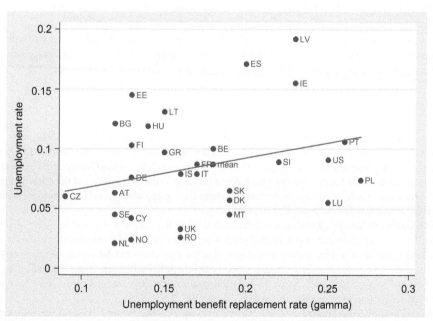

Figure 18.29 Unemployment benefit and unemployment rate—SILC 2010 and PSID 2011.

Still on the side of between-group inequality, we have purposely ignored the functional distribution of income between profit and wages, even though some of these parameters may be correlated to the labor share in the value added. Checchi and Peñalosa (2008) have shown that the same LMI affecting the functional distribution of value added, also affect the distribution of income sources at the individual level, thus modifying income inequality at the aggregate level.

Box 18.1 A model for between-group inequality in earnings

Let us suppose that the workforce has unitary measure and is composed of three groups of individuals:

(i) a fraction $\alpha \in (0,1)$ of the employed is made of skilled workers, earning a wage $w^s = (1+\sigma)w^u$, where $\sigma > 0$ is the skill premium[122];

(ii) a complementary fraction $(1-\alpha)$ is given by unskilled workers, who obtain a wage w^u.

(iii) a fraction u is unemployed and get a benefit $b = \gamma\overline{w}$ where $\gamma \in [0,1]$ is the replacement rate and $\overline{w}$ is the average wage within the employed labor force; skilled and unskilled workers experience the same unemployment rate.[123]

Each economy can be described by two coordinates, the unemployment rate u and the workforce composition α, and can be represented as a point in the unitary simplex. In Figure 18.25 the economy corresponding to point A is characterized by 10% of unemployment, two-thirds of unskilled employees and one-third of skilled ones. The same scheme could be applied to other dual partitioning of the labor force (young/old, male/female, native/foreign, etc.). The actual distribution of the population across different countries in our sample of analysis is reported in Figure 18.26.[124]

Our reference measure of inequality, the Gini concentration index, can provide a measure of the between-group inequality when computed in this simplified population by considering the subgroup differences, obtaining the following expression:

---

[122] We do not consider the presence of a fourth fraction of rich capitalists, as in Alvaredo (2011), who shows that when their population share is negligible (as in the case of top incomes), the Gini inequality index $G_{incomes}$ can be approximated by $G^*_{incomes} \cdot (1-S) + S$, where $G^*_{incomes}$ is the Gini coefficient for the rest of the population and S is the share of total income accruing to the rich fraction of the population. Similarly, the model could be complicated by introducing a third group of workers with an intermediate level of skills, to account for the possibility of polarization.

[123] This simplifies the analysis, avoiding to model relative labor demand, which would allow for modeling a differential impact of institutions on worker subgroups: "Any observer of European labour markets in the last 30 years of the twentieth century would agree that it is a good stylized description of these markets to think of the labour market for high-skill workers as in equilibrium, with wages that adjust to offset demand and supply imbalances, while the low-skill labour market is in disequilibrium, with involuntary unemployment and unresponsive real wages" (Saint-Paul, 2000, 5).

[124] A worker is arbitrarily classified as skilled when possessing a postsecondary school degree. This explains why formerly planned economies exhibit such wide variations in skill endowments.

$$\text{Gini}_{\text{earnings}} = \frac{(1-u)^2\alpha(1-\alpha)[w^s - w^u] + (1-u)\alpha u[w^s - b] + (1-u)(1-\alpha)u[w^u - b]}{2[(1-u)\overline{w} + ub]} \quad (18.1)$$

Using previous definitions, Equation (18.1) can be reexpressed as

$$\text{Gini}_{\text{earnings}} = \frac{(1-u)^2\alpha(1-\alpha)\sigma + (1-u)u(1-\gamma)(1+\alpha\sigma)}{2[1-u(1-\gamma)](1+\alpha\sigma)}$$

$$= \frac{(1-u)^2\dfrac{\alpha(1-\alpha)\sigma}{(1+\alpha\sigma)} + (1-u)u(1-\gamma)}{2[1-u(1-\gamma)]} \quad (18.2)$$

Thus, the (between-groups) inequality in the earnings distribution is parameterized over four characteristics: the employment rate $(1-u)$, the labor force composition α, the skill premium σ, and the generosity of the unemployment benefit γ. It is easy to show that $\frac{\partial \text{Gini}}{\partial \gamma} < 0$ and $\frac{\partial \text{Gini}}{\partial \sigma} > 0$, namely that other things constant, earnings inequality is increasing in skill premium and decreasing in the generosity of the unemployment support scheme. Less clear-cut results obtain with respect to the other two parameters. It can be proved that $\text{sign}\left[\frac{\partial \text{Gini}}{\partial \alpha}\right] = \text{sign}[1 - \alpha(\alpha\sigma + 2)]$, which is positive for $0 \leq \alpha < \frac{\sqrt{1+\sigma}-1}{\sigma}$. Thus, inequality is increasing in the skill composition as long as the initial fraction of skilled worker is small enough and/or not extremely well paid vis-à-vis the other unskilled workers (i.e., the skill premium σ is small). In the case of unemployment tedious calculations[125] prove that

$$\frac{\partial \text{Gini}}{\partial u} > 0 \text{ iff } \frac{1}{1-\gamma}\left(1 - \sqrt{\gamma\frac{A\gamma - (1-\gamma)}{A - (1-\gamma)}}\right) < u < \frac{1}{1-\gamma}\left(1 + \sqrt{\gamma\frac{A\gamma - (1-\gamma)}{A - (1-\gamma)}}\right),$$

$$A = \frac{\alpha(1-\alpha)\sigma}{(1+\alpha\sigma)} < 1$$

Thus, earnings inequality is increasing in unemployment rate in an intermediate range, while it has a negative correlation for high or low values. The Gini surface over the unitary simplex is represented in Figure 18.27: notice that the hump-shape is consistent with the just-mentioned derivative.

So far we have only considered the between-group inequality, ignoring the within-group component, because the former is easier to correlate with LMIs. If we want to take into account both components in an explicit way, we need to resort to a decomposable inequality index, like the generalized entropy index (with $\alpha=0$), known as mean logarithmic deviation $MLD = \frac{1}{n}\sum_{i=1}^{n}\lg\left(\frac{\overline{y}}{y_i}\right)$ (Jenkins, 1995). In the framework of the present model it can be decomposed as

[125] If we rewrite the Gini index as $\text{Gini} = \frac{(1-u)^2 A + (1-u)uB}{2(1-uB)}$ where $A = \frac{\alpha(1-\alpha)\sigma}{1+\alpha\sigma} < 1$ and $B = (1-\gamma) < 1$, then $\text{sign}\left[\frac{\partial \text{Gini}}{\partial u}\right] = \text{sign}[-B(A-B)u^2 + 2(A-B)u + B - A(2-B)]$, which has two real roots under the sufficiency condition that $A > \frac{B}{1-B}$. These roots are given by $u_{1,2} = \frac{(A-B)\pm\sqrt{(A-B)(1-B)(A-B-AB)}}{B(A-B)} = \frac{1}{B}\left(1 \pm \sqrt{\frac{(1-B)(A(1-B)-B)}{(A-B)}}\right)$, which corresponds to what is reported in the text.

$$\text{MLD}_{\text{earnings}} = \underbrace{\alpha(1-u)\cdot\text{MLD}_{\text{skilled}} + (1-\alpha)(1-u)\cdot\text{MLD}_{\text{unskilled}} + u\cdot\text{MLD}_{\text{unemployed}}}_{\text{within-group inequality}}$$

$$\underbrace{+ \alpha(1-u)\cdot\lg\left(\frac{\mu}{w^s}\right) + (1-\alpha)(1-u)\cdot\lg\left(\frac{\mu}{w^u}\right) + u\cdot\lg\left(\frac{\mu}{\gamma\overline{w}}\right)}_{\text{between-group inequality}} \tag{18.3}$$

where μ is the mean income in the population. So far we have neglected the funding of the unemployment benefit scheme (which could derive from profit and rent taxation). In such a case

$$\mu = (1-u)\overline{w} + u\gamma\overline{w} = (1-u(1-\gamma))\overline{w} = (1-u(1-\gamma))(\alpha w^s + (1-\alpha)w^u)$$
$$= (1-u(1-\gamma))(1+\alpha\sigma)w^u$$

On the contrary, if we impose a balanced budget, such that unemployment benefits are to be financed by earnings taxation, we require that $(1-u)t\overline{w} = u\gamma\overline{w}$, where t is the average tax rate. As a consequence

$$\mu = (1-u)\overline{w} + (1-u)t\overline{w} = (1-u)(1+t)(1+\alpha\sigma)w^u \tag{18.4}$$

If we replace definition (18.4) into Equation (18.3) we obtain

$$\text{MLD}_{\text{earnings}} = \underbrace{\alpha(1-u)\cdot\text{MLD}_{\text{skilled}} + (1-\alpha)(1-u)\cdot\text{MLD}_{\text{unskilled}} + u\cdot\text{MLD}_{\text{unemployed}}}_{\text{within-group inequality}}$$

$$\underbrace{+ \alpha(1-u)\cdot\lg\left(\frac{(1-u)(1+t)(1+\alpha\sigma)}{1+\sigma}\right) + (1-\alpha)(1-u)\cdot\lg((1-u)(1+t)(1+\alpha\sigma)) + u\cdot\lg\left(\frac{(1+t)u}{t}\right)}_{\text{between-group inequality}}$$

$$\tag{18.5}$$

It is easy to prove that the between-group component of MLD is increasing in σ and decreasing in γ (under the balanced-budget constraint). In addition, the between-group component is increasing in α for low values, but it changes sign above the threshold defined by $\alpha^* = \frac{1}{\lg(1+\sigma)} - \frac{1}{\sigma}$. The main difference with the Gini measure of inequality is that the gradient of the between-component with respect to the unemployment rate u takes the sign of $\left[1 - \frac{(1+\alpha\sigma)\gamma}{(1+\sigma^\alpha)}\right]$ suggesting that inequality is increasing whenever the replacement rate and/or the wage premium are low.

If we are to check the predictive ability of this simple model, we can use observed sample parameters $(\alpha, \sigma, u, \gamma)$ to predict earnings inequality in each country, well aware that this captures only the between-group component. We define as skilled workers all employees holding a postsecondary degree, and compute the skilled wage as their mean wage. Correspondingly, we define as unskilled all the remaining employees (and obtain their wage); finally, we compute the unemployment share and their mean benefit. The relevant parameters, which are needed for the between-group inequality measures, are reported in Table 18.A4. In column 10, we report the estimated Gini, which has to be compared

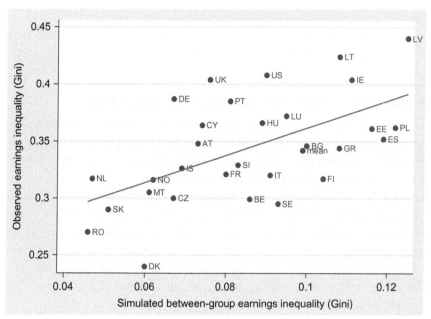

Figure 18.30 The between-group component of earnings inequality—SILC 2010 and PSID 2011.

with the actual one computed on the same data set in column 11. The two coefficients are highly correlated (rank correlation coefficient is 0.57).[126]

Using the Gini index computed over four parameters, we can claim that the between-group component accounts for almost one-third of overall earnings inequality, the remainder being attributable to individual heterogeneity (age, gender, finer partition of educational attainments—including variations of hours). It is rather surprising that such a simple model, based on four parameters only, is able to account for a significant portion of the observed cross-country differences in earnings inequality. Looking at Figure 18.30 we notice that some countries (lying to the right of the regression line) are characterized by higher-than-the-mean between-group inequality (or lower-than-the-mean overall earnings inequality): not surprisingly the Nordic and the Mediterranean countries (except Portugal) are on this side, indicating that in these countries institutions may help to reduce the corresponding within-group inequality. On the left side of the regression line, however, we find the liberal market economies (United States, United Kingdom, and Ireland) and some transition economies (Latvia, Lithuania, and Hungary) as well as some

---

[126] Regressing the observed Gini in labor earnings onto the simulated one computed according to Equation (18.2) yields the following estimation: $\text{Gini}_{\text{observed}} = 0.24 + 1.20 \cdot \text{Gini}_{\text{simulated}}$ with an $\underset{(0.03)}{} \underset{(0.32)}{}$ $R^2 = 0.33$.

continental European country (such as Germany and the Netherlands). These countries are characterized by individual rather than collective wage setting, thus raising the between-group component of earnings inequality.

18.5.2 The Within-Group Inequality and the Role of LMIs

We now consider the within-group component of inequality. To obtain an exact decomposition of earnings inequality for employees, we abstract from self-employment (we think it is potentially affected by existing labor market regulations, but it often also records negative incomes that are not easily dealt by inequality measures), and we restrict ourselves to individuals aged below 55 (to minimize country differences attributable to a different extent of early retirement[127]) who receive either a positive income from dependent employment or from unemployment benefit. Using the mean log deviation to decompose earnings inequality, we find that on average the between-component accounts for one-fifth of the observed inequality, being highest in Portugal (30%), Hungary (28%), and Slovenia (28%) and lowest in Sweden (7%), Norway (8%), and the Netherlands (11%) (see Table 18.3).

The within-group component follows common patterns: inequality is highest among the unemployed,[128] but its contribution to the within-group component is limited, the country average being 16%. Skilled workers are characterized by higher earnings inequality than the unskilled ones, and this is not surprising once we consider that their wage will more frequently be determined by individual bargaining. The unskilled workers (who on average comprise 57% of the workforce) do contribute half of total within-group inequality, and it is here that we may expect to find the strongest impact of LMIs (especially the minimum wage and bargaining activity of unions).[129]

---

[127] The SILC codebook allows for the classification as unemployed of early retired workers if they perceive themselves as such ("Early retirement for economic reasons can be included here according to the respondent's feeling, i.e., a person in early retirement for economic reasons will be included here if he/she classifies him/herself as unemployed" (Eurostat, Description of Target Variables: Cross-sectional and Longitudinal 2010 operation (Version February 2010, 139).

[128] Inequality among (unemployment) benefit recipients is significantly affected by the duration of unemployment spells, by differences in the entitlement rights and in the take-up rates. Although we do not have adequate data to cope with all these factors, if we just replace the current figures for the benefit with its monthly average (simply dividing the yearly received subsidy by months in unemployment) we obtain that the inequality in monthly unemployment benefit significantly declines for some countries (Austria, Czech Republic, Netherlands, Norway) but it increases in others (Estonia, Ireland, Italy), the country average of MLD remains almost unchanged (from 0.388 to 0.381).

[129] Freeman and Schettkat (2001) follow a similar approach when comparing US and German earnings inequality, showing that inequality within each educational group is higher in the former country, and they attribute it to the role of bargaining structures.

Table 18.3 Earnings inequality decomposition—dependent employees or unemployed (mean log deviation)—SILC 2010 and PSID 2011

	Decomposition of total inequality			Decomposition of the within-group component					
	Overall yearly gross earnings inequality	Between group inequality	Within group inequality	Population share of skilled workers	Inequality in yearly gross earnings of skilled workers	Population share of unskilled workers	Inequality in yearly gross earnings of unskilled workers	Population share of unemployed workers (receiving a positive benefit)	Inequality in unemployment benefits (conditional on being unemployed)
Austria	0.234	0.031	0.203	0.321	0.223	0.616	0.181	0.063	0.327
Belgium	0.179	0.048	0.131	0.439	0.124	0.461	0.119	0.100	0.214
Bulgaria	0.241	0.046	0.195	0.225	0.176	0.654	0.161	0.121	0.410
Cyprus	0.263	0.031	0.232	0.391	0.255	0.567	0.214	0.042	0.270
Czech Republic	0.184	0.033	0.151	0.176	0.171	0.764	0.119	0.060	0.494
Denmark	0.129	0.016	0.113	0.376	0.111	0.566	0.101	0.057	0.243
Estonia	0.270	0.033	0.237	0.322	0.200	0.532	0.194	0.145	0.475
Finland	0.204	0.049	0.155	0.434	0.145	0.462	0.132	0.103	0.294
France	0.229	0.031	0.198	0.336	0.197	0.576	0.173	0.087	0.367
Germany	0.334	0.069	0.265	0.454	0.234	0.470	0.276	0.076	0.381
Greece	0.224	0.031	0.193	0.381	0.197	0.522	0.164	0.097	0.328
Hungary	0.250	0.071	0.179	0.273	0.206	0.608	0.150	0.119	0.262
Iceland	0.218	0.027	0.191	0.394	0.169	0.527	0.178	0.079	0.384
Ireland	0.316	0.048	0.268	0.484	0.250	0.361	0.233	0.155	0.406
Italy	0.224	0.027	0.197	0.203	0.205	0.718	0.169	0.079	0.436
Latvia	0.418	0.076	0.342	0.314	0.279	0.495	0.261	0.192	0.653
Lithuania	0.377	0.061	0.316	0.574	0.295	0.296	0.248	0.131	0.566
Luxembourg	0.260	0.060	0.200	0.296	0.205	0.649	0.196	0.055	0.213
Malta	0.199	0.029	0.170	0.242	0.179	0.713	0.150	0.045	0.453
Netherlands	0.200	0.023	0.177	0.432	0.172	0.547	0.167	0.021	0.563
Norway	0.230	0.018	0.212	0.470	0.204	0.505	0.200	0.024	0.605

Continued

Table 18.3 Earnings inequality decomposition—dependent employees or unemployed (mean log deviation)—SILC 2010 and PSID 2011—cont'd

	Decomposition of total inequality			Decomposition of the within-group component					
	Overall yearly gross earnings inequality	Between group inequality	Within group inequality	Population share of skilled workers	Inequality in yearly gross earnings of skilled workers	Population share of unskilled workers	Inequality in yearly gross earnings of unskilled workers	Population share of unemployed workers (receiving a positive benefit)	Inequality in unemployment benefits (conditional on being unemployed)
Poland	0.253	0.038	0.215	0.312	0.226	0.614	0.188	0.074	0.387
Portugal	0.259	0.078	0.181	0.159	0.246	0.734	0.163	0.106	0.204
Romania	0.121	0.032	0.089	0.254	0.111	0.720	0.078	0.026	0.176
Slovak Republic	0.180	0.029	0.151	0.248	0.172	0.687	0.113	0.065	0.476
Slovenia	0.229	0.064	0.165	0.242	0.189	0.669	0.116	0.089	0.471
Spain	0.249	0.057	0.192	0.345	0.177	0.483	0.171	0.171	0.284
Sweden	0.230	0.016	0.214	0.426	0.245	0.530	0.166	0.045	0.484
United Kingdom	0.306	0.058	0.248	0.427	0.261	0.541	0.231	0.033	0.359
United States	0.339	0.045	0.294	0.483	0.310	0.468	0.271	0.049	0.347
Average	0.245	0.044	0.201	0.340	0.203	0.575	0.174	0.085	0.388

If we now consider the potential role of LMI in shaping the wage distribution within workers' types, we do expect a differential impact according to the way in which different workers are affected.[130] We spent some effort to collecting consistent information on institutional variables for the same countries, mostly from various OECD data sets. We tried to build long series in order to match individuals of different age cohorts to the institutional setup prevailing either at the beginning of their work careers or during their entire career. Data sources and descriptive statistics are in Appendix C.

Table 18.4 summarizes our theoretical expectations, mostly deduced from the existing literature. Betcherman (2012) reviews the empirical literature on the correlation between different institutional dimensions and earnings inequality. He concludes that the minimum wage is the less contentious among the institutional impact, being associated to an improvement in the bottom tail of the wage distribution, at least for the formal sector. Neumark and Wascher (2008) do not contest the inequality-reducing impact of minimum wage (by creating a spike at the relevant threshold and/or inducing upward spillover effect across the entire wage distribution), though they stress the contemporaneous disemployment effect on low-wage earners, raising doubts about the overall effect on inequality at household level.[131]

The effect of unions is mixed, combining a reduction of within-group inequality (among formal dependent employment, especially in terms of skill premium—Koeniger et al., 2007) and a potential increase in the wage gap between union-covered sectors and nonunion-covered sectors (including informal employment). Using cross-country data, Visser and Checchi (2009) find that union presence is associated with lower within-group inequality, because both the gender gap and the return to education are negatively correlated with union density.[132,133] As a consequence, the skill premium declines, both as a result of wage compression and as a consequence of the incentives to over-invest in education. In addition, union presence is also associated to

---

[130] Eichhorst et al. (2008) provide a recent review of how LMIs are measured and their impacts on unemployment.

[131] Among the long-run impacts they also list the inhibiting impact on skill acquisition for youngsters, which will split over into greater earnings inequality in the future. Thus, they conclude, "Minimum wages do not deliver on their goal of improving the lives of low-wage workers, low-skill individuals, and low-income families" (p. 293).

[132] The egalitarian attitude of workers' unions has been rationalized by Agell and Lommerud (1992) using the argument that high-productivity risk-adverse workers may prefer pay compression in the absence of a market for private insurance.

[133] We do not consider here that institutions may operate in a complementary way, through interactions. In particular employment protection reinforces the impact of union density on unemployment and wage bargaining (Belot and van Ours, 2004). Fiori et al. (2012) provide an empirical application of Blanchard and Giavazzi (2003), which shows the substitutability of product and labor market reforms in terms of employment impact.

Table 18.4 Theoretical expectations of the effects of institutions on earnings inequality

Labor market institutions	Between groups	Within groups	Overall impact on earnings inequality
Minimum wage (measured by ratio to median wage)	• Raises the bottom tail of hourly wage, mostly for the unskilled	• Raise the bottom tail (typically populated by marginal workers)	• Reducing inequality in hourly wages—overall effects depend on hours dynamics
Union presence (measured by union density, coverage, centralization and/or coordination, strike activity)	• Compresses the skill premium (*equal pay for equal work*) • Expands the union wage gap (between union and nonunion sectors/jobs)	• Reduce inequality in hours (control/opposition to overtime, regulation of part-time, work sharing as alternative to layoffs) • Reduces gender wage gap, thus favoring work-sharing within the family and female participation	• Reducing (ambiguous when unemployment effects are taken into account)
Employment protection (measured by OECD summary index)	• Lowers unskilled wage when inducing people to retain unproductive jobs • Increases long-term unemployment	• Reduces job flows in/out of unemployment • Discourages labor market entry of marginal workers (young, women)	• Ambiguous
Unemployment benefit (measured by replacement rate and public expenditure in passive labor market policies)	• Raises the income of the unemployed • Raises the outside option, thus augmenting the bargaining power of unions • Lowers the incentive to job search	• Potential subsidy traps (especially on second earner, because the reservation wage is positively correlated with first earner)	• Ambiguous

Tax wedge (measured by the ratio between labor cost and take home pay)	• Increases unemployment (if the employer is unable to transfer the burden onto the employee)	• When altering labor cost (if they cannot be shifted to workers), taxes and payroll taxes alter the relative employment of worker subgroups • Even within the household, EITC (earned income tax credit) measures may favor joint participation of spouses to the labor market, especially when part time is easily available	• Increases personal earnings inequality (because presence of part-timers) but may reduce household earnings inequality (because presence of an additional income in the household)
Active labor market policies (measured by public expenditure on GDP) Child/old people care facilities (availability of ECCE facilities, parental leave)	• Reduces unemployment	• Increasing labor market participation, possibly with reduced hours • Increasing female participation, it brings in additional workers into employment	• Ambiguous (due to the combined effect of participation and hours) • Ambiguous (due to a compositional effect)

unemployment, though correlation may go in different directions: union density seems associated with higher unemployment (Bertola et al., 2007; Flaig and Rottmann, 2011; Nickell et al., 2005), and centralized bargaining seems to attenuate this negative effect (Bassanini and Duval, 2006; Nickell, 1997—see also Glyn et al. (2003) for a critical review of these results). Thus, the overall effect of unions on earnings inequality remains uncertain.

The results of employment protection legislation are less clear-cut. OECD (2011, 2012) show that EPL and wage coordination have a negative effect on earning inequality, while tax wage and wage coverage have a positive effect. The proposed rationalization is that unskilled workers are favored by firing restriction, raising their relative bargaining power relative to skilled ones.[134]

Unemployment benefits, active labor market policies, and the tax wedge may play an indirect role, via the impact on aggregate employment (or unemployment). The tax wedge in particular has been found to be significantly and positively correlated to the unemployment rate (Flaig and Rottmann, 2011; Nickell et al., 2005).[135] But these two institutions also affect different groups of workers in different ways, especially along the gender divide (Bertola et al., 2007): as a consequence, they may impact on the household distribution of earnings via changes in the redistribution of work opportunities within the family. In addition, when aiming to decompose the contribution to inequality associated with hourly wages and hours worked, the legal framework (limitation to part-time, family, or individual taxation) may lead to opposite impacts on labor supply, the corresponding employment and wage outcomes. Possibly for these reasons, we have not found consensus on this dimension in the literature, and therefore we will let the data speak.

Work redistribution within the household may also be affected by parental leave opportunities and child care provisions (Thévenon and Solaz, 2013). As long as these institutional dimensions favor female participation, they should reduce earnings inequality measured at the household level, but they may increase inequality at the individual level, owing to a larger fraction of part-timers in the economy. However, these results are conditional on parental leave not exceeding a specific threshold, because otherwise it may produce a reduction in labor supply.[136] In addition, as long-mandated parental leave

---

[134] A similar argument can be found in Koeniger et al. (2007), where employment protection has stronger effect for less-qualified workers.

[135] Flaig and Rottmann (2011, 19) conclude from their cross-country analysis covering 19 OECD countries over the 1960–2000 period that "[a] tighter employment protection legislation, a more generous unemployment insurance system and a higher tax burden of labour income increase the medium term development of the unemployment rate, whereas a higher centralization of the wage bargaining process lowers unemployment. Union density has no clear effect and seems to be unimportant."

[136] Lalive et al. (2011) study the complementarity between job protection associated with parental leave and financial support to new parents, showing that either policy instrument has a detrimental effect on female labor supply in the medium run.

may raise female supply in the labor market, it may also exert a downward pressure on their relative wage, thus contributing to increased inequality (which, however, is not found in the limited data analyzed by Thévenon and Solaz, 2013). Also in such a case, we may let the data speak.

A serious problem in assessing the impact of single institutions on labor market outcomes is that some institutions are likely to interact with each other, in a positive or in a negative way. Consider, for example, the role of workers' unions, which is typically correlated in a negative way to earnings inequality. The presence of unions is strengthened by employment protection legislation, but is weakened by the presence of minimum-wage provisions.[137] Similarly, the tax wedge may have a significant impact on employment in a country where the (after-tax) minimum wage is relatively high because part of the wedge will be passed on to wages at a higher level. In some countries (such as France and Belgium) rebates on payroll taxes for low-wage workers significantly impact on their employability.

Addressing the issue of institutional complementarity opens up another set of literature, which is typically analyzed by political economy (Amable, 2003; Hall and Soskice, 2001). From an empirical point of view it does require a sufficient number of degrees of freedom (either in terms of variety of countries or in terms of repeated observations over the same country). Just as descriptive evidence, the sample bivariate correlations between the inequality measures presented in Table 18.4 and the LMIs described in Appendix C are presented in Table 18.5.[138] Exploiting the decomposability of the Mean Log Deviation, we have considered six dimensions of earnings inequality: its overall measure, the decomposition into between-group and within-group, and the contributions to the within-component attributable to each group of workers (skilled, unskilled, and unemployed).[139]

They confirm that union presence (either measured by union density or by coverage) may contribute to reducing earnings inequality, though in a different way. Union density seems statistically correlated with the between-group component, whereas the coverage of collective agreements (which assures equivalent treatment of all workers) exhibits a negative correlation with the within-component. Similar negative correlations are exhibited by employment protection with respect to the skilled worker group; analogously, parental leave facilities are negatively correlated to skilled wage inequality. It is

---

[137] Checchi and Lucifora (2002) discuss the complementarity/substitutability of LMIs with respect to union density.

[138] A review of existing data sets on LMIs is in Ochel (2005) and Eichhorst et al. (2008).

[139] By considering the contribution to inequality attributable to workers' groups we are combining two sources of variation: the group size and its internal inequality. Although the fraction of unemployed workers may be directly correlated to LMIs (such as unions or unemployment benefit), the skill composition of the labor force may be correlated with the quality and quantity of education available in the country in earlier decades.

Table 18.5 Correlation between labor market institutions (averages 2001–2010) and different component of earnings inequality (MLD)—SILC 2010 and PSID 2011

	Overall yearly gross earnings inequality	Between group inequality	Within group inequality	Inequality in yearly gross earnings attributable to skilled workers	Inequality in yearly gross earnings attributable to unskilled workers	Inequality in unemployment benefits attributable to unemployed
Union density	−0.415★	−0.420★	−0.346★	−0.112	−0.308★	−0.346★
Agreements coverage	−0.601★	−0.3512★	−0.584★	−0.391★	−0.378★	−0.436★
Centralization	−0.099	−0.223	−0.044	−0.036	−0.141	0.083
Strike activity	−0.280	−0.190	−0.268	−0.115	−0.343	−0.144
Minimum wage (Kaitz index)	0.127	0.3219★	0.043	0.026	−0.161	0.216
Employment protection legislation	−0.330	0.074	−0.410★	−0.626★	0.018	0.011
Unemployment benefit	0.125	0.010	0.142	0.061	−0.092	0.327★
Tax wedge	−0.241	−0.023	−0.273	−0.099	−0.316★	−0.188
Social expenditure	−0.229	−0.175	−0.190	0.035	−0.238	−0.267
Child care	−0.179	−0.040	−0.189	−0.252	0.037	−0.109
Parental leave	−0.320	−0.138	−0.318	−0.435★	−0.060	0.040
Tax treatment of household incomes	0.052	−0.170	0.120	0.292	−0.024	−0.117
Active labor market policies	−0.296	−0.222	−0.273	−0.047	−0.322★	−0.255
Passive labor market policies	−0.248	−0.068	−0.266	−0.089	−0.320★	−0.182

30 countries—★significant at 10%.

interesting to note that the generosity of the unemployment benefit seems to contribute positively to the inequality component attributable to the unemployed (even if we are unable to distinguish whether this is due to an increase of the unemployment rate or to a different distribution within the group). Not surprisingly, household or individual taxation does not affect wage inequality, because it may be ineffective in modifying household labor supply (Dingeldey, 2001). Active and passive labor market policies seem mostly effective in reducing the within-component of the earnings inequality of unskilled workers.

Overall these results are not satisfying in terms of statistical significance, suggesting that isolating a single institution at a specific point in time (even though here we are considering a decennial average) may not be the best strategy to investigate the association between inequality and institutions. Though it may sometimes be inevitable for empirical reasons, it does seem advisable to consider the degree of embeddedness of individual institutions in a collection of institutions to see whether one can lay more weight on analytical results obtained for one institution compared to another. For example, the strong legal nature of an institution may enhance its standalone effect. In addition, bivariate correlations are sensitive to the criticism of spurious correlation and also to omitted-variable bias. For this reason we now consider more robust methods to study the impact of institutions on earnings inequality.

18.5.3 Empirical Assessment
18.5.3.1 Cross-Sectional Approach
One crucial issue in the analysis of the role of LMI in shaping earnings inequality is the match of inequality computed from microdata to the corresponding institutional measures. If we correlate current inequality measured over workers of different ages (who therefore have been staying in the labor market for different durations) to the current union density (which is computed over the workers who are currently working) we are simply considering "industrial relations" regimes, without any claim of causality in one direction or the other. Such an exercise is conducted in Table 18.6, in which we consider three different dimensions of inequality (yearly earnings from dependent employment, hourly wages, and worked hours by dependent employees). In accordance with our previous between-group inequality decomposition (see Section 18.5.2), for each dimension we consider two market phenomena that are correlated with market forces: level of qualification of the labor force and level of employment (better captured by the female employment rate).[140] In all cases an increasing level of education in the

---

[140] Actually the skill level of the labor force is the joint outcome of the demand for education of the population and the institutional supply of schooling; however, replacing it with some measure of the strength of the institutional push toward education (such as the years of compulsory education) did not prove statistically significant.

Table 18.6 Gross earnings inequality (SILC 2010–PSID 2011) against market and labor market institutions (2001–2010) Effects—OLS

Dependent variable	Gini of gross annual employee earnings (working more than 1000 h per year)			Gini of gross hourly wages			Gini of employee (all durations)			Correlation of wages and hours		
	1	2	3	4	5	6	7	8	9	10	11	12
Population share with secondary degree	−0.309 [0.073]*	−0.06 [0.091]	−0.086 [0.131]	−0.424 [0.151]**	−0.277 [0.190]	−0.367 [0.259]	−0.233 [0.083]**	−0.139 [0.124]	−0.201 [0.148]	−0.095 [0.262]	−0.139 [0.124]	−0.201 [0.148]
Population share with postsecondary degree	−0.217 [0.059]*	−0.197 [0.067]**	−0.211 [0.095]***	−0.235 [0.085]**	−0.268 [0.100]**	−0.289 [0.158]	−0.19 [0.078]**	−0.189 [0.058]*	−0.189 [0.077]**	0.083 [0.171]	−0.189 [0.058]*	−0.189 [0.077]**
Female employment rate	−0.66 [0.211]*	−0.405 [0.175]**	−0.528 [0.281]***	−0.816 [0.426]***	−0.679 [0.377]***	−0.835 [0.595]	0.208 [0.177]	0.429 [0.115]*	0.564 [0.254]***	0.537 [0.417]	0.429 [0.115]*	0.564 [0.254]***
Union density	−0.078 [0.039]***	−0.125 [0.038]*	−0.19 [0.039]*	−0.048 [0.052]	−0.131 [0.075]	−0.192 [0.099]***	−0.083 [0.037]**	−0.121 [0.036]*	−0.124 [0.057]***	−0.23 [0.147]	−0.121 [0.036]*	−0.124 [0.057]***
Minimum wage/mean wage	−0.064 [0.043]	−0.105 [0.041]**	−0.136 [0.041]**	−0.074 [0.065]	−0.157 [0.065]**	−0.193 [0.093]***	−0.045 [0.040]	−0.072 [0.034]**	−0.088 [0.052]	−0.104 [0.144]	−0.072 [0.034]***	−0.088 [0.052]
Passive labor market policy/gdp (×100)	−0.04 [0.010]*	−0.036 [0.010]*	−0.055 [0.034]	−0.044 [0.015]*	−0.04 [0.016]**	−0.089 [0.067]	0.025 [0.009]**	0.022 [0.010]**	0.045 [0.034]	−0.024 [0.027]	0.022 [0.010]**	0.045 [0.034]

	(1)	(2)	(3)	(4)	(5)	(6)	(7)	(8)	(9)	(10)	(11)	(12)
Employment protection legislation [1–6]		−0.022 [0.010]★★	−0.023 [0.016]		−0.041 [0.022]★★	−0.047 [0.031]		−0.029 [0.006]★	−0.031 [0.007]★		−0.029 [0.006]★	−0.031 [0.007]★
Enrollment rate in early child care and preprimary education		−0.111 [0.032]★	−0.174 [0.042]★		−0.139 [0.064]★★	−0.186 [0.090]★★★		−0.019 [0.037]	−0.002 [0.057]		−0.019 [0.037]	−0.002 [0.057]
Agreements coverage			0.052 [0.056]			0.064 [0.100]			0.051 [0.044]			0.051 [0.044]
Bargaining centralization			−0.056 [0.042]			−0.052 [0.091]			−0.012 [0.050]			−0.012 [0.050]
Active labor market policy/gdp (×100)			0.015 [0.047]			0.078 [0.103]			−0.042 [0.051]			−0.042 [0.051]
Social expenditure/gdp			0.891 [0.937]			−0.632 [1.855]			0.22 [0.711]			0.22 [0.711]
Tax wedge			0.059 [0.091]			−0.031 [0.192]			−0.121 [0.117]			−0.121 [0.117]
Unemployment benefit Replacement rate			0.039 [0.074]			0.042 [0.105]			−0.022 [0.052]			−0.022 [0.052]
Observations (countries)	29	23	23	29	23	23	29	23	23	29	23	23
R-squared	0.66	0.78	0.84	0.46	0.69	0.74	0.47	0.71	0.81	0.31	0.71	0.81

Note: unless specified, all variables are in percent points—★significant at 1%; ★★significant at 5%; ★★★significant at 10%—robust standard errors in brackets—constant included.

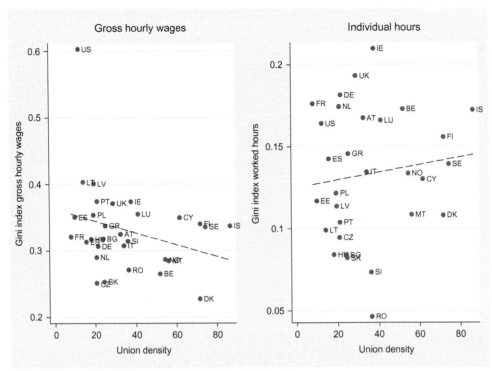

Figure 18.31 Earnings inequality (SILC 2010–PSID 2011) and union density (average 2001–2010).

labor force is negatively and significantly associated with inequality. Similarly, it occurs for wages, but not for hours: not surprisingly, when more women enter the labor market, the working hours regime as a whole becomes more diversified.[141]

When we introduce institutional measures to capture deviations from market equilibrium, we identify a subset of institutions that are significantly correlated with different inequalities (see columns 2–5–8 of Table 18.6). Union density has a negative association with yearly earnings, hourly wages, and hours: this captures different dimensions of union presence (such as coverage or wage centralization, which are not statistically significant[142]). Although the unconditional correlation with worked hours appears positive (see Figure 18.31), once we control for compositional effects it turns negative (despite a rather small magnitude). A second institutional dimension with a statistical negative correlation with earnings inequality is the presence and the level of minimum wages. However, as discussed in Appendix C, this institution is present only in a subset of

---

[141] Additional compositional controls related to the age composition do not come out statistically significant and therefore are left out of the analysis.

[142] Also strike activity is not statistically significant, but in addition it reduces the sample to 18 countries, and therefore is not shown.

countries, while in others this role is played by legislative or judicial extension of the union-bargained wage. In addition, there are often derogations for marginal workers, which are not captured by this measure. Nevertheless, the mere existence of a legal floor to downward flexibility of wages contributes to the containment of inequality.

The third institutional dimension deals with unemployment benefit, whose theoretical expectation is ambiguous due to a potential enhancing effect on the unemployment rate. The replacement rate does not exhibit a statistically significant correlation, whereas the overall public expenditure on passive labor market policies is negatively correlated with earnings and wage inequalities, and positively with hours inequality.[143] This suggests that transferring money to members of the labor force (which constitutes our sample of investigation) reduces inequality in terms of revenues, but on the other side allows for the continuation of unequally distributed job opportunities. A fourth dimension is connected to the employment protection.[144] Not surprisingly, its correlation is strongest with the distribution of work: the more regulated the labor contract, the more equal is the distribution of worked hours. Because employment protection and union activities tend to be complements (Bertola, 2004), it is not surprising to find an analogous negative correlation with earnings and wage inequality, as clearly shown in Figure 18.32.

Still restricting our examination to the subsample of OECD countries, we find some statistical evidence of a negative correlation of earnings inequality with child care attendance, interpreted as a proxy for child care availability. On a theoretical ground, we do expect a larger female participation in the labor market and an evener distribution of external work opportunities in the couple: both should have an impact on the hours inequality, which, however, do not appear in the data. The negative correlation with earnings inequality could capture some unobservable dimension of welfare provision, which is typically associated to lower inequality (though a direct measure of it, given by social expenditure, does not come out statistically significant).[145]

Despite the limited degrees of freedom, these are the only institutional features that correlate with statistical significance with various dimensions of earnings inequality. Against the potential objection of omitted variables, we have also introduced all measures that we have collected (see columns 3–6–9 of Table 18.6), without finding any other statistical correlation. However, despite the richness of the institutional framework, a simple cross-country regression such as the actual one does not provide an incontrovertible evidence of LMIs contributing to shape earnings inequality. To this end, we now move to exploit cohort variation in inequalities.

---

[143] Data on the expenditure on labor market policies are not available in the case of Iceland.

[144] The OECD measure of EPL is not available for non-OECD members (Bulgaria, Cyprus, Latvia, Lithuania, Malta, and Romania). However, in order not to lose these countries in the analysis of other institutions, we have imputed these missing values using the sample mean of nonmissing countries.

[145] If we reduce the number of countries even further (to 21) by introducing measures of parental leave, we find some statistical significance for a negative correlation with inequality in hourly wages (not shown).

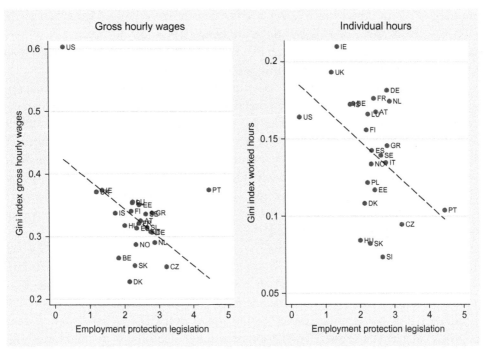

Figure 18.32 Earnings inequality (SILC 2010–PSID 2011) and employment protection (average 2001–2010).

In columns 10–11–12 of Table 18.6 we have considered as a dependent variable the correlation computed at the country level between hourly wages and worked hours, following the idea that higher correlation (in absolute terms) may reduce earnings inequality (as long as this correlation does not simply capture spurious correlation—see again Figure 18.22 and the discussion there). We find a negative correlation with both union density and employment protection legislation, suggesting that in a highly regulated labor market (due to firing restrictions and/or active union presence) the working poor obtain partial compensation of their weak command in the labor market by extended (or just complete) working hours.

18.5.3.2 Longitudinal or Pseudo-Longitudinal Approach

Aiming to obtain more statistically robust results, we need to exploit cross-country and within-country variations of inequality and institutions, to be able to dispense with unobservables by means of appropriate country and time-fixed effects. If data were available, one could take repeated cross sections for each country, compute inequality

Table 18.7 Matching rules between inequality measures and institutional variables

Cohort	Individual birth year	Age in 2010	Matching rule 1a: average institutional measures prevailing when entering the labor market aged 20-year old	Matching rule 1b: average institutional measures prevailing just before the entrance in the labor market (5-year lag)	Matching rule 2: average institutional measures prevailing over the entire working life course
1	1986–1990	20–24	2006–2010	2001–2005	2006–2010
2	1981–1985	25–29	2001–2005	1996–2000	2001–2010
3	1976–1980	30–34	1996–2000	1991–1995	1996–2010
4	1971–1975	35–39	1991–1995	1986–1990	1991–2010
5	1966–1970	40–44	1986–1990	1981–1985	1986–2010
6	1961–1965	45–49	1981–1985	1976–1980	1981–2010
7	1956–1960	50–54	1976–1980	1971–1975	1976–2010
8	1951–1955	55–59	1971–1975	1966–1970	1971–2010
9	1946–1950	60–64	1966–1970	1961–1965	1966–2010

measures of the relevant population in each survey, and match them with the prevailing institutional measures. Unfortunately, cross-country comparable surveys for the countries under analysis do not go back more than a couple of decades, and this has led us to pursue an alternative strategy. Because we need to match individuals belonging to different age cohorts, who entered the labor market in different years, to institutional profiles that are relevant for their wage determination, we need to discuss the appropriate matching rule.

One possibility would match individuals to the institutions prevailing at the time of their entrance into the labor market (see matching rules 1a and 1b in Table 18.7). This implies that the current difference between a person's wage and the wages of his or her coworkers may be affected by the bargaining activity exerted by the unions 30 years ago. As long as wages are highly persistent (due to seniority rules and/or automatic adjustment clauses) this may be considered a viable assumption. An alternative possibility considers both institutional persistence (institutions are slow-changing variables) and different exposure to an institutional environment (variable treatment). In this second perspective, older individuals are supposed to have been exposed to an institutional framework that has been (on average) available over their entire working life (see matching rule 2 in Table 18.7). In such a case, the current difference between someone's wage and the wages of his or her coworkers has been affected by the bargaining activity exerted over the past 30 years. To appreciate differences in the institutional measures according to the different matching rules, Figure 18.33 plots the

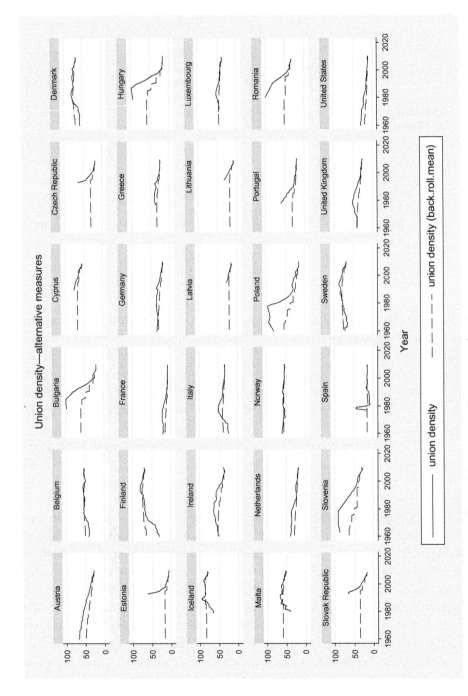

Figure 18.33 Alternative measures of exposition to institutions: union density.

contemporaneous union density (solid line) and the backward (moving) mean according to the third matching rule (dashed line): although the former is more volatile, the latter "keeps" a smoothed memory of past dynamics.

Both strategies are approximations because they induce measurement errors in the dependent variables (measuring wage inequality by age cohort is used as proxy for overall inequality measured in the past). However, they have the advantage of covering a long time span, allowing greater variability in the institutional measures.

Irrespective of the chosen matching, by treating our cross section as a pseudo-panel we significantly augment the degrees of freedom in the estimation. The different time coverage of institutional measures yields an unbalanced panel, where we control for country and cohort fixed effects. The errors are clustered at the country level. As a consequence, our results are more robust than the previous cross-section estimates reported in Table 18.8. As long as the fixed effects clean away all the other sources of confounding variations, we use cross-country and life-cycle variations in inequality for identifying the contribution of institutions to shape the earnings distribution. The contemporaneous insertion of several institutional measures allows for the identification of each specific contribution, other institutions and sample composition kept constant. We have decided to exclude the two oldest cohorts, inasmuch as information on institutions in the 1960s is available only for union density and unemployment benefit. In addition, retirement rules vary across countries, introducing large variations in the employment rate for these age cohorts.[146]

In Table 18.8 we present the estimates corresponding to the matching rule 1a (individual matched to the institutions prevailing when entering the labor market—the other matching rule 1b gives similar results on a shorter sample size, and is not reported for brevity). The structure of Table 18.8 resembles the previous Table 18.6 but leaves out the analysis of the correlation between hours and wages. We consider three measures of inequality (yearly earnings for full-time workers, hourly wages, and hours worked) and for each of them we control for educational attainment in the labor force and female participation. In both cases they exert a negative impact on inequality, despite the weaker statistical significance of education. For each dependent variable we consider three specifications: country fixed effects (columns 1–4–7), country and cohort fixed effects (columns 2–5–8), and country and cohort fixed effects including OECD indicator for employment protection, which excludes non-OECD members (columns 3–6–9).[147]

---

[146] The employment rate for individuals aged 55–64 ranges from 65% in Sweden (or 62% in the United States) to 30% for Italy or Romania.

[147] The first two columns still exclude Iceland, due to the lack of data on labor market policies, while the third excludes non-OECD countries.

Table 18.8 Gross earnings inequality (SILC 2010–PSID 2011) against market and labor market institutions (1975–2010) effects—OLS—longitudinal cohort data (matching rule 1a)

Dependent variable	Gini of gross yearly employee earnings (working more than 1000 h per year)			Gini of gross hourly wages			Gini of employee hours (all durations)		
	1	2	3	4	5	6	7	8	9
Population share with secondary degree	-0.022 [0.165]	0.041 [0.140]	0.028 [0.138]	-0.074 [0.154]	-0.075 [0.159]	-0.093 [0.160]	0.082 [0.104]	0.089 [0.109]	0.093 [0.120]
Population share with postsecondary degree	-0.162 [0.068]*	-0.104 [0.090]	-0.127 [0.091]	-0.18 [0.069]*	-0.239 [0.100]*	-0.285 [0.097]**	-0.084 [0.065]	-0.093 [0.108]	-0.103 [0.101]
Female employment rate	0.309 [0.141]*	-0.01 [0.169]	-0.035 [0.167]	0.315 [0.203]	0.333 [0.211]	0.318 [0.223]	-0.452 [0.121]**	-0.462 [0.202]*	-0.472 [0.220]*
Union density	0.138 [0.055]*	0.053 [0.045]	0.051 [0.046]	0.09 [0.041]*	0.073 [0.060]	0.058 [0.062]	-0.058 [0.033]***	-0.063 [0.037]	-0.076 [0.041]***
Minimum wage/mean wage	-0.127 [0.073]***	-0.136 [0.055]*	-0.149 [0.063]*	0.064 [0.055]	0.066 [0.062]	0.059 [0.070]	-0.053 [0.028]***	-0.049 [0.030]	-0.04 [0.031]
Passive labor market policy/gdp	-0.004 [0.005]	-0.009 [0.006]	-0.007 [0.006]	-0.011 [0.007]	-0.012 [0.008]	-0.009 [0.008]	0.008 [0.004]*	0.007 [0.005]	0.008 [0.005]***
Employment protection legislation			0.026 [0.022]			0.011 [0.026]			-0.022 [0.018]
Observations	130	130	113	130	130	113	130	130	113
Number of countries	29	29	23	29	29	23	29	29	23
R-squared	0.4	0.5	0.56	0.19	0.22	0.28	0.64	0.65	0.67
Country fixed effects	Yes	Yes	Yes	Yes	Yes	Yes	Yes	Yes	Yes
Cohort fixed effects	No	Yes	Yes	No	Yes	Yes	No	Yes	Yes

Robust standard errors clustered by countries in brackets—; *significant at 5%; **significant at 1%; ***significant at 10%.

In this framework we find only partial support to our previous findings with cross-sectional analysis. Focusing on a model that includes both country and cohort fixed effects, there is some evidence of a negative impact of unions on the distribution of work (column 9) and of a stronger impact of the minimum wage on earnings inequality. Contrary to previous results, passive labor market policies do not reach statistical significance for their negative impact on earnings and wage inequality, but register some positive impact on the Gini index for hours worked. Other institutional variables (such as the tax wedge, unemployment benefit, parental leave, and active labor market policies), which are constantly nonsignificant are not reported for brevity.[148] The same results are reinforced when we adopt the second matching rule, as shown in Table 18.9. The different data organization significantly extends the sample, and this allows for a more precise identification of the effects (see, for example, the unconditional correlation with passive labor market policies, depicted in Figure 18.34). Union density is now clearly reducing inequality in hours, and the minimum wage reduces inequality both in earnings and hours. In addition to the negative contribution of passive labor market policies on earnings and wage inequality, we now find that also active labor market policies negatively contribute to inequality reduction, possibly owing to the reduction in unemployment (i.e., more workers become employed earning a wage higher than the benefit).

18.5.4 Discussion

Our empirical results are consistent with the main findings in the literature reviewed in Section 18.4.6.[149] They confirm that the presence and stringency of a minimum wage reduces earnings inequality, also setting an (implicit) control on the distribution of working hours, which seems to be the main channel of inequality reduction of the bargaining activity of unions. Less common in the literature is the finding of a negative impact of both active and passive labor market policies. Here, we surmise that most of this effect works through variations in the unemployment rate: when active labor market policies are effective in pushing the unemployed back to work (at least for some hours) they reduce the bottom tail of the earnings distribution; when the unemployment support becomes more generous and/or more universal (as has happened during the current recession) it reduces the income gap between employed and unemployed, but potentially

---

[148] The other institutional measures appearing in Table 18.7 and not in Table 18.9 (child care, social expenditure, tax wedge) are not reported because they are not available over a longer time span going back to the older cohorts.

[149] Issues of data quality and a review of main findings for cross-country analysis can be found in Eichhorst et al. (2008).

Table 18.9 Gross earnings inequality (SILC 2010–PSID 2011) against market and labor market institutions (1975–2010) effects—OLS—longitudinal cohort data (matching rule 2)

Dependent variable	Gini of gross yearly employee earnings (working more than 1000 h per year)			Gini of gross hourly wages			Gini of employee hours (all durations)		
	1	2	3	4	5	6	7	8	9
Population share with secondary degree	0.018 [0.102]	0.1 [0.089]	0.053 [0.118]	−0.019 [0.089]	0.012 [0.099]	−0.017 [0.137]	0.097 [0.070]	0.092 [0.075]	0.104 [0.088]
Population share with postsecondary degree	−0.12 [0.051]*	−0.052 [0.065]	0 [0.061]	−0.116 [0.047]*	−0.104 [0.060]**	−0.091 [0.076]	−0.053 [0.043]	−0.013 [0.078]	−0.039 [0.095]
Female employment rate	0.283 [0.115]*	−0.116 [0.140]	−0.09 [0.149]	0.314 [0.129]*	0.177 [0.163]	0.218 [0.194]	−0.409 [0.090]***	−0.285 [0.148]**	−0.356 [0.158]*
Union density	0.094 [0.064]	−0.053 [0.035]	−0.042 [0.053]	0.109 [0.053]**	0.067 [0.056]	0.083 [0.088]	−0.137 [0.041]***	−0.082 [0.038]*	−0.123 [0.037]***
Minimum wage/mean wage	−0.226 [0.127]**	−0.22 [0.095]*	−0.259 [0.098]*	0.053 [0.101]	0.063 [0.098]	0.051 [0.105]	−0.102 [0.058]**	−0.119 [0.070]**	−0.101 [0.079]
Active labor market policy/gdp	−0.094 [0.032]***	−0.101 [0.024]***	−0.102 [0.024]***	−0.113 [0.035]***	−0.119 [0.037]***	−0.119 [0.036]***	−0.043 [0.028]	−0.049 [0.026]**	−0.051 [0.024]*
Passive labor market policy/GDP	−0.009 [0.020]	−0.037 [0.014]*	−0.047 [0.014]***	−0.054 [0.017]***	−0.064 [0.017]***	−0.068 [0.020]***	0.007 [0.013]	0.007 [0.013]	0.011 [0.014]
Employment protection legislation			0.035 [0.053]			−0.007 [0.062]			−0.057 [0.046]
Observations	203	203	161	203	203	161	203	203	161
Number of countries	29	29	23	29	29	23	29	29	23
R-squared	0.33	0.48	0.56	0.33	0.37	0.4	0.61	0.65	0.67
Country fixed effects	Yes	Yes	Yes	Yes	Yes	Yes	Yes	Yes	Yes
Cohort fixed effects	No	Yes	Yes	No	Yes	Yes	No	Yes	Yes

Robust standard errors clustered by countries in brackets—*significant at 5%; **significant at 10%; ***significant at 1%.

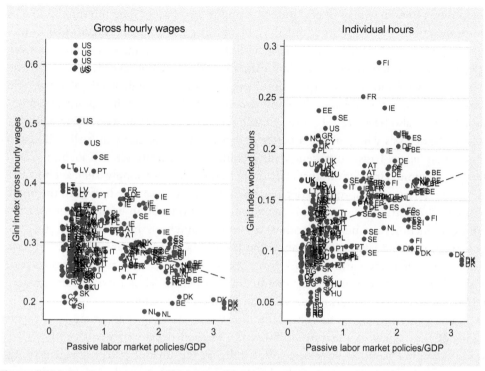

Figure 18.34 Earnings inequality (SILC 2010–PSID 2011) and passive labor market policies, 5-year averages (1975–2010).

raises the unemployment rate. The combined effect of these channels seems to be overall inequality-reduction.

18.6. CONCLUSION AND FUTURE RESEARCH

Putting the literature on the distribution of (individual) wages in the context of the (household) income distribution we are struck by the disconnect between the two. There is an extensive literature with a long tradition on each of them but very little on both, despite the fact that wage earnings are by far the most important source of income in modern society. The strong shift from single-earner to dual-earner households that has come about with the rapid growth of female and in many cases part-time employment and the growing attention paid to the phenomenon of household joblessness make this an important lacuna. Significant policy implications may be suspected. The debate on household joblessness has already put into question the workings of labor market policies. The important debate on job polarization ignores how households may be affected or, alternatively, how they may offer compensation for the process. The interlinking of the two distributions raises doubts about the policies of redistribution. Traditional instruments found on each of the two sides, such as the minimum wage or income taxation, expectedly work out differently in a dual-earner world where household labor supply can involve low-paid jobs or low (part-time) earnings even at high levels of household income. As a result, the effects of these instruments will change and their political support in society may also be altered. Future research will require improved and systematic fact finding, the analysis will generate a better understanding of earnings as well as hours of work on an *annual* basis, consistent with incomes, and also broaden to include other, often newly minted institutions that affect joint household labor supply, such as child care provisions. There is no shortage of detailed research on various issues; however, the broad picture of the distributions as such is lacking. Connections run in both directions, from earnings to incomes as much as the other way around, and household formation and concomitant household labor supply cannot be taken as a given but are affected by both. Importantly, often the national work force has also doubled over recent decades, as a result of rapidly rising educational attainment and female labor market participation, and not only the global work force after the demise of communism.

Subsequently turning to the distribution of wages alone we have gone back to the origins of the debate in the early 1980s and sketched developments toward what is now a large and complex literature. We find that the unanticipated rise in earnings inequality in the United States over the 1970s put LMIs, such as (declining) unionization, as one possible explanation among others, such as demography or deindustrialization, on the research agenda. During the 1990s, the debate gave rise to the thesis of skill-biased technological change but also to international comparisons. The former approach has focused on market forces of supply and demand, the latter deemed those insufficient because of the growing international divergence in wage-inequality trends and has put the limelight on the role of national LMIs. After some leapfrogging of the two approaches from one consensus explanation to another during the 1990s, the two seem to be increasingly growing apart during the 2000s when important new contributions were made to the disadvantage of an integrated approach that could give each its proper place. Both sides may be at risk of creating "Ptolemaic epicycles" aimed to incorporating new observations. The supply-and-demand approach is challenged by the need for finding better empirical measures of technological change aimed at dispelling doubts that the relative demand of skills may be a tautology. It has added "tasks," "offshoring," and even "consumer preferences," which risk being ad hoc additions,[150] without realizing their

---

[150] Compare Autor's (2013, 25) remark "that there are almost as many distinct task classifications as there are papers in the task literature."

institutional preconditions. The institutional approach, on the other side, faces an abundance of institutions and ever new ones are added. It lacks a sufficiently clear-cut concept of institutions, ranging from laws, regulations, and habits to actual policies, and of their interactions—be they mutually reinforcing or compensating—on the one hand, and a clear criterion for delineating the institutional scope on the other hand.

In light of this, the double aim of future work on both sides should be to foster itself and to integrate the other side into its own framework at the same time. Pursuing this may seem more a problem of empirical method for the institutional side, although by contrast on the demand and supply side the problem may be more one of theoretical method as long as institutions keep being viewed as bodies alien to the market and to theorizing. For both sides there is a perspective of work to do at the firm level. Matched employer–employee data can help enlighten the role of both institutions as well as labor supply and demand. Such data are increasingly becoming available. This brings us back to the availability and quality of the data in addition to the earnings/incomes fact-finding already mentioned. Data and analysis shall move beyond the commonly used earnings data for full-time workers only, which are less and less representative especially at the margins of earnings and incomes. Therefore, more needs to be done regarding individuals' and households' work efforts and earning outcomes on an annual basis. In addition, though much attention has been paid to data quality, a better grasp of the customary use of inequality measures—currently, each of the two approaches has its own rather exclusive preferences—seems desirable.

Finally, we have set up a simple model accounting for the correlation of the different components of inequality (between and within) with LMIs. We find indeed that unionized labor markets are ceteris paribus less unequal in terms of annual earnings, because both hourly wages and worked hours are more evenly distributed. We improve on existing approaches with the help of a pseudo-longitudinal approach linking workers cohort-wise to the change in institutions over their working life in three different ways. Empirical results of three cross-country exercises focusing on different inequality measures and covering the United States and all European countries in 2010–2011, suggest inequality-reducing effects of unionization for hours, and of minimum wages for both hours and earnings.

ACKNOWLEDGMENTS

We are grateful to Christina Haas, John Schmitt, Thomas Lemieux, Nicola Fuchs-Schündeln for their help with the data and Anna Salomons for some useful suggestions. We thank in particular our editors, Tony Atkinson and François Bourguignon, for their very helpful comments and suggestions.

APPENDIX A. COUNTRY CODES

ISO alpha-3 and alpha-2 country codes

AUS	AU	Australia
AUT	AT	Austria
BEL	BE	Belgium
BGR	BG	Bulgaria
CAN	CA	Canada (BC: British Columbia, ON: Ontario)
CHE	CH	Switzerland
CYP	CY	Cyprus
CZE	CZ	Czech Republic
DEU	DE	Germany
DEU-W	DE-W	West Germany
DNK	DK	Denmark
ESP	ES	Spain
EST	EE	Estonia
EU		European Union
FIN	FI	Finland
FRA	FR	France
GRC	GR	Greece (also named EL by Eurostat)
HUN	HU	Hungary
IRL	IE	Ireland
ISR	IL	Israel
ITA	IT	Italy
JPN	JP	Japan
KOR	KR	Korea
LTU	LT	Lithuania
LUX	LU	Luxemburg
LVA	LV	Latvia
MLT	MT	Malta
NLD	NL	Netherlands
NOR	NO	Norway
NZL	NZ	New Zealand
POL	PL	Poland
PRT	PT	Portugal
ROM	RO	Romania
SWE	SE	Sweden
SVK	SK	Slovak Republic
SVN	SI	Slovenia
UK	UK	United Kingdom (official code GBR not used)
USA	US	United States

APPENDIX B. DATA SOURCES AND ADDITIONAL TABLES ON EARNINGS

We obtain data from the EUSILC survey conducted in 2010 (ver.1 dated 01/03/12), to which we added populations from Cyprus and Ireland extracted from the 2009 survey (ver.2 dated 01/08/11). Overall among European countries we consider 476,265 observations (of which 9902 Irish and 7557 Cypriots). For these individuals we know relevant demographics (age, gender, education,[151] marital status, birthplace), occupational characteristics (whether employed or self-employed, full-time or part-time, permanent or temporary contract, ISCO occupational code, workplace size, work experience).

We obtain data on the United States from participants to PSID survey conducted in 2011. Basic demographics (age, gender, education,[152] marital status, labor market status) are obtained from individual file (file ind2011er.zip downloaded on 22/07/13), which includes 24,661 observations. Information on labor earnings are collected from one respondent for each of 8907 households (typically a male household head), who responds about wage and hours for himself and his spouse (file fam2011er.zip downloaded on 22/07/13).

We adopt two selection rules:

(a) population in relevant working age, which we define as being between 20 and 64 years old. This is justified to allow for secondary school completion, and to take into account different early retirement rules in different countries. This leads to the exclusion of employed youngsters aged 15–19, a fraction of which is employed with an average hourly wage that is on average half of the average wage in the adult population. Because countries differ in the duration of compulsory education as well as in institutional design, we have preferred to leave the youngster component of the labor force out of our analysis.[153]

(b) population in the labor market, who self-define as either employed (employee or self-employed) or unemployed. This takes as exogenously given the significant cross-country differences in participation/employment rates (see Table 18.A1). These differences are even enhanced when we consider analogous rates computed at household level. Notice the high share of self-employed in Italy and Greece, which are also the countries where the share of top incomes accruing to them is

---

[151] Data on years of education have been computed from maximum educational attainment according to ISCED classification (variable PE040 in SILC) converted into years by using legal duration.

[152] Data on completed years of education are directly reported by the interviewees (variable ER34119 in PSID).

[153] There is an additional reason for excluding these cases as we identify cohabiting couples by taking the two first working members in the household. Retaining these individuals would increase the risk of mixing couples up with single earners and an earning child.

largest. The final sample is made of 264,216 individuals in the labor market, among which 201,500 employees, 33,384 self-employed, and 29,332 unemployed.

The labor earnings variable is defined as either "gross yearly earnings from dependent employment—cash or near cash"[154] or "gross yearly cash benefits or losses from self-employment" (see Table 18.A2 for means and standard deviations).[155] Unemployed subsidies received by (temporarily) unemployed workers are also considered in the computation of earnings inequality.[156]

In order to distinguish between annual earnings and hourly wages, we need information about the number of hours worked. In both survey hours worked are reconstructed thanks combining answers to two questions (weekly hours usually worked in recent months—thus referred to the period of interview—and number of months worked in the previous year).[157] The gross hourly wage rate is then computed dividing the yearly earnings by the hours worked.[158] Descriptive statistics on hours worked and hourly wages are reported in Table 18.A3. Notice that there is a significant loss of information when moving from yearly data (259,500 observations with nonnegative annual earnings) to hourly wage (228,153 observations with nonmissing hourly wages), due to missing information about weekly hours worked. A probit estimate indicates that young uneducated women holding a temporary contract are more likely not to report hours.

---

[154] Our GW variable (earnings from dependent employment) and GSELFW (earnings from self-employment) correspond to PY010G and PY050G variables, respectively, in EUSILC. In the case of PSID labor earnings are obtained from the sum of ER47501, ER47552, ER47582, and ER47612 variables (appropriately converted into yearly values) for the household head and from the sum of ER47752, ER47779, ER47809, and ER47839 variables for the working spouse. They are then separated between dependent employment or self-employment earnings according to the nonnegative value of the ER47495 or ER47752 variables ("how much is your salary").

[155] Negative values on earnings from self-employment are recoded into zeros, because most inequality indices (notably the Gini index) are defined over nonnegative values.

[156] This corresponds to the variable PY090G in EUSILC and to the variables ER48500/ER48619 (converted in annual values) in PSID.

[157] In EUSILC this corresponds to the variable PL060 (number of hours usually worked per week in main job) and the variables PL073-74-75-76-80 (number of months spent at full-time/part-time work as employee/self-employed (including family worker)/unemployed). In PSID this corresponds to the variables ER47456/ER47713 (On average, how many hours a week did (you/he/she) work on (all of) (your/his/her) (job/jobs) during 2010?) multiplied by variables ER47454/ER47711 (weeks employed last year—reconstructed variable from work histories) net of variables ER47633/ER47890 (weeks of vacation).

[158] In EUSILC, data on hourly wages are not fully temporally consistent, because the gross yearly wage and the months of work are referred to 2009, whereas the information about the weekly hours is referred to 2010. In PSID the interviewees directly provide a measure of hourly wage (variables ER47501/ER47758: What is your hourly wage rate for your regular work time?). In the case of the United States, where both measures are available, computed and elicited wages with positive values exhibit a correlation of 0.53.

Table 18.A1 Descriptive statistics computed from microdata—SILC 2010 and PSID 2011—labor market attachment (sample weights)

	Participation rate	Employment rate	Unemployment rate	Share self-employed	Female participation rate
Austria	0.734	0.676	0.079	0.124	0.596
Belgium	0.732	0.650	0.112	0.106	0.597
Bulgaria	0.800	0.670	0.163	0.096	0.620
Cyprus	0.754	0.710	0.058	0.139	0.644
Czech Republic	0.752	0.675	0.103	0.167	0.582
Denmark	0.782	0.715	0.085	0.094	0.702
Estonia	0.783	0.647	0.173	0.074	0.648
Finland	0.765	0.673	0.121	0.135	0.650
France	0.754	0.672	0.109	0.099	0.637
Germany	0.792	0.711	0.102	0.055	0.659
Greece	0.736	0.644	0.125	0.304	0.553
Hungary	0.687	0.595	0.134	0.124	0.542
Iceland	0.789	0.731	0.073	0.125	0.685
Ireland	0.707	0.592	0.162	0.149	0.532
Italy	0.682	0.607	0.109	0.219	0.485
Latvia	0.791	0.602	0.239	0.071	0.593
Lithuania	0.804	0.649	0.193	0.100	0.662
Luxembourg	0.739	0.692	0.063	0.078	0.609
Malta	0.632	0.593	0.063	0.136	0.423
Netherlands	0.760	0.732	0.037	0.154	0.660
Norway	0.797	0.771	0.033	0.073	0.741
Poland	0.716	0.640	0.105	0.214	0.571
Portugal	0.788	0.672	0.148	0.144	0.617
Romania	0.689	0.653	0.053	0.265	0.547
Slovak Republic	0.764	0.660	0.137	0.108	0.603
Slovenia	0.737	0.633	0.141	0.096	0.587
Spain	0.787	0.624	0.207	0.161	0.546
Sweden	0.823	0.776	0.057	0.043	0.751
United Kingdom	0.768	0.728	0.052	0.122	0.677
United States	0.791	0.709	0.104	0.109	0.683
Average	0.752	0.671	0.108	0.138	0.605

Table 18.A2 Descriptive statistics computed from microdata—SILC 2010 and PSID 2011–labor earnings (sample weights)

Country name	Gross earnings from dependent employment (mean)	Gross earnings from dependent employment (SD)	Gross earnings from self-employment (mean)	Gross earnings from self-employment (SD)	No. of observations with nonmissing values on yearly earnings
Austria	26,461.08	25,858.63	4096.55	17,355.84	6116
Belgium	26,723.36	20,772.17	2717.21	11,508.15	6387
Bulgaria	3024.31	2925.93	446.67	2378.81	7731
Cyprus	18,748.41	16,532.35	3139.14	13,762.04	3970
Czech Republic	7499.50	6937.02	1752.81	6380.98	9489
Denmark	38,504.27	26,550.36	2017.71	18,497.89	7005
Estonia	7507.27	6367.43	122.38	959.08	5891
Finland	27,382.17	21,351.46	2076.83	10,272.64	12,705
France	22,219.13	19,263.07	2110.23	15,184.50	11,518
Germany	24,586.15	22,526.16	1968.18	14,598.60	12,693
Greece	12,219.81	14,306.38	5645.76	18,567.37	7163
Hungary	5038.98	5062.23	777.84	3393.05	10,240
Iceland	23,832.86	17,620.38	818.24	3899.32	4075
Ireland	26,624.65	28,929.35	4520.33	19,799.64	4766
Italy	17,593.58	17,522.40	7017.56	24,495.35	19,637
Latvia	5942.19	6430.71	207.53	1370.13	6742
Lithuania	4979.52	5607.18	447.30	2589.25	6097
Luxembourg	42,588.71	38,248.88	2896.52	22,171.74	5717
Malta	13,787.59	11,406.58	2393.88	8493.19	3678
Netherlands	31,138.58	26,156.98	3186.18	16,507.76	11,621
Norway	42,686.63	32,290.34	3409.42	23,335.28	6269
Poland	5567.64	6017.03	1020.09	3613.49	14,693
Portugal	10,768.63	12,283.16	1432.51	6260.98	5655
Romania	2664.20	2452.14	333.46	1338.79	7342
Slovak Republic	6322.45	8057.32	683.42	2971.25	8071
Slovenia	14,493.82	12,900.63	1125.57	4699.40	14,085
Spain	14,620.40	14,235.10	1305.97	7504.83	16,812
Sweden	25,384.12	18,901.72	753.78	5208.48	8355
United Kingdom	24,787.20	28,023.56	3654.77	26,042.01	7818
United States	51,786.79	840,084.88	7103.13	35,807.86	7159
Average	18,819.88	32,903.78	2627.03	16,288.20	259,500

Note: Data in 2010 Euros except US where data are in 2011 US dollars.

Table 18.A3 Descriptive statistics computed from microdata—SILC 2010 and PSID 2011—hours and wages (sample weights)

	Hours worked (mean)	Hours worked (SD)	Hourly wage (mean)	Hourly wage (SD)	No. of observations with nonmissing values of hourly wages
Austria	1801.05	648.58	17.14	25.54	5689
Belgium	1742.40	630.42	18.74	16.46	5662
Bulgaria	1924.69	413.00	1.83	1.67	6381
Cyprus	1844.24	527.32	10.67	8.73	3743
Czech Republic	1979.71	489.53	4.23	3.29	8685
Denmark	1752.24	449.20	24.02	15.45	6615
Estonia	1761.99	498.25	5.22	5.93	4795
Finland	1718.94	558.07	19.46	21.05	11,479
France	1746.34	617.55	15.20	18.75	10,223
Germany	1746.93	619.15	15.24	11.98	11,569
Greece	1829.68	553.70	7.96	8.64	6212
Hungary	1844.58	403.42	3.05	2.71	8876
Iceland	1914.37	642.18	14.38	19.49	3783
Ireland	1637.80	693.63	22.17	29.44	3917
Italy	1829.60	474.38	11.17	10.77	17,248
Latvia	1816.58	487.95	4.07	4.06	5092
Lithuania	1784.31	415.07	3.38	3.41	4995
Luxembourg	1833.12	576.49	25.13	20.55	5311
Malta	1863.97	517.44	8.22	7.08	3353
Netherlands	1582.64	553.61	21.33	19.91	11,212
Norway	1765.72	504.90	25.81	21.14	6043
Poland	1894.65	517.62	3.40	4.36	13,077
Portugal	1866.69	470.88	7.02	7.65	4281
Romania	1950.27	352.44	1.46	1.24	6589
Slovak Republic	1913.54	395.13	3.81	4.11	7180
Slovenia	1897.84	415.46	8.76	7.16	12,131
Spain	1821.19	536.07	10.32	10.42	12,783
Sweden	1516.64	496.22	19.80	24.18	7755
United Kingdom	1785.60	637.22	15.39	19.19	7328
Unites States	1937.14	848.38	8.65	26.66	6146
Average	1793.65	564.99	12.37	15.44	228,153

Note: Data in 2010 Euros except US where data are in 2011 US dollars.

Table 18.A4 Estimates of model relevant parameters—employed or unemployed individuals—SILC 2010 and PSID 2011

	(1)	(2)	(3)	(4)	(5)	(6)	(7)	(8)	(9)	(10)	(11)	(12)	(13)
	Skilled workers	Unskilled workers	Unemployed	Average wage	Unemployment benefit	Replacement rate	Skilled wage	Unskilled wage	Wage premium	Between-group inequality	Overall inequality		
	$\alpha(1-u)$ pct. points	$(1-\alpha)(1-u)$ pct. points	u pct. points	$\bar{w}$ euros/dollars	b euros/dollars	γ pct. points	w^s euros/dollars	w^u euros/dollars	σ pct. points	$\mathrm{Gini_{est}}$	$\mathrm{Gini_{obs}}$	$\Delta\mathrm{Gini}$	$\frac{\mathrm{Gini_{est}}}{\mathrm{Gini_{obs}}}$
AUT	0.321	0.616	0.063	32,205.34	3948.59	0.12	41,021.68	27,604.24	0.49	0.073	0.348	0.28	0.21
BEL	0.439	0.461	0.100	33,006.56	5958.73	0.18	39,378.79	26,940.58	0.46	0.086	0.299	0.21	0.29
BGR	0.225	0.654	0.121	3789.24	449.98	0.12	5186.9	3309.31	0.57	0.100	0.346	0.25	0.29
CYP	0.391	0.567	0.042	21,922.22	2928.37	0.13	28,080.84	17,672.54	0.59	0.074	0.364	0.29	0.20
CZE	0.176	0.764	0.060	9785.79	926.04	0.09	14,118.73	8786.53	0.61	0.067	0.3	0.23	0.22
DEU	0.454	0.470	0.076	47,286.8	6110.35	0.13	55,418.81	41,882.96	0.32	0.067	0.387	0.32	0.17
DNK	0.377	0.566	0.057	8493.88	1626.26	0.19	10,215.24	7451.71	0.37	0.060	0.24	0.18	0.25
EST	0.322	0.532	0.145	34,994.66	4483.46	0.13	42,707.44	27,756.81	0.54	0.116	0.361	0.24	0.32
ESP	0.345	0.483	0.171	25,870.6	5178.83	0.20	32,662.33	21,905.82	0.49	0.119	0.352	0.23	0.34
FIN	0.434	0.463	0.103	30,659.61	3949.61	0.13	38,298.93	23,276.59	0.65	0.104	0.317	0.21	0.33
FRA	0.336	0.576	0.087	19,628.96	3255.67	0.17	23,998.9	16,440.65	0.46	0.080	0.321	0.24	0.25
GRC	0.381	0.522	0.097	6403.25	955.58	0.15	9143.06	5173.97	0.77	0.108	0.344	0.24	0.31
HUN	0.273	0.608	0.119	27,111.2	3831.86	0.14	32,224.25	23,284.92	0.38	0.089	0.366	0.28	0.24
IRE	0.484	0.361	0.155	38,583.85	8978.04	0.23	45,739.25	28,977.96	0.58	0.111	0.404	0.29	0.27
ISL	0.394	0.527	0.079	23,958.99	3936.05	0.16	29,992.45	22,250.91	0.35	0.069	0.326	0.26	0.21
ITA	0.203	0.718	0.079	7518.82	1252.23	0.17	10,476.27	5644.96	0.86	0.091	0.32	0.23	0.29
LTU	0.574	0.296	0.131	6335.65	961.26	0.15	7365.67	4337.72	0.70	0.108	0.424	0.32	0.26
LUX	0.296	0.649	0.055	44,751.21	11,201.46	0.25	67,207.76	34,529.19	0.95	0.095	0.372	0.28	0.25
LVA	0.314	0.495	0.192	16,856.53	3797.42	0.23	22,378.49	14,985.31	0.49	0.125	0.44	0.31	0.28
MLT	0.242	0.713	0.045	37,965.09	7090.32	0.19	47,164.16	30,699.66	0.54	0.061	0.305	0.24	0.20
NLD	0.432	0.547	0.021	48,789.02	6094.77	0.12	56,535.29	41,581.87	0.36	0.047	0.317	0.27	0.15
NOR	0.470	0.505	0.024	7390.9	996.99	0.13	9625.72	6253.77	0.54	0.062	0.316	0.25	0.20
POL	0.312	0.614	0.074	14,248.9	3843.58	0.27	26,901.73	11,502.8	1.34	0.122	0.362	0.24	0.34
PRT	0.159	0.734	0.106	3684.08	966.96	0.26	5262.04	3126.16	0.68	0.081	0.385	0.30	0.21
ROM	0.254	0.720	0.026	7954.01	1245.76	0.16	10,154.17	7159.13	0.42	0.046	0.27	0.22	0.17
SWE	0.426	0.530	0.045	18,068.09	2233.65	0.12	27,336.91	14,716.41	0.86	0.093	0.295	0.20	0.32
SVNI	0.242	0.669	0.089	20,305.54	4503.04	0.22	26,071.97	16,187.4	0.61	0.083	0.329	0.25	0.25
SVK	0.248	0.687	0.065	28,105.98	5413.02	0.19	31,987.71	24,987.56	0.28	0.051	0.29	0.24	0.18
UK	0.427	0.541	0.033	30,438.71	4831.86	0.16	39,293.29	23,445.94	0.68	0.076	0.404	0.33	0.19
United States	0.531	0.378	0.091	39,150.52	9903.6	0.25	47,253.16	27,769.21	0.70	0.090	0.408	0.32	0.22
Mean	0.342	0.571	0.087	23,162.53	4147.73	0.18	31,462.71	18,192.87	0.73	0.099	0.342	0.24	0.29

APPENDIX C. DATA SOURCES AND DESCRIPTIVE STATISTICS ON LMIs

Data on institutional measures were collected over a time interval spanning half a century, from 1960 to 2010.

Union density

It measures the fraction of wage and salary earners who are members of trade unions. It excludes unemployed and retired workers (net version). Source: ICTWSS database version 2 (Database on Institutional Characteristics of Trade Unions, Wage Setting, State Intervention and Social Pacts in 34 countries between 1960 and 2007—see Visser, 2009—variable UD—downloaded on 04/04/13).[159]

Coverage

It measures the fraction of employees covered by wage-bargaining agreements over all wage and salary earners in employment with the right to bargaining. Source: ICTWSS database version 2 (variable ADJCOV).

Wage centralization

It represents a summary measure (ranging between 0 and 1) of centralization and coordination of union wage bargaining, taking into account both union authority and union concentration at multiple levels—source: ICTWSS database version 2 (variable CENT).

Strike activity

It measures the days not worked for strikes and lockouts divided by participant worker—total economy. Source is ILO (downloaded on 04/04/13).

Minimum wage

It takes the ratio of the statutory minimum wage relative to mean wage of full-time workers (sometimes known as "Kaitz index"—see Dolado et al., 1996). However this measure does not consider the possibility of differentiation across workers types. For this reason, Aghion et al. (2011) have combined the ratio of the minimum wage to the GDP per capita with an index of stringency derived from ILO.[160] For this reason, the

---

[159] This measures highly correlates with the OECD corresponding measure (0.95) and with the ILO one (0.99), which is not surprising given the background studies conducted by the same author (Jelle Visser).

[160] This index takes value of 1 if there is a legal statutory minimum wage and if the minimum wage is set at the national level without any derogation, value of 0.5 if there is a legal statutory minimum wage but with derogations by age, qualification, region, sector, or occupation; or if the wage floor is set by collective bargaining but extended to all workers, and a value of 0 if the wage is set by collective bargaining and only applies to the unionized workers. This solution introduces a value of the index even if a country does not have the provision of a minimum wage, because otherwise these countries should be left out of picture. See the ILO TRAVAIL legal databases (http://www.ilo.org/dyn/travail), which however provides only the contemporaneous information (thus preventing us to use the measure for past periods).

variable is set to zero when minimum wage provision is absent. Data are downloaded from the OECD Stats website (except than in the case of Iceland, whose values are taken from Table 5.5 of Danish Technological Institute. *Assessment of the Labour Market in Iceland.* Contract no. VC/2010/038 Final report—Policy and Business Analysis—April 2011).

Employment protection legislation

The measure we use is provided by OECD, which recently have partially revised their country assessment (OECD, 2012).[161] It measures the stringency of firing regulation and is based on eighteen dimensions of the firing procedure.[162] There is a second series provided by World Bank, which has been used among others such as Botero et al. (2004).[163]

Unemployment benefit

Unemployment insurance and unemployment assistance benefits—gross replacement rate (ratio to the average wage) for a full-time adult worker. The source is OECD historical series, which is available in odd years and imputed using intermediate means in even years. It is the average between single worker and one-earner married couple with two children.[164]

---

[161] Data used in the analysis of the main text have been downloaded on 02/08/13. A preliminary download conducted on 4/4/2013 yields a different series for overall EPL, which however exhibit a correlation with the new one of 0.97.

[162] Eight dimensions concern "regular contracts": notification procedures, delay involved before notice can start, length of the notice period at various tenure durations, severance pay at various tenure duration, definition of justified or unfair dismissal, length of trial period, compensation following unfair dismissal, possibility of reinstatement following unfair dismissal. Six dimensions concern "temporary employment": valid cases for use of fixed-term contracts (FTC), maximum number of successive FTC, maximum cumulated duration of successive FTC, types of work for which temporary work agency (TWA) employment is legal, restrictions on number of renewals, maximum cumulated duration of TWA contracts. Four dimensions concern "collective dismissal": definition of collective dismissal, additional notification requirements, additional delays involved before notice can start, other special costs to employers—methodology is accurately described in chapter 2 of OECD, 2004)

[163] The World Bank index measures firing costs in terms of weeks of salary and it is based on three components: the notice period for redundancy dismissal, the severance pay for redundancy dismissal, and the legally mandated penalty for redundancy dismissal.

[164] It combines GRR(APW) until 2001 and GRR(AW) afterward. Eurostat provides a measure of the unemployment benefit net replacement rate for a single worker, which has a correlation index with OECD gross ratio equal to 0.55 and a limited time coverage, because it starts with 2001 and does not cover the United States.

Tax wedge

Average tax wedge (sum of social contributions and income taxes as ratio to the average wage). It considers the average between single worker with no child and one-earner married couple with two children. The source are the estimates from the OECD microsimulation model.

Social expenditure

It measures the expenditure for cash benefits and benefit in kind for social assistance, as percentage of GDP. The source is OECD historical series, which are available on 5-year base, and then interpolated.

Child care

It measures the enrollment rate in early child care and preprimary education (average between age 3, 4, and 5—full- and part-time students) and proxies the availability of child care facilities. Available values for years 2005 and 2010, while intermediate values are interpolated. The source is OECD, *Education at a Glance 2012*, Table C2.1.

Parental leave

It captures the possibility of reconciling work and fertility, by measuring weeks of paid leave for childbirth. The series is available since 1970. The source is Thévenon and Solaz (2013). Further documentation can be found at http://www.oecd.org/social/soc/oecdfamilydatabase.htm

Tax treatment of household incomes

This variable aims to capture the potential favorable tax treatment of working couples vis-à-vis individual taxation. It is constructed as the ratio between the average tax rate of single earner family (earning 170% of average wage) and the average tax rate of a two earners family (main earner at average wage and second earner making 67% of average wage). The reported variable consists of a further averaging between two household situation with respect to children (zero children and two children families). A higher value would indicate a favorable treatment of labor market participation of a second earner. Data available since 2001. The underlying data is obtained from the OECD microsimulation model, available at http://stats.oecd.org/Index.aspx?DataSetCode=FIXINCLSA.

Active and passive labor market policies

It considers the public expenditure on active or passive labor market policies as percentage of GDP. It combines two data sources: when available we have been using

OECD statistics for homogeneity with other series; otherwise we have resorted to Eurostat, which classifies as actives expenditure categories from 2 to 7 (2. Training—3. Job rotation and job sharing—4. Employment incentives—5. Supported employment and rehabilitation—6. Direct job creation—7. Start-up incentives) and passive expenditure categories 8 and 9 (8. Out-of-work income maintenance and support—9. Early retirement).

Overall means and standard deviations for these variables are reported in Table 18.A5. Country means are reported in table with reference to the most recent decade.

Table 18.A5 Descriptive statistics for institutional measures, sample period 1960–2010, 30 countries

Variable	No. of observations	Mean	SD	Minimum	Maximum
Union density	1123	45.99	22.97	6.67	100.00
Coverage	931	70.70	21.74	7.50	100.00
Centralization	1016	0.42	0.19	0.08	0.98
Strike activity	730	5.09	7.29	0.00	61.14
Minimum wage	1179	0.19	0.21	0.00	0.71
Employment protection legislation	506	2.37	0.88	0.26	5.00
Unemployment benefit	918	27.02	15.48	0.00	70.00
Tax wedge	294	25.32	7.75	8.17	41.88
Social expenditure	615	2.07	1.00	0.20	4.40
Child care	144	81.73	16.46	24.70	101.13
Parental leave	887	40.82	43.57	0.00	214.00
Tax treatment of household incomes	228	1.93	1.47	0.26	8.21
Active labor market policies	560	0.70	0.52	0.03	3.04
Passive labor market policies	572	1.25	0.99	0.08	5.45

Table 18.A6 Sample means of institutional measures—recent years (average 2000–2010)

	Union density	Coverage	Central-ization	Strike	Minimum wage	Employment protection legislation	Unemploy-ment benefit	Tax wedge	Social expenditure	Child care	Parental leave	Tax treatment of household incomes	Active labor market policies	Passive labor market policies
Austria	32.37	98.91	0.90	1.03	0.00	2.47	31.67	31.90	2.72	78.00	117.09	0.85	0.66	1.32
Belgium	51.88	96.00	0.46	23.07	0.44	1.82	40.91	36.97	2.63	99.54	28	1.93	1.17	2.23
Bulgaria	24.01	32.50	0.31	na	0.00	na	46.40	21.43	na	na	na	na	0.30	0.25
Cyprus	61.63	57.35	0.25	2.33	0.00	na	60.40	8.50	na	na	na	0.56	0.13	0.58
Czech Republic	20.74	43.77	0.25	na	0.31	3.21	6.14	17.74	1.87	82.01	185.64	0.33	0.23	0.27
Denmark	71.62	81.87	0.47	3.49	0.00	2.13	52.72	39.19	3.55	91.91	48.91	2.26	1.72	2.06
Estonia	9.69	25.06	0.36	0.21	0.30	2.43	50.00	17.60	1.79	87.08	na	0.67	0.11	0.39
Finland	71.84	87.13	0.40	2.16	0.00	2.19	34.56	32.57	2.98	51.29	42.35	2.69	0.90	1.84
France	7.84	90.00	0.21	22.47	0.47	2.42	39.88	24.90	3.02	100.99	32.55	0.69	1.02	1.46
Germany	21.44	64.40	0.48	1.60	0.00	2.80	25.85	36.73	1.96	91.57	60.1	4.11	1.03	1.78
Greece	25.03	65.00	0.34	na	0.33	2.80	14.42	22.77	1.14	72.30	24.09	1.06	0.17	0.44
Hungary	18.01	37.85	0.23	1.36	0.36	2.00	13.31	34.13	3.26	86.86	110	1.11	0.42	0.44
Iceland	86.47	88.02	na	16.74	0.51	1.73	40.76	26.00	3.00	95.44	25.97	3.16	na	na
Ireland	37.55	49.91	0.52	6.20	0.45	1.36	34.95	11.86	2.70	53.51	20.91	2.42	0.75	1.24
Italy	34.01	80.00	0.34	1.01	0.00	2.76	34.64	24.59	1.31	97.71	48	4.05	0.50	0.83
Latvia	19.41	19.41	0.48	4.01	0.33	na	60.00	25.11	na	na	na	1.08	0.19	0.46
Lithuania	13.93	12.16	0.30	2.41	0.36	na	47.62	23.61	na	na	na	2.74	0.18	0.23
Luxembourg	41.00	58.22	0.31	na	0.34	2.25	26.67	19.89	3.36	85.95	42	1.19	0.42	0.60
Malta	56.02	58.26	0.37	1.35	0.00	na	30.63	14.94	na	na	na	1.13	0.04	0.36
Netherlands	20.69	82.63	0.57	2.58	0.43	2.87	41.74	32.36	1.67	68.02	20.73	1.40	1.31	1.74
Norway	54.44	72.94	0.51	11.38	0.00	2.33	51.80	28.46	2.93	91.93	37.91	5.97	0.65	0.44
Poland	19.18	39.00	0.23	3.48	0.34	2.23	10.89	28.74	1.13	49.00	122.55	0.70	0.43	0.74
Portugal	20.92	60.07	0.34	1.35	0.36	4.45	42.23	18.55	1.15	81.19	18.65	1.75	0.64	1.11
Romania	36.28	70.00	0.25	13.27	0.29	na	32.20	27.34	na	na	na	na	0.08	0.38
Slovak Republic	24.34	44.70	0.50	0.01	0.35	2.30	9.50	18.22	1.89	72.53	164	0.99	0.30	0.46
Slovenia	35.96	97.40	0.40	na	0.43	2.65	61.64	29.09	1.07	80.67	na	1.00	0.29	0.41
Spain	15.60	87.84	0.36	2.55	0.34	2.36	34.98	16.41	1.16	98.68	16	0.65	0.79	1.78
Sweden	74.40	93.17	0.51	3.58	0.00	2.62	37.62	31.25	3.29	90.39	59.95	3.50	1.20	1.06
United Kingdom	28.74	34.64	0.11	2.20	0.36	1.20	15.99	25.87	3.14	91.88	28.55	1.84	0.36	0.23
United States	12.07	13.88	0.18	na	0.26	0.26	18.05	18.16	0.70	63.01	0	1.49	0.15	0.49

APPENDIX D. LITERATURE SUMMARY TABLES: HOUSEHOLD INCOMES AND EARNINGS AND WAGE DISPERSION AND INSTITUTIONS[165]

Table 18.A7 Household incomes and Earnings (see Section 18.2)

Authors	Years and countries	Data sets* and sample selection	Method and important variables	Main findings
i. Comparison of aggregate inequality measures				
Atkinson and Brandolini 2006	CAN, DEU, FIN, NLD, NOR, SWE, UK, United States; around 2000.	LIS; sample consecutively extending from employees aged 15–65 to all individuals in households.	International comparisons of earnings dispersion: cross section and trends. Comparison Gini's of wages, earnings of employed 15–64, earnings of all 15–64, income all 15–64, income all, equivalized income all.	They aim to take stock of existing research and conclude to, interalia: – need to model supply and demand and institutional variables in a common framework, linked to an underlying economic model; – differences in definitions and coverage may affect cross-country comparisons and cannot be assumed to be fixed over time. – need for care with different income concepts and different populations. – important interdependences between different explanatory variables.
Brown (1999)	Mainly US studies, from Gramlich 1976 to Neumark and Wascher 1997.		Several simple statistics: poor fraction among low-wage workers: around 20%. Card and Krueger (1995a) argue that other forces have increased the fraction. Probability of low pay among workers in low-income families. But many poor families have no workers. Gains of minimum wage increase comparable across deciles. Small impacts, difficult to find.	Effects of the minimum wage on the wage distribution became clearer with the declining real minimum wage in the 1980s; nevertheless the ability of minimum wages to equalize the distribution of family incomes remains quite limited.
Burtless (1999)	United States; 1979 vs. 1996.	CPS; ages 25–59.	Counterfactuals for Gini coefficient of household–equivalent personal income: holding constant male, female earnings distributions, or partners' earnings correlation.	Much of the rise in overall US inequality is due to family composition shifts and other causes rather than the change in pay patterns. Household income inequality change attributed to 33–44% earnings, shift to single and single-parent households 21–25%, partners' increased earnings correlation 13%.

[165] Tables A7 and A8 make generous use of summaries, abstracts, introduction and conclusions of the underlying papers.

Gottschalk and Smeeding (1997)	AUS, ISR, JPN, NOR, NZL, United States, and most of EU15; 1980s into early 1990s.	National data sets.	Comparison of studies of income inequality with discussion of roles of earnings, demography and social protection. The inclusion of multiple income sources received by multiple individuals thwarts attempts to identify the causal links that led to variations across time and across countries in the distribution of total posttax and transfer family income. Researchers have, therefore, limited themselves largely to purely accounting exercises which decompose changes in overall inequality into a set of component parts that may reflect endogenous as well as exogenous changes.	Better structural models of income distribution and redistribution that can be applied across nations are badly needed. Ideally, an overall framework would simultaneously model the generation of all sources of income (labor income, capital income, private transfers, public transfers, and all forms of taxation) as well as the formation of income sharing units. Although most of the components of such a model were identified as early as the mid-1960s, our progress toward building such a model has been slow. If we are to understand why we observe the extent and pattern of inequality levels and trends that are extant in this review, an overall conceptual framework with empirically testable components is the next big step that must be taken.
Gottschalk and Danziger (2005)	United States; 1975–2002.	CPS; ages 22–62 with positive earnings, males/females separately.	Comparison of wage rates: between/within inequality, and annual hours, family earnings, family incomes and equivalized incomes. No attempt to decompose the change in family income into its component parts because there are many ways to do so and there is no consensus on the most appropriate decomposition.	The similarity in the timing of changes in male wage rate inequality and family income inequality has been used as evidence that increased family income inequality primarily reflects increased inequality of wage rates. Authors show that other important factors were also at work. Female wage inequality actually declined steadily from 1975 through 2002. Although earnings inequality of males grew even more rapidly than wage inequality during the early 1980s, this largely reflects cyclical changes in hours. For females, changes in hours more than offset the rise in wage inequality. The acceleration in male wage and earnings inequality during the early

Continued

Table 18.A7 Household incomes and Earnings (see Section 18.2)—cont'd

Authors	Years and countries	Data sets* and sample selection	Method and important variables	Main findings
Kenworthy (2008)	12: 9 old EU, United States, CAN, AUS; 1980–2005.	LIS for households, OECD for employment.	Cross-country comparison circa 2000 of pretax pretransfer equivalized household income inequality (P75:P25 ratios) to individual earnings inequality, (part-time) employment rate, zero-earner household rate, singles and marital homogamy, and to posttax posttransfer inequality (Gini's).	1980s disappears when earnings of other family members are included. Thus, changes in work hours by other family members seems to have largely offset increased male labor market inequality. Thus, although much of the cross-country variation in levels of posttax–posttransfer income inequality is a product of differences in levels of market inequality, redistribution is also important. For understanding developments over time, redistribution is essential. Thus the focus ought to be chiefly on employment and redistribution, rather than on wage inequality and/or household composition.
Reed and Cancian (2001)	United States; 1969–1999.	March CPS; families with adults aged 25–59.	A new approach to measuring source contributions that has three advantages over inequality decompositions. First, a clear counterfactual, "What would have been the change in family income inequality were it not for the change in the distribution of the income source?" Second, simulation of counterfactual distribution of family income, allowing use of multiple summary measures of inequality and evaluation of impact at various points in the distribution (e.g., the 10th and 90th percentiles). Third, incorporate married-couple and single-person families and account for changes in marriage rate.	Changes in distribution of male earnings account for more of the growth in family income inequality than do changes in any other source of income. Changes in the distribution of female earnings have reduced family income inequality.

				Cross-country differences in individual labor-market earnings inequality are amplified by household combination of labor supply and the correlation of pay between its members. The former effect is always much larger (+99%) than the latter (+11%).
Salverda and Haas (2014)	EU (ex. CYP, MLT); 2010.	SILC 2011; employees in households with main income from earnings and working-age nonstudent head.	Decile comparisons with fixed household rankings of individuals; annual earnings with breakdown by hourly rates and annual hours worked; number of earners in household over deciles of household earnings.	
Večerník (2010)	CZE, HUN, POL, SVK, and AUT, DEU; from late 1980s on for CZE, HUN, POL, SVK, 2007 for all six.	LIS, and SILC for 2007; employees only.	Quintile shares and Gini's. Pearson coefficient correlations of household incomes with personal earnings for males/females; decomposition of Gini's.	Even with the best possible data on personal and household incomes available for analysis, there is still much we do not know about income sources, development and inequality. In fact, we cannot expect that income statistics will ever be capable of describing real incomes and income inequality in full. However, not having any other source of general information about income distribution, we cannot do anything else but examine the surveys from various angles and try, from time to time, to look beyond just data.
Večerník (2013)	CZE; 1988, 1992, 1996, 2002, 2009	National microcensuses and Czech part of SILC.	OLS regressions of contributions by sex, age and education to couples' earnings.	Increasing influence of education is the personal earnings of employees; in couples, education has an important impact on both women's employment and their earnings; the importance of marital partners' education levels on household income grew even more than its effect on earnings.

ii. Decompositions of incomes

Brewer et al. (2009)	UK; 1968–2006.	HBAI; all individuals.	Decomposition: Shorrocks (1982) (Paul, 2004). Incomes: regression-based methodology developed by Fields (2003) and Yun (2006). Incomes: after all direct taxes and all state	Changes in within-group inequality are always the dominant explanatory factor in changes in overall inequality, although between-group effects also contribute significantly in some periods. Changes in relative incomes between groups are the

Continued

Table 18.A7 Household incomes and Earnings (see Section 18.2)—cont'd

Authors	Years and countries	Data sets* and sample selection	Method and important variables	Main findings
			benefits and tax credits. Individual earnings: gross.	major source of this between-group variation, though population changes also have a particularly significant impact in the early 1980s—presumably due to the rising number of workless households. The relative incomes of multi-earner households climbed steadily throughout almost the entire period we study. Income inequality: large unexplained residual term, even more so for change; employment status and occupation is by far the most significant explanatory variable, explaining almost a third of total income inequality in 1972. The residual is also important for earnings though less.
Brewer and Wren-Lewis (2012)	UK; 1968–2009.	HBAI; all individuals.	Three complementary decomposition methods: (1) Decomposition by income source, following Shorrocks (1982); (2) decomposition by population subgroup, following Mookherjee and Shorrocks (1982) and Jenkins (1995); (3) decomposition by factor, following Fields (2003). Because inequality in earnings (among individuals in employment) is an important source of changes in overall income inequality, the second and third decompositions are performed on individual earnings inequality, as well as on household income inequality.	Inequality in gross employment and self-employment income grew but since 1991 effect on inequality in total income almost entirely offset by: (1) declining inequality between those with different employment statuses, primarily due to a fall in unemployed people, (2) mitigation by employment taxes, (3) investment income became less unequal largely due to the decline in its importance, (4) rise in relative incomes of pensioners and households with children under 5.

Study	Country; Period	Data; Sample	Method	Findings
Cancian and Schoeni (1998)	United States; 1968–1995.	March CPS; all persons related and residing are part of the same family, only families with prime-age heads (22–55). Exclude military, farmers, self-employed, students, and those living in group quarters.	Decomposing coefficient of variation. Estimate impact of wives' earnings using four alternative counterfactual reference distributions. If observed distribution of income is more equal than counterfactual distribution, then wives' earnings can be said to be equalizing.	Changes in husbands' earnings are substantially more important in explaining recent trends.
Cancian and Schoeni (1998)	AUS, CAN, FRA, DEU-W, NOR, ISR, SWE, CHE, UK, United States; 1980s.	LIS; husbands and wives.	Splitting CV2 when there are only two components of income: earnings of husband and of wife, into parts. Interest in change in inequality when wives' earnings are included as a source of income, i.e., (CVfamily—CVhead)/CVhead. The key components of this change are the share of total earnings attributable to wives' earnings relative to husbands', the correlation of spouses' earnings, and the dispersion of wives' and husbands' earnings.	Mitigating effect of wives' earnings actually increased slightly in all countries; the correlation of spouses' earnings would have to experience an unprecedented increase in order for wives' earnings to become disequalizing.
Corluy and Vandenbroucke (2013)	EU, 1995–2008.	ELFS and SILC; aged 20–59.	Decomposes household employment rate by individual employment rate, household structure, and jobs distribution over households. Decompose changes in at-risk-of-poverty rates on the basis of changes in the poverty risks of jobless household, and of other (nonjobless) households, and of changes in household joblessness due to individual employment rates, household structures and distribution of employment.	Incorrect to attribute disappointing poverty trends during the EU employment boom years solely to the modest conversion of individual employment successes in household employment successes, or more specifically to ongoing polarization of jobs over households. Complementarity of employment creation and poverty reduction through social transfers and inclusive labor market policies.

Continued

Table 18.A7 Household incomes and Earnings (see Section 18.2)—cont'd

Authors	Years and countries	Data sets* and sample selection	Method and important variables	Main findings
Daly and Valetta (2006)	United States; 1967–1989/ 1989–1998.	March CPS Demographic Supplement; including men with earnings equal to zero to account for the possibility that declining labor force participation by low-wage men contributed to rising inequality in family income. Equivalent family income	Semiparametric density estimation. For complete decomposition, four factors are considered: (i) distribution of men's earnings; (ii) women's labor force participation; (iii) family structure and (iv) underlying family characteristics, in this and by way of sensitivity test also in reversed order. The latter led to a somewhat larger role for residuals.	For the period 1969–1989, the growing dispersion of men's earnings and changing family structure can account for most of the rise in family income inequality. By contrast, the increase in labor force participation by women tended to offset this trend. Inequality grew at a slower rate in the 1990s largely because of stabilization in the relative earnings of men from low-income families. Larger effect found than by Burtless (1999) because of accounting for increasing inactivity. Consistent with "episodic" inequality change (Atkinson, 1997).
Del Boca and Pasqua (2003)	ITA; 1977–1998.	SHIW (and ECHP).	Decomposition of the CV2 of total household income. Three sources of income are considered: husband's earnings, wife's earnings and other sources of income (both from other components and nonlabor income). Simulations of household income distribution that would occur if wives had no earnings.	Total income distribution would have been more unequal without women's labor income.
Johnson and Wilkins (2003)	AUS; 1982–1997/ 1998.	Seven waves of the IDS.	Semiparametric procedure developed by DiNardo et al. (1996).	Changes in the distribution of work across families—for example, an increase in both two-earner families and no-earner families—were the single-most important source of the increase in private income inequality, with such changes on their own accounting for half the increase in inequality.

Karoly and Burtless (1995)	United States; 1959, 1969,1979, 1989.	Census and March CPS; Personal equivalent income distribution.	Decompose changes in Gini coefficient following Lerman and Yitzhaki (1984).	Increase in proportion of single-head families boosted inequality over entire period. Forty percent reduction in income inequality in the 1960s because of the decline in earnings inequality among male heads of families; more than one-third of increase in inequality after 1969 because inequality in male earnings soared. Since 1979 females' gains in earnings have increased inequality because these gains have been concentrated increasingly in families with high incomes.
Larrimore (2013)	United States; 1979–2007	March CPS, <1992 adjusted upward Square root equivalent income.	Shift share decomposition given Cowell-Fiorio's (2011) critique of Dinardo et al. (1996) and Daly and Valetta (2006) decomposition; the data intensity prevents this method from being suitable for all decompositions of interest. In particular, it is limited in its ability to observe how a range of income sources interact to account for changing inequality.	Factors contributing to rapid rise in income inequality in the 1980s differ substantially from those contributing to slower increase since that time. In the 1980s changes in the correlation of spouses' earnings accounted for income inequality growth, but not thereafter. Additionally, the 2000s business cycle is the first full business cycle in at least 30 years where changes in earnings of male household heads accounted for declines in income inequality. Instead, continued growth in income inequality was accounted for primarily by increases in female earnings inequality and declines in both male and female employment.
Lehrer (2000)	United States; 1973, 1992/1993.	NSFH; married couples.	Decompose CV2 of husband's plus wife's earnings.	1973 and 1992–1994 important similarity: spouse's contribution is equalizing in all life-cycle stages (no children, young <6 years, and older children). However, equalizing influence of wife's contribution grew substantially stronger—partly due to a decrease in the dispersion of female earnings relative to that of male earnings.

Continued

Table 18.A7 Household incomes and Earnings (see Section 18.2)—cont'd

Authors	Years and countries	Data sets* and sample selection	Method and important variables	Main findings
Lu et al. (2011)	CAN; 1980, 1995, 2005.	Census; heads 16–64; Census family as <2000 (opposite sex); excl. no earnings; square root equivalent income; head wages >0; full-time ≥30 h.	Semi-parametric decomposition methods Dinardo et al. (1996), closely following the work of Fortin and Schirle (2006). by male and female earnings structure, female EPOP, assortative mating, family compos. and characteristics.	Actual gap between "rich" and "poor" married-couple households, as measured by their income from labor, is narrower than if all wives were out of the labor force. 1980–1995 substantial increases in family earnings inequality, some decrease 1995–2005 although earnings of Top 1% of families increase substantially. Employment rates of men and women, increases in their educational attainment, and decreases in assortative mating had equalizing effects (women coupling below their level); increases in the returns to higher education and in proportion of single individuals and lone-parent families drove increases in family earnings inequality.
Review of Economic Dynamics Special issue 2010: "Cross-sectional economic facts for macro-economists"	Relevant countries: CAN, DEU, ESP, ITA, SWE, UK, United States; 1960s/1970s/1980s/1990s up to mid-2000s.	National data sets on earnings, incomes and expenditures.	Country contributions by Brzozowski et al, Fuchs-Schündeln et al., Pijoan-Mas and Sanchéz-Marcos, Japelli and Pistaferri, Domeij and Floden, Blundell and Etheridge, and Heathcote et al. These document level and evolution, over time and over life cycle, of inequality of wages, labor earnings, income, consumption, and wealth, adopting as much as possible a uniform approach.	Substantial increases in wages and earnings inequality, over the last three decades; experience premium rose and gender premium fell virtually everywhere. Earnings inequality appears to be strongly counter-cyclical. In all countries, government redistribution through taxes and transfers reduced level, trend and cyclical fluctuations in income inequality. The rise in income inequality was stronger at the bottom of the distribution. Consumption inequality increased less than disposable income inequality, and tracked the latter much more closely at the top than at the bottom of the distribution.

| Shorrocks (1983) | United States; 1968–1977. | PSID, households excl. those with change of head. | Empirical approach to decomposition rules proposed by Shorrocks (1982). | Measuring the age profile of inequality is challenging because of the interplay of time and cohort effects. Dollar for dollar, capital income and taxes have more distributional impact than earnings, which in turn exceeds the impact of transfer income (defined to include retirement pensions and annuities). |
| Van Weeren and Van Praag (1983) | BEL, DEU-W, DNK, FRA, ITA, NLD, UK; 1979. | Special survey (van Praag et al., 1982); net household income. | Between-group decomposition of variance of log incomes and Theil index by several socioeconomic characteristics. | In most countries the greatest inequality exists between employment subgroups (employees, self-employed, and not-working). Other important characteristics are age and education of the main breadwinner. The place of living household appeared to be of minor importance, and number of breadwinners is only of secondary importance. |

Table 18.A8 Wage dispersion and the recent polarization and offshorability approaches to supply and demand (see Section 18.4.5)

Authors	Years and countries	Data sets* and sample selection	Method and important variables	Main findings
Acemoglu and Autor (2011)	Mainly United States, going back to around 1960, and 10 EU15 countries, going back to 1992.	Appendix provides detail of US data sources used for depicting trends; Truncate at bottom and top 5% of earnings distribution. Census is used for empirical example.	Takes stock of US trends in wage inequality in detail and adds some detail of polarization in EU countries. Evaluates shortcomings of canonical model explaining those and develops a model with endogenous assignment of three levels of skills to a continuum of tasks and possible substitution of machines for certain tasks previously performed by labor.	Provides a stylized empirical application of the new framework to US data, and suggests further directions for empirical exploration.
Antonczyk et al. (2010)	DEU-W, United States; 1979–2004.	IABS and ORG CPS, full-time working men.	This paper compares trends in wage inequality in the United States and Germany separating age, cohort, and time macro-economic effects. It accounts for potential cohort effects, an issue which is mostly ignored by the recent literature on wage inequality, even though SBTC may have a bias in the age/cohort dimension.	Between 1979 and 2004, wage inequality increased strongly in both the United States and Germany, but there were various country specific aspects of this increase. There is a large role played by cohort effects in Germany, whereas it is only small in the United States. Although there is evidence in both the United States and Germany, which is consistent with a technology-driven polarization of the labor market, the patterns of trends in wage inequality differ strongly enough that technology effects alone cannot explain the empirical findings. Episodic changes resulting from changes in institutional factors such as unionization or the minimum wage may explain the differences.
Autor (2013)	United States	Recent literature.	An emerging literature argues that changes in the allocation of workplace "tasks" between capital and labor, and between domestic and foreign workers, has altered the structure of labor demand in industrialized countries and fostered	The paper concludes with a cautiously optimistic forecast for the potential of the task approach to illuminate the interactions among skill supplies, technological capabilities, and trade and offshoring opportunities, in shaping the aggregate

Continued

			employment polarization—that is, rising employment in the highest and lowest paid occupations. Analyzing this phenomenon within the canonical production function framework is challenging, however, because the assignment of skills to tasks is essentially static. This essay sketches an alternative model of the assignment of skills to tasks based on comparative advantage, reviews key conceptual and practical challenges that researchers face in bringing the "task approach" to the data, and cautions against two common pitfalls that pervade the growing task literature.	demand for skills, the assignment of skills to tasks, and the evolution of wages. For further research the classification of tasks is a challenge as the four task attributes—routine, abstract, manual, offshorable—though broadly distinct show important overlaps which hinder the classification of tasks. It is advisable to use, reuse, recycle, replicate, repeatedly apply existing task classifications, and thus attempt to converge upon a shared and standardized set of task measures. It is mistaken to give up on "middle-skill" education because there is no future for middle-skill jobs, as education is cumulative and middle-skill jobs are not slated to disappear though many middle-skill tasks may.
Autor and Dorn (2013)	United States; 1980–2005.	Census IPUMS and ACS.	The paper offers a unified analysis of the growth of low-skill service occupations and the concurrent polarization of employment and wages. It hypothesizes that polarization stems from the interaction between consumer preferences, which favor variety over specialization, and the falling cost of automating routine, codifiable job tasks. Applying a spatial equilibrium model where local labor markets have differential degrees of specialization in routine-intensive industries, it corroborates four implications of this hypothesis. Local labor markets that specialized in routine tasks differentially adopted information technology, reallocated low-skill labor into service occupations (employment polarization), experienced earnings growth at the tails of the distribution (wage polarization), and received inflows of skilled labor.	The twisting of the lower tail of the employment and earnings distributions is substantially accounted for by rising employment and wages in a single broad category. The paper considers a panoply of alternative explanations including offshoring of jobs tasks, income and substitution effects in high-skill consumption and labor supply, and demographic and economic shifts including immigration, population aging, female labor force entry, and declining manufacturing employment. Many of these alternative explanations receive some empirical support but none appears to play a leading role.

Table 18.A8 Wage dispersion and the recent polarization and offshorability approaches to supply and demand (see Section 18.4.5)—cont'd

Authors	Years and countries	Data sets* and sample selection	Method and important variables	Main findings
Autor et al. (2003)	United States; 1960–1998.	DOT occupational characteristics appended to Census IPUMS 1960–1990 and ORG CPS 1980–1998; employees aged 18–64, FTE weights.	The paper argues that computer capital (1) substitutes for workers in performing cognitive and manual tasks that can be accomplished by following explicit rules; and (2) complements workers in performing nonroutine problem solving and complex communications tasks. Provided that these tasks are imperfect substitutes, the model implies measurable changes in the composition of job tasks.	Within industries, occupations, and education groups, computerization is found to be associated with reduced labor input of routine manual and routine cognitive tasks and increased labor input of nonroutine cognitive tasks. Translating task shifts into education demand, the model can explain 60% of the estimated relative demand shift favoring college labor during 1970–1998. Task changes within nominally identical occupations account for almost half of this impact.
Blinder (2007)	United States; 2004.	O*NET.	Using detailed information on the nature of work done in over 800 BLS occupational codes, this paper ranks those occupations according to how easy/hard it is to offshore the work—either physically or electronically.	Using that ranking, it estimates that somewhere between 22% and 29% of all US jobs are or will be potentially offshorable within a decade or two. Because the rankings are subjective, two alternatives are presented—one objective, the other is an independent subjective ranking. It is found that there is little or no correlation between an occupation's "offshorability" and the skill level of its workers (as measured either by educational attainment or wages). However, it appears that, controlling for education, the most highly offshorable occupations were already paying significantly lower wages in 2004.
Blinder and Krueger (2009)	United States; 2008.	Special survey for Princeton Data Improvement Initiative (PDII).	This paper reports on a pilot study of the use of conventional household survey methods to measure something unconventional: what we call	Offshorability appears to be particularly prevalent in production work and in office and administrative jobs. By industry group, it is most common in manufacturing,

Study	Country; period	Data	Description	Findings
			"offshorability," defined as the ability to perform one's work duties (for the same employer and customers) from abroad. Notice that offshorability is a characteristic of a person's job, not of the person.	finance and insurance, information services, and professional and technical services. More educated workers appear to hold somewhat more offshorable jobs. But differences in offshorability by race, sex, age, and geographic region are all minor. In estimated multivariate econometric models, offshorability does not appear to have consistent systematic effects on either wages or the probability of layoff. union members and people in licensed positions are always less likely to hold offshorable jobs; and, perhaps surprisingly, routine work is no more likely to be offshorable than other work.
Dunne et al. (2004)	United States; 1977 and 1992.	March CPS and LRD; only plants that reported investments.	Using establishment-level data, we shed light on the sources of the changes in the structure of production, wages, and employment that have occurred over recent decades.	The findings are (1) the between-plant component of wage dispersion is an important and growing part of total wage dispersion; (2) much of the between-plant increase in wage dispersion is within industries; (3) the between-plant measures of wage and productivity dispersion have increased substantially over recent decades; and (4) a significant fraction of the rising dispersion in wages and productivity is accounted for by changes in the distribution of computer investment across plants.
Goos and Manning (2007) (see also 2003)	UK; 1976–1999.	NES complemented by for part-time workers.	The more nuanced version of SBTC recently proposed by Autor et al. (2003) makes a different prediction about what is happening to employment in low-wage jobs.	This paper presents evidence that employment in the United Kingdom is polarizing into lovely and lousy jobs in consistence with the nuanced view. Job polarization can explain one-third of the rise in the log(50/10) wage differential and one-half of the rise in the log(90/50).

Continued

Table 18.A8 Wage dispersion and the recent polarization and offshorability approaches to supply and demand (see Section 18.4.5)—cont'd

Authors	Years and countries	Data sets* and sample selection	Method and important variables	Main findings
Goos et al. (2011) (see also 2009 and 2010)	15 EU countries; 1996–2006.	LFS-EU, excl. agriculture and fishing, and OECD STAN	This paper develops a simple and empirically tractable model of labor demand to explain recent changes in the occupational structure of employment as a result of technology, offshoring, and institutions. This framework takes account not just of direct effects but indirect effects through induced shifts in demand for different products.	The routinization hypothesis of Autor et al. (2003) is found to be the most important factor behind the observed shifts in employment but offshoring does also play a role. Shifts in product demand are acting to attenuate the impacts of recent technological progress and offshoring. By implication, wage-setting institutions play little role in explaining job polarization in Europe.
Liu and Grusky (2013)	United States; 1979–2010.	ORG CPS, O*NET; nonmilitary wage and salary workers including part-time, aged 16–65.	Is the third industrial revolution indeed driven by rising payoffs to skill? This simple but important question has gone unanswered because conventional models of earnings inequality are based on exceedingly weak measurements of skill. By attaching occupational skill measurements to the CPS, it becomes possible to adjudicate competing accounts of the changing returns to cognitive, creative, technical, and social skill.	The well-known increase in between–occupation inequality is fully explained when such skills are taken into account, while returns to schooling prove to be quite stable once correlated changes in workplace skills are parsed out. The most important trend, however, is a precipitous increase in the wage payoff to synthesis, critical thinking, and related "analytic skills." The payoff to technical and creative skills, often touted in discussions of the third industrial revolution, is shown to be less substantial.
Mishel et al. (2013)	United States; 1973–2007.	ORG and May CPS (provide an independent test of earlier results based primarily on the decennial census and the American Community Survey);	The influential "skill-biased technological change" (SBTC) explanation claims that technology raises demand for educated workers, thus allowing them to command higher wages—which, in turn, increases wage inequality. A more recent SBTC explanation focuses on computerization's role in increasing employment in both higher-wage and lower-wage occupations,	Principal findings include: 1. Technological and skill deficiency explanations of wage inequality have failed to explain key wage patterns over the last three decades, including the 2000s. 2. History shows that middle-wage occupations have shrunk and higher-wage occupations have expanded since the 1950s. This has not driven any changed

	wage and salary workers aged 18–64.	resulting in "job polarization." This paper contends that current SBTC models—such as the education-focused "canonical model" and the more recent "tasks framework" or "job polarization" approach mentioned above—do not adequately account for key wage patterns (namely, rising wage inequality) over the last three decades.	pattern of wage trends. 3. Evidence for job polarization is weak. 4. There was no occupational job polarization in the 2000s. 5. Occupational employment trends do not drive wage patterns or wage inequality. 6. Occupations have become less, not more, important determinants of wage patterns. 7. An expanded demand for low-wage service occupations is not a key driver of wage trends. 8. Occupational employment trends provide only limited insights into the main dynamics of the labor market, particularly wage trends.
Spitz–Oener (2006)	DEU-W 1979, 1985/1986, 1991/1992, 1998/1999.	A unique data set from West Germany enables looking at how skill requirements have changed within occupations. Two hypotheses are tested: (1) IT is a substitute for routine manual and routine cognitive activities, and (2) IT is complementary to analytic and interactive activities.	Occupations are found to require more complex skills today than in 1979, and the changes in skill requirements have been most pronounced in rapidly computerizing occupations. It occurred within occupations, within occupation-education groups, and within occupation-age groups, changes in skill requirements similar to those in the United States. The question that now arises is why similar changes in skill requirements in all of these countries have not led to similar changes in the structure of wages.

Table 18.A9 Wage dispersion and institutions (see Section 18.4.6)

Authors	Countries and years	Data sets* and sample selection	Methods and important variables	Types of institutions**	Main findings
i. Overviews of the literature					
Blau and Kahn (1999)	13 EU countries and CHE, AUS, CAN, JPN, NZL, United States; 1970s to 1990s.	Draws on existing literature and data sources used there.	This chapter examines the impact of wage-setting institutions and government policies on wages and employment, focusing on the OECD countries.	AP, CP, DI, MW, UB, UD	There is considerable evidence that centralized collective bargaining, minimum wages, and antidiscrimination policies raise the relative wages of the low paid. Evidence of the impact of these institutions and other policies such as mandated severance pay, advance notice or unemployment insurance is more mixed with some studies finding active employment effects while others do not. This may reflect the adoption by many OECD countries of offsetting policies, such as public employment, temporary employment contracts and active labor market programs, which, although they may have reduced the adverse relative employment effects of their less-flexible labor market institutions on the low skilled, appear not to have prevented high overall unemployment.
Blau and Kahn (2009)	IALS: 8 countries; OECD: 12 countries.	IALS, 1994, 200+ annual hours and 10+ annual weeks; OECD Earnings database, 1980, 1990, 2000.	Documents and provides explanations for levels of and trends in earnings inequality, focusing on international (OECD) differences. Distinguishes between wage rates, hours worked, and earnings.	ED, HR, MW, UB	International differences reflect diversity of working population and prices, which in turn are affected by supply and demand as well as institutions. Collective bargaining and the minimum wage bring up the bottom, leading to employment losses. Offshoring deserves further attention (and may actually narrow wage differentials); so do employment protection, product market regulation and norms.

Study	Country	Data	Approach	Topic	Findings
Doucouliagos and Stanley (2009)	United States	Extensive literature search.	Multivariate meta-regression analysis accommodate a potentially complex employment effect, misspecification biases and differential propensities to report adverse employment effects. It uses employment elasticity with respect to the minimum wage as the metric.	MW	Recently developed meta-analysis methods applied to 64 US minimum-wage studies (almost 1500 estimates) show that the minimum-wage effects literature is contaminated by publication selection bias, which is estimated to be slightly larger than the average reported minimum wage effect. Once this is corrected, little or no evidence of a negative association between minimum wages and employment remains. The results confirm those of the meta-analysis of Card and Krueger (1995b).
De Linde Leonard et al. (2013)	UK	Extensive literature search.	Multivariate meta-regression analysis of 236 estimated minimum-wage elasticities and 710 partial correlation coefficients from 16 UK studies.	MW	The study finds no overall practically significant adverse employment effect. Unlike US studies (see Doucouliagos and Stanley, 2009), there seems to be little, if any, overall reporting bias. It identifies several research dimensions that are associated with differential employment effects. In particular, the residential home care industry may exhibit a genuinely adverse employment effect.
Freeman (2005)	OECD	No new empirics.	This paper argues that there are two reasons for inconclusive debate over the claim that labor institutions impair aggregate performance. The first reason is that many adherents to the claim hold strong priors that labor markets operate nearly perfectly in the absence of institutions and let their priors dictate their modeling choices and interpretation of empirical results. The second reason is that the cross-country aggregate data at issue is weak—too weak to decisively reject strong prior views or to convince those with weaker priors.	Various	The debate over the influence of labor market flexibility on performance is unlikely to be settled by additional studies using aggregate data and making cross-country comparisons. Although this approach holds little promise, microanalysis of workers and firms and increased use of experimental methods represent a path forward. Steps along this path could help end the current "lawyer's case" empiricism in which priors dominate evidence.

Continued

Table 18.A9 Wage dispersion and institutions (see Section 18.4.6)—cont'd

Authors	Countries and years	Data sets* and sample selection	Methods and important variables	Types of institutions**	Main findings
Freeman (2007)	OECD	No new empirics.	The paper documents the large cross-country differences in labor institutions that make them a candidate explanatory factor for the divergent economic performance of countries and reviews what economists have learned about the effects of these institutions on economic outcomes. It identifies three ways in which institutions affect economic performance: by altering incentives, by facilitating efficient bargaining, and by increasing information, communication, and trust.	CP, UB	The evidence shows that labor institutions reduce the dispersion of earnings and income inequality, which alters incentives, but finds equivocal effects on other aggregate outcomes, such as employment and unemployment. Given weaknesses in the cross-country data on which most studies focus, the paper argues for increased use of microdata, simulations, and experiments to illuminate how labor institutions operate and affect outcomes.
Katz and Autor (1999)	United States	No new empirics.	The chapter presents a framework for understanding changes in the wage structure and overall earnings inequality. It emphasizes the role of supply-and-demand factors and the interaction of market forces and labor market institutions. Recent changes in the US wage structure are analyzed in detail to highlight crucial measurement issues that arise in studying wage structure changes and to illustrate the operation of the framework. The roles of skill-biased technological	IR, MW, UB, UD	Several directions for future research are suggested: the roles of changes in labor market institutions (the incidence of labor market rents) and changes in competitive supply-and-demand factors. A key issue model is how to model the effects of institutions on employment rates and composition as well as on wages. The extent to which institutional changes reflect exogenous political events as opposed to responses to market forces can help sort out the effects of institutions from supply-and-demand factors. Taking a longer-term historical perspective will also be helpful as the US experience for

			change, globalization forces, changes in demographics and relative skill supplies, industry labor rents, unions, and the minimum wage in the evolution of the US wage structure are examined, as are differences and similarities in wage structure changes among OECD nations.		the 1970s, 1980s, and 1990s illustrates. Cross-country comparative work and differences across regions within a country may also provide useful variation in demand-and-supply shocks and institutional factors.
Kierzenkowski and Koske (2012)	OECD	Recent literature.	Despite a general trend of increasing labor income inequality, there have been differences in the timing, intensity, and even direction of these changes across OECD countries. These stylized facts have led to numerous studies about the main determinants of labor income inequality and, as a result, a significant revision of the previous consensus about the key drivers. The most researched channels include skill-biased technological change, international trade, immigration, education, as well as the role of labor market policies and institutions.	MW, UB	SBTC (canonical view) fails to explain why inequality has diminished at the bottom relative to the median since the late 1980s as well as why within-group wage dispersion has grown substantially and mainly for college-educated workers. SBTC (nuanced view) explains why OECD labor markets have become polarized. International trade seems to have important implications for at least some groups of workers. Immigration has a rather small impact on native workers and sizable adverse wage or employment effects on the cohorts of previous immigrants. Education: Wage inequality is negatively correlated with the average level of educational attainment. Labor market policies and institutions: The impact of declining unionisation and of the lower relative minimum wage is most pronounced at the lower end of the wage distribution while cross-country evidence suggests that government employment reduces wage inequality.
Lemieux (2011)	AUS, CAN, United States; since 1980s.	No new empirics.	Wage inequality has been increasing in most industrialized countries over the last three decades. There are, nonetheless, major differences across	MW, UD, UW	Although demand factors linked to technological change may be a leading factor behind the secular growth in wage inequality (or the more recent polarization of wages), they cannot

Continued

Table 18.A9 Wage dispersion and institutions (see Section 18.4.6)—cont'd

Authors	Countries and years	Data sets* and sample selection	Methods and important variables	Types of institutions**	Main findings
			countries in terms of the timing and magnitude of the growth in inequality. A large number of explanations have been suggested for these observed changes, including technological progress and the computer revolution, labor market institutions and social norms, and changes in the relative supply of highly educated workers. This paper assesses the validity of these explanations in light of the large differences in inequality growth across countries, and the stunning growth in the concentration of income at the top end of the distribution.		account for the large differences in inequality growth observed across countries. Supply factors and institutions are more successful than demand at explaining differences across countries. None provides a compelling answer to the question of why inequality at the very top end of the distribution has increased so much in some countries but not in others. Two main conclusions are, first, that the SDI explanation is still alive and well, in the sense that no single explanation (supply, demand, or institution) can account for all of the changes in wage inequality observed across countries. Second, we still do not understand very well why inequality at the very top end of the distribution has increased so much in countries like the United States, Canada, or Australia.
Machin (1997)	UK; 1979 and 1993.		At the same time as the role of labor market institutions declined very dramatically in Britain there was a very sharp rise in wage inequality. It therefore provides a very good testing ground for evaluating the importance of labor market institutions in explaining the evolution of the wage structure. Regression of wage inequality measures distinguished by Wage Council applicability.	MW, UD	The weakening of unions and minimum wages that have traditionally propped up wage levels at the bottom end of the wage distribution, is found to play an important part in the rise in wage inequality in Britain.

| Machin (2008) | Various. | No new empirics. | The paper describes the origins of the recent work documenting trends in wage inequality, the sizable body of research trying to understand national and international differences, and discuss the directions in which more recent work has moved and where it may go in future. | Various | It is concluded that the evidence shows that the wage distribution has been characterized by long-run growth in the relative demand for skills driven by technological change (rather than trade) and that changes in skill supply and institutional changes have affected the timing of how SBTC impacts on the wage structure in different contexts. Slower inequality growth in the lower tail in the United States and the United Kingdom and rising inequality in previously stable (European) distributions together with a polarization of job growth have refined explanations and added sophistication to the SBTC story. |
| Manning (2011) | International. | No new empirics. | The paper defends the claim that it is simply not true to claim that the perspective of perfect competition tells us all we need to know. There are rents in the typical jobs, though the size and distribution are not well known. | DI, IR, MW, UB, and employer collusion | Many empirical observations (e.g., equilibrium wage dispersion, the gender pay gap, geographical agglomeration, the effect of minimum wages on employment, employers paying for general training, costs of job loss for workers with no specific skills to list only a few) that are puzzles in the perspective of a perfectly competitive labor market are simply what one might expect if one thinks the labor market is characterized by pervasive imperfect competition. Views of the likely effects of labor market regulation should be substantially altered once one recognizes the existence of imperfect competition. However, although imperfect competition can be used as a justification for some regulation on efficiency grounds, it always predicts some limits to regulation with quite what those limits are is left to empirical research to decide. |

Continued

Table 18.A9 Wage dispersion and institutions (see Section 18.4.6)—cont'd

Authors	Countries and years	Data sets* and sample selection	Methods and important variables	Types of institutions**	Main findings
Nickell and Layard (1999)	Various subsets of OECD countries.	Various.	Aims to survey the literature to see propositions such as these depends on which labor market institutions really are bad for unemployment and growth, and which are not.	AP, CP, ED, MW, PM, TA, UB, UD, WE	There is quite strong evidence that the compressed earnings distributions in some OECD countries relative to the United States are a consequence of equally compressed skill distributions. Most of the gross features of unemployment and wage distributions across the OECD in recent years seem explicable by supply-and-demand shifts and the role required of special institutional features such as unions and minimum wages is correspondingly minimal. Labor market institutions on which policy should be focused are unions and Social Security systems. Encouraging product-market competition is a key policy to eliminate the negative effects of unions. For Social Security the key policies are benefit reform linked to active labor market policies to move people from welfare to work. By comparison, time spent worrying about strict labor market regulations, employment protection and minimum wages is probably time largely wasted.
Rogerson and Shimer (2011)	17 OECD countries; 1965 to late-2000s.	LFS–OECD and GGDC.	This chapter assesses how models with search frictions have shaped understanding of aggregate labor market outcomes in two contexts: business cycle fluctuations and long–run (trend)	Various	Results are mixed. Search models are useful for interpreting the behavior of some additional data series, but search frictions per se do not seem to improve our understanding of movements in total hours at either business–cycle frequencies

Study	Region	Coverage	Description	Topics	Findings
			changes (and the shock-and-institutions explanation of international differences). It consolidates data on aggregate labor market outcomes for a large set of OECD countries, and asks how models with search improve our understanding of these data.		or in the long run. Still, models with search seem promising as a framework for understanding how different wage-setting processes affect aggregate labor market outcomes.
Schmitt (2013)	United States	Recent literature since about 2000.	Labor markets have imperfections in the form of inadequate information, uneven bargaining power, limited ability to enforce long-term commitments, and insufficient insurance mechanisms against employment-related risks. Labor policies and institutions can in principle be used to address these imperfections. The report examines recent research on the employment effect of the minimum wage to determine the best current estimates of the impact of increases in the minimum wage on the employment prospects of low-wage workers. In particular, it discusses channels of adjustment to an increase in the minimum wage.	MW	The evidence points to little or no employment response to modest increases in the minimum wage. Evidence on 11 possible adjustments to minimum-wage increases may help to explain why the measured employment effects are so consistently small. The strongest evidence suggests that the most important channels of adjustment are: reductions in labor turnover; improvements in organizational efficiency; reductions in wages of higher earners ("wage compression"); and small price increases. These adjustment mechanisms appear to be more than sufficient to avoid employment losses, even for employers with a large share of low-wage workers.
World Bank (2012)	Worldwide	Recent literature since about 2000.	Labor markets have imperfections in the form of inadequate information, uneven bargaining power, limited ability	AP, CP, MW, TA, UB, WE	Policies should seek to avoid the distortive interventions that stifle labor reallocation and undermine the creation of jobs in functional cities and global value

Continued

Table 18.A9 Wage dispersion and institutions (see Section 18.4.6)—cont'd

Authors	Countries and years	Data sets* and sample selection	Methods and important variables	Types of institutions**	Main findings
			to enforce long-term commitments, and insufficient insurance mechanisms against employment-related risks. Labor policies and institutions can in principle be used to address these imperfections. It is important, then, to understand the role and the impacts of policies and institutions like labor market regulation, collective bargaining, active labor market programs, and social insurance. But the main constraints to the job creation often lie outside the labor market, and a clear approach is needed to support appropriate policy responses.		chains. But policies should also ensure voice and social protection, especially for the most vulnerable. Ideally, policies should aim at removing the market imperfections and institutional failures preventing the private sector from creating more of those jobs. If the constraints cannot be easily singled out or are difficult to remove, offsetting policies may be considered.
ii. Aggregate studies (institutions may be indirect)					
Acemoglu (2003)	AUS, BEL, CAN, DEU, DNK, FIN, ISR, NLD, NOR, SWE, UK, United States; mid-80s to mid-90s.	CPS and LIS; annual earnings of full-time, full-year male household heads aged of 18–64.	Relative-supply-demand model to determine differential effects, followed by a model of Differential Technology. Responses across countries (not tested).	MW, UW, some Demographics	Relative demand for skills increased differentially across countries. Labor market institutions creating wage compression in Europe also encourage more investment in technologies increasing the productivity of less-skilled workers, implying less skill-biased technical change in Europe than the United States.
Alderson and Nielsen (2002)	16 OECD; 1967–1992.	Deininger and Squire (1996) for income inequality.	Gini of incomes regressed on economic aggregate measures.	OP, UD, WE	Direct investment and North–South trade have played a role in the determination of income inequality in the contemporary period; likewise for immigration.

Study	Geography; period	Data	Method	Codes	Findings
Autor et al. (2005)	United States; 1973–2003.	March CPS and May/ORG CPS; real log hourly wages of wage and salary workers.	Extends quantile decomposition that nests DiNardo et al. (1996) in view of more differentiated developments over the earnings distribution after 1990s (as 90/50 and 50/10 trends diverge).	MW	Compositional shifts in labor force have contributed to earnings inequality during the 1990s.
Autor et al. (2008)	United States; 1963–2005.	March CPS, matched with DOT; FTFY workers log earnings. Abstract, routine and manual tasks within occupations.	Kernel reweighting approach of Lemieux used to facilitate a direct comparison. Overall 90/10, 90/50 and 50/10; between-group educational differentials; within-group 90/10, 90/50, and 50/10 residual wage gaps conditioned on measures of education, age/experience, and gender.	ED, occupations by mean years of schooling, MW	Upper-tail (90/50) inequality has increased steadily since 1980 and fluctuations in the real minimum wage are not a plausible explanation; a puzzling deceleration in relative demand growth for college workers in the early 1990s potentially reconciled by a modified version of the skill-biased technical change hypothesis that emphasizes the role of information technology in complementing abstract (high-education) tasks and substituting for routine (middle-education) tasks. Employment and wage growth by skill percentile are found to be positively correlated in each of the last two decades.
Blanchard and Wolfers (2000)	20 OECD; 1960–1995.	Nickell's and OECD institutions data.		AP, CP, ED, MW, PM, TA, UB, UD, WE	Interactions shock and institutions are essential for understanding international differences.
Bedard and Ferrall (2003)	AUS, BEL, CAN–BC/ON, DEU–W, FIN, FRA, JPN, NLD, SWE, UK, United States; 1964/1982 vs. 1969…1992	Wage data from national sources; test data from IME conducted in 1964 and 1982.	Compares test scores at age 13 to wages later in life.	ED	Wage dispersion, as summarized by Gini coefficients, is significantly related to test score dispersion. For the United States, the United Kingdom, and Japan, with more data, evidence of skill-biased changes in wage dispersion between the early 1970s and the late 1980s is found.

Continued

Table 18.A9 Wage dispersion and institutions (see Section 18.4.6)—cont'd

Authors	Countries and years	Data sets* and sample selection	Methods and important variables	Types of institutions**	Main findings
Bertola and Boeri (2003)	EU15; 1982–1995.	OECD, Eurostat, ILO.	Institutions protective of labor serve some intended purpose. More intense competition may increase demand for protection, and certainly calls for reforms. A stylized model of structural change and resulting reform tensions is used to examine recent evidence.	CP, TA, UD, WE	Labor market reforms are becoming relatively more frequent in EMU countries, and many of them reduce welfare system generosity and deregulate labor markets. Most reforms are marginal, however, and in many cases deregulation-oriented reforms are accompanied by measures which appear to try and offset the implications of stronger competition instead. To exploit fully the advantages of economic and monetary integration, the institutional structure of labor and other markets needs to be revised extensively.
Budría and Pereira (2005)	DEU, FIN, FRA, GRC, ITA, NOR, PRT, SWE, UK; 1980s, 1990s.	EDWIN microdata, private-sector males ages 18–60, 35 + hours, nonagricultural employees.	Quantile regression and OLS of returns to education.	ED	Inequality increasing effect of tertiary education, through the "within" dimension, became more acute over last years.
Christopoulou et al. (2010)	AUT, BEL, DEU, ESP, GRC, HUN, IRL, ITA, NLD, 1995 and 2002.	EU-SES 1995, 2002; hourly wage including regular bonuses and payment for overtime.	Split between composition effect and returns effect, and residual.	MW, OP, UB, UD	Wage inequality growth diverges across countries. Only minor contribution of compositional change, but association with technology and globalization, while with immigration wages decline. Mixed effect of labor market institutions.

iii. Specific institutions in more depth (see iv for jobs polarization)

Authors	Countries and years	Data sets* and sample selection	Methods and important variables	Types of institutions**	Main findings
Baccaro (2008)	51 Advanced, Central and Eastern European, Latin	New ILO data set on industrial relations and labor law, various	Between- and within-country regressions.	UB, UD, labor-law compliance	What changes from the 1990s on in advanced countries is the capacity of industrial relations institutions to reduce inequality directly by compressing market earnings. In particular, centralized

Study	Coverage / Sample	Data	Method	Variables	Findings
	American and Asian countries late 1980s to early 2000s; and analysis of 16 Advanced countries from the late 1970s.	dimensions of globalization, and controls for demand and supply of skilled labor.			collective bargaining seems to have become less redistributive than in the past. To the extent that industrial relations institutions continue to support and reproduce the welfare state, they reduce inequality indirectly though this channel.
Barth and Lucifora (2006)	AUT, BEL, DEU, DNK, ESP, FIN, FRA, GRC, ITA, NOR, SWE, UK; 1973...2003.	EDWIN, ECHP; nonagricultural employees 18–64 15+ hours, gross hourly earnings.	Model with supply and demand for different types of labor, as well as institutions affecting the bargained relative wage.	CP, ED, UB, UD	No evidence of increasing "over-education" in Europe. Bargaining coordination and employment protection have compressing effect on wages, but at different points of the wage distribution.
Bassanini and Duval (2006)	21 OECD; 1982–2003.		Aggregate employment and group-specific participation, institutional/policies interactions.	AP, MW, PM, TA, WE	Changes in policies and institutions appear to explain almost two-thirds of noncyclical unemployment changes over the past two decades.
Bassanini et al. (2009)	OECD; 1982–2003.	OECD annual cross-country aggregate data on the stringency of employment protection legislation and industry-level data on productivity.	Examines effect of dismissal regulation on productivity.	CP	Empirical results suggest that mandatory dismissal regulations have a depressing impact on productivity growth in industries where layoff restrictions are more likely to be binding. By contrast, no evidence is found of a productivity effect of regulations concerning temporary contracts, which suggests that partial reforms, facilitating the use of fixed-term and atypical contracts, are unlikely to have an important impact on efficiency and technological change and cannot therefore be a substitute for comprehensive reforms whereby dismissal restrictions for open-ended contracts are also weakened.

Continued

Table 18.A9 Wage dispersion and institutions (see Section 18.4.6)—cont'd

Authors	Countries and years	Data sets* and sample selection	Methods and important variables	Types of institutions**	Main findings
Bertola et al. (2001)	28 OECD countries; 1960–1999.	Database of Blanchard and Wolfers together with wage distributions from OECD Earnings database and labor force and population data from ILO.	Analysis why the United States moved from relatively high to relatively low unemployment over the last three decades. Institutions are largely assumed to be invariant.	AP, CP, TA, UB, UD, WE	Although macroeconomic and demographic shocks and changing labor market institutions explain a modest portion of this change, the interaction of these shocks and labor market institutions is the most important factor explaining the shift in the United States relative unemployment. This is consistent with Blanchard and Wolfers (2000). Controlling for country- and time-specific effects, high employment is associated with low wage levels and high levels of wage inequality. Disaggregating, the employment of both younger and older people fell sharply in other countries relative to the United States since the 1970s, with much smaller differences in outcomes among the prime-aged.
Bičáková (2006)	FRA, UK, United States; 1990–2002.	National LFS; 25–54; incl. self-employed; hourly wages (net in FR); skill groups: sex × age × education.	Focus is changes in the between-group variation in earnings, employment, unemployment, and inactivity; labor supply and demand model with heterogeneous types of labor, using a pseudo-panel of different skill-groups; three equations for wage, employment, and labor force participation as a function of exogenous supply and demand shifters, as implied by the structural model, is estimated by two-way fixed effects on group-level panel data.	Wage rigidity (MW in sideshow)	Trade-off inequality to unemployment for declining demand for low-skilled is found for FRA vs. UK and United States.

Source	Country; Period	Data	Description	Topics	Findings
Bingley et al. (2013)	DNK; 1980–2003.	LFS; males aged 21–55 working full time in private sector.	Investigates the relationship between life-cycle wages and individual membership of unemployment insurance schemes, separating permanent from transitory wages and characterise them using membership of unemployment insurance funds.	WE	Unemployment insurance is associated with lower wage growth heterogeneity over the life cycle and greater wage instability, changing the nature of wage inequality from permanent to transitory. Robustness checks suggest that moral hazard is relevant.
Blau and Kahn (2002) (see also 1996)	OECD; 1979–1999.	Various, both macro and micro.	Discusses the literature and builds on own earlier contributions to compare US labor market performance to other countries.	AP, CP, ED, TA, UB, WE	Interventionist labor market institutions in Europe compress wages and lower wage inequality; however, jobs most be lost for some groups. Institutional and demographic change and macroeconomic policy also differs to the advantage of the United States.
Boeri (2011)	Europe; since 1980.	fRDB-IZA social policy reforms database.	Reviews literature building on institutional reforms as quasi-natural experiments.	AP, CF, CP, TA, UB, WE	Literature is very informative but insufficiently accounts for long-lasting asymmetries between reformed and unreformed segments of the labor market. Extends Mortensen-Pissarides model with this segmentation for a theoretical approach that can help improving the identification of causal effects using reforms. Also gives empirical evidence on reforms.
Boeri and Jimeno (2005)	ITA; 1986–1995.	LFS rotation panel, Italian social security records (INPS archives).	Within-country exemptions to coverage of employment protection provisions allow making inferences on the impact of EPL when assessing the effects on dismissal probabilities and, using a change in EPL in 1990, on the equilibrium size distribution of firms.	CP	Results are in line with predictions of the theoretical model. Workers under permanent contracts in firms with less restrictive EPL are more likely to be dismissed. However, there is no effect on the growth of firms.

Continued

Table 18.A9 Wage dispersion and institutions (see Section 18.4.6)—cont'd

Authors	Countries and years	Data sets* and sample selection	Methods and important variables	Types of institutions**	Main findings
Bryson et al. (2012)	Europe and United States; early 2000s.	GSS 2002 and 2006, EWCS 2000 and 2005; employees with a permanent contract in private sector and in profit oriented firms only excluding managers and CEOs.	Presents new comparable data on the incidence of performance pay schemes. The percentage of employees exposed to incentive pay schemes ranges from around 10–15% in some European countries to over 40% in Scandinavian countries and the United States. Individual pay and profit/gain sharing schemes are widely diffused, whereas share ownership schemes are much less common, particularly in Europe.	UW	A number of empirical regularities are found. Incentive pay is less common in countries with a higher share of small firms. Higher product and labor market regulation are associated with lower use of incentive pay. Capital market development is a necessary requirement for a wider diffusion of incentive pay, particularly sharing and ownership schemes. Controlling for a large set of individual characteristics and company attributes, the probability that a worker is covered by an incentive scheme is higher in large firms and in high-skilled occupations, while it is much lower for females.
Card and DiNardo (2002)	United States; around 1970–2000.	CPS: March, May and ORG; diverging samples are compared.	Extended discussion of the measurement of technological change and of changes in the structure of wages in the U.S. labor market over the past 20–30 years, concluding to myriad shifts.	MW	Viewed from 2002, it now appears that the rise in wage inequality was an episodic event. A key problem for the SBTC hypothesis is that wage inequality stabilized in the 1990s despite continuing advances in computer technology; SBTC also fails to explain the evolution of other dimensions of wage inequality.
Card et al. (2004)	CAN, UK, United States; 1973/ 1984… 2001.	CAN-LFS + supplements, UK-LFS and GHS, May and ORG CPS; hourly wages of employees aged 16–65.	Comprehensive analysis of the evolution of unionization and wage inequality for both men and women in all three countries over the past two to three decades, as a sequel to Freeman (1980) and Freeman and Medoff (1984). The countries collect comparable data and share similar collective bargaining institutions.	UB, UD, MW	Unions reduce male inequality also after controlling for skill; but they increase female inequality; over time the declining unionization has eroded equalization.

Study	Coverage	Data source	Description	Institutions	Findings
Checchi and Garcia Peñalosa (2008)	11 EU countries, AUS, CAN, NOR, CHE and United States; 1969–2004.	LIS; na	Labor market institutions are a crucial determinant of wage inequality, the wage share in aggregate income, and the unemployment rate. Because these variables affect, in turn, the distribution of income across households, the question arises of whether stronger labor market institutions have an impact on income inequality. Institutions can in principle have conflicting effects. This paper examines what is the overall impact of labor market institutions on household income inequality. And counterfactually simulates adoption in other countries of labor standards of United States, UK or EU average.	CP, MW, TA, UB, UD	The evidence indicates that stronger institutions are associated with lower income inequality, but in some cases also with higher rates of unemployment. The magnitude of this trade-off is explored, and the changes in inequality and unemployment are quantified that would be observed if a common labor standard were imposed on members states of the European Union—results are not encouraging as a consequence of a lowering of employment protection; this could be accompanied though by a reinforcement of wage coordination and union density but these are no obvious policy targets.
Checchi and Garcia Peñalosa (2010)	OECD; 1960–2000.	Aggregate data from various sources (see paper's Appendix B).	This paper argues that personal income inequality depends on the wage differential, the labor share and the unemployment rate. Labor market institutions affect income inequality through these three channels, and their overall effect is theoretically ambiguous.	MW, TA, UB, UD	It is found that greater unionization and greater wage bargaining coordination have opposite effects on inequality, implying conflicting effects of greater union presence on income inequality.
Coelli et al. (1994)	14 OECD countries; around 1970–1990.	OECD National accounts sectoral data.	This paper examines the issue of wage flexibility in an international context using sectoral wage dispersion data from 14 OECD countries. It draws comparisons between a	UB	No strong systematic relationship exists between wage dispersion and the degree of centralization of labor market institutions.

Continued

Table 18.A9 Wage dispersion and institutions (see Section 18.4.6)—cont'd

Authors	Countries and years	Data sets* and sample selection	Methods and important variables	Types of institutions**	Main findings
			measure of wage dispersion and the degree of centralization of a country's wage setting institution to determine whether decentralized wage setting institutions are necessarily associated with more flexible wages. Inter–country comparisons are drawn among the levels of wage dispersion over time, and the relationship between wages and demand conditions for labor, including productivity and relative prices, are examined.		
Corsini (2008)	11 EU countries; early 1990s to early 2000s	BHPS, GSOEP and ECHP; employees.	The paper studies the evolution of wage differentials between graduate (skilled) and nongraduate (unskilled) workers. All countries show an increasing relative supply of skilled workers but different behaviors of the wage differentials. The standard explanation for nondecreasing differentials in the face of rising relative supply is that technological progress is skill biased. This in turn would imply that technological progress differs in its magnitude and effects across Europe. Turning	R&D and CP, UD, WE	The findings show that what is relevant in the determination of the differentials it is the pace and intensity at which technological progress takes place. Adding institutions to the role of R&D employment rates of different groups as well as union density and generosity of unemployment benefits are found to be important for explaining the evolution of the wage differentials between skilled and unskilled workers. They do not produce wage compression between skilled and unskilled workers.

Dahl et al. (2011)	DNK; 1992–2001.	IDA, Income Register; full-time workers aged 25–65 years employed in bargaining segments.	then to institutions a model is built of imperfect competition and wage bargaining which relates the differentials to the technological progress but also to several labor market institutions. This paper studies how decentralization of wage bargaining from sector to firm-level influences wage levels and wage dispersion. We use detailed panel data covering a period of decentralization in the Danish labor market. The decentralization process provides variation in the individual worker's wage-setting system that facilitates identification of the effects of decentralization.	UB	We find a wage premium associated with firm-level bargaining relative to sector-level bargaining, and that the return to skills is higher under the more decentralized wage-setting systems. Using quantile regression, we also find that wages are more dispersed under firm-level bargaining compared to more centralized wage-setting systems.
Dinardo et al. (1996)	United States; 1979–1988.	CPS; hourly wages.	This paper presents a semiparametric procedure to analyze the effects of institutional and labor market factors on recent changes in the US distribution of wages. The effects of these factors are estimated by applying kernel density methods to appropriately weighted samples. The procedure provides a visually clear representation of where in the density of wages these various factors exert the greatest impact.	MW, UD	De-unionization and supply-and-demand shocks were important factors in explaining the rise in wage inequality from 1979 to 1988. The decline in the real value of the minimum wage explains a substantial proportion of this increase in wage inequality, particularly for women. Labor market institutions are as important as supply-and-demand considerations in explaining changes in the US distribution of wages from 1979 to 1988.
DiNardo and Lemieux (1997)	CAN, United States; 1981–1988.	CAN-LFS and CPS; men aged 17–64 excl. university	During the period 1981–1988 the decline in the percentage of workers belonging to unions and an increase in hourly wage	MW, UD	Results suggest that much more severe declines in the unionization rate in the United States than in Canada account for two-thirds of the differential growth in

Continued

Table 18.A9 Wage dispersion and institutions (see Section 18.4.6)—cont'd

Authors	Countries and years	Data sets* and sample selection	Methods and important variables	Types of institutions**	Main findings
		graduates 17–19.	inequality were much more pronounced in the United States than in Canada. Study the effect of labor market institutions on changes in wage inequality by computing simple counterfactuals such as the distribution of wages that would prevail if all workers were paid according to the observed nonunion wage schedule.		wage inequality between the two countries.
Dustmann et al. (2009)	DEU-W; mid-1970s to mid-2000s.	IABS 1975–2004, and LIAB 1995–2004; ages 21–60.	Using the kernel reweighting procedure (DiNardo et al., 1996) it is shown that it is important to account for changes in workforce composition, in particular at the upper end of the wage distribution. Fluctuations in relative supply explain the evolution of the wage differential between the low- and medium-skilled very well, but do a poor job in predicting the evolution of the wage differential between the medium- and high-skilled.	UD	Wage inequality in West Germany has increased over the past three decades, contrary to common perceptions. During the 1980s, the increase was concentrated at the top of the distribution; in the 1990s, it occurred at the bottom end as well. Technological change is responsible for the widening of the wage distribution at the top. At the bottom of the wage distribution, the increase in inequality is better explained by episodic events, such as supply shocks and changes in labor market institutions. Occupations with high median wages in 1980 experienced the highest growth rate, whereas occupations in the middle of the 1980 wage distribution lost ground relative to occupations at the bottom.
Eissa and Hoynes (2004)	United States; 1984–1996.	March CPS; married couples residing in the	Simulation of 1984 and 1996 EITC rules on married couples labor participation. Effects estimated using both quasi-	TA	EITC family targeting can disincentivize secondary earners: 1% fall married women, strong increase for single-parent women, slight increase married men.

Study	Country; period	Data; sample	Description	Variables	Conclusion
			experimental and traditional reduced-form labor supply models, with same conclusion.		
Firpo et al. (2011)	United States; 1976/1977, 1988/1990, 2000/2002, 2004/2004, 2009/2010.	same household, ages 25–54, and less than high school in main estimates CPS and O★Net; male employees	Changes in returns to occupational tasks have contributed to changes in the wage distribution over the last three decades. Using a decomposition based on Firpo et al. (2009).	OP, UD	Technological change and deunionization played a central role in the 1980s and 1990s, and offshorability became an important factor from the 1990s onward.
Fortin and Lemieux (1997)	United States; 1979 and 1988.	CPS; workers aged 16–65.	Show what the variance of the (log) wage distribution would have been, if each of the three institutional changes had not happened. Decompose distribution of wages using three elements: the fraction of workers "affected" by the institutional factor of interest; the mean level of log wages among affected and nonaffected workers; and the dispersion of log wages among affected and nonaffected workers. By reverting some of these measures to their previous level, simulate what would have happened if the institutional changes had not taken place.	MW, PM, UB, UD	Historical evidence from the United States, international comparisons among industrialized countries and analyses of US data for the 1980s all yield the same conclusion: institutional forces simply cannot be overlooked in any serious attempt to understand the recent rise in wage inequality in the US labor market.
Golden and Wallerstein (2006)	16 OECD countries; 1980–2000.		Examine three main hypotheses for the rise of pay inequality: postindustrial, globalization, and institutional. Main idea is	OP, UB, UD, WE	Causes for pay inequality are quite different in the 1980s than in the 1990s. In the 1980s, growing wage dispersion is due to changes in the institutions of the labor

Continued

Table 18.A9 Wage dispersion and institutions (see Section 18.4.6)—cont'd

Authors	Countries and years	Data sets* and sample selection	Methods and important variables	Types of institutions**	Main findings
			determinants of wage inequality underwent considerable substantive change over the period. A statistical model uses first differences over 5-year periods, because effects of the explanatory variables are not instantaneous.		market. Declining unionization and declines in the level at which wages are bargained collectively both contribute to widening pay dispersion in the 1980s. In the 1990s, by contrast, increases in pay inequality are due to increasing trade with less developed nations. To the extent that low-pay workers have been protected from rising wage differentials in the 1990s, it has been because of government policy, in the form of social insurance, and not thanks to labor organizations.
Hall and Krueger (2010)	United States; 2008.	Special survey of a representative sample of US workers to inquire about the wage determination process at the time they were hired into their current or most recent jobs.	Some workers bargain with prospective employers before accepting a job. Others face a take-it-or-leave-it opportunity. Theories of wage formation point to substantial differences in labor market equilibrium between bargained and posted wages. A third of the respondents reported bargaining over pay before accepting their current jobs. About a third of workers had precise information about pay when they first met with their employers, a sign of wage posting. About 40% of workers could have remained on their earlier jobs at the time they accepted their current jobs, indicating a more favorable bargaining position than is held by unemployed job-seekers.	UW	Our analysis of the distribution of wages shows that wage dispersion is higher among workers who bargained for their wages. Wages are higher among bargainers than nonbargainers, after adjusting for the differing compositions of the groups. Our results on wages give substantial support to the job-ladder model—workers who had the option to remain at their current jobs when they took their current jobs can earn higher wages than those without that option.

Study	Countries and period	Data	Description	Codes	Findings
Kenworthy (2001)	AUS, AUT, BEL, CAN, CHE, DEU, DNK, FIN, FRA, ITA, JPN, NLD, NOR, SWE, UK, United States	15 Bargaining Indicators found in the literature.	This article offers a survey and assessment of the principal existing measures in the literature: eight measures of wage centralization and seven measures of wage coordination. There are three aims: provide an inventory of existing indicators, examine their features and merits, and assess sensitivity of findings generated by these measures.	UB	The two best available measures of centralization of wage bargaining are the Iversen and Traxler–Blaschke–Kittel indicators. The former is based on structural features, and the latter aims to measure behavior. There is currently only one available measure of wage-setting centralization. The conceptual differences between wage-setting measures lead to some noteworthy differences in scoring of certain countries and years. A potentially problematic gap is the lack of any measure of wage setting at the subnational level.
Koeniger et al. (2007)	AUS, CAN, FIN, FRA, DEU, ITA, JPN, NLD, SWE, UK, United States; 1970s, 1980s, 1990s.	Various.	Variance decomposition of aggregates.	C, MW, U, WE	Institutions explain at least as much as trade and technology.
Kugler and Pica (2008)	ITA; 1986–1995.	Social Security employer–employee panel.	Study effects of the Italian reform of 1990 on worker and job flows, exploiting the fact that this reform increased unjust dismissal costs for businesses below 15 employees, while leaving dismissal costs unchanged for bigger businesses, to set up a natural experiment research design.	CP	The increase in dismissal costs decreased accessions and separations for workers in small relative to large firms, especially in sectors with higher employment volatility, with a negligible impact on net employment. Also some evidence is found suggesting that the reform reduced firms' entry rates and employment adjustments, but had no effect on exit rates.
Lemieux (2008)	United States; 1973–2005.	May and ORG CPS, PSID; mainly males but females partly considered separately.	The paper reviews recent developments in the literature on wage inequality with a particular focus on why inequality growth has been particularly concentrated in the top end of the wage distribution over the	MW, NO, UB, UD, UW	The nature of the changes in inequality has been dramatically altered over the last 15 years. Although the growth in inequality in the 1980s was pervasive, it has been concentrated at the top end of the distribution since then unlike SBTC, the institutional change explanation can

Continued

Table 18.A9 Wage dispersion and institutions (see Section 18.4.6)—cont'd

Authors	Countries and years	Data sets* and sample selection	Methods and important variables	Types of institutions**	Main findings
			last 15 years. Several possible institutional and demand-side explanations are discussed for the secular growth in wage inequality in the United States and other advanced industrialized countries.		help explain why inequality changes became concentrated in the top end after 1990 and why inequality grew more in the United States and the United Kingdom than in other advanced countries. This being said, just like in the 1980s, available estimates indicate that institutional change can only account for about a third of the observed recent changes in wage inequality. However, broadening the traditional institutional explanation to include pay-setting mechanisms such as performance-pay can help explain more of the growth in inequality at the top end. For the time being, however, most of the growth in top-end inequality over the last 15 years remains unaccounted for.
Lemieux et al. (2009)	United States; 1976–1998.	PSID (some robustness test using NLSY); male household heads, aged 18–65, employees in private sector.	An increasing fraction of jobs explicitly pay workers for their performance using bonus pay, commissions, or piece-rate contracts. Variance components analysis.	UD, UW	Compensation in performance-pay jobs is more closely tied to both observed and unobserved productive characteristics of workers than compensation in nonperformance-pay jobs. The return to these productive characteristics increased faster over time in performance-pay jobs. Performance pay provides a channel through which underlying changes in returns to skill get translated into higher wage inequality, accounting for 21% of the growth in the variance of male wages between the late 1970s and the early 1990s and for most of the increase in wage inequality above the 80th percentile over the same period.

Study	Country/Period	Data	Description	Codes	Findings
Leonardi and Pica (2013)	ITA; 1985–1997.	Italian Social Security Institute (INPS) matched employer–employee panel: Veneto Workers History data set; private–sector excluding agriculture, male employees aged 20–55.	This study estimates the effect of employment protection legislation on wages, exploiting the 1990 Italian reform that introduced unjust dismissal costs for firms below 15 employees. It combines a regression discontinuity design (RDD) with a difference–in–difference (DID) approach for identifying the effect.	CP	The slight average wage reduction induced by the reform hides highly heterogeneous effects. Workers who change firm during the reform period suffer a drop in the entry wage, while incumbent workers are left unaffected. Also, the negative effect of the reform is stronger for young blue collars, low-wage workers and workers in low-employment regions. This pattern suggests that the ability of employers to shift firing costs onto wages depends on workers' relative bargaining power.
Levy and Temin (2007)	United States; 1930s to mid-2000s.	Various.	We provide a comprehensive view of widening income inequality in the United States contrasting conditions since 1980 with those in earlier postwar years. We argue that the income distribution in each period was strongly shaped by a set of economic institutions. A Bargaining Power Index is used (percent of output captured by full-time worker's compensation), split by categories of workers.	MW, OP, TA, UB	The early postwar years were dominated by unions, a negotiating framework set in the Treaty of Detroit, progressive taxes, and a high minimum wage—all parts of a general government effort to broadly distribute the gains from growth. More recent years have been characterized by reversals in all these dimensions in an institutional pattern known as the Washington Consensus. Other explanations for income disparities including skill-biased technical change and international trade are seen as factors operating within this broader institutional story.
Manzo and Bruno (2014)	United States construction industry; 2007–2011.	IPUMS data from the ACS, 5.0% sample.	An ordinary least squares (OLS) regression model is run evaluating the effects on decile ratios of income inequality of unionization, distinguishing	UD, UB	The largest contributor to rising income inequality has been the gradual, long-term decline in labor union membership. The union wage premium is between 10 and 17%, helping lower- and

Continued

Table 18.A9 Wage dispersion and institutions (see Section 18.4.6)—cont'd

Authors	Countries and years	Data sets* and sample selection	Methods and important variables	Types of institutions**	Main findings
			between prevailing-wage-law states and right-to-work law states, and controlling for demographic, educational, and work factors, including 24 distinct occupations.		middle-income workers most. Right-to-work laws decrease unionization by between 5% and 8% points and reduce the average construction worker's earnings by 6% in the national economy.
Nunziata (2005)	OECD; 1960–1994.	Various.	An empirical analysis of the determinants of labor cost, with particular reference to the impact of labor market institutions from 1960 to 1994. The paper also discusses the econometric issues related to the estimation of a macro pooled model like ours: among other things, the hypothesis of poolability and the cointegration properties of the model. The explanatory power of the model is finally tested by means of a series of country by country dynamic simulations.	CP, MW, TA, UB, UD, UW, WE	Labor market regulations can explain a large part of the labor cost rise in the last few decades once we control for productivity.
Oliver (2008)	14 OECD countries; 1980–2002.	Unpublished data set from the OECD	With a series of cross-sectional time-series analyses, this article investigates how a particular wage-bargaining institution: the extent to which industrywide wage minima (wage scales) cover both higher and lower skilled workers, mitigates pressures from growing international competition and new production techniques and affects the degree of wage inequality growth.	UW	The results strongly indicate that the presence of industrywide wage scales is a key factor in the evolution of wage inequality across OECD countries.

| Plotnick (1982) | United States; 1957–1977. | Unpublished earnings data Henle and Ryscavage (1980), CPS (unpublished and several specific data sources; males). | This study uses newly available time series data to analyze trends in earnings inequality. It shows that although a human capital approach fits the data well and most of its predictions on signs are correct, the model's more exacting implications are not satisfied. A complementary more ad hoc approach retains variables found to be significant and looks beyond aggregate inequality measures into parts of the distribution which gain or lose. | UD | The major finding is that the observed slow upward trend in earnings inequality is well explained by a small number of plausible economic factors. Earnings inequality is significantly related to the level of unionization, dispersion in weeks worked, the age distribution of workers, and inequality of education. Once such factors are considered, there was no secular trend in earnings inequality over the 1958–1977 period. |
| Scheve and Stasavage (2009) | AUS, CAN, CHE, DEU, FRA, IRL, JPN, NLD, NZL, SWE, UK, United States; 1916–2000. | Top-incomes data, OECD earnings database, Lydall (1968), existing data on political institutions and new political data coded by the authors. | Although explaining post-1970 differences in income inequality between OECD countries is an important task, it is also the case that convincing comparative political economy hypotheses should be able to account as well for inequality trends in earlier time periods. The article considers the correlation of centralized wage bargaining and government partisanship with three separate top incomes fractions. With a longer time span there has been significantly more variation within countries over time than there has been between countries. A longer time span also enables examining whether within-country changes in institutions like wage bargaining centralization have been associated with changes in inequality. | UB | Regression analysis over the 13 countries and the whole period gives little evidence that government partisanship and wage-bargaining centralization can account for variation in inequality over the long run. A test of four individual countries that established a centralized system of wage bargaining in the middle of the twentieth century (DNK, IRL, NLD, SWE) also shows little evidence of an effect on inequality.
This raises questions about the extent to which centralized wage bargaining is an institution that has a causal effect on inequality or alternatively whether centralized bargaining is simply an outcome that has, along with income equality, evolved over time in response to an underlying political or economic process. |

Continued

Table 18.A9 Wage dispersion and institutions (see Section 18.4.6)—cont'd

Authors	Countries and years	Data sets* and sample selection	Methods and important variables	Types of institutions**	Main findings
Schivardi and Torrini (2008)	ITA; 1986–1998.	INPS comprehensive longitudinal matched employer-employees data set.	The paper studies the effects of the more stringent employment protection legislation that applies to firms with over 15 employees. It considers firms' propensity to grow when close to that threshold and changes in employment policies when they pass it. Using a the stochastic transition matrix for firm size.	CP	The probability of firms' growth is reduced by around 2% points near the threshold. The long-run effects of EPL on the size distribution of firms are quantitatively modest. Contrary to the implications of more stringent firing restrictions, workers in firms just above the threshold have on average less stable employment relations than those just below it; this might be because firms above the threshold make greater use of flexible employment contracts, arguably to circumvent the stricter regulation on open-end contracts.
Van der Wiel (2010)	NLD; 1997–2001.	Dutch Socio-Economic Panel SEP1984–2002: five waves containing contractual information.	This paper empirically establishes the effect of notice on the wage level of employees through a fixed effects regression model. The term of notice is defined as the period an employer has to notify workers in advance of their upcoming dismissal. The wages paid during this period are an important element of firing costs and hence employment protection. To find a causal effect, the paper exploits the exogenous change in the term of notice that resulted from the introduction of a new Dutch law in 1999.	CP	Strong evidence is found that a longer "dormant" term of notice leads to higher wages. In the sample used, an additional month of notice increases wages by 3%, ceteris paribus.

REFERENCES

Abowd, John, Kramarz, Francis, Lemieux, Thomas, Margolis, David, 1999. Minimum wages and youth employment in France and the United States. In: Blanchflower, David, Freeman, Richard (Eds.), Youth Employment and Joblessness in Advanced Countries. NBER and University of Chicago Press, Boston/Chicago (Chapter 11).

Acemoglu, Daron, 2003. Cross-country inequality trends. Econ. J. 113, F121–F149.

Acemoglu, Daron, Autor, David, 2011. Skills, tasks and technologies: implications for employment and earning. In: Ashenfelter, Orley, Card, David (Eds.), Handbook of Labor Economics. vol. 4/B. Elsevier, Amsterdam, pp. 1043–1171.

Acemoglu, Daron, Autor, David, 2012. What Does Human Capital Do? A Review of Goldin and Katz's The Race Between Education and Technology, NBER Working Paper 17820.

Agell, Jonas, Lommerud, Kjell Erik, 1992. Union egalitarianism as income insurance. Economica 59 (235), 295–310.

Agell, Jonas, Lommerud, Kjell Erik, 1993. Egalitarianism and growth. Scand. J. Econ. 95 (4), 559–579.

Aghion, Philippe, Algan, Yann, Cahuc, Pierre, 2011. Civil society and the state: the interplay between cooperation and minimum wage regulation. J. Eur. Econ. Assoc. 9 (1), 3–42.

Alderson, Arthur S., Nielsen, François, 2002. Globalisation and the great U-turn: income inequality trends in 16 OECD countries. Am. J. Sociol. 107, 1244–1299.

Alesina, Alberto F., Algan, Yann, Cahuc, Pierre, Giuliano, Paola, 2010. Family Values and the Regulation of Labor, NBER Working Paper 15747.

Allegretto, Sylvia, Dube, Arindrajit, Reich, Michael, 2011. Do minimum wages really reduce teen employment? Accounting for heterogeneity and selectivity in state panel data. Indus. Relat. 50 (2), 205–240.

Alvaredo, Facundo, 2011. A note on the relationship between top income shares and the Gini coefficient. Econ. Lett. 110 (3), 274–277.

Alvaredo, Facundo, Atkinson, Anthony B., Piketty, Thomas, Saez, Emmanuel, 2013. The top 1 percent in international and historical perspective. J. Econ. Perspect. 27 (3), 3–20.

Amable, Bruno, 2003. The Diversity of Modern Capitalism. Oxford University Press, Oxford.

Andersson, Frederik, Freedman, Matthew, Haltiwanger, John, Lane, Julia, Shaw, Kathryn, 2006. Reaching for the Stars: Who Pays for Talent in Innovative Industries? NBER Working Paper 12435.

Antonczyk, Dirk, DeLeire, Thomas, Fitzenberger, Bernd, 2010. Polarization and Rising Wage Inequality: Comparing the U.S. and Germany, Discussion Paper 10-015. ZEW, Mannheim.

Ashenfelter, Orley, Card, David (Eds.), 2011. Handbook of Labor Economics, vol. 4/B. Elsevier, Amsterdam.

Atkinson, Anthony B., 1970. On the measurement of inequality. J. Econ. Theor. 2, 244–263.

Atkinson, Anthony B., 1993. What is happening to the distribution of income in the UK? Keynes lecture in economics 1992. Proc. Br. Acad. 82, 317–351, Oxford University Press.

Atkinson, Anthony B., 1997. Bringing income distribution in from the cold. Econ. J. 107 (441), 297–321.

Atkinson, Anthony B., 1999. Economic Consequences of Rolling Back the Welfare State. MIT Press and CESifo, Munich.

Atkinson, Anthony, 2007a. The long run earnings distribution in five countries: "remarkable stability," U, V or W? Rev. Income Wealth 53 (1), 1–25.

Atkinson, Anthony, 2007b. The distribution of earnings in OECD countries. Int. Labour Rev. 146 (1–2), 41–60.

Atkinson, Anthony B., 2008. The Changing Distribution of Earnings in OECD Countries. Oxford University Press, Oxford.

Atkinson, Anthony B., 2009. Factor shares: the principal problem of political economy? Oxf. Rev. Econ. Pol. 25 (1), 3–16.

Atkinson, Anthony B., Bourguignon, François, 2000. Introduction. In: Handbook of Income Distribution, vol. 1. Elsevier, North Holland.

Atkinson, Anthony, Brandolini, Andrea, 2001. Promise and pitfalls in the use of secondary datasets: income inequality in OECD countries as a case study. J. Econ. Lit. 39, 771–799.

Atkinson, Anthony B., Brandolini, Andrea, 2006. From earnings dispersion to income inequality. In: Farina, F., Savaglia, E. (Eds.), Inequality and Economic Integration. Routledge, London (Chapter 2).

Atkinson, Anthony B., Morelli, S., 2012. Chartbook of Economic Inequality: 25 Countries 1911–2010. http://ineteconomics.org/sites/inet.civicactions.net/files/Note-15-Atkinson-Morelli.pdf.

Atkinson, Anthony B., Piketty, Thomas (Eds.), 2007. Top Incomes Over the Twentieth Century: A Contrast Between Continental European and English-Speaking Countries. Oxford University Press, Oxford.

Atkinson, Anthony B., Piketty, Thomas (Eds.), 2010. Top Incomes. A Global Perspective. Oxford University Press, Oxford.

Atkinson, Anthony B., Rainwater, Lee, Smeeding, Timothy, 1995. Income Distribution in European Countries, Working Paper MU 9506, Department of Applied Economics, University of Cambridge.

Atkinson, Anthony B., Piketty, Thomas, Saez, Emmanuel, 2011. Top incomes in the long run of history. J. Econ. Lit. 49 (1), 3–71.

Autor, David, 2013. The "Task Approach" to Labor Markets: An Overview, NBER Working Paper 18711.

Autor, David, Dorn, David, 2013. The growth of low-skill service jobs and the polarization of the US labor market. Am. Econ. Rev. 103 (3), 1553–1597.

Autor, David, Levy, Frank, Murnane, Richard J., 2003. The skill content of recent technological change: an empirical exploration. Q. J. Econ. 116 (4), 1279–1333.

Autor, David, Katz, Lawrence, Kearney, Melissa, 2005. Rising Wage Inequality: The Role of Composition and Prices, NBER Working Paper 11628.

Autor, David, Katz, Lawrence F., Kearney, Melissa S., 2006. The polarization of the U.S. labor market. Am. Econ. Rev. Papers Proc. 96 (2), 189–194.

Autor, David, Katz, Lawrence, Kearney, Melissa, 2008. Trends in U.S. wage inequality: revising the revisionists. Rev. Econ. Stat. 90 (2), 300–323.

Autor, David, Manning, Alan, Smith, Christopher, 2010. The Contribution of the Minimum Wage to U.S. Wage Inequality Over Three Decades: A Reassessment, NBER Working Paper 16533.

Baccaro, Lucio, 2008. Labour, Globalisation and Inequality: Are Trade Unions Still Redistributive? International Institute for Labour Studies, Discussion Paper 192. ILO, Geneva.

Barth, E., Lucifora, C., 2006. Wage Dispersion, Markets and Institutions: The Effects of the Boom in Education on the Wage Structure, Discussion Paper 2181, IZA, Bonn.

Bassanini, Andrea, Duval, Romain, 2006. The determinants of unemployment across OECD countries: reassessing the role of policies and institutions. OECD Econ. Stud. 2006 (1), 7–86.

Bassanini, Andrea, Nunziata, Luca, Venn, Danielle, 2009. Job protection legislation and productivity growth in OECD countries. Econ. Policy 24 (4), 349–402.

Bauer, Thomas, Bender, Stephan, Bonin, Holger, 2007. Dismissal protection and worker flows in small establishments. Economica 74 (296), 804–821.

Becher, Michael, Pontusson, Jonas, 2011. Whose interests do unions represent? Unionization by income in western Europe. In: Brady, David (Ed.), Comparing European workers part B: policies and institutions. Res. Sociol. Work 22, Emerald, Bingley, pp. 181–211.

Bedard, Kelly, Ferrall, Christopher, 2003. Wage and test score dispersion: some international evidence. Econ. Educ. Rev. 22 (1), 31–43.

Behar, Alberto, 2013. The Endogenous Skill Bias of Technical Change and Inequality in Developing Countries, IMF Working Paper No. 13/50.

Bell, Linda A., Freeman, Richard B., 2001. The incentive for working hard: explaining hours worked differences in the US and Germany. Labour Econ. 8, 181–202.

Belot, Michèle, van Ours, Jan, 2004. Does the recent success of some OECD countries in lowering their unemployment rates lie in the clever design of their labour market reform? Oxford Econ. Papers 56 (4), 621–642.

Benassi, Chiara, 2011. The Implementation of Minimum Wage: Challenges and Creative Solutions, Global Labour University, Working Paper 12, ILO, Geneva.

Bertola, Giuseppe, 2004. A pure theory of job security and labour income risk. Rev. Econ. Stud. 71 (1), 43–61, Oxford University Press.

Bertola, Giuseppe, Boeri, Tito, 2003. Product Market Integration, Institutions and the Labour Markets, Mimeo. http://didattica.unibocconi.it/mypage/upload/48791_20090205_034431_48791_20090116_035648_BOERIBERTOLA14-4-03.pdf.

Bertola, Giuseppe, Blau, Francine, Kahn, Lawrence, 2001. Comparative Analysis of Labor Market Outcomes: Lessons for the US from International Long-Run Evidence, NBER Working Paper 8526.

Bertola, Giuseppe, Blau, Francine, Kahn, Lawrence, 2007. Labor market institutions and demographic employment patterns. J. Popul. Econ. 20 (4), 833–867.

Betcherman, Gordon, 2012. Labour Market Institutions. A Review of the Literature, Policy Research, Working Paper No. 6276, World Bank.

Bičáková, Alena, 2006. Market vs. Institutions: The Trade-Off Between Unemployment and Wage Inequality Revisited, EUI Working Paper ECO No. 2006/31, Florence.

Bingley, Paul, Cappellari, Lorenzo, Westergård-Nielsen, Niels, 2013. Unemployment insurance, wage dynamics and inequality over the life cycle. Econ. J. 123 (568), 341–372.

Blackburn, McKinley, Bloom, David E., 1987. Earnings and income inequality in the United States. Popul. Dev. Rev. 13 (5), 575–609.

Blackburn, McKinley, Bloom, David E., 1995. Changes in the structure of family income inequality in the United States and other industrialized nations during the 1980s. Res. Labor Econ. 14, 141–170.

Blackburn, McKinley, Bloom, David E., Freeman, Richard, 1990. An era of falling earnings and rising inequality? Brookings Rev. 9 (1), 38–43.

Blanchard, Olivier, Giavazzi, Francesco, 2003. Macroeconomic effects of regulations and deregulation in goods and labor markets. Q. J. Econ. 118 (3), 879–907.

Blanchard, Olivier, Tirole, Jean, 2008. The joint design of unemployment insurance and employment protection: a first pass. J. Eur. Econ. Assoc. 6 (1), 45–77.

Blanchard, Olivier, Wolfers, Justin, 2000. The role of shocks and institutions in the rise of European unemployment: the aggregate evidence. Econ. J. 110, C1–C33.

Blanchflower, David, Oswald, Andrew, 2013. Does High Home-Ownership Impair the Labor Market? Mimeo at andrewoswald.com.

Blau, Francine, Kahn, Lawrence, 1996. International differences in male wage inequality: institutions versus market forces. J. Polit. Econ. 104 (4), 791–837.

Blau, Francine, Kahn, Lawrence, 1999. Institutions and laws in the labor market, In: Ashenfelter, Orley, Card, David E. (Eds.), Handbook of Labor Economics. vol. 3A. pp. 1399–1461 (Chapter 25).

Blau, Francine, Kahn, Lawrence, 2002. At Home and Abroad. U.S. Labor Market Performance in International Perspective. Russell Sage, New York.

Blau, Francine, Kahn, Lawrence, 2009. Inequality and earnings distribution. In: Salverda, Wiemer, Nolan, Brian, Smeeding, Timothy (Eds.), The Oxford Handbook of Economic Inequality. Oxford University Press, Oxford, pp. 177–203 (Chapter 8).

Blinder, Alan, 2007. How Many U.S. Jobs Might Be Offshorable? Working Paper 60, Center for Economic Policy Studies, Princeton.

Blinder, Alan, Krueger, Alan, 2009. Alternative Measures of Offshorability: A Survey Approach, Working Paper 190, Center for Economic Policy Studies, Princeton.

Bluestone, Barry, Harrison, Bennett, 1982. The Deindustrialization of AMERICA. Basic Books, New York.

Bluestone, Barry, Harrison, Bennett, 1988. The Great U-Turn: Corporate Restructuring and the Polarizing of America. Basic Books, New York.

Blundell, Richard, Etheridge, Ben, 2010. Consumption, income and earnings inequality in Britain. Rev. Econ. Dyn. 13 (1), 76–102.

Boeri, Tito, 2011. Institutional reforms and dualism in European labor markets. In: Ashenfelter, Orley, Card, David (Eds.), Handbook of Labor Economics. vol. 4B. Elsevier, Amsterdam, pp. 1173–1236 (Chapter 13).

Boeri, Tito, 2012. Setting the minimum wage. Labour Econ. 19 (3), 281–290.

Boeri, Tito, Jimeno, Juan, 2005. The effects of employment protection: learning from variable enforcement. Eur. Econ. Rev. 49, 2057–2077.

Boeri, Tito, van Ours, Jan, 2008. The Economics of Imperfect Labor Markets. Oxford University Press, Oxford.

Botero, Juan C., Djankov, Simeon, La Porta, Rafael, Lopez-de-Silanes, Florencio, Shleifer, Andrei, 2004. The regulation of labor. Q. J. Econ. 119 (4), 1339–1382.

Bound, John, Johnson, George, 1989. Changes in the Structure of Wages During the 1980's: An Evaluation of Alternative Explanations, NBER Working Paper 2983.

Bound, John, Johnson, George, 1992. Changes in the structure of wages in the 1980's: an evaluation of alternative explanations. Am. Econ. Rev. 82 (3), 371–392.

Bourguignon, François, Ferreira, Francisco, Lustig, Nora (Eds.), 2004. The Microeconomics of Income Distribution Dynamics in East Asia and Latin America. World Bank and Oxford University Press, Oxford.

Bowles, Samuel, Park, Yongjin, 2005. Emulation, inequality, and work hours: was Thorsten Veblen right? Econ. J. 115, F397–F412.

Brandolini, Andrea, D'Alessio, Giovanni, 2001. Household Structure and Income Inequality, Working Paper 6/2001. Center for Household, Income, Labour and Demographic Economics CHILD.

Brandolini, Andrea, Rosolia, Alfonso, Torrini, Roberto, 2011. The Distribution of Employees' Labour Earnings in the European Union: Data, Concepts and First Results, Working Paper 2011-198, ECINEQ.

Brewer, Mike, Wren-Lewis, Liam, 2012. Why did Britain's households get richter? Decomposing UK Household Income Growth Between 1968 and 2008–09, Working Paper 2012–08, ISER, University of Essex.

Brewer, Mike, Duncan, Alan, Shephard, Andrew, Suarez, María José, 2006. Did working families' tax credit work? the impact of in-work support on labour supply in Great Britain. Labour Econ. 13, 699–720.

Brewer, Mike, Muriel, Alastair, Wren-Lewis, Liam, 2009. Accounting for Changes in Inequality Since 1968: Decomposition Analyses for Great Britain, Mimeo.

Brown, Charles, 1999. Minimum wages, employment, and the distribution of income. In: Ashenfelter, Orley, Card, David (Eds.), Handbook of Labor Economics. vol. 3. Elsevier, Amsterdam, pp. 2101–2163.

Brügemann, Björn, 2012. Does employment protection create its own political support? J. Eur. Econ. Assoc. 10 (2), 369–416.

Bryson, Alex, Freeman, Richard, Lucifora, Claudio, Pellizzari, Michele, Perotin, Virginie, 2012. Paying for Performance: Incentive Pay Schemes and Employees' Financial Participation, CEP Discussion Paper 1112, LSE.

Brzozowski, Michael, Gervais, Martin, Klein, Paul, Suzuki, Michio, 2010. Consumption, income, and wealth inequality in Canada. Rev. Econ. Dyn. 13 (1), 52–75.

Budría, Santiago, Pereira, Pedro T., 2005. Educational Qualifications and Wage Inequality: Evidence for Europe, IZA Discussion Paper 1763. Bonn.

Burtless, Gary, 1999. Effects of growing wage disparities and changing family composition on the U.S. income distribution. Eur. Econ. Rev. 43, 853–865.

Burtless, Gary, 2009. Demographic transformation and economic inequality. In: Salverda, Weimer, Nolan, Brian, Smeeding, Timothy (Eds.), The Oxford Handbook of Economic Inequality. Oxford University Press, Oxford, pp. 435–454 (Chapter 18).

Butcher, Tim, 2011. Still evidence-based? The role of policy evaluation in recession and beyond: the case of the national minimum wage. Natl. Inst. Econ. Rev. 219, R26–R40.

Butcher, Tim, Dickens, Richard, Manning, Alan, 2012. Minimum Wages and Wage Inequality: Some Theory and an Application to the UK, CEP Discussion Paper 1177, LSE.

Cancian, Maria, Schoeni, Robert, 1998. Wives' earnings and the level and distribution of married couples earnings in developed countries. J. Income Distribut. 8 (1), 45–61.

Card, David, DiNardo, John, 2002. Skill-biased technological change and rising wage inequality: some problems and puzzles. J. Labor Econ. 20 (4), 733–783.

Card, David, Krueger, Alan, 1995a. Myth and Measurement. The New economics of the Minimum Wage. Princeton University Press, Princeton.

Card, David, Krueger, Alan, 1995b. Time-series minimum-wage studies: a meta-analysis. Am. Econ. Rev. 85, 238–243.

Card, David, Lemieux, Thomas, Riddell, Craig, 2004. Unions and wage inequality. J. Labor Res. 25 (4), 519–562.

Cardoso, Ana, 2010. Do firms compress the wage distribution? In: Marsden, David, Rycx, François (Eds.), Wage Structures, Employment Adjustments and Globalization: Evidence from Linked and Firm-level Panel Data. Palgrave Macmillan, Basingstoke, pp. 202–218.

Charles, Kerwin Kofi, Guryan, Jonathan, 2007. Prejudice and the Economics of Discrimination, NBER Working Paper 13661.

Charles, Kerwin Kofi, Guryan, Jonathan, 2008. Prejudice and the economics of discrimination. J. Polit. Econ. 116 (5), 773–809.

Checchi, Daniele, Lucifora, Claudio, 2002. Unions and labour market institutions in Europe. Econ. Policy 17 (2), 362–401.

Checchi, Daniele, Garcia Peñalosa, Cecilia, 2008. Labour market institutions and income inequality. Econ. Policy 56, 600–651.

Checchi, Daniele, Garcia Peñalosa, Cecilia, 2010. Labour shares and the personal distribution of income in the OECD. Economica 77 (307), 413–450.

Cheon, Byung You, Chang, Jiyeun Hwang, Seong Shin, Gyu, Wook Kang, Jin, Wook Lee, Shin, Hee Kim, Byung, Joo, Hyun, 2013. Growing Inequality and Its Impacts in Korea, Country Report to the GINI project, http://gini-research.org/CR-Korea.

Chetty, Raj, 2008. Moral Hazard vs. Liquidity and Optimal Unemployment Insurance, NBER Working Paper 13967.

Christopoulou, Rebekka, Jimeno, Juan F., Lamo, Ana, 2010. Changes in the Wage Structure in EU Countries, Documentos de Trabajo 1017. Banco de España.

Coelli, Michael, Fahrer, Jerome, Lindsay, Holly, 1994. Wage Dispersion and Labour Market Institutions: A Cross Country Study, Research Discussion Paper 9404. Reserve Bank of Australia.

Congressional Budget Office (CBO), 2012. The Distribution of Household Income and Average Federal Tax Rates, 2008 and 2009. Supplemental data, http://www.cbo.gov/publication/43373.

Conyon, Martin, Fernandes, Nuno, Ferreira, Miguel, Matos, Pedro, Murphy, Kevin, 2011. The Executive Compensation Controversy: A Transatlantic Analysis, Fondazione Rodolfo De Benedetti.

Corluy, Vincent, Vandenbroucke, Frank, 2013. Individual Employment, Household Employment and Risk of Poverty in the EU. A Decomposition Analysis, Eurostat.

Corsini, Lorenzo, 2008. Institutions, Technological Change and the Wage Differentials Between Skilled and Unskilled Workers: Theory and Evidence from Europe, IRISS Working Paper 2008-02.

Cowell, Frank, 2000. Measurement of inequality, In: Atkinson, A.B., Bourguignon, F. (Eds.), Handbook of Income Distribution. vol. 1. pp. 87–166, Elsevier, Amsterdam (Chapter 2).

Cowell, Frank, Fiorio, Carlo, 2011. Inequality decompositions—a reconciliation. J. Econ. Inequality 9, 509–528.

Dahl, Christian, le Maire, Daniel, Munch, Jakob, 2011. Wage Dispersion and Decentralization of Wage Bargaining, IZA Discussion Paper 6176.

Daly, Mary, Valetta, Robert, 2006. Inequality and poverty in United States: the effects of rising dispersion of men's earnings and changing family behaviour. Economica 73 (289), 75–98.

De Graaf-Zijl, Marloes, Nolan, Brian, 2011. Household joblessness and its impact on poverty and deprivation in Europe. J. Eur. Soc. Policy 21, 413–431.

De Linde Leonard, M., Stanley, T.D., Doucouliagos, Hristos, 2014. Does the UK minimum wage reduce employment? A meta-regression analysis. Br. J. Indus. Relat. 52 (3), 499–520.

Deininger, Klaus, Squire, Lyn, 1996. A new data set measuring income inequality. World Bank Econ. Rev. 10 (3), 565–591.

Del Boca, Daniela, Pasqua, Sylvia, 2003. Employment patterns of husbands and wives and family income distribution in Italy (1977–98). Rev. Income Wealth 49 (2), 221–245.

DiNardo, John, Lemieux, Thomas, 1997. Diverging male wage inequality in the United States and Canada, 1981–1988: do institutions explain the difference? Indust. Labor Relat. Rev. 50 (4), 629–651.

DiNardo, John, Pischke, Jorn-Steffen, 1997. The returns to computer use revisited: have pencils changed the wage structure too? Q. J. Econ. 112 (1), 291–303.

DiNardo, John, Fortin, Nicole, Lemieux, Thomas, 1996. Labor market institutions and the distribution of wages, 1973–1992: a semiparametric approach. Econometrica 64 (5), 1001–1044.

Dingeldey, Irene, 2001. European tax systems and their impact on family employment patterns. J. Soc. Policy 30, 653–672.

DiPrete, Thomas, 2007. What has sociology to contribute to the study of inequality trends? An historical and comparative perspective. Am. Behav. Sci. 50 (5), 603–618.

Dolado, Juan, Kramarz, Francis, Machin, Stephen, Manning, Alan, Margolis, David, Teulings, Coen, 1996. The economic impact of minimum wage in Europe. Econ. Policy 23, 317–372.

Dolton, Peter, Bondibene, Chiara Rosazza, 2011. An evaluation of the international experience of minimum wages in an economic downturn, Research Report for the Low Pay Commission, University of London, Royal Holloway College.

Domeij, David, Floden, Martin, 2010. Inequality trends in Sweden 1978–2004. Rev. Econ. Dyn. 13 (1), 179–208.

Dooley, Martin, Gottschalk, Peter, 1984. Earnings inequality among males in the United States: trends and the effect of labor force. J. Polit. Econ. 92 (1), 59–89.

Dooley, Martin, Gottschalk, Peter, 1985. The increasing proportion of men with low earnings in the United States. Demography 22 (1), 25–34.

Doucouliagos, Hristos, Stanley, T.D., 2009. Publication selection bias in minimum-wage research? A meta-regression analysis. Br. J. Ind. Relat. 47 (22), 406–428.

Dube, Arindrajit, 2013. Minimum Wages and the Distribution of Family Incomes. https://dl.dropboxusercontent.com/u/15038936/Dube_MinimumWagesFamilyIncomes.pdf (December 30, 2013).

Dube, Arindrajit, Lester, William, Reich, Michael, 2010. Minimum wage effects across state borders: estimates using contiguous counties. Rev. Econ. Stat. 92 (4), 945–964.

Dube, Arindrajit, Lester, William, Reich, Michael, 2012. Minimum Wage Shocks, Employment Flows and Labor Market Frictions. Institute for Research on Labor and Employment, Berkeley, CA.http://escholarship.org/uc/item/76p927ks.

Dunne, Timothy, Foster, Lucia, Haltiwanger, John, Troske, Kenneth R., 2004. Wage and productivity dispersion in United States manufacturing: the role of computer investment. J. Labor Econ. 22 (2), 397–429.

Dupuy, Arnaud, Fernández-Kranz, Daniel, 2011. International differences in the family gap in pay: the role of labour market institutions. Appl. Econ. 43, 413–438.

Dustmann, Christian, Ludsteck, Johannes, Schönberg, Uta, 2009. Revisiting the German wage structure. Q. J. Econ. 124 (2), 843–881.

Eichhorst, Werner, Feil, Michael, Braun, Christoph, 2008. What Have We Learned? Assessing Labor Market Institutions and Indicators, IZA Discussion Paper 3470. Bonn.

Eissa, Nada, Hoynes, Hilary, 2004. Taxes and the labor market participation of married couples: the earned income tax credit. J. Public Econ. 88, 1931–1958.

Eissa, Nada, Hoynes, Hilary, 2006. Behavioral responses to taxes: lessons from the EITC and labor supply. In: Poterba, J.M. (Ed.), Tax Policy and the Economy. MIT Press, Cambridge MA, pp. 73–110 (Chapter 3).

Farber, Henry, Valletta, Robert, 2013. Do extended Unemployment Benefits Lengthen Unemployment Spells? Evidence From Recent Cycles in the US Labour Market, Working Paper 573, Princeton University, Industrial Relations section.

Fields, Gary, 2003. Accounting for income inequality and its change: a new method, with application to the distribution of earnings in the United States. Res. Labor Econ. 22, 1–38.

Fiori, Giuseppe, Nicoletti, Giuseppe, Scarpetta, Stefano, Schiantarelli, Fabio, 2012. Employment effects of product and labour market reforms: are there synergies? Econ. J. 122, F79–F104.

Firpo, Sergio, Fortin, Nicole, Lemieux, Thomas, 2009. Unconditional quantile regressions. Econometrica 77 (3), 953–973.

Firpo, Sergio, Fortin, Nicole M., Lemieux, Thomas, 2011. Occupational Tasks and Changes in the Wage Structure, IZA Discussion Paper 5542. Bonn.

Flaig, Gebhard, Rottmann, Horst, 2011. Labour Market Institutions and Unemployment. An International Comparison, CESifo Working Paper 3558.

Förster, Michael, 1994. Measurement of Low Incomes and Poverty in a Perspective of International Comparisons, OECD Labour Market and Social Policy Occasional Papers 14.

Fortin, Nicole, Lemieux, Thomas, 1997. Institutional changes and rising wage inequality: is there a linkage? J. Econ. Perspect. 1 (2), 75–96.

Fortin, Nicole, Lemieux, Thomas, 2014. Changes in wage inequality in Canada: an interprovincial perspective, First draft, http://faculty.arts.ubc.ca/nfortin/FortinLemieux_Inequality_%20provinces.pdf.

Fortin, Nicole, Lemieux, Thomas, Firpo, Sergio, 2011. Decomposition methods in economics. In: Ashenfelter, Orley, Card, David (Eds.), Handbook of Labor Economics. vol. IIIA. Elsevier, Amsterdam, pp. 1463–1555. (Chapter 1; also NBER Working Paper 16045, 2010).

Fortin, Nicole M., Schirle, Tammy D., 2006. Gender dimensions of changes in earnings inequality in Canada. In: Green, David A., Kesselman, Jonathan R. (Eds.), Dimensions of Inequality in Canada. Vancouver, UBC Press, pp. 307–346.

Freeman, Richard, 1980. Unionism and the dispersion of wages. Ind. Labor Relat. Rev. 34 (2), 3–23.

Freeman, Richard, 1988. Labour market institutions and economic performance. Econ. Policy 3 (6), 63–88.

Freeman, Richard, 1991. How Much Has De-Unionisation Contributed to the Rise in Male Earnings Inequality? NBER Working Paper 3826 (In: Danziger and Gottschalk (Eds.), Uneven Tides, 1992).

Freeman, Richard (Ed.), 1994. Working Under Different Rules. Russell Sage, New York.

Freeman, Richard, 2000. Single Peaked vs. Diversified Capitalism: The Relation Between Economic Institutions and Outcomes, NBER Working Paper 7556.

Freeman, Richard B., 2001. Single Peaked Vs. Diversified Capitalism: The Relation Between Economic Institutions and Outcomes, Working Paper No. 7556, NBER, Boston.

Freeman, Richard, 2005. Labour Market Institutions without Blinders: The Debate over Flexibility and Labour Market Performance, NBER Working Paper 11286.

Freeman, Richard, 2006. The great doubling: the challenge of the new global labor market. http://emlab.berkeley.edu/users/webfac/eichengreen/e183_sp07/great_doub.pdf.

Freeman, Richard, 2007. Labor market institutions around the world, NBER Working Paper 13242.

Freeman, Richard, 2009. Labor Regulations, Unions, and Social Protection in Developing Countries: Market Distortions or Efficient Institutions? NBER Working Paper 14789.

Freeman, Richard, Katz, Lawrence (Eds.), 1995. Differences and Changes in Wage Structures. University of Chicago Press, Chicago.

Freeman, Richard, Medoff, James, 1984. What Do Unions Do? Basic Books, New York.

Freeman, Richard, Schettkat, Ronald, 2001. Skill compression, wage differentials and employment: Germany vs. the US. Oxf. Econ. Pap. 53 (3), 582–603.

Friedman, Milton, 1968. The role of monetary policy. Am. Econ. Rev. 58 (1), 1–17.

Fuchs-Schündeln, Nicola, Krueger, Dirk, Sommer, Mathias, 2010. Inequality trends for Germany in the last two decades: a tale of two countries. Rev. Econ. Dyn. 13 (1), 103–132.

Garnero, Andrea, Kampelmann, Stephan, Rycx, François, 2013. Minimum Wage Systems and Earnings Inequalities: Does Institutional Diversity Matter? DULBEA Working Paper 13-06.

Gautié, Jérôme, Schmitt, John (Eds.), 2010. Low-Wage Work in Wealthy Countries. Russell Sage, New York.

Gindling, Thomas, Terrell, Katherine, 2009. Minimum wages, wages and employment in various sectors in Honduras. Labour Econ. 16 (3), 291–303.

Giuliano, Laura, 2013. Minimum wage effects on employment, substitution, and the teenage labor supply: evidence from personnel data. J. Labor Econ. 31 (1), 155–194.

Glyn, Andrew, 2009. Functional distribution and inequality. In: Salverda, Weimer, Nolan, Brian, Smeeding, Timothy M. (Eds.), Oxford Handbook of Economic Inequality. Oxford University Press, Oxford, pp. 101–126 (Chapter 5).

Glyn, Andrew, Baker, Dean, Howell, David, Schmitt, John, 2003. Labor Market Institutions and Unemployment: A Critical Review of the Cross-Country Evidence, Discussion Paper 168. Department of Economics, University of Oxford, Oxford.

Golden, Miriam, Wallerstein, M., 2006. Domestic and International Causes for the Rise of Pay Inequality: Post -Industrialism, Globalization and Labor Market Institutions. Mimeo.

Golden, Miriam, Wallerstein, Michael, 2011. Domestic and international causes for the rise of pay inequality in OECD nations between 1980 and 2000. In: Comparing European Workers. Part A: Experiences and Inequalities. In: Research in the Sociology of Work, vol. 22. pp. 209–249.

Goos, Maarten, Manning, Alan, 2003. Lousy and Lovely Jobs: the Rising Polarization of Work in Britain. London, LSE, CEP Working Paper 604.

Goos, Maarten, Manning, Alan, 2007. Lousy and lovely jobs: the rising polarization of work in Britain, Rev. Econ. Stat. 89 (1), 118–133.

Goos, Maarten, Manning, Alan, Salomons, Anna, 2009. Job polarization in Europe. Am. Econ. Rev. 99 (2), 58–63.

Goos, Maarten, Manning, Alan, Salomons, Anna, 2010. Explaining Job Polarization in Europe: The Roles of Technology, Globalization and Institutions, CEP Discussion Paper 1026, LSE.

Goos, Maarten, Manning, Alan, Salomons, Anna, 2011. Explaining Job Polarization: The Roles of Technology, Offshoring and Institutions. KU Leuven, Center for Economic Studies, Discussion Paper 11.34.

Goos, Maarten, Manning, Alan, Salomons, Anna, 2014. Explaining job polarization: routine-biased technological change and offshoring. Am. Econ. Rev. 104 (8), 2509–2526.

Gottschalk, Peter, Danziger, Sheldon, 2005. Inequality of wage rates, earnings and family income in the United States 1975–2002. Rev. Income Wealth 51 (2), 231–254.

Gottschalk, Peter, Joyce, Mary, 1998. Cross-national differences in the rise in earnings inequality: market and institutional factors. Rev. Econ. Stat. 80 (4), 489–502.

Gottschalk, Peter, Smeeding, Timothy, 1997. Cross-national comparisons of earnings and income inequality. J. Econ. Lit. 35, 633–687.

Gregg, Paul, Wadsworth, Jonathan, 1996. More work in fewer households? In: Hills, J. (Ed.), New Inequalities. Cambridge University Press, London, pp. 181–207.

Gregg, Paul, Wadsworth, Jonathan, 1998. It Takes Two: Employment Polarisation in the OECD, Discussion Paper 304, Centre for Economic Performance, London.

Gregg, Paul, Wadsworth, Jonathan, 2008. Two sides to every story: measuring polarization and inequality in the distribution of work. J. R. Stat. Soc. Ser. A 171 (4), 857–875.

Gregg, Paul, Scutella, Rosanna, Wadsworth, Jonathan, 2010. Reconciling workless measures at the individual and household level. Theory and evidence from the United States, Britain, Germany, Spain and Australia. J. Popul. Econ. 23, 139–167.

Hall, Robert, Krueger, Alan, 2010. Evidence on the Determinants of the Choice Between Wage Posting and Wage Bargaining, NBER Working Paper 16033.

Hall, Peter, Soskice, David (Eds.), 2001. Varieties of Capitalism: The Institutional Foundations of Comparative Advantage. Oxford University Press, Oxford.

Harrison, Bennet, Tilly, Chris, Bluestone, Barry, 1986. Wage inequality takes a great U-turn. Challenge 29 (1), 26–32, Symposium of the Joint Economic Committee of Congress on the 40th Anniversary of the Employment Act of 1946 (Part 1).

Heathcote, Jonathan, Perri, Fabrizio, Violante, Giovanni, 2010. Unequal we stand: an empirical analysis of economic inequality. Rev. Econ. Dyn. 13, 15–51.

Heckman, James, Sedlacek, Guilherme, 1985. Heterogeneity, aggregation, and market wage functions: an empirical model of self-selection in the labor market. J. Polit. Econ. 93 (9), 1077–1125.

Henle, Peter, 1972. Distribution of earned income. Monthly Labor Rev. 95 (12), 16–27.

Henle, Peter, Ryscavage, Paul, 1980. The distribution of earned income among men and women, 1958–77. Monthly Labour Rev. 103 (4), 3–10.

Heshmati, Almas, 2004. A Review of Decomposition of Income Inequality, Discussion Paper 1221, IZA Bonn.

Hills, John, Brewer, Mike, Jenkins, Stephen, Lister, Ruth, Lupton, Ruth, Machin, Stephen, Mills, Colin, Modood, Tariq, Rees, Teresa, Riddell, Sheila, 2010. An Anatomy of Economic Inequality in the UK: Report of the National Equality Panel. http://sticerd.lse.ac.uk/case/_new/publications/NEP.asp.

Holzmann, Robert, Pouget, Yann, Vodopivec, Milan, Weber, Michael, 2011. Severance Pay Programs around the World: History, Rationale, Status, and Reforms, IZA Discussion Paper 5731.

Hyslop, Dean, 2001. Rising US earnings inequality and family labor supply: the covariance structure of intra-family earnings. Am. Econ. Rev. 91, 755–777.

ILO, 2008. Global Wage Report 2008/09. Minimum Wages and Collective Bargaining: Towards Policy Coherence, Geneva.

ILO, 2010. Global Wage Report 2010/11. Wage Policies in Times of Crisis, Geneva.

Japelli, Tullio, Pistaferri, Luigi, 2010. Does consumption inequality track income inequality in Italy? Rev. Econ. Dyn. 13 (1), 133–153.

Jenkins, Stephen, 1995. Accounting for inequality trends: decomposition analyses for the UK, 1971–86. Economica 62 (245), 29–63.

Jenkins, Stephen, van Kerm, Philippe, 2009. The measurement of economic inequality. In: Salverda, Weimer, Nolan, Brian, Smeeding, Timothy (Eds.), The Oxford Handbook of Economic Inequality. Oxford University Press, Oxford, pp. 40–67 (Chapter 3).

Johnson, David, Wilkins, Roger, 2003. The Effects of Changes in Family Composition and Employment Patterns on the Distribution of Income in Australia: 1982 to 1997–1998, Working Paper 19/03, Melbourne Institute of Applied Economic and Social Research.

Juhn, Chinhui, Murphy, Kevin, Pierce, Brooks, 1993. Wage inequality and the rise in returns to skill. J. Polit. Econ. 101, 410–442.

Kahn, James, 2005. Labor Supply and the Changing Household. Paper presented to Society for Economic Dynamics.

Kampelmann, Stephan, Garnero, Andrea, Rycx, François, 2013. Minimum Wages in Europe: Does the Diversity of Systems Lead to a Diversity of Outcomes? ETUI Report 128, Brussels.

Karabarbounis, Loukas, Neiman, Brent, 2013. The Global Decline of the Labor Share, NBER Working Paper 19136.

Karoly, Lynn, 1988. A Study of the Distribution of Individual Earnings in the United States from 1967 to 1986. PhD Thesis, Yale University.

Karoly, Lynn, 1992. Changes in the distribution of individual earnings in the United States: 1967–1986. Rev. Econ. Stat. 74 (1), 107–115.

Karoly, Lynn, 1993. The trend in inequality among families, individuals and workers in the United States: a twenty-five year perspective, In: Danziger, S., Gottschalk, P. (Eds.), Uneven Tides, Rising Inequality in America. Russell Sage, New York, pp. 19–97 (Chapter 2).

Karoly, Lynn, Burtless, Gary, 1995. Demographic change, rising earnings inequality, and the distribution of personal well-being, 1959–1989. Demography 32 (3), 379–405.

Katz, Lawrence, Autor, David, 1999. Changes in the Wage Structure and Earnings Inequality. In: Ashenfelter, Orley, Card, David (Eds.), Handbook of Labor Economics. vol. IIIA. Elsevier, Amsterdam, pp. 1463–1555.

Katz, Lawrence, Murphy, Kevin, 1992. Changes in relative wages: supply and demand factors. Q. J. Econ. CVII, 35–78.

Kenworthy, Lane, 2001. Wage-setting measures: a survey and assessment. World Polit. 54, 57–98.

Kenworthy, Lane, 2008. Sources of Equality and Inequality: Wages, Jobs, Households, and redistribution, Working Paper 471, Luxembourg Income Study. Chapter 3 of Kenworthy, Jobs with Equality, Oxford University Press, 2008.

Kenworthy, Lane, Pontusson, Jonas G, 2005. Rising inequality and the politics of redistribution in affluent countries. Perspect. Polit. 3 (3), 449–471.

Kierzenkowski, Rafal, Koske, Isabel, 2012. Less Income Inequality and More Growth—Are they Compatible? Part 8. The Drivers of Labour Income Inequality—A Literature Review, OECD Economics Department Working Paper 931, OECD Publishing.

Kimhi, Ayal, 2011. On the interpretation (and misinterpretation) of inequality decompositions by income sources. World Dev. 39 (10), 1888–1890.

Kluve, Jochen, 2010. The effectiveness of European active labor market programs. Labour Econ. 17 (6), 904–918.

Koeniger, Winfried, Leonardi, Marco, Nunziata, Luca, 2007. Labor market institutions and wage inequality. Ind. Labor Relat. Rev. 60 (3), 340–356.

Krueger, Dirk, Perri, Fabrizio, 2006. Does income inequality lead to consumption inequality? Evidence and theory. Rev. Econ. Stud. 73 (1), 163–193.

Kugler, Adriana, Pica, Giovanni, 2008. Effects of employment protection on worker and job flows: evidence from the 1990 Italian reform. Labour Econ. 15 (1), 78–95.

Lalive, Rafael, Schlosser, Analía, Steinhauer, Andreas, Zweimüller, Josef, 2011. Parental Leave and Mothers' Careers: The Relative Importance of Job Protection and Cash Benefits, IZA Discussion Paper 5792, Bonn.

Lane, Julia, 2009. Inequality and the labour market – employers. In: Salverda, Wiemer, Nolan, Brian, Smeeding, Timothy (Eds.), The Oxford Handbook on Economic Inequality. Oxford University Press, Oxford, pp. 204–229 (Chapter 9).

Larrimore, Jeff, 2013. Accounting for United States household income inequality trends: the changing importance of household structure and male and female labour earnings inequality. Rev. Income Wealth 101 (3), 173–177.

Layard, Richard, Nickell, Stephen, Jackman, Richard, 1991. Unemployment. Macroeconomic Performance and the Labour Market. Oxford University Press, Oxford.

Lee, David, 1999. Wage inequality in the United States during the 1980s: rising dispersion or falling minimum wage? Q. J. Econ. 114 (3), 977–1023.

Lehrer, Evelyn, 2000. The impact of women's employment on the distribution of earnings among married-couple households: a comparison between 1973 and 1992–1994. Q. Rev. Econ. Finance 40, 295–301.

Leigh, Andrew, 2009. Top incomes, In: Salverda, Wiemer, Nolan, Brian, Smeeding, Timothy (Eds.), The Oxford Handbook of Economic Inequality. Oxford University Press, Oxford, pp. 150–174 (Chapter 7).

Lemieux, Thomas, 2006a. Postsecondary education and increasing wage inequality. Am. Econ. Rev. 96 (2), 195–199.

Lemieux, Thomas, 2006b. Postsecondary Education and Increasing Wage Inequality, NBER Working Paper 12077.

Lemieux, Thomas, 2006c. Increasing residual wage inequality: composition effects, noisy data, or rising demand for skill? Am. Econ. Rev. 96 (3), 461–498.

Lemieux, Thomas, 2008. The changing nature of wage inequality. J. Popul. Econ. 21 (1), 21–48.

Lemieux, Thomas, 2010. What Do We Really Know about Changes in Wage Inequality?. In: Abraham, Katharine, Spletzer, James, Harper, Michael (Eds.), Labor in the New Economy. NBER Books, University of Chicago Press, Boston/Chicago, pp. 17–59 (Chapter 1).

Lemieux, Thomas, 2011. Wage inequality: a comparative perspective. Aust. Bull. Labour 37 (1), 2–32.

Lemieux, Thomas, Macleod, Bentley, Parent, Daniel, 2009. Performance pay and wage inequality. Q. J. Econ. 124 (1), 1–49.

Lemos, Sara, 2009. Minimum wage effects in a developing country. Labour Econ. 16, 224–237.

Leonardi, Marco, Pica, Giovanni, 2013. Who pays for it? The heterogeneous wage effects of employment protection legislation. Econ. J. 123 (573), 1236–1278.

Lerman, Robert, Yitzhaki, Shlomo, 1984. A note on the calculation and interpretation of the Gini index. Econ. Lett. 15 (3–4), 363–368.

Leuven, Edwin, Oosterbeek, Hessel, van Ophem, Hans, 1997. International Comparisons of Male Wage Inequality; Are the Findings Robust? Tinbergen Institute, Working Paper 97-59, University of Amsterdam.

Leuven, Edwin, Oosterbeek, Hessel, van Ophem, Hans, 2004. Explaining international differences in male skill wage differentials by differences in demand and supply of skill. Econ. J. 114, 466–486.

Levy, Frank, Murnane, Richard, 1992. U.S. earnings levels and earnings inequality: a review of recent trends and proposed explanations. J. Econ. Lit. 30, 1333–1381.

Levy, Frank, Murnane, Richard, 2005. How Computerized Work and Globalization Shape Human Skill Demands, MIT IPC Working Paper IPC-05-006.

Levy, Frank, Temin, Peter, 2007. Inequality and Institutions in 20th Century America, NBER Working Paper 13106.

Liebman, Jeffrey, 1998. The impact of the earned income tax credit on incentives and income distribution. In: Poterba, James (Ed.), Tax Policy and the Economy. vol. 12.

Liu, Yujia, Grusky, David, 2013. The payoff to skill in the third industrial revolution. Am. J. Sociol. 118 (5), 1330–1374.

Lu, Yuqian, Morissette, René, Schirle, Tammy, 2011. The growth of family earnings inequality in Canada 1980–2005. Rev. Income Wealth 57 (1), 23–39.

Lucifora, Claudio, Salverda, Wiemer, 2009. Low pay, In: Salverda, Wiemer, Nolan, Brian, Smeeding, Timothy (Eds.), The Oxford Handbook of Economic Inequality. Oxford University Press, Oxford, pp. 256–283 (Chapter 11).

Lydall, Harold, 1968. The Structure of Earnings. Clarendon Press, Alderley, Gloucestershire.

Machin, Stephen, 1997. The decline of labour market institutions rise in wage inequality in Britain. Eur. Econ. Rev. 41 (3–5), 647–657.

Machin, Stephen, 2008. An appraisal of economic research on changes in wage inequality. Labour 22 (Special issue), 7–26.

Mandel, Hadas, Semyonov, Moshe, 2005. Family policies, wage structures, and gender gaps: sources of earnings inequality in 20 countries. Am. Sociol. Rev. 70, 949–967.

Mandelbrot, Benoit, 1962. Paretian distributions and income maximization. Q. J. Econ. 76 (1), 57–85.

Manning, Alan, 2011. Imperfect competition in the labour market. In: Ashenfelter, Orley, Card, David (Eds.), Handbook of Labor Economics. vol. 4B. Elsevier, Amsterdam, pp. 973–1041.

Manzo IV, Frank, Bruno, Robert, 2014. Which Labor Market Institutions Reduce Income Inequality? Labor Unions, Prevailing Wage Laws, and Right-to-Work Laws in the Construction Industry, Illinois Economic Policy Institute (ILEPI). Research Report.

Martin, John, Scarpetta, Stefano, 2011. Setting It Right: Employment Protection, Labour Reallocation and Productivity, IZA Policy Paper 27, 27.

Martins, Pedro, 2009. Dismissals for cause: the difference that just eight paragraphs can make. J. Labor Econ. 27 (2), 257–279.

Matano, Alessia, Naticchioni, Paolo, 2011. Is there rent sharing in Italy? evidence from employer-employee data. Eur. J. Comp. Econ. 8 (2), 265–279.

Messina, Julian, Vallanti, Giovanna, 2007. Job flow dynamics and firing restrictions: evidence from Europe. Econ. J. 117, F279–F301.

Metcalf, David, 2004. The impact of the national minimum wage on the pay distribution, employment and training. Econ. J. 114, C84–C86.

Mishel, Lawrence, Shierholdz, Heidi, Schmitt, John, 2013. Don't Blame the Robots. Assessing the Job Polarization Explanation of Growing Wage Inequality, Working Paper, EPI, Washington (19 November).

Mookherjee, Dilip, Shorrocks, Anthony, 1982. A decomposition analysis of the trend in UK income inequality. Econ. J. 92 (368), 886–902.

Mortensen, Dale, 2005. Wage Dispersion: Why Are Similar Workers Paid Differently? MIT Press, Cambridge MA.

Mühlau, Peter, Horgan, Justine, 2001. Labour Market Status and the Wage Position of the Low Skilled: The Role of Institutions and of Demand and Supply—Evidence from the International Adult Literacy Survey, Working Paper 5, European Low-wage employment Research network. http://www.uva-aias. net/uploaded_files/regular/05MuehlauHorgan.pdf.

Neal, Derek, Rosen, Sherwin, 2000. Theories of the distribution of earnings, In: Atkinson, A., Bourguignon, F. (Eds.), Handbook of Income Distribution, pp. 379–428, Elsevier, Amsterdam.

Neumark, David, Wascher, William, 2008. Minimum Wages. MIT Press, Cambridge MA.

Neumark, David, Schweitzer, Mark, Wascher, William, 2004. Minimum wage effects throughout the wage distribution. J. Hum. Resour. 39 (2), 425–445.

Neumark, David, Salas, Ian, Wascher, William, 2013. Revisiting the Minimum Wage-Employment Debate: Throwing Out the Baby with the Bathwater? NBER Working Paper 18681.

Nickell, Stephen, 1997. Unemployment and labor market rigidities: Europe versus North America. J. Econ. Perspect. 11, 55–74.

Nickell, Stephen, Layard, Richard, 1999. Labour market institutions and economic performance, In: Ashenfelter, Orley, Card, David (Eds.), pp. 3029–3084 (Chapter 46).

Nickell, Stephen, Nunziata, Luca, Ochel, Wolfgang, 2005. Unemployment in the OECD Since the 1960s. What do we know? Econ. J. 115 (500), 1–27.

Nunziata, Luca, 2005. Institutions and wage determination: a multi-country approach. Oxf. Bull. Econ. Stat. 67 (4), 435–466.

Ochel, Wolfgang. 2005. Concepts and Measurement of Labour Market Institutions. CESifo DICE Report 4/2005, pp. 40–55.

OECD, 2004. Employment Outlook. OECD Publishing, Paris.

OECD, 2009. What Are Equivalence Scales?. OECD Publishing, Paris.

OECD, 2011. Divided We Stand: Why Inequality Keeps Rising. OECD Publishing, Paris.

OECD, 2012. Employment Outlook. OECD Publishing, Paris.

OECD, 2013. OECD Skills Outlook 2013. First Results from the Survey of Adult Skills. OECD Publishing, Paris.

Oliver, Rebecca, 2008. Diverging developments in wage inequality which institutions matter? Comp. Polit. Stud. 41 (12), 1551–1582.

Olivetti, Claudia, Petrongolo, Barbara, 2008. Unequal pay or unequal employment? A cross-country analysis of gender gaps. J. Labor Econ. 26 (4), 621–654.

Oswald, Andrew, 1996. A Conjecture on the Explanation for High Unemployment in the Industrialised Nations, Warwick Economic Research Papers 475.

Paul, Satya, 2004. Income sources effects on inequality. J. Dev. Econ. 73 (1), 435–451.

Peichl, Andreas, Pestel, Nico, Schneider, Hilmar, 2010. Does Size Matter? The Impact of Changes in Household Structure on Income Distribution in Germany, CESifo Working Paper 3219.

Philippon, T., 2001. The impact of differential payroll tax subsidies on minimum wage employment. J. Public Econ. 82, 115–146.

Pierce, Brooks, 2001. Compensation inequality. Q. J. Econ. 116 (4), 1493–1525.

Pierce, Brooks, 2010. Recent trends in compensation inequality. In: Abraham, Katharine, Spletzer, James, Harper, Michael (Eds.), Labor in the New Economy. NBER Books, University of Chicago Press, Boston/Chicago, pp. 63–98 (Chapter 2).

Pijoan-Mas, Josep, Sánchez-Marcos, Virginia, 2010. Spain is different: falling trends of inequality. Rev. Econ. Dyn. 13 (1), 154–178.

Piketty, Thomas, 2003. Income inequality in France, 1901–1998. J. Polit. Econ. 111, 1004–1042.

Piketty, Thomas, Saez, Emmanuel, 2003. Income inequality in the United States, 1913–1998. Q. J. Econ. 118, 1–39.

Piketty, Thomas, Saez, Emmanuel, 2006. The evolution of top incomes: a historical and international perspective. Am. Econ. Rev. 96 (2), 200–205.

Piketty, Thomas, Saez, Emmanuel, 2012. Optimal Labor Income Taxation, NBER Working Paper18521.

Piketty, Thomas, Saez, Emmanuel, 2013. Optimal labor income taxation, vol. 5. In: Auerbach, Alan, Chetty, Raj, Feldstein, Martin, Saez, Emmanuel (Eds.), Handbook of Public Economics. Elsevier, Amsterdam (Chapter 7).

Piketty, Thomas, Saez, Emmanuel, Stantcheva, Stefanie, 2011. Optimal Taxation of Top Labor Incomes: A Tale of Three Elasticities, NBER Working Paper17616.

Plotnick, Robert, 1982. Trends in male earnings inequality. South. Econ. J. 48 (3), 724–732.

Reed, Deborah, Cancian, Maria, 2001. Sources of inequality: measuring the contributions of income sources to rising family income inequality. Rev. Income Wealth 47 (3), 321–333.

Rogerson, Richard, Shimer, Robert, 2011. Search in macroeconomic models of the labor market. In: Ashenfelter, Orley, Card, David (Eds.), Handbook of Labor Economics. vol. 4A. Elsevier, Amsterdam, pp. 619–700.

Rogerson, Richard, Shimer, Robert, Wright, Randall, 2005. Search-theoretic models of the labor market: a survey. J. Econ. Lit. 43 (4), 959–988.

Rosen, Sherwin, 1986. The theory of equalizing differences. In: Ashenfelter, Orley, Layard, Richard (Eds.), Handbook of Labor Economics. vol. 1. Elsevier, North Holland, pp. 641–692.

Rueda, David, Pontusson, Jonas, 2000. Wage inequality and varieties of capitalism. World Polit. 52 (3), 350–383.

Saint-Paul, Gilles, 2000. The Political Economy of Labour Market Institutions. Oxford University Press, Oxford.

Salverda, Wiemer, 2008. Labor market institutions, low-wage work, and job quality, In: Salverda, Weimer, van Klaveren, Maarten, van der Meer, Marc (Eds.), Low-Wage Work in the Netherlands. Russell Sage, New York, pp. 63–131 (Chapter 3).

Salverda, Wiemer, 2009. The bite and effects of wage bargaining in the Netherlands 1995–2005. In: Keune, Maarten, Galgóczi, Béla (Eds.), Wages and Wage Bargaining in Europe; Developments Since the Mid-1990s. ETUI, Brussels, pp. 225–254.

Salverda, Wiemer, 2013. The Evolution of Dutch Top-Income Shares Until 2012 and the Puzzle of Stability, AIAS Working Paper.

Salverda, Wiemer, Atkinson, Anthony B., 2007. Top incomes in the Netherlands over the twentieth century, In: Atkinson, Piketty, (Eds.), (Chapter 10).

Salverda, Wiemer, Haas, Christina, 2014. Earnings, employment and income inequality, In: Salverda, Wiemer, Nolan, Brian, Checchi, Daniele, Marx, Ive, McKnight, Abigail, Gyögy Tóth, István, van de Werfhorst, Herman (Eds.), Changing Inequalities in Rich Countries: Analytical and Comparative Perspectives. Oxford University Press, Oxford (Chapter 3).

Salverda, Wiemer, Haas, Christina, de Graaf-Zijl, Marloes, Lancee, Bram, Notten, Natascha, Ooms, Tahnee, 2013. Growing Inequalities and Their Impacts in The Netherlands, Country Report for The Netherlands. GINI project, http://www.gini-research.org/system/uploads/512/original/Netherlands.pdf?1380138293.

Salverda, Wiemer, Nolan, Brian, Maitre, Bertrand, Mühlau, Peter, 2001. Benchmarking Low-Wage and High-Wage Employment in Europe and the United States, Report to the European Commission DG Employment and Social Affairs. http://www.uva-aias.net/uploaded_files/regular/draftdef0-1-1.pdf Brussels.

Scheve, Kenneth, Stasavage, David, 2009. Institutions, partisanship, and inequality in the long run. World Polit. 61 (2), 215–253.

Schivardi, Fabiano, Torrini, Roberto, 2008. Identifying the effects of firing restrictions through size-contingent differences in regulation. Labor Econ. 15 (3), 482–511.

Schmitt, John, 2013. Why Does the Minimum Wage Have No Discernible Effect on Employment? Center for Economic and Policy Research, CEPR, Washington, DC.

Schwartz, Christine, 2010. Earnings inequality and the changing association between spouses' earnings. Am. J. Sociol. 115 (5), 1524–1557.

Shorrocks, Anthony, 1982. Inequality decomposition by factor components. Econometrica 50 (1), 193–211.

Shorrocks, Anthony, 1983. The impact of income components on the distribution of family incomes. Q. J. Econ. 98 (2), 311–326.

Slonimczyk, Fabián, 2013. Earnings inequality and skill mismatch. J. Econ. Inequal. 11 (2), 163–194.

Slonimczyk, Fabián, Skott, Peter, 2012. Employment and distribution effects of the minimum wage. J. Econ. Behav. Organ. 84 (1), 245–264.

Spitz-Oener, Alexandra, 2006. Technical change, job tasks, and rising educational demands: looking outside the wage structure. J. Labor Econ. 24 (2), 235–270.

Stewart, Mark, 2012. Wage inequality, minimum wage effects, and spillovers. Oxf. Econ. Pap. 64, 616–634.

Sutch, Richard, 2010. The Unexpected Long-Run Impact of the Minimum Wage: An Educational Cascade, NBER Working Paper 16355.

Thévenon, Olivier, 2013. Drivers of Female Labour Force Participation in the OECD, OECD Social, Employment and Migration Working Paper 145, Paris.

Thévenon, Oliver, Solaz, Anne, 2013. Labour Market Effects of Parental Leave Policies in OECD Countries, OECD Social, Employment and Migration Working Paper 141, Paris.

Van der Wiel, Karen, 2010. Better protected, better paid: evidence on how employment protection affects wages. Labor Econ. 17, 16–26.

Van Praag, B., Hagenaars, Aldi, van Weeren, Hans, 1982. Poverty in Europe. Rev. Income Wealth 28 (3), 345–359.

Van Weeren, Hans, Van Praag, Bernard M.S., 1983. The inequality of actual incomes and earning capacities between households in Europe. Eur. Econ. Rev. 24, 239–256.

Večerník, Jiří, 2010. Earnings Disparities and Income Inequality in CEE Countries: An Analysis of Development and Relationships, Working Paper 540, Luxembourg Income Study.

Večerník, Jiří, 2013. The changing role of education in the distribution of earnings and household income. The Czech Republic, 1988–2009. Econ. Transit. 21 (1), 111–133.

Visser, Jelle, 2009. The ICTWSS Database: Database on Institutional Characteristics of Trade Unions, Wage Setting, State Intervention and Social Pacts in 34 Countries Between 1960 and 2007. http://www.uva-aias.net/208.

Visser, Jelle, Checchi, Daniele, 2009. Inequality and the labour market: unions, In: Salverda, Wiemer, Nolan, Brian, Smeeding, Timothy (Eds.), The Oxford Handbook of Economic Inequality. Oxford University Press, Oxford, pp. 230–256 (Chapter 10).

Vlasblom, Jan Dirk, de Gijsel, Peter, Siegers, Jacques, 2001. Taxes, female labour supply and household income: differences between the Netherlands and the Federal Republic of Germany. Appl. Econ. 33, 735–744.

Vroman, Wayne, 2007. Replacement Rates and UC Benefit Generosity, Mimeo.

Wallerstein, Michael, 1999. Wage-setting institutions and pay inequality in advanced industrial societies. Am. J. Polit. Sci. 43 (3), 649–680.

Wood, Adrian, 1995. North–South Trade, Employment and Inequality: Changing Fortunes in a Skill-Driven World. Oxford University Press, Oxford.

World Bank, 2012. World Development Report 2013: Jobs, Washington.

Yun, Myeong-Su., 2006. Earnings inequality in USA, 1969–99: comparing inequality using earnings equations. Rev. Income Wealth 52 (1), 127–144.

CHAPTER 19

Cross-Country Evidence of the Multiple Causes of Inequality Changes in the OECD Area

Michael F. Förster*, István György Tóth[†]
*OECD, Paris, France
[†]Tárki Social Research Institute, Budapest, Hungary

Contents

Handbook of Income Distribution, Volume 2B
ISSN 1574–0056, http://dx.doi.org/10.1016/B978-0-444-59429-7.00020-0

Abstract

This chapter provides a thorough survey of what recent international (i.e., cross-country) studies can tell us about the multiple causes of income inequality in the OECD area with regard to both levels and trends. The survey covers economics literature in particular but also relevant evidence from sociology and political science. We provide an overview of drivers of inequality in six areas: (i) structural macroeconomic sectoral changes, (ii) globalization and technology change, (iii) labor market and other relevant institutions, (iv) politics and political processes, (v) tax/transfer schemes, and (vi) demographic and other microstructural changes. We find that the literature, while extremely rich in partial analysis of all six areas, provides very few analyses with truly multivariate and multicountry specifications for the joint section of the OECD and EU countries. Suggestions include more cross-discipline reflections on various findings. This is now well facilitated by the spectacular development of data, as well as in relation to methodological harmonization across disciplines.

Keywords

Income distribution, Globalization, Labor market institutions, Political economy, Redistribution, Demographic structure, Multivariate models, Cross-country comparisons, OECD countries

JEL Classification Codes

D30, D31, D63, I32, I38, J31, O15

19.1. INTRODUCTION

In their review of income inequality in richer and OECD countries, Brandolini and Smeeding (2009) concluded that "attempts to model and understand causal factors and explanations for differences in level and trend in income inequality across nations is the ultimate challenge to which researchers on inequality should all aspire" (p. 97). This sentence summarizes well the aim of the literature review in this chapter.

The chapter aims to provide a thorough survey of what international (i.e., cross-country) studies can tell us about the drivers and underlying causes of income inequality with regard to levels and, in particular, trends. The survey intends to be interdisciplinary, focusing on economics literature in particular but also on relevant evidence from sociology and political science.[1] While the overview intends to be comprehensive, some important research decisions limit its scope with regard to coverage and focus:

- The geographical coverage of the chapter is limited to the joint set of OECD and EU countries. Driving factors of inequality in emerging and developing countries and issues of world development are covered by Chapters 9, 11 and 20 in this volume.
- The chapter provides an update of existing reviews of literature with mostly recent studies, focusing largely on cross-country analyses that became available since the turn of the century.
- The chapter basically provides a meta-analysis based on review of the relevant literature. It does not produce a new data analysis within the frame of this survey. However, the chapter presents and provides a numerical analysis of the key findings of the literature.
- The focus of the chapter is on inequality of outcomes rather than inequality of opportunity. The analysis of the latter is provided in Chapter 4.
- Research results on determinants of poverty are not reviewed here. While it is acknowledged that (relative) poverty is a feature of inequality, we keep the focus here to studies aiming to explore the determinants of the full range of the dispersion of incomes. On poverty literature, see Nolan and Marx 2009, and Chapters 3, 8, 9, and 23 in this volume.
- When dealing with "inequality," the emphasis is on inequality of household income as much as possible, following the main focus of the Handbook. Given the scope of the empirical literature at hand, results of the determinants of the distribution of income subaggregates such as labor earnings also are reported. The determinants of the distribution of individual wages are, however, discussed in Chapter 18.
- The chapter focuses on the size distribution of personal incomes, leaving the vast range of literature on functional income distribution to other studies.
- While there is a trade-off between country coverage (N) and the length of the time series (T) in an analysis (given the limitations of data for large cross-country data sets for a long time series), the chapter draws practical boundaries here. A large cross-section of countries is relevant, even if only one or a few points in time are covered.

---

[1] The interdisciplinary approach applied here has forced us to make some difficult choices with regard to different methods and approaches applied by various strands of scientific analysis and that are rooted in the history of disciplinary accounts of inequality. Choosing as a starting point a frame that is (mostly) applied by economists might seem procrustean for representatives of other disciplines. With due acknowledgements, though, we hope our approach is useful.

On the other hand, analyses of only a few countries but for a long time series may be relevant for the review. The issue of this trade-off, however, is discussed further later in the chapter.

• The chapter reviews findings on the driving factors of inequality under several aspects: cross sections of within-country inequalities, quasi panels of countries and cross-country comparisons of longitudinal surveys (the data background of the studies is discussed in Section 19.3.2, covering the comprehensive data background of the income distribution literature). We do not include studies of cross-country differentials such as gross domestic product (GDP) convergence.

The structure of the chapter follows a broad classification of research questions of the literature. The chapter ends with a concluding section that attempts to summarize and classify the wealth of findings from the literature and to provide a critical assessment of the findings.

When selecting the empirical studies to be reviewed, we considered four elements as crucial: (i) the analyses had to show empirical results on income (or at least earnings) inequality; (ii) they had to cover a multiple of countries; (iii) they had to be at least multivariate; and (iv) their coverage had to relate to the joint set of OECD and EU countries. This led, obviously, to painful omissions of many excellent reports of driving factors of inequality.[2]

19.2. THE RESEARCH QUESTION AND METHODS TO EXPLAIN INEQUALITY AND ITS CHANGE

This chapter sets out the problem of a multicausal explanation of income inequality in a cross-country context. First we present the structure of the problem and then we provide an outline of the methods used in the literature we review.

19.2.1 The Structure of the Research Question

To understand and place the formulation of the research questions of the literature, it is useful to start with a very general flow chart showing the major elements of inequality formation (see Figure 19.1); this deliberately ignores potential causality directions at this stage. As the figure illustrates, income inequality (at all levels of economic development) is a product of macro processes (such as supply and demand processes, globalization, trade,

---

[2] However, these selection criteria could not always be fully respected. For example, the data background of certain studies we reviewed seemed at first glance to not properly fit the above criteria, for example, when a model of an important political process (such as corporatist agreements) is tested with individual wages rather than incomes. However, the line of argument dealing with the political economy of interest groups remains of interest even if it refers to the effect on wages only. Also, in some cases, especially in the frame of the debate on globalization and technological change, lessons from developing countries may be important for theoretical or methodological reasons, so some of those studies with coverage of countries outside of our prime target have not been excluded. The general guidelines from the above limitations, however, remain to be held.

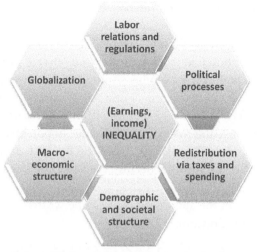

Figure 19.1 Stylized description of determinants of income distribution.

and sectoral change in the economy); structural conditions (in terms of economic and social structures as well); and institutional constructs (political institutions for the aggregation of collective preferences, labor market institutions to assist an efficient utilization of human capital endowments, and tax/transfer schemes for institutionalizing redistribution in society).

Schematically, Figure 19.1 numerates six families of potential key drivers of earnings and income distributions. From left to right, "globalization" is primarily meant to cover the economic dimensions of globalization, such as increased trade integration, outsourcing or financial integration. Technological changes also fall into this family. Next, under the heading "labor relations and regulations," we also discuss institutional features of the labor markets, such as the level of unionization, the potential role of wage-bargaining institutions, or levels of corporatism embedded into the political system. "Political processes" include preference formation (of voters and of parties), political representation, and interest group politics. "Redistribution and tax-transfer policies" involve various policy arrangements aimed at altering the "original" distribution that came about as a result of market processes. "Demographic and societal structure" refers to the way individuals (with their own incomes) combine into families and households (household structure by age, employment, income levels) and how the society is composed of various sociodemographic variables (such as age, gender or education). Finally, the "macroeconomic structure" of societies (characterized by sector distribution of employment, by degrees of labor market attachment, etc.) is of central importance for the determination of overall inequalities. With this schematic we illustrate the complexity of factors that affect income distribution and highlight the partial nature of most empirical analyses we found in our literature search.[3]

The overwhelming majority of the articles we reviewed model inequality (or inequality changes) and regress a chosen inequality measure on selected driver variables, usually among one (rarely more) of the driver families. Among this literature, the list of 48 articles with key features analyzed and that come closest to satisfying the criteria above can be found in Annex Table A19.1. Many of them focus on some particular parts of Figure 19.1. Few of them, however, aim to cover the full range of potential variables explaining changes in income distribution (Cornia, 2012, or OECD, 2011, are among these exceptions; see Annex Table A19.1 for further details). Nevertheless, it is useful to keep the full picture in mind when certain specific parts are analyzed.

A general formulation of the approach taken can be written in the form of a generalized regression equation (Equation 19.1).

$$INEQ_{i,t} = \alpha + \beta * X_{i,t} + \gamma * Z_{i,t} + \lambda * Q_{i,t} + \eta_i + \mu_t + \varepsilon_{i,t} \tag{19.1}$$

where $INEQ_{i,t}$ is a properly chosen measure of inequality of household incomes within country i at a certain point in time t, and $X_{i,t} = \{x_{j,i,t}\}$ is the vector of population characteristics aggregated from individual (or household) attributes (age, education, sex, household type, etc.). On country level these attributes define the structural conditions to inequality development in a certain country. $Z_{i,t} = \{z_{j,i,t}\}$ is the vector of macroeconomic (GDP, trade, financial globalization, technology, etc.) and institutional variables (policies, redistribution, wage-setting mechanisms, etc.). In a cross-country comparison, where the unit of analysis is country, these variables enter as attributes of the macro units (countries); $Q_{i,t} = \{q_{j,i,t}\}$ is the vector of specific historic/contextual variables (history, size location, composition, etc). η_i And μ_t stand for the inclusion of country and time dummies, respectively (these occasionally entail, as fixed effects, a large variety of country-specific attributes and year-specific effects). $\varepsilon_{i,t}$ Represents the error term, i is $1, \cdots, N$ for countries, and t is $1, \cdots, T$ for years. For later use we denote Equation (19.1) as a grand inequality regression equation (GIRE).[4]

---

[3] By nature, our account of the literature—while covering a wide range of areas, as shown in Figure 19.1— remains superficial from a specialist point of view. We are, however, in a favourable position insofar as a number of chapters in this Handbook provide more in-depth detail for all six areas. For instance, although we discuss the effects of labor market institutions on income distribution, some particular elements such as wage policies are further detailed in Chapter 18. Similarly, while we include a discussion of the effects of redistribution and analysis of tax/benefit schemes, these are not exhaustive given that Chapters 24 and 25 are devoted to these issues. Further examples of complementarities could be listed.

[4] Although it looks very general, the way the equation is formulated here is, to some extent, also very specific. More refined formulations, of course, also have to take nonlinearities and potential interactions between explanatory variables into account. We, however, offer the formulation here as a heuristic device only, to help structure the frame for the chapter. Another caveat is that the implications for inequality depend on the specification of the left-hand side. This is discussed later in Section 19.4.

19.2.2 Notes on the Arguments and Parts of the Grand Inequality Regression Equation (GIRE)

Atkinson and Brandolini (2009) advise readers hoping to understand the empirical inequality literature that they should consider theory, data and estimation together, meaning that data have to be sufficient and adequate to theory, and estimation methods have to be adequate to available data. This requirement is key for the interpretations of empirical articles in all disciplines (economic, sociological and political science literature). When going through the various empirical accounts, we focus attention on this requirement.

19.2.2.1 *The Usefulness of the General Formulation*

An important point concerning the regression approach should be addressed at the outset. Some scholars may argue that cross-country regressions fail to capture adequately the cross-country differences because historical and institutional specificities define completely different relationships between dependent and independent variables. Others argue that the relationship between variable X and variable Y will be the same when controlled for all other potential factors. We think that well-specified regressions can help in understanding links (even if not causalities) between various factors, but, at the same time, caution is warranted, and country specificities always have to be taken into account. Classifications of various welfare regimes (going back to the seminal work of Esping-Andersen, 1990, differentiating between the conservative, the liberal and the socialist regimes) or differentiations between such complex settings as varieties of capitalism (Hall and Soskice, 2001) can add important parameters, and they do describe different sets of circumstances, but controlling for them (in an ideal data case) leaves sufficient room for the relationship between X and Y to operate uniformly across countries.[5]

Taking—admittedly—to the extreme the welfare regime literature, however, makes it quite difficult to identify the contribution of the various single factors to income distribution (or a change in it). Given that welfare regimes are defined as a complex interplay and a joint product of the state, the market and the family (Esping-Andersen, 1990; Esping-Andersen and Myles, 2009), the proper methodological analogy would be cluster analysis rather than regression. Clusters built from a wide array of country attributes could show similar and dissimilar country examples of inequality, together with the other observed factors (Kammer et al., 2012 is a prominent example of this type of analysis of welfare regimes). However, no causality directions could even be attempted. Without even hints to any judgments on this, we try to comply with the logic highlighted above to help structure the discussion of determinants of income distributions.

---

[5] In fields where institutional complexities of the subject and the training background of scholars induce widespread use of qualitative methods, an explicit mention of this caveat is important (see, for example, Rueda and Pontusson, 2000 warning for political scientists or Kenworthy, 2007 message to sociologists).

19.2.2.2 The Units of Analysis

In cross-country explanations of inequality drivers, the units of analysis (data points) are countries, characterized by various inequality measures as left-hand variables and other macro characteristics such as GDP, shares of economic sectors, globalization, institutions or redistribution as right-hand variables. In most of these analytic attempts a time dimension is introduced on the right-hand side with the use of multiple data points for various periods. This in some cases allows for a macro-level analysis of changes.[6] Many reviewed studies belong to this class. It would, however, be ideal to have analyses of pooled micro-data to identify cross-country differences of determinants of income inequality. Surprisingly enough, we did not find articles that fit into the latter category.

Another strand of analysis, again using micro rather than macro variables to explain the underlying drivers of inequality (and of changes in inequality), makes use of decomposition methods. Decomposition can be a powerful instrument to disentangle mathematically the different components that make up overall inequality. Decomposition can be used to identify the relative roles of several income sources to overall income inequality (tracing back to Shorrocks, 1982) or else to analyze the contribution of different population subgroups to levels of and trends in inequality.

19.2.2.3 Regression Methodology

The majority of macroeconomic cross-country panel studies reviewed use ordinary least square (OLS) regression with pooled cross sections in a macroeconomic setting to gauge causal factors impeding between- and within-country inequality. However, simple pooled OLS approaches have been judged unsatisfactory by many authors of multicountry studies of trends, especially if the analysis contains a larger sample of countries that differ in a systemic way—either in measuring inequality or in institutional or macroeconomic specificities. For example, there may be unobserved time-invariant, country-specific heterogeneity that forces an error term relating to a same country over time being correlated, leading to biased estimates of traditional OLS methods. Moreover, there may be panel heteroscedasticity because (i) error variances for a given country may display time dependence (i.e., serial correlation) and/or (ii) error variances may systematically

---

[6] When change in country level inequality indexes is of interest, using the notations of Equation (19.1), a the following relationship is estimated:

$$\delta(INEQi) = f(\delta Xi, + \delta Zi, + Qi, + \eta i, + \varepsilon i), \tag{19.2}$$

which should be read that change in inequality (on a country level) is dependent on a specifically weighted portfolio of the following factors:

δX = change in structural attributes (age, education, sex, etc.) from t to $t+1$; and

δZ = change in macro and institutional variables (policies, redistribution, wage-setting mechanisms, etc.) from t to $t+1$.

The other arguments remain the same as in Equation (19.1).

differ across countries. Both patterns would lead to inefficient OLS estimates if not treated properly.

To assign country-specific factors to country-specific intercepts rather than constraining all countries to the same intercept, a large majority of the macroeconomic panel approaches reviewed here apply fixed effects in their models. Gourdon et al. (2008), for instance, put forward as one of their main conclusions that "results from studies that do not control for effects of omitted variables via fixed effects are biased" (p. 352).

However, some authors consider fixed-effects methodology overly conservative because any variation between countries is disregarded in the data and the effect of some factors that are constant over time but differ between countries, such as institutions, are likely to be overlooked. This is the line of argument of, for example, Nielsen and Alderson (1995) and Alderson and Nielsen (2002), who propose as an alternative a random effects model ("random" in the sense that it treats unobserved effects as random variables because they are treated independent of the explanatory variables). Such a model removes only a fraction of the country-specific means, not the whole mean, and is thus considered as "less wasteful of between-country variation" (Alderson and Nielsen, 2002, p. 26).

There also has been more general criticism of the usefulness of time series regression methodology for explaining inequality determinants. One issue is that of identifying long-running relationships and cointegration of series. A problem with the standard panel regression approach is how to account for the timing of the effect of the explanatory variables. Globalization or deregulation, for instance, may well be "significant" factors but they may take some time to affect the distribution; furthermore, the delay may not be the same across countries and across factors. This may be less of a problem if long-enough time series were available, but this is generally not the case.

A related issue is that of the nonstationarity of data points, that is, that they have means and variances that change over time, either in trends, cycles or at random. Parker (2000), for instance, argues that the fact that many explanatory variables are likely to be nonstationary produces spurious regression results in that they may indicate a relationship between two variables where there is none. Further, the power of integration and cointegration tests tends to be low when small sample sizes are used, which is often the case in studies of inequality.[7] One possible solution is to combine OLS with the method of error correction models proposed by Hox (2002) and applied, for instance, by Rohrbach (2009) or Cassette et al. (2012). This method regresses the lowest-level variable on covariates from all other levels simultaneously.

Similarly, Jäntti and Jenkins (2010) argue that direct estimation of parameters in time series analysis can be problematic because of the nonstationarity of both left- and

---

[7] As an alternative going beyond the OLS approach, Parker (2000) proposes turning to decomposition and cross section regression analyses.

right-hand variables. Further, left-hand variables are typically bounded, usually to the unit interval, which involves problems for tests of stationarity and also raises more general issues about the appropriate specification.[8] Jäntti and Jenkins (2010) propose returning to parametric distribution functions instead. Applying the latter approach to UK data, they found a lesser distributive effect of macroeconomic factors than is suggested when commonly used methods are applied.

That said, even if cross-country panel regressions entail a number of interpretational problems and often, taken together, provide inconclusive findings, especially with regard to the role of globalization, much has been learned from the studies undertaken during the past decades. As Eberhardt and Teal (2009) put it (referring to controversial findings of cross-country growth regressions), "the lesson of incomplete success is not to abandon the "quest" but to seek to understand why success has been so limited" (p. 28).

The most common approach to explaining changes in inequality in the studies reviewed is with aggregate inequality measures. By doing so, however, one might miss important changes in the distribution. From that point of view, it may be worth pursuing more comprehensive approaches, such as the reweighting procedure proposed by DiNardo et al. (1996), as well as the recentered influence function regressions by Firpo et al. (2009) for labor market analyses or the microeconometric approach by Bourguignon et al. (2005) to the household income distribution in the microeconomics of income distribution dynamics project. All these approaches aim to shed light on the drivers behind changing income distributions by simulating counterfactual distributions in a controlled manner.

Such approaches remain on a partial equilibrium view. Another challenge today, therefore, is to bring together macro- and micro-based regression methodologies and their findings. To that aim, new tools of macro–micro models have been developed (see Bourguignon et al., 2010). These models analyze, for example, the distributive effect of "macro" events, such as migration, by integrating a macro framework with a microsimulation model that uses household or individual data, either by implementing a sequential approach (e.g., first computing the macroeconomic variables in a computable general equilibrium model and then using estimated values as input for a microsimulation model that distributes the effects of macro changes among micro units), or via full integration of microsimulation models within computable general equilibrium models.

In terms of the presentation of results from cross-country panel regression studies, in addition to indicating the significance of coefficients, many studies try to gauge the *relative* importance of the different variables that have been estimated to affect inequality. Because the variables under examination often are measured in different units, a common approach is to calculate standardised coefficients (which are obtained by first

---

[8] Following Atkinson et al. (1989, p. 324–325), there is a case for using a log-logistic formulation of the type log[$INEQ/(1 - INEQ)$], which allows unbounded variation.

standardizing all variables to have a mean of 0 and a standard deviation of 1). Moreover, simple simulations or a back-of-the-envelope calculation often are used to quantify the effect of an individual factor. For instance, IMF (2007) and Jaumotte et al. (2008) calculated the contributions of various factors to the change in inequality as the annual average change in the respective variable multiplied by the corresponding coefficient, and the averages across country groups were weighted by the number of years available for each country (to increase the weight of countries with longer observation periods in these averages). The OECD (2011) makes use of the same computation approach to show the relative size of the contributions of different factors to the increase in overall earnings inequality.

19.3. DATA SOURCES FOR CROSS-COUNTRY STUDIES

This section provides an overview of data available for multivariate analysis of within-country inequality in an international comparison.

19.3.1 Different Strategies for Multicountry Studies

At the outset, although seldom explicitly, research needs to decide on the precise coverage of a country sample to be analyzed. While this choice may be constrained (but should not be motivated) by the availability of data, two different strategies exist when using multicountry samples to explain variations in inequality. First, the sample may be formed by a set of countries sharing similar systemic characteristics (e.g., the OECD area), a strategy called "most similar design" by Przeworski and Teune (1970). Conversely, the aim can be to test a hypothesis such as the Kuznets-type relationship between development and inequality on a set of countries with a maximum of differing systemic characteristics, a "most dissimilar design" strategy.

While many earlier studies of global causes of inequality aimed to include as many countries as possible to the analyses, they still had an overrepresentation of developed countries in the sample. Coverage of African countries in particular was very low. In a typical study with "universal" coverage of inequality observations in the 1990s and early 2000s, OECD countries represented half up to two-thirds of the whole data set. This has changed in more recent studies, but the OECD area still makes up typically a third of all country observations. While this choice is dictated by data availability, the precision and generalization in the interpretation of empirical results suffers.[9] Depending on the nature of a research question and following a thorough examination of underlying data and their quality, a reduced sample of countries may be a preferred option, or, as Atkinson and

---

[9] A good example is the discussion by Tsai et al. (2012), who replicate the same model on the same data as Zhou et al. (2011) but find different and partly contradictory results by adding dummy variables for developed, transitional and developing countries rather than pooling all 60 countries included in the study.

Brandolini (2006a) propose, "A deeper understanding of national sources · · · may lead us to analyze a carefully matched subset of countries, rather than to seek to maximize their number."

In that sense, even the focus on an apparently more homogenous country panel such as the group of OECD or EU countries may involve interpretational problems, especially if new member countries are included in the analysis. The results from empirical analyses of the importance of sector dualism and sector bias between agriculture and industry as a driver of inequality (see Section 19.3.2) very much depends on how the OECD area and the EU area are defined. Empirical findings may be blurred if these definitions include not only the "traditional" OECD member countries or the "old" EU member states but also newer member countries such as Poland or Mexico, where the share of agricultural employment is still important (more than half the OECD average) and the dualism model may have some salience. In what follows we go through the "menu" of the available data sets for inequality research.

19.3.2 Data Sources: The Fast Development of Data Availability in the Last Decades

In the concluding remarks of his seminal article on economic growth and income inequality, Simon Kuznets (1955) acknowledged that his "paper is perhaps 5 per cent empirical information and 95 per cent speculation" (p. 26). Until the early 1990s, the availability of internationally comparable income inequality data still was scarce. During the past two to three decades, however, a substantive amount of household surveys became available, and much progress in distributional data collection and standardization has been made in OECD countries. The situation is still far from being ideal, but today's research and results may perhaps mirror 50% empirical information and 50% speculation.

This section is about the former 50%. It describes the main sources of data on income inequality and other key variables used in cross-country studies of the drivers of inequality. It reviews international data sets of income inequality: *ex ante* standardized data, ex post standardized data, data standardized on best national sources, and secondary data sets. The review focuses on data sets that include at least most of the group of OECD countries. It will also become clear how some of these new data sources open prospects for new types of research questions and application of new types of analytic methods (notably the use of longitudinal panel data).

19.3.2.1 Standardized Microdata

Despite continuing progress, the availability of comparable primary data sets for inequality research is still limited. The major initial and pioneering effort was launched 30 years ago by the data collection of the Luxembourg Income Study (LIS). Since the mid-2000s, the Statistical Office of the European Union (EUROSTAT) launched a harmonized household survey on income and living conditions (EU-SILC), which is available for the 28 member countries and some additional European countries. Equally, since the mid-2000s, OECD has made available a detailed set of standardized household income and poverty indicators for their 34 member countries.

19.3.2.1.1 Luxembourg Income Study

The LIS, formerly known as the Luxembourg Income Study, is a data archive and research centre dedicated to cross-national analysis (http://www.lisdatacenter.org/). The project collects income microdata from household surveys and standardizes those into a common framework of income, demographic and employment variables. The standardization is undertaken ex post. The key concept is that of disposable income, and detailed income aggregates are available. When the project started, it included data from seven countries. Today, LIS stores microdata for over 40 countries, for 8 points in time, starting with a year around 1980, in approximately 5-year intervals. Access to the LIS microdata is granted to researchers of financially contributing countries and institutions and students worldwide upon registration. Use of the microdata is permitted for scholarly, research or educational purposes but not for commercial purposes.

One of the key assets of the LIS database is that it allows researchers the access to the microdata, via a remote access system. The scrutiny of the ex post standardization also allows a high degree of comparability of the micro variables. One main disadvantage is the somewhat limited geographical and time coverage, although the recent inclusion of a number of middle-income and emerging countries as well as a more frequent update (3-year rather than 5-year intervals) will allow more extensive panel data analysis (http://www.lisdatacenter.org/our-data/lis-database/documentation/list-of-datasets/).

19.3.2.1.2 EU Statistics on Income and Living Conditions

The EU-SILC is an annual survey that collects microdata on income, poverty, social exclusion and living conditions in the 28 EU member countries and 4 non-EU countries. It has been implemented since 2004 for 15 countries and since 2007 for 32 countries (http://epp.eurostat.ec.europa.eu/portal/page/portal/microdata/eu_silc). The EU-SILC surveys are "output" rather than "input" standardized. This implies that the data are not collected with a single survey across all countries; rather, countries are provided a list of variables that they can collect using national surveys and definitions, and the necessary standardization is made on this basis by EUROSTAT. EU-SILC includes longitudinal information insofar as the surveys are based on a rotational panel (usually with a duration of 4 years). In contrast to most other longitudinal surveys, cross sectional and longitudinal data are released separately in the EU-SILC.

Access to the anonymized EU-SILC microdata (the so-called user database) is not granted to individuals but only to research institutions (or similar entities) inside the EU and European economic area countries by means of research contracts. For other kinds of organizations inside the EU and organizations outside the EU, approval for access needs to be requested from the European Statistical System Committee, which takes about 6 months. A detailed set of indicators on incomes and other living conditions from these data is available from the EUROSTAT databank (http://epp.eurostat.ec.europa.eu/portal/page/portal/income_social_inclusion_living_conditions/data/database).

The main assets of the EU-SILC are the high degree of standardization, especially with regard to income concepts; the availability of annual data; and the availability of a longitudinal part of the data. One disadvantage for researchers today is simply the fact that the project is still relatively young: microdata are generally available for less than 10 years, thus preventing the analysis of long-term series.[10] There are also a few remaining problems that have to do with the loss of some information when the wealth of original microdata is transformed into a more restricted final data set for which the underlying methodology of such transformations as well as treatment of data at the national level (e.g., imputation procedures) are not always exhaustively documented. That said, it has been suggested that most of the latter set of problems can be easily overcome with a greater consistency and clarity in documentation in the years to come (Iacovou et al., 2012).

19.3.2.1.3 OECD Data (Income Distribution Database)

The OECD income distribution database (IDD) builds on regular data collection undertaken by the OECD through a network of national consultants who provide standard tabulations from national microdata considered the "most appropriate" data source in each country and are based on comparable definitions and methodological approaches. This is done via a detailed data questionnaire consisting of tabulations on income distribution and poverty indicators, together with standardized terms of references. The main concept of the data collection is that of equivalized household disposable income, including wages and salaries, self-employment incomes, realized property incomes and cash transfers from the general government less taxes and social security contributions paid by households. The definitions used in calculating these income components are based on the recommendations for household income statistics adopted by the Canberra Group (see http://www.unece.org/stats/groups/cgh.html).

A detailed set of variables for the 34 OECD member countries is available from the OECD "data cube" (http://www.oecd.org/social/income-distribution-database.htm). It includes several summary inequality and poverty measures (on a before and after tax/transfer basis) as well as data on income levels and population ventilations. Data

---

[10] Doubts as to the comparability of EU-SILC with a predecessor survey, the European Community Household Panel, which covered 15 EU countries for the years 1994 to 2001, remain. It should also be noted that the current practice of EUROSTAT publications is to report the EU-SILC survey year n for indicators but not the income year, which is $n-1$ in all countries except Ireland and the United Kingdom. This can create confusion when comparing EU-SILC-based indicators with results from other surveys.

are available in approximately 5-year intervals back to the mid-1990s and, for a subset of countries, to the mid-1980s and mid-1970s. From the mid-2000s, data are available on a more frequent basis, depending on the underlying surveys but, in general, annually (for 28 of the 34 countries). Access to these data is free.

The method of data collection used by the OECD IDD allows coverage of the entire region of OECD countries with harmonized data that facilitate cross-country comparison, based on information that is both more up to date relative to that available through other statistical sources and better suited for assessing changes in income distribution over time. However, data are available only on an "equivalized" household basis, which renders comparison with indicators on a "per capita" basis (used in many of the more global data sets) very difficult. The main disadvantage of the OECD database is that it does not allow access to the original microdata, which constrains the analyses that can be performed. In that sense, the OECD income distribution database constitutes its own category between primary and secondary data sets.

19.3.2.2 Secondary Datasets

With regard to the difference of the data sets described above, secondary datasets are based on a collection of published or otherwise available summary key inequality indicators. These usually include the Gini coefficient, quintile share ratios and/or percentile ratios and, more rarely, other summary measures such as the Theil index. Often, alternative series for the same country and year point are proposed alongside recommendations of "preferred" series, along the lines of, for instance, the A–B–C typology used by Atkinson (2008).[11] Typically, such data sets aim to collect indicators for the greatest number of countries. The trade-off is that there is necessarily less room available for verification of data quality and consistency, which leads to issues of data comparability between and within countries.

19.3.2.2.1 The Deininger-Squire Data Set (Measuring Income Inequality Database)

Klaus Deininger and Lyn Squire brought together a large set of worldwide inequality indicators in 1996. Their data set (DS) compiled Gini coefficients and cumulative quintile shares for 138 developed and developing countries, adding summary information on the nature of the data (population coverage, income or consumption base, net or gross income base). Most of the data cover the period between the 1960s and early 1990s.

With regard to earlier data compilations,[12] the DS data set imposed "minimum standards for quality," namely that indicators are based on household surveys, on

---

[11] Atkinson (2008) undertakes an in-depth review of available data sources on earnings inequality and classifies them into three groups: (A) most appropriate, (B) acceptable if not ideal and (C) rejected.

[12] In the early 1970s, the first major improvements of international data comparisons were achieved by Jain (1975) and when Adelman and Morris (1973) and Paukert (1973) tested the Kuznets hypothesis.

comprehensive coverage of the population, and on comprehensive coverage of income sources (Deininger and Squire, 1996, p. 567). On this basis, among the entire data set of 2630 observations, Deininger and Squire identify a subset of "high-quality" observations, with 693 observations for 115 countries. Those observations labelled "accept" in the DS data set nonetheless include indicators based on different definitions and methodologies, which impedes the comparability of these data.[13]

The DS data set is freely available at the World Bank's website (http://go.worldbank.org/UVPO9KSJJ0). It became a major data source for international inequality research during the early 2000s, including many of the cross-country panel studies reviewed in this chapter. While there were further developments on the basis of the DS data sets in the frame of follow-up projects (see 19.3.2.2.2), the above-mentioned version has not been updated or revised for corrections.

19.3.2.2.2 UNU-WIDER Database

In the vein of the DS data set and partly based on it, the United Nations University-World Institute for Development Research (WIDER) World Income Inequality Database (WIID) collects a secondary inequality data set for developed, developing and transition countries. The project started in the late 1990s and led to a first release of data for 155 countries (WIID1), extending the time frame to the early 2000s and augmenting the number of distributional indicators: calculated and reported Gini coefficients, decile and quintile shares, as well as survey means and medians, along with the income shares of the richest 5% and the poorest 5%. In addition to income and consumption, the data set also includes indicators for earnings.

A second and substantially revised version of WIID was compiled in the mid-2000s and resulted in the release of WIID2. The currently available version—World Income Inequality Database V2.0c (May 2008)—proposes data series up to 2006 and is described by the authors as a "new" rather than "updated" data set. It adds, where possible, a second Gini coefficient estimate calculated using a method developed by Shorrocks and Wan (2008) to estimate the Gini coefficient from decile data. An update of the database to WIID3.0 is pending at the time of writing.

---

[13] Deininger and Squire accept both person- and household-based Gini coefficients because the mean difference between these estimates turned out to be not too large (<2 points), and they therefore do not expect a large systematic bias in empirical work. A similar argument leads to the inclusion of both gross income- and net income-based indicators, with an average difference of 3 points found in 19 developed countries, and on the grounds that redistribution is more limited in developing countries. The DS data set also includes both income- and consumption-based indicators because 39 countries (136 observations) report only the latter. Because the bias can be larger in this case, one suggestion was to add the mean difference of 6.6 points found between the expenditure-based and income-based coefficient to the former (Deininger and Squire, 1996, p. 582).

Similar to the DS data set, WIID defines three quality criteria—(i) whether the underlying concepts are known, (ii) coverage of concepts and (iii) survey quality—but provides a more detailed quality ranking from 1 (underlying concepts are known and the quality of the income concept and survey can be judged as sufficient) to 4 (unreliable).[14]

The WIID dataset is freely available at the UNU/WIDER website (http://www.wider.unu.edu/research/Database/). It has been increasingly used in international inequality research and, with the merge with the former DS data set, constitutes the most widely known secondary inequality data set. One of four articles reviewed in Annex Table A19.1 make use of this data set.

19.3.2.2.3 All the Ginis Data Set

The All the Ginis (ATG) data set has been put together by Branko Milanovic from the World Bank since 2004. It includes combined and harmonized Gini coefficients (but no further inequality indicators) from seven original sources: the LIS, the Socio-Economic Database for Latin America, the EU-SILC, the World Bank Europe and Central Asia data set, the World Income Distribution (WYD), World Bank PovCal, and the WIDER.

The most recent version of the ATG data set was released in 2013 and includes close to 4000 Gini observations for 164 countries for the period from 1950 through 2012. Almost 2000 of these observations have been considered "consistent." Rather than classifying observations as "accept" (DS) or "reliable" (WIID), this "consistent" classification is based on an approach described as "choice by precedence." This approach takes the Gini values in overlapping cases in order of preference of the seven data sources, namely in the order as they are listed above.[15] The ATG data set presents the Gini values along with key dummy variables defining the type of welfare aggregate (income or expenditure, net or gross) and recipient unit (household or individual). Another specific feature of the ATD data set is that it includes a variable that allows the survey to be distinguished from the income year.

The ATG data set is freely available in form of a stata file at http://econ.worldbank.org/projects/inequality.

19.3.2.2.4 WYD Data Set (World Bank)

The WYD database was created as part of the World Bank's work on global income distribution. The objective of this work is to gather and analyze detailed household survey data for as many countries as possible for several benchmark years to calculate estimates of global inequality. Currently, data exist for five benchmark years (1988, 1993, 1998, 2002

---

[14] Regarding the difference of the DS data set, there can be more than one observation labelled 1 for the same country and the same year. In some cases there can be up to six observations with label 1, such as in the case of Germany for 1984.

[15] The database allows the user to define any alternative "choice by precedence."

and 2005). The objective of the WYD database was to create "rich" (numerous in terms of countries) and "dense" (ventiles or percentiles for each country's distribution) coverage for the benchmark years, not to maximize the number of Gini observations or provide longer-term series for individual countries. The WYD series are integrated into the ATG data set described earlier.

The WYD data are freely available in form of a stata file at http://go.worldbank.org/IVEJIU0FJ0.

19.3.2.2.5 The PovCal Database (World Bank)
The PovCal database covers the period since 1978 and includes 124 low-income, lower-middle-income and upper-middle-income countries, thus excluding higher-income OECD countries. In general, PovCal shares the same underlying survey data sources as WYD. There are over 800 Gini observations, most of which are calculated from direct access to household surveys. The PovCalNet tool is available at http://iresearch.worldbank.org/PovcalNet/index.htm.

19.3.2.2.6 World Development Indicators (World Bank)
The World Development Indicators (WDI) is the primary World Bank collection of development indicators compiled from officially recognized international sources. These also include the Gini index. However, data on OECD countries are scarce, with many countries missing data in all years. A priori, WDI Ginis also should come from the same underlying microdata used by WYD and PovCal. The data are available at http://databank.worldbank.org/data/home.aspx.

19.3.2.2.7 Sociómetro-BID (Inter-American Development Bank)
Sociómetro-BID is a diverse data set of social indicators derived from national household survey data, covering 21 Latin American and Caribbean countries from 1990 to 2009. While the Sociómetro includes traditional global indicators including the millennium development goals, the database also includes information on Gini coefficients for per capita household income. The data are freely available at http://www.iadb.org/research/sociometroBID/tables.cfm?indicator=4&lang=en.

19.3.2.2.8 TRANS-MONEE Database (UNICEF)
The TransMonEE (Transformative Monitoring for Enhanced Equity) database collects a vast range of data relevant to social and economic issues in 28 countries of Central Eastern Europe and the Commonwealth of Independent States. The database was initiated by the UNICEF Innocenti Research Centre in 1992 and is updated annually. The 2012 version of the database contains 180 economic and social indicators divided into 10 topics (population, natality, child and maternal mortality, life expectancy and adult mortality, family formation, health, education, child protection, crime and juvenile justice, economy).

It includes data on Gini coefficients, covering the period 1989–2009. In general, these data are based on interpolated distributions from grouped data from household budget surveys. The data are freely available at http://www.transmonee.org/.

19.3.2.2.9 International Labor Organization Database

Since 2012, the International Labor Organization (ILO) database provides recent data for over 100 indicators and 230 countries. It includes a series of D9/D1 and D9/D5 percentile ratios for earnings for employees (although the precise definition and concept are not clear from the description). The data are freely available from http://www.ilo.org/ilostat/faces/home/statisticaldata. The former ILO database LABORSTA (http://laborsta.ilo.org/) included both decile values and Gini coefficients for selected years up to the early 2000s.

19.3.2.2.10 The GINI Inequality and Poverty Dataset

The GINI Inequality and Poverty Dataset is a very recent outcome of the "Growing Inequalities' Impacts" (GINI) project completed within the 7th Framework program of the European Commission between 2009 and 2013. The project produced in-depth case studies for the 30 participant countries, which include 25 of the 28 EU countries together with 5 non-European countries: Australia, Canada, Japan, Korea and the United States. The country case studies followed a predetermined template specifying the most important variables to be monitored over a 30-year time span (from 1980 to 2010). The variables related to inequality cover Gini coefficients and relative income poverty. For both Gini coefficients and poverty, the preferred income concept is net/disposable equivalized household income. The income sharing unit is the household, whereas the unit of analysis for the computation of various indexes is the individual member of the household. In each case the figures refer to national coverage and thresholds rather than, for example, regions or specific social groups. For most of the countries and for most of the data points these requirements are met (for further details see Salverda et al., 2014 and Tóth, 2014).

19.3.2.2.11 Chartbook of Economic Inequality Data

Atkinson and Morelli (2014) created a chartbook of economic inequality that includes indicators beyond income inequality measures for 25 countries (of which 17 are OECD countries) and covers series for up to 100 years until the present. These refer to earnings inequality (usually D9/D5 ratios for OECD countries) and overall inequality (usually Gini coefficients of household income) as well as poverty, pretax top income shares and wealth. These series are based on "preferred" definitions, which are documented for each country included in the data. The focus of this data collection is on over-time comparability rather than between-country comparability. The underlying data are freely available at www.chartbookofeconomicinequality.com.

19.3.2.2.12 World Top Incomes Database

Long-run data series on pretax top incomes ranging back 80 years or more have been collected and prepared by Facundo Alvaredo, Tony Atkinson, Thomas Piketty, Emmanuel Saez and various collaborators and are available online (http://topincomes. parisschoolofeconomics.eu/). The database includes information on top income levels and top income shares (such as the top 1%, top 0.1% or top 0.01%) for 27 countries, of which 18 are OECD countries.

Two main limitations of these data sets are that they cannot be used to describe the whole distribution (and hence do not include summary inequality measures) and that data refer to pretax incomes. Further limitations of tax data for inequality analysis are that tax-exempt income is typically not reported and consequently is left out of the indicators; cross-country differences (and changes over time) in the concept of income that is measured; the extent of tax planning and tax evasion; and the definition of the tax unit. For a summary of the main results from analyses of these data and a discussion of the underlying data, see, for instance, Atkinson et al. (2011).

19.3.2.3 Secondary Synthetic Data Compilations

Synthetic data compilations are based on regression-based procedures to estimate time series from existing inequality data sets.

19.3.2.3.1 University of Texas Inequality Project

The University of Texas Inequality Project data set, which is associated with the work of James Galbraith, is based on a project concerned with measuring and explaining movements of inequality in wages and earnings and patterns of industrial change around the world. It uses microdata available based on industrial statistics from the United Nations Industrial Development Organization. The project establishes a relationship between these measures and the broader concepts of inequality, such as income inequality, which is considered reasonably reliable. The data use the Theil's T statistic to compute inequality indexes from industrial, regional and sectoral data. It produces data sets on pay inequality at the global level; at the national level, including data for Argentina, Brazil, Cuba, China, India, and Russia; and at the regional level for Europe. Data on pay inequality were used as an instrument to estimate measures of household income inequality for a large panel of countries from 1963 through 2008. This global data set has around 4000 country-year observations. All data sets are available at http://utip.gov.utexas.edu/data.html.

19.3.2.3.2 SWIID Database

The SWIID database standardizes the WIDER data (described earlier) and other inequality data while minimizing reliance on problematic assumptions by using as much information as possible from proximate years within the same country.[16] It uses the data collected by the LIS as the benchmark standard. The SWIID currently incorporates Gini indexes of gross and net income inequality for 173 countries for as many years as possible from 1960 to the present, as well as estimates standard errors for these statistics. The SWIID data and the procedure used to generate it are available at http://myweb. uiowa.edu/fsolt/swiid/swiid.html and are described by Solt (2009).

There are other, more one-off exercises to build synthetic cross-country data compilations from existing inequality data sets, such as the Standardized Income Distribution Database. This database was created by Babones and Alvarez-Rivadulla (2007) on the basis of the UNU-WIDER dataset (WIID) but is not available online. It can be requested from the authors.

19.3.3 Concluding Remarks

There is no single "ideal" data set for international research on the multiple causes of inequality, despite the rapid development of international data sets of primary and secondary inequality data over the past 20 years. Opting for one or the other of the above-described data sets depends on the nature of the research question as well as on the target group of countries that are to be compared. If a study is confined to the group of EU and/ or OECD countries, one of the primary data sets may reveal the first choice because of their higher degree of standardization. For more global country coverage, secondary data sets provide a necessary starting point but great care needs to be taken, and not all series can be integrated in econometric analysis. In particular, compared with primary data sets, generally fewer resources can be devoted by the suppliers of these data sets to ensure data quality and consistency.

Many of the criticisms regarding quality and consistency in secondary income distribution data put forward by Atkinson and Brandolini (2001) and later by Francois and Rojas-Romagosa (2005) are still valid. More generally, it also has been argued that survey estimates that build the basis for both primary and secondary data sets often only partially portray the income distribution (Pyatt, 2003). In addition, the fact that secondary data sets include indicators based on different concepts and definitions is often tackled by applying "dummy variable" adjustments. Atkinson and Brandolini (2001) conclude that such adjustments are not satisfactory because "differences in methodology may affect not only the level but also the trend of variables (so that it may not be sufficient to apply a fixed-effect correction in panel data estimation)" (p. 295). Rigorous sensitivity analyses are therefore required because data choices can impede both levels and trends in distributional indicators, which in turn can greatly affect the identification and interpretation of causal factors in an internationally comparative context. Primary users of the databases discussed above should not take the series collected at face value; they need to carefully

---

[16] Such a procedure can, however, occasionally result in dubious estimates, especially for earlier periods for which data sources are rare and less comparable.

examine the downloaded data. In turn, secondary users of the research based on one or the other of these databases ("meta-users") need to verify to what extent the researchers validated the data they used.

19.4. DEFINITION OF INEQUALITY MEASURES AND THEIR VARIABILITY
19.4.1 Definition of the Dependent Variable

This section describes how the dependent variable—household income inequality—is measured in the empirical work under review. It is important to note right from the outset that in an overwhelming majority of cases researchers do not have full discretion over which inequality measure they will analyze or include in their models. This is, in most of the cases, limited by the availability of the data, and it is especially so in the case of country-level comparisons of secondary data. The variable list of the large international secondary data sets (such as WIID, for example) hugely constrains the choice. The larger the data set in terms of country coverage, the more this is likely to be the case (because the possibility of having new, harmonized indicators diminishes with the size of the surveys). There are only a few measures usually available, of which the Gini coefficient is by far the most often used, followed by various decile shares (S80/S20 or S90/S10) and, sometimes, percentile ratios such as P90/P10 or ratios of some other percentile values.

None of the above-mentioned measures are overly sensitive to the tails of the income distribution, and therefore the analyses based on them may miss important changes within the distribution. This could partly be overcome by the use of more tail-sensitive measures such as D9/D5 ratios, generalized entropy-type measures of inequality (Theil, MLD), or Atkinson-class measures. However, it also became important to pay attention to polarization measures comparing the values of a comparison distribution to the values of a reference distribution (Alderson and Doran 2013; Handcock and Morris, 1999; Morris et al., 1994; Wolfson 1997). The share of population classified by cutpoints of the comparison distribution can show how it falls in similarly defined categories of the reference distribution, allowing us to compare relative positions of people at various parts of the distribution.[17]

Studies investigating developments of tail-sensitive overall inequality measures or polarization measures, however, remain rare in the literature, given the fact that these measures are, unlike Gini coefficients, much less available for international comparisons.[18] On the

---

[17] For some analyses inequality is measured by the relative welfare-to-material-to-income ratio of various social subgroups (elderly/children, higher educated/lower educated, gender, etc.).

[18] A recent attempt to construct a more tail-sensitive measure is the one suggested by Palma (2011). The Palma index compares the top decile share with the share of the bottom four deciles and is suggested to better reflect developments in the upper tail compared with the majority. However, its calculation requires the availability of decile shares (i.e., generally microdata), and because the top decile average—especially in small samples—is very vulnerable to accidental inclusion of outliers, care is warranted with the Palma index as well.

other hand, using the Gini and other middle sensitive measures does also have advantages, especially when sampling variability due to small sample sizes is an issue.

Further, in some studies, such as, for example, political science explanations, or in analyses of the effects of redistribution, it is not the actual value of the inequality measure such as the Gini coefficient (of net disposable incomes) in itself but the difference between the pre-tax and -transfer Gini on the one hand and the post-tax and -transfer Gini on the other that is used as the dependent variable. This is a measure of redistribution for many analytic papers (e.g., Bradly et al., 2003; Iversen and Soskice, 2006) and a proxy of how politics and policies affect inequalities.

The range of available inequality indicators also constrain the features of inequality that can be analyzed in international comparisons. If only inequality measures insensitive to the tails are available and analyzed, there is a risk that important changes in the income distribution are missed or noticed too late.

19.4.2 Variability of the Dependent Variable

Trends and patterns of inequalities in countries in the OECD area are analyzed in depth in Chapters 7–9 of this volume. Overviews of the developments of income inequality have been presented in a large number of studies; some of the recent core publications include OECD (2008, 2011),[19] Alderson and Doran (2013), Brandolini and Smeeding (2009), Ward et al. (2009), Tóth (2014), Ferreira and Ravallion (2009), Salverda et al. (2014), and Nolan et al. (2014).

One of the most fundamental questions of comparisons of inequality is the variability of the measures used to characterize inequality in society, both across countries and over time as well. The large and rapidly growing income distribution literature (Atkinson and Bourguignon, 2000; Salverda et al., 2009) presents various narratives about the development of income inequality. The major narrative dominating the literature is proposed by the landmark studies of the OECD (2008, 2011) and by various papers based on the data collections of the LIS. According to this, within-country inequalities have increased in a majority of OECD countries since the 1980s, and at least until the breakout of the Great Recession (OECD, 2008, 2011, 2013a; see also Atkinson, Rainwater and Smeeding, 1995; Gottschalk and Smeeding, 2000; Brandolini and Smeeding, 2009; Chapter 8 of this volume). As the most recent OECD (2011) study stresses, in a large majority of OECD countries the income of the richest 10% of households has grown faster than that of the poorest 10%. The Gini coefficient increased on average from 0.286 in the mid-1980s to 0.316 in the late 2000s. Of the 22 countries for which a long time series is available, 17 have witnessed increasing inequality. For seven of these the Gini coefficient increased by more than four points over the period. In only five of these countries

---

[19] For a summary, see Förster (2013).

did inequality not increase or even decline. This is a narrative proposing inequality trends, which are dominant in the era of the "great U-turn" of inequality developments.

After an analysis of the GINI Inequality and Poverty Database, Tóth (2014) concludes that over the past three decades, inequality has indeed increased on average across the countries included in the analysis (25 EU countries, to which the United States, Canada, Korea, Japan and Australia are added); the whole range of Gini coefficients were at a higher level at the end of the period (from a minimum/maximum level of 0.20/0.33 to 0.23/0.37). The above work also stresses that the growth in inequality was far from uniform. In some countries (mostly in continental European welfare states such as Austria, Belgium, France), the level of inequality remained largely unchanged or fluctuated around the same level, whereas in others it increased substantially. The latter trend was experienced by some European transition countries (Bulgaria, Estonia, Lithuania, Latvia, Romania and Hungary) and to a lesser but still a considerable extent by the Nordic countries, most notably Sweden and Finland. It also was found that the pattern of inequality change may sometimes show declines for shorter or for longer periods. Such spells of decline were observed in Estonia, Bulgaria and Hungary, for example, sometimes after sharp increases.

Finally, over time it seems possible indeed that countries shift between inequality regimes (Tóth, 2014). After decades of a gradual but incessant increase of inequality, some of the Nordic countries, for example, while still being part of the group of low-inequality countries, no longer are at the lowest end of the inequality "league table." The United Kingdom moved from being a middle-level inequality country in the 1970s to the group of high-level inequality countries by 1990. Also, some of the transition countries such as the Baltic countries, Romania or Bulgaria witnessed very large changes that have put their inequality levels in a different range (see also Tóth and Medgyesi, 2011). Chapter 8 of this volume provides a more detailed account of post-1970 trends in within-country inequality in OECD and a range of middle-income countries.

19.4.3 Reliability of the Dependent Variable

Population surveys from which data on inequality are computed cover only a sample of the population. Originating basically from this fact, there is always a sampling variance of the statistic chosen to describe features of the distribution. The variability of the sample estimate about its expected value in hypothetical repetitions of the sample (the sampling variance) may be due to sampling and nonsampling errors. Most surveys are based on complex sample design (allowing, for example, a stratification of base populations to draw the sample, of a clustering of cases, of differential techniques providing equal probability of getting into the sample, etc.) Nonsampling errors (of coverage, wording, nonresponse, imputation, weighting, etc.) add to the uncertainty of the selected statistics.

All inequality measures (Gini figures, P90/P10 ratios, etc.) used in international comparisons are estimates from samples that are, in most cases of different designs, based on partially (or not at all) harmonized surveys. In addition, inequality indices are not like simple ratios from samples; for most of them the calculation is based on complicated formulae, leading to nonlinearities of the indexes. It is therefore very important to understand to what extent secondary uses (i.e., multivariate and multicountry analyses of drivers of inequality) can account for such uncertainties.

Inference for inequality and poverty measures calculated from properly documented microdata can be tested by "direct" or formula-based (asymptotic) methods and by experimental methods (based on resampling techniques such as bootstrapping or Jacknife, for example) (see Kovacevic and Binder, 1997; Biewen and Jenkins, 2006; Osier et al., 2013; and others). Both types of methods are used in various research contexts, but none of the results are frequently reported in official statistics and in secondary datasets. While it is shown that the way inference is calculated is important—Davidson and Flachaire, 2007, for example, found that in the case of complex sample design, bootstrapping may lead to not accurate estimates of inference, even for very large samples—sticking to point estimates only is clearly problematic, in part because it creates false images of certainty in inequality statistics and in part because it misguides interpretations of intertemporal change and cross-country differentials. While the degree of accuracy that may be worth pursuing is open to discussion (as Osier et al., 2013 stress, there is need to address a trade-off between statistical accuracy and operational efficiency when choosing estimation methods for standard errors), overlooking the issue is clearly the worst option.

To properly estimate sampling variance, sample design, weighting procedures, imputation practices and the actual computation formula of the statistic is to be taken into account. The effects of these factors are tested in various papers. As Goedemé (2013) and Biewen and Jenkins (2006) stress, ignoring the effect of clustering of individuals in households for poverty indexes (that are derived from incomes measured at the household level but analyzed at the individual level) may lead to a serious underestimation of standard errors for the analyzed poverty measures. Taking clustering into account leads to fairly good proxy of "true" estimations to settings when sample design variables are not missing. Little is known on similar tests for inequality measures.

Van Kerm and Pi Alperin (2013) tested how their measures of inequality reacted to the presence or elimination of extreme values from the surveys they analyzed, and they found their measures were arbitrarily large when they left outliers in their sample. However, other measures such as poverty rates remained more robust for the presence or elimination of extreme values (Van Kerm, 2007).

An essential requirement for computation of variance estimates for inequality measures is that microdata be available for analysis. Most secondary data sets lack any indication of not only the standard error estimates but also essential properties of the samples they have been drawn from. This makes it especially difficult for comparative studies using secondary data sets to assess reliability of their findings.

Further, the Gini coefficient, by construction, is a variable with a relatively small range. Even if inequality may change significantly in the long run, when shorter periods are taken into account and when many data points within the longer period are considered, the adjacent Ginis (in time or across countries) may not (in statistical terms) be significantly different from each other. Therefore, if these values are put into a variable on the left-hand side of a regression, there is a serious risk that a large "noise" enters the estimates.[20]

Also, when using secondary datasets, where there are no microdata at hand the researchers have to apply some rule of thumb to decide what can be considered a "real" change over time. There is no agreement in the literature, however, about how over-time changes or cross-country differences of Gini coefficients (normally arrived at from heterogeneous sample designs and greatly varying samples) could be defined as significant in statistical terms. Bootstrap (or, better, linearization) estimates of confidence intervals of Gini would suggest roughly ±1 Gini point differences in EU-SILC samples to be registered as "significant," but little is known on how this could be applied to changes over time given the lack of information in necessary detail about sample designs.

Atkinson (2008) proposed a simple metric of changes in the case of considering changes in percentiles (relative to the median) over a period of decades. He requires a 5% change to be "registered," a 10% change to be qualified as "significant," and a 20% change to be qualified as "large." The bottom decile falling from 50% to at least 47.5% of the median thus would "register" as a change, be considered "significant" if falling below 45%, and being considered "large" if falling below 40%.

Breaks in series pose a serious challenge for cross-country comparisons as well as for intertemporal tracking of inequality, as already noted (Atkinson and Brandolini, 2001). A break in a series may provide an obvious basis for suspicion if accompanied by a sudden change in the level of inequality that subsequently does not continue in the same direction. However, in other cases one must rely on expert judgements as to whether such breaks have in fact masked an underlying change in inequality.

A way of constructing long-term data series of inequality is to link subsequent data series stemming from different data sources or definitions together with use of information on overlaps of these series (Atkinson and Morelli, 2014; Förster and Mira d'Ercole, 2012), a method often called "data splicing ."[21]

A proper definition of *inequality change* in empirical studies (in addition to knowledge of sample sizes and sample designs) also has to be based on careful examination of annual increments of the inequality measure at hand, on the length of the data spells, and on

---

[20] In general, the articles reviewed do not publish confidence intervals for the inequality measures.
[21] The OECD Income Distribution Database (IDD) described earlier also applies data splicing (when needed) (see OECD, 2013b).

many other "accidental" factors. As Tóth (2014) stresses, a year-to-year difference up to a magnitude of 1 Gini point can be considered as no change, especially if variation in subsequent years go in different directions. However, consistent year-to-year changes, even if small ones (say, half a point) from 1 year to another, may accumulate into a five-point change or more in the Gini over 10 years, which is a substantial change indeed. Such longer-run consistency of increments over time may also change the interpretation of short-term comparisons. Consider long-term fluctuation of the Belgian or the Irish Gini series (resulting in longer periods of "no change" in inequalities) and compare those with the very small but consistent year-to-year increments of Ginis in Sweden or Finland, and it becomes clear how important it is to pay attention to even small and insignificant Gini changes (Tóth, 2014).

Nevertheless, when the Gini index is used as left-hand variable in regressions, spell contexts (as defined above) cannot always be taken into account, and the actual interpretation of the parameter estimates depends heavily on statistical inference. Careful and balanced evaluation: this is the main lesson that can be drawn and the only suggestion that can be given at this stage.

19.5. DRIVERS OF INEQUALITY: MAIN EXPLANATIONS

This section sets out the main arguments of inequality drivers in OECD countries put forward in cross-country studies and reports the results from recent empirical work supporting or not supporting these arguments. We focus our review of the literature including studies undertaken in the past 10–15 years, with no pretention of exhaustiveness. In particular, this review updates Atkinson and Brandolini (2009) and extends the literature review by Chen et al. (2013a).

The section introduces the main factors put forward to explain international differences in levels and trends of income inequality. The discussion is structured along six main headings: structural macroeconomic sectorial changes; globalization and technical change; changes in institutions and regulations; political processes; redistribution via taxes and transfers; and structural societal changes. Annex Table A19.1 gives an account of the wealth of findings for a subset of 48 selected studies that are considered to be the most pertinent ones undertaken in the past 10–15 years. The selection criteria relate to coverage (i.e., the studies should include a critical mass of countries and should focus on the joint OECD and EU areas); multivariate explanations (i.e., monocausal studies were excluded); and timeliness (i.e., preference was given to more recent studies not yet included in literature surveys available elsewhere).

When talking about "main drivers," it is useful first to make a distinction between direct, or proximate, drivers and indirect, or underlying, factors resp. causes behind changes in income distribution (see Cornia, 2012 for the same distinction). Direct drivers can be gauged, for instance, by decomposing summary income inequality measures by income components or by calculating the first-order effect of changing household structures on income distribution, for example, by using shift-share analyses. A variety of such direct factors for growing inequality in OECD countries has been identified by the OECD (2008). While usually analyzed in isolation, such identification of factors—especially if as exhaustive as possible—provides a useful checklist of "hints" (Cornia, 2012) at indirect factors or causes that lie behind inequality changes. In the following subsections, we classify the main underlying factors into six overall headings, following the presentation in Figure 19.1.

The subsections below resume the arguments put forward in the literature and report the results from empirical analyses. The main "culprits" tested in the literature have been subsumed under the different subheadings enumerated above, each observing single sets of drivers of inequality and inequality changes, thus defining more monocausal explanations of inequality. Of course, none of the studies reviewed is monocausal in nature, and all test the significance and relative importance of several drivers, but the point of departure is often related to one particular area, for example, the impact of globalization versus technology or versus institutions.

Our review focuses on OECD and EU countries. The country coverage in some studies is limited to only a subset of OECD countries, whereas many other studies include a larger sample of countries, including notably middle-income and developing countries. Given the focus of this chapter, we review below results pertaining to the OECD area, also when obtained from the second strand of studies insofar as results for OECD countries are reported separately.

Though our preferred explanatory variable is dispersion of household disposable income, we also report findings that explain changes in the distribution of earnings. While the use of one or the other of these two income concepts may alter the findings (net income estimates also are affected by household structure and tax/transfer changes), and definitions within these two aggregates differ (full-time wages or annual earnings; gross or net incomes), a number of studies refer exclusively to the effect on earnings, especially those looking at the causal role of trade and technology. Findings referring to income and earnings are presented separately below.

19.5.1 Structural Macroeconomic Sectoral Changes

For a long time, the quest to identify driving factors of inequality looked primarily at the association between economic development and inequality and was focused on testing the hypothesis that Kuznets (1955) put forward. According to this hypothesis, inequality follows an inverted U-shaped relationship with increased development. This is linked to a sectoral move from a "traditional" sector (agriculture) to a "modern" sector (industry). Insofar as the traditional sector is less productive, it will provide lower wages than the modern sector (sector dualism); it also is expected that the traditional sector has lower inequality within it (sector bias). Consequently, it is expected that development first increases and subsequently decreases inequality.

Usually, economic development is proxied by real income or GDP per capita (y). To capture the parabolic shape of the relationship, the quadratic form of y is added. Following Hellier and Lambrecht (2012), in the frame of a panel of country studies, the relationship can be written as:

$$INEQ_{i,t} = \alpha + \beta_1 y_{i,t} + \beta_2 y_{i,t}^2 + AX_{i,t} + \varepsilon_{i,t} \qquad (19.3)$$

where i and t are country and time, y is per-capita real income (or GDP) and $X_{i,t} = \{x_{j,i,t}\}$ a vector of variables j that affect the inequality measure $INEQ$. These variables seek to control for shocks as well as institutional and regulatory differences across countries. Equation (19.1) is a specific variant of the general regression equation GIRE described earlier in Section 19.2.1. The Kuznets hypothesis then is confirmed if the estimated values β_1 and β_2 are such that $\beta_1 > 0$ and $\beta_2 < 0$. The turning point, where inequality attains its highest value and begins to decrease, can then be estimated to correspond to the period Ω, such that $y_\Omega = y_0 - \beta_1/2\beta_2$ (for a start of the estimation at time $t = 0$ with the income per capital y_0).[22]

Evidence from studies of the inequality/development relationship remains broadly inconclusive. Around half of the studies reviewed by Atkinson and Brandolini (2009) estimate such relationship, with or without other controls. Some of these studies support the Kuznets hypothesis but others reject it. Hellier and Lambrecht (2012) undertake a review of studies testing the Kuznets hypothesis. Studies based on cross-sectional analysis of countries in their majority tended to support the Kuzents hypothesis (although some clearly reject it), whereas the evidence from panel data estimations is more mixed. In a study of the EU member states between 2000 and 2005, Medgyesi and Tóth (2009) suggest absence of a clear relationship between the economic growth rate and inequality within EU member states in the first half of the 2000s. Bourguignon (2005) concludes that, overall, the analyses of the available data at hand "do not suggest any strong and systematic relationship between inequality and the level of development of an economy" (p. 1733).

Empirically, the past 20–30 years were characterized by a considerable increase in earnings and income inequality in a large majority of OECD countries (OECD 2008, 2011), a development that is sometimes called "the great U-turn" (but see Section 19.4.2 on variability of inequality measures). Even if one considers the

---

[22] In discussing the appropriate specification of the Kuznets relationship, Anand and Kanbur (1993) derive functional forms of and conditions for the turning point for six different inequality indexes. They show that under the Kuznets assumptions, different indices of the Lorenz class increase at the start of the development process, but the behaviour at the end of the process—and the existence of a turning point—is ambiguous. Importantly, each index is shown to have its own functional form and turning point condition.

inequality/development relationship to be accurately described as an inverted U-shaped curve, this picture needs to be amended and replaced by an N-shaped (Alderson and Nielsen, 2002) or tilde-shaped (Hellier and Lambrecht, 2012) curve.

Alderson and Nielsen (2002) test the Kuznets hypothesis by applying a measure of sector dualism (shift of employment out of agriculture) for 16 OECD countries for the period 1967–1992. They find that sector dualism has no significant effect on income inequality unless none of the globalization variables are controlled for. At the same time, sector bias (measured as the share of the labor force in agriculture) has a strong and positive effect. The latter surprising positive sign is explained by Alderson and Nielsen by the fact that dualism in agriculture has become less relevant for OECD countries for overall inequality, and its meaning now is more likely to be a measure of agrarian traditionalism than a component of the dualism model.

The "great U-turn" may then better be explained by other phenomena such as globalization or institutional change (see the next section). Still, issues of sector dualism and sector bias can be expected to play an important role when analyzed in terms of a sectoral change from a postindustrialized to a knowledge society. Nollmann (2006) and Rohrbach (2009) propose a model similar to that of Alderson and Nielsen (2002) but focus on sector dualism in terms of the wage differential between the knowledge sector and the remainder of the economy and on sector bias in terms of employment shares in the knowledge sector. For a panel of 19 OECD countries for 1970–2000, Rohrbach finds support for the sector bias hypothesis but no support for sector dualism. Moreover, and in contrast to Alderson and Nielsen (2002), Rohrbach (2009) finds no significant effect of globalization (in terms of trade openness), concluding that factor effects remain central determinants for understanding inequality. This traces back to the original argument by Kuznets that through the segmentation of factor markets sectorial changes can be important drivers of inequality changes. However, while there is some segmentation of the labor market in OECD countries, it does not appear across large sectors of activity. The high-tech/low-tech distinction seems more important but less easy to implement analytically.

19.5.2 Globalization and Technical Change

Since the 1990s, economic globalization has been intensively analyzed as one of the main potential drivers of increased earnings and income inequality in the OECD area. "Globalization" is, however, a multifaceted phenomenon and cannot be reduced to a single variable.[23] There are different aspects of it and they are likely to affect trends in earnings and income inequalities in different ways and in possibly opposing directions:

---

[23] Note that the discussion here and later refers to the "new age" of globalization (or Globalization II). It has been suggested that the distributive effects of the earlier Globalization I during the late nineteenth century up to World War II have been very different (Milanovic 2012).

- trade integration (goods and services mobility)
- financial integration (capital mobility)
- production relocation (firm mobility)
- technology transfers (information mobility)
- political aspects of globalization

The following subsections consider these aspects in turn.[24]

19.5.2.1 Trade

Increased trade integration is often taken as a main sign and sometimes as the sole proxy for the degree of economic globalization. The share of world trade in world GDP has grown from about one third to over half in the past 30 years (IMF, 2007). In most OECD countries, the extent of trade integration has doubled or tripled during this period, and the increase was especially stark during the 1990s (OECD, 2011).[25]

The standard reading of traditional international trade theory is that increased trade integration is associated with higher relative wages of skilled workers in advanced countries, thus contributing to increased inequality in those countries and higher relative wages of unskilled workers in developing countries with an associated decrease in inequality (for a discussion of the relationship between skill differentials and globalization, see, for instance, Krugman, 1995, 2000 and Kremer and Maskin, 2003). This is based on predictions of the Heckscher–Ohlin (HO) model, or variants of it. This model expects that countries export goods that use intensively the factor with which they are most abundantly endowed and import those that intensively use their scarce factors. Advanced countries with abundant highly skilled labor will therefore import products from countries with lower endowments of skills and export products made by skilled workers. Combined with the Stolper–Samuelson theorem, which predicts that trade increases the real returns to relatively abundant factors, increased trade integration should then reduce the demand for less-skilled workers and increase the demand for skilled workers in advanced countries and the inverse in developing countries Heckscher-Ohlin-Samuelson (HOS) model. Second, less-skilled workers are predicted to migrate to advanced countries. Third, capital would flow from advanced countries with large capital-to-labor ratios to developing countries with small capital-to-labor ratios. All three processes are predicted to lead to increased inequality in advanced countries and to decreased inequality in developing countries.

However, most studies found it difficult to reconcile the empirical evidence on earnings and income inequality trends with the traditional HOS model, which typically does not capture technology diffusion. A number of cross-country studies find trade globalization

---

[24] There are additional features of globalization that may have indirect and direct effects on the distribution of income, such as cultural aspects of globalization or migration, which are, however, beyond the scope of the detailed discussion in this chapter. The issue of migration is discussed partially (as a trend having composition effects on societies) in Section 19.5.6.

[25] Note, however, that the increase in the GDP share of trade would be much lower if trade was measured in terms of value added.

to have increased income inequalities in high-wage and low-wage countries alike, which is at odds with traditional trade theory (for a review, see Milanovic and Squire, 2007). Furthermore, all sectors tended to become more skill intensive (as already reported by Krugman, 1995). Chusseau et al. (2008) relate this to the fact that trade between advanced and developing countries still accounts for a lower share than trade between advanced countries, thereby playing a lesser role in the shift of factor demand (Chusseau et al., 2008).

Some of the shortcomings of the traditional HOS model have been put forward by, for instance, Davis and Mishra (2007). The particular assumption of growing capital flows from developed to developing countries and their equalizing impact (in developing countries) has been challenged, notably on the grounds of capital market imperfections (Lucas, 1990; Alfaro et al., 2008). During the past 15–20 years, new approaches in trade models have been developed to overcome analytical shortcomings of the HOS model in several areas. The first one is to take account of heterogeneity of firms within industries in both developed and developing countries based on the development of dynamic industry models, as in the work of Melitz (2003). The coexistence of more productive firms that are expanding and entering the export market and contracting less productive firms within the same industry has an effect on how trade influences the wage and income distribution (Pavcnik, 2011). Exporting firms can employ more productive workers and offer higher wages, with a possible sizeable effect on increased wage inequality within sectors.

This calls into question the assumption of competitive labor markets underlying the HOS model, which expects an equalizing wage distribution in developing countries through higher unskilled wages. Newer trade theories therefore accounted for labor market imperfections by including efficiency wage models or models of fair wages in their framework (e.g., Verhoogen, 2008; Egger and Kreickemeier, 2009, 2010). In a next and complementary step, attempts were made to relate the exporting firms' wage premium to search frictions as a source of labor market imperfection, introducing search and matching models (Helpman et al., 2009). In both streams of work, trade liberalization can be consistent with increasing residual wage inequality, that is, inequality between workers with the same skills and other characteristics.

Empirically, however, both these channels, which are related to the recognition of heterogeneity of firms, can only be observed and analyzed at the micro level, going beyond models based on "representative firms." A number of studies reporting results for particular countries, mainly Latin American countries and Indonesia, were published in the later 2000s. Most of these studies (reviewed by Pavcnik, 2011) suggest that increased export market access was associated with greater wage inequality in a given country. But there are no cross-country studies available so far.

There are channels other than the HOS model through which trade can affect income inequality. One is increased competition, which tends to reduce the relative prices of consumption goods and can also diminish the monopoly position enjoyed by the upper class—both processes would reduce income inequality (Birdsall, 1998). A more indirect argument refers to the second-order effects of decreases in the relative wages of unskilled workers; this may lead to incentives for workers to up-skill and for employers to hire more unskilled labor, leading to lower inequality (Blanchard and Giavazzi, 2003). There are also other theories and models that predict that inequality would decrease in both advanced and developing countries, namely through the effect of specialization; such division of labor could generate increasing returns to scale, whereby labor has a higher marginal productivity (Francois and Nelson, 2003).

In the following, the empirical results of selected pooled cross-country studies are summarized, distinguishing effects of trade globalization on wage dispersion on the one hand and on income inequality on the other. When discussing the effect on wage dispersion, the notions of "wage differential" and "wage distribution" need to be distinguished. The models described above (in particular the HOS theory) yield predictions about the wage differential (i.e., on wage ratios between various skill or occupation groups), but the effect on the distribution of wages also depends on quantities (i.e., the number of people earning these wages). If quantities are fixed (as assumed in a static trade theory), one can read the distribution of wages directly from the wage differential. But if people migrate and change across sectors, one cannot predict distributional effects directly from changing wage differentials. Most of the empirical studies reviewed below test the potential effect of trade integration on wage distribution.

19.5.2.1.1 Wage Dispersion Effects

For a set of 23 OECD countries 1980–2008, OECD (2011) suggests that trade integration[26] has no significant effect on trends in wage dispersion at the aggregate level within countries once the effects of technological change and institutions are controlled for. This result holds for both top and bottom sensitive indicators of earnings (interdecile ratios) and when imports and exports are examined separately. An insignificant distributive effect of trade integration is also estimated for the overall earnings distribution among the entire working-age population (i.e., including the unemployed), insofar as trade had neither a significant positive or negative effect on employment.

On the other hand, Cassette et al. (2012) suggest a positive relationship between trade and wage dispersion for a subsample of 10 OECD countries between 1980 and 2005, which, however, differs between goods and services as well as in short- and long-run estimates. In the short run, wage dispersion is widened by increased trade in goods, whereas trade in services has no effect. That differs from long-run effects, where trade in services increases inequality, in particular at the top of the earnings distribution (i.e., between top and median earnings).

For OECD countries, a subaggregate of total trade may be a more pertinent indicator, namely the share of imports from low-income developing countries (LDCs). However, Rueda and Pontusson (2000) suggest that its increasing share had no effect on wage

---

[26] Trade integration is measured as trade exposure, that is, a weighted average of import penetration and export intensity.

dispersion, at least for the period up to 1995. Similarly, Mahler (2004) shows that, for a subset of 14 OECD countries for the period 1980–2000, imports from LDCs had no significant distributive effects on either earnings or disposable incomes. For the more recent period up to 2008, OECD (2011) reports similar findings, although with nuances: overall the effect of LDC imports is distribution neutral, but considering the institutional context, such imports tend to compress the wage dispersion in countries with stronger employment protection legislation (EPL) but widen it in countries with weaker EPL. For Golden and Wallerstein (2011), however, trade with LDCs is one of the key drivers of increased wage dispersion within 16 OECD countries during the 1990s.[27] Their results distinguish the period of the 1990s from the decade of the 1980s, when trade played no role but institutions did (see Section 19.5.3). Among those finding a moderate disequalizing role of imports from LDCs are Alderson and Nielsen (2002), although their results refer to income rather than earnings inequality.[28]

19.5.2.1.2 Income Distribution Effects
Few studies estimate the effect of trade openness for the group of OECD countries on the distribution of income directly. For the subgroup of advanced countries analyzed by the IMF (2007), economic globalization overall (trade and financial globalization taken together) contributed to increasing income inequality, but this was entirely because of foreign direct investment (FDI) trends, which more than outweighed the equalizing effects of trade: both exports and, in particular, imports from LDCs (but not trends in tariffs) were associated with decreasing income inequality in advanced countries. Similarly, for 24 OECD countries for the period 1997–2007, Faustino and Vali (2012) found that trade liberalization decreases income inequality, making use of both static and dynamic regression estimates. In a study of 16 OECD countries, the ILO (2008) included tariff liberalization as only a proxy for trade openness, finding no significance for an effect on income inequality.

19.5.2.2 Trade Openness and Inequality in an Enlarged Country Sample
There are somewhat more findings attributing distributive effects to increased trade integration when the country sample is enlarged from the group of OECD countries.[29]

---

[27] Their results suggest a one percentage point increase in trade, with LDCs being associated with a one percentage point increase in wage inequality.

[28] Results suggest that increasing LDC import penetration by 1 standard deviation increases the Gini coefficient of income inequality by 0.6 points.

[29] When analysis is restricted to the OECD area, a group of relatively homogenous economies in terms of their development status, it is reasonable to disregard differences in national income levels when assessing the contributions of factors such as trade globalization on the income distribution. Enlarging the country sample, however, needs to take into account that trade and other globalization variables may have different effects on inequality depending on a country's level of development. That is what is at least predicted by the traditional HOS theorem or variations of it. Estimating the effects of globalization on income distribution in both richer and poorer countries together therefore requires analysis of the interaction with GDP/capita and economic growth.

Evidence is mixed, and for a full sample of 129 countries for three points in time in the 1980s and 1990s, Milanovic (2005) suggests that as national income increases, the inequality effects of globalization reverse, enhancing inequality at poorer income levels but dampening inequality at higher levels.[30] This runs counter to the hypotheses of the classical HOS model.

Milanovic and Squire (2007) investigated the effect of trade (measured with the unweighted average tariff rate) on interoccupational and interindustry wage differentials for the period between 1980 and 1999. For both indicators, a decrease in tariff rates tended to have a positive association with wage dispersion in poorer countries but a negative association in richer ones. Institutions (union density and coverage) do not play a role in interoccupational wage disparity but reinforce the disequalizing effect on interindustry wage differentials.

For a panel of 51 countries, Bertola (2008) found that trade openness is positively associated with inequality of both gross income and disposable income (for a smaller set of countries) and that government expenditure is less redistributive in countries with a higher degree of trade openness. Spilimbergo et al. (1999) suggested that the effects of trade openness on inequality depend on factor endowments, increasing income inequality in skill-abundant countries but reducing it in capital-abundant countries. Based on newer data and a larger country sample, Gourdon et al. (2008) nuanced this finding. Measured as a lagged ratio of tariff revenues to imports, they found that trade openness is associated with increases in income inequality in both high skill-abundant and capital-abundant countries. By contrast, IMF (2007) suggests that the role of trade globalization in the last two decades of the twentieth century was insignificant overall, but some elements actually contributed to decreasing income inequality, in particular lower tariffs and higher agricultural exports.

For the specific country group of Latin American countries, Cornia (2012) found, perhaps contrary to expectations, that the gains in terms of trade realized during the 1990s and 2000s contributed significantly, albeit modestly, to the recent decline in income inequality. This is explained by relaxed external constraints on growth and consequently increased incomes, employment, and revenue collection.[31]

19.5.2.3 Financial Openness

There are mechanisms other than trade through which economic globalization can accelerate earnings and income inequality. One such mechanism is cross-border movement of capital, a factor that is overlooked in the basic trade model, which assumes that labor and capital are mobile within a country but not internationally. Factors such as deregulation,

---

[30] Milanovic (2005) identifies the "turning point" as around US$8.000 per capita in 1985 PPPs.

[31] However, the reversal of the skill premium as well as a shift towards more progressive labor and fiscal policies are identified as the main factors for the decrease in inequality (Cornia, 2012).

privatization and advances in technology all contributed to the rapid growth of capital movement, in particular FDI, over the past decades. If the utilization of capital as well as embodied technology requires the use of skilled workers, and capital and skilled labor are complementary, the increase in inward capital will increase demand for skilled workers (Acemoglu, 2002).

Much like HOS models of trade, models of FDI usually predict different effects in advanced and developing countries. If FDI flows are directed to countries with relative abundance of low-skilled labor, this should a priori increase the demand for the abundant factor and hence have an equalizing effect in developing but a disequalizing effect in developed countries. However, less skill-intensive outward FDI from advanced countries can appear as relatively high skill-intensive inward FDI in developing countries. In that case, even when the transferred technology is "neutral," an increase in FDI from advanced to developed countries can increase the demand for skilled labor and contribute to increasing inequality in both advanced and developing countries (Feenstra and Hanson, 2003; Lee and Vivarelli, 2006). Further, there may be indirect disequalizing effects, even if FDI is mainly attracted by low skill-intensive countries and sectors; to attract FDI, countries may relax regulations in the field of employment protection or fiscal parameters, which otherwise would have an equalizing effect (Cornia, 2005).

Endogenous growth models such as those proposed by Aghion and Howitt (1998) or Aghion et al. (1999) assume two stages of development and inequality when new technologies are introduced: in the transition phase skilled labor demand and hence wage inequality increase before decreasing in a second stage. Such models can be adapted in terms of effects of FDI on the availability of new technologies. Figini and Görg (2006), for instance, view FDI as a vehicle for introducing new technologies. They expect that in a first step more FDI will lead to increased inequality between skilled and unskilled workers, with a reversed trend in the second step as domestic firms follow up imitating advance technologies.

19.5.2.3.1 Wage Dispersion Effects

Figini and Görg (2006) wrote one of two articles in our review that use FDI as the main explanatory factor for distributional changes. Their model specifies only the inward component of FDI. For the subsample of 22 OECD countries, they found that higher inward FDI is significantly (at the 5% level) related to lower earnings inequality in the manufacturing sector for the period 1980–2002. Further, this effect seems to be linear. This is in contrast to the results for non-OECD countries, where the inward FDI has a positive though nonlinear association with earnings inequality.

Similar findings are also suggested in the results of OECD (2011) for 23 OECD countries between 1980 and 2008. Although overall FDI turns out to be insignificant, inward FDI has a significant equalizing effect on wage distribution and outward FDI has a disequalizing effect, although the latter effect is rather modest (see the next section). Inward

FDI, however, seems to be correlated with trends in trade integration. Other indicators of financial openness were reported to be insignificant in this study; this concerns cross-border assets and liabilities, foreign portfolio investment, and a de jure measure of FDI restrictiveness, which was the preferred measure of financial openness in this study.[32]

Among more country-specific studies, Taylor and Driffield (2005) found that inward FDI flow can explain, on average, 11% of the increase in wage inequality in United Kingdom between 1983 and 1992. Bruno et al. (2004) examined the effects of inward FDI on relative skilled labor demand and wage differentials in manufacturing in the Czech Republic, Hungary and Poland for the years 1993–2000. They found that FDI did not contribute to increasing wage dispersion in the three countries, although it did contribute to increasing the skill premium in the Czech Republic and in Hungary (but not in Poland). Hijzen et al. (2013) analyzed microeconomic (firm-level) data for three developed and two emerging economies and found that wage premium effects following foreign ownership are larger in developing countries, that the largest effect on wages comes from workers who move from domestic to foreign firms and that employment growth after foreign takeover is concentrated in high-skill jobs.

19.5.2.3.2 Income Distribution Effects

Most studies reviewed found only modest or no significant effects of overall FDI in OECD countries, but there are more significant results when inward and outward FDI are analyzed separately. Using time series data for the period 1960–1996, Reuveny and Li (2003) showed that inward FDI flow for 69 countries is significantly and positively associated with income inequality for both OECD and less developed countries, which were sampled separately. The IMF (2007) reached the same conclusion: for the subsample of advanced countries in the study of trends over 1980–2003, they identified both inward and, in particular, outward FDI as the elements of globalization that most increased income inequality, slightly more than outweighing the equalizing effect of increased trade. For a more recent period, 1997–2007, increased inward FDI was also found to be significantly positively related to income inequality for a sample of 24 OECD countries by Faustino and Vali (2012).[33] This seems to back up the observation that FDI occurs in more skill- and technology-intensive sectors.

The opposite was found by Çelik and Basdas (2010). Their article is the second of the two studies in our review that uses FDI as the main explanatory factor for distributional changes. For a subsample of five developed countries, their analysis suggests that both FDI inflows and FDI outflows are associated with *decreased* income inequality for the period of

---

[32] This is because de facto volume-based measures of financial openness such as FDI or foreign portfolio investment are often endogenously determined by other factors included in the framework, for example, technology or trade, as has been shown above.

[33] The effect of FDI, however, becomes insignificant when the authors control for potential endogeneity by applying generalized methods of moments estimators.

the mid-1990s to mid-2000s. The working hypothesis is that this is attributable to greater redistribution permitted by higher tax revenues from increased employment in the case of FDI inflows and changes in the economic structure with low-skilled labor being pushed to up-skill in the case of FDI outflows. The small number of observations (5 countries for 11 time observations), however, casts some doubts on the robustness of the results.

On the other hand, the ILO (2008) estimates that the inward FDI share in GDP had no effect on income inequality in a sample of 16 OECD countries for the period 1978–2002, as long as the analysis controls for technology (information and communications technology [ICT] share)—otherwise FDI comes out as a significant predictor, suggesting that FDI could act as a proxy for that omitted factor and actually lead to greater demand for skilled labor.

Somewhat more clear-cut results were found for the region of Latin America. Cornia (2012) examined a subsample of 19 Latin American countries for the period from 1990 to 2009. Given the boom in capital inflow, Cornia expects deteriorating effects on income inequality via an appreciation of the real exchange rate and a dampened growth in the labor intensive noncommodity traded sector. Indeed, the FDI stock had a significant and strongly disequalizing effect in all specifications, and the effect is most pronounced among the group of Andean countries (where FDI is particularly important in the mining sector). That said, in this analysis FDI—such as other external economic and demographic variables considered— had a more limited average effect on income inequality than the policy variables.

A more disequalizing effect of FDI also often is found in studies with the broadest possible country coverage. Broadening the analysis to 42 advanced and developing countries, the ILO (2008) found inward FDI to be the only variable among eight economic controls to be robustly positively associated with increased income inequality. This positive association was confirmed by the IMF (2007) for 51 countries, although technology played an even stronger role in the latter study. Higher inward FDI benefits solely the top quintile, whereas income effects for the three bottom quintiles are significantly negative. For a panel for 111 countries from 1970 to 2000, Te Velde and Xenogiani (2007) showed that FDI positively affects skill formation not only within countries but also across countries, especially in countries that are relatively well endowed with skills to start with. On the other hand, in his analysis of 129 countries for three benchmark years (late 1980s, early 1990s, late 1990s), Milanovic (2005) found that FDI has no effect on the income distribution, whether alone or when interacting with income. However, results from analyses that pool developed and developing countries are difficult to interpret because this blurs the channels through which financial openness affects the distribution of incomes, especially when inward and outward FDI are netted out.

19.5.2.4 Outsourcing

Most of the evidence that relates increasing earnings or income inequality on increased trade openness focuses on trade in *final* goods. As shown earlier, a larger part of the literature suggests that trade, measured in these terms, has not been the major driving factor (if at all) of increased inequalities in the OECD area. Such findings, however, neglect that the production of goods itself has become globalized, and outsourcing in terms of increasing trade in *intermediate* products may play a decisive role. It has been estimated that the potential of off-shoring of tasks concerns between 20% and 30% of all jobs in a number of OECD countries, including medium- and high-skilled jobs; however, tradability is determined not only by the technical feasibility of unbundling and digitization but also by transaction costs and the economies of scope of keeping tasks together (Lanz et al., 2011).

Among the first to put forward the outsourcing hypothesis, Feenstra and Hanson (1996) suggested that the rapid development of international production sharing[34] (from home companies to their foreign affiliates) may distort the wage distribution in home countries by moving some of domestic non-skill-intensive activities abroad. Such a move concerns potentially all firms (not only traded industries) as long as business owners find the fragmentation of production more cost-effective. Firms in advanced countries may "outsource" particular stages of production to less developed countries; these stages seem less skill-intensive in the advanced country but relatively skill-intensive in the receiving country. As a result, trade—the outsourcing aspect of it—may reduce the relative demand for unskilled workers and increase employment toward skilled work within industries in *both* countries. This also offers an explanation of why trade could lead to increased relative demand for skilled workers within industries, rather than across industries, as predicted by the traditional HOS theory. Chusseau et al. (2008) and Pavcnik (2011) provide a summary of recent approaches of theoretical outsourcing models.

Various studies have tested the outsourcing hypothesis for single countries. Feenstra and Hanson (1996) found that outsourcing can account for a sizeable share of the increase in the relative demand for skilled workers in manufacturing sectors and for a notable amount of the increase in the relative wage of nonproduction workers in the United States during the 1980s.[35] Using updated data for the United States and measuring outsourcing by intermediate inputs in total materials purchase, Feenstra and Hanson (2003) found that outsourcing can account for half or more of the observed skill upgrading; the other half is contributed by technological change. For the United Kingdom, Hijzen (2007) also found international outsourcing contributing to the increase in wage inequality during the 1990s, although not to the same extent as technological change. Kang and Yun (2008) identified deindustrialization and outsourcing to China as two of the factors of rapidly increasing wage inequality in Korea since the mid-1990s, in addition to human

[34] The definition of outsourcing as "imports of intermediate inputs by domestic firms" is broader than the pure subcontracted part of the production process usually associated with outsourcing (see Chusseau et al., 2008).

[35] Feenstra and Hanson (1999) estimate that outsourcing could explain between 15% and 40% of the increase in wage inequality, depending on the specification.

capital factors and technological change. On the other hand, Slaughter (2000) suggested that outsourcing activities of US multinational enterprises tend to have small, imprecisely estimated effects on US relative labor demand. Similarly, using industrial data for a group of OECD countries, the OECD (2007) also concluded that outsourcing in general has only a rather moderate effect on shifting relative demand away from low-skill workers within the same industry. Lorentowicz et al. (2005), on the other extreme, discovered that outsourcing actually lowered the skill premium in Austria, a skill-abundant country, whereas it increased the wage gap in Poland, a relatively labor-abundant country.[36]

There are, however, few larger cross-county studies that explicitly test the outsourcing hypothesis. Taking outward FDI as a partial proxy for outsourcing, the OECD (2011) found this effect to be only modestly significant for explaining increased wage inequality in a sample of 23 OECD countries and distribution neutral in terms of overall earnings inequality (i.e., when employment effects are included).[37] This result is consistent with the fact that outsourcing activities to developing economies account for a small portion of total outward FDI stock in most OECD countries.[38] Analyzing 16 OECD countries over 1980–2000, Mahler (2004) also found that outward FDI is not significantly related to both household earnings and income inequality in either direction.

19.5.2.5 Technological Change

Next to trade and financial globalization, there are other equally plausible and competing explanations for income distributional changes. One that is often portrayed as an alternative to trade-related explanations is technological progress (e.g., Autor et al., 1998; Berman et al., 1998). Technological change, often described as advances in information and communication technology, is considered skill-biased insofar as it increases the total relative demand for skills for given prices of skilled and unskilled labor. Whether factor- or sector-biased (or indirectly biased via other factors of production), skill-biased technological change (SBTC) tends to increase the wage premium and/or increase unemployment among low-skilled workers and is therefore expected to increase inequality.[39] The wage premium will not increase only if the increase in the relative

---

[36] Some country-specific studies analyze the outsourcing effects on wage dispersion at the firm level. Analyzing data for the United States from 1981 to 2006, Ebenstein et al. (2009) suggested that the location of off-shoring activities matter, and off-shoring to high-wage countries can increase wages (via proliferation of nonroutine tasks), whereas off-shoring to low-wage countries have a negative wage effect.

[37] The same study also tested whether outward FDI has different effects in countries with distinct institutional settings (notably EPL), and found that outsourcing plays a modest role in wage inequality trends regardless of the institutional setting of the country considered.

[38] Intra-OECD investment, in fact, accounts for >75% of total outward FDI stocks in more than half of OECD countries (OECD, 2005).

[39] For the specific subset of central and eastern European transition countries, Vecernik (2010) suggests that differences in wages between skilled and unskilled labor were one of the major determinants of inequality increase after the economic transition in 1989.

demand for skilled labor is offset by a corresponding increase in the endowment with skilled labor.

In most studies, skill bias is identified by looking at changes in the share of skilled workers in sectoral wage bills or employment, and an increase in these shares within selected and defined research and development (R&D) industries or firms often is interpreted as evidence for SBTC.[40] Research that uses direct measures for technological progress such as computer usage or total factor productivity also reaches similar conclusions, although there is still debate over whether it is sector bias or skill bias that determines changes in the wage distribution.[41] The impact of technology seemed to be robust even when broader levels of aggregation were analyzed.

One reason why technological change often has been privileged over trade as the main explanation for increased inequality is the observation that employment shifts toward skilled work happening *within* rather than between sectors (although newer trade theories take this phenomenon into account in the frame of heterogeneity of firms models; see Section 19.5.2.1). Although this finding was confirmed for a sample of 12 OECD countries by the OECD (2011, p. 139), the analysis also highlights the growing wage inequality among workers with *similar* skills. Even after accounting for observable differences across workers, the dispersion of wages has risen, that is, there has been an increase in residual wage variation. The simple distinction between skilled and unskilled workers may not be detailed enough, and technological change, in particular ICT developments, can be accompanied by shifts away from routine and toward nonroutine labor (Autor et al., 2003; Michaels et al., 2010; Goos and Manning, 2007).

Many studies that have put technological change in the forefront of their explanation refer to one single country. Over the years, considerable evidence has been collected for the United Kingdom (e.g., Haskel and Slaughter, 1999; Hijzen, 2007) or for the United States (e.g., Blackburn and Bloom, 1987; Acemoglu, 1988; Card and DiNardo, 2002; Autor et al., 2003; Wheeler, 2005).

Larger cross-country studies including measures of technological progress (usually among the controls) became available more recently. Some studies identified this process as a key driver for inequality: the IMF (2007) finds that, overall (i.e., for the total sample of 51 countries), "technological progress has had a greater impact than globalization on (income) inequality within countries" (p. 31). Looking at the subsample of advanced countries, it turns out that globalization in terms of FDI contributed as much as, if not somewhat more than, technological change to increasing overall income inequality.

---

[40] Machin and Van Reenen (1998) and Autor et al. (1998) showed that such an indirect technology measure (i.e., the share of wage bills or employment) is highly correlated with direct measures of technological changes such as R&D intensity or computers.

[41] Krueger (1993), for instance, measures technology by computer usage, whereas Hijzen (2007) uses total factor productivity growth for skill-biased technical change. For a discussion of sector versus factor bias, see Haskel and Slaughter (2001, 2002).

A higher share of ICT investment also is identified as being strongly and significantly associated with higher inequality in 16 advanced countries by the ILO (2008).

The OECD (2011) also shows a strong and positive effect of technological change (captured by R&D business sector expenditures) on both wage dispersion among workers and overall earnings inequality among the whole working-age population. The second effect arises because technological change had no significant effect on employment rates, and the overall effect was therefore driven by the increased wage dispersion effect. Technological change is further shown to affect mostly the upper part of the distribution (OECD, 2011).

It is, however, in practice extremely difficult to disentangle technological change from other aspects of globalization that increase skill premia.[42] Advances in technology are, for instance, at the origin of the fragmentation of economic activities, outsourcing and off-shoring, or, as Freeman (2009) put it, "offshoring and digitalization go together."

19.5.2.6 Trade-Induced Technological Change or Technology-Induced Trade?

In most studies, technological change is treated as an exogenous variable (e.g., IMF, 2007; ILO, 2008; OECD, 2011). However, developments of technology and trade are not independent. Increased trade openness has contributed to the spread of technology, whereas technological progress has helped widen trade integration. Therefore, the three studies mentioned above recognize that technological change can also be seen as an additional channel through which economic globalization operates.[43,44]

Chusseau et al. (2008) reviewed four studies from the early 2000s, all of which found indications of trade-induced technological change in advanced countries. More recent studies confirm this picture. Bloom et al. (2011) showed that trade with low-wage countries (in particular China) had large effects on technical change in 20 European countries and the United States; it led to within-firm technology upgrading as well as between-firm reallocation of jobs towards more technology-intensive enterprises. Equally, Goldberg and Pavcnik (2007), Verhoogen (2008), and van Reenen (2011) emphasized in their studies that increased trade integration leads to faster technology upgrading.

Another approach to the interaction between globalization and technology has been called "defensive innovation" and goes back to Wood (1994). Firms that faced intensified import competition from developing countries have incentives to engage in more R&D efforts to develop new ways of production to remain competitive. While testing this

---

[42] As Wood (1998) argues for the period between the mid-19670s and mid-1990s, "there is plenty of evidence that skill-biased technical change has raised the relative demand for skilled workers, but much less evidence of an *autonomous* acceleration in its pace over the past two decades" (p. 1478).

[43] As Feenstra and Hanson (2003) put it, "Distinguishing whether the change in wages is due to international trade, or technological change, is fundamentally an empirical rather than a theoretical question" (p. 148).

[44] Institutions-induced technological change also has been proposed (see Chusseau and Dumont, 2012).

hypothesis is complex because it requires the availability of innovation data at the firm level, there are some studies confirming such an effect.[45]

The hypotheses of trade-induced skill-biased technological change SBTC and endogenous SBTC through capital deepening is also backed up by the OECD (2011), which suggested a positive correlation between SBTC, trade and capital flows, pointing to an interplay between globalization and technological change.

19.5.2.7 Education

Access to education and human capital accumulation are important factors that are expected to have an impact on income distribution. A higher average level of education is often expected *ceteris paribus* to reduce income inequality because it allows a greater share of the population to benefit from higher-skill activities (see, e.g., results from Sylwester, 2003 for OECD countries and an enlarged country sample for the period 1970–1990). However, while there is agreement on the existence of positive economic returns on education in terms of earnings levels, the theoretical predictions of the *inequality* effect of changes in education enrolment are not straightforward. Increases in education levels entail both a composition and a wage effect, which can move in different directions: the composition effect increases the share of higher education and initially tends to increase inequality before eventually decreasing it when higher education becomes the majority choice. The wage effect lowers the wage premium as the supply of more highly educated workers increases and thereby decreases inequality (for a discussion, see Bergh and Fink, 2008 or De Gregorio and Lee, 2002).

The important point to retain here is that the education–inequality relationship is neither monotonic nor linear, and the education effect can first be disequalizing and then equalizing, in analogy with the Kuznets process (see also Rehme, 2007). Further, there remains the issue of lagged reversed causality, with inequality levels at time t affecting education enrolment at time $t + 1$.

Human capital can be seen as a complement to technology. Increases in human capital and in the supply of skills are necessary to decrease and eventually reverse the pressure to higher inequality that stems from technological change. The underlying logic is that technological change in the economy drives up the demand for higher-skilled workers, while the overall effect on inequality by and large depends on how elastic the higher education output is in relation to the increased demand. If the response is slow or inadequate, the skill premium of the more highly educated (the incumbent and the inflow as well)

---

[45] Thoenig and Verdier (2003) found support for defensive innovations by looking at the correlation between foreign competition and the share of skilled workers within the firm. Bloom et al. (2011) used technology data at the establishment/firm level for advanced countries and found that Chinese import competition has led to a considerable technological upgrading in European firms through both fast diffusion and innovation. They also showed that both Chinese imports and information technology intensity, in turn, are associated with an increase in the wage share of skilled workers.

increase, implying, by definition, an increase in inequality in a dimension (education) that plays a large role in explaining overall inequality (on this latter relationship see Ballarino et al., 2014). Such a view refers to the model of a "race between technology and education" going back to Tinbergen (1975).[46]

In many of the studies reviewed here, some education variable (e.g., share of adults with secondary or higher education, average school years) is introduced, most often as a control variable to capture human capital development. None of these studies suggest a positive association with inequality, that is, a disequalizing effect of education on earnings or income inequality but in their majority rather an equalizing one. This is particularly the case when the country sample is restricted to the OECD/EU area, and significant coefficients are reported, for instance, by the ILO (2008), OECD (2011), Afonso et al. (2010) and Cassette et al. (2012), as well as Cornia (2012) for Latin American countries. In terms of magnitude, according to the OECD (2011), the growth in average educational attainment over the 1980–2008 period offset to a great extent the disequalizing effect brought on by other factors, in particular SBTC. De Gregorio and Lee (2002), in one of the studies that specify educational factors—attainment and distribution of education—as the main explanatory variable in their models, suggest that these explain some but by no means all of the variation in income inequality across countries and over time. Nonetheless, their analysis confirms a negative relationship between income inequality and higher educational attainment (and a positive one with educational inequality) for a larger sample of around 60 countries.

On the other hand, the IMF (2007) suggests that there is an insignificant association between education and income inequality for both the OECD and an enlarged country sample. Carter (2007) and Bergh and Nilson (2010) even report a positive association, but their studies pool a subset of OECD with a larger number of mostly low-income countries. The point that a more highly educated labor force can contribute to greater income inequality in developing and emerging economies is also made by Carnoy (2011). This is related to increasing returns to university relative to secondary and lower education; decreasing public spending differences between higher and lower education; and increasing differentiation of spending among higher education institutions, with declining spending towards mass universities relative to elite universities.[47]

For the sample of OECD/EU countries, however, it is fair to say that most empirical evidence points to an equalizing effect of educational expansion. These results are also important for policy considerations drawn from cross-country studies of the multiple causes of inequality. If "up-skilling" of the population can indeed provide a most powerful

---

[46] A note of caution is warranted here. While appealing, such a model should not be applied mechanically because it does not take into account dynamics and ignores the interaction with the capital market (Atkinson, 2008).

[47] Carnoy (2011) underlines that some of these features also hold for the United States.

element for countering the trend towards increasing inequality, policy responses that focus on increased access to education will be more promising than those that concentrate on limiting economic globalization (and technological progress). They potentially have a double dividend by contributing to capturing benefits from increased economic integration and by keeping inequality levels lower or actually lowering them (see also Machin, 2009).

19.5.2.8 Going Beyond the Economic Notion of Globalization

Some authors have argued that the pure economic aspects of increased openness—trade, capital flows, foreign investment and so on—do not reflect the whole reality of globalization. Other more social, political and cultural aspects would also merit consideration (e.g., Dreher and Gaston, 2008; Zhou et al., 2011; Atif et al., 2012; Heshmati, 2004). These authors typically construct synthetic measures of globalization along the lines of the Kearney globalization indexes[48] and test their significance and that of their subcomponents for explaining earnings and income inequality.

Interestingly, some of these studies—in particular Heshmati (2004) and Zhou et al. (2011)—find overall globalization to have a *negative* relationship with income inequality.[49] In these cases, investigation of the subcomponents of globalization reveals that the economic aspects (such as trade) tend to have a significant positive relationship, which is, however, more than outweighed by factors such as increased personal contacts/travel and information/Internet use.

While the above two studies of the impact of "overall" globalization are based on a broad country sample of advanced and developing countries (60 and 62, respectively), the Dreher and Gaston (2008) study allows the OECD area to be separated out in their analysis of 100 countries. For the OECD sample, they found overall globalization to have a significant *positive* relationship with inequality, whereby this association is much larger for earnings than for income inequality.[50] Different than the studies mentioned above, the three subdimensions of globalization (economic, political, social) seem to have no systematic relationship with inequality except that none of them have a negative sign in any of the specifications. Bergh and Nilson (2010) are another example of an analysis of the effect of an overall indicator of globalization and its element on net income inequality trends over the past 35 years in around 80 countries. Their results reveal a

---

[48] The Kearney Globalization Index (KGI) (see Kearney, A.T., Inc. and the Carnegie Endowment for International Peace, 2004, 2007) is composed of four major component variables: economic integration, personal contact, technological connections and political engagement. Each of these four component variables is a weighted average of several determinant variables. In a similar vein, Dreher (2006) proposed a composite measure for 123 countries, the KOF index of globalization, which is based on 23 variables that relate to three globalization dimensions: economic integration, political engagement and social globalization (see http://globalization.kof.ethz.ch/).

[49] But see a critical review of their methods and results in Atif et al. (2012) and Tsai et al. (2012).

[50] They estimate that a one-point increase in the overall globalization index increases industrial wage inequality by 26% and household income inequality by 3%.

positive and strong association[51] that is largely driven by the social dimension of globalization. Although the sign and size of the economic and the political dimensions of globalization are similar, their coefficient is not significant.

19.5.3 Changes in Institutions and Regulations

Until 30 years ago, the quest for identifying driving factors of income inequality focused on testing the Kuznet hypothesis (see Section 19.5.1). However, since the 1990s a range of other factors has increasingly been considered. In the context of OECD countries, globalization and technological change became prime candidates for research (many other variables show little variability in the OECD). It is, however, important to also consider the role of institutions, in particular labor market institutions, and changes in regulations (Checchi and Garcia-Penalosa, 2005; Piketty and Saez, 2006; Lemieux, 2008). The increase in wage inequality since the 1980s in several countries coincided with changes in labor market institutions, such as a decline in the importance of unions in setting wages. That labor market institutions and policies have lost redistributive potential in recent times also has been put forward; in particular, trade union density, collective bargaining coverage and centralized collective bargaining were estimated to have become less effective in reducing inequality (Baccaro, 2008). Chapter 18 provides a detailed discussion of the theory and literature that relates labor market institutions to the dispersion of wage earnings and proposes an empirical approach for analysis.

While it is widely recognized that institutions are an important factor for identifying the multiple causes of inequality (e.g., Acemoglu, 2003; Smeeding, 2002), the weight attached to this factor in econometric studies has long been limited. Some papers have argued that, given the relative stability of institutional patterns across countries, including country fixed effects in the analysis would capture a larger part of this factor, at least its time invariant components (e.g., Figini and Görg, 2006). This does not, however, fully reflect development over the past decades, during which some institutions such as union density and coverage or EPL considerably weakened in many countries.

In the earlier studies, the degree of unionization was the main factor used to measure labor market institutions (e.g., Freeman, 1993); union density (share of employees who are members of a trade union) or union coverage (share of employees covered by wage bargaining agreements) are probably more precise indicators. Union density and coverage often are expected to have an equalizing effect on the earnings distribution, not only because unions strive for wage standardization and seek to increase the earnings of their members[52] but also through indirect effects, such as promotion of social expenditures that

---

[51] Their results suggest that the maximum effect of overall globalization would be a 14% increase of the Gini coefficient of income inequality.

[52] The existence of wage premia for union members tends to be equalising if low-wage earners were better organized than high-wage earners, but the opposite may hold if high-paid earners were better organized (Freeman, 1993). Blau and Kahn (2009) argue that the net effect of unions on wage inequality partly depends on which groups have higher labor demand and supply elasticities.

benefit low-income groups as a whole (Mahler, 2004), creation of an institutional environment in which workers care more about wage dispersion because of some shared norm of fairness (Golden and Wallerstein, 2011) or employers following certain pay norms where workers are paid a fraction of their productivity plus a uniform amount (for a discussion of this reputational approach see Atkinson, 2002).

Another factor increasingly analyzed is the impact of wage-setting centralization and coordination. Again, this factor may have both direct and indirect effects on the distribution of earnings: centralized bargaining improves the bargaining position of workers; it may help broaden norms of distributive justice; and it is expected to be economically more efficient, resulting in more resources to be distributed (Mahler, 2004; see also the discussion in sub-section below).

A third factor that is expected to have an important effect on wage dispersion is EPL. EPL is likely to affect employers' costs to hire/dismiss workers. Such policies would compress the wage differential if they are relatively more important for unskilled workers. There may, however, be considerable differences for the effects of changes in EPL for regular versus temporary workers.

Further, there are a number of regulative factors that affect the distribution of earnings, such as minimum wages, unemployment benefits and tax wedges. The working hypothesis here is that minimum wages compress the wage differential, and a decrease in minimum wages contributes to an increase in wage inequality. Higher unemployment benefit replacement rates would increase the reservation wage, with a possible equalizing effect on wage inequality. The distributive effect of tax wedges is a priori ambiguous. Finally, not only labor market institutions and regulations affect the earnings distribution; the observed trend of a large decline in product market regulation (PMR), which precedes the larger trends weakening labor market institutions, also is expected to have a major role (OECD, 2011).

Many of the above aspects of labor market institutions and regulations are, in general, expected to have a more or less equalizing effect on the distribution of wages. This is, however, not necessarily the case when it comes to household earnings or income inequality; the latter also is influenced by trends in employment and unemployment at the household level. Rising employment, for instance, may attenuate growing wage inequality, and the net effect of institutions on household income inequality also depends on their effect on employment. A vast body of empirical evidence points to a significant effect of both institutions and regulations on employment levels (for an overview, see OECD, 2006).[53] Theoretically, the overall impact of institutions and regulations remains ambiguous (Checchi and Garcia-Penalosa, 2008).

---

[53] For evidence on unemployment benefits, see, for instance, Nickell (1998) and Nunziata (2002). For evidence on labor market bargaining models, see Layard et al. (1991) or Pissarides (1990). For evidence on product market regulation, see Blanchard and Giavazzi (2003), Spector (2004), Messina (2003), or Fiori et al. (2007).

The majority of studies reviewed (with the major exception of ILO, 2008) point to a negative association between various aspects of institutional and regulatory change and earnings as well as income inequality. Weakening of institutions has often been identified as a key driver of increasing inequalities.

19.5.3.1 Wage Dispersion Effects

Earlier studies of single OECD countries found that the decline in unionization increased wage inequality (Card, 1996; Machin, 1997). Looking at trends in a cross-country setting up to 1995, Rueda and Pontusson (2000) suggested higher union density is associated with a more compressed wage dispersion independent of the policy "regime" of a country (social, liberal, mixed). For the same set of OECD countries, Golden and Wallerstein (2011) provide newer estimates but make a distinction between the 1980s and the 1990s: in the former decade, decreasing union density and centralization were identified as key factors of increasing wage dispersion, whereas these factors were no longer significant in the 1990s and were replaced by trade and social expenditures as explanatory factors. Cassette et al. (2012) found union density and union concentration to be significantly negatively associated with earnings inequality for a set of 10 countries for a period of 25 years (up to 2005). Such a finding is also reported by Burniaux et al. (2006), although it is limited to particular inequality indexes. On the other hand, Mahler (2004) founds no effect of union density but a significant and negative effect of wage coordination on earnings inequality for a set of 13 OECD countries over the two decades 1980–2000.

Koeninger et al. (2007) found changes in a set of labor market institutions explained as much as trade and technology: EPL, levels and duration of benefit replacement rates, union density and the minimum wage were shown to negatively affect the wage differential. Checchi and Garcia-Penalosa (2005) identified three types of labor market institutions as essential determinants of wage differentials: union density, the unemployment benefit and the minimum wage. Declining minimum wages also have been found to increase wage dispersion, mainly at the lower end of the distribution (Dickens et al., 1999; DiNardo et al., 1996; Lee, 1999).

The OECD (2011) considers a range of labor market institutions and regulations as possible explanatory factors for increased earnings inequality in 23 OECD countries up to 2008. The weakening in these institutions and regulations since the 1980s was shown to widen the wage dispersion among workers: (i) the effect of EPL is entirely driven by weakening EPL for temporary workers, whereas EPL for regular workers had no significant effect. Furthermore, EPL had more of an impact on the lower than the upper half of the earnings distribution; (ii) lower unemployment benefit replacement rates for low-wage workers (but not for average-wage workers); (iii) decreases in union coverage, which predominantly affected the upper half of the earnings distribution; and (iv) and lower taxation of earnings (tax wedge).

Effects of changes in product market regulation are generally not included in analyses of inequality but rather are considered in studies of employment effects (e.g., Nicoletti and Scarpetta 2005; Bassanini and Duval, 2006; Fiori et al., 2007). However, it can be expected that these regulations had a larger role in wage dispersion. The OECD (2011) showed that declining PMR contributed significantly to a wider wage dispersion, in particular at the lower half of it. This is consistent with the view that PMR tends to reduce market rents available for unions to capture through collective bargaining (Nicoletti et al., 2001); this leads to a decline in union power (or more decentralized bargaining), which in turn results in greater wage dispersion.

Combining the results of the effect of institutions on wage dispersion with additional ones on employment, the OECD (2011) estimated the overall effects on earnings distribution among the entire working-age population. It turns out that wage dispersion and employment effects often were off-setting and led to undetermined estimates of the effects of institutions and regulations on overall earnings inequality, with one exception: weaker employment protection among temporary workers, which is estimated to have an overall disequalizing effect.

19.5.3.2 Income Inequality Effects

Some studies provide estimates of the direct effect of institutions on (gross or net) income inequality, in particular Checchi and Garcia-Penalosa (2005, 2008) and the ILO (2008). All three studies cover a set of 16 OECD countries for a period up to the early 2000s. Checchi and Garcia-Penalosa (2005) identify union density, the tax wedge and unemployment benefits as major determinants of higher income inequality, whereas the effect of minimum wages is only marginally significant. The overall effect of stronger institutions is estimated to reduce income inequality, partly through wage compression and partly through a reduction in the rewards for capital. For a smaller sample of seven OECD countries, Weeks (2005) estimated decreasing union density as a strong predictor of increased gross income inequality.

Based on a different set of data that allows several income concepts to be investigated, Checchi and Garcia-Penalosa (2008) suggested only a weak role for institutions in determining factor income inequality. A stronger effect occurs when considering disposable income inequality, particularly for unemployment benefits and EPL (negative) as well as tax wedge (positive), whereas union density, wage coordination and minimum wage remain insignificant. The fact that the tax wedge is estimated to increase income inequality (including factor income inequality) runs counter to some of the evidence summarized earlier. Checchi and Garcia-Penalosa (2008) put forward that high-wage workers may be better able to pass tax increases onto their employers than low-wage workers and that a high tax wedge can increase unemployment.

Results reported by the ILO (2008), based on Baccaro (2008), show that trade unionism and collective bargaining are not significantly associated with within-country inequality, except in the central and eastern European countries.[54] Rather, economic factors such as technology-induced shifts in the demand for skilled labor and increases in FDI shares seem better predictors if increasing inequality. This nonsignificance of institutional factors also holds for the enlarged sample of 51 countries going beyond the subsample of the 16 OECD countries. Evidence for 14 OECD countries, presented by Mahler (2004), is quite the opposite: union density and wage coordination were found to have the strongest negative relationship with disposable income inequality, whereas indicators of economic globalization (imports, outbound investment, financial openness) were found to be insignificant.

19.5.4 Political Processes

A great deal of the political science and of the policy literature is concerned with the effects of inequalities and how they can be mitigated in various societies. For this chapter, however, it is the other direction that is interesting: mechanisms of how various political arrangements (voting, electoral institutions and representation in political parties, interest reconciliation and employer–employee relationships) affect inequality. The core question is, therefore, How and to what extent can political factors account for the variability of inequalities across countries and over time? How much of the cross-country and over-time variance of inequality can be explained by political determinants (agency,[55] institutions or policies)?

The explanation of inequalities by political institutions has to start from the actual level and structure of inequality itself (initial or t_1 distribution). Then the degree of change achieved by institutions and policies—how they modify the social setting and transform it into a new system of inequality (end result or t_2 distribution)—is subject to study here. The assumption is that the objective position in the income distribution defines preferences over redistribution, which is aggregated in the political process, the end of which, in turn, is a change in income distribution. This is, no question, a loop in the line of reasoning, indicating a circularity in the arguments. This is a difficult issue for empirical research and, although recognized by many, few have offered convincing solutions to it.

We classify the channels of this transformation into three groups: (i) democratic representation and partisan politics, (ii) interest groups and lobby organizations and (iii) redistributive policies of the state (governments). From a different angle, we are concerned with the demand for and the supply of policies, mediated by the political process itself. Below we turn to these in detail.

---

[54] Bradley et al. (2003) also report the "absence of any significant effect of wage coordination on pre-tax and transfer inequality" (p. 216) for the 61 countries they investigated.

[55] There is no question that agency (political leadership) may exert influence on the shape of inequality, especially for shorter periods and especially in countries where the political system allows for a larger role of personalities. This happens in fully democratic states, less democratic states and nondemocratic environments, in "normal" democracies and in populist regimes. Nevertheless, dealing with the role of political personalities would stretch beyond the scope of this chapter.

19.5.4.1 Preference Formation and Partisanship
19.5.4.1.1 General Frame of Understanding

The most commonly used general frame for understanding the politics of redistribution in democratic societies is offered by Meltzer and Richard (1981), originating from a Downsian definition of political competition and democracy (Downs, 1957; see also Romer, 1975). In this setting politics is about redistribution only, and the extent of redistribution is defined by electoral politics only. The aim of parties is to win elections. It is assumed that in majority voting systems (where the winner takes all) the party that is able to attract the vote of the median voter—the median being defined in terms of the dimension in which the political agenda stretches the political spectrum (incomes, political opinions, etc.)—wins. For voting on taxes and redistribution, the spectrum is, by definition, defined by the level of incomes/wealth. Voters, who by their material wealth/incomes occupy the full continuum of the income distribution, vote over the general tax rate, which provides resources (public funds) for redistribution. If the pivotal voter is the same as the person with a median income (which is not necessarily the case), on the assumption of self-interest he or she would prefer more redistribution (higher taxes) than a person with an income above the median. An increase in inequality can be gauged by the increased distance between the median and the average income. The demand for redistribution in period t_2, therefore, is assumed to be linked to the extent of inequalities in period t_1. Under the Meltzer and Richard (hereafter MR) paradigm, greater inequality leads to higher social spending and results in larger redistribution. This would imply a higher level of redistribution in countries with greater inequalities to start with. To put it differently, multiparty democracy, as described above, would produce an equalizing self-correction mechanism, leading to larger redistribution in those countries where inequalities are larger. The prediction, therefore, is that the variance of inequalities are, at least to some extent, dependent upon the essential features of democracy.

There have been many tests of this proposition, contrasting levels of inequality with levels of redistribution, with varying results. As an empirical test, for example, Milanovic (2000) found that there is a consistent association between gross household income inequality and more tax/transfer redistribution in a set of 24 democracies in the period of the mid-1970s to the mid-1990s. Also, Mahler (2008) found support for the MR propositions after refining definitions of original inequality and redistribution.[56] Mahler (2010) found a positive relationship between pregovernment inequality and government redistribution on the basis of observations of 13 OECD countries. Mohl and Pamp (2009) stated that there is a nonlinear relationship between the two. They concluded that at very high levels the positive relationship between inequality and redistribution is reversed. The argument for the reversal stresses the role of Director's law, that is, that redistribution

---

[56] When, however, it is not the status (democratic preference aggregation via representative democracy) but the process itself (say, transition from nondemocracy into democracy) that is observed, Nel (2005) did not find support for the median voter hypotheses (despite careful definitions of the variables used).

may go from the ends to the broadly defined middle class (ranging from the 20th to the 80th percentile).[57]

Contrary to the above findings, and partly because of lack of appropriate data or improper specifications, many of the tests of the link between initial inequality and redistribution could not reach conclusive results. (For reviews of various aspects of the MR model and its propositions, see Alesina and Giuliano, 2009; Borck, 2007; Guillaud, 2013; Keely and Tan, 2008; Kenworthy and McCall, 2007; Lübker, 2007; Lupu and Pontusson, 2011; McCarty and Pontusson, 2009; Mohl and Pamp, 2009; Olivera, 2014; Osberg et al., 2004; Senik, 2009.)

A potential reason for the inconclusiveness of the literature may be that, as Robinson (2009) put it, "The model does not predict a simple positive relationship between inequality and redistribution across countries since there are many differences between countries which may be correlated with either the demand or supply of redistribution at a particular level of inequality" (p. 28). Also, it can be expected that in high-inequality countries with badly performing institutions, any income that is taxed away is likely to be wasted by corruption or diverted by elites, and this will reduce the demand for redistribution. Also, in general, MR would mean that extension of the franchise will increase redistribution, that is, democratization of the political regimes brings about lower levels of inequalities. However, while the equalizing effects of democratization seem to be shown in many cases, they might not be automatic (see Galbraith, 2012; Nel, 2005; Robinson, 2009).[58]

In what follows we go through some relevant assumptions and predictions and use the MR proposition to structure the line of reasoning here, acknowledging the fact that some alternative suggested theoretical papers (most notably Iversen and Soskice, 2006 and to some extent Moene and Wallerstein, 2001) suggest different frames and sometimes diametrically different conclusions. We start from the micro (assumptions on the motivational base of voters) and move to the macro level (such as features of electoral systems).

---

[57] When referring to a "pregovernment" situation, one needs to keep in mind that the data relate to incomes before taxes and transfers in the presence of government. The "before redistribution" inequality is affected by the existence of the government, and it is quite possible that this is greater than the inequality that would be found if the government were not present.

[58] A more recent attempt to trace inequality paths among 30 developed societies points out that countries experiencing democratization in central and eastern Europe followed very different paths in terms of inequalities. While all belonged to the lower end of the inequality spectrum in the 1980s, they ended up at very different parts of the European "league table" in the late 2000s: Slovenia and the Czech and Slovak Republics at the bottom and the Baltic states on top, while the rest lie in between. The experiences of Spain, Portugal and Greece, where the ending of the dictatorships went hand in hand with inequality decreases, therefore, have to be balanced against the experiences of the central and eastern European countries in further comparative research (Tóth, 2014). However, a major difference between the Mediterranean and central and eastern European transitions was clearly that, in the latter group of countries, transition also implied marketization and liberalization, in contrast to countries in southern Europe where the role of the state changed albeit less in scope.

A simple presentation of the potential links between inequality, redistribution and intermediate processes is shown in Figure 19.2 (following Tóth et al., 2014). As indicated in Figure 19.2, there are potential mediating mechanisms on both the micro and the macro levels. On the one hand, personal attributes and perceptions might have an effect on individual redistributive preferences and, on the other, the institutional mechanisms that translate preferences to policy actions. Determinants of political participation shape the ratio and the composition of voters, and the activity of the civil society matters a lot in policy decisions. Finally, it is clear that the ways in which (and to what extent) attitudes of voters will, via the machinery of politics, shape policies depend to a large extent on various institutions (political and executive alike).

19.5.4.1.2 Motivations, Expectations and Values of Voters

To understand the mechanisms of the micro determinants of votes over redistribution is crucial and has to be linked more closely to the political science literature. However, a large number of empirical studies are already available and provide more understanding of the characteristics and *motivations* (from the redistribution perspective) of citizens belonging to various parts of the income distribution. Various studies show that although it exists, the correlation linking material position and attitudes regarding the welfare interventions of the state is far from perfect. Some attempts to identify reasons for the

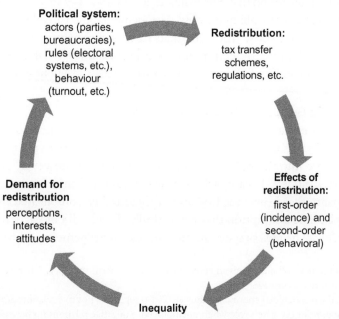

Figure 19.2 Theoretical links of the political processes involved in the determination of income distribution. *Source: Tóth et al. (2014)*

"deviations" (i.e., the observation that some of the relatively richer voters will be pro-redistribution while others with below-median incomes may not be supportive) stress that it is not only the current economic position but also the expectations concerning economic prospects that matter (see Bénabou and Ok, 2001 and Ravallion and Loskhin, 2000 for prospect for upward mobility; see Alesina and Fuchs-Schündeln, 2005, 2005, Piketty, 1995 or Guillaud, 2013 for social mobility experiences and expectations based on these[59]).

Others stress the role of socialization into general *value systems* either in the frame of the overall sociopolitical environment, such as a socialist past, or simply ideological systems or family traditions (Kelley and Zagorski, 2004; Corneo and Grüner, 2002; Fong, 2001, 2006; Alesina and Fuchs-Schündeln, 2005; Gijsberts, 2002; Suhrcke, 2001). These are, in many cases, not temporary but long-lasting cultural differences, sometimes transmitted over generations (Alesina and Fuchs-Schündeln, 2005; Luttmer and Singhal, 2008). Also, the beliefs about the fairness of the economic system and about the rules of the game of "getting ahead" in society seem to be important determinants of the acceptance the actual level of redistribution or a demand for more of it (Fong, 2001, 2006; Alesina and La Ferrara, 2005; Alesina and Glaeser, 2006; Osberg and Smeeding, 2006; for a recent review of the literature on inequality and justice perceptions see Janmaat, 2013).

Finally, it is not simply general views and attitudes but also personality traits that can matter. A hypothesis of how these attitudes come about is presented by Tepe and Vanhuysse (2014). They found that personality traits in some cases strongly determine welfare attitudes, even after controlling for class, sociodemographic variables and even socialization.[60] Moreover, they show that some traits such as conscientiousness, openness and extraversion are conditioned by communist regime socialization (when comparing the Eastern and Western Länder of Germany, similar to Alesina and Fuchs-Schündeln, 2005).

19.5.4.1.3 Reference Groups and Heterogeneity of Voters

Inequality is often measured by various indices reflecting the whole income distribution (most commonly by the Gini coefficient but also by various other variance-based measures). Putting these into the right-hand side of regressions is, however, problematic in political economy models. It cannot be reasonably assumed that voters have the same image of inequality that is provided by any of these rather complicated measures. It is a much more plausible assumption that voters think of social distances, define proximity to other voters, etc. The idea of social affinity (an acknowledgement of those groups who

[59] As for the measurement of and trends in actual income (and social) mobility, Chapter 10 of this book provides an exhaustive overview.

[60] As an example, the research of Tepe and Vanhuysse (2014) suggests a positive relationship between agreeableness and support for the state's role when unemployed, a negative relationship between openness and support for governmental responsibility for the family and a positive association between conscientiousness and governmental responsibility for the elderly.

are the closest to the assumed decision makers) was raised by Kristov et al. (1992). For political economy models of redistribution the idea has been applied by Osberg et al. (2004), Lupu and Pontusson (2011), Finseraas (2008) and Tóth and Keller (2013). Empirical tests show that that the actual level of inequality (and, more importantly, the structure of inequality as measured by the distance between the middle classes and the poor) also drives attitudes towards redistribution. There seem to be convincing examples that the relative position of the middle—which might cover also the pivotal voter in elections—influences public spending priorities (and coalition formation). As Lupu and Pontusson (2011) showed, a greater dispersion in the lower half of the earnings distribution (as measured by the P50/P10 ratios) is consistently associated with less redistribution in a sample of 15 advanced democracies. A more prominent skew of the redistribution (meaning middle classes being positioned closer to the poor) would result in more redistribution in their sample. Osberg et al. (2004) also showed that the structure of redistribution matters, but in a different way: they found that inequality between the top and the middle of the distribution (measured by the 90/50 ratio) has a large and negative effect on social spending, implying that the top may have more room for opting out of public services in the case of larger inequalities.

19.5.4.2 The Issues at Stake: Different Forms of Redistribution

The assumption of the basic MR model is that there is only one type of redistribution (vertically transferring money from the rich to the poor). The original model is even more simplistic: it specifies a uniform tax rate levied on the above-average-income voters on the one hand and a lump sum amount handed over to the lower segments of the distribution. Actual redistribution programs are, however, more sophisticated. As Moene and Wallerstein (2001, 2003) pointed out, distinction between insurance-type programs (in which participants seek provisions against income losses at bad times) and redistribution programs involving taxes on the rich to benefit the poor has to be made. They suggest (and offer empirical evidence to support the suggestion) that while the demand for vertical redistribution is negatively correlated with income, the demand for insurance is positively correlated (and in some situations these two effects might even cancel out each other). This might indeed have a sizeable effect on the actual distributive outcomes.

In his review of the literature, Borck (2007) summarized various types of redistribution and classified the literature according to this differentiation. The first and most obvious direction is redistribution from the rich to the poor; models underlying social preferences, upward mobility and voter mobilization (see above) point to the direction of causation from increased inequality to increased vertical redistribution. There are, however, other types of redistributive mechanisms, such as spending programs, that entail transfers from the poor to the rich. This might be the case when there is public provision of private goods, education or insurance. In these cases the state/public budgets may effectively be subsidized by the poorer income groups. Finally, the public provision of private goods or the operations of public pension schemes might represent a case for the so-called Director's law: when the tails of the distribution are expropriated by the middle (for other reviews, see Mohl and Pamp, 2009; Mahler, 2010; Alesina and Giuliano, 2009).

Another issue regarding the definition of redistribution relates to the income concepts used for measurement. Obviously, simply associating Gini coefficients after taxes and benefits with the size of the public social budgets is erroneous because it conflates the right- and the left-hand sides of the equation. Based on LIS data, Kenworthy and Pontusson (2005) refined the definition of redistribution. They proxy redistribution by a difference between the Gini of disposable household incomes (after taxes and benefits) and the Gini for market incomes (before taxes and benefits). This helps them show (on both cross section and on country time series data) that an increase in market income inequality correlates with an increase in redistribution (see similar results from Immervoll and Richardson, 2011).[61] This finding about the over-time, within-country variation of redistribution as a response to inequality is in broad agreement with what is suggested by the MR proposition. What makes a difference between countries, however, is the elasticity with which the welfare states react during the period they observe (varying spells in the 1980s and 1990s) an inequality increase.[62]

An additional empirical characteristic of electoral politics is that sometimes parties do not simply play the cards of (vertical or insurance-type) redistribution in elections. They often try to make political space multidimensional, sometimes introducing issues that create divisions orthogonal to the vertical income differentiation. Campaigns often are about complex packages, and "issue bundling" might easily place the median voter at a part of the income distribution different from the median income (Roemer, 1998). This might, in concrete circumstances, be a strategy to target parties on the Right of the political spectrum (because they are interested in diverting the electorate away from issues that motivate the lower-income groups), but issue bundling may sometimes also be in the interest of Left parties.[63]

19.5.4.3 *Political Inequality: Unequal Participation in Elections*
The prediction of higher redistribution in the case of higher inequality also assumes full (or at least uniform across income groups) participation in elections. This, however,

---

[61] A special note is needed here. Increased redistributive effects of given welfare state measures may be detected induring periods of increasing market income inequality, even in the absence of any changes in redistribution instruments such as taxes and transfers. We turn back to this in Section 19.5.5.1. Also, see Immervoll and Richardson (2011).

[62] Also the choice of the country universe in this case can clearly make a difference in results. OECD comparisons (see, e.g., OECD, 2011) tend to show a great deal of sensitivity of the results to the inclusion of lower-income OECD countries (such as Mexico or Chile).

[63] A further analysis of issue bundling would reveal how politics and policies that are not directly aiming inequalities could have important effects on actual developments in income distribution. This way of taking account of secondary effects, by-products and unintended consequences of party politics would, however, go beyond the scope of this chapter.

generally does not hold empirically.[64] Therefore, differential voter participation might alter aggregate redistributive preferences. If the middle classes participate more than the poor, then parties may seek to represent the interests of relatively higher-income voters. In another dimension, greater participation of older voters can induce more party promises for pension expenditures compared with family-related expenditures. Therefore, empirics of the actual redistribution might differ from predictions based on uniform participation. (See more on participation in Kenworthy and Pontusson, 2005; Larcinese, 2007; Pontusson and Rueda, 2010.)

An important note by Kenworthy and Pontusson (2005) and, especially, by Pontusson and Rueda (2010) is that the mobilization of voters is a crucial issue in how inequality translates into politics of redistribution. Political inequality (at least in terms of participation in elections) may play a major role in policy formation. Because the low-income voters who might be motivated in larger redistribution may not be sufficiently activated during elections, redistribution might be lower than predicted by "objective" inequality. Pontusson and Rueda (2010) also point out that there is a need to differentiate between core constituencies of the Left (and Right) parties, in addition to the positions of the median voters who, in proportional representative (PR) systems at least, can be considered swing voters. Their major finding is that the extent to which Left parties take up the issue of redistribution also depends on the general mobilization of low-income citizens. To put it differently: if the "demand" for redistribution is represented by a larger appearance of the low-income segments in the polls, the Left will react to it by offering more redistributive policies. This, of course, cannot fully be treated as exogenous; therefore, party politics for differential mobilization of their core constituencies (especially on the Left) might have an important effect on redistribution. This issue is discussed further in the next section (Section 19.5.4.4) on political institutions.

Mahler (2008) introduces two factors into the analysis: the level of electoral turnout and the degree to which turnout is skewed by income. When these factors are taken into account, the predictive power of the MR model is significantly improved. He found the link to be especially strong for the lower and the middle parts of the income distribution and when social transfer policies are at stake as opposed to tax policies. In a later and more refined formulation, Mahler and Jesuit (2013) showed that political participation (most notably union density) is positively related to redistribution, especially when the share gains of the lower middle classes are considered.

---

[64] Full participation should not even be assumed theoretically. Following Downs (1957) and Olson (1965), it is shown and accepted in mainstream political economy thinking that voters are perfectly rational not to participate in elections, while it is also rational for rich voters/small interest groups to lobby and fund parties (see Olson, 1965). For an overview of what political economy reasons can be found behind insufficient performance MR-type and other "economistic" approaches to politics that work via "the market for votes" analogies, see Vanhuysse (2002).

19.5.4.4 Political Regimes and Partisanship

For a broader understanding of the effect of political dynamics on income distributions, it is worth starting with a consideration of the effect of general political regimes—most notably democracy—on inequality. As stated by Galbraith (2012) in a review of many propositions, it is difficult to establish clear conclusions. Classifying political regimes into democracies and nondemocracies does not help much. Some nondemocratic (communist or Islamic) regimes can have more egalitarian distributions than others. Of course, long-serving, established social democratic regimes of the twentieth century are associated with lower-level inequality, but causality may run in either direction. Finally, there are numerous examples when the transition to a more democratic regime is paralleled by an increase rather than a decrease of inequality (consider the case of central and eastern European countries experiencing post-communist transitions) (Galbraith, 2012; Tóth and Medgyesi, 2011; Tóth, 2014).

Second (and more generally), because various "welfare regimes" (the term coined by Esping-Andersen, 1990 in classifying the overall characteristics of the European welfare systems into three types of welfare regimes à 'la Esping-Andersen) are so embedded in general socioeconomic and sociopolitical settings, partisanship (normally meaning parties staying in an executive position for one or two election terms) cannot really achieve fundamental changes in the operation of an overarching institutional setting. Both of these considerations lead us to an analysis of not only the general frames of the political regimes, such as representative democracy, but also to elements of these (such as partisanship, ideologies, corporatist institutional settings).

A large tradition of the political science literature associates redistribution to the relative strength of the parties representing the working class in elections. Social democratic parties have long governed some democracies with large public spending, although their socioeconomic foundations have declined with the large sectoral shifts in economies following the two consecutive crises in the 1970s. However, the power resources theory (PRT) is an influential paradigm in explaining redistribution, arguing that the extension of the welfare state largely depends on the ability of the parties representing labor to mobilise lower-income voters (Korpi, 2006; Korpi and Palme, 2003).

Bradley et al. (2003), using a panel of 19 OECD countries, attempt to explain what determines "initial" income distribution and what are the results of redistribution and provide support for the central hypotheses of the PRT. They stress that high unemployment, low union density and a large proportion of households led by women are associated with high inequality before taxes and transfer. For the reduction of inequality (i.e., the effectiveness of the welfare state redistribution) they identify the existence of Leftist government (either directly or indirectly via other variables related to partisan politics) as statistically significant (and strong). As they conclude, "leftist government very strongly drives the redistributive process directly by shaping the redistributive contours of taxes and transfers and indirectly by increasing the proportion of GDP devoted to taxes and transfers."

Iversen and Soskice (2006) allow for heterogeneity of parties (assuming separate, exclusive representatives of high-, the middle- and the low-income voters). They also allow coalitions between the representative parties, and they differentiate between PR and simple majoritarian electoral systems. Their proposition is that majoritarian systems tend to redistribute less because they tend to favor centre-Right governments (as a result of the interplay of the coalition game under constraints of the potential taxability of the three major income groups). Note, however, that Iversen and Soskice (2006) do not build on assumptions about the relationships of the mean and the median incomes (i.e., about the level of inequalities in the society), nor about the position of the median voter in the income distribution (i.e., about the effect of political mobilization on political coverage of the full income spectrum). Their assumed parties are, however, class parties representing the various income groups. The core element of the argument is the nontaxability of high-income groups and the uncertainty about the potential to enforce pre-election party commitments after a coalition is formed.

Some empirical accounts of the political dynamics and its effects on inequality challenge the usefulness of the traditional notions of Left–Right differentiation, and they also add to a more balanced understanding of the meaning of various "regimes." As Rueda (2008), for example, stresses in his study of 16 OECD countries, in regimes where the underlying socioeconomic structure is characterized by corporatism (a broad, concentrated, institutionalized and informal system of bargaining and interest reconciliation between social partners, state bureaucracies and political parties), a small part of the discretion over, for instance, wage policies remains in the hands of partisan politics—hence the nonsignificance of the partisanship variables in explaining income distribution. In addition (as also put forward by Rueda, 2008), Left parties may (contrary to their general image) not always represent the full "labor side" of the economy. Rather, they may be more concerned with "insiders" (the employed, in this case) of the labor market rather than the "outsiders," who may wish to enter the labor market but are not (yet) there. With outsiders' interests being overlooked, inequality of overall incomes may increase even in periods of Left governments.

Rueda and Pontusson (2000) analyze four relevant political-institutional variables to explain (wage) distribution in a set of advances countries[65]: in addition to the partisan composition of government, they measure unionization rates, centralization of wage bargaining and the size of the public sector. They observe the effect of these variables in two different broad institutional contexts: social market economies (SMEs) and in liberal market economies (LMEs), as defined by Hall and Soskice (2001). The former setting is characterized by comprehensive, publicly funded welfare systems, heavily regulated labor markets and institutionalized wage bargaining systems. They find that these two distinctive general settings do have an effect on wage formation and distribution. Except for

---

[65] To account for broader socioeconomic variables, they control for participation of women in the labor force and unemployment rates.

unionization, for which the above broader institutional settings are not significant (higher unionization has an equalizing effect in both regimes), the effect of the other observed institutional variables differs in the various variations of capitalism (i.e., between SMEs and LMEs). The finding that the effect of a partisan composition of government varies among sociopolitical regimes (it matters in LMEs but not in SMEs) is also important in understanding the working of the median voter theorem, as specified in the previous section.

In a subsequent study Pontusson et al. (2002) also found that higher levels of unionization and wage bargaining and larger shares of public sector employment reach their equalizing effects primarily by improving the relative position of unskilled workers (who constitute the lower tail of the distribution), but partisanship (most notably the participation of the Left in government) has an equalizing effect on the upper end of the distribution by constraining the wage growth of the highly skilled. In centralized wage bargaining systems the Left governments seem to be successful in controlling changes at both the upper (taxation, etc.) and the lower (minimum wages, etc.) tails of the wage distribution.

Reflecting the fact that parties traditionally considered "Left-wing" became increasingly heterogeneous in their ideological beliefs and policies throughout the last decades, Tepe and Vanhuysse (2013) reclassify them by reweighting their nominal positions with their ideological stances/declarations in their party manifestos (data taken from the Comparative Manifesto Project). Also, the same authors aimed to identify strategies of Leftist parties and of trade unions with regard to their effect on EPL (assumed to favor insiders) and active labor market policies (ALMP; assumed to favor outsiders). Analyzing data from a sample of 20 OECD countries between 1986 and 2005, they found (in line with Rueda, 2008) that the Left party power variable has no effect on outsider-favoring ALMP spending in general and a negative effect on job creation programs (which contradicts what PRT theorists suggest). However, as they emphasize, larger and more strike-prone unions tend to increase ALMP spending overall, specifically in those dimensions that help their members: employment assistance and labor market training (Tepe and Vanhuysse, 2013).

19.5.5 Redistribution Via Taxes and Transfers: Technical and Efficiency Aspects

The question of why and in what direction redistribution changes the pre-tax and pre-transfer income distribution depends largely on the interplay of various political forces that are able to influence the political process. The question of how and with what effectiveness it happens is more of a technical nature. This section describes some aspects of effectiveness, many of which are not straightforward right from the outset.

The identification and measurement of redistribution presupposes a counterfactual that exists before the redistributive action of transferring money from taxpayers to benefit recipients takes effect. However, the pretransfer distribution already is influenced by regulatory acts (relating to interhousehold transfers such as alimony and others such payments, to employer–employee relationships such as regulations of wages or working conditions, to supply and demand in various markets such as rent control in housing markets, etc.), the operation of which contributes to the shape taking place before conventionally defined income distribution starts to be measured.[66] Further, the features of "pre-redistribution" are embedded into a broader context such as informal norms of responsibility over the welfare of others (younger or older family or local community members, the poor or the handicapped, etc.); the actual role of such forms of informal solidarity varies across countries. These caveats need to be mentioned at the outset, although no extensive coverage can be given to them in what follows.

Broad forms of redistribution (and of welfare states) can be classified into two categories: the "piggy banks" and the "Robin Hoods" (Barr, 2001). The piggy bank approach puts the focus on smoothing consumption and on insurance against risks prevalent in various stages of the life cycle. In its ideal form it has an effect on life cycle distribution of incomes but does not lead to interpersonal redistribution. The other type (the Robin Hood approach) focuses is on redistribution between various social strata (most commonly from the rich to the poor).

Our image (and, even more, our evaluation) of the extent of redistribution is greatly affected by the perspective from which we see incomes and benefits. Consider the largest item—pensions—as an example. In actuarially fair pension insurance systems there is no interpersonal redistribution involved. Under given parametric regimes of accrual rates, retirement ages, compensation rates, etc., people save for income security during their old age. But putting this income transfer into a cross-sectional frame produces a false impression of the extent of redistribution between richer and poorer segments of the society at a given point in time. In the same vein, the perspective has to be clear when evaluating the redistributive role of sickness insurance, education finance (especially at a higher level), and many other fields.

Furthermore, for cross-country comparisons of income distribution, it should be made clear that countries differ in the mix of the characteristics described above (systems such as the Danish tax-financed welfare states are more the Robin Hood type, whereas Bismarckian systems and to a lesser extent the Beveridgean systems are more piggy bank types), although no really ideal types exist. However, changing the perspective also changes our images of the redistributive effects of the various welfare state arrangements. (See Whiteford, 2008 for more on this.) The extent to which welfare states focus on redistribution among versus between people in a lifetime perspective varies considerably (roughly half in Australia but two-thirds in the United Kingdom and four-fifths in Sweden, taken from a lifetime perspective; see Hills, 2004; Ståhlberg, 2007). This also hints to what extent we can expect welfare states to modify income distribution in a long-term perspective.

---

[66] This "counterfactual problem" in welfare state research has been discussed by Bergh (2005) and Esping-Andersen and Myles (2009). See also Lambert et al. (2010) and Förster and Mira d'Ercole (2012).

For explaining the distribution of current incomes (our focus in this chapter) it is mostly the Robin Hood–type welfare state activity that matters.[67] Among the many related issues (mostly treated in Chapters 23 and 24 on antipoverty policies and micro-simulation, respectively), our focus remains on the effect of redistribution on incomes. We focus on the following questions.

– What overall first-order effect does redistribution have on (initial, cross-sectional, "virgin") income distribution?
– What feedback/secondary effects of redistribution can be identified?

To measure redistribution, setting up a proper income accounting framework is crucial. The commonly used framework (see OECD, 2008, for example, but earlier in Atkinson, 1975) starts from (1) factor incomes (i.e., gross wages, salaries, self-employment and property incomes, adding private occupational pensions to arrive at (2) market incomes, which are supplemented by social benefits, private transfers and miscellaneous cash incomes, resulting in (3) gross income, from which the deduction of various taxes (on wages and/or incomes, by employees and/or employers) results in (4) disposable cash incomes (see Förster and Whiteford, 2009 for more on this framework). Attempts to measure redistribution compare various elements of the above to assess the immediate (direct, first-order) effects of redistribution.[68]

19.5.5.1 Overall, First-Order Effects of Redistribution

After comparing pre-redistribution (market income) inequality to post-redistribution (net disposable income) inequality, Whiteford (2008) concluded that redistribution reduces inequality by roughly one-third of the "original" inequality (ranging between 45% in Denmark, Sweden and Belgium and some 8% in Korea [Whiteford, 2008]). These results refer to the entire population and thus include the effect of public pension transfers, which, as argued earlier, blurs the picture. The OECD (2011, 2013) showed that the redistributive effect of public transfers and taxes for the working-age population—thereby excluding public pensions to a large extent—amounted to, on average, little over a quarter across OECD countries in the late 2000s, reaching close to 40% in some Nordic and continental European countries.

Immervoll and Richardson (2011) showed that redistribution (as measured by the difference between Gini coefficients before and after redistributive measures, whichever is appropriate) increased between the 1980s and the mid-2000s in general across the OECD. However, the pace of increase of market income inequality to a large extent

---

[67] Mostly, but not exclusively. Life cycle income smoothing mechanisms also have cross-sectional income distribution effects. Consider the immediate effect of pensions on the relative position of the elderly. However, social insurance instruments are better judged by their own standards: their ability to smooth consumption over the life cycle.

[68] Most empirical studies are, however, confined to the effect of cash transfers and direct income taxes. Publicly provided services (in-kind transfers) also play an important redistributive role. While the inequality reducing effect in general is lower than that of cash benefits, it is still sizeable and amounts, for instance, to on average 20% of OECD countries in the 2000s (see, e.g., OECD, 2011; Förster and Verbist, 2012).

exceeded the increase of redistribution during the period. Especially during the periods between the mid-1990s and mid-2000s, the redistributive strength of tax benefit systems decreased in many countries (in the latter period the weakening redistribution contributing to inequality increased more than market income inequality increased in itself).

Regarding the redistributive effectiveness of the two sides (taxes on the one hand and expenditures on the other), the OECD (2008) and Whiteford (2008) found redistribution achieved by public cash transfers was twice as large as redistribution achieved by income taxes (except, among the whole OECD country range, the case of the United States, where taxes play a greater role). Immervoll and Richardson (2011) found that the effect of benefits on inequality was much stronger than social contributions or income taxes,[69] despite the fact that taxes and contributions were larger compared with household incomes.[70] Partly relating to this, the overall effect of the tax/benefit system on the various parts of the income distribution was found to be more prevalent in the bottom tail than in the top of the income distribution (Immervoll and Richardson, 2011).

Nevertheless, Fuest et al. (2009) highlighted that the differential effect of taxes and transfers on redistributive outcomes is sensitive to the methods applied. In their study of 25 EU countries on the basis of the 2007 wave of the EU-SILC survey, their analysis, following the traditional redistribution accounting framework (see Förster and Whiteford, 2009), confirms that benefits are the most important inequality-reducing factors. However, when applying factor decompositions described by Shorrocks (1982) (i.e., when determining what roles various factor components play in determining overall inequality), they concluded that benefits play a minor role (if any) in redistribution. This later procedure results in a much larger role for taxes and contributions in inequality reduction in almost all countries (Fuest et al., 2009). Among the explanations, they argue that while in a traditional accounting framework an equally distributed social transfer tends to have a positive effect on final inequality, to achieve a redistributive effect in a decomposition framework requires a definite negative correlation of transfers with incomes. There has, however, been criticism with regard to policy interpretation of results based on the decomposition framework, which estimates the contribution of equally distributed income sources to overall inequality, by definition, as zero. This is regarded as not being intuitive because a flat-rate benefit that is "added" to unequally distributed pre-transfer income would normally be expected to decrease inequality.[71]

---

[69] Similarly, Mahler (2010) also found a much smaller redistributive effect for taxes than for social transfers.

[70] The corresponding effective tax rate is measured by dividing all taxes paid by all pretax income (of households, for both items). The analysis by Immervoll and Richardson (2011) takes into account the country-specific interactions of taxes with benefits and legal differences in sequencing, for example, the fact that some benefits are taxable while others are not.

[71] Another point is that the results by Fuest et al. (2009) are based on the coefficient of variation, which is highly sensitive to outliers at the top, and this mere fact can lead to somewhat misleading interpretations. In addition, the fact that in certain countries the EU-SILC is based on registers that better capture top incomes, the direct cross-country comparison of redistributive effects of benefits estimated by effects on a tail-sensitive measure can be another reason for caution.

Based on LIS data comparisons, Lambert et al. (2010) suggested at the outset that empirical literature on the relationship between income inequality and redistribution is inconclusive. Given the fact that pre-redistribution (i.e., pre-tax and pre-transfer) income inequality can, by definition, be counterfactual only, they suggest a method called "transplant and compare" for measuring the "true" effect of redistribution, independent of the starting level of inequality of the observed countries. When income tax systems are evaluated according to their own pre-tax/-transfer inequality baseline, redistributive effects of personal income taxes seem to be stronger in more unequal countries for most of the measures they applied. When harmonizing the baselines across countries, they found a weaker relationship.

Based on an analysis of an unbalanced panel of 43 upper-middle- and high- income countries for the period 1972–2006, Muinelo et al. (2011) put the issue of redistribution and inequality into a broader context. After estimating structural equations to model the role of fiscal policies in economic growth and inequality, they found that increasing the size of the public sector (defined as direct taxes and expenditures), while decreasing inequality, harms growth. However, the effect of indirect taxes on both growth and inequality was found to be insignificant. Public investment of general government as a share of GDP, however, is shown to have an equalizing effect without harming economic growth. For a more restricted data set (an unbalanced panel of 21 high-income OECD countries for the period 1972–2006) and with a different variables structure for fiscal policies, Muinelo et al. (2013) found a positive correlation between lower levels of inequality and the size of the public sector (defined in terms of expenditures and taxes per the GDP). They also found that an increase of distributive expenditures (public spending on social protection, health, housing and education) to reduce income inequality in high-income welfare states had no a clear harmful effect on growth. At the same time, they found that an increase in nondistributive expenditure (general public services, defence, public order, economic services) decreases economic growth while increasing income inequality, irrespective of the financing sources (direct or indirect taxes) of expenditures.

Afonso et al. (2010) attempted to estimate how effectiveness (success in achieving program objectives) and efficiency (the degree to which the use of available resources maximize their objectives) of public spending programs is achieved in various countries. According to their propositions, higher social spending is associated with a more equal distribution of incomes across the OECD countries. Southern countries are shown to perform less well in terms of efficiency than Nordic countries. For the Anglo-Saxon countries, output efficiency (the degree to which outputs can be maximized with given inputs) tends to be low, whereas input efficiency (the degree to which a given output can be maintained with decreasing inputs) tends to be high.

On the basis of an analysis of 25 OECD countries, Goudswaard and Caminada (2010) found that total public social expenditures have a strong positive effect on redistribution (and inequality reduction). At the same time, countries with higher private social expenditures have lower levels of redistribution. When excluding services (health expenditures in their analysis), social expenditures (public and private) were shown to make a somewhat smaller contribution to inequality reduction. However, the effect of spending on services did not seem to have a strong effect on their results. The various elements of social expenditures have different contributions; public pensions have larger effects and unemployment benefits and labor market programs have smaller but still positive effects. The sign for private pensions was shown to be positive, implying an inequality-increasing effect.

19.5.5.2 Back to Politics: The Paradox of Redistribution

With regard to the effect of welfare spending on poverty and income distribution, an influential article by Korpi and Palme (1998) pointed out an apparent paradox: they found that targeted benefit systems may have achieved less redistribution than more universal ones, based on available data for the 1980s. Kenworthy (2011) confirmed this finding for the original 10 OECD countries Korpi and Palme analyzed for the 1985–1990 time span. However, Kentworthy showed that that this inverse relationship between targeting and redistribution has weakened by the mid-1990s and then disappeared by 2000–2005. With refinements of the measures, extensions of the country coverage and robust checks of sensitivity to alternative income definitions, Marx et al. (2013) argued that the claimed empirical relationship as such no longer holds. On the methodological side they indicated that the outcomes are not only sensitive to operationalization (i.e., definitions of the counterfactual) and data sources (such as differences between LIS and EU-SILC data) but also to the country selection (inclusion of southern and eastern European countries reveals patterns that are different from each other and also from the previously involved country groupings). On the policy side, they argued that the nature and effects of targeted programs also substantially changed as the decades elapsed (with more emphasis on incentives and changed focus targeting in-work groups started to enjoy more support from middle class electorates as well). With better data, more refined analytics and broader coverage, Marx et al. argued that it is the differential efficiency of various targeted programs and of different country experiences that has to be explained in future research.

Identifying and measuring inequality-reducing effects of redistribution may become prohibitively difficult in the frame of understanding of welfare regimes (Esping-Andersen and Myles, 2009). A full analysis should involve an analysis of taxes and transfer schemes and services, all analyzed simultaneously in a complex setting where state activities are embedded into general societal functioning, producing welfare outcomes jointly with the market and the family. Under these circumstances, the same egalitarian commitments of two different states may produce different results (Esping-Andersen and Myles, 2009). This makes systematic accounts very difficult, calling rather for analysis in a case study fashion. It is therefore important to understand the nature and operation of welfare state interventions at a program level before generalizing to the level of welfare regimes.

19.5.5.3 Second-Order Effects of Redistribution: Labor Market Responses

The above findings may, however, misguide us in the understanding of redistribution if we do not pay attention to the fact that there are second-order effects that also have to be specified and analyzed. The immediate effects (as above) are "overnight" hypothetical gains to recipients (say, of social assistance) and costs to contributors (say, taxpayers). Groups on both sides may vary (according to what type of redistribution is at stake). However, redistribution can also induce second-order effects as actors when noticing changes in costs and benefits their actions will adopt (rich people may change the way they receive their incomes to lower their effective tax rates, whereas poor people might change their labor supply, etc.). Regarding second-order effects, there are many assumptions and fewer tests (except, perhaps, tests of the Laffer curve, assuming high elasticity of labor supply to changes in marginal tax rates).

When modelling second-order effects, Doerrenberg and Peichl (2012) found no significance for the progressivity of income taxes, concluding that, for tax variables, the second-order (behavioral) effects might be larger than they are for expenditures. Niehues (2010) concluded that increased specific targeting of low-income groups is not associated with lower postgovernment levels of inequality. From this, her indirect conclusion is that there might be second-order (potential disincentive) effects in the case of means-tested benefits. However, her analysis of the overall effect of social transfers shows strong equalizing effects that largely outweigh second-order effects.

Blundell (1995; and Blundell et al., 2011) examined potential effects of income taxation on labor supply (extensive margin [decisions to enter labor market from the outside] and intensive margin [work effort decisions of those already in the labor market]). They found that labor supply elasticities for women at both margins are larger than elasticities for men. The overview by Blundell (1995) lists a number of factors why individual labor supply responses to changes in marginal tax rates is very complex (fixed costs of work, life cycles aspects of savings, demographics and wealth accumulation, on–the-job human capital and seniority, the role of unions and collective bargaining, as well as benefit usage and effective tax rates). All these elements characterize the actual operation of the redistribution, making generalized judgements of the secondary effects of redistribution almost impossible. It is even more difficult to draw any further conclusions with respect to inequality effects, given the large number of corresponding assumptions in addition to the above (the interplay of behaviors/demographics and of the labor market effects and income effects, etc.).

Starting from the assumptions that labor supply elasticity is higher at the bottom than at the top and that higher redistribution may shift employers away from social responsibility, Doerrenberg and Peichl (2012) expect negative second-round effects of redistribution on inequality, that is, increasing inequality. However, in an unspecified panel of

OECD countries for the period of 1981–2005, they found that redistributive policies' first-order effects (we might call it "overnight incidence") remain dominant when taking into account the offsetting second-order effects (i.e., behavioral repercussions). They concluded that a 1% increase in public social spending reduces inequality in the order of 0.3% in magnitude overall. Care must be taken when interpreting the magnitude of second-order effects when they are attempted to be put into a conventional redistribution framework. Consider for example the case when market income inequality is contrasted with disposable income inequalities. The differences of the Gini coefficients calculated for these two elements may already entail behavioral reactions from the past and they may also provoke reactions in the future. Therefore, introducing the time dimension is important, especially for the understanding of the second-order effects.

19.5.6 Structural Societal Changes

There are a number of reasons why changes in social structure have direct (via changing composition and the changing relative sizes of various societal subgroups) or indirect (via changing behaviors) effects on income distribution. Below is a list of examples of both direct and indirect effects, in the order of the demographic groups in question.

In ageing societies, depending on the concrete institutional arrangements of the pension systems, the growth of the elderly population may contribute to lower aggregate income inequality, given the fact that in most pension systems the inequality between pensioners is smaller than inequality among the active-age population, but it may also contribute to higher inequality because pensioners, on average, have lower relative incomes. Also, the growing imbalance between social insurance recipients and social insurance contributors (or taxpayers) induces shifts in retirement ages—a fact that also has a direct consequence on pensions-to-wages ratios and, through this, on income distribution. Furthermore, the shifting of the age balance of the electorate affects the political power of the elderly who, in elections, may have a stronger voice on public expenditure preferences; this points towards the direction of the relatively better situation of the elderly compared with the income situation of the younger generations.

Another example is that changes in family structures can also have direct and indirect effects. The long-term trend of the breakup process of traditional large families results in a larger number of societal units with a smaller average size. The unit of analysis for income inequality (as opposed to wage inequality) is the household. The changing household structure in a country (decline in household size, breakup of traditional family forms such as the breadwinner model, etc.) affects the unit of measurement, and this may have an immediate effect on household inequality, even if there is no change at all in wage distribution. The same holds for changes in household composition by labor market attachment; for example, an expansion of female participation in the labor force, depending on the distribution of it, will itself alter distribution. In addition, and parallel to the breakup of larger units, an additional strain on the welfare state may arise, given the duties of modern states in taking care of vulnerable citizens (should the breakup take the form of the increase of single-parent families and/or the share of elderly single households).

Further, a general education expansion (which was massive in the past 50 years in the OECD area) not only changes the structure of subgroups with higher and lower skills but also contributes to deeper societal trends: more educated voters might become more interested in politics, with stronger opinions on economic or social policies, etc. Related to this, the emergence of a broader or shrinking middle class not only has a measurement consequence but the middle class change might also induce behavioral and attitudinal consequences.

Finally, the change of the composition of the population by origin of birth as a result of international migration can lead to income distribution changes, depending, of course, on which parts of the income distribution of the recipient country the migrants enter. Also, changes in the attitudes or ethnic composition of societies might urge politicians to reflect these attitudes in changes in their policies.

While there are a large number of studies of some particular aspects of these trends, relatively few systematic accounts of the effects of social structures in income distributions are available. When assessing the role of population structure changes on summary measures of inequality, the OECD (2008) emphasizes that income inequality exists between and within demographic groups (of various ages or by sex, for example). That study presented simulation results, considering population demography as "frozen" at the start of the observation period (mid-1980s or mid-1990s, depending on the country) to show the independent effect of changing population composition on income inequality. This highlights that changes in demography (ageing and household structure change combined) contributed to higher income inequality in most countries. It also showed that the effect of the change of household structure seems to be larger than the effects of ageing. Changes in population structure were driven by the increase of single-parent households, a key trend in determining the overall demographic effects.

The effect of demographic trends on income inequality has been studied by a number of papers in the past two decades (see Burtless, 2009 and OECD, 2011 for an overview), but the number of systematic cross-national accounts is small. It has been shown for the United States (see Karoly and Burtless, 1995; Burtless, 1999) that the increase in the share of single households was an important contributor to the increase of inequality. Similar trends were shown for Germany (Peichl et al., 2010) and Canada (Lu et al., 2011), although the latter was not confirmed by another study of five OECD countries (including Canada) by Jantti (1997).

Marital sorting or "assortative mating," that is, the growing tendency that people are married to spouses with similar earning levels, can also contribute to higher inequality, which has been documented in a number of country-specific studies. Schwartz (2010), for instance, found that, for the United States, assortative mating contributed one-quarter to one-third to higher earnings inequality among married couples, with the main contribution occurring at the top of the distribution. A review of some other country-specific articles by the OECD (2011) lists a number of studies showing that an increased similarity of spouses' earnings in households contributes to widened inequality (OECD, 2011) Cross-country evidence, however, is rare. The role of assortative mating can be illustrated by counterfactual simulations (Burtless, 2009; Chen et al., 2013b). As these simulations show, assortative mating may have nontrivial effects on inequality. The OECD (2011) provides an overview of the literature, which indicates that a number of studies show that increased resemblance of spouses' earnings had an inequality-increasing effect, although there is a wide range of estimates as to the relative weight of this effect.

OECD (2011, chapter 5) looks into this issue from a broader perspective, analyzing the transmission of earnings inequality from individuals to households in 23 countries. Results drawn from primary-order decompositions show that labor market factors outweigh demographic factors for determining increased household earnings inequality by far; the major driver behind household earnings inequality is the increase of male wage dispersion (this contributes one-third to one-half to the overall increase of household earnings inequality). A second major factor, but one that works in the opposite direction, is the increase in women's employment in most of the countries under scrutiny. This had an off-setting, that is, equalizing, effect everywhere. Finally, demographic factors also are shown to contribute to inequality. Both the effects of the more widespread assortative mating and the change of household structure played a role, directing towards a larger inequality, though this effect was assessed (OECD, 2011) to be much more modest than labor market–related changes.[72]

In their recent article, Greenwood et al. (2014) concluded that assortative mating increased between 1960 and 2005 in the United States, with an increasing effect on inequality; comparing inequality figures based on assortative mating with inequality figures based on random matching, the estimated difference increased considerably, implying that part of the inequality increase in the United States can be accounted for by increased marital sorting.

In his LIS-based analysis of 18 rich (mostly OECD) countries, Brady (2006) tested the effect of various structural factors on the lower tail of the income distribution. He found that an increase in employment in general, and female employment in particular, reduces income poverty. After controlling for institutional factors (welfare state variables) and economic factors, this was found to be the largest single item with the largest poverty-reducing impact. On the other hand, the growth in the share of the elderly population and the increase in the share of children in single-mother families had an effect on increasing the poverty headcount. When concluding, however, he stressed that the welfare state has a larger effect than structural factors.

---

[72] The effects of assortative mating and other household structure changes taken together are estimated to count roughly half as much as the effect of increased male wage dispersion alone.

The equalizing effect of women's participation in employment also is documented in other recent cross-country studies. On the basis of a counterfactual analysis of 20 OECD countries, Chen et al. (2014) found that if female labor force participation had not increased in the past 20 years, household income inequality would have increased by 1 point more on average than it actually did.

Esping-Andersen (2009) pointed to the importance of demographic shifts in society, sometimes even counterbalancing the effects of large trends such as globalization and technology. The changing role of women in terms of increased labor market participation, domestic work, marriage and education has a large role in the formation of inequalities. As he argues, the process, characterized by women's commitment to longer work careers and to their increased participation in (higher) education, via more equal division of domestic work between spouses and a greater degree of assortative mating, leads to a lower level of inequality within the family (i.e., among men and women), but it also leads to higher level of overall inequality in the society. The latter trend is induced primarily by the fact that it is the higher-educated and higher-income women among whom the process runs first, leading to widening inequalities between women with higher and lower social status. From this it follows that observed cross-country differentials in income inequality also reflect the state of what he terms the "incomplete revolution" of changing gender roles (Esping-Andersen, 2009). A next step in this reasoning could be that because societies differ according to their dominant family patterns (the two extremes being the male breadwinner model/nuclear family on the one hand and a model characterized by dual earner models and shared domestic work on the other), so too do their inequality patterns differ. This conclusion remains to be proven by further empirical comparisons.

The effect of demographic and household formation changes in households have, in turn, different consequences for inequality and income dynamics, depending on the differential institutional structures in various countries. As DiPrete and McManus (2000) concluded in their US–Germany comparisons, the chances of individuals and households responding to "trigger events" (such as partner losses, unemployment, etc.) are different in institutional settings relying more on the market than in countries having more elaborate welfare arrangements. The effect of shifts in income and material well-being, triggered by household employment and household composition changes, is mediated by tax/transfer schemes as well as by private responses to these events. As DiPrete and McManus highlight, the relative role of labor market events, family change and welfare state policies in income dynamics also depends on gender.

The effect of migration on inequality in donor and in recipient countries depends on the skill composition of migrants and native populations, on the process and speed of integration of migrants into the host labor markets, on differential household composition of migrants and of natives, among other factors. Also, the balance of inward and outward migration and the institutional structure is of major importance. Not only the share but also the skill composition of migrants varies substantially across countries. This makes drawing general conclusions on the effect of migration on income distribution very difficult (if not impossible). The effect—if it exists—is thus very much country and context dependent. The vast empirical migration analysis literature focuses on these elements on various target variables such as labor market outcomes, poverty and tax/benefit systems, but they very rarely have the ambition of modelling the full impact of migration on overall income inequality (Chen, 2013).

A few models, however, are formulated to reach some broad general conclusions. Kahanec and Zimmermann (2009) introduced a model with heterogeneous labor markets. Their prediction is that highly skilled immigration can contribute to a decrease in inequality in the receiving countries. The argument (although with many caveats about complementarities between skilled and unskilled labor and about institutional and social histories of the various country contexts) stresses that, in OECD countries where skilled labor is abundant, the degree of the labor market assimilation of immigrants into the host country is key in determining the true long-term effect of migration on inequality. There is a much less general conclusion that can be offered for unskilled migration. Kahanec and Zimmermann (2009) concluded that the effects can be expected to be ambiguous.

As a conclusion of a thorough literature review, Chen (2013) identified a number of challenges for the assessment of the effect of migration on inequality. As he concludes, most assessments are partial (focus on relative wages rather than on the full distribution) and mostly cross sectional (and, as such, overlook the earnings potential and lifetime earnings of migrants). The review suggests building integrated micro-/macrosimulation models to assess the full effects of migration on income inequality.

19.6. CONCLUSIONS: MAJOR FINDINGS FROM THE LITERATURE SURVEY AND IMPLICATIONS FOR FURTHER RESEARCH

19.6.1 A Summary of Findings and Propositions from the Overview of Studies Providing Multicausal Explanations

This section summarizes the main findings presented above from the most important recent studies that provide multicausal explanations and provides a combined analysis of the relative weights of the various arguments set out in Section 19.5. For the purpose of the summary, we differentiate between three levels of explanatory factors. On the first, broadest level (represented by the diamonds in Figure 19.1), there are six different groups of factors:

1. structural macroeconomic sectoral changes
2. globalization and technology change
3. labor market and other relevant institutions
4. politics and political processes
5. tax/transfer schemes
6. demographic and other microstructural changes

As indicated in Section 19.1, we may think of the above factors as "underlying" causes of inequality change. On the second level, there are elements within each of the six broad groups (such as FDI, technology, trade, etc., for globalization or such as unionization, unemployment benefits, employment protection legislation, etc., for labor market institutions). This second group could be included under the umbrella of "proximate causes" of inequality or "hints" at causes.[73] Finally, there is a third level, on which the various authors operationalize their models, that is, where they chose the appropriate variables for their models, which are, in most cases, necessarily second-best proxies of the second-level factors. In what follows, we summarize the results of the level of abstraction represented by the first level. While doing that, we also report findings for the interactions between the effects of the various variable groupings as far as they are available.

As for the major hypothesis of structural macroeconomic sectoral changes (i.e., sector bias and sector dualism, as proposed by Kuznets), the evidence is inconclusive. A large part of the literature (half of 30 studies reviewed by Atkinson and Brandolini, 2009 and 19 studies in Hellier and Lambrecht, 2012) tests the Kuznets hypothesis, but sector dualism does not seem to find support.[74] Alternative explanations of the great U-turn therefore have been investigated in various articles in the past 15 years. The most influential hypotheses of these alternatives related the reversal of inequality trends to developments of globalization and of trends in skill-biased technology change to changes of (labor market) regulations and institutions.

As for the debate on globalization versus technology, there has been a move away from trade-focused explanations to technology explanations during the 1990s. In the 2000s, several authors changed track from their earlier views that the effect of trade on inequality was modest at best (Krugman, 2007; Scheve and Slaughter, 2007). They now suggest that trade-induced phenomena such as outsourcing may have had a more significant effect on income distribution than formerly assumed. That said, while under the pure aspect of trade costs, off-shoring all tasks that are technically off-shorable may indeed be possible, this will not always make sense from a business point of view, especially when transaction costs and economies of scope are taken into account; the assumed effect of a surge in off-shoring may therefore be exaggerated, as argued by Lanz et al. (2011).

At the same time, technological change now is more often understood as endogenous and interacting with trade. More generally, the key issue today is no longer identifying which trade or technological change was the main culprit in increasing inequality, but rather to identify the channels through which these two operate and interact in their effect on inequality (see Chusseau et al., 2008).

---

[73] These notations follow Cornia (2012).

[74] However, Nollmann (2006) and Rohrbach (2009) propose a focus on knowledge sector dualism and bias.

The effect of *education*—human capital accumulation—on inequality is not linear and, because of different composition and wage premium effects at different times, can first be disequalizing and then equalizing, analogous with the Kuznets process. That said, none of the studies covering the set of OECD/EU countries suggest a disequalizing role for the growth in average educational attainment over the past three decades; on the contrary, in their majority they propose a rather equalizing role. Human capital can be seen as a complement to technology. Increases in human capital and in the supply of skills are necessary to decrease and eventually reverse the pressure to higher inequality that stems from technological change.[75]

While it is widely recognized that institutions matter, the weight attached to this factor in econometric studies has long been limited. A majority of (but not all) studies finds significant negative associations, in particular with wage inequality, through direct or indirect effects of union density/coverage, wage coordination/centralization and EPL. Checchi and Garcia-Penalosa (2005) and the OECD (2011) found the weakening of employment protection and the decline in unionization increased wage dispersion, mostly having effects at the lower ends of the distribution of wages. It has, however, also been emphasized that when observed in a broader context (i.e., concentrating on combined employment and dispersion effects of institutional changes), the results were inconclusive because employment and inequality effects of institutional change tended to net each other out (OECD, 2011). Also, Checchi and Garcia-Penalosa (2008) suggested that the combined effects of institutions on factor income inequality are weak, whereas the income distribution effects of high tax wedges (which could be expected to serve larger redistribution to favor lower segments of the labor markets) also has controversial effects (high-wage workers are able to pass on tax burden to their employers, while the overall tax wedge effects can contain considerable unemployment increases).

All in all, it is shown that for inequality trends, developments in political processes are of key importance. How preferences of the electorate are recognized, processed and translated into policies (which, in turn, shape labor market and welfare state institutions) do play an important role in redistributive institutions and, ultimately, in inequalities. Indirect proof of this is found in the fact that many tests trying to find a direct relationship between initial and post-redistribution inequalities have been shown to be inconclusive. While some of these failures can be explained by problems of specification, of identification of the various factors or of data, there are a number of substantive elements of the political system that may have a special role in defining inequalities. Among these, the

---

[75] It can be suspected, however, that this is conditional on the stage of the "race between education and technology" change (Tinbergen, 1975). Most of the studies reviewed here refer to the OECD area for the 1980–2008 period, a rather fortunate period and set of countries where higher education expansion was to a great extent capable of keeping pace with the upwards pressure of the technology revolution. In different countries and in different periods, the results of this race may be less positive for inequality outcomes.

differential mobilization of voters from various parts of the income scale seems to be of a crucial importance (Pontusson and Rueda, 2010; Mahler, 2008). Also, how the actors of the political arena perceive their core constituencies is important. If the parties from the political Left perceive the mobilization of the poor on the ballots worth going for, they may put the issue of redistribution to the poor at the center of their political agenda.

The identification of the Left and the Right may easily turn out to be problematic, especially when representation of the various labor market segments is taken into account (Rueda, 2008). Given the fact that parties sometimes pick up interests of insiders (such as active earners) as opposed to the interests of outsiders (such as the inactive earners and the unemployed), redistributive outcomes might come about as results of sometimes contradicting tendencies of redistribution from the rich to the poor and of legislation to support the interest of the insiders of the labor markets.

When analyzing actual redistribution processes, the definitions of the pre- and post-redistribution inequality (in other words, the accounting framework in which the redistribution processes are understood and interpreted) has been identified as crucial to the measurement of the effects of redistribution (Whiteford, 2008; Immervoll and Richardson, 2011; Kenworthy and Pontusson, 2005). It also has been emphasized that redistribution might have a number of second-order effects. The results of redistribution analyzes have shown that redistribution reduces inequality overall in all OECD countries, although to a varying extent, depending on concrete institutional settings. It was found that "original" inequality (if it exists at all) is reduced by an order of magnitude of some one-third by redistribution (ranging between 45% in some northern and continental European countries to ~8% in Korea; see Whiteford, 2008; OECD, 2011).

The redistributive effectiveness of the two sides (taxes and benefits) has been shown to be different: cash transfers (in all countries but the United States) are estimated to have much larger first-order effects on inequality than taxes (Whiteford, 2008; Immervoll and Richardson, 2011).[76] Among public social transfers, public pension programmes achieve the largest redistribution; however, the interpretation and evaluation of these differs and is dependent on the chosen perspective of Robin Hood or piggy bank welfare states.

There are second-order effects of redistribution, such as those resulting from behavioral adjustment on the contributor side (taxpayers) or the recipient side (social assistance beneficiaries). Some studies are able to show the existence of second-order responses, the magnitude of which, however, seems to be relatively small (Doerrenberg and Peichl, 2012). The measured effects of taxation on labor supply (which is clearly an important area of potential behavioral repercussions) imply that social embeddedness of institutions is noticeable. Studies by Blundell et al. (2011)

---

[76] This is also confirmed by other studies (Mahler, 2010; Goudswaard and Caminada, 2010). The latter study also shows that countries relying mostly on public social expenditures achieve higher levels of redistribution than countries relying more on private social transfers.

highlighted that behavioral elasticities for women are larger with regard to both decisions about entering the labor markets (extensive margin) and changing work efforts on the labor markets (intensive margins).

An important aspect in redistribution research is how the change in size and techniques of tax transfer schemes have contributed to changes in overall inequality. As highlighted by the OECD (2011), changes in redistribution can be seen as causal factors for increasing inequality during the period before the breakout of the economic recession in 2008. The redistributive power of the welfare state was weakened in the period between the mid-1990s to mid-2000s. While in the period between mid-1980s and mid-1990s the share of increased market income inequality offset by taxes and transfers was measured at a level of almost 60%, this share declined to around 20% by the mid-2000s (OECD, 2011).

The social context can also be captured by the effects of changing demographic composition (by age, household types, etc.) and of changing demographic behavior (household formation, assortative mating, etc.) on inequality. While the (composition) effects of ageing and of household composition are estimated to have an inequality-increasing effect (Lu et al., 2011; OECD, 2011; Peichl et al., 2010), the results of some of the discussed behavioral trends (assortative mating) are less clear-cut, but in general also are shown to have an effect on inequality change, mostly as disequalizing effects. Some scholars present the results of the "incomplete revolution" of women's changing role in labor markets and in families as equalizing *within* the households (because of more equal divisions of domestic labor) but disequalizing *among* households (because of differential behavioral reactions of women with higher and lower status [Esping-Andersen, 2009]). Taken together, when modelling the inequality effects of changes in demographic composition and behavior on the one hand and labor market related changes on the other, the OECD (2011) concludes that the former seems to explain much less of the increase in inequality than the latter.

In a nutshell, this is what we found at the first level of factors identified at the beginning of this section (and in the diamonds of Figure 19.1). To give a brief summary assessment of the results found in the studies published over the past 10–15 years, Figure 19.3 provides an idea of the direction of causal factors of inequality that were identified. This summary remains qualitative and cannot be based on quantitative assessment because the multitude of studies use various and different methodologies, estimation methods and data, as well as varying country coverage. Further, it is in part our own subjective assessment. As a convention, positive/negative association means disequalizing/equalizing. "Significance" has to be understood here (and elsewhere in the text) as a statistically significant association, notwithstanding the relative size of a coefficient. "Inconclusive" means that roughly as many studies report (significantly) positive as negative effects. Further, this assessment is based as much as possible on studies covering the restricted sample of OECD/EU countries.

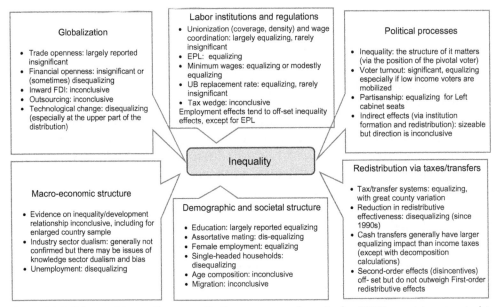

Figure 19.3 Drivers of inequality: a qualitative summary of results for OECD countries reported in recent studies. EPL, employment protection legislation; FDI, foreign direct investment; UB, unemployment benefit.

A first glance at Figure 19.3 reveals that inconclusiveness prevails for many possible drivers of inequality, that is, the large number of recent empirical, cross-country studies report contradicting results, which can often but not always be traced back to different country samples, time periods, data and methodological specifications. In particular, for those factors for which there are more complete and fairly direct measures at hand (such as measures of trade openness or financial openness), there is little clear effect reported, whereas for factors where more proxy-type measures need to be used (such as technology), there seem to be more significant findings. One is tempted to detect some sort of Heisenberg principle: the sharper we can measure a variable, the less effect will be found.

As mentioned above, the summary assessment in Figure 19.3 refers to findings on the different level-one factors separately. To show and interpret the relative strength of the various findings, one would need to refer to studies with a true multivariate design, that is, those covering not only a multitude of countries but also a sufficient number of variables representing *each* of the first-level factors in the models. Because of the complexity of methodological and data requirements, none of the studies attempts to cover all of the first-level factors simultaneously, but a few studies in our literature review were able to cover a multitude of the factors mentioned above.

One of the few examples is OECD (2011), which makes an attempt to study the interactions between four groups of factors: (i) globalization (captured both by trade and financial openness); (ii) SBTC; (iii) institutional and regulatory reforms; and (iv) changes in employment patterns.[77] When explaining the relative weights of these factors within a common analytical framework,[78] the authors conclude that globalization (trade, FDI, financial liberalization) had little effect on wage inequality trends per se once institutional factors are accounted for. However, globalization processes put pressure on policies and institutional reforms to deregularize labor and product markets. Such institutional and regulatory reforms were primarily aimed at promoting growth and productivity, and while they had a positive effect on employment, at the same time they have been associated with increased wage inequality in many countries. What concerns the role of technology development in the period is that it was mostly beneficial for the highly skilled workers, a trend that resulted in larger wage disparities. However, increases in human capital (via mostly large-scale expansion of higher education in most OECD countries) offset much of the drive towards rising inequality.

Another example is Cornia (2012), who examined the explanatory factors of the declining inequality trends in Latin American countries. Among "proximate" causes of inequality, he investigated changes in both factorial and personal distributions of income caused by endowments of unskilled labor, human capital, physical capital, land and nonrenewable assets; their rates of returns also were taken into account. State intervention was measured by taxes and transfers received by households. Household-level income components enter the equation (similar to GIRE), together with macro-level variables such as dependency rates and activity rates. Overall inequality (measured by Gini coefficients) was decomposed into a weighted average of six factors (six different types of income). Results then were put into a broader framework, and changes in proximate causes are interpreted within the frame of changes in underlying causes (these include external conditions such as exports or capital flows, macrovariables related to the balance of payments, nonpolicy endogenous factors such as fertility and activity trends, dependency ratios, etc.), educational achievements and policy factors (related to taxes and transfers policies, wages, labor markets, economic and social policies, etc.). The major conclusion of the paper is that the decline in inequality in Latin America was most importantly due to the reversal of the skill premium (resulting from a massive increase of secondary enrolment), a decrease in the supply of unskilled labor, a return to

[77] In a second step, when moving from explaining individual earnings inequality to explaining household earnings and income inequality, the study adds two additional factors to the framework: (v) changes in family formation and household structures; and (vi) changes in tax and benefit systems. These have been identified as two of the key drivers of the increase in inequality up to the Great Recession, as the redistributive effectiveness tended to decline, mostly starting in the mid-1990s.

[78] For applying a joint framework for capturing the distribution effects on both wages and employment, the study uses a methodological approach proposed by Atkinson and Brandolini (2006b).

collective bargaining and an increase in minimum wages. Other factors such as the improvements in external economic conditions or the endogenous changes in dependency and activity rates played only a minor role in inequality reversal.

A third noticeable example for an attempt to create a broad based modelling of inequality change is Mahler (2010), who sought to explain the determinants and effects of government redistribution on inequality, mostly focusing on the role of taxes and transfers and on the distributive effect of wage bargaining institutions and minimum wages. He tested five alternative explanations from the literature: the median voter argument, the PRT, the political institutional approach, the labor unions approach and the globalization approach. Government redistribution was found to be positively related to pregovernment inequality (as the MR argument predicts), to the level of electoral turnout, to unionization rate and to the presence of proportional electoral systems. Further, a relatively egalitarian distribution of earnings was found to be positively associated with the degree of coordination of wage bargaining. On the other hand, no significant relationship has been found for the measures of globalization in his models.[79] The study also does not find support for the government partisanship hypothesis (share of cabinet positions held by Left parties).

These three examples are quoted here in more detail because they help show how far the various multivariate analyses can take us in understanding the relative weights of the various drivers of inequality. However, for a more encompassing GIRE-type specification and a proper test of it, still better data and larger country coverage are awaited.

19.6.2 Lessons on Methods and Models

We started this chapter with the aim to provide a thorough survey of what international (i.e., cross-country) studies can tell us about the drivers and underlying causes of income inequality with regard to levels and, in particular, trends. In the sections above, we were able to demonstrate how much progress has been made in terms of data availability and use for the countries in the joint set of the EU and the OECD (despite all remaining deficiencies of secondary data sets). A rich literature of studies of various drivers of inequality and their results have been discussed in the chapter. Yet, for the answers to some of the most important questions formulated at the outset, the jury is still out. These relate to

- the influence of the time coverage and geographical coverage of inequality data
- a more precise identification of the relative weights of factors (drivers) of inequality
- the comparability and accuracy of model estimates

---

[79] "Although the prospect that globalization will bid down social transfers and constrain earnings of low income groups looms large in the popular consciousness, it does not appear that a country's integration into the world economy seriously undermines government redistribution in the developed world" (Mahler, 2010, p. 529).

Below we discuss these three aspects in turn.

The articles reviewed in this chapter reveal that there have been quite spectacular developments in data infrastructures for the research on earnings and income inequality. Elements of this development can be summarized as follows:

— First and foremost, some new, large, comparative data collection exercises began. The most prominent one is the EU–SILC, produced annually for all of the member states of the EU and some non-EU countries. This data exercise encompasses a combination of ex ante and ex post harmonized data collection activities (Atkinson and Marlier, 2010).
— The collection of inequality variables in secondary data sets (most recently, the OECD Income Distribution Database, for example) has been accelerated and standardized and moved to annual reporting. In addition, some new secondary data sets have been built (of which the GINI project has most recently provided a rich data set for 30 countries and 30 years; Tóth, 2014).
— For some of the countries, a historical data collection exercise started, which contributes to a much better understanding of long-term trends in inequality (see, e.g., Atkinson and Morelli, 2014 or the long-run data series of the World Top Incomes Database developed by Alvaredo et al.)

In sum, the data situation improved greatly in the past few decades and even since the publication of Volume 1 of the *Handbook of Income Distribution* (Atkinson and Bourguignon, 2000). Simon Kuznets could now perhaps count on a situation where not 5% but maybe 50% of the analysis comes from data and only the other half (rather than 95% in 1955) of the analysis has to rely on speculation. Nevertheless, there are still deficiencies in the data front that impose serious limits on analysis and on a better understanding of the dynamics of inequality from a cross-country perspective.

While there are some data sets covering a large number of countries, there are a few truly longitudinal data sets covering long periods but only a few countries. However, researchers wishing to analyze inequality developments using comparable long-term series of country data will have to make serious compromises.[80] These types of compromises regard coverage (N), the number of data points (t) per country and their combinations as well.

The vast majority of studies reviewed is based on unbalanced panels because they cover different time periods for each country. That means that t has a variance across the cases. If this variance is nonrandom, the estimates may be biased. When missing years correlate in a systematic way with the dependent variable, estimates risk being biased. In addition, for income inequality estimates, annual time series are not available for most

---

[80] As an illustration, in the GINI project, involving hundreds of country experts and producing case studies for 30 countries (27 from the EU as of 2010) over 30 years between 1980 and 2010, only some two-thirds of all the possible cells of the 30 × 30 matrix could be filled with reasonably well-comparable Gini coefficients (Tóth, 2014).

countries and in general not in secondary data sets. Most of the studies summarized in Annex Table A19.1 look at a time period of about 20–30 years, but the number of observations per country differs greatly, from around 3 up to 20.

How serious the issue of unbalanced panels is also depends on the nature of the research question: for some tests of questions, a large N may compensate for a small t, for example, when testing the effect of institutional change (in which case the over-time variance in short periods will be negligible). In other cases, for example, when looking at the effect of macroeconomic changes (where year-to-year fluctuations may be not negligible), it may not.[81]

As we have shown in Sections 19.5.1–19.5.6 (roughly corresponding to the six major "diamonds" in Figure 19.1 representing six different groups of potential drivers of inequalities), studies of inequality identified significant effects of globalization and technical change, of political structures, of redistributive expenditures and some demographic composition changes. However, most models following the structure of Equation (19.3) (GIRE) are partial in the sense that they ask how variable group X affects inequality when controlled for variable groups Z or Q variables. This sometimes can misguide readers when interpreting the relevance of the results. All in all, in the literature there are rare attempts to provide weights to various significant factors; many leave complementary variable sets among the group of omitted variables or assume them to be absorbed by fixed effects.

As an example, studies analyzing the effects of globalization on inequality typically control for sectoral composition of the economy or sometimes for institutional variables (such as unionization or employment protection) but still leave out a great number of variables that could help control for demographic or education structure, for political processes or for redistribution. Similarly, analyses focusing on, for example, politics do account for party structures, electoral systems, voter turnout patterns and the like, sometimes controlling for demographic composition of societies, and so on. However, they also remain "rough," omitting too many variables (related to globalization, sectoral divisions, etc.) and thereby keeping a large part of the unexplained variance in the dark (or gray).

However, when trying to enrich the variable sets on the right-hand side of the GIRE, we run into problems similar to those of growth regressions. This does not come as a surprise because the structure of inequality regressions and those of growth regressions is similar, with just different left-hand variables. As indicated in the literature on economic growth regressions (see Mankiw, 1995; Temple, 2000; Eberhardt and Teal, 2009), part of the problem of inconclusiveness of results stems from a very simple fact: too small a number of countries, too many competing explanations and too short a time series with not many comparable definitions. Mankiw (1995) lists three of these

---

[81] For instance, the U-shaped inequality development in France between 1985 and 2010 (with the lowest point reached in 1998) requires more frequent year observations to perform meaningful econometric analysis.

problems: the problem of simultaneity, the problem of multicollinearity and the problem of degrees of freedom. For inequality regressions, each of these holds equally.

Simultaneity refers to the fact that right-hand variables are, in many cases, not exogenous but products of the same third (sometimes unobserved) factor, which determines inequality, and the chosen right-hand-side variable as well. This problem can also be called the endogeneity problem or reverse causality. Should we find that inefficient redistribution in a country fails to produce the expected inequality reduction, it might easily be that both government inefficiency and the large market income inequality are a product of a third factor, such as bad governance and or distrust in the given country (also on this issue see Robinson, 2009).

Multicollinearity has a similar origin. In many of the models the right-hand variables are correlated. A high level of taxes, for instance, will correlate with high levels of expenditures, especially in countries with higher levels of state employment (which in itself may have a lower level of inequality within this sector). Also, a higher share of more educated people may correlate with higher employment in education, where wage bargaining is more centralized. Inequality regressions need to face these multicollinearities, and researchers need to be innovative in trying to find proper ways to decrease the level of multicollinearity problems.

The third aspect is related to the potential number of explanatory variables. The trade-off here can be summarized as follows. For partial regressions, there may be too much unexplained variance left for the omitted variables. For more comprehensive regressions, the small number of observations limits the options. Given the fact that cross-country comparisons usually cover only a limited number of countries, the increase in the number of independent variables also is constrained. As Mankiw (1995) puts it, "there are too few degrees of freedom to answer all the questions being asked" (p. 306). For a better understanding of how inequalities evolve in a cross section of countries, more data points are needed—but for this we cannot have more countries, only time observations.

Furthermore, with the current amount of information at hand, not all of the complex mechanisms and channels that affect the distribution of earnings and incomes will show up in aggregate inequality regressions. Therefore, attempts to better specify the GIRE need to be complemented with more analysis of the constituent parts of these channels.

A final but important lesson relates to the disciplinary composition of inequality researchers. In our review we covered literature from economics, sociology and political science. Our most important lesson from this was that these disciplines have something to tell and to learn from each other. To share knowledge and discuss results, a common language is needed. As we have seen from scrolling though the literature, it is starting to exist.

As Atkinson and Brandolini (2009) put it, "valuable lessons can be learned but that we require: an integrated approach to theory and estimation; a proper specification of the data employed; and techniques to address the deficiencies of the underlying data" (p. 442). This will help decrease the level of speculation in inequality research—what Kuznets estimated to be 95% and we estimate now to be around 50% because of the fast development of inequality research in the past few decades.

Annex Table A19.1 Summary of multivariate analyses of determinants of cross-country differentials of within-country income distributions

Author, date	Geographical coverage, period and number of inequality observations	Data source for inequality measure	Dependent variable (inequality measure)	Explanatory variables and regressors	Estimation method	Findings with regard to causal factors of inequality	Other main findings
Globalization							
Spilimbergo et al. (1999)	34 Countries (21 OECD countries), 1965–1992, 320 observations	Deininger and Squire (1996 version)	Gini coefficient of personal income distribution	– Endowments: arable land per capita; capital per worker; skill intensity – GDP per capita in PPPs (and squared) – Endowment-corrected measure of trade openness	OLS	– Land- and capital-abundant countries: significant positive – Skill-abundant countries: significant negative – Trade openness (keeping constant factor endowments): significant positive – Trade openness (interacted with factor endowments): significant positive in skill-abundant countries but significant negative in capital-abundant countries	For the subsample of developing countries, coefficient of openness measure itself is negative but not significant
Heshmati (2004)	60 Countries (29 OECD countries); years between 1995 and 2000	WIID1	Gini coefficient of income (concept not specified) for most recent year and average across all available years	– Kearney composite index of globalization (covering economic integration, personal contact, technology and political engagement) – Regional dummies	Cross-sectional OLS	*Overall globalization index:* – Significant negative *Subcomponents of globalization:* – Personal contacts and technology (internet use): significant negative (especially personal contacts) – Economic integration: significant positive (but insignificant when average Ginis are used) – Political engagement: insignificant	Economic integration does not systematically lead to increased income inequality. Overall, globalization explains little of cross-country variations of inequality. Regional heterogeneity captures most of the variation

Study	Sample	Data source	Dependent variable	Independent variables	Method	Results	Notes
Mahler (2004)	14 OECD countries, 59 observations, 1980–2000	LIS	Gini coefficient of households, earnings	– Economic globalization: LDC trade (share in GDP of imports from LDCs), outbound investment flow as percentage of GDP, financial openness (14-point scale) – Domestic factors: ideological balance (5-point scale), electoral turnout, union density, wage coordination (5-point scale), unemployment rate, female participation rate	OLS, fixed effects	– Concerning earnings inequality: financial openness (+), electoral turnout (−), wage coordination (−). – Concerning fiscal redistribution: wage coordination (−) – Concerning disposable income inequality: union density (−), wage coordination (−)	—
Milanovic (2005)	129 Countries, 3 benchmark years (1988, 1993, 1998), 321 observations	WYD	Mean-normalised per capita household income deciles	– Trade openness (exports+imports)/GDP – FDI/GDP *Controls:* – Financial depth (M2/GDP) – Democracy indicator *Extended version:* interest rate and government expenditure/GDP	Pooled cross-sectional OLS for each income decile; GMM instrumental variable estimation	– Increased trade openness: pro-rich in lower-income countries but pro-poor and middle incomes in higher-income countries (from around $8,000 PPP per capita) – FDI: no effect – Financial depth: increases low- and middle-income shares – Higher democracy index: increases middle-income shares – Higher government expenditures: pro-poor – Higher interest rates: pro-rich	Introducing regional dummy variables increases significance of results

Continued

Annex Table A19.1 Summary of multivariate analyses of determinants of cross-country differentials of within-country income distributions—cont'd

Author, date	Geographical coverage, period and number of inequality observations	Data source for inequality measure	Dependent variable (inequality measure)	Explanatory variables and regressors	Estimation method	Findings with regard to causal factors of inequality	Other main findings
Figini and Görg (2006)	107 Countries (22 OECD countries), 1980–2002, 664 (200) observations	UNIDO	Gini coefficient and Theil index of pay dispersion in the manufacturing sector	Inward FDI stock/GDP, squared, and lagged *Controls:* GDP per capita, secondary education enrolment, trade openness	OLS fixed effects GMM	*OECD countries:* – Inward FDI: significant negative – Education, trade: insignificant	– Nonlinearity of FDI effects is rejected when using lagged FDI and with GMM
IMF (2007)	51 Countries (19 OECD countries), 1981–2003, 271–288 observations	PovCal, supplemented by WIID2b (2007 version)	Gini coefficient and quintile shares of per capita income (not defined)	Nonoil exports/GDP Tariff liberalization (100–tariff rate) Inward FDI-stock/GDP *Controls:* ICT share in capital stock; credit to private sector/GDP; education (attainment and average years); agricultural and industry employment share	OLS, fixed effects	*Full sample:* – Technological progress: significant positive (largest contribution to increasing income inequality) – Globalization: small disequalizing effect, (equalizing) effect of trade offset by (disequalizing) effect of inward FDI – Financial depth (credit to private sector): significant positive *Subset of advanced countries:* – Technological progress: significant positive – Globalization: disequalizing (contributed somewhat more than technology); imports from DCs and inward debt significant negative but inward and especially outward FDI significant positive	Using quintile shares as dependent variables confirms findings, but estimates are less precise for tariff liberalization and technological progress

Study	Sample	Data source	Dependent variable	Explanatory variables	Method	Findings	Additional findings
... (2007)	~170 observations (OWW); ~90 countries, 1975–1999, ~170 observations (UTIP)	wages around the world (OWW) (ii) UTIP/UNIDO	...of interoccupation wage inequality; Theil index of inequality for interindustry wages	tariff rate; Import-weighted indicator of presence of trade reforms in country's most important trading partners; GDP per capita; Union density; Coverage of collective agreements/ Social expenditures/ GDP	and regressors in first differences	inequality: – Decrease in tariff rate: significant positive in poorer countries, but significant negative in richer countries – Labor market conditions: insignificant Interindustrial wage inequality: – Decrease in tariffs rate significant positive in poorer countries, particularly in countries with a high density of trade unions; but negative in richer countries – Social expenditures: insignificant	on both interoccupational and interindustry inequality reverses at around the world median level of income ($4000 in 1995 PPPs)
Bertola (2008)	51 countries (14 OECD countries); 1970–2000; 467 observations	WIID1 (2007 version)	Gini coefficient of household income (generally net income; observations for gross income are controlled by dummy variables)	Trade openness (exports + imports)/GDP; Share of government in GDP; Ratio of private credit to GDP; With and without controls for GDP per capita	OLS (fixed effects)	– Trade openness: significant positive – Financial development: significant positive – Government spending: significant negative (estimated by fixed effect regressions)	Government spending is less effective (i.e., less significant negative effect on inequality) if openness is high
Dreher and Gaston (2008)	– 100 countries (27 OECD countries) and 411 (129) observations for earnings – 100 countries (26 OECD countries) and 340 (110) observations for income – 1970–2000, averages of 5 years	UTIP/UNIDO	– Theil index of individual earnings – Gini coefficient of gross household income (estimated from earnings inequality above)	– Synthetic globalization index (KOF) and separately for economic, political and social globalization – Lagged dependent inequality variable; Controls: – GDP per capita and its square – Democracy index	OLS fixed effects and GMM	– Globalization (overall index): significantly positive on earnings and income inequality in OECD countries (GMM: only income inequality) – No systematic evidence for three subdimensions of globalization – Lagged dependent: highly significant positive	– Greater democracy has not decreased earnings or income inequality – Results robust when including additional variables: demography (dependency ration, population growth) and size of government (government consumption expenditure) – Replacing time dummies with a time trend in all models leads to more poorly fitting models

Continued

Annex Table A19.1 Summary of multivariate analyses of determinants of cross-country differentials of within-country income distributions—cont'd

Author, date	Geographical coverage, period and number of inequality observations	Data source for inequality measure	Dependent variable (inequality measure)	Explanatory variables and regressors	Estimation method	Findings with regard to causal factors of inequality	Other main findings
Gourdon et al. (2008)	Dataset 1: 61 countries (22 OECD countries); 1980–2000; 198 observations Dataset 2: 55 countries (20 OECD countries); 1988–1998; 146 observations	Dataset 1: WIID1 (2005 version) Dataset 2: WYD	Gini coefficient of income (generally net household income; observations for gross income, personal income and expenditure are controlled by dummy variables)	– Trade openness: lagged ratio of tariff revenues to imports – Relative factor endowments Controls: – Log GDP per capita in PPPs (if no interaction with factor endowment) – Other controls (inflation, education, ethnicity)	OLS (fixed effects)	– Trade openness (changes in tariffs): significant positive When interacted with factor endowments: – Trade openness: significant positive in capital-abundant and highly skill-abundant countries – Macro stability (reduction in inflation): significant negative	– Analyzing more detailed data (decile data from WYD) but over a shorter time periods shows similar results but estimates often lack precision. – All studies should control for the source of inequality data via dummies and for omitted variable bias via FE.
ILO (2008)	16 OECD countries, 1978–2002, 175 observations	WIID2b, supplemented by LIS, PovCal, SEDLAC and TransMONEE	Gini coefficient of income (not specified but probably both net and gross)	– Globalization: inward FDI, tariff liberalisation, capital account openness – Institutions: union density; collective bargaining coordination – Other controls: ICT share, education years, credit to private sector, public social expenditures	OLS or FGLS (not specified), fixed effects	– Institutions: insignificant – Social expenditures: significant negative – Technology (ICT share): significant positive – Capital openness: significant positive – Education: significant negative	– FDI significant positive only when technology variable is not taken into account – PCA analysis suggests that from 1990s institutions forfeited capacity to reduce market inequality directly and retained indirect influence by virtue of the size of welfare state
Celik and Basdas (2010)	Five developed countries 1995–2007 (FR, GE, NL, UK, US); 5 developing countries 1995–2006 (AG, BZ, CZ, HU, PL); 6 miracle countries 1990/1995–2005 (CH, IN, KO, MA, SI, TH)→8 OECD countries	UNU-WIDER (WIID2), US Census Bureau (USA), EUROSTAT and other statistical departments	Gini index (household, income)	FDI inflows, FDI outflows and trade openness	OLS	– Developed countries: FDI inflows, outflows significant negative, trade openness positive – Developing countries: FDI inflows negative, trade openness positive – Miracle countries: FDI inflows positive, trade openness negative	Results cannot be generalized.

| OECD (2011), Part I | 22 OECD countries, 1979–2008, 333 observations | – OECD earnings database
– LIS (for overall earnings distribution among working-age population) | – Interdecile ratios of full-time earnings: D9/D1, D9/D5, D5/D1
– Employment rate | – Trade exposure and subcomponents
– FDI restrictiveness, inward and outward FDI, FPI, cross-border assets, private credits
– Business sector expenditure on R&D
– Institutional variables: union coverage, EPL (regular and temporary), tax wedge, UI replacement rate of low-wage workers, minimum wage, PMR
Controls:
– Education, sectorial employment share, female employment rate, output gap | OLS fixed effects | *Earnings inequality among workers:*
– Globalization (trade and financial integration): insignificant
– Technology: significant positive
– Institutions/regulations: significant negative
– Education, female employment: significant negative
Overall earnings inequality among working-age population:
– Globalization (trade and financial integration): insignificant
– Technology: positive
– Education: negative
– EPL (temporary): negative
– Other institutions/regulations: undetermined, sign depends on assumption of reservation wage | *Earnings inequality among workers, effects of subaggregates:*
– Imports from low-income DCs: positive in low-EPL countries and negative in high-EPL countries
– Inward FDI: negative, outward FDI: positive
– Distributional effect of EPL is entirely driven by EPL for temporary contracts
– Minimum wage (smaller sample): significant negative
D9/D5 and D5/D1 effects:
– FDI deregulation: reduces dispersion at bottom half and widens it at top
– Technology: positive for D9/D5 only
– PMR and EPL: positive for D5/D1 only
– Union coverage: negative for D9/D5 only
– Education and female employment: negative for both D5/D1 and D9/D5 |

Continued

Annex Table A19.1 Summary of multivariate analyses of determinants of cross-country differentials of within-country income distributions—cont'd

Author, date	Geographical coverage, period and number of inequality observations	Data source for inequality measure	Dependent variable (inequality measure)	Explanatory variables and regressors	Estimation method	Findings with regard to causal factors of inequality	Other main findings
Zhou et al. (2011)	62 countries (24 OECD countries), benchmark year 2000	WIID2b (2004 version)	Gini coefficient of net income (observations on expenditures were increased by 5 points, on gross income decreased by 7.5 points)	– Globalization: equally weighted Kearney index and principal component index – Education level (HDR education index) – Urbanization level	Cross-sectional OLS	– Both overall globalization indices: significant negative – Education: significant negative – Results of globalization are robust to inclusion of education and urbanization	*Subcomponents of globalization:* – International travel and Internet user: significant negative – Trade: significant positive – FDI: insignificant
Cassette et al. (2012)	10 OECD countries (AS, DK, FI, FR, GE, JP, NE, SW, UK, US), balanced panel; 1980–2005; 220–240 observations	OECD earnings database	Interdecile ratios of individual earnings: D9/D1, D9/D5, D5/D1	– Trade openness: total, goods and "other" services *Controls:* – FDI stock – Education (average years of schooling) – GDP per capita – Inflation – Technology (ICT capital/total capital stock) – Institutions (union density and concentration, bargaining level)	Error correction model regression	*Long-run effects:* – Trade in goods: significant positive on D9/D1 and D5/D1 – Trade in services: significant positive on D9/D1, D9/D5 and D5/D1 – FDI, GDP/capita: significant positive *Short-run effects:* – Trade in goods: significant positive on D9/D1 and D5/D1 – Trade in services: insignificant – FDI, GDP: insignificant	Education has a negative effect on inequality (but coefficient not always significant) Union density and union concentration: significant and negative
Faustino and Vali (2012)	24 OECD countries; 1997–2007; 230 observations	WIID2 (2008 version) (missing values imputed)	Gini coefficient of income	– Trade openness: (exports+imports)/GDP – FDI (net inflows/GDP) *Controls:* – GDP/capita, unemployment, LTU, inflation, number of companies	– OLS fixed effects – GMM	*OLS:* – Inward FDI significant positive – Trade openness significant negative *GMM:* – Inward FDI insignificant – Trade openness significant negative	*OLS:* – GDP/capita, unemployment and inflation significant positive, other controls insignificant *GMM:* – GDP/capita significant positive, other controls insignificant

Institutions

Study	Sample	Data source	Dependent variable	Independent variables	Method	Results	
De Gregorio and Lee (2002)	22 countries (1965), 49 countries (1990) (18 OECD)	IMF Government Finance Statistics Yearbook	Gini coefficient and quintile shares (household, income)	Educational inequality, educational attainment, log of GDP/capita, square of log of GDP per capita, social expenditure/GDP, regional dummies	OLS	Nonlinear relationship between educational attainment and educational inequality (inverted *U*-shape)	—
Beck et al. (2004)	For changes in the distribution of income: 52 developing and developed economies with data averaged over the period 1960 to 1999; For changes in poverty: 58 developing countries with data over the period 1980 to 2000	World Development Indicators, Dollar and Kray (2002), PovCal Net	Changes in 4 separate dependent variables: (i) changes in poverty (change in income of each economy's poorest 20%); (ii) changes in income distribution (Gini coefficient); (iii) growth rate of the percentage of population living under 1$ a day (and 2$ in robustness tests); (iv) growth rate of the Poverty Gap (=weighing by distance from the 1$ level)	GDP % of private credit by financial intermediaries to private firms + GDP growth; Instrumental variables: legal origin of the country, latitude of the capital city, natural resource endowments; plus for inequality models: initial (1960) avg schooling, inflation, trade openness; plus for poverty models: initial poverty level	OLS, 2SLS	1. Financial development alleviates poverty and reduces income inequality 2. Countries with better-developed financial intermediaries experience faster declines both in poverty and income inequality	—
Checchi and Garcia-Penalosa (2005)	16 OECD countries, 1960–1996, 210 observations	Deininger and Squire (1998 version) Brandolini (2003)	Gini coefficient of personal incomes	– Labor share – Wage dispersion – Unemployment rate – Unemployment benefit	OLS and IV, fixed effects SLS regressions	– Labor share: significant negative – P9/P1 ratio: significant positive – Unemployment rate: significant positive (insignificant in OLS) – UB benefit: significant negative (indirectly through labor share in SLS) *Reduced form equation:* capital/labor ratio and education have strongest correlation with inequality, followed by union density, tax wedge and UB; minimum wage marginally significant	Labor market institutions (union density, minimum wage, unemployment benefit) are essential determinants of labor market outcomes: labor share, wage differentials, unemployment rates

Continued

Annex Table A19.1 Summary of multivariate analyses of determinants of cross-country differentials of within-country income distributions—cont'd

Author, date	Geographical coverage, period and number of inequality observations	Data source for inequality measure	Dependent variable (inequality measure)	Explanatory variables and regressors	Estimation method	Findings with regard to causal factors of inequality	Other main findings
Weeks (2005)	7 OECD countries (AS, CN, GE, JP, SW, UK, US); 1980–1998; 61 observations	WIID1	Gini coefficient of gross personal income	– Current public expenditure share in GDP – Unemployment rate – Union density rate	OLS (fixed country effects)	– Union density: significant negative – Public expenditure: significant negative – Unemployment: significant positive	Applying the model to two countries with annual time series (UK, US) yield the same strong significance for union density but unemployment and government expenditure (UK only) become insignificant
Carter (2007)	39 countries (20 OECD), 104 observations at all levels of economic development	WIID2b	Gini coefficient	– Economic freedom – Per capita income – Political rights – Civil liberties Controls: – Years of education; percentages of population under 15; over 64; urban; employed in industry; employed in services – Quadratic specification also included	OLS with robust standard errors	Economic freedom lowers equality by reducing income distribution towards the poor – However, if controls and fixed effects are omitted, the estimated trade-off between inequality and economic freedom disappears	–
Checchi and Garcia-Penalosa (2008)	16 OECD countries, 1969–2004, 82 observations	LIS	Gini coefficient of 3 equivalized income definitions for the working-age population: factor income, gross income, disposable income	– Institutions: union density, unemployment benefit, EPL, wage coordination, minimum wage, tax wedge – Controls: – Demography: age of head of household, age of spouse – Tertiary education – Other controls: female employment, investment, openness	OLS, fixed effects	Factor income inequality: – Institutions insignificant, except tax wedge (significant positive) Gross and disposable income inequality: – Unemployment benefit, EPL: significant negative – Tax wedge: significant positive	– Trade-off of unemployment benefit and EPL: both lower inequality but increase unemployment (EPL only without fixed effects) – Weaker effect of institutions on factor income than on disposable income inequality

Study	Sample	Data	Dependent variable	Independent variables / model	Method	Results	
Beramendi and Cusack (2009)	13 countries (all OECD), 41 observations, 1978–2002 (LIS 5-year time periods)	LIS	Gini coefficient for market income inequality, wage inequality and disposable income inequality	– First model (wage inequality): number of manufacturing workers, imports from the Third World (percentage of GDP), female labor force participation rate, proportion of at least college education, union density, government partisanship, economic coordination, interaction of the last two – Second model (market income inequality): wage inequality, stock market capitalization, percentage of population in retirement age – Third model (disposable income inequality): union density, economic coordination, government partisanship	OLS (robust standard errors and panel-estimated standard errors)	First model (effects on wage inequality): female participation (+), percentage of college education (+), union density (−), economic coordination (−), interaction of economic coordination and partisanship (−) Second model (market-based income inequality): stock market capitalization (+), pension-age population (+) Third model (disposable income inequality): market income inequality (+), union density (−), economic coordination (−) Left government inheritance (−)	—
Carnoy (2011)	20 countries (3 OECD); 1960–2003	WDI	Gini coefficient of household, income, highest 20%, lowest 20%	Trends of inequality, distribution of education, private and social returns to education, ratio of public spending	Trend analysis (no regression)	Higher education: greater inequality	Logical chain: higher education + → differentiation + → better (and richer) students to better universities → returns of education differentiate → greater inequality
Golden and Wallerstein (2011)	16 OECD countries (AS, AT, BE, CN, DK, FI, FR, GE, IT, JP, NE, NO, SW, CH, UK, US);	OECD earnings database	Interdecile ratio of individual earnings: D9/D1	First differences over 5-year periods: – Deindustrialization: share of industrial employment	Weighted OLS; separate regression models for 1980s and 1990s; IV (independent variables); extreme	1980s: – Union density and centralisation: negative and highly significant Determinants of earnings inequality are different in 1980s (institutions) and 1990s (trade with LDCs and social	

Continued

Annex Table A19.1 Summary of multivariate analyses of determinants of cross-country differentials of within-country income distributions—cont'd

Author, date	Geographical coverage, period and number of inequality observations	Data source for inequality measure	Dependent variable (inequality measure)	Explanatory variables and regressors	Estimation method	Findings with regard to causal factors of inequality	Other main findings
	1980–2000; around 220 observations			– Globalization: total trade; trade with LDCs – Institutions: union density; centralization *Controls:* – Migrants share in population; Right parties share in parliament; social insurance expenditures/GDP; unemployment rate; female labor force participation	bounds analysis to test robustness	– Trade, deindustrialization: positive but insignificant – Other controls: insignificant 1990s: – Trade with LDCs: positive and significant – Social insurance expenditures: negative and significant – All other regressors and controls: insignificant	expenditures), but in neither period is deindustrialisation significant
Muinelo-Gallo and Roca-Sagalés (2011)	Unbalanced panel of 43 upper-middle- and high-income countries for 1972–2006	WIID2b (Gini coefficients)	(Log of) Gini coefficient (5-year averages) of income	– Civil liberties – Education inequality – Growth – Public investment – Current public expense – Direct taxes – Indirect taxes – Disposable income *Control:* – Dummy for various data sources	– OLS (pooled, one-way random effects models with temporal dummies)	– Increase in civil liberties index reduce income inequality – Increase in educational inequality increase inequality – Current public expenditure has significant and sizeable negative effect on inequality – The direct effect of public investment is not significant (though indirect effects are shown) – Direct taxes have negative and significant (though small) effect – economic growth has a significant negative effect on inequality	– Data source dummy is significant on Gini – Public current expenditures and direct taxation robust in sensitivity estimates

Study	Sample	Data source	Dependent variable	Independent variables	Method	Significant results	Conclusions
Rueda and Jonas Pontusson (2000)	16 OECD countries (1973–1995)	OECD earnings database	Interdecile ratio of individual earnings: D9/D1	Union density, centralization of wage bargaining, the public sector's share of employment, partisan composition of government, social vs. liberal market economy, social spending/GDP, collective bargaining coverage and employment protection	OLS fixed effects	Union density, centralization of wage bargaining, the public sector's share of employment, and government partisanship: significant equalizing effect	The effect of institutional variables differs between the various variations of capitalism (liberal market economies [LMEs] and social market economies [SMEs]).
Bradley et al. (2003)	61 observations from 19 OECD countries, 1967–1997	LIS	Pre-tax, pre-transfer income distribution and proportional reduction in inequality from pre- to post-taxes and transfer inequality (based on household, income Gini coefficients)	Welfare generosity; Leftist party and Christian democratic party share of government; veto points; union membership; bargaining centralization/corporatism + globalization (4 measures); economic development (GDP per capita and agricultural employment); deindustrialization (industrial employment); secondary school enrolment, vocational education; percentage of the unemployed, of female labor force participation, of female-headed households and of population under the age of 15	OLS	Unemployment (+), female-headed family (+) and union density (–); secondary education not significant	Effects on governmental redistribution: taxes, transfers, Leftist government. The hypothesis that the magnitude of taxes and transfers has a strong effect on the reduction of inequality is confirmed
Kenworthy and Pontusson (2005)	11 countries (1979–2000) (all OECD)	LIS	Gini coefficient (household income)	–	Trend analysis	–	Redistribution increased, but the effects were hidden by the even more increasing market inequality. Voter turnout can explain the redistribution paradox (the more inequality the less redistribution).

Continued

Annex Table A19.1 Summary of multivariate analyses of determinants of cross-country differentials of within-country income distributions—cont'd

Author, date	Geographical coverage, period and number of inequality observations	Data source for inequality measure	Dependent variable (inequality measure)	Explanatory variables and regressors	Estimation method	Findings with regard to causal factors of inequality	Other main findings
Iversen and Soskice (2006)	14 countries, 61 observations, 1967–1997 (all OECD)	LIS	Gini coefficient (household, income) before and after tax	Government partisanship, electoral system, pre-tax and tax inequality, constitutional veto points, unionization, voter turnout, unemployment, real per capita income, female labor force participation	OLS	*Effects on redistribution:* Right government (−), veto points (−), unionization (+), female labor force (−), GDP (−), unemployment (+), voter turnout (+)	—
Rueda (2008)	16 OECD countries (1973–1995)	OECD Economic Outlook	Gini coefficient (earnings, individuals)	Cabinet partisanship, unemployment, LDC trade, female labor force participation, private service employment + international and financial openness, government debt, unemployment, GDP growth	OLS fixed effects	*In case of low corporatism:* Left governments increase government employment and minimum wages, but reduce welfare state generosity, with following effects on inequality: employment (significant negative); minimum wages (significant negative); generosity (positive, not significant) *In case of high corporatism:* Left governments reduce government employment, minimum wages and welfare state generosity, which have the following effect on inequality, respectively: − (significant), + (not significant), − (not significant). *In general:* Left governments do not have a significant effect on inequality.	—
Iversen and Soskice (2009)	16 OECD countries, 1880–1990	LIS, Cuzack (2003), Cusack and Fuchs (2002)	Gini coefficient (individual, earnings) before and after tax	Electoral system, degree of nonmarket economic coordination + size of the electorate, size of the elderly population, GDP per capita; interactions of electoral system with decade	OLS (fixed effects)	Electoral system and partisanship: significant effects on redistribution	Proportional representative electoral systems: positive effect on social spending shocks

Mahler (2010)	59 observations in 13 countries (all OECD), 1979–2000	LIS	Gini coefficient and percentiles (upper/lower, upper/middle and middle/lower percentile ratios)	Dependent variable: government redistribution Regressors: electoral turnout, skewness of turnout by income, distribution of pre-government income + share of the population over 65, ideological balance of the governing cabinet, share of imports from less developed countries in GDP, share of outbound FDI in GDP, and a measure of the openness of a country's economy to global financial flows, electoral disproportionality, competitiveness of elections, voter registration	OLS	Voter turnout is positively correlated to government redistribution even after controlling for pregovernment inequality	—
Pontusson and Rueda (2010)	10 OECD countries, 1966–2002	Atkinson (2007)	Share of total income accounted for by the top 1% of income earners (individual)	Voter turnout, effective number of parties, dummy for the existence of Left-wing competitors, median voter, union density	OLS	Left party position reduces inequality, if median voter mobility is high	—

Redistribution

Fuest et al. (2009)	26 EU countries (except Malta), 2007	EU-SILC	Squared coefficient of variation, GE(2)	—	Measurement of the contributions of social policy instruments to redistribution with two methods (standard and decomposition), cluster analysis	- Findings from the standard approach: benefits are the most important source of redistribution - Findings from decomposition approach: taxes are the most important ones (differences can be understood through focusing on the main goal of both approaches)	According to cluster analysis, new EU member countries do not form a distinct group, central eastern European countries tend to show similarities with continental welfare states, whereas the Baltic countries with the Mediterranean ones

Continued

Annex Table A19.1 Summary of multivariate analyses of determinants of cross-country differentials of within-country income distributions—cont'd

Author, date	Geographical coverage, period and number of inequality observations	Data source for inequality measure	Dependent variable (inequality measure)	Explanatory variables and regressors	Estimation method	Findings with regard to causal factors of inequality	Other main findings
Mohl and Pamp (2009)	23 OECD countries, 1971–2005	LIS	5-Year averages of cumulative share-gains of the first, the first to second and the first to fifth deciles and share-gain of second to eighth deciles	– Overall government expenditures – Government social expenditures – Social transfers ratio (average transfers per total disposable income) – Unemployment expenditures – Health expenditures – Gini – Percentiles ratios (P90/P50, P50/P10, median-to-mean ratio) – Left government – Disproportionality of the electoral system – Voter turnout Controls: – GDP growth – Unemployment rate – Population 65+	Panel regressions ($t=7$, $N=23$) with various robustness checks, two-step system GMM	– At very high levels of inequality the positive relationship between inequality and redistribution is reversed (nonlinear relationship) – Redistribution is driven by the P90/P50 ratio and targeted at the middle class (Director's law)	—
Afonso et al. (2010)	26 OECD countries; year around 2000 and average for period 1995–2000	WIID, supplemented by OECD and LIS	– Gini coefficient of household disposable income – Income share of bottom 40% – Per capita income of bottom 20% in PPPs	– Redistributive social spending (transfers, subsidies) – PIT – Education achievement (PISA) – Education spending – Unemployment – GDP per capita in PPPs	– Cross-sectional OLS – DEA for assessing efficiency of public spending – Tobit regressions to capture exogenous nondiscretionary factors in explaining spending efficiency	– Redistributive social spending: highly significant equalizing the distribution (all three inequality indicators) – Education achievement (in particular maths): significantly equalizing – Education spending and PIT: not significant – Only high social spending coupled with good education reduces inequality (Gini)	– DEA suggests low efficiency of public spending with regard to inequality in some southern and continental European and high efficiency in some Nordic countries – Tobit analysis suggests strong indirect role of institutions on distribution, being significantly correlated with spending efficiency

Study	Sample	Data	Dependent variable	Independent variables	Method	Findings	Notes
Goudswaard and Caminada (2010)	25 OECD countries (as in OECD 2008)	OECD (2008) data on income inequality	Redistribution (reduction of Gini coefficient of market income to Gini of disposable household income)	– Public social transfers (and elements such as pensions, active labor market benefits, unemployment benefits) – Spending on public services (health) – Private (pension) social expenditures	OLS	– Higher social spending, higher per capita GDP and lower unemployment: associated with higher income of bottom quintile – Total public expenditure on redistribution: positive – The effect of total social expenditure (public and private) on redistribution: weaker but positive – At program level, pensions have larger effect than unemployment and labor market programs – Excluding health expenditure does not significantly affect the above – Private pensions expenditure on redistribution: negative	
Jesuit and Mahler (2010)	12 OECD countries, 52 observations, 1979–2004	LIS	Gini coefficient of household income	—	Estimating net redistribution (difference between pregovernment and postgovernment Ginis) with three different methods: standard, only pre-pension society, life-cycle based	Intra-individual redistribution arises mostly from government taxes and transfers, but its rate is quite different depending on pension systems and other social policies	Using the alternative method described in the article results in lower values for redistribution than based on the conventional measure
Niehues (2010)	24 EU countries (21 OECD), 183 observations, 1993–2006	European Community Household Panel (1993–2000), EUROMOD (2001), EU–SILC (after 2003)	Gini coefficient of equivalised disposable income	Social spending + lagged dependent variable, macroeconomic factors (GDP per capita, and GDP per capita squared), socioeconomic factors (dependency ratio, percentage of the	Nonparametric analysis, stochastic kernel on dimensional graph + GMM	– Social spending: negative (especially social benefits, unemployment benefits and old age survivor benefits, and not health benefits), – GDP (inverse U-shaped),	—

Continued

Annex Table A19.1 Summary of multivariate analyses of determinants of cross-country differentials of within-country income distributions—cont'd

Author, date	Geographical coverage, period and number of inequality observations	Data source for inequality measure	Dependent variable (inequality measure)	Explanatory variables and regressors	Estimation method	Findings with regard to causal factors of inequality	Other main findings
Immervoll and Richardson (2011)	14 OECD countries, mid-1980s to mid-2000s	LIS	Gini (disposable, market income)	population aged 25–64 with at least secondary education), union density, dummy for post-communist countries Redistribution as instrument to reduce inequality	Trend analysis, decomposition	post-socialism: negative Second-order effects are found to be nonsignificant	– Tax–benefit systems are less effective than they were in the 1980s (despite the fact that they became more redistributive over the whole period). – In general, benefits decreased in real terms, although they were still the major drivers of redistribution. – Taxes contributed less to redistribution. – Redistribution strategies based on government transfers have to be complemented by employment policy
Doerrenberg and Peichl (2012)	Panel of OECD countries (unspecified)	– LIS – WIID – University of Texas Inequality Project (UTIP) – Penn U tables – World Tax Indicators (Sabirianove-Peter et al., 2010) – OECD statistics – WB WDI database	– Gini coefficient of household incomes – Regression estimates of household income inequality from wage inequality data	*Dependent variables (lagged 1 year):* – Government spending (Penn) – Public total social expenditure (OECD Soc exp) – Degree of tax progressivity (WTA) *Controls (lagged 1 year):* – GDP per capita – Squared GDP per capita – Trade openness – Inflation rate	– OLS with country and year fixed effects – 2SLS for instrumental variables	– 1% Increase in government spending decreases inequality by 0,3% – Tax progressivity is insignificant – Social expenditures are more efficient in inequality reduction than taxes – There are indications of second-order effects	– No significance of GDP (as a control variable) for the results – Inflation: slight negative effect – Union density: strong effect on inequality

Study	Sample	Dependent variable	Independent variables	Method	Results	Findings
			– Unemployment rate – Union density – Higher education levels – Index of globalization levels *Instrumental variable:* – 1981 level of policy variables (government spending, government social experiments, progressivity) extrapolated		– Sector bias: significant positive – All 3 globalization indicators: significant positive – All 3 institutional indicators: significant negative – Female labor force participation: significant positive – Secondary school enrolment: significant negative – Other controls: insignificant	– Only modest evidence for inequality trend being inherently linked to postindustrial development – When calculating relative contributions of factors, sector bias has the strongest effect (positive), followed by union density and decommodification (negative), southern import penetration and DI outflow (positive) – When estimating the maximum longitudinal effect (within single countries), sector bias is still dominant, but followed by southern import penetration and FI outflow
Structural and Macro						
Alderson and Nielsen (2002)	16 OECD countries, 1967–1992, 192 observations	Gini coefficient of gross income	– GDP per capita (and squared) – Sector dualism (shift of employment out of agriculture) – Sector bias (share of labor force in agriculture) – Natural rate of population increase – Secondary school enrolment – 3 Globalization variables: DI outflow/labor force, southern import penetration/GDP; net migration rate – 3 Institutional variables: union density, wage setting coordination, decommodification – Female labor force participation – Period indicators (1970s and 1980s)	Random effects		

Continued

Annex Table A19.1 Summary of multivariate analyses of determinants of cross-country differentials of within-country income distributions—cont'd

Author, date	Geographical coverage, period and number of inequality observations	Data source for inequality measure	Dependent variable (inequality measure)	Explanatory variables and regressors	Estimation method	Findings with regard to causal factors of inequality	Other main findings
Rohrbach (2009)	19 OECD countries, 1970–1999, 225 observations	UTIP/UNIDO (EHII data set)	Gini coefficient of gross income (estimated from pay data)	– Sector dualism (knowledge sector wage differential) – Sector bias (employment share in knowledge sector) *Controls:* – Average years of schooling – Natural rate of population growth – Union density – Trade openness (trade/GDP constant prices)	Error Correction Model regression	– Sector bias (income differential in knowledge sector): significant positive – Sector dualism (differential between knowledge sector and other sectors): insignificant	– Average years of schooling lower inequality, in all specifications – No significant effects of demographic change and trade openness – Union density increases inequality
Social Structure							
Brady (2006)	18 Developed countries (mostly OECD)	LIS	Poverty head count Poverty intensity	– Manufacturing employment – Agricultural employment – Female labor force participation, the Elderly population – Children in single-mother families *Control variables:* – Economic development, welfare state	Random effects models and counterfactual simulations	– Manufacturing employment and female labor force participation significantly reduces poverty headcount – Share of elderly population and share of children in single mother families increases poverty headcount – Agricultural employment has no effect on headcount. – None of the explanatory variables are significant for poverty intensity	Welfare state has, in general, larger effect on poverty reduction than any of the structural explanatory variables. Economic development is mostly insignificant for (relative) poverty.
OECD (2011), chapter 5	23 OECD countries, mid-1980s to end of 2000s	LIS	Gini coefficient and D9/D1 ratio (of disposable income in 12 countries and of gross incomes in 11 countries)	– Dispersion of male earnings, male employment rates – Female employment rates – Assortative mating (earnings correlation of spouses)	Conditional reweighting and decomposition (see Chen et al., 2013b for methods)	– Main contributor to household earnings inequality: men's earnings dispersion – Increase in female employment has an equalizing effect in all countries – Change in men's employment has little	– Assortative mating has increased in OECD countries – There is a considerable heterogeneity in the size of unexplained increase in inequality

				– Household composition (five household types)		– effect on household earnings inequality in all but three countries – Assortative mating and household structure changes has inequality increasing effects, but are less sizable than employment effects
General						
Li et al. (1998)	49 developed and developing countries between 1947 and 1994, 573 observations	Deininger and Squire (1996) data set	Gini coefficients (for inequality determinants models: averaged over 5-year periods)	*Dependents for testing cross-country variance:* – Country and years to measure cross- and over-time variance *Dependents for determinants of inequality:* – Political economy variables (political freedom and initial secondary schooling) – Credit market imperfections (measured by land distribution and financial market development index) *Controls:* – Various definitions of Gini (income/consumption, etc.)	– Analysis of variance – OLS with dummies – OLS with instrumental variables	– 90% of total variance of Ginis is explained by variations across countries as opposed to intertemporal variation – 7 of 49 countries show significant decline, 10 show (small) increase in Gini – 65% of the sample of countries show no clear time trend – Financial market imperfection has larger effect on inequality than the political economy variables – Both effects are stronger for the lower 80% than for the top 20% – A more egalitarian distribution of land decreases inequality (benefits the poor more) – Expansion of political liberty, of secondary education and of financial market improvements benefits all and contributes to inequality decrease

Annex Table A19.1 Summary of multivariate analyses of determinants of cross-country differentials of within-country income distributions—cont'd

Author, date	Geographical coverage, period and number of inequality observations	Data source for inequality measure	Dependent variable (inequality measure)	Explanatory variables and regressors	Estimation method	Findings with regard to causal factors of inequality	Other main findings
Cornia (2012)	14 Countries in Latin America, 1990–2009 (2 OECD)	IDLA database	Gini coefficient (household, income)	– External conditions (international terms of trade, migrant remittances, and FDI); – The rate of growth of GDP per capita; – Changes in exogenous factors (the dependency rate and the activity rate); – The distribution of human capital among workers (the ratio of changes over time in the number of adults with secondary and tertiary education divided by changes over time in the number of those with primary or no education); – Fiscal policies (the ratio of direct to indirect taxes, and public expenditure on social security/GDP); – Labor market policies (the minimum wage interacted with the share of formal sector workers); – Macroeconomic policy (the real effective exchange rate and its square); (viii) political variables (the dummies "social democratic" and "radical-populist" and the Polity2 index, which measures the quality of democracy)	OLS, 3SLS, GMM	*Impact on Gini:* Terms of trade (−), remittances (not significant), FDI (+), GDP/c growth rate (−/not significant), dependency ratio (not significant), labor force participation (not significant), education (−), taxes (−), public expenditure (−), exchange rate (−), exchange rate squared (+), minimum wage (−), political variables (−), lagged Gini (++)	—

ACKNOWLEDGMENTS

The authors are grateful to Tony Atkinson, François Bourguignon and Andrea Brandolini for their useful comments and suggestions on earlier drafts of this chapter. The authors also thank Wen-Hao Chen, Tim Goedemé, Alexander Hijzen, Márton Medgyesi and Pieter Vanhuysse for comments and advice on the literature. Numerous comments at the Paris author's conference organized in preparation of this book in April 2013 are much appreciated. The authors also thank Anna B. Kis and Eszter Rékasi for their research assistance. They have no responsibility for any remaining errors. The views expressed are not necessarily those of the institutions with which the authors are affiliated.

REFERENCES

Acemoglu, D., 2002. Technical change, inequality, and the labor market. J. Econ. Lit. XL, 7–72.

Acemoglu, D., 2003. Labor- and capital-augmenting technical change. J. Eur. Econ. Assoc. 1 (1), 1–37, 03.

Acemoglu, 1988. Why do new technologies complement skills? Directed technical change and wage inequality. Q. J. Econ. 113, 1055–1090.

Adelman, I., Morris, C.T., 1973. Economic Growth and Social Equity in Developing Countries. Stanford University Press, Stanford, CA.

Afonso, A., Schuknecht, L., Tanzi, V., 2010. Income distribution determinants and public spending efficiency. J. Econ. Inequal. 8 (3), 367–389.

Aghion, P., Howitt, P., 1998. Endogenous Growth Theory. MIT Press, Cambridge, MA.

Aghion, P., Caroli, E., Garcia-Penalosa, C., 1999. Inequality and economic growth: the perspective of the new growth theories. J. Econ. Lit. 37 (4), 1615–1660.

Alderson, A.S., Doran, K., 2013. How has income inequality grown? The income distribution in LIS countries. In: Gornick, J., Jantti, M. (Eds.), 2013: Economic Disparities and the Middle Class in Affluent Countries. Stanford University Press, Stanford, CA, pp. 51–74.

Alderson, A., Nielsen, F., 2002. Globalization and the great u-turn: income inequality trends in 16 OECD countries. Am. J. Sociol. 107 (5), 1244–1299.

Alesina, A., Fuchs-Schünde ln, N., 2005. Good Bye Lenin (or Not?): The Effect of Communism on People's Preferences. Working Paper 11700, In: National Bureau of Economic Research (NBER), Cambridge, MA.

Alesina, A., Glaeser, E.L., 2006. Fighting Poverty in the US and Europe: A World of Difference. Oxford University Press, Oxford.

Alesina, A., La Ferrara, E., 2005. Preferences for redistribution in the land of opportunities. J. Public Econ. 89 (5–6), 897–931.

Alesina, A., Giuliano, P., 2009. Preferences for Redistribution. Working Paper 14825, National Bureau of Economic Research (NBER), Cambridge, MA.

Alfaro, L., Kalemli-Ozcan, S., Volosovych, V., 2008. Why doesn't capital flow from rich to poor countries? An empirical investigation. Rev. Econ. Stat. 90 (2), 347–368.

Anand, S., Kanbur, S.M.R., 1993. The Kuznets process and the inequality–development relationship. J. Dev. Econ. 40 (1993), 25–52.

Atif, S.M., Srivastav, M., Sauytbekova, M., Arachchige, U.K., 2012. Globalization and Income Inequality: A Panel Data Analysis of 68 Countries. MPRA Paper No. 42385.

Atkinson, A.B., 1975. The Economics of Inequality. Oxford University Press, Oxford.

Atkinson, A.B., 2002. A critique of the transatlantic consensus on rising income inequality. World Econ. 24 (4), 433–452.

Atkinson, A.B., 2007. The distribution of earnings in OECD countries. Int. Labour Rev. 146 (1–2), 41–61.

Atkinson, A.B., 2008. The Changing Distribution of Earnings in OECD Countries. Oxford University Press, Oxford.

Atkinson, A.B., Bourguignon, F. (Eds.), 2000. Handbook of Income Distribution. Elsevier Science B.V., Amsterdam, p. 958.

Atkinson, A.B., Brandolini, A., 2001. Promise and pitfalls in the use of 'secondary' data-sets: income inequality in OECD countries. J. Econ. Lit. 39 (3), 771–799.

Atkinson, A.B., Brandolini, A., 2006a. On data: a case study of the evolution of income inequality across time and across countries. Camb. J. Econ. 33 (3), 381–404.

Atkinson, A.B., Brandolini, A., 2006b. From earnings dispersion to income inequality. In: Farina, F., Savaglio, E. (Eds.), Inequality and Economic Integration. Routledge, London, pp. 35–64 (chapter 2), 335 p.

Atkinson, A.B., Brandolini, A., 2009. The panel-of-countries approach to explaining income inequality: an interdisciplinary research agenda. In: Morgan, S.L., Grusky, D.B., Fields, G.S. (Eds.), Mobility and Inequality: Frontiers of Research in Sociology and Economics. Stanford University Press, Stanford, pp. 400–448.

Atkinson, A., Marlier, E., 2010. Income and Living Conditions in Europe. Eurostat, Luxembourg.

Atkinson, A.B., Morelli, S., 2014. Chartbook of Economic Inequality, ECINEQ WP 2014 - 324. http://ssrn.com/abstract=2422269.

Atkinson, A.B., Gordon, J.P.F., Harrison, A., 1989. Trends in the shares of top wealth-holders in Britain, 1923–1981. Oxf. Bull. Econ. Stat. 51 (3), 315–332.

Atkinson, A.B., Rainwater, L., Smeeding, T., 1995. Income Distribution in OECD Countries: Evidence from the Luxembourg Income Study. OECD Publishing, Paris.

Atkinson, A.B., Piketty, T., Saez, E., 2011. Top incomes in the long run of history. J. Econ. Lit. 49 (1), 3–71.

Autor, D.H., Katz, L.F., Krueger, A.B., 1998. Computing inequality: have computers changed the labor market? Q. J. Econ. 113 (4), 1169–1213.

Autor, D., Levy, F., Murnane, R., 2003. The skill content of recent technological change: an empirical exploration. Q. J. Econ. 118 (4), 1279–1334.

Babones, S., Alvarez-Rivadulla, M.J., 2007. Standardized income inequality data for use in cross-national research. Socio. Inq. 77 (1), 3–22.

Baccaro, L., 2008. Labour, Globalisation and Inequality: Are Trade Unions Still Redistributive? Discussion Paper No. 192, International Institute for Labour Studies, Geneva.

Ballarino, G., Bratti, M., Filippin, A., Fiorio, C., Leonardi, M., Servini, F., 2014. Increasing educational inequalities? In: Salverda, W. et al., (Ed.), Changing Inequalities in Rich Countries: Analytical and Comparative. Oxford University Press, Oxford (Chapter 5).

Barr, N., 2001. The Welfare State as Piggy Bank. Information, Risk, Uncertainty, and the Role of the State. Oxford University Press, Oxford.

Bassanini, A., Duval, R., 2006. Employment Patterns in OECD Countries: Reassessing the Role of Policies and Institutions. OECD Economics Department Working Papers 486, OECD, Economics Department.

Beck, T., Demirguc-Kunt, A., Levine, R., 2004. Finance, Inequality, and Poverty: Cross-Country Evidence. NBER Working Paper No. 10979, http://www.nber.org/papers/w10979.

Bénabou, R., Ok, E., 2001. Social Mobility and the Demand for Redistribution: The POUM Hypothesis. Q. J. Econ. 116 (2), 447–487.

Beramendi, P., Cusack, T.R., 2009. Diverse disparities: the politics and economics of wage, market, and disposable income inequalities. Polit. Res. Q. 62 (2), 257–275.

Bergh, A., 2005. On the counterfactual problem of welfare state research: how can we measure redistribution? Eur. Sociol. Rev. 21, 345–357.

Bergh, A., Fink, G., 2008. Higher education policy, enrollment, and income inequality. Soc. Sci. Q. 89 (1), 217–235.

Bergh, A., Nilson, Th., 2010. Do liberalization and globalization increase income inequality? Eur. J. Polit. Econ. 26, 488–505.

Berman, E., Bound, J., Machin, S., 1998. Implications of skill-biased technological change: international evidence. Q. J. Econ. 113 (4), 1245–1279.

Bertola, G., 2008. Inequality, Globalization, and Financial Development, Conference Paper Globalization and Inequality: Reflections on the Development of a Divided World, European University Institute in Florence.

Biewen, M., Jenkins, S.P., 2006. Variance estimation for generalized entropy and Atkinson inequality indices: the complex survey data case. Oxf. Bull. Econ. Stat. 68 (3), 371–383.

Birdsall, N., 1998. Life is unfair: inequality in the world. Foreign Policy 112, 76–83.

Blackburn, M.L., Bloom, D., 1987. The Effects of Technological Change on Earnings and Income Inequality in the United States, NBER Working Paper No. 2337, Cambridge.

Blanchard, O., Giavazzi, F., 2003. Macroeconomic effects of regulation and deregulation in goods and labor markets. Q. J. Econ. 118 (3), 879–907, MIT Press.

Blau, F.D., Kahn, L.M., 2009. Inequality and earnings distribution. In: Nolan Salverda, W.B., Smeeding, T.M. (Eds.), pp. 177–203 (Chapter 8).

Bloom, N., Draca, M., Van Reenen, J., 2011. Trade Induced Technical Change: The Impact of Chinese Imports on Innovation and Productivity. NBER Working Paper No. 16717, National Bureau of Economic Research, Cambridge, MA.

Blundell, R.W., 1995. The Impact of Taxation on Labour Force Participation and Labour Supply. OECD Jobs Study Working Papers No. 8, OECD Publishing.

Blundell, R., Bozio, A., Laroque, G., 2011. Labour supply and the extensive margin. Am. Econ. Rev. Pap. Proc. 101 (3), 482–486.

Borck, R., 2007. Voting, inequality and redistribution. J. Econ. Surv. 21 (1), 90–109.

Bourguignon, F., 2005. The effect of economic growth on social structures. In: Aghion, P., Durlauf, S. (Eds.), Handbook of Economic Growth, vol 2. Elsevier, North-Holland, Amsterdam, pp. 1702–1747 (Chapter 27).

Bourguignon, F., Ferreira, F., Lustig, N., 2005. The Microeconomics of Income Distribution Dynamics in East Asia and Latin America. The World Bank and Oxford University Press, Washington, DC, 2005.

Bourguignon, F., Bussolo, M., Cockburn, J., 2010. Macro–micro analytics: background, motivation, advantages and remaining challenges. Int. J. Microsimulation 3 (1), 1–7.

Bradley, D., Huber, E., Moller, S., Nielsen, F., Stephens, J., 2003. Distribution and redistribution in post-industrial democracies. World Polit. 55 (January), 193–228.

Brady, D., 2006. Structural theory and relative poverty in rich western democracies, 1969–2000. Res. Soc. Stratif. Mobil. 24 (2), 153–175.

Brandolini, A., 2003. A bird-eye view of long-run changes in income inequality. Bank of Italy, mimeo.

Brandolini, A., Smeeding, T.M., 2009. Income inequality in richer and OECD countries. In: Salverda, W., Nolan, B., Smeeding, T.M. (Eds.), The Oxford Handbook of Economic Inequality, Oxford University Press, Oxford, pp. 71–100.

Bruno, G.S.F., Crino, R., Falzoni, A.M., 2004. Foreign Direct Investment, Wage Inequality, and Skilled Labor Demand in EU Accession Countries, Centro Studi Luca d'Agliano Development Studies Working Papers No. 188, October 2004.

Burniaux, J.M., Padrini, F., Brandt, N., 2006. Labour Market Performance, Income Inequality and Poverty in OECD Countries, OECD Economics Department Working Papers 500.

Burtless, G., 1999. Effects of growing wage disparities and changing family composition on the US income distribution. Eur. Econ. Rev. 43, 853–865.

Burtless, G., 2009. Demographic transformation and economic inequality. In: Salverda, W., Nolan, B., Smeeding, T.M. (Eds.), The Oxford Handbook of Economic Inequality, Oxford University Press, Oxford, pp. 435–454 (Chapter 18).

Card, D., 1996. The effect of unions on the structure of wages: a longitudinal analysis. Econometrica 64 (4), 957–979.

Card, D., DiNardo, J., 2002. Skill Biased Technological Change and Rising Wage Inequality: Some Problems and Puzzles, NBER Working Paper No. 8769.

Carnoy, M., 2011. As higher education expands, is it contributing to greater inequality? Natl. Inst. Econ. Rev. 215, R4.

Carter, J.R., 2007. An empirical note on economic freedom and income inequality. Public Choice 130 (1–2), 163–177.

Cassette, A., Fleury, N., Petit, S., 2012. Income inequalities and international trade in goods and services: short- and long-run evidence. Int. Trade J. 26 (3), 223–254.

Çelik, S., Basdas, U., 2010. How does globalization affect income inequality? A panel data analysis. Int. Adv. Econ. Res. 16 (4), 358–370. Accessed June 19, 2012, http://www.springerlink.com/index/10.1007/s11294-010-9281-0.

Checchi, D., Garcia-Penalosa, C., 2005. Labour Market Institutions and the Personal Distribution of Income in the OECD, IZA Discussion Paper 1681.

Checchi, D., Garcia-Penalosa, C., 2008. Labour market institutions and income inequality. Econ. Policy 23 (56), 601–649, CEPR, CES, MSH.

Chen, 2013. Assessing the Possible Distributional Impact of Migration in OECD Countries—A Scoping Paper, Discussion Paper at the EU/OECD Seminar on Jobs, Wages and Inequality, Paris November 2013, mimeo.

Chen, W.-H., Förster, M., Llena-Nozal, A., 2013a. Globalisation, Technological Progress and Changes in Regulations and Institutions—Which Impact on the Rise of Earnings Inequality in OECD Countries? Luxembourg Income Study Working Paper, No. 597.

Chen, W.-H., Förster, M., Llena-Nozal, A., 2013b. Determinants of Households Earnings Inequality: The Role of Labour Market Trends and Changing Household Structure, Luxembourg Income Study Working Paper, No. 591.

Chen, W.-H., Förster, M., Marshalian, M., Llena-Nozal, A., 2014. Women, Work and Wages: The Gender Aspect of Earnings and Household Income Inequality. OECD Social, Employment and Migration Working Papers, OECD Publishing, Paris (forthcoming).

Chusseau, N., Dumont, 2012. Growing Income Inequalities in Advanced Countries, ECINEQ Working Paper No. 2012-260.

Chusseau, N., Dumont, M., Hellier, J., 2008. Explaining rising inequality: skill-biased technical change and north–south trade. J. Econ. Surv. 22 (3), 409–457.

Corneo, G., Grüner, H.P., 2002. Individual preferences for political redistribution. J. Public Econ. 83, 83–107.

Cornia, G.A., 2005. Policy Reform and Income Distribution, DESA Working Paper No. 3.

Cornia, G.A., 2012. Inequality Trends and their Determinants: Latin America Over 1990–2010. WIDER Working Paper No. 2012/09 appeared under the same title as Chapter 2 in Cornia, G.A. (Ed.), 2014. Falling Inequality in Latin America. Oxford University Press, pp. 23–49.

Cusack, T., Fuchs, S., 2002. Ideology, Institutions, and Public Spending. Discussion Paper P 02 – 903, Social Science Research Center, Berlin.

Davidson, R., Flachaire, E., 2007. Asymptotic and bootstrap inference for inequality and poverty measures. J. Econom. 141 (1), 141–166.

Davis, D., Mishra, P., 2007. Stolper–Samuelson is dead: and other crimes of both theory and data. In: Harrison, A. (Ed.), Globalization and Poverty, University of Chicago Press, Chicago, pp. 87–107.

De Gregorio, J., Lee, J., 2002. Education and income inequality: new evidence from cross country data. Rev. Income Wealth 48 (3), 395–417.

Deininger, K., Squire, -L., 1996. A new data set measuring income inequality. World Bank Econ. Rev. 10 (3), 565–591.

Deininger, K., Squire, L., 1998. New ways of looking at old issues. J. Dev. Econ. 57, 259–287.

Dickens, R., Machin, S., Manning, A., 1999. The effects of minimum wages on employment: theory and evidence from Britain. J. Labor Econ. 17, 1–22.

DiNardo, J., Fortin, N., Lemieux, T., 1996. Labour market institutions and the distribution of wages, 1973–1992: a semi-parametric approach. Econometrica 64, 1001–1044.

DiPrete, Th., McManus, P., 2000. Family change, employment transitions, and the welfare state: household income dynamics in the United States and Germany. Am. Sociol. Rev. 65 (3), 343–370.

Doerrenberg, P., Peichl, A., 2012. The Impact of Redistributive Policies on Inequality in OECD Countries, IZA DP No. 6505.

Dollar, D., Kraay, A., 2002. Growth is good for the poor. J. Econ. Growth 7, 195–225.

Downs, A., 1957. An Economic Theory of Democracy. Harper and Brothers, New York.

Dreher, A., 2006. Does globalization affect growth? Evidence from a new index of globalization. Appl. Econ. 38 (10), 1091–1110.

Dreher, A., Gaston, N., 2008. Has globalization increased inequality? Rev. Int. Econ. 16 (3), 516–536.

Ebenstein, A., Harrison, A., McMillan, M., Phillips, S., 2009. Estimating the Impact of Trade and Offshoring on American Workers Using the Current Population Surveys, NBER Working Paper No. 15107.

Eberhardt, M., Teal, F., 2009. Econometrics for Grumblers: A New Look at the Literature on Cross-Country Growth Empirics, CSAE WPS/2009-07.

Egger, H., Kreickemeier, U., 2009. Firm heterogeneity and the labor market effects of trade liberalization. Int. Econ. Rev. 50 (1), 187–216.

Egger, H., Kreickemeier, U., 2010. Worker-specific effects of globalisation. World Econ. 33 (8), 987–1005.

Esping-Andersen, G., 1990. The Three Worlds of Welfare Capitalism. Princeton University Press, Princeton, NJ.

Esping-Andersen, G., 2009. The Incomplete Revolution: Adapting to Women's New Roles. Polity Press, Cambridge, UK.

Esping-Andersen, G., Myles, J., 2009. Economic inequality and the welfare state. In: Salverda, W., Nolan, B., Smeeding, T. (Eds.), The Oxford Handbook of Economic Inequality. Oxford University Press, Oxford, pp. 639–664.

Faustino, H., Vali, C., 2012. The Effects of Globalisation on OECD Income Inequality: A Static and Dynamic Analysis, School of Economics and Management Working Paper WP 12/2011/DE, Lisbon.

Feenstra, R., Hanson, G., 1996. Globalization, outsourcing, and wage inequality. Am. Econ. Rev. 86, 240–245.

Feenstra, R., Hanson, G.H., 1999. The impact of outsourcing and high-technology capital on wages: estimates for the United States, 1979–1990. Q. J. Econ. 114 (3), 907–940.

Feenstra, R., Hanson, G., 2003. Global production sharing and rising inequality: a survey of trade and wage. In: Choi, E.K., Harrigan, J. (Eds.), Handbook of International Trade. Blackwell, Malden, MA, pp. 146–185.

Ferreira, F.H.G., Ravallion, M., 2009. Poverty and inequality: the global context. In: Salverda, W., Nolan, B., Smeeding, T.M. (Eds.), Chapter 24, pp. 599–636.

Figini, P., Görg, H., 2006. Does Foreign Direct Investment Affect Wage Inequality? An empirical Investigation, IZA Discussion Paper No. 2336.

Finseraas, H., 2008. Income inequality and demand for redistribution: a multilevel analysis of european public opinion. Scand. Polit. Stud. Nord. Polit. Sci. Assoc. 32 (1), 94–119.

Fiori, G., Nicoletti, G., Scarpetta, S., Schiantarelli, F., 2007. Employment Outcomes and the Interaction between Product and Labor Market Deregulation: Are They Substitutes or Complements? IZA Discussion Papers 2770, Institute for the Study of Labor (IZA).

Firpo, S., Fortin, N.M., Lemieux, T., 2009. Unconditional quantile regressions. Econometrica 77 (3), 953–973.

Fong, C.M., 2001. Social preferences, self-interest, and the demand for redistribution. J. Public Econ. 82 (2), 225–246.

Fong, C.M., 2006. Prospective Mobility, Fairness, and the Demand for Redistribution. Department of Social and Decision Sciences Working Paper, Carnegie Mellon University, Pittsburgh, PA.

Förster, M., 2013. Répartition des revenus et inégalités sociales. In: Bontout, O., Hazouard, S., Lasserre, R., Zaidman, C. (Eds.), Les Réformes de la Protection Sociale en Allemagne. CIRAC/DREES, Paris, pp. 237–258.

Förster, M.F., Mira d'Ercole, M., 2012. The OECD approach to measuring income distribution and poverty. In: Besharov, D., Couch, K. (Eds.), Counting the Poor—New Thinking About European Poverty Measures and Lessons for the United States. Oxford University Press, Oxford, pp. 27–58.

Förster, M.F., Verbist, G., 2012. Money or Kindergarten? Distributive Effects of Cash Versus In-Kind Family Transfers for Young Children. OECD Social, Employment and Migration Working Papers No. 135, OECD Publishing.

Förster, M.F., Whiteford, P., 2009. How much redistribution do Welfare States achieve? The role of cash transfers and household taxes. CESifo DICE REPORT J. Inst. Comp. 7 (3), 34–41, Munich.

Francois, J., Nelson, D., 2003. Globalization and Relative Wages: Some Theory and Evidence. GEP Research Paper 03/15, University of Nottingham.

Francois, J., Rojas-Romagosa, H., 2005. The Construction and Interpretation of Combined Cross-Section and Time-Series Inequality Datasets. CEPR Discussion Paper No. 5214.

Freeman, R., 1993. How much has de-unionization contributed to the rise in male earnings inequality?" In: Danziger, S., Gottschalk, P. (Eds.), Uneven Tides: Rising Inequality in America. Russell Sage, New York, NY, pp. 133–163.

Freeman, R., 2009. Globalization and inequality. In: Salverda, W., Nolan, B., Smeeding, T. (Eds.), The Oxford Handbook of Economic Inequality. Oxford University Press, Oxford, pp. 575–589.

Fuest, C., Niehues, J., Peichl, A., 2009. The Redistributive Effects of Tax Benefit Systems in the Enlarged EU. IZA DP No. 4520.

Galbraith, J., 2012. Inequality and Instability. A Study of the World Economy Just Before the Crisis. Oxford University Press, Oxford.

Gijsberts, M., 2002. The legitimation of income inequality in state-socialist and market societies. Acta Sociol. 45 (4), 269–285.

Goedemé, T., 2013. How much confidence can we have in EUSILC? Complex sample designs and the standard error of the Europe 2020 poverty indicators. Soc. Indic. Res. 110 (1), 89–110. http://dx.doi.org/10.1007/s11205-011-9918-2.

Goldberg, P.K., Pavcnik, N., 2007. Distributional effects of globalisation in developing countries. J. Econ. Lit. XLV, 39–82.

Golden, M.A., Wallerstein, M., 2011. Domestic and international causes for the rise of pay inequality in OECD nations between 1980 and 2000. In: Brady, D. (Ed.), Comparing European Workers Part A (Research in the Sociology of Work, Volume 22 Part 1) Emerald Group Publishing Limited, pp. 209–249.

Goos, M., Manning, A., 2007. Lousy and lovely jobs: the rising polarization of work in Britain. Rev. Econ. Stat. 89 (1), 118–133, 01.

Gottschalk, P., Smeeding, T.M., 2000. Empirical evidence on income inequality in industrial countries. In: Atkinson, A.B., Bourguignon, F. (Eds.), Handbook of Incomes Distribution. Elsevier, North-Holland, Amsterdam, pp. 261–307 (Chapter 5).

Goudswaard, K., Caminada, K., 2010. The redistributive effect of public and private social programmes: a cross-country empirical analysis. Int. Soc. Secur. Rev. 63 (1), 1–19.

Gourdon, J., Maystre, N., de Melo, J., 2008. Openness, inequality and poverty: endowments matter. J. Int. Trade Econ. Dev. 17 (3), 343–378.

Greenwood, J., Guner, N., Kocharkov, G., Santos, C., 2014. Marry Your Like: Assortative Mating and Income Inequality, NBER Working Paper No. 19829.

Guillaud, E., 2013. Preferences for redistribution: an empirical analysis over 33 countries. J. Econ. Inequal. 11 (1), 57–78.

Hall, P.A., Soskice, D. (Eds.), 2001. Varieties of Capitalism. The Institutional Foundations of Comparative Advantage, Oxford University Press, Oxford.

Haskel, J.E., Slaughter, M., 1999. Trade, Technology and UK Wage Inequality? CEPR Discussion Paper No. 2091.

Haskel, J.E., Slaughter, M., 2001. Trade, technology and UK wage inequality. Econ. J. 111, 163–187.

Haskel, J.E., Slaughter, M., 2002. Does the sector bias of skill-biased technical change explain changing skill premia? Eur. Econ. Rev. 46, 1757–1783.

Hellier, J., Lambrecht, S., 2012. Inequality, growth and welfare: the main links. In: Hellier, J., Chusseau, N. (Eds.), Growing Income Inequalities: Economic Analyses. Palgrave Macmillan, pp. 274–311, http://www.palgrave.com/page/detail/?sf1=id_product&st1=520792&loc=uk.

Helpman, E., Itskhoki, O., Redding, S., 2009. Inequality and Unemployment in a Global Economy, NBER Working Paper No. 14478, Cambridge, MA.

Heshmati, A., 2004. The Relationship Between Income Inequality, Poverty and Globalisation, IZA Discussion Paper No. 1277.

Hijzen, A., 2007. International outsourcing, technological change, and wage inequality. Rev. Int. Econ. 15 (1), 188–205.

Hijzen, A., Martins, P.S., Schank, T., Upward, R., 2013. Foreign-owned firms around the world: a comparative analysis of wages and employment at the micro-level. European Economic Review 60, 170–188.

Hills, J., 2004. Inequality and the State. Oxford University Press, Oxford.

Hox, J., 2002. Multilevel Analyses. Lawrence Erlbaum Assoc, Mahwaj, NJ.

Iacovou, M., Levy, H., Kaminska, O., 2012. Using EU-SILC Data for Cross-National Analysis: Strengths, Problems and Recommendations. ISER Working Paper No. 2012-03, University of Essex.

ILO, 2008. Labour institutions and inequality. In: ILO, World of Work Report, Volume October 2008. ILO. Geneva, pp. 71–114 (Chapter 3).

IMF, 2007. Globalization and inequality. In: World Economic Outlook, Volume October 2007. IMF, Washington, pp. 31–65.

Immervoll, H., Richardson, L., 2011. Redistribution Policy and Inequality Reduction in OECD Countries: What Has Changed in Two Decades? LIS Working Paper No. 571.

Iversen, T., Soskice, D., 2006. Electoral institutions and the politics of coalitions: why some democracies redistribute more than others. Am. Polit. Sci. Rev. 100, 165–181.

Iversen, T., Soskice, D., 2009. Distribution and redistribution. The shadow of the nineteenth century. World Polit. 61 (3), 438–486.

Jain, S., 1975. Size Distribution of Income. World Bank, Washington.

Janmaat, J.G., 2013. Subjective inequality: a review of international comparative studies on people's views about inequality. Eur. J. Sociol. 54 (03), 357–389. http://dx.doi.org/10.1017/S000397561300020.

Jäntti, M., 1997. The role of demographic shifts, markets, and government policies. Economica 64 (255), 415–440.

Jäntti, M., Jenkins, S., 2010. The impact of macroeconomic conditions on income inequality. J. Econ. Inequal. 8 (2), 221–240, Springer.

Jaumotte, F., Lall, S., Papageorgiou, C., 2008. Rising Income Inequality: Technology, or Trade and Financial Globalization? IMF Working Paper No. WP/08/185.

Jesuit, D.K., Mahler, V.A., 2010. Comparing government redistribution across countries: the problem of second order effects. Soc. Sci. Q. 91 (5), 1390–1404.

Kahanec, M., Zimmermann, K., 2009. International migration, ethnicity, and economic inequality. In: Salverda, W., Nolan, B., Smeeding, T. (Eds.), The Oxford Handbook of Economic Inequality. Oxford University Press, Oxford, pp. 455–490.

Kammer, A., Niehues, J., Peichl, A., 2012. Welfare regimes and welfare state outcomes in Europe. J. Eur. Soc. Policy 22, 455–471.

Kang, B., Yun, M., 2008. Changes in Korean Wage Inequality, 1980–2005, IZA Discussion Paper No. 3780.

Karoly, L., Burtless, G., 1995. Demographic change, rising earnings inequality, and the distribution of personal well-being, 1959–1989. Demography 32 (3), 379–405.

Kearney, A.T., Inc., the Carnegie Endowment for International Peace, 2004. Measuring globalization: economic reversals, forward momentum. Foreign Pol. March/April 2004, 1–12.

Kearney, A.T., Inc., the Carnegie Endowment for International Peace, 2007. The globalization index 2007. Foreign Pol. October/November 2007, 1–12.

Keely, L.C., Tan, C.M., 2008. Understanding preferences for income redistribution. J. Public Econ. 92 (5–6), 944–961.

Kelley, J., Zagorski, K., 2004. Economic change and the legitimation of inequality: the transition from socialism to the free market in Central-East Europe. In: Bills, D.B. (Ed.), Research in Social Stratification and Mobility. vol. 22, Elsevier Ltd, Oxford, pp. 319–364.

Kenworthy, L., 2007. Inequality and sociology. Am. Behav. Sci. 50 (5), 584–602. http://dx.doi.org/10.1177/0002764206295008.

Kenworthy, L., 2011. Progress for the Poor. Oxford University Press, Oxford.

Kenworthy, L., McCall, L., 2007. Inequality, Public Opinion, and Redistribution. Working Paper 459, LIS, Luxembourg.

Kenworthy, L., Pontusson, J., 2005. Rising inequality and the politics of redistribution in affluent countries. Perspect. Polit. 3 (3), 449–471.

Koeninger, W., Leonardi, M., Nunziata, L., 2007. Labour market institutions and wage inequality. Ind. Labour Relat. Rev. 60 (3), 340–356.

Korpi, W., 2006. Power resources and employer-centered approaches in explanations of welfare states and varieties of capitalism: protagonists, consenters, and antagonists. World Polit. 58 (2), 167–206.

Korpi, W., Palme, J., 1998. The paradox of redistribution and strategies of equality. Am. Sociol. Rev. 63, 661–687.

Korpi, W., Palme, J., 2003. New politics and class politics in the context of austerity and globalization: welfare state regress in 18 countries, 1975–95. Am. Polit. Sci. Rev. 97 (3), 425–446.

Kovacevic, M.S., Binder, D.A., 1997. Variance estimation for measures of income inequality and polarization—the estimating equations approach. J. Off. Stat. 13 (1), 41–58.

Kremer, M., Maskin, E., 2003. Globalization and Inequality, Harvard University, Department of Economics. Unpublished Manuscript.

Kristov, L., Lindert, P., McLelland, R., 1992. Pressure groups and redistribution. J. Public Econ. 48, 135–163.

Krueger, A.B., 1993. How computers have changed the wage structure: evidence from microdata, 1984–1989. Q. J. Econ. 108, 33–60.

Krugman, P., 1995. Growing world trade: causes and consequences. Brookings Pap. Econ. Act. 1, 327–377.

Krugman, P., 2000. Technology, trade and factor prices. J. Int. Econ. 50, 51–71.

Krugman, P., 2007. Trade and Inequality, Revisited. http://voxeu.org/index.php?q=node/261.

Kuznets, S., 1955. Economic growth and income inequality. Am. Econ. Rev. 65, 1–25.

Lambert, P., Nesbakken, R., Thoresen, Th., 2010. On the Meaning and Measurement of Redistribution in Cross-Country Comparisons, LIS Working Paper No. 532.

Lanz, R., Miroudot, S., Nordås, H.K., 2011. Trade in Tasks. OECD Trade Policy Working Papers No. 117, OECD Publishing.

Larcinese, V., 2007. Voting over redistribution and the size of the welfare state: the role of turnout. Polit. Stud. 55 (3), 568–585.

Layard, R., Nickell, S., Jackman, R., 1991. Unemployment: Macroeconomic Performance and the Labour Market. Oxford University Press, Oxford.

Lee, D.S., 1999. Wage inequality during the 1980s: rising dispersion or falling minimum wage? Q. J. Econ. 114, 977–1023.

Lee, E., Vivarelli, M., 2006. Understanding Globalization, Employment and Poverty Reduction. Palgrave, Houndmills.

Lemieux, T., 2008. The changing nature of wage inequality. J. Popul. Econ. 21 (1), 21–48.

Li, H., Zou, H., Squire, 1998. Explaining international and intertemporal variations in income inequality. Econ. J. 108, 26–43. http://www.worldbank.org/research/inequality/pdf/squire.pdf.

Lorentowicz, A., Marin, D., Raubold, A., 2005. Is Human Capital Losing from Outsourcing? Evidence from Austria and Poland, Governance and the Efficiency of Economic Systems, Discussion Paper No. 76.

Lu, Y., Morissette, R., Schirle, T., 2011. The growth of family earnings inequality in Canada, 1980–2005. Rev. Income Wealth 57 (1), 23–39.

Lübker, M., 2007. Inequality and the demand for redistribution: are the assumptions of the new growth theory valid? Soc Econ Rev. 5 (1), 117–148.

Lucas, R., 1990. Why doesn't capital flow from rich to poor countries? Am. Econ. Rev. 80 (2), 92–96.

Lupu, N., Pontusson, J., 2011. The structure of inequality and the politics of redistribution. Am. Polit. Sci. Rev. 105 (2), 316–336.

Luttmer, E., Singhal, M., 2008. Culture, Context, and the Taste for Redistribution. Working Paper 14268, National Bureau of Economic Research (NBER), Cambridge, MA.

Machin, S., 1997. The decline of labour market institutions and the rise of wage inequality in Britain. Eur. Econ. Rev. 41 (3–5), 647–657.

Machin, S., 2009. Education and inequality. In: Salverda, W., Nolan, B., Smeeding, T.M. (Eds.), The Oxford Handbook of Economic Inequality. Oxford University Press, Oxford, pp. 261–307 (Chapter 17).

Machin, S., Van Reenen, J., 1998. Technology and Changes in Skill Structure: Evidence from Seven OECD Countries. IFS Working Paper W98/04, Institute for Fiscal Studies.

Mahler, V.A., 2004. Economic globalization, domestic politics, and income inequality in the developed countries: a cross-national study. Comp. Polit. Stud. 37, 1025–1053. http://cps.sagepub.com/cgi/content/abstract/37/9/10257.

Mahler, V.A., 2008. Electoral turnout and income redistribution by the state: a cross-national analysis of the developed democracies. Eur. J. Polit. Res. 47 (2), 161–183.

Mahler, V.A., 2010. Government inequality reduction in comparative perspective: a cross-national study of the developed world. Polity. 42 (4), 511(31) (Report).

Mahler, V., Jesuit, D., 2013. Political sources of government redistribution in high-income countries. In: Gornick, J.C., Jäntti, M. (Eds.), Economic Inequality in Cross-National Perspective. Stanford University Press, Stanford, pp. 145–172.

Mankiw, G., 1995. The growth of nations. Brookings Pap. Econ. Act. 1995 (1), 275–326, 25th Anniversary Issue (1995).

Marx, I., Salanauskaite, L., Verbist, G., 2013. The Paradox of Redistribution Revisited: And that it May Rest in Peace? IZA Discussion Paper 7414 (May 2013). Available at http://www.iza.org/en/webcontent/publications/papers/viewAbstract?dp_id=7414.

McCarty, N., Pontusson, J., 2009. The political economy of inequality and redistribution. In: Salverda, W., Nolan, B., Smeeding, T.M. (Eds.), The Oxford Handbook of Economic Inequality. Oxford University Press, Oxford, pp. 665–692.

Medgyesi, M., Tóth, I.Gy., 2009. Economic growth and income inequalities. In: Ward, T., Lelkes, O., Sutherland, H., Tóth, I.Gy. (Eds.), European Inequalities. Tárki Social Research Institute, Budapest, pp. 131–152 (Chapter 6).

Melitz, M., 2003. The impact of trade on intra-industry reallocations and aggregate industry productivity. Econometrica 71 (5), 1695–1725.

Meltzer, A.H., Richard, S.F., 1981. A rational theory of the size of government. J. Polit. Econ. 89 (5), 914–927.

Messina, J., 2003. The Role of Product Market Regulations in the Process of Structural Change. Working Paper Series, No. 217, European Central Bank.

Michaels, G., Natraj, A., Van Reenen, J., 2010. Has ICT Polarized Skill Demand? Evidence from Eleven Countries over 25 Years, CEPR Discussion Papers 7898, CEPR Discussion Papers.

Milanovic, B., 2000. The median-voter hypothesis, income inequality and income redistribution. Eur. J. Polit. Econ. 16 (2–3), 367–410.

Milanovic, B., 2005. Can we discern the effect of globalization on income distribution? Evidence from household surveys. World Bank Econ. Rev. 191, 21–44.

Milanovic, B. (Ed.), 2012. Globalization and Inequality, Edward Elgar Publishing, Cheltenham, UK.

Milanovic, B., Squire, I., 2007. Does tariff liberalization increase wage inequality. In: Harrison, A. (Ed.), Globalization and Poverty. Chicago University Press, Chicago, pp. 143–181 (chapter 4).

Moene, K.O., Wallerstein, M., 2001. Inequality, social insurance, and redistribution. Am. Polit. Sci. Rev. 95 (4), 859–874.

Moene, K.O., Wallerstein, M., 2003. Earnings inequality and welfare spending: a disaggregated analysis. World Polit. 55 (4), 485–516.

Mohl, P., Pamp, O., 2009. Income inequality & redistributional spending: an empirical investigation of competing theories. Public Finance Manag. 9 (2), 179(56) (Report).

Muinelo-Gallo, l., Roca-Sagalés, O., 2011. Economic growth and inequality: the role of fiscal policies. Aust. Econ. Pap. 50 (2–3), 74–97.

Muinelo-Gallo, l., Roca-Sagalés, O., 2013. Joint determinants of fiscal policy, income inequality and economic growth. Econ. Model. 30, 814–824.

Nel, P., 2005. Democratization and the dynamics of income distribution in low- and middle-income countries. Politikon 32 (1), 17–43. http://dx.doi.org/10.1080/02589340500101675.

Nickell, S., 1998. Unemployment: questions and some answers. Econ. J. Roy. Econ. Soc. 108 (448), 802–816.

Nicoletti, G., Scarpetta, S., 2005. Product Market Reforms and Employment in OECD Countries. OECD Economics Department Working Papers 472OECD, Economics Department.

Nicoletti, G., Haffner, R., Nickell, S., Scarpetta, S., Zoega, G., 2001. European integration, liberalization and labor market performance. In: Bertola, G., Boeri, T., Nicoletti, G. (Eds.), Welfare and Employment in United Europe. MIT Press, Cambridge, MA, pp. 147–236.

Niehues, J., 2010. Social Spending Generosity and Income Inequality: A Dynamic Panel Approach, IZA Discussion Paper Series. Discussion Paper No. 5178.

Nielsen, F., Alderson, A., 1995. Income inequality, development, and dualism: results from an unbalanced cross-national panel. Am. Sociol. Rev. 60, 674–701.

Nolan, B., Marx, I., 2009. Economic inequality, poverty, and social exclusion. In: Salverda, W., Nolan, B., Smeeding, T.M. (Eds.), The Oxford Handbook of Economic Inequality. Oxford University Press, Oxford, pp. 315–341 (Chapter 13).

Nolan, B., Salverda, W., Checchi, D., Marx, I., Mcknight, A., Tóth, I.Gy., van de Werfhorst, H.G. (Eds.), 2014. Changing Inequalities and Societal Impacts in Rich Countries: Thirty Countries' Experiences. Oxford University Press, Oxford.

Nollmann, G., 2006. Erhöht Globalisierung die Ungleichheit der Einkommen? Determinanten von Einkommensverteilungen in 16 OECD-Ländern 1967–2000. Kölner Zeitschrift für Soziologie und Sozialpsychologie 58 (4), 638–659.

Nunziata, L., 2002. Unemployment, Labour Market Institutions and Shocks. Economics Papers 2002-W16, Economics Group, Nuffield College, University of Oxford.

OECD, 2005. Measuring Globalisation. OECD Economic Globalisation Indicators. OECD Publishing, Paris.

OECD, 2006. OECD Employment Outlook - Boosting Jobs and Incomes. OECD Publishing, Paris.

OECD, 2007. Offshoring and Employment: Trends and Impacts. OECD Publishing, Paris.

OECD, 2008. Growing Unequal? Income Distribution and Poverty in OECD Countries. OECD Publishing, Paris, 308 pp.

OECD, 2011. Divided We Stand: Why Inequality Keeps Rising? OECD Publishing, Paris, 386 pp.

OECD, 2013a. Crisis Squeezes Income and Puts Pressure on Inequality and poverty—New Results from the OECD Income Distribution Database. OECD Publishing, Paris.

OECD, 2013b. Quality Review of the OECD Database of Household Incomes and Poverty and the OECD Earnings Database. OECD Publishing, Paris.

Olivera, J., 2014. Preferences for redistribution after the economic crisis. Working Papers, ECINEQ, Society for the Study of Economic Inequality 334, ECINEQ. Society for the Study of Economic Inequality.

Olson, M., 1965. The Logic of Collective Action Cambridge. Cambridge University Press, Cambridge, UK.

Osberg, L., Smeeding, T.M., 2006. 'Fair' inequality? Attitudes toward pay differentials: the united states in comparative perspective. Am. Sociol. Rev. 71 (3), 450–473.

Osberg, L., Smeeding, T.M., Schwabish, J., 2004. Income distribution and public social expenditure: theories, effects, and evidence. In: Neckerman, K. (Ed.), Social Inequality. Russel Sage Foundation, New York, NY, pp. 821–859.

Osier, G., Berger, Y., Goedemé, T., 2013. Standard error estimation for the EU-SILC indicators of poverty and social exclusion. Eurostat Methodologies and Working Papers, Eurostat, Luxembourg, 2013 edition.

Palma, J.G., 2011. Homogeneous middles vs. heterogeneous tails, and the end of the 'inverted-U': it's all about the share of the rich. Dev. Change 42 (1), 87–153.

Parker, S.C., 2000. Opening a can of worms: the pitfalls of time-series regression analyses of income inequality. Appl. Econ. 32 (2), 221–230.

Paukert, F., 1973. Income distribution at different levels of development: a survey of evidence. Int. Labour Rev. 108, 97–125.

Pavcnik, N., 2011. Globalization and within-country income inequality. In: Bacchetta, M., Jansen, M. (Eds.), Making Globalization Socially Sustainable, International Labour Organization and World Trade Organization publication, pp. 233–260 (Chapter 7).

Peichl, A., Pestel, N., Schneider, H., 2010. Does Size Matter? The Impact of Changes in Household Structure on Income Distribution in Germany, IZA DP No. 4770.

Piketty, T., 1995. Social mobility and redistributive politics. Q. J. Econ. 110 (3), 551–584.

Piketty, T., Saez, E., 2006. The evolution of top incomes: a historical and international perspectives. Am. Econ. Rev. 96 (2), 200–205.

Pissarides, C., 1990. Equilibrium Unemployment Theory. Basil Blackwell, Oxford.

Pontusson, J., 2000. Wage inequality and varieties of capitalism. World Polit. 52, 350–383.

Pontusson, J., Rueda, D., 2010. The politics of inequality: voter mobilization and left parties in advanced industrial states. Comp. Polit. Stud. 43 (6), 675–705. http://dx.doi.org/10.1177/0010414009358672.

Pontusson, J., Rueda, D., Way, C.R., 2002. Comparative political economy of wage distribution: the role of partisanship and labour market institutions. Br. J. Polit. Sci. 32 (2), 281–308. http://dx.doi.org/10.1017/S000712340200011X.

Przeworski, A., Teune, H., 1970. The Logic of Comparative Social Inquiry. Wiley-Interscience, New York, 153 p.

Pyatt, G., 2003. Development and the distribution of living standards: a critique of the evolving data base. Rev. Income Wealth 49 (3), 333–358.

Ravallion, M., Loskhin, M., 2000. Who wants to redistribute? The tunnel effect in 1990s Russia. J. Public Econ. 76, 87–104.

Rehme, G., 2007. Education, economic growth and measured income inequality. Economica 74 (295), 493–514.

Reuveny, R., Li, Q., 2003. Economic openness, democracy, and income inequality: an empirical analysis. Comp. Polit. Stud. 36 (5), 575–601.

Robinson, J.A., 2009. The Political Economy of Redistributive Policies, Research for Public Policy, Inclusive Development, ID-09–2009. RBLAC-UNDP, New York.

Roemer, J.E., 1998. Why the poor do not expropriate the rich: an old argument in new grab. J. Public Econ. 70, 399–422.

Rohrbach, D., 2009. Sector bias and sector dualism: the knowledge society and inequality. Int. J. Comp. Sociol. 50 (5–6), 510–536.

Romer, T., 1975. Individual welfare, majority voting, and the properties of a linear income tax. J. Public Econ. 14 (May), 163–185.

Rueda, D., 2008. Left government, policy, and corporatism: explaining the influence of partisanship on inequality. World Polit. 60 (3), 349–389.

Rueda, D., Pontusson, J., 2000. Wage inequality and varieties of capitalism. World Polit. 52, 350–383.

Sabirianova-Peter, K., Buttrick, P., Duncan, D., 2010. Global reform of personal income taxation, 1981–2005: Evidence from 189 countries. Natl. Tax J. 63 (3), 447–478.

Salverda, W., Nolan, B., Smeeding, T. (Eds.), 2009. The Oxford Handbook of Economic Inequality, Oxford University Press, Oxford.

Salverda, W., Nolan, B., Checchi, D., Marx, I., Mcknight, A., Tóth, I.Gy., van de Werfhorst, H.G. (Eds.), 2014. Changing Inequalities and Societal Impacts in Rich Countries: Analytical and Comparative Perspectives, Oxford University Press, Oxford.

Scheve, K.F., Slaughter, M.J., 2007. A new deal for globalization. Foreign Aff. 86 (4), 34–47.

Schwartz, C., 2010. Earnings inequality and the changing association between spouses' earnings. Am. J. Sociol. 115 (5), 1524–1557.

Senik, C., 2009. Income Distribution and Subjective Happiness: A Survey. OECD Social, Employment and Migration Working Paper 96, OECD, Paris, France.

Shorrocks, A., 1982. Inequality decomposition by factor components. Econometrica 50, 193–211.

Shorrocks, A., Guanghua, W., 2008. Ungrouping Income Distributions - Synthesising Samples for Inequality and Poverty Analysis. WIDER Research Paper No. 2008/16.

Slaughter, M.J., 2000. Production transfer within multinational enterprises and American wages. J. Int. Econ. 50, 449–472.

Smeeding, T., 2002. Globalization, inequality, and the rich countries of the G-20: evidence from the Luxembourg Income Study (LIS). In: Gruen, J.L.D., OBrien, T. (Eds.), Globalisation, Living Standards, and Inequality, Recent Progress and Continuing Challenges. J.S. McMillian Printing Group, Lidcombe NSW, Australia, pp. 179–206.

Solt, F., 2009. Standardizing the world income inequality database. Soc. Sci. Q. 90 (2), 231–242.

Spector, D., 2004. Competition and the capital-labor conflict. Eur. Econ. Rev. 48 (1), 25–38, Elsevier.

Spilimbergo, A., Londoño, J.L., Székely, M., 1999. Income distribution, factor endowments, and trade openness. J. Dev. Econ. 59 (1), 77–101.

Ståhlberg, A.C., 2007. Redistribution across the life course in social protection systems. In: OECD (Eds.), Modernising Social Policy for the New Life Course. OECD Publishing, Paris, pp. 201–216, 226 p.

Suhrcke, M., 2001. Preferences for Inequality. East vs. West. Innocenti Working Paper 89, UNICEF International Child Development Centre, Florence, Italy.

Sylwester, K., 2003. Enrolment in higher education and changes in income inequality. Bull. Econ. Res. 55, 249–262.

Taylor, K., Driffield, N., 2005. Wage inequality and the role of multinationals: evidence from UK panel data. Labour Econ. 12, 223–249.

Te Velde, D., Xenogiani, T., 2007. Foreign direct investment and international skill inequality. Oxf. Dev. Stud. Taylor Francis J. 35 (1), 83–104.

Temple, J., 2000. Growth regressions and what the textbooks don't tell you. Bull. Econ. Res. 52 (3), 0307–3378.

Tepe, M., Vanhuysse, P., 2013. Parties, unions, and activation strategies: the context-dependent politics of active labor market policy spending. Polit. Stud. 61 (3), 480–504.

Tepe, M., Vanhuysse, P., 2014. Taking social policy personally: the effect of personality traits and regime socialization on welfare state attitudes in Germany, R&R, European Political Science Review.

Thoenig, M., Verdier, T., 2003. A theory of defensive skill-biased innovation and globalization. Am. Econ. Rev. 93 (3), 709–728.

Tinbergen, J., 1975. Income Distribution: Analysis and Policies. American Elsevier (New York), North-Holland (Amsterdam).

Tóth, I.Gy., 2014. Revisiting grand narratives of growing income inequalities: lessons from 30 country studies. In: Nolan, B., Salverda, W., Checchi, D., Marx, I., Mcknight, A., Tóth, I.Gy., van de Werfhorst, H. G. (Eds.), Changing Inequalities and Societal Impacts in Rich Countries: Thirty Countries' Experiences. Oxford University Press, Oxford, pp. 11–47.

Tóth, I.Gy., Keller, T., 2013. Income distribution, inequality perception and redistributive preferences in European countries. In: Gornick, J.C., Jäntti, M. (Eds.), Economic Inequality in Cross-National Perspective. Stanford University Press, Stanford, pp. 173–220.

Tóth, I. Gy, Medgyesi, M., 2011. Income distribution in new (and old) EU member states in Corvinus. J. Sociol. Soc. Policy 2 (1), 3–31.

Tóth, I.Gy., Horn, D., Medgyesi, M., 2014. Rising inequalities: will electorates go for higher redistribution? In: Salverda, W., Nolan, B., Checchi, D., Marx, I., Mcknight, A., Tóth, I.Gy., van de Werfhorst, H.G. (Eds.), Changing Inequalities and Societal Impacts in Rich Countries: Analytical and Comparative Perspectives. Oxford University Press, Oxford, pp. 195–217 (Chapter 8).

Tsai, P.L., Huangy, C.H., Yang, C.Y., 2012. Impact of globalization on income distribution inequality in 60 countries: comments. Global Econ. J. 12 (3), 1–10. Article 7, http://www.bepress.com/gej/vol12/iss3/7.

Van Kerm, P., 2007. Extreme Incomes and the Estimation of Poverty and Inequality Indicators from EUSILC. IRISS Working Paper Series, CEPS-Instead, Luxembourg, p. 51.

Van Kerm, P., Pi Alperin, M.N., 2013. 2013: inequality, growth and mobility: the intertemporal distribution of income in European countries 2003–2007. Econ. Model. 35, 931–939.

Van Reenen, J., 2011. Wage Inequality, Technology and Trade: 21st Century Evidence. CEP Occasional Paper No. 28, London.

Vanhuysse, P., 2002. Efficiency in politics: competing economic approaches. Polit. Stud. 50 (1), 136–149.

Vecernik, J., 2010. Earnings disparities and income inequality in CEE countries: an analysis of development and relationships. Luxembourg Working Paper, Luxemburg. Retrieved from, http://papers.ssrn.com/sol3/papers.cfm?abstract_id=1806991.

Verhoogen, E., 2008. Trade, quality upgrading and wage inequality in the Mexican manufacturing sector" Q. J. Econ. 123 (2), 489–530.

Ward, T., Lelkes, O., Sutherland, H., Tóth, I.Gy. (Eds.), 2009. European Inequalities: Social Inclusion and Income Distribution in the European Union, Tárki, Budapest, 214 pp.

Weeks, J., 2005. Inequality Trends in Some Developed OECD Countries, DESA Working Paper No. 6, UN.

Wheeler, C.H., 2005. Evidence on wage inequality, worker education, and technology. Fed. Reserve Bank St. Louis Rev. 87 (3), 375–393.

Whiteford, P., 2008. How much redistribution do governments achieve? The role of cash transfers and household taxes. In: OECD, Growing Unequal? OECD Publishing, Paris, pp. 97–121 (Chapter 4).

Wood, A., 1994. North-South Trade, Employment and Inequality: Changing Fortunes in a Skill-Driven World. Clarendon Press, Oxford.

Wood, A., 1998. Globalisation and the rise in labour market inequalities. Econ. J. 108 (450), 1463–1482.

Zhou, L., Biswasy, B., Bowlesz, B., Saunders, P., 2011. Impact of globalization on income distribution inequality in 60 countries. Global Econ. J. 11 (1), 1–16, Article 1.

CHAPTER 20

Globalization and Inequality

Ravi Kanbur
Cornell University, Ithaca, NY, USA

Contents

Abstract

To what extent can increasing inequality be explained by globalization? And if there is a connection, what if anything can and should be done about it? This chapter begins with an overview of how conventional trade theory has fared in predicting changes in inequality and how it has needed to be extended and expanded when, contrary to some received wisdom, greater global integration is associated with increasing inequality in developed and developing countries. From there, the chapter goes well beyond these concerns to take in the effects of crises on inequality, globalization and gender inequality, openness and spatial inequality, and the effect of international migration on inequality. Finally, reviews of the latest developments in the design of national and global policy to address the challenges of globalization and inequality are presented. The literature reviewed is lively and flourishing. Having animated the economic analysis and policy discourse for the past half century, the globalization–inequality nexus seems set to continue in this vein in the coming decades.

Keywords

Globalization, Inequality, New trade theory and inequality, Crises and inequality, Globalization and gender, Spatial inequality, International migration and inequality, National policy, Global policy

JEL Classification Codes

D31, D33, F15, F24, F61, F63, F68, 019, 024

Handbook of Income Distribution, Volume 2B
ISSN 1574-0056, http://dx.doi.org/10.1016/B978-0-444-59429-7.00021-2

20.1. INTRODUCTION

Globalization is the dominant economic phenomenon of the last 30 years. Openness in trade, investment, and financial flows has grown dramatically. Inequalities within countries have also increased significantly during this period.[1] The natural question to ask is whether there is a connection between the two. To what extent can the increase in inequality be explained by globalization? And, if there is a connection, what if anything can and should be done about it?

Any exploration of inequality must begin by specifying inequality of what and inequality between whom. The focus in this chapter is on income inequality, although quite often measurement will be confined to inequality of consumption expenditure. As for inequality between whom, this can be between all individuals in the world, between nations, between individuals within nations, or between broad groupings within the nation. The focus of this chapter is inequality within developing nations. However, this in no way suggests that globalization is unimportant to inequality in developed countries. Evidence on inequality in developed countries is also referred to as relevant throughout this chapter. The inequality considered is primarily between individuals, but inequality between broadly defined groups within the nation (spatial and gender)—will also be discussed. The measure of inequality, which determines what aspect of the income distribution is emphasized, is also a relevant consideration. For the most part, this chapter considers standard measures of inequality such as the Gini coefficient.

A simple framework for linking income distribution and globalization is to write income as derived from different assets and the return on those assets plus net transfers. The transfers can be further disaggregated into private and public transfers. Assets can be disaggregated into basic factors such as land, labor, and capital, although further disaggregation, especially of labor between different skill levels, is also sometimes useful. The assets of an individual are therefore the capital and land that individual owns, plus the human capital embodied in that individual's labor power. The evolution of income distribution can then be decomposed into the evolution of assets, the evolution of rates of return to these assets, and the evolution of public and private transfers.

As noted above, different economic dimensions of globalization can be measured by increases in trade, investment, financial flows, and migration across national borders. These are of course outcome variables, determined by more fundamental causal variables such as natural endowment differences between nations and national and global policy. The literature often slips into the practice of labeling increases in trade, for example, as the causal factor whose consequences for inequality need to be investigated. This chapter is not immune to this tendency, but the caveat must always be borne in mind.

The focus of the large and growing literature that looks to uncover the links between globalization and inequality is primarily through the effects of globalization on rates of

---

[1] Chapter 9 of this volume covers trends in income inequality in developing and emerging economies, while Chapter 8 is devoted to inequality trends in developed countries.

return to assets, holding fixed the asset distributions. Even when assets are considered as mobile, the focus is on the impact of this mobility on returns to assets rather than on the distribution of assets. Within the analysis of returns, the literature is structured around gaps in returns to capital as a whole and labor as a whole, and around the gaps in returns to skilled and unskilled labor. The underlying assumption is that a widening in these gaps will increase interpersonal inequality as measured through standard indices such as the Gini coefficient. Because individuals who get their income primarily from capital generally have higher incomes than those who get their income primarily from labor and because skilled individuals generally have higher incomes than unskilled individuals, this is not an unreasonable assumption to make. However, it should be stressed that one cannot read directly from factor returns to the inequality of personal incomes. The distribution depends not only on factor prices but also on quantities. Nevertheless, in much of the literature, an analysis of inequality is replaced by an analysis of differentials in returns to capital and to labor at different skill levels.

Once the market distribution of income is determined, public and private transfers will contribute to the outcome of the final income distribution. These can be equally important as determinants of inequality, and globalization can affect them as well. First, international remittances, a natural consequence of international migration, can affect inequality in developing countries. Second, the greater ability of capital and high-income labor to cross borders can also have an impact on the progressivity of public tax and transfer regimes and thus on final inequality. This channel from globalization to inequality also needs to be considered.

With this background, the structure and plan of this chapter is as follows: Section 20.2 begins with the state of play in the three decades after World War II, from the 1950s through to the 1970s. The focus here will be on how the distributional predictions of the Hecksher–Ohlin (H–O) model, particularly the Stolper–Samuelson theorem, meshed with the great policy debates of the time, especially around the significance of the East Asian experience. These economies delivered a "growth with equity" miracle in a regime of trade openness at a time when other economies with import substitution regimes were either stagnating with low growth rates (like India) or were growing but with high and rising levels of inequality (like Brazil). This experience was consistent with the prediction that in economies that were abundant in unskilled labor, opening up would lead to a narrowing of the gap between unskilled labor on the one hand, and skilled labor and capital on the other hand. The East Asian experience was crucial to informing the debate and to persuading the international financial institutions and, in turn, many developing country governments to open out their economies in the 1980s and 1990s.

Section 20.3 provides a thumbnail sketch of the evolution of within-country inequality in the 1980s, 1990s, and 2000s, with a particular focus on the impact of openness.[2]

---

[2] This brief review complements the more detailed discussion of post-1970 trends in inequality in developing countries in Chapter 9.

The bottom line is that openness seems to have been associated with increases in pretransfer inequality. Clearly, this pattern from the 1980s onward questions the validity of the basic H–O framework in explaining the inequality consequences of trade, especially because inequality rose both in economies that were relatively labor abundant and in those that were relatively labor scarce. The section then turns to a range of new theories, particularly those emphasizing heterogeneity of workers and firms and market-based selection effects intensified by trade. Such a perspective, it turns out, is more successful in explaining the stylized facts of openness and inequality in the last three decades.

Sections 20.2 and 20.3 focus on a particular notion of openness (greater levels of trade and cross-border investment), a particular entry point to income distribution (differential rates of return to broadly defined factors of production), and a particular notion of inequality (between persons within nations). These are of course major strands in the literature. However, the remaining sections of the chapter take up a number of extensions, modifications, and generalizations that have developed in the last few years from this base.

Section 20.4 focuses on an aspect of globalization that became prominent with the East Asian crisis in 1997 and occupied policy makers' thinking strongly in the 2008 global financial crisis. How do crises induced by globalization of financial flows affect inequality within countries? There is significant literature developed on this topic based on country studies and global analysis for the crises of the 1990s and the 2000s. This section will review this literature and take stock.

Section 20.5 takes up a particular dimension of inequality—gender inequality.[3] This is an important aspect of inequality in its own right, with substantial and significant literature focusing specifically on globalization and gender inequality. For example, the Bangladesh garment sector or the Mexican maquiladoras employ women disproportionately, and there is heated debate about the conditions of work in these sectors and whether the women are better off here compared to the best alternative.[4] The empirical literature matches the policy debate, supporting both sides of the argument, and will bear a systematic review to draw out the main analytical issues and "centre of gravity" of the conclusions.

Section 20.6 addresses a dimension of inequality that is prominent in the policy discourse—spatial inequality within a country. This can be seen merely as a component or a contributor to interpersonal inequality, but doing so would miss important recent analytical and policy strands in the literature—for example, how agglomeration economies interact with openness, or the political economy of uneven development within a country.

Section 20.7 begins the assessment of openness, transfers, and inequality by looking at private transfers through remittances. It also takes up the more general question of the

---

[3] The general question of gender and inequality is taken up in Chapter 12.

[4] This also highlights the difference between income and broader measures of well-being, including for example health and safety standards.

impact of international migration on inequality in developing countries. Can migration and remittances exacerbate domestic inequality? There is some evidence that it can, and this may be a contributory factor in the association between global integration and within-country inequality.

Section 20.8 moves to public transfers and public policy in general and asks how greater mobility of capital and skilled labor in particular may constrain governments from pursuing progressive tax and transfer policies with consequences for inequality in the final distribution of income. This section also takes up the more general question of international coordination of public policy to address the impact of openness on inequality.

Section 20.9 concludes the discussion with suggestions for areas of further research. A final caveat is in order, however. This chapter is about globalization and inequality, and the focus is naturally on the links from globalization to inequality. As such, it may sometimes give the impression that globalization is the main factor behind inequality increase. There are of course other forces affecting inequality, and trade and capital flows may not even be the most important factors, although they surely interact with and influence a range of structural and policy influences on inequality.

20.2. IMMEDIATE POST-WAR THEORIES, PREDICTIONS, AND EVIDENCE

Although economic historians have been interested in the links between globalization and inequality in the nineteenth and early twentieth centuries,[5] we begin this discussion by considering the first three decades after World War II. At the start of this period, much of the development literature was focused away from global opportunities. It was either concerned primarily with domestic processes to the neglect of the global context, or it was suspicious of international trade, investment, and capital flows.

An example of a theory of development that was isolated from global forces is the classic Lewis (1954) surplus labor perspective. In the first part of this paper, Lewis analyzes a pure closed economy in terms of drawing labor away from the traditional surplus labor sector toward modern capitalist forms of production, a process that continues until labor becomes scarce and wages start rising.

What is interesting and not very well appreciated, however, is that the Lewis (1954) paper was in two parts. Part II of the paper deals with the open economy in the phase when surplus labor is exhausted:

When capital accumulation catches up with the labour supply, wages begin to rise above the subsistence level, and the capitalist surplus is adversely affected. However, if there is still surplus labour in other countries, the capitalists can avoid this in one of two ways, by encouraging

---

[5] See for example Lindert and Willamson (2001).

immigration or by exporting their capital to countries where there is still abundant labour at a subsistence wage.

Lewis (1954, p. 176)

Lewis carries out a detailed analysis of a number of archetypical cases of trade and investment. Among his conclusions are the following:

The export of capital reduces capital formation at home, and so keeps wages down. This is offset if the capital export cheapens the things which workers import, or raises wage costs in competing countries. But it is aggravated if the capital export raises the cost of imports or reduces costs in competing countries. . . . The importation of foreign capital does not raise real wages in countries which have surplus labour, unless the capital results in increased productivity in the commodities which they produce for their own consumption. . . . The Law of Comparative Costs is just as valid in countries with surplus labour as it is in others. But whereas in the latter it is a valid foundation of arguments for free trade, in the former it is an equally valid foundation of arguments for protection.

Lewis (1954, p. 189)

This perspective on openness dovetailed with other perspectives such as export pessimism on the demand for products produced by developing countries. Many models of development at this time were built on this foundation. Overall, it would be fair to say that Lewis was indeed suspicious of openness in trade and investment raising wages relative to the return to capital in a country with surplus labor. In addition, in his other writings, he was quite "Kuznetsian" in seeing the initial stages of development as leading to rising inequality because, as he said (Lewis, 1976),

Development must be inegalitarian because it does not start in every part of the economy at the same time. . . . There may be one such enclave in an economy, or several; but at the start development enclaves include only a small minority of the population. (p. 26).

Thus, as opportunities opened up for trade they would be taken by some and not others and this would create inequality. At the same time, surplus labor would prevent the narrowing of the inequality on average between labor and capital. Overall, then, a pessimistic view exists on globalization and inequality.

Counter to this perspective is a view of the world without surplus labor, with trade between economies with different degrees of labor scarcity. This neoclassical H–O model famously leads to the "Stolper–Samuelson" conclusion that opening up of trade will raise the relative return of the relatively abundant factor. Because in developing countries this factor is labor relative to capital, it must follow that opening up will narrow the differential in rates of return to labor and capital. Making the reasonable assumption that owners of capital are richer than those who earn their living through their labor power, it follows that globalization will reduce inequality in developing countries.

These theoretical perspectives corresponded, of course, to policy stances. Most developing countries in the immediate post-war period adopted import substitution strategies—convinced that opening up would be bad for growth and for inequality.

Elaborate multisector planning models, such as those for the first Indian 5-year plans, had these key elements of a focus on domestic markets and domestic industrialization. Latin American countries adopted import substitution strategies, as did the newly independent African countries in the 1960s and 1970s. However, a group of countries in East Asia went against this trend and, from the 1960s onward, pursued policies of integration with the global economy. There is of course a huge debate on the details of these strategies. In particular, there is debate on the extent to which their policies can be classified as "free market" policies. However, there is no question that for three decades after the war, these economies, in contrast to other economies discussed above, did indeed integrate into the world economy in a purposive manner.

The East Asia experience was crucial to the policy debates of the 1970s and 1980s and to the turn in policies that one began to see in the rest of the developing word from the 1980s and 1990s onward. The 1960s and 1970s saw what has been dubbed the "East Asia miracle" of growth with equity. Not only did this group of countries have historically high growth rates, and higher growth rates than their contemporaries, they also managed growth with falling levels of inequality. The combination of high growth and falling inequality meant a sterling record in poverty reduction as well.

Of course the details of the inequality performance are varied and are not quite so uniform across countries and over time. There were periods of increasing inequality in some of the countries, and there were differences between Northeast Asia and Southeast Asia.[6] But there is a general acceptance that the East Asia story is one of growth with inequality kept in check. However, the interpretation of the facts is a different story. Already alluded to is the use of experience to support both the "free market" and the "judicial intervention" strands of the policy debate. The distributional outcomes have similarly been interpreted in different ways. One straightforward interpretation is in terms of support for the neoclassical H–O model with its prediction that opening up would narrow the returns to labor and capital and, with it, bring about a reduction in inequality. Indeed, this was the interpretation that was most used by those urging other countries, like India, to adopt outward-oriented policies. Thus, the classic exposition by Bhagwati and Desai (1970) represents a turning away from the nostrums of the immediate post-war, post-independence consensus in India that equitable development could only be achieved through import substitution and industrial planning. This strand of literature found its apogee in a series of studies by the World Bank in the 1980s, including for example, in Papageorgiou et al. (1990), the capstone to publications entitled the "Liberalizing Foreign Trade Series." The contrast of East Asia with stagnation in India and growth with inequality in Brazil was very much highlighted in this literature. At the same time, the integration of Europe through the European Union, and the success it

---

[6] World Bank (1993) and Jomo (2006).

delivered over a long period of high growth with falling inequality in the immediate post-war decades, was also relevant in the policy discourse.

However, the East Asian experience has also been used to support the thesis that the equity dimensions of outcomes owe a significant amount to other structural and policy features. Among these are the land reforms instituted by the occupying American forces in South Korea in the 1940s and 1950s, which meant that they entered the next phase of development, in the 1960s and 1970s, with supportive initial conditions for equitable development. Further, in these countries and in other East Asian countries, proactive policy had ensured a very wide spread of basic education. Here is how Adelman (n.d.), the leading scholar of South Korean development strategy at that time, sets out these structural factors in the country from the end of World War II until the beginning of the 1960s:

> There were two waves of land reform, in 1947 and 1949. In 1947, the U.S. military government decreed that the land confiscated from Japanese farmers and Japanese corporations should be redistributed to tenants.... The second wave of land reform redistributed the holdings of Korean landlords owning more than 3 chongbo (7.5 acres or about 3 hectares) to tenant farmers and landless farm laborers.... The distribution of land holdings became very even.... The bulk of government investment during this period was on social development...Over this period, the literacy rate increased from 30 to over 80 percent.

These structural factors have to be seen in conjunction with the perspective of Lewis (1976) that initial differences in advantage can be magnified by the appearance of economic opportunity. Thus, perhaps the best interpretation of the East Asia experience is being supportive of both a structuralist view and a neoclassical perspective based on the H–O model. The land reforms and the wide spread of education simultaneously reduced surplus labor while at the same time making the distribution of assets (land and human capital) much more equal. The stage was thus set for an opening up and integration into the global economy to deliver growth with equity. However, the outcome was dependent on the initial conditions at the time of the opening up, conditions that need not necessarily hold in other countries, or at other time periods.

20.3. EXPERIENCE AND NEW THEORY FROM THE 1980s ONWARD

The policy debates of the three decades following World War II influenced and were influenced by the analytical frameworks developed to understand the impact of trade and investment openness on inequality. The experiences of this period, in particular the perceived "growth with equity miracle" of East Asian economies, contrasted with the stagnant or rising inequality in countries such as India (with relatively low growth) or Brazil (with relatively high growth), were particularly important in convincing policy makers to open up their economies from the 1980s onward. However, the importance of structural features such as the low degree of asset inequality in East Asian economies when they launched their drive to openness seems not to have received as much attention. The past three decades have been periods of ever intensifying globalization as measured by trade integration and the magnitude of capital flows. What has been the experience with inequality?

The experience of inequality in the United States (and other developed economies) is interesting because of the possible light it can shed on the predictions of the standard H–O model. The simple model has the powerful prediction that opening up will narrow the returns between labor and capital in countries with a relatively low capital-to-labor ratio, or between skilled and unskilled labor in countries with a relatively low skilled-to-unskilled labor ratio. The observance of these trends in East Asia was read as support for the model. The flip side of this same prediction is that the gap between these returns should widen in countries with relatively high ratios of capital to labor and of skilled labor to unskilled labor. This did not happen in the United States in the 1960s and 1970s, but it has been happening since the 1980s. Now, it can be argued that given the relative size of the U.S. economy, it was only in the 1980s and 1990s, with the opening up of China and India, that the trade effects could be felt strongly enough to impact factor returns. So, the inequality trends in the United States could indeed be claimed as partial support for the H–O model.

There is, however, the issue of how much of the rising inequality in the United States can be attributed to trade, and how much to other factors, specifically to technology. The overview by Pavcnik (2011) captures the recent consensus:

> *A large body of research on this topic finds little support that international trade in final goods driven by relative factor endowment differences can account for much of the observed increase in skill premiums in developed and developing countries.... First, the Stolper–Samuelson mechanism suggests that increased relative demand for skilled labour in countries abundant in skilled labour occurs as a result of shifts in the relative demand for skilled labour across industries.... However, the employment shifts across industries have not been sufficiently large to account for the large increase in wage inequality. Most of the observed increase in demand for educated labour in countries such as the United States is driven by increased relative demand for skilled labour within industries. (p. 242)*

There is significant debate on the relative role of trade. Although Krugman (2008) argues against his own earlier view that trade was a relatively small factor in explaining the rise of inequality compared to technology, there are also criticisms of the "small role of trade" view by Irwin (2008), Katz (2008), and Autor (2010). It would be fair to say that skill-biased technical change is considered to be a major driving force, if not necessarily the dominant force, behind rising inequality.[7] This empirical and policy debate has in turn

---

[7] Of course, this argument on skill-bias depends on the magnitude of the elasticity of substitution between skilled and unskilled labor; Further, as Atkinson (2008) points out, with a supply response a rise in the rate of skill-biased technical progress leads only to a higher level of inequality, not permanently rising inequality.

fed into an emerging literature that goes beyond simple H–O/Stolper–Samuelson formulations to consider within-industry wage differentials between heterogeneous firms
and how these could be affected by trade.

The H–O predictions on trade and inequality could be argued to have been confirmed by the experience of rising trade and falling inequality in East Asia in the
1960s and 1970s. They could equally be argued to have been confirmed by the experience of the rising trade and rising inequality in the United States from the 1990s onward,
although there is consensus that the forces of technology provide stronger explanation.
However, the difficulty for the H–O model is that, contrary to its prediction, and contrary to the experience of East Asia in the 1960s and 1970s, from the 1980s onward, the
experience of Asian economies and that of Latin America until the 2000s has been one of
rising trade and rising inequality. As the comprehensive review by Goldberg and Pavcnik
(2007) concludes:

> The survey of the evidence confirms Wood (1999), who noted that inequality increased in several
> middle-income Latin American countries that liberalized their trade regimes in the 1980s and
> 1990s. It further suggests that this positive relationship holds in the cases of India, China and Hong
> Kong. As noted previously by Wood (1999), the experience of developing countries that globalized
> during the 1980s and 1990s contrast with the experiences of several Southeast Asian countries
> (South Korea, Taiwan, Singapore) that underwent trade reforms in the 1960s and 1970s. The latter
> underwent a decline in inequality as they opened up their economies to foreign markets. (p. 54)

A number of comments are in order before we proceed to discuss the implications of
these facts for the H–O model. First, although the economies of Latin America liberalized
during the 1980s and 1990s, this was also a period of painful macroeconomic adjustments
and slow downs, and this could confound attribution of the causes of inequality. Second,
note that the simple Lewis–Kuznets model discussed in the last section could indeed still
predict an increase in inequality with opening up. Finally, two major further stylized facts
have been established since the Goldberg and Pavcnik (2007) survey. First, inequality also
increased in East Asia in the 1990s and the 2000s.[8] Second, inequality has declined in
Latin America since the 2000s.[9] Both of these are after their major periods of trade liberalization and, particularly in Latin America, have been linked to redistributive policy—
these policy issues will be taken up in a subsequent section.

The basic H–O/Stolper–Samuelson framework is foundational in the discourse on
trade and inequality. However, questions about its validity have been raised by the finding that inequality in many developing countries has increased since the 1980s despite
increases in trade. This disconnect between prediction and outcome has led to a fruitful
search for alternative explanations of why an increase in trade may increase inequality,
and some of the theories advanced have also been helpful in understanding the impact

---

[8] Kanbur and Zhuang (2012).
[9] Lustig et al. (2011).

of trade on inequality in developed countries as well. In this section, we examine a range of such theories as illustration of the direction the literature is taking in light of the experiences of the last three decades.

In the wake of the failure of the basic two goods, two factors H–O model to predict co-movement of trade and inequality, a range of models were developed that vary the technology or number of factors and goods (including the introduction of nontraded goods) in order to derive predictions more consistent with the data. Thus, for example, Wood (1994) moves from the two-factor model with a skilled/unskilled labor division to consider a three-factor model with workers classified as skilled (high education)/ semi-skilled (basic education)/unskilled (no education). Further, there are three types of production—skill-intensive manufacturing, semi-skilled intensive manufacturing, and agriculture. In this setting, for a country with comparative advantage in agriculture we get the standard prediction that opening up will reduce inequality. However, for countries with a relatively large number of semi-skilled workers, opening up will increase their wages relative to the wages of both high-skill and unskilled workers. The effect on inequality is thus ambiguous, and measured inequality could increase. While an interesting extension to the basic H–O model, it is not clear how well this fits the data. After all, East Asia in the 1960s could be argued to be a region with a predominance of basic education, and evidence from the 1980s onward suggests that wages of the highly skilled have risen disproportionately.

In the same spirit, Davis (1996) considers a two-factor (he calls them capital and labor), three-goods H–O model, with market imperfections that prevent factor price equalization and full diversification of production. The three goods differ in the capital intensity of production technology. With countries ranked by capital intensity of factor endowment, the least developed countries will export the least capital intensive commodity and import the next most capital intensive. For these countries, the standard result will hold—opening up will narrow the gap in factor returns. However, for countries with intermediate levels of capital intensity of factor endowment, which will export the commodity with intermediate capital intensity of production and import the commodity with highest capital intensity of production, opening up will have the opposite effect. Of course, for the most developed countries we again have the standard Stolper–Samuelson result. At least for developing economies at intermediate levels of capital intensity, then, this type of theorizing might explain co-movement of trade and inequality. Such countries might, in principle, include East Asia from the 1980s onward and Latin America at the time of its opening up in the 1980s and 1990s.

The papers by Wood (1994) and Davis (1996) are examples of attempts to predict co-movements of trade and inequality within a recognizable H–O framework but with more disaggregated specification of commodities or factors. This trend has continued in the literature, with added complications such as capital-skill complementarity in production—to the point that the discourse of today cannot really be labeled as a

H–O discourse. In what follows, I will consider the literature that highlights heterogeneity of workers, firms, and production processes.

Helpman et al. (2010) bring together several strands of the modern trade literature with a focus on firm and worker heterogeneity and derive predictions on trade and inequality that are consistent with many of the empirical findings of the last 30 years. Following Melitz (2003), the model supposes heterogeneous firms producing differentiated commodities. Firms can enter by paying a fixed cost, but discover their productivity only after paying the sunk cost. The productivities are drawn from a Pareto distribution, an assumption that helps the tractability of the model. After productivity is revealed, firms decide whether and how much to produce for export, for the domestic market, or for both, or they exit altogether. Production involves a fixed cost, and output is a function of firm productivity, number of workers hired, and their average ability. A specific functional form is used for tractability, but the key aspect is that these three elements are complementary to one another.

Worker ability is also assumed to have a Pareto distribution—again for tractability. Search and matching frictions exist in the model, and firms can pay more to match with more workers. Further, among the workers the firm can screen for higher abilities above a cutoff by paying a cost (with a higher cutoff costing more), but it cannot distinguish abilities beyond this cutoff. Thus, all workers in a firm are paid the same wage. The wage is modeled as emerging from the outcome of a bargaining game between the firm and the average worker.

Fixed costs of production, and fixed costs of exporting, mean that firms with very low productivities do not produce at all, while firms with high productivities select exporting because of the existence of a cost of trading. Given costs of search and screening, it can also be shown that firms with higher productivity and revenue search more and use a higher ability cutoff, so that they have higher ability workers on average and thus higher wages. The key point is that exporting firms pay higher wages in equilibrium. Thus, if we start from autarky, where fixed costs of exporting are so high that nobody exports, and reduce these fixed costs in a comparative static manner so that some firms begin to export, wage inequality is introduced where none existed before. This applies to all countries; thus, opening up can increase inequality in all countries—developed and developing—because of the selection effects of exporting.

Verhoogen's (2008) is another example of a similar model where selection effects can explain co-movement of trade and inequality. The idea here is that exporting requires the production of higher quality products and only the most productive will find it profitable to go into exporting. With a mechanism of higher wages in more productive firms, this leads to greater inequality with more openness. It should be noted that the Helpman et al. (2010) model also has an intriguing result at the other end of the spectrum where exporting costs are so low that all firms export. Then, once again, wages are equal. In their model, inequality first increases and then decreases as opening up intensifies—an "inverted-U" relationship between inequality and openness. It is of course an empirical question as to whether the intensified globalization from the 1980s onward has now taken some countries to the point where the model would predict falling inequality. If this was the case for some countries, of course, the model could not explain the co-movement of trade and inequality for those countries, and other explanations would have to be considered.

A selection mechanism of a different sort is present in studies of outsourcing as exemplified by Feenstra and Hanson (1996, 1997), which also relates to a broader literature in outsourcing and FDI in trade. They considered a scenario where the final output is produced using intermediate inputs that are produced using different intensities of skilled and unskilled labor. Consider now two economies with different endowments of skilled and unskilled labor. For any given pattern of trade costs, the skilled labor abundant (developed) economy will use the more skilled intensive production of intermediate inputs. When trade costs are lowered in a comparative static exercise, some of this production is relocated from the developed economy to the developing economy. However, the activity that is relocated is the least-skilled intensive in the developed economy and the most-skilled intensive in the developing economy. This increases skill intensity of production in both the developing and the developed economy and, hence, widens the wage gap between skilled and unskilled labor in both economies. Feenstra and Hanson (1997) show empirical support for this as explaining rising wage inequality in Mexico.

Feenstra and Hanson (1997) highlight an aspect of globalization that has come to the forefront in the last 30 years, namely, foreign direct investment (FDI). The issue of portfolio and financial flows will be discussed in a subsequent section, but longer term FDI has also been important in the recent growth surges in developing countries. What are the implications of FDI for inequality?

The theory of FDI in the simple Lewis model discussed in the previous section suggests that as wages rise in a former surplus-labor economy, capitalists will look to investment opportunities abroad, presumably in economies where wages are lower still. If these economies are themselves in a state of surplus labor then further investment will raise the share of capital and worsen the distribution of income for that reason. However, if the "Lewis turning point" has already been reached in the economy receiving FDI, this investment will raise wages further in that economy, and this could be a channel for reducing inequality.

Modern theories of the impact of FDI build on the H–O framework and then bring in firm and worker heterogeneity, as in the analysis of Feenstra and Hanson (1997). Overall, it would be fair to say that the theoretical conclusions are ambiguous, with some suggestion of FDI contributing to an increase in inequality in developing countries at the start of the process, with a possible turnaround in the later stages. For example, Figini and Gorg (1999) discuss the transition as domestic firms absorb the new technology of the FDI.

Inequalities may be created in the early stages, but are mitigated in later stages as the transition proceeds—an inverted-U relationship has framed much of the empirical work in this area. The large and growing empirical literature also gives mixed results, with perhaps a greater weight to the conclusion that FDI is associated with rising inequality in earlier stages,[10] but that there may be a turnaround, and that the impact is muted or even negative at higher levels of income per capita.[11]

Selection effects as the result of global integration are now central to the trade and FDI literature and, thus, to the attempts to explain co-movement of trade and inequality. They do appear to provide a coherent explanation of increases in inequality in both developed and developing countries, and for this reason, they merit close theoretical and empirical attention in the years to come.[12]

20.4. ECONOMIC CRISIS AND INCOME DISTRIBUTION

It is often said that globalization brings risks as well as opportunities at the macroeconomic level. Greater integration with the global economy can lead to the economy being buffeted by global fluctuations in trade and capital flows. What has been the contribution of openness to macroeconomic volatility? The current consensus and weight of research seems to suggest that openness is associated with greater volatility (Bekaert et al., 2006; Easterly et al., 2001; Kose et al., 2006; Rodrik, 1997).[13] The paper by Di Giovanni and Levchenko (2008) conducts a careful analysis of the channels through which trade openness increases volatility. They test for three channels: (i) increased volatility of individual sectors, (ii) increased co-movement of sectors, and (iii) a more specialized production pattern. They find support for the first and third but find that more openness in a sector

---

[10] Feenstra and Hanson (1997) for Mexico, Figini and Gorg (1999) for Ireland, Taylor and Driffield (2005) for the United Kingdom, Tsai (1995) for a cross-section of 33 countries and Basu and Guariglia (2007) for 8 countries, find the increasing relationship.

[11] Figini and Gorg (2011) find for a cross-section of 100 developing and developed countries that: "Results for developing countries are robust and suggest the presence of a nonlinear effect: wage inequality increases with FDI inward stock, but this effect diminishes with further increases in FDI. For developed countries, wage inequality decreases with FDI inward stock, and there is no robust evidence to show that this effect is nonlinear." (p. 1473)

[12] The literature on heterogeneous workers, heterogeneous firms, and trade is exploding and it would be impossible to do it justice in the space available. The recent surveys by Grossman (2013) and Costinot (2009) are useful. The paper by Costinot essentially generalizes H–O to trade models with heterogeneous workers and firms.

[13] It should be noted that it was concern about exposure to foreign trade fluctuations that was very much behind policy debates about unemployment in the United Kingdom and elsewhere at the end of the nineteenth century, and this led to the introduction of social insurance.

reduces the co-movement of its growth with overall growth in the economy, which tends to reduce aggregate volatility. However, the overall effect of openness on volatility is clear:

> ...moving from the 25th to the 75th percentile in trade openness is associated with an increase in aggregate volatility of about 17.3% of the average aggregate variance observed in the data. The impact of openness on volatility varies a great deal depending on country characteristics, however. For instance, we estimate that an identical change in trade openness is accompanied by an increase in aggregate volatility that is five times higher in the average developing country compared to the average developed country. Lastly, we estimate how the impact of trade changes across decades. It turns out that all three channels, as well as the overall effect, increase in importance over time: the impact of the same trade opening on aggregate volatility in the 1990s is double what it was in the 1970s. (p. 5)

However, a major focus of the last two decades has been volatility and crises induced by financial flows. Financial crises appear to be the new normal in the global economy. Fully fledged global crises, such as the one that occurred in 2008–2009, or the East Asian financial crisis of 1997, which also had global repercussions, are recognized as at least aided by the far greater ease of movement of portfolio capital around the world in the wake of capital account liberalizations from the 1990s onward. These global crises also have implications for national level macroeconomic volatility, which has also been affected by trade openness. Indeed, Hnatkovska and Loayza (2013) argue that the increased volatility can be attributed more to crises ("large recessions") than to the normal economic cycle.

There is now a consensus that volatility is associated with lower growth—Hnatkovska and Loayza (2013) present only the most recent assessment in this vein. However, this section will review the recent discourse on the consequences of economic crisis for the distribution of income—for poverty and for inequality.[14] The literature has set out a range of channels through which a global collapse of the type seen in 2008–2009, or the more limited contagion effects of the crisis in 1997, feeds through into income distribution. Atkinson and Morelli (2011) and Baldacci et al. (2002) highlight the following channels:

1. Economic slowdown. As a "balance sheet adjustment" recession takes hold in originating countries, it is transmitted through trade to other countries. Thus, each country faces an economic slowdown. There is unemployment in the formal sector and consequent downward pressure on earnings in the informal sector. We would expect the impact of economic slowdown to be rising poverty and also rising inequality.

2. Relative prices and sectoral effects. For a particular country, the decline in international demand may be concentrated in specific sectors, with quantity and price effects. Thus, unemployment and wage contraction will have sectoral patterns that differ

---

[14] There is a growing literature on whether inequality breeds crises—a good example of this line of argument is in Rajan (2011). We will not discuss this strand of the literature here.

from country to country. Here, the impact on wage inequality will depend on whether the sectors that are negatively impacted are the ones that were paying higher wages to begin with. If so, crisis could actually reduce inequality through this channel (although poverty would rise).

3. **Asset effects.** Changes in interest rates and revaluation of assets can affect incomes and wealth at the top of the income distribution. If there are major downward valuations and reductions in income from capital, then crises could reduce wealth and income inequality through this channel.

4. **Policy responses.** This includes the consequences of fiscal retrenchment, which will have impacts at the lower tail of the income distribution, or bank bailouts, which will affect the top end of the distribution. In general, fiscal retrenchment through reducing public employment, or support for public works schemes and other forms of unemployment support, would increase poverty and inequality in the social sectors. Bank bailouts would support asset values and incomes at the top end of the income distribution and increase inequality. Finally, an important channel linking crises and distribution is the drastic devaluation most often undertaken as a response to a balance of payment crisis. This is equivalent to a drop in real wages and an increase in profits.

Each of these channels can have multiple impacts on poverty and inequality, so the overall effect is an empirical question. Ravallion and Chen (2009) focus on the 2008 global financial crisis and provide projections of the likely impact on poverty. They estimate that "the crisis will add 64 million people to the population living under a dollar a day." The methodology for doing this, however, assumes no distributional change within a country, based on the observed regularity that "relative inequality falls about as often as it rises during aggregate economic contractions, with zero change on average." Thus, Ravallion and Chen (2009) simply apply projected contraction in total consumption and assume this contraction to be distributionally neutral. They do recognize, however, that "while distribution neutrality is plausible on average, there will be some countries where the poverty impact of the crisis is greater than these calculations suggest, and some where it will be smaller. Country-specific analysis would be needed to determine which countries might have above-average impacts."

An attempt at identifying the impacts of poverty and inequality through cross-country regression techniques is presented by Baldacci et al. (2002). They define crisis episodes, identify appropriate controls of country-time spells, and estimate the impact of crises on different dimensions of income distribution. Not surprisingly, they find that crises are associated with rising poverty. However, in terms of income distribution, they find that "The main losers in terms of changes in income shares are not the poorest (lowest income quintile) but those in the second (lowest) income quintile. The income share of the highest quintile also falls in crisis years relative to pre crisis years." Thus, treating this regression finding as a representation of the average outcome, the results are consistent with the assumptions of Chen and Ravallion who state that crises are, on average, distribution neutral.

The post-1997 crisis experience highlights the country-specific differences that can arise. Hagen (2007) argues that income inequality rose significantly in Korea after the crisis. Similarly, inequality rose in Singapore and Malaysia, but it fell in Indonesia and in Mauritius (Atkinson and Morelli, 2011). Atkinson and Morelli (2011) assess the association between crises and inequality for a large number of crises over a long period of time. They distinguish between banking crises and crises of collapse in consumption. They look at the time path of inequality on either side of the identified crisis. For the former, they conclude that "the empirical evidence suggests that cases in which inequality tend to increase following the crisis are in majority, although we should caution that the sample size is too limited to draw firm conclusions." For the latter, "empirical evidence concerning 'change in direction' suggests that consumption crises are more associated with reduction in inequality. No particular pattern stands out from the analysis of GDP crises."

It would seem, therefore, that no easy generalizations are available for the impact of crises on inequality, as might be expected from the multiple channels through which they can work and how initial conditions in a country can affect the impact. What this means is that we need country-specific modeling to analyze and to predict the impact of crisis on inequality. One such approach is that of a microsimulation model, as in the work of Habib et al. (2010). This approach combines macroeconomic projections with transmission mechanisms to the income distribution:

> *The model focuses on labor markets and migration as transmission mechanisms and allows for two types of shocks: shocks to labor income, modeled as employment shocks, earnings shocks or a combination of both; and shocks to non-labor income, modeled as a shock to remittances. Shocks can be positive or negative depending on the trends outlined by the macroeconomic projections. In most cases labor income and remittances account for at least 75-80% of household income.* (p. 5)

Such country-specific analysis can then be used both to identify early warning indicators and to design possible policy responses. For example, the authors apply the model to Bangladesh and recommend monitoring of remittances and wages by sector as indicators of the need for action.[15] A range of these models and methods is surveyed in Bourguignon and Bussolo (2012), and in Bourguignon et al. (2008). However, an important question arises as to whether we use anonymous distributions before and after crises or whether we use panel data, which follow individuals from before the crisis to after. Then, anonymous distributions can show no change even when there is considerable "churning" as a result of the crisis as pointed out by Robilliard et al. (2008).

---

[15] For an example of a microsimulation model to the impact of crisis on inequality for a developed country, see O'Donoghue et al. (2013).

20.5. GLOBALIZATION AND GENDER INEQUALITY

So far we have analyzed the relationship between globalization and interpersonal inequality without regard to the gender of the persons. Indeed, gender was not present in the classical developments in attempts to link trade theory to theory of income distribution. However, in the past quarter century this issue has come to the fore strongly in the policy and analytical literature. The analytical reasons for this development are related to greater evidence on gender dimensions of inequality and the development of nonunitary models of the household, which allows for the prospect of unequal outcomes within the household. The policy reasons are related to strong debates on whether the global integration of the past 25 years has hurt or helped women.

It is well established that there is a strong gender dimension to interpersonal inequality.[16] This is most easily demonstrated empirically for variables that can be quantified at the individual level. Patterns are country specific, of course. However, in many developing countries, educational attainments are lower for women than for men and especially so at lower incomes. Sex ratios at birth in some countries reveal discrimination against women in sex selection, and maternal mortality rates in many developing countries are at the levels that Sweden attained in 1900. Women earn less than men for similar work, but also women tend to work in sectors and occupations that are low paying.[17]

It is not easy to measure the magnitude of gender inequality along the standard dimension of consumption, because consumption data are usually collected at the household level in surveys. The first cut of measuring gender inequality by inequality between female-headed households and male-headed households is unsatisfactory for obvious reasons. The standard assumption in translating household level information into individual level well-being is to simply divide by household size and allocate per capita consumption of the household to each individual in the household. Of course, this suppresses all intrahousehold inequality including gender inequality. Thus, our standard measures of inequality are underestimates of true inequality because they set gender inequality in consumption within the household to zero. On rare occasions when individual level consumption data is available (for example on food consumption), it has been shown that the standard procedure understates inequality (and poverty) by as much as 25% (Haddad and Kanbur, 1990). Thus, gender inequality, as reflected in intrahousehold inequality, matters.

While it is accepted that gender structures inequality in an economy, there is less consensus on how exactly globalization interacts with this structure. How is the standard analysis of openness and inequality, for example, affected by structuring the economy along gender lines? And, overall, does globalization reduce gender inequality, or increase it?

---

[16] Chapter 12 of this volume is devoted to the topic of gender inequality.
[17] World Bank (2011), p. 74, 78, and 79.

Before looking at some evidence, let us consider how standard theoretical arguments on globalization and inequality could be modified by taking into account the gender dimension of production and income distribution. A standard piece of analysis in open economy macroeconomics is the effect of devaluation on the balance of payments. As is well known, the transmission mechanism is through "expenditure switching" brought about by raising the price of tradables relative to the price of nontradables. The distributional consequences of this have been analyzed in the usual way through the Stolper–Samuelson theorem. If tradables are relatively more intensive in their use of labor, then the relative return to labor will rise. Indeed, this was the argument made by many for the pro-poor and progressive aspects of devaluation.

However, suppose that tradables are actually more intensive in their use of male labor. Then, it is seen that male earnings will be favored. This should not matter much if there is perfect income sharing within the household—the representative household would gain overall if the policy of devaluation was efficient for the economy as a whole. However, if the household is not described by a unitary model, and if, for example, there is bargaining between the man and the woman and their outside options matter for the outcome of bargaining, then, the macro policy of devaluation will have the micro consequence of strengthening the bargaining power of males and will have a type of impact on inequality not contemplated in the classical analysis.[18] Of course, the outcome is context specific—it depends on which sector is male or female labor intensive. The main theoretical point, however, is that gender matters (Haddad and Kanbur, 1994).

The above is in terms of the pure demand for labor. However, there is also evidence that women are paid less for the same job. The impact of globalization on such wage differentials is uncertain. On the one hand, there is the standard argument that greater global competition will reduce the scope for discriminatory wage practices, and this should narrow wage differentials. However, to the extent that mobility of capital reduces bargaining power of workers, and to the extent that women are concentrated in industries where capital is more mobile, greater openness will lead to lower female wages (Seguino, 2007). The effects of this competition in footloose industries might be seen not just in standard wages but also in labor standards (Chau and Kanbur, 2003, 2006). Again, to the extent that women are disproportionately employed in such industries, the impact of globalization will affect them disproportionately.

There are two main empirical strands of the gender and globalization literature. The first is focused on the effects of openness on demand for female labor and on female wages. The second is related to the previous section—how crises affect women relative to men. We take up these strands one at a time.

---

[18] Again, there is considerable evidence that household decision making is not best described by the unitary model. For an early survey of the literature see Alderman et al. (1995). A recent review is provided in Chapter 16 of this volume.

The effects of opening up on the demand for female labor are nuanced and context specific. On the one hand, the demand for female labor rises through expansion of light manufactures. As the World Bank's World Development Report on Gender notes:

> In the Republic of Korea, the share of women employed in manufacturing grew from 6 percent in 1970 to around 30 percent in the 1980s and early 1990s.... Similarly, in Mexico, female employment in manufacturing grew from 12 percent in 1960 to 17 percent in 2008, with 10 times more women in 2008 than in 1960.
>
> **World Bank (2011, p. 256)**

However, this phase contrasts with the next phase as there is a move to the production of more capital intensive goods (Seguino, 2013; Tejani and Milberg, 2010; Van Staveren et al., 2007). What about female-wage differentials? Here again, the evidence reflects the conflicting forces, which are resolved differently in different countries. As Seguino (2013) notes in her overview:

> Evidence of the impact of trade and investment liberalization for gender wage equality is also mixed. Some studies show that gender wage differentials have declined, in large part due to narrowing educational gaps. But in several developing countries, including China and Vietnam, however, the discriminatory portion of gender wage gaps has increased. (p. 15)

A final, newly emergent strand of the literature provides a gender perspective on the selection and heterogeneity models discussed in Section 20.3. The argument put forward by Juhn et al. (2013) builds on the idea that more productive firms enter into export and modernize technologies. If new technologies require less physical strength (the "brains" vs. "brawn" issue, as it is characterized in some circles), we would expect that demand for female labor would rise in blue-collar occupations and not in white-collar occupations. This is because new technology can change the "brain/brawn" mix in blue-collar occupations, but white-collar jobs will be unaffected on this score. The authors find that for Mexico, post-NAFTA tariff reductions are associated with rising female employment and wage shares in blue-collar jobs but not in white-collar jobs.[19]

The various contradictory forces are also highlighted in Bussolo and de Hoyos (2009). On the basis of their studies of Africa and Latin America, they conclude, essentially, that with forces pulling in opposite directions, the net effect of trade openness on gender inequality may well turn out to be fairly weak:

> Overall, the messages of this volume are very clear: trade expansion exacerbates gender disparities in agricultural-based, African economies and reduces it in manufacturing-based economies like Honduras.... Admittedly, the magnitude of the links between trade shocks, producer prices, male versus female bargaining power, consumption decisions, future growth and poverty reduction does not seem too large.... To conclude, trade liberalization brings important gender effects, but the evidence collected here shows that these effects tend to be of a small and sometimes uncertain magnitude.

---

[19] The brain–brawn issue is also discussed in World Bank (2011), p. 259.

While the literature on the trade effects of globalization on gender inequality thus renders a relatively neutral verdict, the same is not true of the literature on the impact of economic crises on women. The effects of economic downturns generally, and economic collapses in particular, are argued to be felt most sharply by women because they tend to be displaced first. In turn, they crowd into the informal sector, pushing down earnings further in that sector, which is in any case disproportionately female in employment (Braunstein and Heintz, 2008; Takhtamanova and Sierminska, 2009). It is further argued that the fiscal retrenchment that accompanies economic crises affects women disproportionately both directly and indirectly, through reducing public services that support women's work, such as health and child care (Seguino, 2013).

There is, finally, an intriguing and important, yet unresolved issue of the effects of globalization on societal norms that determine the structure of gender inequality. Based on the work of Kabeer (1997, 2000) and Hossain (2011), World Bank (2011) argues as follows:

> In Bangladesh, the employment of hundreds of thousands of women in the ready-made garment industry feminized the urban public space, creating more gender-equitable norms for women's public mobility and access to public institutions. In the process, Bangladeshi women had to redefine and negotiate the terms of purdah, typically reinterpreting it as a state of mind in contrast to its customary expression as physical absence from the public space, modest clothing, and quiet demeanor.

How widespread these effects are, and how much they can be attributed to globalization, is still under debate. What is clear is that any discussion of globalization and inequality must go beyond the classical analysis and develop theory and empirical investigation on globalization and the gender dimension of inequality.

20.6. OPENNESS AND SPATIAL INEQUALITY

The spatial dimension of inequality is a key concern in the policy discourse, because it intersects and interacts with disparities between subnational entities and jurisdictions. These entities sometimes have defined ethnic or linguistic characteristics, and in federal structures have constitutional identities that naturally lead to a subnational perspective on national inequality. This section considers the impact of globalization, in particular greater openness in trade, on spatial inequality.

What exactly is spatial inequality? One way of linking standard interpersonal measurement of inequality to regional inequality is to decompose national inequality into a between-region and a within-region component. The share of national inequality accounted for by the between-region component—which would be zero were it not for the fact that average incomes differ across regions—is then a measure of regional inequality. The fraction of total inequality accounted for by variation in average income across regions depends, of course, on the number of regions. The larger the number of regions, the greater the inequality that can be attributed to regional difference in mean income. Estimates vary, but 15–20% of spatial inequality in total inequality is not unusual (see Kanbur, 2006).

An alternative, however, is to consider the disparities in regional mean incomes directly, not weighted by their population. Equal weights correspond to some dimensions of many constitutions, where key elements of political power are divided equally between constituent provinces or states (Kanbur and Venables, 2005). In the case of just two entities, then, this could be simply the ratio of the two means, for example. For more than two entities, other standard measures of dispersion can be used. Yet, other measures are sometimes used in the literature, attempting to capture regional "polarization." However, as Zhang and Kanbur (2001) argue, such measures may not make that much difference in assessing trends.

Kanbur and Venables (2007) review the literature and provide other measures of the level of spatial disparities observed around the world. In particular, they highlight variations in poverty and human development indicators. In Africa, in 6 out of the 12 countries studied, the percentage of people below a poverty line constructed on the basis of information about households' asset holdings is more than 50% greater in rural areas than in urban areas. The smallest rural–urban difference is 30%. Similarly, school enrollments, and the ratio of girls to boys enrolled, is much higher in urban than in rural areas. In Peru, the incidence of poverty in districts at sea level was 46.1% in 1997, while for districts at an altitude greater than 3500 m above sea level it was 63.3%. In Indonesia in 1993, the rural poverty incidence was 46.5% in West Kalimantan, but only 10.7% in Yogyakarta.

However spatial inequality is measured, there are major differences in the literature on how much it should matter in policy design. One strand of the policy discourse can be characterized by the "balanced development" perspective, which holds that too much concentration of economic activity is inimical to equity and to efficiency. However, there is a contrary strand that is best expressed in the World Bank's World Development Report on Economic Geography (World Bank, 2008, p. 73):

> For decades, "spatially balanced growth" has been a mantra of policy makers in many developing countries. It was an obsession of planners in the former Soviet Union.... And it has been the objective of governments of various political hues in the Arab Republic of Egypt, Brazil, India, Indonesia, Mexico, Nigeria, the Russian Federation, South Africa, and other great developing nations. There has even been a strong commitment to spatially balanced development in the economic history of many developed countries.

This strong perspective against "balanced growth" in the conventional sense is important in light of the report's own assessment of evolving economic forces, in particular global integration in the era of globalization:

> Although the basic forces shaping the internal economic geography of developing countries are the same as those that earlier shaped the economic landscapes of today's developed countries,

the magnitudes have changed. Larger international markets, better transportation, and improved communication technologies mean that leading areas in open developing countries have greater market potential than industrial countries did in their early development. So the forces for spatial divergence between leading and lagging areas are now stronger.

World Bank (2008, p. 74)

The above perspective on openness and economic spatial disparity owes much to the burgeoning "new economic geography" literature that brings increasing returns to scale and agglomeration economies center stage in characterizing the development of an economy. In the context of a closed economy with two sectors, one in which ("agriculture") has conventional diminishing returns while the other ("manufacturing") displays firm level costs that fall as the sector as a whole grows, equilibrium can have spatial concentration of economic activity even when there is no "natural" geographic differentiation between the regions.[20] There is thus a distinction between spatial divergence caused by "first-nature geography," natural variations in environmental endowment, and "second-nature geography" that arises out of the self-enforcing feedback loops of agglomeration economies.[21]

What precisely is the impact of greater openness on spatial disparity when played through the forces of agglomeration economies? The World Bank (2008) quote above seems to suggest that spatial disparities will increase. However, the specific theory does not produce quite such a clear-cut answer. Different specifications, modeling different contexts, produce different answers.[22] For example, it matters whether different regions have equal access to the international market. It also matters whether the opening up is only for trade or also for capital mobility. The theoretical ambiguity is emphasized in recent papers by Rodríguez-Pose (2010) and Ottaviano (2009). Ottaviano (2009) summarizes the theoretical conclusions in a series of propositions as follows:

when regions have the same access to foreign markets, international trade liberalization fosters regional disparities and this effect is stronger the more important the foreign market and the more integrated the national market. (p. 7). . .if the smaller region is a gate or a hub, international trade liberalization may reduce regional disparities. (p. 8) International capital mobility amplifies the positive effect of trade liberalization on regional disparities in the smaller country as well as in the larger one. (p. 8).

Given these theoretical ambiguities then, what is the evidence on openness and spatial inequality? Kanbur and Venables (2007) summarize the results of a major project collating country case studies on the evolution of spatial inequality in the last quarter century. For 26 developing and transitioning countries, spatial inequality measures are available for at

---

[20] There is of course by now a huge literature on this. Standard references include Krugman (1991), Fujita et al. (2001), and Ottaviano and Thisse (2004).

[21] Kanbur and Venables (2007).

[22] Compare, for example, Krugman and Livas Elizondo (1996) and Paluzie (2001).

two or more points in time, so that we can get a sense of the time trends. The first and major empirical finding is that spatial inequalities have been rising in the last two to three decades.[23]

The last three decades have also been the period of globalization. Is there then a link between openness on rising spatial inequality? The case studies reported in Kanbur and Venables (2007) seem to support the hypothesis that openness is associated with greater spatial inequality. Thus, Kanbur and Zhang (2005) establish dramatic increases in spatial inequality in China since the start of the reforms in 1978. Their econometric analysis attributes at least part of this increase to the measure of openness (the other factors that are statistically significant include the degree of decentralization). Rodríguez-Pose and Sánchez-Reaza (2005) find greater regional polarization in Mexico comparing the periods before and after the North American Free Trade Agreement (NAFTA). Friedman (2005) identifies an indirect channel for Indonesia, in that openness leads to growth, but more remote areas benefit less from growth in terms of poverty reduction impact. Outside of the country studies reviewed in Kanbur and Venables (2007), Daumal (2008) finds that while for India openness contributes to greater inequality between Indian states, for Brazil the opposite is true. Thus, country context matters.

A number of cross-country regression studies have also focused on the issue of the link between openness and spatial inequality. Barrios and Strobl (2009) regress within country regional inequality against trade openness, with other controls, for 15 European Union countries. They find a positive association between regional inequality and the trade to GDP ratio for a country. Milanovic (2005) considers the evolution of regional inequality over time in China, India, the United States, Indonesia, and Brazil over 1980–2000. He finds a significant causal relationship between measures of openness and measures of regional inequality. Rodríguez-Pose and Gill (2006) analyze regional inequality similarly across country panels for the period 1970–2000. They find that it is the particular interaction of openness with the composition of trade that results in regional inequality impacts.

Perhaps the most recent and comprehensive cross-country study of regional inequality and openness is by Rodríguez-Pose (2010). It uses unbalanced panel data for 28 countries over 1975–2005. Half of these countries are developed countries and the other half are developing or transition economies. The measure of regional inequality used is the Gini coefficient of regional GDP per capita. There is no simple association between openness and regional inequality in these data. However, this is before various controls are introduced, and the panel structure of the data is exploited with appropriate techniques. On the conditioning variables, use is made of the theory referred to earlier, so that "greater trade openness will have a more polarizing effect in countries characterized

---

[23] Examples include Sahn and Stifel (2003) for a range of African countries, García-Verdú (2005) for Mexico, Forster et al. (2005) for Eastern Europe, Friedman (2005) for Indonesia, and Kanbur and Zhang (2005) for China.

by (a) higher differences in foreign market accessibility among its regions and (b) where there is also a high degree of coincidence between the regional income distribution and accessibility to foreign markets" (Rodríguez-Pose, 2010, p. 13). Further, like Kanbur and Zhang's (2005) work on China, it is hypothesized that the degree of decentralization will also matter for regional inequality. A number of other controls are also used, including institutional quality variables.

The overall conclusion of the comprehensive and rigorous analysis by Rodríguez-Pose (2010) is striking:

> By and large, countries in the developing world are characterized by a series of features that are likely to potentiate the spatially polarizing effects of greater openness to trade. Their higher existing levels of regional inequality, their greater degree of sector polarization, the fact that their wealthier regions often coincide with the key entry points to trade, and their weaker state all contribute to exacerbate regional disparities as trade with the external world increases.
>
> *Rodríguez-Pose (2010, p. 26)*

Thus, structural differences in the country at the time of opening up tend to interact with the forces of openness, and in the recent experience at least, this has led to openness contributing to greater regional inequality. Of course, this leaves open the issue of whether this is not just the first-round effects of trade opening and whether it could it be weakened or offset by further geographical adjustments, namely, domestic migration of workers or capital, at a later stage. However, the inequality consequences in the short run will need to be addressed, and the policy implications of these findings will be discussed in a subsequent section.

20.7. INTERNATIONAL MIGRATION, REMITTANCES, AND INEQUALITY

Globalization in its most general terms is the greater integration of global economic activity. This is manifested in larger trade and in freer movement of factors of production. The vastly increased mobility of capital is often commented upon in the discourse. However, larger cross-border movement of population, from low income to high income countries, is also the subject of commentary in the popular discourse. Analytical literature has been developed to assess this phenomenon and to explore its causes and consequences. This section will provide an overview of this literature, focusing in particular on migration from developing to developed countries and on the impact of this migration on inequality in developing countries.

In 2010, the total stock of international migrants in the world (developed and developing countries) was 214 million people, up from 191 million in 2005.[24] This compares to an estimated 749 million for internal migrants. International migration is a significant

---

[24] International Organization for Migration (2011), p. 49.

and growing phenomenon. This is especially true of migration from developing to developed countries. The stock of immigrants in high-income countries increased at about 3% per year from 1980 to 2000. As a share of high-income country population, migrants increased from around 4% to above 8% over this 20-year period. [25]

How might the much higher rate of international migration affect the distribution of income in developing countries in theory? The answer depends on who migrates and what they do with their income after they migrate in terms of remittances to their family. If migration and remittance was representative of the domestic income distribution, then the distribution would not be affected, except for a translation to the right as remittances flowed back. Thus, poverty would decline as a result of international migration.

What if migration was not representative but selective on individual characteristics? Would the poverty results still hold? The impact effect of migration as the result of better income earning opportunities must surely be to reduce poverty at the origin. However, in the next round there is the possibility of externalities kicking in if the migrants are the most highly skilled, with knock on effects on the rest of the economy. This is the famous "brain drain" hypothesis that was popular in the 1970s and 1980s. [26] In recent years, this has been countered by the "brain gain" hypothesis, which is based on the simple idea that the probability of having access to international migration depends on the education level of the prospective migrant. In order to improve this probability, prospective migrants invest in education. Only some of these will be selected for migration, but those left behind will serve to increase the stock of human capital compared to what it would have been without the prospect of migration. [27]

There is some empirical support for the brain gain hypothesis, although others argue that its magnitude is greatly exaggerated. [28] Furthermore, there is considerable evidence for the proposition that international migration reduces poverty in the origin country. In perhaps the most comprehensive such exercise, Adams and Page (2005) asked the question on the impact of international migration on poverty using data from 71 developing countries:

> The results show that both international migration and remittances significantly reduce the level, depth, and severity of poverty in the developing world. After instrumenting for the possible endogeneity of international migration, and controlling for various factors, results suggest that, on average, a 10% increase in the share of international migrants in a country's population will lead to a 2.1% decline in the share of people living on less than $1.00 per person per day. After instrumenting

---

[25] World Bank (2006), p. 27.
[26] See for example Bhagwati and Hamada (1974).
[27] Mountford (1997) and Stark et al. (1997).
[28] See Beine et al. (2008) for support; however, see Schiff (2005) for a skeptical perspective.

*for the possible endogeneity of international remittances, a similar 10% increase in per capita offi-
cial international remittances will lead to a 3.5% decline in the share of people living in poverty.*[29]

Adams and Page (2005, p. 1645)

These results are confirmed by a range of country specific studies on international migration, remittances, and poverty—examples include Acosta et al. (2006) for Latin America,
Lokshin et al. (2007) for Nepal, and Adams(2006) for Ghana.

So much for poverty, where theory and evidence is relatively clear cut. What about
inequality? It should be clear that selectivity of migration and remittances makes this an
intricate question theoretically and empirically. And the question of identifying such selectivity is an important one in the international migration literature. In particular, there is
some debate about whether migrants are selected according to education level. Using data
from Docquier and Abdeslam (2006), Hanson (2010) compares the share of emigrants with
tertiary education to the share of total population with tertiary education. He finds that in
the vast majority of the countries, the former exceeds the latter, indicating positive selection into migration by higher levels of education. Mexico and Puerto Rico appear to be
exceptions to this almost universal phenomenon, but research on migration from those
origins to the United States seems to have had significant weight in the discourse. Hanson
(2010) argues that a larger literature now seems to support selection on education.

What about migration selection based on unobserved variables? McKenzie et al.
(2006) conduct an ingenious exercise using the results of a lottery for emigration from
Tonga to New Zealand. They compare losers in the lottery with nonapplicants, both
groups of course still being in Tonga. They find that the applicants have higher earnings
after controlling for observables; and they conclude therefore, that those desiring to
migrate are selected in terms of higher income earning potential.

If international migrants are selected from households that already have high earnings,
and their migration raises income earning and, through remittances, adds to the income
of the household in the origin area, it should be clear that such migration would tend
to increase inequality in the sending country. However, to the extent that the selection
goes the other way, inequality in the sending country will be mitigated by international
migration. There is now a considerable literature on assessing directly the impact of international migration on inequality, and we now turn to an overview of those studies.

The empirical results on international migration and inequality are inconclusive as a
whole. Barham and Boucher (1998) compare the actual distribution post-migration

---

[29] It should be noted that there is an issue in interpreting these results, which is similar to the problem of the
counterfactual when microsimulating the effects of remittances. In the regression: Poverty $= f$(GDP per
capita, remittances per capita) the net effect of the latter variable should be the estimated coefficient minus
the (negative) change in mean income or GDP per capita due to migration times the coefficient of the
mean income variable. But for this, we need an estimate of the impact of migration on the home country
mean income. If it is assumed to be zero, then it is in effect assumed that migrants' labor supply is fully
compensated by people remaining behind them.

including remittances for Nicaragua, with a counterfactual of what the distribution would have been if the migrants had not left and earned their original income. They found that the Gini coefficient is higher by 12%. Adams (2006) finds a much smaller increase in the Gini coefficient for Ghana—of 3%. The difference made by the counterfactual approach is illustrated by comparing the findings of De and Ratha (2005) and Karunaratne (2008) for Sri Lanka. Using the 2003–2004 Socioecononmic Survey for Sri Lanka, Karunaratne (2008) shows that "income receivers belonging to lowest 10 percent receive 1.3 percent of their income as remittances with the top 10 percent of the income receivers getting 4.6 percent of their income from remittances" (p. 58). He uses this to argue that remittances increase inequality. However, De and Ratha (2005) conduct counterfactual analysis and show that remittance income exceeds the counterfactual loss in income from migrating in the bottom two deciles, while the opposite is true for the top two deciles. Thus, they argue, remittances are equalizing.

A major issue in the empirical literature is the difference between short-term and long-term effects of international migration on inequality. In other words, the issue has to do with comparing changes in inequality in the origin location in the early stages when migration starts with when it has been going on for some time. An early study by Stark et al. (1986) found a positive relationship between remittances and inequality in the short term, but the opposite result in the long run for Mexico.[30] McKenzie and Rapoport (2007) argue that while in the short term, migration selectivity favors the better off because of the costs of migration, in the longer term these costs fall as migration networks form in the destination country. Using again the case of migration from Mexico to the United States, they argue that migration reduces inequality in communities that have experienced high levels of migration in the past. There may thus be an inverse-U relationship between international migration and inequality—first increasing and then decreasing.

Overall, then, the final effect of globalization on inequality in developing countries through the channel of international migration is ambiguous in theory, and this is reflected in the conflicting empirical findings. Of course, the migrants are themselves better off—it is the consequences for those they leave behind that are uncertain. These results pick up on a theme of this chapter as a whole, namely that the consequences for distribution depend on the context and, in particular, on preexisting structural inequalities. When these inequalities are high and interact with the opportunities presented by globalization in such a way as to benefit those who already well off, inequality will increase. The next section turns to the policy implications of these findings.[31]

---

[30] The analysis is based on simulating the effects of increased remittances on inequality for two villages—one of which has longstanding migration patterns to the United States and the other of which does not.

[31] There is much literature on the impact of immigration on inequalities in the host developed countries that is not covered in this chapter. For example, Borjas (2003) is the leading analyst arguing that immigration worsens inequality by lowering the relative wages of domestic low-skilled workers in the United States, while Card (2009) argues that the impact of immigration on relative wages is small, accounting for as little as 5% of the increase in U.S. age inequality between 1980 and 2000.

20.8. NATIONAL AND GLOBAL POLICY RESPONSES

Globalization brings enormous benefits, but in its wake it also brings significant risks. The risk of rising inequality has been ever present in the recent globalization discourse, where the concern has been that far from delivering "growth with equity," as it seems to have done for East Asia in the 1970s and 1980s, the more recent push to global integration has been accompanied by rising inequality. Indeed, those parts of the world that have avoided rising inequality, such as Latin America, seem to have done so through purposive policy intervention. What, then, are the policy implications of the association between globalization and rising inequality? To answer this question, bear in mind that as discussed in previous sections, our understanding of the effects of globalization on inequality, let alone of the quantitative magnitudes, is limited. This hampers policy formulation.

It helps to begin by accepting that inequality is indeed a legitimate concern for policy makers. Although not universal, there appears to be a broad consensus that rising inequality lowers social welfare directly because societies are inequality averse, and it lowers social welfare indirectly because higher inequality can impede investment and growth through a number of channels.[32] This is true of standard interpersonal inequality, as well as inequality between broadly defined groups such as gender, regions, or ethnicities. Policy makers appear to be well aware of and concerned about inequality. For example, in a survey of more than 500 Asian policy makers 44% rated concern in their country about inequality as being "high" or "very high," while 36% rated the concern as being "medium." On the question of whether higher income inequality is acceptable so long as poverty is declining, 52% disagreed or strongly disagreed. Finally, when asked how important it is to have policies in place to prevent rises in inequality in order to maintain stability and sustain growth, 95% said it was "important" or "very important."[33]

The next step in the argument is to understand that the inequality of market outcomes depends on structural inequality and on how these inequalities interact with market processes to exacerbate or mitigate these inequalities. Thus, policy can affect the inequality of final outcomes in three ways—by addressing structural inequality premarket, by addressing the operation of market processes, and by redistributing income generated by structure and market. Viewed in this way, the component parts of globalization—opening up of trade, capital, and labor flows—can be seen as dimensions of market processes. Reversing these processes in order to manage inequality is neither desirable, because it also blocks off a major route to economic growth and efficiency, nor feasible given the instruments that policy makers actually have. Of course, to the extent that the market processes are themselves distorted, for example, preferential access to foreign markets for

---

[32] This chapter is not the place for a review of the vast literature on this topic. A recent representative contribution is by Berg and Ostry (2011). Evidence for the detrimental effect of gender inequality and growth is presented in World Bank (2011). The effects of inequality on growth are covered in Chapter 14 of this volume.

[33] Kanbur and Zhuang (2012), p. 44.

monopolies or for politically favored groups, then addressing these can improve efficiency and equity.[34] However, policy could fruitfully focus on addressing structural inequalities and redistributing market income more equitably. Sometimes these can be combined, and redistribution of market income can be done in such a way as to mitigate structural inequalities as well.

A good entry point into policy is provided by the contrasting experiences of Asia and Latin America in the last 20 years, when both regions have faced the same global economy and increases in global integration. During the 1990s and 2000s, Asia saw sharp increases in inequality. During this period, 83% of developing Asia's population lived in countries with rising inequality, and if the high growth that occurred had taken place without rising inequality, nearly one-quarter of a billion more people would have been lifted out of poverty, according to one estimate.[35] On the other hand, Latin America, which has long been a byword for high inequality, managed to have a remarkable period of declining inequality from the late 1990s onward. This is true of all the major Latin American economies. For example, in Brazil between 1998 and 2009, without the fall in inequality, the same level of poverty reduction would have required a growth rate higher by 4 percentage points[36] Of course, the levels of inequality in Latin America were and still are much higher than those in Asia. However, the difference in trends is remarkable.

Sections 20.3 and 20.4 of this chapter discussed the skill bias that characterizes technical progress today. Demand for skilled labor is rising globally, and openness in trade and investment is transmitting this global demand to the country level. In the absence of policy intervention, these market processes will lead to rising inequality within countries. As discussed earlier, closing off economies in order to block this channel of inequality increase is neither feasible nor desirable. However, Asian economies have tended not to counteract these pressures, either by addressing structural inequalities in skill levels, or by redistributing market income sufficiently to mitigate inequality. However, Latin American economies have purposively redistributed income through cash transfers and have done it in such a way as to help the buildup of human capital through conditioning these transfers on keeping children in school. This is not the place for a full-blown assessment of conditional cash transfers (CCTs), but it does seem as though Latin American countries have found an appropriate intervention to address rising inequality in general but also for the current conjuncture of globalization-led pressures in rising inequality through a rising demand for skilled labor.[37]

---

[34] Inequality of assets can be compounded by inequality in market access creating inequality in the rate of return to assets for certain groups in society. This links to the discourse on inequality of opportunity, which is covered in World Bank (2005) and Chapter 4.

[35] Kanbur and Zhuang (2012), p.41.

[36] Lustig et al. (2011).

[37] For an overview, see Fiszbein and Schady (2009). It is of course clear that CCTs by themselves are not responsible for the trend of inequality in Latin America.

The additional expenditure on conditional cash transfers requires revenues, and the progressivity of the tax system is another major determinant of how globalization related increases in inequality can be mitigated. Progressivity is also important in addressing the rise in very high incomes the world over, especially in Asia. Asian tax systems do not generally score highly on progressivity. In fact, it is argued that raising progressivity of taxation would have a greater impact on inequality in Asia than elsewhere in the world.[38]

The policy discussion above is pertinent to rises in inequality associated with globalization, and it is also valid for increases in inequality from any source. What globalization brings, however, is the easier movement of capital and labor across borders, and this may well constrain government's abilities to raise revenues to address structural inequalities and to redistribute market incomes. There is now vast literature on tax competition and the globalization's role in intensifying the "race to the bottom." Kanbur and Keen (1993) show that tax rates are (i) suboptimal with lack of tax coordination when the tax base is mobile across borders and (ii) the suboptimality increases with the ease of movement of the tax base. With such revenue effects, questions are naturally raised about the sustainability of redistributive expenditure like CCTs in a globalized world. As the title of one paper asks, "Will social welfare expenditures survive tax competition?" (Hines, 2006).[39]

The basic intuitions of the analysis can be applied to progressive income taxation as well as in the context of international migration. The discussion in Section 20.7 of this chapter showed that international migration was unequivocally good for poverty reduction in developing countries, and while there were possible short-term effects raising inequality, these were turned around in the medium term. This would argue for greater freedom of international migration of labor to match the greater ease of movement of goods and capital. However, there is a catch. The possibility of international migration, especially of skilled high-income labor, could constrain the government's abilities to redistribute income within the country through progressive taxation.

The early work of Mirrlees (1982) concluded that "it may well be desirable to institute substantial income taxes on foreign earnings."[40] While this was the solution for a single country's tax design problem when faced with cross-border migration, it also contains within it the seeds of a solution to the coordination problem, whereby countries follow one another down the path of reduced progressivity, exacerbating the inequality impact of greater openness. A similar logic applies to a race to the bottom on labor standards, where countries lower standards or enforcement to gain competitive advantage (Chau and Kanbur, 2003, 2006). The issue has already been alluded to in the context of gender

[38] Asian Development Bank (2012), p. 76.

[39] See also Hines and Summers (2009).

[40] There is now vast literature on migration and optimal income taxation. A recent example that illustrates many of the intricacies is given by Hamilton and Pestieau (2005).

inequality in industries that employ mainly women. Coordination on labor standards is typically conducted through the International Labor Organization, and this mechanism can be strengthened further to address the inequality increasing forces that globalization can bring (Chau and Kanbur, 2001).

Indeed, Basu (2006) goes so far as to propose an international agency to address this issue:

> That there may be coordination problems in trade is well recognized and we have the WTO to help mitigate such problems. That labor market policies need coordination is known and we have the ILO to address this. For environmental problems we have the UNEP or the GEF. But there is nothing comparable to these for anti-poverty and anti-inequality policies. Yet. . .this is an area where the coordination problem may be no less acute. Hence, there is clearly a perceived need for a coordinating agency. (p. 1371)

Leaving to one side the political feasibility or operational practicality of such an agency, the fact that it is being contemplated highlights like nothing else the challenges that globalization poses to policy makers concerned with its effects on inequality.

20.9. CONCLUSION

The effects of globalization on inequality have animated much theoretical, empirical, and policy literature since World War II, but particularly so in the past 30 years when, contrary to some received wisdom, greater global integration was associated with increasing inequality in developed and especially in developing countries. In the wake of the new facts, theory has responded, particularly with a class of models that emphasizes selection mechanisms into production and trade, thereby allowing inequality to increase everywhere with openness. These new models will need to be developed, fleshed out, and applied in different contexts of trade, investment, and outsourcing. Empirical work will depend on the availability of high quality, firm-level, data, and there will need to be considerable investment in the generation of such data, particularly for low-income countries. Further, the empirical work will also need to link the firm data to household data in order to follow through on the implications for the personal distribution. More generally, there is a need to tie together the analysis of factor incomes with the implications for the personal income distribution.

Inequality is not just interpersonal inequality but also involves inequality across broadly defined groups—gender and regional groups being prime examples as well as ethno–linguistic groupings (not covered in this chapter)—adding another dimension of key policy concern. Further empirical work will need to document the impact of different aspects of globalization on these dimensions of inequality, and theorizing will need to extend and modify the standard H–O model, or indeed the more recent selection-based models, to incorporate structural divides along salient socioeconomic groupings.

At the level of national policy, addressing the inequality consequences of globalization is in principle no different than addressing the inequality consequences of other forces, such as technical progress (although global integration tightens the transmission mechanism from technical change in one part of the world to another). However, greater mobility of goods, capital, and labor constrains the freedom of governments to mitigate inequality through redistributive instruments. More research is needed to delineate, in theoretical and empirical terms, the nature of these constraints and the gains of global coordination on tax and expenditure policy and on labor and capital regulation. In the realm of practical policy, there is also a fairly full agenda, ranging from the implementation of redistributive schemes like Conditional Cash Transfers (CCTs) at the national level, and the use of existing global institutions such as the ILO and the WTO to put a floor on a race to the bottom in taxation and redistribution at the international level.

Having animated the economic analysis and policy discourse for the past half century, the globalization-inequality nexus seems set to continue doing so in the coming decades.

REFERENCES

Acosta, P., Fajnzylber, P., Lopez, H., 2006. Remittances and development in latin America. World Econ. 29 (7), 957–987.

Adams Jr., R.H., 2006. Remittances and Poverty in Ghana, World Bank Policy Research Working Paper 3838.

Adams Jr., R.H., Page, J., 2005. Do international migration and remittances reduce poverty in developing countries? World Dev. 33 (10), 1645–1669.

Adelman, I. (nd). Social development in Korea, 1953–1993. http://are.berkeley.edu/~irmaadelman/KOREA.html (accessed 19 March 2013).

Asian Development Bank, 2012. Asian Development Outlook 2012. Asian Development Bank, Manila.

Alderman, H., Chiappori, P.-A., Haddad, L., Hoddinott, J., Kanbur, R., 1995. Unitary versus collective models of the household: is it time to shift the burden of proof? World Bank Res. Obs. 10 (1), 1–19.

Atkinson, A.B., 2008. The Changing Distribution of Earnings in OECD Countries. Oxford University Press, Oxford.

Atkinson, A.B., Morelli, S., 2011. Economic Crises and Inequality, UNDP Human Development Research Paper, 2011/06.

Autor, D., 2010. The Polarization of Job Opportunities in the U.S. Labor Market: Implications for Employment and Earnings, The Center for American Progress and the Hamilton Project Working Paper (Washington, DC).

Baldacci, E., de Mello, L., Inchauste, G., 2002. Financial Crises, Poverty and Income Distribution, IMF Working Paper 02/04.

Barham, B., Boucher, S., 1998. Migration, remittances and inequality: estimating the net effects of migration on income distribution. J. Dev. Econ. 55 (3), 307–331.

Barrios, S., Strobl, E., 2009. The dynamics of regional inequalities. Reg. Sci. Urban Econ. 39 (5), 575–591.

Basu, K., 2006. Globalization, poverty and inequality: what is the relationship: what can be done? World Dev. 34 (8), 1361–1373.

Basu, P., Guariglia, A., 2007. Foreign direct investment, inequality, and growth. J. Macroecon. 29 (4), 824–839.

Beine, M., Docquier, F., Rapoport, H., 2008. Brain drain and human capital formation in developing countries: winners and losers. Econ. J. 118 (528), 631–652.

Bekaert, G., Harvey, C.R., Lundblad, C., 2006. Growth volatility and financial liberalization. J. Int. Money Financ. 25, 370–403.

Berg, A., Ostry, J.D., 2011. Equality and efficiency: is there a tradeoff between the two or do the two go hand in hand? Financ. Dev. 48 (3), 12–15.

Bhagwati, J., Desai, P., 1970. Planning for Industrialization - A Study of Indian Industrialization and Trade Policies (with J. Bhagwati). Oxford University Press, Oxford.

Bhagwati, J., Hamada, K., 1974. The brain drain, international integration of markets for professionals and unemployment: a theoretical analysis. J. Dev. Econ. 1 (1), 19–42.

Borjas, G.J., 2003. The labor demand curve is downward sloping: re-examining the impact of immigration on the labor market. Q. J. Econ. 118 (4), 1335–1374.

Bourguignon, F., Bussolo, M., 2012. Income distribution and computable general equilibrium models. In: Dixon, P.B., Jorgenson, D. (Eds.), Handbook of Computable General Equilibrium Models. Elsevier, Amsterdam. ISBN: 9780444536341.

Bourguignon, F., Silva, L.A., Bussolo, M. (Eds.), 2008. The Impact of Macroeconomic Policies on Poverty and Income Distribution: Macro–Micro Evaluation Tools. World Bank Publications, Washington, DC. ISBN: 0821357786.

Braunstein, E., Heintz, J., 2008. Gender bias and central bank policy: employment and Inflation reduction. Int. Rev. Appl. Econ. 22 (2), 173–186.

Bussolo, M., de Hoyos, R. (Eds.), 2009. Gender Aspects of the Trade and Poverty Nexus: A Micro–macro Approach. Palgrave Macmillan, London.

Chau, N., Kanbur, R., 2001. The Adoption of International Labor Standards: Who, When and Why. Brookings Trade Forum, Brookings, Washington, DC, pp. 113–156 (with N. Chau).

Chau, N., Kanbur, R., 2003. On footloose industries, asymmetric information, and wage bargaining. http://www.arts.cornell.edu/poverty/kanbur/ChauKanWageBarg.pdf.

Chau, N., Kanbur, R., 2006. The race to the bottom, from the bottom. Economica 73 (290), 193–228.

Card, D., 2009. Immigration and Inequality. NBER Working Papers, No. 14683.

Costinot, A., 2009. An elementary theory of comparative advantage. Econometrica 77, 1165–1192.

Daumal, M., 2008. Impact of trade openness on regional inequality and political unity: the cases of India and Brazil. http://www.etsg.org/ETSG2008/Papers/Daumal.pdf.

Davis, D.R., 1996. Trade Liberalization and Income Distribution. National Bureau of Economic Research, Cambridge, MA, NBER Working Paper No. 5693.

De, P., Ratha, D., 2005. Remittance Income and Household Welfare: Evidence from Sri Lanka Integrated Household Survey. Development Research Group, World Bank, Washington, DC, Unpublished paper.

Di Giovanni, J., Levchenko, A., 2008. Trade Openness and Volatility. http://www.imf.org/external/pubs/ft/wp/2008/wp08146.pdf, accessed 11 August 2012. IMF Working Paper, WP/08/146.

Docquier, F., Abdeslam, M., 2006. International migration by educational attainment, 1990–2000. In: Ozden, C., Schiff, M. (Eds.), International Migration, Remittances, and the Brain Drain. World Bank, Washington, DC, pp. 151–200, Palgrave Macmillan, New York.

Easterly, W., Islam, R., Stiglitz, J.E., 2001. Shaken and stirred: explaining growth volatility. In: Pleskovic, B., Stern, N. (Eds.), Annual World Bank Conference on Development Economics.

Feenstra, R., Hanson, G., 1996. Foreign investment, outsourcing and relative wages. In: Feenstra, R.C., et al., (Eds.), Political Economy of Trade Policy: Essays in Honor of Jagdish Bhagwati. MIT Press, Cambridge, MA, pp. 89–127.

Feenstra, R., Hanson, G., 1997. Foreign direct investment and relative wages: evidence from Mexico's maquiladoras. J. Int. Econ. 42 (3–4), 371–393.

Figini, P., Gorg, H., 1999. Multinational companies and wage inequality in the host country: the case of Ireland. Rev. World Econ. 135 (4), 594–612.

Figini, P., Gorg, H., 2011. Does foreign direct investment affect wage inequality? An empirical investigation. World Econ. 34 (9), 1455–1475.

Fiszbein, A., Schady, N., 2009. Conditional cash transfers: reducing present and future poverty: World Bank Policy Research Report. World Bank, Washington, DC.

Forster, M., Jesuit, D., Smeeding, T., 2005. Regional poverty and income inequality in central and eastern Europe: evidence form the Luxembourg income study. In: Kanbur, R., Venables, A.J. (Eds.), Spatial Inequality and Development. Oxford University Press, Oxford.

Friedman, J., 2005. How responsive is poverty to growth? A regional analysis of poverty, inequality and growth in Indonesia, 1984–99. In: Kanbur, R., Venables, A.J. (Eds.), Spatial Inequality and Development. Oxford University Press, Oxford.

Fujita, M., Krugman, P., Venables, A.J., 2001. The Spatial Economy: Cities, Regions and International Trade. MIT Press, Cambridge, MA.

García-Verdú, R., 2005. Income, mortality, and literacy distribution dynamics across states in Mexico: 1940-2000. Cuad. Econ. 42 (125), 165–192.

Goldberg, P., Pavcnik, N., 2007. Distributional Effects of Globalization in developing Countries. NBER Working Papers, No. 12885.

Grossman, G., 2013. Heterogeneous Workers and International Trade, NBER Working Paper No. 18788.

Habib, B., Narayan, A., Olivieri, S., Sanchez-Paramo, C., 2010. Assessing Ex Ante The Poverty and Distributional Impact of Global Crisis in a Developing Country, World Bank Policy Research Working Paper No. 5238.

Haddad, L., Kanbur, R., 1990. How serious is the neglect of intra-household inequality? Econ. J. 100, 866–881.

Haddad, L., Kanbur, R., 1994. Are better off households more unequal or less unequal? Oxford Econ. Pap. 46 (3), 445–458 (with L. Haddad).

Hagen, K., 2007. The changing faces of inequality in South Korea in the age of globalization. Korean Stud. 31, 1–18.

Hamilton, J., Pestieau, P., 2005. Optimal taxation and the ability distribution: implications for migration equilibria. Int. Tax Public Financ. 12, 29–45.

Hanson, G., 2010. International migration and development. In: Kanbur, R., Spence, M. (Eds.), Equity in a Globalizing World. World Bank for the Commission on Growth and Development, Washington, DC.

Helpman, E., Itskhoki, O., Redding, S., 2010. Inequality and unemployment in a global economy. Econometrica 78 (4), 1239–1283.

Hines, J.R., 2006. Will social welfare expenditures survive tax competition? Oxford Rev. Econ. Policy 22 (3), 330–348.

Hines, J., Summers, L., 2009. How Globalization Affects Tax Design. NBER Working Paper No. 14664.

Hnatkovska, V., Loayza, N., 2013. Volatility and Growth. http://www-wds.worldbank.org/external/default/WDSContentServer/WDSP/IB/2004/02/03/000012009_20040203142259/additional/105505322_20041117173010.pdf.

Hossain, N., 2011. Exports, Equity and Empowerment: The Effects of Readymade Garments Manufacturing Employment on Gender Equality in Bangladesh, Background paper for the WDR 2012.

International Organization for Migration, 2011. World Migration Report, 2011.

Irwin, D., 2008. Trade and Wages, Reconsidered: Comments and Discussion. pp. 138–143, Brookings Papers on Economic Activity, Spring.

Jomo, K., 2006. Growth With Equity in East Asia. DESA Working Paper No. 33, http://www.un.org/esa/desa/papers/2006/wp33_2006.pdf.

Juhn, C., Ujhelyi, G., Villegas-Sanchez, C., 2013. Trade liberalization and gender inequality. Am. Econ. Rev. 103 (3), 269–273.

Kabeer, N., 1997. Women, wages and intrahousehold power relations in urban Bangladesh. Dev. Change 28 (2), 261–302.

Kabeer, N., 2000. The Power to Choose: Bangladeshi Women and Labour Market Decisions in London and Dhaka. Verso, London.

Kanbur, R., 2006. The policy significance of inequality decompositions. J. Econ. Inequal. 4 (3), 367–374.

Kanbur, R., Keen, M., 1993. Tax competition and tax coordination when countries differ in size. Am. Econ. Rev. 83 (4), 877–892 (with M. Keen).

Kanbur, R., Venables, A.J., 2005. Spatial Inequality and development. In: Kanbur, R., Venables, A.J. (Eds.), Spatial Inequality and Development. Oxford University Press, Oxford, pp. 3–11 (with A.J. Venables).

Kanbur, R.., Venables, A.J., 2007. Spatial disparities and economic development. In: Held, D., Kaya, A. (Eds.), Global Inequality. Polity Press, Cambridge, pp. 204–215.

Kanbur, R., Zhang, X., 2005. Fifty years of regional inequality in China: a journey through central planning, reform and openness. Rev. Dev. Econ. 9 (1), 87–106.

Kanbur, R., Zhuang, J., 2012. Confronting rising inequality in Asia. In: Asian Development Outlook 2012. Asian Development Bank, Manila.

Karunaratne, H.D., 2008. International labour migration, remittances and income inequality in a developing country: the case of Sri Lanka. Hosei Econ. Rev 75 (3), 21–65. http://repo.lib.hosei.ac.jp/bitstream/10114/1629/1/75-4hettige.pdf.

Katz, L., 2008. Trade and wages, reconsidered: comments and discussion. Brookings Pap. Econ. Act. 2008 (1), 143–149.

Kose, A., Prasad, E., Terrones, M., 2006. How do trade and financial integration affect the relationship between growth and volatility? J. Int. Econ. 69, 176–202.

Krugman, P., 1991. Increasing returns and economic geography. J. Polit. Econ. 99, 483–499.

Krugman, P., 2008. Trade and wages, reconsidered. Brookings Pap. Econ. Act. 39 (1), 103–137.

Krugman, P., Livas Elizondo, R., 1996. Trade policy and the third world metropolis. J. Dev. Econ. 49 (1), 137–150.

Lewis, W.A., 1954. Economic development with unlimited supplies of labor. Manchester Sch. Econ. Soc. Stud. 22, 139–191.

Lewis, W.A., 1976. Development and distribution. In: Cairncross, A., Puri, M. (Eds.), Employment, Income Distribution and Development Strategy: Problems of the Developing Countries (Essays in honour of H.W. Singer). Holmes & Meier Publisheres, Inc., New York, NY, pp. 26–42.

Lindert, P.H., Williamson, J.G., 2001. Does Globalization Make the World More Unequal? NBER Working Paper 8228.

Lokshin, M., Bontch-Osmolovski, M., Glinskaya, E., 2007. Work-Related Migration and Poverty Reduction in Nepal, World Bank Policy Research Working Paper.

Lustig, N., Lopez-Calva, L.F., Ortiz-Juarez, E., 2011. The Decline in Inequality in Latin America: How Much, Since When and Why. http://econ.tulane.edu/RePEc/pdf/tul1118.pdf, accessed April 20, 2013. Tulane Economics Working Paper Series, No. 1118.

McKenzie, D., Rapoport, H., 2007. Network effects and the dynamics of migration and inequality: theory and evidence from Mexico. J. Dev. Econ. 84 (1), 1–24.

McKenzie, D., Gibson, J., Stillman, S., 2006. How Important Is Selection? Experimental Versus Non-Experimental Measures of the Income Gains from Migration, World Bank Policy Research Paper No. 3906.

Melitz, M., 2003. The impact of trade on intra-industry reallocations and aggregate industry productivity. Econometrica 71 (5), 1695–1725.

Milanovic, B., 2005. Worlds Apart: Measuring International and Global Inequality. Princeton University Press, Princeton, NJ.

Mirrlees, J.A., 1982. Migration and optimal income taxes, J. Publ. Econ. 18, 319–341.

Mountford, A., 1997. Can a brain drain be good for growth in the source economy? J. Dev. Econ. 53, 287–303.

O'Donoghue, C., Loughrey, J., Morrissey, K., 2013. Using the EU-SILC to Model the Impact of Economic Crisis on Inequality, IZA Discussion paper no. 7242.

Ottaviano, G., 2009. Trade Liberalization, Economic Integration and Regional Disparities, CAF Working Papers, No. 2009/05.

Ottaviano, G., Thisse, J.-F., 2004. Agglomeration and economic geography. In: Henderson, V., Thisse, J.-F. (Eds.), In: Handbook of Regional and Urban Economics, vol. 4. Elsevier, Amsterdam.

Paluzie, E., 2001. Trade policies and regional inequalities. Pap. Reg. Sci. 80 (1), 67–85.

Papageorgiou, D., Choksi, A., Michaley, M., 1990. Liberalizing Foreign Trade in Developing Countries: The Lessons of Experience. The World Bank, Washington, DC.

Pavcnik, N., 2011. Globalization and within country inequality. In: Bacchetta, M., Jansen, M. (Eds.), Making Globalization Socially Sustainable. WTO/ILO, Geneva, pp. 233–259.

Rajan, R., 2011. Fault Lines: How Hidden Fractures Still Threaten the World Economy. Princeton University Press, Princeton.

Ravallion, M., Chen, S., 2009. The Impact of the global financial crisis on the world's poorest. http://www.voxeu.org/article/impact-global-financial-crisis-world-s-poorest.

Robilliard, A.-S., Bourguignon, F., Robinson, S., 2008. Examining the impact of the Indonesian financial crisis using a macro-micro model. In: Bourguignon, F., Silva, L.A., Bussolo, M. (Eds.), The Impact of Macroeconomic Policies on Poverty and Income Distribution: Macro-Micro Evaluation Tools. World Bank Publications, Washington, DC. ISBN: 0821357786.

Rodríguez-Pose, A., 2010. Trade and Regional Inequality, World Bank Policy Research Working Paper No. 5347.

Rodríguez-Pose, A., Gill, N., 2006. How does trade affect regional disparities? World Dev. 34, 1201–1222.

Rodríguez-Pose, A., Sánchez-Reaza, J., 2005. Economic polarization through trade: trade liberalization and regional inequality in Mexico. In: Kanbur, R., Venables, A.J. (Eds.), Spatial Inequality and Development. Oxford University Press, Oxford.

Rodrik, D., 1997. Has Globalization Gone Too Far? Institute for International Economics, Washington, DC 1997.

Sahn, D., Stifel, D., 2003. Urban-rural inequality in living standards in Africa. J. Afr. Econ. 12 (1), 564–597.

Schiff, M., 2005. Brain Gain: Claims About Its Size and Impact on Welfare and Growth are Greatly Exaggerated, IZA Discussion Paper No. 1599.

Seguino, S., 2007. Is more mobility good? Firm mobility and the low-wage low productivity trap. Struct. Change Econ. Dyn. 18 (1), 27–51.

Seguino, S., 2013. From micro-level gender relations to the macro economy and back again: theory and policy. In: Figart, D., Warnecke, T. (Eds.), Handbook of Research on Gender and Economic Life. Edward Elgar, Northampton, MA.

Stark, O., Edward Taylor, J., Yitzhaki, S., 1986. Remittances and inequality. Econ. J. 96 (383), 722–740.

Stark, O., Helmenstein, C., Prskawetz, A., 1997. Abrain gain with a brain drain. Econ. Lett. 55, 227–234.

Takhtamanova, Y., Sierminska, E., 2009. Gender, monetary policy, and employment: the case of nine OECD countries. Feminist Econ. 15 (3), 323–353.

Taylor, K., Driffield, N., 2005. Wage inequality and the role of multinationals: evidence from UK panel data. Labour Econ. 12 (2), 223–249.

Tejani, S., Milberg, W., 2010. Global Defeminization? Industrial Upgrading, Occupational Segregation, and Manufacturing, SCEPA Working Paper 2010-1.

Tsai, P.L., 1995. Foreign direct investment and income inequality: further evidence. World Dev. 23 (3), 469–483.

Van Staveren, I., Elson, D., Grown, C., Cagatay, N. (Eds.), 2007. The Feminist Economics of Trade. Routledge, London.

Verhoogen, E., 2008. Trade, quality upgrading and wage inequality in the Mexican manufacturing sector. Q. J. Econ. 123 (2), 489–530.

Wood, A., 1994. North-South Trade, Employment and Inequality: Changing Fortunes in a Skill-Driven World. Clarendon Press, Oxford.

Wood, A., 1999. Openness and wage inequality in developing countries: the Latin American challenge to East Asian conventional wisdom. In: Baldwin, R., et al. (Eds.), Market Integration, Regionalism and the Global Economy. Cambridge University Press, Cambridge.

World Bank, 1993. The East Asian Miracle: Economic Growth and Public Policy. World Bank, Washington, DC.

World Bank, 2005. World Development Report 2006: Equity and Development. World Bank, Washington, DC.

World Bank, 2006. Global Economic Prospects 2006. World Bank, Washington, DC.

World Bank, 2008. World Development Report 2009: Reshaping Economic Geography. World Bank, Washington, DC.

World Bank, 2011. World Development Report 2012: Gender and Development. World Bank, Washington, DC.

Zhang, X., Kanbur, R., 2001. What difference do polarisation measures make? An application to China. J. Dev. Stud. 37 (2001), 85–98.

PART IV

Policies

CHAPTER 21

Democracy, Redistribution, and Inequality

Daron Acemoglu*, Suresh Naidu[†], Pascual Restrepo*, James A. Robinson[‡]
*Massachusetts Institute of Technology, Cambridge, MA, USA
[†]Columbia University, NY, USA
[‡]Harvard University, Cambridge, MA, USA

Contents

Abstract

In this paper we revisit the relationship between democracy, redistribution, and inequality. We first explain the theoretical reasons why democracy is expected to increase redistribution and reduce inequality, and why this expectation may fail to be realized when democracy is captured by the richer segments of the population; when it caters to the preferences of the middle class; or when it opens up disequalizing opportunities to segments of the population previously excluded from such activities, thus exacerbating inequality among a large part of the population. We then survey the existing empirical literature, which is both voluminous and full of contradictory results. We provide new and systematic reduced-form evidence on the dynamic impact of democracy on various outcomes. Our findings indicate that there is a significant and robust effect of democracy on tax revenues as a fraction of GDP, but no robust impact on inequality. We also find that democracy is associated with an increase in secondary schooling and a more rapid structural transformation. Finally, we provide some evidence suggesting that inequality tends to increase after democratization when the economy has already undergone significant structural transformation, when land inequality is high, and when the gap between the middle class and the poor is small. All of these are broadly consistent with a view that is different from the traditional median voter model of democratic redistribution: democracy does not lead to a uniform decline in post-tax inequality, but can result in changes in fiscal redistribution and economic structure that have ambiguous effects on inequality.

Keywords

Democracy, Education, Inequality, Political development, Redistribution, Structural transformation

JEL Classification Codes

P16, O10

21.1. INTRODUCTION

Many factors influence the distribution of assets and income that a market economy generates. These include the distribution of innate abilities and property rights, the nature of technology, and the market structures that determine investment opportunities and the distribution of human and physical capital.

But any market system is embedded in a larger political system. The impact of the political system on distribution depends on the laws, institutions, and policies enacted by that system. What institutions or policies a political system generates depends on the distribution of power in society and how political institutions and mobilized interests aggregate preferences. For example, we expect institutions that concentrate political power within a narrow segment of the population—typical of nondemocratic regimes—to generate greater inequality.[1]

---

[1] Nondemocracies tend to be dominated by the rich either because the rich wield sufficient power to create such a regime or because those who can wield power for other reasons subsequently use this power to become rich.

As the literature has shown, there are several theoretical mechanisms through which such an impact might operate. One would be the enactment of policies benefiting the politically powerful at the expense of the rest of society, including policies pushing down wages by repression and other means. In Apartheid South Africa prior to 1994, for example, the political system dominated by the minority white population introduced government regulations on the occupation and residential choices of black Africans in order to reduce their wages (e.g., by reducing competition for white labor and by forcing blacks into unskilled occupations, see Lundahl, 1982; Wilse-Samson, 2013). Another mechanism is the one highlighted by Meltzer and Richard's (1981) seminal paper. Building on earlier research by Romer (1975) and Roberts (1977), they developed a model where extensions of the voting franchise, by shifting the median voter toward poorer segments of society, increase redistribution, and reduce inequality.[2]

Despite these strong priors, the empirical literature is very far from a consensus on the relationship between democracy, redistribution, and inequality. Several works have reported a negative relationship between democracy and inequality using specific historical episodes or cross-national studies. Acemoglu and Robinson (2000) argued this was the case based on the economic history of nineteenth-century Europe and some twentieth-century Latin American examples. An important study by Rodrik (1999) presented evidence from a panel of countries that democracy is associated with higher real wages and higher labor share in national income. Lindert (1994, 2004) provided evidence from OECD countries indicating a linkage between democratization and public spending, particularly on education; Persson and Tabellini (2003) presented similar cross-national evidence; and Lapp (2004) pointed to a statistical association between democratization and land reform in Latin America. Other papers point in the opposite direction, however. Sirowy and Inkeles (1990) and Gradstein and Milanovic (2004) have argued that the cross-national empirical evidence on democracy and inequality is ambiguous and not robust. Scheve and Stasavage (2009, 2010, 2012) have claimed that there is little impact of democracy on inequality and policy among OECD countries, and Gil et al. (2004) have forcefully argued that there is no relationship between democracy and any policy outcome in a cross section of countries (Perotti, 1996, was an earlier important paper with similar negative findings).

In this chapter we revisit these issues in a unified theoretical and empirical framework. Theoretically, we review the standard Meltzer-Richard model and point out why the relationship between democracy, redistribution, and inequality may be more complex than the standard model might suggest. First, democracy may be "captured" or "constrained." In particular, even though democracy clearly changes the distribution of de jure power in society (e.g., Acemoglu and Robinson, 2006), policy outcomes

---

[2] Historically, the fear of expected redistribution has been one of the factors motivating the opposition to democracy (see Guttsman, 1967).

and inequality depend not just on the de jure but also the de facto distribution of power. For example, Acemoglu and Robinson (2008) argue that, under certain circumstances, those who see their de jure power eroded by democratization may sufficiently increase their investments in de facto power (e.g., via control of local law enforcement, mobilization of nonstate armed actors, lobbying, and other means of capturing the party system) in order to continue to control the political process. If so, we would not see an impact of democratization on redistribution and inequality.[3] Similarly, democracy may be constrained by either other de jure institutions such as constitutions, conservative political parties, and judiciaries, or by de facto threats of coups, capital flight, or widespread tax evasion by the elite.

Second, we suggest that democratization can result in "inequality-increasing market opportunities." Nondemocracy may exclude a large fraction of the population from productive occupations (e.g., skilled occupations) and entrepreneurship (including lucrative contracts) as in apartheid South Africa or the former Soviet bloc countries. To the extent that there is significant heterogeneity within this population, the freedom to take part in economic activities on a more level playing field with the previous elite may actually increase inequality within the excluded or repressed group and consequently the entire society.[4]

Finally, consistent with Stigler's (1970) "Director's law", democracy may transfer political power to the middle class rather than to the poor. If so, redistribution may increase and inequality may be curtailed only when the middle class is in favor of such redistribution.

After reviewing the fairly large and heterogeneous prior literature on this topic, the rest of this chapter examines the empirical impact of democracy on tax revenues as a percentage of GDP (as an imperfect measure of redistribution) and on inequality as well as a number of additional macro variables. We evaluate previous empirical claims about the effect of democracy in a consistent empirical framework that controls for a number of confounding variables. Our objective is not to estimate some structural parameters or the "causal" effect of democracy on redistribution, but to uncover whether there is a

---

[3] Relatedly, there could be reasons for dictators to redistribute and reduce inequality to increase the stability of that regime (e.g., Acemoglu and Robinson, 2001; Albertus and Menaldo, 2012, more generally). Plausible cases of this would be the land reform implemented by the Shah of Iran during his White Revolution of 1963 to help him become more autonomous from elites (McDaniel, 1991), the agrarian reforms made by the Peruvian military regime in the early 1970s (chapter 2 of Seligmann, 1995), or the educational reforms in 19th-century oligarchic Argentina (Elis, 2011).

[4] Our data show that inequality has in fact increased in South Africa between 1990 and 2000 (or 2005) and in ex-Soviet countries between 1989 and 1995 (or 2000), periods that bracket their democratic transitions in 1994 and 1989 respectively. This is probably, at least in part, driven by the increase in inequality among previously disenfranchised blacks and repressed citizens (for details on the post-democracy distributions of income see Whiteford and Van Seventer, 2000, for South Africa and Milanovic, 1998, for ex-Soviet countries).

robust correlation between democracy and redistribution or inequality, and to undertake a preliminary investigation of how this empirical relationship changes depending on the stage of development and various other factors potentially influencing how democracy operates.

The previous literature has used several different approaches (e.g., cross-sectional regressions, time-series and panel data investigations) and several different measures of democracy. We believe that cross-sectional (cross-national) regressions and regressions that do not control for country fixed effects will be heavily confounded with other factors likely to be simultaneously correlated with democracy and inequality. We therefore focus on a consistent panel of countries, and investigate whether countries that become democratic redistributed more and reduced inequality relative to others. We also focus on a consistent definition of democracy based on Freedom House and Polity indices, building on the work by Papaioannou and Siourounis (2008). One of the problems of these indices is the significant measurement error, which creates spurious movements in democracy. To minimize the influence of such measurement error, we create a dichotomous measure of democracy using information from both the Freedom House and Polity datasets as well as other codings of democracy to resolve ambiguous cases. This leads to a measure of democracy covering 184 countries annually from 1960 (or post-1960 year of independence) to 2010. We also pay special attention to modeling the dynamics of our outcomes of interest, taxes as a percentage of GDP, and various measures of structural change and inequality.

Our empirical investigation uncovers a number of interesting patterns (why many of these results differ from some of the existing papers in the literature is discussed after they are presented). First, we find a robust and quantitatively large positive effect of democracy on tax revenue as a percentage of GDP (and also on total government revenues as a percentage of GDP). The long-run effect of democracy in our preferred specification is about a 16% increase in tax revenues as a fraction of GDP. This pattern is robust to various different econometric techniques and to the inclusion of other potential determinants of taxes, such as unrest, war, and education.

Second, we find a positive effect of democracy on secondary school enrollment and the extent of structural transformation (e.g., an impact on the nonagricultural share of employment and the nonagricultural share of output).

Third, however, we find a much more limited effect of democracy on inequality. In particular, even though some measures and some specifications indicate that inequality declines after democratization, there is no robust pattern in the data (certainly nothing comparable to the results on taxes and government revenue). This may reflect the poorer quality of inequality data. But we also suspect it may be related to the more complex, nuanced theoretical relationships between democracy and inequality pointed out above.

Fourth, we investigate whether there are heterogeneous effects of democracy on taxes and inequality consistent with these more nuanced theoretical relationships. The evidence here points to an inequality-increasing impact of democracy in societies with a high degree of land inequality, which we interpret as evidence of (partial) capture of democratic decision making by landed elites. We also find that inequality increases following a democratization in relatively nonagricultural societies, and also when the extent of disequalizing economic activities is greater in the global economy as measured by U.S. top income shares (though this effect is less robust). These correlations are consistent with the inequality-inducing effects of access to market opportunities created by democracy. We further find that democracy tends to increase inequality and taxation when the middle class is less prosperous relative to the poor. These correlations are consistent with Director's law, which suggests that democracy often empowers the middle class to redistribute from the rest of society to itself. Our results suggest the need for a more systematic investigation of the conditions under which democracy does indeed reduce inequality and increase redistribution.

The chapter proceeds as follows. In the next section we discuss the theoretical connections between democracy, redistribution, and inequality. In Section 21.3 we provide a survey of the existing empirical literature on the impact of democracy on taxes, redistribution, inequality, and some other reduced-form dependent variables potentially associated with inequality (e.g., average calories per person, life expectancy, and infant mortality). Section 21.4 then describes our econometric methodology and data. Section 21.5 presents our new findings, and Section 21.6 concludes.

21.2. THEORETICAL CONSIDERATIONS

In this section, we illustrate some of the linkages between democracy and inequality that have been proposed in the literature. We begin with the seminal Meltzer and Richard (1981) model, but then alter the set of instruments available to the government to show how the logic of the standard model can be altered and even reversed. We will discuss the impact of democracy, modeled as a broader franchise, relative to a nondemocratic regime modeled as a narrower franchise or controlled by a small group. This broadening of access to political power is what our primary cross-country empirical measures of democracy attempt to capture, and is arguably the most important feature of a democratic regime.

21.2.1 The Redistributive and Equalizing Effects of Democracy

We start with the standard "equalizing effect" of democracy, first emphasized formally in Meltzer and Richard's (1981) seminal study (see also Acemoglu and Robinson, 2006). Democratization, by extending political power to poorer segments of society, will increase the tendency for pro-poor policy naturally associated with redistribution, and thus reduce inequality.

Suppose that society consists of agents distinguished only with respect to their endowment of income, denoted by y_i for agent i, with the distribution of income in the society denoted by the function $F(y)$ and its mean by $\bar{y}$. The only policy instrument is a linear tax τ imposed on all agents, with the proceeds distributed lump–sum again to all agents. We normalize total population to 1 without loss of any generality.

The government budget constraint, which determines this lump–sum transfer T, takes the form

$$T \le \tau\bar{y} - C(\tau)\bar{y}, \tag{21.1}$$

where the second term captures the distortionary costs of taxation. $C(\tau)$ is assumed to be differentiable, convex and nondecreasing, with $C'(0) = 0$.

Each agent's post-tax income and utility is given by

$$\hat{y}_i = (1 - \tau)y_i + \tau\bar{y} - C(\tau)\bar{y}. \tag{21.2}$$

This expression immediately makes it clear that preferences over policy—represented by the linear tax rate τ—satisfy both single crossing and single-peakedness (e.g., Austen-Smith and Banks, 1999). Hence the median voter theorem, and its variants for more limited franchises (see e.g., Acemoglu et al., 2012) hold.[5]

Suppose, to start with, that there is a limited franchise such that all agents with income above y_q, the qth percentile of the income distribution, are enfranchised and the rest are disenfranchised. Consider a "democratization," which takes the form of y_q decreasing, say to some $y_{q'} < y_q$, so that more people are allowed to vote. Let the equilibrium tax rate under these two different political institutions be denoted by τ_q and $\tau_{q'}$, and the resulting post-tax income distribution by F_q and $F_{q'}$. Then from the observation that the median of the distribution truncated at $y_{q'}$ is always less than the median for the one truncated above $y_q > y_{q'}$, the following result is immediate:

Proposition 1
Redistributive Effects of Democracy
Suppose that starting from only those above y_q being enfranchised, there is a further democratization so that now those above $y_{q'} < y_q$ are enfranchised. This democratization leads to higher taxes $(\tau_{q'} \ge \tau_q)$, higher redistribution, and a more equal distribution of post-tax income in the sense that $F_{q'}$ is more concentrated around its mean than F_q.

A few comments about this proposition are useful. First, this result is just a restatement of Meltzer and Richard's (1981) main result. Second, the first part of the conclusion is stated as $\tau_{q'} \ge \tau_q$, since if both y_q and $y_{q'}$ are above the mean, with standard arguments, $\tau_{q'} = \tau_q = 0$. Third, the second part of the conclusion does *not* state that F_q is a

---

[5] Namely, if we assume that policy choices are made by either a direct democracy procedure choosing the Condorcet winner (if one exists) or as a result of competition between two parties choosing (and committing to) their platforms, the equilibrium will coincide with the political bliss point of the median-ranked voter. As Austen-Smith and Banks (1999) discuss in detail, these types of results, though powerful, are rather special and rely, among other things, on the assumption that the policy space is unidimensional.

mean-preserving spread of, or is second-order stochastically dominated by $F_{q'}$, because higher taxes may reduce mean post-tax income due to their distortionary costs of taxation. Instead, the statement is that $F_{q'}$ is more concentrated around its mean than F_q, which implies the following: if we shift $F_{q'}$ so that it has the same mean as F_q, then it second-order stochastically dominates F_q (and thus automatically implies that standard deviation and other measures of inequality are lower under $F_{q'}$ than under F_q).

Finally, the result in the proposition should be carefully distinguished from another often-stated (but not unambiguous) result, which concerns the impact of inequality on redistribution. Persson and Tabellini (1994) and Alesina and Rodrik (1994), among others, show that, under some additional assumptions, greater inequality leads to more redistribution in the median voter setup (which in these papers is also embedded in a growth model). This result, however, is generally not true.[6] It applies under additional assumptions on the distribution of income, such as a log normal distribution, or when the gap between mean and median is used as a measure of inequality (which is rather non-standard). In contrast, the result emphasized here is unambiguously true.

This result of Meltzer and Richard (1981) is the basis for the hypothesis that democracy should increase taxation and income redistribution and reduce inequality. In the model, the only way that redistribution can take place is via a lump-sum transfer. This is obviously restrictive. For example, it could be that individuals prefer the state to provide public goods (Lizzeri and Persico, 2004) or public education. Nevertheless, the result generalizes, under suitable assumptions, to the cases in which the redistribution takes place through public goods or education.

We next discuss another possible impact of democracy and why its influence on redistribution and inequality may be more complex than this result may suggest.

21.2.2 Democracy and the Structural Transformation

The logic of Proposition 1 applies when the main political conflict involves the tax rate but not other policy instruments. One of the most important alternatives, emphasized by Moore (1966) and by Acemoglu and Robinson (2006) in the economics literature, is the combination of policies used to create abundant (and cheap) labor for the rural sector (see also Llavador and Oxoby, 2005). Many nondemocratic agrarian societies use explicit and implicit limits on migration out of the rural sector, together with labor repression, to keep wages low and redistribute income from the population to the politically powerful landed elites. Even industrial sectors in nineteenth century England used the Master and Servant

---

[6] Consider the following counterexample. In society A, 1/3 of the population has income 2, 1/3 has income 3 and the remaining 1/3 has income 7. If everyone is enfranchised, the Condorcet winner is a tax rate $\tau^A > 0$ with $C'(\tau^A) = 1/4$. In society B, 1/3 of the population has income 0, 1/3 has income 4 and the remaining 1/3 has income 8. If everyone is enfranchised, the Condorcet winner is a tax rate $\tau^B = 0$. Society B has a lower tax rate, and hence less redistribution despite being more unequal (the distribution of income in society A second-order stochastically dominates the distribution of society B).

law to prosecute workers and repress trade unions, and it was only repealed following an expansion of the franchise to workers and decriminalization of workers' organizations (Naidu and Yuchtman, 2013). For example, in rural Africa, land is often controlled by traditional rulers and chiefs and not held as private property. People moving away from particular chieftaincies lose rights over land, which inhibits migration. In Sierra Leone, forced labor controlled by chiefs was common in rural areas prior to the civil war in 1991 (e.g., Acemoglu et al., 2014). We may expect that these policies will be relaxed or lifted when political power shifts either to industrialists, who would benefit from migration out of the rural sector into the industrial one, or to poorer segments of society who are bearing the brunt of lower wages (see Acemoglu, 2006, for a political economy analysis of wage repression and the impact of democracy on it).

To model these issues in the simplest possible way, suppose that there is a single policy instrument denoted by $\eta \in \mathbb{R}_+$ capturing the extent of barriers against mobility out of the rural sector. Suppose now that y_i denotes the land endowment of agent i, so that post-policy income (and utility) of an agent is given by

$$\hat{y}_i = \omega(\eta) + \upsilon(\eta)y_i, \tag{21.3}$$

where $\omega(\eta)$ can be interpreted as the impact of this policy on wage income (thus it applies agents with no land endowment) and naturally we assume that $\omega(\eta)$ is decreasing. On the other hand, $\upsilon(\eta)$ is the impact of its policy on land rents, and is thus increasing. This formulation can also be easily extended to include industrialists who may also be opposed to high values of η, which would reduce the supply of labor to their sector.

Inspection of Equation (21.3) immediately reveals that preferences over η satisfy single crossing, and thus the median voter theorem again applies. This leads to the following result:

Proposition 2
Democracy and Structural Transformation
Consider the model outlined in this subsection. Suppose that starting from only those above y_q being enfranchised, there is a further democratization such that now those above $y_{q'} < y_q$ are enfranchised. This democratization leads to lower mobility barriers out of the rural sector ($\eta_{q'} \leq \eta_q$) and a more equal distribution of income (in the sense that $F_{q'}$ is more concentrated around its means than F_q).

This proposition highlights that the same reasoning that leads to the redistributive and equalizing effects of democracy also weighs in favor of lifting barriers that are against the interest of the middle class and the poor. An important implication of this might be a push toward the structural transformation out of agriculture and into industry and cities that might have been partly arrested artificially by the political process before democratization. An illustrative example of this is the impact of the 1832 Reform Act in Britain, which enfranchised urban manufacturing elites in the newly industrializing cities such as Birmingham and Manchester. This led directly to the abolition of the Corn Laws in 1846 which was a huge distortionary subsidy to land-owners (Schonhardt-Bailey, 2006).

It is also straightforward to apply this reasoning to other policies related to redistribution and structural transformation, such as investment in mass schooling, which we may also expect to be boosted by democratization.

21.2.3 Other Considerations

Obviously, the simple model presented in the previous two subsections leaves out many mechanisms which might influence the extent of redistribution in a democracy and other forces that can shape the political equilibrium (Putterman, 1996, provides an overview of many ideas).[7]

Several papers have investigated how social mobility influences the demand for redistribution even in a democracy (Alesina and La Ferrara, 2005; Bénabou and Ok, 2001; Carter and Morrow, 2012; Wright, 1996). When rates of social mobility are high and tax policy is sticky, people who are poor today may not support high rates of taxation and redistribution because they worry that it will negatively impact them should they become rich in the future. Relatedly, Piketty (1995) suggests that different beliefs about distortionary taxation can be self-fulfilling and lead to multiple equilibria, some with low inequality and a lot of redistribution, and others with high inequality and little redistribution (see also Alesina and Angeletos, 2005; Bénabou, 2001, 2008; Bénabou and Tirole, 2006). Thus, a democratic society could result in an equilibrium with little redistribution.

Alternatively, it could be that social cleavages or identities may be such as to reduce the likelihood that a coalition favoring redistribution would form (De la O and Rodden, 2008; Frank, 2005; Lee, 2003; Roemer, 1998; Roemer et al., 2007; Shayo, 2009). For example, in Roemer's model there is a right-wing political party that does not like taxation and redistribution and a left-wing political party that does. People are ideologically predisposed toward one of the parties, but they also care about religion, as do the parties. If the right-wing party is Catholic, a poor Catholic may vote for it even if it does not offer the tax policy that the voter wishes. Another reason that the above model may fail to characterize the political equilibrium accurately is because ethnic heterogeneity limits the demand for redistribution (Alesina and Glaeser, 2004; Alesina et al., 1999). Daalgard et al. (2005) argue that institutions, particularly ones that influence the

---

[7] We have also left out a discussion of several other important issues that have been raised in theoretical analysis of redistribution in democracy. In particular, there is a growing and vibrant literature on redistribution in a dynamic context, including Krusell et al. (1997), Krusell and Ríos-Rull (1999), Hassler et al. (2003), Battaglini and Coate (2008), and Acemoglu et al. (2012). Overviews of other aspects of democratic policy-making are provided in Drazen (2000), Persson and Tabellini (2000), Acemoglu and Robinson (2006), and Besley (2007). The political economy literature on the emergence of democracy is also beyond the scope of our chapter, and we refer the reader to the extensive discussions in Acemoglu and Robinson (2006).

efficiency of the state, will influence the demand for redistribution. Finally, recent work has tied the amount of social capital to the extent of redistribution such as in Scandinavia (Algan et al., 2013).

Another idea, due to Moene and Wallerstein (2001), is that most redistribution under democracy does not take the form of transfers from rich to poor but of social insurance. Moene and Wallerstein develop a model to show that the comparative statics of this with respect to inequality may be very different from the Meltzer-Richard model.

In the rest of this section, we will instead focus on what we view as the first-order mechanisms via which democracy may fail to increase redistribution or reduce inequality.

21.2.4 Why Inequality May Not Decline: Captured Democracy and Constraints on Redistribution

In contrast to Propositions 1 and 2, greater democratization may not always reduce inequality. In this and the next two subsections, we discuss several mechanisms for this.

The first possible reason is that even though democracy reallocates de jure power to poorer agents, richer segments of society can take other actions to offset this by increasing their de facto power. This possibility, first raised in Acemoglu and Robinson (2008), can be captured in the following simple way here. Suppose that the distribution of income has mass at two points, the rich elite, who are initially enfranchised, and the rest of the citizens, who make up the majority of the population and are initially disenfranchised. Suppose, in addition, that the rich elite can undertake costly investments to increase their de facto power (meaning the power they control outside those that are strictly institutionally sanctioned, such as their influence on parties' platforms via lobbying or repression through control of local law enforcement or nonstate armed actors; see Acemoglu and Robinson, 2006, 2008; Acemoglu et al., 2013b,c). If they do so, they will "capture the political system," for example, control the political agenda of all parties or change political ideology via the media. Suppose also that this type of capture is costly, with cost denoted by $\Gamma > 0$. Then clearly, when there is a limited franchise, the elite will not need to incur the cost for doing so. Once there is enfranchisement, if this cost is not too large, they will find it beneficial to incur this cost, and may then succeed in setting the tax rate at their bliss point, rather than putting up with the higher redistribution that the majority of citizens would impose.

This reasoning immediately implies the following result:

Proposition 3
Captured Democracy
Suppose that the elite can control the political system after democratization at cost $\Gamma > 0$. Then if Γ is less than some $\overline{\Gamma}$, they will prefer to do so, and democratization will lead to no change in taxes and the distribution of income.

This proposition, in a simple way, captures the main idea of Acemoglu and Robinson (2008), even though the specific mechanism for capture is somewhat different. In Acemoglu and Robinson, each elite agent individually contributes to their collective de facto power, which needs to be greater in democracy to exceed the increased de jure power of poor citizens. Under some conditions, the main result of Acemoglu and Robinson (2008) is that the probability of the elite controlling political power is invariant to democratization—or more generally may not increase as much as it may have been expected to do owing to the direct effect of the change in de jure power.

A related channel to Proposition 3 is that democracy may be highly dysfunctional, or effectively captured, because its institutional architecture is often chosen by previous restricted franchises or dictatorships. Acemoglu et al. (2011) develop a model where the elite can take control of democracy by forming a coalition in favor of the continuation of patronage, keeping the state weak.

Other mechanisms include de jure constitutional provisions that restrict the scope for redistribution (e.g., a cap on τ) after democratization. For instance, Siavelis (2000) and Londregan (2000) argue that the constitution imposed by the Pinochet government in Chile prior to the transition to democracy was a way to constrain future redistribution. Another is the threat of a future coup preventing democracy from pursuing high redistribution. Ellman and Wantchekon (2000) discuss how fear of a military coup induced voters to support the right-wing ARENA party, taking redistribution off the political agenda, and also suggest that similar forces operated in electing Charles Taylor in Liberia in 1997 (see also Acemoglu and Robinson, 2001). An alternative mechanism is the threat of capital flight increasing the cost of redistribution (in the reduced-form model here, this would mean an increase in $C(\tau)$).[8] Moses (1994) argues that this was the case for Sweden in 1992, as well as Campello (2011) and Weyland (2004), among others, who suggest that capital flight restrained redistribution in new Latin American democracies (see also Acemoglu and Robinson, 2006). Mohamed and Finnoff (2003) similarly argue that capital flight constrained redistribution in post-apartheid South Africa (see also Alesina and Tabellini, 1989; Bardhan et al., 2006). All of these constraints would reduce the potential impact of democracy on inequality.

An implication of Proposition 3 and our discussion is that democracy may change neither fiscal policy nor the distribution of income. Nevertheless, it is also useful to note that a variant of this model can lead to an increase in taxes without a major impact on inequality. Suppose, for example, that the elite can use their de facto power to redirect spending toward themselves (e.g., toward some public goods that mostly benefit the elite such as investments in elite universities rather than in primary or secondary education),

---

[8] A related idea, proposed by Dunning (2008), is that if the main source of tax revenues is from natural resource rents, rather than personal income or wealth taxes, the elite have less incentive to oppose or capture democracy.

but have a more limited ability to control taxes. In that case, a variant of Proposition 3 would apply whereby democracy might be associated with an increase in taxation, but may not have a major impact on inequality. Moreover, in the Acemoglu et al. model mentioned above, democracy may increase taxes in order to use them as payments to state employees, but still not increase redistribution or reduce inequality.

Another variant of this result where elites can block democratization ex-ante, rather than capturing democracies ex-post, shows how selection bias can affect the correlation between democracy and the extent of redistribution observed. If elites can block democratizations that would be highly redistributive, then the only democratizations that are observed would be those that are not particularly redistributive, and we would see no correlation between democracies and increased taxation or redistribution.

A number of studies present empirical evidence consistent with these mechanisms. Larcinese (2011), for example, shows that the democratization of Italy in 1912, though it had a large positive effect on the number of people who voted, had little impact on which parties were represented in the legislature, something he interprets as consistent with the democracy being captured by old elites. Berlinski and Dewan (2011) similarly show that the British Second Reform Act of 1868, though it greatly expanded voting rights, did not have a significant immediate impact on representation.

Anderson et al. (2011) show that in Maharashtra in Western India, areas where the traditional Maratha landlords are powerful as measured by their landholdings, have democratic equilibria that are far more pro-landlord and anti-poor because the Maratha elites control voting behavior via their clientelistic ties to workers. See also Baland and Robinson (2008, 2012) on Chile; McMillan and Zoido (2004) on Peru; Pettersson-Lidbom and Tyrefors (2011) on Sweden; and Albertus and Menaldo (2014) for a cross-country empirical study of how the strength of elites at the time of democratization influences how redistributive democracy is.

There is also qualitative historical evidence on the redistributive constraints faced by democracies. Writers since James Madison have argued that the U.S. constitution is an effective bulwark against redistribution (Beard, 1913; Holton, 2008; McGuire, 2003). Others have noted that the constitution was a large obstacle to slave emancipation (Einhorn, 2006; Waldstreicher, 2009), and Dasgupta (2013) argues that the Indian constitution has been a key component in elites maintaining control of land reform projects.

21.2.5 Why Inequality May Not Decline: Inequality-Increasing Market Opportunities

Our second mechanism for an ambiguous effect of democracy on inequality is inspired by the experiences of South Africa and Eastern Europe. In South Africa, the end of apartheid in 1994 has been associated with an increase in inequality. This is partly because the black majority now takes part in economic activities from which it was previously excluded, and earnings are more dispersed in these activities than the low-skill, manual occupations to which they were previously confined. Likewise in Eastern Europe after 1989, the collapse of communism created new opportunities for people who were previously trapped in sectors of the economy where they could not use their skills and talents optimally (Atkinson and Micklewright, 1992; Flemming and Micklewright, 2000).

To incorporate this possibility, let us return to the model of structural transformation presented above. Suppose that y_i denotes the "skill" endowment of agent i, and is strictly positive for all agents. Now $\eta \in \{0, 1\}$ denotes a policy instrument preventing people from moving into some potentially high-productivity activity, with $\eta = 1$ representing such prevention and $\eta = 0$ as its cessation. Post-policy income of agent i is

$$\hat{y}_i = v(\eta) y_i \mathbf{I}(y_i > y_q) + (1 - \eta) y_i + w_0,$$

where $v(\eta)$ denotes the return to agents above the $q^{th} > 0.5$ percentile of the distribution (e.g., the landowners) from preventing the rest of the population's entrance into the high-productivity activities (e.g., banning black workers in South Africa from skilled occupations). The indicator function $\mathbf{I}(y_i > y_q)$ makes sure that this term only applies to agents above the qth percentile. In view of this, it is natural to assume that $v(\eta = 1) > v(\eta = 0) + 1$ so that the very rich benefit from this policy. In addition, if $\eta = 1$, then the remaining workers just receive a baseline wage $w_0 > 0$. In contrast, if $\eta = 0$, they are able to take part in economic activities, and in this case, some of them, depending on their type, will be more successful than others.

The median voter theorem still applies in this formulation, and following democratization extending the franchise sufficiently, the political process will lead to a switch to $\eta = 0$. However, this formulation also makes it clear that the increased market opportunities for agents below the qth percentile will create inequality among them. This effect can easily dominate the reduction in inequality resulting from the fact that the very rich no longer benefit from restricting access for the rest of the population. We summarize this result in the next proposition:

Proposition 4
Implications of Inequality-Inducing Market Opportunities
In the model described in this subsection, suppose there is an increase in democracy. If a sufficient number of voters are enfranchised, this will lead to a switch from $\eta = 1$ to $\eta = 0$, but the implications for inequality are ambiguous.

21.2.6 Why Inequality May Not Decline: The Middle Class Bias

The third possible reason for a limited impact of democracy on inequality is that, with additional tax instruments, greater democratization may empower the middle class (loosely and broadly defined), which can then use its greater power to redistribute to itself. Suppose society now consists of three groups: the rich elite with income y_r, the middle class with income $y_m < y_r$, and the poor with income $y_p < y_m$. Let the proportions of these three groups be, respectively, δ_r, δ_m, and δ_p. Consider an extension of the baseline model where there are two types of transfers: the lump-sum transfer, T, as before, and a transfer specifically benefiting the middle class, denoted by T_m. The government budget constraint is then

$$T + \delta_m T_m \leq \tau \bar{y} - C(\tau)\bar{y}. \tag{21.4}$$

Now suppose that starting with the rich elite in power there is a democratization, which makes the median voter an agent from the middle class. This will be the case if there is a limited franchise extension only to the middle class and $\delta_r < \delta_m$ (the middle classes are more populous than the rich), or there is a transition to full democracy but the middle class contains the median voter (i.e., $\delta_r + \delta_p < \delta_m$). Clearly, when only the elite are empowered there will be zero taxation (because, given the available fiscal instruments, the elite cannot redistribute to itself). With the middle class in power, there will be positive taxation and redistribution to the middle class using the instrument T_m. The resulting income distribution may be more or less equal (it will be more equal if the middle class is much poorer than the rich, **and less equal if the middle classes are much richer than the poor**).

In this case, the impact of democracy on inequality is generally ambiguous and depends on the specific measure of inequality under consideration, the cost of taxation and the pre-democracy distribution of income. It can be shown that, focusing on the Gini coefficient, when the poor are numerous and not too poor relative to the rich, that is, when

$$\frac{\delta_p}{1 - \delta_p} y_p > \frac{\delta_r}{1 - \delta_r} y_r, \tag{21.5}$$

inequality increases under democracy.[9] Intuitively, in this case, taxes hurt the poor who also do not benefit from the transfers. When the poor are more numerous and richer, they bear more of the burden of taxation, and this can increase inequality.

Furthermore, whether democratization increases or reduces inequality depends on the shares of income accruing to the rich and the poor before democracy. When either

---

[9] In particular, the Gini coefficient under autocracy is

$G^A = \delta_p - \delta_r + s_r(\delta_m + \delta_r) - s_p(\delta_p + \delta_m),$

where the s's denote the income shares of the rich and the poor. The Gini coefficient under democracy can be computed with the same formula but using the post-tax income shares of the rich and the poor, e.g., $\hat{s}_g = s_g(1 - \tau^D)/(1 - C(\tau^D))$, as

$G^D = \delta_p - \delta_r + s_r \frac{1-\tau^D}{1-C(\tau^D)}(\delta_m + \delta_r) - s_p \frac{1-\tau^D}{1-C(\tau^D)}(\delta_p + \delta_m).$

The change in the Gini due to democratization is then

$G^D - G^A = s_p \left(\frac{\tau^D - C(\tau^D)}{1 - C(\tau^D)} \right)(\delta_p + \delta_m) - s_r \left(\frac{\tau^D - C(\tau^D)}{1 - C(\tau^D)} \right)(\delta_m + \delta_r).$

Noting that $\tau^D > C(\tau^D)$, the result follows.

Equation (21.5) holds or when C is sufficiently convex that the tax choice of the middle class is not very elastic, an increase in the share of income of the rich or a decrease in the share of income of the poor makes it more likely that democracy will reduce inequality.[10] These results are summarized in the next proposition.

Proposition 5
Modified Director's Law
In the model described in this subsection, suppose there is limited enfranchisement to the middle class and $\delta_r < \delta_m$, or there is a transition to full democracy and $\delta_r + \delta_p < \delta_m$. Then there will be an increase in taxes but the effect on inequality—measured by the Gini coefficient—is ambiguous. If Equation (21.5) holds, democracy increases the Gini coefficient. Moreover, if either Equation (21.5) does not hold or C is sufficiently convex, then a larger share of income of the rich (which always increases taxes) makes it more likely that inequality will decline under democracy. If either Equation (21.5) holds or C is sufficiently convex, then a larger share of income of the poor (which also always increases taxes) makes it more likely that inequality will increase under democracy.

We refer to this result as the "Modified Director's law" since it relates to an idea attributed to Aaron Director by Stigler (1970) that redistribution in democracy involves taking from the poor and the rich to the benefit of the middle class (one can derive a similar result in a model of probabilistic voting when the middle class has a larger density for the distribution of its valence term, Persson and Tabellini, 2000, section 7.4).

This result is also related to what Aidt et al. (2009) call the "retrenchment effect" of democratization. They show that local franchise expansion in nineteenth-century Britain to the middle class often reduced expenditure on public good provision since the middle class bore the brunt of property taxes which financed local public good provision. In their model, an expansion of voting rights, by reducing public good provision and taxes on the

---

[10] First note that higher shares of income of the rich and the poor always increase the preferred tax rate of the middle class $\frac{d\tau^D}{ds_r} > 0$ and $\frac{d\tau^D}{ds_p} > 0$. Next, following on from Footnote 9, the impact of the share of income of the rich on the change in the Gini is

$$\frac{d}{ds_r}(G^D - G^A) = -H(\tau^D)(\delta_m + \delta_r) + \left[s_p(\delta_p + \delta_m) - s_r(\delta_m + \delta_r) \right] H'^D) \frac{d\tau^D}{ds_r},$$

where $H(\tau) = (\tau - C(\tau))/(1 - C(\tau))$ is the share of revenue taken by the government in taxes, which is increasing provided that $C'(\tau), C(\tau) < 1$, and $\tau > C(\tau)$, which are automatically satisfied when τ is to the right of the peak of the Laffer curve. The first term, corresponding to the incidence of taxation on the rich, is always negative. The second term is also negative when Equation (21.5) does not hold (otherwise higher taxes, creating more resources to be transferred to the middle class, are dis-equalizing), or dominated by the first term when $\frac{d\tau^D}{ds_r} > 0$ is small, which is the case when C is sufficiently convex (so that taxes do not respond significantly to an increase in s_r).

Similarly, the impact of the share of income of the poor on the changing Gini is given by

$$\frac{d}{ds_p}(G^D - G^A) = H(\tau^D)(\delta_p + \delta_m) + \left[s_p(\delta_p + \delta_m) - s_r(\delta_m + \delta_r) \right] H'^D) \frac{d\tau^D}{ds_p}.$$

The first term is now positive because inequality increases when the poor bear more of the tax burden. The second effect is also positive when Equation (21.5) holds, or dominated by the first term when C is sufficiently convex.

middle class, can thus increase inequality. Relatedly, Fernandez and Rogerson (1995) show how an equilibrium like this could arise in a political economy model of taxation and educational subsidies.

An important contrast between this result and Proposition 3 is on taxes. In Proposition 3, democracy neither increases taxes nor reduces inequality (but note the contrast with extended versions of the captured democracy mechanism). Here democracy increases taxes, but because the additional revenue is used for the middle class, it may not reduce inequality.[11]

21.2.7 Discussion and Interpretation

The theoretical ideas presented so far suggest that in the most basic framework, we expect democracy to increase redistribution and reduce inequality. We may also expect a boost to structural transformation from democratization. However, several factors militate against this tendency. The elite—the richer segments of society—who stand to lose from increased redistribution can attempt to increase their de facto power to compensate for their reduced de jure power under democracy. As we have seen, this can limit redistribution and/or the potential reduction in inequality. Alternatively, consistent with Director's law, democracy may indeed increase taxes but use the resulting revenues for redistribution to the middle class, thus not necessarily reducing inequality. Finally, democracy may also be associated with the opening up of new economic opportunities to a large segment of society, which can be an additional source of inequality.

After reviewing the existing empirical literature, we will investigate the impact of democracy on redistribution and inequality. We will, in particular, study whether the effect of democracy on redistribution and inequality is heterogeneous and whether it depends on the economic and political forces we have highlighted in this section. In line with the theoretical mechanisms here, we expect the captured democracy effect to be stronger if the elite have more to lose from democracy, for example, if they are more vested in land or other assets that will lose value when wages increase and nondemocratic policies useful for these assets are lifted. Additionally, we expect the position of the middle class in the distribution of income to shape the type and extent of redistribution observed in democracy. Finally, we also expect the inequality-inducing market opportunity effect to be stronger when frontier technologies and global economic activities are more human or physical capital-biased and when society is more urbanized and presents greater opportunities for entrepreneurship and capitalist development. These are some of the ideas we will investigate in greater detail in the empirical analysis.

---

[11] While we do not explore this in the chapter, this result also suggests that measures of polarization, as discussed in Chapter 5, could be an important source of heterogeneity in the relationship between democracy and redistribution, as the middle class would have more to gain from taxing both the poor and the rich.

21.3. PREVIOUS LITERATURE

In this section, we survey the literature on the effect of democracy on redistribution and inequality. Our emphasis will be on the empirical literature, though we also discuss some of the theoretical ideas that have played an important role in this literature (several theoretical contributions have already been discussed in the previous section).

21.3.1 Democracy, Taxes, and Redistribution

In the basic model of the policy effects of democracy proposed by Meltzer and Richard (1981), an expansion of democracy should lead to greater tax revenues and redistribution. We first consider the tax and spending part of this. While Gil et al. (2004) found no correlation between tax revenues and different components of government spending and democracy in a cross-sectional specification, as we discuss below, there are many studies which do find such results.

This is certainly true of the more historical studies, for example, Lindert (2004), Gradstein and Justman (1999a), and Acemoglu and Robinson (2000). Aidt et al. (2006) and Aidt and Jensen (2009b) examine the impact of democratization measured by the proportion of adults who could vote in a cross-national panel consisting of 12 Western European countries over the period 1830–1938, and in a sample of 10 Western countries over the period 1860–1938, respectively. The latter paper, for example, finds robust positive effects of suffrage on government expenditure as a percentage of GDP and also tax revenues as a percentage of GDP.

One would expect that democracy not only changes the total amount of tax revenues, but also what taxes were used for. For instance, one might expect democracies to move towards more progressive taxation. Aidt and Jensen (2009b) investigated the impact of suffrage on tax incidence. They found, somewhat paradoxically, that suffrage expansion led to lower direct taxes and higher indirect taxes. Aidt and Jensen (2009a) investigated the determinants of the introduction of an income tax. They reported a nonlinear relationship with suffrage, indicating that an expansion of the franchise starting from very restrictive levels reduces the probability that an income tax will be introduced, but also that this probability increases significantly at higher levels of the franchise.

Scheve and Stasavage (2010, 2012) also adopt a long-run approach using data from OECD countries and find no correlation between democracy and either tax progressivity or the rate of capital taxation. Instead, consistent with Tilly (1985) and Besley and Pearson (2011), they emphasize the importance of warfare, a topic to which we return later.

An important study by Lindert (1994) found an impact of democracy on various types of social spending in a panel data consisting of European and North American countries as well as Japan, Australasia, Argentina, Brazil, and Mexico and spanning the period from 1880 to 1930. In his 2004 book, Lindert summarizes his findings as: "Conclusion #1: There was so little social spending of any kind before the twentieth century mainly because political voice was so restricted" (Lindert, 2004, p. 22).

A lot of research is consistent with this. Huber and Stephens (2012) build a panel data-set for Latin America between 1970 and 2007 and measure democracy by the cumulative years a country has been democratic since 1945 and estimate pooled OLS models without fixed effects. They find the history of democracy is significantly positively correlated with education spending, health spending and Social Security, and welfare spending. In a panel data of 14 Latin American countries for 1973–1997, Kaufman and Segura-Ubiergo (2001) show that democracy, as measured by the dichotomous measure introduced by Przeworski et al. (2000), is positively correlated with government expenditure on health and education but not with other components of spending. Brown and Hunter (1999) also focus on Latin America using a panel between 1980 and 1992. They examine the impact of democracy, coded as a dichotomous measure based on Przeworski et al. (2000), on social spending per capita. They also examine various types of interactions between democracy and other variables such as GDP per capita and the growth rate in GDP per capita. Their basic findings suggest that democracies have greater social spending than autocracies.

Using a broader set of countries and a panel between 1960 and 1998, Persson and Tabellini (2003) also find some evidence that democracy, as measured by the Gastil index and the Polity score, has positive effects on government expenditure and government revenues as well as welfare and Social Security spending as percentages of GDP.

Though most studies tend to focus on a broad measure of democracy, an interesting literature has examined female enfranchisement more specifically. The main focus of this research has been on whether enfranchising women has an additional or differential impact on government taxation or spending. Lindert (1994) showed that female enfran-chisement had an independent effect on social spending and this finding has held up well (see Aidt and Dallal, 2008, for similar results for a later period). Lott and Kenny (1999) studied the expansion of women's voting rights in the United States between 1870 and 1940 and found that it coincided with increases in per capita state revenues and expen-ditures. Miller (2008) also examined this process showing that female suffrage increased health spending and led to significant falls in infant mortality.

Of all the research on this topic, only the paper by Aidt and Jensen (2013) provides an identification strategy to tackle the fact that democracy is endogenous. Building on the theoretical ideas in Acemoglu and Robinson (2000, 2006) and their previous work (Aidt and Jensen, 2011), they argue that "revolutionary threat," measured by revolutionary events in other countries, is a viable instrument for democracy in a panel of Western European countries between 1820 and 1913. Using this source of variation, they find that democracy, as measured by the extent of suffrage (proportion of the adult population that is enfranchised), has a robust positive effect on government spending relative to GDP.

In this light, the paper by Gil et al. (2004) appears an outlier in finding no effects of democracy on tax revenues as a percentage of GDP and spending. Nevertheless, there are econometric problems with all of these papers. Specifically, there is little attention to identification problems and most studies that use panel data do not include country fixed effects, thus confounding the effect of democracy with country-specific factors potentially correlated with democracy and redistribution. Though the important study of Aidt and Jensen (2013) moves the literature a long way forward, their empirical model controls for many endogenous variables on the right side and does not deal with the possibility that revolutionary events in other countries might capture other correlated effects impacting the outcomes of interest (see the discussion of this possibility in Acemoglu et al., 2013a).

21.3.2 Democracy and Inequality

There is an even larger reduced-form empirical literature on the relationship between democracy and inequality, most of it by sociologists and political scientists rather than economists. This has typically delivered ambiguous results. Early work, which consisted mostly of simple cross-national regressions of measures of inequality (usually the income Gini coefficient) on various measures of democracy, was surveyed by Sirowy and Inkeles (1990). They concluded "the existing evidence suggests that the level of political democracy as measured at one point in time tends not to be widely associated with lower levels of income inequality" (p. 151).

Much of this literature, however, also suffers from the econometric problems of the type discussed in the last subsection. Most importantly, there is the possibility that omitted factors are affecting both inequality and democracy, and that reverse causation from inequality to democracy may be present (e.g., Muller, 1988).

Muller (1988), using a larger dataset than the previous literature, found that there was a negative correlation between the number of years a country had been democratic and inequality, which he interpreted as evidence that democracy had to be in place for long enough for inequality to fall. Yet the robustness of his results were challenged by Weede (1989) (see the response by Muller, 1989). Others, such as Simpson (1990), Burkhart (1997), and Gradstein and Justman (1999b) claimed that there was a nonlinear reduced-form relationship between democracy and inequality with inequality being low at both low and high levels of democracy and higher for intermediate levels. The plethora of results is what led Sirowy and Inkeles to be skeptical, though they do suggest that there may be some evidence in favor of the relevance of the history of democracy for inequality (Muller's original finding has been replicated in many subsequent studies, e.g., by Huber et al., 2006; Huber and Stephens, 2012, table 5.10). Nevertheless, there are good reasons for being skeptical about these findings, since the impact of the history of democracy is identified in models that do not include fixed effects, and obviously, it will capture the impact of these omitted fixed effects. More generally, this is just a special case of the difficulty of identifying duration dependence and unobserved heterogeneity—a difficulty that this literature neither tackles nor recognizes.

Three more recent studies used better data and exploited the time as well as the cross-sectional dimensions to investigate the impact of democracy on inequality. Rodrik (1999) showed that either the Freedom House of Polity III measure of democracy was positively correlated with average real wages in manufacturing and the share of wages in national income (in specifications that also control for productivity, GDP per capita and a price index). He illustrated this both in a cross section and in a panel of countries using country fixed effects. He also presented evidence that political competition and participation at large were important parts of the mechanisms via which democracy worked.[12] Scheve and Stasavage (2009) used a long-run panel from 1916 to 2000 for 13 OECD countries with country fixed effects and found that universal suffrage, measured as a dummy, had no impact on the share of national income accruing to the top 1%. Perhaps consistent with a variant of the (upper) middle class bias argument we provided above, they found that there is actually a statistically significant positive correlation between the universal suffrage dummy and what they called the "Top10-1" share, which is the share of income accruing to people between the 90th and 99th percentiles of the income distribution divided by the share accruing to the people above the 99th percentile. Finally, Li et al. (1998) used pooled OLS to show that an index of civil liberties is negatively correlated with inequality (greater civil liberties, lower inequality) though they do not investigate the relationship between inequality and more conventional measures of democracy.

Though this research has been dominated by studies that examine the average effect of democracy, Lee (2005) uses a panel data random effects model to argue that there are heterogeneous effects of democracy on inequality. The panel is unbalanced and covers 64 countries between 1970 and 1994. In particular, he argues that there is a significant interaction between the size of government as measured by tax revenues as a percentage of GDP and democracy. The paper finds that, although there is a significant positive correlation between democracy and inequality, the interaction between democracy and the size of government is significant and negative, suggesting that for large enough levels of government, democracy reduces inequality. Lee interprets this as measuring state strength (similarly to Cheibub, 1998 and Soifer, 2013).

21.3.3 Education and Democracy

The impact of democracy on education has also been examined both historically and using contemporary cross-national data and some of the results were noted in the last section. The work of Lindert (2004, chapter 5) is again central and, as with his work on social spending, Lindert presents evidence that the historical emergence of democracy is connected with educational expansion. A complementary historical study by Engerman and Sokoloff (2005, 2011) points out that within the Americas there is a close

---

[12] We will return to Rodrik's study below, and particularly in Appendix A, to explain the contrast between his and our results.

connection between the extent of democracy, measured by voting rights, the proportion of adults that voted and an effective secret ballot, and measures of education such as literacy rates.

A great deal of econometric work supports this research using various measures of education. Baum and Lake (2001), for example, found that secondary-school gross enrollment rates also increased with democracy across the developing world, "particularly among regimes that have experienced large changes in democracy" (p. 613) (see also Baum and Lake, 2003). Brown and Hunter (2004), focusing on 17 Latin American countries between 1980 and 1997, find that the Polity index is positively correlated with total educational expenditures per capita and also with the share of expenditures going into primary education. This finding mirrors the earlier one of Brown (1999) who finds that various dichotomous measures of democracy created from the Polity dataset and the measure of Przeworski et al. (2000) were positively correlated with primary school enrollment. Huber and Stephens (2012) also find robust evidence in Latin America for a positive correlation between the history of democracy and educational spending (see also Avelino et al., 2005).

These issues have also been intensively studied in sub-Saharan Africa. Stasavage (2005a) examined the impact of democratization in the 1990s in Africa on education, using a measure of democracy similar to Przeworski et al. (2000), and presented evidence that democracy increases total educational spending as a percentage of GDP. He also found evidence of increases in spending on primary education as a percentage of GDP, though this was not robust to the use of country fixed effects. Stasavage (2005b) provides a case study of democratization and educational expansion in Uganda. More recent research by Harding and Stasavage (2013) reconfirms the impact of democracy on primary education, this time looking at primary enrollment, and shows that the likely channel runs through a greater probability that democratic governments will abolish primary school fees.

Gallego (2010) presents one of the few attempts to develop an identification strategy to examine the impact of democracy on education. There are many reasons why this is important. Most obviously, there is the issue of whether or not there is reverse causation from education to democracy. Though the results of Acemoglu et al. (2005) reduce this concern, the above papers deal with this at best by using lagged democracy as an explanatory variable. Gallego follows Acemoglu et al. (2001, 2002) and uses their data on the historical settler mortality of Europeans and indigenous population density in 1500 as instruments for democracy and finds that democracy in 1900, measured by the Polity score, has a significant causal effect on primary school enrollment in 1900. Gallego recognizes that the exclusion restriction of his instrument may be violated but provides a very careful discussion of the potential biases that this involves and how this works against the findings he focuses on, arguing that he estimates a lower bound on the effect of democracy on education.

Using a broad sample of over 100 countries between 1960 and 2000, Ansell (2010) uses panel data regressions with and without country fixed effects to examine the impact of democracy, measured by the Polity score, on various components of educational spending. He also instruments for democracy using lagged democracy and the levels of democracy in neighboring countries. He finds that democracy has a positive and significant effect on total educational spending as a percentage of GDP, and on educational spending as a percentage of the government budget. Using cross-national regressions he also finds a negative correlation between democracy and private educational spending as a percentage of GDP and also between democracy and primary school expenditure per student by the government. He argues, contrary to Stasavage, that democracy tilts educational spending away from primary and toward secondary and tertiary education.

The likely reconciliation of all these results is that the type of education democracy produces depends on what forces democracy unleashes and who wields power in democracy. In Uganda, when President Museveni allowed democratization, he did so in a society lacking a large middle class who could dominate educational spending decisions. Hence as Stasavage showed, primary school enrollment increased. But in a large cross-national sample, the relationship may be dominated by dictatorships that spend more on primary schooling and democracies that focus on secondary schooling (see also Gradstein et al., 2004; Ansell, 2010, for relevant models).

This may also account for the results in recent work by Aghion et al. (2012), which uses a long but unbalanced panel of 137 countries between 1830 and 2001 and reports a negative correlation between the Polity score and primary school enrollment.

21.3.4 Democracy and Health Outcomes

There is also some other work on the impact of democracy on health outcomes. These are potentially related to inequality, because rapid improvements in health outcomes tend to come at the bottom of the distribution. Many studies, for example, find that democracy is positively correlated with life expectancy (see McGuire, 2010, for an overview and case study and econometric evidence). Besley and Kudamatsu (2006) show this in a panel data model for the post-war period but without using country fixed effects. Wigley and Akkoyunlu-Wigley (2011) in a complementary study have shown that life expectancy is positively correlated with the history of democracy of a country. Kudamatsu (2012) showed in the context of democratic transitions in Africa that health outcomes improved in countries that democratized compared to those that did not.

Blaydes and Kayser (2011) looked at the relationship between democracy and average calories per capita interpreted as a proxy for inequality, because calories consumed decline very quickly with income. Using a trichotomous measure of democracy based on the Polity IV dataset (where greater than 7 is a democracy, less than −7 is an autocracy, and everything in between a "hybrid regime"), they show in a panel data model with country fixed effects that democracy is positively correlated with average calorie consumption.

Gerring et al. (2012) find using panel data from 1960 to 2000 that, although the current level of democracy, as measured by the Polity score, is not robustly correlated with infant mortality, there is a strong negative correlation between the history of democracy and infant mortality—the more a country has experienced democracy in the past, the lower is infant mortality currently. Contrary to these findings, Ross (2006), using panel data from 1970 to 2000, the Polity score, the Przeworski et al. (2000) dichotomous measure of democracy, and the history of democracy as independent variables, finds no robust correlation between any of them and infant and child mortality. A possible reconciliation of these findings is that, as mentioned above, the history of democracy is nothing but a proxy for the omitted fixed effects, and Ross obtains different results from Gerring et al. because he controlled for fixed effects. Another confounding factor is that this literature in general does not control for the dynamics of democracy and GDP per capita and the endogeneity of democratization (see Acemoglu et al., 2013).

21.3.5 The Intensive Margin

All the papers discussed so far use various national-level measures of democracy, usually based on well-known databases created by political scientists. An important complementary direction is to investigate within-country variation exploiting other measures of "effective" enfranchisement.

In this context, particularly interesting is Fujiwara's (2011) study of changes in the voting technology in Brazil in the 1990s. These, by making it much simpler and easier for illiterate people to vote, massively enfranchised the poor. Fujiwara estimates the effect of this change by exploiting differences in the way the policy was rolled out. He shows that the consequence of the reform was a change in government spending in a pro-poor direction, particularly with respect to health expenditures, and that infant mortality fell as a result. Baland and Robinson (2008, 2012) examine another related reform, the introduction of an effective secret ballot in Chile in 1958. Though they do not directly study any policy outcomes, they do show that the reform led to large increases in the vote share of left-wing parties, which, they argue, is consistent with this democratizing reform moving the political equilibrium towards more pro-poor policies. They also find that land prices fall, which illustrates that the price of land capitalized the value of controlling workers' votes under the open ballot.

Martinez-Bravo et al. (2012) study the effects of elections in China on redistribution and public good provision. They use variation in the introduction of village elections in China, controlling for village and year fixed effects as well as province-level trends. They find that village chairmen experience higher turnover and become more educated and less likely to be Communist Party members following the introduction of elections. They also find that taxes and public goods increase as a result of the elections. In particular, irrigation increases more in villages with more farmland, and public education increases in villages with more children. They also find that income inequality is reduced, and less land is leased to elite-controlled enterprises.

Naidu (2011) examined the impact of the disenfranchisement of blacks in the US South via poll taxes and literacy tests in the period after the end of Reconstruction. He finds that this reversal of democracy reduced the teacher-student ratio in black schools by 10–23%, with no significant effects on white teacher–student ratios. Also, consistent with Baland and Robinson's results, disenfranchisement increased farm values.

Relatedly, using state-level data Husted and Kenny (1997) examine the impact of the abolition of literacy tests and poll taxes in the United States over the period 1950–1988 and find that this was associated with a significant increase in welfare expenditures but not other types of government expenditures. Using county-level data, Cascio and Washington (2012) find that expansion of voting rights in the South resulted in increased state transfers to previously disenfranchised counties. Besley et al. (2010), on the other hand, show that the abolition of literacy tests and poll taxes was associated with increased political competition in US states. Increased political competition between the Republicans and Democrats reduced government tax revenues relative to state income and increased infrastructure expenditure relative to other components of government expenditure.

21.4. ECONOMETRIC SPECIFICATION AND DATA

Given the conflicting results in the theoretical and empirical literature surveyed above, we now present our econometric framework for investigating the relationship between democracy, redistribution, and inequality. We attempt to evaluate the diverse results within a single empirical strategy and sample, and we provide what we view to be some basic robust facts.

In this section, we describe our econometric specifications and our main data. Our approach is to estimate a canonical panel data model with country fixed effects and time effects while also modeling the dynamics of inequality and redistribution. Both fixed effects and allowing for dynamics (e.g., mean reversion) are important. Without fixed effects, as already noted above, several confounding factors will make the association between democracy and inequality (or redistribution) difficult to interpret. Moreover, we will see that there are potentially important dynamics in the key outcome variables, and failure to control for this would lead to spurious relationships (or make it difficult to establish robust patterns even when such patterns do exist).

Some of the papers we mentioned above have adopted a set-up similar to this, for example Rodrik (1999), Ross (2006), Scheve and Stasavage (2009), Aghion et al. (2012), and Aidt and Jensen (2013), but without modeling the dynamics in inequality or redistribution. In addition, several of these papers suffer from the "bad control" problem; for example, Scheve and Stasavage (2009) control for both suffrage and education in their investigation of the determinants of the top income shares. If democracy influences inequality via its impact on education, then such an empirical model is bound to find that democracy is not correlated with inequality. Even the pioneering paper by Aidt and Jensen (2013) controls for many endogenous variables on the right side of the regression including the Polity score of the country.[13]

21.4.1 Econometric Specification

Consider the following simple econometric model:

$$z_{it} = \rho z_{it-1} + \gamma d_{it-1} + \mathbf{x}'_{it-1}\beta + \mu_t + \psi_i + u_{it}, \qquad (21.6)$$

where z_{it} is the outcome of interest, which will be either (log of) tax revenue as a percentage of GDP or total revenue as a percentage of GDP as alternative measures of taxation, education, structural change, or one of several possible measures of inequality. The dependent variables with significant skewness in their cross-country distribution, in particular, tax to GDP ratio, total government revenues to GDP ratio, agricultural shares of employment, and income and secondary enrollment, will be in logs, which makes interpretation easier and allows the impact of democracy to be proportional to the baseline level. All of the results emphasized in this paper also hold in specifications using levels rather than logs, but these are not reported to conserve space. Lags in this specification will always mean 5-year lags: d_{it-1} is democracy 5 years ago. The lagged value of the dependent variable on the right-hand side is included to capture persistence (and mean reversion) in these outcome measures, which may be a determinant of democracy or correlated with other variables that predict democracy. The main right hand side variable is d_{it}, a dummy for democracy in country i in period t whose construction will be described in detail below. This variable is lagged by one period (generally a 5-year interval) because we expect its impact not to be contemporaneous. All other potential covariates, as well as interaction effects which are included later, are in the vector $\mathbf{x}_{it-1}$, which is lagged to avoid putting endogenous variables on the right-hand side of the regression. In our baseline specification, we include lagged log GDP per capita as a covariate for several reasons.[14] First, as we show in Acemoglu et al. (2013), democracy is much more likely to suffer from endogeneity concerns when the lagged effects of GDP per capita are not controlled for. Second, in Acemoglu et al. (2013), we also show that democracy has a

---

[13] A more desirable approach would be to develop an instrument for democracy. We believe that the only credible papers on this topic are Gallego (2010), Aidt and Jensen (2013), and our own work, Acemoglu et al. (2013). We do not pursue these directions as this would take us too far from our purpose of surveying and interpreting the literature and presenting what we believe to be the robust correlations in the data.

[14] We will always use GDP to refer to log GDP per capita.

major effect on GDP per capita and changes in GDP per capita may impact inequality independently of the influence of democracy on this variable. In all cases, we also report specifications that do not control for GDP per capita to ensure that the results we report are not driven by the presence of this endogenous control.

Finally, the ψ_i's denote a full set of country dummies and the μ_t's denote a full set of time effects that capture common shocks and trends for all countries. u_{it} is an error term, capturing all other omitted factors, with $E[u_{it}|z_{it-1}, d_{it-1}, \mathbf{x}'_{it-1}, \mu_t, \psi_i] = 0$ for all i and t. We estimate the above equation excluding the Soviet Union and its satellite countries because the dynamics of inequality and taxation following the fall of the Soviet Union are probably different from other democratizations. In some cases, for example, when using the tax to GDP ratio, this restriction is irrelevant because there is no data for these countries. When there is data, as with inequality, we also report results including these countries.

Our estimation framework controls for two key sources of potential bias. First, it controls for country fixed effects, which take into account that democracies are different from nondemocracies in many permanent characteristics that we do not observe and that may also affect inequality and taxation.[15] Second, it allows for mean-reverting dynamics and persistent effects in the dependent variable that may be endogenous to democracy.[16] This focus on *changes* in democracy ignores variation across countries that never change political institutions, for example, the United States, India, and China, but these observations help us in forming the counterfactual outcome conditional on the right-hand side covariates. Put differently, countries that never change political institutions may still be informative about how taxation and inequality change as a function of past taxation and inequality.

The simplest way of estimating Equation (21.6) is by OLS and imposing $\rho = 0$, and this is the most common regression in the prior literature which has used panel data. But, as already pointed out above, if $\rho > 0$, this specification may lead to biased estimates and will not correctly identify the long-run effect of democracy on the outcome of interest. An alternative method is to estimate this equation by OLS (which is just the standard within–group estimator removing the fixed effects by eliminating the mean of country i). This estimator is not consistent when the number of time periods is finite, because the regressor z_{it-1} is mechanically correlated with u_{is} for $s < t$, and this will induce a downward bias in the estimate of ρ (e.g., Wooldridge, 2002, chapter 11). However, the bias

---

[15] For instance, democracies may have more pluralistic institutions or stronger states, which may independently affect inequality and taxation.

[16] For instance, crisis, turmoil, social unrest, or increases in inequality could trigger a democratization, and also have a persistent effect on the path of our dependent variable. In this case, it becomes important to control for the dynamics of taxes or inequality by adding their lag on the right-hand side.

becomes smaller as the number of periods grows, holding ρ constant, so for large enough T or low enough ρ it becomes negligible (Nickell, 1981).

Our preferred estimation strategy is to deal with this econometric problem using a standard generalized method of moments (GMM) estimator along the lines of Holtz-Eakin et al. (1988) and Arellano and Bond (1991). This involves differencing Equation (21.6) with respect to time

$$\Delta z_{it} = \rho \Delta z_{it-1} + \gamma \Delta d_{it-1} + \Delta \mathbf{x}'_{it-1}\beta + \Delta\mu_t + \Delta u_{it}, \tag{21.7}$$

where the fixed-country effects are removed by time differencing. Although Equation (21.7) cannot be estimated consistently by OLS either, in the absence of serial correlation in the original residual, u_{it} (i.e., no second-order serial correlation in Δu_{it}), z_{it-2} and all further lags, and thus also d_{it-2} and all further lags, are uncorrelated with Δu_{it}, and can be used as instruments for Δz_{it-1}, incorporating them as moment conditions in a GMM procedure.

An alternative procedure removes country fixed effects by taking forward orthogonal differences. In particular, for variable w_{it}, this is given by

$$w_{it}^{\text{fod}} = \sqrt{\frac{T_{it}}{T_{it+1}}} \left(w_{it} - \frac{1}{T}\sum_{s>t} w_{is} \right),$$

where T_{it} is the number of times w_{is} appears in the data for $s > t$. Forward orthogonal differences also remove the fixed effects. In the absence of serial correlation in the original residual, z_{it-1}, d_{it-1}, $\mathbf{x}'_{it-1}$ and all further lags are orthogonal to the transformed error term u_{it}^{fod}, and can be used to form moment conditions in a GMM procedure. Moreover, if the original residuals were i.i.d., then the transformed error term will also be i.i.d.[17]

We will implement this using Arellano and Bond's GMM estimator with different subsets of moments, and after taking first differences or forward orthogonal differences of the data. As Newey and Windmeijer (2009) show, using the full set of moments in two-step GMM may lead to the "too many instruments" bias, since the number of potential moments one could use to estimate the dynamic panel model is quadratic in the time dimension. Thus, we experiment by restricting the number of lags used to form moments in the estimation. In addition to restricting the number of moments, we focus on

---

[17] Estimates of the model obtained by taking forward orthogonal differences are different from the first difference estimates only in unbalanced panels or when not all Arellano and Bond moments are used, in which case different lags give different moments and these may match dynamics differently. Yet another alternative is Blundell and Bond's (2000) system GMM, which works with the level equation (rather than the difference equation as in Equation 21.7 above) and uses first differences of the dependent variable as instruments for the lagged level. For consistency, this estimator thus requires that the initial value of the dependent variable, in this case democracy, is uncorrelated with the fixed effects. This is unlikely to be a good assumption in our context given the historically determined nature of both democracy and inequality/redistribution.

one-step GMM estimators with a naive weighting matrix that assumes the original residuals are i.i.d.[18] Despite the potential loss in efficiency, these estimators have the advantage
of being consistent when T (the time dimension of the panel) and N (the number of
countries) are large, even if the number of moments also becomes large (see Alvarez
and Arellano, 2003).

As the above description indicates, the source of bias in the estimation of Equation (21.6) with OLS is that the persistence parameter ρ is not estimated consistently
when the time dimension does not go to infinity, and this bias translates into a bias in
all other coefficient estimates. If we knew the exact value of ρ and could impose it,
the rest of the parameters could be estimated consistently by OLS. Motivated by this
observation, we also report OLS estimates of Equation (21.6) imposing a range of values
of ρ, which shows that our main results are robust to any value of ρ between 0 and 1,
increasing our confidence in the GMM estimates.

In all cases, we first focus on results using a 5-year panel, where we take an observation
every 5 years from 1960 to 2010. This is preferable to taking averages, which would
introduce a complex pattern of serial correlation, making consistent estimation more difficult. The 5-year panel is a useful starting point since we expect many of the results of
democracy on the tax to GDP ratio (henceforth, short for tax revenue as a percentage of
GDP) and inequality not to appear instantaneously or not even in one or two years. In the
case of inequality measures, this is also the highest frequency we can use.[19] For the tax to
GDP ratio, the annual data are available, and we also estimate annual panels, which are
similar to Equation (21.6) except that in that case we include up to 12 annual lags of both
the lagged dependent variable and the democracy measure on the right-hand side.

Finally, it is worth reiterating that in all of our estimates, if democracy is correlated
with other changes affecting taxes or inequality, our estimates will be biased. The point of
the GMM estimator is to remove the mechanical bias resulting from the presence of fixed
effects and lagged dependent variables, not to estimate "causal effects." This would neces-
sitate a credible source of variation in changes in democracy, which we do not use in this
paper.

21.4.2 Data and Descriptive Statistics

We construct a yearly and a 5-year panel of 184 countries from independence or 1960,
whichever is later, through to 2010, though not all variables are available for all countries

---

[18] When we take first differences of the data, the weighting matrix has 1 on the main diagonal and -0.5 on
   the subdiagonals below and above it. When we take forward orthogonal differences, the weighting matrix
   is the identity matrix.

[19] Our inequality data from SWIID provides yearly observations for the GINI coefficient, but they are
   5-year moving averages of observations around that specific year, making them inappropriate for an
   annual panel.

in all periods. We extend the recent work by Papaioannou and Siourounis (2008) by constructing a new measure of democracy which combines information from Freedom House and Polity IV—two of the more widely used sources of data about political rights and democracy. We create a dichotomous measure of democracy in country c at time t, d_{ct}, as follows. First, we code a country as democratic during a given year if Freedom House codes it as "Free" or "Partially Free," and it receives a positive Polity IV score. If we only have information from one of Polity or Freedom House, we use additional information from Cheibub et al. (2010, henceforth CGV) and Boix et al. (2012, henceforth BMR). In these cases, we code an observation as democratic if either Polity is greater than 0, or Freedom House codes it as "Partially Free" or "Free" *and* at least one of CGV or BMR code it as democratic. We are interested in substantive changes in political power, and so we give priority to the expert codings of Polity and Freedom House, rather than the procedural codings of CGV and BMR.

We omit periods where a country was not independent. Finally, many of the democratic transitions captured by this algorithm are studied in detail by Papaioannou and Siourounis (2008), who code the exact date of the democratization. When we detect a democratization that is also in their sample (in the same country and generally within 4 years of the year obtained by the previous procedure), we modify our democracy dummy to match the date to which they trace back the event using historical sources.

The Papaioannou and Siourounis measure of democracy captures *permanent* changes in political institutions, and they find that this correlates with subsequent economic growth. One limitation of their measure is that they define permanent changes by looking at democratizations that are not reversed in the future, which raises the possibility of endogeneity of the definition of democracy to subsequent growth or other outcomes that stabilize democracy. In addition, it means that they have no variation coming from transitions from democracy to autocracy. Our measure retains the focus on large changes in political regimes while not using any potentially endogenous outcome to classify democratizations.

Our resulting democracy measure is a dichotomous variable capturing large changes in political institutions. Our sample contains countries that are always democratic ($d_{ct}=1$ for all years) like the United States and most OECD countries; countries that are always autocratic ($d_{ct}=0$ for all years) like Afghanistan, Angola, and China; countries that transition once and permanently into democracy like Dominican Republic in 1978, Spain in 1978, and many ex-Soviet countries after 1991. But different from Papaioannou and Siourounis, we also have countries that transition in and out of democracy such as Argentina, which is coded as democratic from 1973 to 1975, falls back to nondemocracy and then democratizes permanently in 1983. For more details on our construction of the democracy measure, see Acemoglu et al. (2013a). In Appendix B, we show robustness of our main results to other measures of democracy constructed by Cheibub et al. (2010) and Boix et al. (2012).

We combine this measure of democratization with national income statistics from the World Bank economic indicators. We use government taxes to GDP and revenues to GDP ratios measures obtained from Cullen Hendrix covering more than 127 countries yearly from 1960 to 2005 (Hendrix, 2010). These data come from a project now updated by Arbetman-Rabinowitz et al. (2011), and puts together in a consistent way information from the World Bank (for 1960–1972), the IMF Government Financial Statistics historical series, the IMF new GFS, and complementary national sources.[20] Other dependent variables we explored include secondary-schooling enrollment, agricultural shares of employment, and GDP from the World Bank; and our inequality data that will be described below.[21]

Our additional covariates include a measure of average intensity of foreign wars over the last 5 years, constructed from Polity IV and ranging from 0 (no episodes) to 10 (most intense episodes); a measure of social unrest from the SPEED project at the University of Illinois averaging the number of events over the last 5 years;[22] and the fraction of the population with at least secondary schooling from the Barro-Lee dataset. In order to explore interactions we use data on the nonagricultural share of employment in 1968 from Vanhanen (2013).[23] We also use the top 10% share of income in the United States from the World Top Incomes Database (Alvaredo et al., 2010).[24] Finally, we construct the average ratio between the share of income held by the top 10% relative to the bottom 50%, and the ratio between the share of income held by the bottom 10 relative to the bottom 50% before 2000 using the World Inequality Indicators Database. From now on we will refer to these measures as the top and bottom shares of income.[25]

There is some debate on the construction and standardization of inequality measures, particularly Gini coefficients, across countries. We use the data in the Standardized World Inequality Indicators Database (SWIID), constructed by Frederick Solt (Solt, 2009). This database uses the Luxembourg Income Study together with the World Inequality Indicators Database in order to construct a comprehensive cross-national panel of Gini coefficients that are standardized across sources and measures. One advantage of this dataset is that it provides both the net Gini, after taxes and transfers, and the gross Gini coefficients. Measuring country-level inequality is very data-demanding, and so no inequality

---

[20] http://thedata.harvard.edu/dvn/dv/rpc/faces/study/StudyPage.xhtml?globalId=hdl:1902.1/16845.

[21] In the Appendix A we consider manufacturing wages, compiled by Martin Rama from UNIDO statistics and averaged over 5-year intervals.

[22] http://www.clinecenter.illinois.edu/research/speed-data.html.

[23] http://www.fsd.uta.fi/en/data/catalogue/FSD1216/meF1216e.html.

[24] http://topincomes.g-mond.parisschoolofeconomics.eu/.

[25] The World Inequality Indicators Database reports income shares created using different proxies for income, including consumption, monetary income, disposable income, and others. We standardized these ratios by regressing them on a full set of dummies for each income concept and using the residuals. The raw ratios are presented only in the summary statistics.

database is completely satisfactory, but we believe the SWIID provides the most comprehensive and consistent measure for the panel regressions we are estimating. We have experimented with a number of other measures of Gini coefficients, but none have the standardized sample coverage of the SWIID. In particular, we also created a panel with data every 5 years using observations for the Gini coefficient from the World Income Inequality Database (WIID) and CEDLAS (for Latin American countries), and obtained very similar results.

Descriptive statistics for all variables used in the main sample are presented in Table 21.1, separately by our measure of nondemocracy and democracy (observations in a country that was nondemocratic at the time or democratic). In each case, we report means, standard deviations, and also the total number of observations (note that our

Table 21.1 Summary statistics

Variable	Nondemocracies			Democracies		
	Mean	Std. Dev.	N	Mean	Std. Dev.	N
Tax revenue as a percentage of GDP	15.82	9.50	660	20.94	9.73	569
Total government revenue as a percentage of GDP	20.74	12.85	660	25.42	11.01	569
Gini coefficient, net income	38.91	10.76	338	36.81	10.19	497
Gini coefficient, gross income	43.92	11.72	338	45.11	7.71	497
Foreign wars (polity)	0.15	0.70	740	0.07	0.39	623
Social unrest (SPEED)	5.35	24.99	927	9.16	35.40	705
Share with secondary enrollmenty (Barro-Lee)	17.59	16.00	745	32.07	19.23	652
Nonagricultural share of population	64.54	28.51	138	81.39	19.55	301
Nonagricultural share of GDP	74.05	16.65	627	86.32	13.47	649
Secondary enrollment	45.95	31.50	492	76.01	29.90	545
Land Gini	59.96	15.21	214	62.96	16.23	399
Nonagricultural share of population in 1968	35.60	20.94	803	56.55	25.30	598
United States top 10% income share	36.03	5.07	1050	39.43	5.47	822
Top share	1.77	1.32	81	1.34	1.06	237
Bottom share	0.10	0.03	81	0.10	0.03	237
GDP per capita in 2000 dollars	2061.78	3838.08	718	8160.03	9415.89	770

Note: Summary statistics broken by observations during nondemocracy (left panel) and democracy (right panel). See the text for a full description of the data.

sample is not balanced). The summary statistics show that democracies tend to be significantly more economically developed than nondemocracies, with much higher GDP per capita, more education, and smaller agricultural shares of employment (both on average in the sample and in 1968) and GDP. These patterns are relatively well known and are sometimes interpreted as support for modernization theory (but see Acemoglu et al., 2008, 2009 on why this cross-sectional comparison is misleading).

The differences in tax to GDP ratios and revenue to GDP ratios are much smaller; both variables are roughly 4 percentage points higher in democracies than nondemocracies, although not significantly so.[26] Consistent with this tax difference reflecting increased redistribution, after-tax inequality, measured by the net Gini, is almost three points lower in democracies, whereas pretax inequality is one point higher (the Gini is measured on a 0- to 100-scale). Figure 21.1 shows the evolution of average democracy in our sample between 1960 and 2010.[27]

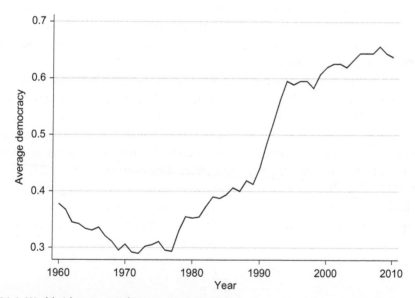

Figure 21.1 Worldwide average democracy since 1960.

[26] This comparison is broadly consistent with the cross-national regressions of Gil et al. (2004), though it is interesting that even in this cross section we do see some differences between democracies and nondemocracies.
[27] Note that democracies appear to be associated with a higher income share of the top 10% in the United States. This is because of the trend shown in Figure 21.1, making democracies more common in the recent past when this variable has also been higher.

21.5. MAIN RESULTS

21.5.1 The Effect of Democracy on Taxes

Our first results are contained in Table 21.2, which reports estimates of Equation (21.6) with the log of tax revenue to GDP ratio (tax to GDP ratio for short) as the dependent variable.

Column 1 is estimated by OLS imposing $\rho = 0$ in Equation (21.6). Though biased when $\rho > 0$, this is a natural benchmark, particularly since it corresponds to a specification often used in the literature. In all columns, we report standard errors corrected for arbitrary heteroskedasticity and serial correlation at the country level. We multiply the coefficient on democracy by 100 to ease interpretation. Throughout, we always report the number of observations, number of countries in the sample, and the number of switches in democracy from 0 to 1 or vice versa in the estimation sample (which is 92 in this case). All models include a lag of GDP per capita as a control, but the coefficients are not reported to save space. The coefficient on the estimated effect of democracy in this column, 15.00 (to two decimal places), implies a 15% increase in the tax to GDP ratio with a standard error of 4.33, and is thus statistically significant at less than the 1% confidence level. This estimate is also economically significant. It indicates that democratization—that is, a change in our democracy dummy—is associated with a 2.4 percentage points increase in the tax to GDP ratio.

Column 2 includes the lag of tax to GDP ratio on the right-hand side, thus relaxing the assumption that $\rho = 0$. The effect of democracy, γ, is now estimated to be 11.7 (approximately 11.7%, with standard error $= 3.38$) and is again statistically significant at less than the 1% level. In the presence of the lagged dependent variable on the right-hand side in this specification, γ is now merely the short-run impact of democracy on the tax to GDP ratio, not the long-run effect. The estimate of ρ is 0.27, and is significant, suggesting that there is indeed some persistence in the dependent variable. To obtain the long-run effect, we set $z_{it} = z_{it-1}$ so that the dynamics in the outcome variable converge to the new "steady state." This gives the long-run effects of a switch to democracy as

$$\frac{\gamma}{1-\rho},$$

and is reported at the bottom, together with the p-value for the hypothesis that it is equal to 0. In Column 2, this long-run effect implies a 16% increase in the tax to GDP ratio from a permanent switch to democracy.

Figure 21.2 shows the effect of democracy on the tax to GDP ratio visually. Here, similar to an event study analysis, we place all transitions to democracy at $t = 0$, and those observations before then (with $t < 0$) show the trends in tax to GDP ratio before democratization, and those with $t > 0$ correspond to changes in the tax to GDP ratio after

Table 21.2 Effects of democratization on the log of tax revenue as a percentage of GDP

	(1)	(2)	GMM (3)	(4)	(5)	Assuming AR(1) coefficient ρ = 0 (6)	ρ = 0.25 (7)	ρ = 0.5 (8)	ρ = 0.75 (9)	ρ = 1 (10)
Democracy lagged	15.00***	11.71***	11.27	18.68**	14.63**	15.00***	11.92***	8.84***	5.77**	2.69
	(4.33)	(3.38)	(7.23)	(8.78)	(5.98)	(4.33)	(3.27)	(2.55)	(2.48)	(3.11)
Dep. Var. lagged		0.27***	0.27***	0.29***	0.33***					
		(0.06)	(0.10)	(0.07)	(0.08)					
Observations	944	944	816	816	816	944	944	944	944	944
Countries	128	128	125	125	125	128	128	128	128	128
Number of moments			81	61	61					
Hansen p-value			0.12	0.05	0.06					
AR2 p-value			0.92	0.83	0.78					
Democracy changes in the sample	92	92	82	82	82	92	92	92	92	92
Long-run effect of democracy	15.00	15.97	15.49	26.35	21.97	15.00	15.89	17.68	23.06	.
p-Value for the long-run effect	0.00	0.00	0.11	0.03	0.01	0.00	0.00	0.00	0.02	.

Note: OLS estimates (Columns 1–2) include a full set of country and year fixed effects. Arellano and Bond's GMM estimators of the dynamic panel model (Columns 3–4) remove country fixed effects by taking first differences of the data, or by taking forward orthogonal differences (Column 5) and then constructing moment conditions using predetermined lags of the dependent variable and democracy. Columns 4 and 5 use up to the fifth lag of predetermined variables to create moments, restricting the number of moments used. Columns 6–10 impose different values for the autocorrelation coefficient in the tax revenue as a percentage of GDP series, and estimates the effect of democracy including a full set of country and year fixed effects. All models control for lagged GDP per capita but this coefficient is not reported to save space. Robust standard errors, adjusted for clustering at the country level, are in parentheses. ★★★: significant at 1%; ★★: significant at 5%; ★: significant at 10%. We do not report long-run effects and their p-values in Column 10 because they are not defined for ρ = 1.

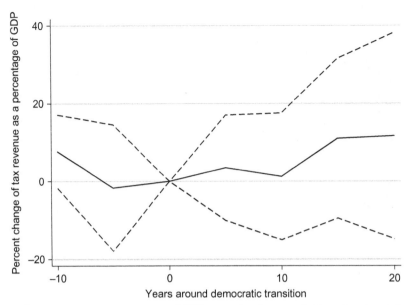

Figure 21.2 Tax revenue as a percentage of GDP around a democratization. Constructed using the 5-year panel.

democratization. The figure shows that there is no discernible change in the tax to GDP ratio before democratization, increasing our confidence in the results concerning the effect of democracy on taxes. It also confirms that the effect of democracy on the tax to GDP ratio evolves only slowly, reaching a maximum 15 years after the democratization takes place. This underscores the role of the lagged dependent variable in our econometric specifications.

As a second diagnostic for our estimates, Figure 21.3 shows a scatterplot of the residuals of the tax to GDP ratio (in logs) on the vertical axis against the residuals of the lag of our democracy measure on the horizontal axis. All covariates, including year and country fixed effects, and the lagged dependent variable, are partialed out. Each point corresponds to a particular country/year observation. The slope of the regression line coincides with our estimated coefficient of 11.7. The figure shows that the estimated relationship does not seem to be driven by any particular outlier. To explore this more formally we removed 49 observations whose Cook distance was above the rule of thumb $4/N$, with N the sample size and reestimated our model. The coefficient of democracy falls to 8.28 with standard error 2.46, and is still significant at the 1% level. The bottom panel of Figure 21.3 shows the scatterplot excluding these outliers. We have experimented with a number of other methods for dealing with outliers, such as Huber M-regressions and excluding outliers with estimated standardized errors > 1.96, and our results on tax to GDP ratios remain generally unchanged.

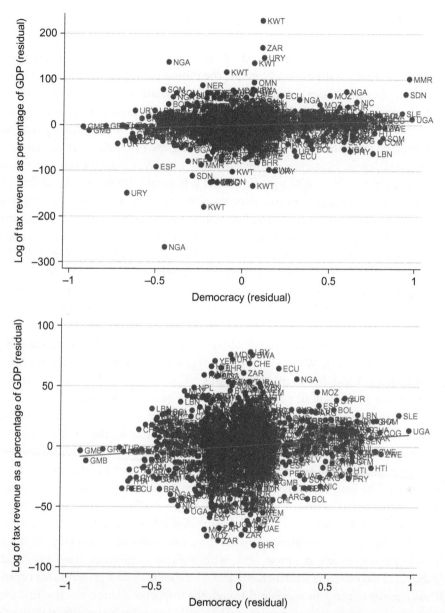

Figure 21.3 Residual of tax revenue as a percentage of GDP (vertical axis) against the residual of our democracy indicator. Each dot is a country/year observation, and there are a total of 975 observations. Bottom figure excludes outliers.

As noted in the previous subsection, the OLS estimator of Column 2 is inconsistent because of the (downward) bias in the estimation of ρ. Column 3 reports the GMM estimator described earlier with the full set of moments (in this case, this corresponds to 82 moments as noted in the table). Notably, the estimate for ρ is identical up to two decimal places, indicating in fact that if there was a downward bias in the estimation of Column 2, it was negligible, suggesting that the large-T assumption (given the low persistence ρ) is a good approximation. The estimate for γ also decreases marginally, but the standard error increases substantially, making the resulting estimate insignificant at conventional levels. However, the long-run impact is very similar to the OLS estimate of approximately 15 (15%), with a p-value of 0.11. It should also be noted that the tests for second-order autocorrelation in the error term and the Hansen's J test for over identification pass comfortably, thus further increasing our confidence in this specification.

Columns 4 and 5 present alternative GMM estimators with fewer moments and with forward-differencing, respectively. Both estimates only use up to the fifth valid lags of democracy and the dependent variable to form moment conditions. The point estimates on both γ and ρ are larger than Columns 2 and 3, and significant at the 5% level, and hence imply the significantly larger long-run effects, 26% and 21%, respectively, reported at the bottom.

Columns 6–10 estimate Equation (21.6), imposing different values for ρ spanning the entire interval from 0 to 1. We use the same sample as in Column 2, which is also the same one as in Column 1 and thus implies that in this case Column 6, which sets $\rho = 0$, is identical to Column 1 (this will not be the case in some of our later tables). As noted above, the problem with the OLS estimation (with fixed effects) stems from the bias in the estimate of ρ, so conditional on the correct value for this variable, the OLS estimate of the impact of democracy is consistent. In almost all cases, with the exception of the last column, there is a statistically and economically significant impact of democracy on the tax to GDP ratio. The long-run impact is smaller when ρ is assumed to take a small value, and comparable to that in Column 2 when we impose $\rho = 0.25$. The coefficient gets smaller and less significant the farther the imposed value of ρ is from the estimated values in Columns 2–5.[28] In sum, the median estimated long-run effect of democracy on the tax to GDP ratio from this table is almost 16%, with estimates that range from 15% to 26%.

Table 21.3 has the same structure as Table 21.2, but uses total government revenue to GDP ratio as the dependent variable. Though the impact of democracy is a little smaller, the pattern is qualitatively very similar, with slightly larger long-run effects in the GMM estimators relative to the OLS estimators. The estimates in Column 2 show that the coefficient of lagged democracy is 7.55 (standard error = 2.35), which is significant at the

---

[28] In Column 10 where we impose $\rho = 1$, we do not compute the long-run impact, since this is undefined in this unit-root specification. The coefficient in this specification is small and insignificant, suggesting that there is not much variation in growth rates of tax to GDP to be explained by democratization.

Table 21.3 Effects of democratization on the log of total government revenue as a percentage of GDP

| | | | GMM | | | | Assuming AR(1) coefficient | | | |
| | | | | | | ρ = 0 | ρ = 0.25 | ρ = 0.5 | ρ = 0.75 | ρ = 1 |
	(1)	(2)	(3)	(4)	(5)	(6)	(7)	(8)	(9)	(10)
Democracy lagged	9.31★★★	7.55★★★	9.37★	11.13★★	10.04★★	9.31★★★	8.06★★★	6.81★★★	5.56★★★	4.31
	(3.44)	(2.35)	(5.01)	(5.58)	(4.37)	(3.44)	(2.60)	(2.08)	(2.15)	(2.76)
Dep. Var. lagged		0.35★★★	0.47★★★	0.52★★★	0.53★★★					
		(0.03)	(0.06)	(0.06)	(0.06)					
Observations	944	944	816	816	816	944	944	944	944	944
Countries	128	128	125	125	125	128	128	128	128	128
Number of moments			81	61	61					
Hansen p-value			0.05	0.04	0.05					
AR2 p-value			0.36	0.39	0.40					
Democracy changes in the sample	92	92	82	82	82	92	92	92	92	92
Long-run effect of democracy	9.31	11.64	17.77	22.96	21.47	9.31	10.74	13.61	22.23	.
p-Value for the long-run effect	0.01	0.00	0.07	0.05	0.03	0.01	0.00	0.00	0.01	.

Note: OLS estimates (Columns 1–2) include a full set of country and year fixed effects. Arellano and Bond's GMM estimators of the dynamic panel model (Columns 3–4) remove country fixed effects by taking first differences of the data, or by taking forward orthogonal differences (Column 5) and then constructing moment conditions using predetermined lags of the dependent variable and democracy. Columns 4 and 5 use up to the fifth lag of predetermined variables to create moments, restricting the number of moments used. Columns 6–10 impose different values for the autocorrelation coefficient in the total government revenue as a percentage of GDP series, and estimates the effect of democracy including a full set of country and year fixed effects. All models control for lagged GDP per capita but this coefficient is not reported to save space. Robust standard errors, adjusted for clustering at the country level, are in parentheses. ★★★: significant at 1%; ★★: significant at 5%; ★: significant at 10%. We do not report long-run effects and their p–values in Column 10 because they are not defined for ρ = 1.

1% level. The long-run effect of democracy is to increase total revenue as a percentage of GDP by 11.64 and is significant at the 1% level. The baseline GMM estimator leads to larger values of ρ and γ, resulting in a larger long-run effect of 17.8%. Figure 21.4 is the analogue of Figure 21.2, but using the total revenue to GDP ratio measure instead, and shows a similar pattern, although there is a slight downward trend prior to democracy in this variable. In sum, the evidence again suggests that democracy results in larger government revenues as a share of GDP.

Table 21.4 estimates Equation (21.6) for the annual panel. Column 1 includes just four (annual) lags of the dependent variable and democracy on the right-hand side, and is estimated by OLS. Even though individual lags of democracy are not significant, they are jointly significant as witnessed by the long-run effect reported at the bottom, which is similar to the OLS long-run effect in Table 21.2. Column 2 adds four more lags and Column 3 adds four further lags, for a total of 12 lags of democracy and the dependent variable on the right-hand side (to economize on space, we only report the p-values for F-tests for the joint significance of these additional lags). The overall pattern and the long-run effects are very similar to Column 1. Columns 4–6 estimate the same models using the Arellano and Bond GMM estimator. The long-run effects are substantially higher and comparable to the one estimated in Columns 3–5 in Table 21.2 using the 5-year panel.

Table 21.5 probes the robustness of the tax to GDP ratio results, focusing on the 5-year panel. Odd-numbered columns report OLS estimates of Equation (21.6), whereas even-numbered columns are for the GMM estimator (equivalent to Column 3 of

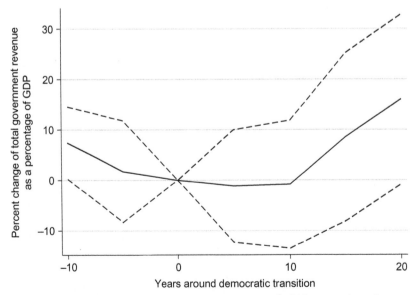

Figure 21.4 Total government revenue as a percentage of GDP around a democratization. Constructed using the 5-year panel.

Table 21.4 Effects of democratization on the log of tax revenue as a percentage of GDP, yearly panel

	OLS			GMM		
	(1)	(2)	(3)	(4)	(5)	(6)
D_{t-1}	3.43	3.45	4.06	5.49	9.49	8.11★
	(2.82)	(2.91)	(3.13)	(3.83)	(5.82)	(4.86)
D_{t-2}	−2.31	−2.01	−2.08	−1.66	−0.67	−1.04
	(2.83)	(2.86)	(3.00)	(2.67)	(2.56)	(2.86)
D_{t-3}	0.66	−0.03	−1.66	1.25	0.53	−0.88
	(2.21)	(2.36)	(2.58)	(2.24)	(2.21)	(2.46)
D_{t-4}	1.65	2.83	3.88★	6.14★★★	3.45★	4.29★★
	(1.63)	(2.03)	(2.14)	(2.32)	(1.81)	(1.93)
p-Value, first four democracy lags	0.02	0.10	0.20	0.06	0.07	0.06
p-Value, second four democracy lags	.	0.61	0.21	.	0.13	0.09
p-Value, third four democracy lags	.	.	0.80	.	.	0.82
y_{t-1}	0.65★★★	0.64★★★	0.62★★★	0.58★★★	0.53★★★	0.52★★★
	(0.04)	(0.04)	(0.05)	(0.05)	(0.04)	(0.06)
y_{t-2}	0.06	0.08	0.09★	0.03	0.04	0.06
	(0.05)	(0.05)	(0.05)	(0.05)	(0.04)	(0.05)
y_{t-3}	0.09	0.10	0.12	0.07	0.07	0.11
	(0.09)	(0.09)	(0.10)	(0.08)	(0.09)	(0.09)
y_{t-4}	−0.00	−0.03	−0.06	−0.03	−0.03	−0.06
	(0.06)	(0.06)	(0.06)	(0.07)	(0.05)	(0.05)
p-Value, first four tax to GDP lags	0.00	0.00	0.00	0.00	0.00	0.00
p-Value, second four tax to GDP lags	.	0.61	0.55	.	0.05	0.19
p-Value, third four tax to GDP lags	.	.	0.51	.	.	0.11
Observations	4434	3925	3425	4306	3799	3301
Countries	128	126	124	128	125	123
Number of moments				373	637	837
Hansen p-value				1.00	1.00	1.00
AR2 p-value				0.30	0.39	0.96
Democracy changes in sample	75	73	69	75	73	68
Long-run effect of democracy	16.49	19.11	12.49	32.38	38.85	25.40
p-Value for long-run effect	0.00	0.00	0.06	0.03	0.01	0.02

Note: OLS estimates (Columns 1–3) include a full set of country and year fixed effects. Arellano and Bond's GMM estimators of the dynamic panel model (Columns 4–6) remove country fixed effects by taking first differences of the data and then constructing moment conditions using as many predetermined lags of the dependent variable and democracy as included in the model. To save space we only report the *p*-value of a joint test of significance for lags 5–8 (second four lags) and lags 9–12 (third four lags). All models control for as many lags of GDP per capita as lags of democracy in the equation, but these coefficients are not reported to save space. ★★★: significant at 1%; ★★: significant at 5%; ★: significant at 10%. We do not report long-run effects and their *p*-values in Column 10 because they are not defined for $\rho = 1$.

Table 21.5 Effects of democratization on the log of tax revenue as a percentage of GDP with different set of controls

	Ex. GDP per capita		Adding other controls							
	OLS	GMM	OLS	GMM	OLS	GMM	OLS	GMM	OLS	GMM
	(1)	(2)	(3)	(4)	(5)	(6)	(7)	(8)	(9)	(10)
Democracy lagged	10.91★★★	12.59★	12.22★★★	12.42★	11.70★★★	10.73	11.59★★★	15.01★★	11.68★★★	15.34★★
	(3.69)	(6.67)	(3.52)	(6.73)	(3.38)	(7.00)	(3.46)	(7.59)	(3.48)	(6.90)
Dep. Var. lagged	0.28★★★	0.31★★★	0.27★★★	0.28★★★	0.27★★★	0.28★★★	0.31★★★	0.32★★★	0.31★★★	0.34★★★
	(0.07)	(0.11)	(0.06)	(0.10)	(0.06)	(0.10)	(0.07)	(0.12)	(0.07)	(0.12)
War lagged			−1.60	−2.38					−2.30	−4.26
			(2.56)	(3.91)					(3.03)	(4.06)
Unrest lagged					0.01	−0.06			0.01	−0.09
					(0.02)	(0.07)			(0.02)	(0.08)
Education lagged							−0.16	0.02	−0.15	−0.30
							(0.19)	(0.63)	(0.20)	(0.69)
Observations	1090	957	889	771	927	802	844	734	803	700
Countries	133	133	118	115	125	122	110	107	103	100
Number of moments		80		82		82		82		84
Hansen p-value		0.22		0.07		0.17		0.15		0.21
AR2 p-value		0.24		0.88		0.91		0.76		0.77
Democracy changes in the sample	101	90	89	80	92	82	77	68	77	68
Long-run effect of democracy	15.22	18.26	16.64	17.27	15.97	14.84	16.76	22.15	16.97	23.17
p-Value for the long-run effect	0.00	0.07	0.00	0.06	0.00	0.12	0.00	0.04	0.00	0.02

Note. OLS estimates (odd columns) include a full set of country and year fixed effects. Columns 3–10 include lagged GDP per capita as a control. Arellano and Bond's GMM estimators of the dynamic panel model (even columns) remove country fixed effects by taking first differences of the data and then constructing moment conditions using predetermined lags of the dependent variable and democracy. Robust standard errors, adjusted for clustering at the country level, are in parentheses. ★★★: significant at 1%; ★★: significant at 5%; ★: significant at 10%.

Table 21.2). The first two columns exclude GDP per capita as a control. Reassuringly, however, our coefficients remain positive and significant, implying a 10–15% increase in the tax to GDP ratio following a democratization. Columns 3 and 4 include the lagged index of foreign wars. This is useful since several authors have claimed that either in history or in the recent past, war has been a major determinant of taxation and redistribution policies. For example, the famous Tilly (1985) hypothesis explains the growth of the state with war and preparation for war (see also Besley and Persson, 2011). More recently, Atkinson et al. (2011) have pointed to large wars and the concomitant economic changes as some of the most significant events correlated with declines of 1% income shares in combatant countries (see also Scheve and Stasavage, 2010, 2012). In contrast to these hypotheses, we do not find any effect of war on the tax to GDP ratio in our post-war panel. The effect of democracy on the tax to GDP ratio remains essentially unchanged when the external war index is included.

Columns 5 and 6 include the lagged measure of social unrest from the SPEED data. This variable is insignificant and has no effect on the coefficient of democracy. Columns 7 and 8 include the stock of education, measured as the fraction of the population with at least secondary schooling from the Barro-Lee dataset, which could be an important determinant of fiscal policy and inequality. Once again, this variable has no major effect on the estimate of the impact of democracy on the tax to GDP ratio and is itself insignificant. Columns 9 and 10 include all three of these variables together, again with a very limited impact on our estimates and no evidence of an effect on war, unrest or the stock of education. The long-run effects at the bottom are very similar to those in Table 21.2 and highly significant.[29]

Overall, the evidence in Tables 21.2–21.5 shows a strong and robust impact of democracy on taxes as measured by the tax to GDP ratio or the government revenue to GDP ratio. This evidence suggests that democracy does lead to more taxes. This evidence is consistent with several of the works discussed above, though it is in stark contrast with Gil et al. (2004). The main difference is the cross-national focus of Gil, Mulligan, and Sala-i-Martin, which contrasts with our econometric approach exploiting the within-country variation (with country fixed effects and also controlling for the dynamics of the tax to GDP ratio). For reasons explained above, we believe that the cross-sectional relationship is heavily confounded by other factors and is unlikely to reveal much about the impact of democracy on redistribution and taxes.

We next investigate whether there is an impact of democracy on inequality.

[29] Another relevant robustness check is to include ex-Soviet countries in the sample. However, fiscal data are only available for Hungary, Poland, and Romania, and then only for the 1990–1995 period, which results in the observations being absorbed by the fixed effects. We thus do not report this robustness check for these specifications (but will report it for our inequality results).

21.5.2 The Effect of Democracy on Inequality

Tables 21.6 and 21.7 turn to the effect of democracy on inequality. Each panel of Table 21.6 mirrors Table 21.2, with the top panel using the net Gini coefficient (after tax and transfers) and the bottom panel using the gross Gini coefficient (before tax and redistribution) as dependent variables.

Though the sample is smaller and data quality may be lower, the most important message from these tables is that there is no consistent evidence for a significant effect of democracy on inequality. Some of our specifications show negative effects of democracy on inequality, particularly on the gross Gini coefficient, but these tend to have large standard errors and are not stable across specifications.

For example, in Table 21.6, most of our estimates suggest there is a negative effect of democracy on the net Gini coefficient, but none of these estimates is statistically significant at the standard levels. For instance, the estimates in Column 3 imply that democracy reduces the Gini coefficient (measured on a 0- to 100-scale) by 2.01 points (standard error $= 1.59$) in the short run, and by 3.1 points in the long run. Given the standard deviation of the net Gini of 10.76 (see Table 21.1), these effects are quantitatively sizable (though they are also smaller in other columns) but also statistically insignificant. The magnitudes for the gross Gini are similar, but a few specifications contain significant results (those with imposed values of $\rho > 0.5$). This may be because there is less measurement error in this measure relative to the net Gini, which does depend on potentially misreported taxes and transfers.

The AR2 test for the GMM estimator for the net Gini suggests there is higher order autocorrelation in the transformed errors, which invalidates the use of second lags as instruments. However, when we only use deeper lags to form valid moment conditions we get very similar results, with smaller effects of democracy on inequality, consistent with the fact that the Hansen overidentification test passes comfortably. The specification tests (AR2 and Hansen J test) for our models using the gross Gini as dependent variable also pass comfortably.

Figure 21.5, which is similar to Figures 21.2 and 21.4, visually shows that there is no substantial fall in inequality following a democratization. There is no pre-trend in inequality. But there is a temporary increase in inequality prior to democratization, which could have persistent effects biasing our estimates unless we control for the dynamics of inequality, further motivating our specifications controlling for such dynamics.

As a second diagnostic of our estimates, Figure 21.6 again shows a scatterplot of the residuals of the net Gini on the vertical axis against the residuals of the lag of our democracy measure on the horizontal axis. All covariates, including year and country fixed effects and the lagged dependent variable, are partialed out. Each point corresponds to a particular country/year observation. The slope of the regression line coincides with our estimated coefficient of -0.744 in Column 2 of the top panel in Table 21.6. The

Table 21.6 Effects of democratization on inequality

			GMM			Assuming AR(1) coefficient				
						ρ=0	ρ=0.25	ρ=0.5	ρ=0.75	ρ=1
	(1)	(2)	(3)	(4)	(5)	(6)	(7)	(8)	(9)	(10)
Dependent variable: Gini coefficient, net income										
Democracy lagged	0.62	−0.74	−2.01	−2.60	−1.60	−0.42	−0.67	−0.92	−1.17	−1.42
	(0.78)	(0.88)	(1.59)	(1.63)	(1.51)	(0.93)	(0.89)	(0.89)	(0.93)	(1.00)
Dep. Var. lagged		0.32★★★	0.35★★★	0.39★★★	0.32★★★					
		(0.07)	(0.10)	(0.12)	(0.12)					
Observations	657	537	420	420	424	537	537	537	537	537
Countries	127	113	100	100	100	113	113	113	113	113
Number of moments			81	61	61					
Hansen p-value			0.60	0.69	0.30					
AR2 p-value			0.02	0.03	0.01					
Democracy changes	65	47	31	31	31	47	47	47	47	47
Long-run effect	0.62	−1.10	−3.12	−4.28	−2.36	−0.42	−0.90	−1.84	−4.67	.
p-Value	0.43	0.40	0.21	0.12	0.30	0.65	0.45	0.31	0.21	.
Dependent variable: Gini coefficient, gross income										
Democracy lagged	−1.22	−1.50	−1.45	−1.88	−1.22	−1.51	−1.50	−1.50★	−1.49★	−1.49
	(0.99)	(0.90)	(1.44)	(1.59)	(1.27)	(1.15)	(1.00)	(0.90)	(0.87)	(0.92)
Dep. Var. lagged		0.50★★★	0.64★★★	0.64★★★	0.76★★★					
		(0.06)	(0.11)	(0.11)	(0.11)					
Observations	657	537	420	420	424	537	537	537	537	537
Countries	127	113	100	100	100	113	113	113	113	113
Number of moments			81	61	61					
Hansen p-value			0.54	0.29	0.37					
AR2 p-value			0.59	0.57	0.48					
Democracy changes	65	47	31	31	31	47	47	47	47	47
Long-run effect	−1.22	−2.98	−3.99	−5.26	−5.15	−1.51	−2.00	−3.00	−5.97	.
p-Value	0.22	0.11	0.36	0.30	0.42	0.19	0.14	0.10	0.09	.

Note: OLS estimates (Columns 1–2) include a full set of country and year fixed effects. Arellano and Bond's GMM estimators of the dynamic panel model (Columns 3–4) remove country fixed effects by taking first differences of the data, or by taking forward orthogonal differences (Column 5) and then constructing moment conditions using predetermined lags of the dependent variable and democracy. Columns 4 and 5 use up to the fifth lag of predetermined variables to create moments, restricting the number of moments used. Columns 6–10 impose different values for the autocorrelation coefficient of the dependent variable, and estimates the effect of democracy including a full set of country and year fixed effects. All models control for lagged GDP per capita but this coefficient is not reported to save space. Robust standard errors, adjusted for clustering at the country level, are in parentheses. ★★★: significant at 1%; ★★: significant at 5%; ★: significant at 10%. We do not report long-run effects and their p-values in Column 10 because they are not defined for ρ=1.

Table 21.7 Effects of democratization on inequality adding controls

	Ex GDP per capita		Baseline sample								Inc. Ex-Soviets	
	OLS	GMM	OLS	GMM	OLS	GMM	OLS	GMM	OLS	GMM		
	(1)	(2)	(3)	(4)	(5)	(6)	(7)	(8)	(9)	(10)	(11)	(12)
Dependent variable: Gini coefficient, net income												
Democracy lagged	−0.87	−2.81**	−0.71	−1.87	−0.75	−2.16	−0.72	−1.46	−0.72	−1.69	−0.26	−1.51
	(0.82)	(1.31)	(0.93)	(1.68)	(0.88)	(1.58)	(1.03)	(1.87)	(1.06)	(1.86)	(0.77)	(1.32)
Dep. Var. lagged	0.33***	0.49***	0.32***	0.34***	0.32***	0.36***	0.32***	0.34***	0.32***	0.33***	0.31***	0.53***
	(0.07)	(0.10)	(0.07)	(0.11)	(0.07)	(0.10)	(0.08)	(0.12)	(0.08)	(0.12)	(0.06)	(0.10)
War lagged			0.12						0.33	0.27		
			(0.28)						(0.28)	(0.49)		
Unrest lagged					−0.01	0.00			−0.00	0.00		
					(0.00)	(0.01)			(0.00)	(0.01)		
Education lagged							−0.02	0.06	−0.02	0.01		
							(0.04)	(0.13)	(0.05)	(0.16)		
Observations	556	435	512	402	523	409	502	399	480	382	611	473
Countries	115	103	106	95	110	97	100	91	95	87	134	121
Number of moments		80		82		82		82		84		81
Hansen p-value		0.82		0.76		0.59		0.67		0.77		0.42
AR2 p-value		0.03		0.04		0.02		0.04		0.04		0.03
Democracy changes	49	34	44	30	47	31	38	28	37	27	61	39
Long-run effect	−1.30	−5.55	−1.06	−2.85	−1.10	−3.39	−1.05	−2.19	−1.06	−2.51	−0.37	−3.23
p-Value	0.29	0.03	0.44	0.26	0.39	0.18	0.48	0.44	0.49	0.37	0.74	0.27
Dependent variable: Gini coefficient, gross income												
Democracy lagged	−1.51*	−2.18*	−1.57*	−1.90	−1.39	−1.39	−1.80*	−1.29	−1.70*	−1.28	−0.97	−0.79
	(0.89)	(1.24)	(0.95)	(1.52)	(0.89)	(1.40)	(1.00)	(1.65)	(1.02)	(1.65)	(0.84)	(1.41)
Dep. Var. lagged	0.53***	0.75***	0.50***	0.60***	0.49***	0.65***	0.49***	0.62***	0.49***	0.62***	0.49***	0.72***
	(0.06)	(0.09)	(0.06)	(0.12)	(0.06)	(0.11)	(0.06)	(0.12)	(0.07)	(0.12)	(0.06)	(0.08)
War lagged			0.06	−0.03					0.21	−0.03		
			(0.26)	(0.44)					(0.27)	(0.46)		

	(1)	(2)	(3)	(4)	(5)	(6)	(7)	(8)	(9)	(10)	(11)	(12)
Unrest lagged					−0.01**	−0.00			−0.01**	−0.00		
					(0.00)	(0.01)			(0.00)	(0.01)		
Education lagged							0.02	−0.02	0.02	−0.00		−0.00
							(0.06)	(0.12)	(0.06)	(0.01)		(0.01)
										−0.02		−0.02
										(0.16)		(0.16)
Observations	556	435	512	402	523	409	502	399	480	382	611	473
Countries	115	103	106	95	110	97	100	91	95	87	134	121
Number of moments		80		82		82		82		84		81
Hansen p-value		0.51		0.70		0.45		0.79		0.84		0.28
AR2 p-value		0.50		0.52		0.45		0.66		0.50		0.50
Democracy changes	49	34	44	30	47	31	38	28	37	27	61	39
Long-run effect	−3.19	−8.69	−3.15	−4.72	−2.75	−3.95	−3.56	−3.38	−3.34	−3.43	−1.91	−2.84
p-Value	0.11	0.13	0.11	0.25	0.13	0.37	0.08	0.46	0.10	0.45	0.26	0.59

Note: OLS estimates (odd columns) include a full set of country and year fixed effects. Columns 3–12 control for lagged GDP per capita. Arellano and Bond's GMM estimators of the dynamic panel model (even columns) remove country fixed effects by taking first differences of the data and then constructing moment conditions using predetermined lags of the dependent variable and democracy. Robust standard errors, adjusted for clustering at the country level, are in parentheses. ★★★: significant at 1%; ★★: significant at 5%; ★: significant at 10%.

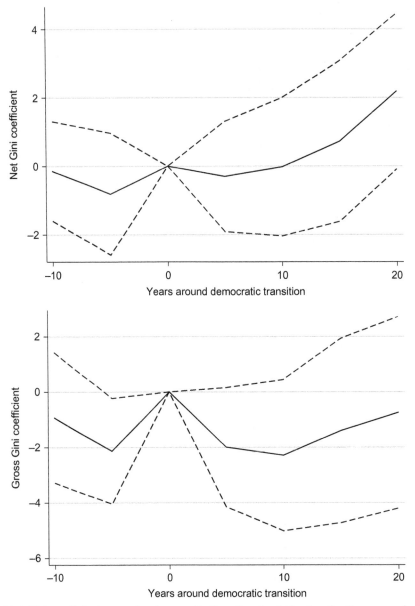

Figure 21.5 Gini coefficient around a democratization. Constructed using the 5-year panel.

figure shows that the estimated relationship does not seem to be driven by any particular outlier. Figure 21.7 shows the same scatterplot, except with gross Gini on the y-axis, and again suggests a negative, if imprecise, relationship. We explored the impact of outliers further, using a procedure similar to the one we used before. We therefore removed observations whose Cook distance was above the rule of thumb 4/N, with N the sample

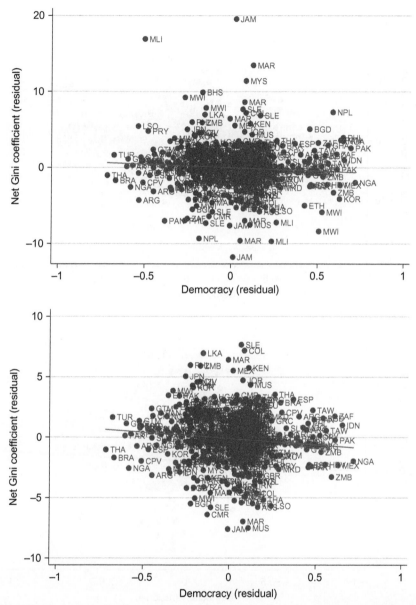

Figure 21.6 Residual of net Gini (vertical axis) against the residual of our democracy indicator. Each dot is a country/year observation, and there are a total of 538 observations. The bottom figure excludes outliers.

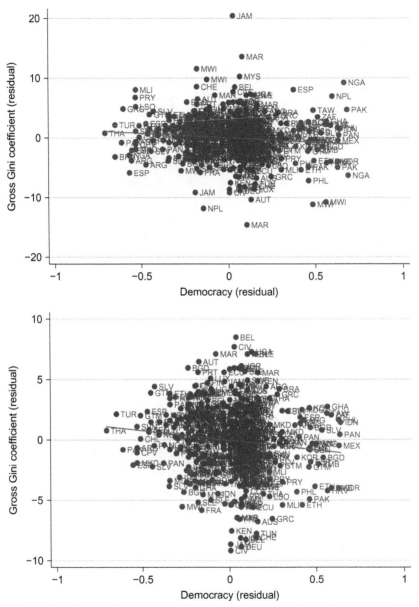

Figure 21.7 Residual of gross Gini (vertical axis) against the residual of our democracy indicator. Each dot is a country/year observation, and there are a total of 538 observations. The bottom figure excludes outliers.

size and reestimated our model. Democracy has no significant effect in this sample without the outliers for the net Gini, but there is a moderately significant effect on the gross Gini in some specifications. In addition, we found a marginally significant effect on both the net and the gross Gini when we used Huber's M estimator. When excluding observations with standardized residuals >1.96, we again found a significant negative effect on the gross Gini but not on the net Gini.

Table 21.7 adds covariates, as in Table 21.5, for the tax variables, and comprises two panels, one for each Gini measure. The only difference is that it adds two columns including ex–Soviet countries in the estimation sample. The addition of controls does not change the patterns shown in Table 21.6, although omitting income as a control does lead to moderately significant negative effects in the GMM estimate on net Gini, and in both the OLS and GMM estimates for gross Gini. This suggests that there may be other forces correlated with GDP and democracy that influence inequality, such as some of the structural transformation variables we examine below. Social unrest is the only variable that has an effect on inequality that is significant in the gross Gini specifications, and our point estimates on democracy are roughly unchanged. The addition of ex–Soviet countries to our estimation sample results in smaller magnitudes of the effect of democracy on inequality, consistent with the idea that inequality went up in these countries following democratization.

We also found (but are not reporting to save space) that democracy does not have any significant effect on other measures of inequality. In particular, in Appendix A we show that, with updated data and our sample, democracy appears to have no effect on the log of industrial wages and explain why this result is different from those of Rodrik (1999).

We have also experimented with other estimates of the Gini using a panel with data every 5 years constructed from the World Income and Inequality Dataset. Controlling for indicators of type of concept used to calculate the Gini (i.e., disposable income, consumption and so on) as well as indicators for data quality, we found broadly similar results, though generally for smaller samples.

Overall, although some specifications do show a negative impact of democracy on inequality, particularly the gross Gini, there is no consistent and robust impact. This contrasts with our results on tax to GDP ratio (or the total government revenue to GDP ratio). Though this could be because of the lower quality of inequality data, it might also reflect some of the theoretical forces we have suggested in the previous section. We will turn to an investigation of some of these channels after looking at the relationship between democracy and structural transformation next.

21.5.3 Democracy and Structural Transformation

While our results above suggest that democracy has little net impact on inequality despite increasing taxation, some of the theoretical models we examined above suggest mechanisms by which democracy could affect inequality independently of government redistribution. (The lowering of barriers to entry, provision of public goods, and the expansion of market opportunities under democracy could be **offsetting** any redistribution accomplished by the fiscal system.) Therefore we examine the effect of democracy on economic structure and education.

Tables 21.8–21.10 look at the impact of democracy on various measures of structural transformation and public goods provision. We focus on the nonagricultural share of employment, nonagricultural share of value added, and secondary enrollment (which is a flow measure, thus better reflecting the effect of democracy on educational investments). Each table has two panels: the top one has the same structure as Table 21.2, whereas the bottom one is similar to Table 21.5 and shows the robustness of the results. Overall, we find significant effects of democracy on these measures of structural transformation.

For example, Tables 21.8 and 21.9 show some significant effects of democratization on the size of the nonagricultural sector.[30] Table 21.8 shows that democratization increases the (log of) nonagricultural share of employment, but this effect is generally only significant at the 10% level in the top panel, and is not completely robust to all exogenously imposed values of ρ in Columns 6–10. The bottom panel shows more consistent and significant estimates, but the coefficients differ substantially between the OLS and GMM estimators. Table 21.9, on the other hand shows that democratization increases the nonagricultural share of GDP. We find significant effects across OLS and most GMM specifications, imposing lower values for ρ, and with various sets of controls. The estimated magnitudes are plausible, with democracy increasing the nonagricultural employment by 4–11% and nonagricultural share of GDP by between 6% and 10% in the long run.

Table 21.10 shows a generally robust long-run effect of democratization on log secondary school enrollment. Although the coefficient magnitudes differ substantially between the GMM and OLS estimators, the long-run effect is uniformly positive and generally significant. Together with the taxation results, this suggests that one important economic change that democracies implement is to tax and provide public goods such as schooling. Our GMM specification in Column 3 of the top panel shows that democracy increases secondary enrollment by 67.6% in the long run, with an associated p-value of 0.07.[31]

---

[30] Bates and Block (2013) find that democratization significantly increased agricultural productivity in Africa, which may also be part of the process of structural change.

[31] The contrast of these results with Aghion et al. (2012), who find that democracy, as measured by the polity score, reduces primary school enrollment, is partly owing to their different sample, dependent variable, and econometric specification. Indeed, Aghion et al. (2012) estimate models without the lagged dependent variable and also include several additional variables on the right-hand side, most notably, military expenditure per capita (which is problematic since it is correlated with democracy, making it a potential "bad control"). They also focus on primary schooling, and according to our discussion above, democracy may have different effects on primary and secondary enrollment depending on the current level of education of the median voter.

Table 21.8 Effects of democratization on the log of the nonagricultural share of population

				GMM					Assuming AR(1) coefficient		
	(1)	(2)	(3)	(4)	(5)	(6)	(7)	(8)	(9)	(10)
						ρ = 0	ρ = 0.25	ρ = 0.5	ρ = 0.75	ρ = 1
Democracy lagged	0.81 (1.74)	0.61★ (0.33)	1.86★ (0.95)	1.71★ (0.92)	1.66★ (0.86)	1.48 (1.63)	1.22 (1.18)	0.96 (0.75)	0.69★ (0.39)	0.43 (0.38)
Dep. Var. lagged	0.83★★★ (0.04)	0.83★★★ (0.05)	0.83★★★ (0.06)	0.83★★★ (0.06)	0.84★★★ (0.06)					
Observations	350	313	252	252	252	313	313	313	313	313
Countries	62	61	60	60	60	61	61	61	61	61
Number of moments			56	40	40					
Hansen p-value			0.33	0.12	0.07					
AR2 p-value			0.10	0.08	0.10					
Democracy changes	23	21	18	18	18	21	21	21	21	21
Long-run effect	0.81	3.59	10.79	9.91	10.09	1.48	1.62	1.91	2.77	21
p-Value	0.64	0.06	0.01	0.02	0.02	0.37	0.31	0.21	0.08	.

	Ex. GDP per capita		Adding other controls							
	(1)	(2)	(3)	(4)	(5)	(6)	(7)	(8)	(9)	(10)
	OLS	GMM	OLS	GMM	OLS	GMM	OLS	GMM	OLS	GMM
Democracy lagged	0.96★ (0.51)	1.34 (1.19)	0.70★ (0.40)	2.24★ (1.19)	0.68★ (0.35)	2.00★★ (0.96)	0.90★ (0.48)	1.60★★★ (0.62)	0.85★ (0.50)	1.38★★★ (0.52)
Dep. Var. lagged	0.83★★★ (0.04)	0.84★★★ (0.05)	0.82★★★ (0.05)	0.81★★★ (0.06)	0.82★★★ (0.05)	0.81★★★ (0.06)	0.79★★★ (0.03)	0.79★★★ (0.04)	0.77★★★ (0.04)	0.77★★★ (0.04)
War lagged			0.09 (0.08)	0.13 (0.17)					0.12 (0.12)	0.50★ (0.28)
Unrest lagged					−0.00 (0.01)	0.01 (0.02)			−0.00 (0.01)	0.03★★ (0.01)
Education lagged							−0.04 (0.03)	−0.06★ (0.03)	−0.03 (0.03)	−0.04 (0.03)
Observations	341	279	229	184	294	237	227	183	189	153

Continued

Table 21.8 Effects of democratization on the log of the nonagricultural share of population—cont'd

	Ex. GDP per capita					Adding other controls				
	OLS	GMM	OLS	GMM	OLS	GMM	OLS	GMM	GMM	
	(1)	(2)	(3)	(4)	(5)	(6)	(7)	(8)	(9)	(10)
Countries	62	61	45	44	57	56	44	43	36	35
Number of moments		55		57		57		52		54
Hansen p-value		0.29		0.81		0.31		0.92		1.00
AR2 p-value		0.82		0.57		0.21		0.23		0.29
Democracy changes	22	19	18	16	21	18	8	6	8	6
Long-run effect	5.72	8.42	3.79	11.87	3.84	10.63	4.20	7.52	3.77	5.90
p-Value	0.04	0.16	0.08	0.03	0.04	0.01	0.07	0.01	0.10	0.01

Notes for top panel: OLS estimates (Columns 1–2) include a full set of country and year fixed effects. Arellano and Bond's GMM estimators of the dynamic panel model (Columns 3–4) remove country fixed effects by taking first differences of the data, or by taking forward orthogonal differences (Column 5) and then constructing moment conditions using predetermined lags of the dependent variable and democracy. Columns 4 and 5 use up to the fifth lag of predetermined variables to create moments, restricting the number of moments used. Columns 6–10 impose different values for the autocorrelation coefficient in the percentage of nonagricultural population series, and estimate the effect of democracy including a full set of country and year fixed effects. Robust standard errors, adjusted for clustering at the country level, are in parentheses. Notes for bottom panel: OLS estimates (odd columns) include a full set of country and year fixed effects. Columns 3–10 include lagged GDP per capita as a control. Arellano and Bond's GMM estimators of the dynamic panel model (even columns) remove country fixed effects by taking first differences of the data and then constructing moment conditions using predetermined lags of the dependent variable and democracy. Robust standard errors, adjusted for clustering at the country level, are in parentheses. ★★★: significant at 1%; ★★: significant at 5%; ★: significant at 10%. We do not report long-run effects and their p-values in Column 10 because they are not defined for ρ=1.

Table 21.9 Effects of democratization on the log of nonagricultural share of GDP

	GMM					Assuming AR(1) coefficient				
	(1)	(2)	(3)	(4)	(5)	(6) ρ=0	(7) ρ=0.25	(8) ρ=0.5	(9) ρ=0.75	(10) ρ=1
Democracy lagged	3.96*** (1.38)	2.49*** (0.95)	2.66* (1.56)	1.58 (2.15)	2.62** (1.31)	4.00*** (1.34)	3.34*** (1.11)	2.68*** (0.95)	2.02** (0.92)	1.36 (1.01)
Dep. Var. lagged		0.57*** (0.05)	0.73*** (0.08)	0.74*** (0.09)	0.73*** (0.07)					
Observations	1033	978	833	833	834	978	978	978	978	978
Countries	147	144	140	140	140	144	144	144	144	144
Number of moments			100	70	70					
Hansen p-value			0.21	0.18	0.08					
AR2 p-value			0.72	0.71	0.40					
Democracy changes	90	88	78	78	78	88	88	88	88	88
Long-run effect	3.96	5.81	9.86	6.14	9.76	4.00	4.46	5.36	8.09	.
p-Value	0.00	0.01	0.10	0.49	0.08	0.00	0.00	0.01	0.03	.

	Ex. GDP per capita					Adding other controls				
	OLS	GMM	OLS	GMM	OLS	GMM	OLS	GMM		
	(1)	(2)	(3)	(4)	(5)	(6)	(7)	(8)	(9)	(10)
Democracy lagged	2.63*** (0.91)	3.61** (1.57)	2.63** (1.01)	3.05* (1.68)	2.43** (0.94)	2.67* (1.54)	2.78*** (1.05)	3.70** (1.66)	2.82*** (1.05)	3.89** (1.67)
Dep. Var. lagged	0.61*** (0.04)	0.78*** (0.07)	0.58*** (0.05)	0.73*** (0.08)	0.58*** (0.05)	0.75*** (0.08)	0.60*** (0.04)	0.76*** (0.07)	0.60*** (0.04)	0.74*** (0.07)
War lagged			-0.45 (0.44)	-1.82** (0.74)					-0.29 (0.43)	-1.79* (0.96)
Unrest lagged					0.00 (0.01)	-0.01 (0.01)			0.00 (0.01)	-0.01 (0.01)
Education lagged							-0.01 (0.04)	-0.15 (0.13)	0.01 (0.05)	-0.10 (0.13)

Continued

Table 21.9 Effects of democratization on the log of nonagricultural share of GDP—cont'd

| | Ex. GDP per capita | | | | | Adding other controls | | | | |
| | OLS | GMM | OLS | GMM | OLS | GMM | OLS | GMM | OLS | GMM |
	(1)	(2)	(3)	(4)	(5)	(6)	(7)	(8)	(9)	(10)
Observations	1010	861	852	730	924	789	823	709	762	658
Countries	148	143	121	117	134	130	113	109	103	99
Number of moments		99		101		101		101		103
Hansen p-value		0.28		0.27		0.30		0.21		0.31
AR2 p-value		0.28		0.52		0.61		0.74		0.64
Democracy changes	91	81	81	74	88	78	70	63	69	62
Long-run effect	6.69	16.61	6.24	11.23	5.78	10.47	7.00	15.39	7.05	14.87
p-Value	0.01	0.08	0.01	0.09	0.01	0.10	0.01	0.02	0.01	0.02

Notes for top panel: OLS estimates (Columns 1–2) include a full set of country and year fixed effects. Arellano and Bond's GMM estimators of the dynamic panel model (Columns 3–4) remove country fixed effects by taking first differences of the data, or by taking forward orthogonal differences (Column 5) and then constructing moment conditions using predetermined lags of the dependent variable and democracy. Columns 4 and 5 use up to the fifth lag of predetermined variables to create moments, restricting the number of moments used. Columns 6–10 impose different values for the autocorrelation coefficient in the nonagricultural share of GDP series, and estimate the effect of democracy including a full set of country and year fixed effects. Robust standard errors, adjusted for clustering at the country level, are in parentheses. *Notes for bottom panel:* OLS estimates (odd columns) include a full set of country and year fixed effects. Columns 3–10 include lagged GDP per capita as a control. Arellano and Bond's GMM estimators of the dynamic panel model (even columns) remove country fixed effects by taking first differences of the data and then constructing moment conditions using predetermined lags of the dependent variable and democracy. Robust standard errors, adjusted for clustering at the country level, are in parentheses. ★★★: significant at 1%; ★★: significant at 5%; ★: significant at 10%. We do not report long-run effects and their p-values in Column 10 because they are not defined for $\rho = 1$.

Table 21.10 Effects of democratization on the log of secondary enrollment

	(1)	(2)	(3)	(4)	(5)	GMM — Assuming AR(1) coefficient (6) ρ=0	(7) ρ=0.25	(8) ρ=0.5	(9) ρ=0.75	(10) ρ=1
Democracy lagged	12.31** (5.17)	12.30*** (4.67)	17.41** (8.21)	20.35** (9.28)	13.39 (8.41)	19.28*** (5.64)	16.25*** (5.00)	13.22*** (4.56)	10.19** (4.40)	7.17 (4.54)
Dep. Var. lagged	0.58*** (0.06)	0.80*** (0.11)	0.74*** (0.12)	0.75*** (0.12)	0.82*** (0.12)					
Observations	825	630	453	453	489	630	630	630	630	630
Countries	150	141	127	127	129	141	141	141	141	141
Number of moments			77	56	57					
Hansen p-value			0.04	0.04	0.12					
AR2 p-value			0.83	0.91	0.79					
Democracy changes	71	51	29	29	29	51	51	51	51	51
Long-run effect	12.31	29.03	67.56	82.43	76.17	19.28	21.67	26.44	40.77	.
p-Value	0.02	0.01	0.07	0.09	0.16	0.00	0.00	0.00	0.02	.

	Ex. GDP per capita (1) OLS	(2) GMM	(3) OLS	(4) GMM	(5) OLS	Adding other controls (6) GMM	(7) OLS	(8) GMM	(9)	(10)
Democracy lagged	11.19** (4.45)	16.77** (8.50)	12.85** (4.98)	21.47** (8.49)	12.81*** (4.70)	19.55** (7.79)	10.92** (5.11)	18.39** (8.67)	11.08** (5.25)	17.36** (8.13)
Dep. Var. lagged	0.58*** (0.06)	0.80*** (0.11)	0.57*** (0.06)	0.72*** (0.12)	0.57*** (0.06)	0.73*** (0.12)	0.61*** (0.06)	0.82*** (0.09)	0.61*** (0.07)	0.81*** (0.09)
War lagged			0.73 (0.98)	-0.07 (1.87)					0.31 (1.01)	-1.21 (1.92)
Unrest lagged					0.04 (0.04)	0.04 (0.06)			0.06 (0.05)	0.12 (0.07)
Education lagged							-0.29* (0.17)	-0.78* (0.42)	-0.32* (0.18)	-0.74* (0.39)

Continued

Table 21.10 Effects of democratization on the log of secondary enrollment—cont'd

| | Ex. GDP per capita | | | | | | Adding other controls | | | |
| | OLS | GMM | OLS | GMM | OLS | GMM | OLS | GMM | OLS | GMM |
	(1)	(2)	(3)	(4)	(5)	(6)	(7)	(8)	(9)	(10)
Observations	686	495	563	411	610	442	553	407	519	385
Countries	151	134	121	111	133	121	116	106	106	99
Number of moments		76		78		78		78		80
Hansen p-value		0.08		0.13		0.04		0.19		0.18
AR2 p-value		0.66		0.67		0.61		0.51		0.59
Democracy changes	54	33	48	29	51	29	43	26	42	26
Long-run effect	26.50	84.72	30.11	76.17	30.04	71.71	28.20	103.65	28.32	93.58
p-Value	0.01	0.11	0.01	0.04	0.00	0.04	0.02	0.04	0.02	0.03

Notes for top panel: OLS estimates (Columns 1–2) include a full set of country and year fixed effects. Arellano and Bond's GMM estimators of the dynamic panel model (Columns 3–4) remove country fixed effects by taking first differences of the data, or by taking forward orthogonal differences (Column 5) and then constructing moment conditions using predetermined lags of the dependent variable and democracy. Columns 4 and 5 use up to the fifth lag of predetermined variables to create moments, restricting the number of moments used. Columns 6–10 impose different values for the autocorrelation coefficient in the secondary enrollment series, and estimate the effect of democracy including a full set of country and year fixed effects. Robust standard errors, adjusted for clustering at the country level, are in parentheses. *Notes for bottom panel*: OLS estimates (odd columns) include a full set of country and year fixed effects. Columns 3–10 include lagged GDP per capita as a control. Arellano and Bond's GMM estimators of the dynamic panel model (even columns) remove country fixed effects by taking first differences of the data and then constructing moment conditions using predetermined lags of the dependent variable and democracy. Robust standard errors, adjusted for clustering at the country level, are in parentheses. ★★★: significant at 1%; ★★: significant at 5%; ★: significant at 10%. We do not report long-run effects and their p-values in Column 10 because they are not defined for $\rho = 1$.

In sum, there is strong evidence that democratization does not just redistribute income, but also results in a degree of structural change of the economy and investment in public goods.[32] As our theoretical discussion implied, this could explain why democratization has a statistically weak effect on inequality. Democracy may be bringing new opportunities and economic change, which may increase inequality, while simultaneously lowering barriers to entry and investing in public goods, which may reduce inequality, and the net result could be either an increase or decrease in inequality, despite the increased taxation documented in Tables 21.2 and 21.3. This reasoning, as well as the theoretical ideas discussed in Section 21.2, underscores the importance of investigating the heterogeneous effects of democracy on inequality, a topic we turn to next.

21.5.4 Investigating the Mechanisms: Heterogeneity

We now turn to heterogeneity in the effect of democracy on inequality. We first consider the effect of democracy interacted with the land Gini, which we take to be a measure of landed elite power, to test the "capture" channel discussed above. We show only effects on net and gross Gini for most of the interactions to save space, and then discuss the heterogeneous effects on tax to GDP and government revenue to GDP ratios in the text.

Table 21.11 shows a positive and generally significant interaction of democracy with land inequality, suggesting that the power of landed elites to capture the state or thwart any redistributive tendencies of democratization results in higher inequality. The magnitudes are sizable, suggesting that a democratization in, say, Myanmar, with the highest land Gini (=77 in a 0- to 100-scale) among nondemocracies in our sample, would increase the after-tax Gini by approximately 0.72–2.42 points and the pretax Gini by 0.2–1.6 points. Our results suggest that democracy may increase inequality in societies with strong landed elites. This could be the case if democracy creates inequality increasing market opportunities while the elite manages to reduce taxation through de facto channels. An alternative explanation is given in Acemoglu and Robinson (2008), where a transition to democracy can lead to more pro-elite policies. The intuition for this somewhat paradoxical result is that the elite invests more in de facto power under democracy because, besides the benefits of being able to impose their favorite economic institutions, investments in de facto power increase the likelihood of a transition to autocracy.

The difference between the net and gross measures may reflect the importance of nonfiscal channels. Consistent with this, we see only moderate attenuation of the effect of democracy on the tax to GDP ratio, and no significant heterogeneity on the government revenue to GDP ratio (omitted to save space). For example, the equalizing effects of lowering barriers to mobility out of the agricultural sector may only be seen in societies

---

[32] Event study figures analogous to Figures 21.2, 21.4, and 21.5 reveal no pre-trends for these variables and an increase after the democratization, but are not included to save space.

Table 21.11 Effects of democratization on inequality (Includes interaction of democracy with Land Gini (averaged over all years with available data))

| | GMM | | | | | Assuming AR(1) coefficient | | | | |
	(1)	(2)	(3)	(4)	(5)	$\rho=0$ (6)	$\rho=0.25$ (7)	$\rho=0.5$ (8)	$\rho=0.75$ (9)	$\rho=1$ (10)
Dependent variable: Gini coefficient, net income										
Democracy lagged	0.29	−0.91	−1.01	−2.44	−1.56	−0.56	−0.81	−1.06	−1.31	−1.57
	(0.90)	(1.02)	(1.31)	(1.86)	(1.46)	(1.04)	(1.02)	(1.05)	(1.12)	(1.22)
Lagged democracy × Land Gini	0.18***	0.11**	0.23**	0.33***	0.27***	0.15***	0.12**	0.09	0.06	0.03
	(0.04)	(0.05)	(0.10)	(0.10)	(0.10)	(0.05)	(0.05)	(0.06)	(0.07)	(0.08)
Dep. Var. lagged		0.35***	0.36***	0.33***	0.34***					
		(0.07)	(0.08)	(0.08)	(0.10)					
Observations	485	407	326	326	329	407	407	407	407	407
Countries	86	78	72	72	72	78	78	78	78	78
Democracy changes in the sample	32	23	16	16	16	23	23	23	23	23
Dependent variable: Gini coefficient, gross income										
Democracy lagged	−2.89**	−2.51**	−2.47*	−4.38**	−2.57**	−2.88*	−2.69**	−2.50**	−2.30**	−2.11**
	(1.32)	(1.04)	(1.28)	(2.07)	(1.29)	(1.48)	(1.21)	(1.03)	(0.96)	(1.05)
Lagged democracy × Land Gini	0.22***	0.18***	0.27***	0.46***	0.29***	0.24***	0.21***	0.18**	0.15**	0.12
	(0.08)	(0.07)	(0.08)	(0.12)	(0.07)	(0.09)	(0.08)	(0.07)	(0.07)	(0.07)
Dep. Var. lagged		0.48***	0.56***	0.49***	0.66***					
		(0.07)	(0.09)	(0.11)	(0.09)					
Observations	485	407	326	326	329	407	407	407	407	407
Countries	86	78	72	72	72	78	78	78	78	78
Democracy changes in the sample	32	23	16	16	16	23	23	23	23	23

Note: OLS estimates (Columns 1–2) include a full set of country and year fixed effects. Arellano and Bond's GMM estimators of the dynamic panel model (Columns 3–4) remove country fixed effects by taking first differences of the data, or by taking forward orthogonal differences (Column 5) and then constructing moment conditions using predetermined lags of the dependent variable, the interaction term and democracy. Columns 4 and 5 use up to the fifth lag of predetermined variables to create moments, restricting the number of moments used. Columns 6–10 impose different values for the autocorrelation coefficient in the tax to GDP series, and estimate the effect of democracy and the interaction term including a full set of country and year fixed effects. All models control for lagged GDP per capita but this coefficient is not reported to save space. Robust standard errors, adjusted for clustering at the country level, are in parentheses. ★★★: significant at 1%; ★★: significant at 5%; ★: significant at 10%.

with politically weak agricultural elites. Although land inequality is potentially correlated with many other economic and social factors that may also mediate the effect of democracy on inequality, we view this as some evidence of the "capture" channel modeled above.

We next consider the effect of democracy depending on the extent of structural transformation, motivated by our hypothesis that democracy induces structural change and may increase inequality by expanding opportunities, such as skilled occupations and entrepreneurship, for previously excluded groups.

Table 21.12 shows the effect of democratization interacted with the share of nonagricultural employment in 1968 as a measure of the extent of structural transformation (results are similar with the 1978 share). We find that democratization *increases* inequality more (or fails to reduce inequality) in places that have smaller agricultural employment shares. This is consistent with democracy expanding access to inequality-increasing market opportunities especially in more urban societies where skilled occupations and entrepreneurship are potentially more important. The magnitudes suggest that democratization in a country that was 10% points less agricultural than the mean in 1968 (measured by the percentage of nonagricultural employment), will bring an increase between 1 and 1.6 net Gini points (1.3 and 2.3 gross Gini points) relative to the average effect in the short run, and between 1.6 and 2.2 net Gini points (2.5 and 5.6 gross Gini points) in the long run. We have also estimated these specifications using our other proxies for structural transformation and obtained uniformly positive, although often imprecise, coefficients on the interaction variables. The results using the gross Gini coefficient show a similar pattern and similar, though slightly larger, estimates.

While we do not show these results for space reasons, there is no significant heterogeneity by nonagricultural employment in the effect of democracy on taxation, and this result is robust to all proxies for the extent of structural transformation we have tried, including the 1970 values of urbanization, education, and nonagricultural share of GDP. This suggests that the mechanisms via which democracy increases inequality in relatively more economically modernized countries has less to do with lowering government redistribution or public good provision, and more to do with other mechanisms emphasized in our discussion of disequalizing market opportunities opened up by democracy for entrepreneurs, educated workers, and capitalists.

Table 21.13 looks further at heterogeneity by the level of potential inequality created by market opportunities. We interact democratization in year *t* with the top 10% share of income in the United States in the same year. This is a proxy (albeit a highly imprecise and imperfect one) for the extent of inequality increasing market opportunities available at the time and their potential to create inequality, shaped by world-level forces such as globalization, technological and organizational changes that either originate or find widespread adoption in the United States (Panitch and Gindin, 2012). We did not find significant interaction effects of this sort on the tax to GDP ratio or the government revenue

Table 21.12 Effects of democratization on inequality (Includes interaction of democracy with the percentage of nonagricultural population in 1968)

| | | | GMM | | | Assuming AR(1) coefficient | | | | |
| | | | | | | $\rho=0$ | $\rho=0.25$ | $\rho=0.5$ | $\rho=0.75$ | $\rho=1$ |
	(1)	(2)	(3)	(4)	(5)	(6)	(7)	(8)	(9)	(10)
Dependent variable: Gini coefficient, net income										
Democracy lagged	0.91	−0.32	−0.45	−1.81	−0.80	−0.05	−0.27	−0.49	−0.71	−0.92
	(0.74)	(0.78)	(1.35)	(1.54)	(1.28)	(0.82)	(0.79)	(0.81)	(0.88)	(0.98)
Lagged democracy × nonagricultural pop. in 1968	0.12★★★	0.11★★	0.16★	0.16★★	0.13★	0.13★★★	0.12★★	0.10★★	0.09	0.08
	(0.03)	(0.05)	(0.08)	(0.07)	(0.07)	(0.05)	(0.05)	(0.05)	(0.06)	(0.06)
Dep. Var. lagged		0.31★★★	0.29★★★	0.29★★★	0.36★★★					
		(0.07)	(0.09)	(0.10)	(0.10)					
Observations	614	506	402	402	406	506	506	506	506	506
Countries	112	100	91	91	91	100	100	100	100	100
Democracy changes in the sample	55	41	29	29	29	41	41	41	41	41
Dependent variable: Gini coefficient, gross income										
Democracy lagged	−0.81	−0.85	−0.40	−1.15	−0.71	−0.72	−0.79	−0.86	−0.92	−0.99
	(0.98)	(0.76)	(1.22)	(1.43)	(1.18)	(0.97)	(0.83)	(0.76)	(0.79)	(0.90)
Lagged democracy × nonagricultural pop. in 1968	0.15★★★	0.13★★	0.21★★★	0.23★★★	0.19★★★	0.17★★★	0.15★★★	0.13★★	0.11★★	0.08★
	(0.05)	(0.05)	(0.08)	(0.08)	(0.07)	(0.07)	(0.06)	(0.05)	(0.05)	(0.04)
Dep. Var. lagged		0.48★★★	0.54★★★	0.55★★★	0.66★★★					
		(0.06)	(0.10)	(0.10)	(0.10)					
Observations	614	506	402	402	406	506	506	506	506	506
Countries	112	100	91	91	91	100	100	100	100	100
Democracy changes in the sample	55	41	29	29	29	41	41	41	41	41

Note: OLS estimates (Columns 1–2) include a full set of country and year fixed effects. Arellano and Bond's GMM estimators of the dynamic panel model (Columns 3–4) remove country fixed effects by taking first differences of the data, or by taking forward orthogonal differences (Column 5) and then constructing moment conditions using predetermined lags of the dependent variable, the interaction term and democracy. Columns 4 and 5 use up to the fifth lag of predetermined variables to create moments, restricting the number of moments used. Columns 6–10 impose different values for the autocorrelation coefficient in the tax to GDP series, and estimate the effect of democracy and the interaction term including a full set of country and year fixed effects. All models control for lagged GDP per capita but this coefficient is not reported to save space. Robust standard errors, adjusted for clustering at the country level, are in parentheses. ★★★: significant at 1%; ★★: significant at 5%; ★: significant at 10%.

Table 21.13 Effects of democratization on inequality (Includes interaction of democracy with share of income held by the top 10 decile in the United States at the time of democratization)

	GMM					Assuming AR(1) coefficient				
						$\rho=0$	$\rho=0.25$	$\rho=0.5$	$\rho=0.75$	$\rho=1$
	(1)	(2)	(3)	(4)	(5)	(6)	(7)	(8)	(9)	(10)
Dependent variable: Gini coefficient, net income										
Democracy lagged	0.68	−0.76	−2.35	−3.06★	−0.88	−0.46	−0.70	−0.94	−1.18	−1.42
	(0.79)	(0.89)	(1.57)	(1.64)	(1.52)	(0.94)	(0.90)	(0.90)	(0.93)	(1.00)
Lagged democracy × Top 10 share in the US	0.22★	0.19★	−0.10	−0.12	0.22	0.27★	0.21★	0.14	0.08	0.01
	(0.13)	(0.11)	(0.19)	(0.19)	(0.17)	(0.15)	(0.12)	(0.10)	(0.09)	(0.10)
Dep. Var. lagged		0.31★★★	0.35★★★	0.36★★★	0.47★★★					
		(0.07)	(0.10)	(0.11)	(0.08)					
Observations	657	537	420	420	424	537	537	537	537	537
Countries	127	113	100	100	100	113	113	113	113	113
Democracy changes in the sample	65	47	31	31	31	47	47	47	47	47
Dependent variable: Gini coefficient, gross income										
Democracy lagged	−1.04	−1.55	−0.68	−0.71	0.44	−1.61	−1.58	−1.54	−1.51★	−1.48
	(0.98)	(0.95)	(1.46)	(1.76)	(1.69)	(1.18)	(1.04)	(0.94)	(0.89)	(0.91)
Lagged democracy × Top 10 share in the US	0.72★★★	0.36★★★	0.25	0.28	0.37★★	0.72★★★	0.52★★★	0.33★★★	0.13	−0.06
	(0.17)	(0.11)	(0.18)	(0.21)	(0.16)	(0.19)	(0.15)	(0.11)	(0.09)	(0.10)
Dep. Var. lagged		0.46★★★	0.61★★★	0.60★★★	0.71★★★					
		(0.06)	(0.11)	(0.11)	(0.11)					
Observations	657	537	420	420	424	537	537	537	537	537
Countries	127	113	100	100	100	113	113	113	113	113
Democracy changes in the sample	65	47	31	31	31	47	47	47	47	47

Note: OLS estimates (Columns 1–2) include a full set of country and year fixed effects. Arellano and Bond's GMM estimators of the dynamic panel model (Columns 3–4) remove country fixed effects by taking first differences of the data, or by taking forward orthogonal differences (Column 5) and then constructing moment conditions using predetermined lags of the dependent variable, the interaction term and democracy. Columns 4 and 5 use up to the fifth lag of predetermined variables to create moments, restricting the number of moments used. Columns 6–10 impose different values for the autocorrelation coefficient in the tax to GDP series, and estimate the effect of democracy and the interaction term including a full set of country and year fixed effects. All models control for lagged GDP per capita but this coefficient is not reported to save space. Robust standard errors, adjusted for clustering at the country level, are in parentheses. ★★★: significant at 1%; ★★: significant at 5%; ★: significant at 10%.

to GDP ratio. However, we do see generally significant impact of this interaction on the gross Gini, which appears to be further increased by democracy when there is greater inequality in the United States. There is also a similar effect on the net Gini but is much weaker and not present when using the GMM estimators. Though on the whole this evidence is on the weak side, it is broadly consistent with a story in which democratization increases inequality at times when the expanded market opportunities available are more disequalizing.

Finally, Tables 21.14–21.17 provide some preliminary evidence on Director's law. Recall from our discussion in Section 21.2, in particular Proposition 5, that our (modified) Director's law implies that the negative effect of democracy on inequality should be visible or greater in places where the rich have a large share of income (Meltzer-Richards also predicts this) and, more uniquely, should be positive where the poor have a higher share of income (which is the opposite of the Meltzer-Richards prediction). Thus, we investigate the heterogeneous effect of democracy depending on the shares of the top and bottom of the income distribution (in each case relative to the share of the middle, i.e., using the top and bottom income shares described above). Recall also that the effect of the income share of the rich on inequality in democracy is related to whether there is capture of democracy by the elite, which provides a reason why this prediction of Proposition 5 may not hold even when a greater share of income of the poor may increase inequality as posited in Proposition 5.

Indeed, Table 21.14 shows that when the top decile is richer relative to the middle, there is no significantly heterogeneous effect on inequality, although coefficients are generally negative. This might be because this estimate is picking up both an elite capture effect (as in the land Gini interaction specifications) as well as additional demand for redistribution by the median voter as in our (modified) Director's law, with higher incidence on the rich. Table 21.15 provides support for the possibility that top tail inequality, as measured by the top share, could be picking up elite capture effects. It shows that the effect of democracy on the tax to GDP ratio is significantly attenuated by income inequality as measured by the top share (but there is no effect on government revenue as a fraction of GDP), contrary to what Meltzer and Richards model or our (modified) Director's law would predict. Our conclusion from this exercise is that our research design does not allow us to separate the effects of democracy through the demand for redistribution and the incidence of taxation emphasized in our modified Director's law from the possibility that democracies with large upper tail inequality are more likely to be captured by the wealthier elite.

Tables 21.16 and 21.17, on the other hand, provide support for the more unique prediction of the (modified) Director's law, that democracy should increase inequality more when the poor are closer to the middle class in nondemocracy. Table 21.16 looks at the interaction of the bottom income share with democracy, and finds that the net Gini does in fact increase with democratization, while there is no effect on the gross Gini. This

Table 21.14 Effects of democratization on inequality (Includes interaction of democracy with the average share of income held by the top decile relative to share of mid 50th earners before 2000)

	(1)	(2)	GMM (3)	(4)	(5)	Assuming AR(1) coefficient ρ=0 (6)	ρ=0.25 (7)	ρ=0.5 (8)	ρ=0.75 (9)	ρ=1 (10)
Dependent variable: Gini coefficient, net income										
Democracy lagged	0.79	−0.54	−1.39	−1.73	−1.24	−0.20	−0.48	−0.76	−1.04	−1.32
	(0.80)	(0.88)	(1.47)	(1.49)	(1.33)	(0.95)	(0.91)	(0.91)	(0.95)	(1.03)
Lagged democracy × Top share	−0.01	−0.01	−0.02	−0.02	−0.01	−0.01	−0.01	−0.01	−0.01	−0.01
	(0.01)	(0.01)	(0.01)	(0.01)	(0.01)	(0.01)	(0.01)	(0.01)	(0.01)	(0.01)
Dep. Var. lagged		0.30★★★	0.29★★★	0.30★★★	0.32★★★					
		(0.07)	(0.08)	(0.08)	(0.08)					
Observations	606	503	397	397	401	503	503	503	503	503
Countries	110	102	93	93	93	102	102	102	102	102
Democracy changes in the sample	55	41	29	29	29	41	41	41	41	41
Dependent variable: Gini coefficient, gross income										
Democracy lagged	−0.76	−1.29	−1.73	−2.30	−1.55	−1.02	−1.16	−1.30	−1.45	−1.59
	(0.93)	(0.85)	(1.31)	(1.41)	(1.30)	(0.98)	(0.89)	(0.85)	(0.88)	(0.97)
Lagged democracy × Top share	−0.00	−0.00	0.00	−0.00	0.00	−0.00	−0.00	−0.00	−0.01	−0.01
	(0.01)	(0.01)	(0.01)	(0.01)	(0.01)	(0.01)	(0.01)	(0.01)	(0.01)	(0.01)
Dep. Var. lagged		0.48★★★	0.52★★★	0.54★★★	0.60★★★					
		(0.06)	(0.08)	(0.08)	(0.08)					
Observations	606	503	397	397	401	503	503	503	503	503
Countries	110	102	93	93	93	102	102	102	102	102
Democracy changes in the sample	55	41	29	29	29	41	41	41	41	41

Note: OLS estimates (Columns 1–2) include a full set of country and year fixed effects. Arellano and Bond's GMM estimators of the dynamic panel model (Columns 3–4) remove country fixed effects by taking first differences of the data, or by taking forward orthogonal differences (Column 5) and then constructing moment conditions using predetermined lags of the dependent variable, the interaction term and democracy. Columns 4 and 5 use up to the fifth lag of predetermined variables to create moments, restricting the number of moments used. Columns 6–10 impose different values for the autocorrelation coefficient in the tax to GDP series, and estimate the effect of democracy and the interaction term including a full set of country and year fixed effects. All models control for lagged GDP per capita but this coefficient is not reported to save space. Robust standard errors, adjusted for clustering at the country level, are in parentheses. ★★★: significant at 1%; ★★: significant at 5%; ★: significant at 10%.

Table 21.15 Effects of democratization on the log of tax and total government revenue as a percentage of GDP (Includes interaction of democracy with the average share of income held by the top decile relative to share of mid 50th earners before 2000)

| | | | GMM | | | | Assuming AR(1) coefficient | | | |
						$\rho=0$	$\rho=0.25$	$\rho=0.5$	$\rho=0.75$	$\rho=1$
	(1)	(2)	(3)	(4)	(5)	(6)	(7)	(8)	(9)	(10)
Dependent variable: Tax revenues as a percentage of GDP										
Democracy lagged	18.75***	14.54***	20.93***	21.97**	19.86**	18.75***	14.50***	10.24***	5.99**	1.74
	(4.88)	(3.72)	(8.02)	(9.86)	(8.55)	(4.88)	(3.46)	(2.48)	(2.52)	(3.54)
Lagged democracy × Top share	−0.10***	−0.08***	−0.22**	−0.19**	−0.20**	−0.10***	−0.08***	−0.06***	−0.03*	−0.01
	(0.04)	(0.03)	(0.09)	(0.08)	(0.10)	(0.04)	(0.03)	(0.02)	(0.02)	(0.02)
Dep. Var. lagged		0.25***	0.23***	0.25***	0.30***					
		(0.06)	(0.09)	(0.08)	(0.08)					
Observations	843	843	730	730	730	843	843	843	843	843
Countries	113	113	110	110	110	113	113	113	113	113
Democracy changes in the sample	72	72	67	67	67	72	72	72	72	72
Dependent variable: Total government revenues as a percentage of GDP										
Democracy lagged	10.56**	8.46***	14.27**	15.50**	13.97**	10.56**	9.09***	7.61***	6.13***	4.66
	(4.03)	(2.43)	(6.11)	(7.07)	(6.86)	(4.03)	(2.81)	(2.02)	(2.19)	(3.17)
Lagged democracy × Top share	−0.03	−0.02	−0.10	−0.11	−0.12	−0.03	−0.02	−0.02	−0.01	−0.00
	(0.03)	(0.02)	(0.06)	(0.07)	(0.08)	(0.03)	(0.02)	(0.02)	(0.02)	(0.02)
Dep. Var. lagged		0.36***	0.43***	0.48***	0.50***					
		(0.04)	(0.06)	(0.06)	(0.06)					
Observations	843	843	730	730	730	843	843	843	843	843
Countries	113	113	110	110	110	113	113	113	113	113
Democracy changes in the sample	72	72	67	67	67	72	72	72	72	72

Note: OLS estimates (Columns 1–2) include a full set of country and year fixed effects. Arellano and Bond's GMM estimators of the dynamic panel model (Columns 3–4) remove country fixed effects by taking first differences of the data, or by taking forward orthogonal differences (Column 5) and then constructing moment conditions using predetermined lags of the dependent variable, the interaction term and democracy. Columns 4 and 5 use up to the fifth lag of predetermined variables to create moments, restricting the number of moments used. Columns 6–10 impose different values for the autocorrelation coefficient in the tax to GDP series, and estimate the effect of democracy and the interaction term including a full set of country and year fixed effects. All models control for lagged GDP per capita but this coefficient is not reported to save space. Robust standard errors, adjusted for clustering at the country level, are in parentheses. ★★★: significant at 1%; ★★: significant at 5%; ★: significant at 10%.

Table 21.16 Effects of democratization on inequality (Includes interaction of democracy with the average share of income held by the bottom decile relative to share of mid 50th earners before 2000)

	(1)	(2)	GMM (3)	(4)	(5)	Assuming AR(1) coefficient $\rho=0$ (6)	$\rho=0.25$ (7)	$\rho=0.5$ (8)	$\rho=0.75$ (9)	$\rho=1$ (10)
Dependent variable: Gini coefficient, net income										
Democracy lagged	0.92	−0.41	−2.11★	−2.64★	−1.93★	−0.07	−0.35	−0.64	−0.92	−1.21
	(0.78)	(0.85)	(1.28)	(1.35)	(1.14)	(0.91)	(0.88)	(0.88)	(0.93)	(1.01)
Lagged democracy × Bottom share	0.52★	0.67★★	0.94★	0.71	0.58	0.71★★	0.68★★	0.65★★	0.62★★	0.59★★
	(0.29)	(0.28)	(0.56)	(0.51)	(0.44)	(0.30)	(0.28)	(0.27)	(0.28)	(0.30)
Dep. Var. lagged		0.30★★★	0.33★★★	0.35★★★	0.43★★★					
		(0.07)	(0.07)	(0.08)	(0.07)					
Observations	606	503	397	397	401	503	503	503	503	503
Countries	110	102	93	93	93	102	102	102	102	102
Democracy changes in the sample	55	41	29	29	29	41	41	41	41	41
Dependent variable: Gini coefficient, gross income										
Democracy lagged	−0.68	−1.24	−1.57	−2.35★	−1.58	−0.95	−1.10	−1.25	−1.40	−1.55
	(0.95)	(0.86)	(1.26)	(1.42)	(1.24)	(1.00)	(0.91)	(0.87)	(0.89)	(0.97)
Lagged democracy × Bottom share	0.29	0.28	−0.08	−0.24	0.09	0.31	0.29	0.28	0.26	0.25
	(0.37)	(0.31)	(0.52)	(0.56)	(0.49)	(0.37)	(0.33)	(0.31)	(0.32)	(0.35)
Dep. Var. lagged		0.48★★★	0.58★★★	0.60★★★	0.66★★★					
		(0.06)	(0.08)	(0.08)	(0.07)					
Observations	606	503	397	397	401	503	503	503	503	503
Countries	110	102	93	93	93	102	102	102	102	102
Democracy changes in the sample	55	41	29	29	29	41	41	41	41	41

Note: OLS estimates (Columns 1–2) include a full set of country and year fixed effects. Arellano and Bond's GMM estimators of the dynamic panel model (Columns 3–4) remove country fixed effects by taking first differences of the data, or by taking forward orthogonal differences (Column 5) and then constructing moment conditions using predetermined lags of the dependent variable, the interaction term and democracy. Columns 4 and 5 use up to the fifth lag of predetermined variables to create moments, restricting the number of moments used. Columns 6–10 impose different values for the autocorrelation coefficient in the tax to GDP series, and estimate the effect of democracy and the interaction term including a full set of country and year fixed effects. All models control for lagged GDP per capita but this coefficient is not reported to save space. Robust standard errors, adjusted for clustering at the country level, are in parentheses. ★★★: significant at 1%; ★★: significant at 5%; ★: significant at 10%.

Table 21.17 Effects of democratization on the log of tax and total government revenue as a percentage of GDP (Includes interaction of democracy with the average share of income held by the bottom decile relative to share of mid 50th earners before 2000)

	(1)	(2)	(3)	(4)	(5)	GMM	Assuming AR(1) coefficient			
						$\rho=0$	$\rho=0.25$	$\rho=0.5$	$\rho=0.75$	$\rho=1$
						(6)	(7)	(8)	(9)	(10)
Dependent variable: Tax revenues as a percentage of GDP										
Democracy lagged	18.72***	14.44***	18.47*	22.49**	17.16**	18.72***	14.42***	10.11***	5.81**	1.50
	(5.18)	(3.98)	(9.43)	(10.35)	(8.34)	(5.18)	(3.70)	(2.61)	(2.49)	(3.45)
Lagged democracy × Bottom share	5.04***	3.88***	7.34	9.31*	6.36	5.04***	3.87***	2.70**	1.54	0.37
	(1.88)	(1.46)	(4.84)	(5.58)	(5.54)	(1.88)	(1.44)	(1.14)	(1.12)	(1.38)
Dep. Var. lagged		0.25***	0.24***	0.24***	0.30***					
		(0.06)	(0.09)	(0.08)	(0.07)					
Observations	843	843	730	730	730	843	843	843	843	843
Countries	113	113	110	110	110	113	113	113	113	113
Democracy changes in the sample	72	72	67	67	67	72	72	72	72	72
Dependent variable: Total government revenues as a percentage of GDP										
Democracy lagged	10.78***	8.30***	13.23*	14.20**	11.74*	10.78***	9.03***	7.29***	5.54**	3.80
	(4.07)	(2.46)	(6.91)	(7.05)	(7.10)	(4.07)	(2.84)	(2.01)	(2.12)	(3.08)
Lagged democracy × Bottom share	1.55	0.74	2.92	4.14	3.37	1.55	0.98	0.40	−0.17	−0.74
	(1.63)	(1.21)	(3.09)	(3.86)	(3.77)	(1.63)	(1.29)	(1.10)	(1.14)	(1.39)
Dep. Var. lagged		0.35***	0.43***	0.47***	0.50***					
		(0.04)	(0.06)	(0.06)	(0.05)					
Observations	843	843	730	730	730	843	843	843	843	843
Countries	113	113	110	110	110	113	113	113	113	113
Democracy changes in the sample	72	72	67	67	67	72	72	72	72	72

Note: OLS estimates (Columns 1–2) include a full set of country and year fixed effects. Arellano and Bond's GMM estimators of the dynamic panel model (Columns 3–4) remove country fixed effects by taking first differences of the data, or by taking forward orthogonal differences (Column 5) and then constructing moment conditions using predetermined lags of the dependent variable, the interaction term and democracy. Columns 4 and 5 use up to the fifth lag of predetermined variables to create moments, restricting the number of moments used. Columns 6–10 impose different values for the autocorrelation coefficient in the tax to GDP series, and estimate the effect of democracy and the interaction term including a full set of country and year fixed effects. All models control for lagged GDP per capita but this coefficient is not reported to save space. Robust standard errors, adjusted for clustering at the country level, are in parentheses. ★★★: significant at 1%; ★★: significant at 5%; ★: significant at 10%.

relative difference between the pre-fiscal and post-fiscal effects suggests that government redistribution may be (part of) the mechanism. Table 21.17 confirms this by showing that the tax to GDP ratio does go up following a democratization in a society where the poor are initially relatively well-off compared to the middle class.

Subject to the major caveats about omitted variables and measurement error, this evidence thus provides some support to our (modified) Director's law: middle classes empowered by democracy appear to be able to use the government to transfer resources from the poor to themselves, increasing post-fiscal inequality. As far as we know, this is the first evidence of this kind on how democracy might redistribute in a way that *increases* inequality.

We have investigated a number of other sources of heterogeneity, including various measures of ethnolinguistic fragmentation, wheat-sugar land suitability ratio (as a measure of the type of agriculture), constitutional provisions against redistribution, and average level of social unrest, and found no robust results.

Overall, the important concerns about endogeneity and measurement error notwithstanding, the results presented in this section paint a picture in which democracy does indeed create greater pressures for redistribution, but the pathways via which these affect inequality are more nuanced than the standard Meltzer-Richard mechanism presumes. In particular, the correlation between democracy and inequality appears to be more limited than one might have at first expected (and more limited than the effect on taxes). On the other hand, the evidence on heterogeneity of effects, even if not as robustly estimated as the impact on taxes, indicates that interactions with elite capture, structural transformation, middle-class bias in redistribution, and the disequalizing market opportunities opened up by democracy might be playing some role in modulating the influence of democracy on inequality.

21.6. CONCLUSION

The effect of democracy on redistribution and inequality is important for understanding how democracies function and use the available policy instruments. Nevertheless, our survey of the relevant literature shows that the social science literature on this topic is far from a consensus or a near-consensus on this topic.

We explained why the baseline expectation in the literature has been that democracy should increase redistribution and reduce inequality (for example, based on Meltzer and Richard's, 1981 seminal paper), and why this expectation may not be borne out in the data because democracy may be captured or constrained; because democracy may cater to the wishes of the middle class; or because democracy may simultaneously open up new economic opportunities to the previously excluded, contributing to economic inequality. This ambiguity may be one of the reasons why the large empirical literature on this topic comes to such inconclusive findings, though the use of datasets with different qualities and different methodologies and econometric practices, many of which are far from satisfactory, are also contributing factors. It may also be that because different researchers have looked at different sets of countries in different periods, the differing results are to some extent picking up situations where one or another of the mechanisms we have identified is more dominant.

The bulk of the chapter empirically investigated the (dynamic) relationship between democracy and various economic outcomes related to redistribution and inequality. Our results, which come from panel data models controlling for the dynamics and persistence in our outcome variables, indicate that democratization does indeed increase government taxation and revenue as fractions of GDP. This confirms the basic prediction of the standard Meltzer-Richard model. In contrast, we have found no robust evidence that democracy reduces inequality, although our estimated coefficients are quite imprecise in this case. Our results also suggest that democracy increases the share of GDP and population not in agriculture, as well as secondary school enrollment. This is consistent with democracy triggering a more rapid structural transformation, for example, because this structural transformation may have been arrested or slowed down by the nondemocratic political system. The relationship between democratic institutions and structural change is worth further investigation.

These patterns suggest that the effect of democracy on redistribution and inequality may be more nuanced than often presumed and highly heterogeneous across societies. We tried to make some tentative progress on this issue by providing additional correlations pertaining to these heterogeneous effects and mechanisms on which they might be based. We found some results suggesting that democratization in the presence of powerful landed elites may increase inequality, and that structural transformation may induce an expansion of opportunities that counteract any additional redistribution, and either of these could explain the absence of an effect on inequality. This interpretation is confirmed by our finding that democracy increases inequality in places that have a lower share of population in agriculture, and at times when the global technological and organizational frontier is more inequality inducing. A natural next step for research is isolating exogenous variation in these heterogeneous effects across democracies and nondemocracies.

In addition, we also found some evidence consistent with a (modified) Director's law, which suggests that democracy redistributes from the rich and the poor to the middle class, and therefore its effect on inequality may depend on the relative position of the middle class vis-a-vis the poor and the rich. Further research on whether and how democracies transfer from the poor to the middle class would be an important contribution.

(Overall, the evidence suggests that to the impact of democracy on inequality is limited, and these limited effects work by altering pre-redistribution market outcomes, while the fiscal mechanisms stressed by the literature play at most a small role in explaining any effect of democracy on inequality, and may in fact be inequality-increasing. We hope that further research on these issues, tackling the first-order endogeneity concerns and exploiting within-country as well as cross-national variation, will more systematically uncover the mechanisms at work.)

ACKNOWLEDGMENTS

We are grateful to the editors for their detailed comments on an earlier draft and to participants in the Handbook conference in Paris, particularly to our discussant José-Víctor Ríos-Rull.

APPENDIX A. COMPARISON TO RODRIK (1999)

This appendix replicates and extends the analysis in Rodrik (1999). At a first glance, the fact that we find no robust effect on net or gross income inequality seems at odds with Rodrik's findings that democracies pay higher real wages in manufacturing. These opposite findings could be explained by a logic similar to the one outlined in Proposition 4. In particular, democracies may increase wages by allowing workers to reallocate to new sectors, but this may also increase inequality if there is sufficient heterogeneity in labor productivity and wages were previously compressed and reduced by labor market institutions. Besides this conceptual difference we also explore the differences between our empirical setting and Rodrik's. We show that while the results are robust to our democracy measure, they are fragile in a number of other directions.

Rodrik's data generating model is given by

$$\log w_{it} = \beta D_{it} + X_{it}\gamma + \delta_i + \delta_t + \Sigma_{it},$$

with w_{it} manufacturing wages from the UNIDO dataset compiled by Martin Rama. However, this model cannot be estimated because wage data comes grouped on averages for the years $t, t+1, t+2, t+3, t+4$ for every 5 years from 1960 onward. Thus, only the average wages between 1960 and 1964, 1965 and 1969, and so on are observed. Thus, Rodrik estimates

$$\log w_{it,t+4} = \beta D_{it,t+4} + X_{it,t+4}\gamma + \delta_i + \delta_t + \epsilon_{it,t+4}. \tag{21.A1}$$

with all variables averaged over 5 year periods (from t to $t+4$), and the model is estimated in a panel covering $1960, 1965, \ldots, 1990$. Though Rodrik presents cross-sectional and panel estimates, we focus on the latter which are the more convincing ones and are also closer to the empirical strategy adopted in this chapter.

In the top panel of Table 21.A1 we present different estimates of Equation (21.A1) using a normalized polity score between 0 and 1, a normalized Freedom House index between 0 and 1 and our democracy measure separately as proxies for democracy. We always control for the log of GDP per capita, the log of worker value added in

Table 21.A1 Replication of Rodrik's results on the log of manufacturing wages

	Original wage data			Updated wage data		
	(1)	**(2)**	**(3)**	**(4)**	**(5)**	**(6)**
Averaging democracy measure over t, $t+4$						
Polity index at t, $t+4$	19.25★★★ (5.72)			14.48★★ (6.00)		
Freedom house index at t, $t+4$		15.78★★ (7.55)			7.60 (8.68)	
Our democracy index at t, $t+4$			8.48★★ (3.66)			6.51 (4.20)
Observations	442	365	468	451	364	467
Countries	93	98	99	90	92	92
Using democracy measure at t						
Polity index at t	8.40 (6.15)			9.01 (5.89)		
Freedom house index at t		11.03 (10.55)			11.52 (9.77)	
Our democracy index at t			1.98 (3.54)			2.89 (3.39)
Observations	429	285	455	437	294	456
Countries	91	96	97	85	87	90

Dependent variable is log of average wages between t and $t+4$.
Note: OLS estimates include a full set of country and year fixed effects. All models control for the log of GDP per capita, log of worker value added and log of the price level, but these coefficients are not reported to save space. Robust standard errors, adjusted for clustering at the country level, are in parentheses. ★★★: significant at 1%; ★★: significant at 5%; ★: significant at 10%.

manufacturing and the log of the price index (from the Penn World Tables) following Rodrik's original setup. The estimates of β are multiplied by 100 to ease their interpretation. The left panel uses Rodrik's original wage data and the right panel uses an updated version. In all models we present robust standard errors adjusting for clustering at the country level, which are reflected in slightly higher standard errors than the ones found by Rodrik.

Our estimates show that democracy, measured by any of the indices, is associated with higher wages using the original wage data, which replicates Rodrik's findings. There are still some small differences caused by updates to Polity and Freedom House, but qualitatively his conclusions hold. In particular, an increase in the polity score from 0 to 1 increases wages by 19.72% (s.e. = 5.98); an increase in the Freedom House index from 0 to 1 increases wages by 20.57% (s.e. = 8.13), and a switch from nondemocracy to democracy in our measure increases wages by 8.54% (s.e. = 3.88). The results using the new wage data are less clear, smaller, and not significant for Freedom House and our democracy measure. The results suggest that the association between democracy and wages is not robust if one uses the updated wage data and the same empirical strategy as Rodrik.

There are two more issues that are important to consider in weighing the importance of Rodrik's evidence. The wage data are in the form of 5-year averages. First, this will tend to induce nontrivial serial correlation in the dependent variable, inducing error in the presence of lagged dependent variables on the right-hand side (which our estimates suggest are present). Second, by averaging the democracy index, Rodrik's specification induces the correlation between wages at t and democracy at $t+1, t+2, t+3$ and $t+4$, which of course does not reflect the effect of democracy on wages, to influence the estimate for β.

To address the second issue and get closer to the empirical strategy we used in this chapter, we can estimate the model

$$\log w_{it,t+4} = \beta D_{it} + X_{it}\gamma + \delta_i + \delta_t + \epsilon_{it}.$$

This model still averages the dependent variable, which cannot be undone given the wage data, but uses the baseline value of the democracy index and the controls for the years $1960, 1965, \ldots, 1990$. The bottom panel in Table 21.A1 presents our results using the original wage data (left panel) and updated wage data (right panel). The estimates for β are significantly smaller and never significant. The comparison between the top panel—which uses Rodrik's original specification—and our preferred specification in the bottom suggests that Rodrik's results are, at least in part, driven by a correlation between wages at t and democracy at $t+1, t+2, t+3$ and $t+4$.

Finally, we present estimates of the model

$$\log w_{it,t+4} = \rho \log w_{it-5,t-1} + \beta D_{it} + X_{it}\gamma + \delta_i + \delta_t + \epsilon_{it}, \tag{21.A2}$$

which comes closest to the empirical specification we used throughout the paper. Table 21.A2 has the same structure as Table 21.2 in the paper and presents several estimates of the dynamic panel model in Equation (21.A1). In this case, the lagged dependent variable also controls for the nontrivial autocorrelation patterns induced by averaging the dependent variable. The results confirm that there is no effect of democracy at time t on average wages between t and $t+4$. Only the GMM estimates show large effects that are almost significant at conventional levels. But these estimates are unreliable because they are significantly above the fixed effect models with different imposed values of ρ (and these estimates should bracket them). Moreover, the estimated ρ is too small compared to the fixed effects estimates (it should typically be larger). We believe that this pattern may be caused by the averaging of the dependent variable, which invalidates the moment conditions of GMM estimation.

Table 21.A2 Effects of democratization on the log of manufacturing wages controlling for worker value added, prices and GDP per capita

	(1)	(2)	GMM			$\rho=0$	$\rho=0.25$	Assuming AR(1) coefficient $\rho=0.5$	$\rho=0.75$	$\rho=1$
			(3)	(4)	(5)	(6)	(7)	(8)	(9)	(10)
Democracy at t	2.89	2.65	15.42	15.91	13.22	3.84	2.65	1.45	0.25	−0.95
	(3.39)	(4.01)	(9.64)	(10.35)	(10.22)	(3.85)	(3.89)	(4.38)	(5.19)	(6.20)
Dep. Var. lagged		0.25★★★	0.20★	0.21★	0.17					
		(0.09)	(0.12)	(0.12)	(0.11)					
Observations	456	384	297	297	298	384	384	384	384	384
Countries	90	86	79	79	79	86	86	86	86	86
Number of moments			40	38	38					
Hansen p-value			0.52	0.44	0.49					
AR2 p-value			0.21	0.21	0.29					
Democracy changes in the sample	47	45	35	35	35	45	45	45	45	45
Long-run effect of democracy	2.89	3.53	19.31	20.01	15.93	3.84	3.53	2.90	1.00	.
p-Value for the long-run effect	0.40	0.50	0.10	0.11	0.19	0.32	0.50	0.74	0.96	.

Dependent variable is log of average wages between t and $t+4$.

Note: OLS estimates (Columns 1–2) include a full set of country and year fixed effects. Arellano and Bond's GMM estimators of the dynamic panel model (Columns 3–4) remove country fixed effects by taking first differences of the data, or by taking forward orthogonal differences (Column 5) and then constructing moment conditions using predetermined lags of the dependent variable and democracy. Columns 4 and 5 use up to the fifth lag of predetermined variables to create moments, restricting the number of moments used. Columns 6–10 impose different values for the autocorrelation coefficient in the tax revenue as a percentage of GDP series, and estimate the effect of democracy including a full set of country and year fixed effects. All models control for the log of GDP per capita, log of worker value added and log of the price level, but these coefficients are not reported to save space. Robust standard errors, adjusted for clustering at the country level, are in parentheses. ★★★: significant at 1%; ★★: significant at 5%; ★: significant at 10%. We do not report long-run effects and their p-values in Column 10 because they are not defined for $\rho=1$.

Rodrik also estimates models using wage data compiled by the Bureau of Labor Statistics for a smaller set of countries. The very small number of democratizations in this sample (only Portugal, South Korea, and Spain) makes these results less reliable. In any case, using Rodrik's original specification, we find that our democracy measure is associated with a 37% increase in wages (standard error $= 14.23$), but when we estimate the specification in Equation (21.6), including the lagged dependent variable, the effect becomes smaller and no longer significant.

APPENDIX B. RESULTS USING OTHER MEASURES OF DEMOCRACY

In this section we study whether our results are driven by our new measure of democracy. In particular we use Cheibub et al. (2010) Democracy-Dictatorship data (CGV) and Boix-Miller-Rosato's Complete Dataset of Political Regimes, 1800–2007 (BMR). Both datasets are different updates and revisions of the Przeworski et al. (2000) measure. We estimate our basic dynamic panel model using the log of tax revenue as a percentage of GDP, and the Gini coefficient for net and gross income as dependent variable. We only report fixed effects estimates and the Arellano and Bond GMM estimates for each of these variables.

The top panel in Table 21.A3 presents the results using Cheibub et al. (2010) democracy measure; while the bottom panel presents the results using Boix et al. (2012) democracy measure. We find a similar pattern and similar magnitudes, though our GMM estimates on the tax to GDP ratio are less precise and not significant. Again, there is

Table 21.A3 Effects of democratization on the log of tax revenue as a percentage of GDP per capita, and Gini coefficient of net and gross income

	Tax ratio		Net Gini		Gross gini	
	OLS	GMM	OLS	GMM	OLS	GMM
	(1)	(2)	(3)	(4)	(5)	(6)
Using Cheibub et al. (2010) democracy measure						
Democracy lagged	9.48**	11.44	−0.55	−1.45	−1.02	−1.56
	(3.80)	(7.58)	(0.89)	(1.77)	(0.81)	(1.26)
Dep. Var. lagged	0.27***	0.28***	0.32***	0.35***	0.49***	0.77***
	(0.06)	(0.10)	(0.07)	(0.10)	(0.06)	(0.09)
Observations	942	814	537	420	537	420
Countries	128	125	113	100	113	100
Number of moments		81		81		81
Hansen p-value		0.17		0.59		0.34
AR2 p-value		0.89		0.02		0.45
Democracy changes in the sample	92	82	47	31	47	31
Long-run effect of democracy	12.98	15.82	−0.80	−2.22	−2.01	−6.87

Continued

Table 21.A3 Effects of democratization on the log of tax revenue as a percentage of GDP per capita, and Gini coefficient of net and gross income—cont'd

	Tax ratio		Net Gini		Gross gini	
	OLS	GMM	OLS	GMM	OLS	GMM
	(1)	(2)	(3)	(4)	(5)	(6)
p-Value for the long-run effect	0.01	0.12	0.53	0.41	0.21	0.24
Using Boix et al. (2012) democracy measure						
Democracy lagged	9.94★★★	10.57	−0.43	−1.99	−1.23	−2.16
	(3.10)	(9.06)	(0.88)	(1.65)	(0.86)	(1.46)
Dep. Var. lagged	0.27★★★	0.28★★★	0.32★★★	0.35★★★	0.49★★★	0.63★★★
	(0.06)	(0.10)	(0.07)	(0.10)	(0.06)	(0.11)
Observations	944	816	537	420	537	420
Countries	128	125	113	100	113	100
Number of moments		81		81		81
Hansen *p*-value		0.16		0.61		0.42
AR2 *p*-value		0.91		0.02		0.64
Democracy changes in the sample	92	82	47	31	47	31
Long-run effect of democracy	13.61	14.66	−0.63	−3.08	−2.42	−5.81
p-Value for the long-run effect	0.00	0.24	0.62	0.22	0.17	0.17

Note: Odd columns present OLS estimates with a full set of country and year fixed effects. Even columns present Arellano and Bond's GMM estimators of the dynamic panel model which remove country fixed effects by taking first differences of the data and then constructing moment conditions using predetermined lags of the dependent variable and democracy. All models control for the lag of GDP per capita but these coefficients are not reported to save space. Robust standard errors, adjusted for clustering at the country level, are in parentheses. ★★★: significant at 1%; ★★: significant at 5%; ★: significant at 10%.

an effect on tax revenue as a percentage of GDP, which holds in a more robust way when we focus on specifications in levels that are not reported here to save space. We also continue to find no robust effect on inequality.

Overall, the results are broadly similar using other measures of democracy, though they are more precise and consistent with our preferred measure—as would be expected if our measure removes some of the measurement error present in other indices. This was one of the main goals for its construction.

REFERENCES

Acemoglu, D., 2006. Modeling inefficient institutions. In: Blundell, R., Newey, W., Persson, T. (Eds.), Advances in Economic Theory. Proceedings of 2005 World Congress. Cambridge University Press, New York, NY.

Acemoglu, D., Robinson, J.A., 2000. Why did the west extend the franchise? Q. J. Econ. 115, 1167–1199.

Acemoglu, D., Robinson, J.A., 2001. A theory of political transitions. Am. Econ. Rev. 91, 938–963.

Acemoglu, D., Robinson, J.A., 2006. Economic Origins of Dictatorship and Democracy. Cambridge University Press, New York, NY.

Acemoglu, D., Robinson, J.A., 2008. Persistence of power, elites and institutions. Am. Econ. Rev. 98, 267–291.

Acemoglu, D., Johnson, S., Robinson, J.A., 2001. The colonial origins of comparative development: an empirical investigation. Am. Econ. Rev. 91 (5), 1369–1401.

Acemoglu, D., Johnson, S., Robinson, J.A., 2002. Reversal of fortune: geography and institutions in the making of the modern world income distribution. Q. J. Econ. 118, 1231–1294.

Acemoglu, D., Johnson, S., Robinson, J.A., Yared, P., 2005. From education to democracy? Am. Econ. Rev. 95, 44–49.

Acemoglu, D., Johnson, S., Robinson, J.A., Yared, P., 2008. Income and democracy. Am. Econ. Rev. 98, 808–842.

Acemoglu, D., Johnson, S., Robinson, J.A., Yared, P., 2009. Reevaluating the modernization hypothesis. J. Monet. Econ. 56, 1043–1058.

Acemoglu, D., Ticchi, D., Vindigni, A., 2011. Emergence and persistence of inefficient states. J. Eur. Econ. Assoc. 9 (2), 177–208.

Acemoglu, D., Egorov, G., Sonin, K., 2012. Dynamics and stability of constitutions, coalitions and clubs. Am. Econ. Rev. 102 (4), 1446–1476.

Acemoglu, D., Naidu, S., Restrepo, P., Robinson, J.A., 2013a. Democracy does cause growth, Unpublished.

Acemoglu, D., Robinson, J.A., Santos, R.J., 2013b. The monopoly of violence: evidence from Colombia. J. Eur. Econ. Assoc. 11 (S1), 5–44.

Acemoglu, D., Robinson, J.A., Torvik, R., 2013c. Why Do voters dismantle checks and balances? Rev. Econ. Stud. 80 (3), 845–875.

Acemoglu, D., Reed, T., Robinson, J.A., 2014. Chiefs: elite control of civil society and economic development in sierra Leone. J. Polit. Econ. 122 (2), 319–368.

Aghion, P., Persson, T., Rouzet, D., 2012. Education and military rivalry. Unpublished, http://scholar.harvard.edu/files/aghion/files/education_and_military_rivalry.pdf.

Aidt, T.S., Dallal, B., 2008. Female voting power: the contribution of women's suffrage to the growth of social spending in Western Europe (1869–1960). Public Choice 134 (3–4), 391–417.

Aidt, T.S., Jensen, P.S., 2009a. The taxman tools Up: an event history study of the introduction of the personal income Tax in western Europe, 1815–1941. J. Public Econ. 93, 160–175.

Aidt, T.S., Jensen, P.S., 2009b. Tax structure, size of government, and the extension of the voting franchise in western Europe, 1860–1938. Int. Tax Public Fin. 16 (3), 362–394.

Aidt, T.S., Jensen, P.S., 2011. Workers of the World Unite! Franchise Extensions and the Threat of Revolution in Europe, 1820–1938. Cambridge Working Papers in Economics 1102, Faculty of Economics, University of Cambridge.

Aidt, T.S., Jensen, P.S., 2013. Democratization and the size of government: evidence from the long 19th century. http://ideas.repec.org/p/ces/ceswps/_4132.html.

Aidt, T.S., Dutta, J., Loukoianova, E., 2006. Democracy comes to Europe: franchise expansion and fiscal outcomes 1830–1938. Eur. Econ. Rev. 50 (2), 249–283.

Aidt, T.S., Daunton, M.J., Dutta, J., 2009. The retrenchment hypothesis and the extension of the franchise in England and Wales. Econ. J 120, 990–1020.

Albertus, M., Menaldo, V., 2012. If you're against them you are with us: the effect of expropriation of autocratic survival. Comp. Polit. Stud. 45 (8), 973–1003.

Albertus, M., Menaldo, V., 2014. Gaming democracy: elite dominance during transition and the prospects for redistribution. Br. J. of Polit. Sci. 44 (3), 575–603.

Alesina, A., Angeletos, G.-M., 2005. Fairness and redistribution. Am. Econ. Rev. 95, 960–980.

Alesina, A., Glaeser, E.L., 2004. Fighting Poverty in the US and Europe: A World of Difference. Oxford University Press, New York, NY.

Alesina, A., La Ferrara, E., 2005. Preferences for redistribution in the land of opportunities. J. Public Econ. 89, 897–931.

Alesina, A., Rodrik, D., 1994. Distributive politics and economics growth. Q. J. Econ. 109, 465–490.

Alesina, A., Tabellini, G., 1989. External debt, capital flight and political risk. J. Inter. Econ. 27 (3), 199–220.

Alesina, A., Baqir, R., Easterly, W., 1999. Pubic goods and ethnic divisions. Q. J. Econ. 114, 1243–1284.

Algan, Y., Cahuc, P., Sangnier, M., 2013. Efficient and Inefficient Welfare States. https://sites.google.com/site/pierrecahuc/unpublished_papers.

Alvaredo, F., Atkinson, A.B., Piketty, T., Saez, E., 2010. The World Top Incomes Database. Available from http://topincomes.g-mond.parisschoolofeconomics.eu/.

Alvarez, J., Arellano, M., 2003. The time series and cross-section asymptotics of dynamic panel data estimators. Econometrica 71 (4), 1121–1159.

Anderson, S., François, P., Kotwal, A., 2011. Clientelism in Indian Villages. http://faculty.arts.ubc.ca/fpatrick/documents/clientAERmay1313.pdf.

Ansell, B., 2010. From the Ballot to the Blackboard: The Redistributive Political Economy of Education. Cambridge University Press, New York, NY.

Arbetman-Rabinowitz, M., Kugler, J., Abdollahian, M., Johnson, K., Kang, K., 2011. Replication Data for: Relative Political Capacity Dataset. http://hdl.handle.net/1902.1/16845 Transresearch Consortium.

Arellano, M., Bond, S.R., 1991. Some specification tests for panel data: Monte Carlo evidence and an application to employment equations. Rev. Econ. Stud. 58 (2), 277–298.

Atkinson, A.B., Micklewright, J., 1992. Economic Transformation in Eastern Europe and the Distribution of Income. Cambridge, Cambridge University Press.

Atkinson, A.B., Piketty, T., Saez, E., 2011. Top incomes in the long Run of history. J. Econ. Liter. 49 (1), 3–71.

Austen-Smith, D., Banks, J.S., 1999. Positive Political Theory I. University of Michigan Press, Ann Arbor, MI.

Avelino, G., Brown, D.S., Hunter, W., 2005. The effects of capital mobility, trade openness, and democracy on social spending in Latin America 1980–1999. Am. J. Polit. Sci. 49 (3), 625–641.

Baland, J.-M., Robinson, J.A., 2008. Land and power: theory and evidence from Chile. Am. Econ. Rev. 98, 1737–1765.

Baland, J.-M., Robinson, J.A., 2012. The political value of land: political reform and land prices in Chile. Am. J. Polit. Sci. 56 (3), 601–619.

Bardhan, P., Bowles, S., Wallerstein, M. (Eds.), 2006. Globalization and Egalitarian Redistribution. Princeton University Press, Princeton, NJ.

Bates, R.H., Block, S.A., 2013. Revisiting African agriculture: institutional change and productivity growth. J. Polit. 75 (2), 372–384.

Battaglini, M., Coate, S.T., 2008. A dynamic theory of public spending, taxation and debt. Am. Econ. Rev. 98 (1), 201–236.

Baum, M.A., Lake, D.A., 2001. The invisible hand of democracy: political control and the provision of public services. Comp. Polit. Stud. 34, 587–621.

Baum, M.A., Lake, D.A., 2003. The political economy of growth: democracy and human capital. Am. J. Polit. Sci. 47, 333–347.

Beard, C.A., 1913. An Economic Interpretation of the US Constitution. The Free Press, New York, NY.

Bénabou, R., 2001. Unequal societies: income distribution and the social contract. Am. Econ. Rev. 90, 96–129.

Bénabou, R., 2008. Ideology. J. Eur. Econ. Assoc. 6, 321–352.

Bénabou, R., Ok, E., 2001. Social mobility and the demand for redistribution: the POUM hypothesis. Q. J. Econ. 116, 447–487.

Bénabou, R., Tirole, J., 2006. Belief in a just world and redistributive politics. Q. J. Econ. 121, 699–746.

Berlinski, S., Dewan, T., 2011. The political consequences of franchise extension: evidence from the second reform Act. Q. J. Polit. Sci. 6 (4), 329–376.

Besley, T.F., 2007. Principled Agents: The Political Economy of Good Government. Oxford University Press, Oxford.

Besley, T.F., Kudamatsu, M., 2006. Health and democracy. Am. Econ. Rev. 96, 313–318.

Besley, T.F., Persson, T., 2011. Pillars of Prosperity. Princeton University Press, Princeton, NJ.

Besley, T.F., Persson, T., Sturm, D., 2010. Political competition, policy and growth: theory and evidence from the United States. Rev. Econ. Stud. 77, 1329–1352.

Blaydes, L.M., Kayser, M., 2011. Counting calories: democracy and distribution in the developing world. Inter. Stud. Q. 55, 887–908.

Blundell, R., Bond, S., 2000. GMM Estimation with persistent panel data: an application to production functions. Econ. Rev. 19 (3), 321–340.

Boix, C., Miller, M., Rosato, S., 2012. A complete data Set of political regimes, 1800–2007. Comp. Polit. Stud. 46 (12), 1523–1554.

Brown, D.S., 1999. Reading, writing and regime type: democracy's impact on primary school enrollment. Polit. Res. Q. 52 (4), 681–707.

Brown, D.S., Hunter, W.A., 1999. Democracy and social spending in Latin America, 1980–92. Am. Polit. Sci. Rev. 93 (4), 779–790

Brown, D.S., Hunter, W.A., 2004. Democracy and human capital formation: educational expenditures in Latin America. Comp. Polit. Stud. 37, 842–864.

Burkhart, R.E., 1997. Comparative democracy and income distribution: shape and direction of the causal arrow. J. Polit. 59 (1), 148–164.

Campello, D., 2011. The great gap: inequality and the politics of redistribution in Latin America. In: Blofield, M. (Ed.), The Politics of Redistribution in Less Developed Democracies: Evidence from Brazil, Ecuador, and Venezuela. Penn State Press, University Park, PA.

Carter, M.R., Morrow, J., 2012. Left, Right, Left: Income Dynamics and the Evolving Political Preferences of Forward Looking Bayesian Voters. http://agecon.ucdavis.edu/people/faculty/michael-carter/docs/nopoumECMA.pdf.

Cascio, E., Washington, E., 2012. Valuing the Vote: The Redistribution of Voting Rights and State Funds Following the Voting Rights Act of 1965. National Bureau of Economic Research, Working Paper No. 17776.

Cheibub, J.A., 1998. Political regimes and the extractive capacity of governments: taxation in democracies and dictatorships. World Polit. 50, 349–376.

Cheibub, J.A., Gandhi, J., Vreeland, J.R., 2010. Democracy and dictatorship revisited. Public Choice 143 (1), 67–101.

Daalgard, C.-J., Hansen, H., Larsen, T., 2005. Income skewness, redistribution and growth: A reconciliation, Unpublished, Department of Economics, University of Copenhagen.

Dasgupta, S., 2013. Legalizing the Revolution. Unpublished, Ph.D. Thesis, Columbia University.

De la O, A.L., Rodden, J., 2008. Does religion distract the poor? Income and issue voting around the world. Comp. Polit. Stud. 41 (4), 437–476.

Drazen, A.M., 2000. Political Economy in Macroeconomics. Princeton University Press, Princeton, NJ.

Dunning, T., 2008. Crude Democracy. Cambridge University Press, New York, NY.

Einhorn, R.L., 2006. American Taxation, American Slavery. University of Chicago Press, Chicago, IL.

Elis, R., 2011. Redistribution Under Oligarchy: Trade, Regional Inequality and the Origins of Public Schooling in Argentina, 1862–1912. Unpublished, Ph.D. Dissertation, Department of Political Science, Stanford University.

Ellman, M., Wantchekon, L., 2000. Electoral competition under the threat of political unrest. Q. J. Econ. 115 (2), 499–531.

Engerman, S.L., Sokoloff, K.L., 2005. The evolution of suffrage institutions in the New World. J. Econ. Hist. 65, 891–921.

Engerman, S.L., Sokoloff, K.L., 2011. Economic Development in the Americas since 1500: Endowments and Institutions. Cambridge University Press, New York, NY.

Fernandez, R., Rogerson, R., 1995. On the political economy of education subsidies. Rev. Econ. Stud. 62, 249–262.

Flemming, J.S., Micklewright, J., 2000. Income distribution, economic systems and transition. In: Atkinson, A.B., Bourguignon, F. (Eds.), Handbook of Income Distribution, first ed. In: vol. 1. Elsevier, Cambridge, pp. 843–918, Chapter 14.

Frank, T., 2005. What's the Matter with Kansas? How Conservatives Won the Heart of America. Holt, New York, NY.

Fujiwara, T., 2011. Voting Technology, Political Responsiveness, and Infant Health: Evidence from Brazil. http://www.princeton.edu/~fujiwara/papers/elecvote_site.pdf.

Gallego, F.A., 2010. Historical origins of schooling: the role of democracy and political decentralization. Rev. Econ. Stat. 92 (2), 228–243.

Gerring, J., Thacker, S., Alfaro, R., 2012. Democracy and human development. J. Polit. 74(1).

Gil, R., Mulligan, C.B., Sala-i-Martin, X., 2004. Do democracies have different public policies than non-democracies? J. Econ. Perspect. 18, 51–74.

Gradstein, M., Justman, M., 1999a. The industrial revolution, political transition and the subsequent decline in inequality in nineteenth century Britain. Explor. Econ. Hist. 36, 109–127.

Gradstein, M., Justman, M., 1999b. The democratization of political elites and the decline in inequality in modern economic growth. In: Breizes, E.S., Temin, P. (Eds.), Elites, Minorities and Economic Growth. Elsevier, Amsterdam.

Gradstein, M., Milanovic, B., 2004. Does liberté=égalité? A survey of the empirical evidence on the links between political democracy and income inequality. J. Econ. Surv. 18 (4), 515–537.

Gradstein, M., Justman, M., Meier, V., 2004. The Political Economy of Education: Implications for Growth and Inequality. MIT Press, Cambridge.

Guttsman, W.L. (Ed.), 1967. A Plea for Democracy: Ad Edited Selection from the 1867 Essays on Reform and Questions for a Reformed Parliament. Macgibbon & Kee, London.

Harding, Robin, Stasavage, David, 2013. What Democracy Does (and Doesn't do) for Basic Services: School Fees, School Inputs, and African Elections. Unpublished, Department of Politics, New York University.

Hassler, J., Storesletten, K., Mora, J.V.R., Zilibotti, F., 2003. The survival of the welfare state. Am. Econ. Rev. 93 (1), 87–112.

Hendrix, C.S., 2010. Measuring state capacity: theoretical and empirical implications for the study of civil conflict. J. Peace Res. 47 (3), 273–285.

Holton, W., 2008. Unruly Americans and the Origins of the Constitution. Palgrave Macmillan, New York, NY.

Holtz-Eakin, D., Newey, W.K., Rosen, H.S., 1988. Estimating vector autoregressions with panel data. Econometrica 56 (6), 1371–1396.

Huber, E., Stephens, J.D., 2012. Democracy and the Left: Social Policy and Inequality in Latin America. University of Chicago Press, Chicago, IL.

Huber, E., Nielsen, F., Pribble, J., Stephens, J.D., 2006. Politics and Inequality in Latin America and the Caribbean. Am. Sociol. Rev. 71 (6), 943–963.

Husted, T.A., Kenny, L., 1997. The effect of the expansion of the voting franchise on the size of government. J. Polit. Econ. 105, 54–82.

Kaufman, R.R., Segura-Ubiergo, A., 2001. Globalization, domestic politics, and social spending in Latin America: a time-series cross-section analysis, 1973–97. World Polit. 53 (4), 553–587.

Krusell, P., Ríos-Rull, J.-V., 1999. On the size of the US government. Am. Econ. Rev. 89 (5), 1156–1181.

Krusell, P., Ríos-Rull, J.-V., Quadrini, V., 1997. Politico-economic equilibrium and growth. J. Econ. Dynam. Control 21 (1), 243–272.

Kudamatsu, M., 2012. Has democratization reduced infant mortality in sub-Saharan Africa? Evidence from micro data. J. Eur. Econ. Assoc. 10 (6), 1294–1317.

Lapp, N.D., 2004. Landing Votes: Representation and Land Reform in Latin America. Palgrave Macmillan, New York, NY.

Larcinese, V., 2011. Enfranchisement and Representation: Italy 1909–1913. Unpublished, Department of Government, London School of Economics, http://personal.lse.ac.uk/LARCINES/enfranchisement_nov11.pdf.

Lee, W., 2003. Is democracy more expropriative than dictatorship? tocquevillian wisdom revisited. J. Devel. Econ. 71, 155–198.

Lee, C.-S., 2005. Income inequality, democracy, and public sector size. Am. Sociol. Rev. 70 (1), 158–181.

Li, H., Squire, L., Zou, H.-f., 1998. Explaining international and intertemporal variations in income inequality. Econ. J. 108 (1), 26–43.

Lindert, P.H., 1994. The rise of social spending, 1880–1930. Explor. Econ. Hist. 31 (1), 1–37.

Lindert, P.H., 2004. Growing Public: Social Spending and Economic Growth since the Eighteenth Century. Cambridge University Press, New York, NY.

Lizzeri, A., Persico, N., 2004. Why Did the elites extend the suffrage? Democracy and the scope of government, with an application to Britain's 'age of reform. Q. J. Econ. 119, 707–765.

Llavador, H., Oxoby, R.J., 2005. Partisan competition, growth, and the franchise. Q. J. Econ. 120, 1155–1192.

Londregan, J.B., 2000. Legislative Institutions and Ideology in Chile. Cambridge University Press, New York, NY.

Lott Jr., J.R., Kenny, L., 1999. How dramatically did women's suffrage change the size and scope of government? J. Polit. Econ. 107 (6), 1163–1198.

Lundahl, M., 1982. The rationale for apartheid. Am. Econ. Rev. 72, 1169–1179.

Martinez-Bravo, M., Padró-i-Miquel, G., Qian, N., Yao, Y., 2012. The effects of democratization on public goods and redistribution: evidence from China. Working Paper.

McDaniel, T., 1991. Autocracy, Modernization and Revolution in Russia and Iran. Princeton University Press, Princeton, NJ.

McGuire, R.A., 2003. To Form a More Perfect Union: A New Economic Interpretations of the United States Constitutions. Oxford University Press, New York, NY.

McGuire, J.W., 2010. Wealth, Health and Democracy in East Asia and Latin America. Cambridge University Press, New York, NY.

McMillan, J., Zoido, P., 2004. How to subvert democracy: montesinos in Peru. J. Econ. Perspect. 4, 69–92.

Meltzer, A.M., Richard, S.F., 1981. A rational theory of the size of government. J. Polit. Econ. 89, 914–927.

Milanovic, B., 1998. Income, Inequality, and Poverty During the Transition from Planned to Market Economy. World Bank, Washington.

Miller, G., 2008. Women's suffrage, political responsiveness, and child survival in American history. Q. J. Econ. 123 (3), 1287–1327.

Moene, K.O., Wallerstein, M., 2001. Inequality, social insurance and redistribution. Am. Polit. Sci. Rev. 95, 859–874.

Mohammed, S., Finnoff, K., 2003. Capital Flight from South Africa, 1980–2000. In: Epstein, G. (Ed.), Capital Flight and Capital Controls in Developing Countries. Edward Elgar Publishing, Inc, Northampton.

Moore, B., 1966. The Social Origins of Dictatorship and Democracy: Lord and Peasant in the Making of the Modern World. Beacon Press, Boston, MA.

Moses, J.W., 1994. Abdication from national policy autonomy: what's left to leave? Polit. Soc. 22 (2), 125–148.

Muller, E.N., 1988. Democracy, economic development, and income inequality. Am. Sociol. Rev. 53 (1), 50–68.

Muller, E.N., 1989. Democracy and inequality. Am. Sociol. Rev. 54 (5), 868–871.

Naidu, S., 2011. Suffrage, Schooling, and Sorting in the Post-Bellum US South. http://tuvalu.santafe.edu/~snaidu/papers/suffrage_may_25_2012_combined.pdf.

Naidu, S., Yuchtman, N., 2013. Coercive contract enforcement: law and the labor market in 19th century industrial Britain. Am. Econ. Rev. 103 (1), 107–144.

Newey, W.K., Windmeijer, F., 2009. GMM estimation with many weak moment conditions. Econometrica 77 (3), 687–719.

Nickell, S., 1981. Biases in dynamic models with fixed effects. Econometrica 49 (6), 1417–1426.

Panitch, L., Gindin, S., 2012. The Making of Global Capitalism. Verso, New York, NY.

Papaioannou, E., Siourounis, G., 2008. Democratisation and growth. Econ. J. 118 (532), 1520–1551.

Perotti, R., 1996. Growth, income distribution and democracy: what the data say. J. Econ. Growth 1, 149–187.

Persson, T., Tabellini, G., 1994. Is inequality harmful to growth? Am. Econ. Rev. 84, 600–621.

Persson, T., Tabellini, G., 2000. Political Economics. MIT Press, Cambridge.

Persson, T., Tabellini, G., 2003. The Economic Effects of Constitutions. MIT Press, Cambridge.

Pettersson-Lidbom, P., Tyrefors, B., 2011. Democracy, Redistribution, and Political Participation: Evidence from Sweden 1919–1938. http://people.su.se/~pepet/democracyFeb2012.pdf.

Piketty, T., 1995. Social mobility and redistributive politics. Q. J. Econ. 110, 551–584.

Przeworski, A., Alvarez, M., Cheibub, J.A., Limongi, F., 2000. Democracy and Development: Political Institutions and Material Well-being in the World, 1950–1990. Cambridge University Press, New York, NY.

Putterman, L., 1996. Why have the rabble not redistributed the wealth? On the stability of democracy and unequal wealth. In: Roemer, J.E. (Ed.), Property Relations, Incentives and Welfare. McMillan, London.

Roberts, K.W.S., 1977. Voting over income tax schedules. J. Public Econ. 8, 329–340.

Rodrik, D., 1999. Democracies pay higher wages. Q. J. Econ. 114, 707–738.

Roemer, J.E., 1998. Why the poor do not expropriate the rich: an old agrument in new garb. J. Public Econ. 70, 399–424.

Roemer, J.E., Lee, W., Van der Straeten, K., 2007. Racism, Xenophobia and Distribution: Multi-Issue Politics in Advanced Democracies. Harvard University Press, Cambridge.

Romer, T., 1975. Individual welfare, majority voting and the properties of a linear income tax. J. Public Econ. 7, 163–168.

Ross, M.L., 2006. Is democracy good for the poor? Am. J. Polit. Sci. 50, 860–874.

Scheve, K., Stasavage, D., 2009. Institutions, Partisanship, and Inequality in the Long Run. World Polit. 61, 215–253.

Scheve, K., Stasavage, D., 2010. The conscription of wealth: mass warfare and the demand for progressive taxation. Inter. Organ. 64, 529–561.

Scheve, K., Stasavage, D., 2012. Democracy, war, and wealth: lessons from two centuries of inheritance taxation. Am. Polit. Sci. Rev. 106 (1), 82–102.

Schonhardt-Bailey, C., 2006. From the Corn Laws to Free Trade: Interests, Ideas, and Institutions in Historical Perspective. MIT Press, Cambridge.

Seligmann, L.J., 1995. Between Reform & Revolution: Political Struggles in the Peruvian Andes, 1969–1991. Stanford University Press, Stanford, CA.

Shayo, M., 2009. A model of social identity with an application to political economy: nation, class, and redistribution. Am. Polit. Sci. Rev. 103 (02), 147–174.

Siavelis, P.M., 2000. The President and Congress in Post-Authoritarian Chile: Institutional Constraints to Democratic Consolidation. Pennsylvania State University Press, University Park, PA.

Simpson, M., 1990. Political rights and income inequality: a cross-national test. Am. Sociol. Rev. 55 (5), 682–693.

Sirowy, L., Inkeles, A., 1990. The effects of democracy on economic growth and inequality: a review. Stud. Comput. Inter. Develop. 25, 126–157.

Soifer, H., 2013. State power and the redistributive threat. Stud. in Comp. Int. Dev. 48 (1), 1–22.

Solt, F., 2009. Standardizing the world income inequality database. Soc. Sci. Q. 90 (2), 231–242.

Stasavage, D., 2005a. Democracy and education spending in Africa. Am. J. Polit. Sci. 49, 343–358.

Stasavage, D., 2005b. The role of democracy in Uganda's move to universal primary education. J. Mod. Afr. Stud. 43 (1), 53–73.

Stigler, G.J., 1970. Director's law of public income redistribution. J. Law Econ. 13, 1–10.

Tilly, C., 1985. Warmaking and state making as organized crime. In: Evans, P., Rueschemeyer, D., Skocpol, T. (Eds.), Bringing the State Back In. Cambridge University Press, Cambridge.

Vanhanen, T., 2013. Democratization and Power Resources 1850–2000. http://www.fsd.uta.fi/en/data/catalogue/FSD1216/meF1216e.html#viittaaminen.

Waldstreicher, D., 2009. Slavery's Constitution: From Revolution to Ratification. MacMillan, New York, NY.

Weede, E., 1989. Democracy and income inequality reconsidered. Am. Sociol. Rev. 54 (5), 865–868.

Weyland, K., 2004. Neoliberalism and democracy in Latin America: a mixed record. Lat. Am. Polit. Soc. 46 (1), 135–157.

Whiteford, A., Van Seventer, D., 2000. Understanding contemporary household inequality in South Africa. Stud. Econ. Econ. 24 (3), 7–30.

Wigley, S., Akkoyunlu-Wigley, A., 2011. The impact of regime type on health: does redistribution explain everything? World Polit. 63 (4), 647–677.

Wilse-Samson, L., 2013. Structural Change and Democratization: Evidence from Apartheid South Africa. Unpublished working paper, Columbia University, http://www.columbia.edu/~lhw2110/research.html.

Wooldridge, J.M., 2002. Econometric Analysis of Cross Section and Panel Data. MIT Press, Cambridge.

Wright, R.D., 1996. Taxes, redistribution and growth. J. Public Econ. 62, 327–338.

CHAPTER 22

The Idea of Antipoverty Policy

Martin Ravallion
Department of Economics, Georgetown University, Washington, DC, USA

Contents

Handbook of Income Distribution, Volume 2B
ISSN 1574-0056, http://dx.doi.org/10.1016/B978-0-444-59429-7.00023-6

Abstract

How did we come to think that eliminating poverty is a legitimate goal for public policy? What policies emerged in the hope of attaining that goal? The last 200 years have witnessed a dramatic change in thinking about poverty. Mainstream economic thinking in the eighteenth century held that poverty was necessary and even desirable for a country's economic success. Today, poverty is more often viewed as a constraint on that success. In short, poverty switched from being seen as a social good to a social bad. This change in thinking, and the accompanying progress in knowledge, has greatly influenced public action, with heightened emphasis on the role of antipoverty policy in sustainable promotion from poverty, as well as protection. Development strategies today typically strive for a virtuous cycle of growth with equity and a range of policy interventions have emerged to help ensure that outcome. An expanding body of knowledge has taught us about how effective those interventions are in specific settings, although many knowledge gaps remain.

Keywords

Poverty, Inequality, Growth, Redistribution, Antipoverty policy

JEL Classification Codes

B00, I38, O15

22.1. INTRODUCTION

The poor . . . are like the shadows in a painting: they provide the necessary contrast.
                    Philippe Hecquet (1740), quoted in Roche (1987, p. 64)

Everyone but an idiot knows that the lower classes must be kept poor or they will never be industrious.
                    Arthur Young (1771), quoted in Furniss (1920, p. 118)

May we not outgrow the belief that poverty is necessary?
                    Marshall (1890, p. 2)

Our dream is a world free of poverty.
                    (Motto of the World Bank since 1990).

It is widely accepted today that eliminating poverty is a legitimate goal of public action, for which governments (in both rich and poor countries) typically take some responsibility. The policy responses include both direct interventions, often put under the heading of "social policies," and various economy-wide policies—overall policies for economic development that have bearing on the extent of poverty. (I will use the term "antipoverty policy" to embrace both sets of policies.) There are essentially three premises to the idea of such policies:

- Premise 1: Poverty is a social bad.[1]
- Premise 2: Poverty can be eliminated.
- Premise 3: Public policies can help do that.

This chapter tries to understand how these three premises came to be broadly accepted and what forms of public action emerged.

Both the differences and the similarities between today's thinking and that of the past are of interest. There are some policy debates that live on and some common themes, such as the role of incentives. However, one is also struck by the differences. Indeed, widespread (though certainly not universal) acceptance of the three premises above appears to be relatively new. Before the late eighteenth century, the dominant school of economic thought saw poverty as a social *good*, essential for economic development. It may well have been granted that, other things being equal, a society with less poverty is to be preferred, but other things were not seen to be equal. Poverty was deemed essential to incentivize workers and keep their wages low, so as to create a strong, globally competitive, economy. Nor did the idea of what constitutes "economic development" embrace poor people as being necessarily among its intended beneficiaries. There was also widespread doubt about the desirability of, or even the potential for, governmental intervention against poverty. In marked contrast, poverty is widely seen today as a constraint on development rather than a precondition for it. And it is now widely (though not universally) agreed, across both rich and poor countries, that the government has an important role in the fight against poverty.

This chapter documents this transition in thinking about poverty and policy. Of course, the interrelationship between thinking and action is complex, and what emerges in the policy arena depends on many things, including technology, public awareness, and political economy. Nonetheless, there is a story to be told about how scholarly and popular thinking has evolved. This helps us understand prevailing views on the distributive role of the state and the specific policies adopted. The change in thinking also teaches us that the progress in knowledge both reinforces and reflects progress in development.

A natural starting point is Fleischacker's (2004) excellent *Short History of Distributive Justice*. Fleischacker defines distributive justice as a situation in which "property is distributed throughout the society so that everyone is supplied with a certain level of material means."[2] He argues that in premodern thought, poverty relief was largely motivated by

---

[1] Poverty can be seen as a social bad either intrinsically (a society with less poverty is preferred) or instrumentally (that a less poor society will be better at other things of value, including its overall economic performance).

[2] Aristotle is widely credited with introducing the term "distributive justice," in the fourth century BC. However, Fleischacker (2004) convincingly argues that Aristotle had something quite different in mind to modern usage. For Aristotle, distributive justice was about assigning political rewards according to "merit."

beneficence—a matter of the donor's personal choice, not a right for poor people, and so quite distinct from justice, which emanates from the secular world of laws and taxes. Most religions see voluntary efforts to help poor people as a virtue.[3] However, such charitable relief is not distributive justice in Fleischacker's eyes. For the birth of that idea, he argues that we need to look to Europe in the late eighteenth century. Fleischacker describes and interprets the development of the idea in philosophical writings. However, what is largely missing from Fleischacker's history is the economics. This is important if we focus on poverty rather than justice. Nor have historians (such as Beaudoin, 2007; Geremek, 1994; Himmelfarb, 1984a,b) given more than passing attention to the economics. And it would be fair to say that economists have paid little attention to the history of thought on poverty and inequality.[4]

The chapter offers an overview of how philosophical and economic thinking on poverty and antipoverty policy has evolved and the types of policies that emerged. The discussion will give less emphasis than Fleischacker on whether poor people were believed to have the legal right to assistance. States can and do ascribe legal rights, but sometimes with little more than symbolic value, given that the administrative capabilities for enforcement are weak, and especially so in poor countries. Instead, the focus here will be on whether (demonstrably or plausibly) public policy helped families permanently escape poverty or merely offered a transient (though potentially important) short-term palliative to protect people from negative shocks. In short, the acid test for a good antipoverty policy will be whether it is aimed at both *promotion* and *protection* (applying a useful distinction made by Drèze and Sen, 1989). This idea of antipoverty policy turns out to be quite recent, with origins in the late nineteenth century, but only emerging with confidence in the late twentieth century.

The chapter begins with a simple characterization of personal wealth dynamics, which will help motivate the chapter's interpretation of past thinking about this class of policies. The bulk of the chapter falls into two parts. The first, comprising Sections 22.3–22.6, traces out the history of thought from mercantilist views on the inevitability of poverty through two main stages of "poverty enlightenment," out of which poverty came to be seen as a social bad (Premise 1). The second part focuses on policies, from economy-wide policies to direct interventions. Sections 22.7 and 22.8 turn to an important aspect of Premise 2, namely, the country's overall development strategy and in particular whether poverty can be eliminated through economic growth and the role played by initial

---

[3] Although with differences in emphasis, both within and between religions. For example, see Kahl's (2005) discussion of the differences between Catholicism, Lutheranism, and Calvinism/Reformed Protestantism.

[4] In one of the few exceptions, Cogneau (2012) discusses the evolution of thought on inequality in a development context. On the neglect of the history of thought by economists, see Blaug (2001).

distribution. Section 22.9 focuses on present-day thinking on specific direct interventions (Premise 3). Section 22.10 concludes the chapter.

22.2. WEALTH DYNAMICS AND ANTIPOVERTY POLICIES

A longstanding explanation heard for poverty is that it stems from the "bad behaviors" of poor people—high fertility, laziness, or bad spending choices, such as excessive consumption of alcohol.[5] It is not that they are in any way constrained to be poor, but that they (implicitly or explicitly) chose to be poor. By this view, the role for antipoverty policy is to ensure behavioral change. We will hear more of these arguments later in this chapter. However, it will be useful to sketch here an alternative model whereby poverty emerges from the wealth dynamics implied by the external constraints facing poor people.

By "wealth" I shall mean both human capital—the accumulated stock of past educational and health inputs, including past nutritional intakes—as well as nonhuman capital, such as industrial or financial capital.[6] To simplify the analysis, however, wealth is treated as a single composite asset. Initial wealth, w_t at date t, is distributed across individuals, some of whom have zero wealth, but may still earn some labor income, consumed fully on their survival needs in each period. A fixed share of current wealth is used for current consumption. Each person has a production function yielding output $h(k)$ from a capital stock k. There is a threshold capital stock needed to produce any output, i.e., $h(k) = 0$ for all $k \leq k^{\min}(>0)$. Once the threshold is reached, output emerges in the next period, though diminishing returns start to set in immediately; in other words, the function $h(k)$ is strictly positive, strictly increasing and strictly concave for all $k > k^{\min}$. Those for whom the threshold has not been reached ($w < k^{\min}$) have no demand for capital as it will not yield any output.

There is more than one interpretation of the threshold. Dasgupta (1993) provides a persuasive argument for its existence based on the biological fact of a positive basal metabolic rate, given that maintaining the human body at rest requires a (substantial) minimum food energy intake, without which no physical work can be done. (Maintenance requirements are 60–75% of food energy intake.) Physiology entails that the set of feasible production activities for an individual is inherently nonconvex. Threshold effects can also reflect nonconvexities in production possibilities associated with minimum schooling needs, the nature of the production technology or from the existence of a lumpy "threshold good" in consumption.[7] In a more elaborate version of this model, one would

[5] See Klebaner (1964), Burnett (1969, Chapter 4), and Wim and Halman (2000).

[6] A good typology is found in Sachs's (2005b, Chapter 13) six types of capital that poor people lack: human capital, business capital, infrastructure, natural capital, public institutional capital, and knowledge capital.

[7] On the latter argument, see Just and Michelson (2007). On other sources of poverty traps, see Azariadis (2006) and other papers in the collection edited by Bowles et al. (2006).

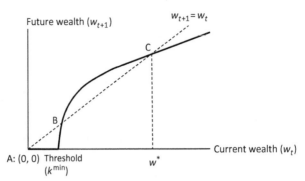

Figure 22.1 Wealth dynamics with a poverty trap.

also want to allow for interaction effects among different dimensions of wealth, such as when poor nutritional status impedes children's learning.

There is another constraint on production possibilities stemming from credit market failures. Because lenders are imperfectly informed about borrowers, a borrowing constraint is imposed, whereby a person can only borrow up to λ times her wealth. Let $k\star$ denote the individual's desired capital stock. Those with wealth sufficient to produce but less than $k\star/(\lambda+1)$ have a desire to invest but are constrained in that, after investing all they can, they still find that the marginal product of capital exceeds the interest rate, given the borrowing constraint. Finally, someone who starts her productive life with sufficient wealth (greater than $k\star/(\lambda+1)$) is able to invest her unconstrained optimal amount, equating the (declining) marginal product of her capital with the prevailing interest rate r (the price of capital), which is taken to be fixed $(h'(k\star)=r)$.[8]

The recursion diagram (the mapping from current wealth to future wealth) then takes the form depicted in Figure 22.1. Future wealth is zero at low levels of current wealth $(w_t < k^{min})$. For levels of initial wealth in the interval $[k^{min}, k\star/(\lambda+1)]$, future wealth is a strictly concave function of current wealth. At higher wealth $(w_t > k\star/(\lambda+1))$, the function becomes linear.

There are potentially three steady-state equilibria (with constant wealth over time) for each individual. Two of these, namely, points A and C in Figure 22.1, are stable while the middle one, at point B, is unstable in that shocks will move those at B toward A or C.[9] In the long run, after repeated small shocks, the economy will settle in a state that can be thought of as having two main classes of people. One class has little or no wealth, given that its members are caught in a *wealth poverty trap*, at point A. There can be many reasons

---

[8] In the special case in which the threshold is not binding, this model is the same as that outlined in Banerjee and Duflo (2003), though with antecedents in the literature.

[9] Imagine someone at point B in Figure 22.1. Any small wealth gain will put her in a region of accumulation (current wealth lower than future wealth) and so the person will progress toward point C. Similarly, a small contraction will put her on a path to point A.

in practice why people are so trapped, including lack of any marketable skills, social exclusion, geographic isolation, debilitating disease, or environmental degradation. The second class comprises people who have settled at point C, at their respective steady-state levels of wealth (w^*). There can still be inequality within each class. There can be inequality of labor earnings among the poorer class, and there can be wealth inequality among the "point C folk," given different steady-state levels of wealth. There can be poverty even if nobody is caught in a poverty trap. The "poor" can be identified as two groups of people, namely, those at point A and the poor among those at point C, that is, those for whom their steady-state level of wealth turns out to be very low, even though they are not caught in a poverty trap.

Although the wealth poverty trap at point A is economically stable for each individual, social and political stability is another matter. The latter types of instability can arise in many ways, defying simple generalizations about its economic causes. However, it is plausible that a large mass of people at point A can threaten social stability, especially if their labor earnings and (hence) consumptions are very low, either in steady state or as a result of some severe shock, and in the latter case the threat to stability may well be even greater.[10]

Motivated by this stylized representation of wealth dynamics, we can think of two broad types of antipoverty policies. There can be policies that provide short-term palliatives, possibly to maintain social stability by assuring that current incomes do not fall below some crucial level, even though poor people remain poor, either because they are caught in a wealth poverty trap or they have a low steady-state level of wealth. These are purely *protection policies*. And there are *promotion policies* that allow poor people to attain the higher level of wealth needed to escape poverty. For those caught in a poverty trap, this will require a sufficiently large wealth gain to put them on a path to eventually reaching their own (higher and stable) steady-state level of wealth. For those not caught in a trap, but still poor, promotion will require some combination of higher wealth and higher returns to their wealth—an upward shift in the recursion diagram in Figure 22.1.

The rest of this chapter will study the origins and nature of both types of policies. It will be argued that, although the idea of some public responsibility for protecting poor people from negative shocks is an old one, the idea of such a role for promotion by relieving the constraints facing poor people (either caught in poverty trap or with low returns to their wealth) is remarkably new. The latter idea came with a significant evolution in thinking about the causes of poverty. The longstanding view that the "moral weaknesses" of poor people caused their poverty implied little scope for public action to promote people from poverty, and rebuffed any calls for taxing the rich to finance such action. It was ultimately up to poor people to escape poverty by changing their behaviors. Public responsibility was largely confined to limited, and highly targeted, protection to address extreme transient poverty and some

---

[10] In *Politics*, Aristotle (350 BC, unnumbered) put the point nicely: "It is a bad thing that many from being rich should become poor; for men of ruined fortunes are sure to stir up revolutions."

efforts at aiding the "moral reform" of poor people. Although one still hears casual claims blaming poor people for their poverty today, across the globe, from the mid-nineteenth century, though not carrying much policy weight until well into the twentieth century, deeper causal understandings of poverty emerged in popular and scholarly writings. These pointed to a new promotional role for public action in fighting persistent poverty.[11] Poverty was seen to reflect in no small measure public failures, including uncorrected market failures.

22.3. THE UTILITY OF POVERTY

For much of the sixteenth through eighteenth centuries, when Western Europe was mired in poverty, the dominant economic theory of the time, mercantilism, saw poverty as a natural state of affairs and, indeed, instrumentally good, as a means of encouraging work effort. The mercantilist goal was to maximize a nation's export surplus—the balance of trade, which was equated with the future prosperity and power of the realm—and the means were cheap production inputs, that is, cheap raw materials (for which colonies proved useful) and cheap, and therefore poor, labor at home. Poverty was not just accepted; it was seen as an essential precondition for a country's economic development. Hunger would encourage work, and lack of it would do the opposite. The seemingly widely held economic premise was that the individual supply curve for unskilled work was negatively sloped—in modern economic terms, that the income effect on demand for leisure dominated the substitution effect. As the Reverend Townsend (1786) put it: "The poor know little of the motives which stimulate the higher ranks to action—pride, honor and ambition. In general, it is only hunger which can spur and goad them onto labor" (p. 23). And so: ". . . in proportion as you advance the wages of the poor, you diminish the quantity of their work" (p. 29).[12]

The idea of a negatively sloped labor supply curve is essentially what Furniss (1920, p. 117) later dubbed "the utility of poverty." The basis for this idea appears to have been little more than casual anecdotes; Furniss (1920, Chapter 6) provides many examples from writings of the time, often with references to the attractions of the alehouse when workers got a wage increase. It was not the last time in the history of thought about poverty that casual incentive arguments resting on little or no good evidence would buttress strong policy positions.

A continuing future supply of cheap labor was also seen to be crucial. Large families were encouraged and good work habits were to be instilled from an early age. Like higher current wages, too much schooling would discourage both current and future work

---

[11] This is not to say that the change in the model of poverty caused the change in policy. To some extent, both changes shared a common causation in broader changes in the economy and society.

[12] Though little known today, Townsend's advocacy of free markets was important in the history of economic thought, with influence on subsequent thinkers (including Malthus and Darwin). For further discussion of Townsend's influence, see Montagu (1971) and Lepenies (2014).

effort. Consistent with this model, few sustainable opportunities were expected to be available to any educated children from poor families. In de Mandeville's (1732, pp. 288–311) mind, the only realistic future prospect for the children of laboring (and hence poor) parents was to be laboring and poor. Poor parents had little realistic hope that their children would be anything but poor; their low aspirations simply reflected and rationalized their lack of opportunity. Small amounts of schooling would have served little purpose. In this view of economic development, there was little or no prospect of reducing wealth poverty—including escaping the poverty trap demonstrated in Figure 22.1. There was little or no perceived scope for upward mobility of working class children. They were born poor and stayed poor.

Modern progressive thinkers may be shocked by de Mandeville's views (and similar views still heard occasionally in modern times), but there may well be an element of cruel truth to them. His claim that a modest amount of extra schooling for working class children is wasted is consistent with the model in Figure 22.1. Suppose that the poor—the working class—are concentrated at the wealth poverty trap (point A in Figure 22.1). A small increase in their wealth, in the form of extra human capital only sufficient to get them to the threshold (say), will not bring any lasting benefit. In due course, the dynamics will push them back to point A. A large gain in schooling is needed.

And de Mandeville's pessimism about schooling would not surprise many poor children in the developing world today. Katherine Boo's (2012) vivid description of life in a Mumbai slum includes a discussion of the choices made by Sunil, a young scavenger who spends long hours collecting whatever he can find of any value in the trash deposits around Mumbai airport. Sunil is clearly very poor. He is also clearly capable of learning and is aware that with sufficient schooling he might escape his wretched life. But how can he finance sufficient schooling? At one point, he spends a few days in a private after-hours school run by a college student who lives in the slum, and after much rote learning he masters the "twinkle-star" song.[13] Boo (2012, p. 68) writes:

> He'd sat in on [the English class taught in the slum] for a few days, mastering the English twinkle-star song, before deciding that his time was better spent working for food.

By interpretation, the modest amount of schooling that Sunil could afford would be insufficient for him to escape poverty. He is better off addressing his current hunger.

22.3.1 Early Social Protection Policies

Recall that the poverty trap in Figure 22.1 has people stuck at zero wealth but they still earn enough to survive (as Sunil does through scavenging). Higher wages or prices for their outputs increase their welfare, and uninsured shocks to their health (say) have the

---

[13] "Twinkle-twinkle little star, how I wonder what you are. Up above the world so high, like a diamond in the sky."

opposite effect. There is space here for social protection policies providing state-contingent income support. Such policies can exist and be seen as reasonably effective without changing the fact that poor people are stuck in the wealth poverty trap.

It has long been argued that governments have a role in social protection from shocks that threaten extreme poverty. For example, around 300 BC, the famous Indian academic and advisor to royalty, Chanakya (also known as Kautilya), recommended that when famine looms a good king should ". . . institute the building of forts or water-works with the grant of food, or share [his] provisions [with the people], or entrust the country [to another king]" (quoted in Drèze, 1990a, p. 75). If one thinks of antipoverty policy primarily in terms of protection from adverse events, then the idea is very old indeed.

Even though mainstream economic thinking has for a long time encouraged a limited role for the state in social protection, more contentious has been the idea of promotion. In the premercantilist feudal and slave economies, the employer had a responsibility for insuring workers, even very poor workers, who may well have faced exploitation but were at least protected to some degree. (This was not necessarily altruistic in any sense; a slave owner had a purely selfish interest in keeping his property alive.) The new elites in the early development of capitalism were keen to see the state take over these roles, but consistently with their economic ideas. The status quo distribution of wealth was seen by its defenders as the outcome of natural processes, which included the competitive market mechanism, and it was not to be tampered with through policy. Persistent poverty was believed to be the natural order of things until modern times. By contrast, transient poverty was seen as a threat to the social order. There was at least an implicit recognition of the limitations of free markets in providing insurance against risk.

The sixteenth and seventeenth centuries saw the emergence of fledgling social policies in Europe in response to rising "pauperism." There were increasing numbers of dislocated and unemployed workers and beggars on city streets. Although the cause was widely seen to be the moral weaknesses of poor people, deeper explanations could be found in changes in the organization of production (including in agriculture with the breakup of feudalism) combined with greater mobility (also with implications for family support of the aged). Although unemployment was not commonly identified as a cause of poverty, work was widely seen as the solution. Publicly financed workhouses were introduced around 1600. Welfare recipients were incarcerated and obliged to work for their upkeep. From the outset, the idea was that the workhouses would be "self-targeting," in that only the poorest would be willing to be so confined, thus providing a cost-effective means of poverty relief (Thane, 2000, p. 115). But the policy was also grounded in the prevailing view that poverty was caused by bad behaviors, which could be controlled and (hopefully) corrected by the workhouses. The workhouses were seen as a cost-effective policy for moral reform.

There was a strong element of protection in the workhouse idea; anyone thrown into poverty by some shock could turn to the workhouse. Was it also a promotional policy?

There is not much discussion in the literature about the promotional value to poor people of the work done beyond the perceived moral value of actually doing work. Advocates might well argue that this was promotion through behavioral change. But it was clearly not promotion by relieving the constraints facing poor people.

22.3.2 England's Poor Laws

A major policy response to poverty emerged in Elizabethan England in the form of the Poor Laws.[14] This was a system of publicly provided insurance against income poverty due to specific sources, notably old age, widowhood, disability, illness, or unemployment. Essentially the central government instructed local parishes to deal with their poverty problem. As a system of protection, the Poor Laws were quite comprehensive and came to be reasonably generous in some places.[15] Arguably the pinnacle of the Poor Laws was the Speenhamland System of 1795 introduced by the justices of Berkshire. This system aimed to ensure a guaranteed minimum income through a sliding scale of wage supplements indexed to the price of bread (Himmelfarb, 1984a; Montagu, 1971).

The antipoverty programs elsewhere in Europe around this time relied heavily on charitable giving and so faced free-rider problems; levels of church and private spending on transfers to poor people were low—well under 1% of national income in most countries (Lindert, 2013). In contrast, the disbursements under the Poor Laws in England and Wales were largely financed by local property taxation. There was evidently some displacement of private charity, though the latter continued to exist (Hindle, 2004; Lindert, 2013). But there can be little doubt that the Poor Laws entailed a net gain in social protection. By the late seventeenth century almost all parishes of England and Wales were covered, and, under the "Old Poor Laws" up to the nineteenth century, all persons were eligible for relief. (New Poor Laws came out of reforms in the 1830s, which I return to later.) The parishes had the responsibility for implementation, subject to monitoring by central authorities. Being based in the parishes was convenient but possibly never ideal as they provided limited scope for pooling risks, and there was undoubtedly considerable horizontal inequity (whereby equally poor people in different parishes fared very differently).[16] Nor could these policies ever be expected to have much impact on the steady-state wealth distribution. However, it is clear that the

---

[14] On the history of the English Poor Laws and their influence, see Mencher (1967), Boyer (2002), and Hindle (2004).

[15] Solar (1995) cites evidence that aggregate disbursements reached 2% of England's national income by the late eighteenth century.

[16] Hindle (2004) notes the large geographic differences in pensions, depending on the economic circumstances of the parishes.

Old Poor Laws did provide a degree of protection from risk, and it has been argued that they helped break the historical link between harvest failures and mortality (Kelly and Cormac, 2010; Smith, 2011).

The Poor Laws appear to have helped ensure a relatively docile and sustained working class, with little threat to the steady-state distribution of wealth. Solar (1995) argues that the Old Poor Laws were crucial to England's long-term social stability, including periods (such as the late eighteenth century) of concern about the possibility of the dramatic instability in France spilling across the English Channel. Broad political support was ensured by the fact that anyone could get relief if needed. For example, widowhood was a threat to many of those who would not normally expect to turn to the parish for relief.[17] As novels of the time often pointed out, even the well-to-do upper middle class family could be vulnerable to poverty (a favorite theme of Charles Dickens).

Fleischacker's (2004, p. 51) discussion of England's Poor Laws argues that they were motivated by the "... virtue of charity rather than the virtue of justice," and as such they did not constitute the beginnings of the modern role for public policy in assuring distributive justice. One can conjecture that the motivation for the Poor Laws was at least as much to do with maintaining social stability as charity or justice. However, whatever may have been the motives of policy makers, the Poor Laws constituted a legally enforceable state policy for limited relief from the specified events, financed by redistributive taxes. And parish residents (though not outsiders) had a legal recourse under the Poor Laws, which is why they could help ensure social stability over some 300 years (Solar, 1995). Against Fleischacker's interpretation, it seems that the Poor Laws came very close to being a premodern example of policies to help ensure distributive justice.

However, an aspect of the Poor Laws that should not be ignored is that they were clearly intended for protection rather than promotion. These laws were an early form of social insurance intended for a world in which the poor and the middle class faced many uninsured risks associated with uncertain employment, health crises, harvest failures, and simple bad luck (Hindle, 2004). Such risks may well have spilled over into production, with adverse long-term consequences. By assuring greater social stability, this, too, may have brought long-term gains. However, it is clear that any longer-term promotional advantages were attained via the enhanced protection that was attained under the Poor Laws. Protection was clearly seen as the main aim of the Poor Laws.

---

[17] Widows were listed as eligible for relief from the earliest Poor Laws, and they are mentioned often in the literature; for example, Hindle's (2004) discussion of parish archival information related to the Poor Laws mentions widows 75 times.

Instead of focusing on whether the motivation was charity or justice, the more important reason why the Elizabethan Poor Laws, or Chanakya's famine relief policy, did not constitute a comprehensive antipoverty policy is that these policies were unlikely to change the steady-state distribution of the levels of wealth. In terms of the model in Section 22.2, what these policies were doing was preventing the consumption levels of those either stuck in the wealth poverty trap or settled at some low steady-state level of wealth from falling too much. They provided a degree of protection but did little to help people permanently escape poverty. By the economic logic of the mercantilists, hunger was a good thing as it motivated poor people to work, with social protection playing a limited and well-defined role. After all, just like the slave owner, mercantilists believed that one must keep the workers alive.

By the late eighteenth century, a significant change in thinking was underway.

22.4. THE FIRST POVERTY ENLIGHTENMENT

The incidence of poverty had clearly been increasing for some time in Britain and much of Europe in the latter part of the eighteenth century, due mainly to falling real wages (Allen, 2007; Tucker, 1975). In Europe and North America, there was mounting concern about prospects for social instability and even rebellion among the working class. There was also frustration among the middle class about the constraints they faced on their upward mobility. And there were clearly some gaping weaknesses in the prevailing mainstream intellectual defenses of the status quo. Inherited inequalities of opportunity and manipulated noncompetitive market processes (sometimes facilitated by government) started to be seen as playing an important role in determining the distribution of wealth, casting doubt on claims that the status quo distribution was some purely natural order emerging from free markets.

The masses started to question longstanding excuses for the deprivations they faced. Of course, there had been sporadic propoor protest movements before. For example, there was the (short-lived) "Levellers" movement for suffrage and religious tolerance in mid-seventeenth-century England, during the Civil War period (Hill, 1972). But the late eighteenth century saw both new thinking and more widespread demands for change across Britain, Europe, and America. Popular politics flourished in the cafés and alehouses of London, Paris, and elsewhere in Europe in the late eighteenth century.[18] The historian Brinton (1934, p. 281) identifies the "essential characteristic" of the change in ideas in the last decade of the eighteenth century in Europe as the transition from the view that ". . . life on this earth is a fleeting transition to eternity, that such life is inevitably

---

[18] The Proceedings of the Old Bailey (2012) contains descriptions for London; an example was the "London Corresponding Society," founded in 1792, and dedicated to expanding working class political representation.

one of misery" to ". . . an assertion of the possibility of the harmonious satisfaction here on earth of what are assumed to be normal human appetites." There was a new mass awareness of the scope for economic and political institutions to serve the material needs of all people. Political representation, notably suffrage, was widely seen to be the key. There was a new questioning of established social ranks, famously so in France in the latter part of the eighteenth century. *The Marriage of Figaro* by Beaumarchais (1778) had Parisian audiences siding with the servants in laughing at the aristocracy and deeply questioning their privileges.[19]

The three words that best capture the spirit of the period are "liberté, égalité, fraternité" (liberty, equality, fraternity)—the motto of the French Revolution (and adopted as France's national motto in the late nineteenth century). Although the first few decades after the French Revolution hardly lived up to these lofty words, and the suffrage that emerged was largely confined to men with property, there can be little doubt that the underlying ideas had lasting impact. "Liberty" was understood in a way consistent with modern usage (as in, say, Rawls, 1971), in that the individual was deemed to have whatever freedoms were consistent with like freedoms for others. "Equality" was not, however, understood as equality of outcomes but was defined in terms of legal rights of *opportunity*—that the law must be the same for everyone and so allow all citizens equal opportunity for public positions and jobs, with the assignment determined by ability. There was little immediate sign of a perceived role for the state in redistribution of rewards, although some calls for this did start to emerge in the 1790s with the left-wing Jacobin Club and (in particular) François-Noël (Gracchus) Babeuf.[20] However, if there was hope for poor people in the mainstream ideas of "liberté, égalité, fraternité," then it was more in "fraternity" than "equality"; as Brinton (1934, p. 283) explains:

> Fraternity had meant to the hopeful eighteenth century the outpouring of its favorite virtue, benevolence, upon all human beings, and especially on the downtrodden and the distant— on peasants, Chinamen and South Sea Islanders.

---

[19] For example, in the fifth act, the servant Figaro asks the Count who employs him, "What have you done to deserve such advantages? Put yourself to the trouble of being born—nothing more. For the rest—a very ordinary man!" Although the play was written in 1778, it was censored by King Louis XVI and was not performed until 1784. It is widely seen as a precursor to the French Revolution.

[20] Fleischacker (2004) gives credit for anticipating the modern concept of distributive justice to Gracchus Babeuf, though he also gives credit to the German philosopher Johann Fichte, a follower of Kant. (A seemingly odd pair: Babeuf is considered a founder of Communism and was executed in 1797 for his rebellious left-wing ideas, while the anti-Semitic Fichte is considered a key influence on the National Socialist movement in Germany.) However, de Montesquieu (1748)) appears to have beaten both to the honor.

Similar views were being heard in America where advocates of a strong state role in fighting poverty saw this as an essential element of what it meant to be "a great friendly society" (Alexander Everett, 1827, quoted by Klebaner, 1964, p. 394).

New philosophical and economic thinking from the mid-eighteenth century had opened the way to this Poverty Enlightenment in the last few decades of that century. Significant cracks had started to appear in mainstream views about the role of the state in influencing the distribution of wealth. A key step in this philosophical thinking was the rejection of the view that prevailing inequalities were inevitable. The social contract approach that emerged in the seventeenth century (often attributed to Thomas Hobbes) asked a fundamental question: How should we decide what constitutes good government? In modern terms, this is a question of evaluation, and the relevant counterfactual was a "natural state" in the absence of government. Like all counterfactuals, the natural state was unknown and open to debate.[21] Hobbes argued that it would be a state of conflict, of "all against all." The question was taken up again in the late eighteenth century by Rousseau, who opened up an important new strain of thinking about the distributive role of the state. In his *Discourse on the Origin of Inequality*, Rousseau argued that, although self-interest was a motivation in the natural state, so, too, was empathy for the situation of others.[22] Human institutions, however, can develop to either support or thwart our natural empathy. Rousseau thus saw poverty and inequality as stemming in no small measure (though not solely) from bad institutions—social arrangements that created ". . . different privileges, which some men enjoy to the prejudice of others, such as that of being more rich, more honored, more powerful or even in a position to exact obedience." Here Rousseau made a key step in recognizing the role played by institutions, including governments, in influencing distribution.[23] Poverty was not then inevitable.

Prominent philosophical writings called for respect for poor people as fellow citizens. Kant (1785, p. 62) put forward the idea that every rational human being must be treated "as an end withal, never as means." This was indeed a radical idea, which gave poor people the same moral worth as rich people. Of course there was some measure of respect for poor people even in (say) de Mandeville's earlier writings, but it was a respect for their labor, consistent with the role assigned to them by their birth. They were merely the means to an end. In Kant, by contrast, there was respect for all rational agents, whatever

---

[21] Rousseau (1754, p. 11) put the point nicely: "The philosophers, who have inquired into the foundations of society, have all felt the necessity of going back to a state of nature; but not one of them has got there."

[22] Rousseau was writing prior to Darwin. Scientific research on animal behavior has revealed strong social and empathic behaviors (de Waal, 2009), suggesting deeper origins for human sociability. It has also been argued that (recently discovered) mirror neurons are the neural foundation of such behavior; see, for example, Keysers (2011).

[23] Rousseau allowed for the existence of what he termed "natural inequality," which would exist in the counterfactual "natural state." Natural inequality reflected innate differences (health, strength, mental ability).

their economic circumstances. This was an essential step for both political equality and comprehensive antipoverty policy, although both were still a long way off.

A longstanding view—often attributed to Cicero in ancient Rome—distinguished justice from beneficence, with only the former entailing a role for the state (Fleischacker, 2004, Chapter 1). Local religious organizations had long been charged with the beneficence role. One crack was opened up by Kant. Theologies have long applauded charity as virtuous. Kant questioned this, arguing that there was an inherently unequal relationship between giver and receiver in charity for poor people; therefore, Kant questioned whether it was "virtuous" to give alms that flatter the giver's pride:

Kant sees moral corruption in the private relationships by which well-off people bestow of their bounty to the needy and looks to the state to provide for a more respectful relationship between rich and poor.

Fleischacker (2004, p. 71).

Such challenges to established thinking about beneficence paved the way for much public debate in Europe and America about the role of the state in fighting poverty and in distribution more broadly, and an eventual shift of responsibilities from religious organizations to the state.

Economic thinking was also advancing. Smith (1776) lambasted the mercantilist view that a country's economic welfare was to be judged by the balance of trade. This had long been questionable (not least for ignoring corrective adjustments through price changes).[24] By arguing for a broader conception of welfare based on the population's command over commodities (including basic consumption goods, not just luxury goods, and also including leisure), Smith opened the way to seeing progress against poverty as a goal for development, rather than a threat to it.[25] Similarly, he argued that higher real wages for workers was a good thing, also in contrast to prevailing mercantilist views (Smith, 1776, Book 1, Chapter 8).

Smith saw the virtue of self-interest—though he did not see it as the sole motive for human behavior (Smith, 1759, Chapter 1, I.I.1)—but only in so far as it advanced social welfare, which depended crucially on the institutional context. And gone was the "utility of poverty," with its negatively sloped individual supply function.[26] Despite the popular characterizations of Smith's noninterventionist views in the twentieth century (Rothschild, 2001), he argued in favor of promotional antipoverty policies, such as limited public subsidies to help cover tuition fees for the basic schooling of the "common people" (Smith, 1776, Book 5, Chapter I, Article 2d). However, on this and other social

---

[24] See Blaug's (1962, Chapter 2) discussion of Smith and the mercantilist doctrines.

[25] See the discussion in Muller (1993, p. 58). Also see Himmelfarb's (1984a,b) discussion of Smith's views relative to others around the same time.

[26] "Where wages are high, accordingly, we shall always find the workmen more active, diligent, and expeditious, than where they are low" (Smith, 1776, p. 72).

issues, Smith was evidently far more progressive than most of his peers. (Note that Smith was writing at roughly the same time as other thinkers such as Joseph Townsend.)

The changes in popular and scholarly thinking around this time came with implications for ongoing policy debates relevant to income distribution. One such debate was on whether income taxes should be progressive and whose incomes should be taxed.[27] The milieu gave impetus to arguments for redistributive taxation. Smith had strongly favored exempting subsistence wages, as did others subsequently, including those who favored proportional taxes above the exemption—implying a progressive tax system overall.

Another policy debate concerned the distribution of the gains from natural resources, notably agricultural land. In a pamphlet (addressed to government of the new French Republic, but with broader relevance), Paine (1797) argued that agricultural land was "natural property," to which every person had a legitimate claim. There was, nonetheless, an efficiency case for its private ownership. So instead of being nationalized, agrarian land should be subject to taxation—a "ground rent," the revenue from which should be allocated equally to *all* adults in society, as all have a claim to that property. (He also made provision for an additional old-age pension.) And this was (explicitly) not to be seen as charity but as a right. Paine's proposal was a comprehensive antipoverty policy; indeed, it appears to have been the first "basic income scheme"—an idea we return to in Section 22.9, but which has not yet seen national implementation in any country.

An important prelude to the eventual emergence of promotional policies came with new thinking on the importance of *schooling*: "Illiteracy had become a stigma instead of an ordinary accompaniment of humble life" (Brinton, 1934, p. 279). Condorcet, the late eighteenth-century French philosopher and mathematician, advocated free universal basic education (though warning against the state instructing on moral or political matters, as he greatly valued diversity in views); Condorcet also advocated equal rights for women and all races (Jones, 2004). However, these were still radical ideas, well ahead of implementation. The classical economists who came to dominate thinking about policy in the nineteenth century also saw education as having the potential to make economic growth more poverty-reducing, notably by attenuating population growth through "moral improvement." But they did not see mass education as having a role in promoting that growth and saw little scope for mass *public* education (Blaug, 1962, p. 216).

An important contribution of the First Poverty Enlightenment was in establishing the moral case for the idea of public effort toward eliminating poverty. That moral case developed out of a new respect for hard-working poor people, as people, on the part of the elites—what de Waal (2009, p. 116) calls "emotional identification." Important new progressive ideas emerged in the writings of Smith, Rousseau, Kant, Fichte, Condorcet, Babeuf, and others. However, we were still a long way from the three premises identified in the introduction. Although the First Poverty Enlightenment brought

---

[27] Musgrave (1985) reviews the history of this and other debates in public finance.

about new thinking relevant to antipoverty policies, it did not mark any dramatic change in the lives of the poor, and they were still being blamed for their poverty; the belief that poor people were to blame for their own poverty persisted into the nineteenth and twentieth centuries.[28] Except for relief under the Poor Laws in England and Wales, neither private assistance nor public support for poor people showed any marked rise in Europe, from their relatively low levels (Lindert, 2013). The main economic beneficiaries of the First Poverty Enlightenment were probably in the middle class, who could now aspire to sources of wealth and power they had previously been excluded from.

22.5. THE LONG GERMINATION OF THE IDEA OF A WORLD FREE OF POVERTY

Although mercantilist ideas lost influence with the emergence of classical economics, mainstream thinking in the nineteenth century still held little prospect for a world free of poverty. A new economic growth path had emerged, starting in England toward the end of the eighteenth century, stemming from the technical innovations of the industrial revolution. However, at the time, it was not widely believed among either supporters of capitalism or its critics that workers would share much in this new growth process. (As we will see in Section 22.7, their pessimism on this point was excessive.) Well beyond the start of the industrial revolution, poverty seemed as plentiful as ever. Social novels (such as Dickens's 1838 classic, *Oliver Twist*) and qualitative observational studies (such as Engels', 1845) described the poor health environments and harsh working conditions of English industrial cities in the mid-nineteenth century. Descriptions of working class diets in England around this time suggest levels of living that would almost certainly be considered "poor" in any developing country today (Ravallion, 2015).[29]

The economics of the time appeared to offer little reason to be hopeful about progress against persistent poverty. The classical theories of wage determination allowed the possibility of a short-term rise in real wage rates through an upward shift in the aggregate demand for labor associated with technical progress. However, the induced growth in the size of the working class due to higher earnings—due either to higher fertility or lower child mortality—would soon bring the wage rate back down to the subsistence level. Thomas Robert Malthus is famous for this argument, but a version is also found in Smith (1776, Book 1, Chapter 8). The induced population growth that was central to such Malthusian dynamics was seen to reflect the "moral weaknesses" of poor people. As Sandmo (2013) notes, the idea that population growth would ensure that real wages

---

[28] See, for example, Klebaner's (1964) descriptions of views of poverty in nineteenth-century America.

[29] For example, Burnett (1969, p. 273) writes that: "The diet of agricultural laborers in mid-century, as of the poorest urban workers throughout the century, consisted essentially of bread—usually white rather than brown because this was more palatable without butter—potatoes, small quantities of tea, cheese and sugar, and meat perhaps once or twice a week."

would stay constant despite technical progress was widely held even to the end of the nineteenth century; see, for example, the writings of Wicksell (1901). The economics was hardly conclusive; lags in the population response and repeated shifts in aggregate demand for labor with technical progress could still yield a secular rise in real wages. The choice-theoretic foundations of the assumed income effect on family size were never clear, but a seemingly common view was that, for poor parents, children were a form of saving for the future. The child wage rate was the return to that saving (net of maintenance costs). A higher wage rate would then be expected to increase the demand for children, thus increasing future labor supply. The classical schema was seen to point to seemingly powerful demographic correctives that would tend to inhibit progress against poverty in a growing economy.

Nor did the most influential classical economists after Smith offer much support for direct public interventions to fight poverty. Indeed, Malthus and David Ricardo were positively hostile to the idea of antipoverty policy, with incentive arguments figuring prominently in their writings. They claimed that such antipoverty policies would discourage work effort and savings and create poverty rather than remove it. Again, the behaviors of poor people were faulted by the elites.[30]

Here, too, it is hardly evident that the economics was decisive one way or the other. Indeed, Malthus (1806) acknowledged that better health and education for working class families could break the brutal population corrective to rising real wages. However, the main interpretation given to the economics of the time was hostile to such policies. In no small measure, this was the intellectual rationalization of a political backlash against the First Poverty Enlightenment, notably among the elites in England who resisted the new liberal ideas that were traveling across the English Channel from France.

22.5.1 The Debate About the Poor Laws

By the early nineteenth century a major public debate about the Poor Laws began (though debates about poverty relief dated back to at least the late seventeenth century). A strong political push for reform came from the landlords, who were financing relief under the Old Poor Laws, who dominated the English parliament around this time, and who were (it seems) no longer worried about impending revolution (Lindert, 2004, Chapter 4). The backlash against the Poor Laws often invoked incentive arguments, and England's classical economists were widely cited by critics of the Poor Laws, including those from America (Klebaner, 1964).

This was a significant debate in the history of thought on poverty. For some time, powerful critics had been concerned about the overall cost of the policy. Labor migration in response to industrialization had meant that local landlords were left to finance a rising

---

[30] Klebaner (1964) points to official claims that 75–90% of pauperism in the United States in the nineteenth century was due to intemperance. Also see Burnett (1969, pp. 274–276) on similar arguments in England.

support bill for children and the elderly (Solar, 1995). Nor was work found by all, and unemployment was causing many in Europe and America to turn to the state for help. But these were not the explanations for the rising relief bill that gained favor. Observers such as de Tocqueville (1835) (in a memoir reporting on a visit to England with the aiming of understanding why there were so many paupers despite the country's affluence) argued that the Poor Laws were a disincentive to work, such that they helped create the poverty problem they aimed to solve. Prominent classical economists, including Malthus (1806, Chapters 5 and 6) and Ricardo (1817), argued for either abandoning the Poor Laws or at least reforming them to ensure better targeting.[31] In an influential earlier pamphlet, *A Dissertation on the Poor Laws*, Townsend (1786, p. 17) wrote that "[t]hese laws, so beautiful in theory, promote the evils they mean to remedy, and aggravate the distress they were intended to relieve." Assumptions about incentives were the core of Townsend's argument. Public relief from chronic hunger would discourage work, and the fiscal burden on the landholding class would discourage the growth of manufacturing and innovation in agriculture (Townsend, 1786, Section V). Ricardo (1817, p. 61) predicted (plainly with huge exaggeration) that the cost of the Poor Laws would rise out of control, that "whilst the present laws are in force, it is quite in the natural order of things that the fund for the maintenance of the poor should progressively increase until it has absorbed all the net revenue of the country." Malthus argued that the Poor Laws encouraged early marriage and high fertility (though counterarguments could also have been made that ensured old-age support would reduce fertility). Moral hazard appears to have been a concern, whereby assistance to those who took high risks, and lost out, would encourage excessively risky behavior. The Poor Laws came to be seen by many as a cause of poverty rather than its cure. Similar debates were also being waged about America's poor laws, with calls for reforms to cut their rising cost (Klebaner, 1964).

However, the evidence was clearly weak for the claims that behavioral responses to the laws were an important cause of the poverty they tried to address. The evidence appears to have been largely based on easily manipulated anecdotes and characterizations, with plainly weak claims of attribution; for example, was the claimed high incidence of intemperance a cause or effect of poverty? Nor was there much recognition that nonintervention could be socially costly, too—that problems of heterogeneous risk and asymmetric information could entail that the private insurance was unavailable,[32] and that uninsured risk could spill over into production and investment decisions of poor people in ways that could impede long-term prospects of escaping poverty. For example, against the concerns that relief would reduce the labor supply, Solar (1995) argues that the Old Poor Laws had the opposite effect, by providing security against the risk of

---

[31] See the discussion of the views of Malthus and Ricardo on this topic in Sandmo (2013).

[32] This economic argument for social insurance was not well developed in the literature until much later, notably by Rothschild and Stiglitz (1976).

unemployment for smallholders who were considering whether to become laborers instead. The type of model, outlined in Section 22.2 (Figure 22.1), motivates social protection even for people at their "high" steady-state equilibrium (point C in Figure 22.1). For example, imagine someone at that equilibrium receiving a sufficiently large negative shock to push them just past the unstable equilibrium. There will be no chance of recovery, and destitution will be the inevitable result. Lack of insurance could well have been a more important reason for poverty than too much insurance.

Although incentive effects and dependency were a legitimate concern, the economic arguments against England's Old Poor Laws may well have been exaggerated to serve political ends (and it was not the first or last time this happened). The "evidence" was weak, and the arguments were somewhat one-sided, with many potential economic benefits of the laws ignored.

Significant reforms to the Poor Laws were implemented in 1834 (including repeal of Speenhamland). Spending was slashed, from a peak of about 2.5% of national income around 1830 to 1% in 1840 (Lindert, 2013, Figure 1). Wider use was made of workhouses. These had long existed, and by the late eighteenth century, 1–2% of the population of London was seeking relief in some 80 workhouses.[33] Their role expanded under the reform effort to ensure better targeting, and the new nineteenth-century workhouses appear to have been even more unpleasant and punitive places than in the past (described well in *London Lives*). Earnings in the workhouse were never to exceed local wages (Beaudoin, 2007, p. 80). The policy became better targeted, but it lost the broad public support of the Old Poor Laws and (indeed) became the subject of intense social criticism. By confining beneficiaries to workhouses, the reformed policy was seen by critics to treat poor people as criminals. The conditions under which inmates were kept became a specific focus of criticism, famously so in the early chapters of Dickens's (1838) *Oliver Twist*. And the criticisms (which started almost immediately) of the New Poor Laws were not just confined to social critics but reached deeply into the leading circles of the Conservative Party, including Benjamin Disraeli (Himmelfarb, 1984a,b).

22.5.2 Utilitarianism

Social contract theory, with its emphasis on rights and freedoms, lost ground in the nineteenth century to a rival school of thought, utilitarianism. This also emerged in the late eighteenth century and over the next 200 years came to have great influence on normative economics—indeed, it became the "official theory of traditional welfare economics" (Sen, 2000, p. 63). Jeremy Bentham, the founding father of utilitarianism, was motivated

[33] See the entry on workhouses in *London Lives 1690–1800*. Also see in Hindle's (2004, p. 176) discussion of the use of encouragements to work under the Old Poor Laws, whereby the church vestry often became a "job-creation service" (p. 176). Workhouses existed elsewhere in Europe, including Holland where they were introduced in Amsterdam around 1600 (Beaudoin, 2007, p. 48).

by practical policy reform, and this led him to reject ideas like "natural rights." (Artz, 1934, p. 83, quotes him as describing the *Declaration of the Rights of Man and of the Citizen* as "a hodge-podge of confusion and absurdity.") Instead, utilitarianism advocated that social choices should maximize the sum of utilities across all individuals, where "utility" was equated with "happiness." Assuming diminishing marginal utility of income, this objective generated a case against *income* inequality because the marginal losses to rich donors of any mean-preserving transfer would be outweighed by marginal gains to poor recipients. This did not, however, open the floodgates of redistributive interventions. Assuming diminishing marginal utility of income and a common utility function only implied that equality of incomes was optimal if total income was invariant to its distribution. The case was unclear if income redistribution lowered overall output, as Bentham expected to be the case. Even aside from incentive effects, merely introducing interpersonal heterogeneity (such that the utility valuation of a given income level varies) upsets the claim that an equal allocation of income maximizes social welfare though this point did not seem to get the same attention as the growth-equity tradeoff.

Bentham and followers had seen government as a necessary evil, and put any actual or contemplated policy effort to the utilitarian test. Some of the literature has (derisively) characterized this as a period of "laissez-faire," although to an economist's eyes it was a welcome discipline in sound policy making, to ensure maximum social welfare. The real issue was what one meant by "social welfare." The influential rights-based thinkers on policy prior to the utilitarians, such as Condorcet, would no doubt have also advocated higher social welfare but would have rejected any attempt to equate welfare with "happiness" or "utility" (Rothschild, 2001).

By the mid-nineteenth century, it was becoming accepted in prominent progressive circles that the state did have a role in ". . . redressing the inequalities and wrongs of nature" (Mill, 1848, p. 805). Even so, it is clear that poverty was still widely accepted as a normal state of affairs. Poor people were still being blamed for their poverty (notably by their reproduction), and there was little role for the state. Even protection was increasingly "targeted" to extreme cases. The best that could be hoped for was that workers would somehow come to see the wisdom of curtailing their desired family sizes. Even among the most progressive utilitarian voices of the time (such as John Stuart Mill), the closest one came to promotional policies would be to point to a role for education of the working class in reducing population growth, but with a strictly limited role for the state.

22.5.3 Schooling Debates

Children from poor families typically started their working lives at an early age; although the evidence is patchy, it was common prior to the mid-nineteenth century for working class children in England to start looking for work from 7 years of age (Cunningham, 1990). The survival of the family often demanded that every able-bodied person worked.

Any skills required would only be those that could be passed on by the family. Idle poor children were abhorrent to the rich; work was the only solution. Child labor was not only condoned but widely seen as desirable; unemployment of poor children was believed to be the bigger social problem (Cunningham, 1990). The idea of mass public schooling appears to have had little support. Indeed, echoing de Mandeville's views, a common view was that mass schooling was wasteful and even dangerous. By the middle of the nineteenth century some 40% of children aged 5–9 in England and Wales were still not in school.[34]

Nor was the state deemed to have an important role in the schooling that was provided. Before the nineteenth century, and well into that century in some countries (including England), almost all schooling received by children from poor families was provided by religious groups. The system of voluntary schooling in England and elsewhere in Europe was clearly highly stratified and unequal. Schooling by religious groups had a mixed record. In England, the church resisted any public role in provision yet also left much unmet demand (Lindert, 2004, Chapter 5). The debate on mass schooling opportunities continued in England until quite late in the nineteenth century, and the country lagged behind much of Europe and North America in schooling attainment, despite its wealth.

Poor families did not always see Church schools as being in their interests. Informal private schools were often more promising for those who could afford them. Van Horn Melton (1988, p. 11) describes the "backstreet schools" in Austria and Prussia that offered more efficient instruction "subordinating religious instruction to the goal of imparting literacy to their pupils," and it appears that these schools were often favored by poor parents who were eager to ensure their children's efficient learning and eventual employability; with reference to Prussia, Van Horn Melton (p. 11) writes that: "... backstreet schools offered poorer families a more cost-effective means of acquiring literacy." This echoes observations of the "backstreet schools" found throughout India today, reflecting evident failures of the state-run schooling system (Probe Team, 1999).

A change in popular views about schooling for poor families started to be evident in much of Europe and North America in the mid-nineteenth century. Mercantilism had lost its influence, and the classical economics that replaced it was not opposed to promotional policies such as public schooling—policies that were capable of a propoor change in the distribution of wealth. The working conditions of children in the factories of the time provided fuel for social novels *and* for the increasingly vocal critics of capitalism, most notably Karl Marx and Friedrich Engels. Prominent calls started to be heard for improving the working conditions of children and for schooling as the better way to

---

[34] This is based on the 1851 census (as reported in Cunningham, 1990, Table 1); 39% of boys and 44% of girls in this age group were not classified as "scholars" (the alternatives being employment or "at home"). The subsequent spread of literacy was also highly uneven geographically (Stephens, 1998).

address unemployment. Schooling for poor children came to be seen as key to their self-improvement and mobility. Mass schooling was also believed to have external benefits, such as reduced crime rates.

National legislation for compulsory schooling had only emerged in a few countries (including Austria and Prussia) toward the end of the eighteenth century but was becoming widespread in Europe and North America by the late nineteenth century.[35] This followed a protracted public debate in Britain, Europe, and North America during the nineteenth century (Weiner, 1991, Chapter 6). Although there were some who argued against almost any intrusion by the state into private decision making,[36] this does not appear to have been the main argument of opponents. Mill's (1859) influential volume *On Liberty* argued that the state had a role in compelling parents to school their children, although Mill did not favor government monopoly in the provision of that schooling. Opponents had long argued that schooling the poor would lead them to unrealistic aspirations (Vinovskis, 1992). As one would expect, the industries that were heavily dependent on child labor lobbied against compulsory schooling although over the course of the nineteenth-century industrial capitalists became more supportive of mass schooling because they wanted to create the more skilled workforce needed for the new technologies (Bowles and Gintis, 1976, with reference to the United States). However, this was not simply a matter of schooling catering to the needs of new technologies developed under capitalism; the debates about schooling were broader socially, and it is not clear that industrial capitalists had that much influence (Vinovskis, 1992). Poor parents and local communities were also increasingly vocal in their demands for mass public schooling. It seems that by the latter half of the nineteenth century the earlier unrealistic aspirations of poor parents for a better life for their children had started to become more realistic. There were also administrative constraints on enforcement to overcome; it was not until birth registration systems had been developed around the mid-nineteenth century that truancy laws could be properly enforced (Weiner, 1991, p. 121).

22.5.4 Socialism

Landauer (1959) identifies the widespread acceptance of poverty in the nineteenth century as one of the factors that led to the emergence of socialism. The leading school of socialist thought, Marxism, saw the root cause of poverty, and most other ills, to be capitalism itself. There was little scope for effective antipoverty policies *within* a capitalist economy; only communism could reliably eliminate poverty. Nor was much value

[35] There were some progressive local initiatives for mass schooling, such as Massachusetts in the late seventeenth century (Weiner, 1991, Chapter 6).

[36] In the United States, one occasionally hears arguments that compulsory schooling is unconstitutional, the reference being to the antislavery amendment introduced near the end of the Civil War on the grounds that (it is claimed) compulsory schooling is "involuntary servitude." See here, for an example.

attached to past philosophical and economic thought on poverty. For example, Marx was as disparaging as Bentham about talk of "rights."[37]

Even so, it is notable that at least a couple of the demands outlined in the *Communist Manifesto* of Marx and Engels (1848) can be recognized today as quite mainstream anti-poverty policies, including progressive income taxation and free education in public schools. Fleischacker (2004) identifies one key influence of Marx's thinking on subsequent non-Marxist thinkers, including Rawls, namely, his insistence that human nature was largely a product of social context. Instead of seeing poverty as the outcome of individual attributes (being lazy is a favorite in some quarters), one should look to social influences on behavior. Of course, this idea also had pre-Marxian antecedents, notably in Rousseau.

22.5.5 Social Research

Much new research on social problems was emerging in the nineteenth century, and poverty was increasingly seen as a social problem. Social research was used to promote better informed public debate on antipoverty policy. Important contributions included Eden's (1797) three-volume tome on poverty in England and Wales in the late eighteenth century, Mayhew's (2008) newspaper reports on London's poor in the 1840s, Frederic Le Play's budget studies of working class families in Europe in the mid-nineteenth century (Brooke, 1998), Mathew Carey's use of data on budgets and wages of poor people to "startle the complacent into giving alms" in Philadelphia in the 1830s (Klebaner, 1964, p. 384), and the work of the German statistician Engel (1857), who studied the relationship between household food expenditures and income, in which he found what came to be known as Engel's Law, namely, that the poorer a family is the higher the share of its budget devoted to food.

Landmarks in the development of modern scientific research on poverty were the (largely independent) studies by Booth (1903) and Rowntree (1902), which documented the living conditions of England's poor (in London and York, respectively) in the late nineteenth century. These were pioneering measurements using seemingly careful household surveys that revealed to nonpoor people how poor people lived. Their work attracted much attention.[38] The English public was shocked that one million Londoners—about one-third of the population—lived below Booth's frugal poverty line of 21 shillings per week for a family. This news came after a period of rising real wages, which added to the shock. Nor could it be said that this was too generous a poverty line.

---

[37] Fleischacker (2004, p. 97) quotes Marx as calling appeals to rights "ideological nonsense."

[38] Booth is often credited with inventing the poverty line. There were also antecedents to the idea of the poverty line in Booth and Rowntree, including the "standard of comfort" proposed by Davies 100 years earlier (Allen, 2013).

By my calculations it was equivalent to 1.5 lb of good wheat per person per day—a frugal line, not very different from (say) India's poverty line in the 1990s.[39]

Booth's research responded to a demand for clarity and data among legislators. His empirical research into old-age poverty and its geographic variation influenced Britain's introduction of a public pension in 1908 (Thane, 2000, Chapter 9) and national insurance in 1911 (Himmelfarb, 1984a,b). The research of Booth and Rowntree also stimulated debates about poverty. For example, 15 years after Booth's books appeared, Alfred Marshall argued that there was even more poverty in Germany than Booth's figures suggested was the case in England; this was in response to Marshall's (1907, p. 12) perception that "one of the few things which every German knows for certain about England is that there are a million people in London living in extreme poverty on the verge of hunger."

The close observational studies of poverty by Booth and Rowntree were influential in social science research. Hunter (1904) followed their lead in studying poverty in the United States. Village studies in India by Mann and collaborators were also influenced by Booth and Rowntree (Thorner, 1967). A long and distinguished tradition of quantitative-economic studies of selected villages followed, including surveys by Askok Rudra and Pranab Bardhan (Bardhan, 1984a), Bliss and Stern (1982), Walker and Ryan (1990), and Lanjouw and Stern (1998). Booth's approach influenced the development of quantitative sociology in both Britain and the United States.[40] Townsend's (1979) empirical study of poverty in England some 80 years later clearly owed much to Booth and Rowntree. So, too, did the Chicago School of Sociology that began studying urban poverty in the United States during the 1930s.

The late nineteenth century saw new questioning of the longstanding idea that poverty was inevitable in any capitalist economy and the emergence of prominent arguments for promotional antipoverty policies in such an economy. Although the late eighteenth century gave birth to the modern idea of distributive justice, it was not until the late nineteenth century that we saw the emergence of the idea of a world free of poverty. By then it had become widely accepted among the "cultivated circles" that a trend rise in the real

[39] Marshall (1907) estimates that 21 shillings was equivalent to three-quarters of a bushel of good wheat. At 13.5% moisture by weight, a bushel of wheat weights 60 lb according to the Wikipedia entry on "bushel." I assume a household of 4.5 people, which is the lower bound of the range 4.5–5 given by Booth (1903, Chapter 4) for the average size of working men's families at the time. Booth's line is thus equivalent to slightly less than 700 g of wheat per person per day. Of course, this is just the wheat equivalent. A reasonable dietary breakdown would be 400 g per person for wheat and the remainder for meat, vegetables, and (very minimal) nonfood needs. This then is similar to India's national poverty line in 1993, which World Bank (1997) calculates to be equivalent to a daily food bundle per person of 400 g of coarse rice and wheat, 200 g of vegetables, pulses, and fruit, plus modest amounts of milk, eggs, edible oil, spices, and tea. After buying such a food bundle, one would be left with about $0.30 per day (at 1993 purchasing power parity) for nonfood items.

[40] On Booth's influence see the Wikipedia entry on Charles Booth and the Archive maintained by the London School of Economics.

wage rate was a sign of overall progress (Daniels, 1898, p. 203). The historian Webb (1974, p. 384) argues that in late nineteenth-century England it came to be recognized that poverty "could and must be eliminated."[41] Near the turn of the century, Marshall's (1890, p. 2) *Principles of Economics* was posing the question quoted at the beginning of this chapter, bemoaning that the children of the poor received too little schooling (p. 467), and sketching policies for fighting poverty (especially., pp. 594–599) that were not just intended as short-term moralistic palliatives but were driven by a recognition that persistent poverty was itself a constraint on wealth generation. Marshall (1890, p. 468) wrote of the "cumulative evil":

> *The worse fed are the children of one generation, the less they will earn when they grow up and the less will be their power of providing adequately for the material wants of their children; and so onto following generation.*

Thus:

> *The inequalities of wealth, and especially the very low earnings of the poorest classes . . . (are) . . . dwarfing activities as well as curtailing the satisfaction of wants (p. 599).*

Marshall's reference here to "dwarfing activities" anticipates a view that is prominent in development thought today whereby certain inequalities are seen as instrumentally important inhibitors of overall economic progress, notwithstanding their intrinsic relevance in "curtailing the satisfaction of wants." Although Marshall was careful to avoid naïve utopianism (see, especially, the comments in Marshall, 1907), his writings reflect a far more optimistic perspective on social policy as a means of expanding opportunities for all to share in the potential of a competitive market economy. Here we had a forthright and prominent advocacy of promotional policies such that ". . . children once born into it [poverty] should be helped to rise out of it" (p. 598).

Importantly, this new optimism was starting to be shared by poor parents, who raised their demand for schooling for their children. By the late nineteenth century, it seems that most poor parents in Europe and North America were anticipating that their children would encounter better economic opportunities than they had. Helped by significant medical and public health advances that were improving child survival rates and raising life expectancy, investing in children's schooling was seen as a far less risky than it had been early in that century (and before then) when the children of the poor working class had little real hope of being anything else than working class and not much chance of being less poor workers than their parents. The demand for mass schooling thus rose along with the supply. Parents were still investing in their children to help secure their own future welfare (formal social security systems were not yet available), but they were investing more in the quality of those children. Fertility rates were falling.

---

[41] Beaudoin (2007, p. 100) gives the idea a more recent origin in the twentieth century, after World War II.

After the First World War, there was a mounting enthusiasm for policy intervention in the West, and there appears to have been broad agreement that greatly reducing, if not eliminating, poverty was a legitimate role for government (Mencher, 1967). In the writings of prominent economists, such as Pigou (1920, Part IV, Chapter 1), it had become accepted that losses to the "national dividend" could be justified by gains to poor people. The incidence of absolute poverty had come to be recognized as an important yardstick for measuring social progress. For example, the eminent statistician Bowley (1915, p. 213) wrote that:

> There is perhaps, no better test of the progress of a nation than that which shows what proportion are in poverty and for watching the progress the exact standard selected as critical is not of great importance, if it is kept rigidly unchanged from time to time.

From around the turn of the twentieth century, statistics was being applied to various social issues, including measuring poverty and inequality. A key methodological issue was whether one could rely on sample surveys (instead of doing a census) and how the sampling was to be done (the choice being between purposive and random sampling). Statisticians such as Bowley, Ronald Fisher, and Jerzy Neyman advanced the theory of statistical inference based on random sampling, although it took a few decades before this became common practice for social and economic surveys.[42] Poverty measurement was a leading application and, in due course, sampling methods were to revolutionize the collection of systematic survey data on poverty and inequality by national statistics offices across the world.

By the interwar period it seems that poverty was no longer being seen in mainstream circles as primarily caused by the bad behavior of poor people, but as reflecting deeper economic and social problems. If nothing else, the observation of mass involuntary unemployment during the Great Depression made that clear. And the observations were carried with force to a broad audience through various media.[43] The period saw massive relief efforts (such as the New Deal in the United States). But these were largely transient efforts for protection rather than promotion (Heclo, 1986).

22.6. THE SECOND POVERTY ENLIGHTENMENT

The period from about 1950 saw a new trajectory of more rapidly declining incidence of absolute poverty in the world, as judged by the standards of what poverty means in the poorest countries.[44] From about the same time, a significant shift in thinking was

---

[42] The two-stage sampling method introduced by Hansen and Hurvitz (1943) was to prove especially useful for countries at all stages of development. On the history of survey sampling methods up to the present, see Bethlehem (2009).

[43] The photos and text of Agee and Evans (1941) describing the living conditions of Southern tenant farmers in the United States in the mid-1930s was an example.

[44] This is shown in Ravallion (2015), drawing on the estimates made by Bourguignon and Morrisson (2002) and Chen and Ravallion (2013).

underway, with bearing on antipoverty policy. This was the Second Poverty Enlightenment, dating from about 1960. Across the globe—including in the newly free countries of the developing world—there was new optimism among policy makers about the scope for fighting poverty. Evidence for the change in public attention to poverty can be found in the striking rise in the incidence of use of the word "poverty" in the writings of the time after 1960. This is evident if one enters the word "poverty" in the *Google Books Ngram Viewer* (the *Viewer* hereafter) (Michel et al., 2010). The *Viewer*'s counts are normalized by the total number of words that year, giving the "incidence" of that word. The upturn in incidence started around 1960. By 2000, the incidence of references to "poverty" reached its highest value in 300 years. And the rise in incidence continued after 2000 and up to the latest year (2008) for which the data are available at the time of this writing; indeed, with moderate smoothing of the time series, in 2008 poverty had the most attention in the literature since 1600.[45] Attention to poverty appears to be higher now than any time since 1800 while the incidence of extreme absolute poverty is at its lowest point since then (Ravallion, 2015).

Similarly to the First Poverty Enlightenment, the Second was a time of radical questioning and instability, although, unlike the First, it did not come in the wake of rising absolute poverty. There were demands for new freedoms across the world. There was social ferment and civil unrest in the rich countries of the world, and newfound political independence combined with much political and economic upheaval in the poor countries of the world.[46] Also similarly to the First Poverty Enlightenment, there was new scholarly thought that had great bearing on antipoverty policy.

In philosophy and economics, the 1960s and 1970s saw renewed questioning of the utilitarian paradigm as a basis for public action against poverty and inequality, and in other domains of public policy. Critics of utilitarianism questioned whether policies that entailed welfare losses to the poorest could ever be justified by sufficiently large gains to the richest. A case was made for the ethical prioritization of helping the poorest first, as in Rawls's (1967, 1971) formulation of the principles of justice, which we return to below. The 1970s saw efforts to generalize the utilitarian schema by embodying an

---

[45] The relevant plot up to 2008 and as far back as possible can be found here. There are two spikes in 1634 and 1659. Naturally, the volume of words in the *Viewer*'s database is low in these earlier years, often with only a few books per year. Each of these spikes largely reflects one or two volumes that used the word "poverty" a lot. This is clearly deceptive. With any smoothing parameter greater than three, the peak year becomes the last year in the series, 2008. Also note that the count is case sensitive. The use of capitalized words mid-sentence was more common in English writing of the seventeenth and eighteenth centuries so it is important to include capitalized words when going back that far. But this matters little after 1800 or so.

[46] Although the 1960s was a famous period in the West, with vocal new movements for peace and racial and gender equity, much was also happening in the developing world. In the 1960s alone, 32 countries in Africa gained independence, though often with contested borders. China's "Cultural Revolution" started in 1966 and wreaked havoc for 10 years. South Asia (Bangladesh and India) and parts of Africa were fighting famines in the 1960s and 1970s, and there was much political instability; even relatively stable India had its share of political upheaval including the "Emergency" in the mid-1970s.

aversion to inequality of utilities, such that the marginal social welfare attached to higher utility fell with the level of utility. In principle, marginal social welfare could then be driven down to virtually zero at a sufficiently high level of utility. Once one made the extra step of allowing the possibility that marginal social welfare could go to zero above some point, prioritizing poverty reduction could be interpreted as the negative of social welfare maximization.[47] Whether or not one took that extra step, there was clearly common ground in these different emerging schools of thought about the social welfare objectives of public policy.

For many economists, the more contentious step (and it is still contentious) was attaching intrinsic value to "rights" and "freedoms." Dissatisfaction with the lack of attention in economics to popular concerns about individual rights and freedoms was evident during the Second Poverty Enlightenment. Of course, the freedom to trade freely was often given high value in economics, but this was an instrumental value—the virtue of competitive exchange was a derived one from longstanding Benthamite or Paretean formulations of policy objectives. The scope for ethically contestable policies was evident if one did not put certain rights above all else.[48] Motivated by such concerns, mainstream thinking about poverty in both scholarly and policy circles was being given to nonutilitarian formulations that put freedom as the central issue, most notably in the writings of Sen (1980, 1985, 1999). The idea that poverty is fundamentally a lack of individual freedom to live the life one wants—a severe deprivation of basic capabilities in Sen's terms—and that such freedom has an overriding ethical merit can be traced back to the Second Poverty Enlightenment.

Many policy issues, including debates on antipoverty policies, call for some form of interpersonal comparison of utility. Yet, in the wake of an influential book by Robbins (1935), the period up to around 1950 saw economists striving to purge welfare economics of interpersonal comparisons—leaving little scope for normative economic analysis of poverty or income distribution more generally.[49] One turning point in thinking on this issue came with Arrow's (1951) famous theorem.[50] In due course, Arrow's theorem and

---

[47] This interpretation is discussed further in Ravallion (1994a), which shows that on introducing inequality aversion into the measure of poverty and allowing for measurement errors in the data on individual economic welfare, the resulting formulation of the objectives of policy in terms of minimizing poverty can essentially be made as close as one likes to the negative of a generalized utilitarian social welfare function.

[48] An example is the various coercive efforts made to encourage poor parents in developing countries to have fewer children; see the examples described by Hartmann (1987).

[49] For an authoritative overview of this and other issues in the history of thought on income distribution, see Sandmo (2013).

[50] Developing arguments first made by Condorcet in 1785, Arrow (1951) established that, under seemingly defensible axioms, a unique social ordering over three or more options that is derived solely from a set of unrestricted individual orderings must be imposed externally.

the work on social choice theory that it stimulated led to a reaffirmation of the need for some form of interpersonal comparability in discussing issues such as antipoverty policy.[51] Ethical considerations soon returned in full force to policy analysis by economists, although it also came to be understood that not all such analyses required fully comparable cardinal utilities (Sen, 1970b). The futility of attempting to infer uniquely comparable utilities solely on the basis of demand behavior also came to be accepted (especially following Pollak and Wales, 1979). The 1970s and 1980s saw new efforts to put poverty and inequality measurement on firmer theoretical foundations.[52] There was an explosion of interest in the measurement of poverty and inequality, both in theory and in practice, starting from around 1970 (Ravallion, 2011).

Other seemingly sacred elements of economics started to be questioned, including whether people were rational, although some of the claims of "irrationality" that emerged from behavioral economics appeared to stem more from limited characterizations of utility functions and/or limited allowances for mistakes (Saint-Paul, 2011). Even the idea that social welfare had to be strictly increasing in all utilities (the Pareto principle) was being questioned as either a sufficient or a morally compelling basis for policy making (as in, for example, Nath, 1969). The Pareto principle was even found to be inconsistent with seemingly mild requirements for personal liberty (Sen, 1970a).

The 1970s also saw a deeper questioning of the efficiency of competitive market allocations. The term "market failure" (introduced by Bator, 1958) had become widely used, and labor and credit markets' imperfections in particular came to be seen as key to understanding poverty. The idea that labor markets were competitive, such that wage rates adjusted to remove any unemployment, had been in doubt since the Great Depression. In understanding poverty in rich countries in the 1960s, the idea of dual labor markets became prominent, following in particular Doeringer and Piore (1971). One segment of the labor market has high wages and good benefits while the second has low wages and little in the way of benefits. Bulow and Summers (1986) showed how this could be an equilibrium given the existence of high costs of monitoring work effort in certain activities, which become the high-wage segment in which profit-maximizing firms pay wages above market-clearing levels (following Shapiro and Stiglitz, 1984). Other activities with low monitoring costs form the competitive segment, which is where the working poor are found.

In another strain of the literature of this period, Akerlof (1970) showed how credit (and other) market failures can arise from asymmetric information, such as when lenders are less well-informed about a project than borrowers, thus constraining the flow of

---

[51] See the discussion in Roemer (1996). Notice, however, that allowing interpersonal comparisons is only one of the possible resolutions of Arrow's dictatorship result (Sen, 1970a,b).
[52] Important contributions came from Watts (1968), Atkinson (1970, 1987), Kolm (1976), Sen (1973, 1976), and Foster et al. (1984).

credit. This helped explain the efficiency role of institutions and governments in facilitating better information signals and broader contract choices. For example, the idea of asymmetric information gave a new perspective on why share-cropping existed (Stiglitz, 1974). Since the work effort of tenants is unobservable by landowners, an optimal contract strikes a balance between risk sharing and incentives for work. Thus, risk is shared between the two parties.

The new economics of information held important implications for understanding poverty. In a perfect credit market, even poor parents will be able to borrow for schooling—to be paid back from children's later earnings. However, if poor parents are more credit constrained than others, then we will see an economic gradient in schooling, whereby the children of poor parents are less schooled.[53] This is indeed what we see, almost everywhere. There will be too much child labor and too little schooling in poor families. Thus, poverty will persist across generations. Risk market failures can have similar implications. Parents will under-invest in their kid's schooling when they cannot insure against the risk of a low economic return from that schooling.

In due course, this new strain of economic thinking would point to important ways in which inequalities in the initial distribution of wealth could persist and impede overall economic progress; Section 22.8 returns to this issue. The economics also pointed to the scope for promotional antipoverty policies—policies that essentially aimed to compensate for the credit and risk market failures, such as by compulsory schooling laws and public support for schooling, especially for children from poor families. Section 22.9 will return to such policies.

22.6.1 Rawls's Principles of Justice

If there is a single philosophical landmark of the Second Poverty Enlightenment, it must be Rawls's (1971) *Theory of Justice*. Borrowing from early formulations of social contract theory (back to Hobbes), Rawls proposed that the principles of justice should be the social contract agreed to among equals in a veil of ignorance about where they would find themselves in the real world. (The veil of ignorance was a thought device to ensure that morally irrelevant—inherited or acquired—advantages in the real world did not color judgments about distributive justice.) Rawls argued that two principles would emerge. First, each person should have an equal right to the most extensive set of liberties compatible with the same rights for all; this borrowed the idea of liberty that had emerged in the late eighteenth century, famously so in the French Revolution. Second, subject to the constraint of liberty, social choices should only permit inequality if it was efficient to do so—that a difference is only allowed if both parties are better off as a result; this is what Rawls called the "difference principle."

---

[53] This was postulated in an important economic model of how poverty could persist; see Loury (1981).

This second idea was more radical in its egalitarianism than the French Revolution's motto. However, it was not the kind of radical egalitarianism that said that equality always trumped efficiency. Indeed, society A, with a great deal of inequality, would be preferred by this moral principle to society B, with no inequality, if the poorest were better off in society A. Thus, the principle amounts to maximizing the advantages of the worst off group and hence became known as "maximin." This was explicitly not a proposal to maximize the lowest income, as it is sometimes interpreted, but rather to maximize the welfare of the worst off group in society. The "worst off" people were to be identified by what Rawls called their command over "primary goods." These are all those things needed to ensure that one is free to live the life one wants. This is a broader category than what are often called "basic needs" as it includes social inclusion needs and basic liberties—in short, rights as well as resources.

As Rawls recognized, one will need an index for determining the least advantaged. Possibly because of his evident desire to break all ties with utilitarianism, Rawls avoided using the term "utility function" (or "welfare function"), but this is evidently what he has in mind in his discussions of the "index problem" (especially, Rawls, 1971, pp. 90–95)— namely, a function that expresses the accepted tradeoffs. And Rawls agreed that it is also compelling that those tradeoffs be consistent with individual preferences over primary goods (Rawls, 1971, p. 94). However, he argues that we need not be concerned with the preferences of the nonpoor under the assumption that their primary good vectors are bound to dominate those of the poor.[54] (This is an empirical question, but a plausible assumption in the absence of data.) Thus, the utility function of the worst off person should be decisive in aggregations across primary goods.[55]

The Second Poverty Enlightenment had intellectual roots in the First. Rawls saw his difference principle as an interpretation of "fraternity" (as in the French Revolution's motto): "[T]he idea of not wanting to have greater advantages unless this is to the benefit of others who are less well off." This was a natural step (though it took a long time) from the aspirations for fraternity in the First Poverty Enlightenment. Utilitarianism was seen to be in conflict with fraternity as it could justify losses to the individual in the name of total utility. There would always be some gain to the richest person that could justify a loss to the poorest. The individual is subordinated to the common good, as measured by the sum of utilities. This Rawls rejected.

Rawls saw his theory as a reinterpretation of Kant. Poor people should have the right to veto any scheme that brings gains to the well-off at their expense. In direct

---

[54] More generally, the partial ordering of vectors of primary goods required by Rawls's maximin principle need not require a mathematically precise aggregation function; a sufficient partial ordering may be possible by only specifying certain generic properties of that function; for further details, see Atkinson and Bourguignon (1982).

[55] "The only index problem that concerns us is that for the least advantaged group" (Rawls, 1971, p. 93).

contradiction to the dominant view 200 years earlier, poverty for some was judged to be unacceptable as the means to others' prosperity. Utilitarianism (by contrast) could not guarantee a satisfactory minimum.[56] And only if a satisfactory minimum was ensured would the social contract be "stable" in that "the institutions that satisfy it will generate their own support" (Rawls, 1967).

The reasoning here was that, as long as the worst off group was happy with the social arrangement, then the rest (all doing better than the worst off group) would have nothing to complain about (Cohen, 1989b). Of course, this reasoning is questionable in the real world as those not in the poorest stratum could be expected to have a different counter-factual in mind when assessing any policy to that of being the worst off. But recall that the social contract was being formed in the absence of information about real-world positions. Rawls argued that maximin was more likely to emerge from rational choice behind the veil of ignorance.

Rawls's theory of justice has stimulated much debate. Harsanyi (1975) questioned whether maximin was a more plausible choice for a social contract than maximizing average utility even behind the veil of ignorance. Roemer (1996, Chapter 5) also questioned whether maximin would emerge as the solution. These critiques rested on the assumption that agents behind the veil would maximize expected utility, which depends solely on their own consumption (and leisure). This requires that subjective probabilities can be assigned to all states behind the veil, which Rawls (1971) questioned.[57] Introducing social preferences could also upset these critiques.

Other critiques of Rawls's theory emerged. Soon after the publication of *Theory of Justice*, Nozick (1974) published a libertarian critique. Nozick gave primacy to historical property rights above all else, although it was never clear on ethical grounds why property rights were never to be questioned.[58]

Sen (1980) took issue with Rawls's concept of primary goods, arguing that this idea does not adequately reflect the freedoms that people have to pursue their goals, recognizing the heterogeneity in the ability of people to transform primary goods into freedoms. This critique led to Sen's (1985) conceptualization of welfare in terms of primary "capabilities"—"what people are able to be and do (rather than in terms of the means they possess)" (Sen, 2000, p. 74).

As Pogge (1989) argues, one can defend the key aspects of Rawls's principles of justice without accepting his rationale in terms of a social contract. Roemer (2013) argues for a

---

[56] Although, as Dasgupta (1993, Chapter 2) points out, classical utilitarianism can be modified to incorporate constraints such that no utility is allowed to fall below some stipulated minimum. But this was never done to my knowledge.

[57] Though see the response in Harsanyi (1975).

[58] Pogge (1989) reviews this and other critiques of Rawls's principles of justice and provides a reinterpretation and (vigorous) defense of Rawls's original arguments.

version of maximin but from a different starting point, namely, the desire to equalize opportunities in society. This is premised on the view that poverty reflected exogenous circumstances facing individuals, as well as personal efforts. Severe empirical challenges remain in cleanly separating efforts from circumstances, but the conceptual distinction has bearing on thinking about antipoverty policy (as has long been recognized in policy debates reviewed below). In striving to equalize opportunities, we would not want to bring everyone down to a common but low level of opportunity. Instead, Roemer advocates that policy choices stemming from an "equal opportunity ethic" should maximize the welfare assigned to the worst off group, defined by a vector of exogeneous "circumstances"—those things that cannot be traced back to the choices made by the individual.[59]

Rawls opened the way to new nonutilitarian thinking on the conceptual foundations of antipoverty policy. This marked a return to the themes that emerged in the First Poverty Enlightenment, although these found more complete and rigorous formulations in the wake of the Second Poverty Enlightenment. Rather than being blamed solely on the bad behaviors of poor people, poverty came to be seen as stemming in large part from circumstances beyond their control, given circumstances of birth and market and governmental failures. This perspective gave promotional policies a deeper conceptual foundation. It was still granted that there was an important role for individual responsibility—that poverty did sometimes stem from bad choices. But this had ceased to be the dominant model. Careful opportunity-based formulations emerged in the writings of both philosophers (such as Cohen, 1989a and Arneson, 1989) and economists (including Roemer, 1998 and Fleurbaey, 2008).

So far the discussion has focused on the new philosophical and economic thinking of the Second Poverty Enlightenment. No less important to policy making were the new data, the new empirical research on those data, and the more popular writings and social movements of this time. We now turn to these.

22.6.2 The Rediscovery of Poverty in America

The industrialized world saw a boom in social spending in the second half of the twentieth century (Lindert, 2004). The new public attention to antipoverty policies is evident in the marked increase in references to "antipoverty," "poverty alleviation," and "redistribution" in the *Viewer* (Ravallion, 2011). References to "redistribution" peaked around 1980. "Redistribution of wealth" was often mentioned in the Great Depression, but use of this term declined during World War II and after until about 1960 when a new upsurge of interest emerged.

---

[59] This assumes that a unique vector exists, dominated by all others. Given that choices (efforts) vary, Roemer proposes to maximize the average welfare level of the worst off group, averaged across levels of effort.

The change in popular thinking was especially evident in the United States. In the wake of the civil rights movement (starting around 1955), the rediscovery of poverty in the midst of affluence was stimulated by important social commentaries, including Galbraith's (1958) *The Affluent Society* and Harrington's (1962) *The Other America*, both bestsellers at the time.[60] The success of Harrington's book was clearly a surprise; the first print-run was only 2500 copies, but by the mid-1990s it had sold 1.3 million copies.

Knowledge made this new awareness of poverty possible. The First Poverty Enlightenment lacked the theories and data that we take for granted today in measuring poverty, reckoning its costs, and informing public action. Nor was there much sign yet of the theories and movements that could represent the interests of poor people. That had changed by the 1950s. Authors like Harrington and Galbraith could formulate accessible knowledge-based arguments, including measurements from sample surveys. Many people were shocked in the early 1960s when the official calculations indicated that almost one-in-five Americans lived in poverty.

Although the type of quantification initiated by Booth and Rowntree 70 years earlier had been crucial, credibly reported qualitative observations in the media and popular books also had a huge influence, including on policy making at the highest levels. Many people were influenced by Harrington's efforts to "describe the faces behind the statistics" (p. 17). This was research aimed squarely at promoting change through knowledge. In an introduction to a 1993 reprint of *The Other America*, Howe (1993, p. xii) describes its central premise: ". . . that if only people *knew* the reality they would respond with indignation, that if people became aware of 'the invisible poor' they would act to eliminate this national scandal."

Galbraith and Harrington described a new "minority poverty" in America. A long period of poverty reduction had meant that the poor were now a minority, albeit a sizeable one. Although overall economic growth had allowed many of the "old poor" to move into the new middle class, others were left behind or thrown into poverty from which they could not escape. Widely held views about upward mobility and equality of opportunity in America also came into question based on empirical studies showing how much parental income and schooling affects the life chances of children (Duncan et al., 1972; Bowles and Gintis, 1976).

There were differences between Galbraith and Harrington in their understanding of this new poverty in America. Galbraith identified two reasons why so many of the old poor were unable to participate in the new opportunities. The first was physical or mental disability—what Galbraith called "case poverty"—while the second was that some were trapped in geographic pockets of poverty (his "insular poverty"). Although not rejecting these categories, Harrington argued that this was incomplete in that many of the minority poor had been negatively impacted by the same economic expansion that had benefited

---

[60] References to both books in the *Viewer* skyrocketed from the 1960s; the graph can be found here.

so many others. Significant economic change had created their poverty, and they were unable to recover. Here, Harrington is making an important point—that even propoor overall progress comes with losers as well as winners. And his description sounds a lot like the model of wealth dynamics in Section 22.2, whereby large negative shocks create persistent poverty, and recovery to get back on track is no small thing.

The political response in the United States included new social programs, notably under the Economic Opportunity Act of 1964, popularly known as the Johnson administration's War on Poverty (Sundquist, 1968). From early on, this policy effort was framed in nonutilitarian and nonwelfarist terms, especially emphasizing opportunities. The new programs included Head Start, which continues today (and is discussed further in Section 22.9). Data and knowledge to support the War on Poverty was provided by (among other bodies) a new national institute created in 1966, The Institute for Research on Poverty at the University of Wisconsin–Madison. This organization was charged with studying the causes of poverty in the United States and evaluating antipoverty programs.[61]

The War on Poverty was not, it seems, prompted by a mass shift in American public opinion; indeed, Heclo (1986) refers to US polls indicating that the public was evenly divided on whether welfare spending should increase. It seems that the political response was motivated by evidence and ideas, not attracting voters. Although causality is unclear, it is notable that the US poverty rate fell between the years 1960 and 1980 (Meyer and Sullivan, 2012).[62]

Similar to the First Poverty Enlightenment, a backlash emerged in due course. An influential counterattack came from Murray's (1984) *Losing Ground*. As was the case with the backlash from Malthus and others around the turn of the nineteenth century, concerns about adverse incentive effects on behavior returned to loom large, such as claims that welfare benefits to single mothers encouraged families to break up. However, as in the debates on the Old Poor Laws, rather little credible supportive evidence was presented, and evidence to the contrary could be cited (Ellwood and Summers, 1986; Hoynes, 1997). Yet reforms followed in the United States during the 1990s; 30 years after declaring a "War on Poverty," the American government declared a "War on Welfare."[63]

Although (again) the attribution to social policies alone can be questioned, it is notable that the decline in US income poverty rates up to about 1980 stalled, and even reversed after that. Also notable is that this came with a marked shift in the demographic

---

[61] A good history of the Institute can be found on their website.

[62] This is true for both incomes and consumptions; income poverty rates crept back up after 1980 though consumption-based measures continued to fall. On the choice between these measures, see Slesnick (2001).

[63] The latter term was used by Katz (1987); also see Albelda et al. (1996).

profile of US poverty, favoring the elderly. Indeed, the incidence of poverty continued to fall among the elderly in the United States after 1980, albeit at a slower rate. Lindert (2013) attributes this difference to a bias in US social spending in favor of the elderly over the young, in common with other rich countries.

In attempting to explain America's poverty amidst affluence, the ideas of a "culture of poverty" and an "underclass" that emerged in the 1960s were much debated. Echoing the debates of prior times (reviewed earlier), critics saw these ideas as blaming poor people for their poverty and ignoring more deep-rooted "structural" inequalities (Gans, 1995; O'Connor, 2002). In some versions of the "underclass" idea, such as in Wilson's (1987) *The Truly Disadvantaged*, a "culture of poverty" was seen to stem from structural inequalities and so was part of their explanation; echoing Harrington, Wilson emphasized macroeconomic factors, including structural changes in the economy, urban structural changes, and aggregate unemployment rates.

Although the debate continues about whether there is space for policy intervention aimed at changing culture,[64] looking back over 200 years, it is clear that there has been a significant shift in thinking about poverty, from primarily blaming poor people to identifying deeper factors beyond their control, yet amenable to public action. This new view did not deny personal responsibility or the scope for mistakes or seemingly irrational behaviors.[65] In due course, evidence also emerged that the stresses of poverty diminished cognitive ability (Mani et al. 2013), again clouding the issue of cause and effect. But the key point to emerge was that "bad choices" was a dangerously incomplete explanation of poverty. As Shipler (2005, p. 6) put it with reference to America's working poor: "Each person's life is the mixed product of bad choices and bad fortunes, of roads not taken and roads cut off by the accident of birth or circumstances."

22.6.3 Relative and Subjective Poverty

Before the Second Poverty Enlightenment, poverty was mainly seen in absolute terms.[66] This changed radically in many of the rich countries of the world from around 1960.[67] The Second Poverty Enlightenment saw a new concept of "relative poverty" in both America and Western Europe, where the idea attained widespread official acceptance. By this view, the definition of poverty was contingent on the average standard of living

---

[64] See, for example, Steinberg's (2011) comments on Small et al. (2010).

[65] Behavioral explanations of poverty have drawn some support from experiments suggesting that people do not always behave rationally, although the experiments are often open to other interpretations, notably about the nature of the optimizing behavior (Saint-Paul, 2011).

[66] By "absolute poverty," I mean a poverty line that is fixed in real terms over time.

[67] Doron (1990, p. 30) describes this change in the 1960s: "The reformers of the period, and certainly the radicals among them, rejected the absolute approach, which contents itself with guaranteeing a minimum of subsistence . . . The needs of men are not stable and absolute but relative and related to the circumstances of the society in a particular period of time."

in the society one was talking about and so could be expected to evolve with the average.[68] Fuchs (1967) appears to have been the first to propose the sharpest version of this idea: that the poverty line should simply be set at 50% of the current median income. For a reason that will soon be clear, I will call these "strongly relative measures."

Although all the debates in the United States that were reviewed earlier in this section were echoed across the Atlantic, this new idea of strongly relative poverty had more influence in Western Europe than in America, and it carried little or no weight in the developing world. In due course, the most widely used definition of poverty in Western Europe followed Fuchs's suggestion, with national poverty lines often set at a constant proportion of the current mean (or median). Eurostat (2005) has produced such relative poverty measures across European countries and over time, as has the influential Luxembourg Income Study (LIS), which started in the mid-1980s and uses a poverty line set at 40–60% of the median in its summary statistics at country level. An immediate implication of these measures is that, when all income levels rise by the same proportion, the measure of poverty remains unchanged.

There were antecedents to the idea of relative poverty in the First Poverty Enlightenment. As Himmelfarb (1984a,b) and others have observed, Adam Smith held a conception of poverty that was socially specific. In a famous passage in *The Wealth of Nations* (1776, Book 5, Chapter 2, Article 4), Smith pointed to the social role of a linen shirt in eighteenth-century Europe.[69] Smith, it seems, wanted the poverty line to be relevant to its context.

That is what we see across countries. The average poverty line rises from $1.25 a day for the poorest countries to $30 a day in the richest (Ravallion, 2012a). At around $13 per person per day, the official poverty line in the United States is far higher than the poverty lines found in poor countries (though below average for rich countries). However, strongly relative lines go further in that they are changing over time in direct proportion to the mean or median, that is, with an elasticity of unity. It is not clear that Smith had in mind such a definition of poverty. One might argue that the poverty line should be relative between countries but absolute for a given country. The official poverty line in the United States is still an absolute line over time (with fixed real value),[70] as are almost all poverty lines in developing countries (Ravallion, 2012a). Logically, however, a poverty line that is fixed in real terms cannot remain relevant to prevailing living standards

---

[68] The period also saw efforts to anchor poverty measures to governmental assistance thresholds; an early example was Abel-Smith and Townsend (1966) describing poverty in Britain. For further discussion of this and other approaches, see Atkinson (1991).

[69] In more recent times, a number of studies have also pointed to the social roles played by festivals, celebrations, and communal feasts; see, for example, Rao (2001), Banerjee and Duflo (2007), and Milanovic (2008).

[70] This has been set at three times the cost of an adequate diet, following Orshansky (1963). Supplementary measures have been introduced in recent years (Johnson and Timothy, 2012).

indefinitely in growing economies. Indeed, as Fuchs (1967) points out, the US poverty line in the 1930s was probably substantially lower in real terms than that of the 1960s.[71] Some gradient over time is clearly called for.

Although the idea of relative poverty goes back to the First Poverty Enlightenment (though largely dormant between the two Enlightenments), explicitly relative measures were a product of the Second Poverty Enlightenment. However, there has been much debate, and it continues today. Some observers have been concerned about unequal treatment of people at similar levels of real income. The advocates of relative poverty lines for rich countries would not presumably have been comfortable in applying the same idea in comparing poverty measures between the majority population and minorities within one country; indeed, the Second Poverty Enlightenment started to see a breakdown of past discriminatory practices in this respect. There were clearly (though rarely explicit) moral bounds to relativism. However, the case for relative poverty lines rested on the view that poverty must be seen as absolute in the space of welfare, whether defined in terms of utility or capabilities; as Sen (1983, p. 163) put it: "... an absolute approach in the space of capabilities translates into a relative approach in the space of commodities."

The more difficult issue was why the poverty line should be strongly relative, that is, proportional to the mean or median. If we consider more closely the two most common arguments made in favor of relativism, neither is compelling in this respect. The first argument concerns *social inclusion*. A linen shirt in eighteenth-century Europe is an example of what can be termed a "social inclusion need." The existence of such needs has been the primary justification given for the Western European relative poverty lines. However, the cost of that shirt will be roughly the same for the poorest person as the richest. More generally, the cost of social inclusion cannot be expected to go to zero in the limit, as mean income goes to zero, as implied by strongly relative lines. That would almost certainly understate the costs of social inclusion in poor countries.

The second argument made for the strongly relative measures is that they allowed for *relative deprivation*—that people care about their income relative to the mean or median of their country of residence.[72] However, this, too, is not so convincing on closer scrutiny. As long as we think that poverty is absolute in the space of welfare (or capabilities) one can only derive these strongly relative poverty measures if welfare *only* depends on relative income (own income relative to the median) (Ravallion, 2012a). In other words, one needs to assume that welfare does not depend on own income at given relative income. This must surely be considered a very strong assumption.

---

[71] Fuchs bases this claim on a necessarily rough calculation, asserting that if the 1960s standard in the United States was applied to the 1930s, then two-thirds of the US population would have been deemed poor as compared to President Roosevelt's estimate that "one-third of the nation" was poor in the 1930s.

[72] The sociologist Runciman (1966) was an influential advocate of this view.

None of this denies the welfare-relevance of social inclusion needs or relative deprivation. Arguably the case is now stronger than ever for incorporating relativist concerns in poverty measurement. Rather the issue is how best to do that. To allow for a (positive) minimum cost of social inclusion one requires what Ravallion and Chen (2011) dub "weakly relative measures."[73] These have the feature that the poverty line will not rise proportionately to the mean but with an elasticity less than unity for all finite mean incomes.[74] Consistent with the national poverty lines, Ravallion and Chen (2013) propose global poverty measures using a schedule of weakly relative poverty lines that contain the absolute lines (typical of poor countries) and relative lines (typical of rich ones) as the limiting cases.

Another strain of the new literature on poverty measurement emphasized the scope for calibrating welfare and poverty measures to subjective questions in surveys. These could take the form of a ladder (from "poor" to "rich" say),[75] or a more general question on satisfaction with life or happiness. Alternatively, the survey questions asked what income level corresponded to specific subjective welfare levels, following Van Praag (1968). A special case was the "minimum income question" that derived the monetary poverty line as the fixed point in the regression function relating personal subjective minima to actual incomes. In other words, the poverty line was drawn such that people with an income below it tended to think their income was inadequate for meeting their needs, while those above the line tended to think their own income was adequate. Alternatively, the poverty line could be identified as the fixed point of adequacy across multiple dimensions of welfare, following Pradhan and Ravallion (2000).[76]

22.6.4 The Rich World's Rediscovery of Global Poverty

A further surge of attention to poverty in the popular and scholarly literature in the late twentieth century stemmed from the Western public's increasing awareness of the existence of severe and widespread poverty in the developing world. Poverty and inequality in developing countries started to attract substantial mainstream scholarly attention in the West from the late 1960s.[77] GDP per capita was no longer seen as the sole metric for

---

[73] A weakly relative line was proposed earlier by Foster (1998). This was given by the weighted geometric mean of an absolute and a strongly relative line. Although this is also weakly relative, it has a constant elasticity, whereas the elasticity rises from zero to unity in the Ravallion and Chen (2011) proposal—consistent with the data on national lines.

[74] It can be argued that a globally relevant schedule of poverty lines should also have this property, and global measures following this approach are available in Ravallion and Chen (2013).

[75] These came to be known as Cantril ladders following Cantril (1965).

[76] For a critical survey of the various approaches found in this literature, see Ravallion (2014).

[77] Important contributions included Dandekar and Rath (1971), Adelman and Morris (1973), Chenery et al. (1974), Lipton (1977), World Bank (1980), Fields (1980), Kakwani (1980), Sen (1981a), Anand (1983), Bardhan (1984a), and Kanbur (1987).

judging success; for example, in his foreword to an overview by the World Bank of 25 years of development, the Bank's first Chief Economist, Hollis Chenery (Chenery (1977, p. v)), wrote that "... economic growth is a necessary but not sufficient condition for social progress and that more direct attention should be given to the welfare of the poorest groups."

For most of the developing world, poverty was "majority poverty"—in marked contrast to Galbraith's characterization of "minority poverty." Travel and visual media made it visible to those living in the West though it was already evident to almost everyone in the developing world. And poverty data were playing an important role in the post-Independence policy debates in some poor countries, including India, notably through its National Sample Surveys, which began in 1950.[78] As was the case with the poverty research by Booth and Rowntree in late nineteenth-century England, around 1990 many people were shocked to learn that there were about one billion people in the world living on less than $1 per day, at purchasing power parity (PPP) (Ravallion et al., 1991; World Bank, 1990)—an explicitly frugal line anchored to the national poverty lines found amongst the world's poorest countries.[79] Since 1990 there has been a massive expansion in survey data collection and availability and refinements to the methodology; the original estimates by Ravallion et al. (1991) used data for 22 countries, with one survey per country, while the latest estimates in Chen and Ravallion (2010) are based on survey data for 125 countries with more than six surveys per country on average. The efforts of country statistics offices—often with support from international agencies such as the UNDP, the World Bank, and the International Comparison Program—to collect household survey data and price data have provided the empirical foundation for domestic and international efforts to fight poverty since the 1980s. Public access to such data was crucial and gradually improved with help from efforts such as the World Bank's Living Standards Measurement Study (LSMS), which facilitates the collection of household-level survey data in developing countries, and the LIS, which facilitates access to harmonized micro data, though mostly for rich countries.

The World Bank's (1990) *World Development Report: Poverty* was influential in development policy circles, and soon after a "world free of poverty" became the Bank's overarching goal. A large body of empirical research on poverty followed in the 1990s, helped by a number of texts that provided useful expositions for practitioners of relevant theory and methods.[80] The UNDP's *Human Development Reports* began in 1990, and they have

---

[78] India was an early leader globally in the application of random sampling in economic and social statistics, notably through the Indian Statistical Institute, founded by the eminent statistician Prasanta Mahalanobis, which led in due course to India's National Sample Surveys, which are still used for measuring poverty in India.

[79] The $1 a day line was chosen as a typical poverty line for low-income countries. It was never exactly $1 a day, and the latest line (based on a much larger and more representative sample of national lines) is $1.25 a day at 2005 PPP (Ravallion et al., 2009).

[80] Examples include Ravallion (1994b), Sadoulet and de Janvry (1995), Deaton (1997), and Grosh and Glewwe (2000).

consistently argued for public action to promote basic health and education in developing countries. The importance to human development of combining poverty reduction with better access to basic services came to be appreciated (Anand and Ravallion, 1993). Sri Lanka's longstanding emphasis on basic health and education services had been shown to bring a large dividend in longevity and other human development indicators relative to countries at a similar level of average income (Sen, 1981b). The emphasis most East Asian countries have long given to broadly shared investments in human development also came to be recognized in the 1990s as a crucial element to their economic success, even though the role played by some other elements of the East Asian policy package remained contentious (Fishlow and Gwin, 1994; Rodrik, 1994; World Bank, 1993). It is clear that by the late twentieth century there had been a complete reversal in policy thinking about poverty, from the view 200 years earlier that human capital development for poor families was a waste of public resources to the view that it is an essential precondition for growth and development.

The period also saw a broadening of the range of policies under consideration, especially in the developing world. There was a new political will for antipoverty policy in many of the newly independent, postcolonial, states, although with mixed success. Policies for promoting economic growth came to be seen and judged by their efficacy in promoting (among other goals) poverty reduction (World Bank, 1990). (The next section will return to this point.) By the 1990s, it seems that nothing in the policy arena was off-limits in discussing impacts on poverty. This brought a new danger too. Without some degree of separability, allowing instruments to be tied to goals risked policy paralysis. But economic analysis and a measure of good sense could often be trusted to guide effective policy action, recognizing the tradeoffs. And the shift in focus from protection to promotion is also evident in the types of policies being tried within the subclass of direct interventions, as we will see in Section 22.9.

By the turn of the twenty-first century, a new optimism about the scope for global poverty reduction had emerged. The Millennium Development Goals (MDGs) were ratified in 2000 at the Millennium Assembly, a meeting of world leaders at the United Nations. The first MDG was to halve the developing world's 1990 "$1 a day" poverty rate by 2015. Sachs (2005b, p. 1) wrote a *New York Times* bestseller, *The End of Poverty*, outlining his personal vision of how "[o]ur generation can choose to end that extreme poverty by the year 2025." Some of this optimism was well founded in subsequent events. Using the $1.25-a-day poverty line based on 2005 prices, the first MDG was attained in 2010, a full 5 years ahead of the goal (Chen and Ravallion, 2013). Even so, that important achievement leaves over one billion people living in extreme poverty, as judged by the standards of the poorest countries. But continuing the success of the fight against extreme poverty begun in 2000 will lift one billion people out of extreme poverty by 2030 (Ravallion, 2013). Progress in reducing global relative poverty will be slower; today over 2.5 billion people remain poor by standards typical of the country they live in (Ravallion and Chen, 2013). However, national poverty elimination targets have emerged in many countries, both rich and poor. In 2010, the European Union adopted its Europe 2020 poverty reduction target to reduce by 25% the numbers of Europeans living below national poverty lines.

Some of the debates of 200 years ago survive today. For example, at the time of this writing, the US Congress was implementing substantial cuts to the Supplementary Nutrition Assistance Program (Food Stamps). During the relevant House of Representatives Committee Meeting, a Congressman was quoted as saying that "[w]hile it was a Christian duty to care for the poor and hungry, it was not the government's duty" (Fifield, 2013). One heard such claims often 200 years ago. The difference today is that the vast majority of people clearly do not agree.

Although there is continuing debate about the causes of poverty and policy prescriptions, modern writings are invariably based on the premise that poverty is something that can be greatly reduced and, indeed, eliminated with the right economic and social policies. By this view, poverty is in no small measure a *global public responsibility*, and governments and the economy are to be judged (in part at least) by the progress that is made against poverty.

22.7. THE IDEA OF A PROGRESSIVE MARKET ECONOMY

Until the late twentieth century, the prevailing view was one of skepticism that poor people would benefit much from economic growth in a capitalist economy. Well into the 1980s, it was common to hear in both popular and scholarly writings that economic growth was expected to largely bypass poor people in both rich and poor countries. Where did this skepticism come from, and was it justified?

By one view, poverty is likely to persist in a growing economy because poverty is relative (Section 22.6). Strictly, poverty could still be eliminated when using a strongly relative poverty line set at a constant proportion of the mean with sufficient redistribution in favor of poor people. Growth in the mean will not eliminate poverty without a change in relative distribution. However, the past explicit acceptance of poverty among economists and noneconomists alike does not appear to be the product of such a relativist view. In fact the latter is a modern idea, which appears to have emerged much later, in the 1970s (Section 22.6). Using absolute or weakly relative poverty measures, sufficient inequality-neutral growth will eliminate poverty.[81]

But growth was not expected to be inequality-neutral. Most classical and Marxist economic thinkers saw little hope that even a growing capitalist economy would deliver

---

[81] For any linear schedule of relative poverty lines as a function of the mean, and all standard measures of poverty, saying that there is a positive lower bound to the cost of social inclusion is essentially equivalent to saying that inequality-neutral growth in the mean will reduce the measure of poverty (Ravallion and Chen, 2011).

rapid poverty reduction or even *any* poverty reduction. Although Smith was optimistic about the potential for a progressive, poverty-reducing, market economy, the prominent classical economists who followed, including Malthus and Ricardo, were more pessimistic about the prospects for higher real wages and (hence) less poverty, suggesting that they anticipated rising inequality from a growing capitalist economy. As discussed in Section 22.5, demographic responses to rising wages were expected to play a key role in attenuating the poverty impact of growth. The socialist movement that emerged toward the middle of the nineteenth century shared the same pessimistic view about the prospects for poverty reduction but took it to be a damning criticism of capitalism. The thirst for profits to finance capital accumulation, combined with the large "reserve army" of unemployed, was seen as the constraint on rising real wage rates rather than population growth.

Distributional dynamics has long been a central theme of development economics. Poverty was a concern for the postcolonial governments of the newly independent countries, but the earliest policy-oriented discussions were pessimistic about the prospects of economic growth bringing much benefit to poor people. It was widely believed that growth in low-income countries was bound to be inequitable, and that view is still heard today.

A foundation for this view was provided by Kuznets (1955), and came to be known as the "Inverted U Hypothesis," whereby inequality first increases with economic growth in a poor country but falls after some critical income level is reached.[82] Although there are other theoretical models in the literature that can generate such a relationship, in the Kuznets formulation, the economy is assumed to comprise a low-mean, low-inequality rural sector and a high-mean, high-inequality urban sector, and growth is assumed to occur through the migration of workers from the former environment to the latter. This growth is assumed to entail that a representative "slice" of the rural distribution is transformed into a representative slice of the urban distribution, preserving distributions within each sector. An inverted U can then be derived linking certain indices of inequality and the population share of the urban sector (Anand and Kanbur, 1993; Robinson, 1976).

Some policy makers appear to have incorrectly inferred that this model also implied that economic growth in poor countries would bring little benefit to poor people. (This sometimes reflected a longstanding confusion between the ideas of "poverty" and "inequality" in development policy discussion.) It is easy to show that for all additive poverty measures, if poverty is initially higher in the rural sector, then aggregate poverty must fall under the Kuznets process of migration described above. Not for the last time,

---

[82] Also see Adelman and Morris (1973), Robinson (1976), Ahluwalia (1976), Ahluwalia et al. (1979), and Anand and Kanbur (1993).

thinking about how the overall development strategy might allow more rapid poverty reduction was led astray by misunderstandings of a theoretical model.

The economic history of today's rich countries has often been seen as a source of lessons for the developing world. Contrary to the expectations of both the nineteenth-century supporters and critics of capitalism, Britain's industrial revolution, which had started around 1760, almost certainly reduced poverty through rising real wage rates. But there was a long lag. Just how long depends on the position one takes in the debate about price indices. Clark's (2005) discussion of builders' real wage rates in England suggests that workers earned higher wages from about 1800, while Allen (2007, 2009) argues that the increase started closer to 1830. Either way the pessimists appear to have been right that for at least a few decades after the technical innovations, real wages did not increase.[83] Real wages in Britain did start to rise in the nineteenth century despite continuing population growth. Falling food prices in Europe due to refrigeration and lower freight transport costs also helped increase real wages later in that century (Williamson, 1998). And there is evidence that the gains in real wages for the working class from the mid-nineteenth century came hand-in-hand with improved nutrition.[84]

The lag in the real wage rate response to the industrial revolution is suggestive of the model by Lewis (1954) in which a surplus of labor in the rural economy keeps wages at a low level until that surplus is absorbed by the economy's modern (urban) sector, as this expands due to technical progress. Allen (2009) offers an alternative explanation whereby the extra demand for capital due to technical progress could only be met by savings from nonlabor income, under the assumption that workers were too poor to save. Then profits had to rise to finance the investments needed, and only when sufficient capital had accumulated did real wages rise. In short, high poverty rates had to persist for some time, despite growth, because poor people simply could not generate the savings required to support that growth. However, even a small amount of savings by each of a large number of workers could have helped finance capital accumulation provided that those savings could be mobilized. Financial underdevelopment may then be seen as a factor in the lag.

The empirical foundations for the expectation that inequality would inevitably rise in growing developing countries were not particularly secure at the time the Kuznets hypothesis was influential. There was not much data to draw on. A debate in the early 1970s on the distribution of the gains from economic growth in Brazil left an appetite for better survey data for measuring poverty and inequality.[85] As better evidence from household surveys accumulated, it was revealed that very few low-income countries have

---

[83] Also see Williamson (1985) and O'Rourke and Williamson (1997).

[84] See the Fogel et al. (1983) series on mean height of working class boys in London, which tracks quite closely Tucker's (1975) series on real wages of London artisans. However, Cinnirella (2008) puts the turning point (after which mean height rose) much later, around the mid-nineteenth century.

[85] Contributions to this debate were made by Fishlow (1972), Fields (1977), and Ahluwalia et al. (1980).

developed over time in a manner consistent with the Kuznets hypothesis, as is shown by Bruno et al. (1998) and Fields (2001). We have learned that growth in developing countries tends to be distribution-neutral on average, meaning that changes in inequality are roughly orthogonal to growth rates in the mean (Dollar and Kraay, 2002; Ferreira and Ravallion, 2009; Ravallion, 1995, 2001). Distribution-neutral growth implies that the changes in any standard measure of either absolute or weakly relative poverty will be negatively correlated with growth rates in the mean.

There is also evidence of inequality convergence, whereby inequality tends to increase in low inequality countries and decrease in high inequality countries (Bénabou, 1996; Ravallion, 2003). This is consistent with neoclassical growth theory, which shows that a fully competitive market economy contains forces for reducing inequality, as demonstrated by Stiglitz (1969) and Bénabou (1996). As Ravallion (2003) argues, the evidence we see of inequality convergence can also be explained by how economic policy convergence in the world during the 1990s interacted with prereform differences in the extent of inequality. To see why, suppose that reforming developing countries fall into two categories: those in which prereform controls on the economy were used to benefit the rich, keeping inequality artificially high (arguably the case in much of Latin America up to the 1980s), and those in which the controls had the opposite effect, keeping inequality low (as in Eastern Europe and Central Asia prior to the 1990s). Then liberalizing economic policy reforms may well entail sizable redistribution between the poor and the rich, but in opposite directions in the two types of countries.

The periods of global trade openness fostered some progress toward convergence of living standards across countries. Although much attention has been given to the current globalization period, Williamson (1998) argues that the prior period of globalization, 1870–1914, fostered economic expansion and convergence within the "Atlantic economy." This globalization almost certainly reduced poverty globally.

Post-Independence policies in most developing countries strived for economic growth, facilitated by government planning in relatively closed economies, although capabilities for effective implementation were often weak. India's Second and Third Plans, as well as many other planning documents, aimed for growth through accelerated capital accumulation and industrialization. These plans were influenced by classical economics and the Harrod–Domar equation, although here, too, policy makers misinterpreted the implications of the model.[86] The prioritization given to the capital-goods sector in India's Second Plan was directly influenced by a two-sector growth model in Mahalanobis (1953), although there were dissenters at the time (including Vakil and Brahmanand, 1956), and subsequent research in growth economics did not find any robust implication to justify this prioritization. As Lipton (1977) points out, the planners also ignored Adam Smith's warning that the food supply would constrain urban

---

[86] See the insightful discussion of the history of thought on economic growth in Ray (1998, Chapter 3).

growth in a closed economy. And poor people were financing the industrialization push, which typically depended on extracting a surplus from agriculture, which provided most of their incomes.[87] The plans were overly optimistic about rapid industrialization and about their potential to raise the demand for labor and so reduce poverty. And the industrialization push displaced other policies; for example, rural infrastructure (electrification and roads) took a back seat.

China's enormous progress against absolute poverty since around 1980, alongside rising inequality, might superficially be seen as testimony to the idea that the country has been in the rising segment of the Kuznets inverted U. However, here, too, the model just does not fit the facts. For one thing, inequality is lower in urban China than rural China, unlike the case assumed by Kuznets (1955), although this is not necessary for an inverted U; see Robinson (1976). More importantly, neither analytic decompositions of the changes in poverty nor regression-based decompositions suggest that the Kuznets process of growth through modern sector enlargement was the main driver of growth and poverty reduction in China (Ravallion and Chen, 2007). One must look elsewhere, notably to the initial agrarian reforms—including the massive land reform when the land of the collectives was assigned to individual farmers—and market liberalization more broadly, for an explanation of China's rapid poverty reduction in the 1980s.[88] Manufacturing growth came to play an important role later though that success was based in part on favorable initial conditions, notably the legacy of investments in human development, including in rural areas. Unlike many developing countries, there was a large literate rural population to draw on as the workforce for China's labor-intensive modern sector enlargement.

In thinking about policies for fighting poverty, the role played by the rural sector has been much debated. The sequence in China was roughly right: In the reform period from 1978, initial attention was given to the rural sector, and agrarian reforms to restore farmer incentives (in land allocation and prices) were crucial to ensuring a sustainably propoor development path, as had been the case elsewhere in East Asia.[89] Few other countries got the sequence right, and China's experience contains an important lesson for Africa today (Ravallion, 2009).

There were efforts to reprioritize development policy in the 1970s and 1980s. World Bank President Robert McNamara's 1973 "Nairobi speech" signaled such an effort from the international development institutions. In development thinking, "urban bias" was increasingly recognized as bad for growth as well as for poverty reduction, though it reflected political structures in much of the developing world (Lipton, 1968, 1977). However, the

---

[87] Even now, three-quarters of the developing world's poor live in rural areas (Ravallion et al., 2007).

[88] Similarly, in Taiwan and South Korea, the initial conditions for more propoor growth were laid by radical redistributive land reform, which led to productive and dynamic owner-farmed smallholdings.

[89] Given that the rest of the economy was growing rapidly, China could delay reforms to its state-owned enterprises (SOEs). Indeed, it was not until the late 1990s (20 years after the agrarian reforms began) that China started reforming its SOEs. Some observers have suggested that this should have happened sooner.

temptation to industrialize rapidly—"run before you have walked"—was strong. Combined with huge inequities in access to finance and human development, the subsequent growth paths were disappointing, both in growth and (especially) poverty reduction.

The debt crises of the 1980s brought a wave of structural adjustment programs supported by the international financial institutions (IFIs) that attempted to restore macroeconomic balances and promote economic growth. Given that the World Bank had produced *Redistribution with Growth* 10 years earlier (Chenery et al., 1974), it is surprising that its own adjustment programs in the early and mid-1980s gave little serious attention to the impacts on poor people though this neglect was consistent with the broader 1980s backlash in the Anglo-Saxon world against the distributional focus of the 1960s and 1970s. The Bank and Fund programs were much criticized for their neglect of distributional impacts, and the criticisms stuck. A progressive recovery in thinking within the IFIs was underway by the late 1980s, and add-on programs to "compensate the losers from adjustment" were soon common. Today, it is widely recognized that poverty and inequality mitigation has to be designed into economy-wide reform programs from the outset.

By the turn of the twenty-first century, enough evidence had accumulated for economists to be confident that higher growth rates tended to yield more rapid rates of absolute poverty reduction.[90] A more poverty-reducing process of global economic growth emerged after 2000, and not just because of China's growth. The trend rate of decline in the "$1.25-per-day" poverty rate for the developing world outside China rose from 0.4% points per year from 1980 to 2000 to 1.0% points per year after that period (Ravallion, 2013).

The poverty impact of a given rate of growth depends in part on the initial distribution.[91] Intuitively, when inequality is high, poor people will tend to have a lower share of the gains from growth. Ravallion (1997a, 2007) confirmed this using household survey data over time.[92] Easterly (2009) conjectured that the initial poverty rate is likely to be the better predictor of the elasticity than initial inequality though no evidence was provided. Ravallion (2012b) provided that evidence, and it compellingly shows that it is not high initial inequality that impedes the pace of poverty reduction at a given rate of growth, but high poverty.

Saying that growth typically reduces poverty does not, of course, mean that any growth-promoting policy will do so or that everyone will benefit. That depends on

---

[90] See Ravallion (1995, 2001, 2007), Fields (2001), Dollar and Kraay (2002), Kraay (2006), and World Bank (1990, 2000). Also see the review of the arguments and evidence on this point in Ferreira and Ravallion (2009).

[91] See Ravallion (1997a, 2007, 2012b), World Bank (2000, 2006), Bourguignon (2003), and Lopez and Servén (2006).

[92] Ravallion (1997a) did not find that the elasticity of poverty to growth varied systematically with the mean, although if incomes are log-normally distributed, then such a variation is implied theoretically (Bourguignon, 2003; Lopez and Servén, 2006).

the distribution—horizontally as well as vertically—of the gains and losses from that policy. There may be vertical inequalities—between people at different levels of mean income—generated in the process that mitigate the gains to poor people from growth. And there can be horizontal inequities, whereby people at the same initial levels of income fare very differently, and some poor people may well lose from a policy that reduces poverty in the aggregate. (Recall that Harrington (1962) emphasized this point in describing the new "minority poverty" in the "other America.")

This point has been clearest in the literature on external trade and poverty. A number of studies have found support for the view that trade openness—typically measured by trade volume as a share of GDP—promotes economic growth.[93] It is unclear that trade volume can be treated as exogenous in these cross-country regressions; higher trade volume may be a response to growth rather than a cause. The policy implications are also unclear since trade volume is not a policy variable; see the discussion in Rodrik (1994) and Rodriguez and Rodrik (2001). But, putting this issue to one side, what about the distributional effects? A number of studies have combined survey-based measures of income inequality at country-level with data on trade and other control variables to assess the distributional impacts of trade openness, as reviewed in Winters et al. (2004). The evidence is mixed. Dollar and Kraay (2004) find little or no effect of trade volume on inequality. Other studies have reported adverse effects. Lundberg and Squire (2003) find evidence that higher trade volume tends to increase inequality. On balance, Ravallion (2006) reports little or no correlation between greater trade openness and the pace of poverty reduction in developing countries.

However, there can be winners and losers at all levels of living, even when a standard measure of inequality or poverty is unchanged. There are many sources of heterogeneity, yielding horizontal impacts of reform. Geographic disparities in access to human and physical infrastructure affect prospects for participating in the opportunities created by greater openness to external trade. Differences in household demographic composition influence consumption behavior and hence the welfare impact of the shifts in relative prices associated with trade openness. Ravallion (2006) reports on two case studies of this heterogeneity in the welfare impacts of liberalizing trade reform, for China and for Morocco. The results indicate a sizable, and at least partly explicable, variance in impacts across households with different characteristics—differences that influenced their net trading positions in the relevant markets.

Where does all this leave us? The antitrade policies (on quotas, tariffs, and exchange rates) of the post-Independence development policy regimes were unlikely to bring

---

[93] In a metastudy of all the cross-country growth regressions with an average of seven regressors (chosen from 67 candidates drawn from the literature on cross-country growth regressions), Sala-I-Martin et al. (2004) report that trade volume is a significant factor in two-thirds of the regressions, though it is not among their subset of 18 robust predictors of economic growth.

much benefit to poor people, the bulk of whom produced tradable goods from primarily nontradable inputs. Although this remains a plausible generalization, there is likely to be considerable heterogeneity across countries in such effects, and one might be skeptical of basing policy advice for any specific country on generalizations from either standard Stolper–Samuelson arguments or cross-country regressions (Ravallion, 2006). For example, some studies have found evidence that higher trade volume increases inequality in poor countries but that the reverse holds true at a higher mean income (Milanovic, 2005; Ravallion, 2001). The macro perspective, focusing on impacts on an aggregate measure of poverty or inequality, hides potentially important horizontal impacts with implications for other areas of policy, notably social protection efforts that may well be needed to complement the growth-promoting reforms. (Section 22.9 discusses these policies further.)

Trade policies have also played a role in social protection, though this, too, has been much debated. Governments of food-exporting but famine-affected areas have often implemented food export bans in the hope of protecting vulnerable citizens. Classical economists were influential in arguing against such policies in favor of free trade. For example, Aykroyd (1974) describes how the Governor of Bombay in the early nineteenth century quoted Smith's *The Wealth of Nations* when defending his policy stance against any form of trade intervention during the famines that afflicted the region. Various "Famine Commissions" set up by the British Raj argued against the trade interventions that were being called for to help protect vulnerable populations. Similarly, Woodham-Smith (1962) describes the influence that Smith and other classical economists had on British policy responses to the severe famines in Ireland in the mid-nineteenth century. In modern times, free trade has been advocated as a means of stabilizing domestic food consumption in the presence of output shocks (World Bank, 1986). Other economists have been less supportive. Sen (1981a) and Ravallion (1987) pointed to the possibility that real income declines in the famine-affected areas can generate food exports while people starve.[94] Regulated trade through taxes or even export bans may then be a defensible policy response to help vulnerable groups relative to feasible alternatives (Ravallion, 1997b).

Critics of trade intervention for the purpose of protection from external price shocks (such as in the period from 2007 to 2011) have pointed out that such a policy can exacerbate the problem of price volatility (Martin and Anderson, 2012). However, in the absence of better options for aggregate intertemporal smoothing, the optimal nontrade protection policy would entail transfers between net food producers and net consumers, to coinsure. And this, too, would exacerbate the price volatility, as shown by Do et al.

---

[94] The analysis of the time series data for famines in British India in Ravallion (1987) indicated that the aggregate income effects were not strong enough to undermine the consumption-stabilizing effects of unrestricted trade.

(2013). So one cannot simply argue that external trade intervention is an inferior form of social protection; any such protection would have a similar feature. Trade interventions will probably entail some price distortions, which must be evaluated against the distortions generated by alternative schemes. There are situations in which trade insulation dominates feasible options for protection (Do et al., 2013).

The key point here is to avoid sweeping generalizations about policies. To take another example (possibly even more contentious than trade policy) consider active industrial policies—the effort to encourage selected promising sectors or firms using tariffs, subsidies, or tax breaks.[95] Advocates point to the successes of some East Asian countries with these policies, though sometimes downplaying the failures of other countries with similar policies. Instead of arguing for or against such policies in the abstract, the focus should be on understanding under what conditions these, or other interventions, work.

Possibly any country will have a good chance of success with a reasonably wide range of policies in a context of macroeconomic stability and a capable public administration that can pragmatically choose sensible interventions and minimize the damage from mistaken ones. But will that be enough? The next section turns to another set of potentially important initial conditions related to the distribution of wealth and income.

22.8. THE FINAL BLOW TO THE IDEA OF THE UTILITY OF POVERTY?

A strain of thought dating back to the mercantilists has essentially argued that, whatever moral position one takes about poverty, a more unequal initial distribution of income allows a higher long-run mean income for any given initial mean. Since higher inequality at a given initial mean almost certainly entails higher poverty (by any standard measure) this amounts to an instrumental excuse for higher poverty now. In other words, by this view, one need not worry about poverty today as it will come with higher growth and (hence) less poverty in the future.

The precise form of this argument evolved over time, although incentives always played a role. Mercantilists worried about adverse effects of higher wages on work effort and export competitiveness. Later arguments switched to the idea that aggregate savings constrained growth. By this view, in a fully employed (closed) economy, capital accumulation was constrained by aggregate domestic savings, and saving is something rich people naturally do more of than poor people. Thus—the argument went—efforts to redistribute income in favor of the poor risked retarding growth and (hence) had ambiguous implications for poverty reduction.

---

[95] A good review of this class of policies and the debate surrounding them can be found in Harrison and Rodríguez-Clare (2010). Supportive discussions can be found in Rodrik (2004) and Lin (2012); a more critical perspective can be found in Pack and Saggi (2006).

The neoclassical theory of economic growth, as represented by the Solow (1956) model, was interpreted by some observers as implying that there was an automatic self-correcting process whereby a high initial level of poverty would eventually be reduced by economic growth. By this argument, countries starting out with a low mean income (and hence high absolute poverty rate) would tend to have a higher marginal product of capital (given that they had so much less capital per worker and that there are diminishing returns), which would entail a higher rate of economic growth when compared to growing high income countries with a similar rate of investment. And so the initially poorer country would eventually catch up. This was strictly a process of dynamic transition, not a model for explaining differences in the steady-state level of income. However, with suitable controls for the latter, a body of empirical work confirmed the prediction of conditional convergence, following an influential early contribution by Barro and Sala-i-Martin (1992).

Because the Solow model is an aggregate model, with no heterogeneity, it was questionable to use it to argue that poverty would be self-correcting. There was no inequality in this model.[96] And, even in his aggregate model, Solow was well aware of the potential for a "poverty trap" (though he did not use that term). Indeed, the original (1956) paper outlined one possible trap, arising from assumed nonlinearities in how population growth rates depend on mean income, with population growth falling at low incomes but rising with higher incomes, then tapering off at higher incomes. A country in a stable equilibrium but at low income would then need a large gain in capital per worker to escape the trap and move to a sustainably positive growth path.

The twentieth century saw another set of ideas, which challenged the "utility of poverty." (Recall that there was an early hint of this challenge in Marshall (1890)). It appears to have been long understood that rich people saved a greater share of income than poor people, who were often assumed to save nothing (as in the models of Kalecki, 1942 and Kaldor, 1955). It would then have been only a small step to the conclusion that a higher poverty rate at a given mean income would yield lower aggregate savings and (hence) a lower growth rate in any economy for which aggregate savings constrained growth. But that conclusion was never drawn to my knowledge. It was, however, understood at least starting in the 1930s that the same property of the savings function implied a growth-equity tradeoff, whereby higher inequality would generate higher savings and (hence) higher growth. Keynes (1936, Chapter 24) questioned the existence of such a tradeoff. His interpretation of the causes of unemployment predicted that it was lack

---

[96] There was much debate around this time concerning the assumption of an aggregate neoclassical production function, such as in the Solow model, which ignored the heterogeneity of capital. Defenders of that assumption argued that it was an analytically useful simplifying assumption, albeit an assumption that became a workhorse of modern macroeconomics. There is an insightful discussion of this debate in Bliss (1975, Chapter 8).

of consumption that prevented full employment, and so a higher share of national income in the command of poor people would promote growth until full employment was reached.

In the 1990s, a new set of ideas emerged that seriously questioned the instrumental case for poverty *and* inequality even in a fully employed economy. By this view, poor and/or unequal societies stifled investment, invention, and reform.[97] These ideas opened up a new window to the potential role of antipoverty policies in economic development.

One argument about why poverty would self-perpetuate in the absence of effective policies related to the idea that poverty would foster a high rate of population growth which would (in turn) entail lower growth. The last step in this argument is an implication of the Solow model discussed above. In that model, a higher rate of growth of the labor force dilutes the capital stock. A higher rate of population growth thus acts in a similar way to a higher rate of depreciation in lowering the steady-state level of capital per worker and (hence) mean income.[98] But what about the first step? The modern version of this argument emphasizes the role played by inequality. An undeniably important dimension of inequality in the world is that people living in poorer families tend to be less healthy and to die sooner. This and other factors—including a dependence on children for old-age support and inequalities in maternal education—play a key role in generating another socioeconomic gradient: fertility rates tend to be higher in poor families. On balance, the natural rate of population growth also tends to be higher for the poor. Thus, we can expect lower rates of progress against poverty in countries with higher population growth rates, and there is some supportive evidence for this view.[99]

An influential strain of thought in the late twentieth-century literature also pointed to the implications of borrowing constraints associated with asymmetric information and the inability to write binding enforceable contracts. Credit market failure leaves unexploited opportunities for investment in physical and human capital, and there is assumed to be a diminishing marginal product of capital. (This idea can also be extended to embrace technical innovation, assuming that everyone gets new ideas, but that the poor are more constrained in developing these ideas.) Then higher current inequality implies lower future mean wealth at a given value of current mean wealth.[100]

---

[97] See Loury (1981), Banerjee and Newman (1993), Perotti (1996), Hoff (1996), Aghion et al. (1999a,b), Bardhan et al. (2000), Ghatak and Jiang (2002), Banerjee and Duflo (2003), Azariadis (2006), and World Bank (2006, Chapter 5). Voitchovsky (2009) provides a survey of the arguments and evidence for how the initial level of inequality influences the subsequent growth rate.

[98] Evidence of an adverse effect of population growth on GDP per capita growth can be found in Kelley and Schmidt (1995, 2001) and Williamson (2001).

[99] Evidence can be found in Eastwood and Lipton (1999, 2001), who regressed changes over time in poverty measures for a cross section of countries on the fertility rate (with various controls) and found an adverse demographic effect on poverty. Using time series data for India, Datt and Ravallion (1998) found evidence that higher rates of population growth increased poverty.

[100] Models with such features include Loury (1981), Galor and Zeira (1993), Bénabou (1996), Aghion and Bolton (1997), and Banerjee and Duflo (2003).

The model outlined at the beginning of this chapter illustrates this point well in the special case in which the distribution of wealth (given production technologies) is such that the threshold is not binding ($w_t > k^{min}$ for everyone). Mean future wealth in a growing economy is then a weakly quasi-concave function of the distribution of current wealth. By standard properties of such functions, a mean-preserving increase in wealth inequality will entail lower mean wealth in the future, that is, a lower growth rate (Banerjee and Duflo, 2003). This is no longer true in general when the threshold is binding. Then there will exist increases in inequality embracing the lower end of the wealth distribution (below k^{min}) that can increase the growth rate of wealth. Thus, the type of model illustrated by Figure 22.1 has ambiguous implications for how much an exogenous reduction in inequality will promote overall growth. That depends crucially on precisely *where* in the distribution the reduction in inequality occurs.

Borrowing constraints is not the only way that inequality can matter to growth. Other models have also been proposed, implying that high inequality leads democratic governments to implement distortionary redistributive policies, as in the model of Alesina and Rodrik (1994). Another class of models is based on the idea that high inequality restricts efficiency-enhancing cooperation, such that key public goods are underprovided, or desirable economic and political reforms are blocked.[101] Rajan (2009a,b) provides an interesting analysis of how the two main types of economic reforms that are widely seen as key to poverty reduction, namely, making markets more competitive and expanding access to education, can be blocked in a democracy in which three classes—the rich oligopolists who benefit from market distortions, an educated middle class, and the uneducated poor supplying unskilled labor—strive to preserve their rents in the status quo. The model helps us understand the observations of Weiner (1991) and others about India's relative lack of progress in attaining mass literacy.

A new interpretation of the long-term impacts of colonialism has identified adverse effects of initial inequality on policies and institutions; Engerman and Sokoloff (2006) provide an overview. The essence of this argument is that the geographic patterns of colonialism (notably between North and South America) implanted greater initial inequality and population heterogeneity in some colonies than others. The main colonial origin of inequality is seen to have been the creation of European enclaves in the colonies that were greatly advantaged over the natives. The more unequal colonies had a harder time developing promotional antipoverty policies (such as mass schooling) that were favorable to both long-term growth and poverty reduction.

But is it inequality that matters to growth and poverty reduction or something else, such as poverty, the size of the middle class, or the extent of polarization? Inequality is obviously not the same thing as poverty; inequality can be reduced without a lower poverty measure by redistributing income among the nonpoor, and poverty can be reduced

---

[101] Arguments along these lines include Bardhan et al. (2000), Banerjee and Iyer (2005), Acemoglu and Robinson (2006), Rajan (2009a,b), and Stiglitz (2012).

without lower inequality. (Similarly, efforts to help the middle class may do little to relieve current poverty.) In fact, there is another implication of credit market failures that has received less attention until recently. Although the literature has emphasized that higher inequality in such an economy implies lower growth, so, too, does higher current wealth poverty for a given mean wealth.[102] Again, the point can be illustrated using the model outlined in Section 22.2. Plainly, a larger density of people near the zero wealth equilibrium will entail lower subsequent growth. What if the threshold is not binding? It is assumed that the poverty line does not exceed $k\star/(\lambda+1)$, and we can let H_t^* denote the poverty rate (headcount index) at this maximum poverty line. Now consider the growth effect of a mean-preserving increase in the poverty rate. I assume that H_t^* increases and that no individual with wealth less than $k\star/(\lambda+1)$ becomes better off. If this holds true, then we can say that poverty is unambiguously higher. Then the credit constraint implies that unambiguously higher poverty incidence—defined by any poverty line up to the minimum level of initial wealth needed to not be liquidity constrained—yields lower growth at a given level of mean current wealth. As this point does not appear to have been made in the literature, the Appendix demonstrates the point more formally.

This theory implies an aggregate efficiency cost of a high incidence of poverty. But note that the theoretical prediction concerns the level of poverty at a *given* initial value of mean wealth. Without controlling for the initial mean, the sign of the effect of higher poverty on growth is ambiguous (see the Appendix). Two opposing effects can be identified. The first is the conditional convergence property described above, whereby countries with a lower initial mean (and hence higher initial poverty) tend to have higher subsequent growth in a neoclassical growth model. Against this, there is an adverse distributional effect of higher poverty. Which effect dominates is an empirical question, which we will return to later in the chapter.

Credit market imperfections are not the only argument suggesting that poverty is a relevant parameter of the initial distribution. Lopez and Servén (2009) introduce a subsistence consumption requirement into the utility function in the model by Aghion et al. (1999a) and show that higher poverty incidence (failure to meet the subsistence requirement) implies lower growth. Another example can be found in the theories that have postulated impatience for consumption (high time preference rates possibly associated with low life expectancy) and hence low savings and investment rates by poor people (see, for example, Azariadis, 2006). Here, too, although the theoretical literature has focused on initial inequality, it can also be argued that a higher initial incidence of poverty means a higher proportion of impatient consumers and hence lower growth.

The potential inefficiency of poverty is starkly obvious when one considers how work productivity is likely to be affected by past nutritional intakes, as these determine the stock

---

[102] Ravallion (2001) argued intuitively that poverty retards growth when there are credit market failures.

of human capital.[103] As noted in Section 22.2, only when nutritional intake is high enough will it be possible to do any work, but diminishing returns to work will set in later; see the model in Dasgupta and Ray (1986). Poverty's effects on the nutrition of young children in poor families are also of special concern. A sizable body of research suggests that poor nutrition (both food energy intakes and micronutrients) in the early years of life retards children's growth, cognitive and learning abilities, schooling attainment, work productivity, and likely earnings in adulthood.[104] The health environment also matters. Chronic undernutrition in children can stem from either low nutritional intake or low nutritional absorption due to constant fecal–oral contamination,[105] such as due to the lack of clean drinking water. This can mean that direct nutritional supplementation does little or nothing to improve children's nutritional status (such as measured by stunting) until the health environment improves.[106] This type of argument can be broadened to include other aspects of child development that have lasting impacts on learning ability and earnings as an adult (Cunha and Heckman, 2007). And the handicap of poverty can emerge in the prenatal period. Maternal and prenatal conditions are now also thought to matter to child development and (hence) economic outcomes later in life (Currie, 2011; Dasgupta, 2011). By implication, having a larger share of the population who were born in and grow up in poverty (including living in poor health environments) will have a lasting negative impact on an economy's aggregate output. Poverty will perpetuate.

In another strain of thinking about how poverty can perpetuate, Mani et al. (2013) present evidence from both experimental and observational studies, suggesting that poverty reduces cognitive ability. The evidence is consistent with the view that, given that human cognitive capacity is physically limited, the concerns generated by poverty crowd out thinking about other things relevant to personal economic advancement.

There are also theoretical arguments involving market and institutional development, although this is not a topic that has received as much attention in the literature. Although past theories have often believed credit market failures to be exogenous, poverty may well be a deeper causative factor in financial development (as well as an outcome of the lack of financial development). For example, given a fixed cost of lending (both for each loan and for setting up the lending institution), liquidity constraints can emerge as the norm in very poor societies.

Some of the theoretical literature has also pointed to the possibilities for multiple equilibria associated with a nonconvexity in the production possibility set, as in Figure 22.1. As noted already, in poor countries, the nutritional requirements for work

---

[103] Strauss and Thomas (1998) review evidence of this relationship. A useful overview of the biomedical arguments and evidence can be found in Dasgupta (2011).

[104] For useful overviews of the evidence, see Alderman et al. (2006), Benton (2010), and Currie (2011).

[105] This is known as environmental enteropathy (see, for example, Korpe and Petri, 2012).

[106] Kinsey (2013) identifies this as one possible reason why the incidence of chronic undernutrition has not fallen in his panel data for Zimbabwe.

can readily generate such nonlinearity in the dynamics, as argued by Dasgupta (1997). Such a model predicts that a large exogenous income gain may be needed to attain a permanently higher income and that seemingly similar aggregate shocks can have dissimilar outcomes; growth models with such features are also discussed in Day (1992) and Azariadis (1996, 2006) among others. Sachs (2005a,b) has invoked such models to argue that a large expansion of development aid would be needed to ensure a permanently higher average income in currently poor countries.

Some of the empirical literature on economic growth has found that higher initial inequality impedes growth.[107] And the effect is quantitatively large, as well as statistically significant. Consider the two most recent published studies at the time of this writing. Herzer and Vollmer (2012) find that a 1% point increase in the Gini index results in a decrease in long-term mean income of 0.013%; when normalized by standard deviations, this is about half the growth impact of the investment share. Berg et al. (2012) also find that more unequal countries tend to have less sustained spells of growth, and this effect is also quite large; a 1% point higher Gini index is associated with a decline in the length of the growth spell of 11–15%.

Not all the evidence has been supportive.[108] The main reason why some studies have been less supportive appears to be that they have allowed for additive country-level fixed effects in growth rates. This specification addresses the problem of time-invariant latent heterogeneity in growth rates. However, it may well have little power to detect the true relationships given that the changes over time in growth rates will almost certainly have a low signal-to-noise ratio. Simulation studies have found that the coefficients on growth determinants are heavily biased toward zero in fixed-effects growth regressions (Hauk and Wacziarg, 2009).

There are a number of remaining issues in this literature. The bulk of the literature has used consumption or income inequality measures. Theoretical arguments based on borrowing constraints point to the importance of asset inequality, not income inequality *per se*. There is evidence of adverse effects of asset inequality on growth.[109]

The aspect of initial distribution that has received almost all the attention in the empirical literature is inequality, as typically measured by the Gini index of (relative) inequality. The popularity of the Gini index appears to owe more to its availability in secondary data compilations on income and consumption inequality measures than to any intrinsic relevance to the economic arguments.[110] However, as Lopez and Servén

---

[107] See Alesina and Rodrik (1994), Rodrik (1994), Persson and Tabellini (1994), Birdsall et al. (1995), Clarke (1995), Perotti (1996), Deininger and Squire (1998), Knowles (2005), Voitchovsky (2005), Herzer and Vollmer (2012), and Berg et al. (2012).

[108] See Li and Zou (1998), Barro (2000), and Forbes (2000).

[109] See Rodrik (1994), Birdsall and Londono (1997), and Deininger and Olinto (2000), all using cross-country data, and Ravallion (1998), using regional data for China.

[110] The compilation of Gini indices from secondary sources (not using consistent assumptions) in Deininger and Squire (1996) led to almost all the tests in the literature since that paper was published.

(2009) observe, the significance of the Gini index in past studies may reflect an omitted variable bias, given that one expects that inequality will be highly correlated with poverty at a given mean.

There are also issues about the relevant control variables when studying the effect of initial distribution on growth. The specification choices in past work testing for effects of initial distribution have lacked clear justification in terms of the theories predicting such effects. Consider three popular predictors of growth, namely, human development, the investment share, and financial development. Of the first predictor, basic schooling and health attainments (often significant in growth regressions) are arguably one of the channels linking initial distribution to growth. Indeed, that is the link in the original papers of Loury (1981) and Galor and Zeira (1993).[111] The second predictor, one of the most robust predictors of growth rates, is the share of investment in GDP (Levine and Renelt, 1992); yet, arguably one of the main channels through which distribution affects growth is via aggregate investment, and this investment is one of the channels identified in the theoretical literature. Finally, consider private credit (as a share of GDP), which has been used as a measure of "financial sector development" in explaining growth and poverty reduction (Beck et al., 2000, 2007). The theories discussed above based on borrowing constraints suggest that the aggregate flow of credit in the economy depends on the initial distribution.

Although the theories and evidence reviewed above point to inequality and/or poverty as the relevant parameters of the initial distribution, yet another strain of the literature has pointed to various reasons why the size of a country's *middle class* can matter to the fortunes of those not (yet) so lucky to be middle class. It has been argued that a larger middle class promotes economic growth by fostering entrepreneurship, shifting the composition of consumer demand, and making it more politically feasible to attain policy reforms and institutional changes conducive to growth.[112] This has been an issue in India, where, since the 1970s, it has been argued that "inequality" constrained the growth of the manufacturing sector by limiting the size of the domestic market for consumer goods; see, for example, the discussion in Bardhan (1984b, Chapter 4). Here, too, it can be argued that it was not inequality *per se* that was the culprit but the relatively small middle class, or (more or less equivalently) the extent of absolute poverty that generated the domestic demand constraint in a relatively closed economy. The argument has been heard less in the more open economies. However, the Indian middle class has also been seen to promote reform (Sridharan, 2004). Using cross-country regressions, Easterly (2001) finds

---

[111] More recently, Gutiérrez and Tanaka (2009) have shown how high initial inequality in a developing country can yield a political economy equilibrium in which there is little or no public investment in basic schooling; the poorest families send their kids to work, and the richest turn to private schooling.

[112] Analyses of the role of the middle class in promoting entrepreneurship and growth include Acemoglu and Zilibotti (1997) and Doepke and Zilibotti (2005). Middle class demand for higher quality goods plays a role in the model of Murphy et al. (1989). Birdsall et al. (2000) conjecture that support from the middle class is crucial to reform.

that a larger income share controlled by the middle three quintiles is a significant predictor of rates of economic growth.

So we have three main contenders for the distributional parameter most relevant to growth: inequality, poverty, and the size of the middle class. The fact that very few encompassing tests are found in the literature and that these different measures of distribution are not independent, leaves one in doubt about what aspect of distribution really matters. As already noted, when the initial value of mean income is included in a growth regression alongside initial inequality, but initial poverty is an excluded but still relevant variable, the inequality measure may pick up the effect of poverty rather than inequality *per se*. Similarly, the main way the middle class expands in a developing country is almost certainly through poverty reduction, so it is unclear whether it is a high incidence of poverty or a small middle class that impedes growth. Similarly, a relative concept of the "middle class," such as the income share of middle quintiles, will probably be highly correlated with a relative inequality measure, clouding the interpretation.

Possibly, the strongest evidence to date to support the view that it is poverty not inequality *per se* that impedes growth in developing countries comes from an observation made by Ravallion (2012b), namely, that we see convergence in average living standards among developing countries and greater progress against poverty in faster growing economies, yet we do not see poverty convergence; the poorest countries are not enjoying higher proportionate rates of poverty reduction. Ravallion resolves this paradox by arguing that a high initial incidence of poverty, at a given initial mean, impedes subsequent growth (this theory is compatible with a number of the theories outlined above). This is shown to be consistent with data for almost 100 developing countries, which reveal an adverse effect on consumption growth of high initial poverty incidence at a given initial mean. Ravallion finds that high poverty at a given initial mean matters more than inequality or measures of the middle class or polarization. Also, starting with a high incidence of poverty limits progress against poverty at any given growth rate. For many poor countries, the growth advantage of starting out with a low mean is lost due to their high poverty rates. That does not, however, imply that any antipoverty policy will promote growth. That will depend on many factors, as discussed in the next section.

The arguments summarized above about why poverty can bring lasting efficiency costs do not require the existence of a poverty trap. However, when a poverty trap is present, the cost of poverty can rise greatly. So it is important to ask whether such traps have economic significance. On *a priori* grounds, it is highly plausible that threshold effects exist. Biology alone makes this plausible; unless one can support the nutritional needs of the body at rest, it will be impossible to do any work. Whether this is of economic significance in practice (even in poor economies) is another matter. As Deaton (2006) points out (in reviewing Fogel, 2004), human caloric requirements can be covered with seemingly modest spending on food staples.[113] However, this is not conclusive. Environmental enteropathy can generate quite low nutrition absorption rates given the persistent fecal–oral contamination of the environments in which many people live. In effect, the implicit price of an absorbed calorie capable of fueling work effort is higher, possibly far higher, than the nominal price. Furthermore, we have also learned that work productivity depends on the personal history of nutrition and health, as argued by Dasgupta (2011). Someone whose growth is stunted due to a long history of undernutrition—low intakes and/or low absorption—can be in current nutritional balance (able to afford current food energy requirements) but have such low productivity that a poverty trap emerges. It may not be a strict threshold, as in Figure 22.1, but a smoother, S-shaped function.

Other sources of threshold effects are also plausible on *a priori* grounds, such as the fact that a minimum level of schooling is essential before schooling can be a viable route out of poverty (recalling the story of Sunil in Boo, 2012). One can also interpret the aforementioned arguments about how poverty reduces cognitive functions as stemming from biological threshold effects—that a minimum level of time not worrying about the financial and other stresses created by poverty is needed to escape poverty (Mani et al., 2013).

In testing for threshold effects, some of the literature has looked for lumpiness in non-human capital requirements. The results have been mixed. Mesnard and Ravallion (2006) find evidence of nonlinear wealth effects on new business start-ups in Tunisia, but they do not find signs of thresholds effects. Nor do McKenzie and Woodruff (2006) find any sign of nonconvexities in production at low levels among Mexican microenterprises. In one of the few studies using wealth data, Barrett et al. (2006) do find evidence of the nonconvexity in asset data for rural Kenya and Madagascar.[114]

It can also be difficult to detect theoretically plausible threshold effects on dynamics in standard microdata sets (Day, 1992). For one thing, depending on the frequency of the observations over time in the data, the existence of the unstable "middle" equilibrium (point B in Figure 22.1) can generate attrition—the destitute simply drop out of the data (including by becoming homeless) (Lokshin and Ravallion, 2004). Also, there will be high social returns and risk-sharing arrangements to prevent most people falling into the trap. The trap is still there, but it may only be evident in extreme situations when those social relationships break down, as Ravallion (1997b) argues is the case during famines.

A testable implication of the models based on credit market failures is that individual wealth should be an increasing concave function of its own past value. In principle, this

---

[113] Subramanian and Deaton (1996) calculate that nutritional requirements can be met with a small fraction of the daily wage rate, using data for India. Similar reasoning leads Swamy (1997) to question the nutrition-based efficiency wage hypothesis.

[114] Also see the discussion in Carter and Barrett (2006).

can be tested on suitable micropanel data, though most data sets only show consumption or income, not wealth. Lokshin and Ravallion (2004) provide supporting evidence of concavity in panel data on incomes for Hungary and Russia while Jalan and Ravallion (2004) do so using panel data for China. These studies do not find the threshold properties in the empirical income dynamics that would be needed for a poverty trap. Using similar methods, but arguably a better identification strategy, Dercon and Outes (2013) find evidence of a low, unstable equilibrium in the income dynamics for a long panel of households in rural India.

Microempirical support for the claim that there are efficiency costs of poor nutrition and health care for children in poor families has come from a number of studies. In a recent example, an impact evaluation by Macours et al. (2008) of a conditional cash transfer (CCT) scheme in Nicaragua found that randomly assigned transfers to poor families improved the cognitive outcomes of children through higher intakes of nutrition-rich foods and better health care. This echoes a number of findings about the benefits to disadvantaged children of efforts to compensate for family poverty.[115]

The upshot of all this data is that present-day thinking is both more optimistic about the prospects of eliminating poverty through an expanding economy and more cognizant of the conditionalities in the gains to poor people from economic growth. Under the right conditions, growth can be a powerful force against poverty. Those conditions pertain in large part to aspects of both the initial distribution and how it evolves. As we will see in the following section, the focus of much antipoverty policy has shifted over time toward efforts to ensure that the conditions in place will allow poor people to contribute to an expanding overall economy, and so escape poverty permanently.

22.9. DIRECT INTERVENTIONS IN MODERN TIMES

If all incomes are observable and there are no behavioral responses, then guaranteeing a minimum income is straightforward—one simply makes transfers sufficient to bring everyone up to that minimum. Administrative capabilities, constraints on information, and incentive effects have meant that the practice of social policy is far more complicated. A range of interventions has emerged. This section discusses some generic issues—information, incentives, and policy design—before reviewing the main types of direct interventions found today.[116]

22.9.1 Generic Issues

The stage of development influences the types of policies needed. Poor places tend as a rule to have weaker administrative capabilities, which tends to mean less reliable

---

[115] For reviews of this literature, see Currie (2001, 2012).

[116] This section summarizes material from a much fuller discussion of antipoverty policy in Ravallion (2015).

information for deciding who should receive help. More universal (probably state-contingent) and/or self-targeted policies can thus have greater appeal in developing countries (including when the rich countries of today were developing), notably when there is a large informal sector. By contrast, the income tax system and means-tested transfer payments that require formalization tend to dominate in rich countries.

The existence of a large informal sector is associated with both information and incentive constraints on social policy in developing countries. The information constraints are obvious, given that informality essentially means that one has little systematic data about actual or potential beneficiaries. The incentive constraint comes from the fact that the informal sector is a feasible option for anyone in the formal sector (though the converse is less true). Thus, a social policy that can apply only to a formal-sector worker will have an added efficiency cost (through the scope for substitution) that would not be the case in a purely formal, developed economy.[117]

Incentive effects have figured in the debates about all forms of targeted direct interventions across all settings. A perfectly targeted set of transfers to poor families in the imaginary world of complete information—meaning that the transfers exactly fill the poverty gaps and so bring everyone up to the desired minimum income—would impose 100% marginal tax rates on recipients. This is very unlikely to be optimal from the point of view of poverty reduction given labor supply responses. One hundred and forty years after the famous debates over the reforms to England's Poor Laws, a rigorous formulation of the problem of redistributive policy with incentive effects was finally available in the form of Mirrless's (1971) optimal tax model. The Mirrless objective function was utilitarian, but his approach could also be adapted to an explicit poverty reduction objective. The simulations by Kanbur et al. (1994) suggested that marginal tax rates around 60–70% would be called for in an optimal antipoverty policy using transfers, allowing for incentive effects.[118]

At the opposite extreme to perfect targeting one can imagine a *basic income scheme*, which provides a fixed cash transfer to every person, whether poor or not.[119] This has been advocated by (among others) Paine (1797), Rhys-Williams (1943), Meade (1972), Raventós (2007), and Bardhan (2011). The idea has spanned both rich and poor countries, and the political spectrum from left to right. There are no substitution effects of the transfers because there is no action that anyone can take to change their transfer receipts, but there will be income effects (including higher demand for leisure, though how much so is unclear). There is no stigma associated with participation, given that there is no purposive targeting to poor people. A complete assessment of the implications

---

[117] Similarly, informal sector firms can evade taxation by resorting to cash (Gordon and Li, 2009).

[118] Also see Kanbur and Tuomala (2011) on alternative characterizations of the policy objective.

[119] This has been called many things including a "poll transfer," "guaranteed income," "citizenship income," and an "unmodified social dividend."

for efficiency (and equity) must take account of the methods of financing the scheme. The administrative cost would probably be low though certainly not zero given that some form of personal registration system would probably be needed to avoid "double dipping" and to ensure that larger households receive proportionately more money. Proposals in developed countries have typically allowed for financing through a progressive income tax (such as in Meade, 1972), in which case the idea becomes formally similar to the Negative Income Tax (Friedman, 1962) though the mode of administration may differ. Atkinson and Sutherland (1989) demonstrate that a basic income scheme can be devised as a feasible budget-neutral way of integrating social benefits and income taxation in Britain. In poor countries, a basic income scheme could be costly, depending on the benefit level and method of financing, although there may well be ample scope for financing by cutting current subsidies favoring the nonpoor, as Bardhan (2011) argues is the case for India. This type of scheme would appear to dominate many policies found in practice today; for example, it would clearly yield a better incidence than subsidies on the consumption of normal goods, which is a type of policy still found in a number of countries. However, as yet there have been very few examples of universal uniform cash transfer schemes in practice. (An example in Bolivia is discussed below.)

The bulk of the direct interventions found in practice fall somewhere between the above extremes of "perfect targeting" and a basic income with no targeting. In countries where income means testing is a feasible option (mostly rich countries), the benefit level can be progressively phased out as income rises above some level, below which some guaranteed support is provided. The rate of benefit withdrawal depends on the strength of the expected labor supply response. With the better data and analytic tools available today, it can be hoped that future policy debates will be better informed about actual behavioral responses. However, from what we know already about labor supply responses, it is evident that poor people gain significantly from transfers in a country such as the United States (Saez, 2006).

The recent emphasis on targeting in many countries (both rich and poor) has typically been defined as avoiding "leakage" of benefits to the nonpoor, implicitly downplaying concerns about coverage of the poor (as pointed out by Cornia and Stewart, 1995). Readily measurable proxies for poverty are widely used for such targeting in settings in which income means-testing of benefits is not an option. Efficiency considerations point to the need to use indicators that are not easily manipulated by actual or potential beneficiaries, although this is rarely very clear in practice. Geographic proxies have been common, as has gender of the recipient, family size, and housing conditions.[120] These targeting methods can be thought of as a "proxy means test" (PMT) in which transfers are allocated on the basis of a score for each household that can be interpreted as predicted

---

[120] Grosh et al. (2008) provide a useful overview of the targeting methods found in practice in developing countries, with details on many examples.

income or consumption, based on readily observed indicators. Depending on how it is designed, this type of scheme can have better incentive effects than perfect means testing and have a higher impact on poverty for a given outlay than a poll transfer. The main alternative method of targeting found in practice uses communities themselves to decide who is in greatest need. This exploits local information that is not normally available for the PMT, but it does so at the risk of exploitation by local elites.[121] However, policy advisors and policy makers sometimes appear to have treated "better targeting" as the objective of the policy design problem, forgetting that it is really only an instrument, and not necessarily the best instrument given the aforementioned costs and the political economy response to targeting, whereby finely targeted programs can undermine the political support for social policies.[122]

22.9.2 State-Contingent Transfers Financed by Taxation

Recall that the essential idea of England's Old Poor Laws was state-contingent transfers financed by taxation. There was little effort at explicit targeting of relief (before the 1834 reforms, which we return to later), although there was some degree of self-targeting given that relatively well-off families would be reticent to turn to the parish for assistance after some economic shock.

   The idea of untargeted state-contingent transfers (as in the Old Poor Laws) reemerged in twentieth century Britain in the form of the *Beveridge Report* (Beveridge, 1942), which outlined detailed proposals for social insurance, whereby all those of working age would be obliged to pay a national insurance contribution to finance state-contingent transfers to the unemployed, the sick, the elderly, or widowed. However, unlike the Old Poor Laws, this was to be a national scheme rather than implemented locally. Two other elements completed the social protection policy. First, family allowances were proposed, to cover the costs of dependent children (after the first). Second, an income top-up was proposed for those who fell below absolute standards taking account of all income sources.[123] Although the aim of these proposals was squarely to eliminate poverty, Beveridge was opposed to means-testing—universal provision at a flat-rate was seen to avoid the costs of targeting and to encourage social cohesion.[124] The past, deliberately stigmatizing,

---

[121] Discussions of community-based targeting can be found in Alderman (2002), Galasso and Ravallion (2005), Mansuri and Rao (2012), and Alatas et al. (2012). The latter paper compares this form of targeting with PMT for a cash transfer program in Indonesia. The study finds that PMT does somewhat better at reaching the poor, but community-based targeting better accords with local perceptions of poverty and is better accepted by local residents.

[122] For further discussion, see van de Walle (1998), De Donder and Hindriks (1998), and Gelbach and Pritchett (2000).

[123] This came to be known as the "Supplementary Benefit" and became more important in practice than Beveridge envisaged; see the discussion in Meade (1972).

[124] There is an interesting discussion of Beveridge's arguments in Thane (2000, especially, Chapter 19).

approach typified by the workhouses was to be abandoned. Beveridge's plan formed the basis for the policies of the new Labour government elected in 1945; the Conservative resistance to the (popular) Beveridge plan helped ensure a Labour victory (Thane, 2000, p. 369).

America's Social Security system had also grown out of prior relief efforts (notably those established during the depression) and came to provide fairly comprehensive state-contingent transfers, financed by taxation, soon after World War II. As with the Poor Laws, there was much debate about these policies. (America's Social Security system was, and still is, decried as "socialism" in some quarters.) Similar to the 1834 reforms to the Poor Laws, calls for targeting have become common since 1980 in an attempt to reduce the fiscal cost of social insurance.

Uniform but state-contingent transfers are not common in developing countries today. It seems that developing countries have largely skipped this stage in the history of social policy. However, it is not entirely clear why this is the case or that it is a good idea from the point of view of sound policy making. To explain why uniform state-contingent transfers of the social insurance type are not used, it is sometimes claimed that such policies are unsuitable to poor economies; they would be too costly, and targeting is needed. Although the fiscal burden of social policies must never be ignored, it is notable that the Old Poor Laws were invented in what was clearly a poor economy by today's standards. For some 300 years, the Old Poor Laws provided a degree of social protection and stability at a seemingly modest cost (Solar, 1995).

As we will see, although better targeting may help, finely targeted policies have costs that are often hidden but must be considered in any proper evaluation of the policy options.

22.9.3 Workfare

The workhouses that emerged in Europe around 1600 can be interpreted as a means of getting around the information and incentive problems of targeting. Design features encouraged those truly in need of help to turn to the workhouse *and* encouraged them to leave it when help was no longer needed, given that there were better options in the rest of the economy. This solves the information problem of targeting. However, it does so by imposing costs on participants, notably the forgone earnings and the welfare costs of stigma and subjugation (as Oliver Twist experienced). A truly utilitarian–welfarist assessment relative to untargeted transfers would clearly be ambiguous without further evidence. Arguably England's workhouses of the nineteenth century went too far in imposing costs, which came to be widely seen as objectionable, on participants to ensure self-targeting. But the idea of self-targeting had lasting influence.

The workhouses are an example of a class of direct interventions often called today "workfare schemes"—schemes that impose work requirements on welfare recipients as a means of ensuring incentive compatibility. Though not involving workhouses, this idea was embodied in the Famine Codes introduced in British India around 1880, and the idea has continued to play an important role to this day on the subcontinent (Drèze, 1990a). Such schemes have helped in responding to, and preventing, famines, including those in Sub-Saharan Africa (Drèze, 1990b). Workfare was also a key element of the New Deal introduced by US President Roosevelt in 1933 in response to the Great Depression.

An important subclass of workfare schemes has aimed to guarantee employment to anyone who wants it at a predetermined (typically low) wage rate. Employment Guarantee Schemes (EGSs) have been popular in South Asia, notably (though not only) in India where the Maharashtra EGS, which started in 1973, was long considered a model. In 2005, the central government implemented a national version, the Mahatma Gandhi National Rural EGS. This promises 100 days of work per year per rural household to those willing to do unskilled manual labor at the statutory minimum wage listed for the program. The work requirement is (more or less explicitly) seen as a means of ensuring that the program reaches India's rural poor.[125]

These schemes can be interpreted as attempts to enforce a minimum wage rate in situations in which there is no other means of legal enforcement. Minimum wages appeared in the late nineteenth century, with the first minimum wage law introduced by New Zealand in 1894. Critics have long pointed to concerns about negative effects on overall employment of minimum wages rates, although advocates have pointed out that those effects may be small in practice and even positive in monopsonistic labor markets. However, enforcement of minimum wage legislation has been famously weak in developing countries with large informal sectors (including traditional farming). For example, Murgai and Ravallion (2005) show that in 2004–2005, three-quarters of India's casual labor was paid less than the country's (state-level) statutory minimum wage rates. In an EGS, anyone who wants work can (in theory) get it provided they are willing to do unskilled manual labor at the statutory minimum wage rate in agriculture.

An important difference between an EGS and minimum wage legislation is that an EGS aims to provide comprehensive insurance for the able-bodied poor, in that anyone who needs work can get it, at least on paper. Eligibility is open to all, so that a farmer who would not need the scheme in normal times can turn to it during a drought (say). This concept was explicit from the outset of the idea of an EGS (as it developed in Maharashtra in the early 1970s). Whether this insurance function is served in practice is another matter; Dutta et al. (2012) find evidence of considerable rationing on India's national EGS. The rationing tends to be greater in poorer states, which may well reflect their weaker administrative capabilities to implement a complex program such as India's national EGS.

---

[125] Dutta et al. (2013) provide an assessment. Also see Jha et al. (2012), Gaiha (1997), and Imbert and Papp (2011).

These schemes illustrate that even a well-targeted transfer scheme can be dominated by untargeted transfers when one takes account of all the costs involved, such as income forgone or other costs in complying with the conditionalities imposed. Ravallion and Datt (1995) and Murgai et al. (2013) provide evidence that in both the Maharashtra EGS and India's new national scheme, an untargeted basic income scheme would have been more cost-effective in directly transferring incomes to poor people.

Workfare schemes have typically been seen as short-term palliatives—a form of social insurance. In principle, a workfare scheme can also directly serve promotional goals. One way is by generating assets that could change the wealth distribution or shift the production function, which could also allow people to break out of the poverty trap illustrated in Figure 22.1. In practice, asset creation has not been given much weight in these schemes in South Asia, although it seems to have greater weight elsewhere, including in Latin America (such as Argentina's Trabajar Program).

Another way that workfare programs can better serve the promotional goal is by tying benefits to efforts to enhance human capital through training. Welfare reforms in many rich countries since the early 1990s have aimed to make transfers conditional on investments in human capital and to incentivize searching for and finding private employment.[126] This form of workfare does not actually provide employment, as in the public works form of workfare. Training and encouragements for private-sector employment using wage subsidies have also been used to encourage the transition from public employment in workfare schemes to private employment.[127]

Next we turn to a policy for which the creation of human wealth is seen as crucial to poverty reduction.

22.9.4 Schooling for Children from Poor Families

Children from poor families tend to get less schooling. This "economic gradient" in schooling persists to this day almost everywhere and has long been seen as a factor that perpetuates poverty across generations—a potential source of a poverty trap. As noted in Section 22.5, the inability of poor families to finance their children's schooling given credit market failures came to be recognized as a key factor in perpetuating poverty and entailing that a more unequal initial wealth distribution will generate aggregate efficiency costs.[128] Thus, policies that can promote the schooling of children from poor families can be seen as an important part of social policy that could improve both equity and efficiency, and credibly allow people to escape poverty permanently.

---

[126] Hemerijck (2014) provides an overview of such reforms in Europe.

[127] An example is the Proempleo scheme in Argentina studied by Galasso et al. (2004).

[128] Physical accessibility is sometimes identified as another factor. However, the simulations by Filmer (2007) do not suggest that this is a major factor in the schooling gap between rich and poor in developing countries; Filmer finds that very large reductions in distance to school would be needed to close the gap.

Such policies are a modern idea, advocated at times but little known in practice before the nineteenth century (see Section 22.5). Past and ongoing policy debates over mass education have raised many issues, but a fundamental one is whether compulsory schooling is even in the interest of poor families, for it was typically their children who were unschooled. Opponents (on both the left and right) of compulsory schooling pointed to the costs (primarily their forgone earnings) to poor families of sending their children to school. While compulsory schooling could break the poverty trap, a short-term trade-off was created by the costs to poor families. Advocates argued, in effect, that the longer-term benefits from breaking out of a poverty trap outweighed these costs.

After much debate, compulsory schooling emerged in virtually all industrialized countries by the early twentieth century, with a significant state role in both public provision and support for private schooling. In England, the Elementary Education Act of 1870 was a breakthrough law that established a secular public sector institutional framework, including democratic school boards. Implementation was uneven geographically, and there was a continuing struggle for control of schools between the democratically elected local bodies and religious organizations (Stephens, 1998). It was not until the 1880 act of the same name that education was compulsory in England for children aged 5–10. A similar act was passed in France about the same time. In the United States, 34 states had compulsory schooling laws by 1900, 30 of which required attendance until at least age 14. Japan in the Meiji period (1868–1912) was not behind the West in promoting mass education, which was virtually universal by the end of the period. Mass public education (with tertiary education left largely to the private sector) was given high priority throughout developing East Asia, with educational attainments far surpassing those of most developing countries and even some developed countries.

The payoffs from mass public education were huge. Equitable, broad-based education has been identified by Goldin and Katz (2008) as a key factor in the US record of relatively equitable and rapid economic growth in the period 1940–1980. The ability of the school system to support a relatively rapid increase in education attainments in the United States in this period (though slowing down greatly after 1980) meant that the supply of skilled workers kept up with the extra demand stemming from new technologies—what Tinbergen (1975) dubbed the "race between education and technology"—thus attenuating the inequality-increasing effects of technical progress favoring demand for relatively skilled labor. The fact that American educational expansion was so broad-based in this period was key. A more elitist school system would have entailed a more unequal distribution of the gains from growth. And Goldin and Katz argue that rising inequality in the United States since 1980 stems in large part from the fact that the education system has not allowed the supply of the types of skilled labor required for the new technologies of the time to keep up with the demand. And it tends to be children from poor families who are most disadvantaged in this race.

Broad-based education has also been identified as a key factor in East Asia's relatively equitable growth. Using a regression of GDP per capita growth rates from 1960 to 1985 on primary and secondary education attainments in 1960—with controls for initial GDP per capita, population growth, and the share of investment in GDP—an influential report by the World Bank (1993) identified primary education as the most important single factor, accounting for somewhere between 58% (Japan) and 87% (Thailand) of GDP growth. Of course, such calculations can be sensitive to model specification; the education variables could well be correlated with other omitted factors. However, it is nonetheless striking that primary education is found to account for a greater share of the variance in growth rates than private (nonhuman) investment.

There is also evidence that education attainments have interacted strongly with India's growth process in determining the impact of that growth on poverty. This was demonstrated by Ravallion and Datt (2002) by comparing rates of poverty reduction among India's states. While the elasticities of measured poverty to farm yields did not vary significantly across states, those for nonfarm output did. The nonfarm growth process tended to reduce poverty more significantly in states with initially higher literacy rates, and interstate differences in literacy rates were the dominant factor among those identified by Ravallion and Datt. The importance of mass education has long been acknowledged in principle in India. A "directive principle" of state policy in the 1949 Constitution was free compulsory education to the age of 14.[129] However, implementation of this policy has lagged considerably, with large interstate differences and often poor quality schooling across the country (Probe Team, 1999). The state that has made the most progress in mass public education is Kerala. Expanding literacy to the whole population was a high priority of the state government from the 1950s (building on a history of prior successes in schooling provided by Christian missionaries dating back to the early nineteenth century). The results of Ravallion and Datt (2002) indicate that Kerala's success in mass schooling has generated a far more propoor process of nonfarm economic growth than is found in other states.

Bans on child labor have often been proposed and legislated. Hazan and Berdugo (2002) model an interesting version of a poverty trap in which, at the early stage of development, child labor is abundant while fertility is high, and mean output is low. With economic growth stemming from technical progress, the returns to schooling rise, making child labor less attractive and also lowering fertility. In this model, the economy eventually converges to a new equilibrium in which child labor has vanished. Hazan and Berdugo show that an effective ban on child labor will speed up the transition to this new equilibrium.

However, in economies with large informal sectors, the enforcement of such bans is difficult. Legislation to set a minimum working age was introduced in some countries

---

[129] A Right to Education Act was passed by India's parliament in 2009, essentially ratifying the Constitution.

from the late nineteenth century, although it is unclear how much this helped reduce the incidence of child labor; Moehling's (1999) analysis suggests this legislation had little effect. Basu (1999) argues that compulsory schooling is a better way of implementing a ban on child labor than an actual ban, and compulsory schooling can also break the poverty trap.

22.9.5 Policy Incentives for Schooling

Although out-of-pocket expenses and the forgone earnings of children figured in the nineteenth-century debates about the idea of compulsory education, there was not much discussion of the obvious policy response: a bursary, or scholarship grant, for poor families. Smith (1776) and Mill (1859, Chapter 5) had advocated tuition subsidies for children from poor families. Marshall (1890, p. 594) took a less sympathetic attitude and proposed instead penalizing poor parents (a public policy of "paternal discipline") who neglected to send their children to school or to care for their health. Educational institutions have for a long time subsidized tuition fees and other costs for selected students, often based on some sort of means test. England's 1870 Elementary Education Act recommended tuition subsidies for children from poor families (Gillie, 1996). However, implementation of public policies providing any form of schooling incentive for poor parents had to wait until the middle of the twentieth century, after which it started to become common practice to build in incentives for children from poor families to stay in school. Britain's 1942 *Beveridge Report* recommended a universal child allowance paid up to the age of 16 if the child stayed in school.[130] Australia had a school bursary program from the 1960s that essentially paid parents from poor families to keep their children in school beyond the age the children would normally leave school as long as the children passed a special exam. It is common today for various forms of education subsidies (scholarships, tuition subsidies, subsidized loans) to be means-tested.

In the development literature in the 1990s, targeted bursaries came to be known as CCTs.[131] The idea was the same: a monetary incentive for poor parents to keep their children in school. Transfers are made under the condition that the children of the recipient family demonstrate adequate school attendance (and health care in some versions of the policy). Plainly, the promotion benefits of these programs rest on ensuring that the transfers go to poor families, presuming that the children of the nonpoor will already be in school. Thus, targeting has been instrumentally important to both the protection and promotion benefits. The promotion benefits also depend on designing the conditions so that the required level of schooling would not be attained in the absence of the program. Early influential examples of these programs in developing countries were

---

[130] Similarly, the US Earned Income Tax Credit (introduced in 1975) gives different age cut offs for full-time students.

[131] Most other direct interventions also have conditions; for example, workfare entails a work requirement.

Mexico's PROGRESA program (now called Oportunidades) and Bolsa Escola in Brazil. Another early example was the Food-for-Education Program in Bangladesh for which the transfers (targeted to poor families) were made in kind but were also conditional on school attendance. Bolivia's CCT, Bono Juancito Pinto, introduced in 2006, is an example of a universal (untargeted) transfer program, for which every child enrolled in public school is eligible, irrespective of family income. More than 30 developing countries now have CCT programs, and the number is growing (World Bank, 2014). And other countries have similar policies that are not called CCTs; for example, in an attempt to ensure that poverty did not constrain schooling, since 2002 China has had a "two exemptions, one subsidy" policy for students from poor rural families; the exemptions are for tuition fees and textbooks, and the subsidy is for living costs.

These programs are clearly designed with a view to breaking the poverty trap stemming from the aforementioned economic gradient in human development. If the sole concern was with current income gains to participating households, then a policy maker would not impose schooling requirements, which entail a cost to poor families by incentivizing them to withdraw children or teenagers from the labor force, thus reducing the (net) income gain to poor people. The idea of these programs is to strike a balance between protection and promotion, based on the presumption that poor families cannot strike the socially optimal balance on their own. The program's incentive effect on labor supply (previously seen as an adverse outcome of transfers) is now judged to be a benefit—to the extent that a well-targeted transfer allows poor families to keep the kids in school, rather than sending them to work. Concerns about distribution *within* households underlie the motivation for such programs; the program's conditions entail that relatively more of the gains accrue to children. Some advocates of CCTs have also claimed that they would reduce child labor, although the economic data are unclear about whether such a policy will work for this purpose; Ravallion and Wodon (2000a) show that, under standard assumptions, a tuition subsidy will increase children's amount of schooling but has theoretically ambiguous effects on the supply of child labor; empirically, the authors find that a tuition subsidy has little effect on child labor in Bangladesh.

There is evidence from impact evaluations that these schemes bring nonnegligible benefits to poor households, in terms of both current incomes and future incomes, through higher investments in child schooling and health care.[132] The conditions change behavior. In the United Kingdom, means-tested grants paid to secondary students have been found to very effectively reduce the number of school drop outs from poor families (Dearden et al., 2009). The various evaluations of Mexico's PROGRESA/Oportunidades program have been positive; see the survey in Fiszbein and Schady (2010). Baird et al. (2011) found sizeable gains from the schooling conditions in a Malawi CCT. In a

---

[132] Fiszbein and Schady (2010) provide a comprehensive review. Also see the discussion in Das et al. (2005).

study for Burkina Faso, Akresh et al. (2013) found that the conditionality mattered more in encouraging the school enrollment of children who were initially less likely to go to school, including girls—children who are less likely to receive investments from their parents. Cameron (2002) found that a CCT program in Indonesia, Jaring Pengamanan Sosial, had the greatest impact at the lower secondary school level where children are most susceptible to dropping out. The design features have also been critically assessed. A series of papers on PROGRESA revealed that a budget-neutral switch of the enrollment subsidy from primary to secondary school would have delivered a net gain in school attainments by increasing the proportion of children who continue onto secondary school.[133] Although PROGRESA had an impact on schooling, it could have had a larger impact. However, it should be recalled that this type of program has two objectives: promotion by increasing schooling (reducing future poverty) and protection by reducing current poverty through the targeted transfers. To the extent that refocusing the subsidies on secondary schooling would reduce the impact on current income poverty (by increasing the forgone income from children's employment), the case for this change in the program's design would need further analysis.

Impact evaluations have also pointed to high returns for early childhood interventions in some settings. The experimental Perry Preschool Program in the United States in the 1960s provided schooling and home visits for poor children aged 3–4. The benefits included higher adult earnings and reduced crime, and the benefit-cost ratio (even without putting greater weight on the propoor distribution of the gains) was estimated to be more than eight to one (Heckman, 2006). Head Start (also begun in the 1960s as part of the United States's War on Poverty) was a similar national preschool program, which targeted a package of education, health, and nutrition services to poor families; the program continues at the time of this writing and, as of 2005, some 22 million preschool children had participated in Head Start programs. Head Start has also been found to generate sizeable long-term gains in schooling, earnings, and reduced crime (Garces et al., 2002). The aggregate benefits from Head Start also appear likely to exceed the cost, even without distributional weights (Ludwig and Phillips, 2007). There is also evidence of significant long-term gains in adult health indicators from an intensive preschool program launched in the United States during the 1970s, the Carolina Abecedarian Project (Campbell et al., 2014). There is a great deal of interest in how effective early childhood interventions might be devised for developing countries.

All these interventions require complementary efforts on the supply side, through effective (public or private) service delivery. This has been an important concern in many developing countries; World Bank (2004) reviews the evidence and discusses how better incentives for service delivery might be developed.

---

[133] See Todd and Wolpin (2002), Attanasio et al. (2004), and de Janvry and Sadoulet (2006).

22.9.6 Microfinance Schemes

As we have seen, credit market failures have been identified as a cause of poverty and a reason why poverty can be costly to overall economic performance. In addition to long-standing moral arguments, transfers to poor people can be interpreted as a means of relieving the constraints stemming from such market failures. But there is another option, namely, policies that aim to make financial institutions for saving and borrowing work better for poor people. Microfinance programs aspiring to support small-scale credit and savings transactions by poor people have attracted a great deal of interest since the idea emerged in the late 1970s, and there are now many examples of such programs in the developing world.

The classic argument is about promotion, namely, that relaxing borrowing constraints faced by poor people allows them to invest and so eventually escape poverty by their own means. Credit and savings are also potentially important instruments for protection, by allowing poor households to more effectively smooth their consumption in the face of income fluctuations.

Much of the early (and ongoing) enthusiasm for microfinance was really little more than advocacy, with weak conceptual and empirical foundations. In recent times, there has been a rise in popular concern in the media (in South Asia especially) about over-borrowing by poor people once they are given access to microfinance. Much of this concern appears to stem from anecdotes, and the debate has also become politicized. Positive average impacts do not, of course, mean that there are no losers among the recipients. This is probably true of all antipoverty policies, but it is especially so in the case of credit-based interventions. Risk is not eliminated, shocks do occur, and mistakes are made, such as due to faulty expectations. There will be both winners and losers in these types of interventions.

The earliest and still most famous example of this class of policies is Bangladesh's group-based lending scheme, Grameen Bank (GB). GB has made a conscious effort to reach the poor both through their eligibility criteria and their branch location decisions, which (in contrast to traditional banks) have favored areas where there are unexploited opportunities for poor people to switch to nonfarm activities (Ravallion and Wodon, 2000b). Research on GB has indicated that the scheme has helped in both protection and promotion; in the former case, by facilitating consumption smoothing and, in the latter, by helping to build the physical and human assets of poor people.[134] This result was found by Pitt and Khandker (1998), who exploited the design features of GB, notably that it is targeted to the landless, to identify effects. Given that access to GB raises the returns of being landless, the returns of having land will be higher in villages that do not have access to GB credit. Thus, comparing the returns of having land between

---

[134] An early contribution to knowledge about GB was made by Hossain (1988).

villages that are eligible for GB and those that are not (with controls for other observable differences) reveal the impact of access to GB credit. Put another way, Pitt and Khandker measure the effect by the mean gain among households that are landless from living in a village that is eligible for GB, less the corresponding gain among those that have land. They found positive impacts on measures relevant to both protection and promotion. This was confirmed in a subsequent study by Khandker and Samad (2014) using survey data on 3000 households spanning 20 years. The success of GB has led to a proliferation of microfinance schemes in Bangladesh, with over 500 providers at the time of this writing.

Even careful observational studies such as that by Pitt and Khandker require identifying assumptions that can be questioned, and there has been some debate about the robustness of their results.[135] This is a type of policy intervention for which it will inevitably be hard to convince everyone of the validity of the identifying assumptions given the likelihood of unobservable factors jointly influencing acceptance and effects. Experimental evaluations relying on randomized assignment (typically at the community level) have offered the hope of more robust results, and there have been some interesting examples. A study by Banerjee et al. (2009) of the impacts of opening new microfinance branches in slums of Hyderabad in India found that overall borrowing, business start-ups, and spending on consumer durables (but not nondurables) increased in the areas that were randomly assigned the new branches relative to the control areas. However, the study did not find evidence of positive impacts on health, education, or women's self-efficacy. Heterogeneity was the focus of a recent experimental evaluation of access to micro-credit by working-age women in Mexico (under the Compartamos Banco scheme) by Angelucci et al. (2013). The authors found positive average effects in a number of dimensions. There was heterogeneity in the impacts, but they found little evidence of significant losses, including among poor borrowers. More research on the benefits and costs of microfinance schemes can be expected.

It is clear that we have seen a shift in thinking about this class of policies over the last 200 years; in the days when poor people were routinely blamed for their poverty, giving them a loan would not have made sense. Of course, identifying credit market failures as one cause of poverty does not imply that credit for the poor will solve the problem. But well-designed programs do have a role, as a complement to other policies for protection and promotion.

22.9.7 Poor-Area Development Programs

Almost all countries have their well-recognized "poor areas," in which the incidence of absolute poverty is unusually high by national standards. We would hope, and under certain conditions expect, that the growth process will help these poor areas catch up.

---

[135] See Morduch (1999) and Roodman and Morduch (2009) as well as the latest detailed rejoinder in Pitt and Khandker (2012).

But this process often appears to be slow, and geographic divergence has sometimes been evident. This has led to antipoverty policies focused on lagging poor areas. "Poverty maps" are widely used in geographic targeting, and the method proposed by Elbers et al. (2003) has facilitated many applications.

Lagging poor areas have prompted poor-area development projects—one of the oldest forms of development assistance, though under various headings (including "Integrated Rural Development Projects" and "Community Driven Development"). Extra resources are channeled to the targeted poor areas for infrastructure and services and developing (farm and nonfarm) enterprises. Emphasis is often given to local citizen participation in decision making, although a survey of the available evaluative research by Mansuri and Rao (2012) found somewhat mixed success given the scope for exploitation by local elites.

It is widely agreed that poor areas are typically characterized by low capital-to-labor ratios, but there is less agreement about the right policy responses, such as efforts to augment local capital—investing in lagging poor areas—versus policies to encourage out migration. Geographic externalities clearly play an important role, but this role is still poorly understood because of a lack of convincing empirical research.

In the case of China, where poor area development has been the main form of direct intervention against poverty since the mid-1980s, there is evidence of pervasive geographic externalities, whereby households living in poor areas have lower growth prospects than seemingly identical households living in well-off areas (Jalan and Ravallion, 2002; Ravallion, 2005). This suggests that there is scope for poor-area development as a means of ensuring longer-term promotion from poverty, as well as protection. However, here, too, the evidence for the success of the policies currently in practice is mixed.[136]

The main concerns about the incentive effects of poor-area programs have related to the responses of local governments to external aid and to migration. An example of the former is found in Chen et al. (2009), who demonstrate that local government spending allocations changed in response to efforts by higher levels of government to target poor villages in rural China, dampening the targeting outcomes. Regarding migration, there appears to be a widely accepted assumption that there is limited intrarural mobility in developing countries, sometimes reflecting institutional and policy impediments (such as local administrative powers for land reallocation, as in China). It is not clear how confident we can be in making that assumption.

There is still much we do not know about the impacts of poor-area development efforts, especially over the long term, and the tradeoffs faced by policy options. Although local infrastructure development is clearly crucial to fighting poverty, it has not attracted the degree of attention in evaluative research that has been generated by social policies. Here, an important factor is the extent to which "development impact" is challenged by

---

[136] For example, contrast the findings of Jalan and Ravallion (1998) with Chen et al. (2009) on poor-area programs in China.

donors and citizens. "Impact" is too often taken for granted with infrastructure develop-ment. By contrast, the "softer" social policies have had to work hard to justify themselves, and evaluative research has served an important role. If the presumption of impact is rou-tinely challenged by donors, aid organizations, and citizens, then we will see stronger incentives for learning about impact and fewer knowledge gaps.

22.9.8 Information Campaigns

There has been recent interest in the scope for using information-based interventions because lack of information is a decisive factor inhibiting poor people from successfully participating in actions to get the services to which they are entitled. There are some signs of support for this premise from past research. Strömberg (2004) reports evidence that US antipoverty programs have worked better in places with greater access to radios. Besley and Burgess (2003) found that the governments of Indian states where newspaper circu-lation is greater are more responsive in their efforts to mitigate negative agricultural shocks. Reinikka and Svensson (2005) found significant effects of information through a newspaper campaign on school outcomes in Uganda.

There have been some evaluations of information interventions. The results so far seem mixed. Focusing on one country and one sector, Pandey et al. (2009) report that a community-based information campaign led to short-term gains in schooling out-comes, while the findings of Banerjee et al. (2010) are less encouraging about the scope for using information interventions to improve the monitoring of education service pro-viders in India. In rich countries facing concerns about the rising incidence of obesity, there have been efforts to post information on the "calorie prices" of food.[137] A recent review of both experimental and nonexperimental evaluations found mixed evidence of effectiveness (Swartz et al., 2011).

Mixed results of this sort might not be surprising. Three observations can be made. First, public information about a program may well discourage participation; for some people, learning about the program may have the opposite effect; see, for example, Hertel-Fernandez and Wenger (2013), with regard to an information campaign for a US program. Second, incomplete information is only one of the possible reasons why poor people do not access services (Keefer and Khemani, 2005; Cappelen et al., 2010). Third, mixed results might also stem from heterogeneity in the quality of the information intervention itself. Also, for India, Ravallion et al. (2013) report success in changing public awareness of rights and rules under India's EGS using an entertaining and high-quality fictional movie that can be shown in villages. However, the results also warn that informing poor people of their rights is not sufficient for positive change. Public awareness can be improved, but this must be combined with effective responses on the supply side.

[137] For example, US legislation in 2010 requires restaurant chains with 20 or more outlets to post calorie counts for all food items sold.

22.10. CONCLUSIONS

This chapter has tried to describe and better understand how the idea of antipoverty policy emerged and has evolved over the last 200 years. It has been argued that we have transitioned from one view of poverty to another, radically different view of poverty. In the first, there was little reason to think that poor people had the potential to be anything else than poor. Poverty would inevitably persist, and, indeed, it was deemed necessary for economic expansion, which required a large number of people eager for work; avoiding hunger was seen as the necessary incentive for poor people to do that work. Social policy had a role in ensuring social stability—most importantly, a generally docile working class willing to work for low wages—and successfully so it seems in the case of England's Poor Laws. Promotional antipoverty policies would probably not have made much sense to those in power, although the need for protection from economic shocks would have been more evident and appears to have had reasonably broad support from the elites even when mass chronic poverty was taken for granted. However, beyond short-term palliatives to address shocks, there was little or no perceived scope for public efforts to permanently reduce poverty. And a world free of poverty was unimaginable—after all, who then would be available to farm the land, work the factories, and staff the armies?

In the second, modern, view, poverty is not only seen as a social ill that can be avoided through public action, but such action is seen as perfectly consistent with a robust growing economy. Indeed, the right antipoverty policies are expected to contribute to development by removing material constraints on the freedom of individuals to pursue their own interests.

Granted, such a public commitment is not universal today in any country. Some observers still point to behaviors of poor people as causes of their poverty, while others point to constraints beyond their control. Advocates against poverty are often frustrated by the setbacks. However, the progress that has been made in both the idea of antipoverty policy and its effective implementation is undeniable. Recognizing such a marked transition in mainstream thinking over 200 years makes one more optimistic that the idea of eliminating poverty can be more than a dream.

Progress has been uneven over time. Two key historical steps in the transition can be identified, dubbed here as the First and Second Poverty Enlightenments. The First, taking place just before the turn of the nineteenth century, saw the emergence of a new respect for poor people as people—no longer the "shadows in a painting" or objects that served some purely instrumental role as means of production. Instead, the economy itself came to be seen as a means to promote human welfare, including that of poor people. The Second Poverty Enlightenment, in the latter part of the twentieth century, came with the strongest case yet for antipoverty policy, which saw poverty as a severe constraint on freedom and personal self-fulfillment. A consensus emerged that poverty was morally unacceptable, though with continuing debates on what to do about it.

Although the foundation for this change was laid in the First Poverty Enlightenment—notably in seeing all human beings as morally equal, with legitimate desires for freedom and self-fulfillment—it was really only by the time of the Second Poverty Enlightenment that it came to be understood that freedom and self-fulfillment required (among other things) that people were not constrained by poverty. The state was seen to have a role in ensuring that all individuals had access to the material conditions for their own personal fulfillment—arguably the most important requirement for equity, but also the key to breaking out of poverty traps. Antipoverty policy came to be seen as a matter of both promotion and protection. Along with rising real wages and (hence) savings by poor people, public education systems, sound health care systems, and reasonably well-functioning financial markets came to be seen as crucial elements for the next generation of poor families to escape poverty for good.

Once it started to be widely accepted that those born poor could in fact escape poverty, public action against poverty became more acceptable, and more people joined political coalitions or struggles toward that end. Once successful promotion policies had been initiated, the fiscal burden of providing relief to those who remained poor started to fall. This was probably reinforced by new political support for action and moral conviction about its need, stemming from the world's (now much expanded) middle class. Beyond some point, a self-reinforcing cycle emerged in the successful countries to help ensure a sustained and (over time) more rapid escape from poverty. The cycle has been broken at times; the history of thinking and action on poverty gives ample illustration of the fragility of the progress we have seen. Each Poverty Enlightenment was followed by a backlash in thinking and policy making. But we have seen progress.

ACKNOWLEDGMENTS

This chapter's title owes a debt to Gertrude Himmelfarb's (1984) text, *The Idea of Poverty: England in the Early Industrial Age*. For comments the author thanks Robert Allen, Tony Atkinson, Pranab Bardhan, Francois Bourguignon, Denis Cogneau, Jean-Yves Duclos, Sam Fleischacker, Pedro Gete, Karla Hoff, Ravi Kanbur, Charles Kenny, Sylvie Lambert, Philipp Lepenies, Peter Lindert, Michael Lipton, Will Martin, Alice Mesnard, Branko Milanovic, Johan Mistiaen, Berk Ozler, Thomas Pogge, Gilles Postel-Vinay, Henry Richardson, John Roemer, John Rust, Agnar Sandmo, Amartya Sen, Dominique van de Walle, and participants at presentations at the World Bank, the Midwest International Economic Development Conference at the University of Wisconsin–Madison, the Paris School of Economics, the Canadian Economics Association, the 12th Nordic Conference on Development Economics, Lancaster University, and the World Institute for Development Economics Research.

APPENDIX

This Appendix proves the claim made in Section 22.8 about the properties of the characterization of wealth dynamics in Section 22.2. The claim in Section 22.8 referred to a situation in which the threshold is not binding, giving the Banerjee and Duflo (2003) model. The latter paper shows that higher initial wealth inequality lowers future growth in wealth. Here, we focus instead on the implications of high initial wealth poverty.

Initial wealth, w_t for date t, is distributed across individuals according to the cumulative distribution function, $F_t(w)$, giving the population proportion with wealth lower than w, and let $H_t = F_t(z)$ denote the headcount index of poverty (poverty rate) when the poverty line is z. (It will be analytically easier to work with the inverse of $F_t(w)$, namely, the quantile function, $w_t(p)$.) If credit is constrained ($w_t \le k^\star/(\lambda+1)$), then output at $t+1$ is limited by the amount of capital available at time t, which is given by own–wealth plus maximum borrowing, yielding an output of $h((\lambda+1)w_t)$. The recursion diagram for the credit-constrained individual then takes the form:

$$w_{t+1} = \varphi(w_t) = \beta[h((\lambda+1)w_t) - r\lambda w_t] \quad \text{for} \quad w_t \le k^*/(\lambda+1) \tag{23.1}$$

By contrast, the following recursion diagram holds for the unconstrained person (who is free to implement the optimal capital stock $k^\star$ at which point $h'(k^\star) = r$):

$$w_{t+1} = \beta[h(k^*) + r(w_t - k^*)] \quad \text{for} \quad w_t > k^*/(\lambda+1) \tag{23.2}$$

Here, β is the fixed share of current wealth that is not currently consumed. Plainly, $\varphi(w_t)$ is strictly concave up to $k^\star/(\lambda+1)$ and linear above that point. It is assumed that $z \le k^\star/(\lambda+1)$. Let $H_t^* \equiv F_t[k^\star/(\lambda+1)]$. Mean future wealth is:

$$\mu_{t+1} = \int_0^\infty \varphi[w_t(p)]\mathrm{d}p \tag{23.3}$$

By standard properties of concave functions, we can readily verify that an inequality-increasing spread in the wealth distribution in this economy will reduce mean future wealth at a given level of mean current wealth, that is, reduce the growth rate, as in Banerjee and Duflo (2003).

What about the impact on growth of higher initial poverty at a given initial mean? Using Equations (23.1) and (23.2), we can rewrite Equation (23.3) as:

$$\mu_{t+1} = \beta \int_0^{H_t^*} [h((\lambda+1)w_t(p)) - \lambda r w_t(p)]\mathrm{d}p + \beta \int_{H_t^*}^1 [h(k^*) + (w_t(p) - k^*)r]\mathrm{d}p \tag{23.4}$$

Consider the growth effect of a mean-preserving increase in the poverty rate. It is assumed that H_t^* increases and that no individual with wealth less than $k^\star/(\lambda+1)$ becomes better off, implying that $\partial w_t(p)/\partial H_t^* \le 0$ for all $p \le H_t^*$. If this holds true, then we can say that poverty is unambiguously higher. Note that the function φ is continuous at $k^\star/(\lambda+1)$. Then it is readily verified that:

$$\frac{\partial \mu_{t+1}}{\partial H_t^*} = \beta \int_0^{H_t^*} [h'((\lambda+1)w_t(p))(\lambda+1) - \lambda r]\frac{\partial w_t(p)}{\partial H_t^*}\mathrm{d}p + \beta r \int_0^{H_t^*} \frac{\partial w_t(p)}{\partial H_t^*}\mathrm{d}p \tag{23.5}$$

The sign of this expression cannot be determined under the assumptions so far. It may be noted that, if there is (unrestricted) first-order dominance, whereby $\partial w_t(p)/\partial H_t^* \leq 0$ for all $p \in [0, 1]$, then $\partial \mu_{t+1}/\partial H_t^* \leq 0$. However, first-order dominance is ruled out by the fact that the mean is held constant; there is a redistribution from the "wealth poor" to the "wealth nonpoor." On imposing a constant initial mean, $\mu_t = \bar{\mu}$, Equation (23.5) simplifies to:

$$\left[\frac{\partial \mu_{t+1}}{\partial H_t^*}\right]_{\mu_t = \bar{\mu}} = \beta \int_0^{H_t^*} [h'((\lambda + 1)w_t(p)) - r](\lambda + 1)\frac{\partial w_t(p)}{\partial H_t^*}dp < 0 \qquad (23.6)$$

Thus, we find that an unambiguously higher initial headcount index of poverty holding the initial mean constant implies a lower growth rate, as claimed in Section 22.8.

REFERENCES

Abel-Smith, B., Townsend, P., 1966. The Poor and the Poorest, a New Analysis of the Ministry of Labour's Family Expenditure Surveys of 1953–54 and 1960. Bell, London.

Acemoglu, D., Robinson, J., 2006. Economic Origins of Dictatorship and Democracy. Cambridge University Press, Cambridge, England.

Acemoglu, D., Zilibotti, F., 1997. Was Prometheus unbound by chance? J. Polit. Econ. 105 (4), 709–751.

Adelman, I., Morris, C.T., 1973. Economic Growth and Social Equity in Developing Countries. Stanford University Press, Stanford.

Agee, J., Evans, W., 1941. Let Us Now Praise Famous Men, the American Classic, in Words and Pictures, of Three Tenant Families in the Deep South, Houghton Mifflin edition, Boston, MA, 2000.

Aghion, P., Bolton, P., 1997. A theory of trickle-down growth and development. Rev. Econ. Stud. 64, 151–172.

Aghion, P., Caroli, E., Garcia-Penalosa, C., 1999a. Inequality and economic growth, the perspectives of the new growth theories. J. Econ. Lit. 37 (4), 1615–1660.

Aghion, P., Banerjee, A., Piketty, T., 1999b. Dualism and macroeconomic volatility. Quart. J. Econ. 114 (4), 1359–1397.

Ahluwalia, M.S., 1976. Inequality, poverty and development. J. Dev. Econ. 3, 307–342.

Ahluwalia, M.S., Carter, N.G., Chenery, H.B., 1979. Growth and poverty in developing countries. J. Dev. Econ. 6, 299–341.

Ahluwalia, M.S., Duloy, J., Pyatt, G., Srinivasan, T.N., 1980. Who benefits from economic development? Comment. Am. Econ. Rev. 70 (1), 242–245.

Akerlof, G., 1970. The market for lemons, quality uncertainty and the market mechanism. Quart. J. Econ. 84, 485–500.

Akresh, R., de Walque, D., Kazianga, H., 2013. Cash Transfers and Child Schooling, Evidence from a Randomized Evaluation of the Role of Conditionality, Policy Research Working Paper 6340, World Bank.

Alatas, V., Banerjee, A., Hanna, R., Olken, B.A., Tobias, J., 2012. Targeting the poor, evidence from a field experiment in Indonesia. Am. Econ. Rev. 102 (4), 1206–1240.

Albelda, R., Folbre, N., The Center for Popular Economics, 1996. The War on the Poor. A Defense Manual. The New Press, New York.

Alderman, H., 2002. Do local officials know something we don't? Decentralization of targeted transfers in Albania. J. Pub. Econ. 83, 375–404.

Alderman, H., Hoddinott, J., Kinsey, B., 2006. Long-term consequences of early childhood malnutrition. Oxf. Econ. Pap. 58 (3), 450–474.

Alesina, A., Rodrik, D., 1994. Distributive politics and economic growth. Quart. J. Econ. 108, 465–490.

Allen, R., 2007. Pessimism Preserved, Real Wages in the British Industrial Revolution, Oxford University Department of Economics Working Paper 314.

Allen, R., 2009. Engels' pause technical change, capital accumulation, and inequality in the British industrial revolution. Explor. Econ. Hist. 46, 418–435.

Allen, R., 2013. Poverty Lines in History, Theory, and Current International Practice. Nuffield College, Oxford, Mimeo.

Anand, S., 1983. Inequality and Poverty in Malaysia. Oxford University Press, Oxford.

Anand, S., Kanbur, R., 1993. The Kuznets process and the inequality-development relationship. J. Dev. Econ. 40, 25–52.

Anand, S., Ravallion, M., 1993. Human development in poor countries, on the role of private incomes and public services. J. Econ. Perspect. 7 (Winter), 133–150.

Angelucci, M., Karlan, D., Zinman, J., 2013. Win Some Lose Some? Evidence from a Randomized Microcredit Program Placement Experiment by Compartamos Banco. mimeo.

Aristotle, 350BC, Politics Book 2 (B. Jowett, Trans.). http://classics.mit.edu/Aristotle/politics.2.two.html.

Arneson, R., 1989. Equality and equal opportunity for welfare. Philos. Stud. 56 (1), 77–93.

Arrow, K.J., 1951. Social Choice and Individual Values. John Wiley, New York.

Artz, F.B., 1934. Reaction and Revolution, 1814–1834. Harper and Row, New York.

Atkinson, A.B., 1970. On the measurement of inequality. J. Econ. Theory 2, 244–263.

Atkinson, A.B., 1987. On the measurement of poverty. Econometrica 55, 749–764.

Atkinson, A.B., 1991. Comparing poverty rates internationally, lessons from recent studies in developed countries. World Bank Econ. Rev. 5 (1), 3–21.

Atkinson, A.B., Bourguignon, F., 1982. The comparison of multi-dimensional distributions of economic status. Rev. Econ. Stud. 49, 183–201.

Atkinson, A.B., Sutherland, H., 1989. Analysis of a partial basic income scheme. In: Atkinson, A.B. (Ed.), Poverty and Social Security. Harvester Wheatsheaf, Hertfordshire.

Attanasio, O., Meghir, C., Santiago, A., 2004. Education Choices in Mexico, Using a Structural Model and a Randomized Experiment to Evaluate PROGRESA. Working Paper EWP04/04, Institute of Fiscal Studies, London.

Aykroyd, W.R., 1974. The Conquest of Famine. Chatto and Windus, London.

Azariadis, C., 1996. The economics of poverty traps. Part one: complete markets. J. Econ. Growth 1, 449–486.

Azariadis, C., 2006. The theory of poverty traps, what have we learned? In: Bowles, S., Durlauf, S., Hoff, K. (Eds.), Poverty Traps. Princeton University Press, Princeton.

Baird, S., McIntosh, C., Ozler, B., 2011. Cash or condition? evidence from a cash transfer experiment. Quart. J. Econ. 126 (4), 1709–1753.

Banerjee, A., Duflo, E., 2003. Inequality and growth, what can the data Say? J. Econ. Growth 8 (3), 267–299.

Banerjee, A., Duflo, E., 2007. The economic lives of the poor. J. Econ. Perspect. 21 (2), 141–167.

Banerjee, A., Iyer, L., 2005. History, institutions and economic performance, the legacy of colonial land tenure systems in India. Am. Econ. Rev. 95 (4), 1190–1213.

Banerjee, A., Newman, A., 1993. Occupational choice and the process of development. J. Polit. Econ. 101 (2), 274–298.

Banerjee, Abhijit, Duflo, Esther, Glennerster, Rachel, Kinnan, Cynthia, 2009. The Miracle of Microfinance? Evidence from a Randomized Evaluation, BREAD Working Paper No. 278, BREAD.

Banerjee, A., Banerji, R., Duflo, E., Glennerster, R., Khemani, S., 2010. Pitfalls of participatory programs, evidence from a randomized evaluation in education in India. Am. Econ. J. Econ. Policy 2 (1), 1–30.

Bardhan, P., 1984a. Land, Labor and Rural Poverty, Essays in Development Economics. Columbia University Press, New York.

Bardhan, P., 1984b. The Political Economy of Development in India. Basil Blackwell, Oxford.

Bardhan, P., 2011. Challenges for a minimum social democracy in India. Econ. Pol. Wkly. 46 (10), 39–43.

Bardhan, P., Bowles, S., Ginitis, H., 2000. Wealth inequality, wealth constraints and economic performance. In: Atkinson, A.B., Bourguignon, F. (Eds.), In: Handbook of Income Distribution, vol. 1. North-Holland, Amsterdam.

Barrett, C.B., Marenya, P.P., McPeak, J.G., Minten, B., Murithi, F.M., Oluoch-Kosura, W., Place, F., Randrianarisoa, J.C., Rasambainarivo, J., Wangila, J., 2006. Welfare dynamics in rural Kenya and Madagascar. J. Dev. Stud. 42 (2), 178–199.

Barro, R., 2000. Inequality and growth in a panel of countries. J. Econ. Growth 5 (1), 5–32.

Barro, R., Sala-i-Martin, X., 1992. Convergence. J. Polit. Econ. 100 (2), 223–251.

Basu, K., 1999. Child labor, cause, consequence and cure, with remarks on international labor standards. J. Econ. Lit. 37, 1083–1119.

Bator, F.M., 1958. The anatomy of market failure. Quart. J. Econ. 72 (3), 351–379.

Beaudoin, S., 2007. Poverty in World History. Routledge, New York.

Beaumarchais, P., 1778. La Folle Journée ou Le Mariage de Figaro. Nathan, Paris, 2007.

Beck, T., Levine, R., Loayza, N., 2000. Finance and the sources of growth. J. Financ. Econ. 58, 261–300.

Beck, T., Demirguc-Kunt, A., Levine, R., 2007. Finance, inequality and the poor. J. Econ. Growth 12, 27–49.

Bénabou, R., 1996. Inequality and growth. In: Bernanke, B., Rotemberg, J. (Eds.), National Bureau of Economic Research Macroeconomics Annual. MIT Press, Cambridge.

Benton, D., 2010. The influence of dietary status on the cognitive performance of children. Mol. Nutr. Food Res. 54 (4), 457–470.

Berg, A., Ostry, J.D., Zettelmeyer, J., 2012. What makes growth sustained? J. Dev. Econ. 98, 149–166.

Besley, T., Burgess, R., 2003. The political economy of government responsiveness, theory and evidence from India. Quart. J. Econ. 117 (4), 1415–1451.

Bethlehem, J., 2009. The Rise of Survey Sampling, Statistics Netherlands Discussion Paper 09015, Amsterdam.

Beveridge, W., 1942. Social Insurance and Allied Services. His Majesty's Stationary Office, London.

Birdsall, N., Londono, J.L., 1997. Asset inequality matters, an assessment of the world Bank's approach to poverty reduction. Am. Econ. Rev. 87 (2), 32–37.

Birdsall, N., Ross, D., Sabot, R., 1995. Inequality and growth reconsidered, lessons from east Asia. World Bank Econ. Rev. 9 (3), 477–508.

Birdsall, N., Graham, C., Pettinato, S., 2000. Stuck in the Tunnel, Is Globalization Muddling the Middle Class? Center on Social and Economic Dynamics, Working Paper 14, Brookings Institution, Washington, DC.

Blaug, M., 1962. Economic Theory in Retrospect. Heinemann Books, London.

Blaug, M., 2001. No history of ideas, please, we're economists. J. Econ. Perspect. 15 (1), 145–164.

Bliss, C., 1975. Capital Theory and the Distribution of Income. North-Holland, Amsterdam.

Bliss, C., Stern, N., 1982. Palanpur, The Economy of an Indian Village. Clarendon Press, Oxford.

Boo, K., 2012. Behind the Beautiful Forevers. Random House, New York.

Booth, C., 1903. Life and labour of the people of London. Second Series: Industry, vol. 5. Macmillan and Co., London.

Bourguignon, F., 2003. The growth elasticity of poverty reduction, explaining heterogeneity across countries and time periods. In: Eicher, T., Turnovsky, S. (Eds.), Inequality and Growth Theory and Policy Implications. MIT Press, Cambridge.

Bourguignon, F., Morrisson, C., 2002. Inequality among world citizens, 1820–1992. Am. Econ. Rev. 92 (4), 727–744.

Bowles, S., Gintis, H., 1976. Schooling in Capitalist America, Educational Reform and the Contradictions of Economic Life. Routledge and Kegan Paul, London.

Bowles, S., Durlauf, S., Hoff, K., 2006. Poverty Traps. Princeton University Press, Princeton.

Bowley, A.L., 1915. The Nature and Purpose of the Measurement of Social Phenomena. P.S. King and Sons, London.

Boyer, G., 2002. English poor laws. In: Whaples, R. (Ed.), EH.Net Encyclopedia.

Brinton, C., 1934. A Decade of Revolution 1789–1799. Harper and Row, New York.

Brooke, M.Z., 1998. Le Play Engineer and Social Scientist. Transaction Publishers, New Brunswick.

Bruno, M., Ravallion, M., Squire, L., 1998. Equity and growth in developing countries, Old and New perspectives on the policy issues. In: Tanzi, V., Chu, K.-y. (Eds.), Income Distribution and High-Quality Growth. MIT Press, Cambridge.

Bulow, J., Summers, L., 1986. A theory of dual labor markets with application to industrial policy, discrimination and Keynesian unemployment. J. Labor Econ. 4 (3), 376–414.

Burnett, J., 1969. A History of the Cost of Living. Penguin Books, Harmondsworth, England.

Cameron, L., 2002. Did Social Safety Net Scholarships Reduce Drop-Out Rates during the Indonesian Economic Crisis? Policy Research Working Paper 2800, World Bank.

Campbell, F., Conti, G., Heckman, J., Moon, S.H., Pinto, R., Pungello, E., Pan, Y., 2014. Early childhood investments substantially boost adult health. Science 343, 1478–1485.

Cantril, H., 1965. The Pattern of Human Concerns. Rutgers University Press, New Brunswick.

Cappelen, A., Mæstad, O., Tungodden, B., 2010. Demand for childhood vaccination-insights from behavioral economics. Forum Dev. Stud. 37 (3), 349–364.

Carter, M., Barrett, C., 2006. The economics of poverty traps and persistent poverty, an asset-based approach. J. Dev. Stud. 42 (2), 178–199.

Chen, S., Ravallion, M., 2010. The developing world is poorer than we thought, but no less successful in the fight against poverty. Quart. J. Econ. 125 (4), 1577–1625.

Chen, S., Ravallion, M., 2013. More relatively poor people in a less absolutely poor world. Rev. Income Wealth 59 (1), 1–28.

Chen, S., Ren, M., Ravallion, M., 2009. Are there lasting impacts of aid to poor areas? J. Pub. Econ. 93, 512–528.

Chenery, H., 1977. Forward to David Morawetz, Twenty-Five Years of Economic Development. World Bank, Washington, DC.

Chenery, H., Ahluwalia, M.S., Bell, C., Duloy, J., Jolly, R., 1974. Redistribution with Growth. Oxford University Press, Oxford.

Cinnirella, F., 2008. Optimists or Pessimists? A Reconsideration of Nutritional Status in Britain, 1740–1865. Eur. Rev. Econ. Hist. 12, 325–354.

Clark, G., 2005. The condition of the working class in England 1209–2004. J. Polit. Econ. 113, 1307–1340.

Clarke, G.R.G., 1995. More evidence on income distribution and growth. J. Dev. Econ. 47, 403–428.

Cogneau, D., 2012. The Political Dimension of Inequality during Economic Development. Région et Développement 35, 11–36.

Cohen, G., 1989a. On the currency of egalitarian justice. Ethics 99 (4), 906–944.

Cohen, J., 1989b. Democratic equality. Ethics 99 (4), 727–751.

Cornia, Giovanni, Stewart, Frances, 1995. Two errors of targeting. In: van de Walle, Dominique, Nead, Kimberly (Eds.), Public Spending and the Poor. Johns Hopkins University Press for the World Bank, Baltimore.

Cunha, F., Heckman, J., 2007. The technology of skill formation. Am. Econ. Rev. 97 (2), 31–47.

Cunningham, H., 1990. The employment and unemployment of children in England c.1680-1851. Past Present 126, 115–150.

Currie, J., 2001. Early childhood development programs. J. Econ. Perspect. 15 (2), 213–238.

Currie, J., 2011. Inequality at birth, some causes and consequences. Am. Econ. Rev. 101 (3), 1–22.

Currie, J., 2012. Antipoverty programs for poor children and families. In: Jefferson, P.N. (Ed.), The Oxford Handbook of the Economics of Poverty. Oxford University Press, Oxford.

Dandekar, V.M., Rath, N., 1971. Poverty in India. Indian School of Political Economy, Pune.

Daniels, W., 1898. The bearing of the doctrine of selection upon the social problem. Inter. J. Ethics 8 (2), 203–214 (now called Ethics).

Das, J., Do, Q.-T., Ozler, B., 2005. A welfare analysis of conditional cash transfer schemes. World Bank Res. Obs. 20 (1), 57–80.

Dasgupta, P., 1993. An Inquiry into Well-Being and Destitution. Oxford University Press, Oxford.

Dasgupta, P., 1997. Poverty traps. In: Kreps, D.M., Wallis, K.F. (Eds.), Advances in Economics and Econometrics, Theory and Applications. Cambridge University Press, Cambridge.

Dasgupta, P., 2011. Personal Histories and Poverty Traps. In: Annual World Bank Conference on Development Economics. World Bank, Washington, DC.

Dasgupta, P., Ray, D., 1986. Inequality as a determinant of malnutrition and unemployment. Econ. J. 96, 1011–1034.

Datt, G., Ravallion, M., 1998. Farm productivity and rural poverty in India. J. Dev. Stud. 34 (4), 62–85.

Day, R.H., 1992. Complex economic dynamics, obvious in history, generic in theory, elusive in data. J. Appl. Econ. 7, S9–S23.

De Donder, P., Hindriks, J., 1998. The political economy of targeting. Public Choice 95, 177–200.

De Janvry, A., Sadoulet, E., 2006. Making conditional cash transfer programs more efficient, designing for maximum effect of the conditonality. World Bank Econ. Rev. 20 (1), 1–29.

De Mandeville, B., 1732. An essay on charity and charity schools. In: The Fable of the Bees, Or, Private Vices, Publick Benefits, sixth ed. Oxford University Press, London, Oxford, 1957 (reprint).

de Montesquieu, C., 1748. The Spirit of Laws (T. Nugent, Trans.). G. Bell and Sons, London (1914 edition).

De Tocqueville, A., 1835. Memoir on Pauperism, Does Public Charity Produce and Idle and Dependent Class of Society? Cosimo Classics edition, New York, 2005.

de Waal, F., 2009. The Age of Empathy. Nature's Lessons for a Kinder Society. Three Rivers Press, New York.

Dearden, L., Emmerson, C., Frayne, C., Meghir, C., 2009. Conditional cash transfers and school dropout rates. J. Hum. Res. 44 (4), 827–857.

Deaton, A., 1997. The Analysis of Household Surveys: A Microeconometric Approach to Development Policy. World Bank, Washington, DC.

Deaton, A., 2006. The great escape, a review of Robert Fogel's the escape from hunger and premature death, 1700–2100. J. Econ. Lit. 44, 106–114.

Deininger, K., Olinto, P., 2000. Asset Distribution, Inequality and Growth, Policy Research Working Paper 2375, World Bank.

Deininger, K., Squire, L., 1996. A New data set measuring income inequality. World Bank Econ. Rev. 10, 565–591.

Deininger, K., Squire, L., 1998. New ways of looking at old issues, inequality and growth. J. Dev. Econ. 57 (2), 259–287.

Dercon, S., Outes, I., 2013. The Road to Perdition, Rainfall Shocks, Poverty Traps and Destitution in Semi-Arid India. Oxford University, mimeo.

Dickens, C., 1838. Oliver Twist. Richard Bently, London, Penguin edition, 2003.

Do, Q.-T., Levchenko, A., Ravallion, M., 2013. Copying with food price volatility, trade insulation as social protection. In: Chavas, J.-P., Hummels, D., Wright, B. (Eds.), The Economics of Food Price Volatility. University of Chicago Press, forthcoming.

Doepke, M., Zilibotti, F., 2005. Social class and the spirit of capitalism. J. Eur. Econ. Assoc. 3 (2–3), 516–524.

Doeringer, P., Piore, M., 1971. Internal Labor Markets and Manpower Analysis. Sharpe, New York.

Dollar, D., Kraay, A., 2002. Growth is good for the poor. J. Econ. Growth 7 (3), 195–225.

Dollar, D., Kraay, A., 2004. Trade, growth and poverty. Econ. J. 114 (493), F22–F49.

Doron, A., 1990. Definition and measurement of poverty—the unsolved issue. In: Social Security, Journal of Welfare and Social Security Studies, 2, pp. 27–50, Special English Edition.

Drèze, J., 1990a. Famine prevention in India. In: Drèze, Sen (Eds.), In: The Political Economy of Hunger, vol. 2. Oxford University Press, Oxford.

Drèze, J., 1990b. Famine prevention in Africa, some experiences and lessons. In: Drèze, J., Sen, A. (Eds.), The Political Economy of Hunger. vol. 2. Oxford University Press, Oxford.

Drèze, J., Sen, A., 1989. Hunger and Public Action. Oxford University Press, Oxford.

Duncan, O., Featherman, D., Duncan, B., 1972. Socioeconomic Background and Achievement. Seminar Press, New York.

Dutta, P., Murgai, R., Ravallion, M., van de Walle, D., 2012. Does India's employment guarantee scheme guarantee employment? Econ. Pol. Wkly. 48 (April 21), 55–64.

Dutta, P., Murgai, R., Ravallion, M., van de Walle, D., 2013. Right-to-Work? Assessing India's Employment Guarantee Scheme in Bihar. World Bank, Washington, DC.

Easterly, W., 2001. The middle class consensus and economic development. J. Econ. Growth 6 (4), 317–335.

Easterly, W., 2009. How the millennium development goals are unfair to Africa. World Dev. 37 (1), 26–35.

Eastwood, R., Lipton, M., 1999. The impact of changes in human fertility on poverty. J. Dev. Stud. 36 (1), 1–30.

Eastwood, R., Lipton, M., 2001. Demographic transition and poverty, effects via economic growth, distribution and conversion. In: Birdsall, N., Kelley, A., Sinding, S. (Eds.), Population Matters. Oxford University Press, Oxford.

Eden, Frederick Morton, 1797. The State of the Poor. J. Davis, London.

Elbers, C., Lanjouw, J., Lanjouw, P., 2003. Micro-level estimation of poverty and inequality. Econometrica 71 (1), 355–364.

Ellwood, D., Summers, L., 1986. Poverty in america, is welfare the answer or the problem? In: Danziger, S., Weinberg, D. (Eds.), Fighting Poverty, What Works and What Doesn't. Harvard University Press, Cambridge.

Engel, E., 1857. Die Productions- und Consumtionsverhältnisse des Königreichs Sachsen. Zeitschrift des statistischen Bureaus des Königlich Sächsischen Ministerium des Inneren 8–9, 28–29.

Engels, F., 1845. The Condition of the Working Class in England. Oxford University Press, Oxford, 1993 edition.

Engerman, S.L., Sokoloff, K., 2006. Colonialism, inequality and long-Run paths of development. In: Banerjee, A., Benabou, R., Mookherjee, D. (Eds.), Understanding Poverty. Oxford University Press, Oxford, pp. 37–62.

Eurostat, 2005. Income poverty and social exclusion in the EU25, Statistics in Focus 03/2005, Office of Official Publications of the European Communities, Luxembourg.

Ferreira, F.H.G., Ravallion, M., 2009. Poverty and inequality, the global context. In: Salverda, W., Nolan, B., Smeeding, T. (Eds.), The Oxford Handbook of Economic Inequality. Oxford University Press, Oxford.

Fields, G.S., 1977. Who benefits from economic development? a reexamination of Brazilian growth in the 1960's. Am. Econ. Rev. 67 (4), 570–582.

Fields, G.S., 1980. Poverty Inequality and Development. Cambridge University Press, Cambridge.

Fields, G.S., 2001. Distribution and Development. Russell Sage Foundation, New York.

Fifield, A., 2013. Starved of healthy options. Financ. Times, 9, June 14.

Filmer, D., 2007. If You build It, will they come? school availability and school enrolment in 21 poor countries. J. Dev. Stud. 43 (5), 901–928.

Fishlow, A., 1972. Brazilian size distribution of income. Am. Econ. Rev. 62, 391–402.

Fishlow, A., Gwin, C., 1994. Overview, Lessons from the East Asian Experience. In: Fishlow, A., Gwin, C., Haggard, S., Rodrik, D., Wade, R. (Eds.), Miracle or Design? Lessons from the East Asian Experience. Overseas Development Council, Washington, DC.

Fiszbein, A., Schady, N., 2010. Conditional Cash Transfers for Attacking Present and Future Poverty. World Bank, Washington, DC.

Fleischacker, S., 2004. A Short History of Distributive Justice. Harvard University Press, Cambridge, MA.

Fleurbaey, M., 2008. Fairness Responsibility and Welfare. Oxford University Press, Oxford.

Fogel, R.W., 2004. The Escape from Hunger and Premature Death, 1700–2100. Cambridge University Press, Cambridge.

Fogel, R.W., Engerman, S., Floud, R., Friedman, G., Mango, R., Sokoloff, K., Steckel, R., Trussell, J., Villaflor, G., Watchter, K., 1983. Secular change in American and British stature and nutrition. In: Rotberg, R., Rabb, T. (Eds.), Hunger in History. Cambridge University Press, Cambridge.

Forbes, K.J., 2000. A reassessment of the relationship between inequality and growth. Am. Econ. Rev. 90 (4), 869–887.

Foster, J., 1998. Absolute versus relative poverty. Am. Econ. Rev. 88 (2), 335–341.

Foster, J., Greer, J., Thorbecke, E., 1984. A class of decomposable poverty measures. Econometrica 52, 761–765.

Friedman, M., 1962. Capital and Freedom. University of Chicago Press, Chicago.

Fuchs, V., 1967. Redefining poverty and redistributing income. Public Interest 8, 88–95.

Furniss, E., 1920. The Position of the Laborer in a System of Nationalism. A Study in the Labor Theories of the Later English Mercantilists. Houghton Mifflin, Boston and New York.

Gaiha, R., 1997. Rural public works and the poor, the case of the employment guarantee scheme in India. In: Polachek, S. (Ed.), Research in Labour Economics. JAI Press, Connecticut.

Galasso, E., Ravallion, M., 2005. Decentralized targeting of an antipoverty program. J. Pub. Econ. 89, 705–727.

Galasso, E., Ravallion, M., Salvia, A., 2004. Assisting the transition from workfare to work: Argentina's Proempleo Experiment. Ind. Labor Relat. Rev. 57 (5), 128–142.

Galbraith, J.K., 1958. The Affluent Society. Mariner Books, Boston.

Galor, O., Zeira, J., 1993. Income distribution and macroeconomics. Rev. Econ. Stud. 60 (1), 35–52.

Gans, H., 1995. The War Against the Poor. Basic Books, New York.

Garces, E., Thomas, D., Currie, J., 2002. Longer term effects of head start. Am. Econ. Rev. 92 (4), 999–1012.

Gelbach, J., Pritchett, L., 2000. Indicator targeting in a political economy, leakier can be better. J. Policy Reform 4, 113–145.

Geremek, B., 1994. Poverty. A History. Blackwell, Oxford.

Ghatak, M., Jiang, N.N.-H., 2002. A simple model of inequality, occupational choice, and development. J. Dev. Econ. 69 (1), 205–226.

Gillie, A., 1996. The origin of the poverty line. Econ. Hist. Rev. 49 (4), 715–730.

Goldin, C., Katz, L.F., 2008. The Race Between Education and Technology. Harvard University Press, Cambridge.

Gordon, R., Li, W., 2009. Tax structures in developing countries, many puzzles and a possible explanation. J. Pub. Econ. 93 (7–8), 855–866.

Grosh, M., Glewwe, P., 2000. Designing Household Survey Questionnaires for Developing Countries. Lessons from 15 Years of the Living Standards Measurement Study, 3 vols. World Bank, Washington, DC.

Grosh, M., del Ninno, C., Tesliuc, E., Ouerghi, A., 2008. For Protection and Promotion, the Design and Implementation of Effective Safety Nets. World Bank, Washington, DC.

Gutiérrez, C., Tanaka, R., 2009. Inequality and education decisions in developing countries. J. Econ. Inequal. 7, 55–81.

Hansen, M.H., Hurvitz, W.N., 1943. On the theory of sampling from a finite population. Ann. Math. Stat. 14, 333–362.

Harrington, M., 1962. The Other America, Poverty in the United States. Macmillan, New York.

Harrison, A., Rodríguez-Clare, A., 2010. Trade, foreign investment, and industrial policy for developing countries. In: Handbook of Development Economics. vol. 5. North Holland, Amsterdam.

Harsanyi, J., 1975. Can the maximin principle serve as a basis for morality? A critique of john Rawls's theory. Am. Polit. Sci. Rev. 69 (2), 594–606.

Hartmann, B., 1987. Reproductive Rights and Wrongs, the Global Politics of Population Control and Contraceptive Choice. Harper and Row, New York.

Hauk, W.R., Wacziarg, R., 2009. A Monte Carlo study of growth regressions. J. Econ. Growth 14 (2), 103–147.

Hazan, M., Berdugo, B., 2002. Child labour, fertility, and economic growth. Econ. J. 112 (482), 810–828.

Heckman, J., 2006. Skill formation and the economics of investing in disadvantaged children. Science 30, 1900–1902.

Heclo, H., 1986. The political foundations of antipoverty policy. In: Danziger, S., Weinberg, D. (Eds.), Fighting Poverty, What Works and What Doesn't. Harvard University Press, Cambridge.

Hemerijck, A., 2014. The reform capacities of European welfare states. In: Cantillon, B., Vandenbroucke, F. (Eds.), Reconciling Work and Poverty Reduction. How Successful are European Welfare States? Oxford University Press, Oxford.

Hertel-Fernandez, A., Wenger, J.B., 2013. Taking Up Social Benefits, A Cautionary Tale from an Unemployment Insurance Survey Experiment, Available at SSRN, http://ssrn.com/abstract=2341885 or http://dx.doi.org/10.2139/ssrn.2341885.

Herzer, D., Vollmer, S., 2012. Inequality and growth, evidence from panel cointegration. J. Econ. Inequal. 10, 489–503.

Hill, C., 1972. The World Turned Upside Down, Radical Ideas During the English Revolution. Maurice Temple Smith, London.

Himmelfarb, G., 1984a. The Idea of Poverty, England in the Early Industrial Age. Faber and Faber, London.

Himmelfarb, G., 1984b. The idea of poverty. Hist. Today 34 (4). http://www.historytoday.com/gertrude-himmelfarb/idea-poverty.

Hindle, S., 2004. On the Parish? The Micro-Politics of Poor Relief in Rural England 1550–1750. Oxford University Press, Oxford.

Hoff, K., 1996. Market failures and the distribution of wealth, a perspective from the economics of information. Polit. Soc. 24 (4), 411–432.

Hossain, M., 1988. Credit for Alleviation of Rural Poverty, the Grameen Bank in Bangladesh: IFPRI Research Report 65. International Food Policy Research Institute, Washington, DC.

Howe, I., 1993. Introduction to Michael Harrington's, the Other America. 1993 Reprinting, Touchstone, New York.

Hoynes, H., 1997. Does welfare play any role in female headship decisions? J. Publ. Econ. 65, 89–117.

Hunter, R., 1904. Poverty. MacMillan Company, London.

Imbert, C., Papp, J., 2011. Estimating leakages in India's employment guarantee. In: Khera, R. (Ed.), The Battle for Employment Guarantee. Oxford University Press, New Delhi, pp. 269–278.

Jalan, J., Ravallion, M., 1998. Are there dynamic gains from a poor-area development program? J. Pub. Econ. 67 (1), 65–86.

Jalan, J., Ravallion, M., 2002. Geographic poverty traps? A micro model of consumption growth in rural China. J. Appl. Econ. 17 (4), 329–346.

Jalan, J., Ravallion, M., 2004. Household income dynamics in rural china. In: Dercon, S. (Ed.), Insurance Against Poverty. Oxford University Press, New York, pp. 107–123.

Jha, R., Gaiha, R., Pandey, M.K., 2012. Net transfer benefits under India's rural employment guarantee scheme. J. Policy Model 34 (2), 296–311.

Johnson, D., Smeeding, T., 2012. A Consumer's Guide to Interpreting Various U.S. Poverty Measures, Fast Focus No. 14, Institute for Research on Poverty, University of Wisconsin.

Jones, G.S., 2004. An End to Poverty? A Historical Debate. Columbia University Press, New York.

Just, D., Michelson, H., 2007. Wealth as welfare, Are wealth thresholds behind persistent poverty? Appl. Econ. Perspect. Policy 29 (3), 419–426.

Kahl, S., 2005. The religious roots of modern poverty policy, catholic, Lutheran, and reformed protestant traditions compared. Eur. J. Sociol. 46, 91–126.

Kakwani, N., 1980. Income Inequality and Poverty, Methods of Estimation and Policy Applications. Oxford University Press, Oxford.

Kaldor, N., 1955. Alternative theories of distribution. Rev. Econ. Stud. 23 (2), 94–100.

Kalecki, M., 1942. A theory of profits. Econ. J. 52, 258–267.

Kanbur, R., 1987. Measurement and alleviation of poverty. IMF Staff. Pap. 36, 60–85.

Kanbur, R., Tuomala, M., 2011. Charitable conservatism, poverty radicalism and inequality aversion. J. Econ. Inequal. 9, 417–431.

Kanbur, R., Keen, M., Tuomala, M., 1994. Labor supply and targeting in poverty alleviation programs. World Bank Econ. Rev. 8 (2), 191–211.

Kant, I., 1785. Fundamental Principles of the Metaphysic of Morals. In: Kingsmill Abbott, T. (Ed.), 10 ed, Project Gutenberg.

Katz, M.B., 1987. The Undeserving Poor, From the War on Poverty to the War on Welfare. Pantheon Books, New York.

Keefer, P., Khemani, S., 2005. Democracy, Public Expenditures, and the Poor, Understanding Political Incentives for Providing Public Services. World Bank Res. Obs. 20 (1), 1–28.

Kelley, A., Schmidt, R., 1995. Aggregate population and economic growth correlations, the role of the components of demographic change. Demography 32 (4), 543–555.

Kelley, A., Schmidt, R., 2001. Economic and demographic change, a synthesis of models, findings and perspectives. In: Birdsall, N., Kelley, A., Sinding, S. (Eds.), Population Matters. Oxford University Press, Oxford.

Kelly, M., Cormac, Ó.G., 2010. Living Standards and Mortality since the Middle Ages, Working Paper 201026, School Of Economics, University College Dublin.

Keynes, J.M., 1936. The General Theory of Employment, Interest and Money. Macmillan Press, London.

Keysers, C., 2011. Empathic Brain. How the Discovery of Mirror Neurons Changes our Understanding of Human. Social Brain Press, Nature.

Khandker, S., Samad, H., 2014. Dynamic Effects of Microcredit in Bangladesh. Policy Research Working Paper 6821, World Bank, Washington, DC.

Kinsey, B., 2013. The excluded generations, questioning a leading poverty indicator. In: Paper presented at the UNU-WIDER conference "Inclusive Growth in Africa, Measurement, Causes, and Consequences.

Klebaner, B.J., 1964. Poverty and its relief in American thought, 1815–61. Soc. Serv. Rev. 38 (4), 382–399.

Knowles, S., 2005. Inequality and economic growth, the empirical relationship reconsidered in the light of comparable data. J. Dev. Stud. 41 (1), 135–159.

Kolm, S.-C., 1976. Unequal inequalities. I. J. Econ. Theory 12 (3), 416–442.

Korpe, P., Petri, W., 2012. Environmental enteropathy, critical implications of a poorly understood condition. Trends Mol. Med. 18 (6), 328–336.

Kraay, A., 2006. When is growth Pro-poor? Evidence from a panel of countries. J. Dev. Econ. 80, 198–227.

Kuznets, S., 1955. Economic growth and income inequality. Am. Econ. Rev. 45, 1–28.

Landauer, C., 1959. European Socialism, a History of Ideas and Movements from the Industrial Revolution to Hitler's Seizure of Power. University of California Press, Berkeley.

Lanjouw, P., Stern, N., 1998. Economic Development in Palanpur over Five Decades. Clarendon Press, Oxford.

Lepenies, P.H., 2014. Of goats and dogs, Joseph Townsend and the idealisation of markets—a decisive episode in the history of economics. Camb. J. Econ. 38, 447–457.

Levine, R., Renelt, D., 1992. A sensitivity analysis of cross-country growth regressions. Am. Econ. Rev. 82, 942–963.

Lewis, A., 1954. Economic development with unlimited supplies of labor. Manchester Sch. Econ. Soc. Stud. 22, 139–191.

Li, H., Zou, H.-f., 1998. Income inequality is not harmful to growth, theory and evidence. Rev. Dev. Econ. 2 (3), 318–334.

Lin, J.Y., 2012. New Structural Economics, a Framework for Rethinking Development and Policy. World Bank, Washington, DC.

Lindert, P.H., 2004. Growing Public: The Story, Social Spending and Economic Growth since the Eighteenth Century, vol. 1. Cambridge University Press, Cambridge.

Lindert, P.H., 2013. Private welfare and the welfare state. In: Neal, L., Williamson, J. (Eds.), The Cambridge History of Capitalism. Cambridge University Press, Cambridge.

Lipton, M., 1968. Urban bias and rural planning, strategy for agriculture. In: Streeten, P., Lipton, M. (Eds.), The Crisis in Indian Planning. Oxford University Press, Oxford.

Lipton, M., 1977. Why Poor People Stay Poor, Urban Bias and World Development. Temple Smith, London.

Lokshin, M., Ravallion, M., 2004. Household income dynamics in two transition economies. Stud. Nonlinear Dyn. Econom. 8 (3), 1–33.

Lopez, H., Servén, L., 2006. A Normal Relationship? Poverty, Growth and Inequality, Policy Research Working Paper 3814, World Bank.

Lopez, H., Servén, L., 2009. Too Poor to Grow, Policy Research Working Paper 5012, World Bank.

Loury, G., 1981. Intergenerational transfers and the distribution of earnings. Econometrica 49, 843–867.

Ludwig, J., Phillips, D.A., 2007. The Benefits and Costs of Head Start, NBER Working Paper 12973.

Lundberg, M., Squire, L., 2003. The simultaneous evolution of growth and inequality. Econ. J. 113, 326–344.

Macours, K., Schady, N., Vakis, R., 2008. Cash Transfers, Behavioral Changes and Cognitive Development in Early Childhood. Policy Research Working Paper 4759, World Bank, Washington, DC.

Mahalanobis, P.C., 1953. Some observations on the process of growth. Sankhya 12, 307–312.

Malthus, T.R., 1806. An Essay on the Principle of Population, 1890 ed. Ward, Lock and Co., London.

Mani, A., Mullainathan, S., Shafir, E., Zhao, J., 2013. Poverty impedes cognitive function. Science 341, 976–980.

Mansuri, G., Rao, V., 2012. Localizing Development, Does Participation Work? World Bank, Washington, DC.

Marshall, A., 1890. Principles of Economics. Macmillan, London (8th ed., 1920).

Marshall, A., 1907. Some possibilities of economic chivalry. Econ. J. 17 (65), 7–29.

Martin, W., Anderson, K., 2012. Export restrictions and price insulation during commodity price booms. Am. J. Agr. Econ. 94 (2), 422–427.

Marx, K., Engels, F., 1848. Manifesto of the Communist Party, London.

Mayhew, H., 2008. London Labour and the London Poor. Wordsworth Classics, London (reprinting a selection of newspaper articles from the 1840s).

McKenzie, D., Woodruff, C., 2006. Do entry costs provide an empirical basis for poverty traps? Evidence from Mexican microenterprises. Econ. Dev. Cult. Change 55 (1), 3–42.

McNamara, R., 1973. Address to the Board of Governors at the 1973 Annual General Meeting. World Bank, Washington DC.

Meade, J., 1972. Poverty in the welfare state. Oxf. Econ. Pap. 24, 289–326.

Mencher, S., 1967. Poor Law to Poverty Program, Economic Security Policy in Britain and the United States. University of Pittsburgh Press, Pittsburgh.

Mesnard, A., Ravallion, M., 2006. The wealth effect on new business startups in a developing economy. Economica 73, 367–392.

Meyer, B.D., Sullivan, J., 2012. Consumption and income poverty in the United States. In: Jefferson, P.N. (Ed.), The Oxford Handbook of the Economics of Poverty. Oxford University Press, Oxford.

Michel, J.-B., Shen, Y.K., Aiden, A.P., Veres, A., Gray, M.K., The Google Books Team, Pickett, J.P., Hoiberg, D., Clancy, D., Norvig, P., Orwant, J., Pinker, S., Nowak, M.A., Aiden, E.L., 2010. Quantitative analysis of culture using millions of digitized books. Science, 16 December.

Milanovic, B., 2005. Can we discern the effect of globalization on income distribution? World Bank Econ. Rev. 19 (1), 21–44.

Milanovic, B., 2008. Qat expenditures in Yemen and Djibouti, an empirical analysis. J. Afr. Econ. 17 (5), 661–687.

Mill, J.S., 1848. Principles of Political Economy, 1965 ed. A.M. Kelly, New York.

Mill, J.S., 1859. On Liberty, Dover Thrift Edition, Toronto2002.

Mirrlees, J., 1971. An exploration in the theory of optimum income taxation. Rev. Econ. Stud. 38, 175–208.

Moehling, C.M., 1999. State child labor laws and the decline of child labor. Explor. Econ. Hist. 36 (1), 72–106.

Montagu, A., 1971. Forward, in the 1971 reprint of Townsend (1786).

Morduch, J., 1999. The role of subsidies in microfinance, evidence from the Grameen Bank. J. Dev. Econ. 60, 229–248.

Muller, J.Z., 1993. Adam Smith in his Time and Ours, Designing a Decent Society. Princeton University Press, Princeton.

Murgai, R., Ravallion, M., 2005. Is a Guaranteed Living Wage a Good Antipoverty Policy? Policy Research Working Paper 3460, World Bank.

Murgai, R., Ravallion, M., van de Walle, D., 2013. Is Workfare Cost-Effective against Poverty in a Poor Labor-Surplus Economy? Policy Research Working Paper, World Bank.

Murphy, K., Schleifer, A., Vishny, R., 1989. Industrialization and the big push. J. Polit. Econ. 97 (5), 1003–1026.

Murray, C.A., 1984. Losing ground: American Social Policy 1950–1980. Basic Books, New York.

Musgrave, R., 1985. A brief history of fiscal doctrine. In: Auerbach, A.J., Feldstein, M. (Eds.), In: Handbook of Public Economics, vol. 1. North-Holland, Amsterdam.

Nath, S.K., 1969. A Reappraisal of Welfare Economics. Routledge and Kegan Paul, London.

Nozick, R., 1974. Anarchy, State and Utopia. Basic Books, New York.

O'Connor, A., 2002. Poverty Knowledge, Social Science, Social Policy, and the Poor in Twentieth-Century U.S. HistoryPrinceton University Press, Princeton.

O'Rourke, K., Williamson, J., 1997. Globalization and History, the Evolution of the Nineteenth Century Atlantic Economy. MIT Press, Cambridge, MA.

Orshansky, M., 1963. Children of the poor. Soc. Secur. Bull. 26, 3–29.

Pack, H., Saggi, K., 2006. The Case for Industrial Policy, a Critical Survey. Policy Research Working Paper 3839World Bank, Washington, DC.

Paine, T., 1797. Agrarian Justice, 2004 edition published with Common Sense by Penguin.

Pandey, P., Goyal, S., Sundararaman, V., 2009. Community participation in public schools, impacts of information campaigns in three indian states. Educ. Econ. 13 (3), 355–375.

Perotti, R., 1996. Growth, income distribution and democracy, what the data say. J. Econ. Growth 1 (2), 149–187.

Persson, T., Tabellini, G., 1994. Is inequality harmful for growth? Am. Econ. Rev. 84, 600–621.

Pigou, A., 1920. The Economics of Welfare, Fourth ed. Macmillan, London, 1971.

Pitt, M., Khandker, S., 1998. The impact of group-based credit programs on poor households in Bangladesh, does the gender of participants matter? J. Polit. Econ. 106, 958–996.

Pitt, M., Khandker, S., 2012. Replicating Replication Due Diligence in Roodman and Morduch's Replication of Pitt and Khandker (1998). Policy Research Working Paper 6273, World Bank, Washington, DC.

Pogge, T.W., 1989. Realizing Rawls. Cornell University Press, Ithaca.

Pollak, R., Wales, T., 1979. Welfare comparison and equivalence scale. Am. Econ. Rev. 69, 216–221.

Pradhan, M., Ravallion, M., 2000. Measuring poverty using qualitative perceptions of consumption adequacy. Rev. Econ. Stat. 82 (3), 462–471.

Probe Team, 1999. Public Report on Basic Education in India. Oxford University Press, New Delhi.

Proceedings of the Old Bailey., 2012. London, 1760–1815. Web Site, London.

Rajan, R., 2009a. Rent preservation and the persistence of underdevelopment. Am. Econ. J. Macroecon. 1 (1), 178–218.

Rajan, R., 2009b. Saving growth from unequal influence. In: Levy, S., Walton, M. (Eds.), No Growth without Equity? Inequality, Interests and Competition in Mexico. World Bank, Washington, DC.

Rao, V., 2001. Poverty and public celebrations in rural India. Ann. Am. Acad. Pol. Soc. Sci. 573 (1), 85–104.

Ravallion, M., 1987. Trade and stabilization: another look at British India's controversial foodgrain exports. Explor. Econ. Hist. 24, 354–370.

Ravallion, M., 1994. Measuring social welfare with and without poverty lines. Am. Econ. Rev. 84 (2), 359–365.

Ravallion, M., 1995. Growth and poverty, evidence for developing countries in the 1980s. Econ. Lett. 48, 411–417.

Ravallion, M., 1997a. Can high inequality developing countries escape absolute poverty? Econ. Lett. 56, 51–57.

Ravallion, M., 1997b. Famines and economics. J. Econ. Lit. 35 (3), 1205–1242.

Ravallion, M., 1998. Does aggregation hide the harmful effects of inequality on growth? Econ. Lett. 61 (1), 73–77.

Ravallion, M., 2001. Growth, inequality and poverty, looking beyond averages. World Dev. 29 (11), 1803–1815.

Ravallion, M., 2003. Inequality convergence. Econ. Lett. 80, 351–356.

Ravallion, M., 2005. Externalities in rural development, evidence for China. In: Kanbur, R., Venables, T. (Eds.), Spatial Inequality and Development. Oxford University Press, pp. 137–162.

Ravallion, M., 2006. Looking beyond averages in the trade and poverty Debate. World Dev. 34 (8), 1374–1392.

Ravallion, M., 2007. Inequality is bad for the poor. In: Micklewright, J., Jenkins, S. (Eds.), Inequality and Poverty Re-Examined. Oxford University Press, Oxford.

Ravallion, M., 2009. Are there lessons for Africa from China's success against poverty? World Dev. 37 (2), 303–313.

Ravallion, M., 2011. The two poverty enlightenments, historical insights from digitized books spanning three centuries. Poverty Public Policy 3 (2), 1–45.

Ravallion, M., 2012a. Poverty lines across the world. In: Jefferson, P.N. (Ed.), The Oxford Handbook of the Economics of Poverty. Oxford University Press, Oxford, pp. 75–104.

Ravallion, M., 2012b. Why don't we see poverty convergence? Am. Econ. Rev. 102 (1), 504–523.

Ravallion, M., 2013. How long will it take to lift one billion people out of poverty? World Bank Res. Obs. 28 (2), 139–158.

Ravallion, M., 2014. Poor, or just feeling poor. In: Clark, A., Senik, C. (Eds.), Subjective Wellbeing in Developing Countries. Oxford University Press, Oxford, pp. 140–174.

Ravallion, M., 2015. The Economics of Poverty: History, Measurement and Policy. Oxford University Press, New York.

Ravallion, M., Chen, S., 2007. China's (uneven) progress against poverty. J. Dev. Econ. 82 (1), 1–42.

Ravallion, M., Chen, S., 2011. Weakly relative poverty. Rev. Econ. Stat. 93 (4), 1251–1261.

Ravallion, M., Chen, S., 2013. A proposal for truly global poverty measures. Glob. Policy 4 (3), 258–265.

Ravallion, M., Datt, G., 1995. Is targeting through a work requirement efficient? Some evidence for rural India. In: de Walle, D., Nead, K. (Eds.), Public Spending and the Poor: Theory and Evidence. Johns Hopkins University Press, Baltimore.

Ravallion, M., Datt, G., 2002. Why has economic growth been more pro-poor in some states of india than others? J. Dev. Econ. 68, 381–400.

Ravallion, M., Wodon, Q., 2000a. Does child labor displace schooling? Evidence on behavioral responses to an enrolment subsidy. Econ. J. 110, 158–176.

Ravallion, M., Wodon, Q., 2000b. Banking on the poor? Branch location and non-farm rural development in Bangladesh. Rev. Dev. Econ. 4 (2), 121–139.

Ravallion, M., Datt, G., van de Walle, D., 1991. Quantifying absolute poverty in the developing world. Rev. Income Wealth 37, 345–361.

Ravallion, M., Chen, S., Sangraula, P., 2007. New evidence on the urbanization of global poverty. Popul. Dev. Rev. 33 (4), 667–702.

Ravallion, M., Chen, S., Sangraula, P., 2009. Dollar a day revisited. World Bank Econ. Rev. 23 (2), 163–184.

Ravallion, M., van de Walle, D., Dutta, P., Murgai, R., 2013. Try Telling People their Rights? On Making India's Largest Antipoverty Program work in India's Poorest State. Department of Economics, Georgetown University, Washington, DC.

Raventós, D., 2007. Basic Income, the Material Conditions of Freedom. Pluto Press, London.

Rawls, J., 1967. Distributive justice. In: Laslett, P., Runciman, W.G. (Eds.), Philosophy, Politics and Society. In: Series III, London.

Rawls, J., 1971. A Theory of Justice. Harvard University Press, Cambridge, MA.

Ray, D., 1998. Development Economics. Princeton University Press, Princeton, New Jersey.

Reinikka, R., Svensson, J., 2005. Fighting corruption to improve schooling, evidence from a newspaper campaign in Uganda. J. Eur. Econ. Assoc. 3 (2–3), 259–267, Papers and Proceedings of the Nineteenth Annual Congress of the European Economic Association.

Rhys-Williams, J., 1943. Something to Look Forward To. MacDonald, London.

Ricardo, D., 1817. Principles of Political Economy and Taxation, Everyman Edition, London, 1911.

Robbins, L., 1935. An Essay on the Nature and Significance of Economic Science, London.

Robinson, S., 1976. A note on the U-hypothesis relating income inequality and economic development. Am. Econ. Rev. 66, 437–440.

Roche, D., 1987. The People of Paris, an Essay in Popular Culture in the Eighteenth Century. University of California Press, Berkeley.

Rodriguez, F., Rodrik, D., 2001. Trade Policy and Economic Growth, A Sceptic's Guide to the Cross-National Evidence. NBER Macroeconomic Annual 2000MIT Press, Cambridge, pp. 261–324.

Rodrik, D., 1994. King Kong meets Godzilla, The World Bank and The East Asian Miracle. In: Fishlow, A., Gwin, C., Haggard, S., Rodrik, D., Wade, R. (Eds.), Miracle or Design? Lessons from the East Asian Experience. Overseas Development Council, Washington, DC.

Rodrik, D., 2004. Industrial Policy for the Twenty-First Century, Kennedy School of Government Working Paper RWP04-047, Harvard University.

Roemer, J., 1996. Theories of Distributive Justice. Harvard University Press, Cambridge.

Roemer, J., 1998. Equality of Opportunity. Harvard University Press, Cambridge, MA.

Roemer, J., 2013. Economic Development as Opportunity Equalization, Policy Research Working Paper 6530, World Bank.

Roodman, D., Morduch, J., 2009. The Impact of Microcredit on the Poor in Bangladesh, Revisiting the Evidence, Working Paper 174, Center for Global Development.

Rothschild, E., 2001. Economic Sentiments, Adam Smith, Condorcet, and the Enlightenment. Harvard University Press, Cambridge, MA.

Rothschild, M., Stiglitz, J., 1976. Equilibrium in competitive insurance markets, an essay on the economics of imperfect information. Quart. J. Econ. 90 (4), 629–650.

Rousseau, J.-J., 1754. Discourse on the Origin of Inequality, a Discourse on a Subject Proposed by the Academy of Dijon, What is the Origin of Inequality Among Men, and is it Authorised by Natural Law. Translated by G. D. H. Cole.

Rowntree, B.S., 1902. Poverty, a Study of Town Life. Macmillan, London.

Runciman, W.G., 1966. Relative Deprivation and Social Justice, a Study of Attitudes to Social Inequality in Twentieth Century England. Routledge and Kegan Paul.

Sachs, J., 2005a. Investing in Development, A Practical Plan to Achieve the Millennium Development Goals. United Nations Millennium Project, vol. 1, New York.

Sachs, J., 2005b. The End of Poverty. Economic Possibilities for Our Time. Penguin Books, New York.

Sadoulet, E., de Janvry, A., 1995. Quantitative Development Policy Analysis. The Johns Hopkins University Press, Baltimore.

Saez, E., 2006. Redistribution toward low incomes in rich countries. In: Banerjee, A., Benabou, R., Mookherjee, D. (Eds.), Understanding Poverty. Oxford University Press, Oxford.

Saint-Paul, G., 2011. The Tyranny of Utility. Behavioral Social Science and the Rise of Paternalism. Princeton University Press, Princeton.

Sala-I-Martin, X., Doppelhofer, G., Miller, R., 2004. Determinants of long-term growth, a Bayesian averaging of classical estimates (BACE) approach. Am. Econ. Rev. 94 (4), 813–836.

Sandmo, A., 2015. Income distribution in the history of economic thought. Handbook of Income Distribution, vol. 2A (Atkinson, A.B., Bourguignon, F. Eds.). Elsevier Science, Amsterdam (Chapter 1).

Sen, A.K., 1970a. Collective Choice and Social Welfare. Holden Day, San Francisco.

Sen, A.K., 1970b. Interpersonal aggregation and partial comparability. Econometrica 38 (3), 393–409.

Sen, A.K., 1973. On Economic Inequality. Clarendon Press, Oxford.

Sen, A.K., 1976. Poverty, an ordinal approach to measurement. Econometrica 46, 437–446.

Sen, A.K., 1980. Equality of what? In: McMurrin, S. (Ed.), Tanner Lectures on Human Values. Cambridge University Press, Cambridge.

Sen, A.K., 1981a. Poverty and Famines. Oxford University Press, Oxford.

Sen, A.K., 1981b. Public action and the quality of life in developing countries. Oxf. Bull. Econ. Stat. 43 (4), 287–319.

Sen, A.K., 1983. Poor, relatively speaking. Oxf. Econ. Papers 35 (2), 153–169.

Sen, A.K., 1985. Commodities and Capabilities, North-Holland, Amsterdam.

Sen, A.K., 1999. Development as Freedom. Alfred Knopf, New York.

Sen, A.K., 2000. Social Justice and the distribution of income. In: Atkinson, A.B., Bourguignon, F. (Eds.), Handbook of Income Distribution. In: vol. 1. Elsevier Science, Amsterdam.

Shapiro, C., Stiglitz, J., 1984. Involuntary unemployment as a worker discipline device. Am. Econ. Rev. 74 (3), 433–444.

Shipler, D., 2005. The Working Poor. Invisible in America. Vintage, New York.

Slesnick, D., 2001. Consumption and Social Welfare. Cambridge University Press, Cambridge.

Small, M.L., Harding, D.J., Lamont, M., 2010. Reconsidering culture and poverty. Ann. Am. Acad. Pol. Soc. Sci. 629, 6–29.

Smith, A., 1759. The Theory of Moral Sentiments. A. Millar, London.

Smith, A., 1776. An Inquiry into the Nature and Causes of the Wealth of Nations. Electronic Classic Edition, Pennsylvania State University, Pittsburgh.

Smith, R.M., 2011. Social security as a development institution? The relative efficacy of poor relief provisions under the english old poor law. In: Bayly, C.A., Woolcock, M., Szreter, S., Rao, V. (Eds.), History, Historians and Development Policy, A Necessary Dialogue. Manchester University Press, Manchester.

Solar, P.M., 1995. Poor relief and english economic development before the industrial revolution. Econ. Hist. Rev. 48, 1–22.

Solow, R., 1956. A contribution to the theory of economic growth. Quart. J. Econ. 70 (1), 65–94.

Sridharan, E., 2004. The growth and sectoral composition of India's middle class, its impact on the politics of economic liberalization. India Rev. 3 (4), 405–428.

Steinberg, Stephen, 2011. Poor Reason, Culture Still Doesn't Explain Poverty, Boston Review January 13.

Stephens, W.B., 1998. Education in Britain 1750–1914. Macmillan, London.

Stiglitz, J.E., 1969. Distribution of income and wealth among individuals. Econometrica 37 (3), 382–397.

Stiglitz, J.E., 1974. Incentives and risk sharing in sharecropping. Rev. Econ. Stud. 41, 219–255.

Stiglitz, J.E., 2012. The Price of Inequality. W.W. Norton & Co., New York.

Strauss, J., Thomas, D., 1998. Health, nutrition and economic development. J. Econ. Lit. 36 (2), 766–817.

Strömberg, D., 2004. Radio's impact on new deal spending. Quart. J. Econ. 119 (1), 189–221.

Subramanian, S., Deaton, A., 1996. The demand for food and calories. J. Polit. Econ. 104 (1), 133–162.

Sundquist, J.L., 1968. Politics and Power, the Eisenhower, Kennedy and Johnson Years. Brookings, Washington, DC.

Swamy, A., 1997. A simple test of the nutrition-based efficiency wage model. J. Dev. Econ. 53, 85–98.

Swartz, J., Braxton, D., Viera, A.J., 2011. Calorie menu labeling on quick-service restaurant menus, an updated systematic review of the literature. Int. J. Behav. Nutr. Phys. Act. 8, 135.

Thane, P., 2000. Old Age in English History. Oxford University Press, Oxford.

Thorner, D., 1967. Social and economic studies of Dr Mann. Econ. Pol. Wkly. 2 (13), 612–645.

Tinbergen, J., 1975. Income Distribution, Analyses and Policies, Amsterdam, North-Holland.

Todd, P., Wolpin, K., 2002. Using a Social Experiment to Validate a Dynamic Behavioral Model of Child Schooling and Fertility, Assessing the Impact of a School Subsidy Program in Mexico, Penn Institute for Economic Research Working Paper 03–022, Department of Economics, University of Pennsylvania.

Townsend, Joseph, 1786. A Dissertation on the Poor Laws by a Well-Wisher to Mankind, Reprint: University of California Press, Berkeley and Los Angeles, 1971.

Townsend, P., 1979. Poverty in the United Kingdom, a Survey of Household Resources and Standards of Living. Penguin Books, Harmonsworth.

Tucker, R.S., 1975. Real wages of artisans in London, 1729–1935. In: Taylor, A.J. (Ed.), The Standard of Living in the Industrial Revolution. Methuen, London.

United Nations Development Programme, 1990. Human Development Report. Oxford University Press for the UNDP, New York.

Vakil, C.N., Brahmanand, 1956. Planning for an Expanding Economy. Vora and Company, Bombay.

van de Walle, D., 1998. Targeting revisited. World Bank Res. Obs. 13 (2), 231–248.

Van Horn Melton, James, 1988. Absolutism and the Eighteenth Century Origins of Compulsory Schooling in Prussia and Austria. Cambridge University Press, Cambridge.

Van Praag, B., 1968. Individual Welfare Functions and Consumer Behavior, Amsterdam, North-Holland.

Vinovskis, M., 1992. Schooling and poor children in 19th-century America. Am. Behav. Sci. 35 (3), 313–331.

Voitchovsky, S., 2005. Does the profile of income inequality matter for economic growth? J. Econ. Growth 10, 273–296.

Voitchovsky, S., 2009. Inequality and economic growth. In: Salverda, W., Nolan, B., Smeeding, T. (Eds.), The Oxford Handbook of Economic Inequality. Oxford University Press, Oxford.

Walker, T.S., Ryan, J.G., 1990. Village and Household Economies in India's Semi-Arid Tropics. Johns Hopkins University Press, Baltimore.

Watts, H.W., 1968. An economic definition of poverty. In: Moynihan, D.P. (Ed.), On Understanding Poverty. Basic Books, New York.

Webb, R.K., 1974. Modern England from the 18th Century to the Present. Dodd, Mead and Company, New York.

Weiner, M., 1991. The Child and the State in India. Princeton University Press, Princeton.

Wicksell, K., 1901. Lectures on Political Economy. Routledge and Kegan Paul, London, 1934 English Edition.

Williamson, J., 1985. Did British Capitalism Breed Inequality? Routledge, London.

Williamson, J., 1998. Globalization and the labor market, using history to inform policy. In: Aghion, P., Williamson, J. (Eds.), Growth, Inequality and Globalization. Cambridge University Press, Cambridge.

Williamson, J., 2001. Demographic change, economic growth and inequality. In: Birdsall, N., Kelley, A., Sinding, S. (Eds.), Population Matters. Oxford University Press, Oxford.

Wilson, W.J., 1987. The truly disadvantaged, the inner city, the underclass and the truly disadvantaged. Chicago University Press, Chicago.

Wim, V.O., Halman, L., 2000. Blame or fate, individual or social? An international comparison of popular explanations of poverty. Eur. Soc. 2 (1), 1–28.

Winters, L.A., McCulloch, N., McKay, A., 2004. Trade liberalization and poverty, the evidence so far. J. Econ. Lit. 42 (March), 72–115.

Woodham-Smith, C., 1962. The Great Hunger, Ireland 1845–9. Hamilton, London.

World Bank, 1980. World Development Report, Poverty and Human Development. Oxford University Press, New York.

World Bank, 1986. Poverty and Hunger, Issues and Options for Food Security in Developing Countries. World Bank, Washington, DC.

World Bank, 1990. World Development Report, Poverty. Oxford University Press, New York.

World Bank, 1993. The East Asian Miracle, Economic Growth and Public Policy. Oxford University Press, New York.

World Bank, 1997. India, Achievements and Challenges in Reducing Poverty: Report No. 16483-IN. World Bank, Washington, DC.

World Bank, 2000. World Development Report, Attacking Poverty. Oxford University Press, New York.

World Bank, 2004. World Development Report, Making Services work for the Poor. Oxford University Press, New York.

World Bank, 2006. World Development Report, Equity and Development. Oxford University Press, New York.

World Bank, 2014. Conditional Cash Transfers. http://web.worldbank.org/WBSITE/EXTERNAL/TOPICS/EXTSOCIALPROTECTION/EXTSAFETYNETSANDTRANSFERS/0,contentMDK:20615138~menuPK:282766~pagePK:148956~piPK:216618~theSitePK:282761,00.html

CHAPTER 23

The Welfare State and Antipoverty Policy in Rich Countries

Ive Marx*,†, Brian Nolan‡, Javier Olivera§
*Herman Deleeck Centre for Social Policy, University of Antwerp, Antwerp, Belgium
†Institute for the Study of Labor, IZA, Bonn, Germany
‡Department of Social Policy and Intervention and Institute for New Economic Thinking at the Oxford Martin School, University of Oxford, UK
§Institute for Research on Socio-Economic Inequality, RU INSIDE, University of Luxembourg, Luxembourg, Luxembourg

Contents

Abstract

The aim of this chapter is to highlight some key aspects of recent economic research on the welfare state and antipoverty policy in rich countries and to explore their implications. We begin with the conceptualization and measurement of poverty before sketching out some core features and approaches to the welfare state and antipoverty policies. We then focus on the central plank of the modern welfare state's efforts to address poverty—namely, social protection, discussing in turn the inactive working-age population, child income support, in-work poverty, and retirement and old-age pensions. After that we discuss social spending other than cash transfers, the labor market, education, training and activation, and, finally, intergenerational transmission, childhood, and neighborhoods. We also discuss the

Handbook of Income Distribution, Volume 2B
ISSN 1574-0056, http://dx.doi.org/10.1016/B978-0-444-59429-7.00024-8

welfare state and antipoverty policy in the context of the economic crisis that began in 2007–2008 and the implications for strategies aimed at combining economic growth and employment with making serious inroads into poverty. We conclude with directions for future research.

Keywords

Poverty, Antipoverty policy, Redistribution

JEL Classification Codes

I3, I38, D63

23.1. SETTING THE SCENE

23.1.1 Introduction

Seen by some as primarily a manifestation of inequality in the distribution of income and wealth and by others as a distinctive phenomenon, poverty continues to represent a core challenge for rich countries and their welfare states. This is reflected in the substantial body of research on poverty in industrialized countries, both country-specific and comparative, which seeks to capture the extent of poverty and how it is changing over time, understand its nature, and assess the effectiveness of policies and strategies aimed at addressing it. Poverty is widely regarded as a key social concern in most rich countries, not only in terms of the quality of life of those affected but also in terms of their wasted potential, as well as the risks to the social fabric and to social cohesion more generally. (Chapter 22 by Martin Ravallion argues that the notion that poverty should and can be eliminated in such countries is a relatively recent development and also discusses in depth the links between poverty and macroeconomic performance.) While the nature of poverty and how best to tackle it remain hotly contested at a political and ideological level, the focus of research has increasingly been on the effectiveness of antipoverty policies and strategies, which the recent economic crisis has served only to reinforce.

The aim of this chapter is to highlight some key aspects of recent economic research on the welfare state and antipoverty policy in rich countries and to explore their implications. A core theme will be that the way poverty is conceptualized and measured has fundamental implications for how antipoverty policy is thought about, designed, and implemented. We therefore begin Section 23.1 with a discussion of conceptualization and measurement and key patterns and trends (see also Jäntti and Danziger, 2000), before sketching out some core features and approaches to the welfare state and antipoverty policies. Section 23.2 focuses on the central plank of the modern welfare state's efforts to address poverty—namely, social protection, discussing the inactive working-age population, child income support, in-work poverty, and retirement and old-age pensions. Section 23.3 looks beyond social protection to discuss social spending on other than cash transfers, the labor market, education, training, and activation. Finally, intergenerational transmission, childhood, and neighborhoods are addressed. Section 23.4 discusses the welfare state and antipoverty policy in the context of the economic crisis that began in 2007–2008 and the implications for strategies aimed at combining economic growth and employment with making serious inroads into poverty. Finally, Section 23.5 highlights directions for future research.

23.1.2 Conceptualizing and Measuring Poverty

The definition of poverty underpinning most recent research in Europe relates to exclusion from the ordinary life of the society due to lack of resources, as spelled out, for example, in the particularly influential formulation by Townsend (1979). This has also been very influential from a policy-making perspective as evidenced by the definition adopted by the European economic communities in the mid-1980s:

> The poor shall be taken to mean persons, families and groups of persons whose resources (material, cultural and social) are so limited as to exclude them from the minimum acceptable way of life in the Member State in which they live.

Poverty from this starting point has two core elements: It is about inability to participate, and this inability to participate is attributable to inadequate resources. Most economic research then employs income to distinguish the poor, with a great deal of research and debate on how best to establish an income cutoff for that purpose. There are also substantial theoretical and empirical literatures on concepts such as social exclusion (Kronauer, 1998) and on the "capabilities" approach pioneered by Sen (1980, 1993), which have implications for how one thinks about and measures poverty. Indeed, a concern with "poverty" *per se* may predominantly be seen as an Anglo-Saxon concern, with concepts such as deprivation and social exclusion more often the focus in countries such as France or Germany and with the "level of living" approach to living standards and well-being of central importance in the Nordic countries (and having much in common with Sen's capabilities approach in general orientation, on which see for example Erikson, 1993).

In comparative analysis, the most common approach to deriving income thresholds has been to calculate them as proportions of median income in the country in question, with 50% or 60% of the median being the most widely used metric. The underlying rationale is that those falling more than a certain "distance" below the average or normal income in their society are unlikely to be able to participate fully in that society, and notable examples from a very large literature adopting this approach are Atkinson et al. (1995) and the OECD's recent studies *Growing Unequal?* (Whiteford, 2008) and *Divided We Stand* (OECD, 2011a). Such research, like that on income inequality, was for many years bedeviled by differences in definition and measures in the data available for different countries, but sources such as the Luxembourg Income Study (LIS) micro database, the figures produced by Eurostat from micro data for the EU countries, and the database of aggregate poverty (and inequality) estimates assembled by the OECD have greatly improved this situation. Differences across countries and trends over time in relative income poverty measured in this fashion have played a central role in European research and policy debate. Chapter 8 in this volume by Morelli et al. presents evidence on trends in such measures to which we will return below.

This approach to deriving income thresholds can be contrasted with the approach taken by the United States, where the existence of a long-standing official poverty line has fundamentally influenced how poverty is debated and how research is carried out. That standard goes back to the 1960s when it was originally based on the cost of a nutritionally adequate diet, multiplied by a factor to take account of nonfood spending, but its key feature is that it has subsequently been uprated in line with consumer prices, rather than linked to average income or living standards. To characterize this contrast as between "relative" versus "absolute" notions of poverty would be to oversimplify, because above subsistence-level notions of what constitutes poverty inevitably reflect prevailing norms and expectations. The key issue in making comparisons over time is whether the poverty standard is fixed in terms of purchasing power—that is, "anchored" at a point in time or increases as average living standards rise. As Lampman (1971) put it in a U.S. context, in fighting a "War on Poverty" one may want to monitor how well one is doing in meeting a fixed target rather than redefining the target as income changes. However, over any prolonged period where average living standards are rising, this may lose touch with the everyday understanding of poverty in the society. Thus, an influential expert panel reviewing the U.S. official measure saw poverty in terms of insufficient resources for basic living needs, "defined appropriately for the United States today" (Citro and Michael, 1995).

The fact that the "anchored" measure has continued to be seen as relevant in the United States—for all its well-recognized and analyzed technical limitations—is in itself a reflection of the fact that growth in median real incomes has been modest there. In Europe, the set of poverty and social inclusion indicators adopted by the European Union (EU) since 2001 have supplemented purely relative income poverty thresholds with ones anchored at a point in time some years earlier and uprated in line with prices. The onset of the economic crisis from 2007 to 2008, when median income and relative income thresholds actually fell in some countries, proved a salutary reminder of the value of such anchored thresholds. Similar arguments apply in making comparisons across countries at rather different levels of average income: Neither purely country-specific relative measures nor common thresholds tell the whole story with respect to poverty. In a European context, this was brought to the fore by the accession to the EU in 2004 and 2007 of new eastern countries with much lower levels of average income than the "old" member states.

Alternative ways of establishing an income poverty threshold in a rich country have been proposed, for example, by reference to what it costs to buy a specified basket of goods and services, to ordinary expenditure patterns, to standards implicit in social security support rates, or to views in the population about, for example, the income needed to "get by." This continues to represent a significant theme in poverty research literature, as shown by recent attempts to apply the "basket of goods" approach in a consistent fashion across a variety of European countries (for a discussion of strengths and limitations of these alternatives see Nolan and Whelan, 1996). However, the extent to which this research has affected policy formulation and debate remains quite limited, with the relative and anchored income lines dominating. One suspects this is because of their reasonably straightforward empirical derivation.

In a similar vein, the way household size and composition are taken into account in applying those income lines is, for the most part, rather straightforward. The household is conventionally taken as the income recipient unit, as in the study of income inequality more broadly, assuming that income is shared so members reach a common standard of living. The fact that the types of household identified as poor (much more than the overall poverty rate) can be highly sensitive to the precise equivalence scale employed has been known for some time (Buhmann et al., 1987; Coulter et al., 1992), but in the absence of a more satisfactory alternative emerging from research practice, one has to rely on several commonly used scales (the square root of household size, the "OECD scale," and the "modified OECD scale") and (at best) present results with more than one so that this sensitivity can be assessed. While a number of studies have sought to open up the household "black box" from a poverty perspective, a subset of the research on intra-household inequality, more broadly discussed in Chapter 16 of this volume by Chiappori and Meghir, has had little impact on practice in empirical analysis and policy formulation.

The same could be said of the extensive literature on how best to capture the extent of poverty in a single summary indicator, where despite the considerable literature developing sophisticated indicators the most commonly used measure remains the simple headcount. As long ago as in the mid-1970s, Amartya Sen highlighted how the policy maker is faced with the perverse incentive to target the least poor, and Sen's (1976) and alternative ways of incorporating the "poverty gap" and inequality among the poor have been debated, often derived from a set of axioms representing *a priori* notions of the properties such a measure should have. The Foster et al. (1984) class of poverty measures, for example, are additively decomposable and, additionally, allow for different judgments regarding the importance attached to the extent on inequality among the poor. Such poverty measures that capture poverty intensity also suffer from greater sensitivity to measurement error, especially in the presence of extreme low incomes, which often reflects misreporting,[1] and as Myles (2000) argues, their mathematical representation may have made their meaning obscure to potential users. The robustness of poverty

---

[1] The poverty gap measure advanced by Hills (2002), based on the distance between the threshold and the median income of the poor, is one response to that problem.

orderings has also been a long-standing concern in the literature (Atkinson, 1987; Zheng, 2000), and dominance approaches developed for income inequality comparisons have been adapted for use in the poverty context (see Duclos and Makdissi, 2005), but once again this has not entered mainstream empirical practice, where the comparison of poverty headcounts over time or across countries on the basis of one or, at most, a very limited set of thresholds and equivalence scales remains the norm. An awareness of the importance of measurement error and the need to take statistical confidence intervals seriously in such comparisons does appear to be increasing, however (see Goedemé, 2013). There have also been significant improvements in the quality and comparability of income data for poverty analysis in recent years (as is the case for the analysis of income inequality more generally, as brought out in Morelli et al.'s Chapter 8 and in Tóth, 2014), largely due to the efforts of organizations such as the OECD, the LIS, and Eurostat as well as national statistics offices.

A substantial strand in recent research on poverty that is increasingly influencing practice has focused instead on questioning what economic research had tended to take for granted: that current income is the most satisfactory, or least bad, yardstick available for identifying the poor. It has instead been argued forcefully that low-income fails in practice to distinguish those experiencing poverty and exclusion, because current income does not capture the impact of savings, debt, previous spending on consumer durables, owner-occupied housing, goods and services provided by the State, work-related expenses such as transport and child care, and geographical variation in prices, because needs also differ in ways missed by conventional equivalence scales (for example in relation to disability), and because income from self-employment, home production, and capital are particularly difficult to measure accurately. One response is to measure financial poverty in terms of consumption rather than income, on the basis that the transitory component is a great deal smaller, but expenditure as measured in household budget surveys often covers only a short period and is not the same as consumption, while low expenditure may be associated with saving and does not necessarily capture constrained resources. Other avenues explored in research have been to impute income from durables, owner-occupied housing and noncash benefits, to broaden the needs incorporated into equivalence scales and to combine survey and other data to improve the measurement of income.

The exploitation of longitudinal data has also been a significant contributor to income-based poverty research. Poverty measures are often based on the income of the household in a specific week, month, or year, but (even if measured accurately) income at a particular point in time may not be representative of the usual or longer term income of the household. Longitudinal data tracking households and their incomes have now become much more widely available, allowing those who move in and out of low income to be distinguished from those who are persistently of low income, and a dynamic perspective on income now plays a central role in research on poverty. Bane and Ellwood

(1986) pioneered research on the length of spells in poverty in the United States, and cross-country analysis was pioneered by Duncan et al. (1993). Comparative studies of income poverty dynamics since then include OECD (2001), Whelan et al. (2003), Fouarge and Layte (2005), and Valletta (2006). Movements in and out of poverty are special cases of more general income mobility, discussed in Chapter 10 by Jäntti and Jenkins in this volume. Available studies show what the OECD (2001) has summarized as the seeming paradox that poverty is simultaneously fluid and characterized by long-term traps. Many spells in poverty are short and represent only transitory setbacks, and considerably fewer people are continually poor for an extended period of time than are observed in poverty at a point in time, but on the other hand, the typical year spent in poverty is lived by someone who experiences multiple years of poverty; comparison across countries has found poverty persistence to be particularly high in the United States and much lower in countries with lower cross-sectional poverty rates. The EU's social inclusion indicators now include a measure of persistent poverty, the percentage below the relative poverty threshold in the current year and at least two of the three previous years. More generally, this aspect of poverty research, with its emphasis on trying to understand not only once-off poverty entries and escapes but also the cumulative experience of poverty over years, has had a major impact on the way policy effectiveness is thought about and assessed.

As well as broadening the measurement of income/financial resources and their dynamics, a parallel development in recent poverty research has sought to go beyond income, with a view to:

- identifying the poor more accurately and understanding the causal processes at work,
- capturing the multidimensional nature of poverty, and/or
- encompassing social exclusion conceived as something broader than "financial poverty."

Nonmonetary indicators of deprivation have been used for quite some time to directly capture different aspects of living standards and social exclusion (either on their own or combined with low income), to validate an income poverty threshold, and/or to bring out graphically what it means to be poor; the review of the literature on measures of material deprivation in OECD countries by Boarini and Mira d'Ercole (2006) listed more than 100 studies. Over the past decade or more, nonmonetary indicators measured at micro levels are also increasingly being used to capture the multidimensional nature of poverty and of social exclusion more broadly—especially in Europe, where the concepts of social exclusion and social inclusion have come to be widely used alongside poverty in research and policy circles, unlike in the United States where they have so far had little purchase. Comparative analysis of datasets such as the European Community Household Panel Survey (ECHP) organized by Eurostat and carried out in most of the (then) EU-member states from the mid-1990s to 2001, and the EU-Statistics on Income and Living Conditions (EU-SILC) data-gathering framework, which replaced it, has identified distinct dimensions of disadvantage (see Eurostat, 2005; Guio, 2009; Guio and Macquet, 2007; Nolan and Whelan, 2010, 2011; Whelan et al., 2001), bringing out that low income alone is not enough to predict who experiences poor housing, neighborhood deprivation, poor health and access to health services, and low education. The measurement of multidimensional poverty and inequality, discussed in Chapter 3 of this volume by Aaberge and Brandolini, raises complex issues not only about the best way to identify and empirically capture particular dimensions, but also about how information about different aspects of deprivation or exclusion is best summarized across those dimensions (see Aaberge and Peluso, 2012; Atkinson, 2003; Bourguignon and Chakravarty, 2003; Tsui, 2002).

The focus on multidimensionality has gone well beyond a purely academic concern to also influence the way poverty reduction targets have been framed, both nationally and at EU level. The national poverty reduction target adopted in Ireland in the 1990s, for example, was framed in terms of the combination of low income and "basic" deprivation, and lively debates about how best to frame targets for child poverty in the United Kingdom have centered on the role of multidimensionality. Since 2001 the EU's social inclusion process has at its core a set of indicators designed to monitor progress and support mutual learning that is explicitly and designedly multidimensional, including but going beyond income-based poverty indicators, including indicators of material deprivation and housing deprivation (see Atkinson et al., 2002; Marlier et al., 2007; Nolan and Whelan, 2011; Chapter 3). Even more strikingly, when in 2010 the EU adopted the *Europe 2020* strategy for jobs and growth, which for the first time included poverty reduction among its high-level targets, the target population for poverty reduction was identified as those:

- below the 60% of national median threshold relative income threshold, and/or;
- above the material deprivation threshold, and/or;
- in a jobless household.

A total of 23% of EU citizens were identified as "at-risk-of-poverty and social exclusion," as this was labeled, significantly more than the 16% below the "headline" 60% of median relative income threshold, and EU leaders pledged to bring at least 20 million of these people out of poverty and exclusion by 2020. While once can readily criticize the logic and implications of this precise combination of elements (on which see Nolan and Whelan, 2011), it represents a powerful illustration of the role that multidimensional measures, and direct measures of material deprivation as a central component, have come to play in framing European antipoverty policy.

The European poverty target evolved from a process of development and adoption of social inclusion indicators at EU level over the previous decade (see Atkinson et al., 2002), which has had a significant influence on data and analyses of poverty and antipoverty policy in Europe, and indeed on the way poverty is thought about and research is framed. This serves as an important example of the broader point that a good deal of research on poverty is carried out or sponsored by bodies—national or international—that have an interest in demonstrating that particular sets of policies or orientations toward antipoverty strategy are or are likely to be successful. In a more subtle way, their perspectives will influence the data and indicators available to researchers, and thus the analyses that can be readily undertaken. There have been enormous advances in the availability of accessible micro data in recent years, which has fundamentally influenced poverty research and helped to "democratize" it, but the influence of national governments and international organizations remains substantial.

Finally, in discussing how poverty research is approached, differences in disciplinary perspectives are also important. For example, researchers from an economics perspective are generally more comfortable with financial indicators of living standards and exclusion, and highlight the role of economic incentives in understanding and tackling poverty, whereas sociologists have often been more open to employing nonmonetary measures and highlight the role of social stratification and social context. Having said that, there has been significant blurring of disciplinary boundaries, and poverty research has become a site for particularly fruitful collaborations between *inter alia* economists, sociologists, social policy analysts, geographers, anthropologists, educationalists, epidemiologists, psychologists, and indeed geneticists and neuroscientists, of which this chapter can only give a flavor, concentrating for the most part on the economics literature.

23.1.3 Key Patterns and Trends

As the previous section highlighted, the most common practice in comparative research on poverty remains the application of relative income poverty thresholds and comparisons of headcounts of the proportions falling below those thresholds in different countries. On that basis, poverty rates for various OECD countries based on the data in the LIS have been compared in, for example, Atkinson et al. (1995) and Fritzell and Ritakallio (2004). The OECD has assembled estimates for many of its member countries at intervals from 1980, which have underpinned its important studies in this area (notably OECD, 2008, 2011a) and annual estimates are also now produced by Eurostat for all the member states of the EU. This, together with national data, provides a substantially improved evidence base for the study of poverty across countries and over time.

Chapter 8 in this volume by Morelli et al. summarizes broad trends in relative income poverty over time, with figures from the LIS suggesting that from the mid-1980s to mid-2000s relative income rates generally rose or stayed stable, with very few examples of significant falls. The OECD's analysis of the estimates of relative income poverty it assembled, as examined in Burniaux et al. (1998), Förster and Pearson (2002), Förster and Mira d'Ercole (2005), *Growing Unequal?* (Whiteford, 2008), and *Divided We Stand* (OECD, 2011a), highlighted that the most common direction of change in those figures was upward. The corresponding data produced by Eurostat covers only (most of) the countries in the EU-15 for the period from the mid-1990s to 2001, based on the ECHP, while the expansion of the Union to 27 member states was accompanied by the development of a new statistical apparatus underpinning these estimates, EU-SILC, from about 2004; this means that trends before 2004 can be assessed only for the "old" member states and, for many of these, with a break in the series in the early 2000s, which affects comparability. Nonetheless, the feature displayed by these figures highlighted by a number of studies is the disappointing progress in bringing relative income poverty rates down despite strong growth in employment in some countries over the decade to the mid-2000s (see, for example, Cantillon, 2011).

It is important to note, however, that there is considerable variability in country experiences and that the stability in the overall poverty rate can mask major underlying shifts for different groups. The OECD's studies, for example, show that the trend in relative income poverty for working-age people in the second half of the 1990s and into the 2000s was generally upward, often reflecting a decline in the poverty-reducing impact of taxes and transfers, but pensioners saw sizeable declines in many countries. So policies operating with respect to one important target group—such as older persons—could be having substantial success in reducing poverty while that is obscured by the impact of changes for other groups. In a similar vein, child poverty—the focus of particular attention from policy makers in recent years—may not necessarily move in the same direction as the overall poverty rate, with the U.K. providing an example where trends in child versus overall poverty have deviated substantially over the past two decades.

The OECD has also usefully documented trends in overall poverty taking a threshold "anchored" at 50% of the median in the mid-1980s and then indexed to price changes. On this measure, all OECD countries achieved significant reductions in "absolute" poverty up to year 2000. In countries like Ireland and Spain, which experienced very rapid income growth, poverty in 1995 measured this way was one-sixth the level of 10 years earlier. The U.S. poverty rate on this basis shows a decline from the mid-1980s up until 2000, though smaller than the average decline of the 15 OECD countries included in the study (Förster and Mira d'Ercole, 2005). In a similar vein, it is striking that some countries where relative income poverty remained quite stable or even rose have seen very marked falls in levels of material deprivation, notably some of the lower-income countries joining the EU from 2004 as the common indicators of material deprivation now also produced by Eurostat serve to demonstrate. The evolution of alternative measures of poverty since the onset of the economic crisis across the OECD from 2007 to 2008 is also of central relevance, as we discuss in detail in the final section of this chapter.

National studies for various countries also shed light on poverty trends and the factors at work, though given differences in methods and approaches, it is more difficult to generalize from them. In the United States, for example, most analyses of long-term poverty trends focus on the official poverty rate, which is not linked to average or median income (see Hoynes et al., 2006; Meyer and Wallace, 2009; Smeeding and Thompson, 2013). This (and variants of it) was higher in the 1980s than in the 1970s but despite subsequent falls was still as high in the mid-2000s as it had been in the mid-1970s. Stagnant median wage growth, rising inequality, and the evolution of unemployment have been highlighted in studies, with the changing wage distribution assigned a central role in explaining poverty trends. Studies of poverty trends in the United Kingdom, by contrast, have generally focused on relative income poverty and have highlighted the role of changes in the transfer and direct tax systems in the increase recorded in the 1980s and into the 1990s and then stabilization from the late 1990s. However, as Dickens and Ellwood (2003) emphasize in a comparative study of Britain and the United States, the factors influencing poverty trends can differ substantially between absolute and relative measures as well as countries, and it is hazardous to generalize.

Trends in poverty over time, overall, and for specific subgroups offer one important window into the causal factors involved and into "what works" in addressing poverty, especially in terms of the impact of changes made in social protection and tax systems. It is also striking that the ranking of countries in terms of relative income poverty rates tend to be fairly stable over time. Table 23.1 shows the percentage of people in households falling below 50% and 60% of median (equivalized) disposable household income in 25 OECD countries around the mid-2000s. The simple fact that there is considerable cross-country variation in poverty measured this way—with some countries displaying percentages below 60% of the median as low as 11–12% and at the other extreme countries having figures twice that high—and that the ranking of countries tends to be reasonably stable over time, suggests that there are important structural factors at work from which antipoverty strategies have much to learn.

A similar point is brought home by reference to the variation across countries in relative income poverty rates for specific population subgroups. Table 23.2 illustrates this with the rates for children and older persons falling below 50% of national median income, compared with the population as a whole. Children have above-average rates in about half the countries shown, with the gap being particularly wide in the United Kingdom and the United States, but in a substantial minority, their rate is below average. The elderly have an above-average rate in most countries, with substantial variation in the size of the gap, and there are some instances where their rate is well below the average. A similar comparison across the EU 27 using data from EU-SILC shows similar patterns. So, this reinforces the notion that there is much to be learned in policy terms from analysis of the situation and treatment of similar groups in different countries.

The same is true of other groups that are generally thought of as vulnerable. For example, the unemployed face a significantly heightened risk of relative income poverty virtually everywhere, but the gap between them and the employed varies widely across countries. Similarly, single parents often face much higher risks of poverty than couples with one or two children, but that gap varies a great deal. As OECD (2005) points out, in

Table 23.1 Income poverty rates in OECD countries, mid-2000s

Country	% below 50% of median income	% below 60% of median income
Australia (2003)	12.3	20.4
Austria (2004)	7.1	13.4
Belgium (2000)	8.1	16.1
Canada (2007)	11.9	18.7
Czech Republic (2004)	5.8	11.4
Denmark (2004)	5.6	13.2
Estonia (2004)	12.8	20.4
Finland (2004)	6.6	13.7
France (2005)	8.5	14.9
Germany (2007)	8.4	14.6
Greece (2004)	11.9	19.6
Hungary (2005)	7.4	12.5
Ireland (2004)	13.2	22.0
Italy (2008)	11.9	19.7
Luxembourg (2004)	8.9	13.8
Mexico (2004)	18.3	25.5
Netherlands (2004)	6.3	11.8
Norway (2004)	7.1	12.8
Poland (2004)	10.7	17.2
Slovenia (2004)	7.1	11.7
Spain (2007)	13.7	20.3
Sweden (2005)	5.6	12.0
Switzerland (2004)	8.0	14.8
UK (2004)	11.2	19.0
USA (2007)	17.7	24.4

Source: LIS downloaded.

many countries it is not living in single-parent households *per se* that increases risk, but rather the likelihood that the parent is not at work. As we shall see, this type of comparative analysis plays a central role in research aimed at informing antipoverty policies and strategies.

It is also worth noting that although relative income poverty measures are sometimes dismissed as really only capturing inequality, in fact a country (or group within it) can have zero poverty despite substantial inequality. To give concrete examples, in both the Netherlands and New Zealand the incidence of relative poverty among the elderly (with the 50% of median threshold) is close to zero, although there is substantial income inequality among their elderly populations. The redistributive effort required to truncate the distribution at a widely used poverty threshold like 50% of median equivalent income is in fact a fraction of the actual redistributive flows that take place in most countries. In practice, as Figure 23.1 shows, broadly speaking, where inequality in disposable income is

Table 23.2 Income poverty rates for children and elderly in OECD countries, mid-2000s

Country	% of below 50% of median income		
	Children	Elderly (65+)	All
Australia (2003)	14.0	22.3	12.3
Austria (2004)	6.8	9.4	7.1
Belgium (2000)	7.2	15.4	8.1
Canada (2007)	15.0	8.3	11.9
Czech Republic (2004)	10.2	2.1	5.8
Denmark (2004)	3.9	8.5	5.6
Estonia (2004)	15.4	13.5	12.8
Finland (2004)	4.1	10.3	6.6
France (2005)	10.2	7.4	8.5
Germany (2007)	9.3	9.0	8.4
Greece (2004)	12.4	18.8	11.9
Hungary (2005)	9.9	4.0	7.4
Ireland (2004)	15.9	23.8	13.2
Italy (2008)	17.1	11.0	11.9
Luxembourg (2004)	13.5	4.7	8.9
Mexico (2004)	22.2	27.1	18.3
Netherlands (2004)	9.2	2.4	6.3
Norway (2004)	5.3	8.5	7.1
Poland (2004)	15.6	3.5	10.7
Slovenia (2004)	5.5	16.4	7.1
Spain (2007)	17.3	20.7	13.7
Sweden (2005)	4.7	6.6	5.6
Switzerland (2004)	9.3	15.1	8.0
UK (2004)	13.0	16.3	11.2
USA (2004)	22.0	24.2	17.7

Source: LIS downloaded.

high relative income poverty rates tend to be high as well, but similar inequality levels can be associated with quite different levels of relative income poverty.

23.1.4 The Welfare State and Poverty

As Barr (2001) put it, the welfare state combines the role of piggy bank and Robin Hood, providing collective insurance against social risks while also aiming to ameliorate need and poverty. Redistribution can be horizontal, across the life cycle, or vertical between higher and lower incomes. Poverty reduction is by no means the sole criterion against which the success of welfare state institutions would or should be judged—whether at a point in time or over the life cycle—but it would be widely accepted as among the core aims. Research aimed at assessing success or failure in those terms can focus at the aggregate level, at specific population subgroups, or at particular institutional

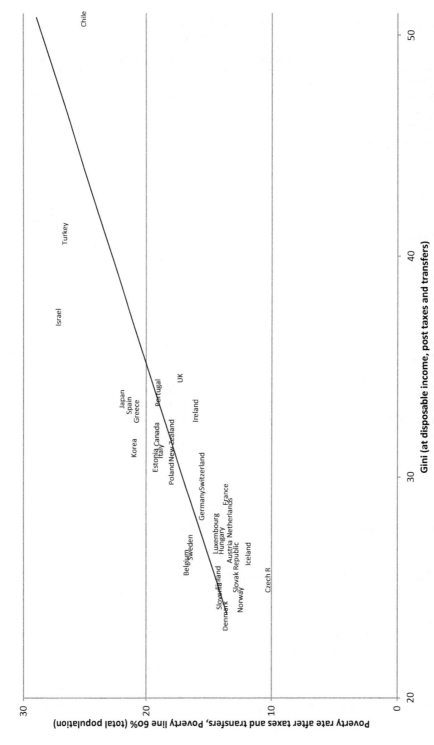

Figure 23.1 Gini coefficient for disposable income and relative income poverty (60% median), 2009, OECD. *Source: OECD income distribution database.*

structures, interventions, or innovations and can be for a particular country or from a comparative perspective.

The nature of that research is also multifaceted. At one end of the spectrum one can locate studies of the effectiveness of very particular aspects of institutional structures or changes in those structures on the target population to whom they are directed. Such evaluation studies employ a wide variety of analytical and technical approaches, which have been the subject of intensive development in the economics literature in recent years. While the outcome studied is occasionally whether people are lifted out of poverty, there is a much more extensive literature focusing on effectiveness in getting unemployed persons into employment, improving performance in school, keeping people out of jail or improving their health, all of which may be expected to impact on poverty status. While randomized controlled trials are recently in vogue in this context—though the negative income tax experiments conducted in the United States and Canada in the 1970s provide early large-scale examples[2]—more commonly, assessments are not based on such an approach. The methods employed include reduced form or limited information models (including least squares, matching methods including propensity score matching, instrumental variable analysis or the closely related regression discontinuity design approach, and difference in difference estimation) versus the estimation of structural models/parameters.[3] Such methods are discussed extensively in other books in this series (notably those focused on labor economics, since assessing the impact of labor market programs has been a particularly fertile field of application); purely from the point of view of research on poverty, though, while influencing specific national reform efforts they have had much less impact on the way antipoverty policy is thought about more broadly.

In that respect, comparative analysis of poverty outcomes and redistributive effort across countries over time continues to dominate (see Cantillon et al., 2014). This is underpinned by the fact that the direct effect of transfers and direct taxes on measured poverty is seen to differ very substantially across countries. OECD analysis concludes that the best-performing countries succeed in lifting about two-thirds of their pre-tax/transfer poor above the threshold, while others only manage to move one-quarter above. Recent EU statistics tell a similar story, as Table 23.3 illustrates: Welfare systems reduce the risk of poverty by 38% on average across the EU, but this impact varies from under 15% to more than 60% across the member states. Some countries achieve better "efficiency" (i.e., reduce poverty more for each euro or dollar spent) through targeting low-income groups, and the role of means-testing is one of the most hotly debated aspects of antipoverty policy to which we return below. However, the prior point to be made here is that

---

[2] See for example Levine et al. (2005).

[3] For discussion of the advantages and disadvantages of alternative approaches see Chetty (2009), Deaton (2010), Heckman and Urzúa (2010), Imbens (2010), and Heckman (2010).

Table 23.3 Income poverty rates pre- and post-transfers in EU countries, 2007

Country	Pre-transfer poverty %	Post-transfer poverty %	Reduction in poverty % point	%
Belgium	27.5	15.2	12.3	44.7
Bulgaria	25.5	22	3.5	13.7
Czech Republic	20.1	9.6	10.5	52.2
Denmark	27.1	11.7	15.4	56.8
Germany	24.8	15.2	9.6	38.7
Estonia	25.2	19.4	5.8	23
Ireland	33.1	17.2	15.9	48
Greece	23.7	20.3	3.4	14.3
Spain	23.9	19.7	4.2	17.6
France	26.4	13.1	13.3	50.4
Italy	24.1	19.8	4.3	17.8
Cyprus	21	15.5	5.5	26.2
Latvia	27.2	21.2	6	22.1
Lithuania	25.5	19.1	6.4	25.1
Luxembourg	23.4	13.5	9.9	42.3
Hungary	29.3	12.3	17	58
Malta	21.2	14.8	6.4	30.2
Netherlands	20.6	10.2	10.4	50.5
Austria	24.7	12	12.7	51.4
Poland	26.5	17.3	9.2	34.7
Portugal	24.2	18.1	6.1	25.2
Romania	30.9	24.8	6.1	19.7
Slovenia	23.1	11.5	11.6	50.2
Slovakia	18.2	10.6	7.6	41.8
Finland	28.9	13	15.9	55
Sweden	27.5	10.5	17	61.8
UK	29.7	18.6	11.1	37.4

Source: Eurostat downloaded.

the pattern of incomes from the market, taken as the baseline for comparison, will itself be very much influenced by social transfers and indeed by welfare state institutions more broadly. The existence of social transfers allows substantial numbers of households to have no income from the market, which would not be sustainable otherwise, and the welfare state also affects incentives to work and save in many other ways: the "no welfare state" counterfactual is not known.

A favored mode of analysis in comparative studies is to take a set of countries—at a point in time or pooling cross-sections over time—and assess the relationship between poverty outcomes and a wide set of independent variables reflecting population structures, welfare spending levels and aspects of labor market and welfare state institutions. (These parallel, and sometimes overlap, similar studies employing income inequality as dependent variable reviewed in depth in Chapter 19 of the current volume by Förster and Tóth.) Particularly, influential studies in this vein include Korpi and Palme (1998), Moller et al. (2003), and Kenworthy (2011). In such comparative analysis, countries may be taken as individual units of observation, or they may be grouped together into different "welfare regimes," designed to capture key commonalities/differences in welfare state institutions. Esping-Andersen's (1990) distinction of three distinct regimes has been highly influential: the liberal/Anglo-Saxon countries with minimal public intervention and a preference for targeting and reliance on the market, the social democratic/ Nordic countries with comprehensive social entitlements, and the continental welfare states with conservative origins built around social insurance but often along narrowly defined occupational distinctions and a significant degree of reliance on the family (see also Esping-Andersen, 1999, 2009). A fourth "southern" regime is also generally distinguished (Ferrera, 1996), and the treatment of the formerly communist countries of eastern Europe is also a matter for debate. The relationship between aggregate social spending and poverty levels looks systematically different for the countries that joined the EU in 2004 versus the "old" 15 members (see Tsakloglou and Papadopoulos, 2002), but treating them as a single "regime" may not be satisfactory. Many empirical studies have brought out the extent to which conventional indicators of (relative income) poverty vary systematically across welfare regimes (for a recent example see Whelan and Maitre, 2010), and highlight the consistently low rates found in Nordic countries compared with the generally high (though varying) ones seen in the liberal and southern European countries. Looking in some detail at the make-up of household income by source, Maitre et al. (2012) show that countries in the Anglo-Saxon/liberal regime were distinctive in the extent to which low-income households were dependent on social transfers, and also in the extent to which that dependence served as a predictor of material deprivation. The social democratic and corporatist regimes were characterized by a more modest degree of welfare dependence among low-income households, while in the southern Mediterranean countries welfare was not strongly associated with low income and was a particularly poor predictor of deprivation.

Aggregate-level comparative analysis of this type suggests that while transfer and tax systems are undoubtedly key in underpinning variations in poverty levels, other institutional features also contribute in the best performers, notably high levels of minimum wage protection and strong collective bargaining compressing wages, more extensive public and subsidized employment as well active labor market programs, higher levels of public spending on education, and so forth (see also Chapter 19 in this book). Disentangling the effect of these various factors is inherently fraught with difficulties, and that is where simulation via tax-benefit models, discussed in detail in Chapter 24 of this volume by Figari et al. may be particularly helpful. The Euromod research program in particular has enabled comparative tax-benefit simulation analysis across the EU (Figari and Sutherland, 2013; Immervoll et al., 2006) with major implications for policy. To take just one example, Cantillon et al. (2003) showed that simply increasing spending on transfers would have a limited impact on poverty in some EU countries because much of it would go to those already above the poverty line, particularly in the southern European welfare states where pensions dominate.

Another central strand of comparative poverty research has focused on analysis of the characteristics associated with being in poverty and the underlying processes involved, employing micro data. This has been the subject of a very wide variety of studies covering many countries, both descriptive and econometric. Broadly speaking, the types of individual or household seen as at particular risk of poverty include those with low levels of education and skills, the low paid, the unemployed, people with disabilities, single parents, large families, the elderly, children, ethnic minorities, migrants, and refugees. However, there is substantial variation across countries in the patterning of risk, with major implications for how the underlying processes are understood and for policy. The extent to which individual characteristics, qualifications, or experiences manifest themselves in high-poverty rates is clearly seen to depend on the household, labor market, and institutional settings in which those "disadvantages" are experienced. To take one example, the poverty risk for the unemployed compared with others is seen to depend on whether they have dependants, whether there are others in the household at work, and how the welfare state and its institutions try to cushion the impact of unemployment, most importantly through social protection. Strikingly, a high employment rate is clearly not a sufficient condition for low poverty among the working-aged population, which as we discuss below is of central relevance when boosting labor market participation is at the heart of antipoverty policy in many countries.

Finally, the availability of longitudinal data has also allowed the development of econometric modeling of poverty dynamics, which seeks to link observed movements into or out of poverty over time to changes in the earnings, labor force participation, and composition of the household. Duncan et al. (1993) were the first to do so in a comparative setting. A distinction is often made in such dynamic analyses between income "events," such as changes in earnings or benefits, and demographic "events," such as the arrival of a new child, partnership formation, death, marital dissolution, or offspring leaving home. The comparative dynamic analysis by OECD (2005) suggests that changes in household structure may be less important in poverty entries and escapes in European countries than in the United States, with changes in transfers as well as earnings seen to be important in the EU and to a lesser extent in Canada, but much less so in the United States.

23.2. SOCIAL PROTECTION AND REDISTRIBUTION

23.2.1 Introduction

Cash spending as a percentage of GDP is the most widely used measure of how much "effort" is being made to directly redistribute income. Despite its widespread use, this measure has some well-documented shortcomings. First, it ignores the need to jointly analyze benefit and tax policies. Conventional measures of (gross) social expenditure tend to overestimate the cost of welfare in Denmark, Finland, and Sweden, where a substantial amount of benefit spending is clawed back through taxation. Conversely, in the Czech Republic and Slovenia, a substantial share of social spending takes the form of tax breaks for social purposes rather than cash transfers (Adema et al., 2011). Another widely acknowledged weakness of this measure is that it is a very imperfect indicator of policy intent and policy design. A high level of spending may result from very generous benefits flowing to small numbers of people and not necessarily people occupying the bottom end of the distribution—for example, government elites. Yet it may also result from relatively small benefits flowing to a large number of people (De Deken and Kittel, 2007).

Yet, several studies have established a strong empirical relationship at country level between the overall level of social spending and various measures of inequality and inequality reduction, including (relative) poverty. This is arguably one of the more robust findings of comparative poverty research over the past decades (Atkinson et al., 1995; Ferrarini and Nelson, 2003; Gottschalk and Smeeding, 1997; Immervoll and Richardson, 2011; Kenworthy, 2004, 2008, 2011; Kraus, 2004; Nolan and Marx, 2009; OECD, 2008; Pestieau, 2006). Notable in these analyses is that no advanced economy achieved a low level of inequality and/or relative income poverty with a low level of social spending, regardless of how well that country performed on other dimensions that matter for poverty—namely, employment. Contrarily, countries with relatively high social spending tended to have lower inequality and poverty. Here the extent of cross-country variation is always more significant, with some countries achieving more limited inequality/poverty reductions despite high social spending.

The number of countries for which internationally comparative data are available has increased over recent years recently. As Figure 23.2 shows, there are now a number of countries (Czech Republic, Slovakia, Slovenia, as well as Korea) that do combine fairly low levels of social expenditure with low relative poverty rates and income inequality. For the Central European countries, part of the explanation may lie in a reliance on tax breaks as social policy tools, which are not captured in gross social spending indicators. More generally, the redistributive impact of taxes is not captured here (Verbist, 2004; Verbist and Figari, 2014).

This relatively strong relationship between social spending and poverty at the country level probably does not simply reflect the direct impact of transfers only: High-spending countries have other institutional features that contribute, notably high levels of minimum wage protection and strong collective bargaining compressing wages (hence limiting overall inequality), more extensive public and subsidized employment as well active labor market programs, higher levels of public spending on education, and so forth. Disentangling the effect of these various factors is inherently fraught with difficulties. There may in fact be mechanisms of mutual reinforcement between these factors

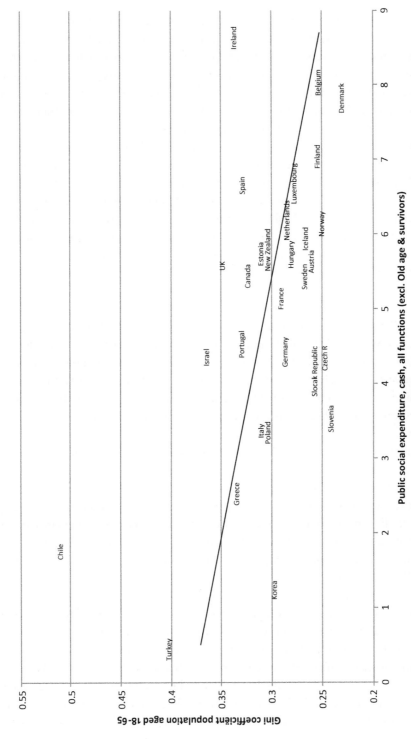

Figure 23.2 Cash public social expenditure and income inequality on the working age in OECD countries, 2009. *Note: Gini coefficient of equivalized disposable household income among the population aged 18–65. Source: OECD Divided We Stand (Gini); OECD SOCX (social expenditure).*

Public social expenditure, cash, all functions (excl. Old age & survivors)

Gini coefficient population aged 18-65

Chile

Israel

Ireland

Turkey

Greece

Italy
Poland

Portugal

UK

Spain

Belgium

Denmark

Finland

Korea

Germany

Canada

Estonia
New Zealand

Hungary Netherlands
Luxembourg

Norway

France

Sweden Iceland
Austria

Slocak Republic
Czech R

Slovenia

(Beramendi Alvarez, 2001). Barth and Moene (2009) argue that a more equal wage distribution leads to welfare generosity through a process of political competition. In turn, more income redistribution produces more equality. The authors hypothesize that this "equality multiplier" operates mainly through the bottom of the income distribution: The amplification occurs where wages near the bottom of the distribution are compressed, not where higher incomes are compressed. They find empirical support in their analyses on 18 OECD countries over the years 1976–2002.[4]

While in theory, low or moderate levels of social spending could produce low poverty rates if resources were well targeted, the reality remains that almost no advanced economy achieves a low (relative) poverty rate, or a high level of redistribution, with a low level of social spending. Large, universal welfare systems, while on paper being least distributive, distribute in fact the most. Systems that by design strongly target resources to toward the poorest tend to be in fact less redistributive. Korpi and Palme (1998) have called this the "paradox of redistribution."

There is a long-standing controversy in welfare state literature on the question of whether targeting benefits toward the bottom part of the income distribution actually enhances the redistributive impact of welfare state policies, especially of social transfer policies. This issue is of far more than academic importance. In its 2011 *Divided We Stand?*, the OECD states that "redistribution strategies based on government transfers and taxes alone would be neither effective nor financially sustainable." In this context, the OECD (2011a) calls for "well-targeted income support policies." Organizations like the IMF and the World Bank have long advocated targeted benefits. The issue of targeting will probably gain even more poignancy in a post-crisis period marked by continued and, in some cases, increased budget austerity.

The debate on targeting is still marked by opposed views. On the one side there are those who believe that a welfare state can only fight poverty effectively and efficiently (i.e., cost-effectively) when benefits are mainly targeted to those most in need—that is, when benefits are selective. The straightforward argument here is that selective benefit systems are cheaper because fewer resources are "wasted" on people who are not poor. Lower public expenditures imply lower taxes, which in turn are said to be conducive to economic growth. Economic growth, the argument proceeds, benefits the poor directly (although not necessarily proportionally so) and increases at the same time the fiscal base for redistributive policies.

This view of selectivity has never been commonly shared. Two sorts of arguments underpin this more critical stance. First, there are technical considerations. Van Oorschot (2002) sums up the most important dysfunctions of means-testing. First, these

---

[4] There is a sizeable political economy literature on this issue. McCarty and Pontusson (2009) review a number of political economy theories with regard to voter behavior under different conditions of economic inequality.

include higher administrative costs. Establishing need or other relevant criteria require monitoring, whereas universal benefits allow for less complex eligibility procedures. Furthermore, means-tested benefits are subject to higher non-take-up, partly because of stigmatization issues. Finally, and perhaps most importantly, targeted benefits can give rise to poverty traps, where benefit recipients have little incentive to work because this would entail loss of benefits.

A second line of counterargument is that proponents of selectivity pursue a "mechanical" economic argument that makes abstraction of the political processes, which determine how much is actually available for redistribution. The reasoning is that, paradoxically, in countries with selective welfare systems fewer resources tend to be available for redistribution because there is less widespread and less robust political support for redistribution. As a consequence, the redistributive impact of such systems tends to be smaller. To put it differently, some degree of redistributive "inefficiency" (the Matthew-effect) is said to foster wider and more robust political support for redistribution, including to the most needy. This follows from the fact that a universal welfare state creates a structural coalition of interests between the least well-off and the politically more powerful middle classes (median voter theorem). By contrast, a selective system entails an inherent conflict between the least well-off, by definition the sole recipients of social transfers, and the better-off, who fund the system without the prospect of getting much out of it.

The juxtaposition outlined above forms the starting point for Korpi and Palme's highly influential "Paradox of Redistribution," a paper in which they claim that more selective systems, paradoxically, have a smaller redistributive impact than universal systems offering both minimum income protection as well as income security and cost compensations (for children) in a broader sense. Korpi and Palme (1998) find that, in effect, this relationship is mediated by the relative size of available means for redistribution. Countries with selective redistribution systems, they argue, spend less on redistribution, at least in the public sector. In essence, selective systems are generally smaller systems.

The degree of redistribution is measured here by comparing the actually observed income inequality or at-risk-of-poverty rate with a rather unsophisticated "counterfactual" distribution (Bergh, 2005). In theory this counterfactual ought to accurately reflect the income distribution that would prevail in the absence of social transfers. However, the construction of this counterfactual is hampered by theoretical and practical problems. In most cases, including in Korpi and Palme's paper, pre-transfer income is simply calculated by deducting observed social transfers and re-adding observed taxes. Full abstraction is thus made of any behavioral effects that a change in transfer/tax regime would entail. While patently less than perfect, the reality is that no satisfactory method exists to adequately model such behavioral effects. Many studies have pursued similar empirical approaches—for example, Nelson (2004, 2007).

Another critique has been formulated by Moene and Wallerstein (2003) who have argued that analyses of redistribution need to be done at a more disaggregated level than "the welfare system" because the determining redistributive principles may differ substantially for, say, unemployment, health care, or pensions. Some schemes may rest heavily on the insurance principle, while others may put more weight to the need principle. Universality and selectivity can coexist within one system. Yet, Moene and Wallerstein (2001) also conclude that universal provisions provoke the largest political support because of the higher chance of middle-class citizens to become a beneficiary. Some opinion-based studies also confirm that universal welfare schemes enjoy broader support (Kangas, 1995).

Some recent studies, however, claim that the link between redistribution and universal provision has substantially weakened, or even reversed over time. Kenworthy (2011) reproduces and updates Korpi and Palme's analyses, which related to the situation in 11 countries as of 1985. Kenworthy's findings confirm that countries with more universal benefits achieved more redistribution (measured in the size of redistributive policies in the budget) for the period from 1980 to 1990. By 1995, the image becomes less clear. Data for 2000 and 2005 seem to indicate that there is no longer any association (either positive or negative) between the two variables. Evidently, the findings are based on a small number of cases, which make them particularly sensitive to outliers. A trend toward more targeting in Denmark, in conjunction with an evolution toward more universal benefits in the United States, is largely responsible for the shift in conclusions. Moreover, the new findings may be driven to some extent by the growing share of pensions in social spending. Kenworthy (2011, p. 58) writes about this: "This by no means settles the question, but it does suggest additional reason to rethink the notion that targeting is an impediment to effective redistribution."

Figure 23.3, taken from Marx et al. (2013b), strengthens the finding that the relationship between the extent of targeting and redistributive may have weakened considerably. Here targeting is captured through the concentration index. This is calculated in a similar way as the Gini coefficient. The more negative the concentration coefficient, the more targeted the transfers, whereas the closer the concentration coefficient is to the Gini, the more universal the transfers are distributed. Australia, the United Kingdom, and Denmark have most negative concentration coefficients and can be characterized as strongly pro-poor. Negative concentration coefficients are found in the majority of the countries, pointing to a substantial degree of targeting. Note however that the term "targeting" suggests that outcomes are due to the characteristics of the system, but this need not be the case. Moreover, the outcomes of a system are highly dependent on the characteristics of the underlying population in terms of sociodemographic characteristics, income inequality, composition of income, and so forth. If, for instance, a benefit is designed in such a way that all children are eligible, but all children are situated in the bottom quintile, then this policy measure may appear as targeted in its outcomes, even though its design may

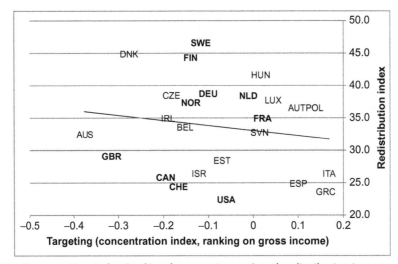

Figure 23.3 Concentration index (ranking by gross income) and redistributive impact, mid-2000s. *Notes: (1) for Belgium, France, Greece, Hungary, Slovenia, and Spain calculations are based on disposable incomes instead of gross incomes due to data availability. (2) The countries included in Korpi and Palme (1998) are in bold. Source: Marx et al. (2013a,b) on the basis of the Luxembourg Income Study.*

not include any means-testing or needs-based characteristics. This means that strictly speaking we cannot derive from the concentration coefficient how pro-poorness of a transfer comes about.

Redistribution refers to the impact of taxes and transfers on income inequality. It is measured by the difference between the Gini coefficients with and without tax-transfers relative to pre-transfer income; this corresponds in this analysis to the difference of the Gini coefficients of market and disposable income relative to that of market income. The impact on inequality is driven by the size of transfers, as well as by their structure, whether these transfers are going relatively more to lower or higher incomes.

Looking more closely at this graph, at the left-hand side are Australia, the United Kingdom, and Denmark, all characterized by having benefit systems that are the most strongly pro-poor of all countries. Yet, the redistributive impact in Denmark appears to be much stronger. Similarly, looking at the countries with still strong pro-poor spending (concentration indices between −0.2 and 0), the corresponding redistributive impact differs a great deal. Some of the countries with the strongest redistributive tax/transfer systems are to be found here (Sweden and Finland), together with some countries with the weakest (the United States, Canada, Israel, and Switzerland). On the right-hand side of the graph—the countries with positive targeting coefficients—the relationship does become consistently negative, especially in the countries with the weakest pro-poor spending (Greece, Spain, and Italy).

Why does a similar degree of strong targeting, as captured by the concentration index, produce stronger redistributive outcomes in Denmark as compared to the United Kingdom and Australia? Similarly, why do similar (quasi) universal systems yield such different redistributive outcomes across countries? This strongly suggests that design features matter. It is notable that one relationship remains fairly strong: the one between the extent of targeting and the size of the system. However, there are exceptions here: A country like Denmark does combine a strong degree of targeting with a high level of social spending.

The strongest redistributive impact is achieved by countries that combine moderate (Sweden and Finland) to strong targeting (Denmark) with comparatively high levels of spending. This suggests that the most redistributive systems are characterized by what is called "targeting within universalism"—that is, systems in which many people receive benefits but where the poorest get relatively more.

It is interesting to note that the very strong relationship between the extent of targeting and the size of the spending has weakened, as is documented by Kenworthy (2011). One of the factors that arguably made targeted systems less politically robust and prone to spending cuts in the 1980s was the fact that strongly targeted (means-tested) benefits entailed strong work disincentives and also (perceived) family formation incentives. The last decades have seen an intensified attention to this issue. To reduce work disincentives, earnings disregards have been introduced for people who make a (partial) transition from complete benefit dependency to part-time work.

Most importantly perhaps, means-tested benefits are no longer exclusively aimed at people not in work, but also at those in work in low-paying jobs. The French RSA (Revenu de Solidarité Active) scheme is a good example of a new style means-tested benefit scheme that offers integrated support for the nonemployed and (part-time) low-paid workers alike. The scheme also has entirely different work incentives. The RSA was introduced in France in 2008 with the specific aim of remodeling the incentive structure social assistance beneficiaries, and particularly to make work or returning to education a more lucrative financial prospect. The previous minimum income system (Minimum Integration Income) was based on a one-for-one trade-off of benefit for earned income. Under RSA, a 62% slope is applied. Efforts have also been made to encourage beneficiaries of RSA into employment, for example, with assisted employment contracts and (improved) insertion mechanisms. In addition, the RSA has simplified the provision of social protection by combining several previously separate schemes into a single sum. A household with no earned income is eligible for the "basic RSA," which is defined at the household level and takes into account the composition of the household. The "in-work RSA" acts as a top-up for people paid less than the national minimum wage (SMIC).

The point here is that targeted, means-tested systems look totally different today from the systems in place in the 1980s. Whereas the old systems were the focus of harsh welfare critiques, especially from the right, the new targeted systems are lauded as gateways of welfare to work. They enjoy broad partisan support, as is evident in the United Kingdom where the working tax credit (WTC), implemented by the Labor government, building on a scheme implemented under a Conservative one, is again expanded by the current Conservative one. Similarly, in France, the newly elected socialist government has no intentions for a major overhaul of the RSA, introduced by the Fillon/Sarkozy government.

In the United States, the earned income tax credit (EITC)—a transfer program for households of low earnings—has become the country's preeminent welfare program (Kenworthy, 2011). The system appears to enjoy far broader and more robust political support than earlier U.S. antipoverty programs. The system also is less strongly targeted than earlier provisions, and it caters to larger sections of the electorate, including the (lower) middle class, which may account for that expansion. However, an equally if not more important factor may well be the fact that the system is perceived to encourage and reward work.

23.2.2 Cash Transfers for the Inactive Working-Age Population

Much comparative poverty research that has sought to link observed variation in income inequality and poverty across countries to policy has relied on government (social) spending statistics as indicators of policy "effort." As we have seen, the relationship across countries between the level of social spending as a percentage of GDP, or some related indicator, and observed inequality or poverty levels is in fact by and large a rather strong one. This is in a way surprising because the level of spending is as much reflective of the number of people receiving benefits than it is of the level and thus potential adequacy of those benefits. Likewise, measured outcomes, for example, pre- versus post-transfer differences in inequality or poverty also depend on a host of factors that are independent or only indirectly influenced by policy: contextual and compositional factors, including labor market conditions (unemployment, employment patterns, and wages), household composition (patterns of cohabitation, marriage, divorce, childbirth, etc.), and policies that influence these dynamics (e.g., ALMPs and child care).

If we want to understand variations in outcomes we need more sophisticated and accurate measures of policy effort and policy design than spending indicators. So-called institutional indicators aim to be directly reflective of policy intent and design. Replacement rates for various branches of social insurance are commonly applied indicators of social protection. They are intended to express the level of benefit generosity within a particular provision, for example unemployment or disability insurance. The OECD has been compiling such time series for a considerable length of time. Academic databases have been compiled by, among others, the Swedish Institute of Social Research (the SCIP database) and the University of Connecticut (Scruggs database).

While such indicators are more directly reflective than spending-based measures of what actually happens at policy levels, they are not without their drawbacks. One is that replacement rates are generally expressed as a proportion of a reference wage. This is problematic for various reasons. With the growth of part-time and temporary employment, it has become increasingly difficult to specify a consistent wage denominator on the basis of available data. More importantly, wages have generally not evolved in line with the standard of living (and thus the relative poverty threshold). In many countries the standard of living has increased thanks to the proliferation of dual income families rather than through real wage growth. The mere fact that benefits follow wages says little about the potential adequacy of benefits in terms of poverty relief. A second important problem is that replacement rates, for example, within the systems of unemployment insurance or invalidity, do not capture the entitlement criteria applied, nor do they adequately express the entitlement periods. Nonetheless, there are strong indications that these are precisely the areas where policy makers have intervened the most. Unemployment benefit entitlement, for example, is now linked more strongly with job-search intensity. A third important issue is that replacement rates are based on a narrow rationale and tend to be calculated on a purely individual basis. For example, unemployment benefits may be combined with (increased) child benefit and other allowances. Additionally, of course, there may be the income of other household members, including its impact on benefit entitlement and vice versa. Also relevant in this context is the role of taxation. In most instances, the level of income protection that people actually receive in various situations is determined by a complex interaction between social security, social assistance, and taxation.

It is nevertheless interesting and relevant to consider trends. OECD time series on net replacement rates for the unemployed provide strong indications of reduced cash support for the unemployed between 1995 and 2005 (Immervoll and Richardson, 2011). Seven of the 10 countries recorded declining NRRs. Finland and Germany saw the biggest reductions in net replacement rates. Changes for the unemployed in most countries tended to be less damaging (or, sometimes, more beneficial) for families with children. The largest relative income drop was generally faced by long-term unemployed job seekers who mostly rely on unemployment assistance or social assistance for income support.

In the remainder of this section, we will focus in somewhat more detail on institutional indicators of minimum income protection because adequate protection against severe financial poverty is arguably the first duty of the welfare state and also because poverty relief is the prime focus of this chapter. Such a focus is further desirable because the design features of tax and benefits systems, and especially the way various programs interact in specific situations, tend to be so complex that they are not accurately and validly captured in a limited number of parameters. Minimum income protection provisions also mark the ground floor of other income maintenance provisions; minimum social insurance levels and minimum wages are almost always above the level of the social safety net. In that sense, indicators of minimum income protection also tell us something about the generosity of other income maintenance provisions (Marx and Nelson, 2013).

We draw on the CSB minimum income protection indicators (MIPI) dataset. In this dataset net income packages are calculated using the so-called model family approach, where the income package of households in various situations (varying by household composition and income levels) in simulated, taking into account all relevant benefits for which such households are eligible and also taking into account taxes. The MIPI database is among the most comprehensive databases available in terms of geographic and longitudinal scope, as well as in terms of the range of household situations and income components. It is worth pointing out that such institutional indicators have their limits too. They are calculated for a limited number of family types and situations. The assumption is that there is full take-up of benefits and that people effectively and immediately receive what they are entitled to. In the case of minimum wages, the assumption is these are fully enforced. However, this is not always the case and this is one reason why the observed relationship between generosity levels, as reflected in these indicators and outcomes, is relatively weak.

Van Mechelen and Marchal (2013) have analyzed patterns and trends in the level of minimum income protection for able-bodied citizens in the European countries. The chief focus is on means-tested benefits providing minimum income protection, usually in the form of social assistance. These general means-tested benefits provide cash benefits for all or almost all people below a specified minimum income level. In some countries separate schemes exist for such groups as newly arrived migrants or the disabled. The empirical analyses use data from the CSB-MIPI and cover social assistance developments in 25 European countries and three U.S. states. The study shows that the minimum income benefit packages for the able-bodied in Europe have become increasingly inadequate in providing income levels sufficient to raise households above the EU at-risk-of-poverty rate, defined as 60% of median equivalent income in each country (Figure 23.4). The overall tendency for the 1990s was one of almost uniform erosion of benefit levels, relative to the development of wages. This downward trend in the relative income position of families in receipt of social assistance changes somewhat in the 2000s, when the erosion of the level of benefit packages came to a halt in a number of countries. In a few countries, there is even evidence of a partial reversal of the declining trend, thus somewhat strengthening the income position of able-bodied persons that are in receipt of social assistance benefits. During the crisis period in particular, a small number of countries took extra steps to increase protection levels (Marchal et al., 2014). Despite a number of positive developments, net incomes of minimum income recipients continue to fall well short of the EU's at-risk-of-poverty threshold in all but a few EU countries. The size of the gap between the level of the social safety net and the poverty threshold varies across countries and family types, but it is generally quite substantial.

While the erosion of minimum income protection levels seems to have slowed, the fact remains that Europe's final safety nets offer inadequate protection in all but a handful of countries. This begs the question: Why are social safety nets not more adequate? Let

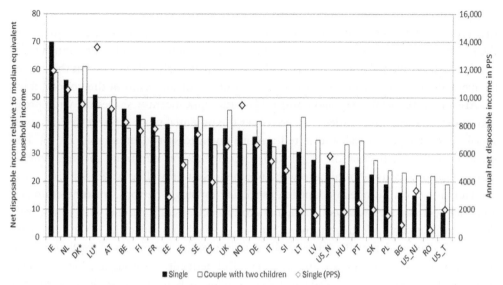

Figure 23.4 The level of the social safety net in the EU and three U.S. states, 2012. *Notes: In some countries, such as the United States, Italy, and Bulgaria, time limits apply, either formal or discretionary. In order to avoid additional assumptions, the levels displayed do not take these time limits into account. Source: CSB-MIPI (Eurostat; US Bureau of the Census and Bureau of Labor Statistics; Van Mechelen et al., 2011).*

us briefly consider two potential impediments: first, "adequate social safety nets are not affordable" and second, "adequate social safety nets undermine the work ethic and people's willingness to work."

Are adequate social safety nets too costly? Final safety net provisions (social assistance schemes) generally constitute only a fraction of total social transfer spending (typically well below 2.5% of GDP in Europe, except in Ireland and the UK), with the bulk of outlays going to pensions, unemployment and disability insurance, child benefits, and other benefits. Vandenbroucke et al. (2013) have made tentative calculations showing that the redistributive effort required to lift all equivalent household incomes to the 60% level would be below 2.5% of aggregate household income in most European countries and nowhere higher than 3.5%. The countries that would have to make such a relatively great effort are all southern and eastern member states. Vandenbroucke et al. (2013) also show that it is not the case that being poor in GDP per capita always implies a great redistributive effort to close the poverty gap. The Czech Republic and Hungary are relatively poor in terms of GDP per capita, but closing the poverty gap would require relatively little effort. On the other hand, Denmark and the United Kingdom have much higher living standards, yet they would have to make a relatively sizeable effort to close the poverty gap. Such a mechanical calculation ignores incentive effects and behavioral change (more poor people may prefer social assistance to low-paying jobs; the nonpoor may reduce their work effort). The real cost of such an operation is probably higher than the mechanical effect and the calculation may be seen as indicating a lower boundary for the distributive effort that is required. Still, the calculation also illustrates that the cost of an adequate social safety net is not necessarily outside of the realm of the conceivable.

Are adequate social safety nets compatible with work incentives? Despite widespread and sometimes strongly worded concerns over the potential work disincentive effects of social safety nets, empirical studies tell a more nuanced story (Immervoll, 2012). The income gap between situation of full-time dependence on minimum income benefits and a full-time job at the minimum wage (or the lowest prevailing wage) is in fact quite substantial in most European countries, especially for single persons. In some countries and under certain circumstances, particular groups such as single parents with young children gain relatively little from moving into a low-paid job, especially when child care costs are accounted for. Partial transitions into work—moving to a small part-time job—also do not pay in certain circumstances. But generally speaking it is hard to argue that long-term dependence on social assistance benefits is an attractive financial proposition in most of Europe. The hypothetical Europe-wide introduction of social assistance minimums equal to 60% of median income would, however, create a financial inactivity trap in many countries, as is also brought out in the paper by Vandenbroucke et al. (2013). In countries such as Bulgaria, Estonia, Slovenia, and Lithuania, the net income of a single benefit recipient would be between 25% and 30% higher than the equivalent income of a single person working at minimum wage; in Spain and the Czech Republic, the relative advantage of the benefit claimant would amount to around 15%. This implies that if such countries would wish to move toward better final safety net provisions then minimum income floors would have to be raised at least in step.

This would require quite substantial increases in minimum wages. In 2013, 20 member states of the EU had a national minimum wage set by government, often in cooperation with or on the advice of the social partners, or by the social partners themselves in a national agreement. As is illustrated in Figure 23.5, presenting figures for 2010, only for single persons and only in a number of countries do net income packages at minimum wage level (taking into account taxes and individual social security contributions, but also social benefits) reach or exceed the EU's at-risk-of-poverty threshold, as in all graphs set at 60% of median equivalent household income in each country. For single parents and sole breadwinners with a partner and children to support, net income packages at minimum wage are below this threshold almost everywhere, usually by a wide margin. This is the case despite shifts over the past decade toward tax relief and additional income support provisions for low-paid workers (Marx et al., 2013a).

When it comes to the question of whether and to what level minimum wages and hence minimum income benefits in general could be increased, opinions clearly diverge. Concerns about the work disincentive effects of social safety nets are legitimate, as are

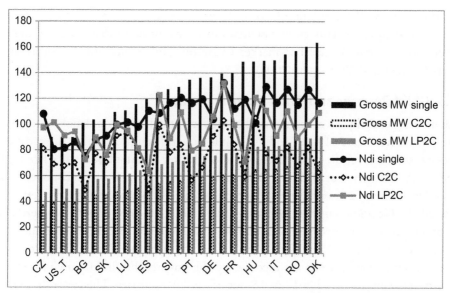

Figure 23.5 Gross minimum wages and net incomes at minimum wage as a percentage of the relative poverty threshold, 2012, selected EU-member states plus the United States (New Jersey). *Source: CSB-MIPI (Eurostat, 2011; US Census Bureau, 2003; Van Mechelen et al., 2011).*

concerns over potential negative employment effects of minimum wages, especially if these were to be set at levels high enough to keep households solely reliant on that wage out of poverty. The fact remains, however, that countries such as Denmark or the Netherlands combine what are comparatively among the highest levels of minimum protection for workers and nonworkers alike with labor market outcomes that on various dimensions are also among the best in the industrialized world. The Netherlands and Denmark enjoy among the highest employment rates in Europe and the lowest (long-term) unemployment rates.

Elaborate active labor market policies, specifically activation efforts directed at social assistance recipients, coupled with intensive monitoring and noncompliance sanctioning, appear to play a key role here. But it appears that the strength of overall labor demand is a key contextual factor for such associated policies and practices to effectively result in low levels of long-term dependence. Moreover, in terms of quality of employment, Denmark and the Netherlands are clearly among the best performers in Europe with relatively few workers in low-quality jobs (European Commission, 2008). Replicating the activation, empowerment, and sanctioning aspects associated with comparatively generous systems may well be difficult enough in itself. Replicating a context where job growth is strong and where jobs are sufficiently rewarding and attractive may be even more difficult.

Relatively elevated social safety nets and other income protection systems can be compatible with well-functioning labor markets. In fact, such systems may actually be conducive to well-functioning labor markets. Flexicurity proponents identify adequate social security benefits as an essential flexicurity pillar in that adequate benefits stimulate and accommodate labor market transitions and reduce risk aversion among workers (Bekker and Wilthagen, 2008).

23.2.3 Child Poverty and Child Cash Transfers

Children are generally at a higher risk of poverty than the population as a whole (Atkinson and Marlier, 2010). In addition, child poverty trends have, for the most part, not been favorable over the past decade (see also Chapter 8 in this book). The latest 2010 EU-SILC data shows that between 2005 and 2010 the at-risk-of-child-poverty rate increased in 17 out of 29 countries (EU27 plus Iceland and Norway). Child poverty rates rose in all the Nordic countries, Germany, and France. In most countries where child poverty fell this was in part the result of a fall in the 60% of median income threshold due the recession (Czech Republic, Estonia, Ireland, Lithuania, Poland, and Portugal). Poverty gaps (the gap between net income and the poverty threshold) for children have also risen between 2005 and 2010 in 15 out of the 29 countries. This deteriorating situation is of course the result of rising unemployment. However, in 2010, the majority of countries in the EU have more than 20% of poor children living in households with all working-age members in employment (work intensity of 1) and all but Belgium, Bulgaria, Czech Republic, Finland, Hungary, Ireland, and the UK have more than half of their poor children living in households with a work intensity of 0.5 or more (Van Mechelen and Bradshaw, 2013).

There are a number of reasons why children are living in poverty when their parents are employed. One explanation is that parental earnings are too low either because they are working part time and/or full-time but their wage is low. The second explanation is that families may be taxed into poverty. The direct taxes taken in income tax and social insurance contributions reduce gross incomes so much that they fall below the poverty threshold. The third explanation is that the cash benefits paid by the state to help parents with the costs of raising children are inadequate. Finally, the reason why a child with a working parent may be poor is that after having paid for housing and other charges the resources available for consumption are too little.

Countries use different mixes of tax benefits and cash benefits for delivering help to families with children. One can distinguish between income-related and universal— that is, non-income-related—cash benefits. Income-related benefits aim to target direct cash transfers to low-income families. Governments may decide to target benefits to other specific groups, for example, single parents or disabled children. Tax instruments are also used to redistribute income from childless families to families with dependent children—either in the form of tax allowances or tax credits specifically aimed at families with children. Tax allowances are deducted from taxable income whereas tax credits are subtracted from the amount of tax due. Tax credits may be wasteable or nonwasteable. Nonwasteable or refundable tax credits are tax benefits that can be paid as cash transfer to the taxpayer whenever the benefit exceeds tax liability. Wasteable tax credits can only be used if tax liability is positive. Both cash and tax benefits tend to vary by the age and the number of children (Bradshaw and Finch, 2002; Van Lancker and Ghysels, 2012).

Child benefit packages, as a whole, play an important role in preventing financial poverty. Nevertheless, in many countries child benefit packages fail to protect low-wage earners against poverty. In all countries the incomes of single-earner couples on minimum wages is below the poverty line. The child benefit package for a lone parent is more generous in most countries. However, how and whether child care costs are subsidized makes a big difference to the package, especially for lone parents. The costs of child care can undermine the value of the package in some countries. Whereas during the 1990s child benefit packages have been able to escape welfare erosion, over the past decade the value of the package relative to median equivalized income has fallen in more countries than it has increased (Van Mechelen and Bradshaw, 2013). This trend of decreasing child benefits has affected both low-paid families and the better-off.

Various studies have looked in detail at the structure of the child benefit package (e.g., Bradshaw, 2010; Bradshaw and Finch, 2002; Corak et al., 2005; Matsaganis et al., 2005; Van Lancker and Ghysels, 2012) and have documented the adequacy of child support arrangements in terms of poverty alleviation using empirical income surveys. Corak et al. (2005) find that universal child-related benefits that also have some degree of targeting at the poorest protect best against poverty. Their conclusion that targeting within universalism yields the best outcomes is echoed by Van Mechelen and Marchal (2013). They find that cross-country variation in the level of child-benefit packages for single-earner families on low pay largely overlaps with the degree of low-income targeting. Model family-type simulations suggest that comparatively generous packages for low-paid workers are to be found in countries where financial help for families with children is well targeted at low-income households by means of income-related cash benefits, refundable income-related tax credits, or social assistance top-ups. However, model family-type simulations effectively assume full take-up of benefits and full granting of rights. In reality, selective benefit systems may be quite ineffective with regard to poverty alleviation due to take-up problems and labor market disincentives (Deacon and Bradshaw, 1983; Gassmann and Notten, 2008). Van Mechelen and Bradshaw (2013) also show that child benefit packages are often also above average in countries with universal cash benefits but are combined with income-related cash benefits, housing allowances, or supplementary benefits from social assistance (Ireland, France, Austria, and Finland). This finding may in effect confirm and reinforce the assertion in empirical literature that targeting may be not so bad, if embedded in a universal social insurance context (Kenworthy, 2011; Skocpol, 1991; Van Lancker and Ghysels, 2012; Whiteford, 2008).

23.2.4 The Working Poor and Combating In-Work Poverty

The issue of in-work poverty has received increased attention recently (Andreß and Lohmann, 2008; Crettaz, 2011; Fraser et al., 2011; Lohmann, 2009; Maitre et al., 2012; Marx and Nolan, 2013; OECD, 2008). It is usually linked to the growth of low-paid insecure employment in the service sector. The contrast is often drawn with the golden years of welfare capitalism when the manufacturing industry provided stable, well-paid employment even for those with little or no formal education. As Esping-Andersen et al. (2002) put it: "We no longer live in a world in which low-skilled workers can support the entire family. The basic requisite for a good life is increasingly strong cognitive skills and professional qualifications . . . Employment remains as always the sine qua non for good life chances, but the requirements for access to quality jobs are rising and are likely to continue to do so." By the same token, Bonoli (2007, p. 496) states, "Postindustrial labour markets are characterized by higher wage inequality with the result that for those at the bottom end of the wage distribution, access to employment is not a guarantee of a poverty-free existence."

At the same time that good jobs for the less skilled are becoming scarcer, an increased policy emphasis on activation has become evident in many European countries, certainly at the level of rhetoric, and gauging by some indicators also in terms of actual policy (Barbier and Ludwig-Mayerhofer, 2004; Digeldey, 2007; Eichhorst et al., 2008; Kenworthy, 2008; OECD, 2007a,b). Within the broad set of activation strategies deployed, an important number specifically target the long-term unemployed, including social assistance recipients. And within this set, an important number of measures are aimed at stimulating these people, who generally have low levels of educational attainment, into relatively low-paid/minimum-wage level jobs.

So has in-work poverty become more prevalent? The literature on the working poor employs a variety of definitions based on different approaches of what is meant by "poor" and by "working" (for an overview see Crettaz, 2011; Nolan and Marx, 2000). The working poor are conventionally defined and measured as those individuals who have been mainly working during the reference year (either in employment or self-employment) and whose household equivalized disposable income is below 60% of the median in the country in question. It is widely recognized that analysis of in-work poverty needs to distinguish between employees and the self-employed, both because of their differing nature and because survey information on self-employment income is normally less reliable than wages and salaries, and also between full-time and part-time workers, which is another important distinction. In fact, with the growth of part-time work, zero-hour contracts, internships, and so forth, "being employed" has become a very fuzzy heterogeneous concept indeed. Moreover, combining two levels of analysis—the individual's labor market status and the household's income (adjusted for household size)—inherently complicates interpretation, because the labor market status of other persons in the household, rather than that of the individual being considered, may be crucial, as may the number of dependent children if any. Using a year as the reference period for labor market status and income position also complicates interpretation. Those working for part but not all of the year may be in poverty on an annual basis for that reason even if they were not poor while working, and how much of the year does one have to work to be counted as "working"? For these and other reasons, this definition/measure makes it difficult to identify the different factors potentially underlying the phenomenon and thus the locus or loci of policy failure, which could include: low (household) work intensity; inadequate out-of-work benefits; inadequate earnings; inadequate earnings supplements, the number of dependent people (children) relative to income, and so on.

Data from the EU-SILC database clearly shows that in-work poverty is a Europe-wide phenomenon. The prevalence of in-work poverty varies across EU countries; the extent of in-work poverty ranges from a low of 4–5% in Austria, Belgium, the Czech Republic, Finland, the Netherlands, and Slovenia up to 13–14% in Greece and Spain and 17% in Romania. On the basis of Eurostat figures, which combine data from ECHP and SILC, we can seek no general tendency for in-work poverty to have risen since the start of the century. Taking the time span from 2000 to 2010, in-work poverty is seen to have increased over the decade in countries such as Denmark, Germany, Spain, Luxembourg, Romania, and Sweden, but fell in as many countries. Abstracting altogether from the crisis period, a comparison of 2000 with 2006 also fails to show a marked rise in in-work poverty in many countries. The common presumption of a rising trend is therefore not supported by this data and indicator. However, the fact that the sources of data for 2000, unlike the later years, are not EU-SILC means that the trends shown have to be treated with some caution.

It is useful to relate these figures and trends to analysis by the OECD, providing a point of comparison and covering the decade from the mid-1990s to the mid-2000s (see OECD, 2009). Drawing on a variety of sources but seeking to apply a uniform methodology, the OECD found in-work poverty to have increased substantially in EU countries such as Germany, the Netherlands, and Luxembourg over this decade, but declined substantially in some other countries such as Italy. The OECD figures also draw on different data sources and employ a different definition—namely, in-work poverty being measured as households below 50% (rather than 60%) of median poverty threshold (with a different equivalence scale), and with "working" being captured at household rather than individual level by the presence of at least one person in work in the household. The study by Airio (2008) of the period 1970–2000 covering six OECD countries (and mostly based on data from the LIS) concludes that it is difficult to find any common trend on in-work poverty. These differences illustrate the care that must be exercised in drawing strong conclusions about levels and trends in in-work poverty across countries, because definitions, data, and period covered can all affect the outcome.

Which policy action, or set of policy actions, is most appropriate cannot be seen as entirely independent from normative notions that underlie the various ways the causes of working-age poverty in relation to work can be construed. Take for example a dual adult household with only one working adult and three dependent children. The male breadwinner has a low-paid job, yet is paid well above the minimum wage. Child benefits are limited. Whether their at-risk-of-financial-poverty status is construed as a problem of insufficient breadwinner earnings, or as a problem of partner nonparticipation, or as a problem of insufficient child support makes a fundamental difference as to what type of policy action is to be examined and possibly favored. In the case of traditional breadwinner-type households with insufficient earnings, the preponderance of opinion in Europe appears to be that this is to be seen as a matter of partner nonparticipation or underparticipation. But other cases may be less clear-cut. Even if in-work poverty is construed as largely a problem of low-household work intensity, the question arises what can be deemed as sufficient level of work intensity. It is not self-evident that this is to equal all working age, work-capable adults in the household to be in full-time work the whole year round. Societal norms may differ across countries. In the Netherlands, for example, a four-fifths job per adult appears to be closer to the norm of full-work intensity. Also, household composition may be deemed to matter. It is not self-evident that a lone parent with young children is expected to work full-year, full-time before additional income support is to be considered legitimate if his or her earnings fall short of the poverty threshold.

Poverty is, to a large extent, far from exclusively associated with low-work intensity at the household level (see Corluy and Vandenbroucke, 2013; De Graaf-Zijl and Nolan, 2011). This brings into view a wide variety of potential policies that can help households to increase if not maximize their work intensity. These include policies aimed at boosting the demand for workers, and particularly the demand for people with low levels of education or weak work experience. Employer subsidies or reductions in employers' social security contributions are an example here. At the supply side, policy can stimulate (e.g., through fiscal reform) or support (e.g., through child care) people to take-up work or to increase working hours. What mix of policies will work best in a given context will depend on the composition of the low-work-intensity population and on the underlying causes of low-work intensity.

Yet, and this is crucial, it must be recognized that even if such policies succeeded in getting every single nonemployed person into work, or every household to a level of full-work intensity for that matter (and all empirical evidence to date suggests this to be highly unlikely), this would not guarantee the elimination of poverty. What policy can do to help households in these circumstances is again likely to depend on such factors as the institutional and policy context in place, labor market conditions, and the profile of the population in need of support.

In some EU countries, and certainly outside of the EU, minimum wages remain nonexistent or low relative to average wages, but in a range of others they do suffice to keep single persons reliant on them out of poverty. Thus, it would appear sensible for countries with nonexistent or very low minimum wages to contemplate introducing or increasing these. However, the route of introducing or boosting minimum wages to the upper ranges currently prevailing in Europe (relative to average earnings) would, even in the absence of negative employment effects, not be sufficient to eradicate in-work poverty. Even in countries where minimum wages are comparatively high they do not suffice to keep sole-breadwinner households out of poverty, especially when there are dependent others or children. Minimum wages have probably become inherently constrained in providing minimum income protection to sole-breadwinner households, especially in countries where relative poverty thresholds have become essentially determined by dual earner living standards.

For low-earnings households, only direct household income supplements may offer a reasonable prospect to a poverty-free existence, especially when there are dependent children. Such "in-work benefits" are now often associated with Anglo-Saxon-type "tax credits" such as the EITC in the United States and the WTC in the United Kingdom. It is increasingly argued that more effective redistribution will not come from augmenting/expanding the traditional channels of income support, for example, more generous social insurance or social assistance levels, or from higher minimum wages. These are seen not only as failing to address today's social risks and needs, but also as exacerbating underlying problems such as exclusion from the labor market and entrapment in passive benefit dependency. Worse, these are considered as standing in the way of innovative mechanisms of social protection that are proactive and self-sufficiency enhancing, such as active labor market policies and services such as child care and improved education and training.

The options to consider, then, are other forms of (targeted) income supplements for households that provide some level of income protection and that are also conducive to labor market participation. As Kenworthy (2011) puts it, "Given the importance of employment and working hours for the market incomes of low-end households, policy makers must guard against programs that provide attractive benefits without encouraging or requiring employment. An ideal transfer would be one that both boosts the incomes of low-earning households and promotes employment by able working-aged adults. As it happens such a program exists. Referred to variously as 'in-work benefit' or 'employment-conditional earnings subsidy', it is best exemplified by the Working Tax Credit (WTC) in the United Kingdom and the Earned Income Credit (EITC) in the United States" (p. 44).

Under these schemes households with low earnings do not pay taxes but instead they receive additional money through the tax system. In the United States, the 1993 expansion of the EITC created the country's preeminent antipoverty program for families of working age. The United Kingdom has also implemented and extended several schemes (and in fact did so earlier than the United States), culminating in the Universal Credit.

Clearly, Anglo-Saxon-style negative income taxes have been garnering increased interest of late. As Immervoll and Pearson (2009) note, "Even in the mid-1990s, twenty years after such schemes were first introduced in the United Kingdom and the United States, such schemes were seen as interesting but unusual [. . .] it seems reasonable to conclude that IWB schemes are now mainstream policies in many countries."

That is perhaps somewhat of an overstatement. Several European countries have contemplated introducing Anglo-Saxon-style tax credits, or have done so in some form. Examples here include the "Prime Pour l'Emploi" (PPE) and the Revenue de Solidarité Active (rSa) in France, the "Combination Credit" in the Netherlands, and a "Low Wage Tax Credit" in Belgium. Yet, the reality is that most of these schemes exhibit only a faint resemblance to the EITC or the WTC. Sweden has a scheme that goes by the same name in English as its U.S. counterpart, EITC. It was introduced in 2007, and was reinforced in 2008, 2009, and 2010. The stated motive for the reform was to boost employment; in particular, to provide incentives for individuals to go from unemployment to, at least, part-time work. The scheme is different from the U.S. scheme in that it is a nonrefundable tax credit. Also, because the tax unit in Sweden is the individual and not the household it works in effect as a tax relief on low individual earnings. In that respect it is similar to personal social security contributions relief measures elsewhere.

While tax-channeled in-work benefits targeted at households with low-earnings remain of limited significance in most European countries, it is of course the case that many countries have child benefit systems that provide an additional income to workers and their families (Van Mechelen and Bradshaw, 2013). Child benefits have generally lost ground. For a couple with two children, the size of the child benefits package, expressed as a percentage of the gross minimum wage, declined in the majority of countries awarding these benefits. For single parents with two children the trend was somewhat more favorable in a number of countries. The decline of child cash benefits, both in value as in their importance in net disposable income, is discussed more extensively in Van Mechelen and Bradshaw (2013). Interest in EITC type schemes remains strong, however, in the public debate and in the academic literature (Aaberge and Flood, 2013; Allègre and Jaehrling, 2011; Crettaz, 2011; Kenworthy, 2011; Marx et al., 2012a). This interest seems entirely legitimate. The empirical evidence shows the U.S. EITC, in combination with other policy reforms and several increases in the minimum wage, to have produced some significant results, including marked increases in labor market participation and declines in poverty among some segments of the population, especially single-parent households (Eissa and Hoynes, 2004; Hotz and Scholz, 2003). It needs to be noted, however, that these initial results occurred in favorable economic circumstances, including strong labor demand and low unemployment. The relatively strong increases in labor supply of single mothers in the U.S. setting also resulted from welfare reform—notably, the transformation of the social assistance scheme into a temporary support system with time limits on the duration of benefits. This clearly provided a strong push incentive, with the EITC acting as pull incentive. Not all who were forced out of passive dependence found their way to work (Grogger, 2003, 2004). In addition, as the survey by Holt (2011) reveals, there is considerable evidence of incomplete take-up (around 75% according to some estimates), although exact estimates are hampered by the fact that there is no systematic tracking.

There are potential downsides to subsidizing low-paid work. While EITC is intended to encourage work, EITC-induced increases in labor supply may drive wages down, shifting the intended transfer toward employers. Rothstein (2010) simulates the economic incidence of the EITC under a range of supply and demand elasticities and finds that in all scenarios a substantial portion of the intended transfer to low-income single mothers is captured by employers through reduced wages. The transfer to employers is borne in part by low-skill workers who are not themselves eligible for the EITC. There is some empirical evidence that corroborates the potential wage erosion effect of EITC (Chetty et al., 2013; Leigh, 2010).

Yet, whether EITC type schemes can work elsewhere, as Kenworthy (2011) and others suggest, is not self-evident. The sociodemographic make-up of the United States differs from that in most European countries; there are more single adult (and parent) households and also more multi-earner households. The dispersion in earnings is also much more compressed in most European countries, where, in addition, benefits are generally higher relative to wages (including minimum wages) and less subject to means-testing if they derive from social insurance. This also implies that benefit entitlements of household members are less interdependent, possibly weakening the potential impact on labor supply. Many countries have individual taxation, and the trend is moving away from joint taxation of couples.

In order to be effective as an antipoverty device and at the same time affordable within reasonable limits, such measures need to be strongly targeted. However, strong targeting at households with low earnings is bound to create mobility traps, which can only be avoided if taper-off rates are sufficiently flat. That comes at a very considerable cost if the lower end of the household earnings distribution is densely populated, as is the case in many European countries. This cost can only be avoided by making the amount of the tax credit itself smaller, but in that case the antipoverty effect is reduced. Simulations by Bargain and Orsini (2007) for Germany, France, and Finland, by Figari (2011) for four southern European countries (Italy, Spain, Portugal, and Greece) and by Marx et al. (2012a) for Belgium, shed doubt over the applicability of EITC type systems in other settings. In an earlier study, Bargain and Orsini (2007) investigated the effects on poverty of the hypothetical introduction of the British scheme (as it was in place in 1998) in Germany, France, and Finland, using EUROMOD for 2001. They found that the antipoverty effects of a U.K.-type tax credit (similar in design and relative overall spending) would be very small in these countries, especially relative to the budgetary cost. For Belgium, the hypothetical introduction of the United Kingdom's WTC is shown to yield a limited reduction in poverty at the cost of possible weakened work incentives for second earners (Marx et al., 2012a). Figari (2011) notes that the presence of extended families in southern Europe does not allow for such policies to be well targeted at the very poorest. Bargain and Orsini (2006) have concluded that "interest in such schemes is destined to fade away." Whether this is true remains uncertain and indeed doubtful, but EITC type negative tax credits are not obviously suitable for wholesale emulation throughout continental Europe. In Germany, for example, the labor market has undergone some profound changes over the past decade. Low-paid employment has become far more prevalent and in-work poverty seems to have increased. It is not unlikely that a simulation such as the one performed by Bargain and Orsini on 2001 data would yield different results today. A recent study by Giannelli et al. (2013) analyzes the quality of new jobs created in Germany between 1998 and 2010 and find that the reforms of the 2000s (Hartz reforms) reinforced an existing trend of increasing wage inequality and lower wages among the least advantaged individuals. Although, as found by Card et al. (2013), a great deal of the increase of wage inequality in Germany for the period 1985–2009 is due to the increasing heterogeneity in job premiums and the raise of assortativeness in the matching between workers and establishments.

Clearly, simulations demonstrate that in-work benefit schemes that work well in certain settings do not necessarily perform equally well in a different context. Family composition, individual earnings distributions, and family income structures drive outcomes in a very substantial way. It remains to be explored whether alternative designs are conceivable that have better outcomes in continental European settings and that are realistically affordable.

23.2.5 Pensions

The terminology "pillars" is widely employed (Holzmann and Hinz, 2005) to capture the different elements of pension systems, as they operate within, for example, Bismarckian or Beveridgean welfare states. Bovenberg and Van Ewijk (2011) offer a typology of four models of pension systems based on the dimensions of governance (private vs. public) and individual choice (mandatory vs. voluntary), which are related to the classification of welfare states by Esping-Andersen (1990). As pension systems in rich economies have, simultaneously or not, characteristics of social insurance and poverty prevention, and different forms to finance benefits, a more flexible taxonomy of pension systems is used by the OECD (see Figure 23.6).

There are three main visible tiers forming the retirement-income system. The first one is intended to prevent old-age poverty and is publicly financed. Within this tier there are basic benefits paid at a flat rate, resources-tested (means and assets) benefits, and minimum pensions. The second tier is composed by mandatory schemes that can be public or

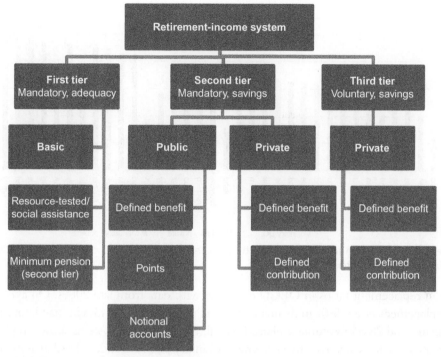

Figure 23.6 Taxonomy of different types of retirement-income systems. *Source: OECD (2011b).*

private. The public schemes offer defined benefits (DB) where the pension entitled is a function of individual contributed years and income. A system of points earned with each year income and accrued up to retirement age is also possible (e.g., occupational plans in France). A third plan under the public provision of the second tier is the Notional Defined Contributions, which is used in Italy, Norway, Poland, and Sweden. Under this plan, the individual contributions are recorded by the pension institution and offered a return rate. Once the retirement age is reached, such contributions are converted into pensions through an actuarial formula. The second tier also includes compulsory private (occupational) managed pensions, which can be DB or defined contribution (DC) types. Finally, the third tier is composed by voluntary private plans.

The composition of each plan within and between countries varies to a great extent. From 34 OECD countries, 14 have mandatory private schemes, 12 have public resources-tested benefits, 13 have basic flat rate benefits, and 18 have minimum pensions. Furthermore, DB pensions are present in 20 countries while DC pensions exist in 11 economies. For more details about the composition of pension plans by county, see section II.1 of OECD (2011a).

The adequacy of pension benefits is broadly measured by the replacement rate—namely, the ratio between pensions and average wages. Figure 23.7 reports the net

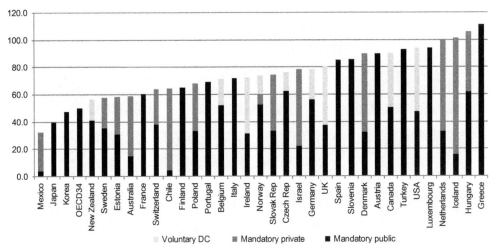

Figure 23.7 Net pension replacement rates by pension schemes in OECD countries. *Source: OECD (2011b). Authors' elaboration.*

pension replacement ratios in OECD countries with data from late 2000s. On average, the replacement rate is 50% in mandatory public plans while it is 43% in mandatory private plans, and 28% in voluntary plans. Overall, the mandatory systems show a replacement rate of 68%, which rises to 77% when voluntary plans are added. Furthermore, one can observe that adequacy differs significantly among countries and pension schemes. For example, in Japan, Korea, and Mexico the overall net replacement rate is lower than 50% while in 13 of 34 countries this figure is above 80%. All of the replacement ratio figures are lower when gross income and pensions are considered because income taxation burden for retirees is milder than for the working population. The mandatory systems have a gross replacement ratio of 57% and this reaches 64% when voluntary plans are included.

Typically, individuals at the beginning and the end of the life cycle face higher poverty rates. This U-shaped relationship by age groups has been maintained during the last decades, but the poverty rates have shifted impressively in favor of the elderly and in detriment of children and the young. Figure 23.8 from the OECD's *Unequal Growing?* shows clearly the sharp reduction of poverty risk for old-age individuals between the 1970s and the 2000s in OECD countries. Moreover, women report more poverty rates than men. The poverty gap by gender significantly increases for older ages. As explained in OECD (2008), Smeeding and Sandstrom (2005), and Vignoli and De Santis (2010), the risk of living in poverty is higher for elderly women because they have gained less pension rights during their working life, and they are more likely to live alone after the death of their spouses. In this regard, studies from Burtless (2009) and Vignoli and De Santis (2010) alert on the trends of new living arrangements (shrinking of the household size of the elderly) that jeopardize the living conditions of the elderly and increase the risk of falling into poverty. As a feedback mechanism, the larger participation of the elderly in pensions

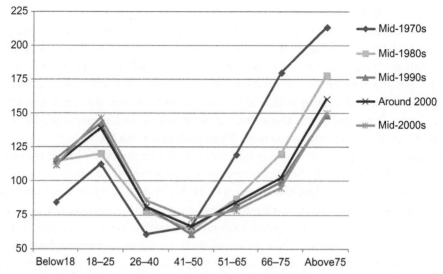

Figure 23.8 Risk of relative poverty by age of individuals in OECD-7 countries (poverty rate of the entire population in each year = 100). *Notes: Relative poverty risk is the age-specific poverty rate divided by the poverty rate for the entire population times 100. The poverty threshold is set at 50% of median income of the entire population. OECD-7 is the average for Canada, Finland, Greece, the Netherlands, Sweden, the United Kingdom, and the United States. Source: OECD (2008).*

and transfers will allow them to live alone without the need of other relatives, increasing in this way the risk of poverty. McGarry and Davenport (1998) are also aware of the effects of survivorship benefits for pensions on the poverty rates of U.S. widows given the scarcity of pension wealth of women.

The role of pensions in reducing poverty is particularly important due to the large share of old-age income coming from social security. On average, public transfers (earnings-related pensions, resource-tested benefits, etc.) to people over 65 during the mid-2000s represent 60% of their incomes. In some countries this figure reaches 80% or more (France, Hungary, Slovak Republic, and Belgium). The rest of the sources are divided in-work income (21%) and capital income (19%). The shares of incomes from work are large in Japan, Turkey, Mexico, and Korea where those represent about 50%. The average share of capital income for the elderly in Netherlands, United Kingdom, Switzerland, Canada, Australia, Denmark, and the United States is about 41%. Note that occupational plans are included in capital income sources, so that this component includes pension incomes. All these figures by country can be consulted in OECD (2011a). It is also observed that the reduction of market income poverty attained with transfers and taxes is greater for old-age people than for working-age people (OECD, 2008).

A number of recent studies have sought to measure the contribution of pensions in reducing old-age poverty across countries. Smeeding and Williamson (2001) use LIS data to estimate the effect of public pensions on poverty rates of the elderly in eight developed economies for mid-1990s: Australia, Canada, France, Germany, the Netherlands, Sweden, the United Kingdom, and the United States. The poverty rate for old-age people would be 84% in average if only market income is considered. This is reduced to 71.8% when occupational pensions are added, and then this falls to 21.2% when universal and social incomes are included. With social safety net transfers, the average poverty rate drops up to 13.2%. Different from the English-speaking countries, the greatest redistributive effects are found in France, Germany, the Netherlands, and Sweden. Similar trends are found when Smeeding and Sandstrom (2005) analyze data for the early 2000s. In both works, it is found that pensions are more effective to reduce poverty of old-age males than in old-age females. With early 2000s data, pensions, income social transfers, and safety net transfers reduce poverty of elderly women up to 24.3% while that figure is reduced up to 13.3% for both sexes. As women participate to less extent in the pension system, the safety net transfers are more important for them to reduce their risk of poverty, and the contrary holds for occupational pensions in the case of men. In a similar exercise by Lefebvre (2007), it is found that poverty alleviation due to pensions is less effective for the very old (75 +) than for the old (65–74). This feature combined with gender depicts a very negative picture for very old women, who in turn, represent the majority of members in the oldest old cohort. Moreover, micro-simulation models like the one implemented by Dang et al. (2006) arrive at similar conclusions. Chapter 24 of this book shows other relevant micro-simulation models.

There is concern about the sustainability of public pension expenditures due to the accelerated aging process in developed economies; and, in particular, there is a legitimate worry about the effects of the reforms aiming to attenuate it on old-age poverty and inequality (Arza and Kohli, 2008; Börsch-Supan, 2012; Burtless, 2006). Although, as indicated in the reports by Zaidi et al. (2006a,b) the pension reforms promoted by the World Bank were mainly driven by financial sustainability issues, and little concern was put on the effects on the living standards of the retirees. These reports offer an important effort to estimate the long-term effects of a variety of pension reforms in EU countries—undertaken between the 1990s and the 2000s—on the poverty and living standards of the elderly. In Zaidi et al. (2006b), the authors find a strong negative relationship between the generosity of public pensions and the at-risk-of-poverty rates among the 65 and older, and they foresee a decline of the pension generosity (for years 2025 and 2050) on the basis of the analysis of each pension reform. These two combined findings will result in an increase of the poverty rate for the vast majority of countries analyzed (Estonia, Malta, Austria, Italy, Belgium, Denmark, Spain, France, Latvia, Lithuania, Portugal, Slovenia, Finland, and Sweden). Only Ireland and Cyprus appear to have a reduction of the 65 and older poverty rates. However, as warned by the authors, these results have to be taken with caution as no behavioral responses are considered.

In a more static framework, Van Vliet et al. (2012) estimate the effects of pension reform on poverty and inequality in European countries. They acknowledge that recent shifts from public to private provision in pensions are still limited in Europe but that this is important for some countries. They estimate the effects of those changes on old-age inequality and poverty with OLS panel data regressions, but they do not find substantial effects on those variables. Nonetheless, they cast the limitation of their analysis by indicating that the reforms may be affecting only to new and future retirees.

Looking at the effects of public transfers and taxes in a more general way, some authors appeal for a rebalance of the spending from pension programs toward programs aimed to prime-age people and their children at the bottom of the income scale, which could reduce poverty rates to a greater extent (OECD, 2008). As pointed out by Dang et al. (2006), social protection systems are very old-age oriented in the EU with the elderly receiving much more cash transfers than the working population. They show that even high old-age spending countries can leave significant pockets of elderly in poverty while others with lower expenditures in old-age can be more successful at limiting the risk of poverty. Furthermore, their simulations indicate that there is scope to reorient the expenditures from old-age to working population and rebalance the tax liabilities in favor of the working population. These changes will not jeopardize the living standards of the elderly if the reforms include proper safety net measures.

The role of public pensions in reducing inequality can be very large because these pensions represent a large fraction on income in old-age. During the mid-2000s, public cash benefits accounted for 70% of income of retirement-age individuals in 24 OECD countries, and in many of them the figure was above 80% (OECD, 2008). In countries where public pensions are important, the effect of re-ranking when one uses the distribution of market or disposable income as the counterfactual can be large. Mahler and Jesuit (2006) find a sizeable effect of pensions (public and private) in reducing the Gini coefficient on 13 rich countries during the period 1980–2000. On average, the Gini is reduced from 0.43 to 0.27 when all taxes and transfers are considered, with a reduction of 0.039 points from taxes and 0.121 from transfers of which 0.068 comes from pensions, 0.013 from unemployment transfers, and 0.040 from other transfers. In Belgium, Sweden, and France, the reduction in the Gini is about 0.10 points due to pensions, while in the United States, Canada, and Australia it is only about 0.04 points. Lefebvre (2007) computes the marginal contribution of earnings, property income, private pensions, and public transfers on total inequality in 19 EU countries. It is found that public pensions decrease inequality in all countries and that private pensions increase inequality in all countries except in Ireland and France. Similarly, Caminada et al. (2012) disentangle the changes of contributions of different income components in reducing inequality between the mid-1980s and mid-2000s in 12 LIS countries. Around 1985, the primary income Gini falls 0.139 points after transfers and taxes, while around 2005 this drop is about 0.163 points. The authors estimate that this increase in redistribution is mainly due to the state old-age and survivor benefits, which account for 60% of the total change. Different designs of pension systems have diverse effects on inequality. For example, Benedict and Shaw (1995) with data from the early 1980s, find that private pensions in the United States increase inequality among unionized workers by 21% with respect to observed wage inequality. On the reforms undertaken in Europe since the mid-1990s, Van Vliet et al. (2012) do not find evidence of important effects of those reforms on income inequality.

In general, the assessment of inequality is made in one single year, but studies such as Burtless (2006) emphasize that this approach can overestimate the redistributive impact of pensions. This is related to the question of what is the proper counterfactual distribution to use when one analyzes the impact of pensions. If pensions are simply absent, it is expected that individuals will look for other forms of savings to afford their old-age. Different living arrangements can also be different if pensions would be nonexistent or less generous, which will cause other redistributive effects (Burtless, 2006, 2009). In this regard, some authors favor the estimation of the distribution of lifetime income (e.g., Deaton et al., 2002; Liebman, 2002) although the data requirements are more demanding. This approach shares features with a growing literature studying lifetime income inequality (see for instance Aaberge and Mogstad, 2012) which highlights a life-cycle bias that overestimates income inequality when only one or a few years are analyzed.

23.3. BEYOND SOCIAL PROTECTION
23.3.1 Noncash Social Spending and Poverty

While cash transfers form a substantial proportion of overall social expenditure and have a pronounced impact on household incomes and poverty, other forms of social expenditure—such as health, housing, and perhaps education (which is sometimes included as "social" spending and sometimes not)—may also have substantial direct and indirect effects. Table 23.4 shows spending on cash transfers and on other forms of social expenditure—which one can think of as benefits in kind from a household perspective—based on the OECD's social expenditure database before the onset of the economic crisis in 2007–2008, which has boosted expenditure on cash transfers in many countries. This shows that in about half the countries shown, cash transfers significantly outweighed such benefits in kind—notably, in the "continental/corporatist" countries like France, Germany, Belgium, and Luxembourg; in the southern countries of Italy, Spain, and Greece; and in Poland. However, in many of the other OECD countries, overall social spending was fairly evenly balanced between cash transfers and other spending. This is using a definition of social expenditure that does not include education, so if one adds education spending, the relative importance of noncash spending is even more obvious, as brought out in Marical et al. (2008). They conclude that public spending on health, education, and "other services" in the OECD social expenditure database represents an amount comparable to public cash transfers, exceeding those transfers in 11 OECD countries.

The impact of such noncash spending on poverty is difficult to assess for various reasons (see for example Currie and Gahvari, 2008; Garfinkel et al., 2006). One approach

Table 23.4 Social expenditure distinguishing cash and noncash benefits as percentage of GDP in OECD countries, mid-2000s

Country	Cash transfers % of GDP	Noncash social benefits % of GDP
Australia	8.1	6.7
Austria	18.4	8.2
Belgium	16.2	9.1
Canada	8.8	9.4
Czech Republic	11.4	7.8
Denmark	13.8	11.8
Finland	15.3	9.9
France	17.5	10.8
Germany	15.9	9.9
Greece	13.4	7.1
Hungary	13.8	8.7
Ireland	8.4	7.7
Italy	16.7	7.7
Japan	10.2	8.1
Luxembourg	13.9	8.8
Netherlands	11.1	8.5
New Zealand	9.7	8.4
Norway	10.9	10.1
Poland	15.7	4.9
Slovak Republic	10.2	6.1
Spain	13.1	7.4
Sweden	14.5	13.6
Switzerland	11.8	7.8
UK	10.3	10.5
USA	8.0	7.0

Source: OECD social expenditure database.

employed in comparative studies (Callan et al., 2008; Marical et al., 2008; Paulus et al., 2010; Smeeding et al., 1993) and in national studies (Aaberge and Langørgen, 2006; Callan and Keane, 2009; Harding et al., 2006; Nolan and Russell, 2001; Wolff and Zacharias, 2007) is to use micro data to assess who is benefiting from such expenditure and to what extent, and to compare overall inequality and (sometimes) poverty levels when this noncash income is included. With some studies this also means allocating indirect taxes to households and deducting them to arrive at a "final" income concept. Major decisions have to be made about how to value the benefits to users of services as has been debated in the literature for three decades. The empirical studies have shown that these can have a marked impact on the measured outcomes—notably, in the case of health spending where particularly challenging conceptual issues have to be addressed.

One complication is that services, which in principle are provided free or in subsidized fashion to everyone, may actually be readily available only in certain areas or to certain groups, or even if available may be taken up to a varying degree by those with higher versus lower levels of income or education. Information on actual use patterns may not always be available, and attributing a common value across a particular age group, for example, may be misleading. Empirical studies thus make use, where possible, of information—generally from household surveys—of actual usage patterns for the range of services involved, but this may not cover all the areas of expenditure one wants to include.

Difficulties then arise, though, first of all because one does not know whether households would have bought the same amount of the goods or services in question if those were not provided free or at a subsidized rate. Recipients may place a value on noncash benefits that is less than what they would have to pay for the good or service in the market, because the recipient has no choice in its allocation. However, a U.S. study of food stamps suggested that where the item is a basic necessity and the in-kind transfer is smaller than the amount the household would normally spend on that good, the value to the recipient may be very close to the market price (Moffit, 1989). Unlike food, what is meant by market price for many of the services provided by the state may itself be unclear since they are not available in the market—the most obvious examples being defense or law enforcement. If one takes the supply price (i.e., the cost to government) as the point of reference, the optimal level of provision will equate the marginal benefit with this price times the marginal cost of public funds. In any case, the widely used approach in empirical studies is simply to assume that the value of a particular (unit of a) service is equal to the average cost of producing it. Use of such an average may mask variations in quality of the service provided to different socioeconomic groups—for example, in the quality of the health care provided to the rich versus the poor—and that is another important aspect that is very difficult to capture empirically.

The second general issue arises where the noncash benefit covers something like health care, which is required to meet a specific contingency affecting only some households in a given year. In those circumstances, if we simply add the cost of the free or subsidized services supplied to the households consuming them, sick people will be richer than the healthy at any cash income level. One can in those circumstances attempt to also take the additional "needs" of such persons into account by elaboration of the equivalence scales employed—drawing on, for example, recent studies focused on the costs associated with disability such as in Jones and O'Donnell (1995) and Zaidi and Burchardt (2005)—but this remains underdeveloped. A more widely employed approach is that instead of basing values on the household's own consumption, one attributes to all those eligible for state provision an extra income equal to the insurance premium they would have to pay to obtain the same level of cover in the market. Even assuming the cost of this cover can be established satisfactorily, a serious problem remains. Even the insurance value could be worth enough by itself to bring a household above the poverty threshold when it might still have insufficient cash income to buy enough food, clothing, or shelter, reinforcing the point that the in-kind transfer does not represent command over resources in the same way that cash income does. Furthermore, even with the insurance approach, the fact that different households have different underlying needs should be taken into account in arriving at conclusions about the welfare implications of in-kind benefits (see Aaberge et al., 2010).

The final, and fundamental, issue to be noted relates to the time-period employed. In measuring poverty and income inequality annual income is most often the focus, but in thinking about the consumption of education or health care and the value of the in-kind benefit they represent it would be natural to take a life-cycle approach, since the benefits are often long-term rather than confined to the point of use. Such an approach is very demanding in data terms and involves a wide range of assumptions for which it is difficult to find a robust empirical basis.

The results of recent empirical studies on this topic are of significant interest in the broader context of welfare state institutions and policies and their impact on poverty. Marical et al. (2006—and also chapter 9 in OECD, 2008) look at the impact of public spending on health, education, and social housing on income inequality in OECD countries, concluding that they generally contribute to narrowing inequality, though not usually by as much as cash transfers and direct taxes combined; they do not look at corresponding results for poverty. Paulus et al. (2010) on the other hand assess the impact of valuing noncash or in-kind benefits from public housing subsidies, education, and health care in five European countries, recalculating both inequality and relative poverty measures when this value is added to cash income. In such an exercise, the relative income poverty threshold—in this case 60% of median equivalized income—is itself recalculated, rising by between about one-fifth and one-third in value when in-kind benefits are included. The proportion of persons falling below that threshold is found to be much lower than the corresponding figure based on cash income in all five countries, with reduction being greatest in the United Kingdom where the poverty rate falls by half and least in Greece where it still falls by one-third. There are also major effects on the composition of those falling below the threshold, with the reduction in poverty rate greatest for children and older people (since the incidence of spending on education and health care is particularly concentrated on them). This pattern is familiar, having featured strongly in Smeeding et al.'s (1993) early comparative study covering seven countries based on data in LIS.

Sutherland and co-authors caution that "it is doubtful whether these results should be interpreted as having any bearing on the assessment of poverty or inequality from a welfare perspective" (p. 259), being mainly of interest in showing the scale of noncash incomes relative to cash incomes, but without taking into account the needs of individuals for health care or education. The study goes on to attempt to take the variation in those needs into account via modifying the equivalence scales employed. It finds that the distributional effects of noncash transfers on several summary income inequality measures are then far more modest; corresponding results for poverty rates are not reported, but it seems likely that the same would be true in that case. It is also worth highlighting the argument by Bourguignon and Rogers (2007) that once the intertemporal or intergenerational nature of the effects of many social expenditures are recognized, it is no longer possible to assume that they are equivalent to cash transfers, food subsidies, and other programs of direct redistribution. Education spending is an investment in future generations and may have redistributive effects for these generations, but may worsen distribution initially. Moral hazard makes it infeasible to borrow against the human capital of one's descendants, so an increase in public education expenditures financed by an increase in a neutral tax may actually be regressive for the generations with school-age children. Poor households in this generation pay the tax and receive no benefit, whereas rich households pay the tax but may recover it through intergenerational reallocation of consumption (that is, smaller bequests to their children). Intergenerational accounting may then be necessary to more fully capture the redistributive and poverty-related effects.

23.3.2 The Labor Market, Education, and Active Labor Market Policy

Income derived from the labor market is central to the overall distribution of income and to poverty and disadvantage at household level (see for example OECD, 2008). Even for those not currently earning (via employment or self-employment), previous labor market experience may determine current entitlement to social protection or to occupational pensions. A wide variety of studies on poverty in individual countries, both descriptive and econometric, find that those in work are much less likely to be poor than the unemployed or working-age inactive. Cross-country differences in labor market performance and structure then seem a natural starting point in seeking to understand cross-country variation in poverty rates (Burniaux et al., 1998; Förster and Mira d'Ercole, 2005). The poverty rate among the working-age population varies greatly across OECD countries and is indeed the main contributor to overall poverty headcounts (see for example OECD, 2009). However, at the country level working-age poverty—overall or for specific groups—is not in fact strongly linked to employment rates. Burniaux et al. (2006) report some relationship between female participation rates and poverty rates across OECD countries, but it is not particularly strong. Poverty rates are generally lower in low unemployment countries and vice versa, but there are notable exceptions. High employment rate is not a sufficient condition for low poverty among the working-aged population (see also the simulations in Marx et al., 2012b). At the aggregate level, then, employment performances are not the main driver of cross-country differences in the overall poverty risk among the working-age population (OECD, 2009).

There is thus a contrast between micro studies on poverty and the labor market in individual countries, which tends to focus on the labor market situation and experience of individuals and their households and the characteristics associated with good rather than bad labor market outcomes for them, and comparative studies at the aggregate level, which focus on labor market institutions and performance. The relationship between individual characteristics and labor market outcomes is of course a core concern of labor market research, as is the structure of earnings in terms of overall dispersion and differentials. (For reviews see the Handbook of Labour Economics; Ashenfelter and Card, 1999, 2011; Ashenfelter and Layard, 1987; Blau and Kahn, 2008; and Chapter 18 of this volume by Checchi and Salverda.) The extent to which individual disadvantage and relatively bad labor market outcomes manifest themselves in high-poverty rates depends on the household, labor market, and institutional settings in which those disadvantages are experienced. Comparative studies of the relationship between poverty and the labor market at the aggregate level include collective bargaining structures, the role of unions, minimum wages, and so forth, in the explanatory variables employed as key aspects of labor market institutions (see, for example, Burniaux and Mira d'Ercole, 2006). These may often be embedded in wider sets of variables covering, for example, welfare spending and structures, intended not only to serve as controls but also to capture broader concepts of the welfare state "regime," as discussed in Section 23.1.4. This reflects a recognition that labor market institutions, while central, are inextricably bound up with the broader welfare state, and that the impact on poverty of, for example, a minimum wage will vary depending on that broader context—as brought out in our discussion of in-work poverty and social protection transfers in Section 23.2.4.

A core element of that broader welfare state, strongly linked to the labor market, is the education system and educational spending. Once again a contrast may be drawn between micro studies on the relationship between educational attainment, earnings, and poverty at individual or household level, and studies at the aggregate level that focus on the education system and spending and their impact on economic performance and poverty. The relationship between educational attainment and earnings/labor market outcomes for individuals has been a major preoccupation of labor market research since the earnings equation first derived by Mincer (1958) became a basic tool of analysis, but the broader role of education as a facilitator or engine of economic growth is also a major focus of research. The concept of "human capital" has become embedded since the "Chicago School" of economics (see especially Becker, 1964; Mincer, 1958), with human capital seen as similar to physical means of production in that investment in enhancing capacities and skills, notably through education and training, also increases future productive capacity. Microeconomic investigation of this relationship via estimation of the returns accruing to the individual in terms of earnings is the topic of a vast array of empirical economic research, including investigation of the extent to which the positive earnings differentials for the more educated may be interpreted as a causal impact of education itself rather than selection (on which see for example Card, 1999; Machin, 2008). The impact of educational attainment on the likelihood of being in poverty is also a consistent finding from microeconometric analysis of individual OECD countries and holds whether poverty is measured in terms of low annual income, persistent low income, or levels of deprivation (see for example Fouarge and Layte, 2005; Layte and Whelan, 2002), though the relative and absolute "penalty" paid for low educational attainment in terms of enhanced poverty risk varies substantially across countries.

The implications of this individual-level link between educational attainment and poverty risk for aggregate performance and for policy is not as straightforward as it is often taken to be, and requires further research. Improving the education and skills of the workforce has assumed a central role in strategies to promote economic growth and tackle poverty and exclusion. This is illustrated by the European Union's, 2013 *Social Investment Package*, which focuses on policies designed to strengthen people's skills and capacities, including education and child care as well as active labor market policies (see European Commission, 2013), or in a U.S. context by the Obama administration highlighting that "To prepare Americans for the jobs of the future and help restore middle-class security, we have to out-educate the world and that starts with a strong school system."[5] This reflects, in particular, the concern that the low-skilled in advanced economies are being left behind by rapid technological change in a globalized world economy, as discussed in depth in Freeman (2008) and Chapter 20 by Kanbur in this volume. On the role of education in this context, OECD (2011a) concludes that between the mid-1980s and the mid-2000s the sizeable disequalizing effect on earnings of factors such as technological change, more flexible labor market regulation, and less generous unemployment insurance was largely offset by growth in average educational attainment, up-skilling serving to reduce wage dispersion among workers and increase employment rates.

However, the corollary is not that continued expansion in education *per se* will be effective as an equalizing or antipoverty policy. As Checchi et al. (2014) emphasize, increasing average levels of educational attainment was associated with reducing dispersion in attainment in many OECD countries over the twentieth century, but with completion rates at second level approaching saturation in many rich countries, the main issue facing educational policies in most OECD countries now is whether they should pursue further expansion at tertiary level. Such expansion, depending on how it is brought about and underpinned, may not benefit those from poorer backgrounds, as we discuss in the context of intergenerational transmission of disadvantage in the next section. Research on how best to enhance skills in the middle and bottom parts of the distribution in secondary school, including performance in mathematics and languages, as well as issues of

---

[5] http://www.whitehouse.gov/issues/education, downloaded July 25, 2013.

school system structures, tracking, and early childhood education, discussed in the next section are thus also central to the research agenda from a poverty perspective.

Training and skill enhancement, as well as matching, are important components of the active labor market programs and activation strategies that are now widely seen as at the core of antipoverty policies (see European Commission, 2013; OECD, 2009). These have been the subject of a very substantial research literature, covering the evaluation of the impact of specific interventions and of active labor market policies more broadly. For reviews see Heckman et al. (1999), OECD (2005, 2007b), Card et al. (2010), and Kluve (2010). The general thrust of these evaluations, when carried out rigorously, was not particularly positive for a time, as reflected in Richard Freeman's summary that "Random assignment social experiments analysed with care .... have shown us that one favourite solution to labour market problems—training and other active labour market measures—have at best only modest effects on outcomes" (Freeman, 1998, p. 16). More recent evaluations have been more positive in tone, with OECD (2009), for example, concluding that activation programs can have a significant impact on unemployment. Card et al.'s (2010) meta-analysis of microeconometric evaluations yields particularly interesting findings from both a substantive and methodological point of view. They find subsidized public sector employment programs to have the least favorable impact estimates, whereas job-search assistance programs have relatively favorable short-run impacts, classroom and on-the-job training programs tend to show better outcomes in the medium-run than in the short-run, and programs for youths are less likely to yield positive impacts than untargeted programs. Methodologically, they find that—controlling for the outcome measure and the type of program and participants—experimental and nonexperimental studies have similar impact estimates, suggesting that the research designs used in recent nonexperimental evaluations are unbiased. They also note that the outcome variable used to measure program effectiveness matters, with evaluations based on registered unemployment durations being more likely to show favorable short-term impacts. The outcome variable is also clearly very important from a poverty perspective: It cannot be taken for granted that success in terms of a transition from unemployment into employment, even if sustained, leads to an escape from poverty because not all those benefiting may have been in poverty when unemployed. For those who were in poverty, the increase in income involved after taxes and withdrawal of benefits may not suffice to lift the household above a poverty threshold, as discussed at some length in Section 23.3. The rigorous evaluation of active labor market programs in terms of their impact on poverty remains a major gap to be filled.

As is noted in Card et al.'s (2010) work, active labor market programs are widely diverse. An effort to categorize these policies in relation to their political determinants is made by Bonoli (2010) on the basis of national variation across OECD economies. However, Bonoli found little regularity over time in these determinants, with a mix of leftist and centrist political parties in each period advocating active labor market policies. Moreover, Bruno and Rovelli (2010) compare and document differences in labor market policies in EU countries in 2000s and find that, in general, higher rates of employment are associated with more expenditure on active labor market programs for countries with a larger share of the population embracing pro-work attitudes. Recently, an OECD (2013) study analyzing activation programs in OECD countries and with more detail in Ireland, the United Kingdom, Japan, Norway, Finland, Switzerland, and Australia brings out the different responses of expenditures on activation programs after the economic crisis, finding it difficult to establish a common pattern.

23.3.3 Intergenerational Transmission, Childhood, and Neighborhoods

The intergenerational transmission of poverty and disadvantage continues to be a core concern for research and policy. Research on income mobility across the distribution is the topic of Chapter 10 by Jäntti and Jenkins, but here it is important to reiterate that there is substantial evidence from country-specific studies that mobility is particularly limited toward the bottom of the socioeconomic hierarchy, so that poverty is to a significant degree inherited across generations. Examples from research in the United States include Wilson (1987), Gottschalk et al. (1994), Duncan et al. (1994, 1998), Duncan and Brooks-Gunn (1997), and Corcoran (2001); for Canada, see Corak (2001); for recent U.K. studies include Sigle-Rushton (2004) and Blanden and Gibbons (2006), and similar studies that trace current poverty or disadvantage to conditions in childhood that exist for other rich countries. The likelihood of being a welfare recipient is also seen to be associated across generations—see, for example, Corak (2004) for Sweden and Canada and Page (2004) for the United States.

OECD (2009) concludes that variation in the strength of transmission of poverty across countries cannot reliably be assessed with the available evidence. However, the findings of Jäntti et al. (2006) showing considerably greater upward mobility in individual earnings from the bottom quintile in the Scandinavian countries than in the United Kingdom and especially the United States, and those of Raaum et al. (2007) that the intergenerational transmission of family earnings is also significantly stronger in the United Kingdom and even more so the United States than in the Scandinavian countries, are suggestive (see also Aaberge et al., 2002). Furthermore, recent studies by Esping-Andersen and Wagner (2010) and Whelan et al. (2013) have been able to exploit the availability of harmonized data from a special module on intergenerational transmission attached to EU-SILC in 2005. Esping-Andersen and Wagner estimate the impact of economic hardship during childhood on both educational attainment and adult income (controlling *inter alia* for lone motherhood and parents' education) in Denmark, Norway, France, Italy, Spain, and the United Kingdom. They conclude that economic hardship in childhood has no direct effects on adult income in any of the countries, but it does have powerful indirect effects via children's educational attainment; this effect disappears among the youngest cohorts in both Denmark and Norway but not in the other countries, leading the authors to conclude that the Scandinavian countries are more recently succeeding in minimizing the adverse consequences of economic want in childhood. This is consistent with Whelan, Nolan, and Maitre's study, which included a broader range of EU countries and found that factors such as parental class, parental education, and childhood economic circumstances/hardship had less influence on income poverty and a broader, multidimensional measure of vulnerability in social democratic countries than in countries in the liberal and southern European welfare regimes.

Understanding the mechanisms at work is clearly vital in designing strategies aimed at reducing the extent to which poverty is handed down from one generation to the next, and both causal channels and policy responses have been the subject of substantial bodies of literature (for reviews see D'Addio, 2007; Esping-Andersen, 2004a,b; Nolan et al., 2011). Studies focused on the United States show that the inheritance of poverty is connected with substantially less schooling (on average, poor children will have 2 years fewer schooling than nonpoor children), poor health, and crime (Duncan and Brooks-Gunn, 1997; Mayer, 1997), and similar if less dramatic effects have been documented for the United Kingdom (Gregg et al., 1999) and France (CERC, 2004; Maurin, 2002). Gregg et al.'s (1999) study controls for the child's abilities (via cognitive test scores at age seven), and still finds strong poverty effects. U.S. and British studies demonstrate strong negative effects of lone motherhood on child outcomes, but also suggest that the main reason has to do with poor economic conditions (Biblarz and Raftery, 1999; Gregg et al., 1999; McLanahan and Sandefur, 1994), while selection into lone parenthood may also be a factor (Piketty, 2003). Interestingly, Esping-Andersen and Wagner's (2010) multicountry study found no significant effects of lone motherhood on educational attainment or adult income having controlled for mother's education and childhood financial hardship.

The impact of genes/nature versus nurture and the interactions between them have been the topic of much debate in the broader intergenerational mobility literature, as discussed in Jäntti and Jenkins' Chapter 10. (See also Chapter 18 by O'Donnell, Van Doorslaer and Van Ourti for a detailed discussion on health and inequality.) From the point of view of transmission of poverty and disadvantage, the key thrust of recent findings is that cognitive skills and family finances matter, but so do noncognitive abilities, social skills, cultural resources, motivation and, more generally, the familial "learning milieu." Cognitive and noncognitive skills are influenced by family endowments that are neither strictly financial or genetic. Heckman and Lochner (2000) and Carneiro and Heckman (2003) have been influential studies, with their "learning-begets-learning" model stressing the fundamental causal importance of conditions in the preschool years, especially those related to behavioral and cognitive development. There is growing consensus in the literature that conditions when children are under age 6, or even 3, are decisive for their cognitive skills, sense of security, and ability and motivation to learn (Danziger and Waldfogel, 2000; Duncan and Brooks-Gunn, 1997). Substantial differences in children's cognitive abilities by parents' socioeconomic status emerge at early ages and carry through to subsequent achievements in education and earnings (e.g., Cunha and Heckman, 2007); poverty in early childhood has strong adverse effects on these later outcomes, partly because of parental traits such as poor cognitive and noncognitive skills and the effects of family "culture," in particular in terms of how it influences parenting behavior and child stimulation (de Graaf et al., 2000; Esping-Andersen, 2007).

This has significantly influenced thinking about the role of education in seeking to reduce intergenerational transmission of poverty. Mounting evidence suggests that differences in the design and financing of education systems *per se* seem to matter rather less than had been thought. There appears to be a broad consensus that early tracking according to ability reduces educational mobility across generations (see Hanushek and Woessmann, 2006), with the abolition of early tracking and the introduction of comprehensive school systems seen to have boosted educational attainment among the least privileged social strata in Sweden, Finland, and Norway. Since these are also countries in which welfare state redistribution increased substantially over the same period, it is difficult to identify how much of it was education reform or income equalization that produced higher mobility. However, Blanden et al.'s (2005) U.K. analyses suggest that education reform that delayed tracking produced a substantial increase in intergenerational mobility there, primarily to the benefit of children from low-income families, which cannot be ascribed to an increase in welfare state redistribution because over the period in question income inequality actually grew. More broadly, though, it has become increasingly clear that generalized policies promoting the attainment of higher levels of education by increasing the proportion going on to third level—assigned a central role in strategies aimed at improving equality of opportunity in many countries—may not be adequate if the aim is to address the disadvantages that children from poorer backgrounds face from the outset.

This has served to reinforce the emphasis in recent literature arguing for an early childhood focus, and that high-quality early childhood programs can significantly improve both cognitive and noncognitive outcomes for disadvantaged children (Carneiro and Heckman, 2003; Currie, 2001; Karoly et al., 2005; Waldfogel, 2006). Heckman's work has been particularly influential in demonstrating that investing in early childhood is a cost-effective policy (though the broader implications in terms of later interventions have been hotly debated). The core evidence that underpins Heckman's work comes from early intervention programs in the United States, but Esping-Andersen (2004a,b) relates the significant decline in social inheritance effects for the Nordic countries to the introduction of universal, high-quality child care. Schütz et al. (2005) in their cross-sectional comparison across countries report an inverted U-shaped relationship between family background effect and preschool enrolment, which suggests that early education may reduce the extent to which family background shapes life chances. OECD (2009) concludes that good quality care in early childhood, preschool, and also school years, are essential tools for promoting intergenerational mobility.

Going beyond education, the extent and nature of the welfare state itself can clearly affect the intergenerational transmission of poverty, indeed this is often articulated as a core aim in terms of equalizing children's life chances and avoiding wasted potential. One might expect that social policies that reduce child poverty (such as effective income support and promoting maternal employment, as discussed earlier—see UNICEF, 2007; Whiteford and Adema, 2007) would also promote more intergenerational inequality, but directly demonstrating that link is less straightforward. Mayer (1997), for example, argued that low income in itself is less important than parental characteristics such as low skills, poor health, or deviance, which affect the likelihood of being poor. In a comparison across the United States, though, Mayer and Lopoo (2008) find that in high-spending states the difference in mobility between advantaged and disadvantaged children is smaller than in low-spending states. It has been calculated that the risk of child poverty falls by a factor of four when mothers are employed (Esping-Andersen, 2009). There is also some evidence that intergenerational transmission of welfare dependency may be related to program design, with Corak et al.'s (2004) comparison of cash support schemes in North America and Sweden suggesting that passive programs are more likely to promote the transmission of welfare dependency than active ones. More generally, benefit systems that rely heavily on means-testing are more likely to create the poverty and unemployment traps that make it more likely that poverty and welfare dependency persist into subsequent generations.

Finally, still focusing on children and the transmission of poverty, an issue that has received considerable attention in the research literature is the potential effect of living in a "bad" neighborhood. Some studies suggest that local conditions can help explain the intergenerational transmission of income (OECD, 2008), although their impact may be relatively weak even in the United States. The range of U.S.-focused studies reported in Brooks-Gunn et al. (1997) suggested that neighborhood does matter for child and youth development, having greatest impact in early childhood and late adolescence and less in between, but the size of these effects was usually much smaller than those of family-level conditions. Solon et al. (2000) used the cluster sampling design of the Panel Study of Income Dynamics to estimate both sibling and neighborhood correlations on years of schooling and found sibling correlations of around 0.5, whereas their neighborhood estimates were as low as 0.1. Raaum et al. (2003) used Norwegian census data and concluded likewise that neighborhood correlations were small compared to sibling correlations, both for educational attainment and long-run earnings. This is consistent with the findings of U.S. experiments where families living in public housing were assigned housing vouchers by lottery encouraging them to move to neighborhoods with lower poverty rates; the results reported in Sanbonmatsu et al. (2006) show no significant effects on test scores. Looking beyond educational attainment to a broader set of poverty-related outcomes, the difficulties in adequately characterizing neighborhoods in terms of all their potentially relevant characteristics, and of distinguishing their effects on poverty and related outcomes from those of individual/family characteristics—taking into account that there may be interactions between them—have also been emphasized in research outside the United States (see Lupton, 2003).

23.4. THE WELFARE STATE, ANTIPOVERTY POLICY, AND THE ECONOMIC CRISIS OF THE LATE 2000s

23.4.1 Poverty, Income Inequality, and the Economic Crisis

The economic crisis experienced by the OECD countries since 2007–2008 has been the most serious since the Great Depression of the 1930s in terms of its impact on output and growth and is central to the ways in which poverty and antipoverty policies are now being thought about, studied, and debated. The crisis has affected poverty directly, as we will discuss, but it also has altered the context in which welfare states are currently operating and perspectives on how they are and should be evolving in the medium term. Here, we look first at the evidence on the immediate impact of the crisis, and then at the medium-term context for antipoverty policy.

The immediate impact of the crisis on income inequality and poverty has been the subject of a number of national and comparative studies, including Matsaganis and Leventi (2013), Callan et al. (2011), Figari et al. (2011), and Jenkins et al. (2013). Jenkins and colleagues adopt a comparative perspective, looking at aggregate indicators across the OECD and at six case-study countries in depth. Their central conclusion is that the immediate impact of the crisis on income inequality and income poverty in most countries was much more modest than the dramatic experience of the Great Depression, although not so different from more recent recessions, such as the Nordic crisis of the early 1990s. They stress that a striking feature of the crisis from 2007 to 2008 has been the extent to which its macroeconomic impact varied across countries: in some there were major declines in economic activity and sharply rising unemployment, but in others there was much more modest changes in growth and employment (see also Lane and Milesi-Ferretti, 2012). The peak-to-trough fall in quarterly GDP was substantially larger than the average fall during recessions over the previous 50 years almost everywhere but ranged, nonetheless, from zero in Australia to nearly 13% in Ireland. Another feature highlighted is that GDP declines were not fully transmitted into falls in the real disposable income of households, which were protected by both automatic stabilizers and additional support of governments through the tax and benefit system. The immediate response of employment to the fall in GDP was also frequently smaller than in previous recessions, though this was not the case in countries such as Ireland, Spain, and the United States where a boom–bust pattern in the housing market played an important role in the recession. Large falls in individual employment were also accompanied by significant rises in household worklessness in countries such as Ireland, Spain, and the United States, but not in some others—notably, Denmark and Finland where the workless household rate fell despite relatively large increases in the individual nonemployment rate, cushioning the impact on poverty. Another feature of the immediate onset of the crisis was the decline in income from capital, concentrated among richer households.

Looking at available poverty indicators up to 2009 compared with pre-crisis, Jenkins and colleagues found that relative income poverty rates typically fell in European countries, whereas absolute poverty rates (using "anchored" income thresholds indexed to prices) tended to fall slightly in Europe while rising modestly in the United States (as measured with the U.S. official poverty line), but in both cases these rates fell for the elderly. The six countries they studied in detail—Germany, Ireland, Italy, Sweden, the United Kingdom, and the United States—experienced differing macroeconomic shocks, with Germany recovering very rapidly, Sweden seeing a large decline in GDP but relatively rapid recovery, the United States experiencing marked contraction followed by some recovery, Italy and the United Kingdom seeing major downturns, and Ireland experiencing the largest GDP decline among OECD countries. Germany saw little change in employment, whereas in Ireland and in the United States at the other extreme, unemployment rose rapidly. The short-run impact on household income inequality and poverty was relatively modest. In Germany, the proportion of persons with a household income less than 60% of the contemporary median income declined marginally, and the proportion in households below such an income threshold held fixed in purchasing power at its 2007 level also fell. Chapter 2 shows that median income, inequality, and relative poverty all rose slightly in 2010. In the United Kingdom, the number falling below 60% of median income fell by more than 1 percentage point, and a fixed real threshold showed a larger decline in poverty. In Sweden, the proportion falling below 60% of median income increased, although when a threshold fixed in purchasing power terms is employed the increase was a good deal smaller. In Ireland, relative income poverty declined between 2007 and 2009 while the proportion below a fixed real income threshold remained stable. In Italy, the buffering role of social transfers was relatively limited, although the consequent increase in poverty might be considered modest given the scale of the initial macroeconomic shock. Finally, in the United States, the relative poverty rate declined modestly, reflecting a decline in real median income, whereas the official poverty rate (calculated using a low-income cut-off held fixed in real terms) increased. In all six case-study countries, elderly people were relatively well protected, compared with children and individuals of working age.

The variation in the distributional impact of the crisis to date across countries reflects not only differences in the nature of the macroeconomic downturn but also differences in how cash transfers and direct taxes cushioned household net incomes from the full effects of what was happening to market incomes. To some extent, these are differences in automatic stabilization and so they vary with the generosity and comprehensiveness of social safety nets and the structure and levels of direct taxes and social insurance contributions. However, policy responses and choices as the recession impacted have also been important (for a discussion of EU government's initial responses to the crisis see Marchal et al., 2014).

More recent poverty indicators for European countries produced by Eurostat, up to 2011, also show that experiences have been quite varied. As shown in Table 23.5, between 2007 and 2011 the proportion falling below 60% of median income rose by 1 percentage point or more in eight countries, fell by that amount in seven countries, and was stable in the rest. The average relative income poverty rate across the EU 27 was 16.5% in 2007 and 16.9% in 2011. Income poverty rates "anchored" at the 2008 60% of median threshold and then indexed to prices showed a good deal more variability over time across EU countries, as Table 23.6 shows. This rose in 13 countries, sometimes by a remarkably large amount—by 11 percentage points in Latvia and Lithuania and almost 14 percentage points in Iceland; however, it fell in another 10 countries, so that the overall average across the EU rose only from 16.4% to 17.5%. It is interesting to compare this with the trend in material deprivation over the same period, as measured by the EU's severe material deprivation indicator: Table 23.7 shows that this rose between 2008 and 2011 in 13 countries while falling in 6; the average across the EU rose marginally. Among countries particularly hard hit by the crisis, deprivation rose sharply in Ireland, Spain, Greece, and Italy, as well as in Latvia and Lithuania, but fell in Portugal.

23.4.2 The Crisis and Antipoverty Policy in the Medium Term

The immediate impact of the onset of the crisis from 2007 to 2008 on living standards and poverty was cushioned, at least to some extent, by welfare state institutions and in particular by social protection and tax systems. The medium-term impact of the crisis on poverty depends not only on developments in the macroeconomy and in employment, but also on the policies adopted with respect to the welfare state broadly conceived and to transfers most particularly. The effects of the crisis on the public finances are dominant in framing the context in which these choices are being made. The need—or perception of such a need—to consolidate public finances plays a central role in debates about responding to the crisis, with tackling poverty often relegated to a more modest role. This could lead to changes to welfare state systems and parameters that will take many years to work their way through, continuing to have an impact on poverty long after economic growth has resumed and the recession is considered to have ended from a purely macroeconomic perspective. (The fairness of fiscal consolidation programs may itself affect the likelihood of them being successful, as analyzed by Kaplanoglou et al. (2013) for 29 OECD countries over the period 1971–2009; their results suggest that programs improving the targeting of

Table 23.5 Relative income poverty rates (60% of median threshold), European Union countries 2007–2011

Country	2007 (%)	2008 (%)	2009 (%)	2010 (%)	2011 (%)
Belgium	15.2	14.7	14.6	14.6	15.3
Bulgaria	22.0	21.4	21.8	20.7	22.3
Czech Republic	9.6	9.0	8.6	9.0	9.8
Denmark	11.7	11.8	13.1	13.3	13.0
Germany	15.2	15.2	15.5	15.6	15.8
Estonia	19.4	19.5	19.7	15.8	17.5
Ireland	17.2	15.5	15.0	16.1	–
Greece	20.3	20.1	19.7	20.1	21.4
Spain	19.7	19.6	19.5	20.7	21.8
France	13.1	12.7	12.9	13.3	14.0
Italy	19.8	18.7	18.4	18.2	19.6
Cyprus	15.5	15.9	15.8	15.1	14.5
Latvia	21.2	25.6	25.7	21.3	19.1
Lithuania	19.1	20.0	20.6	20.2	20.0
Luxembourg	13.5	13.4	14.9	14.5	13.6
Hungary	12.3	12.4	12.4	12.3	13.8
Malta	14.8	15.0	15.3	15.0	15.4
Netherlands	10.2	10.5	11.1	10.3	11.0
Austria	12.0	12.4	12.0	12.1	12.6
Poland	17.3	16.9	17.1	17.6	17.7
Portugal	18.1	18.5	17.9	17.9	18.0
Romania	24.8	23.4	22.4	21.1	22.2
Slovenia	11.5	12.3	11.3	12.7	13.6
Slovakia	10.6	10.9	11.0	12.0	13.0
Finland	13.0	13.6	13.8	13.1	13.7
Sweden	10.5	12.2	13.3	12.9	14.0
United Kingdom	18.6	18.7	17.3	17.1	16.2
Iceland	10.1	10.1	10.2	9.8	9.2
Norway	11.9	11.4	11.7	11.2	10.5
Switzerland	–	16.2	15.1	15.0	15.0
Croatia	18	17.3	17.9	20.5	21.1
European Union (27 countries)	16.5	16.4	16.3	16.4	16.9

Notes: The household income statistics in Eurostat are mainly produced with EU-SILC data, which reference period is a fixed 12-month period (such as the previous calendar or tax year) for all countries except the United Kingdom for which the income reference period is the current year and IE for which the survey is continuous and income is collected for the last 12 months.
Source: Eurostat (downloaded March 20, 2013).

social transfers and their effectiveness in poverty alleviation, increasing spending on training and active labor market policies, and even reducing value-added taxes on necessities, enhance the probability of successful adjustment while promoting social cohesion.)

In such a context, the pressure to increase the targeting of cash transfers is likely to intensify, although that can run the risk of worsening poverty and unemployment

Table 23.6 Anchored income poverty rates (60% of median threshold in 2008, indexed to consumer prices subsequently), European Union countries 2008–2011

Country	2008 (%)	2009 (%)	2010 (%)	2011 (%)
Belgium	14.7	13.1	13.0	13.5
Bulgaria	21.4	16.1	14.8	17.8
Czech Republic	9.0	8.1	7.8	8.6
Denmark	11.8	13.1	12.6	12.2
Germany	15.2	16.0	15.8	15.9
Estonia	19.5	18.9	19.7	23.9
Ireland	15.5	15.4	22.8	–
Greece	20.1	18.9	18.0	24.9
Spain	19.6	20.2	22.3	25.7
France	12.7	12.7	12.3	13.9
Italy	18.7	19.9	19.3	21.4
Cyprus	15.9	16.3	16.2	14.4
Latvia	25.6	26.0	33.0	36.2
Lithuania	20.0	18.6	28.4	30.8
Luxembourg	13.4	15.5	14.4	14.6
Hungary	12.4	11.8	13.7	14.7
Malta	15.0	14.3	16.5	15.9
Netherlands	10.5	10.6	10.0	11.0
Austria	12.4	11.4	11.0	10.5
Poland	16.9	13.7	13.0	11.9
Portugal	18.5	18.1	16.1	17.9
Romania	23.4	18.2	16.2	17.9
Slovenia	12.3	10.2	12.1	13.0
Slovakia	10.9	7.8	7.3	7.0
Finland	13.6	13.0	12.0	12.3
Sweden	12.2	11.7	11.2	11.6
United Kingdom	18.7	20.4	21.4	21.8
Iceland	10.1	9.8	16.7	23.7
Norway	11.4	10.2	9.6	8.9
Switzerland	16.2	13.8	13.8	13.1
European Union (27 countries)	16.4	16.3	16.4	17.5

Notes: The household income statistics in Eurostat are mainly produced with EU-SILC data, which reference period is a fixed 12-month period (such as the previous calendar or tax year) for all countries except the United Kingdom for which the income reference period is the current year and IE for which the survey is continuous and income is collected for the last 12 months.
Source: Eurostat (downloaded March 20, 2013).

"traps" and undermining the bases for social solidarity and political support for relatively generous provision. The notion of "social investment" has come to play a major part in debates about the role of social spending and the future of welfare states in rich countries, particularly in Europe where the language of social investment has become embedded in EU discourse since the adoption of the Lisbon Agenda in 2000. A number of important

Table 23.7 Severe material deprivation rate, European Union countries 2008–2011

Country	2007 (%)	2008 (%)	2009 (%)	2010 (%)	2011 (%)
Belgium	5.7	5.6	5.2	5.9	5.7
Bulgaria	57.6	41.2	41.9	45.7	43.6
Czech Republic	7.4	6.8	6.1	6.2	6.1
Denmark	3.3	2.0	2.3	2.7	2.6
Germany	4.8	5.5	5.4	4.5	5.3
Estonia	5.6	4.9	6.2	9.0	8.7
Ireland	4.5	5.5	6.1	7.5	–
Greece	11.5	11.2	11.0	11.6	15.2
Spain	3.0	2.5	3.5	4.0	3.9
France	4.7	5.4	5.6	5.8	5.2
Italy	6.8	7.5	7.0	6.9	11.2
Cyprus	13.3	9.1	9.5	10.1	10.8
Latvia	24.9	19.0	21.9	27.4	31.4
Lithuania	16.6	12.3	15.1	19.5	18.5
Luxembourg	0.8	0.7	1.1	0.5	1.2
Hungary	19.9	17.9	20.3	21.6	23.1
Malta	4.2	4.0	4.7	5.7	6.3
Netherlands	1.7	1.5	1.4	2.2	2.5
Austria	3.3	6.4	4.8	4.3	3.9
Poland	22.3	17.7	15.0	14.2	13.0
Portugal	9.6	9.7	9.1	9.0	8.3
Romania	36.5	32.9	32.2	31.0	29.4
Slovenia	5.1	6.7	6.1	5.9	6.1
Slovakia	13.7	11.8	11.1	11.4	10.6
Finland	3.6	3.5	2.8	2.8	3.2
Sweden	2.2	1.4	1.6	1.3	1.2
United Kingdom	4.2	4.5	3.3	4.8	5.1
Iceland	2.1	0.8	0.8	1.8	2.1
Norway	2.3	2.0	2.2	2.0	2.3
Switzerland	–	2.2	2.1	1.7	1.0
Croatia	–	–	–	14.5	14.8
European Union (27 countries)	9.1	8.4	8.1	8.3	8.8

Source: Eurostat (downloaded March 20, 2013).

recent contributions have highlighted the potential of social investment as a new perspective on or a paradigm for social policy in the context of the economic crisis and to the demand of the knowledge-based economy more broadly, as an alternative to neoliberal responses focusing on retrenchment in social spending, and as a key ingredient in responding to the macroeconomic/Euro crisis (see the contributions to Hemerijck and Vandenbroucke, 2012; Morel et al., 2011; Vandenbroucke et al., 2011). Others have sought to assess the extent to which recent directions in social policies and spending patterns could be characterized as moving toward a social investment strategy and whether disappointing outcomes in terms of poverty can be seen as a failure of such a strategy (Cantillon, 2011; Vandenbroucke and Vleminckx, 2011; van Kersbergen and Hemerijck, 2012). The EU is paying serious attention to this debate, as evidenced by the establishment by DG Employment, Social Affairs and Equal Opportunities of an expert group on Social Investment for Growth and Cohesion in autumn 2012 as input to a major initiative envisaged in the area of social policies.

"Social investment" may be viewed in a number of distinct ways, as Nolan (2013) discusses: as a paradigm and strategy for social policies and spending, as a conceptual base and analytical framework, and/or as a platform for political engagement in both a narrow and broad sense. Whether social investment can credibly be presented as the paradigm most likely to underpin economic growth or employment is open to debate and merits further research, even if—as Nolan (2013) argues—the distinction between social "investment" and other social spending is not particularly robust, conceptually and empirically. Highlighting that distinction may not in any case be the most useful and productive way to frame the debate about the future of social spending, where concentration on a narrow economic argument runs the risk of obscuring normative choices and the broader case for social spending.

Finally, it is important to note that an economic crisis of the depth and nature of the one that began in 2007–2008 may also have major implications for intergenerational equity, especially if it continues to be the case that the elderly are relatively well-cushioned from its effects compared to younger people; sustained high unemployment in particular may well result in long-term "scarring" of those affected, with the risk that their disadvantage is transmitted to the next generation.

23.5. FUTURE RESEARCH DIRECTIONS

We conclude with a brief discussion of priorities for research on poverty and antipoverty policy. The key challenges lie in deepening understanding of the processes at work in creating and perpetuating poverty at individual, household, national, and cross-national level. While much has been learned about the characteristics associated with poverty in different countries, the fact that this differs so widely across countries provides a window into the nature of the underlying processes that has not been fully exploited. In the same vein, studying the factors associated with change over time in a specific country is valuable but putting these changes in a comparative perspective adds another dimension. So a panel-of-countries approach has increasing potential as the statistical underpinning in terms of comparable data continues to be built. This can be complemented by continued development of the potential to carry out micro-simulation analysis in a comparative perspective; the challenge of incorporating behavioral responses into such analysis remains substantial (Immervoll et al., 2007). Exploiting the potential of panel data will continue to be a priority to reliably distinguish those data genuinely and persistently on low income and understanding the barriers to income smoothing facing those on low income more transiently. Increasing recognition of the multidimensional nature of poverty and social exclusion points to the need to deepen understanding of the linkages between different forms of deprivation and exclusion, moving beyond descriptive analysis of the extent to which they go together to study the processes that underpin the underlying relationships between them—where once again a comparative perspective is invaluable—while also addressing the difficult conceptual issues involved.

There also remains a substantial research agenda in the field of antipoverty policy. Not many countries have made very substantial progress in reducing relative poverty as conventionally measured in recent years, though material deprivation and absolute poverty have generally declined up to the crisis from 2008. While some progress has been made in understanding the factors at work, many of the deeper causal questions remain largely unsettled. Changes in the distribution of income from the market may have made reducing relative poverty more difficult, and the redistributive impact of tax and benefit systems may have declined, and each needs to be much better understood. A key question is whether the apparent failure of many governments to maintain or to improve the antipoverty impact of their tax and benefit systems is a consequence of lack of effective political will (voter preferences) or reflects instead (or as well) systemic limits and/or external constraints. Important items on the policy research agenda include:

- Can more be done with less? There is a continuing controversy over targeting and cost-effectiveness of public social expenditure. With ageing populations and rising needs due to sociodemographic and economic trends, this question is bound to remain at the forefront of the research agenda.
- Why are antipoverty provisions in many countries so manifestly inadequate? Are there systemic limits to incrementalism in redistributive policy? That is to say: are there really limits to what improvement can be achieved by strengthening the existing main pillars of redistribution: wage and broader market force regulation, social insurance, social assistance, and taxes? What promise do new redistributive mechanisms and programs offer? Negative income taxes and associated systems are seen as the way forward by some, but short-term issues, such as take-up and long-term effects on wages and human capital formation, earnings mobility, and so forth are not well understood.
- What is the optimal balance between direct redistribution and "social investment"— that is, expenditures that seek to generate lasting effects through improvements in skills and capabilities? To what extent can social investment act as a substitute for direct "compensatory" redistribution, or is there complementarity? If so, what is the optimal balance?
- Making cash benefits and services conditional on certain behavioral requirements and conditions is a policy strategy that is gaining increased attention, part of a broader

current toward more micro intervention in social policy, and informed by social experiments (see Bastagli, 2011; Medgyesi and Temesváry, 2013). Is such a shift from the macro to the micro level really the way forward, and what, if any, are the limits there?

Finally, we should note that while this survey has focused on the "rich world" (as it is conventionally understood), some of the most innovative antipoverty policy is being conceived, implemented, and analyzed outside of that area, with a number of South American and Asian countries standing out in this respect. An important task for future research is to integrate these rich but largely parallel streams of poverty research.

ACKNOWLEDGMENTS

We thank the participants at the April 2013 Conference "Recent Advances in the Economics of Income Distribution" held at the Paris School of Economics and organized by A.B. Atkinson and F. Bourguignon. Particularly, thanks go to Rolf Aaberge, who served as the main discussant of this chapter.

REFERENCES

Aaberge, R., Flood, L., 2013. U.S. versus Sweden: the effect of alternative in-work tax credit policies on labour supply of single mothers: IZA Discussion Papers 7706. Institute for the Study of Labor (IZA), Bonn.

Aaberge, R., Langørgen, A., 2006. Measuring the benefits from public services: the effects of local government spending on the distribution of income in Norway. Rev. Income Wealth 52 (1), 61–83.

Aaberge, R., Mogstad, M., 2012. Inequality in current and lifetime income: Discussion Papers 726. Research Department of Statistics Norway.

Aaberge, R., Peluso, E., 2012. A counting approach for measuring multidimensional deprivation: IZA Discussion Papers 6589. Institute for the Study of Labor (IZA), Bonn.

Aaberge, R., Björklund, A., Jäntti, M., Palme, M., Pedersen, P., Smith, N., Wennemo, T., 2002. Income inequality and income mobility in the Scandinavian countries compared to the United States. Rev. Income Wealth 48 (4), 443–469.

Aaberge, R., Bhuller, M., Langørgen, A., Mogstad, M., 2010. The distributional impact of public services when needs differ. J. Public Econ. 94 (9–10), 549–562.

Adema, W., Fron, P., Ladaique, M., 2011. Is the European Welfare State Really More Expensive? Indicators on Social Spending, 1980–2012; and a Manual to the OECD Social Expenditure Database (SOCX). OECD Publishing, Paris.

Airio, I., 2008. Change of Norm? In-Work Poverty in a Comparative Perspective: Studies in Social Security and Health 92. Kela Research Department, KELA, Helsinki.

Allègre, G., Jaehrling, K., 2011. Making work pay for whom? Tax and benefits impacts on in-work poverty. In: Fraser, N., Gutiérrez, R., Peña-Casas, R. (Eds.), Working Poverty in Europe: A Comparative Approach. Palgrave Macmillan, Basingstoke, pp. 278–303.

Andreß, H.-J., Lohmann, H., 2008. The Working Poor in Europe: Employment, Poverty and Globalization. Edward Elgar, Cheltenham.

Arza, C., Kohli, M., 2008. Changing European Welfare: The New Distributional Principles of Pension Policy. Routledge, New York.

Ashenfelter, O., Card, D., 1999. first ed. Handbook of Labor Economics, vol. 3. Elsevier/North Holland, Amsterdam.

Ashenfelter, O., Card, D., 2011. first ed. Handbook of Labor Economics, vol. 4. Elsevier/North Holland, Amsterdam.

Ashenfelter, O., Layard, R., 1987. first ed. Handbook of Labor Economics, vol. 2. Elsevier/North Holland, Amsterdam.

Atkinson, A.B., 1987. On the measurement of poverty. Econometrica 55 (4), 749–764.

Atkinson, A.B., 2003. Multidimensional deprivation: contrasting social welfare and counting approaches. J. Econ. Inequal. 1 (1), 51–65.

Atkinson, A.B., Marlier, E., 2010. Income and Living Conditions in Europe. Eurostat, Luxembourg.

Atkinson, A., Rainwater, L., Smeeding, T., 1995. Income Distribution in OECD Countries. OECD, Paris.

Atkinson, T., Cantillon, B., Marlier, E., Nolan, B., 2002. Social Indicators: The EU and Social Inclusion. Oxford University Press, Oxford.

Bane, M.J., Ellwood, D., 1986. Slipping in and out of poverty: the dynamics of poverty spells. J. Hum. Resour. 12, 1–23.

Barbier, J.-C., Ludwig-Mayerhofer, W., 2004. Introduction: the many worlds of activation. Eur. Soc. 6 (4), 423–436.

Bargain, O., Orsini, K., 2006. In-work policies in Europe: killing two birds with one stone? Labour Econ. 13 (6), 667–697.

Bargain, O., Orsini, K., 2007. Beans for breakfast? How exportable is the British workfare model? In: Bargain, O. (Ed.), Microsimulation in Action. Policy Analysis in Europe using EUROMOD. Research in Labour Economics, vol. 25. Elsevier, Oxford.

Barr, N., 2001. The Welfare State as Piggy Bank: Information, Risk, Uncertainty and the Role of the State. Oxford University Press, Oxford.

Barth, E., Moene, K., 2009. The equality multiplier: NBER Working Paper 15076. National Bureau of Economic Research, Cambridge, MA.

Bastagli, F., 2011. Conditional cash transfers as a tool of social policy. Econ. Polit. Wkly XLVI, 61–66.

Becker, G., 1964. Human Capital: A Theoretical and Empirical Analysis, with Special Reference to Education. University of Chicago Press, Chicago.

Bekker, S., Wilthagen, A.C.J.M., 2008. Flexicurity: a European approach to labour market policy. Intereconomics 43 (2), 68–73.

Benedict, M.E., Shaw, K., 1995. The impact of pension benefits on the distribution of earned income. Ind. Labor Relat. Rev. 48 (4), 740–757.

Beramendi Alvarez, P., 2001. The politics of income inequality in the OECD. The role of second order effects: Luxembourg Income Study Working Paper No. 284.

Bergh, A., 2005. On the counterfactual problem of welfare state research: how can we measure redistribution? Eur. Soc. Rev. 21 (4), 345–357.

Biblarz, T., Raftery, A., 1999. Family structure, educational attainment, and socioeconomic success: rethinking the "pathology of matriarchy" Am. J. Soc. 105, 321–365.

Blanden, J., Gibbons, S., 2006. The Persistence of Poverty Across Generations: A View from Two Cohorts. Policy Press, Bristol.

Blanden, J., Gregg, P., Machin, S., 2005. Educational inequality and intergenerational mobility. In: Machin, S., Vignoles, A. (Eds.), What's the Good of Education? Princeton University Press, Princeton, NJ.

Blau, F., Kahn, L., 2008. Inequality and earnings distribution. In: Salverda, W., Nolan, B., Smeeding, T. (Eds.), The Oxford Handbook of Economic Inequality. Oxford University Press, Oxford.

Boarini, R., Mira d'Ercole, M., 2006. Measures of Material Deprivation in OECD Countries: OECD Social, Employment and Migration Working Papers 2006(6). OECD, Paris.

Bonoli, G., 2007. Time matters. Postindustrialisation, new social risks and welfare state adaptation in advanced industrial democracies. Comp. Polit. Stud. 40, 495–520.

Bonoli, G., 2010. The political economy of active labour market policies. Polit. Soc. 38, 435–457.

Börsch-Supan, A.H., 2012. Entitlement reforms in Europe: policy mixes in the current pension reform process: NBER Working Paper No. 18009.

Bourguignon, F., Chakravarty, S., 2003. The measurement of multidimensional poverty. J. Econ. Inequal. 1 (1), 25–49.

Bourguignon, F., Rogers, F.H., 2007. Distributional effects of educational improvements: are we using the wrong model? Econ. Educ. Rev. 26 (6), 735–746.

Bovenberg, L., van Ewijk, C., 2011. The future of multi-pillar pension systems: Netspar Discussion Papers DP 09/2011-079.

Bradshaw, J., 2010. An international perspective on child benefit packages. In: Kamerman, S., Phipps, S., Ben-Arieh, A. (Eds.), From Child Welfare to Child Well-Being: An International Perspective on Knowledge in the Service of Policy Making. Springer, Berlin, pp. 293–307.

Bradshaw, J., Finch, N., 2002. A comparison of child benefit packages in 22 countries: Research Report 174. Department for Work and Pensions, Norwich.

Bradshaw, J., et al., 2008. A Minimum Income Standard for Britain. What People Think. Joseph Rowntree Foundation, York.

Brooks-Gunn, J., Duncan, G.J., Aber, J.L., 1997. Neighborhood Poverty. Context and Consequences for Children, vol. 1 Russell Sage Foundation, New York, NY.

Bruno, R., Rovelli, R., 2010. Labour market policies and outcomes in the enlarged EU. J. Common Market Stud. 48, 661–685.

Buhmann, B., Rainwater, L., Schmaus, G., Smeeding, T., 1987. Equivalence scales, well-being, inequality and poverty: sensitivity estimates across ten countries using the Luxembourg income study (LIS) database. Rev. Income Wealth 34, 115–142.

Burniaux, J.-M., Mira d'Ercole, M., 2006. Labour market performance, income inequality and poverty in OECD countries: OECD Economics Department Working Paper 500. OECD, Paris.

Burniaux, J., Padrini, F., Brandt, N., 2006. Labour Market Performance, Income Inequality and Poverty in OECD Countries. OECD Economics Department Working Papers, No. 500, OECD Publishing.

Burniaux, J.-M., Dan, T.-T., Fore, D., Förster, M., Mira d'Ercole, M., Oxley, H., 1998. Income Distribution and Poverty in Selected OECD Countries: OECD Economics Department Working Paper 189. OECD, Paris.

Burtless, G., 2006. Poverty and inequality. In: Clark, G.L., Munell, A.H., Orszag, J.M. (Eds.), The Oxford Handbook of Pensions and Retirement Income. Oxford University Press, Oxford.

Burtless, G., 2009. Demographic transformation and economic inequality. In: Salverda, W., Nolan, B., Smeeding, T.M. (Eds.), The Oxford Handbook of Economic Inequality. Oxford University Press, Oxford.

Callan, T., Keane, C., 2009. Non-cash benefits and the distribution of economic welfare. Econ. Soc. Rev. 40 (1), 49–71.

Callan, T., Smeeding, T., Tsakloglou, P., 2008. Short-run distributional effects of public education transfers to tertiary education students in seven European countries. Educ. Econ. 16 (3), 275–288.

Callan, T., Nolan, B., Walsh, J., 2011. The economic crisis, public sector pay, and the income distribution. In: Immervoll, H., Peichl, A., Tatsiramos, K. (Eds.), In: Research on Labor Economics, vol. 32. Emerald, Bingley, pp. 207–225.

Caminada, K., Goudswaard, K., Wang, C., 2012. Disentangling income inequality and the redistributive effect of taxes and transfers in 20 LIS countries over time: LIS Working Paper Series Luxembourg Income Study (LIS) No. 581.

Cantillon, B., 2011. The paradox of the social investment state: growth, employment and poverty in the Lisbon era. J. Eur. Soc. Policy 21 (5), 432–449.

Cantillon, B., Marx, I., Van den Bosch, K., 2003. The puzzle of egalitarianism: the relationship between employment, wage inequality, social expenditure and poverty. Eur. J. Soc. Secur. 5 (2), 108–127.

Cantillon, B., Van Mechelen, N., Pintelon, O., van den Heede, A., 2014. Social redistribution, poverty and the adequacy of social protection in the EU. In: Cantillon, B., Vandenbroucke, F. (Eds.), Reconciling Work and Poverty Reduction: How Successful Are European Welfare States? Oxford University Press, Oxford, pp. 157–184.

Card, D., 1999. The causal effect of education on earnings. In: Ashenfelter, O., Card, D. (Eds.), In: Handbook of Labor Economics, vol. 3. Elsevier/North Holland, Amsterdam.

Card, D., Kluve, J., Weber, A., 2010. Active labor market policy evaluations: a meta-analysis. Econ. J. 120, F452–F477.

Card, D., Heining, J., Kline, P., 2013. Workplace heterogeneity and the rise of West German wage inequality. Q. J. Econ. 128 (3), 967–1015.

Carneiro, P., Heckman, J., 2003. Human capital policy. In: Heckman, J., Krueger, A. (Eds.), Inequality in America. MIT Press, Cambridge, MA.

CERC, 2004. Child Poverty in France. Conseil de L'Emploi, des Revenues et de la Cohesion Sociale, Paris.

Checchi, D., van de Werfhorst, H., Braga, M., Meschi, E., 2014. The policy response: education. In: Salverda, W., Nolan, B., Checchi, D., Marx, I., McKnight, A., Tóth, I., van de Werfhorst, H. (Eds.), Changing Inequalities and Societal Impacts in Rich Countries: Analytical and Comparative Perspectives. Oxford University Press, Oxford.

Chetty, R., 2009. Sufficient statistics for welfare analysis: a bridge between structural and reduced-form methods. Ann. Rev. Econ. 1 (1), 451–488.

Chetty, R., Friedman, J.N., Saez, E., 2013. Using differences in knowledge across neighborhoods to uncover the impacts of the EITC on earnings: NBER Working Paper 18232.

Citro, C., Michael, R., 1995. Measuring Poverty: A New Approach. National Research Council, National Academy Press, Washington, DC.

Corak, M., 2001. Are the kids all right? Intergenerational mobility and child well-being in Canada: Analytical Studies Branch Research Paper Series 2001171e. Statistics Canada, Ottawa.

Corak, M., 2004. Generational income mobility in North America and Europe: an introduction. In: Corak, M. (Ed.), Generational Income Mobility in North America and Europe. Cambridge University Press, Cambridge.

Corak, M., Gustafsson, B., Österberg, T., 2004. Intergenerational influences on the receipt of unemployment insurance in Canada and Sweden. In: Corak, M. (Ed.), Generational Income Mobility in North America and Europe. Cambridge University Press, Cambridge.

Corak, M., Lietz, C., Sutherland, H., 2005. The impact of tax and transfer systems on children in the European Union: IZA Discussion Paper 1589. Institute for the Study of Labor, Bonn.

Corcoran, M., 2001. Mobility, persistence, and the consequences of poverty for children: child and adult outcomes. In: Danziger, S., Haveman, R. (Eds.), Understanding Poverty. Russell Sage Foundation/Harvard University Press, Cambridge, MA.

Corluy, V., Vandenbroucke, F., 2013. Household joblessness. In: Cantillon, B., Vandenbroucke, F. (Eds.), Reconciling Work and Poverty Reduction. How Successful Are European Welfare States? Oxford University Press, Oxford.

Coulter, F., Cowell, F., Jenkins, S., 1992. Equivalence scale relativities and the extent of inequality and poverty. Econ. J. 102, 1067–1082.

Crettaz, E., 2011. Fighting Working Poverty in Post-Industrial Economies. Causes, Trade-Offs and Policy Solutions. Edward Elgar, Cheltenham, UK/Northampton, MA, USA.

Cunha, F., Heckman, J., 2007. The technology of skill formation. Am. Econ. Rev. 97 (2), 31–47.

Currie, J., 2001. Early childhood intervention programs. J. Econ. Perspect. 15 (2), 213–238.

Currie, J., Gahvari, F., 2008. Transfers in cash and in-kind: theory meets the data. J. Econ. Lit. 46 (2), 333–383.

D'Addio, A.C., 2007. Intergenerational transmission of disadvantage: mobility or immobility across generations? A review of the evidence for OECD countries: Social, Employment and Migration Working Papers No. 52. OECD, Paris.

Dang, T.-T., Immervoll, H., Mantovani, D., Orsini, K., Sutherland, H., Dang, T.-T., Immervoll, H., Mantovani, D., Orsini, K., Sutherland, H., 2006. An age perspective on economic well-being and social protection in nine OECD countries: IZA Discussion Papers 2173. Institute for the Study of Labor (IZA), Bonn.

Danziger, S., Waldfogel, J., 2000. Securing the Future: Investing in Children From Birth to College. Russell Sage Foundation, New York.

De Deken, J., Kittel, B., 2007. Social expenditure under scrutiny: the problems of using aggregate spending data for assessing welfare state dynamics. In: Clasen, J., Siegel, N.A. (Hg.), Investigating Welfare State Change: The "Dependent Variable Problem" in Comparative Analysis. Edward Elgar Publishing, Cheltenham, pp. 72–104.

De Graaf, N.D., de Graaf, P., Kraaykamp, G., 2000. Parental cultural capital and educational attainment in The Netherlands: a refinement of the cultural capital perspective. Soc. Educ. 73 (2), 92–111.

De Graaf-Zijl, M., Nolan, B., 2011. Household joblessness and its impact on poverty and deprivation in Europe. J. Eur. Soc. Policy 21 (5), 413–431.

Deacon, A., Bradshaw, J., 1983. Reserved for the Poor: The Means Test in British Social Policy. Robertson, Oxford.

Deaton, A., 2010. Instruments, randomization, and learning about development. J. Econ. Lit. 48, 424–455.

Deaton, A., Gourinchas, P.-O., Paxson, C., 2002. Social security and inequality over the life cycle. In: Feldstein, M., Leibman, J. (Eds.), The Distributional Effects of Social Security Reform. Chicago University Press for NBER, Chicago, pp. 115–148.

Dickens, R., Ellwood, D.T., 2003. Child poverty in Britain and the United States. Econ. J. 113 (488), F219–F239.

Digeldey, I., 2007. Between workfare and enablement—the different paths to transformation of the welfare state: a comparative analysis of activating labour market policies. Eur. J. Polit. Res. 46 (6), 823–851.

Dolls, M., Fuest, C., Peichl, A., 2011. Automatic stabilizers, economic crisis and income distribution in Europe. In: Immervoll, H., Peichl, A., Tatsiramo, K. (Eds.), Who Loses in the Downturn? Economic Crisis, Employment and Income Distribution. In: Research in Labor Economics, vol. 32. Emerald Group Publishing Limited, Bingley, pp. 227–255.

Dolls, M., Fuest, C., Peichl, A., 2012. Automatic stabilizers and economic crisis: US vs. Europe. J. Pub. Econ. 96, 279–294.

Duclos, J.-Y., Makdissi, P., 2005. Sequential stochastic dominance and the robustness of poverty orderings. Rev. Income Wealth 51 (1), 63–87.

Duncan, G.J., Brooks-Gunn, J., 1997. Consequences of Growing Up Poor. Russell Sage Foundation, New York.

Duncan, G., Gustafsson, B., Hauser, R., Schmaus, G., Messinger, H., Muffels, R., Nolan, B., Ray, J.-C., 1993. Poverty dynamics in eight countries. J. Popul. Econ. 6 (3), 215–234.

Duncan, G.J., Brooks-Gunn, J., Klebanov, P.K., 1994. Economic deprivation and early childhood development. Child Dev. 65 (2), 296–318.

Duncan, G.J., Yeung, W.J., Brooks-Gunn, J., Smith, J.R., 1998. How much does childhood poverty affect the life chances of children? Am. Soc. Rev. 63, 406–423.

Eichhorst, W., Gienberger-Zingerle, M., Konle-Seidl, R., 2008. Activation policies in Germany: from status protection to basic income support. In: Eichhors, O., Kaufmann, O., Konle-Seidl, R. (Eds.), Bringing the Jobless into Work? Experiences with Activation Schemes in Europe and the US. Springer, Berlin.

Eissa, N., Hoynes, H., 2004. Taxes and the labor market participation of married couples: the earned income tax credit. J. Public Econ. 88 (9–10), 1931–1958.

Erikson, R., 1993. Descriptions in inequality: the Swedish approach to welfare research. In: Nussbaum, M.C., Sen, A. (Eds.), The Quality of Life. Clarendon Press, Oxford.

Esping-Andersen, G., 1990. The Three Worlds of Welfare Capitalism. Polity Press, Cambridge, UK.

Esping-Andersen, G., 1999. Social Foundations of Postindustrial Economies. Oxford University Press, Oxford.

Esping-Andersen, G., 2004a. Unequal opportunities and the mechanisms of social inheritance. In: Corak, M. (Ed.), Generational Income Mobility in North America and Europe. Cambridge University Press, Cambridge.

Esping-Andersen, G., 2004b. Untying the Gordian knot of social inheritance. Res. Soc. Stratif. Mobil. 21, 115–139.

Esping-Andersen, G., 2007. Sociological explanations of changing income distributions. Am. Behav. Sci. 50 (5), 639–658.

Esping-Andersen, G., 2009. The Incomplete Revolution: Adapting to Women's New Roles. Polity Press, Cambridge.

Esping-Andersen, G., Wagner, S., 2010. Asymmetries in the opportunity structure: intergenerational mobility trends in Scandinavia and Continental Europe: Department of Sociology Working Paper. UPF, Barcelona.

Esping-Andersen, G., Gallie, D., Hemerijck, A., Myles, J., 2002. Why We Need a New Welfare State. Oxford University Press, Oxford.

EU Commission, 2013. Communication from the Commission: Towards Social Investment for Growth and Cohesion – including implementing the European Social Fund 2014–2020. COM(2013) 83 final, European Commission, Brussels.

European Commission, 2008. Employment in Europe. Publications Office of the European Communities, Luxembourg.

European Union, 2013. Social Investment Package. European Union, Brussels.

Eurostat, 2005. Material Deprivation in the EU, Statistics in Focus, Population and Social Conditions, 21/2005. Statistical Office of the European Communities, Luxembourg.

Ferrarini, T., Nelson, K., 2003. Taxation of social insurance and redistribution: a comparative analysis of ten welfare states. J. Eur. Soc. Policy 13 (1), 21–33.

Ferrera, M., 1996. The 'southern model' of welfare in social Europe. J. Eur. Soc. Policy 6 (1), 17–37.

Figari, F., Sutherland, H., 2013. EUROMOD: the European Union tax-benefit microsimulation model. J. Microsimul. 6 (1), 4–26.

Figari, F., Salvatori, A., Sutherland, H., 2011. Economic downturn and stress testing European welfare systems. In: Immervoll, H., Peichl, A., Tatsiramos, K. (Eds.), Who Loses in the Downturn? Economic Crisis, Employment and Income Distribution. In: Research in Labor Economics, vol. 32. Emerald Group Publishing Limited, Bingley, pp. 257–286.

Förster, M., Mira d'Ercole, M., 2005. Income Distribution and Poverty in OECD Countries in the Second Half of the 1990s: OECD Social Employment and Migration Working Papers No. 22. OECD, Paris.

Förster, M., Pearson, M., 2002. Income distribution and poverty in the OECD area: trends and driving forces. OECD Econ. Stud. 34, 7–39.

Foster, J., Greer, W.J., Thorbecke, E., 1984. A class of decomposable poverty indices. Econometrica 52, 761–766.

Fouarge, D., Layte, R., 2005. Welfare regimes and poverty dynamics: the duration and recurrence of poverty spells in Europe. J. Soc. Policy 34, 1–20.

Fraser, N., Gutiérrez, R., Peña-Casas, R., 2011. Working Poverty in Europe: A Comparative Approach. Palgrave Macmillan, Basingstoke.

Freeman, R., 1998. War of the models: which labour market institutions for the 21st century? Labour Econ. 5, 1–24.

Freeman, R., 2008. Globalization and inequality. In: Salverda, W., Nolan, B., Smeeding, T. (Eds.), The Oxford Handbook of Economic Inequality. Oxford University Press, Oxford.

Fritzell, J., Ritakallio, V.-M., 2004. Societal shifts and changed patterns of poverty: Luxembourg Income Study Working Paper No. 393. LIS, Luxembourg.

Garfinkel, I., Rainwater, L., Smeeding, T., 2006. Wealth and Welfare States: Is America a Laggard or Leader? Oxford University Press, Oxford.

Gassmann, F., Notten, G., 2008. Size matters: poverty reduction effects of means-tested and universal child benefits in Russia. Eur. J. Soc. Policy 18 (3), 260–274.

Giannelli, G.C., Jaenichen, U., Rothe, T., 2013. Doing Well in Reforming the Labour Market? Recent Trends in Job Stability and Wages in Germany: IZA Discussion Paper No. 7580. Institute for the Study of Labor, Bonn.

Goedemé, T., 2013. How much confidence can we have in EU-SILC? Complex sample designs and the standard error of the Europe 2020 poverty indicators. Soc. Indic. Res. 110 (1), 89–110.

Gottschalk, P., Smeeding, T., 1997. Cross-national comparisons of earnings and income inequality. J. Econ. Lit. XXXV, 633–687.

Gottschalk, P., McLanahan, S.S., Sandefur, G.D., 1994. The dynamics and intergenerational transmission of poverty and welfare participation. In: Danziger, S.D., Sandefur, G.D., Weinberg, D.H. (Eds.), Confronting Poverty: Prescription for Change. Harvard University Press, Cambridge.

Gregg, P., Harkness, S., Machin, S., 1999. Child Development and Family Income. Joseph Rowntree Foundation, York.

Grogger, J., 2003. The effects of time limits, the EITC, and other policy changes on welfare use, work, and income among female-headed families. Rev. Econ. Stat. 85 (2), 394–408.

Grogger, J., 2004. Welfare transitions in the 1990s: the economy, welfare policy, and the EITC. J. Policy Anal. Manage. 23 (4), 671–695.

Guio, A.-C., 2009. What can be learned from deprivation indicators in Europe?: Eurostat Methodologies and Working Paper. Eurostat, Luxembourg.

Guio, A.-C., Maquet, E., 2007. Material deprivation and poor housing. Comparative EU Statistics on Income and Living Conditions: Issues and Challenge. Office for Official Publications of the European Communities, Eurostat, Luxembourg.

Hanushek, E., Woessmann, L., 2006. Does educational tracking affect performance and inequality? Differences-in-differences evidence across countries. Econ. J. 116 (510), C63–C76, 03.

Harding, A., Warren, N., Lloyd, R., 2006. Moving beyond traditional cash measures of economic well-being: including indirect benefits and indirect taxes: NATSEM Discussion Papers, Issue 61/2006. NATSEM, Canberra.

Heckman, J.J., 2010. Building bridges between structural and program evaluation approaches to evaluating policy. J. Econ. Lit. 48 (2), 356–398.

Heckman, J., Lochner, L., 2000. Rethinking education and training policy. In: Danziger, S., Waldfogel, J. (Eds.), Securing the Future. Russell Sage Foundation, New York.

Heckman, J.J., Urzúa, S., 2010. Comparing IV with structural models: what simple IV can and cannot identify. J. Econ. 156 (1), 27–37.

Heckman, J., Lalonde, R., Smith, J., 1999. The economics and econometrics of active labor market programs. In: Ashenfelter, O., Car, D. (Eds.), In: Handbook of Labour Economics, vol. 3. Elsevier/North Holland.

Hemerijck, A., Vandenbroucke, F., 2012. Social investment and the euro crisis: the necessity of a unifying social policy concept. Intereconomics 47 (4), 200–206.

Hills, J., 2002. Comprehensibility and balance: the case for putting indicators in baskets. Polit. Econ. 1, 95–98.

Holt, S., 2011. Ten Years of the EITC Movement: Making Work Pay Then and Now. Brookings Metropolitan Policy Program, Washington, DC.

Holzmann, R., Hinz, R., 2005. Old-Age Income Support in the 21st Century: The World Bank's Perspective on Pension Systems and Reform. The World Bank, Washington, DC.

Hotz, V.J., Scholz, J.K., 2003. The earned income tax credit. In: Moffit, R. (Ed.), Means-Tested Transfer Programs in the U.S. University of Chicago Press, Chicago, IL.

Hoynes, H., Page, M., Stevens, A., 2006. Poverty in America: trends and explanations. J. Econ. Perspect. 20, 47–68.

Imbens, G., 2010. Better LATE than nothing: some comments on Deaton (2009) and Heckman and Urzua (2009). J. Econ. Lit. 48 (2), 399–423.

Immervoll, H., 2012. Minimum-income benefits in OECD countries: policy design, effectiveness and challenges. In: Besharov, D., Couch, K. (Eds.), Measuring Poverty, Income Inequality, and Social Exclusion. Lessons from Europe. Oxford University Press, Oxford.

Immervoll, H., Jacobsen Kleven, H., Thustrup Kreiner, C., Saez, E., 2007. Welfare reform in European countries: a microsimulation analysis. Econ. J. 117 (516), 1–44.

Immervoll, H., Pearson, M., 2009. A good time for making work pay? Taking stock of in-work benefits and related measures across the OECD: OECD Social, Employment and Migration Working Papers No. 81. OECD, Paris.

Immervoll, H., Richardson, L., 2011. Redistribution policy and inequality reduction in OECD countries: what has changed in two decades? IZA Discussion Papers 6030. Institute for the Study of Labor (IZA).

Immervoll, H., Levy, H., Lietz, D., Mantovani, D., Sutherland, H., 2006. The sensitivity of poverty rates in the European Union to macro-level changes. Cambridge J. Econ. 30, 181–199.

Jäntti, M., Danziger, S., 2000. Income poverty in advanced countries. In: Atkinson, A.B., Bourguignon, F. (Eds.), Handbook of Income Distribution. Elsevier, Amsterdam.

Jäntti, M., Bratsberg, B., Roed, K., Raaum, O., Naylor, R., Österbacka, E., Björklund, A., Eriksson, T., 2006. American exceptionalism in a new light: a comparison of intergenerational earnings mobility in the Nordic countries, the United Kingdom and the United States: IZA Discussion Paper No. 1938. Institute for the Study of Labor, Bonn.

Jenkins, S.P., Brandolini, A., Micklewright, J., Nolan, B., 2013. The Great Recession and the Distribution of Household Income. Oxford University Press, Oxford.

Jones, A., O'Donnell, O., 1995. Equivalence scales and the costs of disability. J. Public Econ. 56 (2), 273–289.

Kangas, O., 1995. Attitudes to means-tested social benefits in Finland. Acta Sociol. 38, 299–310.

Kaplanoglou, G., Rapanos, V., Bardakas, I., 2013. Does fairness matter for the success of fiscal consolidation?: Working Paper, Available at SSRN: http://ssrn.com/abstract=2267831 or http://dx.doi.org/10.2139/ssrn.2267831.

Karoly, L., Kilburn, R., Cannon, J., 2005. Early Childhood Interventions. Rand Corporation, Santa Monica, CA.

Kenworthy, L., 2004. Egalitarian Capitalism? Jobs, Incomes and Inequality in Affluent Countries. Russell Sage Foundation, New York.

Kenworthy, L., 2008. Jobs with Equality. Oxford University Press, Oxford.

Kenworthy, L., 2011. Progress for the Poor. Oxford University Press, Oxford.

Kluve, J., 2010. The effectiveness of European active labor market programs. Labour Econ. 17 (6), 904–918.

Korpi, W., Palme, J., 1998. The paradox of redistribution and strategies of equality: welfare state institutions, inequality, and poverty in the western countries. Am. Sociol. Rev. 63 (5), 661–687.

Kraus, M., 2004. Social security strategies and redistributive effects in European social transfer systems. Rev. Income Wealth 50 (3), 431–457.

Kronauer, M., 1998. 'Social Exclusion' and 'Underclass'—new concepts for the analysis of poverty. In: Andreß, H.-J. (Ed.), Empirical Poverty Research in Comparative Perspective. Ashgate, Aldershot.

Lampman, R., 1971. Ends and Means of Reducing Income Poverty. Markham, Chicago.

Lane, P.R., Milesi-Ferretti, G.M., 2012. External adjustment and the global crisis. J. Int. Econ. 88 (2), 252–265, Elsevier.

Layte, R., Whelan, C.T., 2002. Cumulative disadvantage or individualization: a comparative analysis of poverty risk and incidence. Eur. Soc. 4 (2), 209–223.

Lefebvre, M., 2007. The redistributive effects of pension systems in Europe: a survey of evidence: LIS Working Paper Series. Luxembourg Income Study (LIS) No. 457.

Leigh, A., 2010. Who benefits from the earned income tax credit? Incidence among recipients, coworkers and firms. B.E. J. Econ. Anal. Policy, 10 (1), Berkeley Electronic Press.

Levine, R.A., Watts, H., Hollister, R., Williams, W., O'Connor, A., Widerquist, K., 2005. A retrospective on the negative income tax experiments: looking back at the most innovative field studies in social policy. In: Widerquist, K. (Ed.), The Ethics and Economics of the Basic Income Guarantee. Ashgate, Aldershot.

Liebman, J.B., 2002. Redistribution in the current U.S. social security system. In: Feldstein, M., Liebman, J.B. (Eds.), The Distributional Aspects of Social Security and Social Security Reform. University of Chicago Press, Chicago.

Lohmann, H., 2009. Welfare states, labour market institutions and the working poor: a comparative analysis of 20 European countries. Eur. Soc. Rev. 25 (4), 26.

Lupton, R., 2003. Neighbourhood Effects: Can We Measure Them and Does It Matter?: CASE Paper 73. Centre for the Analysis of Social Exclusion, London School of Economics, London.

Machin, S., 2008. Education and inequality. In: Salverda, W., Nolan, B., Smeeding, T. (Eds.), The Oxford Handbook of Economic Inequality. Oxford University Press, Oxford.

Mahler, V.A., Jesuit, D.K., September, 2006. Fiscal redistribution in the developed countries: new insights from the Luxembourg Income Study. Soc. Econ. Rev. 4, 483–511.

Maitre, B., Nolan, B., Whelan, C.T., 2012. Low Pay, In-Work Poverty and Economic Vulnerability: A Comparative Analysis Using EU-SILC. Manchester School 80 (1), 99–116.

Marchal, S., Marx, I., Van Mechelen, N., 2014. The great-wake up call? Social citizenship and minimum income provisions in times of crisis. J. Soc. Policy 43 (2), 247–267.

Marical, F., Mira d'Ercole, M., Vaalavuo, M., Verbist, G., 2006. Publicly-Provided Services and the Distribution of Resources. OECD Social, Employment and Migration Working Papers No. 45, OECD, Paris.

Marical, F., Mira d'Ercole, M., Vaalavuo, M., Verbist, G., 2008. Publicly-provided services and the distribution of households' economics resources. OECD Econ. Stud. 44 (1), 9–47.

Marlier, E., Atkinson, A.B., Cantillon, B., Nolan, B., 2007. The EU and Social Inclusion: Facing the Challenges. Policy Press, Bristol.

Marx, I., Nelson, K., 2013. Minimum Income Protection in Flux. Palgrave Macmillan, Basingstoke.

Marx, I., Nolan, B., 2013. In-work poverty. In: Cantillon, B., Vandenbroucke, F. (Eds.), Reconciling Work and Poverty Reduction: How Successful Are European Welfare States? Oxford University Press, Oxford.

Marx, I., Vanhille, J., Verbist, G., 2012a. Combating in-work poverty in continental Europe: an investigation using the Belgian case. J. Soc. Policy 41 (1), 19–41.

Marx, I., Vandenbroucke, P., Verbist, G., 2012b. Will rising employment levels bring lower poverty: regression based simulations of the Europe 2020 target. J. Eur. Soc. Policy 22 (5), 472–486.

Marx, I., Marchal, S., Nolan, B., 2013a. Mind the gap: net incomes of minimum wage workers in the EU and the US. In: Marx, I., Nelson, K. (Eds.), Minimum Income Protection in the Flux. Palgrave MacMillan, Basingstoke.

Marx, I., Salanauskaite, L., Verbist, G., 2013b. The paradox of redistribution revisited, and that it may rest in peace?: IZA Discussion Paper Series, vol. 7414. Institute for the Study of Labor, Bonn.

Matsaganis, M., Leventi, C., 2013. The distributional impact of the Greek crisis in 2010. Fisc. Stud. 34 (1), 83–108.

Matsaganis, M., et al., 2005. Child poverty and family transfers in Southern Europe: IZA Discussion Paper Series, No. 1509. Institute for the Study of Labor, Bonn.

Maurin, E., 2002. The impact of parental income on early school transitions. J. Public Econ. 85 (3), 301–332.

Mayer, S., 1997. What Money Can't Buy. Harvard University Press, Cambridge, MA.

Mayer, S., Lopoo, L., 2008. Government spending and intergenerational mobility. J. Public Econ. 92 (1–2), 139–158.

McCarty, N., Pontusson, J., 2009. The political economy of inequality and redistribution. In: Salverda, W., Nolan, B., Smeeding, T. (Eds.), The Oxford Handbook of Economic Inequality. Oxford University Press, Oxford, 2008.

McGarry, K., Davenport, A., 1998. Pensions and the distribution of wealth. In: Wise, D.A. (Ed.), Frontiers in the Economics of Aging. University of Chicago Press, Chicago.

McLanahan, S., Sandefur, G., 1994. Growing Up with a Single Parent. Harvard University Press, Cambridge.

Medgyesi, M., Temesváry Z., 2013. Conditional cash transfers in high-income OECD countries and their effects on human capital accumulation. GINI Discussion Paper #84, Amsterdam.

Meyer, D., Wallace, G., 2009. Poverty levels and trends in comparative perspective. Focus 26 (2), 7–13, Madison: Institute for Research on Poverty.

Mincer, J., 1958. Investment in human capital and personal income distribution. J. Polit. Econ. 66 (4), 281–302.

Moene, K., Wallerstein, M., 2001. Inequality, social insurance and redistribution. Am. Polit. Sci. Rev. 95 (4), 859–874.

Moene, K., Wallerstein, M., 2003. Earnings inequality and welfare spending: a disaggregated analysis. World Polit. 55 (4), 485–516.

Moffit, R., 1989. Estimating the value of an in-kind transfer: the case of food stamps. Econometrica 57 (2), 385–409.

Moller, S., Huber, E., Stephens, J., Bradley, D., Nielsen, F., 2003. Determinants of relative poverty in advanced capitalist democracies. Am. Sociol. Rev. 68 (1), 22–51.

Morel, N., Palier, B., Palme, J., 2011. Towards a Social Investment Welfare State? Ideas, Policies and Challenges. Policy Press, Bristol.

Myles, J., 2000. Poverty indices and poverty analysis. Rev. Income Wealth 46, 161–179.

Nelson, K., 2004. Mechanisms of poverty alleviation: anti-poverty effects of non-means tested and means-tested benefits in five welfare states. J. Eur. Soc. Policy 14 (1), 371–390.

Nelson, K., 2007. Universalism versus targeting: the vulnerability of social insurance and means-tested minimum income protection in 18 countries, 1990–2002. Int. Soc. Sec. Rev. 60, 33–58.

Nolan, B., 2013. What use is social investment? J. Eur. Soc. Policy 23 (5), 459–468.

Nolan, B., Marx, I., 2000. Low pay and household poverty. In: Gregory, M., Salverda, W., Bazen, S. (Eds.), Labour Market Inequalities: Problems and Policies of Low-Wage Employment in International Perspective. Oxford University Press, Oxford, pp. 100–119.

Nolan, B., Marx, I., 2009. Inequality, poverty and social exclusion. In: Salverda, W., Nolan, B., Smeeding, T. (Eds.), Oxford Handbook of Economic Inequality. Oxford University Press, Oxford.

Nolan, B., Russell, H., 2001. Non-Cash Benefits and Poverty in Ireland: Policy Research Series Paper No. 39. The Economic and Social Research Institute, Dublin.

Nolan, B., Whelan, C.T., 1996. Resources, Deprivation and Poverty. Clarendon Press, Oxford.

Nolan, B., Whelan, C.T., 2010. Using non-monetary deprivation indicators to analyze poverty and social exclusion: lessons from Europe? J. Policy Anal. Manage. 29 (2), 305–325.

Nolan, B., Whelan, C.T., 2011. Poverty and Deprivation in Europe. Oxford University Press, Oxford.

Nolan, B., Esping-Andersen, G., Whelan, C.T., Maitre, B., Wagner, S., 2011. The role of social institutions in intergenerational mobility. In: Erikson, R., Jantti, M., Smeeding, T. (Eds.), Persistence, Privilege, Policy and Parenting: The Comparative Study of Intergenerational Mobility. Russell Sage Foundation, New York.

OECD, 2001. When Money is Tight: Poverty Dynamics in OECD Countries. Chapter 3 of Economic Outlook, OECD, Paris.

OECD, 2005. Labour Market Programmes and Activation Strategies: Evaluating the Impacts: OECD Employment Outlook 2005. OECD, Paris (Chapter 4).

OECD, 2007a. Benefits and Wages. OECD, Paris.

OECD, 2007b. Activating the Unemployed: What Countries Do: OECD Employment Outlook 2007. OECD, Paris (Chapter 5).

OECD, 2008. Growing Unequal: Income Distribution and Poverty in OECD Countries. OECD, Paris.

OECD, 2009. Employment Outlook: Tackling the Jobs Crisis: Is Work the Best Antidote to Poverty? OECD, Paris, pp. 165–210 (Chapter 3).

OECD, 2011a. Divided We Stand. Why Inequality Is Rising. OECD, Paris.

OECD, 2011b. Pensions at a Glance 2011. Retirement Income Systems in OECD and G20 Countries. OECD, Paris.

OECD, 2013. Activating Jobseekers: Lessons from Seven OECD Countries: OECD Employment Outlook 2013. OECD, Paris.

Olivera, J., 2012. Preferences for Redistribution in Europe: Working Papers 2012/25. Geary Institute, University College Dublin.

Page, M.E., 2004. New evidence on the intergenerational correlation in welfare participation. In: Corak, M. (Ed.), Generational Income Mobility in North America and Europe. Cambridge University Press, pp. 226–244.

Paulus, A., Sutherland, H., Tsakloglou, P., 2010. The distributional impact of in-kind public benefits in European countries. J. Policy Anal. Manage. 29 (2), 243–266.

Pestieau, P., 2006. The Welfare State in the European Union. Oxford University Press, Oxford.

Piketty, T., 2003. The impact of divorce on school performance. Evidence from France, 1968–2002: CEPR Discussion Paper 4146. CEPR, London.

Raaum, O., Salvanes, K., Sørensen, E., 2003. The impact of a primary school reform on educational stratification: a Norwegian study of neighbour and school mate correlations. Swedish Econ. Policy Rev. 10 (2), 143–169.

Raaum, O., Bratsberg, B., Røed, K., Österbacka, E., Eriksson, T., Jäntti, M., Naylor, R., 2007. Marital sorting, household labor supply, and intergenerational earnings mobility across countries. B.E. J. Econ. Anal. Policy 7 (2) (Article 7).

Rothstein, J., 2010. Is the EITC as good as an NIT? Conditional cash transfers and tax incidence. Am. Econ. J. Econ. Policy 2 (1), 177–208.

Sanbonmatsu, L., Kling, J., Duncan, G., Brooks-Gunne, J., 2006. Neighborhoods and academic achievement: results from the moving to opportunity experiment. J. Hum. Res. 41 (4), 649–691.

Schütz, G., Ursprung, H., Woessmann, L., 2005. Education policy and equality of opportunity: IZA Discussion Paper No. 1906. Institute for the Study of Labor, Bonn.

Sen, A., 1976. Poverty: an ordinal approach to measurement. Econometrica 44, 219–231.

Sen, A., 1980. Equality of what. In: McMurrin, S.M. (Ed.), Tanner Lectures in Human Values I. Cambridge University Press, Cambridge.

Sen, A., 1993. Capability and well-being. In: Nussbaum, M., Sen, A. (Eds.), The Quality of Life. Oxford University Press, Oxford.

Sigle-Rushton, W., 2004. Intergenerational and life-course transmission of social exclusion in the 1970 British Cohort Study: Centre for Analysis of Social Exclusion Discussion Paper No. 78. London School of Economics and Political Science, London.

Skocpol, T., 1991. Targeting within universalism: politically viable policies to combat poverty in the United States. In: Jencks, C., Peterson, P.E. (Eds.), The Urban Underclass. The Brookings Institution, Washington, DC, pp. 411–436.

Smeeding, T., Sandstrom, S., 2005. Poverty and income maintenance in old age: a cross-national view of low income older women. Fem. Econ. 11 (2), 163–174.

Smeeding, T., Thompson, J., 2013. Inequality and Poverty in the United States: the Aftermath of the Great Recession, Finance and Economics Discussion Series 2013–51. Federal Reserve Board, Washington.

Smeeding, T., Williamson, J., 2001. Income maintenance in old age: what can be learned from cross-national comparisons: LIS Working Paper No. 263. Luxembourg Income Study, Luxembourg.

Smeeding, T.M., Saunders, P., Coder, J., Jenkins, S.P., Fritzell, J., Hagenaars, A.J.M., Hauser, R., Wolfson, M., 1993. Poverty, inequality, and family living standards impacts across seven nations: the effect of noncash subsidies for health, education, and housing. Rev. Income Wealth 39, 229–256.

Solon, G., Page, M., Duncan, G., 2000. Correlations between neighboring children in their subsequent educational attainment. Rev. Econ. Stat. 82 (3), 383–392.

Tóth, I., 2014. Revisiting grand narratives of growing inequalities: lessons from 30 country studies. In: Nolan, B., Salverda, W., Checchi, D., Marx, I., McKnight, A., Tóth, I.G., van de Werfhorst, H. (Eds.), Changing Inequalities and Societal Impacts in Rich Countries: Thirty Countries' Experiences. Oxford University Press, Oxford.

Townsend, P., 1979. Poverty in the United Kingdom. Penguin, Harmondsworth.

Tsakloglou, P., Papadopoulos, F., 2002. Aggregate level and determining factors of social exclusion in twelve European countries. J. Eur. Soc. Policy 12 (3), 209–223.

Tsui, K., 2002. Multidimensional poverty indices. Soc. Choice Welfare 19, 69–93.

UNICEF, 2007. Child poverty in perspective: an overview of child well-being in rich countries: Innocenti Report Card 7. UNICEF, Florence, Italy.

US Census Bureau, 2003. Dynamics of Economic Well-Being: Poverty 1996–1999. US Census Bureau, Washington, DC.

Valletta, R., 2006. The ins and outs of poverty in advanced economies: government policy and poverty dynamics in Canada, Germany, Great Britain, and the United States. Rev. Income Wealth 52, 261–284.

van Kersbergen, K., Hemerijck, A., 2012. Two decades of change in Europe: the emergence of the social investment state. J. Soc. Policy 41, 475–492.

Van Lancker, W., Ghysels, J., 2012. Who benefits? The social distribution of subsidized childcare in Sweden and Flanders. Acta Sociol. 55, 125–142.

Van Mechelen, N., Bradshaw, J., 2013. Child poverty as a government priority: child benefit packages for working families, 1992–2009. In: Marx, I., Nelson, K. (Eds.), Minimum Income Protection in Flux. Palgrave Macmillan, Basingstoke.

Van Mechelen, N., Marchal, S., Goedemé, T., Marx, I., Cantillon, B., 2011. The CSB Minimum Income Protection Indicators dataset (CSB-MIPI). CSB Working Paper, Herman Deleeck Centre for Social Policy, Antwerp.

Van Mechelen, N., Marchal, S., 2013. Struggle for life: social assistance benefits, 1992–2009. In: Marx, I., Nelson, K. (Eds.), Minimum Income Protection in Flux. Palgrave Macmillan, Basingstoke.

Van Oorschot, W., 2002. Targeting welfare: on the functions and dysfunctions of means-testing in social policy. In: Townsend, P., Gordo, D. (Eds.), World Poverty: New Policies to Defeat an Old Enemy. The Policy Press, Bristol.

Van Vliet, O., Been, J., Caminada, K., Goudswaard, K., 2012. Pension reform and income inequality among older people in 15 European countries. Int. J. Soc. Welf. 21, S8–S29.

Vandenbroucke, F., Vleminckx, K., 2011. Disappointing poverty trends: is the social investment state to blame? J. Eur. Soc. Policy 21, 432–449.

Vandenbroucke, F., Hemerijck, A., Palier, B., 2011. The EU Needs a Social Investment Pact: OSE Paper Series, Opinion Paper No. 5. Observatoire Social Europeene, Brussels.

Vandenbroucke, F., Cantillon, B., Van Mechelen, N., Goedemé, T., Van Lancker, A., 2013. The EU and minimum income protection: clarifying the policy conundrum. In: Marx, I., Nelson, K. (Eds.), Minimum Income Protection in Flux. Palgrave MacMillan, Basingstoke.

Verbist, G., 2004. Redistributive effect and progressivity of income taxes: an international comparison across the EU using EUROMOD: EUROMOD Working Paper EM5/04. Microsimulation Unit, Cambridge University, Cambridge.

Verbist, G., Figari, F., 2014. The redistributive effect and progressivity of taxes revisited: an international comparison across the European Union. FinanzArchiv 70, 1–25.

Vignoli, D., De Santis, G., 2010. Individual and contextual correlates of economic difficulties in old age in Europe. Popul. Res. Policy Rev. 29, 481–501.

Waldfogel, J., 2006. What Children Need. Harvard University Press, Cambridge, MA.

Whelan, C.T., Maitre, B., 2010. Welfare regime and social class variation in poverty and economic vulnerability in Europe: an analysis of EU-SILC. J. Eur. Soc. Policy 20 (4), 316–332.

Whelan, C.T., Layte, R., Maître, B., Nolan, B., 2001. Income, deprivation and economic strain: an analysis of the European community household panel. Eur. Soc. Rev. 17 (4), 357–372.

Whelan, C.T., Layte, R., Maître, B., 2003. Persistent income poverty and deprivation in the European Union. J. Soc. Policy 32 (1), 1–18.

Whelan, C.T., Nolan, B., Maître, B., 2013. Analysing intergenerational influences on income poverty and economic vulnerability with EU-SILC. Eur. Soc. 15 (1), 82–105.

Whiteford, P., 2008. How much redistribution do governments achieve? The role of cash transfers and household taxes. In: OECD (Ed.), Growing Unequal? OECD, Paris.

Whiteford, P., Adema, W., 2007. What works best in reducing child poverty: a benefit or work strategy?: OECD Social Employment and Migration Working Papers, No. 51. OECD, Paris.

Wilson, W.J., 1987. The Truly Disadvantaged: The Inner City, The Underclass and Public Policy. University of Chicago Press, Chicago.

Wolff, E., Zacharias, A., 2007. The distributional consequences of government spending and taxation in the U.S., 1989 and 2000. Rev. Income Wealth 53 (4), 692–715.

Zaidi, A., Burchardt, T., 2005. Comparing incomes when needs differ: equalization for the extra costs of disability in the U.K. Rev. Income Wealth 51 (1), 89–114.

Zaidi, A., Makovec, M., Fuchs, M., Lipszyc, B., Lelkes, O., Grech, A., Marin, B., de Vos, K., 2006a. Poverty of elderly people in EU25: Report submitted to the European Commission. European Centre for Social Welfare Policy and Research, Vienna.

Zaidi, A., Marin, B., Fuchs, M., 2006b. Pension policy in EU25 and its possible impact on elderly poverty and appendices: Report Submitted to the European Commission. European Centre for Social Welfare Policy and Research, Vienna.

Zheng, B., 2000. Poverty orderings. J. Econ. Surv. 14, 427–466.

CHAPTER 24

Microsimulation and Policy Analysis

Francesco Figari*,†, **Alari Paulus**†, **Holly Sutherland**†
*University of Insubria, Varese, Italy
†Institute for Social and Economic Research (ISER), University of Essex, Colchester, UK

Contents

Handbook of Income Distribution, Volume 2B
ISSN 1574-0056, http://dx.doi.org/10.1016/B978-0-444-59429-7.00025-X

Abstract

We provide an overview of microsimulation approaches for assessing the effects of policy on income distribution. We focus on the role of tax-benefit policies and review the concept of microsimulation and how it contributes to the analysis of income distribution in general and policy evaluation in particular. We consider the main challenges and limitations of this approach and discuss directions for future developments.

Keywords

Microsimulation models, Income distribution, Tax-benefit policies

JEL Classification Codes

C81, D31, H30, I30

24.1. INTRODUCTION AND OVERVIEW

24.1.1 What is Microsimulation?

Microsimulation methods are increasingly used to evaluate the effects of policies on income distribution. Microsimulation refers to a wide variety of modeling techniques that operate at the level of individual units (such as persons, firms, or vehicles), with rules applied to simulate changes in state or behavior. These rules may be deterministic or stochastic, with the result being an estimate of the outcomes of applying these rules, possibly over many steps involving many interactions. These estimates are also at the micro level, allowing analysis of the distribution of the outcomes and changes to them, as well as the calculation of any relevant aggregate.[1]

In the social sciences, Guy Orcutt and his colleagues pioneered microsimulation models in the 1950s as a new approach to analyzing the impact of social and economic policies, which accounted for the characteristics and behavior of the microlevel units

---

[1] Adapted from the definition provided by the International Microsimulation Association (http://microsimulation.org/). Broadly speaking, microsimulation modeling could also cover agent-based simulation (ABS), though they have remained very distinct fields in the literature with microsimulation methods drawing heavily on micro-data (Spielauer, 2011).

under investigation (Orcutt, 1957; Orcutt et al., 1961). Microsimulation is commonly applied to many areas relevant to public policy, such as transportation, location planning for public services and commercial developments, and demand for health care and long-term care.[2] The microsimulation approaches considered here are those that primarily address questions related to the impact of tax-benefit policies on income distribution. Models simulating the effects of social and fiscal policies on household income were first developed in the 1980s when the essential inputs—micro-data from household surveys and accessible computing power—began to be made available.

These early tax-benefit microsimulation models were arithmetic, recalculating the components of household disposable income (usually cash benefits, direct taxes, and social contributions) for each household in a representative microdataset under different sets of policy rules. They could answer "what if" questions about the effects of specific policy reforms on each household's income and hence on the overall income distribution and the aggregate public budget. Some early studies include Atkinson et al. (1983) and Betson et al. (1982). These models could also readily be used to calculate indicators of work incentives on the intensive margin (Atkinson and Sutherland, 1989; Bourguignon et al., 1993). Since then, this "static" modeling approach has not only proliferated, but it has also been refined in a number of directions, influenced by developments in data availability, methodology, speed, capacity of accessible computing power, and the demands made by policymaking and policy analysis.

Microsimulation models are often categorized as "static," "dynamic," or "behavioral" (see Harding, 1996a). The first type applies purely deterministic policy rules to microdata in combination with data adjustments such as reweighting. The characteristics of the micro units stay constant. Dynamic models, on the other hand, "age" the micro units through time, changing their characteristics in response to natural processes and the probabilities of relevant events and transitions (Li and O'Donoghue, 2013). Behavioral models use microeconometric models of individual preferences to estimate the effects of policy changes on behavior, often in terms of labor supply. In practice the distinction between modeling approaches is no longer necessarily useful because modern microsimulation analysis often combines elements of each type, according to the question being addressed. For example, labor supply models require the calculation of budget sets (household income under alternative labor supply scenarios) for individuals, and these are usually generated by static tax-benefit models. Behavioral reactions, as well as static calculations, are relevant in dynamic microsimulations. In seeking to simulate the effects of policy changes in a variety of economic environments, so-called static models may borrow elements from dynamic model methodology, and in seeking to simplify the dynamic modeling process, the reverse can also be true (Caldwell, 1990). In practice,

---

[2] There are extensive literatures covering each area. See, for example, Dowling et al. (2004), Waddell et al. (2003), and Gupta and Harding (2007).

dynamic models mainly address questions about the effects of policies that take time to evolve, such as pensions (e.g., Borella and Coda Moscarola, 2010; Dekkers et al., 2010; Flood, 2007) and long-term care reform (e.g., Hancock, 2000; Hancock et al., 2013), often focusing on the cost, winners, and losers, as well as questions about intrapersonal redistribution over the lifecycle (Harding, 1993).

Without tax-benefit microsimulation modeling, and before it was widespread, analysis of the effects of taxes and benefits on household income, as well as calculation of work incentive indicators, was limited to "model family" calculations for stylized households, sometimes referred to as "tax-benefit models." These calculations are carried out, for example, by the Organization for Economic Cooperation and Development (OECD) for the purpose of making cross-country comparisons (OECD, 2007), but, depite being useful for understanding the net effects of policies in particular standardized cases, such models cannot give full information about impacts on income distribution.

This chapter provides an overview of microsimulation approaches for exploring the effects of policy on income distribution, and it highlights some particular state-of-the-art or innovative studies that have been carried out in this area. The main emphasis is on static modeling methods, though we also consider extensions accounting for behavioral reactions (Section 24.3.3) and highlight the main modeling features of dynamic modeling (Section 24.5.2), referring to the existing reviews. We have not attempted to create a comprehensive review of the models themselves. Their proliferation would make such a task not only daunting, but quickly out-of-date. There are already a number of reviews and collections describing the models and the analyses using them, a selection of which we summarize below.

24.1.2 Microsimulation in the Economic Literature

There are several distinct motivations for using a microsimulation model to simulate the impact of a given policy on income distribution. Microsimulation can be used to quantify the role of *existing* policies on income inequality or poverty in a given context. More importantly, it is a tool to aid the design of new policies with particular objectives and to evaluate actual or proposed *reforms* in dimensions that were not taken into account in the original design. Moreover, it can also be used to show how alternative approaches could result in better outcomes in some respect. From a practical policy perspective, one of the main uses of microsimulation modeling for the design of policy is to assess the approximate budgetary cost of a new policy given its objectives, such as the desire to reduce the poverty gap or to increase work incentives for particular groups. Such analysis rarely sees the light of day except in its final form as a costed reform proposal.

Evidence from microsimulation modeling is also used to inform academic economic debates about the impact of policy reforms and the optimal design of policy (Blundell, 2012). In general terms, a microsimulation approach allows the researcher to conduct a controlled experiment by changing the parameters of interest while holding everything else constant and avoiding endogeneity problems in identifying the direct effects of the policy under analysis (Bourguignon and Spadaro, 2006). The use of tax-benefit micro-simulation models to calculate counterfactual states and scenarios underpins much micro-economic analysis of the causal impact of fiscal policy reforms. A prime example is the use of the Institute of Fiscal Studies tax-benefit microsimulation model, TAXBEN for the UK, to provide empirical evidence for the arguments about tax design put forward in the authoritative Mirrlees Review (Mirrlees et al., 2010). Moreover, the counterfactuals shed light on the potential ingredients of optimal tax analysis, which cannot be derived in a quasiexperimental setting. This is demonstrated by the developments of the computational optimal income taxation theory, applied by Aaberge and Colombino (2013) to Norway and by Blundell and Shepard (2012) to the UK.

Microsimulation modeling is increasingly recognized as part of the policy evaluation literature, in which it is one of the key ingredients of a careful, evidence-based evaluation of the design of tax-benefit reforms. Although, in general, this literature has been more focused on ex-post analysis, Keane (2010) and Blundell (2012), among others, have underlined the need to consider both ex-ante and ex-post approaches to study the effects of policy changes. In this context, tax-benefit microsimulation models can offer insights in two ways. First, they are unique tools for conducting ex-ante analysis through the simulation of counterfactual scenarios reflecting alternative policy regimes. Such counterfactuals are needed both for the "morning-after" evaluation of tax-benefit reforms and for more complex structural models that reveal individual behavioral changes based on simulated budget constraints and an estimated model of individual and family choices (see Section 24.3.3). Second, by developing a counterfactual scenario, tax-benefit microsimulation models enable the researcher to disentangle ex-post what would have happened without a given policy. Although ex-post analysis is typically conducted by means of quasiexperimental approaches, based on difference-in-difference, matching, and selection estimators, the cross-fertilization between ex-ante and ex-post approaches has contributed to the increasing credibility of analysis based on detailed microsimulation models, making them a core part of the causal policy evaluation literature. A prime example is the quasiexperimental analysis used to validate structural models of labor supply that use microsimulation models to derive the budget sets faced by individuals (see, among others, Blundell, 2006).

Furthermore, microsimulation features in the strain of literature that involves micro–macro linkage, aiming to measure the effects of macroeconomic changes (including macroeconomic policy) on income distribution. More specifically, the linkage of microsimulation models to macroeconomic models allows one to consider the interactions of macroeconomic policies or shocks with the tax-benefit systems (see Section 24.3.4). Ignoring the tax-benefit policy effects on income distribution can be justifiable in some circumstances, for example, when analyzing their impact in developing countries, because they may be very limited in size, and reform to social expenditures or macroeconomic shocks could be much more relevant for redistribution, but it is more problematic in the context of mature welfare states (Bourguignon and Bussolo, 2013).

The literature on microsimulation has expanded enormously in the last 20 years, along with the spread and development of this methodology. An attempt to cover all relevant publications would be a daunting task, and, therefore, we aim to provide some of the most important methodological references with relevant illustrations in the rest of this chapter. For further and broader material, we refer the reader to a number of reviews and workshop and conference volumes that provide good surveys, both of model applications and of models themselves, reflecting how state-of-the-art modeling has evolved since the beginning of the 1990s: Harding (1996b), Gupta and Kapur (2000), Mitton et al. (2000), Gupta and Harding (2007), Harding and Gupta (2007), Lelkes and Sutherland (2009), Zaidi et al. (2009), Dekkers et al. (2014), and O'Donoghue (2014).[3] For surveys of the models themselves, see Merz (1991), Sutherland (1995), Klevmarken (1997), Gupta and Kapur (2000), O'Donoghue (2001), Zaidi and Rake (2001), Gupta and Harding (2007), Urzúa (2012), and Li and O'Donoghoue (2013). In addition, several books focus on specific models, providing excellent examples of opening the "black box" often associated with complex economic models. For example, Harding (1993) describes the details of her dynamic cohort microsimulation model used to evaluate lifetime income distribution and redistribution for Australia; Redmond et al. (1998) provide an extensive discussion of the inner workings of POLIMOD, a static tax-benefit model for the UK; and Bargain (2007) offers a collection of applications using EUROMOD, the EU tax-benefit model. Furthermore, the microsimulation community established the International Microsimulation Association (IMA) in 2005, and since 2007, it has been possible to follow the latest developments in the field through the *International Journal of Microsimulation*, a refereed online journal published under the auspices of the IMA.[4]

24.1.3 Summary of Chapter

The remainder of this chapter is structured as follows. Before getting into the ways in which microsimulation can be used to understand the effects of policy changes, Section 24.2 describes how it can be used to improve the information generally available for the analysis of income distribution and redistribution. Simulated estimates of tax liability and benefit entitlement can be used alongside the values recorded in survey and administrative microdatasets to understand and improve on the deficiencies in the latter (e.g., to impute gross income from net if the former is not available or measured satisfactorily in the source data). Furthermore, indicators that cannot be collected in surveys or through administrative processes but are of value in understanding the

---

[3] For older conference volumes and reviews, see literature references given in these collections.

[4] See http://www.microsimulation.org/ijm/.

relationships between policy and income distribution, such as indicators of work incentives, can be calculated using microsimulation models.

Throughout the chapter we provide some empirical illustrations drawing mainly on analysis using the EU-wide tax-benefit model EUROMOD (Sutherland and Figari, 2013). Covering 27 countries and made generally accessible, this has become one of the most widely used models. We have chosen to highlight EUROMOD at least partly because it is generally available to use, and readers can reproduce, update, and extend the chapter's examples of analysis with relative ease. More information about EUROMOD is provided in Box 24.1.

Box 24.1 EUROMOD—A tax-benefit microsimulation model

EUROMOD is the tax-benefit microsimulation model of the European Union. It simulates individual and household tax liabilities and cash benefit entitlements according to the policy rules in place, and reforms to them, in each member state. It has two main distinguishing features. First, it covers many countries within the same framework, enabling a wide range of applications and comparability of results. Generally, EUROMOD is much more flexible than national microsimulation models in order to ensure consistency of results and transferability of tax-benefit system components across countries. Second, it is intended to be openly accessible: use is not restricted to the owners of the model. The calculations carried out by EUROMOD for any one country are in other respects quite typical of all tax-benefit microsimulation models, at least for developed countries. The description below is therefore generally applicable.

EUROMOD combines information on policy rules with detailed and nationally representative microdata on individual and household circumstances drawn from household income surveys and other data sources. The rules for each policy instrument are applied arithmetically to the characteristics of each individual, resulting in the amount of tax liability or benefit entitlement. For example, in the case of the simplest universal child benefit, the number of children within the eligible age range in the family is counted and the benefit amount per child is multiplied by this number to give the family's entitlement. Further issues complicate the calculation: "child" and "family" need to be defined, and the interaction of the child benefit amount with the rest of the tax-benefit system needs to be accounted for. This illustrative calculation is taken further in Appendix A by considering the effects of a change in policy.

The results of the calculations for each household are stored at the micro level and can be analyzed with any statistical software. At their simplest they may be weighted to population level, and the weighted change in income can be added up to provide an estimate of the budgetary effect of the policy change, or it can be analyzed in relation to any characteristics provided in the data: for example, to show the proportion of households gaining and losing by income quantile, region, or household type. The micro-outputs from alternative policy or labor market scenarios can also be used as the basis for calculating indicators of work incentives or for modeling changes in labor supply or other behavior.

Continued

EUROMOD aims to simulate as many of the tax and benefit components of household disposable income as possible, and generally, the following instruments are simulated: income taxes, social insurance contributions, family benefits, housing benefits, social assistance, and other income-related benefits. Instruments that are not simulated are taken directly from the data. These include most contributory benefits and pensions (due to the lack of information on previous employment and contribution history) and disability benefits (because of the need to know the nature and severity of the disability, which is also not present in the data).

EUROMOD input data for most countries are derived from the European Union Statistics on Income and Living Conditions (EU-SILC). In common with most sources of microdata used as input into microsimulation models, the EU-SILC was not designed for this purpose (Figari et al., 2007). A significant amount of preparation of the data, including imputing necessary information that is missing, needs to be done. For example, if gross income values are not directly recorded during the data collection operations and are imputed in an unsatisfactory way, a net-to-gross procedure is applied to the net income variables in order to derive the gross values used in the policy simulation.

EUROMOD includes some simple adjustments for the non-take-up of some benefits and evasion of taxes in some countries. In common with other adjustments and assumptions (e.g., the updating of nonsimulated incomes to a more recent point in time than the data income reference point) these can be changed or "switched off" by the user, depending on the analysis being done.

Baseline systems in EUROMOD have been validated and tested at the micro level (i.e., case-by-case validation) and the macro level. For each system simulated in EUROMOD, Country Reports are available on the EUROMOD web pages with background information on the tax-benefit system(s), a detailed description of all tax-benefit components simulated, a general overview of the input data, and an extended summary of the validation process.

For more information about EUROMOD and its applications, see the official website (https://www.iser.essex.ac.uk/euromod) and Sutherland and Figari (2013).

The primary motivation for building a tax-benefit microsimulation model is to be able to analyze the effects of policy changes on income distribution. Section 24.3 starts with a description of the basic process and explains the need to carry out microlevel calculations in order to capture the effects due to the complexity of tax-benefit systems. However, in any microsimulation analysis, the modeler must choose which dimensions to focus on and which to hold constant. Most studies do not set out their specific choices in formal terms. Section 24.3.2 provides a formal framework applicable to most tax-benefit microsimulation analyses. The following four subsections focus on some of the major and commonly applied extensions to the basic approach. Section 24.3.3 discusses how individual behavioral responses to policy changes are estimated and focuses on labor supply responses. This is followed in Section 24.3.4 by a review of the ways changes in income distribution can be linked to macroeconomic processes. Section 24.3.5 covers the use of microsimulation, in conjunction with macrolevel statistics or forecasts, to provide estimates of income distribution for periods beyond those covered by the latest microdata. These projections might be for the current situation (nowcasting) or sometime in the future (forecasting). Finally, Section 24.3.6 focuses on the ways in which microsimulation can be used to inform cross-country comparisons of the effects of policies.

Of course, there are many remaining challenges to providing estimates of the effects of policy and policy changes that can be used with confidence within policy analysis, and Section 24.4 considers three major ones. First, Section 24.4.1 considers the issues around reconciling the simulated income distribution and that measured using the original microdata (from surveys particularly, but also administrative sources). A major difference between the two distributions can undermine confidence in microsimulation results but has a number of interrelated causes, some of which can point to problems in survey data (e.g., income underreporting), and can be mitigated using information from simulations, and others that cannot (e.g., small and unrepresentative samples of high-income earners). Simulations can overestimate income if the non-take-up of benefits is not accounted for and also distorted if there is tax evasion. These issues, and how they may be accounted for in microsimulation models, are discussed in Section 24.4.2. Finally, it is important that the reliability of microsimulation estimates is possible to ascertain. This applies both in terms of how well point estimates match up to information from other sources (validation) and the need for statistical reliability indicators that can be applied to microsimulation estimates. Section 24.4.3 considers these issues.

Although the main focus of this chapter is the contribution to policy analysis of (direct) tax and (cash) benefit microsimulation of household incomes at the national level at a given point in time, Section 24.5 considers a somewhat broader scope, in some dimensions. Section 24.5.1 discusses a broadening of the outcome income measure to include the effect of noncash benefits and, particularly, indirect taxes. Section 24.5.2 reviews the main features of dynamic microsimulation models used in analyzing the long-term redistributive effects of policies and the incidence of tax-benefit systems over the lifetime rather than cross-sectionally at a point in time. Section 24.5.3 discusses the use of microsimulation to explore the effects of policies at a lower level than that of the nation (e.g., Spanish regions or US states) and at a higher level (e.g., the European Union or world regions such as southern Africa).

The final section concludes by first summarizing our view of the achievements of microsimulation for policy analysis to date and then by exploring the outlook for the future along two dimensions: the need for data improvements and methodological developments and the need to consider ways to organize development, maintenance, and access to microsimulation models for policy analysis purposes.

24.2. WHAT DOES MICROSIMULATION ADD TO ANALYSIS OF INCOME DISTRIBUTION AND REDISTRIBUTION?

24.2.1 Enriching Existing Microdata

Although the most obvious application of the microsimulation method is assessing the effects of tax-benefit policy *changes* on income distribution, it can be also useful for analyzing the existing income distribution and redistribution. Compared to research on income distribution directly utilizing only survey or administrative data, fiscal microsimulation can complement and improve such analysis by (i) adding further information, (ii) checking the consistency of the collected data, and (iii) allowing for greater flexibility with respect to the unit of analysis.

24.2.1.1 Adding Information

Simulations allow the generation of data that may be too difficult or expensive to collect directly or accurately from individuals. A common use of microsimulation in the processing of income survey data is deriving gross incomes from the net values that are collected, or vice versa. Compared to other methods such as statistical imputation, microsimulation accounts for the full details of the tax-benefit rules that are applicable for a given individual or household. Hence, it provides more accurate results, but may also require more effort to develop and keep up-to-date. Specific microsimulation routines are often built for this purpose. Among others, see Betti et al. (2011) on the Siena Microsimulation Model, which is used for conversions between net and gross income variables for several countries in the European Union Statistics on Income and Living Conditions (EU-SILC) survey, and Jenkins (2011) on the derivations of net income variables for the British Household Panel Survey (BHPS).

Such gross-to-net conversion routines naturally follow the logic of full-scale tax-benefit models, though they may still have notable differences. For example, tax-benefit models typically deal with the final tax liability (i.e., aiming to account for all tax concessions and considering the total taxable income), but taxes withheld on specific income sources are often more relevant for gross/net adjustments in a survey. For net-to-gross conversions, there are two microsimulation-related approaches. One is to apply inverted statutory tax rules and the other is to use gross-to-net routines in an iterative procedure to search for the corresponding gross value for a given net income, as suggested in Immervoll and O'Donoghue (2001). The first approach can be more straightforward if tax rules are relatively simple and analytical inversion is feasible, while the second approach allows the use of already existing tax-benefit models. The latter approach has also been used in the Siena model and related applications, as discussed by Rodrigues (2007).

If a tax-benefit model is applied to income data that contain imputed gross values, it is important to ensure that the net-to-gross conversion is consistent with the tax-benefit model calculations because otherwise simulated net incomes will not match the observed values. This source of bias is easy to overlook, and consistency is often difficult to establish because the documentation of net-to-gross derivations carried out by survey data providers often lacks sufficient details for tax-benefit modeling purposes.

Microsimulation methods can be also used to obtain more detailed tax information compared to what is usually available in the surveys (if any at all). For example, the Current Population Survey (CPS), one of the main household surveys in the US, provides such information through the Annual Social and Economic Supplement (ASEC), which includes simulated direct taxes and imputed employer's contributions for health insurance (Cleveland, 2005). Alternatively, surveys could be combined with detailed tax information from administrative records, though in practice this is still underdeveloped due to limitations on access to administrative records. Furthermore, microsimulation models can extend the scope of income information by simulating employer social insurance contributions and indirect taxes, which are usually not captured in income (and expenditure) surveys, even though their economic incidence is typically considered to be borne by individuals (Fullerton and Metcalf, 2002) and hence relevant for welfare analysis.

Although benefit information tends to be more detailed in income surveys, there are applications in which microsimulation methods can still provide further insights. Specifically, microsimulation allows the assessment of the intended effect of transfers (by calculating benefit eligibility) and contrasts it with reported outcome (i.e., observed benefit receipt), which is influenced by individual compliance behavior (see more in Section 24.4.2) and the effectiveness of benefit administrations, among other factors.

Of course, it is possible to carry out analysis of the redistributive effect of taxes and benefits only using survey information directly. For example, Mahler and Jesuit (2006), Immervoll and Richardson (2011) and Wang et al. (2012) use household survey data from the Luxembourg Income Study (LIS) to analyze redistributive effects in the OECD countries, and Fuest et al. (2010) and Atta-Darkua and Barnard (2010) use the SILC data for EU countries. However, microsimulation methods can often add to the scope and detail of the analysis. For example, Immervoll et al. (2006a), Paulus et al. (2009), Jara and Tumino (2013) use tax and benefit data simulated with EUROMOD for EU countries, and Kim and Lambert (2009) analyze redistribution in the US on the basis of the CPS/ASEC. Wagstaff et al. (1999) specifically analyze the progressivity of personal income taxes in the OECD countries also using the LIS data, and Verbist and Figari (2014) carry out similar analysis for EU countries, relying on EUROMOD simulations, allowing them to extend the analysis with social insurance contributions as well. Piketty and Saez (2007) use the TAXSIM[5] model to compute US federal individual income taxes and analyze their progressivity. Furthermore, Verbist (2007) employs EUROMOD to consider the distribution and redistributive effects of replacement incomes, taking into account interactions with taxes and social contributions, and Hungerford (2010) uses simulations to examine certain federal tax provisions and transfer programs in the US. Decoster and Van Camp (2001), O'Donoghue et al. (2004), and Decoster et al. (2010) are examples of studies simulating and analyzing the effects of indirect taxes across the distribution of income.

Microsimulation can additionally help to detect inconsistencies and potential measurement errors in the existing data. An obvious example is cross-checking whether gross and net income values (if both are reported) correspond to each other. As benefit income tends to be underreported in survey data (Lynn et al., 2012; Meyer et al., 2009), use of simulated benefits has the potential to improve the accuracy of income information (see more in Section 24.4.1). However, the quality of input data is also critical for the simulated results themselves, and there could be other reasons for discrepancies between observed and simulated income apart from underreporting (see Figari et al., 2012a).

24.2.1.2 The Unit of Analysis

Microsimulation can also offer some flexibility in the choice of unit of analysis. In any analysis of distribution, the unit of measurement is an important issue. Income is often measured at the household level, aggregating all sources across all individuals. Income surveys may not facilitate analysis at a lower level (e.g., aggregating within the narrow family or the fiscal unit) because some or all income variables are provided only at the household level. This is the case, for example, for the microdata provided by Eurostat from the European Statistics on Income and Living Conditions (EU-SILC). However, considering the effect of policy on the incomes of subunits within households may be relevant in a number of ways. The assumption of complete within-household sharing of resources deserves to be questioned, and its implications made clear. For example, assessments of poverty risk among pension recipients might look quite different if

---

[5] TAXSIM is the NBER microsimulation model that calculates US federal and state income taxes (http://www.nber.org/taxsim/). It covers the federal tax system from 1960 and the state systems from 1977 up to the current year. Model calculations are done in the TAXSIM server on the basis of survey data provided by the users in the required format containing different sources of income, deductions, and personal characteristics used to calculate tax liabilities. The program, written in FORTRAN, reads the input data sent by the user through a web application, calculates tax liabilities, and loads the results on the user's computer. Recent applications are based on the March Current Population Survey, the Survey of Consumer Finance, the Consumer Expenditure Survey, and the Panel Study of Income Dynamics, and a library of scripts used to derive the input data from different sources is made available by previous users. See Feenberg and Coutts (1993) for more information.

researchers did not assume that they shared this income with coresident younger generations, and vice versa. Furthermore, it may be particularly relevant to consider the effects of policy in terms of the particular unit of assessment, rather than the household as a whole. Minimum income schemes use a variety of units over which to assess income and eligibility, and these are often narrower than the survey household. A flexible microsimulation model is able to operate using a range of units of analysis, as well as units of assessment and aggregation, because they are able to assign income components, or shares of them, to the relevant recipient units within the household. Examples of microsimulation studies that consider units of analysis apart from the household are Decoster and Van Camp (2000) in relation to tax incidence at the household or fiscal unit level, Figari et al. (2011a) who analyze income within couples, and Bennett and Sutherland (2011) who consider the implications of means-testing at the family-unit level for receipt of benefit income by individuals.

24.2.2 Microsimulation-Based Indicators

The microsimulation method is also used to construct various indicators to measure the extent to which household disposable income reacts to changes in gross earnings or individual or household characteristics through interactions with the tax-benefit system. The two main groups of such indicators reflect individual work incentives and automatic adjustment mechanisms built into fiscal systems. This subsection gives an overview of these indicators and provides some examples, and a more formal presentation can be found in Section 24.3.2.

24.2.2.1 Indicators of Work Incentives

Marginal effective tax rates and participation tax rates are indicators of work incentives for the intensive (i.e., work effort) and the extensive labor supply margin (i.e., decision to work), respectively. Marginal effective tax rates (METR) reflect the financial incentive for a working person to increase his work contribution marginally either through longer hours or higher productivity (increasing the hourly wage rate). They show the proportion of additional earnings that is taxed away, taking into account not only the personal income tax but also social contributions as well as interactions with benefits, including withdrawal of means-tested benefits as private income increases. As such, METRs indicate more accurately the actual tax burden on additional income compared to statutory marginal income tax rates. Given that taxes and benefits form a complex nonlinear system, it is usually not feasible to obtain METRs in the form of analytical derivatives of the overall tax-benefit function. Instead, METRs are estimated empirically by incrementing gross earnings of an employed person by a small margin (e.g., 1–5%) and recalculating disposable income, as discussed by Immervoll (2004), Adam et al. (2006b), and Jara and Tumino (2013). Figure 24.1 provides an example from the last of these showing the extent to which average METRs and their distributions vary across the European

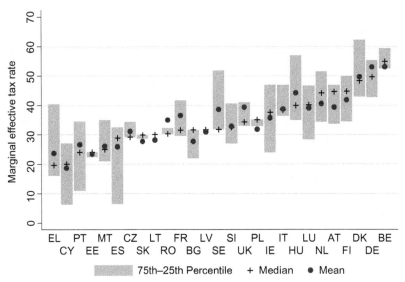

Figure 24.1 Marginal effective tax rates across the EU, 2007 (%). *Notes: Countries are ranked by median METR. Source: Jara and Tumino (2013), using EUROMOD.*

Union.[6] The scope of these calculations is usually limited to direct taxes and (cash) benefits and current work incentives, though extensions also account for consumption taxes and taking a life-cycle labor supply perspective (see Kotlikoff and Rapson, 2007). Graphically, METRs can be illustrated with a budget constraint chart that plots net income against gross earnings (or hours worked) (see Adam et al., 2006b; Morawski and Myck, 2010), as the slope of this line corresponds to $1 - \text{METR}$ which is the proportion of additional gross earnings retained by the individual.

Participation tax rates (PTR) are conceptually very similar, indicating the effective tax rate on the extensive margin, or the proportion of earnings paid as taxes and lost due to benefit withdrawal if a person moves from inactivity or unemployment to work. METRs and PTRs are typically between 0% and 100%, with higher rates implying weaker incentives to work (more). Because of nonlinearities and complex interactions in the tax-benefit systems, however, individuals facing greater than 100% (or negative) tax rates may also be found. These often expose unintended effects built into the tax-benefit system. More generally, relatively high values indicate situations that can constrain labor supply and trap people at certain income/employment levels. Marginal effective tax rates

---

[6] In Figure 24.1 and elsewhere we use the official country acronyms for the EU countries. These are (using the official country ordering): Belgium (BE), Bulgaria (BG), Czech Republic (CZ), Denmark (DK), Germany (DE), Estonia (EE), Ireland (IE), Greece (EL), Spain (ES), France (FR), Italy (IT), Cyprus (CY), Latvia (LV), Lithuania (LT), Luxembourg (LU), Hungary (HU), Malta (MT), Netherlands (NL), Austria (AT), Poland (PL), Portugal (PT), Romania (RO), Slovenia (SI), Slovakia (SK), Finland (FI), Sweden (SE), United Kingdom (UK).

and participation tax rates are hence useful indicators to assess whether the tax-benefit system may limit employment for certain individuals. These are also central parameters in assessing optimal tax design. See Immervoll et al. (2007) and Brewer et al. (2010) for empirical applications. Figure 24.1 illustrates how in many countries there is a considerable spread in the value of the METRs even before considering the extremes of the distributions. This demonstrates how an analysis using work incentive indicators based on calculations for average or representative cases may be quite misleading.

Replacement rates (RR) complement participation tax rates, showing the level of out-of-work income relative to in-work disposable income (see, e.g., Immervoll and O'Donoghue, 2004). High replacement rates also reflect low financial incentives to become (or remain) employed. Compared to METRs and PTRs, negative values are even more exceptional (though not ruled out altogether). RRs are often calculated separately for the short-term and long-term unemployed to reflect differences in the level of unemployment benefits depending on unemployment duration. As work incentive indicators, PTRs and RRs are calculated for nonworking persons for whom potential employment income is not observed, and, hence, the latter must be either predicted or assumed.[7]

Although PTRs and RRs both describe work incentives on the extensive margin, they have a different focus and characteristics (Adam et al., 2006a). For instance, if taxes and benefits are changed so that net income increases by the same amount for the out-of-work and in-work situation (e.g., corresponding to a lump-sum transfer), then the replacement rate would typically increase while the participation rate remained unchanged. This is because the tax burden on additional income does not change while, in relative terms, working becomes less attractive. On the other hand, RRs remain constant if out-of-work and in-work net income increase by the same proportion (but for PTRs this is not the case).

Although these three indicators are used to measure work incentives for a particular individual by changing *individual* gross earnings (and labor market status), the effect on disposable income is assessed at the *household* level because this is usually considered to be the more relevant unit of assessment for benefits and unit of aggregation when measuring living standards.[8] Each measure can be also decomposed to show the effect of specific tax-benefit instruments, for example, income taxes, social insurance contributions, and benefits.

24.2.2.2 Indicators of Automatic Stabilization

Another closely related group of indicators characterize how tax-benefit systems act as automatic stabilizers for income or unemployment shocks, as indicated by the extent to which (aggregate) household income or tax revenue fluctuations are moderated

---

[7] For example, OECD calculates these indicators assuming various income levels in the range of 33–150% of average wage (AW).

[8] In principle other units of aggregation within the household could be specified.

without direct government action. These focus on exogenous shocks rather than individual incentives to alter labor supply. Apart from this, the calculations are technically very similar to the previous group, with the main differences related to interpretation.[9]

Estimates based on microdata go back at least to Pechman (1973), who simulated income tax revenues in the US for 1954–1971 and showed how much tax liabilities change in absolute terms compared to changes in income (at the aggregate level), characterized as built-in flexibility. Although this is very similar to marginal effective tax rates, the interpretation is different and focused on the macro-level and government revenue side rather than at the individual. A closely related measure captures the elasticity of tax liability with respect to changes in incomes, or percentage increase in taxes for a 1% change in income, though as Auerbach and Feenberg (2000) point out, this mainly reflects the progressivity of taxes because it does not capture whether the tax burden is high or low.

More recently, Auerbach and Feenberg (2000) estimate the aggregate change in taxes when increasing all (taxable) income (and deductions) for each individual by 1% to measure the responsiveness of tax revenues to income changes for the US. They find that, over the period 1962–1995, income taxes offset between 18% and 28% of variation in before-tax income (at the aggregate level). Similarly, Mabbett and Schelke (2007) simulate a 10% increase in individual earnings for 14 EU countries and estimate both the responsiveness (i.e., elasticity) of various tax-benefit instruments and the overall stabilization effect of the system. According to their estimates, the latter varies from 31% in Spain to 57% in Denmark.

Dolls et al. (2012) model a *negative* income shock in which household gross incomes fall by 5% and an unemployment shock with household income at the aggregate level decreasing also by 5%, covering both the US and a large number of the EU countries. Although the proportional income shock is distribution-neutral, the unemployment shock is asymmetric because not all households are affected. They find that tax-benefit systems absorb a greater proportion of income variation in the EU compared to the US— 38% (EU) versus 32% (US) of the income shock and 47% (EU) versus 34% (US) of the unemployment shock (see Figure 24.2). This difference is largely explained by the higher coverage and generosity of unemployment benefits in Europe. Automatic stabilizers in the case of an unemployment shock are basically replacement rates for a transition from employment to nonwork at the aggregate level. Rather than work incentives (as discussed in the previous section), they reflect how much the tax-benefit system absorbs (market) income losses due to becoming unemployed or exiting the labor market altogether.

Instead of focusing on aggregate stabilization, Fernández Salgado et al. (2014) analyze the distribution of replacement rates when simulating the unemployment shock in six EU

---

[9] One technical nuance concerns the treatment of multiperson households. Although work incentives are typically estimated for each household member separately, holding earnings of other household members constant, in the case of automatic stabilizers, changes are simulated for all of the relevant population at once.

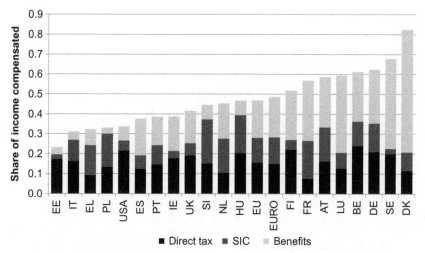

Figure 24.2 Share of income compensated by the tax benefit system in the case of an unemployment shock. *Notes: The unemployment shock corresponds to an increase in the unemployment rate such that the total household income decreases by 5%. Countries are ranked by the share of income compensated. EU and EURO are the population-weighted averages of 19 EU and 13 eurozone countries, respectively, included here. Estonia joined the eurozone later and is here excluded from that group. Source: Dolls et al. (2012), using EUROMOD and TAXSIM.*

countries due to the Great Recession. They distinguish between short- and long-term unemployment, and their findings confirm higher replacement rates in the short term and point to serious challenges for minimum income schemes to cope with the consequences of this crisis in the longer term. They also highlight the important role of incomes of other household members in boosting replacement rates.

24.2.2.3 Indicators of Household Composition Effects

Another type of indicator based on microsimulation captures the effect of changes in household sociodemographic characteristics in order to identify the marginal effect of the tax-benefit system due to particular household configurations. For example, Figari et al. (2011b) apply this approach to calculate "child contingent" incomes estimated as the change in household disposable income for families with children as if they did not have children. They argue that "child-contingent" incomes, capturing not only transfers net of taxes but also tax concessions, account more precisely for the full net support provided through tax-benefit systems to families with children, as compared to simply considering (gross) benefit payments labeled explicitly for children or families, as is typically the case using the information directly available from the survey data. As shown in Figure 24.3, the net value can be greater than the gross if there are tax concessions or child supplements in benefits labeled for other purposes, and the gross value can be greater than the net if the benefits are taxed or reduced because of other interactions.

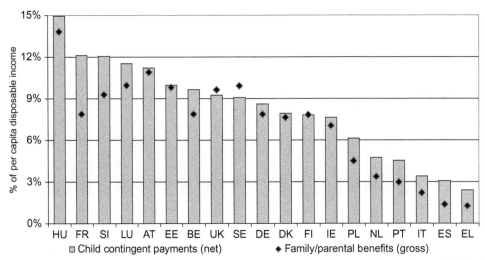

Figure 24.3 Total net child-contingent payments versus gross family/parental benefits per child as a percentage of per capita disposable income. *Notes: Countries are ranked by total net child-contingent payments. Source: Figari et al. (2011b), using EUROMOD.*

24.3. THE EFFECTS OF POLICY CHANGES ON INCOME DISTRIBUTION

24.3.1 A Basic Example

The simplest use of a tax-benefit microsimulation model involves calculating the effects of a policy change on household income, without changing any of the characteristics of the household members. An example might be an increase in the amount of an existing universal child benefit. The model would take account of the increase in payment per eligible child, any clawback through the system of means-tested benefits (if the child benefit is included in the income assessment for these benefits), any clawback if the benefit is taxed or included in the base for contributions, and any other relevant interaction with the rest of the tax-benefit system. Even a simple reform involves quite complicated arithmetic and ignoring the interactions would give misleading results. This is illustrated in Appendix A with a concrete example comparing the effects of doubling the UK child benefit at two points in time: 2001 and 2013. Although the structure of child benefit itself has remained the same, the net effect of changes to it is quite different because of changes to the interactions with the rest of the tax-benefit system. The interactions matter and need to be accounted for in understanding the effects of policy changes and in designing policy reforms.

The financing of such a reform would also need to be considered. For example, if the net cost was met by a percentage point increase in all rates of income tax, this increase might also have knock-on effects (e.g., if the assessment of any means-tested benefits depended on after-tax income), and then iterations of the model would be needed to find a revenue-neutral solution to the tax rate increase. The "revenue neutral" package could then be evaluated relative to the prereform situation, in terms of its effect on the income distribution and an analysis of gainers and losers.

Of course, in the new situation some people affected will wish to change their behavior in response to the change in some way and at some point in time. One might expect labor supply and fertility to be affected and, depending on the specifics of the system and the change in it, so might other dimensions of behavior. As Bourguignon and Spadaro (2006) point out, it is important to be clear about when these second order effects can, and cannot, be neglected. We return to this issue in Section 24.3.3.

In any case, an "overnight" or "morning after" analysis, as the pure arithmetic effect is often called, is clearly of value in its own right as the immediate effect might be relevant to a particular research question. Moreover, the mechanics of the way in which policy reforms impact on incomes are relevant for improving design, and it will often be important to identify how much of the overall effect on income can be attributed to the direct effect.

24.3.2 Formal Framework
24.3.2.1 Decomposing Static Policy Effects

Tax-benefit models provide information on the distribution of household disposable income and its components under various policy scenarios, allowing the effects of policies to be inferred from a comparison of different scenarios. As such, the application of the microsimulation method starts by defining an appropriate baseline and a counterfactual scenario. The latter corresponds to the state *after* policy changes (i.e., how the world would look after implementing new policies) in forward-looking analysis or the state *before* policy changes (i.e., how the world would have looked without new policies or what would happen if policy changes where rolled back) in the case of backward-looking analysis.

Drawing on Bargain and Callan (2010) and Bargain (2012a), we provide a formal framework for decomposing changes in household income to separate the effects of policy changes.[10] Mathematical formulation helps to avoid ambiguities about how exactly a counterfactual scenario is defined, which often arise in empirical microsimulation applications relying only on textual descriptions. Furthermore, full decomposition (rather than only focusing on the role of policy changes) has clear advantages by drawing attention to the fact that the (marginal) contribution of a given component is evaluated conditional on the values of other components, and, hence, the overall change in income can be decomposed in multiple ways. Decomposing all components (at once) also helps to ensure that

---

[10] There is a notable strand in the economic literature focusing on the decomposition of income distributions, reviewed recently in Fortin et al. (2011). This, however, is primarily concerned with wage distributions, ignoring the role of tax-benefit policies.

these are consistently derived. Apart from small technical modifications,[11] we closely follow Bargain and Callan's original approach but broaden its scope by showing that a wider range of applications can be interpreted within the same framework.

Let us denote household sociodemographic (and labor market) characteristics with a vector c and household original income[12] (i.e., income before adding cash benefits and deducting direct taxes) with a vector x. The net transfer via the tax-benefit system k (i.e., total cash benefit entitlement less total direct tax liability) for a household with characteristics c and income x is denoted as a function $f_k(c, x, m_k)$, where, following Bargain and Callan (2010), we distinguish between the structure of the tax-benefit system f_k and the various monetary parameters m_k it takes as arguments (e.g., tax brackets, benefit amounts). $f_k(c, x, m_k)$ is positive if public pensions and cash benefits received by a given household exceed direct taxes for which the household is liable, and it is negative if the opposite holds. Household disposable income y is then

$$y_k(c, x, m_k) = x + f_k(c, x, m_k). \tag{24.1}$$

In the simplest case, where original income and household characteristics can be assumed to remain constant, the effect of policy changes $(A \rightarrow B)$ on disposable income is

$$\Delta y = y_B(c, x, m_B) - y_A(c, x, m_A). \tag{24.2}$$

This corresponds to how the effects of proposed or hypothetical tax-benefit reforms are typically studied, as "morning-after" changes with the policy rules before and after referring (implicitly) to the same time period. There are numerous examples of such exercises (e.g., Callan and Sutherland, 1997; Figari, 2010; Matsaganis and Flevotomou, 2008; Matsaganis et al., 2006; Paulus and Peichl, 2009).

Next, let us consider the case of analyzing the effect of policy changes over time. Accounting explicitly for the time span over which policy changes are considered introduces additional complexities for defining an alternative scenario. It is important to ensure that the baseline and the counterfactual refer to the same time period, and if there is a time gap between the existing policies and the counterfactual, then one or the other must be adjusted to reflect that. For example, when analyzing the effect of policy change in $t+1$, it may not be sufficient to assume that the alternative would have been simply period t policies continuing (in nominal terms) in period $t+1$, even though this is often

---

[11] We carry out decomposition in steps starting from the policy effects—our key interest—and other effects, then introducing further splits. Such nesting helps to ensure consistency between the various components and across different combinations. We also distinguish sociodemographic characteristics (c) from original incomes (x).

[12] This includes market incomes from employment, self-employment, property and investments, and other nonpublic income sources such as private pensions and transfers between households. It is also known as "pretax and pretransfer income" in the literature.

implicitly done. One should consider how existing policies in nominal terms *would* have evolved otherwise, given the legal rules or usual practice of indexation of policy parameters, or *should* have evolved. The importance of the time factor becomes even more obvious when considering policy changes over a longer period. We will return later to the question of what is an appropriate basis for indexing monetary parameters in the counterfactual scenario, but for now we simply denote such a factor as p.

First, the total change in disposable income for a given household can be decomposed to show first order policy effects (or mechanical effects) *conditional* on household characteristics and original incomes in the end-period B (denoting the start-period with A):

$$
\begin{aligned}
\Delta y &= y_B(c_B, x_B, m_B) - y_A(c_A, x_A, m_A) \quad \text{(total change)} \\
&= y_B(c_B, x_B, m_B) - y_A(c_B, x_B, pm_A) \quad \text{(policy effect)} \\
&\quad + y_A(c_B, x_B, pm_A) - y_A(c_A, x_A, m_A) \quad \text{(other effect)} \\
&= \Delta y_I^P + \Delta y_I^O
\end{aligned}
\tag{24.3}
$$

Here we are implicitly assuming that we are dealing with panel data, with characteristics and original income for the same household being observed in several periods. The total change for the same household cannot be observed with multiple waves of cross-sectional datasets; however, as explained further below, the same decomposition approach can be also applied at the group-level (e.g., the bottom decile group) or to statistics summarizing the whole income distribution (such as various inequality indices). Importantly, household characteristics are only required at a single point in time to calculate the policy effect (in absolute terms).

Noting the symmetry of the decomposition, the other effect can be decomposed further into two subcomponents separating the impact of change in household characteristics and nominal levels. The effect due to changes in characteristics can be measured either in end-period income levels:

$$
\begin{aligned}
\Delta y_I^O &= y_A(c_B, x_B, pm_A) - y_A(c_A, px_A, pm_A) \quad \text{(change in characteristics)} \\
&\quad + y_A(c_A, px_A, pm_A) - y_A(c_A, x_A, m_A) \quad \text{(change in nominal levels)}
\end{aligned}
\tag{24.4}
$$

or start-period incomes

$$
\begin{aligned}
\Delta y_I^O &= y_A(c_B, x_B, pm_A) - y_A(c_B, p^{-1}x_B, m_A) \quad \text{(change in nominal levels)} \\
&\quad + y_A(c_B, p^{-1}x_B, m_A) - y_A(c_A, x_A, m_A) \quad \text{(change in characteristics)}
\end{aligned}
\tag{24.5}
$$

The term capturing the effect of "change in nominal levels" measures how household disposable income is affected if original income and all money-metric policy parameters change in the same proportion. As Bargain and Callan (2010) pointed out, tax-benefit systems are typically homogenous of degree 1, meaning that in such a case, household disposable income would also change by the same factor:

$$
py(c, x, m) = y(c, px, pm)
\tag{24.6}
$$

They illustrate this with a hypothetical example involving a basic income and a flat tax and find empirical support for Ireland and France.[13]

In principle, the term reflecting the impact of changes in characteristics could be split further, distinguishing between changes in sociodemographic (and labor market) characteristics c and movements in original incomes x. Again, there would be two possible combinations that could be obtained by introducing a new term—either $y_A(c_B, px_A, pm_A)$ or $y_A(c_A, x_B, pm_A)$ with Equation (24.4).

Second, the change in disposable income can be decomposed to assess policy effects conditional on household characteristics and original incomes in the start-period A:

$$\Delta y = y_B(c_B, x_B, m_B) - y_B(c_A, x_A, p^{-1}m_B) \quad \text{(other effect)}$$
$$+ y_B(c_A, x_A, p^{-1}m_B) - y_A(c_A, x_A, m_A) \quad \text{(policy effect)} \qquad (24.7)$$
$$= \Delta y_{II}^O + \Delta y_{II}^P$$

The other effect can be now decomposed again such that the effects due to changes in characteristics are measured in end-period incomes:

$$\Delta y_{II}^O = y_B(c_B, x_B, m_B) - y_B(c_A, px_A, m_B) \quad \text{(change in characteristics)}$$
$$+ y_B(c_A, px_A, m_B) - y_B(c_A, x_A, p^{-1}m_B) \quad \text{(change in nominal levels)} \qquad (24.8)$$

or start-period incomes

$$\Delta y_{II}^O = y_B(c_B, x_B, m_B) - y_B(c_B, p^{-1}x_B, p^{-1}m_B) \quad \text{(change in nominal levels)}$$
$$+ y_B(c_B, p^{-1}x_B, p^{-1}m_B) - y_B(c_A, x_A, p^{-1}m_B) \quad \text{(change in characteristics)} \qquad (24.9)$$

Altogether there are four ways to decompose the overall change in income, given the initial split into the direct policy effect and the other effect.

Until now, we have focused on a single household, though it is straightforward to derive the aggregate change in disposable income by summing income differences (and subcomponents) across all households:

$$\Delta Y = \sum_i \Delta y^i \qquad (24.10)$$

Decomposition can also be applied to any distributional statistic D calculated for a specific subgroup, as with average income among households with elderly, or summarizing the whole income distribution, $(\mathbf{y})$, as with the Gini coefficient or the headcount poverty ratio. For example, Equation (24.3) would then become (indicating vectors in bold):

---

[13] Bargain and Callan (2010) refer to the personal income tax in Germany as one of the few examples for which this property does not hold, due to its unique quadratic functional form.

$$\Delta D(y) = D[y_B(c_B, x_B, m_B)] - D[y_A(c_A, x_A, m_A)] \quad \text{(total change)}$$
$$= D[y_B(c_B, x_B, m_B)] - D[y_A(c_B, x_B, pm_A)] \quad \text{(policy effect)} \quad (24.11)$$
$$+ D[y_A(c_B, x_B, pm_A)] - D[y_A(c_A, x_A, m_A)] \quad \text{(other effect)}$$

In the case of scale-invariant distributional measures (see Cowell, 2000) and linearly homogenous tax-benefit systems, the decomposition of other effects (Equations 24.4, 24.5, 24.8, 24.9) simplifies because the effect of a change in nominal levels becomes (approximately) zero at the population level.[14] Furthermore, Equation (24.4) is now equivalent to Equation (24.5), and Equation (24.8) is equivalent to Equation (24.9), reducing the overall number of combinations from four to two.

We now return to what would be an appropriate basis for choosing the indexation factor p. Bargain and Callan (2010) have argued for using the growth of average original incomes, expressed as $p = \overline{x}_B / \overline{x}_A$, to obtain a "distributionally neutral" benchmark. This would broadly ensure that aggregate disposable income rises (or falls) in proportion to an increase (or a decrease) in aggregate original incomes; in other words, the overall tax burden and expenditure level remain constant in relative terms.[15] Nevertheless, disposable income for a given household could still grow at a higher (or lower) rate than their original income if the latter grows less (or more) than on average. However, there are alternatives ways of choosing p, depending on the chosen conception of "neutrality." For example, basing it on a consumer price index would be appropriate if the point was to ensure a constant absolute standard of living (on average). Clark and Leicester (2004) contrast price-indexation with indexation based on the nominal GDP, and they show that the choice matters for results. There is no clear consensus in the literature on decomposition regarding the most appropriate choice of index.

Finally, there is the issue of how to deal with path dependency and multiple combinations for decomposition. Can some combinations be preferred over others or can different combinations somehow be brought together? In some cases, one might be limited to specific combinations by data constraints. The prime example here is ex ante analysis of (implemented) policy changes before microdata of actual postreform incomes become available (e.g., Avram et al., 2013). Relying on estimates for p, one could already quantify the effect of policy changes (with Equation 24.7), but both start- and end-year datasets are needed to assess other effects. Given that there are no clear arguments for preferring one particular combination over another, all variants should be covered. Bargain and Callan (2010) adopt the Shorrocks–Shapley approach (Shorrocks, 2013) to summarize various combinations, essentially averaging the effect of a given component

---

[14] Notice that, with each subcomponent aggregated separately (rather than aggregating the differences between various components), it is possible to carry out such exercise on two waves of cross-sectional data without necessarily using panel data.

[15] This holds for linearly homogenous tax-benefit systems, but nonlinear elements make this an approximation. Nevertheless, as demonstrated in Callan et al. (2007) for Ireland, the bias would typically be small.

across all combinations. In this way, results conditional on household characteristics in each period are given equal weights.

Other examples where such decomposition has been used explicitly include Bargain (2012b), Bargain et al. (2013b), and Creedy and Hérault (2011). In addition, there is a large literature that documents similar assessments within less formal frameworks (for example, see Clark and Leicester, 2004; Thoresen, 2004).

24.3.2.2 Specific Applications
24.3.2.2.1 Actual Versus Counterfactual Indexation of Policy Parameters

Any system which is not fully indexed with respect to growth in (average) private incomes or prices would result in the erosion of the relative value of benefit payments and increased tax burden through so-called bracket creep (or fiscal drag). Furthermore, it is essential to acknowledge that keeping a tax-benefit system unchanged also impacts household incomes (unless the distribution of household original income is also constant over time). Let us consider the change in household disposable income in such a case using our notation from above:

$$\Delta y = y(c, x_B, m) - y(c, x_A, m) \tag{24.12}$$

Following the decomposition framework in the more general case above, Equation (24.12) can be split again into three terms: the policy effect, changes in original incomes, and the change in nominal levels (i.e., change in disposable income if both original incomes and policy parameters were scaled up by the same factor). The policy effect would now reflect the outcome of keeping policy parameters constant in nominal terms and can be calculated as $y(c, x_B, m) - y(c, x_B, pm)$ or $y(c, x_A, p^{-1}m) - y(c, x_A, m)$. In a typical case, p is positive, reflecting growth in private incomes (or consumer prices), and, hence, the policy effect would be negative (i.e., income-reducing). This is because a positive p implies higher benefit amounts and tax bands in the counterfactual scenario and translates into higher disposable incomes (for the same original incomes) compared to disposable incomes under tax-benefit rules when these are kept nominally constant. This has been studied, for example, by Immervoll (2005), Immervoll et al. (2006b) and Sutherland et al. (2008). It is also important to realize that if p is negative, meaning average original incomes (or prices) fall, and a tax-benefit system is kept nominally constant, then households' tax burdens fall in relative terms.

24.3.2.2.2 Policy Swaps

An analogous type of exercise to that comparing the effects of policies across time in one country involves assessing the effects of policies from one country (A) when simulated in another (B), the so-called policy swaps. The starting point is again Equation (24.3), but instead of comparing the effects of two different national policy regimes on the same population and distribution of original incomes, the aim is to compare the effects of a particular set of "borrowed" policies on different populations and income distributions. Some studies focus on the effects of several alternative systems in one particular country (one-way swaps), and others carry out two-way swaps sometimes involving more than two countries in a series of swaps. Section 24.3.6 discusses some examples of such studies. Instead of growth in income over time and the relative movement in tax-and benefit parameters, the nature of p has to do with difference in nominal levels of original income across countries. Often there are additional complexities involved in maintaining correspondence with original policies, especially if more than one pair-wise comparison is made. Attempts so far have aimed to keep the values of parameters fixed in relative terms, for example, in connection to average income or in order to maintain budget neutrality.

24.3.2.2.3 Microsimulation-Based Indicators

The same framework can be used to describe microsimulation-based indicators, designed to capture some inherent characteristics of a given tax-benefit system, which are not directly observable. The nature of these was already explained in Section 24.2.2, and here we formalize the key definitions. Overall, these indicators show how household disposable income reacts to changes in people's gross earnings and circumstances (for a given tax-benefit system):

$$\Delta y = y(c_B, x_B, m) - y(c_A, x_A, m) \qquad (24.13)$$

Using our notation, we can express marginal effective tax rates (METR) as follows:

$$\text{METR} = 1 - [y(c, x + d, m) - y(c, x, m)]/d \qquad (24.14)$$

where the change in household disposable income is divided by the margin (d) used to increment gross earnings (x) of a given household member, yielding a relative measure. This is further deducted from one to show the part of additional earnings which is taxed away.

In the case of participation tax rates (PTR), both earnings (x) and other household characteristics (c) are adjusted to reflect the change in labor market status, as with the change from inactivity or unemployment (A) to work (B):

$$\text{PTR} = 1 - [y(c_B, x_B, m) - y(c_A, x_A, m)]/(x_B - x_A) \qquad (24.15)$$

The relative income change is again deducted from one to reflect the effective tax rate at this margin. (Note that this could be further simplified as $x_A = 0$.) Replacement rates (RR) are simply calculated as the ratio of out-of-work disposable income (A) to in-work disposable income (B):

$$\text{RR} = y(c_A, x_A, m)/y(c_B, x_B, m) \qquad (24.16)$$

Finally, indicators based on counterfactuals reflecting only changes in household sociodemographic characteristics (c) can be calculated as $\Delta y = y(c_A, x, m) - y(c_B, x, m)$.

For example, "child-contingent" incomes would show the change in household disposable income for families with children (A) compared to the income if they did not have children (B).

24.3.2.3 Decomposition With Labor Supply Changes

So far we have focused on the static effects of policy changes, whereby potential behavioral reactions have been absorbed by the component capturing changes in household characteristics more generally. Following Bargain (2012a), we now extend the previous case and explicitly account for behavioral changes in the form of labor supply adjustments due to policy changes. For this purpose, we slightly change the notation from x_k to x_k^l, which refers to original incomes by population with characteristics c_k based on labor supply choices made under the policy system l. (As such, the meaning of x_k^k is exactly the same as x_k before and, hence, will be shortened to the latter.) This allows the term "changes in characteristics" to be further split into two components—labor supply adjustments following changes in policy rules ($A \rightarrow B$) and other effects due to changes in the population structure c (assumed to be exogenous to tax-benefit policy changes, at least in the short and the medium term). We can now express the overall change in household disposable income as a sum of four components: direct (or mechanical) policy effect, labor supply reactions, change in nominal levels, and change in characteristics.

Decomposing Equation (24.4) and combining it with Equation (24.3), we can separate the behavioral effects comparing disposable income with labor supply under the initial and the new policy rules, expressed in terms of initial policy rules (y_A, pm_A) and either start-period household characteristics c_A:

$$
\begin{aligned}
\Delta y = {} & y_B(c_B, x_B, m_B) - y_A(c_B, x_B, pm_A) \quad \text{(direct policy effect)} \\
& + y_A(c_B, x_B, pm_A) - y_A(c_A, px_A^B, pm_A) \quad \text{(change in characteristics)} \\
& + y_A(c_A, px_A^B, pm_A) - y_A(c_A, px_A, pm_A) \quad \text{(behavioral effects)} \\
& + y_A(c_A, px_A, pm_A) - y_A(c_A, x_A, m_A) \quad \text{(change in nominal levels)}
\end{aligned}
\tag{24.17}
$$

or end-period household characteristics c_B

$$
\begin{aligned}
\Delta y = {} & y_B(c_B, x_B, m_B) - y_A(c_B, x_B, pm_A) \quad \text{(direct policy effect)} \\
& + y_A(c_B, x_B, pm_A) - y_A(c_B, x_B^A, pm_A) \quad \text{(behavioral effects)} \\
& + y_A(c_B, x_B^A, pm_A) - y_A(c_A, px_A, pm_A) \quad \text{(change in characteristics)} \\
& + y_A(c_A, px_A, pm_A) - y_A(c_A, x_A, m_A) \quad \text{(change in nominal levels)}
\end{aligned}
\tag{24.18}
$$

Decomposing Equation (24.8) instead and combining it with Equation (24.7) allow the behavioral effects to be expressed in terms of new policy rules (y_B, m_B) and, again, start-period household characteristics c_A:

$$\Delta y = y_B(c_B, x_B, m_B) - y_B\left(c_A, px_A^B, m_B\right) \quad \text{(change in characteristics)}$$
$$+ \, y_B\left(c_A, px_A^B, m_B\right) - y_B(c_A, px_A, m_B) \quad \text{(behavioral effects)}$$
$$+ \, y_B(c_A, px_A, m_B) - y_B(c_A, x_A, p^{-1}m_B) \quad \text{(change in nominal levels)} \quad (24.19)$$
$$+ \, y_B(c_A, x_A, p^{-1}m_B) - y_A(c_A, x_A, m_A) \quad \text{(direct policy effect)}$$

or end-period household characteristics c_B[16]:

$$\Delta y = y_B(c_B, x_B, m_B) - y_B\left(c_B, x_B^A, m_B\right) \quad \text{(behavioral effects)}$$
$$+ \, y_B\left(c_B, x_B^A, m_B\right) - y_B(c_A, px_A, m_B) \quad \text{(change in characteristics)}$$
$$+ \, y_B(c_A, px_A, m_B) - y_B(c_A, x_A, p^{-1}m_B) \quad \text{(change in nominal levels)} \quad (24.20)$$
$$+ \, y_B(c_A, x_A, p^{-1}m_B) - y_A(c_A, x_A, m_A) \quad \text{(direct policy effect)}$$

Modeling behavior and in particular labor supply is discussed in more detail in the next section.

24.3.3 Modeling Behavioral Changes

24.3.3.1 Accounting for Individual Reactions

The impact of policies on individual behavior, through incentives and constraints, is at the core of economics, and behavioral microsimulation models are valuable tools for providing insights into the potential behavioral reactions to changes in the tax-benefit system and, consequently, on their effect on economic efficiency, income distribution, and individual welfare (Creedy and Duncan, 2002). Nevertheless, it is important to be clear when the second-order effects can, and cannot, be neglected. To capture the individual effect of reforms, it is not always necessary to quantify behavioral responses, on the assumption that the effects of the policy changes are marginal to the budget constraint (Bourguignon and Spadaro, 2006).

Of course, it is not possible to judge a priori whether the behavioral response is large or ignorable. Judgments must necessarily be made on an *ad hoc* basis, using available evidence and related to the context of the analysis and how results are to be interpreted. If behavior is known to be constrained (e.g., in the case of labor supply adjustments at times of high unemployment), then behavioral responses might be ignored, and it is sufficient to consider the results of the analysis in terms of changes in income (rather than welfare). If static indicators of work incentives, such as marginal effective tax rates and participation tax rates, change very little as a result of a policy change, then one can assume that labor supply responses driven by substitution effects will be small. If the change in income with and without modeled behavioral response is expected to be rather similar, then given the error in the modeling of behavior and in the static microsimulation estimates themselves,

---

[16] We skip decompositions based on Equations (24.5) and (24.9) because the terms for behavioral effects and change in characteristics are simply scaled down by p (if the homogeneity property holds), compared to Equations (24.4) and (24.8), respectively.

going to the trouble of modeling responses may not be worthwhile (Pudney and Sutherland, 1996).

Moreover, being clear about the relevant time period is important. From a policy-making viewpoint, it is the effect on the income distribution and on the public budget in the year of the reform that often matters. Most tax and benefit policy changes are made year to year and are fine-tuned later if necessary. On the one hand, behavior takes time to adapt to changing policies, partly because of constraints, adjustment costs, and lack of information or understanding. This applies most obviously to fertility but also to labor supply in systems where full information about the policy rules is not available until the end of the year (after labor supply decisions have already been acted on). On the other hand, changes in behavior may also happen in anticipation of the policy being implemented, with short-term responses larger than long-terms effects. This may apply particularly to tax planning behavior and is well-illustrated by the case of an announcement in the UK in 2009 of a large increase in the top rate of tax on high incomes in the 2010–2011 tax year. Major forestalling of income by those who would pay the additional tax and were in a position to manipulate the timing of their income resulted in an unexpected increase in tax revenue in the 2009–2010 tax year and a corresponding reduction in the following year (HMRC, 2012).

In some situations the morning-after effect is the most relevant when considering short-term policy adjustments and equilibrium (or partial equilibrium) considerations are not particularly relevant. Furthermore, if indicative results are needed quickly because reform is imperative, then in the absence of an already-estimated and tested behavioral model, static results with the appropriate "health warnings" are still more informative than nothing at all.

Nevertheless, it is widely recognized that, depending on the policy change being analyzed, ignoring behavioral reactions can lead to misleading estimates of the impact of the policy reform on the income distribution and the macroeconomic consequences (Bourguignon and Spadaro, 2006), as is also illustrated by the tax-planning example.

At the other extreme, modeling behavioral responses in the case of very large changes to policy poses challenges for the empirical basis of behavioral modeling. For example, replacing an existing tax-benefit system with a combination of a basic income and a flat tax such that no income fell below the poverty threshold would presumably result in large changes in many dimensions of behavior which are unlikely to be correctly captured by the labor supply models that are used traditionally.

Despite the long tradition of modeling behavior in economics, the behavioral reactions to changes in the tax system that are most commonly analyzed are related to labor supply (starting with the seminal contributions of Aaberge et al., 1995 and van Soest, 1995) and program participation (Keane and Moffitt, 1998), feeding into a growing literature, which is characterized by an increasing level of econometric sophistication. The same level of development does not yet apply to other research areas in which microsimulation models have been used, such as investigating the potential effects of tax policies on consumption (Creedy, 1999b; Decoster et al., 2010), saving (Boadway and Wildasin, 1995; Feldstein and Feenberg, 1983), and housing (King, 1983), at least partly due to a lack of suitable data.

24.3.3.2 Labor Supply Models

There is a general consensus in the literature about using (static) discrete choice models to simulate the individual labor supply reactions to changes in the tax-benefit system.[17] Such models are structural because they provide direct estimations of preferences over income and hours of work, through the specification of the functional form of the utility function. Discrete choice models belong to the family of random utility maximization models (McFadden, 1974) that allow the utility function to have a random component (usually following the extreme value distribution), affecting the optimal alternative in terms of utility level associated with each choice.

The discrete choice character of the models is due to the assumption that utility-maximizing individuals and couples choose from a relatively small number of working hour combinations, which form the personal choice set. Each point in the choice set corresponds to a certain level of disposable income given the gross earnings of each individual (derived using the observed or predicted wage), other incomes, and the tax-benefit system rules simulated by means of a tax-benefit microsimulation model taking into account the sociodemographic characteristics of the family. The nonlinear and nonconvex budget sets determined by complex tax-benefit systems provide a primary source of identification of the model itself. Most of the discrete choice models based on the van Soest (1995) approach assume that the same choice sets are defined and available for each individual and that an individual has the same gross hourly wage for each such alternative. Ilmakunnas and Pudney (1990) is one of the few exceptions in the literature, allowing the hourly wage to be different according to the number of hours offered by each individual. Aaberge et al. (1995) provide a more flexible specification that defines the alternatives faced by the individuals in terms of a set of a wage rate, hours of work, and other job-related characteristics. The wage rate can differ for the same individual across alternatives, the hours of work are sampled from the observed distribution, and the availability of jobs of different types can depend on individual and institutional characteristics.

Regardless of the econometric specifications, the sample is usually restricted to individuals who are considered "labor supply-flexible" in order to exclude individuals whose labor choices are affected by factors that are not or cannot be controlled for in the labor supply model. Examples of these factors include disability status, educational choices, early retirement, and self-employment status. This represents a limit in the use of the

---

[17] See Creedy and Kalb (2005) for an extensive review of modeling strategies.

estimated labor supply responses to analyze changes in overall income distribution because, for the individuals not covered by the labor supply models, the behavior is assumed to be inelastic. In most applications, working age individuals within the family are allowed to vary their labor supply independently of each other, and the utility maximization takes place at the family level, considering the income of both partners subject to a pooled income constraint, in line with the unitary model of household behavior. Blundell et al. (2007) provides an example of the structural model of labor supply in a collective setting, excluding the effects of taxes.

Figure 24.4 depicts the main components of a standard labor supply model that uses a static tax-benefit algorithm to generate input for the labor supply estimation and to evaluate the labor supply reactions to policy reforms.

In the prereform scenario (left panel of Figure 24.4), the labor supply model is estimated on the budget set providing a direct estimate of the preferences over income and hours. In the postreform scenario (right panel of Figure 24.4), a new budget set for each family is derived by the tax-benefit model applying the new tax-benefit rules following the simulated reform. Assuming that individual random preference heterogeneity and observable preferences do not vary over time, labor supply estimates from the prereform scenario are used to predict the labor supply effects and the second-round redistributive effects (i.e., when labor supply reactions are taken into account) of the simulated policy reforms. Such effects might come out of an iterative procedure calibrating the policy parameters to ensure revenue neutrality once the labor supply reactions and their effects on tax revenue and benefit expenditure are taken into account.

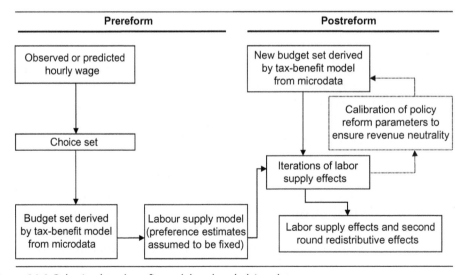

Figure 24.4 Behavioral tax-benefit model and underlying data.

Applications of discrete choice behavioral models are too numerous to be surveyed in this context. Along with many applications focused on the potential effects of specific tax-benefit policies (among others, see Brewer et al. (2009) for a review of analysis of the effects of in-work benefits across countries), labor supply models based on microsimulation models provide labor supply elasticities that can be used in other tax policy research (e.g., Immervoll et al., 2007). Using EUROMOD and TAXSIM, Bargain et al. (2014) provide the first large-scale international comparison of labor supply elasticities including 17 EU countries and the US. The use of a harmonized approach provides results that are more robust to possible measurement differences that would otherwise arise from the use of different data, microsimulation models and methodological choices. Figure 24.5 shows the estimated own-wage elasticities for single individuals and individuals in couples, which suggest substantial scope for the potential impact of tax-benefit reforms on labor supply and hence income distribution, though the differences across countries are found to be smaller with respect to those in previous studies. Bargain et al. (2014) also show the extent to which labor supply elasticities vary with income level which has important implications for the analysis of the equity-efficiency trade off inherent in tax-benefit reforms. To this aim, labor supply models can be used to implement a computational approach to the optimal taxation problem, allowing the empirical identification of the optimal income tax rules according to various social welfare criteria under the constraint of revenue neutrality (Aaberge and Colombino, 2013).

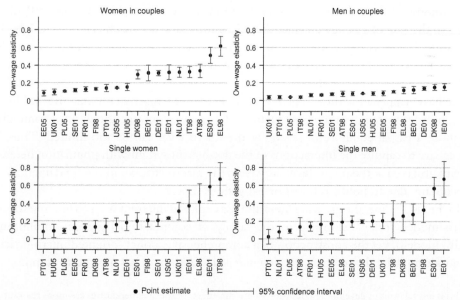

Figure 24.5 Europe and United States: Own-wage elasticities. *Source: Bargain et al. (2014), using EUROMOD and TAXSIM.*

The rapid dissemination of labor supply models, no longer restricted to the academic sphere and increasingly used to inform the policy debate, has been accompanied by a continuing refinement of the econometric specifications. Nevertheless, further improvements are still necessary to model the labor market equilibrium that can emerge as a consequence of a policy simulation (Colombino, 2013), to take into account demand side constraints (Peichl and Siegloch, 2012) and to exploit the longitudinal dimension of micro-data, where this is available, in order to avoid labor supply estimates being potentially biased by individual unobserved characteristics and to consider the state dependence in the labor supply behavior (Haan, 2010).

24.3.4 Macroeconomic Effects

In a basic application of a static microsimulation model, labor market conditions and levels of market income are taken from the underlying data without further adjustments. However, these conditions may change due to policy, and economic and institutional changes, and in order to assess the social consequences of macroeconomic changes, it is important to consider the interactions of the tax-benefit system with new conditions in the labor market and with other macroeconomic effects in general. On the one hand, micro-oriented policies can have a second round effect due to micro-macro feedbacks: for example, a generous income support scheme can have effects on labor market and saving behaviors. On the other hand, macro-oriented policies or exogenous shocks have a redistributive impact that needs to be assessed if the potential implications for the political economy of the reforms is to be understood (Bourguignon and Bussolo, 2013).

As in the case of a policy change, the microsimulation approach can offer insights in two ways. First, it can provide, in a timely fashion, an ex-ante assessment of how individuals are affected by the macroeconomic changes, either actual or hypothetical. Second, it can be used to develop a counterfactual scenario to disentangle ex-post what would have happened without a given component of the macroeconomic shock. However, in order to capture the consequences of a macroeconomic shock on income distribution, a partial equilibrium setting at the micro level can be too limited. Thus, it is necessary to capture the interactions of the tax-benefit system with population heterogeneity observed at the micro level, as well as the macro changes in the fundamentals of an economy due to policy reforms or exogenous shocks.[18]

In the last decade, the growing literature has explored different ways to link micro and macro models (often belonging to the family of computational general equilibrium (CGE) models), yet the construction of a comprehensive, policy-oriented micro–macro economic model still faces many challenging issues. Although it is now quite common to

---

[18] This is less relevant in developing countries where the effects of social expenditures are more relevant in shaping the income distribution than tax-benefit systems, but it cannot be ignored in mature welfare states and in emerging countries due to the increasing use of conditional cash transfer programs.

see disaggregated information from micro-level data used in a macro model (i.e., using the parameters of behavioral models or the effective tax rates simulated by microsimulation models in CGE models), it is rarer to see a fully developed microsimulation model being integrated with a macro model. See Bourguignon and Bussolo (2013) for an excellent review of the different approaches.

The simplest and widely implemented way to combine micro and macro models is the top-down approach. Robilliard et al. (2008) provide an example of sequentially combining a microsimulation model with a standard multisector CGE model, not only focusing on the labor markets but also on the expenditure side taking into account the heterogeneity of consumption behavior of individuals. First, the macro model predicts the linkage variables, such as new vectors of prices, wages, and aggregate employment variables that are the consequences of a macroeconomic shock or a new policy. Second, the microsimulation model generates new individual earnings and employment status variables consistent with the aggregates from the macro model and hence simulates a new income distribution. In such a top-down approach, the potential macro feedback effects of the new situation faced by the individual are not taken into account specifically, but only through the representative households embedded in the macro model. Because it depends on the aggregation of behavior at the individual level, this approach can only provide the first-round effects of the exogenous (policy) change. Bourguignon et al. (2005) extend the top-down approach by including in the microsimulation model the behavioral reactions of individuals to the price changes predicted by the macro model.

In contrast, in the bottom-up approach, the individual behavioral changes due to a policy reform are simulated at the micro level and then aggregated to feed into the macro model as an exogenous variation in order to analyze the overall effect on the economy. Any feedback effect from the macro model back into the microeconomic behavior is ignored in this setting (Brown et al., 2009).

A more complete recursive approach is given by the combination of the two approaches through a series of iterations until effectively no further adjustments are observed, in order to take into account the feedbacks that would otherwise be ignored and to arrive at a fully integrated macro–micro model. In the macro part of such a model, the household sector is not given by a few representative households but by the micro-level sample of households representative of the whole population. Aaberge et al. (2007) is an example of the integration between a labor supply microsimulation model and a CGE model in order to assess the fiscal sustainability of the aging population in Norway. Peichl (2009) uses the same approach to evaluate a flat tax reform in Germany.

Considering the efforts needed to develop a fully integrated model, the choice of the appropriate approach depends on the research or policy question at hand, and more parsimonious models can do the job in many circumstances. Notwithstanding, a fully integrated micro–macro model, as suggested by Orcutt et al. (1976), would be an incredibly powerful tool for building counterfactuals taking into account feedback effects between the micro and macro levels and for disentangling the effect of a given macro change on individual resources and hence on income distribution.

24.3.5 Predicting Income Distribution

Using microsimulation to predict income distribution is an area of work that is fueled by the need of policymakers to have more up-to-date estimates of poverty and inequality and the effects of policy than can be supplied directly from micro-data that are usually 2–3 years out of date.

This need is particularly acute if indicators of income distribution are to be taken into account in assessments of economic and social conditions alongside aggregate economic indicators, which are generally available in a more timely way (Atkinson and Marlier, 2010; Stiglitz, 2012). Furthermore, the practice of setting targets for the future achievement of social goals is becoming more widespread. In relation to poverty and income distribution, this applies particularly in the European Union through the Europe 2020 targets for the risk of poverty and social exclusion,[19] and in the developing world through the UN Millennium Development Goal for the eradication of hunger and extreme poverty.[20] Predictions of the current situation, known as "nowcasts," are valuable indicators for measuring the direction and extent of movement toward the associated targets, along with predictions for the target date at some future point (i.e., forecasts).

The approaches for predicting income distribution also depend on the time framework of the analysis. Methods for nowcasting and forecasting are distinct in the sense that the latter must rely on assumptions or other forecasts about the economic and demographic situation, as well as the evolution of policies, rather than recent indicators, data, and known policy parameters. However, the choice of techniques is common to both, and before discussing the two time frameworks in turn, the next subsection considers a key issue: how to model changes in labor market status.

24.3.5.1 Modeling Changes in Labor Market Status

In order to capture the effects of exogenous changes in economic status on income distribution, two techniques can be implemented at the micro level. One approach is to reweight the data (Creedy, 2004; Gomulka, 1992; Merz, 1986), and another approach is to model transitions from one status to another at the individual level (Fernández Salgado et al., 2014).

Reweighting is commonly used because it is relatively straightforward to carry out and to test the effects of alternative specifications. For example, to model an increase in the unemployment rate (Immervoll et al., 2006b), the survey weights of households containing unemployed people at the time of the survey must be increased, and the

---

[19] http://ec.europa.eu/europe2020/targets/eu-targets.
[20] http://www.un.org/millenniumgoals/.

weights of other similar households reduced, in order to keep demographic characteristics and household structures constant in other relevant dimensions. Following this approach, Dolls et al. (2012) simulate a hypothetical unemployment shock in 19 European countries and the US in order to analyze the effectiveness of the tax and transfer systems to act as an automatic stabilizer in an economic crisis.

However, the main disadvantage of the reweighting approach, especially in the context of a rapidly changing labor market, is that it assigns the characteristics of the "old" unemployed (in the original data) to the "new" unemployed (corresponding to the current period). To the extent that the unemployed in the data were long-term unemployed, this will underestimate the number of new unemployed in receipt of unemployment insurance benefits, which are time-limited in most countries, and overestimate the extent to which incomes are lowered by unemployment. Furthermore, the unemployment shock may have affected certain industries and occupations more than others.

Another drawback of reweighting is that it can result in very high weights for some observations, which can distort the results of simulations affecting dimensions not controlled for. In addition, although the implications of alternative formulations for the empirical results are straightforward to explore, it is far less straightforward to assess the statistical properties and reliability of the weights themselves, given that for any one set of weights satisfying the calibration constraints, there are also others (Gomulka, 1992).

Moreover, reweighting does not permit the modeller to account for the interactions between changes in the individual status and different tax-benefit instruments, for example, to analyze to what extent the welfare system counterbalances income losses specifically for those who became unemployed, rather than at the aggregate level. This is possible with the second approach, which involves explicit modeling of transitions at the individual level, making use of external information about the changes occurring in a given dimension. In principle, the full range of relevant characteristics of the people affected can be taken into account. An explicit simulation allows for the detailed effects of tax and benefit policy to be captured for those making the transition. In other words, it allows the production of quasi "panel data" that tracks the same individual before and after a given change, disentangling what would have happened without the change and highlighting the interactions of the tax-benefit system with the individual sociodemographic characteristics.

Following this approach, Fernández Salgado et al. (2014) simulate individual transitions from employment to unemployment at the onset of the Great Recession in six European countries. As a consequence of the macroeconomic shock, household incomes of individuals who lose their jobs are predicted, considering the direct cushioning effect of the tax-benefit systems and the way they depend on the market income of other household members and personal/household characteristics. The comparison between incomes before and after the shock provides a way to stress-test the tax-benefit systems, assessing the relative and absolute welfare state resilience.

To date there have been few systematic comparisons of reweighting versus the explicit simulation of individual transitions. Hérault (2010) provides a comparison of results using the two methods on South African data and concludes that "the reweighting approach can constitute a good alternative when data or time constraints do not allow the use of the behavioral approach and when the production of individual level transition matrices in and out of employment is not essential" (p. 41).

24.3.5.2 Nowcasting

Tax-benefit microsimulation models have for many years been used to simulate the effects of the most recent policies so that ex ante analysis of policy reforms can take the current situation as the starting point. In doing this, it is necessary to update the input micro-data to reflect current economic and social conditions. This might be done with varying degrees of sophistication depending on the question at hand and the amount of change in relevant dimensions between the reference period of the micro-data and the reference year of the policy. Usually, information in the data on original income is updated using appropriate indexes. In addition, the sample might be reweighted to account for certain demographic and economic changes (see section 24.3.5.1). The simulated distribution of household disposable income, based on adjusted population characteristics, updated original income, and simulated taxes and benefits using current rules, is then assumed to be a reasonable representation of the current income distribution.[21]

However, in times of rapid change, two factors suggest that this approach may not be adequate. First, simple reweighting cannot generally capture major changes accurately, and income growth may vary greatly around the mean, requiring a disaggregated approach. Most obviously this applies in the case of an economic downturn and a sudden increase in unemployment with its asymmetric effects, or an upturn and an increase in employment, when, as is typically the case, the impact is uneven across the population. Secondly, it is at times of rapid change or economic crisis that policymakers particularly need to know about very recent movements in the income distribution and the current situation rather than those a few years previously. The same applies in times of growth if policymakers are concerned about some sections of the population being left behind. Furthermore, in times of crisis, fiscal stimulus or fiscal consolidation policies may play a particularly important role in reshaping income distribution. A microsimulation approach has particular advantages because it captures the specific impact of the components of these policy packages that have a direct effect on household incomes, as well as their interactions with changing market incomes. In times of rapid growth, fiscal drag will typically have distributional consequences (see Section 24.3.2.2), which will be important for policymakers to anticipate if they wish to prevent relative poverty from rising (Sutherland et al., 2008).

[21] See for example Redmond et al. (1998) and Callan et al. (1999).

Borrowing the term nowcasting from macroeconomics (see, for example, Banbura et al., 2011) the use of an extended and refined set of microsimulation methods in combination with timely macroeconomic statistics is able to provide estimates of the current income distribution using micro-data on household income which are typically 2 or more years out of date. These methods include: (a) updating market incomes from the income data year to current (or latest), using published indexes with as much disaggregation as these statistics allow and from the latest to "now" according to macro-level forecasts or assumptions; (b) simulating policy changes between the income data year to those prevailing currently; (c) adjusting data to account for important dimensions of actual labor market change between the data year and the most recently available information; (d) adjusting data to account for actual and projected demographic and other compositional changes (e.g., household composition) between the data year and "now."[22]

An early attempt to use these methods to update poverty statistics for the UK is provided by de Vos and Zaidi (1996). More recently, these methods have been used to nowcast the policy effects of the crisis in Ireland (Keane et al., 2013); to examine the distributional effects of the crisis in Greece (Matsaganis and Leventi, 2013); and to nowcast the income distribution in Ireland (Nolan et al., 2013), the UK (Brewer et al., 2013), and Italy (Brandolini et al., 2013). They have also been used for eight European Union countries to nowcast the risk of poverty, using EUROMOD (Navicke et al., 2014).[23]

A key issue for all the studies that aim to nowcast income distribution in (or on the way out of) the Great Recession, using prerecession data, is to capture labor market changes with sufficient precision. The same would apply during a period of increasing employment rates. Most of the studies cited above use reweighting to adjust for both demographic and labor market changes. The study by Navicke et al. (2014) is an exception. Holding demographic factors constant, it used explicit simulation of labor market transitions to capture the very specific and varied incidence of unemployment across the eight countries considered in the relevant period. The method is based on that employed by Figari et al. (2011c), using Labor Force Survey (LFS) statistics to establish the required number of transitions of each type according to personal characteristics. The microsimulation model, in this case EUROMOD, then selects from the available pool of people with these characteristics in the input database and changes their status accordingly. Incomes are simulated, accounting for the new status, for example, by calculating

---

[22] Some studies also make specific data adjustments that are relevant to the effect of policies in the projection period, such as increasing the pension age (Brewer et al., 2011).

[23] In the US, where there is also an interest in predicting current indicators, child poverty has been nowcast using a simple econometric model based on state-level current and lagged economic indicators and benefit receipt statistics (Isaacs and Healy, 2012). This is a feasible approach, rather than using microsimulation, because in the US the poverty threshold is not a function of the income distribution, as it is in the EU, and because welfare benefit receipt is in itself a good predictor of poverty, which is not the case in the EU or elsewhere in the OECD.

eligibility and entitlement to unemployment benefits for those making the transition from employment to unemployment.

24.3.5.3 Forecasting

Although nowcasts can make use of very recent indicators of economic and labor market conditions and typically project forward by only a few years, allowing slowly changing factors such as demographic composition to stay the same, forecasts project further in time and must rely on assumptions and predictions from other models. In this sense they are usually better seen as drawing out the implications for the income distribution of a particular economic/demographic scenario. For example, Marx et al. (2012) explore the implications of meeting the Europe 2020 targets for employment for indicators of risk of poverty and social exclusion, finding that the composition of any new employment is a key factor. The World Bank (2013) uses a similar approach to exploring the implications of meeting both the education and employment targets for the poverty indicators in the countries of Eastern Europe. In both cases there is no tax-benefit microsimulation, and it is assumed that tax-benefit effects are the same as those in the underlying micro-data. This is justified on the grounds that future policy reforms are difficult to predict. However, this approach neglects any interactions between sociodemographic and labor market characteristics and the tax-benefit system. Microsimulation can take account of these and, even assuming a constant tax-benefit policy structure and a constant relationship between income levels and tax-benefit parameters, would allow the automatic effects of policies on changing market incomes to be captured.

Nevertheless, as explained in Section 24.3.2.2, it is important to be aware that assumptions about the indexation of current policies can have a major effect on distributional outcomes (Sutherland et al., 2008). In some situations enough is known about the probable evolution of policies to include the discretionary tax-benefit reform effects in the predictions, as well as the automatic effects driven by changes in the circumstances of households. In the UK not only are policy reforms often announced several years in advance, but also there is detailed information available about indexation assumptions that are built into official public finance forecasts (HM Treasury, 2013; Table A1), as well as regular and detailed growth and inflation forecasts (OBR, 2013; Table 2.1) that can together be used as baseline assumptions for defining policies in the forecast year. Brewer et al. (2011) have forecast child poverty in 2020, using a combination of these types of assumptions, reweighting, and tax-benefit microsimulation. Such an approach not only provides a prediction (in this case that, given the assumptions, the UK will not meet its target for child poverty reduction in 2020) and allows the drivers of the prediction to be identified (through sensitivity analysis), but it also allows a "what would it take?" analysis to suggest what combinations of reforms and other changes would be needed to meet the target.

24.3.6 Cross Country Comparisons Using Microsimulation

Cross-country comparisons of the effects of policies naturally add value to what can be said about a single country because the broader perspective helps to provide a sense of scale and proportion. They provide the basis for assessing the robustness of results and generalizing conclusions. In addition, considering several countries within the same analysis provides a kind of "laboratory" in which to analyze the effects of similar policies in different contexts or different policies with common objectives (Sutherland, 2014). Comparisons can take several forms. At their simplest the effects of different policies or policy reforms in different countries can be analyzed side-by side. Bargain and Callan's (2010) decomposition analysis for France and Ireland is one example of this approach. Another is Avram et al. (2013) who analyze the distributional effects of fiscal consolidation measures within a given period in nine countries.

A second approach is to contrast the effects of a common, hypothetical policy reform in several countries, highlighting the relevance of the interactions of a specific policy design with population characteristics and economic conditions. Often the "reform policy" is designed to highlight features of the existing national system that it replaces or supplements. Examples include Atkinson et al. (2002) and Mantovani et al. (2007) for minimum guaranteed pensions, Levy et al. (2007a) for universal child benefits, Callan and Sutherland (1997) for basic income, Bargain and Orsini (2007) and Figari (2010) for in-work benefits, Matsaganis and Flevotomou (2008) for universal housing transfers, Figari et al. (2012b) for the taxation of imputed rent, and Paulus and Peichl (2009) for flat taxes. This type of analysis is usually complicated by the need for the reform policy to be scaled somehow if it is to have an equivalent effect in countries with different levels of income, and because of the need to consider how the reform policies should be integrated with existing national policies. Given that the starting points are different (e.g., the tax systems may treat pensions differently) the net effects will differ, too.

A third approach, which was introduced in Section 24.3.2.2, is to swap existing policies across countries in order to explore how their effects differ across different populations and economic circumstances. Examples of this kind of "policy learning" experiment include a comparison of the effectiveness of benefits for the unemployed in Belgium and the Netherlands (De Lathouwer, 1996), as well as many studies of the effectiveness of public support for children and their families: Atkinson et al. (1988) for France and the UK; Levy et al. (2007b) for Austria, Spain and the UK; Levy et al. (2009) for Poland, France, Austria, and the UK; Salanauskaite and Verbist (2013) for Lithuania, Estonia, Hungary, Slovenia, and the Czech Republic; and Popova (2014) who compares Russia with four EU countries.

Policy swap analysis can, in principle, be done using a set of national microsimulation models, side by side. But Callan and Sutherland (1997) found that the task of making models produce comparable results was formidable, even for just two (arguably) relatively similar countries (Ireland and the UK). This justified the construction of EUROMOD as a multicountry model that now covers all EU member states (see Box 24.1).

Indeed, with some exceptions, many of the studies referred to above make use of EUROMOD. As intended, this greatly facilitates cross-country comparability (particularly of the concepts used), the implementation of common reforms using common code and the mechanics of carrying out policy swaps (transferring coded policies from country A to country B). EUROMOD is designed to be as flexible as possible, allowing a huge range of assumptions to be made about cross-country equivalence of different aspects of policy simulation. One example is the treatment of non-take-up of benefits (see Section 24.4.2), and another is the default indexation of policies each year (see Section 24.3.2.2). Thus policy swapping is not a mechanical procedure. Each exercise has its own motivation and corresponding decisions to be made about which aspects of policy (and assumptions driving its impact) are to be "borrowed" from elsewhere and which are to be retained from the existing local situation.

Here, we give two empirical examples. The first is an example of side-by-side cross-country analysis using EUROMOD from Avram et al. (2013). This compares the distributional effects of the fiscal consolidation measures taken in nine European countries in the period up to 2012 from the start of the financial and economic crisis. Figure 24.6 shows the percentage change in average household income due to the measures across the (simulated) 2012 income distribution. The measures include different mixes of increases in income tax and social contributions and cuts in public pensions, other cash benefits, and public sector pay.

Four things are striking about this figure and serve to demonstrate the added value of cross-country comparisons of this type, relative to single country studies. First, the scale of the effect varies greatly across the countries (noting that the country charts are drawn to different scales, but the grid interval is uniformly 2% points), ranging from a drop in income on average from 1.6% in Italy to 11.6% in Greece. Second, the choices made by governments about which instruments to use differ across countries. Third, the incidence of the particular changes is not necessarily as one might expect a priori. For example, increases in income tax have a roughly proportional effect in many countries and are concentrated on higher-income households only in Spain and the UK, as might be expected a priori. Cuts in (contributory parental) benefits in Latvia particularly target the better off. Finally, the overall distributional effects range from broadly progressive in Greece, Spain, Latvia, and the UK to broadly regressive in Estonia.

The second example is of a policy swap, showing what would happen to child poverty in Poland under a range of child and family tax-benefit arrangements, as compared with the actual 2005 system, including a reform introduced in 2007 and the revenue-neutral alternatives offered by scaled-down versions of the Austrian, French, and UK systems of child and

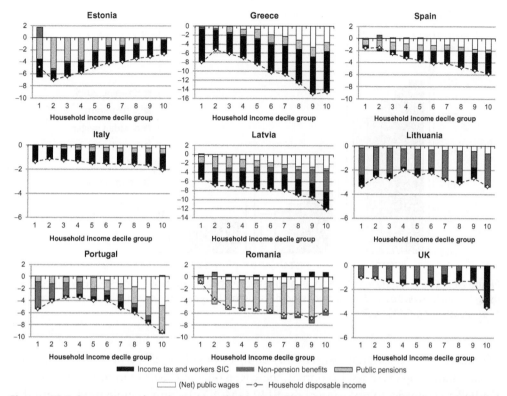

Figure 24.6 Percentage change in household disposable income due to fiscal consolidation measures 2008–2012 by household income decile group. *Notes: Deciles are based on equivalized household disposable income in 2012 in the absence of fiscal consolidation measures and are constructed using the modified OECD equivalence scale to adjust incomes for household size. The lowest income group is labeled "1" and the highest "10." The charts are drawn to different scales, but the interval between gridlines on each of them is the same. Source: Avram et al. (2013), using EUROMOD.*

family support (Levy et al., 2009). As Figure 24.7 shows, any of the alternative policy systems would have reduced child poverty by more than the actual 2007 reform (costing the same). The French and UK systems would perform especially well from this perspective.

In addition to EUROMOD, other multicountry initiatives have constructed and used microsimulation models. These include a Latin American project that built separate models using a range of software and approaches for Brazil, Chile, Guatemala, Mexico, and Uruguay (Urzúa, 2012). A WIDER project has constructed models that are available in simplified form on the web for 10 African countries.[24] To our knowledge, neither set

---

[24] http://african-models.wider.unu.edu/.

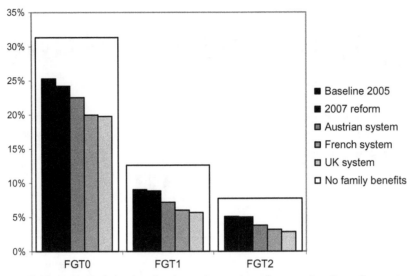

Figure 24.7 Child poverty in Poland under alternative tax-benefit strategies. *Notes: Poverty is measured using FGT indexes and 60% of median household disposable income as the poverty threshold. Source: Levy et al. (2009) using EUROMOD.*

of models has been used for cross-country comparisons of the effects of common reforms or for policy swap exercises. In contrast, there is an ongoing collaboration among some of the Balkan countries to make use of the EUROMOD platform to build models with the explicit intention of using these models for cross-country comparisons. The Serbian model SRMOD is the first completed step in this process (Randelović and Rakić, 2013), followed by the Macedonian model, MAKMOD (Blazevski et al., 2013). Similarly, the South African model, SAMOD, again using the EUROMOD platform, (Wilkinson, 2009) has been joined by a sister model for Namibia, NAMOD, with the aim, among other things, of modeling "borrowed" policies that have been successful in a South African context (Wright et al., 2014).

24.4. CHALLENGES AND LIMITATIONS

24.4.1 Reconciling Simulated Income with Recorded Income and Macro Statistics

A common problem when using micro-data from surveys for the analysis of policies and income distribution is that aggregate values (e.g., gross earnings or income taxes) do not match estimates from national accounts or other sources of macroeconomic statistics. This problem also applies to microsimulation studies based on survey data, with one exception. Tax-benefit model calculations of benefit entitlements may match administrative totals *better* than information on recorded receipt in the data, if there is a problem of underreporting of these sources of income in the survey.

Chapter 11 considers the reconciliation of household surveys and national accounts. Here, we focus on a somewhat different issue, also related to the plausibility and usability of empirical findings. This is that the simulated income distribution is not identical to the income distribution that is measured by directly using the underlying survey (or register) micro-data. Typically, measures of income inequality in microsimulated estimates, using the same micro-data and the relevant policy year, are lower. Adjustments in the simulations for the non-take-up of benefits and for tax evasion go some way to reducing the discrepancy, and these issues are discussed in Section 24.4.2. However, they appear not to be the full explanation, and it is clear that the contributory factors differ across countries. Indeed, in some countries for particular datasets and policy years, the differences are small: for example, Figari et al. (2012a) show this to be the case for four EU countries, using data from the EU Statistics on Income and Living Conditions (EU-SILC) and EUROMOD. However, this is by no means always or even often the case, and reconciling simulated and recorded estimates is an important component of both the process of building a tax-benefit model and validating the content of micro-data from surveys.

As alluded to above, there is evidence that some surveys underreport recipients of some major cash benefits, when compared with administrative statistics.[25] If the reason for this is failure to report these sources of income by recipients, then simulated benefits may perform better, generally leading to higher incomes at the bottom of the distribution and suggesting that the survey overestimates income inequality. An illustration from the UK is provided in Box 24.2.

Box 24.2 Benefit recipients in the UK: Comparing microsimulation estimates with survey responses and administrative statistics

The UK Family Resources Survey (FRS) data, which is used as input by all the main UK tax-benefit models, underestimates recipiency of some benefits by as much as 30% in the case of the pension credit, as shown in the table below.[26] Simulations using the UK component of EUROMOD based on the same data halve the scale of the discrepancy for Pension Credit. The simulations account for non-take-up by applying official estimates for each benefit and client group. Simulations are also closer to the administrative data values in the case of Housing Benefit, for which the shortfall is 2% compared with 19% in the data, but in the case of Working Tax Credit, the simulated

Continued

---

[25] For the UK see http://statistics.dwp.gov.uk/asd/frs/2008_09/frs_2008_09_report.pdf, Table M.6. The increasingly used practice of linking surveys to administrative sources of income data should reduce the prevalence of this problem.

[26] After adjusting the administrative statistics for recipients not living in UK private households in the case of the pension credit.

shortfall is larger. The entitlement here mainly depends on being in low paid work over the year, allowing families to meet the eligibility criteria for the working tax credit for short periods, which is not captured by the simulations based on current income and circumstances. For the other two payments shown in the table, EUROMOD over- rather than underestimates recipiency. The overestimation of Child Tax Credit recipients is to some extent explained by the administrative statistics not containing some long-term recipients of income support, whose child payments are still waiting to be migrated to the tax credit system. Most simulated and nonsimulated benefits are included in the means-test for Council Tax Benefit: its overestimation is expected to the extent that some nonsimulated benefits are underreported and tax credits are undersimulated.

Clearly, simulating receipt is not a solution in itself, and a comprehensive reconciliation needs other benefit-specific factors to be taken into account.

Numbers of recipients of selected UK benefits in the 2009–2010 tax year: estimates from Family Resources Survey (FRS), EUROMOD, and administrative statistics (thousands)

	FRS	EUROMOD	Administrative statistics	Ratio FRS/ external	Ratio EUROMOD/ external
Working Tax Credit	1,800	1,615	2,240	0.80	0.72
Child Tax Credit	3,700	4,951	4,090	0.90	1.16
Pension Credit	1,800	2,337	2,580	0.70	0.85
Housing Benefit	3,700	4,474	4,550	0.81	0.98
Council Tax Benefit	5,100	6,331	5,570	0.92	1.14

Source: EUROMOD version F6.20 with adjustments for non-take-up, using Family Resources Survey 2009/10 updated to 2010–2011 incomes.

Shortfalls in the reported receipt of means-tested welfare benefits compared with administrative information are also found in US surveys on a larger scale (Meyer et al., 2009). Wheaton (2007) uses microsimulation to calculate entitlement and then to calibrate the numbers of recipients so that they match administrative statistics. The result is a large increase in the estimated extent of poverty reduction due to the programs in question.

However, as illustrated in Box 24.2, underreporting of benefit income may not be the only source of the problem. If part of the reason for the shortfall in the survey is that benefit recipients are more likely to be nonrespondents, then microsimulation of eligibility and entitlement is unlikely to solve the problem on its own, and benefit recipiency estimates will still not match administrative information. In this case recalculation of the survey weights, including controls for characteristics that are correlated with benefit receipt and also underrepresented in the survey, may in principle provide a solution, if such characteristics can be identified and external information is available to control the process. This is not often the case.

There are many possible reasons for discrepancies in each simulated income component. Here we discuss income tax as an important example. First, survey estimates of income tax may not relate to the current year or may include only withholding taxes. Second, survey gross incomes (and hence taxes) may have been imputed from net income (see also Section 24.2.1), but their quality and consistency with calculations in the tax-benefit model are usually difficult to establish due to detailed documentation not being made available. We might also expect some discrepancies when the values are compared with fiscal data. Such comparisons need to take national specifics into account, including the nature of the tax structure and administration, as well as the questions asked in the survey. The nature of the comparison and the conclusions that are drawn also depend on whether fiscal data are available at the micro level and whether they can be matched to the survey. In addition, the fiscal data may not provide a fully reliable benchmark, especially if they are based on samples of administrative data or if the administrative process that generates them is not comprehensive or consistent. We provide a case study in Appendix B based on a published table of fiscal statistics for the UK.

Microsimulation estimates of income taxes may be over- or underestimated relative to what is shown by fiscal data. For example, income tax may be underestimated because the market incomes that make up the tax base are underreported or the survey does not adequately represent high-income taxpayers. In this case estimates of income distribution are sometimes adjusted by inflating incomes at the top of the distribution, informed by fiscal data. This is the case for the official estimates of poverty and income distribution produced by the UK Department of Work and Pensions (DWP, 2013), though the same adjustment is not (to our knowledge) applied in UK tax-benefit models. In contrast, the French model TAXIPP merges micro-data and statistics from many sources for its input database.[27] This includes information on top incomes specifically used to correctly capture the very top of the distribution and particularly the taxes paid by that section of the population (Bozio et al., 2012).

Income tax may be overestimated because of tax evasion that has not been modeled (see Section 24.4.2) or because it is not possible to model or measure the size of some tax reliefs and common avoidance measures. It may also be under- or overestimated in line with other simulated income components that are taxable. Combinations of these factors may occur, and indeed it is possible for the simulated tax aggregate to match well that from fiscal data but for the distribution of tax paid to be very different—see Appendix B for an example of this. In addition, estimates of gross income and tax liability from fiscal data may be subject to error due to tax evasion.

Time periods for income assessments are also important. In surveys that collect current income (as in the UK), which mainly use a reference time period of a month, the simulation of income tax must assume that the same monthly income was received

---

[27] http://www.ipp.eu/en/tools/taxipp-micro-simulation/.

all year and will not identify cases with tax liability for part of the year. However, the survey response for those with part year incomes will, at least in principle, indicate the correspondingly lower or higher tax payments, already adjusted for part-year incomes. The UK is unusual in collecting short-period current income. Most income surveys ask about annual income (in the previous year), which is the appropriate reference time period for the calculation of tax liabilities. However, it must also be used to simulate the income assessment of social assistance and other means-tested benefits for which the relevant period is generally much shorter than 1 year. This leads to fewer households being simulated to receive these benefits than shown in the data.

Generally, simulations are only as good as the underlying micro-data and, in the cases where they are necessary, as good as the imputations and adjustments that must be carried out in the absence of all the necessary information. This in turn depends on the specifics of the national benefit and tax systems as well as the quality of the data. In some circumstances it might be appropriate to calibrate and reweight to try and adjust the baseline simulated distribution of income and its components to match that given by the data directly. Generally, however, such an approach will distort the estimates of *change* due to a policy reform. A better approach is to try and understand the source of each problem and to make adjustments that can be applied in a consistent way, and with transparent assumptions, across policy scenarios. This highlights the importance not only of validation and adjustment but also of documenting the process so that users of the models and readers of model applications can make their own assessment, based on the research questions at hand.

24.4.2 Modeling Non-Take-Up and Noncompliance

One particular challenge arises with benefit non-take-up and tax noncompliance.[28] There is no natural data source with explicit information about these phenomena, and modeling each is highly context-specific. Accounting for take-up and noncompliance behavior in tax-benefit models is important because it affects estimates of fiscal aggregates (i.e., total benefit expenditures and tax revenues), but even more importantly, it can affect various parts of the income distribution in a different way. Furthermore, take-up and compliance behavior are likely to be affected by tax-benefit policy reforms and, hence, are themselves endogenous factors in the analysis. Even if microsimulation models commonly assume full take-up and compliance, this has an important implication for cross-national comparisons as results are unlikely to be consistent, as long as the prevalence and patterns of non-take-up and noncompliance vary across countries.

Benefit non-take-up refers to the situation in which those eligible for a given benefit do not successfully claim it for various reasons. This could simply be due to people not being aware of their entitlement (or even the existence of a particular form of public

---

[28] Benefit take-up is also referred to as welfare participation, especially in studies on the US.

support), being put off by a complex or time-consuming claiming process, or related to social stigma, such as not wanting to appear vulnerable and dependent on others' support. In an economic context, these factors can be summarized as implied costs related to take-up (Hernandez et al., 2007). Another likely key determinant is the size of the entitlement (Blundell et al., 1988), both in absolute terms and relative to other income sources and wealth of the claimant. Benefit take-up tends to be higher for universal benefits because the claiming process is simpler and the associated social stigma lower. Arguably, people are most likely to claim contributory benefits (e.g., for old age and maternity) because these are directly linked to their own previous contributions and, hence, entitlement is perceived to be more justified, while take-up of means-tested benefits tends to be lower. Therefore, assuming full take-up can distort comparisons between various benefits and make some benefits seem more effective than in fact they are. It also matters how extensive and long-established the benefit scheme is, because the benefit's scale and longevity contribute to the spread of knowledge among the population. A related phenomenon is benefit leakage, meaning that a benefit is received by those who should not be eligible. This could either indicate an unintentional error on behalf of the benefit administrator or claimant, or benefit fraud.

Studies estimating the scale and determinants of benefit take-up require information on eligibility for a given benefit and actual benefit awards. Because benefit eligibility is not directly observed (for a wider population), it must be inferred from relevant individual and household characteristics on the basis of benefit rules, and as such, it constitutes a microsimulation exercise in itself. Depending on the nature of the rules, especially when means-testing is involved, there can be complex interactions with other tax-benefit instruments, as well as with tax compliance. It is difficult to overemphasize the importance of data quality in this context, and most precise estimates can presumably be obtained with administrative data providing information as close as possible to that used by the welfare agencies, as well as actual benefit receipt (e.g., Bargain et al., 2012). For this to cover all potentially eligible people and not just claimants, it implies that agencies rely (mainly) on information from existing registries (e.g., tax records) rather than data collection from the claimants. Even then, there can still be some scope for simulation error if the claiming process involves factors such as discretion on behalf of officials awarding benefits. For example, in some countries, local social welfare offices are given a considerable level of discretion in deciding who is in greater need and, hence, more qualified for public support. On the other hand, there could be also errors made by the program administrators in the assessment of the eligibility, resulting in incorrect approval or rejection of the claim.

This type of administrative data, if it exists, is usually not accessible, and most empirical studies have relied on survey data instead. There are, however, additional challenges with survey data due to potential measurement error in the observed benefit receipts and other characteristics affecting the eligibility and the entitlement calculation (see

Section 24.4.1). For example, survey respondents may have simply forgotten the receipt of a particular benefit, associated it with an incorrect period or benefit type, or intentionally left it unreported (e.g., because of social stigma). Often, there is also a time delay between becoming entitled and receiving a first payment. Therefore, a careful assessment and cleaning of benefit data are usually required (e.g., Hancock and Barker, 2005; Matsaganis et al., 2010). Similarly, individual and household characteristics relevant for determining benefit eligibility and entitlement might be reported with error, especially other income sources and/or assets in the case of means-tested benefits. There have been only a few attempts to model the various errors explicitly (Duclos, 1995, 1997; Hernandez and Pudney, 2007; Zantomio et al., 2010).

The modeling of benefit take-up becomes even more complicated when considering the receipt of multiple benefits (e.g., Dorsett and Heady, 1991; Hancock et al., 2004), interactions with labor supply (e.g., Bingley and Walker, 1997, 2001; Keane and Moffitt, 1998; Moffitt, 1983) or dynamics in take-up behavior (e.g., Anderson and Meyer, 1997; Blank and Ruggles, 1996). Analyses combining several of these aspects are rare (e.g., Chan, 2013), and avoiding behavioral responses in other dimensions, such as labor supply, is one reason why many of the recent advances in take-up modeling have concentrated on take-up among the retired or others unable to work (e.g., Hernandez and Pudney, 2007; Pudney et al., 2006; Zantomio et al., 2010). Much of the applied research has been done for the UK and US (see above), but, among others, there are also studies for Canada (Whelan, 2010), Finland (Bargain et al., 2012), Germany (Bruckmeier and Wiemers, 2012; Riphahn, 2001), Greece and Spain (Matsaganis et al., 2010).[29] For recent reviews, see Hernanz et al. (2004) and Currie (2004).

Despite general progress with modeling take-up, it remains a challenge to deal with in microsimulation models due to the data requirements and complexities involved. Ideally, tax-benefit models should treat take-up endogenously in simulations, because policy reforms can change take-up behavior (e.g., Zantomio et al., 2010). Such attempts remain scarce (see Pudney et al., 2006). A second best approach is to predict the probability of take-up conditional on personal characteristics that are not affected by policy changes and hence remain constant in policy simulations. To predict take-up on the basis of previously estimated statistical models, the same explanatory variables need to be present in the data used for the tax-benefit model. Furthermore, take-up is highly circumstantial, and a prediction model developed for one benefit in one country is unlikely to perform satisfactorily for other benefits or countries. A simpler approach commonly used to account for incomplete benefit take-up in tax-benefit models is to assign take-up randomly among the group of eligible units for a given benefit such that the aggregate

---

[29] A number of US studies have focused on noncash programs such as Food Stamps (e.g. Daponte et al., 1999; Haider et al., 2003) or The Special Supplemental Nutrition Program for Women, Infants, and Children (e.g., Bitler et al., 2003).

take-up rate matches that in official statistics or previous studies (e.g., Hancock and Pudney, 2014; Redmond et al., 1998; Sutherland et al., 2008). This is obviously a rather crude approach because some people are more likely to claim than others, and, hence, it may not be sufficient to align aggregate benefit expenditure with official statistics, particularly if take-up is correlated with the level of entitlement. Another option is to link benefit entitlement to the observed receipt, which, however, seriously limits the scope for simulations.

Tax noncompliance (or tax evasion) is the other side of the coin and refers to intentional effort to lower tax liability in unlawful ways. In the context of tax-benefit models, this primarily concerns income tax and payroll tax evasion, in the form of underreporting taxable income or overreporting (income tax) deductions. Compared to benefit non take-up, this is an even more challenging issue for several reasons. First, take-up is binary by nature (i.e., an eligible person either claims or not), but tax compliance is often partial. Second, there is no single data source that would allow the precise measurement of tax evasion. Although tax records contain income reported to the tax authority, "true" income remains unobserved. Third, evading taxes may also affect how related incomes are reported to surveys. These constraints point towards the need to combine and utilize multiple data sources to study tax evasion and help to explain why hard empirical evidence at the individual level is very scarce.

Studies estimating the extent and determinants of tax noncompliance by individuals have mainly relied on audited tax records (e.g., Clotfelter, 1983; Erard, 1993, 1997; Erard and Ho, 2001; Feinstein, 1991; Martinez-Vazquez and Rider, 2005). Although tax audits are designed to detect tax noncompliance, these are not often carried out randomly and target those more likely to evade on the basis of initial screening. Repeated and extensive random tax audits, from which insights into tax evasion can be inferred for a broader population, have been primarily carried out in the US. However, even audits are unable to detect all noncompliance, especially income underreporting in which cash transactions are involved, and usually have very limited information on individual characteristics.

Surveys offer a much richer set of information on individuals but usually lack a good measure of noncompliance. Some surveys include explicit questions on compliance (e.g., Forest and Sheffrin, 2002), but given its sensitivity, the reliability of such self-reported data is unclear (Elffers et al., 1992). On the other hand, studies such as Pissarides and Weber (1989), Lyssiotou et al. (2004), and Hurst et al. (2014) have relied on indirect methods, employing econometric models that contrast surveyed income and consumption. These, however, are inevitably cruder and allow for a less detailed analysis of compliance.

Finally, laboratory experiments are common in tax compliance research, (Alm et al., 1992, 2009, 2012; Laury and Wallace, 2005). Although experiments allow one potential determinant to be isolated from the rest and for clearer conclusions to be drawn about causality, it is unclear how well conditions in the laboratory reflect actual behavior, not least as the subjects are typically students without substantial experience paying taxes.

Overall, there is substantial evidence on factors influencing people's decision to evade taxes. There are also studies showing that tax noncompliance is more prevalent for income sources that are less easily tracked by the tax authority (see Klepper and Nagin, 1989; Kleven et al., 2011). For example, the extent of underreporting income from self-employment is notably higher compared to wages and salaries because the latter are usually subject to third-party reporting (i.e., by employers), which reduces opportunities for evasion (though it does not necessarily eliminate these). Fewer studies have focused on the distributional implications of tax noncompliance (e.g., Doerrenberg and Duncan, 2013; Johns and Slemrod, 2010), some in combination with microsimulation modeling (Benedek and Lelkes, 2011; Leventi et al., 2013). For reviews of theoretical and empirical literature on tax evasion, see Andreoni et al. (1998), Slemrod (2007) and Alm (2012).

However, given the highly specific datasets that are often involved in the study of tax compliance, it is not straightforward to utilize previous findings in tax-benefit models, nor is it easy to provide one's own estimates with the type of data commonly used for microsimulation. This helps to explain why attempts to account for tax noncompliance in tax-benefit models seem to remain very limited (e.g., Ceriani et al., 2013; Matsaganis and Leventi, 2013). On the other hand, this may also reflect the fact that microsimulation studies lack details on such adjustments. Therefore, the first step towards improving the modeling of tax noncompliance (as well as benefit take-up) is increasing transparency about how this is handled (if at all) in existing models and studies.

24.4.3 Assessing the Reliability of Microsimulation Estimates

The overall credibility of a microsimulation model in simulating the effects of a given tax-benefit policy encompasses different aspects, some of which are interrelated, and include the application of "sound principles of inference in the estimation, testing and validation" (Klevmarken, 2002).

First, the reliability of a microsimulation model is closely tied to its validation and transparency, which are indicated by the extent to which solid documentation exists for the internal features of the model and the validation of the results against external statistics. Unfortunately, a high level of transparency does not characterize many of the microsimulation models used in the academic and policy literature, which tend to be "black boxes." Good practice is to provide a detailed description of all tax-benefit components simulated, including details of assumptions used, as well as information about the input data and related transformations or imputations. Documented validation of the output against external statistics on benefit recipients and taxpayers and total expenditure/revenue is also an important component of the informed use of microsimulation models.

Nevertheless, such validation is not a comprehensive assessment for three reasons. First, as illustrated in Section 24.4.1, microsimulation estimates and the information available in official statistics may not be comparable conceptually. Second, in some countries, limited external information is available, and in all it is rarely available without a time delay. Third, although it is possible to validate results for existing and past systems, it is usually not possible to find independent estimates of the effects of policy reforms. A correct baseline does not ensure that the model or its input data can correctly estimate the effect of a reform.

In addition, as mentioned by Wolf (2004), a persistent failure of most microsimulation applications is the lack of recognition of the degree of statistical uncertainty associated with the results, some of which is inherent in the sampling process that underlies the input micro-data and some of which is propagated from simulation errors and estimated parameters. The accuracy of the underlying data, the correct and detailed representation of the tax-benefit rules, and the actual implementation of the policy parameters in the simulation code determine the point-estimate of the simulated policy. Nevertheless, the correct interpretation of the results should take into account their statistical inference—an aspect often neglected in the microsimulation literature—which also depends on the nature of the model and whether it is purely deterministic or also involves probabilistic or econometric specifications.

To start with, simulations are subject to the same degree of sampling error, measurement error, and misreporting as any other analysis based on survey data. On the one hand, as discussed in Section 24.4.1, simulations can improve the accuracy of results by simulating the exact rules rather than relying on observed values that might be misreported. On the other hand, the simulation process can introduce other sources of errors due to, for example, approximations in the simulation of tax benefit rules, adjustments for noncompliance or non-take-up, updating of monetary parameters and sociodemographic characteristics to the simulation year, or ignoring behavioral responses or market adjustments.

In the case of simulation of the first-order effects of policy changes, Goedemé et al. (2013) argue that the lack of attention to the statistical significance of the results is undesirable and unjustified due to the availability of standard routines embedded in most standard statistical software. Moreover, when comparing the statistics related to different scenarios, they show the importance of taking into account not only the sampling variance of the separate point estimates but also the covariance between simulated and baseline statistics which are based on the same underlying sample. This can lead to a generally high degree of precision for estimates of the effects of a reform on a particular statistic of interest.

The situation is much less straightforward in the case of more complex simulations involving revenue-neutral reforms or behavioral reactions that add additional sources of uncertainty due to the use of estimated wage rates for constructing the budget set and the preference parameters estimated using econometric models. Despite the growing literature on estimating the labor supply effects of policy changes (see Section 24.3.3), there are only a few examples of studies focusing on the analytical properties of the sampling distribution of the microsimulation outcomes that are affected by simulation uncertainty and estimation uncertainty. The former stems from the simulated choice set that can be different from the one that an agent would choose in reality. The estimation variability comes from the sampling variability of the estimated parameters of the labor supply model (Aaberge et al., 2000). Pudney and Sutherland (1994) derived the asymptotic sampling properties of the most important statistics usually reported in microsimulation studies, taking into account the additional uncertainty introduced by the imposition of revenue neutrality in the construction of the confidence intervals. Pudney and Sutherland (1996) augmented the previous analysis, deriving analytically the asymptotically valid confidence intervals of a number of statistics, allowing for errors associated with sampling variability, econometric estimation of parameters of a multinomial logit model of female labor supply, and stochastic simulation in the calculations. They concluded that sampling error is the largest source of uncertainty, but parameter estimation errors may add additional uncertainty that undermines the practical use of such behavioral models.

The complexity of the analytical solution associated with very detailed microsimulation models, rather complex policy simulation and sophisticated econometric models, has lead to the use of more tractable empirical approaches. Creedy et al. (2007) opted for a simulation approach to approximate the sampling distribution of statistics of interest based on the sampling distribution of the estimated parameters. The approach relies on a number of draws from the parameter distribution of the underlying behavioral model. Moreover, they suggest a simpler and more practical approach in which the functional form of the sampling distribution is assumed to be normal, requiring a small number of draws from the parameter distribution and leading to generally accurate results.

Furthermore, to avoid having to assume the normal distribution for stochastic terms, and exploiting the increasingly available computer power, assessing the statistical reliability of the estimates now commonly relies on resampling methods such as the bootstrap, which allows one to obtain a set of replicated econometric estimates used in one or more simulation runs. The variance of the replicated estimates is then used to capture the variability of the statistics of interest. Although the additional uncertainty added by behavioral modeling is not found to be critical for most analysis (e.g., Bargain et al., 2014), there are reasons for concern when the estimates refer to specific small demographic groups, and further developments in this research area are needed.

24.5. BROADENING THE SCOPE

24.5.1 Extended Income, Consumption and Indirect Taxes

Although disposable income is the most-used indicator of living standard, it is widely recognized that economic well-being is a multidimensional concept (see Chapter 2).

The economic value of the consumption of goods and services, including interhousehold transfers, in-kind benefits, and homeowners' imputed rent related to the main accommodation, is often considered a better indicator than income when measuring individual well-being on both theoretical and pragmatic grounds (Meyer and Sullivan, 2011). The exclusion of consumption expenditure and noncash income from empirical studies of the redistributive effect of tax-benefit systems might also hamper cross-country comparison given the different degree of monetization of the economy across countries. Moreover, the distributional impact of policy changes may be rather different if noncash incomes and indirect taxes are included, with important implications for the design of policies aiming to fight poverty and social exclusion, because such an omission may lead to imperfect targeting and misallocation of resources. Notwithstanding their importance, most microsimulation models do not include either in-kind benefits or indirect taxes, mainly due to data limitations.

In European countries, in-kind benefits, such as services related to child and elderly care, education, health, and public housing, represent about half of welfare state support and contribute to reducing the inequality otherwise observed in the cash income distribution. The economic value of public in-kind benefits can be imputed at individual and household levels on the basis of per capita spending, considering the average cost of public services (such as providing care and education services), the gain from paying below-market rent or no rent at all for public housing, or the risk-related insurance value approach that considers public health care services equivalent to purchasing an insurance policy with the same cost for individuals who have the same sociodemographic characteristics. See Aaberge et al. (2010b) and Paulus et al. (2010) for empirical evidence across European countries and for methodological insights on the derivation of needs-adjusted equivalence scales that are more appropriate for extended income. However, survey data usually do not include enough information to simulate changes in the value of the benefit due to policy reforms, nor do they take into account the real utilization by the individual, the quality of the public service, or the discretion in the provision usually applied by local authorities (Aaberge et al., 2010a).

A more comprehensive measure of individual command over resources should include the income value of home ownership as well. This is because the consumption opportunities of homeowners (or individuals living in reduced or free rent housing) differ from those of other individuals due to the imputed rent that represents what they would pay if they lived in accommodation rented at market prices. The inclusion of imputed rent in microsimulation models is becoming more common due to the refinement of different methods for deriving a measure of imputed rent (Frick et al., 2010) and also a renewed interest in property taxation. From a cross-country perspective, Figari et al. (2012b) analyze the extent to which including imputed rent in taxable income affects the short-run distribution of income and work incentives, showing a small inequality-reducing effect together with a nontrivial increase in tax revenue. This offers the opportunity to shift the fiscal burden away from labor and to increase the incentive for low-income individuals to work.

Indirect taxes typically represent around 30% of government revenue. With only a few exceptions, household income surveys providing input data for microsimulation models do not include detailed information on expenditures either, preventing micro-level analysis of the combined effect of direct and indirect taxation. The solution usually adopted to overcome this data limitation is to impute information on expenditures into income surveys (Sutherland et al., 2002). Decoster et al. (2010, 2011) provide a thoughtful discussion of the methodological challenges and a detailed explanation of the procedure implemented in the context of EUROMOD for a number of European countries. Detailed information on expenditure at the household level is derived from national expenditure surveys, with goods usually aggregated according to the Classification of Individual Consumption by Purpose (COICOP), identifying, for example, aggregates such as food, private transport, and durables. The value of each aggregate of expenditure is imputed into income surveys by means of parametric Engel curves based on disposable income and a set of common socioeconomic characteristics present both in income and expenditure datasets. In order to prevent an unsatisfactory matching quality in the tails of the income-expenditure distributions, a two-step matching procedure can be implemented by first estimating the total expenditures and total durable expenditures upon disposable income and sociodemographic characteristics and then predicting the budget share of each COICOP category of goods. Moreover, the matching procedure takes into account the individual propensity for some activities, such as smoking, renting, using public transportation, and education services, which are not consumed by a large majority of individuals. Individual indirect tax liability is then simulated according to the legislation in place in each country, considering a weighted average tax rate for each COICOP category of goods imputed in the data.

Most microsimulation models that include the simulation of indirect taxes rely on the assumption of fixed producer prices, with indirect taxes fully passed to the final price paid by the consumer. To relax such an assumption one should go beyond a partial equilibrium framework and link the microsimulation models to macro models (see Section 24.3.4) in order to consider the producer and consumer responses to specific reforms or economy-wide shocks. There is some variety in the ways in which the models deal with the estimation of changes in spending patterns due to the simulated reforms (Capéau et al., 2014). Some models simulate only a nonbehavioral first round impact (i.e., quantities or expenditures are kept fixed at the initial level), and others estimate partial behavioral reactions taking into account the income effect on demand for goods and services by means of Engel curves (Decoster et al., 2010) or even full demand systems accounting for the real income effect and the relative price effects (Abramovsky et al., 2012).

The inclusion of indirect taxes also raises the question of how to measure their incidence. Table 24.1 shows the incidence of indirect tax payments for three European

Table 24.1 Incidence of indirect tax payments

Income decile	As % of disposable income			As % of expenditures		
	Belgium	Greece	UK	Belgium	Greece	UK
1	15.3	37.7	20.2	11.3	13.5	13.9
2	12.0	23.4	13.5	11.8	13.9	14.0
3	11.7	19.8	12.6	12.1	14.3	13.8
4	11.6	18.4	12.4	12.5	14.2	13.8
5	11.4	17.6	11.8	12.7	14.2	14.1
6	11.0	16.0	11.6	12.8	14.1	14.3
7	10.9	16.0	11.1	13.1	14.6	14.5
8	10.8	14.9	10.7	13.3	14.2	14.7
9	10.5	14.2	9.9	13.5	14.3	14.6
10	9.9	11.9	8.2	13.9	14.1	14.4
Total	11.1	16.0	10.8	12.9	14.2	14.3

Notes: Decile groups are formed by ranking individuals according to equivalized household disposable income, using the modified OECD equivalence scale.
Source: Figari and Paulus (2013), based on EUROMOD.

countries expressed as a percentage of disposable income and as a percentage of expenditure, by decile of equivalized disposable income. In the first case (see the left panel of Table 24.1), the regressivity of indirect tax payments is clear: poorer individuals pay a larger proportion of their income in indirect taxes compared to richer individuals, mainly due to a larger propensity to consume or even dissaving reflected by average expenditures exceeding incomes for the individuals at the bottom of the income distribution (Decoster et al., 2010). However, survey data might suffer from measurement error, in particular from income underrecording (Brewer and O'Dea, 2012), which could give a misleading snapshot of the income-consumption pattern at the bottom of the income distribution. In the second case (i.e., the right panel of Table 24.1), indirect tax payments are progressive, and poorer individuals pay a slightly smaller proportion of their total expenditure in VAT and excises compared to richer individuals. The main reason for this is that the goods that are exempt from VAT or subject to a lower rate (e.g., food, energy, domestic fuel, children's clothing) represent a much larger share of the total spending of poorer individuals than of richer individuals (Figari and Paulus, 2013). The distributional pattern of the indirect taxes being regressive with respect to disposable income and proportional or progressive with respect to expenditure reinforces, on empirical grounds, the importance of the choice of the measurement stick that should be used as a benchmark in the welfare analysis (Capéau et al., 2014; Decoster et al., 2010).

The potential of microsimulation models that are capable of simulating direct and indirect taxes within the same framework is reinforced by the renewed interest in the tax shift from direct to indirect taxation in order to enhance the efficiency of the tax system (Decoster and Van Camp, 2001; Decoster et al., 2010). In particular, microsimulation models have been used to assess the distributional consequences of a "fiscal devaluation," a revenue-neutral shift from payroll taxes toward value-added taxes that might induce a reduction in labor costs, an increase in net exports, and a compression of imports, with an overall improvement in the trade balance (de Mooij and Keen, 2013; European Commission, 2013).

Two general considerations arise from the use of microsimulation models for the analysis of the redistributive effects of indirect taxes. On the one hand, the actual degree of regressivity of indirect taxes might be less than that observed if surveys tend to underreport income more than consumption at the bottom of the income distribution (Brewer and O'Dea, 2012; Meyer and Sullivan, 2011). On the other hand, a more systematic use of simulated income values, as generated by a microsimulation model rather than as observed in the data, can help in solving the underreporting of income values, closing the gap between reported income and consumption and providing a more robust indicator of living standards for those with a low level of resources.

24.5.2 Dynamic Microsimulation and Lifetime Redistribution

The importance of investigating the "long-range character" of public policies was already highlighted by Guy Orcutt in the 1950s (Orcutt, 1957) and pioneered through his work in the 1970s on DYNASIM, a dynamic microsimulation model of the US designed to analyze the long-term consequences of retirement and aging issues (Orcutt et al., 1976). A number of reviews survey the existing dynamic microsimulation models, the methodological challenges, and the types of uses, providing an overall picture of the evolution of the state of play and future research directions for interested readers (Gupta and Harding, 2007; Harding, 1993, 1996b; Harding and Gupta, 2007; Li and O'Donoghoue, 2013; Mitton et al., 2000).

Dynamic microsimulation models extend the time frame of the analysis in order to address the long-term distributional consequences of policy changes, widening the perspective of the effects of the policies to encompass the individual lifetime and addressing questions about intrapersonal redistribution over the lifecycle (Harding, 1993). Dynamic microsimulation models typically aim to capture two main factors that shape the income distribution in a long-term perspective. First, they cover the changing structure of the population due to evolving individual and household characteristics (e.g., age, education, household composition) and life events (e.g., marriage, household formation, birth, migration). Second, they capture the interaction of market mechanisms (e.g., labor market participation, earnings levels) and the tax-benefit system with such characteristics in each point in time.

In particular, they are useful tools to analyze: (i) the performance of long-term policies such as pensions and other social insurance programs such as health and long-term care, (ii) the consequences of different demographic scenarios, (iii) the evolution of intertemporal processes and behaviors such as wealth accumulation and intergenerational transfers, and (iv) the geographical trend of social and economic activities if dynamic microsimulation models are supplemented with spatial information (Bourguignon and Bussolo, 2013; Li and O'Donoghoue, 2013).

The methodological challenges behind a microsimulation model depend on the scope of the events taken into account and the methodology used to age the population of interest through the period of analysis. The aging process can be either static or dynamic. With the static aging method, the individual observations are reweighted to match existing or hypothetical projections of variables of interest. The approach is relatively straightforward, but it can become unsatisfactory if the number of variables to be considered simultaneously is large or if one is interested in following individual transitions from one point in time to the next (see also Section 24.3.5.1). The dynamic aging method builds up a synthetic longitudinal dataset by simulating individual transition probabilities conditioned on past history and cohort constraints that take into account the evolution of the sociodemographic characteristics of interest through the time horizon of the analysis (Klevmarken, 2008). The major source of information for the estimation of the dynamic processes is derived from longitudinal data available in most developed countries, although often the duration of the panel is not long enough to observe transitions for large samples of individuals, the main exceptions being the long panel data available in Australia, Germany, the UK, and the US. Transitions can be estimated through reduced form models that incorporate deterministic and stochastic components, or they can be simulated, taking into account behavioral reactions of individuals to other changes that occurred at the same time, based on individual preferences estimated through structural models that take into account the endogeneity of some individual transition probabilities (see Section 24.3.3).

The aging of individual and household characteristics can be implemented as a discrete or continuous process. The former is usually built around yearly time intervals; it is more straightforward but implies that some simulated events might not respect the real sequence. The latter is based on survival functions that consider the joint hazard of occurrence of the simulated events.

In principle, dynamic microsimulation models allow for analysis that is more in line with the theoretical arguments in favor of a lifetime approach to the analysis of the redistributive effects of tax-benefit systems, as developed in the welfare economics literature (Creedy, 1999a). Nelissen (1998) is one of the few examples where the annual and lifetime redistributive effects of the social security system (here for the Netherlands) are analyzed simultaneously, making use of the same microsimulation model that guarantees comparable simulations of the tax-benefit system in place over a long period of time. In line with other research (e.g., Harding, 1993), Nelissen (1998) finds that the lifetime redistributive effect is considerably smaller than the annual incidence, with important policy implications due to the different incidence of various pension schemes on different generations.

Due to the complexity of the aging process, early dynamic microsimulation models tended not to address the long term implications of policy and policy change on income distribution as a whole (i.e., population-based models) but rather focused on specific cohorts of the population (cohort models). Nowadays such a distinction is less significant due to the improvements in the modeling set up as well as major improvements in available computing power. However, despite the improvements in dynamic microsimulation modeling, such models are often perceived as black boxes, making it difficult to understand and appreciate their properties. In particular, the lack of good economic theory and sound econometric inference methods are thought to contribute to a sceptical view of these models by the economics profession (Klevmarken, 2008).

Two particular research developments characterize the dynamic microsimulation field. First, this is an area where international collaborations are emerging in an attempt to reduce the efforts needed to build very complex models. The Life-Cycle Income Analysis Model (LIAM) stands out as a viable option to provide a general framework for the construction of new dynamic microsimulation models (O'Donoghue et al., 2009) and to be linked to EUROMOD (and other modular-based microsimulation models) in order to exploit the existing parameterization of tax-benefit systems for the European countries (Liégeois and Dekkers, 2014). Second, most dynamic microsimulation models do not include macro feedback effects and do not have market clearing mechanisms that would require ambitious links to macro models (Bourguignon and Bussolo, 2013). However, due to the number and complexity of the interactions between many social and economic variables involved in the modeling, the integration between dynamic micro and macro models could introduce too much uncertainty in the results to make them useful in a policy context (Li and O'Donoghoue, 2013).

24.5.3 Crossing Boundaries: Subnational and Supranational Modeling

The natural territorial scope for a microsimulation model is a country or nation. This is because in most countries some or all of the tax-benefit system is legislated and administered nationally; the micro-data used as an input dataset are representative at the national level; the other data used to update, adjust, and validate the model are usually made available at national level; and the economy and society are usually assumed to exist and operate at this level. However, in some countries, policies can vary across regions, sometimes following from (or accompanied by) major differences in politics, history, and economic and social characteristics. In some cases, the data that are especially suitable as the basis for microsimulation modeling are only available for one region. For these reasons, models may exist for single regions, or national models may be able to capture regional differences in policy. Examples of regional or subnational models include Decancq et al. (2012) for Flanders (Belgium) and Azzolini et al. (2014) for Trentino (Italy); both are based on the EUROMOD framework, and the latter exploits a rich dataset that combines administrative and survey data. Examples of national modeling exercises that capture extensive regional differences in policies include Cantó et al. (2014) for Spain.

If the micro-data are representative of each region, then the national model can operate as a federation of regional models, also capturing any national policy competencies. As well as simulating the appropriate policy rules regardless of location (many models for countries with regional policy variation simply opt to simulate policies from a single "representative" region), these federal models can identify the implied flows of resources (redistribution) between regions as well as within them, given budget constraints at either national or regional levels. In the US, the most comprehensive in terms of policy coverage is the long-standing microsimulation model, TRIM3, which simulates welfare programs, as well as taxes and regional variation in programs, making use of a common national input dataset: the Current Population Survey (CPS) Annual Social and Economic Supplement (ASEC).[30] See, for example, Wheaton et al. (2011) who compare the effects of policies on poverty across three U.S. states. For Canada, the microsimulation model SPSD/M has been linked to a regional input-output model in order to capture some of the indirect effects of national or provincial tax-benefit policy changes at the provincial level (Cameron and Ezzeddin, 2000).

In the European Union, policies in the 28 member states vary in structure and purpose to a much greater degree than they do across US states. Although the EU-SILC data is output-harmonized by Eurostat, it is far from ideal as an input database for a microsimulation model (Figari et al., 2007), and significant amounts of nationally specific adjustments are needed to provide the input data for EUROMOD, the only EU-wide model (see Box 24.1). Indeed, although the supranational administration of the EU has no relevant policy-making powers (at the time of writing), analysis that considers the EU (or the eurozone) as a whole is highly relevant to approaching the design of tax-benefit policy measures to encourage economic stabilization and social cohesion. Analogously to regionalized national models, EUROMOD is able to draw out the implications of potential EU-level policy reforms for both between- and within-country redistribution (Levy et al., 2013), policy harmonization, and stabilization (Bargain et al., 2013a), as well as for the EU income distribution.

At the other extreme, microsimulation methods have been used to estimate income distribution and other indicators for small areas. This relies on spatial microsimulation techniques (Tanton and Edwards, 2013) or, more commonly, reweighting national or regional micro-data so that key characteristics match those from census data for the small area (Tanton et al., 2011). In the developed world, policymakers generally use these models to predict the demand for services such as care facilities (for example, Lymer et al. (2009) for Australia and Wu and Birkin (2013) for the UK). In circumstances where the census data provide a good indication of income levels, such as in Australia, they have

---

[30] http://trim3.urban.org.

also been used to provide small area estimates of income distribution and its components (Tanton et al., 2009). Linkage of the census with household budget survey data in the UK has been used to estimate the small area effects of an increase in VAT (Anderson et al., 2014). A similar method known as "poverty mapping" has been applied to developing countries by Elbers et al. (2003), using household budget surveys and census micro-data in order to monitor the geographic concentration of poverty and to evaluate geographic targeting of the poor as a way of rebalancing growing welfare disparities between geographic areas. For the use of the model for Vietnam, see Lanjouw et al. (2013).

24.6. CONCLUSIONS AND OUTLOOK FOR THE FUTURE

24.6.1 What Has Been Achieved So Far?

Tax-benefit modeling is now in widespread use to provide evidence in the policy-making process. Tax-benefit models are used within governments to provide costings of policy reforms and impact assessments of distributional and incentive effects. They are used to assess progress towards meeting targets within relevant policy domains (and may be used to set feasible targets in the first place). They are used to explore the implications of alternative reform options. Other participants in the policy-making process (opposition political parties, special interest groups, NGOs, international organizations, and civil society generally) may also put forward their own perspectives and alternative proposals on the basis of microsimulation analysis. All of them may draw on the growing body of microsimulation-informed economic analysis from academic research. Within academia, microsimulation is also an accepted and recognized part of the toolbox in applied public economics, other branches of applied economics, and other disciplines, such as quantitative social policy, sociology, and political science. Evidence for this is provided by the increasing frequency of publication of articles making use of microsimulation in mainstream journals, as is clear from the references included in this chapter, and reliance on microsimulation analysis in the economic debate, as illustrated by Mirrlees et al. (2010).

Microsimulation modeling provides an opportunity for fruitful links between the policy-making and academic communities. There are many instances in which methodological developments within academic policy-focused research have provided new and more sophisticated tools that can be adopted for use by policy-making institutions. One example is the modeling of labor supply responses, which is increasingly included in microsimulation models used by government agencies. There are also instances in which innovation has taken place within government agencies in response to particular policy needs, as well as instances of the analytical needs of policymakers providing the impetus for academic developments. One example from the European Union is the adoption of social targets for Europe 2020 and the need to develop methods of forecasting micro-level indicators. Forging such links can bring additional benefit in the form of more open channels of communication with the official producers and providers of micro-data about the data requirements of microsimulation models and the potential benefits for policy-making.

In our view there are four major strands of technical/methodological achievement and ongoing progress in the use of tax-benefit microsimulation for the analysis of policy and income inequality. A *formal framework* for disentangling the effect of policies on income distribution is an important step toward better understanding how various studies have approached measuring these effects and their consistency. A coherent framework can no doubt greatly increase the clarity and transparency of microsimulation studies and facilitate links with other relevant methodological literature. The devil is in the details and microsimulation modeling offers these in abundance.[31]

Behavioral microsimulation is no longer limited to the academic sphere, and it has an increasing impact on policy-motivated analysis. Further developments of behavioral models in terms of policy scope (e.g., extending economic modeling to cover areas such as housing, mobility, and saving) and their robustness based on the comparison with ex-post evaluation studies may strengthen their role in the policy and economic debate. Moreover, the cross-fertilization between the analytical and the computational approach to the optimal taxation problem based on behavioral microsimulation models could reinforce the link between public finance theory and applied research.

The analysis of tax-benefit policies with a clear impact on the labor market participation and the evaluation of the impact of macroeconomic shocks would clearly benefit from the availability of counterfactuals that consider *feedback effects between the micro and macro level*. A fully integrated micro–macro model, although daunting in terms of the time and resources required to create it, is potentially an incredibly powerful tool for moving beyond the partial equilibrium framework in which microsimulation models operate, for disentangling the effects of macro changes on individual resources, and for extending the policy scope of the analysis through the linkage to environmental models. However, the practical, conceptual, and methodological challenges are formidable. Even so, falling short of full model integration, improving methods of linking microsimulation analysis to macroeconomic data in various ways has been, and remains, an important part of the developing toolbox.

Cross-country comparisons of policy effects, and especially policy swap analysis, inform our understanding of the variation in the effects of policies in different economic and sociodemographic contexts, and, at the same time, these comparisons offer the opportunity for cross-country "policy learning." The development of EUROMOD, and other multicountry models, has facilitated this type of analysis, while maintaining comparability of concepts and measurement and consistency in the operation of policy rules. There is

---

[31] Furthermore, as Spielauer (2011, p. 18) has reflected: "If beauty is to be found in simplicity and mathematical elegance (a view not uncommon in mainstream economics), microsimulation models violate all rules of aesthetics."

potential to extend the approach to global regions other than the EU, such as southern Africa, Latin America, or the Balkan region (where, arguably, policy learning is most relevant). There is also potential to extend beyond the EU to include all OECD countries to aid comparisons, for example, between the EU and the US.

There is room for improvement and for development in two key areas. The first relates to the data and methods that are available for input into and adoption by microsimulation models. Our understanding of how available micro-data may be improved and reconciled with other information, as well as the potential of new forms and sources of data that may improve the quality and scope of simulation or facilitate linkage with other models (macro, environmental, etc.), are areas for attention. In terms of methodological improvements, more attention is clearly needed to assess statistical significance and reliability of results obtained with microsimulation models drawing on various statistical methods.

The second area for improvement relates to the organization of microsimulation activities. There is much duplication of effort (with many models doing the same or similar things in some countries), combined with problems of lack of transparency (i.e., lack of documentation, results that are not reproducible by others). Furthermore, most existing models are not made available or accessible to the people who might make use of them. The final two subsections explore the outlook for microsimulation and policy analysis along these two dimensions.

24.6.2 Data and Methodological Developments

Microsimulation models require access to appropriate and good quality micro-datasets that are themselves well-documented and validated against independent information. The trend toward making more use of register (administrative) data to supply information on income receipt (and in some cases many other variables) is welcome in the sense that it reduces measurement problems and underreporting and potentially frees up resources (e.g., survey interview time) for the collection of more or better quality data in other dimensions. At the same time, such linkage may introduce new problems. It may delay the delivery time of the micro-data if there are limits on the speed of obtaining and processing administrative information. Use of administrative information may also raise new concerns about data confidentiality, which may result in additional restrictions on the ways in which the datasets can be accessed and by whom. There seem to be trade-offs between using high-precision data and widespread access.

Technological developments may offer possible ways around these trade-offs, if models and their micro-level data (both input and output) are housed on a suitably secure server and accessed remotely. This is a mode of working that was pioneered for income distribution analysis by LIS[32] and, in spite of the additional complexities associated with

---

[32] http://www.lisdatacenter.org/.

microsimulation modeling, has also been successfully deployed in a few other cases. These include the WIDER African models, as well as two adaptations of national components of EUROMOD: Mefisto for Flanders (Decancq et al., 2012) and Soresi for Austria.[33] In each of these cases, the broad aim of the models is to provide access to modeling capacity by civil society, with the simulation and output options offered to users structured and restricted accordingly. More critically in this context, in each case the providers of the input micro-data have given permission for such access over the web. It remains to be seen whether it will be possible to make use of high-precision administrative data in this way. Even so, there would be other technical and pedagogical challenges to be overcome in offering to the public the full flexibility of a model like EUROMOD using remote access.

More generally there is potential to extend the policy scope and applicability of microsimulation models through the statistical linkage of data from different sources. Given the increasing complexity of tax-benefit systems that operate through direct and indirect taxes, wealth and property taxes, and cash and noncash benefits, microsimulation models can help in understanding the overall effect on individual material well-being only if more comprehensive surveys become available, cross-links between various administrative datasets are utilized further, or systematic and rigorous matching procedures are implemented and documented. A prime example is the analysis of the effects of indirect taxes, because any conclusion about the incidence and regressivity of taxes can be easily biased by the data inconsistency observed, in particular, at the tails of the income distribution (see Decoster et al., 2010; Brewer and O'Dea, 2012).

Finally, making progress on many of the technical challenges associated with microsimulation modeling, most notably the modeling of take-up and compliance behavior, is also inhibited by lack of suitable data. For example, nonreceipt of a benefit entitlement may be explained in many ways, ranging from (among other causes) measurement error in the survey responses, lack of information about eligibility on the part of a nonclaimant, or a decision not to claim due to the costs of claiming. It is likely that the relative importance of each factor varies with national context and specific benefit. Accurate modeling of the probability of taking up (i.e., receiving, given positive entitlement) a particular benefit, in principle, needs to take any one or many possible causes into account, which would typically be demanding in terms of the data requirements. Modeling of tax noncompliance at the individual level is even more demanding given the concealed nature of such activities and a potentially wider range of possible factors and interactions at play. Progress in these areas can therefore be expected to be patchy and uneven, depending on the specific problems and the data possibilities.

---

[33] http://soresi.bmask.gv.at/Mefisto/.

24.6.3 The Case for a Collaborative Approach

Few models are accessible beyond their producers. This leads to a proliferation of many similar models and the (largely wasteful) duplication of effort that this involves. It also limits access to models because building from scratch is time-consuming and requires specialist skills; there are significant barriers to entry. Furthermore, the need to provide in the public domain documentation or validation of models that are essentially private to their producers is rarely acted upon. This lack of transparency inhibits proper evaluation of microsimulation-based studies, and lack of access inhibits the reproducibility of microsimulation analyses. Together, these factors may reduce the chances of microsimulation-based studies being published in the top scientific journals. As Wolfson (2009, p. 29) says:

> .... microsimulation modelling still has not achieved the kind of scientific status it deserves. One reason is that many potential users are concerned about the 'black box' nature of microsimulation models. An important step, therefore, is for microsimulation modelling to become a 'glass box' activity, including for example public availability of the model and open source code.

Models are also expensive to maintain and keep up to date. If there were fewer, better models that were made generally accessible, this would improve efficiency and quality. A collaborative approach would also bring the various types of use and user closer together and, with the appropriate level of (technical) model flexibility, could also facilitate innovations such as model linkages. EUROMOD and TAXSIM provide two rather different examples of models that already take this approach. EUROMOD makes available both tax-benefit codes and input data to anyone with permission to access the original micro-data sources, while TAXSIM provides online access to the tax calculator that may be linked to input data of the user's own choosing.[34]

Of course, there are also good reasons why microsimulation models are developed as individually or institutionally private investments. In some cases the necessary micro-data cannot be made available more widely (e.g., in the case of government models, especially those using administrative data). In the academic sphere, there are few incentives to share technical developments as public goods in the matter suggested, especially if they embody a large time investment and if they do not themselves attract academic reward.

If the benefits of an open and collaborative approach are to be realized the main challenges are to find ways of organizing and funding arrangements that account for the long-term investment aspect, due to the need to maintain models, as well as engage in initial construction. This would include developing an incentive structure that recognized the academic value of the work done on the "public good" research infrastructure, while

---

[34] In addition, there are the web-based, simplified models referred to above, as well as other web-based developments, including the French model OpenFisca http://www.openfisca.fr/.

eliciting contributions in some form from the users of the models who might otherwise "free ride." In the end, cooperation within the microsimulation community and particularly between academic researchers and policy makers will contribute to the integration of microsimulation for policy analysis into the mainstream of economic policy-making (Atkinson, 2009).

ACKNOWLEDGMENTS

We wish to thank Tony Atkinson, François Bourguignon, and Brian Nolan for their comments and suggestions on the early drafts of this chapter. We are also grateful to Paola De Agostini, John Creedy, Mathias Dolls, Carlo Fiorio, Horacio Levy, Marcello Morciano, Andreas Peichl, Iva Tasseva, and Alberto Tumino for comments and useful discussions, as well as information or permission to make use of their analysis. Paulus and Sutherland acknowledge the support for this work from the core funding of the Research Centre on Micro-Social Change and from the UK Economic and Social Research Council (grant RES-518-28-001).

APPENDIX A. INCREASING UK CHILD BENEFIT IN 2001 AND 2013: THE NET EFFECTS

In both 2001 and 2013, the UK Child Benefit was delivered as a universal benefit for all children under the age of 19 in full-time nonadvanced education. In both years there were two rates, one for the oldest child (£15.50 and £20.30 per week, respectively) and one for any other children (£10.35 and £13.40 per week, respectively). As an illustration, we double these values and use EUROMOD to calculate the net budgetary cost after the operation of the rest of the tax and benefit systems, and we also show how the gain per child would vary across the household income distribution.

In 2001, Child Benefit was disregarded by the income tax system but was taken into account for the assessment of Income Support (and income-related Job Seeker's Allowance), Housing Benefit, and Council Tax Benefit, some of the main UK means-tested benefits for working-age people and their families. (The Working Families Tax Credit disregarded Child Benefit.) As the table shows, although the gross cost of the increase in Child Benefit is estimated at £8.85 billion per year, once the reduced entitlements to these benefits are taken into account, the net cost falls to £7.01 billion or 79% of the gross.

In contrast, in the 2013 system, the Child Benefit is disregarded in the assessment of all means-tested payments, but higher-income parents who pay income tax at the 40% (or higher) marginal rate have the value of their Child Benefit included in their tax calculation. Thus, as shown in the table, the cost of the increase in Child Benefit is offset to a small extent by an increase in income tax liabilities. In addition, in 2013, there was a cap on the overall sum of benefits that could be received by families in some circumstances. This would result in some families not receiving all or any of their Child Benefit increase. In 2013, the gross cost of the increase in Child Benefit is estimated at £11.55 billion per year, and once the reduced entitlements to these benefits are taken into account, the net cost falls to £11.14 billion or 96% of the gross.

Gross and net cost of doubling Child Benefit, 2001 and 2013

| | 2001 | | 2013 | |
	£ Million per year	% of Gross cost	£ Million per year	% of Gross cost
Child Benefit	*8,850*	*100*	*11,549*	*100*
Income Tax	0	0	−290	−3
Income Support	−1,606	−18	0	0
Housing Benefit	−152	−2	0	0
Council Tax Benefit	−81	−1	0	0
Benefit cap	0	0	−123	−1
Net cost	*7,011*	*79*	*11,136*	*96*

Source: EUROMOD version F6.20, using Family Resources Survey data for 2008–2009, adjusted to 2001 and 2013 prices and incomes.

There are different distributional consequences of these differences between gross and net effects, as shown in Figure 24.A1 below. This shows the average net weekly increase in income per child by decile group of equivalized household income under the 2001 and 2013 policy systems. Under the 2001 system, those in the lower income groups receive less, because some of the additional income is withdrawn as reduced entitlement to the means-tested benefit. (This applies to a lesser extent in the bottom decile group in which families simulated to not take-up their entitlements to means-tested benefits are mainly located.) In 2013, however, it is children in higher income households who benefit to a lesser extent, due to the clawback through income tax (the effect of the benefit cap is small and concentrated in the lower-middle of the distribution).

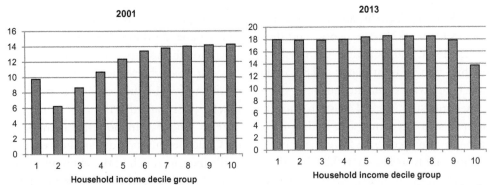

Figure 24.A1 Doubling Child Benefit in the UK: Average net gain per child in £ per week. *Notes: Deciles are based on equivalized household disposable income in the respective years and are constructed using the modified OECD equivalence scale to adjust incomes for differences in household size and composition. The lowest income group is labeled "1" and the highest "10." Source: EUROMOD version F6.20, using Family Resources Survey data for 2008–2009, adjusted to 2001 and 2013 prices and incomes.*

The point of this illustration is to demonstrate how the interactions matter and need to be understood when designing policy scenarios. Similarly, the policy analyst needs to account for the interactions in order to understand the effects of policy changes. If policy-makers wanted to double the payment made to all children in 2001, they would have needed to increase child amounts within the other benefits as well as in Child Benefit. On the other hand, if the goal had been to reduce the number of families subject to means tests (without anyone losing), then the illustrative reform would have done just that (for example, reducing the number of all households receiving Council Tax Benefit). If the goal in 2013 had been to reduce the reach of means-testing, the means-tested payment rates for children would have needed to be reduced at the same time as Child Benefit increase.

APPENDIX B. COMPARISON OF SIMULATED ESTIMATES OF INCOME TAX WITH ADMINISTRATIVE STATISTICS, UK 2010–2011

Here we illustrate the type of validation of simulated income tax that can be carried out using published tables from administrative data of tax revenues. The exercise also suggests ways in which the input micro-data might be adjusted, or not. In this exercise, the input data are the UK Family Resources Survey (FRS) 2009–2010 updated to 2010–2011 incomes and prices.

Simulated income tax liabilities are compared with statistics on income tax paid by band of taxable income, published by the HM Revenue and Customs (HMRC, Table 3.3). The first point to note is that the tax paid in any year may not match the liability for tax on income earned in that year, because of adjustments carried over from previous years.

The first row in the top panel of the table below shows the ratio of microsimulation model (EUROMOD) estimates to those of HMRC in three dimensions: the number of taxpayers (defined as individuals with positive taxable income before deduction of any personal allowances), their total taxable income (before deduction of allowances), and the total tax liability/revenue. The number of taxpayers is underestimated by 7% and taxable income by more: 13%. Also shown are the ratios for the lowest taxable income group (under £10,000 per year) and highest income group (over £150,000).[35]

---

[35] The HMRC statistics provide more detail for top incomes (the top two groups being £0.5 million to £1 million and £1 million+). However, although the overall sample size of the FRS is large by international standards (31,644 individuals in 2009/10), the numbers with very high incomes are too small to analyze. There are 99 observations with taxable incomes in excess of £150,000, including 13 with more than £500,000 and just 2 with more than £1 million (after adjustment to 2010–2011 income levels). As explained in the main text, this is partly due to underrepresentation of, or underreporting by, people with very high incomes in the survey. However, even if their incomes were properly represented, based on the HMRC statistics, there would still be fewer than 30 observations with incomes above £500,000 in a sample of this size.

Ratio of EUROMOD estimates to HMRC statistics

	Taxpayers	Taxable income	Tax revenue
EUROMOD			
All	0.93	0.87	0.85
Taxable income <£10K	0.99	0.98	0.76
Taxable income £150K+	0.46	0.42	0.46
EUROMOD with proportional adjustment to number of taxpayers (adj1)			
All	1.00	0.93	0.91
Taxable income <£10K	1.06	1.05	0.82
Taxable income £150K+	0.50	0.45	0.49
EUROMOD with adjustment to number of taxpayers by income band (adj2)			
All	1.00	0.98	1.05
Taxable income <£10K	1.00	1.00	0.79
Taxable income £150K+	1.00	0.89	0.98

Notes: EUROMOD-adj1 makes a proportional adjustment to the number of taxpayers, to match the total number in HMRC. EUROMOD-adj2 adjusts the number of taxpayers in each income group to match those given by HMRC.
Sources: EUROMOD version F6.20, using Family Resources Survey 2009–2010 updated to 2010–2011 incomes. HMRC http://www.hmrc.gov.uk/statistics/income-by-year.htm%202010-11%20Table%203.3.

The low-income group and their taxable income is well-represented by the FRS data, but the tax revenue simulated by EUROMOD is too low by 24%. The difference in tax liability based on current year incomes (EUROMOD calculations) and tax revenue (HMRC) can arise if the latter contains taxes due on higher previous-year incomes, for example, by the self-employed. The symmetrical effect (revenue smaller than liability, as incomes rise), which in general is equally likely, is not observable because it is distributed throughout the rest of the distribution of taxable income.

The high-income group of taxpayers and their income and tax paid are all underrepresented by more than 50%. This is consistent with either or both the underrepresentation of very high income-earners in the survey or the underreporting of high incomes.

More detail of the pattern of tax revenue by range of taxable income can be seen in Figure 24.B1 below. The black bars show the HMRC estimates, and the white bars show the estimates using EUROMOD simulations. EUROMOD shows some shortfall in most income ranges, but the effect is concentrated in the highest-income group.

The overall shortfall in taxpayers might be explained by the underreporting of income by the whole distribution or parts of it, or by the fact that a proportion of UK income-tax payers are not resident in UK households and hence not captured by the survey data.[36]

---

[36] We do not pursue this second possibility further.

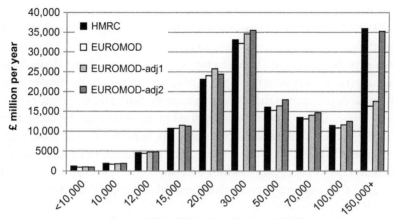

Range of taxable income (lower limit) £ per year

Figure 24.B1 Estimates of income tax revenue by range of taxable income 2010–2011. *Notes: EUROMOD-adj1 makes a proportional adjustment to the number of taxpayers in each income group to match HMRC. EUROMOD-adj2 adjusts the number of taxpayers in each income group to match those given by HMRC. Sources: EUROMOD version F6.20, using Family Resources Survey 2009–2010 updated to 2010–2011 incomes. HMRC http://www.hmrc.gov.uk/statistics/income-by-year.htm%202010-11%20Table%203.3.*

We carry out two adjustments to the comparison of EUROMOD and HMRC statistics (not to the micro-data) in order to explore these possibilities. First, (adj1) we make a proportional adjustment to the three statistics reported in the table such that the total number of taxpayers matches that given by HMRC (i.e., an increase of 7% in the EUROMOD statistic). The middle panel in the table shows that this has the effect of reducing the overall shortfall in taxable income and tax revenue by almost half but does little to rectify the shortfalls in the top income group. The effect on tax revenue in each income group is shown by the pale gray bars in Figure 24.B1. This suggests that a general tendency to underreport is part of the explanation for the shortfall in tax revenue, but it is not the whole story.

A second adjustment accounts for the shortfall in taxpayers within each income group. The effect of this is shown by the darker-gray bar in the figure and the bottom panel in the table. The overall shortfall in taxable income all but disappears, but tax revenue is overestimated by 5%. The shortfall in taxable income in the top income group is greatly reduced to 11%, but tax revenue almost matches that in HMRC statistics for this group. The remaining shortfall in taxable income at the top suggests that there is a problem of lack of response by high-income earners. The relative overestimation of tax revenue suggests that the simulation of tax liability is missing the effect of some tax reliefs and deductions that cannot be simulated due to lack of information in the data. Tax evasion is also a possible explanation. From the figure, it seems that these effects are more important at higher incomes.

To summarize, the validation exercise of the simulated income tax in the UK component of EUROMOD provides some useful insights that should be considered in interpreting microsimulation results for other countries as well, although, of course, the specific explanations may differ, and additional factors may be present. The UK FRS data appear to (a) underrepresent people with high taxable incomes and (b) underreport taxable incomes to some degree, across the whole distribution, although, in countries characterized by large tax evasion, the taxable income reported in the survey can be larger than the one reported in the tax revenue statistics. Simulated tax liabilities do not match tax revenue statistics because of between-year adjustments. The income tax simulations do not account for all reliefs and deductions. Nor do they account for tax evasion, and this may lead to overestimation of tax payments, particularly towards the top of the distribution.

REFERENCES

Aaberge, R., Colombino, U., 2013. Designing optimal taxes with a microeconometric model of household labour supply. Scand. J. Econ. 115 (2), 449–475.

Aaberge, R., Dagsvik, J.K., Strøm, S., 1995. Labour supply responses and welfare effects of tax reforms. Scand. J. Econ. 97 (4), 635–659.

Aaberge, R., Colombino, U., Strøm, S., Wennemo, T., 2000. Joint labour supply of married couples: efficiency and distribution effects of tax and labour market reforms. In: Mitton, L., Sutherland, H., Weeks, M. (Eds.), Microsimulation Modelling for Policy Analysis: Challenges and Innovations. Cambridge University Press, Cambridge, pp. 269–291 (Chapter 13).

Aaberge, R., Colombino, U., Holmoy, E., Strøm, B., Wennemo, T., 2007. Population ageing and fiscal sustainability: integrating detailed labour supply models with CGE models. In: Harding, A., Gupta, A. (Eds.), Modelling Our Future: Population Ageing, Social Security and Taxation. International Symposia in Economic Theory and Econometrics, vol. 15. Elsevier, Amsterdam, pp. 259–290 (Chapter 10).

Aaberge, R., Bhuller, M., Langørgen, A., Mogstad, M., 2010a. The distributional impact of public services when needs differ. J. Public Econ. 94 (9–10), 549–562.

Aaberge, R., Langørgen, A., Lindgren, P., 2010b. The impact of basic public services on the distribution of income in European countries. In: Atkinson, A.B., Marlier, E. (Eds.), Income and Living Conditions in Europe. Eurostat Statistical Books, Publications Office of the European Union, Luxembourg, pp. 329–344 (Chapter 15).

Abramovsky, L., Attanasio, O., Phillips, D., 2012. Demand responses to changes in consumer prices in Mexico: lessons for policy and an application to the 2010 Mexican tax reforms. Conference paper presented at the 2012 Annual Conference of the Royal Economic Society, University of Cambridge.

Adam, S., Brewer, M., Shephard, A., 2006a. Financial work incentives in Britain: comparisons over time and between family types, IFS Working Papers 20, The Institute for Fiscal Studies.

Adam, S., Brewer, M., Shephard, A., 2006b. The Poverty Trade-off: Work Incentives and Income Redistribution in Britain. The Joseph Rowntree Foundation, The Policy Press, Bristol.

Alm, J., 2012. Measuring, explaining, and controlling tax evasion: lessons from theory, experiments, and field studies. Int. Tax Public Financ. 19, 54–77.

Alm, J., McClelland, G.H., Schulze, W.D., 1992. Why do people pay taxes? J. Public Econ. 48 (1), 21–38.

Alm, J., Deskins, J., McKee, M., 2009. Do individuals comply on income not reported by their employer? Public Financ. Rev. 37 (2), 120–141.

Alm, J., Cherry, T.L., Jones, M., McKee, M., 2012. Social programs as positive inducements for tax participation. J. Econ. Behav. Organ. 84 (1), 85–96.

Anderson, P.M., Meyer, B.D., 1997. Unemployment insurance takeup rates and the after-tax value of benefits. Q. J. Econ. 112 (3), 913–937.

Anderson, B., Agostini, P.D., Lawson, T., 2014. Estimating the small area effects of austerity measures in the UK. In: Dekkers, G., Keegan, M., O'Donoghue, C. (Eds.), New Pathways in Microsimulation. Ashgate, Farnham, pp. 11–28 (Chapter 2).

Andreoni, J., Erard, B., Feinstein, J., 1998. Tax compliance. J. Econ. Lit. 36 (2), 818–860.

Atkinson, A.B., 2009. An enlarged role for tax-benefit models. In: Lelkes, O., Sutherland, H. (Eds.), Tax and Benefit Policies in the Enlarged Europe: Assessing the Impact with Microsimulation Models. Ashgate, Vienna, pp. 33–46 (Chapter 2).

Atkinson, A.B., Marlier, E., 2010. Living conditions in Europe and the Europe 2020 agenda. In: Atkinson, A.B., Marlier, E. (Eds.), Income and Living Conditions in Europe. Eurostat Statistical Books, Publications Office of the European Union, Luxembourg, pp. 21–35 (Chapter 1).

Atkinson, A.B., Sutherland, H., 1989. Scaling the "poverty mountain": methods to extend incentives to all workers. In: Bowen, A., Mayhew, K. (Eds.), Improving Incentives for the Low Paid. NEDO, Macmillan, London.

Atkinson, A.B., King, M.A., Sutherland, H., 1983. The analysis of personal taxation and social security. Natl. Inst. Econ. Rev. 103, 63–74.

Atkinson, A.B., Bourguignon, F., Chiappori, P.-A., 1988. What do we learn about tax reform from international comparisons? France and Britain. Eur. Econ. Rev. 32 (2–3), 343–352.

Atkinson, A.B., Bourguignon, F., O'Donoghue, C., Sutherland, H., Utili, F., 2002. Microsimulation of social policy in the European Union: case study of a European minimum pension. Economica 69, 229–243.

Atta-Darkua, V., Barnard, A., 2010. Distributional effects of direct taxes and social transfers (cash benefits). In: Atkinson, A.B., Marlier, E. (Eds.), Income and Living Conditions in Europe. Eurostat Statistical Books, Publications Office of the European Union, Luxembourg, pp. 345–368 (Chapter 16).

Auerbach, A.J., Feenberg, D., 2000. The significance of federal taxes as automatic stabilizers. J. Econ. Perspect. 14 (3), 37–56.

Avram, S., Figari, F., Leventi, C., Levy, H., Navicke, J., Matsaganis, M., Militaru, E., Paulus, A., Rastrigina, O., Sutherland, H., 2013. The distributional effects of fiscal consolidation in nine EU countries. EUROMOD Working Paper EM2/13, University of Essex, Colchester.

Azzolini, D., Bazzoli, M., De Poli, S., Fiorio, C., Poy, S., 2014. TREMOD: A Microsimulation Model for the Province of Trento (Italy), EUROMOD Working Paper EM15/14. University of Essex, Colchester.

Banbura, M., Giannone, D., Reichlin, L., 2011. Nowcasting. In: Clements, M.P., Hendry, D.F. (Eds.), The Oxford Handbook of Economic Forecasting. Oxford University Press, Oxford.

Bargain, O. (Ed.), 2007. Micro-Simulation in Action: Policy Analysis in Europe Using EUROMOD. Research in Labor Economics, vol. 25. Elsevier, Oxford.

Bargain, O., 2012a. Decomposition analysis of distributive policies using behavioural simulations. Int. Tax Public Financ. 19 (5), 708–731.

Bargain, O., 2012b. The distributional effects of tax-benefit policies under New Labour: a decomposition approach. Oxf. Bull. Econ. Stat. 74 (6), 856–874.

Bargain, O., Callan, T., 2010. Analysing the effects of tax-benefit reforms on income distribution: a decomposition approach. J. Econ. Inequal. 8 (1), 1–21.

Bargain, O., Orsini, K., 2007. Beans for breakfast? How portable is the British workfare model? In: Bargain, O. (Ed.), Micro-Simulation in Action: Policy Analysis in Europe Using EUROMOD. Research in Labor Economics, vol. 25. Elsevier, Oxford, pp. 165–198.

Bargain, O., Immervoll, H., Viitamäki, H., 2012. No claim, no pain. Measuring the non-take-up of social assistance using register data. J. Econ. Inequal. 10 (3), 375–395.

Bargain, O., Dolls, M., Fuest, C., Neumann, D., Peichl, A., Pestel, N., Siegloch, S., 2013a. Fiscal union in Europe? Redistributive and stabilizing effects of a European tax-benefit system and fiscal equalization mechanism. Econ. Policy 28 (75), 375–422.

Bargain, O., Dolls, M., Immervoll, H., Neumann, D., Peichl, A., Pestel, N., Siegloch, S., 2013b. Partisan tax policy and income inequality in the U.S., 1979–2007, IZA Discussion Paper 7190.

Bargain, O., Orsini, K., Peichl, A., 2014. Comparing labor supply elasticities in Europe and the US: new results. J. Hum. Resour. 49 (3), 723–838.

Benedek, D., Lelkes, O., 2011. The distributional implications of income under-reporting in Hungary. Fisc. Stud. 32 (4), 539–560.

Bennett, F., Sutherland, H., 2011. The importance of independent income: understanding the role of non-means-tested earnings replacement benefits. ISER Working Paper 2011-09, University of Essex, Colchester.

Betson, D., Greenberg, D., Kasten, R., 1982. A simulation analysis of the economic efficiency and distribution effects of alternative program structures: the negative income tax versus the credit income tax. In: Garfinkel, I. (Ed.), *Income Tested Transfer Programs: The Case For and Against*. Academic Press, New York, pp. 175–203 (Chapter 6).

Betti, G., Donatiello, G., Verma, V., 2011. The Siena Microsimulation Model (SM2) for net-gross conversion of EU-SILC income variables. Int. J. Microsimulation 4 (1), 35–53.

Bingley, P., Walker, I., 1997. The labour supply, unemployment and participation of lone mothers in in-work transfer programmes. Econ. J. 107 (444), 1375–1390.

Bingley, P., Walker, I., 2001. Housing subsidies and work incentives in Great Britain. Econ. J. 111 (471), C86–C103.

Bitler, M.P., Currie, J., Scholz, J.K., 2003. WIC eligibility and participation. J. Hum. Resour. 38, 1139–1179.

Blank, R.M., Ruggles, P., 1996. When do women use aid to families with dependent children and food stamps? The dynamics of eligibility versus participation. J. Hum. Resour. 31 (1), 57–89.

Blazevski, N.M., Petreski, M., Petreska, D., 2013. Increasing labour market activity of the poor and females: Let's make work pay in Macedonia. EUROMOD Working Paper EM16/13, University of Essex, Colchester.

Blundell, R., 2006. Earned income tax credit policies: impact and optimality. The Adam Smith Lecture, 2005. Labour Econ. 13 (4), 423–443.

Blundell, R., 2012. Tax policy reform: the role of empirical evidence. J. Eur. Econ. Assoc. 10 (1), 43–77.

Blundell, R., Shepard, A., 2012. Employment, hours of work and the optimal taxation of low income families. Rev. Econ. Stud. 79, 481–510.

Blundell, R., Fry, V., Walker, I., 1988. Modelling the take-up of means-tested benefits: the case of housing benefits in the United Kingdom. Econ. J. 98 (390), 58–74.

Blundell, R., Chiappori, P., Magnac, T., Meghir, C., 2007. Collective labour supply: heterogeneity and nonparticipation. Rev. Econ. Stud. 74, 417–445.

Boadway, R., Wildasin, D., 1995. Taxation and savings: a survey. Fisc. Stud. 15 (3), 19–63.

Borella, M., Coda Moscarola, F., 2010. Microsimulation of pension reforms: behavioural versus non behavioural approach. J. Pension Econ. Financ. 9 (4), 583–607.

Bourguignon, F., Bussolo, M., 2013. Income distribution in computable general equilibrium modelling. In: Dixon, P.B., Jorgenson, D.W. (Eds.), Handbook of Computable General Equilibrium Modelling. vol. 1B. Elsevier, Amsterdam, pp. 1383–1437 (Chapter 21).

Bourguignon, F., Spadaro, A., 2006. Microsimulation as a tool for evaluating redistribution policies. J. Econ. Inequal. 4 (1), 77–106.

Bourguignon, F., Chiappori, P.A., Hugounenq, R., 1993. Exploring the distribution and incentive effects of tax harmonization. In: Heimler, A., Meulders, D. (Eds.), Empirical Approaches to Fiscal Policy Modelling. Chapman and Hall, London, pp. 235–250 (Chapter 11).

Bourguignon, F., Robilliard, A.S., Robinson, S., 2005. Representative versus real households in the macroeconomic modelling of inequality. In: Kehoe, T.J., Srinivasan, T.N., Whalley, J. (Eds.), Frontiers in Applied General Equilibrium Modelling. Cambridge University Press, Cambridge, pp. 219–254 (Chapter 10).

Bozio, A., Fabre, B., Goupille, J., Lafféter, Q., 2012. Le modéle de micro-simulation TAXIPP—version 0.2. Institut des Politiques Publique, Paris.

Brandolini, A., D'Amuri, F., Faiella, I., 2013. Country case study—Italy. In: Jenkins, S.P., Brandolini, A., Micklewright, J., Nolan, B. (Eds.), The Great Recession and the Distribution of Household Income. Oxford University Press, Oxford, pp. 130–152 (Chapter 7).

Brewer, M., O'Dea, C., 2012. Measuring living standards with income and consumption: evidence from the UK. ISER Working Paper 2012-05, University of Essex, Colchester.

Brewer, M., Francesconi, M., Gregg, P., Grogger, J., 2009. In-work benefit reform in a cross-national perspective—introduction. Econ. J. 119 (535), F1–F14.

Brewer, M., Saez, E., Shephard, A., 2010. Means-testing and tax rates on earnings. In: Mirrlees, J., Adam, S., Besley, T., Blundell, R., Bond, S., Chote, R., Gammie, M., Johnson, P., Myles, G., Poterba, J. (Eds.), Dimensions of Tax Design: The Mirrlees Review. Oxford University Press, Oxford, pp. 90–173, (Chapter 2).

Brewer, M., Browne, J., Joyce, R., 2011. Child and working-age poverty from 2010 to 2020. IFS Commentary C121, The Institute for Fiscal Studies, London.

Brewer, M., Browne, J., Hood, A., Joyce, R., Sibieta, L., 2013. The short- and medium-term impacts of the recession on the UK income distribution. Fisc. Stud. 34 (2), 179–201.

Brown, L.J., Harris, A., Picton, M., Thurecht, L., Yap, M., Harding, A., Dixon, P.B., Richardson, J., 2009. Linking microsimulation and macro-economic models to estimate the economic impact of chronic disease prevention. In: Zaidi, A., Harding, A., Williamson, P. (Eds.), New Frontiers in Microsimulation Modelling. Ashgate, Vienna, pp. 527–555 (Chapter 20).

Bruckmeier, K., Wiemers, J., 2012. A new targeting: a new take-up? Non-take-up of social assistance in Germany after social policy reforms. Empir. Econ. 43 (2), 565–580.

Caldwell, S.B., 1990. Static, Dynamic and Mixed Microsimulation. Department of Sociology, Cornell University, Ithaca.

Callan, T., Sutherland, H., 1997. The impact of comparable policies in European countries: Microsimulation approaches. Eur. Econ. Rev. 41 (3-5), 627–633.

Callan, T., Nolan, B., Walsh, J., 1999. Income tax and social welfare policies. In: Budget Perspectives 1999. ESRI, Dublin.

Callan, T., Coleman, K., Walsh, J.R., 2007. Assessing the impact of tax-transfer policy changes on poverty: methodological issues and some European evidence. In: Bargain, O. (Ed.), Micro-Simulation in Action: Policy Analysis in Europe Using EUROMOD. Research in Labor Economics, vol. 25. Elsevier, Oxford.

Cameron, G., Ezzeddin, R., 2000. Assessing the direct and indirect effects of social policy: integrating input-output and tax microsimulation models at Statistics Canada. In: Mitton, L., Sutherland, H., Weeks, M. (Eds.), Microsimulation Modelling for Policy Analysis: Challenges and Innovations. Cambridge University Press, Cambridge, pp. 42–65 (Chapter 3).

Cantó, O., Adiego, M., Ayala, L., Levy, H., Paniagua, M., 2014. Going regional: The effectiveness of different tax-benefit policies in combating child poverty in Spain. In: Dekkers, G., Keegan, M., O'Donoghue, C. (Eds.), New Pathways in Microsimulation. Ashgate, Farnham, pp. 183–202 (Chapter 12).

Capéau, B., Decoster, A., Phillips, D., 2014. Micro-simulation models of consumption and indirect taxation. In: O'Donoghue, C. (Ed.), Handbook of Microsimulation Modelling. Emerald, Bingley (forthcoming).

Ceriani, L., Fiorio, C.V., Gigliarano, C., 2013. The importance of choosing the data set for tax-benefit analysis. Int. J. Microsimulation 6 (1), 86–121.

Chan, M.K., 2013. A dynamic model of welfare reform. Econometrica 81 (3), 941–1001.

Clark, T., Leicester, A., 2004. Inequality and two decades of British tax and benefit reforms. Fisc. Stud. 25 (2), 129–158.

Cleveland, R.W., 2005. Alternative income estimates in the United States: 2003, Current Population Reports P60-228, U.S. Census Bureau.

Clotfelter, C., 1983. Tax evasion and tax rates: an analysis of individual returns. Rev. Econ. Stat. 65 (3), 363–373.

Colombino, U., 2013. A new equilibrium simulation procedure with discrete choice models. Int. J. Microsimulation 6 (3), 25–49.

Cowell, F.A., 2000. Measurement of inequality. In: Atkinson, A.B., Bourguignon, F. (Eds.), Handbook of Income Distribution. vol. 1. Elsevier, Amsterdam, pp. 87–166 (Chapter 2).

Creedy, J., 1999a. Lifetime versus annual income distribution. In: Silber, J. (Ed.), Handbook on Income Inequality Measurement. Kluwer Academic Publishing, Dordrecht, pp. 513–533 (Chapter 17).

Creedy, J., 1999b. Modelling Indirect Taxes and Tax Reform. Edward Elgar, Northampton.

Creedy, J., 2004. Survey reweighting for tax microsimulation modelling. Res. Econ. Inequal. 12, 229–249.

Creedy, J., Duncan, A., 2002. Behavioural microsimulation with labour supply responses. J. Econ. Surv. 16 (1), 1–39.

Creedy, J., Hérault, N., 2011. Decomposing inequality and social welfare changes: the use of alternative welfare metrics, Melbourne Institute Working Paper 8/11, University of Melbourne.

Creedy, J., Kalb, G., 2005. Discrete hours labour supply modelling: specification, estimation and simulation. J. Econ. Surv. 19 (5), 697–734.

Creedy, J., Kalb, G., Kew, H., 2007. Confidence intervals for policy reforms in behavioural tax microsimulation modelling. Bull. Econ. Res. 59 (1), 37–65.

Currie, J., 2004. The take up of social benefits, NBER Working Paper 10488.

Daponte, B.O., Sanders, S., Taylor, L., 1999. Why do low-income households not use Food Stamps? Evidence from an experiment. J. Hum. Resour. 34 (3), 612–628.

De Lathouwer, L., 1996. A case study of unemployment scheme for Belgium and the Netherlands. In: Harding, A. (Ed.), Microsimulation and Public Policy. Contributions to Economic Analysis, vol. 232. North-Holland, Amsterdam, pp. 69–92 (Chapter 4).

de Mooij, R., Keen, M., 2013. 'Fiscal devaluation' and fiscal consolidation: the VAT in troubled times. In: Alesina, A., Giavazzi, F. (Eds.), Fiscal Policy After the Financial Crisis. University of Chicago Press, Chicago, pp. 443–485 (Chapter 11).

de Vos, K., Zaidi, A., 1996. The use of microsimulation to update poverty statistics based on household budget surveys: a pilot study for the UK. In: Harding, A. (Ed.), Microsimulation and Public Policy. Contributions to Economic Analysis, vol. 232. North-Holland, Amsterdam, pp. 111–128 (Chapter 6).

Decancq, K., Decoster, A., Spiritus, K., Verbist, G., 2012. MEFISTO: a new micro-simulation model for Flanders, FLEMOSI Discussion Paper 14.

Decoster, A., Van Camp, G., 2000. The unit of analysis in microsimulation models for personal income taxes: fiscal unit or household? In: Mitton, L., Sutherland, H., Weeks, M. (Eds.), Microsimulation Modelling for Policy Analysis: Challenges and Innovations. Cambridge University Press, Cambridge, pp. 15–41 (Chapter 2).

Decoster, A., Van Camp, G., 2001. Redistributive effects of the shift from personal income taxes to indirect taxes: Belgium 1988–93. Fisc. Stud. 22 (1), 79–106.

Decoster, A., Loughrey, J., O'Donoghue, C., Verwerft, D., 2010. How regressive are indirect taxes? A microsimulation analysis for five European countries. J. Policy Anal. Manage. 29 (2), 326–350.

Decoster, A., Loughrey, J., O'Donoghue, C., Verwerft, D., 2011. Microsimulation of indirect taxes. Int. J. Microsimulation 4 (2), 41–56.

Dekkers, G., Buslei, H., Cozzolino, M., Desmet, R., Geyer, J., Hofmann, D., Raitano, M., Steiner, V., Tanda, P., Tedeschi, S., Verschueren, F., 2010. The flip side of the coin: the consequences of the European budgetary projections on the adequacy of social security pensions. Eur. J. Soc. Secur. 12 (2), 94–121.

Dekkers, G., Keegan, M., O'Donoghue, C. (Eds.), 2014. New Pathways in Microsimulation. Ashgate, Farnham.

Doerrenberg, P., Duncan, D., 2013. Distributional implications of tax evasion: evidence from the lab. Public Financ. Rev. (forthcoming).

Dolls, M., Fuest, C., Peichl, A., 2012. Automatic stabilizers and economic crisis: US vs. Europe. J. Public Econ. 96 (3–4), 279–294.

Dorsett, R., Heady, C., 1991. The take-up of means-tested benefits by working families with children. Fisc. Stud. 12 (4), 22–32.

Dowling, R., Skabardonis, J., Halkias, J., McHale, G., Zammit, G., 2004. Guidelines for calibration of microsimulation models: framework and applications. Transport. Res. Rec. 1876 (1), 1–9.

Duclos, J.-Y., 1995. Modelling the take-up of state support. J. Public Econ. 58 (3), 391–415.

Duclos, J.-Y., 1997. Estimating and testing a model of welfare participation: the case of supplementary benefits in Britain. Economica 64 (253), 81–100.

DWP, 2013. Households below average income: an analysis of the income distribution 1994/95–2011/12. Department for Work and Pensions, London.

Elbers, C., Lanjouw, J., Lanjouw, P., 2003. Micro-level estimation of poverty and inequality. Econometrica 71 (1), 355–364.

Elffers, H., Robben, H.S., Hessing, D.J., 1992. On measuring tax evasion. J. Econ. Psychol. 13 (4), 545–567.

Erard, B., 1993. Taxation with representation: an analysis of the role of tax practitioners in tax compliance. J. Public Econ. 52 (2), 163–197.

Erard, B., 1997. Self-selection with measurement errors. A microeconometric analysis of the decision to seek tax assistance and its implications for tax compliance. J. Econ. 81 (2), 319–356.

Erard, B., Ho, C.-C., 2001. Searching for ghosts: who are the nonfilers and how much tax do they owe? J. Public Econ. 81 (1), 25–50.

European Commission, 2013. Study on the impacts of fiscal devaluation. Number 36 in Taxation Papers, Publications Office of the European Union, Luxembourg.

Feenberg, D.R., Coutts, E., 1993. An introduction to the TAXSIM model. J. Policy Anal. Manage. 12 (1), 189–194.

Feinstein, J.S., 1991. An econometric analysis of income tax evasion and its detection. RAND J. Econ. 22 (1), 14–35.

Feldstein, M.S., Feenberg, D.R., 1983. Alternative tax rules and personal saving incentives: microeconomic data and behavioral simulations. In: Feldstein, M.S. (Ed.), Behavioral Simulation Methods in Tax Policy Analysis. Chicago, London.

Fernández Salgado, M., Figari, F., Sutherland, H., Tumino, A., 2014. Welfare compensation for unemployment in the Great Recession. Rev. Income Wealth 60, S177–S204.

Figari, F., 2010. Can in-work benefits improve social inclusion in the southern European countries? J. Eur. Soc. Policy 20 (4), 301–315.

Figari, F., Paulus, A., 2013. The distributional effects of taxes and transfers under alternative income concepts: the importance of three 'I's. Public Financ. Rev. (forthcoming).

Figari, F., Levy, H., Sutherland, H., 2007. Using the EU-SILC for policy simulation: prospects, some limitations and suggestions. In: Comparative EU Statistics on Income and Living Conditions: Issues and Challenges. Eurostat Methodologies and Working Papers, Office for Official Publications of the European Communities, Luxembourg, pp. 345–373.

Figari, F., Immervoll, H., Levy, H., Sutherland, H., 2011a. Inequalities within couples in Europe: market incomes and the role of taxes and benefits. East. Econ. J. 37, 344–366.

Figari, F., Paulus, A., Sutherland, H., 2011b. Measuring the size and impact of public cash support for children in cross-national perspective. Soc. Sci. Comput. Rev. 29 (1), 85–102.

Figari, F., Salvatori, A., Sutherland, H., 2011c. Economic downturn and stress testing European welfare systems. In: Immervoll, H., Peichl, A., Tatsiramos, K. (Eds.), Who Loses in the Downturn? Economic Crisis, Employment and Income Distribution. Research in Labor Economics, vol. 32. Emerald Group Publishing Limited, Bingley, pp. 257–286.

Figari, F., Iacovou, M., Skew, A.J., Sutherland, H., 2012a. Approximations to the truth: comparing survey and microsimulation approaches to measuring income for social indicators. Soc. Indic. Res. 105 (3), 387–407.

Figari, F., Paulus, A., Sutherland, H., Tsakloglou, P., Verbist, G., Zantomio, F., 2012b. Taxing home ownership: distributional effects of including net imputed rent in taxable income. EUROMOD Working Paper EM4/12, University of Essex, Colchester.

Flood, L., 2007. Can we afford the future? An evaluation of the new Swedish pension system. In: Harding, A., Gupta, A. (Eds.), Modelling Our Future: Population Ageing, Social Security and Taxation. International Symposia in Economic Theory and Econometrics, vol. 15. Elsevier, Amsterdam, pp. 33–54 (Chapter 2).

Forest, A., Sheffrin, S.M., 2002. Complexity and compliance: an empirical investigation. Natl. Tax J. 55 (1), 75–88.

Fortin, N., Lemieux, T., Firpo, S., 2011. Decomposition methods in economics. In: Ashenfelter, O., Card, D. (Eds.), Handbook of Labor Economics. vol. 4, Part A. Elsevier, Amsterdam, pp. 1–102 (Chapter 1).

Frick, J.R., Grabka, M.M., Smeeding, T.M., Tsakloglou, P., 2010. Distributional effects of imputed rents in five European countries. J. Hous. Econ. 19 (3), 167–179.

Fuest, C., Niehues, J., Peichl, A., 2010. The redistributive effects of tax benefit systems in the enlarged EU. Public Financ. Rev. 38 (4), 473–500.

Fullerton, D., Metcalf, G.E., 2002. Tax incidence. In: Auerbach, A.J., Feldstein, M. (Eds.), Handbook of Public Economics. vol. 4. Elsevier, Amsterdam, pp. 1787–1872 (Chapter 26).

Goedemé, T., Van den Bosch, K., Salanauskaite, L., Verbist, G., 2013. Testing the statistical significance of microsimulation results: a plea. Int. J. Microsimulation 6 (3), 50–77.

Gomulka, J., 1992. Grossing up revisited. In: Hancock, R., Sutherland, H. (Eds.), Microsimulation Models for Public Policy Analysis: New Frontiers. London School of Economics, London, pp. 121–132 (Chapter 6).

Gupta, A., Harding, A. (Eds.), 2007. Modelling Our Future: Population Ageing, Health and Aged Care. International Symposia in Economic Theory and Econometrics, vol. 16. Elsevier, Amsterdam.

Gupta, A., Kapur, V. (Eds.), 2000. Microsimulation in Government Policy and Forecasting. Contributions to Economic Analysis, vol. 247. North-Holland, Amsterdam.

Haan, P., 2010. A multi-state model of state dependence in labour supply. Labour Econ. 17 (2), 323–335.

Haider, S.J., Jacknowitz, A., Schoeni, R.F., 2003. Food stamps and the elderly: why is participation so low? J. Hum. Resour. 38, 1080–1111.

Hancock, R., 2000. Charging for care in later life: an exercise in dynamic microsimulation. In: Mitton, L., Sutherland, H., Weeks, M. (Eds.), Microsimulation Modelling for Policy Analysis: Challenges and Innovations. Cambridge University Press, Cambridge, pp. 226–237 (Chapter 10).

Hancock, R., Barker, G., 2005. The quality of social security benefit data in the British Family Resources Survey: implications for investigating income support take-up by pensioners. J. R. Stat. Soc. Ser. A Stat. Soc. 168 (1), 63–82.

Hancock, R., Pudney, S., 2014. Assessing the distributional impact of reforms to disability benefits for older people in the UK: implications of alternative measures of income and disability costs. Ageing Soc. 34 (2), 232–257.

Hancock, R., Pudney, S., Barker, G., Hernandez, M., Sutherland, H., 2004. The take-up of multiple means-tested benefits by British pensioners: evidence from the Family Resources Survey. Fisc. Stud. 25 (3), 279–303.

Hancock, R., Malley, J., Wittenberg, R., Morciano, M., Pickard, L., King, D., Comas-Herrera, A., 2013. The role of care home fees in the public costs and distributional effects of potential reforms to care home funding for older people in England. Health Econ. Policy Law 8 (1), 47–73.

Harding, A., 1993. Lifetime Income Distribution and Redistribution. Application of a Microsimulation Model. Contributions to Economic Analysis, vol. 221. North-Holland, Amsterdam.

Harding, A., 1996a. Introduction and overview. In: Harding, A. (Ed.), Microsimulation and Public Policy. Contributions to Economic Analysis, vol. 232. North-Holland, Amsterdam, pp. 1–22 (Chapter 1).

Harding, A. (Ed.), 1996b. Microsimulation and Public Policy. Contributions to Economic Analysis, vol. 232. North-Holland, Amsterdam.

Harding, A., Gupta, A. (Eds.), 2007. Modelling Our Future: Population Ageing, Social Security and Taxation. In: International Symposia in Economic Theory and Econometrics, vol. 15. Elsevier, Amsterdam.

Hernandez, M., Pudney, S., 2007. Measurement error in models of welfare participation. J. Public Econ. 91 (1–2), 327–341.

Hernandez, M., Pudney, S., Hancock, R., 2007. The welfare cost of means-testing: pensioner participation in income support. J. Appl. Econ. 22 (3), 581–598.

Hernanz, V., Malherbet, F., Pellizzari, M., 2004. Take-up of welfare benefits in OECD countries: a review of the evidence, Social, Employment and Migration Working Papers 17, OECD, Paris.

HM Treasury, 2013. Budget 2013: policy costings, London.

HMRC, 2012. The Exchequer effect of the 50 per cent additional rate of income tax. HM Revenue & Customs, London.

Hérault, N., 2010. Sequential linking of computable general equilibrium and microsimulation models: comparison of behavioural and reweighting techniques. Int. J. Microsimulation 3 (1), 35–42.

Hungerford, T.L., 2010. The redistributive effect of selected federal transfer and tax provisions. Public Financ. Rev. 38 (4), 450–472.

Hurst, E., Li, G., Pugsley, B., 2014. Are household surveys like tax forms: evidence from income under-reporting of the self-employed. Rev. Econ. Stat. 96 (1), 19–33.

Ilmakunnas, S., Pudney, S., 1990. A model of female labour supply in the presence of hours restrictions. J. Public Econ. 41 (2), 183–210.

Immervoll, H., 2004. Average and marginal effective tax rates facing workers in the EU: a micro-level analysis of levels, distributions and driving factors, Social, Employment and Migration Working Papers 19, OECD, Paris.

Immervoll, H., 2005. Falling up the stairs: the effects of 'bracket creep' on household incomes. Rev. Income Wealth 51 (1), 37–62.

Immervoll, H., O'Donoghue, C., 2001. Imputation of gross amounts from net incomes in household surveys: an application using EUROMOD. EUROMOD Working Paper EM1/01, University of Cambridge.

Immervoll, H., O'Donoghue, C., 2004. What difference does a job make? The income consequences of joblessness in Europe. In: Gallie, D. (Ed.), Resisting Marginalisation: Unemployment Experience and Social Policy in the European Union. Oxford University Press, Oxford, pp. 105–139 (Chapter 5).

Immervoll, H., Richardson, L., 2011. Redistribution Policy and Inequality Reduction in OECD Countries: What has Changed in Two Decades?, Social, Employment and Migration Working Papers 122. OECD Publishing, Paris.

Immervoll, H., Levy, H., Lietz, C., Mantovani, D., O'Donoghue, C., Sutherland, H., Verbist, G., 2006a. Household incomes and redistribution in the European Union: quantifying the equalizing properties of taxes and benefits. In: Papadimitriou, D. (Ed.), The Distributional Effects of Government Spending and Taxation. Palgrave Macmillan, Basingstoke, pp. 135–165.

Immervoll, H., Levy, H., Lietz, C., Mantovani, D., Sutherland, H., 2006b. The sensitivity of poverty rates to macro-level changes in the European Union. Camb. J. Econ. 30 (2), 181–199.

Immervoll, H., Kleven, H.J., Kreiner, C.T., Saez, E., 2007. Welfare reform in European countries: a microsimulation analysis. Econ. J. 117 (516), 1–44.

Isaacs, J.B., Healy, O., 2012. The recession's ongoing impact on children, 2012. The Urban Institute.

Jara, H.X., Tumino, A., 2013. Tax-benefit systems, income distribution and work incentives in the European Union. Int. J. Microsimulation 6 (1), 27–62.

Jenkins, S.P., 2011. Changing Fortunes: Income Mobility and Poverty Dynamics in Britain. Oxford University Press, Oxford.

Johns, A., Slemrod, J., 2010. The distribution of income tax noncompliance. Natl. Tax J. 63 (3), 397–418.

Keane, M.P., 2010. Structural vs. atheoretic approaches to econometrics. J. Econ. 156 (1), 3–20.

Keane, M.P., Moffitt, R., 1998. A structural model of multiple welfare program participation and labor supply. Int. Econ. Rev. 39 (3), 553–589.

Keane, C., Callan, T., Savage, M., Walsh, J., Timoney, K., 2013. Identifying policy impacts in the crisis: microsimulation evidence on tax and welfare. J. Stat. Soc. Inquiry Society Ireland 42, 1–14.

Kim, K., Lambert, P.J., 2009. Redistributive effect of U.S. taxes and public transfers, 1994–2004. Public Financ. Rev. 37 (1), 3–26.

King, M.A., 1983. The distribution of gains and losses from changes in the tax treatment of housing. In: Feldstein, M. (Ed.), Behavioural Simulation Methods in Tax Policy Analysis. University of Chicago Press, Chicago, pp. 109–137 (Chapter 4).

Klepper, S., Nagin, D., 1989. The anatomy of tax evasion. J. Law Econ. Organ. 5 (1), 1–24.

Kleven, H.J., Knudsen, M.B., Kreiner, C.T., Pedersen, S., Saez, E., 2011. Unwilling or unable to cheat? Evidence from a tax audit experiment in Denmark. Econometrica 79 (3), 651–692.

Klevmarken, N.A., 1997. Behavioral modeling in micro simulation models. A survey. Department of Economics, Uppsala University, Working Paper 31.

Klevmarken, N.A., 2002. Statistical inference in micro-simulation models: incorporating external information. Math. Comput. Simul. 59 (1–3), 255–265.

Klevmarken, N.A., 2008. Dynamic microsimulation for policy analysis: problems and solutions. In: Klevmarken, A., Lindgren, B. (Eds.), Simulating an Ageing Population: A Microsimulation Approach Applied to Sweden. Contributions to Economic Analysis, vol. 285. Emerald Group Publishing Limited, Bingley, pp. 31–53 (Chapter 2).

Kotlikoff, L.J., Rapson, D., 2007. Does it pay, at the margin, to work and save? Measuring effective marginal taxes on Americans' labor supply and saving. Tax Pol. Econ. 21, 83–143.

Lanjouw, P., Marra, M., Nguyen, C., 2013. Vietnam's evolving poverty map: patterns and implications for policy. Policy Research Working Paper 6355, The World Bank, Washington, DC.

Laury, S., Wallace, S., 2005. Confidentiality and taxpayer compliance. Natl. Tax J. 58 (3), 427–438.

Lelkes, O., Sutherland, H. (Eds.), 2009. Tax and Benefit Policies in the Enlarged Europe: Assessing the Impact with Microsimulation Models. Public Policy and Social Welfare, vol. 35. Ashgate, Vienna.

Leventi, C., Matsaganis, M., Flevotomou, M., 2013. Distributional implications of tax evasion and the crisis in Greece. EUROMOD Working Paper EM17/13, University of Essex, Colchester.

Levy, H., Lietz, C., Sutherland, H., 2007a. A guaranteed income for Europe's children? In: Jenkins, S.P., Micklewright, J. (Eds.), Inequality and Poverty Re-Examined. Oxford University Press, Oxford.

Levy, H., Lietz, C., Sutherland, H., 2007b. Swapping policies: alternative tax-benefit strategies to support children in Austria, Spain and the UK. J. Soc. Policy 36, 625–647.

Levy, H., Morawski, L., Myck, M., 2009. Alternative tax-benefit strategies to support children in Poland. In: Lelkes, O., Sutherland, H. (Eds.), Tax and Benefit Policies in the Enlarged Europe: Assessing the Impact with Microsimulation Models. Public Policy and Social Welfare, vol. 35. Ashgate, Vienna, pp. 125–151 (Chapter 6).

Levy, H., Matsaganis, M., Sutherland, H., 2013. Towards a European Union child basic income? Within and between country effects. Int. J. Microsimulation 6 (1), 63–85.

Li, J., O'Donoghue, C., 2013. A methodological survey of dynamic microsimulation models. Int. J. Microsimulation 6 (2), 3–55.

Liégeois, P., Dekkers, G., 2014. Combining EUROMOD and LIAM tools for the development of dynamic cross-sectional microsimulation models: a snack preview. In: Dekkers, G., Keegan, M., O'Donoghue, C. (Eds.), New Pathways in Microsimulation. Ashgate, Farnham, pp. 203–216 (Chapter 13).

Lymer, S., Brown, L., Harding, A., Yap, M., 2009. Predicting the need for aged care services at the small area level: the CAREMOD Spatial Microsimulation Model. Int. J. Microsimulation 2 (2), 27–42.

Lynn, P., Jäckle, A., Jenkins, S.P., Sala, E., 2012. The impact of questioning method on measurement error in panel survey measures of benefit receipt: evidence from a validation study. J. R. Stat. Soc. Ser. A Stat. Soc. 175 (1), 289–308.

Lyssiotou, P., Pashardes, P., Stengos, T., 2004. Estimates of the black economy based on consumer demand approaches. Econ. J. 114 (497), 622–640.

Mabbett, D., Schelke, W., 2007. Bringing macroeconomics back into the political economy of reform: the Lisbon Agenda and the 'fiscal philosophy' of EMU. JCMS 45 (1), 81–103.

Mahler, V.A., Jesuit, D.K., 2006. Fiscal redistribution in the developed countries: new insights from the Luxembourg Income Study. Soc. Econ. Rev. 4 (3), 483–511.

Mantovani, D., Papadopoulos, F., Sutherland, H., Tsakloglou, P., 2007. Pension incomes in the European Union: policy reform strategies in comparative perspective. In: Bargain, O. (Ed.), Micro-Simulation in Action: Policy Analysis in Europe using EUROMOD. Research in Labor Economics, vol. 25. Elsevier, Oxford, pp. 27–71.

Martinez-Vazquez, J., Rider, M., 2005. Multiple modes of tax evasion: theory and evidence. Natl. Tax J. 58 (1), 51–76.

Marx, I., Vandenbroucke, P., Verbist, G., 2012. Can higher employment levels bring down relative income poverty in the EU? Regression-based simulations of the Europe 2020 target. J. Eur. Soc. Policy 22 (5), 472–486.

Matsaganis, M., Flevotomou, M., 2008. A basic income for housing? Simulating a universal housing transfer in the Netherlands and Sweden. Basic Income Stud. 2 (2), 1–25.

Matsaganis, M., Leventi, C., 2013. The distributional impact of the Greek crisis in 2010. Fisc. Stud. 34 (1), 83–108.

Matsaganis, M., O'Donoghue, C., Levy, H., Coromaldi, M., Mercader-Prats, M., Rodrigues, C.F., Toso, S., Tsakloglou, P., 2006. Reforming family transfers in Southern Europe: is there a role for universal child benefits? Soc. Policy Soc. 5 (2), 189–197.

Matsaganis, M., Levy, H., Flevotomou, M., 2010. Non-take up of social benefits in Greece and Spain. Soc. Policy Adm. 44 (7), 827–844.

McFadden, D., 1974. Conditional logit analysis of qualitative choice behaviour. In: Zerembka, P. (Ed.), Frontiers in Econometrics. Academic Press, New York, pp. 105–142 (Chapter 4).

Merz, J., 1986. Structural adjustment in static and dynamic microsimulation models. In: Orcutt, G.H., Merz, J., Quinke, H. (Eds.), Microanalytic Simulation Models to Support Social and Financial Policy. North-Holland, Amsterdam, pp. 423–446.

Merz, J., 1991. Microsimulation—a survey of principles, developments and applications. Int. J. Forecast. 7 (1), 77–104.

Meyer, B.D., Sullivan, J.X., 2011. Further results on measuring the well-being of the poor using income and consumption. Can. J. Econ. 44 (1), 52–87.

Meyer, B.D., Mok, W.K.C., Sullivan, J.X., 2009. The under-reporting of transfers in household surveys: its nature and consequences, NBER Working Paper 15181.

Mirrlees, J., Adam, S., Besley, T., Blundell, R., Bond, S., Chote, R., Gammie, M., Johnson, P., Myles, G., Poterba, J. (Eds.), 2010. Dimensions of Tax Design: The Mirrlees Review. Oxford University Press, Oxford.

Mitton, L., Sutherland, H., Weeks, M. (Eds.), 2000. Microsimulation Modelling for Policy Analysis: Challenges and Innovations. Cambridge University Press, Cambridge.

Moffitt, R., 1983. An economic model of welfare stigma. Am. Econ. Rev. 73 (5), 1023–1035.

Morawski, L., Myck, M., 2010. 'Klin'-ing up: effects of Polish tax reforms on those in and on those out. Labour Econ. 17 (3), 556–566.

Navicke, J., Rastrigina, O., Sutherland, H., 2014. Nowcasting indicators of poverty risk in the European Union: a microsimulation approach. Soc. Indic. Res. 119 (1), 101–119.

Nelissen, J.H., 1998. Annual versus lifetime income redistribution by social security. J. Public Econ. 68 (2), 223–249.

Nolan, B., Callan, T., Maître, B., 2013. Country case study—Ireland. In: Jenkins, S.P., Brandolini, A., Micklewright, J., Nolan, B. (Eds.), The Great Recession and the Distribution of Household Income. Oxford University Press, Oxford, pp. 113–129 (Chapter 4).

OBR, 2013. Fiscal Sustainability Report. The Stationery Office, London.

O'Donoghue, C., 2001. Dynamic microsimulation: a methodological survey. Braz. Electron. Econ. J. 4, 1–77

O'Donoghue, C. (Ed.), 2014. Handbook of Microsimulation Modelling. Emerald, Bingley (forthcoming).

O'Donoghue, C., Baldini, M., Mantovani, D., 2004. Modelling the redistributive impact of indirect taxes in Europe: an application of EUROMOD, EUROMOD Working Paper EM7/01, University of Cambridge.

O'Donoghue, C., Lennon, J., Hynes, S., 2009. The Life-Cycle Income Analysis Model (LIAM): a study of a flexible dynamic microsimulation modelling computing framework. Int. J. Microsimulation 2 (1), 16–31.

OECD, 2007. Benefits and Wages 2007. OECD, Paris.

Orcutt, G.H., 1957. A new type of socio-economic system. Rev. Econ. Stat. 39 (2), 116–123.

Orcutt, G.H., Greenberger, M., Korbel, J., Rivlin, A., 1961. Microanalysis of Socio-Economic Systems: A Simulation Study. Harper and Row, New York.

Orcutt, G.H., Caldwell, S., Wertheimer, R., 1976. Policy Explorations Through Microanalytic Simulation. The Urban Institute, Washington, DC.

Paulus, A., Peichl, A., 2009. Effects of flat tax reforms in Western Europe. J. Policy Model 31 (5), 620–636.

Paulus, A., Čok, M., Figari, F., Hegedüs, P., Kralik, S., Kump, N., Lelkes, O., Levy, H., Lietz, C., Mantovani, D., Morawski, L., Sutherland, H., Szivos, P., Võrk, A., 2009. The effects of taxes and benefits on income distribution in the enlarged EU. In: Lelkes, O., Sutherland, H. (Eds.), Tax and Benefit Policies in the Enlarged Europe: Assessing the Impact with Microsimulation Models. Public Policy and Social Welfare, vol. 35. Ashgate, Vienna, pp. 65–90 (Chapter 4).

Paulus, A., Sutherland, H., Tsakloglou, P., 2010. The distributional impact of in-kind public benefits in European countries. J. Policy Anal. Manage. 29 (2), 243–266.

Pechman, J.A., 1973. Responsiveness of the federal individual income tax to changes in income. Brook. Pap. Econ. Act. 2, 385–427.

Peichl, A., 2009. The benefits and problems of linking micro and macro models—evidence from a flat tax analysis. J. Appl. Econ. 12 (2), 301–329.

Peichl, A., Siegloch, S., 2012. Accounting for labor demand effects in structural labor supply models. Labour Econ. 19 (1), 129–138.

Piketty, T., Saez, E., 2007. How progressive is the U.S. federal tax system? A historical and international perspective. J. Econ. Perspect. 21 (1), 3–24.

Pissarides, C.A., Weber, G., 1989. An expenditure-based estimate of Britain's black economy. J. Public Econ. 39, 17–32.

Popova, D., 2014. Distributional impacts of cash allowances for children: a microsimulation analysis for Russia and Europe. EUROMOD Working Paper EM2/14, University of Essex, Colchester.

Pudney, S., Sutherland, H., 1994. How reliable are microsimulation results? An analysis of the role of sampling error in a U.K. tax-benefit model. J. Public Econ. 53 (3), 327–365.

Pudney, S., Sutherland, H., 1996. Statistical reliability in microsimulation models with econometrically-estimated behavioural responses. In: Harding, A. (Ed.), Microsimulation and Public Policy. Contributions to Economic Analysis, vol. 232. North-Holland, Amsterdam, pp. 473–503 (Chapter 21).

Pudney, S., Hancock, R., Sutherland, H., 2006. Simulating the reform of means-tested benefits with endogenous take-up and claim costs. Oxf. Bull. Econ. Stat. 68 (2), 135–166.

Randelović, S., Rakić, J.Ž., 2013. Improving work incentives in Serbia: evaluation of a tax policy reform using SRMOD. Int. J. Microsimulation 6 (1), 157–176.

Redmond, G., Sutherland, H., Wilson, M., 1998. The Arithmetic of Tax and Social Security Reform. A User's Guide to Microsimulation Methods and Analysis. Cambridge University Press, Cambridge.

Riphahn, R.T., 2001. Rational poverty or poor rationality? The take-up of social assistance benefits. Rev. Income Wealth 47 (3), 379–398.

Robilliard, A.-S., Bourguignon, F., Robinson, S., 2008. Examining the social impact of the Indonesian financial crisis using a macro-micro model. In: Bourguignon, F., Bussolo, M., Pereira da Silva, L.A. (Eds.), The Impact of Macroeconomic Policies on Poverty and Income Distribution: Macro-Micro Evaluation Techniques and Tools. The World Bank and Palgrave Macmillan, New York, pp. 93–118 (Chapter 4).

Rodrigues, C.F., 2007. Income in EU-SILC—net/gross conversion techniques for building and using EU-SILC databases. In: Comparative EU, Statistics on Income and Living Conditions: Issues and Challenges. Eurostat Methodologies and Working Papers, Office for Official Publications of the European Communities, Luxembourg, pp. 157–172.

Salanauskaite, L., Verbist, G., 2013. Is the neighbour's grass greener? Comparing family support in Lithuania and four other New Member States. J. Eur. Soc. Policy 23 (3), 315–331.

Shorrocks, A., 2013. Decomposition procedures for distributional analysis: a unified framework based on the Shapley value. J. Econ. Inequal. 11 (1), 99–126.

Slemrod, J., 2007. Cheating ourselves: the economics of tax evasion. J. Econ. Perspect. 21 (1), 25–48.

Spielauer, M., 2011. What is social science microsimulation? Soc. Sci. Comput. Rev. 29 (1), 9–20.

Stiglitz, J.E., 2012. The Price of Inequality. W. W. Norton & Co., New York.

Sutherland, H., 1995. Static microsimulation models in Europe: a survey. Working Papers in Economics 9523, University of Cambridge.

Sutherland, H., 2014. Multi-country microsimulation. In: O'Donoghue, C. (Ed.), Handbook of Microsimulation Modelling. Emerald, Bingley (forthcoming).

Sutherland, H., Figari, F., 2013. EUROMOD: the European Union tax-benefit microsimulation model. Int. J. Microsimulation 6 (1), 4–26.

Sutherland, H., Taylor, R., Gomulka, J., 2002. Combining household income and expenditure data in policy simulations. Rev. Income Wealth 48 (4), 517–536.

Sutherland, H., Hancock, R., Hills, J., Zantomio, F., 2008. Keeping up or falling behind? The impact of benefit and tax uprating on incomes and poverty. Fisc. Stud. 29 (4), 467–498.

Tanton, R., Edwards, K.L. (Eds.), 2013. Spatial Microsimulation: A Reference Guide for Users. Springer, New York.

Tanton, R., McNamara, J., Harding, A., Morrison, T., 2009. Small area poverty estimates for Australia's Eastern Seaboard in 2006. In: Zaidi, A., Harding, A., Williamson, P. (Eds.), New Frontiers in Microsimulation Modelling. Ashgate, Vienna, pp. 79–95 (Chapter 3).

Tanton, R., Vidyattama, Y., Nepal, B., McNamara, J., 2011. Small area estimation using a reweighting algorithm. J. R. Stat. Soc. Ser. A Stat. Soc. 174 (4), 931–951.

Thoresen, T.O., 2004. Reduced tax progressivity in Norway in the nineties: the effect from tax changes. Int. Tax Public Financ. 11 (4), 487–506.

Urzúa, C.M. (Ed.), 2012. Fiscal Inclusive Development: Microsimulation Models for Latin America, Instituto Tecnológico y de Estudios Superiores de Monterrey (ITESM). International Development Research Centre, United Nations Development Programme.

van Soest, A., 1995. Structural models of family labor supply: a discrete choice approach. J. Hum. Resour. 30 (1), 63–88.

Verbist, G., 2007. The distribution effect of taxes on pensions and unemployment benefits in the EU-15. In: Bargain, O. (Ed.), Micro-Simulation in Action: Policy Analysis in Europe using EUROMOD. Research in Labor Economics, vol. 25. Elsevier, Oxford, pp. 73–99.

Verbist, G., Figari, F., 2014. The redistributive effect and progressivity of taxes revisited: an international comparison across the European Union. FinanzArchiv (forthcoming).

Waddell, P., Borning, A., Noth, M., Freier, N., Becke, M., Ulfarsson, G., 2003. Microsimulation of urban development and location choices: design and implementation of UrbanSim. Netw. Spat. Econ. 3 (1), 43–67.

Wagstaff, A., van Doorslaer, E., van der Burg, H., Calonge, S., Christiansen, T., Citoni, G., Gerdtham, U.-G., Gerfin, M., Gross, L., Häkinnen, U., John, J., Johnson, P., Klavus, J., Lachaud, C., Lauridsen, J., Leu, R.E., Nolan, B., Peran, E., Propper, C., Puffer, F., Rochaix, L., Rodríguez, M., Schellhorn, M., Sundberg, G., Winkelhake, O., 1999. Redistributive effect, progressivity and differential tax treatment: personal income taxes in twelve OECD countries. J. Public Econ. 72 (1), 73–98.

Wang, C., Caminada, K., Goudswaard, K., 2012. The redistributive effect of social transfer programmes and taxes: a decomposition across countries. Int. Soc. Secur. Rev. 65 (3), 27–48.

Wheaton, L., 2007. Underreporting of means-tested transfer programs in the CPS and SIPP. In: 2007 Proceedings of the American Statistical Association, Social Statistics Section. American Statistical Association, Alexandria, VA, pp. 3622–3629.

Wheaton, L., Giannarelli, L., Martinez-Schiferl, M., Zedlewski, S.R., 2011. How do States' safety net policies affect poverty? Working Families Paper 19, The Urban Institute, Washington, DC.

Whelan, S., 2010. The take-up of means-tested income support. Empir. Econ. 39 (3), 847–875.

Wilkinson, K., 2009. Adapting EUROMOD for use in a developing country—the case of South Africa and SAMOD. EUROMOD Working Paper EM5/09, University of Essex, Colchester.

Wolf, D.A., 2004. Book review of Microsimulation in Government Policy and Forecasting (2000). In: Gupta, A., Kapur, V. (Eds.), Journal of Artificial Societies and Social Simulation 7, (1).

Wolfson, M., 2009. Preface—Orcutt's vision 50 years on. In: Zaidi, A., Harding, A., Williamson, P. (Eds.), New Frontiers in Microsimulation Modelling. Ashgate, Vienna, pp. 21–29.

World Bank, 2013. Poverty prospects in Europe: assessing progress towards the Europe 2020 poverty and social exclusion targets in New European Union Member States. Report no: ACS4943, Human Development and Poverty Reduction and Economic Management Units.

Wright, G., Noble, M., Barnes, H., 2014. NAMOD: a Namibian tax-benefit microsimulation model. EUROMOD Working Paper EM7/14, University of Essex, Colchester.

Wu, B., Birkin, M., 2013. Moses: a dynamic spatial microsimulation model for demographic planning. In: Tanton, R., Edwards, K.L. (Eds.), Spatial Microsimulation: A Reference Guide for Users. Understanding Population Trends and Processes, vol. 6. Springer, New York, pp. 171–194.

Zaidi, A., Rake, K., 2001. Dynamic microsimulation models: a review and some lessons for SAGE. SAGE Discussion Paper 2, London School of Economics.

Zaidi, A., Harding, A., Williamson, P. (Eds.), 2009. New Frontiers in Microsimulation Modelling. Public Policy and Social Welfare, vol. 36. Ashgate, Vienna.

Zantomio, F., Pudney, S., Hancock, R., 2010. Estimating the impact of a policy reform on benefit take-up: the 2001 extension to the minimum income guarantee for UK pensioners. Economica 77 (306), 234–254.

INDEX

Note: Page numbers followed by *b* indicate boxes, *f* indicate figures and *t* indicate tables.